Eighth Edition

Occupied America

A History of Chicanos

Rodolfo F. Acuña

Emeritus California State University at Northridge

PEARSON

Boston   Columbus   Indianapolis   New York   San Francisco   Upper Saddle River

Amsterdam   Cape Town   Dubai   London   Madrid   Milan   Munich   Paris   Montréal   Toronto

Delhi   Mexico City   São Paulo   Sydney   Hong Kong   Seoul   Singapore   Taipei   Tokyo

FEB 5 2019

Editor in Chief: *Ashley Dodge*
Editorial Assistant: *Amandria Guadalupe*
Managing Editor: *Denise Forlow*
Program Manager: *Kathy Sleys*
Project Manager: *Bonnie Boehme*
Senior Operations Supervisor: *Mary Fischer*
Operations Specialist: *Mary Ann Gloriande*
Art Director: *Jayne Conte*
Cover Designer: *John Christiana*

Cover Image: *Malaquias Montoya*
Director of Digital Media: *Brian Hyland*
Digital Media Project Management: *Learning Mate Solutions, Ltd*
Digital Media Project Manager: *Tina Gagliostro*
Full-Service Project Management and Composition: *Raghavi Khullar*
  Cenveo® Publisher Services
Printer/Binder: *R. R. Donelley*
Cover Printer: *R. R. Donelley*
Text Font: *Minion Pro*

Credits and acknowledgments borrowed from other sources and reproduced, with permission, in this textbook appear on appropriate page within text.

Library of Congress Cataloging-in-Publication Data

Acuña, Rodolfo.
  Occupied America : a history of Chicanos / Rodolfo F. Acuña, Emeritus, California State University at Northridge. — Eighth edition.
    pages cm
  ISBN 978-0-205-88084-3
  1. Mexican Americans—History. I. Title.
  E184.M5A63 2014
  973'.046872—dc23

                                                              2013048339

ISBN 10: 0-205-88084-3
ISBN 13: 978-0-205-88084-3

CONTENTS

CHAPTER 6   Sonora Invaded: The Occupation of Arizona   111

CHAPTER 11 World War II: The Betrayal of Promises 244

CHAPTER 12 "Happy Days": Chicano Communities under Siege 271

CHAPTER 13 Goodbye America: The Chicana/o in the 1960s 295

CHAPTER 15 Becoming a National Minority: 1980–2001 360

CHAPTER 16 Losing Fear: Decade of Struggle and Hope 397

PREFACE

History can either oppress or liberate a people. Generalizations and stereotypes about the Mexican have been circulated in the United States for over 124 years. ... Incomplete or biased analyses by historians have perpetuated factual errors and created myths. The Anglo-American public has believed and encouraged the historian's and social commentator's portrayal of Mexicans as "the enemy." The tragedy is that the myths have degraded the Mexican people—not only in the eyes of those who feel superior, but also in their own eyes.

—Rodolfo Acuña, *Occupied America: The Chicano's Struggle Toward Liberation* (San Francisco: Canfield Press, 1972), p. 1.

The first edition of *Occupied America* was published in 1972. I intended it to be a monograph that explained historical events leading up to the 1970 Chicano Moratorium and the murder of Rubén Salazar, a former *Los Angeles Times* reporter and news director for the Spanish language television station KMEX in Los Angeles. My intention was to publish one edition, and then move on to my area of specialization—the history of northern Mexico. I had a contract to publish my dissertation on nineteenth-century Sonora, Mexico, and a verbal commitment to publish another book on "Los Hombres del Norte," the Sonoran leaders of the Mexican Revolution—Álvaro Obregón, Plutarco Elías Calles, and Adolfo de la Huerta.

That was my intention. However, as Albert Einstein once said, "Information is not knowledge. The only source of knowledge is experience." My experiences at San Fernando Valley State College, now known as California State University Northridge, and the growth of Chicana/o Studies changed my trajectory and my life. The experiences were unique, and teaching at a teacher's college shaped my priorities, which were in teaching, not research.

I came out of a public school teaching background. I was influenced by theorists such as John Dewey who cautioned that education was about teaching the child and not the subject. The question was therefore how to improve the teaching of Chicano history. For many teachers a textbook is a partner with whom they often do not agree but which they use as a tool to fill in the spaces and cover the basics of the course. The truth be told, new fields of study are products of scholarly articles, monographs, and teaching. The textbook summarizes them. So in my case the glove fit, and the evolution of *Occupied America* was a natural next step.

I had taught hybrid survey courses on the Chicano as early as 1966. Consequent to publishing *Occupied America* I published three K–12 books:[1] *The Story of the Mexican Americans* and *Cultures in Conflict* for elementary grades; *The Mexican American Chronicle* was a textbook for high school and community college students. In the introduction to the first edition of *Occupied America* (1972) I laid out the thesis of the internal colony. To my surprise it was successful—to the point that many people believe that I should have left it at that, and I probably would have if it were not for my teaching. The truth be told, to this day I have remained a frustrated eighth grade teacher and I take the questions raised by students seriously.

After a decade of teaching from the first edition of *Occupied America*, , I decided to change it to a textbook. By this time the book had acquired a cachet so it seemed dumb to change horses in midstream and begin from scratch. Besides, the title "Occupied America" said it all; I liked it. Students have to understand the subject in order to be able to identify patterns and make comparisons. So the main objective of the second edition of *Occupied America* was to systematize the learning of the essentials of Chicano history. This was no small task. One of the difficulties is that when a scholar writes Chicano history, she or he must constantly correct the errors of Euro-American historians, and at the same time form the field's identity.

The textbook helps the student organize and analyze. The objective is to understand the historical processes. It keeps them on track, constantly asking, What is behind the story? Historical vignettes are offered to encourage the readers to question what happened. Deduction is a very important part of historical analysis; it should encourage inductive thinking, which is where the instructor comes in.[2]

Over the past 40 years, I have repeatedly corrected the previous editions. Each subsequent edition raised new questions and added new sources. My tenure at a teaching institution, however, had its drawbacks: Aside from growing the Chicano Studies Department, I taught 12 units a semester, was active in community and labor struggles, wrote columns for major newspapers, did research and published other books and revised the various editions of *Occupied America*. This all had to fit into my available time. I am not complaining because this pried me out of the library.

This edition of *Occupied America* takes into account new trends in education. In California education is undergoing a crisis. Tuition has mushroomed to the point that many students cannot afford it. The community colleges are jammed, and it is projected that at least one-third of their offerings will be online in the near future. Corporate America has refused to pay the social cost of production, shifting the entire burden to the middle class and the poor. In January 2012, "Gov. Jerry Brown . . . announced his plan last week to pressure state colleges and universities to expand their online offerings and reduce costs."[3] Online classes save the cost of classroom construction and maintenance.

This brings me to the question that many of you will ask and certainly one that I have asked. Why another edition? I wanted the opportunity to develop the student/teacher manual, which I believe is necessary.

Another reason is that since the last edition, a lot has happened. The immigration question came to a head in 2006 and 2010, and so did the reaction from racist forces who threw reason to the wind. Incredibly, they want to control the border by deporting 12 million undocumented workers and their families, an act that if taken to its logical conclusion would bankrupt the country. They don't consider the economic and human costs of rounding up 12 million people. They don't ask who would replace them in lower-paying jobs. How many teachers and merchants would be displaced if we lost 12 million people? It is the same sort of idiocy that got us to invade Afghanistan and Iraq while lowering taxes on the rich, running the country on a credit card and plunging the country into a depression.

The reelection of President Barack Obama in 2012 was a milestone for Latinos. Without over 70 percent of Latinos voting for Obama, it is doubtful that he would have been reelected. Consequent to the election, more attention is being paid to Latinos and immigration than ever before. Many wonder in contrast to Arizona punished the Republican Party. Since California voters in 1994 passed the Republican-sponsored draconian Proposition 187, Republicans have not been able to elect a statewide candidate. The Latino electorate there is a firewall that checks the manufactured crisis.

This is the eighth edition of *Occupied America*; throughout its history, I have attempted to make each edition less imperfect than the last. As mentioned, this edition was in part prompted by Arizona, but it was also a result of the entire decade: Gore v. Bush (2000), the Middle Eastern Wars, the great recession beginning in 2008, the irrational and unrelenting racist nativism beginning in the early 1990s, the crisis in education, and the shutdown of higher education as a stairway to the middle-class heaven. On a positive note the decade produced the Dream Act movement that built on the work of the Chicana/o generation in support of the foreign born.

This edition is more Internet course friendly. There are links to maps, and a skills section. The book has numerous hyperlinks to sources on the Internet. Every link was tested, but as we know, links often become obsolete. We encourage the readers to use their browsers and check for new web addresses in the event that any we give are not functional. The Internet is not static, and many sites are renamed or dropped frequently.

New to This Edition

- The text covers history from pre-Columbian civilization to the 2012 presidential election.
- New historical material, texts, and scholarship have been taken into account.
- Individual women have been given a bigger share of the narrative alongside organizational development.
- The Preface and the Epilogue have been completely revised.
- Chapters 15 and 16 have been rewritten and revised and emphasis is placed on the role of population growth in forming priorities.
- Special note is made of the heavy immigration of groups other than those of Mexican origin, beginning in the 1980s.
- The Student/Teacher Manual—or, as I call it, the "Mini-book"—is over 100 pages and is designed to accompany *Occupied America*. It is in chapter format with an introduction, hyperlinks, and discussion questions. The manual makes *Occupied America* more online friendly for teachers and students. It is available free of charge at http://forchicanachicanostudies.wikispaces.com/—click on the link "Occupied America Manual" and on the link for Center for the Study of the Peoples of the Americas http://www.csun.edu/cespa/Acuna%20Manual%20Binder.pdf Chapter summaries and overviews have been expanded or added where space allowed.

This text is available in a variety of formats—digital and print. To learn more about pricing options, and customization, visit www.pearsonhighered.com.

Acknowledgments

I thank Chicana/o Studies at California State University, Northridge. It has allowed me to teach part time into my eightieth birthday, giving me contact with 130 students per semester, which has extended my life. It gives me a sense of community and a feeling for what is continuously changing. Aside from the students in my classes I am always thankful to the Movimiento Estudiantil de Aztlán (MEChA) that has kept the flame of activism and caring alive. Because of my students, teaching is not just a vocation; it is a way of life. I would like to thank the teachers, students, and supporters of the Tucson Unified School District for showing us that history is important and worth fighting for. Los Angeles is my hometown: I was born here, and I only left it for the 19 months of my tour in the army. I love LA, smog and all.

Thanks to the founding students of Chicana/o Studies, they founded CHS; it was not the faculty nor I and certainly not the CSUN administration. My good friend José Luis Vargas, director of the Educational Opportunity Programs (EOP), reminds me, EOP was there first and students created and sustained EOP and Chicana/o studies. Thanks are due to Mary Pardo, Jorge García, Gabriel Gutiérrez, and David Rodríguez, who find time to discuss history. I'd like to thank Benjamin Torres; he has been a good friend and supporter throughout the years. I am grateful to the members of the For Chicana/Chicano Studies Foundation and for their support of undocumented students. To the Dreamers who demand their rights as human beings: hopefully their appreciation of history will expand. I would like to thank the Pearson editor, Ashley Dodge. I also appreciate the contribution of the reviewers: James Barrera, South Texas College; Maria Eva Flores, Our Lady of the Lake University; Laura Larque, Santa Rosa Junior College; Manuel F. Medrano, University of Texas at Brownsville; and Mary Ashley Riley Sousa, West Valley College.

Not least, thanks to my sons, Frank and Walter, and my granddaughters and grandsons. My daughter Angela Acuña who I hope never loses her love of animals and maintains her principles; I admire her greatly and love her more. My life would not be the same without her. I just underwent the first of two eye operations and say that my wife, Lupita Compeán, literally es mis ojos. I could not have accomplished a tenth of what I have without her. My writing in newspapers, four of my books, six editions of *Occupied America*, and my suit against the University of California have all occurred on her watch. In addition, we co-edited a three-volume anthology with some 425 documents, and have accomplished much more. I owe her an intellectual and moral debt. I always feel safe because I know she has my back.

Rodolfo F. Acuña, Professor Emeritus of Chicana/o Studies
California State University at Northridge

Notes

1. *The Story of the Mexican Americans: The Men and the Land* (New York: American Book Company, 1969). *Cultures in Conflict: Problems of the Mexican Americans* (New York : Charter School Books, 1970]. *A Mexican American Chronicle* (New York: American Book Company, 1971).

2. Paulo Freire, *Pedagogy of the Oppressed* (New York: Continuum Publishing Company, 1970). Edwin Fenton, *Teaching the New Social Studies in Secondary Schools: An Inductive Approach* (New York: Holt, Rinehart and Winston, 1966).

3. David Siders, "Jerry Brown Carries the Day on Online Classes at UC, CSU," *Sacramento Bee* (Jan. 17, 2013).

CHAPTER 1

Not Just Pyramids, Explorers, and Heroes

LEARNING OBJECTIVES

- Interpret the evolution of Mesoamerican civilizations via a timeline through their Preclassical and Postclassical periods.
- Show the movement of the different Indian societies/civilizations in the context of the spread of corn.
- Explain the evolution of agricultural innovations, urban centers, architecture, calendars, and mathematical and literary achievements.

- Trace the changes in the development of classes and gender differences as the populations grew from villages to chiefdoms, to urban centers, and trace the evolving modes of production.
- Analyze and contextualize the world system, placing the disparate Mesoamerican civilizations within this model.

The primary culture of Mexico and the Americas is Indian. Because this fact challenges the legitimacy of the conquest, many Western scholars minimize this truism and they disrespect or slight the histories of the Indians. Mesoamerican and Andean civilizations did not need the Europeans to give them civilization; they are two of the world's cradles of civilization rivaling other great civilizations in China, the Indus Valley, the Middle East, and Africa. The Mesoamerican and Andean civilizations shared with them similar features. All of the cradles of civilization had a stable food source—this provided the people with an adequate supply of food to fuel a population explosion. In the Eastern Hemisphere, the *basic grains* were wheat, rice, rye, oats, millet, and barley. In North America, corn was developed at least 9,000 years ago in what is today central Mexico, spreading to what is now North America and the Andean region of South America. Corn was essential to the evolution of indigenous cultures, so much so that indigenous peoples worshipped maize. Corn made possible the changes in modes of production and helped mobilize labor to meet the challenges of population growth and cope with environmental change. Corn, like the pyramids, was a product of human labor and ingenuity.

40,000 BC	8000 BC	2000 BC	AD 200	AD 900	AD 1519

Stages of Development		
40,000 BC–8000 BC	*Paleoindian*	*Hunting and Gathering.* Characterized by bands of hunters and by seed and fruit gatherers.
8000 BC–2000 BC	*Archaic*	Incipient agriculture. Domestication of maize and other plants. Earliest corn grown in Tehuacán circa 5000 BC.
2000 BC–AD 200	*Formative Preclassic*	Intensification of farming and growth of villages. Olmeca chiefdom stands out. Reliance on maize and the spread of a religious tradition that focuses on the earth and fertility. Organizational evolution, 1200–400 BC: numerous chiefdoms evolve through Mesoamerica. The Maya appear during this period. Monte Albán is established circa 400 BC–AD 200. Rapid population growth, a market system, and agricultural intensification occur. Development of the solar calendar. Villages grow into centers.
AD 200–900	*Classic*	*The Golden Age of Mesoamerica.* The evolution of state-level societies. The emergence of kings. Priests become more important. Complex irrigation, population growth, and highly stratified society. Excellent ceramics, sculpture, and murals. Building of huge pyramids. Teotihuacán had more than 150,000 people, the largest city outside China.
AD 900–1519	*Postclassic*	*Growth of City-States and Empires.* Civil, market, and commercial elements become more important. The Azteca and Tarascan empires emerge as dominant powers. Cyclical conquests. Use of metals, increased trade, and warfare.

Sources: Robert M. Carmack, Janine Gasco, and Gary H. Gossen, *The Legacy of Mesoamerica: History and Culture of a Native American Civilization* (Upper Saddle River, NJ: Prentice Hall, 1996), 48–49; also see Michael C. Meyer, William L. Sherman, and Susan M. Deeds, *The Course of Mexican History*, 6th ed. (New York: Oxford University Press, 1998), 4.

The Cradles of Civilizations

Worldwide people began settling in sedentary societies around 8000 BC as agriculture became more common. Populaces formed laws based on mores and folkways. Slowly six cradles of civilization formed: China, the Indus Valley, Mesopotamia, the Nile, the Andean region of South America, and Mesoamerica.[1] Food surpluses made possible "specialization of labor" and the development of complex social institutions such as organized religion and education. Trade and a writing system facilitated the cross-fertilization of cultures. The interactive map and timeline at the following website shows the formation of such civilizations.

Time is very important in understanding history. It determines the questions we ask. Time represents the knowledge a people have accumulated. To gain more understanding of the science of time, go to the end of the book and read "Creating a Timeline." Correlate this discussion with the online maps (cited in the text and in The Map Room at the end of the book) and with the timeline above, which shows the stages of cultural evolution in Mesoamerica.

The Corn People: An Overview

When the first modern humans migrated to what are called the Americas is not known precisely but is estimated to be about 20,000–30,000 years ago. Their migration into Western Europe began about 30,000 years ago. By some accounts, the New World was inhabited by about 15,000 BC. However, these are theories and some linguists have raised the notion that language spread from south to north instead of from north to south.[2] There is the probability that some of these early people may well have migrated back to Asia from the Americas, with the last migrations ceasing when the Bering Strait's ice bridge melted around 9000 BC.

The earliest known villages in the Americas appeared along the coasts as early as 12,500 years ago.[3] But it was not until around 7000 BC, when the hunters and fruit gatherers began to farm, that they began to alter or control their environment. In the Valley of Mexico, the climate changed, and water sources, game, and flora became scarce. As the population grew, the people were forced to turn to agriculture or perish. The evolution of this civilization was made possible by the cultivation of maize (corn). The origin appears to be the central valley of Mexico as early as 9,000 years ago. Corn became the primary dietary staple throughout Mesoamerica and then spread northward and southward.[4] Native Americans commonly planted maize, beans, and squash, which formed the basis of their diet.

Maize unified Native American cultures. Recent studies show that people traveled with the seed to various places in the Americas. Archaeologists discovered the remains of the largest human settlement in the American Southwest dating from 760 BC to 200 BC, which included evidence of maize farming. The completeness of the maize culture supports the theory that Mesoamerican farmers brought corn into the Southwest.[5] Corn spread a culture that extended along what today is U.S. Interstate Highway 10 into the eastern half of the United States, eventually becoming a staple throughout much of North America.[6] The symbolic significance of maize and its role can be found in ceremony and ritual throughout Mesoamerica and the Southwest. The presence of maize was also found in modern-day Peru as early as AD 450.[7]

The European invasion put the corn cultures in danger of extinction. This threat continues today in places like the remote mountains of Oaxaca, Mexico, where traces of genetically modified organisms (GMOs) are invading the native corn. Mexico, which banned the commercial planting of transgenic corn in 1998, imports about 6.2 million tons of corn a year, mostly from the United States. About a quarter of the U.S. commercial corn crop contains GMOs, and after harvest it is mixed with conventional corn. As a result, much of the Mexican corn is now considered to contain low levels of "background" GMOs. This concerns Mexicans since GMO foods and seed are an environmental threat to wild plants and species such as the monarch butterfly.[8]

The Olmeca 1500 BC–500 BC

Around 3000 BC, a qualitative change took place in the life of the corn people. The agriculture surpluses and concentration of population encouraged specialization of labor. Shamans became more important in society. Tools became more sophisticated and pottery more crafted. History shows the development of civilization occurring at about the same time as in North Africa and Asia, where the "cradle of civilization" is traditionally believed to have been located. Mesoamerican identity had already begun to form, marked by a dependence on maize agriculture and a growing population.[9]

Because the Olmeca civilization was so advanced, some people speculate that the Olmeca suddenly arrived from Africa—or even from outer space! Most scholars, however, agree that Olmeca, known as the mother culture of Mexico, was the product of the cross-fertilization of indigenous cultures that included other Mesoamerican civilizations.[10] The Olmeca "built the first kingdoms and established a template of world view and political symbolism the Maya would inherit."[11]

One of a few known primary civilizations in the world—that is, state-like organizations that evolved without ideas taken from other systems—the Olmeca culture is one of the world's first tropical lowland civilizations, an antecedent to later Mayan "Classic" culture. The Olmeca settled villages and cities in the Gulf Coast lowlands, mostly in present-day southeastern Veracruz and Tabasco, and in northern Central America.

Around 2000 BC, the production of maize and other domesticated crops became sufficient to support whole villages. A second breakthrough occurred with the introduction of pottery throughout the region. The earliest pottery came from the Oco, who populated the Pacific coast of Chiapas and Guatemala. Although not much is known about the Oco, their pottery is found from Veracruz to El Salvador and Honduras. The development of pottery allowed the storage of food surpluses, encouraging the Olmeca and other Mesoamerican people to form small villages. Little evidence of social ranking and craft specialization has been found in the early villages, which evolved from an egalitarian community into a hierarchical agrarian society of toolmakers, potters, and sculptors. As they evolved, the Olmeca became more patriarchal, and they probably excluded women from production outside the home.

The Olmeca began to build villages on the Gulf Coast as early as 1500 BC. By 1150 BC the Olmeca civilization formed settlements of thousands of people; constructed large formal temples built on earthen mounds; and carved colossal nine-foot-high stone heads. San Lorenzo was one such settlement, an urban center with public buildings, a drainage system, and a ball court.

La Venta (population 18,000), a major ceremonial site in Tabasco, eclipsed San Lorenzo (2,500) as the center of the Olmeca civilization in about 900 BC.[12] Tres Zapotes (3,000) would eventually overtake La Venta. By the Middle Formative period, other chiefdoms emerged throughout Mesoamerica. Trade networks linked the Olmeca with contemporaries in Oaxaca and Central Mexico. In the Valley of Oaxaca, San José Mogote functioned as a primary center, as did Chalcatzingo in the present-day state of Morelos. Priestly elite dominated the primary Olmeca settlements. As time marched on, the shaman class played an ever-increasing role in the lives of the people. From these centers, they ruled dispersed populations of farmers, who periodically assembled at the ceremonial and trade sites to meet labor obligations, attend ceremonies, and use the marketplace. The elite had greater access to valuable trade goods and occupied larger homes than the common people. The elite were even buried in larger tombs.

The Olmeca left behind archaeological evidence of their hieroglyphic script and the foundations for the complex Mayan and Zapotecan calendars. The Olmeca developed three calendars: a ritual calendar with a 260-day cycle that was used for religious purposes; a solar calendar with 18 months of 20 days, plus 5 days tacked on (corresponding to our 365-day calendar); and a combination of the two calendars in which religious days determined tasks such as the naming of a newborn infant. In any case, the Olmeca used a more accurate calendar before the time of Christ than the West uses today.[13]

The development of the calendar required a sophisticated knowledge of mathematics. There is considerable difference of opinion about whether the Olmeca or the Maya discovered the concept of the number *zero* circa 200 BC.[14] (The Hindus discovered the zero in the fifth century AD, and not until AD 1202 did Arab mathematicians export the concept to Europe.) Pre-Columbian astronomy, too, was far ahead of Europe's. The writing system of the Olmeca is still being deciphered. These hieroglyphic texts represent more than a history; they also constitute literature.[15] Other Olmeca legacies are the ball game and the feathered-serpent cult of Quetzalcoatl that they shared with most Mesoamerican cultures.

The growth of agricultural surpluses increased trade, which gave the Olmeca the luxury of developing advanced art forms. Although they are best known for the massive carved full-rounded heads, they also crafted smaller figurines of polished jade. Religion and the natural world inspired the subject matter for Olmeca art.

The Olmeca culture passed its organizational forms, religion, and art to the Maya, Teotihuacán, and later Azteca societies. About 300 BC, Olmeca civilization supposedly mysteriously vanished. In truth, it continued to exist from 150 BC to AD 450, in what some scholars call the Epi-Olmec period.[16]

The Maya

Mayan agricultural villages appeared about 1800 BC. The Maya formed a trade network that interacted with other chiefdoms in the Gulf Coast, Oaxaca, and Central Mexico. Merchants from Teotihuacán lived in Maya centers such as Tikal from at least the first century AD.[17] The Maya experimented with advanced forms of agriculture, dug irrigation canals, and reclaimed wetlands by constructing raised fields. As their population increased, they built larger ceremonial centers. At this point, as in the case of other Mesoamerican societies, rulers took control of religious rituals and the belief system.

From AD 250 to 900, the Maya lived in an area roughly half the size of Texas (today the Mexican states of Yucatán, Campeche, Quintana Roo, part of Chiapas, Tabasco, as well as Guatemala, Belize, western Honduras, and El Salvador). The divine *ahauob*, the "divine lord," ruled millions of farmers, craftsmen, merchants, warriors, and nobles and presided over capitals studded with pyramids, temples, palaces, and vast open plazas serviced by urban populations numbering in the tens of thousands.[18] Agriculture and trade produced prosperity and gave the Maya the ability to build temple-pyramids, monuments, and palaces of limestone masonry in dozens of states. They also used their astronomy skills to link earthly events to those of the heavens. Their calendars were a product of time science.[19]

In the ninth century AD, the Maya Classic culture began to decline, probably because of revolts, warfare, disease, and/or crop failure. Overpopulation explains the internal strife and dissatisfaction with their leadership and is a possible explanation for their decline. But the Maya left many examples of their accomplishments. In a limestone cavern in northern Guatemala, through narrow tunnels frequented 12 centuries ago, there are black carbon images of a sacred ball game, musicians, dwarfs contemplating shells, homosexual lovers locked in embrace, and columns of intricately entwined hieroglyphs.

The decipherment of the glyphs raises many questions. For example, little doubt exists about the presence of homosexuality; the question is how society formed attitudes toward homosexuality.[20] Research in this area is just beginning and, like past literature on the subject, it comes from highly biased sources. One of the most interesting accounts is by Richard Trexler, who argues that Spaniards would often feminize their enemies in warfare, calling them sodomites and pederasts. Trexler says that European notions form much of what we know about homosexuality. In the case of the invasion and subjugation of the Mesoamericans, the Spaniards' homophobia suggested to them their own moral supremacy. Sodomy "was seen as either a sign of insufficient civilization or a sign of moral decay."[21]

Maya Hieroglyphic Writing

The decipherment of hieroglyphic writing is leading to a greater understanding of the Maya culture, including the identification of dynasties of rulers and an understanding of how the various people interacted.[22] Direct evidence from bones of the ancient Maya suggests that the common people seldom lived beyond the age of 40—many died in infancy and early childhood. Men and women in the ruling class were physically larger than others—as much as four inches taller. Furthermore, evidence from bones and inscriptions shows that the ruling class sometimes lived remarkably long lives. One of the greatest rulers of the ancient city of Yaxchilán, Shield Jaguar, lived almost 100 years.

Maya glyphs suggest that a ball game, played throughout Mesoamerica, served as a means to communicate with the gods. It also enhanced social and economic organization and was a substitute for war.[23] Revered by both the Maya and the Azteca, the game possessed deep religious significance. The object of the game, which was played by small groups in an outdoor stone court, was to pass a large rubber ball through a stone ring at opposite ends of the court.[24]

The Maya based their numerical system on counting on the fingers and toes; for example, in Quiché, a branch of Maya culture, the word for the number 20 symbolized "a whole person." This method of counting is also reflected in the decimal divisions. The Maya used a system based on the number 20, with only three symbols: a bar for *five*, a dot for *one*, and a stylized shell for *zero*. As we have discussed above, the Maya, if not the Olmeca, were probably the first people to develop the mathematical concept for zero.[25]

Their knowledge of mathematics allowed the Maya to develop an advanced calendar. The astronomy of the Maya was not limited to observation of the stars and approximate predictions of the movements of the heavenly bodies. Using sophisticated numerical systems and various tabular calculations in conjunction with the hieroglyphic script, Maya astronomers calculated figures running into the millions.[26]

At the time of the Spanish conquest, the Maya still wrote glyphs—not only on stone slate but in handmade books. In 1566 in the Yucatán, Friar Diego de Landa read a great number of Maya books. According to him, because the books were about the indigenous antiquities and sciences, which he believed were based on nothing but superstitions and falsehoods of the devil, he burned them. However, not all of the Maya books were burned; some were sent to Europe as part of the booty seized by Cortés from the Native Americans. The Spaniards could not decipher them, and over the years, most crumbled into dust or were thrown out as trash.

Maya Society

Like other Mesoamerican societies, the Maya lived within the matrix of the community. They organized themselves into extended families in which there was a patrilineal descent. Multiple generations of a clan that had a common ancestor resided in one household compound. The inheritor of supreme authority was established through primogeniture, which resulted in the rule of clan elders. Kings also based their legitimacy on their membership in a clan. The kings erected monuments to commemorate their victories and to record their lineage.[27]

During the Late Classic period, Tikal, a kingdom of around 500,000 people, was the largest known Maya center. It covered about 14 square miles and included more than 3,000 structures. It made alliances with other city-states but also often used force to expand its territory.[28]

The glyphs on a prominent Tikal building reveal the names of notable women such as Bird Claw, Jaguar Seat, Twelve Macaw, and the Woman of Tikal.[29] These women, although buried in honored places, were present only through a relationship with an important male. The differences between males and females changed with time. Scholars suggest that there was more equality before AD 25 than after. As in most advanced civilizations, class differences existed and over time, one's position in society became hereditary. Therefore, a distinct divide between high-ranking members of Tikal society and the poor existed, and this widened over time.

The glyphs reveal few actual women rulers among the Maya. In Palenque during the sixth and seventh centuries, there were only two women rulers, Lady Kanal-Ikal and Lady Zac-Kuk. Both were the descendants of kings and thus legitimate rulers. They inherited the throne and passed it on to their children. Lady Zac-Kuk was the granddaughter of Lady Kanal-Ikal and was the mother of the Great Pacal, who built grand buildings as testimony to her greatness. Indeed, Pacal got his legitimacy through his mother's line of ancestry. She enjoyed great prestige because she lived for 25 years into his rule. Pacal died in his nineties.[30]

The Decline of Mayan Civilization

After AD 909 the Maya built few new temples, and even fewer cities, except in the northern Yucatán at sites such as Chichén Itzá and Tulum. Chichén Itzá was first founded about AD 400 and was governed by priests. The architecture reflects this religious dominance and there are many representations of the god Chaac, the Maya rain god, on the buildings. With the arrival of the Itzá from Central Mexico about AD 850, the city was rebuilt and images of the god Kukulcán, the plumed serpent, became numerous. The Itzá were politically and commercially aggressive rulers.[31] Chichén Itzá, the dominant Maya center in the Yucatán Peninsula during the early Postclassic period, was closely linked to the Tula people in the north, and was greatly influenced by that culture. The importance of the center declined after the late twelfth century, when a rival Maya group sacked it. Tulum and other coastal cities were important centers for sea-based commerce.[32]

Glyphs may someday answer many questions about the Maya, who built their civilization in a hostile and fragile rain forest. How did 6 million Maya coexist in this difficult environment? For a time, these civilizations met the challenge, and they developed a sophisticated knowledge of astronomy and mathematics that allowed them to increase production of food and other necessities. They constructed a mosaic of sunken gardens, fruit trees, and terraces—a system that used the rainfall, fertile soil, and shade of the jungle to their advantage without permanently harming it. Maya farmers dug canals and built raised fields in the swamps for intensive agriculture.[33] Until recently, archaeologists assumed the Maya used a slash-and-burn method in which farmers cut and burned the jungle-planted crops for a few years and then moved on when nutrients were depleted.[34] A true slash-and-burn method would have supported only about 65 people per square mile. However, the Maya population density had already reached about 125 people per square mile by AD 600.

We can speculate that engineering projects like canals, reservoirs, and the terraced fields came about at the cost of human labor. After hundreds of years of relative prosperity and power, the urban infrastructure of many Maya cities broke down. The drop in the food supply increased between the lower and the elite classes and between city-states. Today, Mesoamerican scholars generally agree that no single factor caused this fall. But, by the Late Classic period, populations suffered from malnutrition and other chronic diseases. The environment simply could not support the large population indefinitely.[35]

Surely, class oppression and war played a role in the decline. The common person labored in the fields, maintaining a complex agricultural network, while priests resided in empty ceremonial centers. The nobles plainly oppressed the commoner—the warrior, temple builder, and farmer. The Maya organized construction crews of *corvee*, or unpaid labor, and the growth of this system magnified class hostilities over time. In addition, evidence shows a sharp decrease in rainfall between the years AD 800 and 1000—one of the most severe climate changes in 10,000 years—at roughly the time of the Maya decline in the ninth century. The drought caused tensions: the result was that cities, villages, and fields were burned and wars increased.[36]

Although the cities of the Maya lowlands shared a common culture, they were not politically unified. Each region had a capital city and numerous smaller subject cities, towns, and villages. Furthermore, increased trade and competition led to warfare. The Maya civilization, however, endured for more than 1,000 years during what is known as the "golden age of Mesoamerica." In the Postclassical period, the Maya experienced a gradual breakdown of their social structures, marked by a decline of the priest class and the growing political and cultural influences of a rising merchant class.[37]

Until recently, scholars described the Maya society as peaceful. Decoded glyphs, however, suggest another view of the Maya, revealing the practice of human sacrifice and bloodletting.[38] The Maya believed that the gods controlled the natural elements, and that the gods demanded bloodletting. Human sacrifice was mostly limited to prisoners, slaves, and orphaned or illegitimate children purchased for the occasion. Generally, it was more common to sacrifice animals. This bloodletting and human sacrifice placated the gods and assured the Maya that their crops would grow and their children would be born healthy. As drought and the resulting drop in the food supply took its toll, there was a corresponding increase in both human sacrifice to appease the gods and warfare. (An analogy can be made between human sacrifice and war.)

Teotihuacán

Teotihuacán, the "city of the gods," located in the Valley of Teotihuacán in a pocket-like extension of the Valley of Mexico, became the primary center of Mesoamerican civilization around 200 BC. Like the other city-states, by the end of the Formative Preclassic period, it concentrated sufficient authority and technology to make a quantitative and qualitative leap from a loose collection of settlements to a unified empire.[39] The civic–religious complex laid the foundation for this development. At its height, at the end of the sixth century AD, Teotihuacán covered about eight square miles. It may have housed more than 150,000 inhabitants, making it the largest city in the world outside China.[40]

In the Early Classic period, the people of Teotihuacán lived in apartment compounds, with some larger than others. There were more than 2,000 separate residential structures within the city. Built by the rural peasants, the outlying villages were linked to the core city by commerce. As with peasants of other societies, these workers contributed labor, food, and other products for urban elites and state institutions. A strong central government gave administrators control over peasants in the city and countryside; they often treated the peasants like subjects. The ruling elite forcibly moved the rural peasants into the city during the Early Classic period, leaving some scattered villages. Teotihuacanos, aided by a highly centralized state, conquered an empire that covered most of the central Mexican highlands.

Urbanism and Trade

Teotihuacán was a major manufacturing center in the Early Classic period. The products of its craft workers spread over much of Mesoamerica, as far south as Honduras. The pottery, especially, represents Teotihuacán's highest achievement as a city and empire. Its hallmark feature is the cylindrical vessel with three slab legs and a cover. Vessels shaped like modern flower vases and cream pitchers graced the city. Artifacts from other civilizations were also present, adding to the city's splendor. So fabled was Teotihuacán that Azteca royalty annually made pilgrimages to the city.[41]

Teotihuacán civilization was contemporary with the Maya Classic period and acted as the hub of trade networks from Central America to today's southwestern United States. Without trade, the Maya culture would have remained at the chiefdom stage instead of evolving into a sophisticated world system that stressed material production and common ideas. It grew to a population of 100,000–200,000.

Teotihuacán suffered from internal civil strife in the seventh century, and again at the beginning of the tenth century. In about AD 600–650, unknown invaders burned the civic ceremonial center of the city, marking a turning point in its history. From Teotihuacán emanated a network of societies such as in the city of Xochicalco, later associated with the Tolteca people. It also remained a center of long-distance trade, continuing its history of robust mercantile contact with other regions.[42] Even after its decline, Teotihuacán continued to be a great city of 30,000 inhabitants until about AD 950. However, without its authority, Mesoamerican societies were less centralized, breaking up into dozens of city-states, which competed for trade and influence.

The Tolteca

The Postclassic period is characterized by a secularization of Mesoamerica. Although religion remained important to the Mesoamerican peoples, the civil and commercial sectors of society became more important, and their rise led to the expansion of market systems and long-distance exchange. The Tolteca emerged in what is today central Mexico in about the tenth century AD.

The Tolteca were a dominant force during this period (from about AD 900 to 1150). A subgroup of the Chichimeca, a Nahua-speaking people from the northern desert, the Tolteca controlled the Valley of Mexico.[43] Their capital was Tula (Tollan), about 40 miles north of present-day Mexico City. Founded in the ninth century, Tula incorporated part of the heritage of Teotihuacán, although it is generally associated with Tolteca culture. After Teotihuacán's fall in AD 700, Tolteca refugees migrated there from northern Teotihuacán and adopted many of its cultural features. Topiltzin Ce Acatl Quetzalcoatl (Our Prince One-Reed Feathered Serpent) ruled Tula from AD 923 to 947. Ce Acatl is often confused with the Azteca deity Quetzalcoatl, the feathered serpent who for 1,000 years was part of Mesoamerican mythology.

The Tolteca developed a system of cosmology, practiced religious rites, including human sacrifice, and built grand temples to their gods. In the courtyards of Tula, supporting the roof of the great Temple of Quetzalcóatl, stood 15-foot columns in the form of stylized human figures, specifically, enormous statues of warriors standing stiffly under the weight of their weapons and wearing rigid crowns of eagle feathers. Processions or military marches, and eagles and jaguars devouring human hearts are portrayed. The Plumed Serpent, formerly interpreted in Teotihuacán as the benevolent divinity of agricultural plenty, in Tula became a god of the Morning Star, the archer-god with fearsome arrows.

Little evidence exists that the Tolteca built an empire. Tula, for instance, was not at the crossroads of the international trade networks of the time. In the mid-1100s, the Tolteca collapsed, perhaps under attack by nomadic tribes, and Tula was abandoned. By that time the Tolteca had extended their sphere of influence into what is now Central America. This culture was transposed to Yucatán, where it was superimposed on Maya tradition, evolving and becoming more flexible and elegant. A hybrid art form of dazzling brilliance developed and lasted for two centuries. The Tolteca influence can be seen in a cross-cultural fusion of deities depicted in Mayan glyphs, frescos, and designs.

Tula was the axis of the Tolteca civilization. It controlled most of central Mexico, the Yucatán Peninsula, and the Gulf Coast, and it is speculated that its interests extended to Chiapas and the Pacific coast. The Tolteca also expanded trade with people as far away as Zacatecas, Veracruz, and Puebla; New Mexico and Arizona; and Costa Rica and Guatemala. They assimilated with many of the peoples that they cultivated ties with. An example is the important Mayan ceremonial center of Chichén-Itzá. By the end of the ninth and the beginning of the tenth century, the Mayan culture was in decline. The Itzá stepped into the void and began to substitute their gods and architectural styles. The Toltecas added the Observatory, Kukulcán's Pyramid, the Temple of the Warriors, the Ball Court, and the Group of the Thousand Columns. Judging by the architecture and artifacts, there was considerable cross-fertilization between the two cultural areas.[44]

Other Corn Civilizations

The Zapoteca were the original occupants of the Valley of Oaxaca. About 4,000 years ago, Oaxaca's people settled in agricultural villages. Interaction with common ancestors played an important role in integrating autonomous villages. Between 500 BC and 100 BC, a highly centralized, urbanized state emerged with Monte Albán as its principal center.[45] Great plazas, pyramids, a ball court, and underground passageways graced the city. Some evidence exists that the Zapoteca and the Olmeca engaged in long-distance trading that dates to the time of San Lorenzo, and that the Zapoteca later enjoyed good relations with the city of Teotihuacán.

As with the Maya, Zapoteca society was religious; it held that a supreme being created everything, although not by himself, and there was no beginning and no end of the universe. Like other Mesoamerican societies, the Zapoteca wrote in hieroglyphics and were obsessed with astronomical observation. Their 365- and 260-day calendars set a rhythm for their lives, with the latter serving as a religious guide and marking the birthdays of its adherents.

After AD 650, Monte Albán began to decline as other strong city-states emerged in the valley. Mitla, in the eastern part of the Oaxacan valley, took on greater importance.[46] Mitla is the best-known Postclassic site, continuously occupied since the Early Formative period, and is thought to have been a Zapoteca religious center. Despite the growth of other societies, the Zapoteca remained a major player in the region.

Meanwhile, in the highlands, the Mixteca increased their influence, and by the eleventh century they interacted with the Zapoteca-speaking people of the valley. There was a high degree of assimilation and intermarriage between the Mixteca and the Zapoteca nobility. The Mixteca, like the Azteca, are known to have engaged in a highly ritualized form of warfare and they were known for military prowess. Despite their influence, the Mixteca, like the Zapoteca before them, were not a dominant imperial power. They established the kingdom of Tututepec on the coast, which was important enough to garner tribute from other kingdoms. The Mixteca expanded their power by establishing strong bonds with other city-states through extensive intermarriage and war.[47]

The Mixteca developed their own art style, influenced by the Zapoteca, and the two cultures created a synthesis. The creations of their goldsmiths and their manuscript illuminations are exceptional. Mixteca manuscripts or codices constitute an illustrated encyclopedia, reflecting religious beliefs and rites and the history of the aboriginal dynasties and national heroes. The style and color range of the illustrations, as well as the symbols linked to the ritual calendar, are also found in their murals.[48] The history depicted in the codices is a holy history, showing an abundance of deities and rituals. The Mixteca also excelled in ceramics, which became the most highly prized ware in fourteenth- and fifteenth-century Mexico.

The Tarasco

By the twelfth century, the Tarasco people, also known as the Purépecha, ruled a vast territory in west Mexico, centered in present-day Michoacán. Their exact origin is unknown. Most probably, they were part of the Chichimeca migration. The Chichimeca were supposedly uncivilized natives from the north that the Tolteca were once part of. Nomadic groups along the northern frontier of civilization migrated to what is today central Mexico. The Azteca were part of the later wave of Chichimeca. They, along with the Tarascans, formed the Nahuas. The Tarascan civilization was originally formed through political unification of some eight city-states located within the Párzcuaro basin. The Tarasco occupied the region for more than 1,600 years (150 BC–AD 1530). Their development resembled that of other Mesoamerican cultures. Ceramic artifacts link the Tarasco to the old traditions of Chupicuaro (present-day Guanajuato). Their pottery and metalwork styles are unique, although they borrowed heavily from surrounding societies. This borrowing was common. For example, ceramics found in the present-day northern Mexican states of Zacatecas and Durango bear resemblance to the Hohokam ceramic found in what is today Arizona.

The capital city of the Tarasco was Tzintzuntzán, built on the shores of Lake Pátzuaro and dominated by a huge platform that supported five round temples. The Tarasco raised a well-trained army and from Tzintzuntzán forged an empire. However, Tarasco military prowess did not tell the whole story. Their language and culture almost totally dominated the region, with many of the surrounding villages assimilating into it. They were excellent craftspeople, and they invaded other peoples for honey, cotton, feathers, copal, and deposits of salt, gold, and copper. Tarasco lords were placed in conquered lands and collected tributes in goods.

Unlike other Mesoamericans, the Tarasco were not well-known traders. Nevertheless, it is speculated that they did engage in some long-distance trading, even by sea, reaching South America. Tarasco society was socially stratified, with nobility, commoners, and slaves. The capital city dominated the area, although most people lived in rural settlements.

The Tarasco had many deities who, among other things, were associated with animals and calendrical days. Ceremonial dances affirmed their connection with ancestral gods. Enemies of the Aztecs, the Tarascans flourished from AD 1100 to 1530. The Azteca attempted to conquer the Tarasco but failed. In AD 1478, 24,000 Azteca retreated in the face of a Tarasco army of 40,000 warriors. But because the Tarasco did not leave a written language, scholars know relatively little about them.

The Azteca

Between AD 1325 and 1345, the Azteca founded their capital of Tenochtitlán on an island in Lake Texcoco (later drained to build Mexico City). The Azteca confederation of city-states reached a population of more than 350,000. Part of the Chichimeca[49] arrived from the north, they were from a legendary place today called Aztlán.[50] (Some Chicanos say that it was in what is today the southwestern United States; others, in northern Mexico, in the area of Zacatecas.) A network of trade routes linked the high plateau of central Mexico with Maya territories, reaching as far as the most remote northern districts of the empire, in what is now the southwestern United States.[51]

The Azteca farm surpluses underwrote a highly advanced craft-manufacturing economy. The Azteca excelled in the building arts and supplied food for large cities. The growth of market systems gave the Azteca more opportunities to exchange their goods as well as access to other people. The society was stratified, with the elites extracting tribute and the commoners paying it. The peasants seem to have fared better under the Azteca than in Teotihuacán. They lived in small adobe houses with stone roofs and had more access to material goods.

The Azteca benefited from their highly productive agricultural infrastructure. They farmed on raised fields, or *chinampas*, fashioned by piling earth over the natural growing surface, as a way of reclaiming swampland for cultivation.[52] They stacked flat mounds of fertile river sediment and then deepened the ditches or canals around them to create a waffle-like pattern. The advantage of raised fields was that they could be cultivated year-round, even during the dry season, because swamp water percolated up into the nutrient-rich soil. Five hundred acres of fields could have fed up to 5,200 people.[53]

The Azteca assimilated the cultural experiences of generations of native peoples. For example, Mixteca art played an important role in Azteca artistic skill development. Azteca sculpture displayed technical perfection and powerful symbolism. The Azteca knew and appreciated the masterpieces of the civilizations that preceded them and those of contemporaries such as in Monte Albán. They had a well-defined literature, some of which has been preserved through oral testimony. Much of this tradition was conserved in codices, which consist of a combination of pictographs and ideographs. Religious and cosmological themes dominate the manuscripts.

They also had two kinds of schools—one for commoners, the other for nobility. In both, boys and girls were taught rhetoric, history, ritual dancing, and singing; in the Calmecac School for future leaders, the curriculum included law, architecture, arithmetic, astronomy, and agriculture. The poets were frequently kings or military captains from satellite principalities.[54]

Although a lot is known about the work performed by women, relatively little is known about cultural attitudes toward them. Some scholars assume that Azteca society was rigidly patriarchal, and it became increasingly so with the militarization of society. Another viewpoint is that the "prehispanic Azteca gender system appears to have combined gender parallelism (where men and women played different but parallel and equivalent roles) with gender hierarchy. Gender parallelism was rooted in the kinship structures and in religious and secular ideology. Men and women were genealogically and structurally equivalent."[55]

The lower classes, as in most societies, bore the burden of class oppression. Lower-class women did embroidering, which they often sold in the *mercado* (marketplace). Generally, a woman's caste determined her occupation, and she was schooled to play that role. Women could enter the priesthood, and although there were female goddesses, women could not become the musicians or poets who honored goddesses in public. Furthermore, they could not engage in violent activities or participate directly in mercantile caravans. Women had few options, and circumstances often forced them into prostitution. The woman who worked outside the sphere of male control was suspect. According to Irene Silverblatt, "class and social standing critically shaped the social experiences of Mexica men and women."[56]

Anthropologist June Nash's "The Aztecs and the Ideology of Male Dominance"[57] describes the transformation of the Azteca society from a kinship-based society to a class-structured empire, claiming that there was a diminution of the power of women beginning in AD 830 and continuing to the fifteenth century. Despite this, women enjoyed equal rights under the law and could participate in the economy. According to Nash, women were active producers as well as vendors. They could hold property—but whether they did and how much depended on social class.

The Azteca were the beneficiary of Tolteca culture, and many Azteca males took Tolteca wives, which quickened the assimilation process. According to Nash, polygamy "weakened the role of women in royal families since their sons were not guaranteed succession as in the past." "[The] division of labor by sex had been well established by the late fifteenth century. The codices show men teaching boys to fish, cultivate, and work metal and women teaching girls to weave, tend babies, and cook." According to Nash, sacrificial ceremonies glorified the cult of male dominance.[58]

While Azteca society may have ignored forms of male homosexuality, lesbians were disdained as lower than prostitutes. Contradictorily, there were male transvestite performers, who are said to have been bisexual, and they enjoyed access to male privileges.[59] In short, Azteca culture appears to have been highly puritanical, militaristic, and male-centered. Among men, power came with age, which brought privileges.

As with other Mesoamerican civilizations, human sacrifice and war were interwoven into Azteca religious practice. The Azteca justification for human sacrifice was a cosmic view that encompassed the demands of their god Huitzilopochtli, lord of the sun and god of war. The Azteca placed their faith in their priests, who revealed that the sun and the earth had been destroyed four times; the present era was known as *el quinto sol*, "the fifth sun," the final destruction of which was imminent. Only special intervention through Huitzilopochtli would save them.[60]

The religious system legitimized the authority and the tributary rights of its leaders. Blood sacrifice was necessary to preserve the sun, and the whole structure of the universe, from the threat of cosmic destruction. The logic was that the sacrifices appeased the Sun: it was based on the cyclical belief that the sun provided food and the sacrifices fed the sun. The need for sacrifices was made even more imperative after the drought of 1450 ravaged central Mexico. The Azteca and others believed that too few victims having been offered to the gods caused the calamities of 1450. The Azteca rationalized war, which was the result of politics and trade, in much the same way as the Christians, Jews, and Muslims rationalized their holy wars.

Every aspect of Azteca life, from the birth of a young warrior to a woman's continuous sweeping of dust from the house, symbolized the intricacy of war as well as their advanced society. Azteca society was well-ordered and highly moralistic, treating commoners with "consideration, compassion, and mercy,"[61] while also demanding from them moral conformity. Medical treatment was on a par with Europe's, and life was less harsh than it was in Europe at the time of the arrival of the Spaniards.

Los Norteños

Mesoamerican culture spread beyond what is considered its traditional boundaries; defining these boundaries is arbitrary. Its influence spread from what is today Central America in the south to what are today northern Mexico and the U.S. Southwest.[62] Corn is bound to the rise of Mesoamerica and sustained the northern people. Mexico's north had varied societies, most of which lacked sufficient water to sustain large populations. Nevertheless, the Southwest outside of Mesoamerica and northern Mexico has the longest continuous history of habitation. The indigenous populations of the Southwest shared an agricultural tradition revolving around corn and the use of ceramics. Unlike Mesoamerica, most of the Southwest is believed to have lacked state-level societies and urban centers.

People arrived in what is now the Southwest between 23,000 BC and 10,000 BC.[63] About 4,000 years ago, corn was brought to the region by Mesoamericans. Similar to what is present-day northern Mexico, many formed homes in villages or *rancherías* or remained hunters. Agriculture transformed the lives of the people and by 500 BC corn, squash, and beans were grown and pottery was crafted. The cultivation of corn is estimated to have occurred from 1100 BC to 500 BC.[64] This led to complex social and economic systems among the northern peoples, namely the Hohokam, the Mogollon, and the Anasazi. *Ranchería* populations comprised of Opata and Pima Altos lived in northern Sonora. Band tribes such as the Apache also struggled in proximity to these populations.

Carlos Vélez-Ibañez writes, "A triad of complex agriculturally based societies that included the Hohokam of Southern Arizona and Sonora, perhaps the Mogollon of Casas Grandes, Chihuahua, Mexico, and to a lesser extent the Anasazi of Chaco Canyon and Mesa Verde who inhabited the Four Corners area of New Mexico, Arizona, Utah, and Colorado, lived in the region." One of the most successful civilizations was the Hohokam beginning with their transformation about 300 BC, although, as with the Mesoamerican civilizations, the process began hundreds of years before this date. According to anthropologist Vélez-Ibáñez, the Hohokam were probably migrants from Mesoamerica.[65] For nearly 1,700 years, they flourished along the Desert Rivers before vanishing in the fifteenth century AD.

During the Formative period, the Hohokam lived mainly in flask-shaped huts set in shallow pits, plastered with mud over a framework of poles and woven twigs. Early villages were loose clusters of houses separated by stretches of packed clay.[66] After about AD 1000 Hohokam villages took on a more urban aspect. Each contained several "great houses," typically three or four stories high, and numerous smaller dwellings similar to the early pit houses. One city stretched for a mile and included at least 25 compounds of buildings. A vast irrigation network consisting of more than a thousand miles of canals crisscrossed an area of some 10,000 square miles.[67]

Archaeologists estimate that at least 100,000 and possibly a million people lived in these ancient cities. They subsisted on the barren desert, making the desert productive through irrigation and by breeding a variety of drought-tolerant corn that would grow from planting to harvest on a single watering. In addition, they cultivated squash, beans, tobacco, and cotton. Acid-etched shells suggest that the Hohokam traded with tribes a thousand miles to the east.

By 1450, Hohokam civilization vanished. Legend has it that raiders from the east swept down on the Hohokam, destroying homes and fields. The invaders killed or enslaved the inhabitants of the great cities. Some Hohokam escaped, but upon returning they never rebuilt the cities or canals. Some archaeological authorities believe the demise of the Hohokam came after a gradual transition. They theorized that the Hohokam never left, but abandoned most of their villages in the Salt and Gila River valleys, around AD 1450. The theory is that Hohokam society collapsed because of internal conflicts brought about by environmental pressures and they taxed the land's capacity to feed the people. The floods during the late fourteenth century most probably damaged the Hohokam canal systems. These disasters weakened the control and authority of the secular or theocratic elite. This did not happen overnight but was a process that lasted several generations. Another theory is that the Salado, a mixture of Anasazi and Mogollon cultures, simply migrated in and took over, blending with the Hohokam and diffusing them out of existence. Further evidence suggests that the long-term effects of irrigation contributed to the Hohokam demise. River water carries dissolved minerals. As this water evaporates from irrigated fields, it leaves behind mineral residues—usually alkali salts that gradually make the soil unfit for plants.

The Anasazi (meaning "ancient ones" in the Navajo language), who neighbored the Hohokam, settled in the Four Corners region in about AD 100–1300. Ancestors of Pueblo Indians now living in New Mexico and Arizona, the Anasazi farmed and produced fine baskets, pottery, cloth, ornaments, and tools. Villages evolved in caves that consisted of an array of semi-subterranean houses. Houses in the open also consisted of chambers below and above ground. Pit houses, known as *kivas*, served ceremonial purposes; these were community structures with up to a thousand rooms. Multistoried pueblos like Chaco Canyon and cliff dwellings like Betakin and Mesa Verde are examples. The Anasazi abandoned the cliff houses in the late thirteenth century, possibly because of a severe drought between AD 1276 and 1299, and because of pressure from the Navajo and the Apaches. The Anasazi were the ancestors of today's Hopis, Zunis, and Rio Grande Pueblo peoples.[68]

The Mogollon lived in the southeastern mountains of Arizona and southwestern New Mexico between 200 BC and AD 1200. In all probability, the Mogollon made the first pottery in the Southwest. They depended on rain and stream diversions for their farming, a technique that influenced the Anasazi or Pueblan culture. From about AD 700 on, the Mogollon in New Mexico were greatly influenced by the neighboring Anasazi.

According to Vélez-Ibáñez, Casas Grandes in Chihuahua was a Mogollon city.[69] Also called Paquime, it was a major trading and manufacturing center on the northern frontier within the Mesoamerican world system, from which Mesoamerican culture was dispersed. A link is made between Casas Grandes and the Mimbres culture of southwestern New Mexico, a branch of the Mogollon peoples, who produced painted pottery between AD 800 and 1150 similar to that found in the Casas Grandes area. Other scholars call Paquime an outpost for Mesoamerican traders controlling trade between the Southwest and Mesoamerica, while still others link it with the Anasazi.

Present-day Casas Grandes is set within a vast network of ancient ruins that was once the heart of one of the Southwest's largest trading centers. The area is still being excavated, and much remains unknown about this center. Small villages surrounded the city of Paquime, which evolved into a sophisticated center with an irrigation system that included dams, reservoirs, and *trincheras* (stone ditches). It had warehouses, ball courts, ceremonial structures, plazas, and steam rooms. By the late thirteenth or early fourteenth century, the area began to stagnate. Climatic change, environmental degradation, sociopolitical conflict, and shifting trade patterns all took their toll on the Mogollon people.[70]

By this point in the chapter, hundreds of tribes with different cultures and linguistic dialects in northern Mexico and the Southwest have been omitted because of the lack of space. For example, Texas natives lived in camps perhaps as early as 37,000 years ago.[71] They went through the evolutionary cycle as with other Indian tribes, at first surviving primarily on wild game and then turning to agriculture. In fertile East Texas, the tribes built permanent villages and had well-developed farms and political and religious systems. These tribes formed a loose federation, known as the Caddo confederacies, to preserve the peace and provide mutual protection. This ancient culture originally occupied the Red River area in what is now Louisiana and Arkansas. Semi-sedentary agricultural people, these tribes grouped around ceremonial mounds that resembled temples. Some scholars speculate that these skillful potters and basket makers were linked to the Mesoamerican cultures of the South.[72]

Thousands of miles to the west, present-day Alta California had one of the largest concentrations of native peoples by the latter part of the eighteenth century, in the range of 300,000 to 500,000 indigenous folk. Dozens of tribes adapted to its varied climate and topography. Mostly California had a mild climate and an abundance of food. Like Hawaii, it had an abundance of game, wild fruits and plants, and fish, and most tribes did not have to farm. They supplemented these by trade with the native people to the east and among themselves. Their habitation of central California began between 12,000 and 10,000 BC, and their evolutionary cycles resembled those of other native peoples. They left their artifacts, traditions, and their descendants.

Edward H. Spicer's book *Cycles of Conquest* is one of the most important studies of the native peoples in northern Mexico who at one point were part of the Mesoamerican sphere of influence.[73] The Pima, Opata, and the Tohono O'odham did not have a border marking Mexico and the Southwest. They used the resources of the land to their fullest, building *rancherías* and in some cases small villages. Notable among the tribes were the Cáhita, who spanned northern Sinaloa to central Sonora. Among the Cáhita were the Yaquí: they had a strong sense of identity with the Yaquí River, one of the great waterways of North America.[74] Unlike other people of the desert, they had use of a fast-flowing river that allowed them to form villages of up to 3,000 villagers. Their lives differed from the Tarahumara (Raramuri) and the Conchos, who lived on the eastern slopes and to the east of the Sierra Madre. Although these tribes numbered in the tens of thousands, they traveled in bands of 30 or fewer people, farming, hunting, and gathering to survive. When the sun got blistering hot, they migrated to the headwaters of the sierras to farm; in the harsh winters they migrated to lower altitudes to hunt and gather.

The indigenous people to the north did not build great cities, but like other peoples, they were bound together by corn and they traded intensely. They endured frequent droughts, often warred with each other, and they endured.

Conclusion: The World System in 1519

Mesoamerica was an interconnected world that was integrated and in which events taking place in one social unit affected those in another over an extended region. It was composed of large towns and their dependent rural communities. The rural communities consisted mostly of patrilineal kinship groups; the nobles and other elites lived in the large centers, exercising authority over the commoners. The forms of government varied from chiefdoms to fully developed states. In the Valley of Mexico, there were about 50 city-states with rulers or joint rulers appointed by the "royal" lineage as the supreme authority. They called the supreme ruler a *tlatoani*, "he who speaks," or in the case of joint rulers, *tlatoque*. In the highlands of Guatemala, the Maya called the ruler *ajpop*, "he of the mat." The Azteca Empire was a loose coalition of subject city-states that paid tribute to an imperial center.

Scholars are split on whether or not the Azteca attempted to impose their culture on their subject peoples. One thing is certain: There was considerable ethnic diversity among the people of Mesoamerica. The dominant cultures influenced some, while others remained segregated as distinct cultures. Mesoamerica, although influenced by the dominant world systems of the Maya, Tolteca, and other cultures, was not under the political control of a single power.

The Core Zones

Mesoamerica, meaning "Middle America,"—located between North and South America—was divided into multiple core zones, of which Central Mexico was the most prominent. The exchanges between the core, periphery, and semi-periphery were important in determining the flow of luxury goods—cotton garments, jade, cacao beans, hides, feathers, and gold ornaments. The core—through conquest, tributary demands, or trade activities—often obtained the goods that in great part were a product of its demands.[75]

We have identified the core zones as Central Mexico, West Mexico, Oaxaca, and the Maya zone. Tenochtitlán was the capital of the Central Mexico zone, inhabited by some 200,000 persons. The Azteca Empire ruled over approximately 300 city-states and over another 100 or so client states throughout the Central Mexico core zone. The Azteca appointed administrators to oversee the states and in other instances cemented alliances through marriage between Azteca and other elites. Considerable cultural and linguistic diversity existed within this core.

The Tarasco held sway over the West Mexico core zone. The Tarasco zone, more centralized and militaristic than the Azteca, held a tighter grip over its city-states. But the Tarasco did not have the same impact that the Azteca did on Mesoamerica.

The Oaxaca core zone was less integrated than the previous two zones. This zone consisted of 50 small kingdoms in which the dominant languages were Zapoteca and Mixteca. However, as in the other zones, multiple languages coexisted with the dominant languages. At the time of the Spanish invasion, the Mixteca states enjoyed considerable unity, forged by intermarriage between the ruling families. Trade took place within and outside the core. Intermarriage also occurred between the Mixteca and Azteca, who had significant cultural exchange.

The Maya core zone structurally resembled that of Central Mexico. Maya language and culture dominated the zone, although there was little unity between the highland and the lowland core states. Moreover, Maya had multiple dialects and non-Maya speakers also lived within the zone. The city-states competed with one another and some, like Quiché, incorporated approximately 30 tribute-paying provinces. The smaller zones within the main core zone were densely populated, and trade and warfare existed between them. Tensions also existed between many Maya and the Azteca cores.

The Semi-Peripheral Zones

The semi-peripheral zones, regions that mediated between the core and the periphery, were important to the exchange network, especially when dealing among competing core states. They assimilated much of the trade and the religion of the core and the periphery. Casas Grandes, in what is now the state of Chihuahua, was one such semi-peripheral region (although it did not exist at the time the Spaniards arrived). The Mexican state of Tabasco on the Gulf Coast was also an important semi-peripheral zone. Many of these regions were port-of-trade societies, and centers such as Xicalanco were quite cosmopolitan. They organized the governing classes, comprised of merchants, into political councils, in which women could reach high positions of authority. The south Pacific coast region is less well known. The Azteca and Quiché Maya vied for control of the Xoconusco area, which ultimately became a tributary province of the Azteca. The Caribbean coast, including the Yucatán Peninsula and the Central American isthmus, was another important semi-peripheral zone. Among the most important of these semi-peripheral centers was the island of Cozumel, which was run by merchants who invested in massive temples, shrines, and palaces. These port towns bordered the Caribbean all the way to Panama.

The Mesoamerican Periphery

The zones of the Mesoamerican periphery actively participated in the economic, political, and cultural life of the Mesoamerican world. However, the people in the periphery played a subordinate role. They were unequal, and often subject provinces. The periphery should not be confused with frontier zones, from which the Azteca originally came. The periphery extended to Mexico's northwest, from Colima to Culiacán and well into Sonora. In the northeastern part of what is now Mexico, the Huaxteca played a peripheral role. Its people had no writing system, and tension existed between them and the Azteca. Southeastern Central America was also a peripheral zone, occupied mainly by people speaking Pipil, which is closely related to Nahuatl. The Lenca language was also spoken in this peripheral zone. This peripheral zone was especially rich with diverse peoples, who interacted with the Maya and were organized into simple city-states or chiefdoms.

It is important to reiterate that contact also existed with what is now the U.S. Southwest. This contact varied, but was most intense with the descendants of the Hohokam and other sedentary populations. Distance played a role in how much influence the core had. Frontier people such as the Azteca were eventually integrated into the core. The main point is that the diverse peoples of Mesoamerica were unified under a vast, well-defined world system, in many ways more distinct than the European world system.

Although there has to be more research, it is highly probable that a trade structure existed that integrated the disparate regions. Exotic commodities from Mesoamerica have been found, and it is probable that they were circulated through local native trade networks.[76] Turquoise was an important trade item, and long-distance trade between the Zuni and Sonora existed. There was also a high use of turquoise in Mesoamerica. Trade contributed to the evolution of the division of labor; it led to the evolution of state systems in Mexico proper, and it was a mechanism of economic integration. The population of what is today Mexico and Central American had reached 25–38 million by the arrival of the Spanish and because of the population explosion in what is the Mesoamerican region, it is probable that contact with the Spanish would have increased the quest for water.

Notes

1. Scholars have presumed that agriculture is essential for the development of village life and the evolution of civilizations. The following article describes the building of a massive worship center 11,000 years ago, centuries before intensive farming. This discovery upends the conventional theory that agriculture was necessary before labor could be organized in this fashion. Andrew Curry, "Gobekli Tepe: The World's First Temple?" *Smithsonian*, November 2008, http://www.smithsonianmag.com/history-archaeology/gobekli-tepe.html.

2. "The First Americans," *The Economist* (February 21, 1998): 79. See also Virginia Morell, "Genes May Link Ancient Eurasians, Native Americans," *Science* 280, no. 5363 (April 24, 1998): 520. Ruben Bareiro Saguier, "The Indian Languages of Latin America," *UNESCO Courier* (July 1983): 12. "First Americans Arrived as Two Separate Migrations, According to New Genetic Evidence," *Science Daily*, January 21, 2009, http://www.sciencedaily.com/releases/2009/01/090108121618.htm. Some experts say that humans were in the Americas at least 40,000 years ago. See Patricia McBroom, "Incredible Journeys of Our Native Tongues," *Berkleyan* (March 11, 1998), http://

www.berkeley.edu/news/berkeleyan/1998/0311/linguistics.html, "Bering Strait Theory," http://www.native-languages.org/bering.htm.

3. Robert J. Sharer, *The Ancient Mayan*, 6th ed. (Stanford, CA: Stanford University Press, 1994), 4.

4. Louis Grivetti, Jan Corlett, and Cassius Lockett, "Food in American History, Part 1: Maize: Bountiful Gifts: America on the Eve of European Colonization (Antiquity to 1565)," *Nutrition Today*, 36, no. 1 (January 2001): 20. Temma Ehrenfeld, "Prehistoric Farming (Origin of Maize)," *Newsweek International* (November 24, 2003): 59.

5. Mark Muro, "New Finds Explode Old Views of the American Southwest (Findings of a Primitive Culture)," *Science* 279, no. 5351 (January 30, 1998): 653–54. J. Brett Hill, Jeffery J. Clark, William H. Doelle, and Patrick D. Lyons, "Prehistoric Demography in the Southwest: Migration, Coalescence, and Hohokam Population Decline," *American Antiquity* 69, no. 4 (October 2004): 689–707. Paul Mirocha, "Corn's Journey to North America," Corn's Journey, http://paulmirocha.com/projects/corns-journey/.

6. Kristen J. Gremillion, "Corn and Culture in the Prehistoric New World," *American Antiquity* 60, no. 3 (July 1995): 553–54. Michael W. Diehl, "The Intensity of Maize Processing and Production in Upland Mogollon Pithouse Villages A.D. 200–1000," *American Antiquity* 61, no. 1 (January 1996): 102–15.

7. Sissel Johannessen and Christine A. Hastorf, "Corn and Culture in Central Andean Prehistory," *Science* 244, no. 4905 (May 12, 1989): 690–92. "Ancient Popcorn Discovered in Peru," *Science Daily* (January 18, 2012), http://www.sciencedaily.com/releases/2012/01/120118143624.htm. states "People living along the coast of Peru were eating popcorn 1,000 years earlier than previously reported and before ceramic pottery was used there . . ." This suggests there was contact with Mesoamerica. Corn cobs have been founded that suggest the cultivation of corn much earlier.

8. Claire Hope Cummings, "Risking Corn, Risking Culture," *World Watch* 15, no. 6 (November–December 2002): 8–18ff. Elizabeth Fitting, "Importing Corn, Exporting Labor: The Neoliberal Corn Regime, GMOs, and the Erosion of Mexican Biodiversity," *Agriculture and Human Values* 23 (2006): 15–26.

9. Sharer, *The Ancient Mayan*, 58. Michael C. Meyer, William L. Sherman, and Susan M. Deeds, *The Course of Mexican History*, 6th ed. (New York: Oxford University Press, 1999), 6–7. Karl Cole, "Colossal Head." *School Arts* Sept. 1999: 29.

10. Some African American scholars say that there was African contact. They point to the massive Olmeca stone heads as proof of this. However, this is not a view held by most Mesoamerican scholars. Robert M. Carmack, Janine Gasco, and Gary H. Gossen, *The Legacy of Mesoamerica: History and Culture of a Native American Civilization* (Upper Saddle River, NJ: Prentice Hall, 1996), 26. William F. Rust and Robert J. Sharer, "Olmec Settlement Data from La Venta, Tabasco, Mexico," *Science* 242, no. 4875 (October 7, 1988): 102–03. Claims that the Olmeca were from Africa are mostly based on the facial characteristics of the artifacts, especially the Olmeca stone heads. See The Olmec—Ancient Mexico, http://www.youtube.com/watch?v=lKo9mUeIueM. There is no scientific evidence that the Olmeca are not part of the Amerindian family.

11. Linda Schele and David Freidel, *A Forest of Kings: The Untold Story of the Ancient Mayan* (New York: Quill William Morrow, 1990), 56. Carmack et al., *The Legacy*, 52.

12. Olmec Civilization, http://www.crystalinks.com/olmec.html. Maria del Carmen Rodríguez Martínez et al., "Oldest Writing in the New World," *Science* 313, no. 5793 (September 2006): 1610–14.

13. Carmack et al., *The Legacy*, 53.

14. Anna Blume, "Maya Concepts of Zero," *Proceedings of the American Philosophical Society* 155, no. 1 (March 2011): 51–88.

15. Meyer et al., *Course of Mexican History*, 14. Schele and Freidel, *Forest of Kings*, 55.

16. Robert N. Zeitlin, "Ancient Chalcatzingo," *Science* 241, no. 4861 (July 1, 1988): 103ff. John S. Justeson and Terrence Kaufman, "A Decipherment of epi-Olmec Hieroglyphic Writing," *Science* 259, no. 5102 (March 19, 1993): 1703ff. Scott Faber, "Signs of Civilization—epi-Olmec Hieroglyphics Deciphered—1993—The Year in Science—Column," *Discover* 15, no. 1 (January 1994): 82ff.

17. Schele and Freidel, *Forest of Kings*, 159. Tikal dates to the Middle Formative (about 800 BC), and it was occupied to about AD 900. The Ruins of Tikal, http://www.youtube.com/watch?v=lOvYZiMvZ1Y.

18. Schele and Freidel, *Forest of Kings*, 17.

19. YouTube has a comprehensive 16-part series on the Mayan Calendar Explained (Part 1 of 16)—Ian Xel Lungold, http://www.youtube.com/watch?v=jEyZFbkvJjw. The Mayan Calendar, http://www.youtube.com/watch?v=BeE-3BBqG58. Raymond E. Crist and Louis A. Paganini, "The Rise and Fall of Maya Civilization," *American Journal of Economics and Society* 39, no. 1 (January 1980): 23–30.

20. Virginia Morell, "The Lost Language of Coba," *Science* 86, no. 7 (March 1986): 48ff. Francis Mark Mondimore, *A Natural History of Homosexuality* (Baltimore: Johns Hopkins University Press, 1997). Louis Crompton, "'An Army of Lovers': The Sacred Band of Thebes (Homosexual Soldiers in Ancient Greece)," *History Today* 44, no. 11 (November 1994): 23ff. See Colin Spencer, *Homosexuality in History* (Harcourt Brace, 1996).

21. Pete Sigal, "Ethnohistory and Homosexual Desire: A Review of Recent Works," *Ethnohistory* 45, no. 1 (Winter 1998): 139.

22. Norman Scribes Hammond, "Warriors and Kings: The City of Copan and the Ancient Mayan," *History Today* 43 (January 1993): 54ff. See Maya Writing, http://www.youtube.com/watch?v=u9LRbLXMzyM&feature=related.

23. See Vernon L. Scarborough and David R. Wilcox, eds. *The Mesoamerican Ballgame* (Tucson: University of Arizona Press, 1991). Vernon L. Scarborough, "Courts in the Southern Mayan Lowlands: A Study in Pre-Hispanic Ballgame Architecture," Vernon L. Scarborough and David R. Wilcox, eds. *The Mesoamerican Ballgame* (Tucson: The University of Arizona Press, 1991), 129–44. The following has three parts: Mayan Ball Game, http://www.youtube.com/watch?v=zcal8GcS41I. A brief tour of Chich'en Itza, Yucatan, México, focusing on the ball court, http://www.youtube.com/watch?v=hobmU4Y8-8I.

24. Karl A. Taube, "The Mesoamerican Ballgame," *Science* 256, no. 5059 (May 15, 1992): 1064ff. Theodore Stern, *The Mesoamerican Ballgame* (Tucson: University of Arizona Press, 1991). Google lists several excellent sites on the Mesoamerican ball game.

25. Meyer et al., *Course of Mexican History*, 361. Mayan Numbers Lesson, http://www.youtube.com/watch?v=W-om9DkpvgA or Mayan Counting System, http://www.youtube.com/watch?v=0Mon20Zf56U.

26. Mayan Prophecy for December 21, 2012—End of Time, http://www.youtube.com/watch?v=QEJ8C2qw5FM&feature=PlayList&p=B2878C04EE3C336D&playnext=1&playnext_from=PL&index=37. 2012 Mayan Prophecy End of an Age Part 1. http://www.youtube.com/watch?v=cH6ig9Xgq3s. The Actual Astronomy of 2012—Absolutely Amazing http://www.youtube.com/watch?v=cGPcjMe6Qlw.

27. Schele and Freidel, *Forest of Kings*, 84–85.

28. See Tikal, A Place of Remembered Voices, http://mayaruins.com/tikal.html. Also Mystery of Tikal, http://www.youtube.com/watch?v=Prtjff2ftjM. See "Maya Trade and Economy,"

Authentic Maya, Guatemala, Cradle of Maya Civilization, http://www.authenticmaya.com/maya_trade_and_economy.htm.

29. Schele and Freidel, *Forest of Kings*, 57. Carmack et al., *The Legacy*, 323.

30. Palenque, Pacal's Mystery, http://www.youtube.com/watch?v=TBI-BWiatRo. Schele and Freidel, *Forest of Kings*, 221–305. Anahuac Civilizations: A Focus on Women, http://www.youtube.com/watch?v=zBIYpRW9fgU&feature=related.

31. Palenque—Mexico, http://www.youtube.com/watch?v=Wq-yZzy-cTk.

32. Mayan Ruins at Tulum (YouTube Edition), http://www.youtube.com/watch?v=Y9Vy06GIVMo&feature=related.

33. Meyer et al., *Course of Mexican History*, 14. Thomas O'Toole, "Radar Used to Discover Mayan Irrigation Canals," *Washington Post*, June 3, 1980.

34. The use of radar technology and photographs taken by satellites has revised estimates based on newly discovered evidence. "Science/Medicine: Developments in Brief; NASA Images Aid in Mayan Research," *Los Angeles Times*, March 1, 1987.

35. Vilma Barr, "A Mayan Engineering Legacy—Coba (Includes Related Article on Acid Rain Effects)," *Mechanical Engineering-CIME* 112, no. 2 (February 1990): 66ff. Alison Bass, "Agriculture: Learning from the Past," *Technology Review* 87 (July 1984): 71ff. Carmack et al., *The Legacy*, 63.

36. Carmack et al., *The Legacy*, 61. Morell, "Lost Language of Coba," 48ff. Frank J. Greene, "Smile—You May Be on Candid Satellite," *San Diego-Union-Tribune*, May 10, 1986. "Satellite Discovers Lost Mayan Ruins," *New York Times*, June 19, 1984. "What Killed the Mayas: War or Weather?; A Global Weakening of the Ties...," Outlook; Science & Society, *U.S. News & World Report* 118, no. 23 (June 12, 1995): 10ff.

37. Schele and Freidel, *Forest of Kings*, 321–22. Overpopulation was one of the major problems. As the population grew, it became more difficult to eke out a living. The best farmland rested under many of the newly built buildings in places like Yax-Pac, where the ball court area alone had over 1,500 structures. An estimated 3,000 people per square kilometer lived there. Deforestation also led to other problems such as erosion and affected climate and rainfall.

38. British scholar Eric Thompson was responsible for the myth of the peaceful people. Alfredo Lopez Austin, Leonardo López Luján, and Bernard R. Ortiz De Montellano, *Mexico's Indigenous Past* (Norman: University of Oklahoma Press, 2005), 137. However, it is important to note that no empire has ever been peaceful. The Old Testament is not a peaceful story, nor is the history of the United States. Likewise, it is difficult to get beyond the sensational on YouTube or most articles, scholarly and popular.

39. Pirámides de Teotihuacan, México. 1 de 5, http://www.youtube.com/watch?v=mP5TYm1uQKI Pyramids of Teotihuacan, Outside Mexico City, Mexico, http://www.youtube.com/watch?v=zV-sBJaqo-Q. Teotihuacan, http://www.youtube.com/watch?v=D7nbKa5__XM.

40. Rene Millon, "The Beginnings of Teotihuacan," *American Antiquity* 26, no. 1 (July 1960): 1–10.

41. Meyer et al., *Course of Mexican History*, 11. Carmack et al., *The Legacy*, 57, 60, 77.

42. Carmack et al., *The Legacy*, 33. Kenneth Hirth, "Xochicalco: Urban Growth and State Formation in Central Mexico," *Science* 225 (August 10, 1984): 579.

43. Carmack et al., *The Legacy*, 71. Jacques Soustelle, *Daily Life of the Aztecs on the Eve of the Spanish Conquest* (Stanford, CA: Stanford University Press, 1961).

44. The lecture about Maya Toltec History in Chichen Itza, Mexico, http://www.youtube.com/watch?v=mror2p7qm1o. Second Life—Chichén Itzá Mexico, http://www.youtube.com/watch?v=PPI8s4JZnDg. Chichen Itza—Wonder of the World http://www.youtube.com/watch?v=kuSvd1TEHXo&feature=fvw.

45. Zapotec and Mixtecan Culture at Monte Alban, http://www.youtube.com/watch?v=EfJd4_LA4vg. Early Astrology at Monte Alban, http://www.youtube.com/watch?v=z2EgwqyFDDg&feature=related. Zapotec Ruins of Monte Alban, http://www.youtube.com/watch?v=qBEUrd2Jbbc.

46. Mitla, http://www.youtube.com/watch?v=6q_IQZr-ZvI&feature=related. Mitla, Mexico, http://www.youtube.com/watch?v=Q_SormLIGQI&feature=related.

47. Joyce Marcus and Kent V. Flannery, *Zapotec Civilizations: How Urban Society Evolved in Mexico's Oaxaca Valley* (London: Thames & Hudson, 1996), 12, 20, 84. Carmack et al., *The Legacy*, 73, 91. Matt Krystal, "Conquest and Colonialism: The Mixtec Case," *Human Mosaic* 26, no. 1 (1992): 55. Cultura Mixteca y Zapoteca, http://www.youtube.com/watch?v=wnUmY0Ak5VA

48. Mixtecs, http://www.latinamericanstudies.org/mixtec.htm. Maarten Jansen, "The Search for History in Mixtec Codices," *Ancient Mesoamerica* 1 (1990): 99–109.

49. The Azteca called nomadic tribes north of central Mexico Chichimeca. The name generally meant barbarians. They were different and varying ethnic and linguistic groups.

50. See Richard Townsend, *The Aztec* (Thames & Hudson, 1992). The concept of Aztlán is controversial among right-wing scholars and nativist groups who claim that it is an example of Chicano sentiment to retake the Southwest. It simply states that the Azteca came from a place called Aztlán, which has been documented to have existed. It is not a matter of faith, and it is a process of deductive reasoning, based on early maps. Journalist Roberto Rodríguez and Patrisia Gonzales have done serious research into its existence. The Azteca probably did come from the Southwest. A wider view of indigenous culture comes from an understanding of the corn culture that bonded the peoples of the Americas. "Ancient Maps and Corn Help Track the Migrations of Indigenous People," *University of Wisconsin-Madison NEWS* (June 15, 2004), http://www.news.wisc.edu/9892.

51. Peter W. Rees, "Origins of Colonial Transportation in Mexico," *Geographical Review* 65, no. 3 (July 1975): 323–34. Spanish transportation followed the corridors established by the Azteca and other Mesoamerican merchants who established the first El Camino Reals.

52. Las Chinampas, http://www.youtube.com/watch?v=Q4yO31tpG0Y. Xochimilco canals Mexico City, http://www.youtube.com/watch?v=_TDXbmiCG80.

53. Carmack et al., *The Legacy*, 77–78. Ross Hassig, *Trade, Tribute, and Transportation: The Sixteenth-Century Political Economy of the Valley of Mexico* (Norman: University of Oklahoma Press, 1985).

54. Miguel León-Portilla, *El destino de la palabra: De la oralidad y los códices mesoamericanos a la escritura alfabética* (México, DF: Fonda de la cultura, 1996), 45. Miguel León-Portilla, *Toltecáyotl: Aspectos de la cultura náhuatl* (México, DF: Fonda de la cultura, 1995). Rozanne Dunbar Ortiz, "Aboriginal People and Imperialism in the Western Hemisphere," *Monthly Review* 44, no. 4 (September 1992): 1ff.

55. Carmack et al., *The Legacy*, 324.

56. Inga Clendinnen, *Los Aztecas: Una interpretación* (México, DF: Editorial Patria, 1998), 205–77, or *Aztecs: An Interpretation* (New York: Cambridge University Press, 1991). Irene Silverblatt, "Lessons of Gender and Ethnohistory in Mesoamerica," *Ethnohistory* 42, no. 4 (Fall 1995): 643.

57. June Nash, "The Aztecs and the Ideology of Male Dominance," *Signs* 4, no. 2 (1978): 349–62.

58. Ibid., 355–56, 359.

59. Clendinnen, *Los Aztecas: Una nterpretación*, 225, makes the point that it is unknown in what context the transvestite was portrayed—in a comedy or drama or perhaps a cult. Meyer et al., *Course of Mexican History*, 64. Carmack et al., *The Legacy*, 116. Soustelle, *Daily Life of the Aztecs*, 101–2.

60. Aztec Legend of the Fifth Sun, http://www.youtube.com/watch?v=eFJKzz-eolg&translated=1. Leyenda Azteca, Tenochititlan, http://www.youtube.com/watch?v=6Ado6TVJaU8&translated=1.

61. Clendinnen, *Los Aztecas: Una interpretación*, 155–89. Meyer et al., *Course of Mexican History*, 70.

62. Kay Almere Read and Jason J. Gonzalez, *Mesoamerican Mythology: A Guide to the Gods, Heroes, Rituals, and Beliefs of Mexico and Central America* (Oxford University Press, 2002), 7–8.

63. Barry M. Pritzker, *A Native American Encyclopedia: History, Culture, and Peoples* (USA: Oxford University Press, 2000), 3.

64. Timothy A. Kohler, Matt Pier Glaude, Jean-Pierre Bocquet-Appel, and Brian M. Kemp, "The Neolithic Demographic Transition in the U.S. Southwest," *American Antiquity* 73, no. 4 (2008): 645–69. http://libarts.wsu.edu/anthro/pdf/Kohler%20et%20al%20SW%20NDT%20AAq.pdf states "maize reached northeastern Arizona by 1940 B.C. which is almost as early as the southern Arizona dates. More lag can be seen in its subsequent eastwest spread—for example, it reached the Northern Rio Grande in New Mexico by about 1200 B.C."

65. Carlos G. Vélez-Ibáñez, *Border Visions: Mexican Cultures of the Southwestern United States* (Tucson: University of Arizona Press, 1996), 20–23, 29. James M. Bayman, "The Hohokam of Southwest North America," *Journal of World Prehistory*, 15, no. 3 (2001): 257–311.

66. Nearly two dozen large towns were constructed in or around what is now Phoenix. Vélez-Ibáñez, *Border Visions*, 20–55.

67. Daniel B. Adams, "Last Ditch Archeology," *Science 83*, no. 4 (December 1983): 28ff.

68. Thomas E. Sheridan, "The Limits of Power: The Political Ecology of the Spanish Empire in the Greater Southwest," *Antiquity* 66 (1992): 156.

69. Vélez-Ibáñez, *Border Visions*, 20–23, 29. Paul E. Minnis and Michael E. Whalen, "The Local and the Distant in the Origin of Casas Grandes, Chihuahua, Mexico," *American Antiquity* 68, no. 2 (2003): 314–332.

70. Harold S. Colton, "Reconstruction of Anasazi History," *Proceedings of the American Philosophical Society* 86, no. 2: 264–69. Hector Neff, Daniel O. Larson, and Michael D. Glascock, "The Evolution of Anasazi Ceramic Production and Distribution: Compositional Evidence from a Pueblo III Site in South-Central Utah," *Journal of Field Archaeology* 24, no. 4 (Winter, 1997): 473–92.

71. "Texas: Early history," *Encyclopedia Britannica*, http://www.britannica.com/EBchecked/topic/589288/Texas/79043/History. Gunnar Brune, "Major and Historical Springs of Texas," *Texas Water Development Board, Report 189* (Austin: Texas Water Development Board, March 1975), 5, https://www.twdb.texas.gov/publications/reports/numbered_reports/doc/R189/R189.pdf.

72. Donald E. Chipman, *Spanish Texas, 1519–1821* (Austin: University of Texas, 1992).

73. Edward H. Spicer, *Cycles of Conquest: The Impact of Spain, Mexico, and the United States on Indians of the Southwest, 1533–1960* (Tucson: University of Arizona Press, 1961). Rodolfo F. Acuña, *Corridors of Migration: The Odyssey of Mexican Laborers, 1600–1933* (Tucson: University of Arizona Press, 2007).

74. Rio Yaqui—Life and Death, http://www.youtube.com/watch?v=K0JAWRGVyyk&translated=1. Yaqui Ritual Performance Mexico, http://www.youtube.com/watch?v=hCIfVH7CskY.

75. Dirk Raat, "World History, MesoAmerica, and the Native American Southwest," *History Compass* 10, no. 7 (2012): 537–48.

76. Jonathon E. Ericson and Timothy G. Baugh, *The American Southwest and Mesoamerica: Systems of Prehistoric Exchange* (New York: Springer, 1993), 12–13.

CHAPTER 2

The Occupation of Middle America

LEARNING OBJECTIVES

- Point out the location of the Iberian Peninsula and describe the different peoples who settled there.

- Show the importance of the Muslim invasion in forming Spanish identity.

- Explain the role of slavery in the preparations for Christopher Columbus's voyage to the Americas, and its role in the exploitation of the native people.

- Describe the conquest of the Caribbean and Mexico.

- Discuss the decline of the Indian population and its effect on the race mixture in Mexico.

- Interpret the role of silver mining in the Spaniards' conquest of Mexico.

- Summarize the state of New Spain/Mexico on the eve of the War of Independence.

What Drove the Conquest

Spain's occupation of Mesoamerica violently disrupted the latter's evolution, destroying Mesoamerican social institutions, religion, and infrastructure. Within 80 years, 1519–1600, the native population fell from at least 25 million to about a million. What followed was 300 years of colonial rule, accompanied by political

1480	1492	1519	1521	1600	1700	1810	1821

Note the timeline. Although it runs some 300 years, it is thousands of years shorter than the habitation of the Mesoamerican people of what are today Mexico and Central America. The timeline was not begun in 1492 because events were in motion before the actual beginning of the occupation of the Americas. As you read the chapter, keep in mind the timeline and how it relates to the discussion.

and economic exploitation, the categorization of people by color, and the projection of the dominant class's worldview. It pulled Spain and, ultimately, all of Europe out of the dark ages and allowed them to buy into a world market dominated by China.

The Asian market's demand for silver in the early 1500s contributed to the growth of mining districts such as Zacatecas. In the early 1500s, the gold/silver ratio was 1:6 in China; in Europe it hovered around 1:12, in Persia 1:10, and in India 1:8. Thus, with six ounces of silver, merchants could buy a full ounce of gold in China. In Europe, the same six ounces had a purchasing power of one-half ounce of gold. This trade put a premium on silver. In 1571, the Spaniards founded the city of Manila, Philippines, and it became a global center of substantial and continuous trade across the Pacific Ocean. Through the seventeenth century, Pacific galleons transported more than 50 tons in silver annually from Acapulco to Manila where Chinese merchants would ship the cargo to the mainland. Trade with the Orient pushed demand for Mexican bullion as the Chinese population zoomed from 55 million in 1500 to 231 million in 1600 and 268 million in 1650. By the next century, the Chinese comprised more than one-third of the world's population.[1] Zacatecas and the northern periphery of New Spain depended on the demand for silver in the Orient.

Africa Begins at the Pyrenees

French novelist and playwright Alexandre Dumas (1802–1870) wrote, "Africa begins at the Pyrenees." Iberia (modern-day Spain and Portugal) was much more a part of the ancient glories that were Phoenicia, Carthage, Greece, Rome, and the Muslim world than it was of Western Europe. The intermingling of the races began in about 35,000 BC. By 5000 BC, the Basque people lived in the north, in the Pyrenees region. Between 4000 and 3500 BC, the Iberians entered from North Africa. The Celtics arrived through the Pyrenees from 900 to 650 BC, bringing knowledge of iron metallurgy. Around 1100 BC, Phoenician merchants from present-day Lebanon established trading posts in Cadiz and elsewhere along the Spanish coast. Greeks traded along the northeastern coast and Jewish merchants from North Africa settled on the Iberian Peninsula.[2] The Phoenician colony of Carthage in what is modern-day Tunisia rose in power and displaced the Lebanese Phoenicians. Iberia came under the rule of Carthage, but Rome displaced it following the Punic Wars (264–246 BC), laying the foundations for Spanish language and culture.[3]

Following the fall of the Western Roman Empire in the fifth century AD, the Visigoths, a Germanic people from central Europe, ruled Spain. In 711, the Muslims of northern Africa launched an invasion across the Strait of Gibraltar, occupying most of the peninsula. The African presence lasted more than seven centuries.[4] Under Muslim rule, Spain was a center of learning and art. The Muslims preserved the writings of many Greek, Roman, and Middle Eastern intellectuals—writings that otherwise surely would have been lost. Muslims brought improved irrigation methods, food strains (e.g., oranges and other fruits and vegetables), rice, sugar cane, and cotton. The Africans also brought other breeds of animals; using stock from the Muslims and Moors, the Spaniards developed a better breed of horse, which they adapted to an arid climate. They developed strategies to travel long distances, herding African cattle and churro sheep.[5]

Meanwhile, the Christian kingdoms to the north regained power in holy wars known as *la Reconquista* (the Reconquest), driving the Moors southward. By the 1000s, Christians were gaining an upper hand, and by the 1200s, they had driven the Muslims into the Granada region of the peninsula. In 1479, the marriage of Queen Isabela and King Fernando united the kingdoms of Castile and Aragón, and in 1492, they conquered the last Moorish kingdom, Granada (the eastern half of present-day Andalusia).[6] That same year they expelled between 120,000 and 150,000 Spanish Jews. These events set the stage for "Occupied America."[7]

The Spanish Conquest

Who was this man, Cristóbal Colón or Christopher Columbus?[8] He is claimed by Italians, Jews, Spaniards, and Catalans. No one really knows. DNA tests are being conducted at this very moment, as linguists examine his writings. The only ones who do not claim Columbus are the Native Americans, who prefer to call him "colon," with a small "c" and without an accent mark.

What is pertinent to this narrative? In 1492, Columbus landed in what are now the islands of the Caribbean. When he could not find sufficient gold and wealth, he turned to trading in slaves. In 1495, he rounded up 1,500 Tainos (Arawaks), selected 500 of the best specimens, and set sail for Spain. Only 300 of those natives survived the trip. Because of the Spanish conquest, by 1650 few Tainos or Caribs—who occupied most of the Lesser Antilles, the Virgin Islands, and Vieques Island—remained alive.[9]

By the early 1500s, sugar-growing plantations emerged on the islands. The plantation system was not new to Columbus. The Arabs had initiated it on the Mediterranean islands of Cyprus and Sicily, and it required an immense captive labor force of African slaves. By the 1440s, the Portuguese, through "raid and trade" techniques, expanded down the West African coast. When the Spaniards decimated the native populations, much the same as the Portuguese did on the Atlantic islands, the Azores, the Canaries, the Cape Verde Islands, São Tomé, and Madeira, they too imported African slaves.

Columbus had trained in the Madeira sugar trade. On his second voyage of 1493, he introduced sugar cane plants to the Caribbean. Columbus knew that sugar and slavery were inseparable and that tremendous profits could be gotten from sugar. By the early sixteenth century the sugar industry thrived on Santo Domingo, then on Cuba, and soon after on Puerto Rico. Simultaneously, the Spaniards almost wiped out the native population through warfare, overwork, and disease.[10]

The Pope condemned the Portuguese practice of the plunder and enslavement of human beings along the coast of Africa. However, he left a loophole. The natives could be enslaved if they were cannibals. Columbus himself justified the enslavement of the indigenous people, claiming they were cannibals. The Spaniards repeated this pretext throughout the colonial period. In Central America, they captured and sold tens of thousands of natives as slaves. They shipped Nicaragua natives to Peru to work in the mines and *haciendas*, plantation-like estates.[11]

Faith versus Rationality

Apologists for Columbus say that he did not invent the institution of slavery. They say that Spain tried to control slavery, and that the crown promulgated the Laws of Burgos in 1512 that included regulations protecting indigenous labor and ensuring their Christianization. They argue that Dominicans Antonio de Montesinos and Bartolomé de las Casas vigorously defended the rights of the Native Americans.[12] But the Laws of Burgos were almost never enforced, and the famed national debate over whether or not the natives had rational souls did not occur until six decades after the initial contact in the Caribbean and three decades after the fall of the Azteca Empire.

The debate between Bartolomé de las Casas and the renowned Spanish scholar Juan Ginés de Sepúlveda took place in 1550–1551 in Valladolid, Spain. Sepúlveda based his arguments on Aristotle's doctrine of natural slavery: "that one part of mankind is set aside by nature to be slaves in the service of masters born for a life of virtue free of manual labor." Sepúlveda wrote a treatise justifying war against the natives. According to him, the Spaniards had the right to rule the "barbarians" because of their superiority. He compared the natives to wild beasts.[13] The judges in the debate never reached a decision as to the validity of the arguments of Sepúlveda or Las Casas.

The Spanish Invasion of the Mexica

The Spaniards slowly explored the Caribbean coastline of Middle America, gathering information. By 1511, the invaders conquered Cuba, and in the late 1510s, Hernán Cortés landed on the mainland that was to become Mexico. On the island of Cozumel, Cortés encountered the Maya. In 1519, Cortés sailed to what today is Veracruz, and within two years Cortés's forces conquered the great Azteca Empire and began the colonization of what they later called New Spain.

Throughout the advance to the Azteca capital of Tenochtitlán, gunpowder, horses, snarling dogs, and glistening armor helped the Spaniards. Unlike the invaders, the indigenous warriors did not intend to kill their enemies, hoping to wound and capture and use them as sacrifices to the gods. The Azteca also stopped fighting periodically to remove their dead and wounded from the battlefield. At close range, the

Native Americans used wooden clubs ridged with razor-sharp obsidian—vicious weapons against other indigenous people, but weapons that shattered against Spanish helmets.[14] The double-bladed swords of the Spaniards in close combat slashed left and right, killing or maiming. Their armament allowed them to drive directly at warriors clustered around their leaders. When the Spaniards captured or killed a local chief, the chief's warriors fell back. In the battle for Tenochtitlán, this weaponry gave the Spaniards a strategic advantage over the Azteca.

The Azteca were not immune to smallpox and other European diseases, so outbreaks of these diseases had the effect of germ warfare. At a critical moment, when it seemed as if the Azteca might drive out Cortés's men, a smallpox epidemic ravaged the native population.[15]

The Colonization of Native Mesoamerica

After the conquest of the Azteca, the Spaniards—through looting and torturing—conquered the Tarasco; they executed the Cazonci, the Tarascan ruler, by dragging him through town behind a horse and burning him at the stake. Cortés's men also subdued the natives of Oaxaca, but the conquest of the Maya proved more arduous. Many Maya fled to the dense forests and remained out of the control of the Spaniards for 200 years.

Smallpox and Other Plagues

The distinguishing characteristic of the subjugation of the Mesoamerican native populations was its genocidal proportion. The term *genocide* is used here because when people lose 90 plus percent of their population, millions of lives, an explanation must be forthcoming. As with a nuclear disaster, saying it was accidental is no excuse. After the conquest of Tenochtitlán, smallpox and other epidemics spread throughout the countryside, subsiding and recurring, until eventually as many as 24 million died in what is Mexico. Certainly, the smallpox, measles, and influenza outbreaks hit urban areas hardest because of the population concentration. (These three diseases are highly communicable, being transmitted mainly by air.)[16]

There were four major epidemics in the first 60 years of Spanish occupation. Smallpox caused the first epidemic of 1520–1521, the second year after Spanish contact. Azteca medicine could not stop its spread, and untold thousands died. The second epidemic of smallpox (possibly combined with measles) broke out in 1531. The Azteca called it *tepiton zahuatl*, or "little leprosy." The third epidemic began in 1545 and lasted three years. The Azteca called this *cocoliztli*, or "pest," thought today to have been hemorrhagic fever. A fourth epidemic, again named cocoliztli, lasted from 1576 to 1581, and an estimated 300,000–400,000 Native Americans died of it in New Spain.[17]

Apologists argue that it was the Indians' predisposition to diseases that made them vulnerable to European diseases; they theorize that the native peoples were vulnerable to these diseases because their slow trek across the Bering landmass more than 15,000 years before created a biologic selector and "cold screen" that eliminated harmful bacteria and viruses from their bodies. A more plausible explanation is that the lack of larger-sized domesticated animals shielded the natives from diseases carried by animals.[18] The introduction of domestic animals, accordingly, contributed to the spread of diseases to the natives.

The Columbian Exchange refers to widespread exchange of animals, plants, culture, human populations that included slavery, communicable disease, and ideas between Spain and the New World. Some put a positive spin on the enrichment that occurred in these areas. However, they forget the cost in lives and the destruction of cultures. They forget about the Atlantic slave trade, the enslavement of Indians, and the diseases that killed millions of Native Americans. The Spaniards brought gunpowder, the horse, and the Catholic Church to the Americas. The Americas as part of the exchange sent corn, the potato, the tomato, peppers, pumpkins, squash, pineapples, cacao beans (for chocolate), and the sweet potato and animals such as turkeys. The Europeans brought livestock such as cattle, pig, and sheep and grains such as wheat. They brought the onion, citrus fruits, bananas, coffee beans, olives, grapes, rice, and sugar cane from other parts of the world. But they also brought smallpox, influenza, malaria, measles, typhus, and syphilis. The exchange wiped out the indigenous peoples' religions, submerged their languages, and tried to blank out their history. It introduced a European construct of race that lasts to this day.[19]

The Conquest of Race and Labor in Mesoamerica

The conquerors practiced a "scorched-earth" strategy, causing widespread environmental destruction and social disorganization. Large numbers of displaced, disoriented, and depressed refugees roamed the countryside, suffering severe nutritional deficiency and often starving to death. Illness often prevented many natives from caring for their crops or from processing corn into tortillas. The acute food shortage resulted in starvation, and contaminated food and water spread other diseases. Meanwhile, the Spaniards forcefully herded natives into new farming schemes. Alcoholism took an additional toll with the distilling of native drinks. Before the invasion, *pique*, which was low in alcoholic content and rich in vitamins, was used for religious purposes. It resembled beer rather than hard liquor. When the Spaniards introduced distilled alcohol, it became an escape, and addiction was common.[20] Urban resettlement plans only reinforced substantial crowding and lack of hygiene, and native centers became breeding grounds for epidemics.

Indigenous Labor   A "viceroy," or vice-king, governed New Spain, ruling the colonial government that was subdivided into smaller administrative units. The crown gave former *conquistadores** (meaning "leaders of the crusades") *encomiendas*, large tracts of land with native subjects, an institution that was established in Spain during the Reconquista and also used in the Caribbean islands. The *encomendero* received tribute from a village along with Indian labor. In principle, encomenderos would protect the natives under their care and supervise their conversion to Catholicism.[21] In reality the conquerors often maltreated and abused the natives, keeping them in a state of serfdom.

Theory versus Practice   Throughout the colonial period, Spain passed legislation supposedly to protect the natives. In theory, the Laws of Burgos, passed in 1512 as *Recopilación de las Leyes de los Reynos de las Indias* (Compilation of the Royal Laws of the Indies), protected the natives. Spain strengthened the laws in 1542, eliminating the right of encomenderos to unlimited use of indigenous labor. Occasionally, the natives successfully sued; some used the laws to protect their lands or personal labor. However, there was a difference between what the law said and how it was enforced. Justice rarely went beyond an occasional victory in the courts.[22]

The Spanish Crown abolished indigenous slavery and the encomienda in the 1550s. Yet they flourished on the peripheries and frontiers of New Spain well into the nineteenth century. The *repartimiento*, requiring a native community to provide labor for public projects, agriculture, and mines and as carriers of goods was practiced into the eighteenth century. Although the system made wages for the natives mandatory, the employers often ignored the provision. The repartimiento was not limited to labor; it also included the requirement that natives purchase goods from Spanish authorities.

Structural Controls   The native communities endured the catastrophes of the invasion and colonization of Mesoamerica, but not before Spaniards dramatically changed them. In order to control them, colonial authorities grouped native communities into *municipios,* townships. The largest town of the municipios was the *cabecera*, or head community. While this structure led to the survival of the native community, it strengthened colonial control of the native village. The purpose was to isolate natives in order for them to identify with the local village rather than forming class or ethnic identities. This division made it difficult for the different communities to unite against Spanish rule, destroying intercommunity regional networks and the pre-invasion world system. This concentrated power in the hands of Indian *caciques*, chiefs, who ran the local system, and were loyal to the Spaniards.

The Spaniards allowed the indigenous peoples to retain their languages, but Spanish was the official language. All official government business was conducted in Spanish. If the native or the *casta*, of mixed race, spoke Spanish, he or she was considered superior to those who did not. The Catholic Church was the state religion, and the Christian God supplanted the indigenous gods.[23] The paternalism of the Spanish friars was racist, and they saw the natives as being childlike. They believed that the natives lacked the spiritual

---

* The name *conquistador* expresses the similarity of conquests in the New World and the conquest of the Moors in Spain. It is similar to a knight who participated in the crusades or the Reconquista.

and mental capacity to understand Catholicism. During the early colonial period the Spanish crown did not allow natives to become priests or nuns.[24]

The religious conquest was administered from Spain; most members of the hierarchy were on the peninsula. The monarchy and the Church were one with the crown appointing the bishops—a right generally reserved to the pope. Influenced by the Spanish Reconquista, they were intolerant and hostile toward any person who was non-Catholic. To hold office or be a noble, the nominee was required to prove a *limpieza de sangre* (purity of blood), that is, that they were not of Jewish or Moorish blood.[25] The intolerance extended to Spain's colonies. To further consolidate its power, Spain imposed a caste system based on race that designated an individual's rank according to color. Spanish priests listed racial classification on baptismal certificates. There were four main categories of race: the "peninsular," or Spaniard born in Spain; the "criollo/a," a person of Spanish descent born in Mesoamerica; the "indio/a," or native; and the "negro/a," of African slave descent. Innumerable subcategories of hybrids developed over time.[26] This complex system, used for social control, lasted in various forms throughout the colonial period, although it became more difficult to keep track of one's class position as the castas (those of mixed race) moved north. Distance allowed them to fudge on their race. The advantage of moving up in race is obvious: The more Spanish one looked and claimed to be, the more privileges the person enjoyed.[27]

Women in Colonial Mesoamerica

During the colonial period, criollo culture, literally built on the ruins of the indigenous past, flourished. Although there were women such as Sor Juana Inés de la Cruz (1651–1695), an intellectual whose genius was suppressed because of her gender, in this section we focus on a discussion of women from the indigenous classes, on whose backs society had the luxury of the development of the arts. From riches extracted from the labor of the Indian, colonial society could afford to produce literature and the arts, giving birth to geniuses like Sor Juana. As important as the expressions of criollo women were to Colonial Mexican society, and as outstanding as the writings of Sor Juana are, we focus on women from the indigenous classes, for any discussion on women in this period depends greatly on ethnicity and class.[28] This caveat also applies to males during the colonial period whose genius was possible because of the labor and often the exploitation of others.

The Changing Roles of Women

The social and economic roles of women varied between pre-colonial and colonial societies. Women were the victims of rape, the ultimate symbol of subordination, and the economy opened only limited opportunities for them. In Yucatán the introduction of sheep led to the commercial production of wool. Women were generally responsible for making woolen goods, thus allowing their participation in the wool trade. This was not entirely positive since the repetitive motions in textile work resulted in physical ailments.

Azteca women were recognized as adults. They had rights before the law and society, although this status varied greatly according to their class. Under Spanish rule, their standing was weakened, although Spanish law allowed them to litigate inheritance and land rights in court. Nahua women took advantage of these rights, and they actively litigated and testified on their own behalf in the colonial courts. This activity became less frequent in the seventeenth century, as Nahua husbands and fathers increasingly represented the women in court. Native women were not always recognized as *hijas del pueblo*, daughters or citizens of the town, with communal land rights. Women's rights to property narrowed under colonialism, and their participation changed as commercial agriculture put pressure on *los de abajo* (the poor and powerless) to abandon or sell their land.[29]

Institutionalizing Inequality   Before the arrival of the Spaniards, women generally married when they were about 20 years of age. After the arrival of the Spaniards, however, Church friars encouraged females to marry at 12 or 14. Early reproduction often resulted in health disorders, including anemia. Society was patriarchal, and men received preferential treatment in nutrition.[30] Even in death, men received favored treatment, as they were more likely than women to be buried within the church courtyard. In sum, the colonization worsened the status of women and increased violence toward them.

The family structure also changed during the colonial period. For a time, the native nobility kept much of their prestige. But the colonization led to the breakdown of the traditional indigenous family framework, which was based on an extended family rather than the highly patriarchal nuclear family that the Spaniards favored. According to Carmack and his colleagues, "Colonial authorities believed that the Indians would be easier to supervise and control if divided into small nuclear households," which not only reduced the authority of the elders but also removed the support network for women within the clan.

Early marriage also influenced gender relations and increased the power of the male within the nuclear family, reducing the authority of native women within the clan. The age difference between male and female spouses favored the male. A 20-year-old male who married a 14-year-old girl held much more power than he would if both were 20 years old.[31]

The Assimilation of Native Women

Native women, according to some sources, experienced a diminished participation in traditional social domains. The Catholic Church promoted rigid attitudes toward women, making women the scapegoats for its failures in converting the natives. Priests blamed Indian mothers for not assimilating their children, although little attention was paid to educating Indian women and children. There were few religious schools for women in colonial society. By contrast, during the pre-conquest period, women worked as marketers, doctors, artisans, and priests, and perhaps occasionally as rulers. The opportunities for life outside the home were based on class: Native noble women who married the conquerors and brought a dowry were more readily assimilated and acculturated than the poor.[32]

The Myth of Passivity   Native women were anything but passive or invisible, however. By the end of the eighteenth century, they accounted for one-third of the Tenochtitlán, or Mexico City, workforce. (Tenochtitlán had become the capital of New Spain and was renamed "Mexico City.") A sizable number of native, African, and mixed-race women worked outside the home. In Mexico City, 46 percent of native women and 36 percent of women from *las castas* (mixed races) engaged in work outside the home, whereas only 13 percent of the Spanish or criollas worked outside the home in the labor force. Most women found employment as domestic servants. We can deduce that native women and women from the castes performed the menial work while middle-class women pursued some education.[33]

Native women also were far from docile; legal documents show many examples of resistance. Take the case of Josefa María Francisca, a *cacica*, or noblewoman, who for some 30 years played a leading role in Tepoztlán, near Cuernavaca. Francisca did not know how to read or write and probably was unable to speak Spanish; nevertheless, her fiery temperament made her a respected ally and a feared opponent.[34] What angered Francisca was the repartimiento, which forcefully took the village's men to the hated mines of Taxco. In 1725, when authorities arrested repartimiento workers, she led an assault on the jail and freed them. In September a group of 100 women broke into the sacristy, liberated the ornaments and vestments, and sold them to pay for litigation. Angelina María Francisco, the wife of Miguel Francisco, Francisca's lover for 30 years, led the revolt and authorities sentenced her to one year in an *obraje*—a sweatshop—and six months at the *hospital de indios*. They later commuted her sentence.

In the winter of 1797–1798, as typhus ravaged the Maya village of Ixil, the women feared that the royal administrators would tax the village based on its pre-epidemic population. The fact that Spanish authorities violated the tradition of burying local Maya within the church compound and ordered that typhus victims be buried outside the church boundaries infuriated them. The Maya women locked the doctor and the priest in the church and made their release contingent on proper interment of the deceased.[35] Throughout the colonial period, women lodged complaints against clergy for sexual improprieties. This was no small feat considering they were appealing to a patriarchal structure.

Agent of Social Control or Liberator   For many Mexicans today, the appearance of the *Virgen de Guadalupe* to an indigenous person is proof of the Church's benevolence. For others Guadalupe is the symbol of Spanish social control, representing a passive female role model, subservient to male authority. According to critics, the supposed appearance of the Virgin Mother to Juan Diego[36] at Tepeyac in 1531 is an example of a substitution by church authorities of the Virgin of Guadalupe for the indigenous goddess Tonantzin, mother of gods. Like many narratives, the story of the Virgin of Guadalupe may be the product of "the invention of tradition" rather than historical fact. Today, however, the Virgen de Guadalupe has become a Chicana cultural expression that gives strength to women and unifies and defines Mexican culture. For many, she has become a liberator, a symbol of hope and liberation for her community. Sandra Cisneros and Gloria Anzaldúa have underscored the indigenous roots of the Virgin and her symbol as a source of inspiration.[37]

Vincential Father Stafford Poole, C.M., in his book, *Our Lady of Guadalupe*, traces the making of the Mexican tradition of Guadalupe based on documents produced in the colonial period. According to Poole's evidence, most authorities and priests did not know about the Tepeyac shrine representing the Virgin's appearance for some 20 years after the Virgin supposedly appeared to Juan Diego. Spaniards confused her with the medieval Spanish Lady of Guadalupe shrine (in Extremadura, Spain), and venerated the Virgin. Not until the seventeenth century, when the criollo population began to celebrate her, did she become popular among native populations. Indigenous peoples during this time greatly identified with local religious symbols, which had played a central role in the development of their own religious practices. Consequently, by the mid-1600s, the Church was able to baptize most natives in central Mexico.[38] Far from bringing about a native spontaneous upsurge, however, during the sixteenth and seventeenth centuries, Guadalupe was more a symbol of criollo nationalism than an Indian icon, according to Poole. He argues that even the story of the apparition appears to have changed during the colonial era as did the tradition itself, until Father Miguel Hidalgo used her as a symbol of Mexican independence in 1810. Today the Virgen de Guadalupe has taken on different dimensions, symbolizing for many Mexicans and Latin Americans a "renewal and rebirth as a people. Guadalupe stands for both transformation and continuity in Mexican religious and national life."[39]

Al Norte: God, Gold, Glory, Silver, and Slaves

The Spaniards sent expeditions from Colonial Mexico in every direction searching for riches. A Cuban-based expedition in 1565 planted one of the oldest European colonies in the United States near present-day St. Augustine, Florida. Meanwhile, the viceroy sent scouting expeditions from central Mexico to investigate rumors of another Tenochtitlán to the north. In 1533 Diego de Guzmán, a slave trader, penetrated as far as Yaqui Valley, in what today is Sonora, Mexico. In 1540 Francisco Vázquez de Coronado, in search of Cibola, the legendary city of gold, led an army of mostly Native Americans and five Franciscan friars as far as the Grand Canyon and across the central plains to Kansas before retreating to Mexico without finding a trace of gold.[40]

Unlike the Azteca and the natives of central New Spain, many natives of the north did not live in concentrated areas. Some lacked the complex social and political organization of the towns of south-central New Spain. Nevertheless, the northern tribes resisted the Spanish encroachments, and the Spaniards called them *indios bárbaros*, or barbaric Indians. In short, the conquistadores felt entitled and were offended that the Indians did not meet them with open arms.

Meanwhile, the Spanish named the colonial administrative region in western Colonial Mexico "Nueva Galicia"; it made up roughly the present states of Jalisco, Nayarit, and south Sinaloa. Guadalajara was its administrative capital and base of operations for expeditions into the northwestern frontier. An expedition led by Governor Nuño de Guzmán left a trail of depredations, enslavement, and mistreatment of natives as the Spaniards explored and secured the area as far north as Sinaloa. The most notable of the native rebellions were those of the Tepeque and Zacatecos Indians at Tepechitlán.

Clearly, *bonanzas*, or large mining strikes, energized the pull north. They made possible the exploitation of river valleys and the establishment of haciendas, missions, and settlements. The move to the north was not easy, as the northern tribes resisted the encroachment. It was not until after the 1541 Mixtón Rebellion that the Spanish were able to open the mines of Zacatecas, which, at their height, produced one-third of Mexico's silver and employed 5,000 workers. The bonanza drew prospectors and Christian natives to the mines. It generated institutions such as the hacienda and the mission. Bonanzas in Guanajuato (1548) and Real del Monte (1552) followed Zacatecas. The Chichimeca, sometimes called Otomí or Zacatecos, and their allies fought the advance of the Spaniards throughout the 1560s and 1570s, with Spanish settlements forming a large triangle between Guadalajara, Saltillo, and Querétero.[41]

The Decimation of the Indigenous Population

The Spaniards' arrival on the northern frontier, with natives from the interior and domesticated animals, devastated the native ecology and intensified competition for rivers and valleys. They pushed the native peoples off their lands. The Spanish authorities responded to native resistance by organizing *presidios*, forts, which became an integral part of the invasion after the Chichimeca war of the 1560s. As with the Mesoamerican civilizations, the numbers of natives fell drastically during the Spanish occupation. The Greater Southwest, according to Thomas Sheridan, encompassed "that vast arid convulsion of deserts and mountains north of Mesoamerica," with an estimated population of around 1,700,000 in 1519, plummeting to 165,000 by 1800.[42]

The Living Patterns of the Northern Corn People   Most natives lived in *rancherías*, semi-fixed farming settlements. Three-quarters of all indigenous ranchería natives were Uto-Aztecan. But they varied greatly as to their population density, mode of living, and organization, depending on rainfall and the flow of rivers. For example, at the time of the arrival of the Spaniards, fixed villages did not exist in Chihuahua; instead, natives moved in search of water. In the spring they would travel to the headwaters in the sierras, farm, and live there for the summer, and then migrate east to the deserts during the winter where they would subsist on desert vegetation. This pattern of migration meant that the size of the ranchería was smaller than a traditional native village, numbering between 30 and 50.

The Tarahumara people of modern Chihuahua/Durango lived over a large area; they would come together at *tesgüinadas*, festivals during which the Tarahumara practiced rituals that included imbibing corn beer. In Sonora, the Pima and the Yaqui lived in areas that were more compact. Their rivers, such as the Great Rio Bravo or Grande, gave life to villages of thousands and complex social and political systems. The Pueblo people, found mostly in what is today New Mexico, Colorado, Arizona, and Texas, also lived in villages. In comparison, the nomadic people were still in the process of migration when the Spanish arrived.

The Changing Order

The mining city of Zacatecas was a melting pot of varied races and people. Near the mines, *haciendas* for cattle raising sprang up, which caused tensions with the native populations in these valleys as the newcomers usurped the best land and believed themselves entitled to native labor. As in the south, the Spanish elites considered themselves conquistadores entitled to encomiendas of natives.

Slowly, the Spanish imperial system moved up the Pacific coast to Culiacán, and, simultaneously, up the Zacatecas trail to Durango and Chihuahua. The Spaniards established presidios, missions, haciendas, and pueblos (Indian villages or towns). Because of the lack of population and capital, Catholic missions played an essential role in extending the empire's borders and congregating, forging a native workforce and religious presence on the frontier. The demands on native labor occurred both inside and outside the mission orbit: The growth of the mining industry increased the need for food production, forcing the natives to work longer hours, while the mines and the haciendas pressured the missionaries to provide more native workers. These demands, along with the frequent droughts and epidemics that depopulated the region, made the natives restless. Their frequent uprisings made the Franciscan and Jesuit missionaries, as well as the outside settlers, increasingly dependent on the presidios to maintain order by force.[43]

Meanwhile, the missions profoundly changed the lives of indigenous people. For example, while life had always been harsh for women, often subjected to the raiding and enslavement due to intertribal warfare, they always held strong roles in their communities. Females and males seem to have inherited wealth equally, and women were involved in the trades of weaving and pottery. Both men and women could marry multiple times before they found the ideal mate.[44] A native woman had the choice of abortion, and women participated in ceremonies, although their religious roles were subordinate to those of males. Pre-conquest women shared these cultural memories and religious values; however, the missions ended these choices, as they imposed the attitudes and values of Spanish society on the natives. A hierarchical structure made clear distinctions between the male and female spheres. Finally, Spanish institutions such as the repartimiento shifted women to work that men had previously done.

The Bonanzas

The mining bonanzas forged the *Camino Real* (Royal Road) from Mexico City to Zacatecas, then through today's Durango to Chihuahua, and then to New Mexico. Natives from central Mexico as well as Africans, Spaniards, mestizos, and the castas were drawn over this road to the mines. The conquerors uprooted Native Americans from their villages and destroyed their institutions. Consequently, natives caught in a work-or-starve situation formed a large sector of the wage earners. Dozens of small and large ore strikes brought these workers through Durango to Santa Bárbara and then to Parral in 1631.[45]

By the turn of the sixteenth century, Spain made attempts to expand its dominion into present-day New Mexico, where it anticipated another bonanza. In 1598 Don Juan de Oñate, whom the viceroy had appointed governor of the territory of New Mexico, set out with a party of some 500 colonists, including 10 Franciscans and hispanicized Tlazcala and Tarasco natives, many of whom were from central Mexico, to establish a colony. Juan de Oñate's father had been a prominent mine owner, one of the founders of Zacatecas. The younger Oñate, married to a granddaughter of Cortés and a great-granddaughter of Mocteczuma, financed the operation. When Oñate and his party failed to find gold or silver, he returned to Mexico City in disgrace.[46] However, Oñate did manage to plant a small agricultural and trading colony along the Rio Grande in New Mexico.

For most of the seventeenth century, New Mexico was an outpost. The land between Santa Bárbara/Parral and New Mexico had few villages. Continuous small mining strikes filled this space during the century. However, the northern expansion did not come without cost as the Indians resisted the encroachment as well as enslavement and other forms of forced labor. Due to war and epidemics, the indigenous populations of Chihuahua and New Mexico dwindled radically. For example, the native population in New Mexico numbered more than 60,000 at the time of the Spanish arrival. By 1800 the population fell to 9,000. Throughout the frontier, from 1560 to 1650 the population declined by 50 percent. The population fell 90–95 percent by 1678. Frequent smallpox epidemics brought heightened competition for farm labor in the north; those in 1639–1640, the 1640s, and 1650s were especially severe. In the 1690s, yet another epidemic of measles broke out.[47] Droughts and labor shortages affected the supply of food. Due to these tensions, frequent revolts spread throughout northwestern New Spain during the 1600s.

Forced Labor

Coercion was part of the colonial process. Government officials in collusion with the agricultural establishment perceived the indigenous populations as key to production.[48] Landowners and miners could avoid restrictions on forced labor due to their distance from central government. They sought arrangements that bound natives without being required to pay wages or credit advances. The repartimiento was the optimal form of labor because it improved reliability. The types of labor varied in the mines, and haciendas used mixed crews of wage laborers of all races who worked alongside African and indigenous slaves.

Periodic bonanzas increased demand for labor. Mine owners and *hacendados* pressured the missions for workers. The mission congregation almost invariably followed the establishment of Spanish mining camps and estates. The earliest encomiendas drew workers from the native rancherías; encomenderos competed with the missions and Indian villages for workers. The encomenderos were in full control of the native population under their charge, often abusing the natives' "trust" by renting "their" natives to mine owners and other hacendados. Colonial elites also used native caciques to furnish workers, further stressing the native population.

The repartimiento, although primarily used for agricultural labor, was sometimes used for the mines. The repartimiento as an institution continued long after "free" wage labor was employed in the mines and hacienda. The forced labor draft was crucial to agriculture. In addition, repartimientos were used for maintaining public works. An overlapping progression from slavery to encomienda, to repartamiento, to free labor operated often simultaneously. In this scheme, the missions were training schools, often supplying the haciendas and mines with skilled workers.[49]

The Northern Corridor

Nueva Vizcaya was the "heartland" of the northern frontier for some 250 years. It encompassed the area north of Zacatecas and included most of the modern Mexican states of Chihuahua and Durango, and, at different times, parts of Sinaloa, Sonora, and Coahuila. The capital of the province was Durango. Exploratory and missionary expeditions launched from Nueva Vizcaya resulted in the settlement of New Mexico, Parras and Saltillo, and Sonora and Sinaloa.

The first colony to be settled north of Nueva Vizcaya in what is today the United States was Nuevo México where, as mentioned, the Spaniards hoped to find gold or silver. However, its existence and prosperity rested on the waters of the Rio Grande that ran from the Rocky Mountains down through the center of the province. Because of large numbers of sedentary natives, there was also a ready supply of labor that made possible the development of large haciendas and trade with various other indigenous people.

In New Mexico, the Spanish settlers repeated the patterns of exploitation described in Nueva Vizcaya and Sonora. The use of bonded servants was widespread. New Mexican colonists used fictions such as indios *de depósito* to forcibly place natives in Christian households under the pretense that they would receive a Christian education. Forced indigenous labor was so widespread in New Mexico that the colonists had no need to import expensive black slaves. Indeed, New Mexico was a net exporter of slaves to the mines of Parral and elsewhere.[50]

The Pueblo people had lived in this region since at least AD 1 and shared the traditional indigenous perceptions of the world of nature, only differing in language. The Pueblos also shared a theocratic lifestyle that interrelated their kinships and religious groups with the world of nature. The members of each village organized themselves to cope with their particular environment. Survival conditioned them to note even the minutest variations in climate and topography—the amount and seasonal rhythm of precipitation, the form of flood plain, or the erosion of a temporary stream.

The Pueblo social grouping was matrilineal, that is, they grouped kinship around the core of blood-related women. The Pueblo people conceived kinship as timeless, extending back into the remote past and extending forward through generations of unborn. Thus, they related the kinship system symbolically beyond the human community into the world of nature, using animals and plants as symbols for different clans.

The colonists established Santa Fe as the capital of the province in 1610. During these early years, the hispanicized population of the province increased from a few hundred to a few thousand who were dispersed in isolated farms, ranches, and hamlets.[51] Spanish settlers and their livestock encroached on native fields. Although tensions existed, there is evidence that the newcomers commingled with the natives and often intermarried.

However, tensions mounted as encroachment on native lands, forced labor, a prolonged drought in the region, and Apache raids contributed to the Pueblo Revolt of 1680. Popé of the San Juan pueblo led the rebellion, joined by some mestizos and mulatos. The natives drove the colonists from New Mexico, the bulk of whom did not return until the 1690s.[52]

The 1680 Revolt spread and affected the whole of Nueva Vizcaya and Sonora; it became known as the "Great Northern Revolt." In New Mexico, the revolt had millenarian trappings. The natives washed off the stains of baptism, annulled Catholic marriages, and destroyed churches. The New Mexicans wanted the Spaniards and their God out of their space and wanted to return to the old ways.[53]

Slavery as well as other abuses must have taken their toll. According to Ramón Gutiérrez, "Within New Mexican households slave treatment ran the gamut from the kind neglect of some to the utter sadism of others."[54] At the time of the revolt, 426 slaves were dispersed among the Hispanic households. Some 56 percent of the households had one or more slaves. In this system, female slaves were worth more than males and were sold openly at fairs, as females were valued as household servants and for bearing children, who would also be born into this class. The Spanish merchants also marched New Mexican slaves to Parral to work in the silver mines. Some ended up in the plantations of Veracruz and, after 1800, in Havana, Cuba, and Yucatán. When the Spanish army put down the rebellion, military authorities tried the rebels in Spanish courts and sentenced them to hanging, whipping, dismemberment of hands or feet, or slavery.

The Decline of the Native Population

Constant warfare reduced the Pueblo population from 17,000 in 1680 to 14,000 in 1700. Many Pueblos went into exile with the Apache, Navajo, and Hopi. After the colonists returned to New Mexico, the encomienda system was replaced by the repartimiento. The excessive use of the repartimiento system had a devastating impact on the indigenous people, depriving the native communities of labor for their own crops, which caused a shortage of food, and ultimately malnutrition.[55]

By the end of the eighteenth century, New Mexico society was entrenched: only 68 of some 16,000 persons had been born outside New Mexico, with two born in Spain. The landed peasants, mostly mestizos, lived above Santa Fe in areas they called *Rio Arriba* and *Rio Abajo.* Until the mid-eighteenth century, land grants were largely private grants. After this point, colonial authorities parceled out community grants—that is, community land grants that included common pasture lands and common rights for using land—to buttress the haciendas of the elite in the south of Rio Abajo from native attacks. Most of the mestizo colonists were of humble birth, although they fashioned themselves Spaniards to distance themselves from the *indios* and other lower castas.

The Rio Arriba and Abajo villages were self-sufficient. As a group, the villagers were distinct from the hacendados. Both the Pueblo Indians and the villagers were at a disadvantage compared with the hacendados. However, according to Roxanne Dunbar Ortiz, "Though Pueblos and Hispano villages had no political or economic power during the eighteenth century, the elite, on the other hand, never gained the necessary economic prosperity to affect the predominant village life of the province nor to change land tenure patterns radically during the colonial period." Still, considerable tension existed between the Pueblo population and the colonial administration; as late as 1793, the governor jailed the caciques of various Tewa pueblos for holding "seditious" meetings.[56]

The Colonization of Texas

Texas natives lived in camps perhaps as early as 13,500 years ago and subsisted primarily on wild game. In fertile east Texas the tribes built permanent villages and had well-developed farms and political and religious systems. These tribes formed a loose federation, known as the Caddo confederacies, to preserve the peace and provide mutual protection. This ancient culture originally occupied the Red River area in what is now Louisiana and Arkansas. As semi-sedentary agricultural people, they grouped around ceremonial mounds that resembled temples. Some scholars speculate that as skillful potters and basketmakers, they were probably related to the Mesoamerican cultures of the south.[57]

Because of the vastness and remote location of what eventually became Texas, it took the Viceroyalty of New Spain hundreds of years to occupy it. While on the periphery of the viceroyalty, it had been fully explored. But unlike other parts of the viceroyalty, there was no evidence of mineral wealth to attract expeditions and adventurers from the south. Its occupation came from three directions. El Paso del Norte belonged to New Mexico and was a corridor to Chihuahua and Sonora. East of El Paso, where the Rio Grande joined the Conchos River at La Junta de los Ríos, the Spanish founded missions in Nueva Vizcaya.

The Conchos River was a corridor into west Texas and the area along the Rio Grande. The coastal region from the Nueces River to the Rio Grande and upstream to Laredo was settled from the province of Nuevo Santander after 1749. The movement into Texas came from these areas.

By the eighteenth century, Spain entered a period of declining revenues and defense of its territories. Spain was a declining power and the expenses of the missions and presidios drained the royal treasury. Hence, the crown encouraged the establishment of self-sufficient pueblos, consisting of castas and a sprinkling of Spanish peasants. Unlike Nueva Vizcaya and Sonora, where mining drew settlers, the occupation of Texas was more a matter of holding on to frontier territory.

The Rio Grande played a key role, seen by many as the answer to the development of New Mexico and much of northern Mexico. The river had the potential of an all-water route to the Gulf of Mexico. Plans to exploit the river and navigate it never fully developed—Spain just did not have the resources. But the importance of the Rio Bravo did not escape the early colonists, who recognized the interdependence of the frontier colonies in what today is called the American Southwest and northern Mexico.[58]

El Paso del Norte

The oldest Spanish settlements in Texas were in the El Paso area. The first Spanish entry into the El Paso area took place in 1581 with the Rodríguez-Sánchez expedition, consisting primarily of natives from Mexico. They passed through two mountain ranges rising out of the desert with a deep gap between them at the crossing of the Rio Bravo (Grande), which they named El Paso del Norte. (El Paso refers not to a passage through the mountains but rather to the crossing of the river.) Oñate's expedition also passed through there near today's San Elizario in 1598, when Oñate claimed the entire territory drained by the Rio Bravo. It was not until 1659 that Fray García de San Francisco founded Nuestra Señora de Guadalupe Mission. The Pueblo Indian Revolt of 1680 drove Spanish colonists, Franciscan missionaries, and Pueblo and Tigua natives from northern New Mexico (who sided with the Spaniards) to the Paso del Norte. South of the river, some 12 miles from today's downtown El Paso, the refugees settled Santisimo Sacramento, later known as Ysleta del Sur. Two years later, construction of a mission began there and was completed in 1692.

By 1682, the Spanish crown had founded the missions and settlement of El Paso del Norte, San Lorenzo, Senecú, Ysleta, and Socorro, all south of the river. This cluster of settlements became a trade and farm center on the Camino Real. Throughout the colonial period, this area was more properly part of New Mexico, Chihuahua, and the northwest Mexican territory than of Texas, with some elite families from other provinces moving there.[59]

The Tlaxcalán and the Castas

As with New Mexico, natives from central Mexico played an important role in the colonizing of Texas proper. According to Carlos Vélez-Ibáñez, the Tlaxcalán initially served as scouts and auxiliary soldiers on various expeditions. In 1688, the Tlaxcalán participated in the building of the presidio of San Juan Bautista near today's Eagle Pass. In response to French exploration along the Mississippi River Valley, Spanish friars established six missions along New Spain's eastern frontier in 1690. The missions' isolation—a three-month journey away from the capital in Mexico City—left the missions vulnerable.

Spanish friars planted Mission San Antonio de Valero, now known as the Alamo, as a way station on the San Antonio River in 1718. The following year the French that were active in present-day northwest Louisiana forced the Spaniards to abandon the east Texas missions, and the missionaries took refuge at Mission San Antonio. By 1731, a chain of five missions (three of which had moved from east Texas), populated by indigenous recruits from Texas, operated along the San Antonio River. Mission San José, founded in 1720, quickly grew prosperous and became the largest of the Texas missions. An *acequia*, an irrigation ditch, boosted agricultural production, and the mission sold the surplus to the growing settlements around the military presidio and the villa of San Antonio. The mission's holdings included El Rancho Atascoso, about 30 miles to the south, where native *vaqueros*, or cowboys, tended 1,500 cattle, 5,000 sheep and goats, and herds of mules and horses.[60]

The Importance of San Antonio and Links to the Rio Bravo

The area that is present-day San Antonio was vital to the future of this frontier. In the early 1730s, a contingent of 55 peasants arrived from the Canary Islands. The colonists revived the villa of San Antonio. The Canarians joined the descendants of the first colonists and friars to form a community, depending on the local garrison for trade and outside merchandise. The population increased slowly but began to prosper somewhat by the 1770s when the community developed new markets in Louisiana and in the El Paso area.[61]

Spain chose to colonize the rich valleys of the upper Rio Grande and the mining districts of Nuevo León and Coahuila to prevent French encroachment into this area. The incentive for this expansion was the need for more pasturage for their herds and the growing demand for cattle and their by-products by the mines. The colony of Nuevo Santander included the Mexican state of Tamaulipas and south Texas. Tomás Sánchez and other hacendados established the colony of Laredo in 1755, downstream from Sánchez's *Hacienda de Dolores*, where some 30 families lived.[62] As in other areas, the natives resisted Spanish encroachments.

By 1767, Laredo had a population of 186 persons. The 1789 census listed 45.3 percent of Laredo's residents as *españoles*, 17.2 percent as mestizos, 17.2 percent as mulatos, and 15.6 percent as indios. However, only 6.7 percent of the married persons said they were intermarried. Illegitimacy was the highest between the mulatos and the indios. Tejano historian Gilberto Hinojosa writes that the Spanish population increased to 57.2 percent of the population by 1820 and that the non-Spanish population seemed to have fallen by 23.9 percent. He speculates that the indios may have moved back to their ranchería settlements. A more plausible explanation is that colonists self-identified themselves as Spanish.[63] The population grew to 2,052 in 1828. In 1824, Laredo had 700 sheep; four years later, it had 3,223. Wool became Laredo's chief export, traded with Mexican merchants from the interior. Racial divisions that existed in 1789 persisted in the 1835 census.

Meanwhile, the population of Nuevo Santander grew from 31,000 in 1794 to 56,937 in 1810. (The Native American population in Nuevo Santander was estimated at 190,000 in 1519; by 1800 it fell to 3,000.) By 1820, despite the turmoil of the Mexican War of Independence from Spain, the colony had grown to 67,434. The combined population of Reynosa, Camargo, Mier, Revilla, Laredo, and Matamoros, on both sides of the Rio Bravo, numbered 1,479 in 1749; by 1829, it had increased to 24,686. The administrative structure of the colony was stratified into large landholders, high government officials, and merchants. The rancheros made up a middle group along with artisans, while the natives and servants lingered at the bottom of the social ladder. Seventeen haciendas and 437 ranchos dotted Nuevo Santander by 1794. As in other provinces, the presidio played an important role in the order and brought in government revenue. Ranching and commerce became the main economic pursuits in the Lower Rio Grande.[64]

The Occupation of Alta California: Paradise Lost

The colonization of *Alta*, or Upper, California began in 1769. Upper California had been one of the most densely populated regions in what is now the United States, with a native population of nearly half a million. The population fell to half that number during the Spanish colonial period. The Franciscans led the colonization of Alta California where they established 21 missions. At the height of their influence, the missions had 20,000 natives living under their control.

Los Indios

From south to north the missions housed the Diegueño, Juaneño, Gabrieliño, Chumash, and Costanoan peoples. Inhabiting the coastland, they were skilled artisans who fashioned sea vessels out of soapstone and used clamshell-bead currency. These tribes bore the brunt of missionary activity.

The Spaniards never missionized the Yokut, who lived in settlements that ran the length of the San Joaquín Valley and the western foothills of the Sierra Madre just south of present-day Fresno. They were divided into as many as 50 tribelets, each with their own dialect. The Yokut, also known as Mariposan, spoke a Penitian language. Master hunters and food gatherers, the Yokut lived in communal houses inhabited by as many as 10 persons. Chiefs or co-chiefs headed the tribes; these were hereditary positions that women could inherit. The women also had a wealth of knowledge about religious questions.

The Yokut carried on extensive trade with other California natives. They harbored runaway mission natives, and thus tension existed between them and Spanish authorities. Like native peoples elsewhere, a large number (75 percent) of the Yokut died because of epidemics, the most devastating event occurring in 1833.[65]

The Missions: Myth and Reality

In principle, the missions were supposed to prepare the natives for a self-rule. This did not happen in the Spanish or Mexican periods. Because of the friars' puritanism and harsh treatment, they drove the indigenous populations to rebellion.[66] Critics point to the falling birthrate among the indigenous people during the mission period. Furthermore, work was associated with a complex system of punishments and rewards. The indigenous people in California were not used to the type of confined physical labor found in the missions.

Alongside the missions, presidios and pueblos were built to consolidate Spanish rule. Mostly mixed-race colonists from Sonora and Sinaloa settled the pueblos. Spanish officials granted many former presidio soldiers land, known as *ranchos*, where they raised cattle and sheep. Some received larger grants for haciendas. The California natives did most of the labor, usually trained by the missions to be vaqueros, soap makers, tanners, shoemakers, carpenters, blacksmiths, bakers, cooks, servants, pages, fishermen, farmers, and carpenters, as well as a host of other occupations.

Ample evidence exists as to tension between military and ecclesiastical authorities over the soldiers' mistreatment of the indigenous women; historian Antonia I. Castañeda says that we can assume that this was the case in other provinces of New Spain as well. Father Junípero Serra, himself a severe taskmaster, often complained about soldier misconduct, saying that the indigenous people resisted missionization and sometimes became warlike and hostile "because of the soldiers' repeated outrages against the women." Serra lamented, "Even the children who came to the mission were not safe from their baseness."[67] Evidence suggests that offenses against women were not remedied; rape and even murder went unpunished. Military officials assumed a "boys-will-be-boys" attitude, although the official policy prohibited such abuses.

In 1785, natives from eight rancherías united and attacked Mission San Gabriel, killing all the Spanish settlers. Toypurina, a 24-year-old medicine woman, persuaded six of the eight villages to join the rebellion. The soldiers captured and punished her along with three other leaders.

Conclusion: On the Eve of the Mexican War of Independence

By the eve of the Mexican War of Independence, a complex society had evolved on the northern frontier of New Spain. Although they were isolated, there was considerable interaction between the different regions in northern New Spain. The nonindigenous settlers tapped into a network of routes used before their arrival by the natives. The Chihuahua Trail, part of the Camino Real, was the trade route linking Santa Fe to Chihuahua and Mexico City. After Taos, New Mexico, was founded in the 1790s, they extended this trail to its plaza. A major part of the trail within New Mexico was a river road, following the Rio Grande. Caravans traveled this road and brought imported goods and luxuries to the settlements of the Rio Grande as they had to the mining camps of Nueva Vizcaya. Exchanges would include ore, slaves, and other goods. There were also well-established routes connecting Alta California, Sonora, New Mexico, and Texas.[68]

We should not romanticize this society as egalitarian. Though most of the inhabitants were non-European, the elites in these societies were recently immigrated Spaniards and/or their criollo children. The vast numbers of subjects were castas, those of mixed race, which had limited access to land. Indeed, the 1793 census shows the dynamic race mixture that was taking place in New Spain. A word of caution would be that although there was diversity, race established privilege, and the more Spanish the subject appeared the more privileges that person had.

Race by the nineteenth century was based more on sight than on the rigid categories of the sixteenth century. What would become the Mexican (and Central American) was a conglomerate of people whose racial identity could change from generation to generation—it went beyond the mestizo paradigm popularly portrayed. For instance, the 1810 census suggests that more than 10 percent of the population were Afromestizos, a classification that generally meant they looked mulato or more African than Spanish.[69] Over generations, those who were originally African or native looked *or wanted to look* more like Spaniards.

As has been mentioned throughout the chapter, forced labor, the wars, the enslavement of the natives, and droughts and plagues had taken their toll on the native population. Either they had become hispanicized, or they perished or were forced into exile. In some cases, like that of the Tarahumara, a large portion of them retreated further into the Sierra Madres. The Yaqui, who had warred with the Spaniards, were later drawn into battle with the Mexicans in the 1920s in defense of their homeland. The Mexicans' justification was that they were *gente de razón* (people of reason), or better still, Christians, and those who opposed them were *indios bárbaros*.

On the eve of the Mexican Revolution, Mexico did not yet have a set national identity. As the reader can deduce from the chart below, the new nation was racially diverse. The new nation was predominantly Indian, and Africans were at least 10 percent of the population. Given the 300-year tradition of lying about race in order to gain category, it can be speculated that as many as 20 percent of the population had some African blood and less than stated were full-blooded Spaniards.[70] The colonial mentality and racial ambivalence are a factor even today among the Mexican people. Yet, it is clear from current population data that most miscegenation took place after independence with the mestizo population going from 10 percent in 1810 to about 60 percent today; on the downside the indigenous population fell from 60 percent to 30 percent.

Population of Mexico in 1810

Racial Category	Number	Percentage
Indians	3,676,281	60
Europeans (peninsulares)	15,000	0.3
Criollos (Euromestizos)	1,092,397	18
Mestizos (Indiomestizos)	704,245	11
Mulatoes and zambos (Afromestizos)	624,461	10
Blacks	10,000	0.2

Sources: Austín Cue Cánovas, Historia social y económica de México (1521–1854) (Mexico, 1972), p. 134, adapted in Meyer and Sherman, p. 218.

The population of Mexico in 1810 consisted of 3,676,281 Indians, which were 60 percent of the nation. In contrast, there were only 15,000 (0.3 percent) Europeans or peninsulares. According to estimates, criollos (Euromestizos) numbered 1,092,397 (18 percent). Mestizos (Indiomestizos) or, better still, a mixture of Spanish and Indian numbered only 704,245 (11 percent), mulatos and zambos (Afromestizos) comprised 624,461 (10 percent); and pure-blooded blacks, 10,000 (0.2 percent). The problem with the data is that race was largely self-reporting, and therefore the Indian and black populations would be under-reported because of the social stigma.[71]

Three hundred years of mercantilism had left New Spain without its own commercial or manufacturing infrastructure. Spanish capital fled the country and the mainstays of its economy—agriculture, ranching, and mining—went bankrupt. The Spanish tightly ruled New Spain because it was Spain's most valuable commodity, giving the castas little experience in self-rule. Indeed, the castas as a group would continue to be excluded from the governance of the republic after independence. For example, Mexico did not have a professional civil service bureaucracy. In addition, Mexico experienced a long war of independence (1810–1821), losing an estimated 10 percent of its population, worsening Mexico's serious underpopulation that resulted from the mass migrations to the northern frontier.[72]

On the positive side, influenced by Enlightenment thinking and representative constitutionalism, many of Mexico's new leaders wanted a modern society based on reason rather than theology. However, Mexicans had to overcome 300 years of Spanish colonialism, which was no small order. On the negative side, the secularization and modernization meant not only the privatization of property belonging to the Catholic Church, but elimination of feudalism that meant the privatization of Indian land. To build their own nation, they had to create a new identity for themselves. A crucial part of creating a new identity and nation building was replacing the old saints with new, secular heroes—heroes who would call on the people to celebrate Mexico and everything it meant to be Mexican.[73] Within this was interwoven the acceptance of the Indian heritage, a process that really did not begin until a hundred years later with the Second Mexican Revolution.[74]

Notes

1. Dennis O. Flynn and Arturo Giráldez, "Cycles of Silver: Global Economic Unity through the Mid-Eighteenth Century," *Journal of World History* 13, no. 2 (2002): 391–427. The first chapter of Rodolfo F. Acuña, *Corridors of Migration: The Odyssey of Mexican Laborers, 1600–1933* (Tucson: University of Arizona Press, 2007) discusses the topics in this chapter in greater detail.

2. Jane S. Gerber, *The Jews of Spain: A History of the Sephardic Experience* (New York: Free Press, 1992), 3. The Jews lived not as isolated individuals but as organized communities in Spain.

3. Punic Wars, http://www.youtube.com/watch?v=ARF2r3Ol80Y&feature=related.

4. Gerber, *The Jews of Spain*, 18–19.

5. W. Montgomery Watt and Pierre Cachia, *A History of Islamic Spain* (Garden City, NY: Anchor Books, 1967), 40.

6. Ibid. Islamic Spain: A Golden Age? (1/1), http://www.youtube.com/watch?v=o8rGNBHdmdQ. Ibid. (2/2), http://www.youtube.com/watch?v=hahOI9LKw2Y.

7. Many—not all—of the YouTube clips are in Spanish; in most cases a translation to English can be obtained from the YouTube site. Reconquista Española, http://www.youtube.com/watch?v=ci2jTnI2qqk&feature=channel. When the Moors Ruled in Spain (1 of 11), http://www.youtube.com/watch?v=wBsDDGCIFLQ&feature=related. S. Alfassa Marks, "The Jews in Islamic Spain: Al Andalus," *Foundation for the Advancement of Sephardic Studies and Culture*, http://www.sephardicstudies.org/islam.html.

8. Christopher Columbus, http://www.youtube.com/watch?v=0YjngFYwX1s. William Bigelow, "Once upon a Genocide: Christopher Columbus in Children's Literature," *Language Arts* 69, no. 2 (1992): 112–20. David E. Stannard, "Columbus's Legacy: Genocide in the Americas," *The Nation* 255, no. 12 (October 19, 1992): 430–33.

9. Jalil Sued-Badillo, "Christopher Columbus and the Enslavement of the Amerindians in the Caribbean; Columbus and the New World Order 1492–1992," *Monthly Review* 44, no. 3 (July 1992): 71ff. This article shows the involvement of the Genoese in the spread of sugar production and slavery and their involvement in the Azores and other islands of the Atlantic coast including the Canary Islands, where they experimented with mercantile capitalism. John H. Elliot, *Imperial Spain 1469–1716* (New York: A Mentor Book, 1966), 56–57. Robert M. Carmack, Janine Gasco, and Gary H. Gossen, *The Legacy of Mesoamerica: History and Culture of a Native American Civilization* (Upper Saddle River, NJ: Prentice Hall, 1996), 131. Peter Muilenburg, "The Savage Sea: The Indians Who Gave Their Name to the Caribbean Stopped at Nothing to Satisfy Their Appetite for Adventure—and Human Flesh," *Sun-Sentinel* (Fort Lauderdale, April 25, 1993), is an example of a popular article repeating myths about the Caribs. Claudius Fergus, "Why an Atlantic Slave Trade?" *Journal of Caribbean History* 42, no. 1 (2008): 1–22.

10. Sued-Badillo, "Columbus and the Enslavement," 71ff. From 1494 to the turn of the century about 2,000 slaves were taken to Castile. Kirkpatrick Sale, "What Columbus Discovered," *The Nation* 251, no. 13 (October 22, 1990): 444–46. Vincent Villanueva Mayer, Jr., "The Black Slave on New Spain's Northern Frontier: San Jose De Parral 1632–76" (PhD dissertation, University of Utah, 1975). The Spaniards imported slaves from China, Cambodia, Java, Siam, Bengal, Persia, and the Philippines who entered through Acapulco on the yearly Manila galleon. These slaves were designated as chinos and esclavos de la India de Portugal. Helen Nader, "Desperate Men, Questionable Acts: The Moral Dilemma of Italian Merchants in the Spanish Slave Trade," *Sixteenth Century Journal* 33, no. 2 (Summer 2002): 402–22.

11. Slave traders transported at least 10 million Africans to the Americas during the colonial period. They sold over 5 million to the Guianas and the Caribbean islands, almost 4 million to Brazil, some 600,000 to mainland Spanish holdings, and the remaining 900,000 to the British colonies in North America and

to Europe in roughly equal shares. Sued-Badillo, "Columbus and the Enslavement," 71. The Spaniards also sold Indians in the slave markets of Havana, Mexico City, and even Manila.

12. Digital Story—Bartolome de las Casas, http://www.youtube.com/watch?v=kAkY0u6aH20. United Methodist Women, "Reformations: 1453–1800," The Bible: The Book That Bridges the Millennia, http://gbgm-umc.org/umw/bible/ref.stm.

13. Carmack et al., *The Legacy of Mesoamerica*, 132–36. Lewis Hanke, *Aristotle and the American Indians: A Study in Race Prejudice in the Modern World* (Chicago, IL: Henry Regnery Company, 1959), 13, 33, 45.

14. Charles L. Mee, Jr., "That Fateful Moment When Two Civilizations Came Face to Face; Spaniards and Aztecs," *Smithsonian* 23, no. 7 (October 1992): 56ff.

15. Tenochtitlan, http://www.youtube.com/watch?v=F3QA2J9UxJE. La Noche Triste, http://www.youtube.com/watch?v=lJA_tYOIBaY&feature=related.

16. Noble David Cook, *Born To Die: Disease and New World Conquest* (New York: Cambridge University Press, 1998), 206. Francis J. Brooks, "Revising the Conquest of Mexico: Smallpox, Sources, and Populations," *Journal of Interdisciplinary History* 24, no. 1 (Summer 1993): 1–29. David Henige, *Numbers from Nowhere: The American Indian Contact Population Debate* (Norman: University of Oklahoma Press, 1998).

17. Susan Kellogg, "Hegemony Out of Conquest: The First Two Centuries of Spanish Rule in Central Mexico," *Radical History Review* 53 (1991): 32. Gunter B. Risse, "What Columbus's Voyages Wrought; Editorial," *Western Journal of Medicine* 160, no. 6 (June 1994): 577ff.

18. Kellogg, "Hegemony Out of Conquest," 29. Alfred W. Crosby, Jr., *The Columbian Exchange: Biological and Cultural Consequences of 1492* (Westport, CT: Greenwood Press, 1972), 48–58. See Cook, *Born to Die*, 132, 139, 140, 168, 170, 193, for table summaries of epidemics in Mexico and Guatemala. G. B. Risse, "What Columbus's Voyages Wrought," *Western Journal of Medicine* 160, no. 6 (June 1994): 577–79. "The Spread of Disease in the New World," 123HelpMe.com (November 19, 2013), http://www.123HelpMe.com/view.asp?id=21528.

19. Nathan Nunn and Nancy Qian, "The Columbian Exchange: A History of Disease, Food, and Ideas," *Journal of Economic Perspectives* 24, no. 2 (Spring 2010): 163–88.

20. Neil Robert Kasiak, "Fermenting Identities: Race and Pulque Politics in Mexico City between 1519 and 1754" (Master of Arts thesis, Eastern Kentucky University, 2012).

21. Michael C. Meyer, William L. Sherman, and Susan M. Deeds, *The Course of Mexican History*, 6th ed. (New York: Oxford University Press, 1999), 130–32. Jason Edward Lemon, "The encomienda in early New Spain" Ph.D. dissertation, Emory University, 2000.

22. Hanns J. Prem, "Spanish Colonization and Indian Property in Central Mexico, 1521–1620," *Annals of the Association of American Geographers* 82, no. 3 (September 1992): 446.

23. C. Haring, *The Spanish Empire in America* (New York: Harcourt, Brace & World, 1963). Carmack et al., *The Legacy of Mesoamerica*, 166, quote "[N]ative people had no concept of a 'religion' or a 'faith' as such a clearly defined entity separable from the rest of culture, and they did not comprehend what it was they were supposed to be giving up and taking on."

24. James Lockhart, *The Nahuas After the Conquest: Social and Cultural History of the Indians of Central Mexico, Sixteenth Through Eighteenth Centuries* (Stanford, CA: Stanford University Press, 1992), 14–58, 62, 428, argues that many aspects of the Azteca system remained intact, especially during the first 50 years after the invasion. His account, based on Nahuatl sources, is intriguing, if not always persuasive.

25. María Elena Martínez, *Genealogical Fictions: Limpieza de Sangre, Religion, and Gender in Colonial Mexico* (Stanford, CA: Stanford University Press, 2011). Patricia Lopes Don, "Franciscans, Indian Sorcerers, and the Inquisition in New Spain, 1536–1543," *Journal of World History* 17, no. 1 (March 2006): 27–49.

26. Marcela Tostado Gutiérrez, *El álbum de la mujer de las mexicanas. Volumén II/Época colonial* (México, DF: Instituto Nacional de Antropología é Historia, 1991), 109. Most racial designations were not used after the sixteenth century. The mixed races were referred to as castas. *Diccionario Porrúa: Historia, Biografía y Geografía De México* Quinta Edición (México DF: Editorial Porrúa, S. A., 1986), 535 lists the categories. Adrian Bustamante, "The Matter Was Never Resolved: The Casta System in Colonial New Mexico, 1693–1823," *New Mexico Historical Review* 66, no. 2 (April 1991): 143–63, on page 144 presents another variation. Castas, http://faculty.smu.edu/bakewell/BAKEWELL/thinksheets/castas.html.

27. Pinturas de Castas, Painting of Castes, http://www.youtube.com/watch?v=ZMjO2Ckc1iE. D. A. Brading, "Source," *Hispanic American Historical Review* 53, no. 3 (August 1973), 389–414. Stafford Poole, "Church Law on the Ordination of Indians and Castas in New Spain," *Hispanic American Historical Review* 61, no. 4 (November 1981): 637–50.

28. Strategically, many of the *conquistadores* married the daughters of the nobles and the caciques, who enjoyed the privileges of their class. Some inherited property and even went to Spain to live. There is a rich bibliography on Sor Juana. One of the best known is that by Octavio Paz, *Sor Juana or, the Traps of Faith*, trans. by Margaret Sayers Peden (Cambridge: Harvard University Press, 1988). Sor Juana Inés de la Cruz, http://www.youtube.com/watch?v=4tdNcjFWM9Q. Shorter translated version, http://www.youtube.com/watch?v=uzjp01ECRF4&translated=1.

29. Irene Silverblatt, "Women, Power, and Resistance in Colonial Mesoamerica," *Ethnohistory* 42, no. 4 (Autumn 1995): 639–50. Indian women fared worse on the frontier: Juliana Barr, "From Captives to Slaves: Commodifying Indian Women in the Borderlands," *Journal of American History* 92, no. 1 (June 2005): 18–46.

30. Marie Elaine Danforth, Keith Jacobi, and Mark Nathan Cohen, "Gender and Health Among the Colonial Mayan of Tipu, Belize," *Ancient Mesoamerica* 8, no. 1 (Spring 1997): 1, 15.

31. Carmack et al., *The Legacy of Mesoamerica*, 181–83. Linda Schele and David Freidel, *A Forest of Kings: The Untold Story of the Ancient Mayan* (New York: Quill William Morrow, 1990), 40–41.

32. Louise Burkhart, "Mexica Women on the Home Front: Housework and Religion in Aztec Mexico," in Susan Schroeder, Stephanie Wood, and Robert Haskett, eds., *Indian Women of Early Mexico* (Norman: University of Oklahoma Press, 1997), 25–27. Susan Kellogg, "From Parallel and Equivalent to Separate but Unequal: Tenocha Mexica Women, 1500–1700," in Susan Schroeder, Stephanie Wood, and Robert Haskett, eds., *Indian Women of Early Mexico* (Norman: University of Oklahoma Press, 1997), 123–37. Pedro Carrasco, "Indian-Spanish Marriages in the First Century of the Colony," in Schroeder et al., *Indian Women of Early Mexico*, 87–89, 93, 97.

33. Carmack et al., *The Legacy of Mesoamerica*, 330.

34. Robert Haskett, "Activist or Adulteress: The Life and Struggle of Doña Josefa María of Tepoztlán," in Schroeder et al., *Indian Women of Early Mexico*, 147–53.

35. Silverblatt, "Lessons of Gender and Ethnohistory," 641, 645–46. Javier Pérez Escohotado, *Sexo e Inquisición en España* (Madrid: Ediciones Termas Hoy, 1998), 173–90, deals with the Inquisition in Spain and homosexuality. Laura A. Lewis, "The 'Weakness' of Women and the Feminization of the Indian in Colonial Mexico," *Colonial Latin American Review* 5, no. 1 (June 1996): 73–95. Douglas Richmond, "The Legacy of African Slavery in Colonial Mexico, 1519–1810," *Journal of Popular Culture* 35, no. 2 (Fall 2001): 1–16.

36. Juan Diego was canonized in 2002.

37. Eric Hobsbawm and Terence Ranger, eds., *The Invention of Tradition* (London: Cambridge University Press, 1983). Sandra Cisneros, "Guadalupe as the Sex Goddess," in Ana Castillo, ed., *Goddess of the Americas: Writing on the Virgin of Guadalupe* (New York: Riverhead Books, 1996), 49–50. Gloria Anzaldúa, *Borderlands/La Frontera: The New Mestiza* (San Francisco, CA: Aunt Lute Books, 1987), 27. Stafford Poole, C. M., *Our Lady of Guadalupe: The Origins and Sources of a Mexican National Symbol, 1531–1797* (Tucson: University of Arizona Press, 1995). Carmack et al., *The Legacy of Mesoamerica*, 191–92.

38. Poole, *Our Lady of Guadalupe*. Carmack et al., *The Legacy of Mesoamerica*, 191–92.

39. Poole, *Our Lady of Guadalupe*, 5.

40. Map of Spanish Exploration and Early Colonization Activities in North America, 1513–1607, http://www.artifacts.org/conquest.htm.

41. Thomas P. Moore, "A Brief History of Early Silver Mining in Spanish America," *Mineralogical Record*, 39, no. 6 (November–December 2008): 5–21.

42. Thomas E. Sheridan, "The Limits of Power: The Political Ecology of the Spanish Empire in the Greater Southwest," *Antiquity* 66 (1992): 153, 164, 167.

43. David J. Weber, *The Spanish Frontier in North America* (New Haven: Yale University Press, 1992), 94, 118. Kellogg, "Hegemony Out of Conquest," 29. See Chapter 1 in Acuña, *Corridors of Migration*, especially the footnotes and bibliography.

44. Susan M. Deeds, "Double Jeopardy: Indian Women in Jesuit Missions of Nueva Vizcaya," in Schroeder et al., *Indian Women of Early Mexico*, 255–59, 263. Catholic divorce or annulment was practically unavailable to indigenous women.

45. Florence C. Lister and Robert H. Lister, *Chihuahua: Storehouse of Storms* (Albuquerque: University of New Mexico Press, 1966), 15–20. Carmack et al., *The Legacy of Mesoamerica*, 5. Acuña, *Corridors of Migration*, 12–14.

46. Tina Griego, "A Foot Note to History; Amputation of N.M. Statue Underlines 400-Year-Old Grudge," *Rocky Mountain News* (Denver, CO, June 21, 1998). Just prior to the 400th anniversary, the *Cuarto Centenario* of Oñate's conquest of New Mexico, someone expertly cut the right foot off a bronze statue of Oñate. During Oñate's conquest of New Mexico, the people of Acoma Pueblo resisted the invasion and Oñate punished the people by condemning 24 Acoma men to the amputation of a foot and banished their women and children into slavery.

47. See Susan M. Deeds, "Rural Work in Nueva Vizcaya: Forms of Labor Coercion on the Periphery," *Hispanic American Historical Review* 69, no. 3 (August 1, 1989): 425–49.

48. Deeds, "Rural Work," 435. Acuña, *Corridors of Migration*, 13–14, 37, 71. Estevan Rael-Galvez, "Identifying Captivity and Capturing Identity: Narratives of American Indian Slavery. Colorado and New Mexico, 1776–1934" (PhD dissertation, University of Michigan, 2002).

49. Jeremy Baskes, "Coerced or Voluntary? The Repartimiento and Market Participation of Peasants in Late Colonial Oaxaca," *Journal of Latin American Studies*, 28, no. 1 (February 1996): 1–28.

50. Weber, *The Spanish Frontier in North America*, 128.

51. Angelina F. Veyna, "Women in Early New Mexico: A Preliminary View," in Teresa Córova et al., eds., *Chicana Voices: Intersections of Class, Race, and Gender* (Austin, TX: Center for Mexican American Studies, 1986), 120–35.

52. "The Pueblo Revolt of 1680," *Native Peoples Magazine*, http://worldhistoryproject.org/1680/8/21/pueblo-indians-capture-santa-fe-from-the-spanish. Jack D. Forbes, *Apache, Navaho and Spaniard* (Norman, OK: University of Oklahoma Press, 1960), 200–24. Luis Aboites Aguilar, *Breve Historia de Chihuahua* (Mexico City: Fondo de Cultura Economica, 1994), 42–44; Susan M. Deeds, *Defiance and Deference in Mexico's Colonia North: Indians under Spanish Rule in Nueva Vizcaya* (Austin, TX: University of Texas Press, 2003), 87.

53. The 1680 Revolt inspired indigenous revolts throughout present-day Chihuahua, Durango, and Sonora. Acuña, *Corridors of Migration*, 4–17. Earlier drafts in Acuña Collection, CSUN, have more extensive treatments.

54. Ramón A. Gutiérrez, *When Jesus Came, the Corn Mothers Went Away: Marriage, Sexuality, and Power in New Mexico, 1500–1846* (Stanford, CA: Stanford University Press, 1991), 171. Roxanne Amanda Dunbar, "Land Tenure in Northern New Mexico: An Historical Perspective," (PhD dissertation, University of California, Los Angeles, 1974), 6. Jonathan Hass, "Warfare among the Pueblos: Myth, History, and Ethnography," *Ethnohistory* 44, no. 2 (Spring 1997): 235–61. Also

see Jonathan Haas, "Warfare and the Evolution of Tribal Politics in the Prehistoric Southwest," in Jonathan Haas, ed., *Anthropology of War* (New York: Cambridge University Press, 1990), 171–89, quote 182. Weber, *The Spanish Frontier in North America*, 122.

55. Gutiérrez, *When Jesus Came, the Corn Mothers Went Away*, 159, 174. Angelina F. Veyna, "A Look at Colonial Nueva Mexicanas through Their Testaments," in Adela de la Torre and Beatríz M. Pesquera, eds., *Building with Our Hands New Directions in Chicana Studies* (Berkeley, CA: University of California Press, 1993), 91–108. Weber, *The Spanish Frontier in North America*, 125. Also see Bustamante, 1991, 145–47, which points out that many of the census and parish records were destroyed during the 1680 Pueblo Revolt.

56. Dunbar, "Land Tenure in Northern New Mexico," 15–17, 97, 107, quote, 133. Gutiérrez, *When Jesus Came, the Corn Mothers Went Away*, 150, 162.

57. Donald E. Chipman, *Spanish Texas, 1519–1821* (Austin: University of Texas, 1992). Handbook of Texas Online, Spanish Texas, http://www.tshaonline.org/handbook/online/articles/nps01. "Old Records and Archeological Remains: Making Sense of the Evidence," Texas Beyond History, University of Texas, http://www.texasbeyondhistory.net/plateaus/peoples/records.html.

58. Jesús E. De La Teja, *San Antonio De Béxar: A Community on New Spain's Northern Frontier* (Albuquerque: University of New Mexico Press, 1995), 3–5.

59. For example, Francisco Elías González de Zayas, the founder of the Elías family of Sonora, was a presidio captain, rancher, and miner; he had arrived at Alamos, Sonora, from La Rioja, Spain, in 1729. He was captain of the Presidio of Terrenate in 1768, lived in Arizpe, founded by his family, and died in Paso del Norte, Chihuahua, Mexico, in 1790 as a merchant.

60. Carlos Vélez-Ibáñez, *Border Visions: Mexican Cultures of the Southwest United States* (Tucson: University of Arizona Press, 1996), 47–48. Weber, *The Spanish Frontier in North America*, 179.

61. Weber, *The Spanish Frontier in North America*, 193–95.

62. Gilberto Miguel Hinojosa, *A Borderlands Town in Transition: Laredo, 1755–1870* (College Station: Texas A&M University Press, 1983), 3. Armando C. Alonzo, *Tejano Legacy: Ranchers and Settlers in South Texas, 1734–1900* (Albuquerque: University of New Mexico Press, 1998), 31. An often overlooked book is Reymandlo Ayala Vallejo, *Geografía Histórica De Parras: El Hombre Cambia a la Tierra* (Saltillo, Coahuila: Sandra de la Cruz González, 1996), 52–55. Tlaxcalans were very important in the colonization of the area as were black slaves who were brought into the area by the *hacendados*, missionaries, and mine owners. From 1 to 30 percent of the population was either black or mulato.

63. Hinojosa, *A Borderlands Town in Transition*, 18, 33.

64. Sheridan, "The Limits of Power," 167. Alonzo, *Tejano Legacy*, 67, 160–61.

65. Brooke S. Arkush, "Yokuts Trade Networks and Native Culture Change in Central and Eastern California," *Ethnohistory* 40, no. 4 (Fall 1993): 619–40.

66. Sherburne F. Cook, *The Conflict Between the California Indian and White Civilization*, Vol. I (Berkeley: University of California Press, 1943), 11–157.

67. Antonia I. Castañeda, "Sexual Violence in the Politics and Policies of Conquest: Amerindian Women and the Spanish Conquest of Alta California," in Adela de la Torre and Beatríz M. Pesquera, eds., *Building with Our Hands: New Directions in Chicana Studies* (Berkeley: University of California Press, 1993), 15–33.

68. David J. Weber, *The Mexican Frontier 1821–1846: The American Southwest Under Mexico* (Albuquerque: University of New Mexico Press, 1982), 1. Armando Miguélez, "La trémula luz del relámpago: Lenguaje metafórico en El Clamor Público," Trabajo presentado en la conferencia El Clamor Público: 150 Years of Latino Newspapers in Southern California, the Huntington Library, San Marino, California, 28 de octubre de 2005. Rodolfo F. Acuña, "El Clamor Público: The Sonora Connection (rough draft)," Paper presented at the conference *El Clamor Público*: 150 Years of Latino Newspapers in Southern California, the Huntington Library, San Marino, California, October 28, 2005.

69. Note that Chihuahuans, like New Mexicans, took great pride in so-called racial purity. See examination of censuses for Santa Bárbara, Chihuahua, Padrón de Santa Bárbara, Chihuahua 1778 (AGI indiferente 102), Padrones de Cusiguriachic 1778 (Archivo General de Indias), and various others. Compiled by Sylvia Magdaleno of *La Familia* Ancestral Research Association. The compilation explodes the myth of racial purity. The various *castas* are represented in different censuses. "The El Paso Del Norte: Nuestra Señora de Guadalupe Marriage and Death Records, 1728–1775," extracted by Aaron Magdaleno, of *La Familia* Ancestral Research Association, January 1998, also shows that although race is not designated in every case, there is substantial mixing.

70. In 1560, blacks and mulatos outnumbered Spaniards in Mexico City; Africans came to Mexico in greater numbers than whites until the 1700s.

71. Meyer et al., *The Course of Mexican History*, 218.

72. *Diccionario Porrúa: De Historia, Biografiá y Geografía* Quinta Edición, Vol. I (México DF: Editorial Porrúa, 1986), 876–77, has an interesting summary of demographic patterns in Mexico.

73. The Mexican census of 1921 shines a bright light on the question of identity. See John P. Schmal, "Racial Makeup of Native-Born Mexicans (from the 1921 Census)," *The Hispanic Experience*, http://www.houstonculture.org/hispanic/census-table.html and Schmal, "Indigenous Identity in the Mexican Census," *The Hispanic Experience*, http://www.houstonculture.org/hispanic/census.html.

74. Readers are encouraged to explore the following archive. Wallace L. McKeehan, "Mexican Independence," Sons of Dewitt Colony Texas http://www.tamu.edu/ccbn/dewitt/dewitt.htm. See Pilar Gonzalbo, "La familia en México colonial: Una historia de conflictos cotidianos," *Mexican Studies/Estudios Mexicanos* 14, no. 2 (Summer 1998), 389–406.

CHAPTER 3

Legacy of Hate: The Conquest of Mexico's Northwest

LEARNING OBJECTIVES

- Show the interrelationship between the treaties of 1819 through 1848 and motives for the American encroachment on Texas and the invasion of Mexico.

- Discuss the role of slavery in motivating the Euro-American Texas filibusters.

- Analyze who was to blame for the Mexican-American War.

- Demonstrate an understanding of maps and documenting archival sources.

- Identify what Mexico lost and what the United States gained as a result of the war.

- Explain the Treaty of Guadalupe Hidalgo and its lasting effect on relations between Mexico and the United States.

The purpose of the timeline is to give a context for the history that led to the United States' invasion of Mexico's northern territory. The narrative begins in 1613 with theologian Alexander Whitaker expressing the notion that God brought the Virginia colonists to the Americas. Whitaker was known as "The Apostle of Virginia."[1] Seven years later the Puritans founded Massachusetts Bay Colony, and its first governor John Winthrop continued the theme of a New Israel, saying that "God hath opened this passage unto us."[2] In 1767 Benjamin Franklin articulated this notion of the entitlement of British colonists; in 1776 Franklin and Thomas Jefferson wanted to include an image of the Promised Land on the new nation's Great Seal.[3] Claims of being the chosen people can be plotted on a timeline leading up to the invasions of Texas in 1836 and Mexico in 1847.

1613	1620	1767	1776	1803	1819	1821	1823	1824	1832	1836	1845	1848[4]

Who Started the War?

The notion that the United States invaded Mexico often offends Euro-Americans. I remember the late University of California Santa Barbara historian Robert L. Kelley in 1992 accusing me of lying because I wrote that the United States invaded Mexico. More recently Arizona Attorney General Tom Horne was pressed about why *Occupied America* was banned and answered that it was because it said that the United States had invaded Mexico. According to Kelley and Horne, I lied.[5] However, contemporaries of the war, such as U.S. President Ulysses S. Grant (1822–1885), share my opinion that the United States was an aggressor in these wars. Grant wrote, "For myself, I was bitterly opposed to the measure, and to this day regard the war (with Mexico) . . . one of the most unjust ever waged by a stronger against a weaker nation. It was an instance of a republic following the bad example of European monarchies, in not considering justice in their desire to acquire additional territory." Grant added, "Texas was originally a state belonging to the republic of Mexico. . . . [The American] colonists paid very little attention to the supreme government, and introduced slavery into the state almost from the start, though the constitution of Mexico did not, nor does it now, sanction that institution." Of the annexation of Texas, Grant said, "The occupation, separation and annexation were, from the inception of the movement to its final consummation, a conspiracy to acquire territory out of which slave states might be formed for the American Union." Grant concluded, "Even if the annexation itself could be justified, the manner in which the subsequent war was forced upon Mexico cannot."[6] This view was shared by Illinois Congressman Abraham Lincoln.[7]

Mexican Independence from Spain

Father Miguel Hidalgo y Costilla sparked a social revolution on September 16, 1810, made up of *los de abajo*, the underdogs. Under the banner of the Virgen de Guadalupe, the movement's ranks swelled to some 80,000. Despite the fervor the revolutionary army was ill-prepared, and in early 1811, the Spanish royal troops captured and executed Hidalgo. José María Morelos y Pavón, an indigenous priest with African blood, took up the banner and led a better-organized army with a wider social base. The mostly native army also recruited African Americans and mulatos from the sugar plantations. After the death of Morelos in 1815, revolutionary bands formed smaller forces under leaders like Guadalupe Victoria and Vicente Guerrero, an indo-mulato, who waged guerrilla warfare.[8]

Guerrero joined Agustín de Iturbide, the commander of the royalist forces, and drew up the Plan of Iguala, which offered guarantees of religion, independence, and union. The Plan called for respect for the church, and equality between Mexicans and peninsulars. It won the support of many criollos, Spaniards, and even former rebels. In 1822, Iturbide became Agustín I, Emperor of Mexico. A year later, Guadalupe Victoria overthrew Iturbide. Most of Central America broke from Mexico, catapulting Antonio López de Santa Anna to the center stage of Mexican politics.[9]

The Mexican state was bankrupt, with little chance for stability. The challenge was to form a nation-state that would integrate the new nation's varied population and regions and create an overriding identity.[10] The long and arduous process of state building proved chaotic, and the state formation was not completed until the 1890s.[11] Unlike the newly born United States, the Mexican nation was made up of different races, including a majority of Native Americans, which made nation building harder. The Texas (1836) and Mexican (1845–1848) wars further delayed the process of state formation.

From 1800 through 1819, the United States expanded dramatically through a series of purchases and aggressions. In 1803, the Louisiana territory added 820,000 square miles to the new nation. In 1819, U.S. aggressions in Florida amassed another 58,664 square miles. This crossing of borders took a dramatic turn in 1821 as Mexico gained its independence from Spain. It now bordered the United States in Texas and New Mexico, among other northern Mexican lands. Euro-Americans had acquired an enhanced sense of uniqueness and entitlement. They believed that Texas once belonged to them and that moving the U.S. border south was a reannexation of what was already theirs. This set the stage for the crossing of borders and the "reannexation" of another 261,797 square miles as the borders crossed river valleys.[12]

The United States could not claim that it needed the land. Much of the Louisiana Purchase, central Illinois, southern Georgia, and West Virginia lay vacant. Hence, the wars were for profit, with the United States seizing over half of Mexico.[13] These invasions contributed to the further bankruptcy of Mexico and continued its dependence on military leaders, whom the Mexican people desperately wanted to believe would bring order.

Background to the Invasion of Texas

In the United States, the word *filibuster* refers primarily to the U.S. Senate, where senators use a tactic to delay debate or block legislation. The word originally referred to the buccaneers, the pirates infesting the high seas. For Latin Americans and Mexicans, filibuster has more sinister meanings. *Filibuster* refers to an adventurer who preys on a foreign country with a private military. Thus, Mexicans call the Stephen Austins and Sam Houstons of this world filibusters. Filibustering or freebooting was quite common in the nineteenth century when many Americans wanted to be Sam Adams (a leader of the American Revolution). These wannabes staked out foreign territories for U.S. expansion. The most popular example is William Walker who in the 1850s invaded Lower California, Sonora, and Nicaragua.

Florida set the pattern for the Texas filibusters. In 1818, U.S. troops seized several posts in east Florida, an act that was never officially condemned by the United States. In the Adams-Onis, or Transcontinental, Treaty (1819), Spain ceded Florida to the United States and the United States in turn, renounced its claim to Texas, a part of Coahuila. Notwithstanding this agreement, many North Americans still argued that Texas belonged to the United States, repeating Jefferson's claim that Texas's boundary extended to the Rio Grande and that it was part of the Louisiana Purchase. Euro-Americans made forays into Texas similar to those they had made into Florida. In 1819, James Long led an abortive invasion to establish the "Republic of Texas." He long believed that Texas belonged to the United States and that the Congress of the United States did not have the right or power to sell Texas.[14]

Despite the hostility, the Mexican government opened Texas to Euro-American colonization. Spain had given Moses Austin permission to settle in Texas. After he died Mexico gave his son Stephen permission to settle in Texas, and in December 1821, Stephen founded the colony of San Felipe de Austin. Large numbers of colonists from the United States entered Texas in the 1820s as refugees from the Depression of 1819. By 1830 about 20,000 colonists had settled in Texas along with some 2,000 slaves.[15]

Broken Promises

The preponderance of evidence shows that the early Euro-American settlers intended to obey Mexican laws just so long as the laws did not interfere with their property rights—which meant their right to own slaves—and they reacted negatively to Mexico's attempts to enforce its laws.[16] Euro-American colonists had agreed to obey the conditions set by the Mexican government that all immigrants to Texas become Catholics and that they take an oath of allegiance to Mexico. However, the newcomers became resentful when Mexico tried to enforce the agreements. Mexico, in turn, grew increasingly alarmed at the flood of immigrants from the United States.[17]

Euro-American logic considered the native Mexicans to be the intruders. The Hayden Edwards affair is a case in point: Edwards arbitrarily attempted to evict colonists from his land grant before Mexican authorities had the opportunity to resolve conflicting claims. As a result, the Mexican government nullified his contract and ordered him out of the territory. On December 21, 1826, Edwards and his followers seized the town of Nacogdoches, declaring it the "Republic of Fredonia." Mexicans put down the Edwards revolt with the support of Stephen Austin. A number of U.S. newspapers portrayed the rebellion as "200 Men Against a Nation!" and described Edwards and his followers as "apostles of democracy crushed by an alien civilization."[18]

Events in the United States encouraged the arrogance of the Euro-American colonists in Texas. In 1823, President James Monroe proclaimed that European powers were not permitted to colonize the Americas or interfere with the affairs of its sovereign nations.[19] Critics have said that this proclamation suggested that the "Americas" were for the United States of America only. A year later, Secretary of State John Quincy Adams pressured Mexico to readjust its borders. The United States was not satisfied with the

Sabine River as the border and wanted to push the boundary to the Rio Grande.[20] Two years later Adams, now president, offered to buy Texas for $1 million. When Mexican authorities refused the offer, the United States launched an aggressive diplomatic campaign, attempting to coerce Mexico into selling Texas.

Slavery gave North Americans a huge economic advantage, helping to create a privileged class of plantation owners. North Americans in Texas protected this privilege. When Mexico abolished slavery on September 15, 1829, slave owners circumvented the law by "freeing" their slaves and then signing them to lifelong contracts as indentured servants. The North American elite resented the Mexican order and considered the abolishment of slavery an infringement on their personal liberties. In 1830, Mexico prohibited further North American immigration. Meanwhile, Andrew Jackson increased tensions by attempting to purchase Texas for as much as $5 million. Mexican authorities reacted to the threat by moving troop reinforcements into Coahuila, which Euro-Americans viewed as an act of provocation.[21]

Follow the Money: The Land Companies and Trade

United States-based land companies worsened the strained relations between the United States and Mexico by lobbying for Washington, D.C., to intervene.[22] In the rush to occupy Texas, the land companies began feverishly issuing landscrips, certificates representing entitlement to landownership in Texas. According to Mexican-American historian Dr. Carlos Castañeda:

> *The activities of the "Land Companies" after 1834 cannot be ignored. Their widespread promotion of cheap land and indiscriminate sale of "landscrip" sent hundreds, perhaps thousands, to Texas under the impression that they had legitimate title to lands equal to the amount of scrip bought. The Galveston Bay and Texas Land Company, which bought the contracts of David S. Burnet, Joseph Vahlein, and Lorenzo de Zavala, and the Nashville Company, which acquired the contract of Robert Leftwitch, are the two best known. They first sold scrip at from one to ten cents an acre, calling for a total of seven and one-half million acres. The company was selling only its permit to acquire a given amount of land in Texas, but since an empresario contract was nontransferable, the scrip was, in fact, worthless.[23]*

That is, the scrip was worthless as long as Texas belonged to Mexico.

The North Americans saw the separation of Texas from Mexico and eventual union with the United States as the most profitable political arrangement. Castañeda notes that "Trade with New Orleans and other American ports had increased steadily." This strengthened economic ties with the United States rather than with Mexico. Castañeda continues, "Juan H. Almonte in his 1834 report, estimated the total foreign trade of Texas—chiefly with the United States—at more than 1,000,000 pesos, of which imports constituted 630,000 and exports, 500,000." The exportation of cotton by the colonists reached approximately 2,000 bales in 1833.[24] Colonel Almonte's report recommended concessions to the dissidents but also urged that Mexico be prepared.

Wanna-Be Sam Adamses

The die was cast by 1830; the Mexican government was taking measures to tighten control of Texas and the white colonists reacted harshly.[25] The colonists refused to pay customs to Mexico, abetting smuggling activities. When the "war party" rioted at Anáhuac in December 1831, it had the popular support among white colonists. One of its leaders, Sam Houston, according to historian Eugene C. Barker, "was a known protégé of Andrew Jackson, now president of the United States . . . Houston's motivation was to bring Texas into the United States."[26] The next summer, Mexican troops routed a group of Euro-Americans who attacked a garrison. Matters deteriorated when the colonists convened at San Felipe in October 1832 and drafted resolutions calling for more autonomy for Texas. They sent the demands to the Mexican government and to the state of Coahuila. The secessionists held a second convention in January 1833. Not one Mexican pueblo supported either convention, branding the act seditious. The war party had achieved its purpose. The members elected Houston to lead the army and appointed Austin to take their grievances and resolutions to Mexico City.[27]

The Point of No Return

In Mexico City, Austin pressed for lifting restrictions on Euro-American immigration and for separate statehood. The slave issue also burned in his mind. Austin wrote, anything but conciliatory, to a friend, "If our application is refused . . . I shall be in favor of organizing *without it.* I see no other way of saving the country from total anarchy and ruin. I am totally done with conciliatory measures and, for the future, shall be uncompromising as to Texas."[28]

On October 2, 1833, Austin wrote to the San Antonio *ayuntamiento* (municipal government), urging it to declare Texas a separate state. Austin later said that he had done so "in a moment of irritation and impatience"; yet his actions were not those of a moderate. Contents of the note fell into the hands of Mexican authorities, who questioned Austin's good faith and imprisoned him. Meanwhile, the U.S. minister to Mexico, Anthony Butler, crudely attempted to bribe Mexican officials into selling Texas to the United States. Butler offered one Mexican official $200,000 to "play ball."[29]

On July 13, 1835, a general amnesty released Austin from prison. While en route to Texas, he wrote to a cousin from New Orleans that Texas should be Americanized, saying that Texas would one day come under the American flag. Austin called for a massive immigration of Euro-Americans to Texas, "each man with his rifle," who he hoped would come with "passports or no passports, *anyhow.*" He continued, "For fourteen years I have had a hard time of it, but nothing shall daunt my courage or abate my . . . object . . . to *Americanize* Texas."[30]

On September 19, 1835, Austin concluded, "War is our only recourse. There is no other remedy."[31] Euro-Americans enjoyed huge advantages. They were defending terrain that they were familiar with, and they were receiving arms from the United States. The overwhelming majority of the 5,000 Mexicans living in Texas stayed loyal to Mexico, but the Euro-American population totally eclipsed the Mexican population, their numbers having swelled to almost 30,000. Politically, Mexico was divided: Mexico's independence was just over a dozen years old and Mexico City was thousands of miles from the center of Texas.

The Invasion of Texas

In the United States, many opposed the war and saw the Texas revolution as a disgraceful affair promoted by slaveholders and land speculators. U.S. historians such as Eugene Barker blame Mexico, arguing that the immediate cause of the war was Antonio López de Santa Anna's overthrow of "the nominal republic and the substitution of centralized oligarchy." Barker ignores or denies that slavery was a main issue. He draws parallels between the Texas filibuster and the American Revolution, arguing that the general cause of revolts was "sudden effort to extend imperial authority at the expense of local privilege." Barker posits that "Texans saw themselves in danger of becoming the alien subjects of a people to whom they deliberately believed themselves morally, intellectually, and politically superior." Barker says that the Mexicans also mistrusted the Euro-Americans on racial grounds. According to Baker, when Mexican authorities took drastic measures to keep the American colonists in line, the Euro-American Texans believed that their liberty was endangered and they revolted.[32] But what Barker and others forget is that most of the leaders and their followers in the revolt were outsiders. None of them had been born in Texas, for instance.

The Pretext: Myths of the Alamo

Historical myths are often a combination of fiction and half-truth, justifying the actions of the actors in certain events. Myths are common in history and often become legends taken as truth. In the case of the Texas filibuster, a score of popular books have been written about Mexican cruelty at the Alamo and about the heroics of the doomed men, producing the Alamo myth, which justifies the Texas insurrection. Like so many myths, the story of the Alamo is a distortion of reality, with its exaggeration of 187 filibusters standing against the barbarians at the gates of civilization. Here the "defenders" allegedly barricaded themselves in the Alamo in defiance of Santa Anna's force, which, according to Mexican sources, numbered 1,400, and the Mexicans eventually triumphed.[33]

Many U.S. historians have riddled the myths of the Alamo with dramatic half-truths, portraying those in the mission as selfless heroes who sacrificed their lives to buy more time for their comrades-in-arms. Walter Lord, in an article entitled "Myths and Realities of the Alamo," broke with the Texas story, which portrays the defenders of the Alamo as freedom-loving Texans who were protecting their homes.[34] Actually, two-thirds of the so-called defenders had recently arrived from the United States, and only a half dozen had been in Texas for more than six years. The filibusters were adventurers who were spoiling for a fight.

The Defense of the Mexican Homeland

Santa Anna led an army of about 6,000 soldiers into Texas. The truth is that Mexicans were defending the homeland—of which Texas was a part. Many of Santa Anna's soldiers had been forcefully conscripted into the army and then marched hundreds of miles over hot, arid desert land. They were largely poorly equipped Maya natives who did not speak Spanish. In February 1836, the main contingent arrived in Texas sick and ill-prepared to fight. In San Antonio, the filibusters took refuge in a former mission, the Alamo. The siege began in the first week of March. In the days that followed, the defenders inflicted heavy casualties on the Mexican forces, but the Mexicans eventually won.

Those inside the Alamo were hardly legendary characters. William Barret Travis had fled to Texas after killing a man and abandoning his wife and two children. James Bowie, an infamous brawler who had made a fortune running slaves, had wandered into Texas searching for lost mines and more money. The aging Davy Crockett, a legend in his own time, fought for the sake of fighting. Most of the filibusters had come to Texas for riches and glory, hardly the sort of men whom we could say were peaceful colonists protecting their homes.

As the story goes, William Barret Travis told his men that they were doomed and drew a line in the sand with his sword, saying that all who crossed it would elect to remain and fight to the last. Supposedly, all the men valiantly stepped across the line, with an old man in a cot begging to be carried across the line. Countless Hollywood movies have continued to support the myth by dramatizing the bravery of the defenders.[35]

In reality, while the Alamo had little strategic value, it was the best-protected fort west of the Mississippi, and the men fully expected help. The defenders had 21 cannons to the Mexicans' 8 or 10, and were expert shots equipped with rifles with a range of 200 yards, while the inadequately trained Mexicans were armed with smoothbore muskets with a range of only 70 yards. The walls of the mission protected the Euro-Americans, while the Mexicans advanced in the open and fired at concealed targets. In short, ill-prepared, ill-equipped, and ill-fed Mexicans attacked well-armed, professional soldiers. Moreover, from all reliable sources, it is doubtful whether Travis ever drew a line in the sand. San Antonio survivors, females and noncombatants, did not tell the story until many years later, when the story had gained currency and the myth became legend. Probably the most widely circulated story was that of the last stand of the aging Davy Crockett, who fell "fighting like a tiger," killing Mexicans with his bare hands. The truth is that seven of the defenders surrendered, and Crockett was among them. The Mexican force executed them, and one man, Louis Rose, escaped.[36]

Travis's stand delayed Santa Anna's timetable by only four days, as the Mexicans took San Antonio on March 6, 1836. At first, the stand at the Alamo did not even have propaganda value. Afterward, Houston's army dwindled, with many volunteers rushing home to help their families flee from the advancing Mexican army. Most Euro-Americans realized that they had lost at the Alamo. Nevertheless, the Alamo battle and the Mexican victory at Goliad resulted in massive aid from the United States as volunteers, weapons, and money entered Texas. The cry of "Remember the Alamo" became a call to arms for Euro-Americans in both Texas and the United States.

Mexicans Win the Battles but Lose the War

After the Alamo and the defeat of another garrison at Goliad on March 20, 1836, southeast of San Antonio, Mexican troops under General José Urrea defeated troops under James W. Fannin, who surrendered to Urrea. On March 27 on the orders of Santa Anna, 342 prisoners were executed at Goliad, an act that most Mexican commanders condemned. Santa Anna was in full control; defiantly cries went up, "Remember Goliad."[37] The Mexican army ran Sam Houston out of the territory northwest of the San Jacinto River and then camped an army of about 1,100 men near San Jacinto. There, Santa Anna skirmished with Houston on April 20, 1836, but did not follow up his advantage. Predicting that Houston would attack on April 22, Santa Anna and his troops settled down and rested for the anticipated battle. The filibusters, however, attacked during the siesta hour on April 21. Santa Anna knew that Houston had an army of 1,000, yet the surprise attack caught him totally off guard. Shouts of "Remember the Alamo! Remember Goliad!" filled the air. Houston's men captured Santa Anna, who signed the territory away. The Mexican Congress rejected the treaty; however, it did not have the resources to pursue its claim because sending more troops to Texas would have surely brought the full force of the U.S. army into the war. Meanwhile, Houston was elected president of the Republic of Texas.[38]

Houston's men took few Mexican prisoners at the battle of San Jacinto. Those who surrendered "were clubbed and stabbed, some on their knees. The slaughter . . . became methodical: the Texan riflemen knelt and poured a steady fire into the packed, jostling ranks." The final count of the dead was 630 Mexicans but only 2 Texans.[39]

The victory paved the way for the Mexican-American War. Officially, the United States did not take sides, but men, money, and supplies poured into Texas to aid fellow Euro-Americans. U.S. citizens participated in the invasion of Texas with the open support of their government. According to Lota M. Spell, Manuel Eduardo Gorostiza, Mexico's minister to the United States, protested the "arming and shipment of troops and supplies to territory that was part of Mexico, and the dispatch of United States troops into territory clearly defined by treaty as Mexican territory." President Andrew Jackson sent General Edmund P. Gaines, Southwest commander, into western Louisiana on January 23, 1836; shortly thereafter he crossed into Texas, which Mexicans interpreted as U.S. support for the filibusters. In and out of Texas, U.S. citizens loudly applauded Jackson's actions. The Mexican minister resigned his post in protest.[40]

The Invasion of Mexico

Another continuing myth is that the United States won the war in a fair fight—and, therefore, has no culpability. The reality is that in the mid-1840s, the U.S. population of 17 million people of European extraction and 3 million slaves was much larger than Mexico's 7 million, of which 4 million were indigenous, and 3 million mestizo, Afro-mestizo, and European. The United States acted arrogantly in foreign affairs, partly because it had a homogeneous people who believed in their cultural and racial superiority. On the other hand, financial problems, internal ethnic conflicts, poor leadership, and anarchy plagued Mexico and retarded the nation's development.[41]

The war with Mexico pushed the border further south, crossing people, rivers, and other resources. The U.S. admission of Texas on March 1, 1845, was a provocation for war. Even if Mexico had accepted the loss of Texas, there was the question of the border.

The Manufactured War

By 1845 war with Mexico over Texas and the Southwest was only a matter of time. James K. Polk, who strongly advocated the annexation of Texas and expansionism in general, won the presidency by only a small margin, but he interpreted his election as a mandate for national expansion. Outgoing President Tyler called upon Congress to annex Texas by joint resolution; Congress passed the measure a few days before the inauguration of Polk. He accepted the annexation, and in December 1845, Texas became a state. Mexico promptly broke off diplomatic relations with the United States, and Polk ordered General Zachary Taylor into Texas to "protect" the border, whose location both sides disputed. Mexico claimed the Nueces River that was 150 miles north of the Rio Bravo (Rio Grande) as Mexican. Using the Treaty of Velasco of 1836 as its authority, the United States claimed the Rio Grande as the boundary. The United States pushed for the war that cost Mexico more than 500,000 square miles of territory.[42]

In November 1845, Polk sent John Slidell on a secret mission to Mexico to negotiate for the disputed area. The presence of Euro-American troops between the Nueces and the Rio Grande and the annexation of Texas made negotiations an absurdity. The Mexican government refused to accept Polk's minister's credentials, although they did offer to give him ad hoc status.[43] Slidell declined anything less than full recognition and returned to Washington in March 1846, convinced that Mexico would have to be "chastised" before it would negotiate. By March 28, Polk ordered Taylor to the Rio Grande with an army of 4,000. Polk was incensed at Mexico's refusal to meet with Slidell on his terms and at General Mariano Paredes's reaffirmation of his country's claims to all of Texas. When the president learned of the Mexican attack on Taylor's troops in the disputed territory, he seized the opportunity and began to draft a declaration of war, which claimed among other things that Mexico had attacked the United States and had "shed American blood upon the American soil." On May 13, 1846, Congress declared war and authorized the recruitment and supplying of 50,000 troops.[44]

An Unwarranted Aggression

General Ulysses S. Grant wrote to his fiancée Julia Dent that President Polk provoked the war and that the annexation of Texas was, in fact, an act of aggression. Grant agonized, "I had a horror of the Mexican War . . . only I had not moral courage enough to resign . . . I considered my supreme duty was to my flag."[45] Grant was not alone in his opposition to the war. When Congress declared war on Mexico in May 1846, northern Whigs feared victory would add more slave states to the United States. Whig Congressman Abraham Lincoln demanded to know the spot on American soil where American blood was shed. Sixty-seven Whig representatives voted against mobilization and appropriations for a war, and Ohio senator Tom Corwin accused Polk of involving the United States in a war of aggression.[46] Intellectuals such as Ralph Waldo Emerson bitterly opposed any move toward annexation of Texas; Henry David Thoreau opposed the war by committing civil disobedience.

The Pretext for Conquest

There is no doubt that Polk sent General Zachary Taylor to the contested region between the Rio Grande and the Nueces Rivers, knowing that the army's presence would provoke the Mexicans. Polk had already planned to ask Congress for a declaration before the Euro-American public knew of the Mexican soldiers' gunfire against Zachary Taylor's troops in the disputed territory. The words of Polk's war message of May 11, 1846, should be carefully read since they laid out his pretext for the war:

> The strong desire to establish peace with Mexico on liberal and honorable terms, and the readiness of this Government to regulate and adjust our boundary and other causes of difference with that power on such fair and equitable principles as would lead to permanent relations of the most friendly nature, induced me in September last to seek reopening of diplomatic relations between the two countries.

The United States, Polk continued, had not wanted to provoke Mexico, but the Mexican government refused to receive the U.S. minister. Polk concluded,

> As war exists, and notwithstanding all our efforts to avoid it, exists by the act of Mexico herself, we are called upon by every consideration of duty and patriotism to vindicate with decision the honor, the rights, and the interests of our country.[47]

Religious Justifications for War

The tone for the war was later pronounced by Euro-American poet Walt Whitman in his *Leaves of Grass*, 1855. A romantic, Whitman alleged the greatness and superiority of the American nation was based on the notion of American exceptionalism. Whitman spoke of his belief in the uniqueness (exceptionalism) of the Euro-American people in his poem "Song of Myself." Whitman saw *America* as the prime mover of human history—a belief that most Euro-Americans shared at this time.[48] This feeling of being exceptional has carried with it feelings of moral superiority. In his *Origins of the War with Mexico: The Polk-Stockton Intrigue*, Glenn W. Price writes, "Americans have found it rather more difficult than other peoples to deal rationally with their wars. We have thought of ourselves as unique, and of this society as specially planned and created to avoid the errors of all other nations."[49]

In their belief of American exceptionalism, a substantial segment of U.S. historians dismisses the war with Mexico as simply a "bad war," which took place during the era of Manifest Destiny, a nebulous doctrine, which is much like someone blaming bad conduct on "youthful indiscretions." In reality, Manifest Destiny is a religious doctrine with roots in Puritan ideas which continue to influence U.S. policy to this day.[50] According to the theory of Manifest Destiny, the United States was the embodiment of the City of God on earth and the European race were chosen people predestined for salvation. Most Euro-Americans believed that God had made them custodians of democracy and that Euro-Americans had a mission—that is, that God had predestined Western Europeans to spread his principles to the "New World." Their mission, their destiny made manifest, was to spread the principles of democracy and Christianity to the unfortunate people of the hemisphere. By dismissing the war simply as part of the era of Manifest Destiny, apologists for the war ignored the consequences of those inherently unjust and racist beliefs.[51]

In spite of all of the doublespeak, most Euro-Americans knew that the acquisition of Mexican land was the primary motive for the war. Some feared that the acquisition of more territory would tip the balance of power to the favor of the Northern States and bring into the nation large numbers of nonwhites. U.S. Sen. John C. Calhoun (D-South Carolina) advocated the annexation of Texas in 1836. However, he grew suspicious of President James K. Polk's intrigues and was fearful that the president's intentions of acquiring significant territory below the Rio Grande would hurt the slave states since it would be incorporating a nonwhite people. He argued "To incorporate Mexico, would be the very first instance of the kind of incorporating an Indian race for more than half of the Mexicans are Indians, and the other is composed chiefly of mixed tribes. I protest against such a union as that! Ours, sir, is the Government of a white race."[52]

History as Propaganda

In 1920, Justin H. Smith received the Pulitzer Prize in history for a work blaming the war on Mexico. What is amazing is that Smith allegedly examined more than 100,000 manuscripts, 120,000 books and pamphlets, and 200 or more periodicals to come to this conclusion. He was rewarded for relieving the Euro-American conscience. Smith, in his two-volume "study," entitled *The War with Mexico*, argues that the Mexicans were at fault for the war:

> *At the beginning of her independent existence, our people felt earnestly and enthusiastically anxious to maintain cordial relations with our sister republic, and many crossed the line of absurd sentimentality in the cause. Friction was inevitable, however. The Americans were direct, positive, brusque, angular and pushing; and they would not understand their neighbors in the south. The Mexicans were equally unable to fathom our goodwill, sincerity, patriotism, resoluteness and courage; and certain features of their character and national condition made it far from easy to get on with them.*[53]

Smith's account reflected the post–World War I jingoism of Americans who believed that Mexicans crossed by the border should have been grateful that they now had the benefits of American democracy and were liberated from their tyrannical past. This in their eyes justified the war.

Many Euro-Americans conveniently develop historical amnesia and forget that the United States conducted a violent and brutal war against Mexico as it did against the Native Americans. Anti-Catholicism and racism went a long way in driving the fervor of North Americans during this war. General Zachary Taylor's artillery had leveled the Mexican city of Matamoros, killing hundreds of innocent civilians with *la bomba* (the bomb). Many Mexicans jumped into the Rio Grande, relieved of their pain by a watery grave.[54] The occupation that followed was even more terrorizing. Taylor was unable to control his volunteers:

> *The regulars regarded the volunteers, of whom about two thousand had reached Matamoros by the end of May, with impatience and contempt. . . . They robbed Mexicans of their cattle and corn, stole their fences for firewood, got drunk, and killed several inoffensive inhabitants of the town in the streets.*[55]

Numerous eyewitness accounts to these incidents exist. For example, on July 25, 1846, Grant wrote to Julia Dent:

> *Since we have been in Matamoros a great many murders have been committed, and what is strange there seems [sic] to be very week [sic] means made use of to prevent frequent repetitions. Some of the volunteers and about all the Texans seem to think it perfectly right to impose on the people of a conquered City to any extent, and even to murder them where the act can be covered by dark. And how much they seem to enjoy acts of violence too! I would not pretend to guess the number of murders that have been committed upon the persons of poor Mexicans and our soldiers, since we have been here, but the number would startle you.*[56]

On July 9, 1846, George Gordon Meade, who, like Grant, later became a general during the U.S. Civil War, wrote,

> *They [the volunteers] have killed five or six innocent people walking in the street, for no other object than their own amusement. . . . They rob and steal the cattle and corn of the poor farmers, and in fact act more like a body of hostile Indians than civilized Whites. Their officers have no command or control over them.*[57]

Taylor knew of the atrocities, and Grant acknowledged that Taylor did not restrain his men. In a letter to his superiors, Taylor admitted, "there is scarcely a form of crime that has not been reported to me as committed by them."[58] Taylor requested that they send no further troops from the state of Texas to him.

Violent acts were not limited to Taylor's men. The cannons from U.S. naval ships destroyed much of the civilian sector of Vera Cruz, leveling a hospital, churches, and homes. U.S. troops destroyed almost every city they invaded and then plundered it. Euro-American volunteers showed little respect for anything, desecrating churches and abusing priests and nuns.

Peacemakers Expose the Violence of War

War goes beyond battles and combat strategies.[59] For Mexicans, the U.S. invasion and occupation left a legacy of bitterness and a memory of U.S. abuses in Mexico. The war reinforced Mexican mistrust of Euro-Americans, just as the easy victory of the United States reinforced its people's negative view of Mexicans as weak. However, many Euro-Americans heroically stood up to the hysteria of the moment and condemned this aggression, flatly accusing U.S. leaders of being insolent, arrogant, and land-hungry, and of manufacturing the war. Abiel Abbott Livermore, in *The War with Mexico Reviewed*, accused his country, writing:

> *Again, the pride of race has swollen to still greater insolence the pride of country, always quite active enough for the due observance of the claims of universal brotherhood. The Anglo-Saxons have been apparently persuaded to think themselves the chosen people, anointed race of the Lord, commissioned to drive out the heathen, and plant their religion and institutions in every Canaan they could subjugate. . . . Our treatment both of the red man and the black man has habituated us to feel our power and forget right. . . . The god Terminus is an unknown deity in America. Like the hunger of the pauper boy of fiction, the cry had been, 'more, more, give us more.'*[60]

The American Peace Society awarded Livermore's work, published in 1850, the American Peace Society prize for the best review of the Mexican War and the principles of Christianity.

Without a doubt, the most inspiring speech against the war was given by Illinois Representative Abraham Lincoln. He exploded the myths that the Rio Grande was the boundary and that the United States or Texas had legal title, and he questioned the veracity of Polk.[61] Lincoln questioned the U.S. role in the Mexican-American War and said that its purpose was to seize Texas, California, and other Southwest land areas. According to Lincoln, James K. Polk lied and took the nation into a war of aggression against Mexico to support the South's expansionist goals. Lincoln said that clear and simple, the war supported the ambitions of the slave states. God had nothing to do with the war—American greed did.[62]

The San Patricio Battalion

The conquering army captured soldiers and executed them while also hanging civilians for cooperating with the guerrillas. A sizable number of Irish immigrants, as well as some other Euro-Americans, deserted to the Mexican side, forming the San Patricio Battalion. Many of the Irish were Catholics, and Irish Catholics resented the Protestants' ill treatment of Catholic priests, nuns, churches, and other institutions. As many as 260 Euro-Americans fought on the Mexican side at Churubusco in 1847, many of whom were captured:

> Some eighty appear to have been captured. . . . A number were found not guilty of deserting and were released. About fifteen, who had deserted before the declaration of war, were merely branded with a "D," and fifty of those taken at Churubusco were executed.[63]

Others received 200 lashes and were forced to dig graves for their executed comrades.[64]

These acts were similar to those George Meade described in Monterrey on December 2, 1846:

> They plunder the poor inhabitants of everything they can lay their hands on, and shoot them when they remonstrate; and if one of their number happens to get into a drunken brawl and is killed, they run over the country, killing all the poor innocent people they find in their way to avenge, as they say, the murder of their brother.[65]

The lack of coverage of the atrocities during the war by historians is disturbing. Meade was certainly not a compromised source. Meade in that same December 2 letter writes,

> The volunteers have been creating disturbances, which have at last aroused the old General so much that he has ordered one regiment, the First Kentucky foot, to march to the rear, as they have disgraced themselves and their State . . . [Taylor] impressed upon the officers the necessity of controlling the men and putting a stop to these outrages, which would inevitably end in the massacre of many innocent persons . . . [The Kentuckians] vowing their intention of killing Mexicans, to revenge their murdered comrades, and the same day one man, a Mexican, was shot within a hundred yards of the camp, and a little boy of twelve years of age, who was cutting cornstalks to bring to the camp for sale, was shot in the field and his leg broken. This poor little fellow, all bleeding and crying, was brought by his relatives and laid down in front of the General's tent, and he called out to look at him.[66]

As General Winfield Scott's army left Monterrey, soldiers under his command shot Mexican prisoners of war.[67]

The War Crimes

Memoirs, diaries, and news articles written by Euro-Americans document the reign of terror. Samuel E. Chamberlain's *My Confessions* is a record of Euro-American racism and destruction. Chamberlain was only 17 when he enlisted in the army to fight the "greasers." At the Mexican city of Parras, he wrote,

> We found the patrol had been guilty of many outrages. . . . They had ridden into the church of San José during Mass, the place crowded with kneeling women and children, and with oaths and ribald jest had arrested soldiers who had permission to be present.[68]

On another occasion, Chamberlain described a massacre by volunteers, mostly from Yell's Cavalry, at a cave:

> *On reaching the place we found a "greaser" shot and scalped, but still breathing; the poor fellow held in his hands a Rosary and a medal of the "Virgin of Guadalupe," only his feeble motions kept the fierce harpies from falling on him while yet alive. A Sabre thrust was given him in mercy, and on we went at a run. Soon shouts and curses, cries of women and children reached our ears, coming apparently from a cave at the end of the ravine. Climbing over the rocks we reached the entrance, and as soon as we could see in the comparative darkness a horrid sight was before us. The cave was full of our volunteers yelling like fiends, while on the rocky floor lay over twenty Mexicans, dead and dying in pools of blood. Women and children were clinging to the knees of the murderers shrieking for mercy. . . . Most of the butchered Mexicans had been scalped; only three men were found unharmed. A rough crucifix was fastened to a rock, and some irreverent wretch had crowned the image with a bloody scalp. A sickening smell filled the place. The surviving women and children sent up loud screams on seeing us, thinking we had returned to finish the work! . . . No one was punished for this outrage.*[69]

Chamberlain accused General Taylor not only of forcefully collecting more than $1 million (from the Mexican people), but also of letting "loose on the country packs of human bloodhounds called Texas Rangers," who committed wanton acts of cruelty.[70]

Mexicanas on the Front Lines

The violence of the war was not limited to adult males. "Mexican women likewise were drawn into the conflict, and some found themselves thrust suddenly into combat roles."[71] The Mexican army traveled with a large contingent of *soldaderas*, the female camp followers, wives, daughters, or lovers, who marched with the soldiers and carried their packs. At the Battle of Bracito, north of El Paso, in March 1847, Colonel Alexander W. Doniphan's men observed Mexican women fighting beside the male soldiers, attending the Mexican cannon. That same spring, after the Battle of Cerro Gordo, northwest of Veracruz, women were found among the casualties. They were also prominent in the defense of Mexico City and Monterrey where they were engaged in street fighting.[72]

Finally, there is the story of Dos Amades, as Mexicans know her, who commanded a company of lancers. Dos Amades donned a captain's lancers uniform and swore that she would not yield until the Mexicans drove the "Northern barbarians" from Mexico. Dos Amades survived the war and returned to her home, never to be heard of again. Monterrey also produced a martyr in María Josefa Zozaya, who was killed carrying food to the soldiers and tending to their wounds.[73]

The Prosecution of the War

The poorly equipped and poorly led Mexican army had stood little chance against the expansion-minded Euro-Americans. Even before the war, President Polk had planned the campaign in stages: (1) Mexicans would be cleared out of Texas; (2) the United States would occupy California and New Mexico; and (3) U.S. forces would march to Mexico City to force the beaten government to make peace on Polk's terms.[74] In the end, at a relatively small cost in men and money, the war netted the United States huge territorial gains. In all, the United States took over a half million square miles from Mexico.[75]

Mexico did not have the factories or the money to pay for a professional navy or even good uniforms. In addition, Mexico did not fight an intelligent war. Part of the problem was its commander Santa Anna, who had returned to Mexico from exile and recruited a new army of more than 20,000 men whom he hardly trained; the result was the loss of several major battles. The most that can be said of the Mexican army was that it did not give up. On the other hand, the United States had advantages such as a professional navy, which allowed the largest amphibious landing in history up to that time—General

Scott and his 12,000 men, at Veracruz. The Mexicans were successful only when they conducted guerrilla operations, but Santa Anna did that only infrequently. He had learned very little from Mexico's War of Independence when the rag-a-muffin rebels had not beaten the Spaniards but had just worn them down.

By late August 1847, the war was almost at an end. Scott's defeat of Santa Anna in a hard-fought battle at Churubusco put U.S. troops at the gates of Mexico City. Santa Anna made overtures for an armistice that broke down after two weeks, and the war resumed. On September 13, 1847, Scott marched into the city. Although Mexicans fought valiantly, the battle left 4,000 dead, with another 3,000 taken prisoner. On September 13, before the occupation of Mexico City began, *Los Niños Héroes* (The Boy Heroes) leaped to their deaths from Chapultepec Hill in Mexico City rather than surrender. These teenage cadets—Francisco Márquez, Agustín Melgar, Juan Escutia, Fernando Montes de Oca, Vicente Suárez, and Juan de la Barrera— became "a symbol and image of this unrighteous war."[76] Francisco Márquez, the youngest, was 13 and the squadron leader, Juan de la Barrera, was the oldest, 20.

The Mexicans continued fighting while Manuel de la Peña, the presiding justice of the Supreme Court, assumed the presidency. De la Peña knew Mexico had lost and the chief justice wanted to salvage as much as possible, as U.S. troops took control of much of Mexico. Meanwhile, the United States lost 13,780 men and many more were wounded. Mexico lost at least double that number.[77]

The Treaty of Guadalupe Hidalgo

Nicholas Trist, sent to Mexico to act as peace commissioner, arrived in Veracruz on May 6, 1847, but controversy with General Scott over Trist's authority delayed an armistice and hostilities continued. After the fall of Mexico City, Secretary of State James Buchanan ordered Trist to break off negotiations and return home.[78] President Polk wanted to secure more land from Mexico than originally planned, and he wanted to replace Trist with a tougher negotiator. Trist, however, with the support of General Winfield Scott, decided to ignore Polk's order and began negotiations on January 2, 1848, on the original terms. Mexico, badly beaten, her government in a state of turmoil, had no choice but to agree to the U.S. proposals. The negotiations were difficult for Trist. He was aware of the Mexicans' humiliation and felt a strong sense of embarrassment. Trist himself knew that the war had been a pretext to seize Mexican land.[79]

On February 2, 1848, the Mexican Congress ratified the Treaty of Guadalupe Hidalgo, with Mexico accepting the Rio Grande as the Texas border and ceding almost half of its territory (which incorporated the present-day states of California, New Mexico, Nevada, and parts of Colorado, Arizona, Utah, and even Oklahoma) to the United States in return for $15 million.[80]

A furious Polk considered Trist "contemptibly base" for having ignored his orders. Yet he had no choice but to submit the treaty to the Senate. With the exception of Article X, which concerned the rights of Mexicans in ceded territory, the Senate ratified the treaty on March 10, 1848, by a vote of 28 to 14. To insist on more territory would have meant more fighting, and both Polk and the Senate realized that the war was already unpopular in many circles. The United States sent the treaty to the Mexican Congress for ratification. The Congress had difficulty forming a quorum, barely ratifying the treaty by a 52-to-35 vote on May 19.[81] Hostilities between the two nations officially ended. Polk, disappointed with the settlement, branded Trist as a "scoundrel," however. In fact, there had been considerable support in the United States for acquisition of all Mexico.[82]

The Controversy

During the treaty talks Mexican negotiators expressed great reservations about Mexicans living in the lost territory being forced to "merge or blend" into Euro-American culture. Mexican negotiators protested the exclusion of provisions that protected Mexican citizens' rights, land titles, and religion.[83] They wanted to protect their rights by treaty.

Articles VIII, IX, and X specifically referred to the rights of Mexicans in what became the United States. Under the treaty, they had one year to choose whether to return to Mexico or remain in "occupied Mexico." About 2,000 elected to leave; most remained in what they considered *their* land.

Article IX of the treaty guaranteed Mexicans "the enjoyment of all the rights of citizens of the United States according to the principles of the Constitution; and in the meantime shall be maintained and protected in the free enjoyment of their liberty and property, and secured in the free exercise of their religion without restriction."[84] Lynn I. Perrigo, in *The American Southwest*, summarizes the guarantees of Articles VIII and IX: "In other words, besides the rights and duties of American citizenship, they [the Mexicans] would have special privileges derived from their previous customs in language, law, and religion."[85]

The Deception

The omitted Article X had comprehensive guarantees protecting "all prior and pending titles to property of every description." When the U.S. Senate deleted Article X, Mexican officials protested. Emissaries from the United States reassured them by drafting a Statement of Protocol on May 26, 1848:

> *The American government by suppressing the Xth article of the Treaty of Guadalupe Hidalgo did not in any way intend to annul the grants of lands made by Mexico in the ceded territories. These grants . . . preserve the legal value which they may possess, and the grantees may cause their legitimate (titles) to be acknowledged before the American tribunals.*
>
> *Conformable to the law of the United States, legitimate titles to every description of property, personal and real, existing in the ceded territories, are those which were legitimate titles under the Mexican law of California and New Mexico up to the 13th of May, 1846, and in Texas up on the 2nd of March, 1836.*[86]

Considering the Mexican opposition to the treaty, it is doubtful whether the Mexican Congress would have ratified the treaty without this clarification. The vote was close—it passed by only one vote.

The importance of the Statement of Protocol was that it proved the bad faith of Polk and U.S. authorities. Even as they were selling the statement to Mexican authorities, they called it worthless in the United States because Trist did not have the authority to sign the treaty. What is amazing is that Polk's diary clearly shows that he considered the treaty valid. The fact was that the validity of Article X depended on the good faith of the United States—without that good faith, the letter of protocol was meaningless. Armando Rendón in *Chicano Manifesto* writes that the omission of Article X resulted in the federal government's seizing millions of acres of land from the states, impacting the descendants of the Mexicans and Native Americans left behind. In New Mexico alone the federal government seized 1.7 million acres of communal land.[87]

A letter of protocol assured that the omission of Article X would not affect the validity of most land titles protected by the words, "the legal value which they *may* possess."[88] It threw Mexicans at the mercy of U.S. courts. In practice, they ignored the treaty, and during the nineteenth century most Mexicans in the United States were considered as a class apart from the dominant race.[89] The United States violated nearly every one of the obligations discussed above, confirming the prophecy of Mexican diplomat Manuel Crescion Rejón, who, at the time the treaty was signed, commented:

> *Our race, our unfortunate people will have to wander in search of hospitality in a strange land, only to be ejected later. Descendants of the Indians that we are, the North Americans hate us, their spokesmen depreciate us, even if they recognize the justice of our cause, and they consider us unworthy to form with them one nation and one society, they clearly manifest that their future expansion begins with the territory that they take from us and pushing [sic] aside our citizens who inhabit the land.*[90]

The Honorable Man

Upon returning to the United States, Trist wrote in detail about his experience. In a letter to a friend of the family he wrote:

If those Mexicans . . . had been able to look into my heart at that moment, they would have found that the sincere shame I felt as a North American was stronger than theirs as Mexicans. Although I was unable to say it at the time, it was something that any North American should be ashamed of.

Following the Texas and Mexican-American wars and the U.S. aggressions, the occupation of conquered territory began. In material terms, in exchange for 12,000 lives and more than $100 million, the United States got a colony two and a half times as large as France, containing rich farmlands and natural resources such as gold, silver, zinc, copper, oil, and uranium, which would make possible its unprecedented industrial boom.[91] It got ports on the Pacific that generated further economic expansion across that ocean. The two Mexican wars gave U.S. commerce, industry, mining, agriculture, and stock raising a tremendous stimulus. "The truth is that [by the 1840s] the Pacific Coast belonged to the commercial empire that the United States was already building in that ocean."[92] Mexico was left with its shrunken resources to face the continued advances of the United States. In the next century, it would be severely hindered in its ability to build a strong economic infrastructure to keep up with the population growth that began to approach pre-conquest levels.

Conclusion: The Border Crossed Us: In the Entrails of the Monster

Apart from the impact of the loss of over half of Mexico's territory, the Mexicans lost a measure of dignity. Moreover, the wars left a legacy of hate. To this day, the lack of enforcement of the Treaty of Guadalupe Hidalgo remains an issue between Euro-Americans and Chicanos, although with time the Mexican government has opportunistically made adjustments, such that enforcement of the treaty is a moot issue. The reality is Mexican officials treat their history as a political commodity that the Mexican government barters for trade and other concessions. For example, after the passage of the North American Fair Trade Agreement (NAFTA) in late 1993, it became expedient for Mexico to rewrite its history and downplay the war and the theft of half of Mexico's territory. Not too surprisingly, the treaty is an expendable item of history.

The consequences of the wars went far beyond the immediate losses, still affecting the lives of Mexicans today. The oil of Texas and California alone would have made Mexico a major power. Moreover, Mexico lost major rivers such as the Rio Grande, and the Gila and Colorado Rivers. Even if the boundary had been the Nueces, the Rio Grande would have run through the center of Mexico. The lack of arable land and resources forces the migration of millions of Mexicans and Central Americans north in search of survival. The treaty itself is symbolic of the illusive relations between Mexican Americans and Euro-Americans. The treaty gives the illusion that it protects Mexican Americans while the courts interpret the treaty in favor of special interests. Thus, getting justice from the courts has been nearly impossible.

Caution should, however, be taken not to romanticize the treaty, which is after all a document negotiated and signed by the ruling elites of two nation-states. Consequently, there are troubling aspects about the Treaty of Guadalupe Hidalgo. For instance, the treaty recognizes the Spanish and Mexican governments' right of prior conquest. The treaty also imposes on the United States the duty to control by force *los indios bárbaros.* The treaty pretended to protect the land rights of Mexicans and Native Americans left behind (most indigenous peoples were considered Mexican citizens). In reality, the treaty reduced the rights of some native tribes, penalizing tribes that had suffered multiple conquests—first by Spain and Mexico, and later by the United States. They lost rights to which they might otherwise be entitled under federal Indian policy. This breach should certainly be considered in any discussion of the treaty.

University of Texas anthropologist Martha Menchaca makes a persuasive argument that the United States' violation of the treaty racialized the status of Mexicans and Native Americans.[93] She argues that because the treaty "was broken and they did not give Mexicans the political rights of White citizens a legacy of racial discrimination followed." Instead of a template for interracial harmony, Menchaca cites a history of segregation of public facilities, housing, poll taxes, and other instances of unequal access, which to her and others shows that the Treaty of Guadalupe was and continues to be violated and the legacy of hate the wars left continues to impact our lives.

Notes

1. Alexander Whitaker, "Good News from Virginia," in Conrad Cherry, ed., *God's New Israel: Religious Interpretations of American Destiny* (Englewood Cliffs, NJ: Prentice Hall, Inc., 1971), 33. Alexander Whitaker, "Good News from Virginia sent to the Counsell and Company of Virginia, resident in England First Hand Accounts of Virginia, 1575–1705," Virtual Jamestown Project, http://etext.lib.virginia.edu/etcbin/jamestown-browse?id=J1024. America: The New Israel, http://gbgm-umc.org/UMW/joshua/manifest.html.

2. John Winthrop, "Model of Christian Charity," in Cherry, 43. Document also in the Hanover Historical Texts Project, http://history.hanover.edu/texts/winthmod.html.

3. Frederic Cople Jaher, *A Scapegoat in the New Wilderness: The Origins and Rise of Anti-Semitism in America* (Cambridge, MA: Harvard University Press, 1996), 100.

4. This chapter emphasizes the use of documents. Primary sources are usually contemporary and eyewitness accounts, reports, maps, and the like. They are original or first-hand accounts; secondary sources are also included. Second-hand, published accounts are called secondary sources because they are not as strong as primary. They are based on primary sources. We use them to form a historical narrative. The reader can go to the Internet to find out more about the distinction between the two categories of documents. I have included a mixture of primary and secondary sources in order to acquaint the reader with them. In the case of the primary sources such as treaties and eyewitness accounts and the like, for the reader's convenience, I have included links showing where the documents are housed. Remember it is the task of the historian to examine the evidence. The timeline lines up the argument.

5. Robert Kelley's deposition is housed in the Rodolfo F. Acuña Collection in Special Collections at the California State University Northridge Library. Gabriel Buelna, "Outlawing Shakespeare: The Battle for the Tucson Mind" (2012), http://www.youtube.com/watch?v=anChx_9TF-Q.

6. Ulysses S. Grant, *Personal Memoirs of U.S. Grant* (New York: Charles L. Webster & Co., 1885), 22–24, quoted in http://www.sewanee.edu/faculty/Willis/Civil_War/documents/Grant.html. Ibid., http://www.bartleby.com/1011/.

7. Printed Resolution and Preamble on Mexican War: "Spot Resolutions," The Abraham Lincoln Papers at the Library of Congress, http://memory.loc.gov/cgi-bin/query/r?ammem/mal:@field(DOCID+@lit(d0007000)). Rodolfo F. Acuña and Guadalupe Compeán, eds., *Voices of the U.S. Latino Experience*, Vol. I (Westport: Greenwood Books, 2008), 89–90.

8. Josefina Zoraida Vázquez, "The Mexican Declaration of Independence," *Journal of American History* 85, no. 4 (March 1999): 1362–69. Beau D.J. Gaitors, "The Afro-Mexican Presence in Guadalajara at the Dawn of Independence" (Master of Arts Thesis, Purdue University, 2010).

9. An excellent source of primary documents translated into English can be found in the papers of the Sons of the De Witt Colony Texas, http://www.tamu.edu/ccbn/dewitt/mexicanrev.htm. Rodolfo F. Acuña and Guadalupe Compeán, eds.,

Voices of the U.S. Latino Experience, 3 Vols. (Westport, CT: Greenwood, 2008): 11–13. In e-book form.

10. For general discussions see David Held, *Political Theory and the Modern State: Essays on State, Power, and Democracy* (Stanford, CA: Stanford University Press, 1989), and *Models of Democracy* (Stanford, CA: Stanford University Press, 1987). Michael Mann, *Sources of Social Power, Vol. II: The Rise of Classes and Nation-States, 1760–1914* (Cambridge: Cambridge University Press, 1993). Nora Hamilton, *Modern Mexico, State, Economy, and Social Conflict* (Thousand Oaks, CA: Sage Publications, 1986).

11. Andrés Reséndez, "National Identity on a Shifting Border: Texas and New Mexico in the Age of Transition, 1821–1848," in *Rethinking History and the Nation State: Mexico and the United States*, A Special Issue of the *Journal of American History*, http://www.journalofamericanhistory.org/issues/862/. Marina Iris Mercado-Mont, "Origins of State Formation in Mexico" (PhD dissertation, New School for Social Research, 1988).

12. There are several excellent sites for the original treaties. Avalon Project, Yale University, http://avalon.law.yale.edu/default.asp. *Modern History Sourcebook: United States— Spain: Treaty of 1819*, http://www.fordham.edu/halsall/mod/1819florida.html. Acuña and Compeán, *Voices of the U.S. Latino Experience*, 1–24.

13. Richard W. Johannsen, *To the Halls of the Montezumas: The Mexican War in the American Imagination* (New York: Oxford University Press, 1985). Norman E. Tutorow, *Texas Annexation and the Mexican War* (Palo Alto, CA: Chadwick House, 1978).

14. Richard W. Van Alstyne, *The Rising American Empire* (New York: Norton, 1974), 101. T. R. Fehrenbach, *Lone Star: A History of Texas and the Texans* (New York: Macmillan, 1968), 128. Carlos Castañeda, *Our Catholic Heritage in Texas, 1519–1933*, Vol. 6, *Transition Period: The Fight for Freedom, 1810–1836*, 160–62.

15. See Andrés Tijerina, *Texanos under the Mexican Flag, 1821–1836* (College Station: Texas A&M University Press, 1994), 3–24. Lester G. Bugbee, "Slavery in Early Texas," *Political Science Quarterly* XIII, no. 3 (1898), http://www.tamu.edu/faculty/ccbn/dewitt/slaverybugbee.htm. Fane Downs, "The History of Mexicans in Texas, 1820–1845," (PhD dissertation, Texas Tech University, 1970), 1, 5–6. Stephen Austin boasted that within one year that San Antonio would be transformed beyond recognition. This has good descriptions of different Texas settlements in 1820 including Tejanos. Tina Laurel Meacham, "The Population of Spanish and Mexican Texas, 1716–1836" (PhD dissertation, University of Texas at Austin, 2000), vii, sets me off when she quotes David Weber's "to populate is to govern," and she concludes that Spain or Mexico were willing to spend the monetary resources to bring this about. It sounds like a quote out of Walter Prescott Webb. It is essentially a demographic study, and as such it is helpful.

16. Letter written by Stephen F. Austin, as testified by Guy M. Bryan: "This is a true copy of the letter, recd from S. F. Austin.

Received from Mrs. Bell and I presume was addressed to her husband Josiah H Bell," Sons of DeWitt Colony Texas, http://www.tamu.edu/ccbn/dewitt/slaveryletters.htm. Petition Concerning Slavery, June 10, 1824, Sons of DeWitt Colony Texas, http://www.tamu.edu/ccbn/dewitt/slaveryletters.htm#petitioncongress. Lester G. Bugbee, "Slavery in Early Texas," *Political Science Quarterly* III, no. 3 (1898), reproduced at Sons of DeWitt Colony Texas, http://www.tamu.edu/faculty/ccbn/dewitt/slaverybugbee.htm. Index of Correspondence regarding Slavery in Texas, http://www.tamu.edu/faculty/ccbn/dewitt/slaveryletters.htm. Acuña and Compeán, *Voices of the U.S. Latino Experience*, 25–41. Linda Myers Purcell, "Slavery in the Republic of Texas" (Master of Arts thesis, North Texas State, Denton, 1982). Abigail Curlee, "The History of a Texas Slave Plantation," *Southwestern Historical Quarterly* 26, no. 1 (July 1922–April 1923): 79–127.

17. Walter Prescott Webb, *The Texas Rangers: A Century of Frontier Defense* (Austin: University of Texas Press, 1965), 21–22. Tijerina, *Tejanos under the Mexican Flag*, 25–45. Letter from Gen. Manuel de Mier y Terán to Lucás Alamán, "¿En qué parará Texas? En lo que Dios quiera." ("What is to become of Texas? Whatever God wills."), July 2, 1832, Sons of DeWitt Colony Texas, http://www.tamu.edu/ccbn/dewitt/teranmanuel.htm.

18. Fehrenbach, *Lone Star*, 163–64. Hayden Edwards & The Fredonian Rebellion, 1826–1827, http://www.tamu.edu/ccbn/dewitt/fredonian.htm.

19. The Monroe Doctrine, December 2, 1823, http://avalon.law.yale.edu/19th_century/monroe.asp.

20. Van Alstyne, *The Rising American Empire*, 101.

21. Tijerina, *Tejanos under the Mexican Flag*, 65–78. Laws of Coahuila y Texas 1825, http://www.tamu.edu/ccbn/dewitt/cololaws.htm#coahuila. Colonization Law of 1832, http://www.tamu.edu/ccbn/dewitt/lundy5.htm#cololaw1832. Andrew Jonathan Torget, "Cotton Empire: Slavery and the Texas Borderlands, 1820–1837" (PhD dissertation, University of Virginia, 2009), 195, 197, makes the point that Texas managed to carve out a slaveholding region in northeastern Mexico. He makes the point that slavery exists because it is state sanctioned and therefore it is essential to the slaveholders to control government.

22. Nathaniel W. Stephenson, *Texas and the Mexican War: A Chronicle of the Winning of the Southwest* (New York: United States Publishing, 1921), 52. The Galveston Bay and Texas Land Company of New York, acting to protect its investments, worked through its agent Anthony Butler to lobby for U.S. cooperation. Francis W. Wilson and Dorcas Baumgartner, The Tennessee-Texas Land Company, http://www.tamu.edu/ccbn/dewitt/tenntexland.htm. Colony Expansion: The Burkets, Kents, and Zumwalts, http://www.tamu.edu/ccbn/dewitt/expansion.htm#titles; DeWitt Land Grants, 1825–1832, http://www.tamu.edu/ccbn/dewitt/landgrants.htm.

23. Castañeda, *Our Catholic Heritage in Texas, 1519–1933*, Vol. 6, 217–18.

24. Castañeda, *Our Catholic Heritage in Texas, 1519–1933*, Vol. 6, 240–41. Fehrenbach, *Lone Star*, 180. Juan Nepomuceno Almonte 1803–1869, http://www.tamu.edu/ccbn/dewitt/almontejn.htm. Juan Almonte's Report on Texas Spring/

Summer 1834 (Published January 1835), http://www.tamu.edu/ccbn/dewitt/almonterep.htm.

25. Bustamante's Decree of 1830, http://www.tamu.edu/ccbn/dewitt/consultframe.htm San Felipe de Austin, October 4, 1832, To the Federal Congress of Mexico, http://www.tamu.edu/ccbn/dewitt/consultframe.htm. See DeWitt Papers for other documents. Also see "Archivo Digital de Documentos Sobre la Guerra de Texas, 1835, y la Guerra Mexico-Estados Unidos, 1846–1848," http://www.sre.gob.mx/acervo/index.php?option=com_content&view=article&id=65&Itemid=343. http://forchicanachicanostudies.wikispaces.com/Archival+Research.

26. Eugene C. Barker, *Mexico and Texas, 1821–1835* (New York: Russell & Russell, 1965), 52, 74–80, 80–82. David J. Weber, ed. *Foreigners in Their Native Land* (Albuquerque: University of New Mexico Press, 1973), 89. Quoted in Fehrenbach, *Lone Star*, 182. Leroy Graf, "The Economic History of the Lower Rio Grande, 1820–1870" (PhD dissertation, Harvard University, 1942), 91. Sam Houston Letter to Andrew Jackson, Natchitoches, Louisiana, February 13, 1833, http://www.sonofthesouth.net/texas/sam-houston-letters-jackson.htm. Torget, "Cotton Empire," 203–6, fn 4, dissects Barker's argument that slavery played no part in the rebellion.

27. Castañeda, *Our Catholic Heritage in Texas, 1519–1933*, Vol. 6, 252–53. Fehrenbach, *Lone Star*, 181. Tijerina, *Tejanos under the Mexican Flag*, 113, sheds light on these politics. See Stephen F. Austin, Texas State Library & Archives Commission, http://www.tsl.state.tx.us/treasures/giants/austin/austin-01.html.

28. Stephenson, *Texas and the Mexican War*, 51. Graf, "The Economic History of the Lower Rio Grande, 1820–1870," 111. Austin was involved in opening this trade to non-Mexican vessels. Ironically, there was little trade between the Valley and central and northern Texas. Torget, "Cotton Empire," 207; Austin actively played the cotton market.

29. Stephenson, *Texas and the Mexican War*, 52. Barker, *Mexico and Texas, 1821–1835*, 128. Castañeda, *Our Catholic Heritage in Texas, 1519–1933*, Vol. 6, 234. Gene M. Brack, *Mexico Views Manifest Destiny, 1821–1846: An Essay on the Origins of the Mexican War* (Albuquerque: University of New Mexico Press, 1st ed., 1975).

30. Fehrenbach, *Lone Star*, 188. C. Alan Hutchinson, "Valentín Gomez Farías: A Biographical Study" (PhD dissertation, University of Texas at Austin, 1948), 6. Address of the Honorable S. F. Austin, Louisville, Kentucky, March 7, 1836, The Avalon Project, http://avalon.law.yale.edu/19th_century/texind01.asp.

31. Fehrenbach, *Lone Star*, 189. See The Texas Revolution: Part A (September–October 1835), http://www.tshaonline.org/lshl/texhisdocs04a.html. Austin, September 19, 1835, letter, http://www.tsl.state.tx.us/treasures/giants/austin/austin-safety-1.html.

32. Barker, *Mexico and Texas, 1821–1835*, 146, 147, 162. Barker, on Stephen Austin, http://www.tamu.edu/ccbn/dewitt/austinbio.htm.

33. The DeWitt Colony Alamo Defenders Index, http://www.tamu.edu/ccbn/dewitt/gonreliefframe.htm; http://www.tamu.edu/ccbn/dewitt/dewitt.htm. The DeWitt Papers function as genealogy pointing the reader to the genealogy of those inside the Alamo; only the Mexicans were from Texas. Mary Ann Cooper,

"Remember the Alamo? Maybe Not," *The Hispanic Outlook in Higher Education* 15, no. 2 (October18, 2004): 9.

34. Walter Lord, *A Time to Stand: The Epic of the Alamo* (Lincoln, NE: Bison Books, 1978), 213–20. Jeff Long's *Duel of Eagles: The Mexican and U.S. Fight for the Alamo* (New York: William Morrow, 1990). Walter Lord, "Myths and Realities of the Alamo," *The American West* 3 (May 1964), 18–25. Stephen Hardin, *Texian Iliad: A Military History of the Texas Revolution* (Austin: University of Texas Press, 1996). Tijerina, *Tejanos under the Mexican Flag, 1821–1836.* Timothy M. Matovina, *The Alamo Remembered: Tejano Accounts and Perspectives* (Austin: University of Texas Press, 1995).

35. Archie P. McDonald, "William Barret Travis 1809–1836," http://www.tamu.edu/ccbn/dewitt/adp/history/bios/travis/travis.html. William Barret Travis' Letter from the Alamo, http://www.freedomdocuments.com/Travis/enlarge.html.

36. Lord, "Myths and Realities of the Alamo," 18, 20, 24. Ramón Martínez Caro, "A True Account of the First Texas Campaign," in Carlos E. Castañeda, ed., *The Mexican Side of the Texas Revolution* (Dallas, TX: L. Turner Co., 1928), 103.

37. Fannin's Fight & The Massacre at La Bahia (Goliad), http://www.tamu.edu/ccbn/dewitt/goliadmassacre.htm Goliad Region January–March 27, 1836, Johnson & Grant & Colonel James Fannin's Command, http://www.tamu.edu/ccbn/dewitt/goliadmenframe.htm. Archival Communications Fannin and Goliad August 1835–March 1836, http://www.tamu.edu/ccbn/dewitt/goliadofficial.htm, June 16, M. B. Lamar, S. Whiting, and J. W. J. Niles, "No. 746 Oak Grove June 16, 1838," in Charles Adams Gulick, Jr., and Katherine Elliott, eds., *The Papers of Mirabeau Buonaparte Lamar*, Vol. II (Austin: A. C. Baldwin & Sons Printer, 1922), 167–68.

38. Explore documents such as Santa Anna's account. Victory at San Jacinto, Sons of the DeWitt Colony, http://www.tamu.edu/ccbn/dewitt/dewitt.htm. José Enrique de la Peña, *With Santa Anna in Texas: A Personal Narrative of the Revolution*, trans. Carmen Perry (College Station: Texas A&M University, 1997), 53.

39. Carlos Castañeda, *Our Catholic Heritage in Texas, 1519–1933*, Vol. 7, *The Church in Texas Since Independence, 1836–1950*, 5. Sam Houston's Copy of His Official Report of the Battle of San Jacinto, http://www.tsl.state.tx.us/treasures/republic/sanjacinto/report-01.html.

40. Lota M. Spell, "Gorostiza and Texas," *Hispanic American Historical Review* 37, no. 4 (November 1957): 446. Brack, *Mexico Views Manifest*, 74–75. Burl Noggle, "Anglo Observers of the Southwest Borderlands, 1825–1890: The Rise of a Concept," *Arizona and the West* 1, no. 2 (Summer 1959): 122. Treaty of Velasco, May 14, 1836, Courtesy of the Yale University Law School Library. The Avalon Project, http://avalon.law.yale.edu/19th_century/velasco.asp. The Treaty of Velasco was negotiated between officials of the interim government of the Republic of Texas and General Antonio López de Santa Anna (1794–1876) about three weeks after his capture on April 22, 1836. Santa Anna did not have the authority to negotiate the treaty that gave Texas to the United States.

41. Manual Medina Castro, *El Gran Despojo: Texas, Nuevo México, California* (México, DF: Editorial Diogenes, 1971), 9. Castañeda, *Our Catholic Heritage in Texas, 1519–1933*, Vol. 6, 74. Charles A. Hale, *Mexican Liberalism in the Age of Mora, 1821–1853* (New Haven, CT: Yale University Press, 1968), 11–12, 16.

42. On March 1, 1845, Congress passed the joint resolution, but it was not until July 1845 that a convention in Texas voted to accept annexation to the United States. The political maneuverings behind annexation in the U.S. Congress document the economic motive underlying it. Van Alstyne, *The Rising American Empire*, 104. José María Roa Barcena, *Recuerdos de la Invasión Norte Americana (1846–1848)*, I. Antonio Castro Leal, ed. (México, DF: Editorial Porrúa, 1947), 25–27. For the Mexican reaction see José Joaquín de Herrera, "A Proclamation Denouncing the United States' Intention to Annex Texas," June 4, 1845, in Steven R. Butler, ed., *A Documentary History of the Mexican War* (Richardson, TX: Descendants of Mexican War Veterans, 1995), 5, http://www.dmwv.org/mexwar/documents/herrera.htm.

43. Albert C. Ramsey, ed. and trans., *The Old Side or Notes for the History of the War Between Mexico and the United States*, reprinted (New York: Burt Franklin, 1970), 28–29. Ramón Alcaraz et al., *Apuntes para la Historia de la Guerra Entre México y los Estados Unidos* (México, DF: Tipografía de Manuel Payno, Hiho, 1848), 27–28. For an excellent account of Slidell's mission, see Dennis Eugene Berge, "Mexican Response to United States Expansion, 1841–1848" (PhD dissertation, University of California, Los Angeles, 1965).

44. James. D. Richardson, *A Compilation of the Messages and Papers of the Presidents*, 10 vols. (Washington, DC: Government Printing Office, 1905), 4, 428–42, quoted in Arvin Rappaport, ed., *The War with Mexico: Why Did It Happen?* (Skokie, IL: Rand McNally, 1964), 16. President James Polk's State of the Union Address, December 2, 1845. Joint Session of Congress, State of the Union Address, 29th Congress, First Session, December 2, 1845, http://www.presidentialrhetoric.com/historicspeeches/polk/stateoftheunion1845.html. James K. Polk, Message on War with Mexico, May 11, 1846, http://www.pbs.org/weta/thewest/resources/archives/two/mexdec.htm.

45. Grady McWhiney and Sue McWhiney, eds., *To Mexico with Taylor and Scott, 1845–1847* (Waltham, MA: Praisell, 1969), 3. Letter from Ulysses S. Grant to Fiancée Julia Dent, July 25, 1846, in John Y. Simon, *The Papers of Ulysses S. Grant*, Vol. 1 (London: Feffer & Simons, 1967), 102.

46. Abraham Lincoln's "Spot Resolutions," Resolution and Preamble on Mexican War: "Spot Resolutions," *The Abraham Lincoln Papers at the Library of Congress*, December 22, 1847, http://quod.lib.umich.edu/cgi/t/text/text-idx?c=lincoln;rgn=div1;view=text;idno=lincoln1;node=lincoln1%3A434.

47. Rappaport, *The War with Mexico*, 16.

48. Walt Whitman, *Leaves of Grass* (Brooklyn, NY: Gabriel Harrison daguerreotype, 1855), iii, iv, xi. I.

49. Glenn W. Price, *Origins of the War with Mexico: The Polk-Stockton Intrigue* (Austin: University of Texas Press, 1967), 7.

50. As noted, the belief that Americans are the chosen people is part of the formation of the American image of themselves. The term Manifest Destiny was written by John O'Sullivan in 1839. "The Great Nation of Futurity," *The United States Democratic Review* 6, no. 23 (November 1839): 426–30. Cornell

University Library, http://cdl.library.cornell.edu/cgi-bin/moa/sgml/moa-idx?notisid=AGD1642-0006-46; http://www.mtholyoke.edu/acad/intrel/osulliva.htm.

51. For a good discussion of Calvinist Europe, see Richard van Dulmen, *Los Incicios de la Europa Moderna 1550–1680* (México: Siglo XXI, 1990), 246–63.

52. John C. Calhoun, Conquest of Mexico. TeachingAmericanHistory.org http://teachingamericanhistory.org/library/document/conquest-of-mexico/. Daniel Alejandro Garza, "So Easily Misunderstood: U.S.-Mexican War Soldiers' Motivation, Experience, and Memory, (1846–1890)" (Master of Arts thesis, Southern Methodist University, 2010).

53. Justin H. Smith, *The War with Mexico*, Vol. 2 (New York: Macmillan, 1919; reprint, Gloucester, MA: Peter Smith, 1963), 310 (1919 printing also available online at Internet Archive, The War With Mexico Vol. II, https://archive.org/stream/warwithmexicovol010848mbp#page/n310/mode/1up).

54. T. B. Thorpe, *Our Army on the Rio Grande*, quoted in Abiel Abbott Livermore, *The War with Mexico Reviewed* (Boston: American Peace Society, 1850), 126. A reviewer questioned claims of the incessant bombing of Matamoros. The following memo appears to support this event. Congratulatory Orders. 151. Head-Quarters, Army Of Occupation, Resaca de la Palma, May 11, 1846. By order of Brigadier-General Taylor. "While the main body of the army has been thus actively employed, the garrison left opposite Matamoros has rendered no less distinguished service, by sustaining a severe cannonade and bombardment for many successive days." In Nathan Covington Brooks, *Complete History of the Mexican War: Its Causes, Conduct, and Consequences: Comprising an Account of the Various Military and Naval Operations, from Its Commencement to the Treaty of Peace* (Philadelphia: Grigg, Elliot & Co., 1849), 151.

55. Alfred Hoyt Bill, *Rehearsal for Conflict* (New York: Knopf, 1947), 122.

56. John Y. Simon, *The Papers of Ulysses S. Grant*, Vol. 1 (London and Amsterdam: Feffer & Simons, 1967), 102.

57. William Starr Meyers, ed., *The Mexican War Diary of General B. Clellan*, Vol. 1 (Princeton, NJ: Princeton University Press, 1917), 109–10.

58. Quoted in Livermore, *The War with Mexico Reviewed*, 148–49.

59. Brack, *Mexico Views Manifest*, 10, states that the general view has been that Mexico erred because it chose to fight rather than "negotiate."

60. Livermore, *The War with Mexico Reviewed*, 8, 11, 12.

61. Abraham Lincoln's Speech to Congress against Seizing Mexican Territory, January 12, 1848, United States House of Representatives. The Abraham Lincoln Papers at the Library of Congress. Series 1. General Correspondence. 1833–1916. Library of Congress, http://memory.loc.gov/cgi-bin/query/r?ammem/mal:@field(DOCID+@lit(d0007400)) . In January 1848 he opposed seizing Mexican territory and laid out the causes for the war. Acuña and Compeán, *Voices of the U.S. Latino Experience*, 95–100.

62. Shelley Streeby, "American Sensations: Empire, Amnesia, and the US-Mexican War," *American Literary History* 13, no. 1 (Spring 2001): 1–40.

63. Smith, *The War with Mexico*, Vol. 2, 385, n. 18. Justin Harvey Smith, 1857–1930, *The War with Mexico* (Gloucester, MA: Peter Smith, 1963 [c1919] Vol. 1, 550, n. 6.]) The Saint Patrick's Battalion (Batallón de San Patricio), http://www.youtube.com/watch?v=WiogUx5h28c. Batalla de Monterrey 1846, http://www.youtube.com/watch?v=5-KYgBW_RBA.

64. Livermore, *War with Mexico Reviewed*, 160. Mark R. Day, "Los San Patricios: La Trágica Historia del Batallón de San Patricio" (Vista, CA: San Patricio Productions, 1997), is a video documentary on the San Patricios. The video is also available in English. Clips of the movie can be found on YouTube.

65. Meyers, The Mexican War Diary of General B. Clellan, Vol. 1, 161–62.

66. George Gordon Meade, Monterey, December 2, 1846, George Gordon Meade, *The Life and Letters of George Gordon Meade: Major-General United States Army*, Vol. 1 (New York: Charles Scribner's Sons, 1913), 160–61.

67. Winfield Scott, *Memoirs of Lieut.-General Scott*, Vol. 2 (New York: Sheldon, 1864), 392. Timothy A Garvin, "'An Immortal Band of Rouges': Immigrant Disaffection and the San Patricio Battalion in the United States-Mexican War, 1846–1848" (Master of Arts thesis, California State University, Long Beach, 2004).

68. Samuel E. Chamberlain, *My Confessions* (New York: Harper & Row, 1956), 75.

69. Chamberlain, *My Confessions*, 87, 88.

70. Stephen B. Oates, "*Los Diablos Tejanos*: Texas Rangers," in Odie B. Faulk and Joseph A. Stout, Jr., eds., *The Mexican War: Changing Interpretations* (Chicago: Sage, 1973), 121. Paul Foos, *Short, Offhand, Killing Affair: Soldiers and Social Conflict During the Mexican-American War* (New York: Scholarly Books, 2002). Foos uses soldiers' diaries and letters. He relies largely on U.S. sources for American atrocities against Mexican civilians. Foos raises the question of widespread discontent within the Euro-American forces. Depredations against Mexicans were based on feelings of racial superiority. Judah Swann, "The Texas Rangers in the Mexican War" (Master of Arts thesis, California State University, Dominguez Hills, 2000).

71. Johannsen, *To the Halls of the Montezumas*, 137. Elizabeth Salas, *Soldaderas in the Mexican Military: Myth and History* (Austin: University of Texas Press, 1990). Peggy Mullarkey Cashion, "Women and the Mexican War, 1846–1848" (Master of Arts thesis, University of Texas Arlington, 1990).

72. Johannsen, *To the Halls of the Montezumas*, 137.

73. Pablo Ramos Benitez y Ahmed Valtier, "Maria Josefa Zozaya, La Heroína de la Batalla de Monterrey," *Revista Atisbo*, No. 10 (December 2007–February 6, 2008). Daniel Walker Howe, *What Hath God Wrought: The Transformation of America, 1815–1848* (New York: Oxford University Press, 2007), 778–79. Christopher Conway, "Sisters at War: Mexican Women's Poetry and the U.S.-Mexican War," *Latin American Research Review* 47, no. 1 (2012): 3–13.

74. Peter J. Michel, "No Mere Holiday Affair: The Capture of Santa Fe in the Mexican-American War," *Gateway Heritage Quarterly* 9, no. 4 (Spring 1989): 12–25. Joseph G. Dawson III, "'Zealous for Annexation': Volunteer Soldiering, Military Government, and the Service of Colonel Alexander Doniphan

in the Mexican-American War," *Journal of Strategic Studies* 19, no. 4 (December 1, 1996): 10–36. Randy L. Yoder, "Rackensackers and Rangers: Brutality in the Conquest of Northern Mexico, 1846–1848" (Master of Arts thesis, Oklahoma State University, 2006).

75. Brack, *Mexico Views Manifest*, 2.

76. Alonso Zabre, *Guide to the History of Mexico: A Modern Interpretation* (Austin, TX: Pemberton Press, 1969), 300. For the Mexican side of the war, Ramón Alcaraz et al., eds., *The Other Side: Or Notes for the History of the War between Mexico and the United States Written in Mexico*, Albert C. Ramsey, trans. (New York: John Wiley, 1850), 33–38, 45–50, 122–29, 208–14, 353–65.

77. George Lockhart Rives, *The United States and Mexico: A History of the Relations Between the Two Countries from the Independence of Mexico to the Close of the War with the United States*, Vol. II (New York: Charles Scribner's Sons, 1913), 584–86). Los Ninos Heroes Mexico City's Boy Heroes, http://www.youtube.com/watch?v=x5yAeE1MuMo), Los Niños Héroes, http://www.youtube.com/watch?v=xP6PLFG_b8Y.

78. Dexter Perkins and Glyndon G. Van Deusen, *The American Democracy: Its Rise to Power* (New York: Macmillan, 1964), 273.

79. Alejandro Sobarzo, *Deber y consciencia: Nicolás Trist, el negociador norteamericano en la Guerra del 47* (México: Fondo de Cultura Económica, 1996), 283–85.

80. The treaty drew the boundary between the United States and Mexico at the Rio Grande and the Gila River, for a payment of $15,000,000. The United States received more than 525,000 square miles (1,360,000 square kilometers) of land (now Arizona, California, western Colorado, Nevada, New Mexico, Texas, and Utah). In return it agreed to settle the more than $3,000,000 in claims made by U.S. citizens against Mexico. The treaty was a cause of civil war in both Mexico and the United States. The expansion of slavery in the United States supposedly had been settled by the Missouri Compromise (1820). The addition of the vast Mexican tract as new U.S. territory reopened the question. Attempts to settle it led to the uneasy Compromise of 1850.

81. Robert Self Henry, *The Story of the Mexican War* (New York: Ungar, 1950), 390. Treaty of Guadalupe Hidalgo, 1848, Treaty of Guadalupe Hidalgo, February 2, 1848. The Avalon Project at Yale Law School, http://avalon.law.yale.edu/19th_century/guadhida.asp.

82. See John D. Fuller, *The Movement for the Acquisition of All Mexico* (New York: DaCapo Press, 1969). Netzahualcoyotl Avelar, "A Critical Analysis of the 1848 Treaty of Guadalupe Hidalgo Between the United States of America and the Republic of Mexico: Educational Implications" (Doctor of Education dissertation, University of San Francisco, 1993).

83. Letter from Commissioner Trist to Secretary Buchanan, Mexico, January 25, 1848, *Senate Executive Documents*, no. 52, 283.

84. Wayne Moquin et al., eds., *A Documentary History of the Mexican American* (New York: Praeger, 1971), 185. Irving W. Levinson, "The causes, course, and settlement of the Mexican-American War" (Master of Arts thesis, University of Houston, 1997).

85. Lynn I. Perrigo, *The American Southwest* (New York: Holt, Rinehart and Winston, 1971), 176.

86. *Compilation of Treaties in Force* (Washington, DC: Government Printing Office, 1899), 402, quoted in Perrigo, *The American Southwest*, 176. The Querétaro Protocol, May 26, 1848, Protocol of Querétaro, in Rodolfo F. Acuña and Guadalupe Compeán, eds., *Voices of the U.S. Latino Experience* [Three Volumes] (Westport: Greenwood, 2008), 113–14. The following shows Polk's duplicity: President James K. Polk (1795–1849) on Article X of the Treaty of Guadalupe Hidalgo, February 22, 1848, U.S. Senate, 30th Cong., 1st Sess., Executive Order 68, *Congressional Record*.

87. Armando B. Rendón, *Chicano Manifesto* (New York: Collier Books, 1970), 75–78. Article X from the Treaty of Guadalupe Hidalgo, 1848. Deleted Article X from the Treaty of Guadalupe Hidalgo, 1848, Article X, Treaty of Guadalupe Hidalgo, http://www.loc.gov/rr/hispanic/ghtreaty/ President James K. Polk (1795–1849) on Article X of the Treaty of Guadalupe Hidalgo, February 22, 1848, U.S. Senate, 30th Cong., 1st Sess., Executive Order 68. *Congressional Record.*

88. Rendón, *Chicano Manifesto*, 78.

89. Weber, *Foreigners in Their Native Land*, 14, states that the Supreme Court in *McKinney v. Saviego*, 1855, found that the treaty did not apply to Texas.

90. Antonio de la Peña y Reyes, *Algunos Documentos Sobre el Tratado de Guadalupe-Hidalgo* (México, DF: Sec de Rel. Ext., 1930), 159, quoted in Richard Gonzales, "Commentary on the Treaty of Guadalupe Hidalgo," in Feliciano Rivera, ed., *A Mexican American Source Book* (Menlo Park, CA: Educational Consulting Associates, 1970), 185.

91. Leroy B. Hafen and Carl Coke Rister, *Western America*, 2nd ed. (Englewood Cliffs, NJ: Prentice-Hall, 1950), 312.

92. Van Alstyne, *The Rising American Empire*, 106.

93. Martha Menchaca, "A History of Colonization and Mexican American Education," Paper Presented for a Conference, Harvard Educational Review, March 9, 1998, at the University of California, Irvine.

The Border Crossed Us

The U.S.–Mexican border is where the first world ends and the third begins. Historians differ on the causes of tension between people on the north and south of this 2,000-mile border line. In order to find the answer, we should perhaps ask why historians have so many conflicting interpretations of history. It is because historians often read different sources, which influence their conclusions. For example, a person who bases his or her knowledge on faith generally comes to a different conclusion than one who bases it on science. How we get knowledge determines our historical view. The differences in how we look at things are often called epistemological gulfs.[1]

Some Americans take offense at the notion of an American Empire; many liberal historians, for example, believe that the notion of an American Empire came about in the aftermath of the Spanish–American War of 1898. They are reluctant to accept the fact that the United States was an aggressor nation, and to avoid this conclusion they use many euphemisms such as the Mexican War or the Westward Movement to refer to the U.S. invasion of Mexico, and the theft of half of its territory. Mexicans counter this perception through the use of words such as *intervention,* if they are polite, or *the American Invasion of Mexico,* if they are blunt. Standing in the way of a full confession by the United States is the notion of reannexation, which we discussed in Chapter 3. Amidst all this, theorists quibble over the definition of empire, which also obscures the truth, dampening our ability to make a clearer interpretation.

In order to determine whether the U.S. invasion of Mexico was "an imperialist war," we must look at U.S. leaders' motivations. Was the United States spreading democracy to Mexico based on idealistic motives? Were the motives in 1836 or 1847 any different than those in 1898 or the present when, according to some Americans, they want to spread their values throughout the world? Or does it come down to what J. William Fulbright called in 1966 "The Arrogance of Power"?[2]

There is documentary evidence that Euro-Americans' interests in Latin American countries did not begin or end with the acquisition of Florida and the Mexican cession. Yet these events forged the notion of empire. Even before the "Mexican adventure," Euro-Americans sought to secure their interests in the Caribbean and Central America; situations in these areas were ripe for American "reannexation," and the territories themselves were key to the construction of a "U.S." inter-ocean canal. It was rationalized that the Caribbean was paramount to the defense of U.S. interests in the region. The Cuban Question—whether the U.S. should annex Cuba— was heatedly debated in the U.S. Congress and the media in the 1850s as slave interests pressed for another Texas American–like filibuster.[3]

After the signing of the Treaty of Guadalupe Hidalgo, some Euro-American politicos were not satisfied with the border: Texas claimed the Rio Grande as its western boundary, which included half of New Mexico; expansionists wanted the reannexation of more Mexican land that they believed was their land anyway. Almost immediately the North and the South sought to further their interests in the newly acquired territory. The South wanted slavery legalized, but the North wanted exactly the opposite—to exclude slavery. Before going to war, Congress had passed the Wilmot Proviso (1846) as an amendment to a House of Representatives bill. It prohibited slavery in any land acquired from Mexico. However, once the war was over, discontent among slave interests was on the rise and a crisis similar to the one that led to the Missouri Compromise of 1820 broke out.[4] There were also politicos claiming that the border was further south.[5] Tellingly, the border was referred to as the Mexican border, not the American border, as if it applied only to Mexico.

If truth be told, the border meant little to the people. A person would have been hard put to distinguish between the Lower Rio Grande Valley and Mexico. As commercial agriculture on the U.S. side developed, and African American labor was freed, thousands of Mexican laborers and their families crossed the border. Industrial capitalism in the United States and population growth in Mexico uprooted thousands more.

The following four chapters of this book discuss how the events unfolded in the four states—Texas, New Mexico, Arizona, and California—that formed the center of Mexican life in the United States. To assist the reader in better understanding the topics discussed, the following wheel model has been developed, which will be helpful to connect the events and data to the timeline.

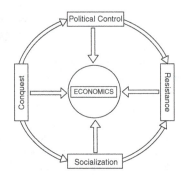

In the wheel, *Economics* is the hub, the center of activity, binding everything together. It is what makes the wheel go round, and determines how each of the other variables is defined. The word *Conquest* does not exist in a vacuum, and there were distinct motives for the conquest in each of the four states or territories. Once the land and other resources are taken, the people must come under *Political Control*, that is, police powers, government, courts, and so forth. Laws set norms essential to social control. Persons either appointed by the conquering people or elected by the conquered people fill these administrative and judicial posts. The courts interpret the law, which is backed by "legitimate" force. People are not easily controlled, and violence or police powers only go so far in keeping people in their place. They undergo *Socialization* through schooling, media, religion, etc. to accept the legitimacy and common codes of conduct of the ruling elite. However, in colonial situations, as in every other situation, people resist. This *Resistance* manifests in the form of social banditry and mob rebellions, and in milder forms such as opposition newspapers and other media.

But history is not static. New memories are constantly being added and older ones revised, and individuals and groups go on adapting to the changes in the modes of economic production. For instance, before 1821 the economy of the Southwest was localized and revolved around subsistence farming. Although trade existed between nonindigenous peoples and the natives, and between regions, life was rather region-centered. After 1821, although transportation was cumbersome, trade and merchants assumed greater prominence. Around 1880, railroad networks connected the Southwest to the more densely populated eastern United States, and the large-scale commercial agriculture and mining began producing such massive quantities as to affect the economy of the entire nation. Such pursuits demanded large amounts of capital and human labor. These changes determined how ordinary people made their living, what relationship they had with the elites, and how they organized to bring about change.

Notes

1. Simon Baatz, "Leopold and Loeb's Criminal Minds," *Smithsonian* (August 2008), http://www.smithsonianmag.com/history-archaeology/criminal-minds.html. The interpretation of psychiatric evidence leads to different conclusions. Neurologists differed from psychoanalysts. The article deals with how historians get their knowledge, how they are trained, and their life experiences, and determines how we know what we know. Hence, the reader must be skeptical about claims made by different sources of knowledge.

2. J. William Fulbright, *The Arrogance of Power* (New York: Random House, 1966).

3. Rodolfo F. Acuña and Guadalupe Compeán, eds., *Voices of the U.S. Latino Experience*, 3 vols. (Westport, CT: Greenwood, 2008), 215–71. *The United States Magazine and Democratic Review* 25, no. cxxxv (September 1849): 197, 198, 200, 203, 205. Letter from U.S. Secretary of State James Buchanan to R. M. Saunders, June 17, 1848, 193–204, http://cdl.library.cornell.edu/cgi-bin/moa/moa-cgi?notisid=AGD1642-0025&byte=226352056. Clayton-Bulwer Treaty, 1850, http://avalon.law.yale.edu/19th_century/br1850.asp. Ostend Manifesto, October 18, 1854, http://xroads.virginia.edu/~HYPER/HNS/OSTEND/ostend.html. Speech Given by William Walker in New Orleans, May 30, 1857, "Filibusterism," *New York Daily Times* (June 8, 1857), 2. The *New York Times* is full of articles on the Cuban Question during the 1850s.

4. Compromise of 1850, January 29, 1850, http://www.loc.gov/rr/program/bib/ourdocs/Compromise1850.html

5. Governor William Carr Lane's Manifesto Regarding the Drawing of the Boundary Between Mexico and the United States, *New York Daily Times* (June 20, 1853), 3. Commissioner James Bartlett's Reply to William Carr Lane, "The Mesilla Valley," *New York Daily Times* (May 5, 1853), 6.

CHAPTER 4

Remember the Alamo:
The Colonization of Texas

LEARNING OBJECTIVES

- Discuss race relations between the conquerors and the conquered.

- Show class divisions within the Mexican-Texas community.

- Analyze the violence toward Mexicans in the context of social banditry, mob rebellions, and other forms of social resistance.

- Describe the role of the Texas Rangers and lynching in Texas.

- Interpret the role of the Rio Grande River.

- Discuss commercialization of agriculture and the impact of the railroad on the Texas economy and Mexicans.

1819	1836	1846	1847	1848	1859	1863	1880	1900

The Years between 1836 and 1845

Aside from the desire for land and harbors for cotton production and trade, a primary motivation for the invasion and conquest of Texas was to control the Rio Grande and the trade of northern Mexico. The Euro-Americans' obsession with controlling the then mighty Rio Grande was similar to their fixation with dominating the mouth of the Mississippi, which resulted in the United States establishing its supremacy over the entire Mississippi delta. (Both these rivers emptied into the Gulf of Mexico.) Thus, not surprisingly, Texas pressed its claim to the length of the river—all 1,885 miles, from southern Colorado to the Gulf of Mexico. Euro-Americans used south Texas as their base of operation.[1]

The strategic and economic importance of the Rio Grande did not escape the Spaniards and the Mexicans before them. According to David Montejano,

> *The commercial importance of the Rio Grande did not lie simply with the distant Santa Fe trade. What is usually overlooked but proved to be critical and more directly related to the outbreak*

of hostilities was the port trade of Matamoros on the lower end of the Rio Grande. In the late 1820s, silver bullion, lead, wool, hides, and beef tallow from Monterey, Saltillo, and San Luis Potosí were all passing through Matamoros, with silver constituting 90 percent or more of the value of the exports.[2]

This trade generated a large part of the Lone Star State's prosperity. Border towns sprang up on the north side of the Rio Grande and linked northern Mexico to San Antonio and the rest of Texas. San Antonio was a Tejano (Texas Mexican) city; between 1836 and the Civil War, Mexicans made up most of the city's population. Numbers gave Tejanos the illusion that they were part of the governance process and would be part of its future. However, independence brought a decline in the number of Tejano office holders; in 1837, 41 Spanish-surnamed candidates ran for office in San Antonio; a decade later the number had come down to only five. The aldermanic council included only one or two Mexicans between 1848 and 1866. The loss of symbolic power accompanied an erosion of the peaceful accommodation that had characterized relations between Mexican and Euro-American elites. Racism united Euro-Americans and gave them an advantage. At the same time, racial divisions divided Mexicans and took their toll in reducing the Tejano elites' influence.[3]

The hue of one's skin color played a huge role initially in the relations between the two peoples. Often their acceptance depended on whether Mexicans looked Caucasian or "colored." On this point, University of Texas professor Neil Foley writes that although the new republic adopted liberal land policies, only white heads of household were eligible to receive land, which meant Texas whites and "Spanish" Mexicans who aided in the Texas revolt.[4] Whiteness, according to Foley, increasingly became a litmus test that most Mexicans could not pass. By the 1840s, the new republic's racist policies had forced at least 200 old "Spanish" families in San Antonio to move to Mexico. "Juan Seguin, captain in the Texas army, hero of San Jacinto, and [until recently] the last Mexican mayor of San Antonio" was forced to flee Mexico in 1842.[5]

It did not help matters that most Euro-American immigrants were from southern states; over time their racist attitudes were accepted as the norm. The antipathy toward Mexicans was irrational—considering they were just over 2 percent of the population by the 1850s. Frederick Law Olmsted observed during his stay in San Antonio a Mexican being caught attempting to steal a horse. The Mexican, according to Olmstead, would have been lynched had it not been for the intervention of an outraged Mexican public. Nevertheless, trying to take advantage of the crisis, the sheriff used it as a pretext to raise a posse of 500 men to drive Mexicans out of the neighborhood.[6]

Memories of the war fanned the animosities between the two peoples. Each incoming wave of U.S. colonists internalized the war; thus the myth of the Alamo became part of Texas lore. Mexico refused to recognize the Republic of Texas. Mexican prisoners of war, for example, suffered untold indignities including being held in cages, with many dying of starvation. In the years before annexation to the United States, the Texan wannabes actively warred on Native Americans and stepped up their diplomatic front against Mexico.[7] Meanwhile, the estimated population of 35,000 in Texas in the fall of 1835 grew to more than 100,000 by 1845. Most of the newcomers considered themselves pioneers entitled to pushing the old *Tejano* families aside—after all, "Americans" had paid for Texas with their blood. Not surprisingly, many Mexican Americans resented their subservient status.[8]

The Texas Mexican population was concentrated in the San Antonio region, the Rio Grande Valley, and the El Paso area. Although many families left Texas for Mexico, the Mexican population grew during this period, increasing from just over 4,000 in 1836 to over 14,000 in 1850. As towns grew on both sides of the Rio Grande, Mexican American and Euro-American merchants cultivated commercial ties with Mexican merchants, who were drawn to the area from the Mexican Border States and the Mexican interior. U.S. merchants assumed an air of superiority, and soon, through political and social connections, they monopolized a disproportionate amount of land and resources.[9] Before 1848, the valley of the Rio Grande supported cattle towns, such as Laredo, Guerrero, Mier, Camargo, and Reynosa. These self-reliant communities raised corn, beans, melons, and vegetables and also tended sheep and goats. Commerce between the people on both sides of the river bound them together by necessity. Alongside this commercial activity, the elites competed for land. Armando Villarreal y Talamantes writes that between "1837 and 1842, 14 upper class

Mexicans bought a total of 278,769 acres from 67 Mexican landowners. During the same period, American buyers purchased 1,368,574 acres from 358 Mexicans, four times the amount purchased by their Mexican counterparts."[10] It is assumed that many of the Mexicans selling their land repatriated to Mexico in search of better opportunities.

Worsening the situation was the resumption of Comanche and Lipan Apache raids during the 1830s, unsettling conditions in south Texas. The *ranchos* (ranches), especially those around Laredo, bore the brunt; raids of these band tribes sharply cut the number of livestock in the valley. Nevertheless, ranching remained the principal activity of Mexican settlers, mainly because farming was uncertain without extensive irrigation projects, which were not common until the end of the century.[11]

Euro-Texans and a number of their Tejano cohorts entertained illusions of empire. The Republic of Texas's Georgia-born president Mirabeau Buonaparte Lamar, who in 1835 had immigrated to Texas, trying to take advantage of Mexico's problems with France, in 1839 pressed for a settlement of the boundary question, offering Mexico a $5 million bribe if it would accept the Rio Grande (Bravo) as the territorial border. This would have given Texas half of New Mexico. In 1841, Lamar dispatched the ill-fated Santa Fe Expedition into New Mexico with the end of adding the area to the republic.[12]

The imperialistic ventures of Euro-Texans continued throughout the nineteenth century. As mentioned, Texas's antipathy toward Mexicans was passed on to succeeding generations and exported to other states as Euro-Texans moved west in search of opportunities. The continuous exodus of white Texans can be tracked through the censuses and the literature of the time. Texan antipathy toward Mexicans was often the source of violence in many mining camps and ranches throughout the Southwest.[13]

Crossing the Northwest Texas-Mexican Border

Even among rich Mexicans, accommodation to the new order was difficult. Most of the Mexican population was poor and dark and had fewer options, so they suffered blatant discrimination and exploitation. Discontent with the new regime was widespread. For example, the northeastern Texas border had separated Spanish-speaking from the French and, later, Mexico from the United States; since the early eighteenth century, there were border tensions over trade and other matters. French and later the Euro-Americans from Natchitoches and New Orleans, Louisiana, used Nacogdoches as a gateway for smuggling. Since the early 1820s, tension had increased between the Mexican old-timers and the newly arrived white Americans who were pushing them aside. According to Janice Elaine Watkins, from the beginning, "Nowhere would the lack of respect for and noncompliance to authority be more apparent than in Nacogdoches. Distance enabled the Nacogdoches land men to ignore orders and conduct their land schemes without interference, and their actions and reactions affected the subsequent Texas revolution." Also from the beginning, there was competition and scheming for land among the Euro-Americans, who were often joined by Mexicans.[14]

By the end of the 1830s, an estimated 1,000 Euro-Americans per month entered Texas by way of Brazos River. There were various factions that often crossed racial lines.[15] In 1835, Vicente Córdova, a native-born Texan, was the alcalde of Nacogdoches. However, within a year he was replaced by a white alcalde as the white population overwhelmed Mexican Nacogdoches. Córdova became captain of the military district.

As the hostilities between Euro-Americans and Mexicans came to a head, Córdova was pressured to take sides, which he refused to do. After the Texas war, the republic sought revenge upon those who had not supported the filibusters. Some Native Americans with long-standing friendships with Mexicans joined Córdova in revolting against the Lone Star Republic.[16] According to oral tradition, one of the rebels, Guillermo Cruz, in response to his employer's question about why Mexicans were revolting, replied, "they were going to fight for their rights, they had been dogs long enough." Córdova undoubtedly expected help from Mexico, but it was not forthcoming. Against all odds, the rebels fought the Republic of Texas in a spirited defense of their cause until 1839, when the rebel band dwindled to fewer than 75 Tejanos, blacks, and Native Americans. The wounded Córdova retreated to Matamoros, and the families of the surviving east Texas Mexicans fled to the woods. Texas authorities tried 33 Tejanos for treason. They found only one, Antonio Menchaca, guilty and sentenced him to be hanged. President Mirabeau B. Lamar of the Texas Republic commuted his sentence, banishing Menchaca and his family from Texas. Authorities used the revolt as a pretext to remove the Cherokee, Delaware, Shawnee, and other tribes from Texas. From Mexico, Córdova continued his war against the Republic of Texas, attracting native, Mexican, black, and even white followers.[17]

The Mexican Corridor

Tensions over Mexico's harboring of runaway slaves continued through the Civil War. By 1855, some 4,000 fugitive slaves had escaped to northern Mexico.[18] Texas authorities estimated that plantation owners lost $3.2 million and alleged that Mexican authorities encouraged slaves to escape. When slave owners demanded their return, Mexican officials refused and Euro-Texans led several expeditions to recover runaways, greatly increasing border tensions. White Texans suspected all Mexicans of aiding blacks.[19] In 1853, the federal government stationed 2,176 soldiers in the state of Texas (from a standing U.S. army of 10,417). The next year, the town of Seguín passed an ordinance forbidding Mexicans from entering the county or associating with blacks. According to James Marten, Mexicans were suspected of not only disloyalty but inciting slaves. Vigilantism increased, and in 1854 "a vigilance committee in Austin expelled at least twenty Mexican families, and Austin businessmen pledged not to hire Mexican laborers," claiming that they gave African slaves a "false notion of freedom."[20] In east Texas a vigilante group called the Moderators harassed the Mexican population.

Even so, not all Mexicans sympathized with the escaped slaves. Some supported the slave plutocracy, considering themselves different from the slaves and the darker-skinned Mexicans. Consider the case of the enigmatic José Antonio Navarro of San Antonio, who matriculated his son Angel at Harvard University. Although Navarro, as a representative to the state constitutional convention, helped secure the vote for Mexicans and, in the 1850s, fought the Know-Nothing Party, he sided with pro-slavery interests and his sons fought for the confederacy. Navarro led white supremacists during post–Civil War Reconstruction.[21]

Control of the Corridor

Charles Stillman arrived in the valley in 1846. Beginning as a merchant in Matamoros, he anticipated the Euro-American occupation, and he and other merchants began to buy property on the U.S. side of the river. In 1848 he established a trading post in a cotton field across the river from Matamoros. Within four years, the lucrative trade with Mexico developed the town of Brownsville. This boom drove land prices up and attracted more Euro-Americans.[22]

A direct link existed between the Mexican War and the origins of the Euro-American mercantile elite. Many of these merchants were camp followers or former soldiers. In 1850, Euro-Americans composed slightly over half of Brownsville's population. Because Euro-Americans controlled the government, they were able to set the rules; racism conditioned them to believe that their authority was part of the natural law. Moreover, Euro-Americans occupied 80 percent of the professional, mercantile, and government positions. Upriver, Laredo, Eagle Pass, and Del Rio were also trade centers where merchants made fortunes from the commercial links with Mexico. With profits from these ventures, merchants monopolized the land, which they purchased or stole from Mexican landowners. Lawyers abetted the process by manipulating government officials. As a consequence of their control of the political and social processes, Euro-Americans had an economic edge.

Stillman was the leader of the white cabal and he masterminded the theft of the prime lands held by the old Mexican families. Initially, Stillman and his cohorts feared that the state of Texas would protect Mexican land claims, so the cabal flirted with the idea of secession from Texas and creating their own state. They enlisted the support of powerful congressmen such as Henry Clay and William Seward. Stillman, Richard King, James O'Donnell, Captain Mifflin Kenedy, and Sam Belden led the separatists and recruited Mexicans to their cause. When the scheme failed, Stillman turned to more familiar means of acquiring land—he stole it.[23]

Stillman's trading post stood on the *Espíritu Santo* grant, belonging to the descendants of Francisco Cavazos. Stillman confused the title by moving squatters onto the Cavazoses' land and then purchasing their claims. Based on these claims, he challenged Cavazos's title. Although a magistrate ruled for the Cavazoses,

Stillman threatened to appeal, so the Cavazoses agreed to take $33,000 for the grant, although it was worth $214,000.[24] The agreement was made with Stillman's attorneys who promptly transferred the title to Stillman. The law firm soon afterward went bankrupt without paying the Cavazoses a cent.

Stillman's associate, Richard King, amassed over 600,000 acres of land during his lifetime, and his widow increased the family holdings to more than 1 million acres. The King Ranch Corporation commissioned a professional author and artist, Tom Lea, to memorialize Richard King in a two-volume work entitled *The King Ranch*, in which Lea portrays King as a tough-minded, two-fisted Horatio Alger who brought prosperity to south Texas. According to Lea, King was as pure as the driven snow and never harmed anyone, except in self-defense. Lea ignores or denies the allegations that King evicted small Mexican ranchers by force. When referring to Mexican resentment toward Euro-Americans like King, Lea describes it as jealousy.

Richard King was born in 1824 in New York City to poor Irish immigrant parents; as a youth, he ran away to sea, and become a pilot on a steamboat mastered by Mifflin Kenedy. The Mexican American War brought them to the Rio Grande, where they stayed on after the war. King ran a flophouse at Boca del Rio and later bought a vessel from the U.S. government and went into the freighting business. In his early career he smuggled goods to the Mexican ranchers and miners in northern Mexico.[25]

Stillman, King, and Kenedy in 1850 formed a business alliance, which prospered and soon monopolized the waterborne trade of northern Mexico. In 1852, King purchased the *Santa Gertrudis* grant's 15,500 acres, which cost him less than 2 cents an acre. During the Civil War, King was a Confederate and made a fortune in war profiteering, selling cattle, horses, and mules to Confederate troops and running cotton to Mexican markets. Flying the Mexican flag, he ran Union blockades. The robber barons made huge fortunes during the Civil War. In 1866, Stillman left the border area, and King and Kenedy took over his operations.

Trade Wars and the Rise of Juan Cortina

Competition for this trade in the 1850s transformed the border into a battleground; Euro-Americans went on the offensive, and in 1855 U.S. merchants lynched 11 Mexicans along the Nueces River. In Helena, in August 1857, 40 masked Euro-American freighters, enraged by Mexicans transporting goods cheaper and more quickly, attacked 17 carts transporting goods from the Texas coast to San Antonio, brutally killing 65-year-old Antonio Delgado. Vigilantes, mostly operating in Goliad, literally ran Mexican cartmen out of the San Antonio area. The white freighters attacked the Mexican cartmen, murdering at least 75 of them. In the same year, residents of Uvalde County passed a resolution prohibiting Mexicans from traveling through the county unless the Mexicans had a passport. At Goliad, the townspeople killed several Mexicans when the cartmen used public roads. The Cart War took place about the time of the rise of the Know-Nothing Party and the national hysteria over the foreign-born, which in this case was based on greed—the vigilantes resented the economic competition.[26]

Even though the city of the Alamo did not have access to the U.S. and world markets comparable to that Houston and Galveston had, San Antonio merchants profited handsomely from the smuggling trade— it was the gateway to Mexico. After the U.S. invasion, San Antonio prospered as a service and distribution center for the western movement. By 1850, the population of San Antonio was nearly 3,500, and by the eve of the Civil War it had climbed to more than 8,000.

In 1858, Governor Ramón Guerra of Tamaulipas created *La Zona Libre*, a free zone that protected Mexican merchants from federal tariffs (they paid only small municipal taxes and an administrative fee). The purpose of La Zona was to rein in the rampant smuggling favoring U.S. merchants. The law exempted Matamoros, Reynosa, Camargo, Mier, Guerrero, and Nuevo Laredo from taxes altogether. In 1861, Mexican federal law extended the zone from the Gulf of Mexico to the Pacific within 12.5 miles of the border with the United States. U.S. merchants claimed that they lost $2 million to $6 million annually because of trade advantages given by the Mexican government to its merchants. Brownsville business leaders pressured the U.S. government to intervene and to invade Mexico to force it to get rid of *La Zona Libre*.[27]

Violence, which is an essential part of gaining social control, was on the rise. According to William D. Carrigan and Clive Webb, the lynching of Mexicans was commonplace. Between 1848 and 1928, mobs lynched at least 597 Mexicans in the United States. Clearly the Mexican population suffered lynching in lesser numbers than did the African Americans, whose population was much larger. However, Carrigan and Webb state that proportionately the number of Mexicans lynched was striking. For instance, between 1848 and 1879 "Mexicans were lynched at a rate of 473 per 100,000 of population. During these years, the highest lynching rate for African Americans was in Mississippi, with 52.8 victims per 100,000 of population."[28]

Enter "Cheno" Cortina

Juan "Cheno" Cortina, a product of Mexico's northern frontier, was born on May 16, 1822, in Camargo, on the Mexican side of the river. His parents were upper class, and his mother owned a land grant near Brownsville, where the family moved during the War of 1846.[29] Cortina, a regionalist, identified with northern Mexico; he had fought to defend it from the Euro-Americans. Many U.S. historians have labeled Cortina an outlaw, portraying him as an illiterate rogue who was from a good family but had "turned bad." Lyman Woodman, a retired military officer, wrote a biography of Cortina, describing him as a "soldier, bandit, murderer, cattle thief, mail robber, civil and military governor of the State of Tamaulipas, and general in the Mexican army" who was, in short, a gringo hater.

In the period after 1848, Cortina was hardly the poster child for a revolutionary: he backed the filibustering expeditions in 1851, led by José María Cabajal in 1851 and supported by white merchants and ranchers such as King and Kenedy, who wanted to separate the Rio Grande Valley from Texas to form the Republic of the Sierra Madre. Cortina also rustled cattle belonging to Mexicans, in partnership with the nefarious German Adolphus Glavecke. By 1859 this alliance had ended, and Glavecke and Cortina were bitter enemies. Glavecke carried a personal vendetta against Cortina, and he played a major role in building the legend of Cortina as a dangerous bandit.

Cortina's career as a revolutionary began accidentally on a hot July morning in 1859. While returning to his mother's ranch, Cheno saw Marshal Bob Spears pistol-whipping a Mexican who was drunk.[30] The victim had worked for Cheno's mother, so Cortina offered to take responsibility for the prisoner. But Spears replied, "What is it to you, you damned Mexican?" Cortina first fired a warning shot and then shot the marshal in the shoulder; he then rode off with the victim.

With a fair trial being impossible, Cheno prepared to leave for Mexico. Before his departure with 50–60 followers, Cortina rode into Brownsville and raised the Mexican flag. Cortina's detractors claim that he plundered the city—a charge that his supporters denied. According to these sources, his men attacked only those who had blatantly mistreated Mexicans, killing the jailer and four other men, two of whom had murdered innocent Mexicans.[31]

Cortina had no plans to lead a revolution when, from his mother's Rancho del Carmen, he published a circular justifying his actions by citing the injustices suffered by his people. He appealed to the U.S. government to bring the "oppressors of the Mexicans" to justice and not to protect them. Cortina, after issuing his statement, once again prepared to immigrate to Mexico.[32]

Cortina's war began in earnest when Brownsville citizens took as prisoner Tomás Cabrera, a man of advanced age and a friend of Cortina. Cortina responded by recruiting an army of about 1,200 men and demanding the old man's release. He threatened to burn Brownsville. The Brownsville Tigers (the local militia) and the Mexican army at Matamoros attacked Cortina. He defeated them; but by that time they lynched Cabrera.[33]

Radicalized by the events, Cortina exhorted for the liberation of Mexicans and the extermination of the "tyrants," calling them "flocks of vampires, in guise of men," continuing, "My part is taken; the voice of revelation whispers to me that to me is entrusted the work of breaking the chains of your slavery, and that the Lord will enable me, with powerful arm, to fight against our enemies."[34]

A state commissioner wrote to Governor Sam Houston, "The Mexicans are arming everything that can carry a gun, and I anticipate much trouble here. I believe that a general war is inevitable. . . . New arms have been distributed to all the *rancheros*, so I apprehend trouble." Houston asked the federal government for assistance and wrote to the secretary of war for help. Meanwhile, state and national press propagated the myth of the Cortina menace.

In February 1860, President James Buchanan sent Robert E. Lee to Texas to find the elusive Cortina. Mexican authorities cooperated with Lee. However, till the end of March, Lee could not catch Cortina and began referring to "that myth Cortina." By May, Lee believed that Cortina had left Texas. But Cortina had merely shifted his base of operations. "Even after the outbreak of the Civil War, unrest and insecurity prevailed along the Rio Grande, and we can only speculate how long it would have been before another showdown would have come had it not been for the prosperity the war brought, even to the poorest."[35] A reign of terror followed that is difficult to assess because of sensationalizing and outright lies by the press. Merchants and business elites used Cortina as a pretext for violence against Mexicans to attract contracts. Robert Taylor, a commissioner sent by Houston to investigate conditions on the border, filed a confidential report: "I am sorry to say a good many . . . who have been Burning and Hanging and shooting Mexicans without authority by law are more dreaded than Cortina."[36] Cortina went to Tamaulipas, where, from 1861 to 1867, he defended the state against the French intervention. Cortina became for a time its military governor as well as a general in the Mexican army. From his Mexican base, Cortina allegedly led rustling operations against Euro-Americans.[37]

The Civil War

The Mexican elite often acted as mediators for the new Euro-American ruling elite and helped control the Mexican masses. They were important in giving the illusion of democracy. In Brownsville, men like Francisco Ytúrria (1830–1912), Jeremiah Galván, and the Spaniard José San Román (1822–1895) amassed fortunes by allying themselves with Charles Stillman. Montejano writes, "In the Lower Valley, the conservative upper class, fearful of outright confiscation of their property, was divided in the response to the Anglo presence."[38] In San Antonio, the Canary Islanders continued to live apart, harboring the illusion of their racial purity. Through cooperation, the Mexican elites benefited from the system.

By 1860 a few Euro-Americans completely dominated the Texas economy. A census taken in that year showed that 263 Texans—presumably mostly male—owned more than $100,000 apiece in real property. Fifty-seven of them were wealthy individuals who lived in southeast Texas; only two were of Mexican extraction, with their holdings in Cameron County. Bexar County had seven wealthy Texans, not one of whom was Mexican. Of significance is the fact that the real property value and the personal worth of the 261 Texans were roughly in balance, while the two Mexicans' personal worth was far below their real wealth.[39] Despite this inequity, a number of Mexicans continued to own large- and medium-size ranches and commercial houses.

Texas Ranger "Rip" Ford estimated that as much as $10 million to $14 million passed through the Rio Grande annually. During the Civil War, merchants amassed large fortunes by running cotton through Mexico, making possible the expansion of the cotton industry as well as the commercial houses.[40] The population of Matamoros mushroomed to 50,000 by the end of 1862. The town was an international marketplace, with an estimated weekly trade of $2 million throughout the 1850s. Merchants on both sides of La Línea vied for this trade, and the Mexican government feared the dominance of U.S. merchants who avoided paying import taxes by smuggling and underselling Mexican merchants, who had to pay taxes.

Despite the alleged sympathy of Tejanos for the confederacy, James Marten makes the point that "despite family and social pressures, hundreds of Texans, including a large number of Mexican-Americans, signed on with the Union army. . . ." Euro-Americans comprised 46.3 percent, Germans 13.1 percent, and Mexicans 40.6 percent of Texas Union Regiment. Proportionately, the Mexican share was much higher than their part of the state's population.

The story of Colonel Santos Benavides is a popular example of a Mexican fighting for the confederacy. Benavides was a wealthy Mexican-born rancher, merchant, and power broker in the Valley. Santos had come to the Nueces Valley during the Euro-American invasion; when the Euro-Americans occupied the strip, he became a U.S. citizen—it was good for business. In 1863 he led troops against both the Union army and Juan Cortina.[41]

Another example, though less important, is the story of Adrián J. Vidal. Some say he was the son of a Mexican woman and a white merchant. He was actually the stepson of Mifflin Kenedy. Adrián was born in Monterrey, Nuevo León, Mexico, in 1840 to Colonel Luis Vidal and Petra Vela. After the death of his father, the family moved to Mier, where Petra met Kenedy, and then to Brownsville, where Adrián Vidal learned about steamboats and the region. He enlisted as a private in the Confederate army, but within a year, he was promoted to captain because of his knowledge of the border. In 1863 he killed two confederate couriers, which some speculate was because of a remark made about his race and implying that he was a half-breed. Vidal deserted, taking 89 men with him. He went over to the Union side when they occupied the Valley, but again deserted, crossing the border to fight against Emperor Maximilian and the French. The Imperialists captured and executed him.[42]

Throughout the war, the Union sought to shut down the Mexican corridor. However, with the support of Santos Benavides and Mexican merchant allies on both sides of the border, the Confederacy was successful in keeping it open. After the Civil War, Kenedy and King returned with full pardons, resuming trade with the Mexican side and seeking to gain special privileges. Other changes took place as Euro-Americans, Germans, and French outnumbered the Tejanos in San Antonio. The Mexican elite's prestige fell further with this decline in Mexican population, and the newcomers became politically and socially dominant as they monopolized the banks and commercial houses. Racial and social segregation also increased. Three factors would contribute to the dramatic transformation of Texas and Euro-American–Mexican relations: barbed wire, irrigation, and the railroad that, by 1877, linked San Antonio and the rest of Texas to the U.S. markets.[43]

The Transformation

The economic transformations after the Civil War brought the Reconstruction Era that pitted the different races against each other. Texas had escaped the economic ravages of the war, but that did not prevent the Euro-Americans from acting more confederate than those in the Deep South. Losing the war worsened the bravado of many Euro-Texans and rather than muting their racism, the loss made them more chauvinistic. It did not matter that many Mexicans fought on the confederate side. The large presence of Mexicans posed a threat to southern institutions and to the white communities in which they lived.

Although the Mexican population of Texas grew to 20,000 in 1860, it remained small in comparison with 600,000 Euro-Americans and 182,000 blacks. Before the Civil War, slave labor lessened the dependence on Mexican workers, and Euro-Americans were able to limit them mostly to south Texas. After the War, the emancipation of the slaves changed the Texas economy by freeing its captive labor force, whereupon Mexicans were imported to create a labor surplus pool. By the 1870s, Mexicans worked alongside blacks in the Brazos area. A revolution in transportation and the increased appetite for beef in the domestic and world markets led to the expansion of stock raising after the War. In addition, by the 1880s, cotton production reached an all-time high. The demand for more workers and reduction of the African American labor force dramatically increased the pull of Mexican laborers to the Lone Star State.[44]

Texas agriculture restructured in other ways in response to the loss of slave labor, and by 1870, share-cropping became more common. (In sharecropping, an owner lends land to tenants, who usually give back to the landlord one-half to two-thirds of the crop.) Railroad expansion led to land speculation and a flood of Euro-Americans migrated to Texas. Even in some border counties, the number of white people equaled the number of Mexicans.[45] By 1890, the open range gave way to mechanization and irrigation, changing production methods and increasing the demand for Mexican labor.

Planters on the Colorado River—near Bastrop in San Marcos and Navidad, Lavaca County—who had threatened and expelled Mexican workers before the Civil War, were now desperate for their labor. The solution was to attract more Mexicans who would work for long hours and at low wages. Mexican migration to Texas accelerated in the 1880s and fanned out throughout the Lone Star State.

Working and competing for work worsened tensions between Mexicans and African Americans. In August 1894, African Americans attacked Mexicans at Beeville, Texas, where growers agitated antagonism between the races. The growers had brought Mexicans into Beeville to drive down wages of blacks. African Americans, blaming the Mexicans rather than the growers for their depressed standard of living, raided the Mexican quarter. The two peoples were played off against each other in other ways as well. The federal government, for instance, encouraged animosity by stationing black soldiers in Mexican areas, using them to control the Mexican population. At Fort McIntosh in Laredo, the Tenth Cavalry, a black unit, was used to police the Mexican population.[46]

Hang 'em High!

On the frontier, U.S. merchants made fortunes supplying to military installations. The merchants and the townspeople lived in fear of the removal of these forts and often exaggerated the threat of Mexican bandits and/or Indian "savages" as a pretext for having large numbers of U.S. troops along the border. The forts meant soldiers, horses, and government contracts. These government contracts and the soldiers' spending was a bonanza for the merchants and cattle dealers along the border. A withdrawal of troops would mean economic hardships for merchants and ranchers, who relied on the forts and soldiers as a source of revenue. The merchants and the townspeople protected this source of income at any cost. Hence the threat of the Mexican population that often dwarfed the white population was used as a pretext; troops gave white settlers a sense of security by keeping the Mexican majority in its place.[47]

From 1869 to 1872, King and Kenedy allegedly lost 200,000 heads of cattle and 5,300 horses; the loss was blamed on Cortina. Rip Ford wrote, "Cortina hates Americans, particularly Texans. . . . He has an old and deep-seated grudge against Brownsville."[48] The Cortina menace was used as a ploy to attack innocent Mexicans. Vigilantes took the law into their hands, spreading terror. Merchants also used it as an opportunity to call for even more federal troops and demand that the United States take over northern Mexico to the Sierra Madres. This ushered in the second Cortina war, known as the "Skinning Wars." Beef prices fell to 62.5 cents a cow, and hides sold for $4.50; this increased competition and disputes over ownership. Raids followed as Euro-Americans formed minute companies (private militia) and vigilance committees. Under the cover of a crisis, Corpus Christi cowboys raided Mexicans, driving the small operators out of business and fencing their ranches.[49]

The Cortina menace also gave an excuse for the passage of the Frontier Protection Act of 1874 that reestablished the Rangers, and six mounted battalions of 75 men each roamed the region.[50] During the spring and summer of that year, a race war raged. Euro-American ranchers had the support of the Rangers in these wars.[51] During the 1870s, as U.S. political influence on the Mexican government increased, pressure was brought on to eliminate Cortina as a threat. In 1875, Mexican authorities exiled Cortina to Mexico City and jailed him on charges of cattle rustling. Cortina did not return to the border until the spring of 1890, when he visited the area for a brief time, receiving a hero's welcome. Cortina's career had transformed him from a social bandit to a revolutionary.

Meanwhile, in 1874 in Goliad County a mob lynched Juan Moya and his two sons. The Moyas had allegedly killed a white family. Authorities later apprehended the real killers, whom they did not prosecute. In April 1877 Andrés Martínez and José María Cordena were arrested in Collins County, Texas, charged with horse stealing. Instead of receiving a trial, they were seized by 10 masked men and hanged. In July of that same year, whites in Nueces County, Texas, randomly slaughtered as many as 40 Mexicans allegedly to revenge the death of one of their white friends.

In the 1870s, a Mexican Border Commission report claimed that Mexicans had raided the Nueces area to retrieve their stolen cattle. Richard King had been branding calves "that belonged to his neighbors' cows."[52] The report charged that King employed known cattle rustlers, such as Tomás Vásquez and Fernando López, to steal cattle and horses from Mexican ranchers. Other prominent Texans, such as Thadeus Rhodes, a justice of the peace in Hidalgo County, were also implicated in cattle rustling, making huge profits from this illicit trade.[53] The report was based on extensive interviews and public records. The Boundary Commission accused King's cabal of funding separatists such as José María Cabajal in 1851, in his war to form the Republic of the Sierra Madre.[54]

It is not surprising that King became president of the Stock Raisers Association of Western Texas, formed by Texas ranchers to protect the "interests" of the big ranchers. The Association organized a private militia, called "minute companies," to fight the so-called Mexican bandits. When the minute companies disbanded, Ranger Captain Leander McNeely carried on the fight. In 1875, McNeely ignored a federal injunction prohibiting him from entering Mexican territory; with a troop of Rangers, he crossed the border and tortured and murdered four innocent Mexicans. King rewarded McNeely's men with a $500 bonus.[55]

In March 1881, Rangers arrested Onofrio Baca *in Mexico* on a charge of murder. He was brought back illegally and lynched by a mob on the cross beams of the gate of the court house. In August 1883, Captain Juan Cárdenas in San Antonio led a protest march on San Pedro Park because Fred Kerble, the lessee, on the orders of the town council, had excluded Mexicans from using the dance floor. A reign of terror punctuated by lynchings ran Mexicans out of the Fort Davis area the next year.[56]

The Historian as an Agent of Social Control

As one researches the history of the Texas Rangers, it is puzzling why Mexican Americans have not reacted more vigorously to the naming of a major league team after the Texas Rangers. What would be the reaction of the Jewish community if a team were called the Hitler All Stars? Part of the explanation is that historians often mythicize the truth. By doing this, historians play a crucial role in socializing the public and inventing an accepted truth.

For example, the so-called "founders of American industry" were called "robber barons," a pejorative reference to industrialists who accumulated huge fortunes and power at the expense of the public. At the time, critics perceived them as unscrupulous highwaymen and books were written blaming them and their monopoly of resources for the misery and poverty of the masses. In the early twentieth century, the industrialists moved to clean up this image through philanthropic ventures. They funded revisionist historians who wrote books arguing that the robber barons were essential to the transformation of the nation into a world power. Instead of robber barons, they rechristened the hated industrialists "captains of industry," changing the public perception.

Racism, racial stereotypes, and fear of the other are important instruments of social control. The Spaniards disciplined the disparate populations through racial categorization (see Chapter 2). In the United States, race defined access to political and economic power and justified inequality. Laws designed to institutionalize racism perpetuated white rule. At each stage, whiteness was the standard of goodness and was rewarded by privileges. In the United States, there has been a stricter categorization applying a black–white standard; in Mexico and Latin America, racial categories form a continuum—racism exists, but there are more exceptions. Unfortunately for Mexicans the Euro-American standard for race was enforced.

Controlling Mexicans

From multiple accounts and documents, it can be seen that the Texas Rangers were in many cases paid assassins. But how did they become the nice guys? Walter Prescott Webb, a professor of the history faculty at the University of Texas at Austin and past president of the American Historical Association, memorialized the Rangers in his books such as *The Texas Rangers*, *The Great Plains*, and *Divided We Stand*, portraying them as bringing civilization to the frontier.[57] This was so even though Webb admitted that the Rangers' actions were often excessive and brutal. After he published an article, "The Bandits of Las Cuevas," in *True West* in October 1962, he received a letter from Enrique Mendiola of Alice, Texas, whose grandfather owned the ranch that the Rangers, under McNeely, mistakenly attacked. Mendiola stated,

> Most historians have classified these men as cattle thieves, bandits, etc. This might be true of some of the crowd, but most of them, including General Juan Flores, were trying to recover their own cattle that had been taken away from them when they were driven out of their little ranches in South Texas. They were driven out by such men as Mifflin Kenedy, Richard King and [the] Armstrongs.[58]

Webb's reply to Mendiola was revealing:

> To get a balanced account, one would need the records from the south side of the river, and these are simply not available.... The unfortunate fact is that the Mexicans were not as good at keeping records as were the people on this side.... I have often wished that the Mexicans, or someone who had their confidence, would have gone among them and got their stories of the raids and counter raids. I am sure that these stories would take on a different color and tone.[59]

But Mexicans did record their story in *corridos* (ballads), which celebrated the deeds of men who stood up to the oppressors. These corridos are still sung in the Rio Grande Valley and elsewhere in the Southwest.

Corridos were dedicated to Juan Cortina because Cortina resisted the gringo in the 1850s through mid-1870s. From those early times to the present, corridos have recorded Mexicans' struggle against racism and injustice.[60] They are uniform in their portrayal of the Rangers as assassins, whom they viewed in much the same way as Jews saw the Gestapo.

Like all history, there are two sides to the story. Rip Ford, a Ranger himself, expressed the Euro-American view of the Texas Ranger, writing, "A Texas Ranger can ride like a Mexican, trail like an Indian, shoot like a Tennessean, and fight like the very devil!"[61] Not surprisingly, most contemporary studies of the Rangers mimic Webb, who wrote,

> When we see him at his daily task of maintaining law, restoring order, and promoting peace— even though his methods be vigorous—we see him in the proper setting, a man standing alone between a society and its enemies.[62]

Webb posited,

> Without disparagement it may be said that there is a cruel streak in the Mexican nature, or so the history of Texas would lead one to believe. This cruelty may be a heritage from the Spanish of the Inquisition; it may, and doubtless should, be attributed partly to the Indian blood.[63]

Webb's influence on historians and the public cannot be exaggerated—even today hundreds of thousands cheer for the Texas Rangers baseball team without knowing or caring about their atrocities.

Américo Paredes describes the Rangers as the puppets of Euro-American ranchers and merchants who controlled the Rio Grande Valley. Their commitment was to keep order for a Euro-American oligarchy. Violence served the interests of Texas capitalists in maintaining a closed social structure that excluded Mexicans from all but the lowest levels. They recruited gunslingers who burned with a hatred of Mexicans, shooting first and asking questions afterward. Paredes writes, "That the Rangers stirred up more trouble than they put down is an opinion that has been expressed by less partisan sources."[64]

Paredes's research was based on oral traditions and documents, and his findings refuted Webb's distortion of reality. For example, concerning the murder of the Cerdas, a prominent family near Brownsville in 1902, Paredes wrote,

> The Cerdas were prosperous ranchers near Brownsville, but it was their misfortune to live next to one of the "cattle barons" who was not through expanding yet. One day three Texas Rangers came down from Austin and "executed" the elder Cerda and one of his sons as cattle rustlers. The youngest son fled across the river, and thus the Cerda ranch was vacated. Five months later the remaining son, Alfredo Cerda, crossed over to Brownsville. He died the same day, shot down by a Ranger's gun.[65]

Paredes documents his report not only on official sources but also on eyewitness accounts. Marcelo Garza, Sr. of Brownsville, a respected businessman, had told Paredes that a Ranger shot the unarmed Alfredo, stalking him "like a wild animal."

On the other hand, Webb's version was based exclusively on Ranger sources. According to Webb, Baker, a Ranger, surprised Ramón De La Cerda branding a calf that belonged to the King Ranch. De La Cerda shot at Baker, and the Ranger shot back, killing Ramón in self-defense. The Ranger was cleared at an inquest. Nevertheless, Mexicans, not accepting this verdict, disinterred De La Cerda's body and conducted their own inquest. They found

> "evidence"... to the effect that De La Cerda had been dragged and otherwise maltreated. Public sentiment was sharply divided.... The findings of the secret inquest, together with wild rumors growing out of it, only served to inflame the minds of De La Cerda's supporters.[66]

Webb ignored the fact that the Cerdas were a well-known and respected family whose land the Kings coveted. "Captain Brooks reported that Baker made bail in the sum of ten thousand dollars, and that he was supported by such people as the Kings, Major John Armstrong—McNeely's lieutenant—and the Lyman Brothers."[67] Further, Webb did not question the financial support of the Kings for the Rangers and especially for Baker. The Cerda affair exposed both the use of violence to take over land and legalizing murder through the court system. It was not an isolated incident; it represented the activities of Rangers throughout the century.

Politics of Race and Gender

There were other forms of social control. When the Spaniards conquered Mexico, Cortés married his officers to the daughters of the Azteca nobles, thus consolidating his control of the vanquished people. Euro-Americans followed this pattern in Texas, where intermarriage between the native aristocracy and the white ruling elite was common for a variety of reasons: there was a lack of white women; intermarriage often gave access to old money; and through their family networks the wives helped control the native population. Captain Mifflin Kenedy's marriage to the wealthy widow Petra Vela de Vidal has already been discussed.[68]

When convenient, the Euro-Americans would identify certain Mexican women as white. During the nineteenth century, it was popular to speak about the "dark-eyed *señoritas*." "There existed at least some indication that Mexican women could have been accepted by whites in Texas under certain circumstances without reservation."[69] Occasionally, they compared Mexican women with the ideal southern belle, and they especially praised *Las Güeras* (the blondes). Euro-American males described these light-skinned Mexicans as of pure Spanish descent from northern Spain with "faultlessly white" flesh and blue eyes. It must be remembered that, in general, intermarriage among different ranks suggests a weakening of ethnic identities and allegiances. As more women of their own race moved into the area, Euro-Americans' infatuation with the whitest of Mexican women cooled, intermarriage dropped, and racially mixed couples became subject to social disapproval and, eventually, persecution.[70]

> *906 Mexican women wed Mexican men, while only 88 chose to marry Anglo-Americans. But of those Anglo-Mexican unions almost half, or 42, involved women from high status families. The significance of those interracial marriages goes far beyond their numbers, since at least one daughter from every rico family in San Antonio married an Anglo.*[71]

Scholars have documented only five unions between Mexican males and Euro-American females.

As with Spanish colonialism, skin color determined social status. In a letter to his cousin John Donelson Coffee, Jr., dated January 20, 1855, R. W. Brahan, Jr., referred to contacts with women of Castilian blood whose "parents avowed their determination to have them wed to genuine Americans."[72] Brahan dwelt on Mexican women's color and said, "Their complexion is very fair," but distinguished poorer Mexican women as "styled greasers." Brahan concluded, "many of these 'greasers,' of fine figures & good features, the color of a mulato, are kept by votaries of sensuality." As with the blacks in the South, the dominant society fabricated sexual myths about Mexicans such as those "suggesting that, if Mexican women easily lapsed from propriety, they especially coveted the company (and intimacy) of white men."[73]

In turn, intermarriage fed the racial and class pretensions of elite Mexican families. Through intermarriage, Mexican elites got a son-in-law whose skin looked white. The Mexican family also received a measure of legal protection and freedom from the stigma of disloyalty, while the Euro-American got a wife and her property, since, under the law, daughters inherited property on an equal basis with their brothers. Intermarriage accelerated "civilization," and although youngsters maintained strong Mexican influences "during their early childhood," they strongly identified with the father's ethnic group. For instance, the daughters of Antonio Navarro became Methodists, which is in itself an indication of assimilation, and affiliation with English-speaking Roman Catholic parishes by the mixed couples was common.

This is not to say that the *ricos* (the rich Mexicans) escaped discrimination; even rich Tejanos were victims of racism. Most of San Antonio's Mexicans during the nineteenth century, even if Americanized, were not treated as equals. "Only the women and children with Anglo surnames, light skins, and wealth had a reasonable chance to escape the stigma attached to their Mexican ancestry."[74] Even the choice of intermarriage, however, was a decision made by the male head of the family based on class interests.

Resistance

As we saw with Colonial Mexico, rebellions were a frequent occurrence. The rebellion often took the form of the so-called bandit activity, which often was just that: banditry. However, when there are divisions between people because of unequal power relations, bandit activity can assume the form of primitive rebellion. The British historian E. J. Hobsbawm, in his *Primitive Rebels*, makes the point that in colonial situations dissidents are commonly labeled bandits; for example, the British called George Washington a bandit. Hobsbawm writes, "in one sense [banditry was] . . . a primitive form of organized social protest, perhaps the most primitive we know."[75] Social bandits rebel against an injustice, and the people of their race or class support them, often covertly. These primitive rebels have no intention of transforming or leveling society; they have simply had enough. Social bandits differ from revolutionaries, who have a trajectory, wanting to change power relationships.

The People's Revolt

Salt, like water, is essential for life in arid environments. But while the Southwest is replete with stories of range wars over water, there are few stories of the usurpation of the Mexican settlers' access to necessary minerals, rangeland, or the forests. Salt is essential for one's health, helping the body to retain fluids; in the nineteenth century, it was used as a preservative, in the absence of refrigeration.

In the late 1860s, a power struggle broke out over control of the salt deposits located in the Guadalupe Mountains 110 miles east of El Paso. Mexicans had ridden out there in search of free salt, which they either used or sold. The salt beds supplied all of western Texas, southern New Mexico, and Mexico. The competition between W. W. Mills, Albert J. Fountain, and Louis Cardis to acquire title to the salt deposits evolved into a bitter struggle that led to bloody battles in the 1870s as a Salt Ring comprised of influential Euro-American politicos led the monopolists. Two factions vied to control the salt beds for commercial purposes, and soon the events deteriorated into a race war.

Hostilities were centered in the small town of San Elizario, near present-day El Paso, Texas, in 1877. One faction was led by the Salt Ring, and the other by Father Antonio Borrajo and the Italian Cardis, a local politico. Charles Howard, a Missouri lawyer and former Confederate officer, at first supported the Borrajo–Cardis faction. In 1872, fighting broke out as Cardis and Howard tried to break the Republican machine's control of the Salt Ring. But this alliance was short lived as Howard betrayed Cardis and took control of the salt flats in 1877. The sides polarized when Howard shot and killed Cardis. This enraged Borrajo, who in turn agitated his Mexican parishioners. Howard, a former Texas Ranger, enlisted the support of the Rangers, and a troop of 20 Texas Rangers rode into San Elizario. Governor Richard B. Hubbard had ordered Major John B. Jones of the Texas Rangers to the El Paso area to put down the rebellion. When the Rangers sided with Howard, Borrajo told the Mexican people, "Shoot the *gringo* [Howard] and I will absolve you."[76]

Francisco "Chico" Barela, an Ysleta farmer, then organized a group of 18 Mexicans and shot Howard. Several days of fighting followed, during which Rangers and vigilantes indiscriminately attacked Mexican residents. Governor Hubbard sent to Silver City for 30 hired gunmen, who, under Sheriff Charles Kerner, committed "rapes, homicides, and other crimes." Mexican families fled to Mexico, where many did not survive the brutal winter.[77]

A report by W. M. Dunn found that

> The outbreak [of the Salt War] was, it is believed, the result of a desire for revenge for the murder of [Louis] Cardis, a crime which had no justification, which was deliberate and brutal, and which exasperated the people beyond control. [Charles] Howard was brought before a justice of the peace for the murder, but was released at once on bail, in violation of law, and as not long

before he had caused the arrest and imprisonment of two men for the mere offense of saying that
they meant to get salt from the ponds, law or no law, the Spanish–American populace naturally
thought they saw that there was no equality of justice, and felt compelled to take the law into
their own hands.[78]

A letter from Colonel John H. King to the Bureau of Military Justice also found that "No evidence taken substantiates the report heretofore prevalent, that the people coming from Mexico and taking part in these criminal proceedings were an organized body previously drilled and disciplined by officers of the Mexican Army."[79]

The Ballad of Gregorio Cortez

Social banditry is a phenomenon that goes back to the Spanish conquest and before. It is common and even natural for people to rebel when unpopular governments impose their will on the general population. Many in the general population vicariously live out their grievances through the rebellion of the bandit who is outside the law. In this way, the support of the social bandit becomes a form of protest. In the case of the Mexicans in Texas and elsewhere, the deeds of the social bandit are memorialized by ballads.

Banditry in Texas was caused in great part by racism and brutality. Mexican laborers did not escape this racism by moving into central and northern Texas. A group called the "white caps" that believed Mexicans were depressing wages in 1897 sent warnings to farmers not to employ Mexicans or blacks. William Carrigan and Clive Webb quoted a warning from a vigilante group the following year in Gonzalez: "Hell, Texas, Feb. 16. Notice to the Mexicans: You all have got then days to leave in. Mr. May Renfro and brother get your Mexicans all off your place. If not, you will get the same that they do. Signed Whitecaps." Vigilantism in central and northern Texas revolved around labor competition whereas in south Texas it was more about property and jealousy that Mexicans owned any; lynching was a method of extracting the property from them. An example of this was the hanging of seven of Toribio Lozano's sheepherders in 1873. Lozano had a large ranch in the Mexican state of Nuevo León and regularly grazed sheep on the U.S. side of the border. Lozano led a torturous fight for compensation for the workers' dependents, enlisting the support of Mexican diplomats.[80]

Without a doubt because of these injustices, there were dozens of Mexican bandits in Texas, which registered more instance of mob violence than any other state. As in other places, the bandit was often idolized. The fact that the Texas Rangers and local enforcement authorities refused to help find or prosecute the perpetrators heightened the sense of injustice. As discussed, Juan Cortina was not in a strict sense a social bandit; he had a political plan. A better example of a social bandit is Gregorio Cortez, who was considered a hero by the Mexicans and a "sheriff killer" by whites. Cortez was a border Mexican who worked on ranches in Gonzales and Karnes counties, and in the surrounding areas.

On June 12, 1901, Karnes County Sheriff W. T. "Brack" Morris went to the Cortez farm to investigate a horse theft. Deputy Boone Choate, acting as interpreter, misunderstood Cortez's answers to Sheriff Morris's question whether he had recently acquired a *caballo*, which means stallion in Spanish. Cortez answered that he had bought a *yegua*, a mare.[81] Believing that Cortez was lying, Morris drew his gun and shot Cortez's brother, provoking Cortez, who shot the sheriff. The incident made Cortez an outlaw, and he was hunted by several posses comprised of hundreds of men. The Mexican population in Karnes County and throughout Texas supported Cortez, who became a border hero. For 10 days, this army chased Cortez over 500 miles; during this pursuit, the dreaded cowboys hounded his supporters and his family members.

A posse surrounded the home of Refugia Robledo, where Cortez was hiding, driving her husband, sons, and Cortez out of the house, while Refugia remained trapped inside with three children. A deputy entered the house, shooting down young Ramón Rodríguez, as Refugia shielded the other two children with her body. The posse arrested Refugia, her two sons, and the wounded Ramón and charged her with the murder of the sheriff, who had been killed in the shootout. She was released only after she said that Cortez had killed the sheriff.[82]

Betrayed by a friend, Cortez was captured on June 22, 1901, after which he faced numerous trials. Cortez was finally convicted and sentenced to 50 years imprisonment for second-degree murder. While his case was on appeal, a mob of 300 white men threatened to lynch him. The Texas Court of Criminal Appeals reversed the verdict, and he was retried; he was again convicted. In 1913, Cortez was pardoned. Meanwhile, countless corridos memorialized Cortez and his war with the gringos.

Boss Rule

The post–Civil War period saw the rise of boss rule in Texas, which involved a cabal of powerful white leaders in collusion with local Mexican elites who manipulated the votes of Mexican majorities. They resembled eastern machines like Tammany Hall of New York City. Often the machines shielded Mexican immigrants with unofficial welfare services and gave them the illusion that they had palanca[83] or influence with those in power. These machines controlled the patronage system and secured jobs and favors from local and state governments, thus centralizing their power.

In south Texas the machines engaged in graft, and played all sides—often selling out the welfare of their constituents. As in other places in the Southwest, the leadership was composed of attorneys who represented the interests of the landed elites. The bosses often lobbied on behalf of the Texas Rangers, which they used to keep order and control Mexicans. On the other hand, while the bosses formed alliances with the Rangers, they also restricted them when they went too far. The bosses catered to land speculators, developers, bankers, and merchants and promoted development. It was a paternalistic arrangement with many bosses acting like modern-day hacendados, who would go to baptisms, marriages, and funerals.

By the mid-1880s, Bryan Callagan II, whose mother was from an elite Mexican family and who spoke fluent Spanish, organized a political machine in San Antonio. Callagan's power was based on his control of the Mexican wards that supported the machine because it gave the residents a measure of protection, patronage, and the illusion of political participation. The machine handed out patronage—city jobs, contracts, franchises, and public utilities. The bosses won elections by turning out the Mexican vote. In the border towns, the machines also controlled the customhouses.

Characteristically, the poor had few options, and the ricos rarely sided with the Mexican masses. They often displayed attitudes and interests that favored their class and racial category. Many members of old Mexican families openly sympathized with the Ku Klux Klan; in San Antonio Alejo Ruiz, Vicente Martínez, John Barrera, Rafael Ytúrris, and José Antonio Navarro allied themselves with ultraconservative factions. After the Civil War, they even campaigned for white supremacist southern Democrats. Through all this, Mexican elites seemed oblivious to the persecution of their fellow Mexicans. By avoiding an advocacy role, Mexican merchants profited and maintained valuable business contacts.

Attorneys made fortunes representing Mexicans. Stephen Powers of Brownsville, an expert on Spanish and Mexican land grant law, defended some Mexican elites, giving him entrance to that community. Powers accumulated 44,000 acres and built vast political power. When Powers died, his junior associate James B. Wells inherited his law practice and his connections, and "a substantial number of Tejano land holdings in much of the Lower Valley."[84]

From 1882 to 1920, the machine controlled several counties; its people transported Mexican voters to the polls and marked their ballots for them. Arnold De León states that in the border areas, whites employed Mexicans to cross into Mexico to recruit people whom the bosses paid to vote for selected candidates. Hundreds of Mexicans were marched to the county clerk's office and naturalized for the modest sum of 25 cents.[85]

Wells had political power because he delivered the Mexican vote, which he garnered by playing godfather to the Mexican people. Wells shared his power with the Klebergs, who owned the King Ranch, and had satellite rings headed by Ed Vela from Hidalgo and the Guerra family of Starr County. The Guerras, along with the Yzaguirre and Ramírez families, owned most of Starr County. Manuel Guerra, a banker and rancher, became Jim Wells's right arm and was the political boss of the Democratic Party in Starr County.[86]

The Guerras controlled Starr County into the 1940s, an arrangement that remained untouched by state authorities. Even Judge J. T. Canales of Brownsville, a maverick, often cooperated with the machine. He had served in the state legislature from 1909 to 1911, in 1917, and in 1919, and was the county judge in

1914. (In Texas, the county judge was, and still is, the most powerful local official.) Along with Alonso Perales, Manuel González, Ben Garza, Andrés de Luna, and Dr. George I. Sánchez, he represented the so-called progressive Tejano movement of the times.[87]

In his book *Boss Rule in South Texas*, Evan Anders attributes machine politics, in part, to the history of the Spanish patron–peon relationship. However, he oversimplifies the phenomenon, since "boss rule" in south Texas resembled political machines in eastern U.S. cities. An important difference between bossism in south Texas and the East was that the Texas machine had fewer constitutional restraints. Moreover, Tejanos had limited access to organizational alternatives, such as trade unions.[88]

In 1890, North American reformers, blaming Mexicans for corrupt political machines, attempted to end bossism by disenfranchising Mexicans. According to Anders, they passed a constitutional amendment requiring foreigners "to file for citizenship six months before the election."[89] Then, in 1902, the reformers passed a poll tax to further discourage the Mexican vote. Both these measures failed to limit the power of the bosses. The Jim Wells machine remained intact until the 1920s, and its end in part can be attributed to Wells's failure to check the extreme violence of the Texas Rangers in south Texas in 1915 and 1917.[90]

The Railroad and the Advent of Industrial Capitalism

Key to Texas's economic and social transformation was the railroad. By the 1880s, railroads crisscrossed Texas, making possible the commercialization of agriculture and further incorporating the state into world markets. Mexicans constituted most of the workers on the Texas and Mexican Railroad as well as on other lines. In addition to the arrival of the railroad, the expansion of the agriculture industry was made possible by the expansion of banking and speculation in the area. Credit became increasingly essential as producers had to purchase land, sink wells, build miles of fences of plank and wire, and finance stock improvement programs to compete. The 1890s saw the arrival of eastern, British, and Scottish syndicates, much the same way as they moved into Arizona and other western states to exploit mining and agriculture. Meanwhile, Kenedy sold his 242,000-acre plantation for $1.1 million.

Between 1865 and 1885, San Antonio's population increased by 208 percent to 37,000. The railroad played an essential role in the rapid development of San Antonio and south Texas after the Civil War. In the 1870s, San Antonio merchants and business leaders financed a line between their city and Galveston. By 1885, two more lines passed through the city connecting it with north Texas and Mexico. Along with the development of the railroads came the growth of the cattle trade in south Texas and the tourist trade in San Antonio.

Four million head of cattle were driven north to market between 1866 and 1880. Land companies ended the open range by building barbed wire fences, displacing small cattlemen and cowboys. Racism increased as ranchers segregated Mexican cowboys and white cowhands in central and south Texas. Most small Mexican operators went out of business because these new operations required large amounts of capital. Adding to the problems of small cattlemen, during the 1880s, were the overproduction in the cattle industry, overgrazing, droughts, quarantine laws, and closing of the cattle trails.[91]

Mexico Comes to Texas

The development of commercial agriculture broke up the provincial cattle-based economy, favoring the expansion of cotton and vegetable production. The new labor market demanded armies of migrant workers. In the 1880s, the United States controlled some 40 percent of Mexico's export trade; by the turn of the century it controlled over 70 percent of this trade, eclipsing British interests. The railroad also made it easier for Mexicans in the Border States to reach U.S. markets than the interior of Mexico. The Mexican population growth and the inability of the Mexican economic infrastructure to absorb this growth heightened tensions, and Mexican migration to the United States increased.

This population shift was also caused by the commercialization of Mexican cotton production in places like Coahuila and eastern Durango during the 1880s. The Laguna district of western Coahuila attracted an industrial labor force of an estimated 30,000 workers from the interior of Mexico. After the harvest season, they would migrate to Texas to pick cotton there. The exchange marked transferences of ideas and labor strategies.

Meanwhile, the commercialization of agriculture in Texas brought about a deterioration in the old way of life and changed the mode of production. While farmers had been relatively prosperous during 1860–1890, the mechanization of agriculture made heavy outlays of capital essential. The changes brought about the creation of factory farms that drove small producers out of business. The Mexicans were a symptom of this change, not the cause. However, small farmers and workers blamed the Mexicans for the decline or the end of small farms, the loss of year-round jobs, and the lowering of wages.[92] Within this new world order, labor organizations either ignored the Mexicans or excluded them.

The abandoned Mexican laborers turned to their own devices. The proliferation of *mutualistas*, or mutual aid societies, in Texas began in the 1870s. These societies, popular in Mexico since the 1860s, promoted identity and provided death benefits, loans, and financial assistance.[93] They were organized to soften the shock of urbanization and industrialization on artisans and other workers, and were important in uniting Mexican people and maintaining Mexican culture. The middle class furnished the leadership of many of these groups, and their political orientation greatly depended on the ideology of these leaders, which was sometimes radical and sometimes quite conservative. The Mexican government at first sponsored the *mutualistas,* since the self-help philosophy took the pressure off the newly emerging capitalist class to furnish social benefits. However, this changed as radicals used the societies to criticize and organize against the state.

Reform Politics and Mexicans

By the late 1880s, both Populists and Republicans pushed for the disenfranchisement of all Mexicans. The Populist, or People's, Party, while fighting the spread of agribusiness and demanding reforms in government, scapegoated Mexicans, blaming them for the decline of small farms and the demise of rural America. Mexicans fought back. In San Antonio, A. L. Montalvo vowed to fight for civil rights and condemned the Populists for attempting to reduce the Texas Mexicans "to the category of pack animals, who may be good enough to work, but not good enough to exercise their civil rights."[94]

Although many of the People's Party's interests were compatible with those of the Mexican workers, the party regarded them as its enemy. The Texas Populists forged alliances with black workers, while attacking Mexicans and threatening to deport them. The Populists used the pretext that the Democratic Party manipulated their vote. Instead of organizing progressive elements within the Mexican community and attempting to check the machines, the Populists made Mexicans their scapegoats, popularizing crass racist arguments.[95]

The Growth of the Mexican Population

The 1880 Census counted about 43,000 Mexicans in Texas. Most lived in the southern part of the state, where Mexicans remained the overwhelming majority until the arrival of large numbers of North Americans in the 1890s. The white newcomers formed their own neighborhoods, strictly segregating Mexicans to the older parts of the town. Increase in the number of North Americans strengthened their control of the political, social, and economic institutions. Mexicans as a community were too poor to support independent political movements and depended on their Mexican bosses for whatever influence they had.

By 1900, the total population of Texas reached 3,048,710; there were 620,722 African Americans. The Mexican population was not officially counted in the census. Texas Mexicans lived largely in rural areas and numbered about 70,000 statewide; unofficially the number was closer to 165,000. Mexicans, however, were less than 5 percent of the population in Texas—blacks were the state's largest minority.[96] Demographic changes in the last two decades of the nineteenth century, along with the spread of cotton and commercial agriculture, set the stage for the modernization of the Texas economy in the next century. Land companies and irrigation projects put enormous tracts of land into production, increasing the demand for Mexican labor. The majority of Mexicans continued to live in *jacales* (shacks).

The Growth of Racist Nativism

Euro-American nativists saw Mexicans, whether born in the United States or Mexico, as aliens. Through the courts, nativists attempted to exclude them from citizenship. By inference, the Treaty of Guadalupe Hidalgo (1848) made Mexicans white, without which status they could not be equal or immigrate to the United States. In 1897, Richard Rodríguez, who was born in Mexico, applied for citizenship, which was denied because immigration authorities said he was an Indian. Rodríguez had lived in Texas for 10 years. Federal attorneys argued against his eligibility on the grounds that Rodríguez was "not a white person, not an African, nor of African descent." U.S. District Judge Thomas Maxey held that because Rodríguez knew "nothing of the Aztecs or Toltecs," he was not an Indian and thus had the right to become a naturalized citizen. This issue would continue to plague Mexican Americans throughout the twentieth century.

As late as 1895, a mob lynched Cotula jailer Florentino Suaste.[97] In January 1896, authorities found the mutilated body of Aureliano Castellón in San Antonio. He had made the mistake of courting Emma Stanfield, a white girl, over the objections of her brothers. He was shot eight times and his body was burned. On June 30, 1896, the *San Antonio Express* published a note entitled "Slaughter the *Gringo*," signed by 25 Mexicans. The signers allegedly threatened to kill only gringos and Germans, exempting blacks, Italians, and Cubans.[98]

Two years later, the Spanish–American War spread fear among Euro-Americans, who believed that Mexicans would ally themselves with Spain and begin border raids. In places such as San Diego, Texas, Euro-Americans formed Minute Men companies to "protect" themselves. Although they soon learned that Mexicans had little empathy with Spain and the uprisings never took place, the situation gave racists an excuse to persecute all Mexicans.

The White Cap movement of south Texas in the late 1890s aggravated conditions. (Texas White Caps should not be confused with the Mexican *Gorras Blancas*, White Caps of New Mexico; see Chapter 5.) Texas White Caps were a vigilante group that demanded that white planters refuse to rent to blacks and Mexicans and fire Mexican field hands. White Cap activity centered in Wilson, Gonzales, and DeWitt counties, where its members terrorized Mexicans. "Astonishing numbers of Mexicans in the nineteenth century fell victim to lynch law and cold-blooded deaths at the hands of whites who thought nothing of killing Mexicans."[99] Social attitudes reinforced by violence froze Mexicans into a caste system that facilitated exploitation of their labor in the twentieth century.

Mexican Resistance

Despite discrimination, Mexicans were quite active in politics. For example, by 1900, Mexicans numbered 24,033 or 55.5 percent of the population of El Paso County.[100] Victor L. Ochoa in April 1891 gave a speech calling on Mexicans to organize and promote self-help. He wanted the people to pressure government not to award public works contracts to firms that hired workers directly from Mexico and lobbied to create an office of a superintendent of public works who would hire Mexicans from El Paso. Ochoa advocated equal pay for Mexican American police and other Mexican American public employees, who were then paid less than whites.[101]

Ochoa, along with revolutionary and spiritualist Lauro Aguirre, was among those participating in the plots against Mexican dictator Porfirio Díaz. They had contact with Mexican revolutionaries in the Guerrero, Chihuahua, region. Guerrero was a transition zone between ranching country and Sierra, the location of native villages, mine settlements, and logging camps. The arrival of the Mexican Central Railroad in 1884, the telegraph, and the elimination of the Apache had fanned tensions in Chihuahua and the situation was ripe for a revolution. El Paso Mexican leaders formed ties with the dissidents. Ochoa in 1892 and his circle condemned federal troops for the slaughters of innocent people at Tomochic and Santo Tomas in 1892.

In November 1893, the *revoltosos* (revolutionaries) assaulted the border town of Palomas. The *El Paso Evening Tribune* reported that 3,000 rebels were marching on Guerrero, which was defended by 800 Mexican soldiers. At Palomas, the rebels under the command of Valente García and Ochoa, then only 23 and editor of *The Hispano Americano*, occupied the customhouse. Only three, including Ochoa, made it back to the United States. Ochoa was charged with violating the U.S. neutrality laws.[102]

The rebels made another abortive strike on January 15, 1894. Ochoa escaped, dressed in the clothes of a Mexican soldier, made his way to El Paso, and was arrested in October for filibustering. The U.S. government had no difficulty in proving its case. The sheriff, at the insistence of the Mexican government, held him at Fort Stockton while it attempted to extradite him. They intended to kidnap him and take him to Mexico. Ochoa was convicted and sent to the Kings County Penitentiary.[103] After his release from prison, Ochoa continued his anti-Díaz activities. In October 1915, Ochoa, along with José Orozco and E. L. Holmdahl, was again convicted of conspiring to violate neutrality laws and was sentenced to 18 months in Leavenworth.[104]

Meanwhile, the political consciousness of Mexicans in the United States had grown. By the 1870s and 1880s, many Spanish-language newspapers in Texas catered to the Mexican populace. After the 1880s, a constant in-migration of political exiles from Mexico, voluntary and involuntary, was witnessed in San Antonio, El Paso, and along the Rio Grande. These exiles often furnished leadership to workers, and they integrated themselves into the Tejano society via the *mutualistas* and other institutions. In 1885, Catarino Garza, a journalist, traveling salesman, and former Mexican consul at St. Louis, Missouri, organized *mutualistas* in the valley and exhorted Mexicans to unite and fight racism. Garza accused a U.S. customs inspector, Victor Sebree, of assassinating Mexican prisoners who actively opposed Díaz; in 1888, on the streets of Rio Grande City, Sebree shot and wounded Garza.

Garza soon became a leader of the anti-Díaz movement. Garza recruited adherents through *La Sociedad Mexicana*, which was founded by Dr. Ignacio Martínez, who like Garza was once a supporter of the Mexican president. Journalist Paulino Martínez also supported Garza as did powerful generals in Mexico, among them Sostenes Rocha, Francisco Naranjo, Sebastian Villareal, Francisco Estrada, Luis E. Torres, and Luis Terrazas.

In 1891, Garza led an abortive armed attack on Mexican territory in an effort to incite a revolution. On three other occasions that year, Garza crossed into Mexico only to be chased by the U.S. cavalry, sheriffs, and marshals. U.S. military authorities asked for an additional 10,000 troops to put down the revolt, claiming that Garza had cost the Mexican government $2 million. Sensational newspaper accounts raised concerns that Mexicans would arm themselves, rekindling old fears of a Mexican revolt. Also rumored was that General Juan Cortina would soon return to Texas from Mexico City to lead the revolution. The pursuit forced Garza to flee to Key West, Florida, where he helped Cuban exiles fight for their independence. He then went to Central America, where he fought for liberal causes.[105] Garza died in 1895, killed by Colombian troops after joining Colombian rebels. By 1896 Lauro Aguirre was residing in El Paso, where he allied with other dissidents including Victor Ochoa, Pedro García de Lama, Manuel Flora Chapa, and Teresa (Teresita) Urrea. The cabal led several abortive forays into Mexico.[106]

Conclusion: The Return of the Mexicano

By 1900, mass migration from Mexico to Texas worsened racism despite the fact that there was a booming economy that mostly benefited whites. The number of farms swelled from 12,000 in 1850, to 340,000 by 1900. One-third of the Mexican population was employed in agriculture; most were farm hands. Their wages declined an estimated 30 percent, while urban wages increased, contributing to a flight to the cities. Moreover, child labor was more common in agriculture, further encouraging migration to urban areas.[107]

The foreign-born Mexican population climbed from 47.1 percent in 1850 to 61.2 percent in 1900, while the white foreign-born population declined from 44.8 percent to 24.3 percent among workers in central Texas, the Lower Rio Grande Valley, and the El Paso region. By 1900, 85 percent of the population in south Texas was of Mexican extraction. Significantly, literacy declined among Mexicans from 25.1 percent to 13.0 percent while among whites it increased from 86.6 percent to 92.2 percent.[108] This was a transitional period of changing identities among Mexican-origin peoples in the Lower Rio Grande Valley, as Trinidad Gonzales writes. According to Gonzales, in 1900 Valley Mexicans considered the area "Occupied Mexico, but within two decades they recognized it as American territory. They held on to the Mexican culture, *lo mexicano*, with a Tejano identity emerging." A similar process would happen throughout the Southwest.[109]

Notes

1. By 1826 Euro-Americans dominated commerce along the lower Rio Grande, changing the economic face of the region. Commercial farming and land transactions transformed New Mexico and Texas. Because the Mexican government threatened those economic interests, the time of the Texas revolt in 1836 was moved up. Andres Reséndez, "National Identity on a Shifting Border: Texas and New Mexico in the Age of Transition, 1821–1848," *Journal of American History* 86, no. 2 (September 1999): 679, 681, 683.

2. David Montejano, *Anglos and Mexicans in the Making of Texas, 1836–1986* (Austin: University of Texas Press, 1987), 16. A substantial number of the Mexican or Tejano elite supported the Euro-Americans. See Memoirs of Antonio Menchaca, Yanaguana Society, San Antonio, 1937. Courtesy of Wallace L. McKeehan, Sons of DeWitt Colony Texas, http://www.tamu.edu/ccbn/dewitt/menchacamem.htm. José María Salomé Rodríguez, *The Memoirs of Early Texas*, 1913, Sons of DeWitt Colony Texas, http://www.tamu.edu/ccbn/dewitt/rodmemoirs.htm. José Antonio Navarro's Letter to the Editor of the San Antonio *Ledger* (October 30, 1853), http://www.tamu.edu/ccbn/dewitt/navarromem1.htm. Armando Villarreal y Talamantes, "Intervention and Conflict in the Trans-Nueces, 1755–1850" (Master's thesis, University of Texas at Arlington, 2003), 7.

3. David R. Johnson, John A. Booth, and Richard J. Harris, eds., *The Politics of San Antonio* (Lincoln: University of Nebraska Press, 1983), 5. Montejano, *Anglos and Mexicans in the Making of Texas, 1836–1986*, 26–27. Gilberto Miguel Hinojosa, *A Borderland Town in Transition: Laredo, 1755–1870* (College Station: Texas A&M University Press, 1983), 35. Raúl A. Ramos, *Beyond the Alamo: Forging Mexican Ethnicity in San Antonio, 1821–1861* (Chapel Hill: University of North Carolina Press, 2008), 171, 174. There were individual exceptions; José Antonio Navarro was elected to the state legislature, and Seguín was a state senator.

4. Neil Foley, *The White Scourge: Mexicans, Blacks, and Poor Whites in Texas Cotton Culture* (Berkeley: University of California Press, 1997), 19–20.

5. Montejano, *Anglos and Mexicans in the Making of Texas, 1836–1986*, 26–27. Hinojosa, *A Borderland Town in Transition*, 59. Juan Seguín's Address to the Texas Senate, February 1840, The Seguin Family Historical Society, "The Original and Official Seguín Family Organization and Web Site," http://www.seguinfamilyhistory.com/index.html#address. Ramos, *Beyond the Alamo*, 167–68, 177–78; soon after the arrival of more Euro-Americans the window of opportunity closed. As tensions with Mexico increased, the Tejanos were looked at as a suspect class.

6. Frederick Law Olmsted, *Journey Through Texas* (New York: Dix, Edwards & Co., 1857), 164–65.

7. T. R. Fehrenbach, *Lone Star: A History of Texas and the Texans* (New York: Macmillan, 1968), 245. Donald E. Chipman, *Spanish Texas, 1519–1821* (Austin: University of Texas Press, 1992). Andrés Tijerina, *Tejanos & Texas under the Mexican Flag, 1821–1836* (College Station: Texas A&M University Press, 1994), 137–44. Michael Paul Rogin, *Fathers and Children: Andrew Jackson and the Subjugation of the American Indian* (Edison, NJ: Transaction Press, 1991), 306. President Andrew Jackson reacting to Goliad said he would have killed every Mexican prisoner, one by one. James Alan Marten, *Texas Divided: Loyalty and Dissent in the Lone Star State, 1856–1874* (Lexington: University Press of Kentucky, 1990), 12, 19, 29.

8. Important research is being conducted on Mexicans in Texas. Two very good dissertations are Allison Brownell Tirres, "American Law Comes to the Border: Law and Colonization on the U.S./Mexico Divide, 1848–1890" (PhD dissertation, Harvard University, Cambridge, 2008), 8–9, which concentrates on El Paso. Euro-Americans there found themselves isolated from their culture and adopted a hybrid legal structure. The other is J. Edward Townes, "Invisible Lines: The Life and Death of a Borderland" (PhD dissertation, Texas Christian University, Fort Worth, 2008). The Townes dissertation is on the Natchitoches border area, which has a longer history of Euro-American–Mexican conflict than that of the Rio Bravo. The racism is also documented in Olmsted, *Journey Through Texas*; eyewitness accounts capture the antipathy toward Mexicans.

9. Arnold De León, *The Tejano Community, 1836–1900* (Albuquerque: University of New Mexico Press, 1982), 20. Montejano, *Anglos and Mexicans in the Making of Texas, 1836–1986*, 31. Hinojosa, *A Borderland Town in Transition*, 65–6. Stephen L. Moore, *Savage Frontier: 1840–1841: Rangers, Riflemen, and Indian Wars in Texas*, Vol. 3 (Denton: University of North Texas Press, 2007), 289. Paul Horgan, *Great River: The Rio Grande in North American History, Vol. 1. Indians and Spain, Vol. 2. Mexico and the United States*, 2 vols. (New York: Rinehart, 1954).

10. Villarreal y Talamantes, "Intervention and Conflict in the Trans-Nueces, 1755–1850," 33.

11. Armando Alonzo, *Tejano Legacy: Rancheros and Settlers in South Texas 1734–1900* (Albuquerque: University of New Mexico Press, 1998), 85–86, 93.

12. Letter from Texas President Mirabeau B. Lamar to the People of Santa Fé, April 14, 1840, Courtesy of Sons of DeWitt Colony Texas, and President M.B. Lamar Address to the People of Santa Fé, June 5, 1841, http://www.tamu.edu/ccbn/dewitt/santafeexped.htm. Mirabeau B. Lamar to James Webb, February 23, 1842, http://www.tsl.state.tx.us/treasures/giants/lamar/lamar-webb-1.html. Moore, *Savage Frontier*, 275, said that Lamar "hoped to cash in on the trade value of the profits now going to St. Louis and Mexican towns. Claiming this territory would add to the international prestige of Texas."

13. Glen Sample Ely, "Gone from Texas and Trading with the Enemy: New Perspectives on Civil War West Texas," *Southwestern Historical Quarterly* CX, no. 4 (April 2007): 439, 440. In the spring of 1864, many Euro-Texans left the Lone Star State for a fresh start in California. John Chisum and other

Texas ranchers had to look westward for new sales. See Rodolfo F. Acuña, *Corridors of Migration: The Odyssey of Mexican Laborers, 1600–1933* (Tucson: University of Arizona Press, 2007), 87, 207; "In the 1870s, Texans who had migrated to nearby Tombstone began to hound and rob Mexicans on both sides of the border." Their antipathy was noted during the 1917 Copper strikes and the 1933 Cotton Strike.

14. Janice Elaine Watkins, "Nacogdoches Land Men and the Texas Revolution" (Master of Arts thesis, Stephen F. Austin State University, 2009), 1, 5, 34–37. The Euro-Americans who settled in this area knew that they had broken Mexican law. Many had been involved in filibustering activities during the Spanish period, and had been joined by Spanish subjects.

15. Ibid., 46.

16. Townes, "Invisible Lines," 208, 214–17.

17. Paul D. Lack, "The Córdova Revolt," in Gerald R. Poyo, ed., *Tejano Journey, 1770–1850* (Austin: University of Texas Press, 1996), 89–109. Letter from Vicente Córdova to Manuel Flores, July 19, 1838, Texas Indian Papers, Vol. 1, no. 2. Archives and Manuscripts, Texas State Library and Archives Commission, www.tsl.state.tx.us/exhibits/indian/early/cordova-1838.html. John Henry Brown, "Vicente Córdova and the Córdova Rebellion," *From History of Texas*, http://www.tamu.edu/ccbn/dewitt/cordovavicente.htm#brown. J. W. Wilbarger, *The Córdova Fight, From Indian Depredations in Texas*. Wilbarger, The Flores Fight and Archival Correspondence, http://www.tamu.edu/faculty/ccbn/dewitt/cordovavicente2.htm. Mike Coppock, "The Forced Expulsion of the Texas Cherokees: Houston Supported Them but Not Lamar," *Wild West* 21, no. 2 (August 2008): 22–23.

18. Testimonies of fugitive slaves can be found at "Fugitive Slave Cases, 1862," May 15–19, 1862, Transcribed from National Archives Microfilm Publication M433 "Records of the United States District Court for the District of Columbia Relating to Slaves, 1851–1863, Roll 3." See Christine's Genealogy Website, http://ccharity.com/contents/fugitive-slave-cases-1862-may-15-19-1862/fugitive-slave-cases-1862-may-15-19-1862-0/.

19. Jack C. Vowell, "Politics at El Paso: 1850–1920" (Master's thesis, Texas Western College, El Paso, 1952), 145. De León, *The Tejano Community, 1836–1900*, xvi. José Antonio Navarro, 1795–1871, biography, autobiography and letter to Stephen Austin, Sons of DeWitt Colony Texas, http://www.tamu.edu/ccbn/dewitt/Navarro.htm.

20. Ronnie G. Tyler, "The Callahan Expedition of 1855: Indians or Negroes?" *Southwest Historical Quarterly* 70, no. 4 (April 1967): 575, 582. Arnoldo De León, "White Racial Attitudes toward Mexicanos in Texas, 1821–1920" (PhD dissertation, Texas Christian University, Fort Worth, 1974), 141.

21. Marten, *Texas Divided*, 13. Alberto Rodríguez, "Ethnic Conflict in South Texas: 1860–1930" (Master of Arts thesis, The University of Texas Pan American, Edinburg, 2005), 2–5, 8, 21, 30, 36. King Cotton conditioned Tejano–African American relations. Rodríguez says that Mexicans reacted to white attitudes of social class by siding with whites and negotiating their whiteness, while poor Mexicans sympathized with blacks and in some cases cohabitated with African Americans crossing over into Mexico and becoming Mexicans. Between 1820 and 1860 Mexico was a safe haven for runaway slaves.

22. Vowell, "Politics at El Paso." De León, *The Tejano Community, 1836–1900*, xvi. José Antonio Navarro, 1795–1871, biography, autobiography and letter to Stephen Austin, Sons of DeWitt Colony Texas, http://www.tamu.edu/ccbn/dewitt/Navarro.htm.

23. LeRoy P. Graf, "The Economic History of the Lower Río Grande Valley, 1820–1875" (PhD dissertation, Harvard University, Cambridge, 1942), 212, 236, writes that by December 1849 Brownsville was a boomtown. Montejano, *Anglos and Mexicans in the Making of Texas, 1836–1986*, 41–43. The Mexican War had brought unprecedented prominence to Matamoros, but the founding of Brownsville siphoned off the prosperity of the Mexican city.

24. Hinojosa, *A Borderland Town in Transition*, 65. Alonzo, *Tejano Legacy*, 99. Montejano, *Anglos and Mexicans in the Making of Texas, 1836–1986*, 42–43. Graf, "The Economic History of the Lower Río Grande Valley, 1820–1875," 212. Clarence C. Clendenen, *Blood on the Border: The United States Army and the Mexican Irregulars* (New York: Macmillan, 1969), 18.

25. Alonzo, *Tejano Legacy*, 146–52. "Investigating Commission of the Northern Frontier," in Carlos E. Cortés, ed., *The Mexican Experience in Texas* (New York: Arno Press, 1976). Charles W. Goldfinch, *Juan Cortina, 1824–1892: A Re-Appraisal* (Brownsville, TX: Bishop's Print Shop, 1950), 21, 31.

26. Tom Lea, *The King Ranch, 2 vols.*, Vol. 1 (Boston: Little, Brown, 1957), 457. Graf, "The Economic History of the Lower Río Grande Valley, 1820–1875," 192. James Arthur Irby, "Line of the Rio Grande: War and Trade on the Confederate Frontier, 1861–1865" (PhD dissertation, University of Georgia, Athens, 1969), v, xi. Author reviewed book in manuscript form. William D. Carrigan and Clive Webb, *Forgotten Dead: Mob Violence against Mexicans in the United States, 1848–1928* (New York: Oxford University Press, 2013), 64–66, makes the case that Mexican foreign officials continuously intervened on behalf of victims in cases of violence and lynching. In regards to the Cart War, Texas Governor Elisha Pease got the state legislature to pay for militia to protect Mexican teamsters. However, Mexican cartmen had already bypassed Goliad. John Salmon Ford in Stephen B. Oates, ed., *Rip Ford's Texas* (Austin: University of Texas Press, 1963), 467. Frank H. Dugan, "The 1850 Affair of the Brownsville Separatists," *Southwestern Historical Quarterly* 61, no. 2 (October 1957): 270–73. Marten, *Texas Divided*, 30; the violence drove the cartmen out of San Antonio. *Report of the Mexican Commission on the Northern Frontier Question, Investigating Commission of the Northern Frontier* (New York: Baker & Godwin Printer, 1875), 130–32, condemned the atrocities committed.

27. Edward H. Moseley, "The Texas Threat, 1855–1860," *Journal of Mexican American History* 3 (1973): 89–90. De León, "White Racial Attitudes toward Mexicanos in Texas, 1821–1920," 7, 147. David J. Weber, ed., *Foreigners in Their Native Land* (Albuquerque: University of New Mexico Press, 1973), 155–56. Jerry Thompson, *Cortina: Defending the Mexican Name in*

Texas (College Station: Texas A&M Press, 2007), 9, 12. Juan Cortina's father Trinidad Cortina was the alcalde of Camargo. Cortina had a strong sense of family background. In 1844 he was a member of Los Defensores del Pueblo in Matamoros, Mexico. He served on the Mexican side during the Mexican American War. Although the book is interesting, it has the basic problem that the author makes a lot of suppositions.

28. William D. Carrigan, Clive Webb, "The Lynching of Persons of Mexican Origin or Descent in the United States, 1848 to 1928," *Journal of Social History* 37, no. 2 (Winter 2003): 411–38. This excellent article has been expanded to a book: Carrigan, Webb, *Forgotten Dead*. On page 7 the authors include an inventory of 547 victims, slightly revising the number. However, the number is conservative and based on what the authors could find. The book is a major contribution.

29. Michael Gordon Webster, "Texan Manifest Destiny and Mexican Border Conflict, 1865–1880" (PhD dissertation, Indiana University, Bloomington, 1972), 30, 74–76. Graf, "The Economic History of the Lower Rio Grande Valley, 1820–1875," 664–65, makes the point that the full impact of the Free Zone was not felt in the Valley during the first years because of internal disorders and the relatively insecure status of the zone. *Report of the Mexican Commission on the Northern Frontier*, 208. Moore, *Savage Frontier*, 293. The role of the Rangers in maintaining control through brutality is well documented. "Capt. Richard Roman's men captured about 10 Mexican traders, whom they herded back toward Victoria. En route, they stopped to divide the traders' effects, [and] . . . robbed them and took horses."

30. Goldfinch, *Juan Cortina, 1824–1892*, 1–3, 17. José T. Canales, *Juan N. Cortina Presents His Motion for a New Trial* (San Antonio, TX: Artes Gráficas, 1951), 6.

31. Graf, "The Economic History of the Lower Río Grande Valley, 1820–1875," 375–401.

32. Juan Nepomuceno Cortina to the inhabitants of the State of Texas, and especially to those of the city of Brownsville (September 30, 1859). To the Mexican inhabitants of the State of Texas: Proclamation (November 23, 1859). (TEXT: U.S. Congress, House, Difficulties on the Southwestern Frontier, 36th Congress; 1st Session, 1860, H. Exec. Doc. 52, 70–82), http://www.pbs.org/weta/thewest/resources/archives/four/cortinas.htm#0959.

33. Walter Prescott Webb, *The Texas Rangers: A Century of Frontier Defense* (Austin: University of Texas Press, 1965), 176. Lyman Woodman, *Cortina: Rogue of the Rio Grande* (San Antonio, TX: Naylor, 1950), 8. Graf, "The Economic History of the Lower Río Grande Valley, 1820–1875," 320–22. Space constraints prevent an in-depth presentation of this revolt. José María Carbajal, born in San Antonio, was educated in the United States. He married the daughter of empresario Martín de León. He fled Texas during the so-called Revolution, returning in 1839 to recruit troops for the federalist cause in Mexico. Carbajal fought in the Mexican army against invading U.S. forces. His original demand was the decentralization of government. Northern Mexico was feeling the impact of state building, and the residents were discontent over central government's attempts to end certain aspects of their independence. Many at first supported Carbajal, only to become disaffected when he attracted remnants of recently disbanded Texas Rangers, adventurers, and rich Euro-American merchants. As a result, he failed to attract the mass support he needed. James LeRoy Evans, "The Indian Savage, the Mexican Bandit, the Chinese Heathen: Three Popular Stereotypes" (PhD dissertation, University of Texas, El Paso, 1967), 107, 118. *Report of the Mexican Commission on the Northern Frontier*, 28–29.

34. Webb, *The Texas Rangers*, 178. Goldfinch, *Juan Cortina, 1824–1892*, 44–45. Webster, "Texan Manifest Destiny and Mexican Border Conflict, 1865–1880," 18. Evans, "The Indian Savage, the Mexican Bandit, the Chinese Heathen," 107, 121. *Report of the Mexican Commission on the Northern Frontier*, 137–39.

35. Wayne Moquin et al., eds., *A Documentary History of the Mexican American* (New York: Praeger, 1971), 207–9. For the complete text of the speech, delivered on November 23, 1859, see *Report of the Mexican Commission on the Northern Frontier*, 133, n. 62.

36. Graf, "The Economic History of the Lower Río Grande Valley, 1820–1875," 397. See Angel Navarro to Houston (January 26, 1860). Texas State Library and Archives Commission, http://www.tsl.state.tx.us/governors/earlystate/houston-navarro-1.html.

37. Evans, "The Indian Savage, the Mexican Bandit, the Chinese Heathen," 127.

38. Montejano, *Anglos and Mexicans in the Making of Texas, 1836–1986*, 36. Woodman, *Cortina*, 53, 55, 59, 98–99. Evans, "The Indian Savage, the Mexican Bandit, the Chinese Heathen," 105, 111, 113, 308–9. Report of Major Samuel P. Heintzelman to Colonel Robert E. Lee (March 1, 1860). In Troubles on Texas Frontier, House of Representatives, 36th Congress, 1st Session, Ex. Doc. No. 81, Letter from the Secretary of War, 2–14. This congressional report is full of primary documents on Cortina.

39. Montejano, *Anglos and Mexicans in the Making of Texas, 1836–1986*, 36. Ford, *Rip Ford's Texas*, 467.

40. Ralph Wooster, "Wealthy Texans," *Southwestern Historical Quarterly* (October 1967): 163, 173. Irby, "Line of the Rio Grande," 3, 13, 63. Kenedy in 1860 listed his real-estate holdings at $50,000 and his personal estate at $50,000. José San Ramón, another merchant, listed his real-estate holdings at $50,000 and personal estate at $200,000. Stillman had a modest $13,000 in real estate and $600 in personal holdings.

41. Jeffrey William Hunt, *The Last Battle of the Civil War: Palmetto Ranch* (Austin: University of Texas Press, 2002), 17–20. Mary Margaret McAllen Amberson, "The Politics of Commerce: Merchants' and Military Officials' Machinations to Prolong Civil War Turmoil Along the Lower Rio Grande, 1865–1867" (Master's thesis, University of Texas, San Antonio, 2007), 3.

42. Marten, *Texas Divided*, 93, 32, 77, 123, 125. Irby, "Line of the Rio Grande," 34, 142. Ranger Rip Ford had relations with many of the elite Mexican families in the Valley. For instance,

he refused to extradite his friend Juan María Carbajal to Mexico. Captain Santos Benavides aided the Euro-American campaigns against Juan Cortina, a bitter enemy of Ford. Col. Santo Benavides, http://www.37thtexas.org/html/Santosbio.html. Confederates in Mexico, http://www.youtube.com/watch?v=QQQ5S33XUCM. Mexican Confederates, http://www.youtube.com/watch?v=X79xmf7B7pg. Mexican Texans in the Civil War, http://www.tshaonline.org/handbook/online/articles/pom02. Jerry D. Thompson ed., *Tejanos in Gray: Civil War Letters of Captains Joseph Rafael de la Garza and Manuel Yturri* (College Station, Texas: Texas A&M University Press, 2011).

43. Marten, *Texas Divided*, 126. Brewster Hudspeth, "The Short but Eventful Life of Adrián J. Vidal 1840–1865," http://www.texasescapes.com/FallingBehind/Short-but-Eventful-life-of-Adrian-J-Vidal.htm. Richard Nelson Current, *Lincoln's Loyalists: Union Soldiers from the Confederacy* (Boston: Northeastern University Press, 1992), 99–102, 137. "Nearly three times as many Mexican-Texans served the Rebels as served the Yankees." A recent biography was published on Petra Kenedy's life: Jane Clements Monday and Frances Brannen Vick, *Petra's Legacy: The South Texas Ranching Empire of Petra Vela and Mifflin Kenedy*, 1st ed. (College Station: Texas A&M University Press, October 30, 2007).

44. Tina N. Cannon, "Bordering on Trouble: Conflict between Tejanos and Anglos in South Texas, 1880–1920" (Master of Arts, Baylor University, Waco, College Station, 2001), 28, 32, 33, 36. Introduction of barbed wire placed Mexicans and Euro-Texans at odds: reduced payrolls and long drives. Railroads brought an end to long drives. Barbed wire, irrigation, and railroads encouraged immigration to south Texas. Railroads took off in the 1870s; in 1881 Texas and Pacific gained charter from the state. Amberson, "The Politics of Commerce," 4, 6, 13, 18, 21. Alberto Rodriguez, "Ethnic Conflict in South Texas: 1860–1930" (Master of Arts hesis, Pan American University, 2005), 5: the black population went from 58,161 in 1850 to over 82,000 in 1860. King Cotton dominated the economy. Jesse Dorsett, "Blacks in Reconstruction Texas, 1865–1877" (PhD dissertation, Texas Christian University, Abilene, 1981).

45. De León, *The Tejano Community, 1836–1900*, 63. Alonzo, *Tejano Legacy*, 169.

46. Fehrenbach, *Lone Star*, 678–79. Weber, *Foreigners in Their Native Land*, 146, states that 11,212 Mexicans lived in Texas in 1850, constituting only 5 percent of the population. John R. Scotford, *Within These Borders* (New York: Friendship Press, 1953), 35. Montejano, *Anglos and Mexicans in the Making of Texas, 1836–1986*, 172–76. John Solomon Otto, *The Final Frontiers, 1880–1930: Settling the Southern Bottomlands* (Portsmouth, NH: Greenwood Press, 199), 101. World of the Tenant Farmer, Texas Beyond History, University of Texas, http://www.texasbeyondhistory.net/osborn/world.html.

47. De León, "White Racial Attitudes toward Mexicanos in Texas, 1821–1920," 140, 238, 239.

48. Ford, *Rip Ford's Texas*, 371. Webster, "Texan Manifest Destiny and Mexican Border Conflict, 1865–1880," 76. James LeRoy

Evans, "The Indian Savage, the Mexican Bandit, the Chinese Heathen," vii. Alonzo, *Tejano Legacy*, 163–65.

49. Ford, *Rip Ford's Texas*, 371.

50. *Report of the Mexican Commission on the Northern Frontier*, 154–55. Webster, "Texan Manifest Destiny and Mexican Border Conflict, 1865–1880," 79–80. Montejano, *Anglos and Mexicans in the Making of Texas, 1836–1986*, 53.

51. An Act to Provide for the Protection of the Frontier, 1874. Texas Ranger Research Center, http://www.texasranger.org/ReCenter/org1874.htm.

52. Leonard Morris, "The Mexican Raid of 1875 on Corpus Christi," *Texas Historical Association Quarterly* 55, no. 2 (October 1900): 128.

53. Lea, *The King Ranch*, 2 vols., 275.

54. *Report of the Mexican Commission on the Northern Frontier*. This report is an indictment of U.S. merchants and ranchers.

55. Graf, "The Economic History of the Lower Río Grande Valley, 1820–1875," 320–22.

56. *Report of the Mexican Commission on the Northern Frontier*, 29–30, 62, 105. Alonzo, *Tejano Legacy*, 142. Montejano, *Anglos and Mexicans in the Making of Texas, 1836–1986*, 38. Meanwhile, the state adjudicated the 350 Tamaulipas and Coahuila land grants. In 1853 the state legislature confirmed some 200 titles. Of the 14 Chihuahua land grants, only 7 were confirmed. After 1901, 50 more were confirmed. Many of these titles had already passed to Euro-American owners. The role of the Rangers in giving Euro-Americans hegemony over the corridor is obvious in various accounts. Moore, *Savage Frontier*, 289, 293.

57. De León, "White Racial Attitudes," 159–61, 172, 239. De León, *The Tejano Community, 1836–1900*, 18–19, 33–34. Carrigan and Webb, "The Lynching of Persons of Mexican Origin," 413–14, 416–18, 425. There were Mexicans in the Rangers, http://www.texasranger.org/ReCenter/hispanic_indian_rangers.htm. "A Little Standing Army in Himself": N. A. Jennings Tells of the Texas Rangers, 1875, http://historymatters.gmu.edu/d/6534.

58. Larry McMurtry, *In a Narrow Grave* (Austin, TX: Encino Press, 1968), 40, underscores the inconsistencies of Webb's description of the Rangers' role in the siege of Mexico City.

59. Llerena B. Friend, "W. Webb's Texas Rangers," *Southwestern Historical Quarterly* 74, no. 3 (January 1971): 321.

60. Ibid.

61. [quote] Editorial by John Salmon Ford in the *Texas Democrat*, September 9, 1846; quoted in Fehrenbach, *Lone Star*, 465. [contextual] Américo Paredes, *With a Pistol in His Hand* (Austin: University of Texas Press, 1958). Alonzo, *Tejano Legacy*, 75–76.

62. Editorial by John Salmon Ford in the *Texas Democrat* (September 9, 1846) quoted in Fehrenbach, *Lone Star*, 465.

63. Webb, *The Texas Rangers*, xv.

64. Paredes, *With a Pistol in His Hand*, 31.

65. Paredes, *With a Pistol in His Hand*, 31. Julian Samora, Joe Bernal, and Albert Peña, *Gun Powder Justice: A Reassessment of the Texas Rangers* (Notre Dame: University of Notre Dame Press, 1979), 56–57. "De La" means "of the." Paredes uses just

Cerda, while Webb uses "De La." It is the same family. It was probably used interchangeably. Samora et al. use it the same way as I do.

66. Paredes, *With a Pistol in His Hand*, 29.
67. Webb, Texas Rangers, 464.
68. Cynthia E. Orozco, "Kenedy, Petra Vela de Vidal," Handbook of Texas Online (http://www.tshaonline.org/handbook/online/articles/fkerl), accessed November 21, 2013. Published by the Texas State Historical Association. The revisionism is evident in the biography by Monday and Vick, *Petra's Legacy*, 250–51, writing how King memorialized McNeely. Teresa Palomo Acosta and Ruthe Winegarten, *Las Tejanas: 300 Years of History* (Austin: University of Texas Press, 2003), 45–68.
69. De León, "White Racial Attitudes," 112–13, 115, 116, 122.
70. De León, "White Racial Attitudes," [quote] 126;112–13, 115, 116, 122. E. Larry Dickens, "Mestizaje in 19th Century Texas," *Journal of Mexican American History* 2, no. 2 (Spring 1972): 63.
71. Jane Dysart, "Mexican Women in San Antonio, 1830–1860: The Assimilation Process," *Western Historical Quarterly* 7, no. 4 (October 1976): 370.
72. Dysart, "Mexican Women," 370.
73. Quoted in Aaron M. Boom, ed., "Texas in the 1850's as Viewed by a Recent Arrival," *Southwestern Historical Quarterly* 70, no. 2 (October 1966): 282–85.
74. De León, "White Racial Attitudes," 126. [quote] Dysart, "Mexican Women," 375.
75. Eric J. Hobsbawm, *Primitive Rebels: Studies in Archaic Forms of Social Movement in the 19th and 20th Centuries* (New York: Norton, 1965), 13.
76. Webb, *The Texas Rangers*, 360–61. Vowell, "Politics at El Paso," 69–70. "A Little War on the Border," *New York Times* (October 22, 1877), 4. Oscar J. Martinez, *Troublesome Border* (Tucson: University of Arizona Press, 1995), 85–86.
77. Leon Metz, "Atrocities, Plunder Mark End of El Paso Salt War," *El Paso Times* (March 17, 1974). Vowell, "Politics at El Paso," 65–66, 69, 72–73. Fehrenbach, *Lone Star*, 289. Carey McWilliams, *North from Mexico* (New York: Greenwood Press, 1968), 110. Webster, "Texan Manifest Destiny and Mexican Border Conflict, 1865–1880," 234.
78. W. M. Dunn's Report to War Department, Bureau of Military Justice (April 19, 1878), "El Paso Troubles in Texas," Letter from the Secretary of War, House of Representatives, 45th Cong., 2d. Sess., Ex. Doc. No. 93 (May 28, 1878), 3–5.
79. Letter from Colonel John H. King, Secretary of War, House of Representatives, to the Bureau of Military Justice (April 19, 1878), "El Paso Troubles in Texas," 13–18. Webster, "Texan Manifest Destiny and Mexican Border Conflict, 1865–1880," 238. Salt Trade, Trails, and Wars, http://www.texasbeyondhistory.net/trans-p/images/he3.html. Webb, *The Texas Rangers*, 350.
80. Carrigan and Webb, *Forgotten Dead*, 26–29, 67, 86–89 (Manuscript).
81. W. M. Dunn's Report to War Department, Bureau of Military Justice (April 19, 1878). Letter from Colonel John H. King, Secretary of War, "El Paso Troubles in Texas," 45th Cong., 2d. Sess., Ex. Doc. No. 93 (May 28, 1878), 13–18.

82. *The Ballad of Gregorio Cortez* [the movie], http://www.youtube.com/watch?v=FsApt0st_u4. Los Alegres De Teran—Gregorio Cortez, http://www.youtube.com/watch?v=jj4-6ZCc7i4.
83. Palanca also refers to the voting booth lever that voters pulled.
84. Alonzo, *Tejano Legacy*, 161. Montejano, *Anglos and Mexicans in the Making of Texas, 1836–1986*, 43–44. Robert J. Rosenbaum, *Mexicano Resistance in the Southwest* (Austin: University of Texas Press, 1981), 55.
85. De León, "White Racial Attitudes," 164. O. Douglas Weeks, "The Texas-Mexican and the Politics of South Texas," *American Political and Social Science Review* 24 (August 1930): 611–13.
86. Edgar Greer Shelton, Jr., "Political Conditions among Texas Mexicans Along the Río Grande" (Master's thesis, University of Texas, 1946), 26–28, 32–36. By the early 1920s Wells lost control, but the machine stayed intact, with power divided among his lieutenants. He died in 1922. O. Douglas Weeks, "The Texas-Mexican and the Politics of South Texas," *American Political and Social Science Review* 24 (August 1930): 611–13. De León, "White Racial Attitudes," 164.
87. Shelton, "Political Conditions," 26–28, 32–36. By the early 1920s, Wells had lost control, but the machine stayed intact, with power divided among his lieutenants. He died in 1922. The patriarch was José Alejandro Guerra, a surveyor for the Spanish crown in 1767. He had received *porciones* in the valley, which his heir Manuel Guerra inherited. Manuel started a mercantile house in Roma, Texas, in 1856. He married Virginia Cox, daughter of a Kentuckian father and Mexican mother.
88. Evan Anders, *Boss Rule in South Texas* (Austin: University of Texas Press, 1982).
89. Ibid., 283.
90. Shelton, "Political Conditions," 36–37, 90, 98, 123. At one point Canales quarreled with the Guerras in Starr County, and in 1933 he organized a new party to oppose them.
91. Anders, *Boss Rule in South Texas*, 283.
92. De León, *The Tejano Community, 1836–1900*, 90. Montejano, *Anglos and Mexicans in the Making of Texas, 1836–1986*, 62–63. Hector R. Pérez, "The Parrs: Patrones of Duval County, Texas, 1905–1975" (Master of Arts thesis, Texas A&M University, Kingsville, 2003): 1. The Parr machine evolved, according to Pérez, from the patron system.
93. Emilio Zamora, *The World of the Mexican Worker in Texas* (College Station: Texas A&M Press, 1993), 16, 34.
94. De León, "White Racial Attitudes," 166, 168. Zamora, *The World of the Mexican Worker*, 92–93.
95. Robert Miller Worth, "Building a Progressive Coalition in Texas: The Populist-Reform Democrat Rapprochement, 1900–1907," *Journal of Southern History* 52, no. 2 (May 1986): 163–182. The Populists were not progressive when it came to immigrants. Zamora, *The World of the Mexican Worker*, 92–93.
96. Fehrenbach, *Lone Star*, 627. Rupert N. Richardson, *Texas: The Lone Star State*, 2d ed. (Englewood Cliffs, NJ: Prentice-Hall, 1958), 271, 274.
97. De León, *The Tejano Community, 1836–1900*, 20–22. Donald W. Meinig, *Imperial Texas* (Austin: University of Texas Press, 1969), 65.

98. Carrigan and Webb, "The Lynching of Persons of Mexican Origin."

99. De León, "White Racial Attitudes," [quote 192], 186–87, 226–27, 232.

100. Ibid., 192–93, 267–68.

101. De León, *The Tejano Community, 1836–1900*, 43.

102. Ochoa, once had a $50,000 price on his head, Smithsonian, http://www.smithsonianeducation.org/scitech/impacto/graphic/victor/revolutionary_arrested.html.

103. "Mexican Revolt," *El Paso Evening Tribune* (April 18, 1893). "More Fighting," *El Paso Evening Tribune* (April 19, 1893). "All Quiet on Potomac," *El Paso Evening Tribune* (April 20, 1893). "The Chihuahuan Troubles," *El Paso Evening Tribune* (April 24, 1893). "Alarma Infundada," *El Norte*, Vol. iii, no. 130, Chihuahua, Chi. (November 13, 1893). "El Robo a la Aduana de Palomas," *El Norte: Bisenanario de Información* Año III, no. 129, Chihuahua, Chi. (November 19, 1893). "Rebelión de Palomas y el Manzano, 1893–1894," *Archivo General de la Nación* (Mexico City) (AGN MGR), Vol. 8. "Rebels Again Take Palomas," *El Paso Times* (November 16, 1893). "Perez Issues Manifesto," *El Paso Times* (December 3, 1893). Santana Pérez, a rebel leader in western Chihuahua, calls Díaz a traitor. "Rebels Hang Federal General," *El Paso Times* (December 13, 1893). "Charged with Aiding Rebels; Mexican Vice Consul Causes the Arrest of an American Citizen," *New York Times* (December 1, 1893). "Los Sucesos de Tomochic," Vol. 7, Ramo Gobernación, Paquete # 590, Exp 13. This section has all of the primary documents on the siege of Tomóchic, Vol. 8 El Estado de Chihuahua. XVII, # 320 (February 3, 1894). "Rebelión de Palomas y El Manzo: Años de 1893 y 1894," Periódico Oficial, 11 bandidos in District of Bravo, march on rebels. "Fighting Near Colonia Juarez," *El Paso Times* (December 14, 1893); 100 rebels, 17 hours of fighting.

104. "To Mexico for Revenge," *New York Times* (August 17, 1895). Francisco R. Almada, *Diccionario Historia Geografía y Biografía Chihuahuenses* Segunda Edición (Cd. Juárez: Universidad de Chihuahua, 1968), 33. "Something Wrong," *Los Angeles Times* (January 20, 1894). A dispatch from the mayor of Juárez said revolutionists attacked west side of town. Federal garrison responded. Masses of people were in sympathy with Santana Pérez, "Charged with Aiding Rebels," *New York Times* (December 1, 1893). "Simón Analla [sic] reported dead," *El Paso Times* (May 2, 1893).

105. "Sentence Carranza Agents," *New York Times* (October 21, 1915).

106. De León, *The Tejano Community, 1836–1900*, 30, 45, 48. De León, "White Racial Attitudes," 234–35, 263–64. Emilio Zamora, "Mexican Labor Activity in South Texas, 1900–1920" (PhD dissertation, University of Texas, Austin, 1983), 86–87. Celso Garza Guajardo, *En busca de Catarino Garza, 1859–1895* (Nuevo León: Atonoma de Nuevo León, 1989), contains his memoirs. "Another Fight in Texas," *New York Times* (January 4, 1892). M. Romero, "The Garza Raid and Its Lessons," *North American Review* (Spring 1892): 327. *New York Times* (November 18, 1893).

107. Paul J. Vanderwood, *The Power of God Against the Guns of Government: Religious Upheaval in Mexico at the Turn of the Nineteenth Century* (Stanford, CA: Stanford University Press, 1998), 291–92. Ochoa in 1890 organized *la Union Occidental Mexicana*. De León, *The Tejano Community, 1836–1900*, 130, 196.

108. Kenneth L. Stewart and Arnold De León, *Not Room Enough: Mexicans, Anglos, and Socio-economic Change in Texas, 1859–1900* (Albuquerque: University of New Mexico Press, 1993), 21, 23, 26, 29, 33, 35–36. De León, *The Tejano Community, 1836–1900*, 73, 107. Alonzo, *Tejano Legacy*, 110. David M. Vigness and Mark Odintz, "Rio Grande Valley," Handbook of Texas Online. The Texas State Historical Association. "The Valley" encompasses Starr, Cameron, Hidalgo, and Willacy counties. Large-scale irrigation was introduced in 1898 and the railroad linked the Valley to markets in 1904. By 1930 the population of the four lower Rio Grande Valley counties exceeded 176,000.

109. Trinidad Gonzales, "The World of Mexico Texanos, Mexicanos and Mexico Americanos: Transnational and National Identities in the Lower Rio Grande Valley during the Last Phase of United States Colonization, 1900–1930" (PhD dissertation, University of Houston, 2008), 5–6. Rodolfo F. Acuña, *Corridors of Migration: The Odysssey of Mexican Laborers, 1600–1933* (Tucson: University of Arizona Press, 2007), goes into the transnational character of migration. It was part of developing a Mexican identity on both sides of the border. Rodolfo F. Acuña, *Anything but Mexican: Chicanos in Contemporary Los Angeles* (London: Verso, 1996), deals with identity in the City of Los Angeles where similarities and differences have occurred throughout the city.

CHAPTER 5

Freedom in a Cage: The Colonization of New Mexico

LEARNING OBJECTIVES

- Discuss the importance of land and the Rio Grande to the conquest and development of New Mexico.

- Explain the significance of the Santa Fe Trail and the arrival of the Euro-American merchants.

- Describe the differences in the development of Rio Abajo and Rio Arriba and how they related to the perpetuation of the myth of whiteness.

- Describe the role of the Santa Fe Ring in the New Mexican land grabs and resulting wars.

- Explain the reasons behind the resistance to American rule.

- Analyze the illusion of the inclusion of Spanish Americans in the governance of New Mexico.

The wheel revolves around an Economic hub which is the axis for the other variables. The below timeline is your story board that you should be able to fill in after reading the chapter.

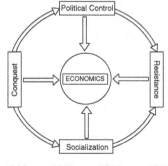

| 1803 | 1821 | 1836 | 1841 | 1846 | 1847 | 1848 | 1861 | 1863 | 1880 | 1912 |

The motivation for the *conquest* of New Mexico was profit. How? *Political control* furthered these ends by giving and maintaining the privilege of a few largely Euro-American males and their Mexican cohorts. *Socialization* was necessary to reinforce a structure and taught values and justified or explained these values. But like the old Mexican proverb says, *No hay mal que dure cien años, ni cuerpo que lo resista.* (There is no pain [or injustice] that lasts 100 years, nor a [human] body that can endure it.) When a system or society is flawed and causes injustices, there is bound to be *resistance.*

On the Frontier

Before Mexican Independence in 1821, New Mexico was on the periphery, the northern frontier, of New Spain.[1] The original Spanish settlement began in 1598 and after years of clash and adjustment the original settlement grew. In 1796 there were about 23,648 Hispanos and 10,557 Native Americans in the province. By the 1820s, El Paso, Santa Fe, and Albuquerque were all towns of several thousand dwellers.[2] During the Spanish period, a safe zone formed the so-called Rio Abajo, the middle Rio Grande Valley, with its center in Albuquerque. New Mexico's northern boundary was Santa Fe and Belén, the southern. Rio Arriba was the upper portion of the river.[3] When the Spanish settlers arrived, Rio Abajo was heavily settled by Pueblo people displaced in many cases by Hispano farm settlements. Over time large estates, haciendas, squeezed the villagers and the natives in the Rio Abajo area.

The different Indian tribes joined by the pueblos revolted in 1680 and drove the Spanish colonists out of New Mexico. The revolt affected tribes in Chihuahua and Sonora by driving the settlers to those provinces.[4] After the 1680 revolt, the crown built presidios from Sonora to Texas because the rebellion encouraged the Apache to also revolt. In the 1690s, some Spanish settlers returned, although many New Mexican families remained in Sonora and Chihuahua, increasing contact between the northern provinces. The returning settlers slowly reconquered the province and fortified Rio Abajo. In 1720, the Spanish Crown began to distribute other kinds of grants to encourage the settlement of the northern frontier, Rio Arriba. It conferred town ownership grants, community grants, and ranch grants.[5] As with other parts of northern Mexico, some Rio Arriba families earned their livelihood by grazing livestock on common lands.[6]

The increased population further stressed the Pueblo and nomadic Indians that rebelled. In response to the Indian hostilities, the Spaniards set up colonies in Rio Arriba to act as a buffer between the hacendados (owners of large haciendas), the Rio Abajo colonists, and the natives. Authorities distributed both private and communal land grants during the eighteenth and nineteenth centuries. The communal grants were helpful in encouraging the population of the frontier. Throughout the province, many of the poor depended on *partido* contracts—raising sheep for a large owner and taking half the increase in stock. While the Spanish elites continued to form large sheep- and cattle-ranching operations, the poor survived through subsistence farming supplemented by sheep grazing.

Some northern New Mexican villagers coexisted with the Pueblo natives—trading and occasionally intermarrying and struggling for land and water. Denise Holladay Damico writes "'Hispanos,' grew the same crops as Pueblo Indians and, like the people of the Pueblos, used irrigation ditches," while emphasizing that there were also differences.[7] Alien trappers and traders periodically intruded on the life of what was Mexico's northernmost and isolated province. Mexican Independence led to the destruction of this way of life as the North American penetration, infiltration, and conquest took their toll.[8] Increased population and privatization of existing resources strained the infrastructure. Meanwhile, trade caravans along the Camino Real linked New Mexico to Chihuahua and the rest of Mexico. By 1804, exports to Chihuahua reached 60,000 pesos per annum.

Land and water were New Mexico's principal resource; they were at the heart of the Pueblo Indians' grievances against the Spaniards, many of whom, according to Roxanne Dunbar Ortiz, attempted to "build large hereditary estates using Pueblo lands and labor."[9] The peoples were bound together by the Rio Grande, which begins its 1,800-mile trek in the mountains of Colorado.[10] The Rio Grande furnished a good part of the water that formed farm communities along the Rio and its tributaries.

Josiah Gregg wrote in the early 1840s about New Mexico's irrigation system:

One acequia madre (mother ditch) suffices generally to convey water for the irrigation of an entire valley. Or at least for all the fields of one town or settlement . . . Where there is not a superabundance of water, which is the case on the smaller streams, each farmer has his day, or portion of a day allotted to him for irrigation; and at no other time is he permitted to extend water from the acequia madre.[11]

It was not a perfect society but there was some blending.

The Santa Fe Trail: The Trojan Horse

North Americans began regular contact with New Mexico in the 1820s when they initiated the Santa Fe Trail. North Americans had secretly traded with New Mexicans since the Louisiana Purchase of 1803. Eighteen years later, when Mexico won its independence, it liberalized its trade policies. The following year, St. Louis merchants began their annual caravan from Missouri to Santa Fe. Meanwhile, North American commercial interests headquartered their operations at Taos. Charles Bent, the leader of the area's Euro-Americans, built Bent's Fort near Taos. Bent married a prominent Mexican woman, establishing ties with New Mexican merchants and elites.[12] These changes produced an exchange of money and allowed for the amassing of greater amounts of New Mexican capital. According to Deena González, "In the 1820s, as many as one hundred Euro-American merchants resided in Santa Fe [alone] and by the 1830s, another hundred had arrived."[13] By the late 1840s, Santa Fe was a town of 2,000–6,000 inhabitants. El Paso del Norte, established in 1659 on the south side of the river, by 1805 had a population of over 6,000 (shortly afterwards El Paso was no longer counted as part of New Mexico).[14]

At first, the trade with the indigenous peoples was almost exclusively in the hands of Mexican merchants. This control changed after Bent monopolized the traffic. Nevertheless, economic self-interest brought North American and Mexican closer, and by the 1840s, Mexican merchants were sending their children to parochial schools in St. Louis and to business houses (as apprentices).[15]

Before the Santa Fe Trail came about, New Mexicans traded almost exclusively with Chihuahua, whose merchants controlled the commerce between the two provinces. Since its first days as a Spanish colony, New Mexico's and Chihuahua's histories were interwoven; they jointly warred against the Apache, and Indian prisoners of war were often sold as slaves in the slave market of Parral, Chihuahua. The trade in Apaches enriched New Mexican governors such as Luis de Rosas.[16] The growth of trade between the two provinces led to the expansion of the El Paso del Norte area where merchants from Sonora and Chihuahua migrated. After 1826, New Mexicans organized their own caravans to Chihuahua. U.S. economic infiltration set a pattern, as explorers and traders paved the way for the invasion of New Mexico. The route was the old Camino Real, which ran from Chihuahua to Santa Fe, where it was linked to St. Louis via the Santa Fe Trail. This route would fall to Euro-American merchants before the U.S. military entered Santa Fe in 1846.[17]

The opening of the Santa Fe Trail proved disastrous for the self-sufficient northern villages. It strengthened the capitalist class, and it increased the gap between *los ricos* and the poor villagers. By the 1830s, a growing number of New Mexicans worked in mercantile activities such as the sale of livestock, trade with native communities, and mercantile stores. These allowed them to expand their property holdings at the expense of subsistence farmers. Ten years later the Euro-American presence had grown even more, and they began to directly control property in Santa Fe.

The Santa Fe Trail trade increased from $15,000 worth of goods in 1822 to $90,000 four years later to a quarter of a million dollars annually by the early 1830s. In 1846, the Santa Fe Trail carried a million dollars' worth of merchandise. Although North Americans made the major share of the profits, a handful of New Mexicans capitalized handsomely. By 1844, the wealthy New York merchant Edwin Norris and the wealthy German Albert Speyer were doing business directly with New Mexicans.[18]

Anti-American Sentiment

The racism and monopolistic tendencies of Euro-Americans in Texas did not go unnoticed in New Mexico. Many locals felt threatened and resented the governor giving generous grants to the newcomers—prominent among the critics was Fray Antonio José Martínez.[19] In addition, they felt threatened by partnerships between Euro-Americans and influential New Mexicans. Further, they were becoming more wary of the imperial designs of the Texas Republic, which claimed as its western boundary the Rio Grande.

New Mexican angst increased in 1841, as General Hugh McLeod led an expedition of about 300 Texans into New Mexico. Governor Manuel Armijo sounded the alarm; Armijo tricked the Texans into believing he had a large army, bluffing them into surrendering. McLeod claimed he was leading a trading expedition. Conspiracy was rife and New Mexicans blamed Bent and his party for the invasion and imprisoned him in Santa Fe. A mob attacked the house of U.S. consul Manuel Alvárez, who was accused of complicity with the Texans; Alvárez was a close ally of Charles Bent.

Euro-Americans retaliated, and a nasty guerrilla war that had racial overtones followed. During 1842 and 1843, clashes between antagonists became more frequent. New Mexicans accused Bent of contraband, theft, and collusion with the Texans, harboring thieves, and selling firearms to natives, and he was temporarily banished from New Mexico. In 1843, Colonel Jacob Snively raided a New Mexican caravan, shooting 23 Mexicans. That year Padre Antonio José Martínez, a leader in the anti-American party, wrote to Antonio López de Santa Anna, warning him of U.S. encroachments and the construction of forts on the Arkansas and Platte Rivers.[20]

The Euro-American Invasion

In June 1846, Colonel Stephen Watts Kearny led the Army of the West into New Mexico. As Kearny approached New Mexico, he sent the well-known merchant James W. Magoffin to Governor Armijo with an ultimatum. U.S. authorities would not disturb them if they would surrender; if they did not, they would suffer the consequences.[21]

By August Kearny captured Las Vegas, New Mexico, and positioned his troops to attack Santa Fe. Armijo fled south without firing a shot, allowing the Army of the West to enter the capital without resistance. Some sources claim that negotiators bribed Armijo to sell out the province. On August 22, Kearny issued a proclamation to the people of New Mexico, announcing his intention of occupying the province as a permanent possession of the United States. This was the first statement revealing that the real purpose of the war was acquisition of territory. Believing that New Mexican resistance had been broken, Kearny left for California on September 25; in mid-December, Colonel Alexander W. Doniphan was sent south to conquer Chihuahua. He wrote, "A people conquered but yesterday could have no friendly feeling for their conquerors, who have taken possession of their country, changed its laws and appointed new officers, principally foreigners."[22]

The Taos Revolt: The Myth of the Bloodless Conquest

Many elite New Mexicans were unhappy with Mexican rule and sought greater autonomy and opportunities by siding with the Euro-Americans. Yet the harshness of the U.S. occupation was unexpected, driving many influential New Mexicans to conspire to drive the Euro-American troops out of the province; among them were Tomás Ortiz, Colonel Diego Archuleta, Padre Antonio José Martínez, and Reverend Juan Felipe Ortiz, vicar general of the diocese and brother of Tomás. The plan was to ambush U.S. authorities during the Christmas season. Meanwhile, Charles Bent, who had been appointed the governor, uncovered the plot through his spies.[23]

Soon afterward, on January 19, 1847, Pablo Montoya, a Mexican peasant, and Tomasito Romero, a Pueblo Indian, attacked the Euro-Americans, killing Governor Bent and five other important members of the American bloc.[24] Nearly every village in the Rio Arriba area supported the revolt. The rebel army numbered over 1,000 rebels. The role of Padre Martínez is unclear; his brother Pascual allegedly took part in the revolt.[25] However, Padre Martínez apparently attempted to restrain the rebels; a realist, he knew that an unorganized revolt would fail and that the consequences would be disastrous.

U.S. Colonel Sterling Price and his army retaliated and attacked some 4,500 Mexicans and Pueblo Indians. The army slaughtered rebels on the snow-covered ground outside the insurgent capital of Taos. Meanwhile, Rio Abajo elites supported Price. The rebels retreated to the pueblo's church, defending themselves from intense artillery fire. During the brutal attack the U.S. troops killed some 150 Mexicans, firing squads shot down and captured another 25 or 30 prisoners, and other rebels were publicly flogged.

The trial was a farce. According to Hubert Howe Bancroft, "One of the judges was a close friend of the slain governor and the other's son had been murdered by the rebels. The George Bent, the brother of the slain governor, was foreman of the grand jury and one of the jurors a relative of the slain sheriff." One Euro-American eyewitness reported hearing a French juror who did not speak English ask the Euro-American jury foreman what he should do: "Why, hang them, of course; what did you come here for?" The tribunal sentenced 15 rebels to death—1 for high treason.[26] The despotism of Colonel Price's occupation fanned the resentment, and Manuel Cortés, a fugitive of the Taos rebellion, led the guerrilla warfare. The military occupation of New Mexico ended in 1851, although, according to the new governor, James S. Calhoun, "treason is rife."[27]

Incredibly, many New Mexicans invented the myth of the "bloodless conquest of New Mexico"—that is, that New Mexicans welcomed the North American troops as liberators. This myth survives in face of the fact that most of the more than 60,000 people living in New Mexico were not enthusiastic about the U.S. invasion; considerable anti-American feelings existed that were a reaction to Euro-American feelings of racial superiority. New Mexico Professor of Law Laura Gómez writes that these feelings ran so deep that many Euro-American soldiers believed that New Mexicans belonged to a mongrel nation whose women would contaminate Euro-American soldiers upon contact.[28]

Inventing Whiteness

Most of New Mexico's early colonizers were descendants of people recruited from the interior of Mexico and Zacatecas, and they were related to Mexican families in Chihuahua and Sonora. Most did not immigrate to New Mexico directly from Spain. Yet many New Mexicans chose to call themselves *Hispanos*, or Spanish Americans, rather than Mexicans. They rationalized that New Mexicans were descendants of the original settlers, who were Spanish conquistadores, and, according to them, New Mexico was isolated from the rest of the Southwest and Mexico during the colonial era, so New Mexicans remained racially pure and were Europeans, in contrast to the mestizo (half-breed) Mexicans.[29]

New Mexicans were under the illusion that they could distance themselves from the intense racism and hatred toward Mexicans, allowing them to better their economic and, sometimes, their social status by separating themselves from the Mexican label. Most New Mexicans are not descendants of the original colonists who arrived with Oñate in 1598. Over the years, many mixed with the Pueblo Indians and with Mexican natives who settled in the area. New Mexican scholar Nancie González writes that it was not until the twentieth century that New Mexicans denied their Mexican identity.

During the 1910s and 1920s, an influx of Mexican laborers entered New Mexico, converging with white Texans, Oklahomans, and other southerners who settled in the eastern plains. The latter brought their prejudices of color, intensifying discrimination against Mexicans. According to González, some New Mexicans did what was expedient and rationalized to the Euro-Americans, "You don't like Mexicans, and we don't like them either, but we are Spanish-Americans, not Mexicans." By this simple denial of their ethnicity, New Mexicans thought they could escape discrimination and qualify for higher-paying jobs, which in most cases did not happen.

However, the *manitos'* (from *hermanitos*, or "little brothers") state of mind cannot solely be attributed to U.S. racism. New Mexicans had their share of racial prejudices that were deeply rooted in the Spanish conquest and colonization. "Thinking white" was encouraged by the Spanish colonial pecking order (see Chapter 2). Thinking white was a state of mind, which facilitated the exploitation of the castas. Color determined purity and was a sign of prominence and/or insignificance. That is why, between Mexicans and people of color overall, a bleaching-out took place, a phenomenon that encourages individuals to consciously or unconsciously marry "up"—that is, marry someone lighter than they are.[30]

Circumstances made New Mexicans feel like strangers in their own land; consequently many returned to their Mexican homeland. According to Samuel E. Sisneros,

> *Beginning in 1849, more than 150 families from central and southern Texas, a small group from California, close to 4,000 people from Nuevo México, along with approximately seven hundred people from the present El Paso Lower Valley (Socorro, Ysleta and San Elizario), chose to retain their Mexican citizenship and emigrate. They followed the receding and consequently redrawn border dividing México and the United States and crossed over to the Republic of México.[31]*

The Mexican government actively recruited Mexicans to return to the homeland, and, according to a Mexican commissioner, many New Mexicans agreed. Undoubtedly, more would have returned if New Mexican authorities had not placed obstacles in their way, violating the Treaty of Guadalupe Hidalgo.[32] Later in the decade, New Mexican officials retaliated against those who had not surrendered their Mexican citizenship and would not allow them to reverse their decisions, or to hold public office. For instance, in 1855 Miguel A. Otero successfully challenged the election of Father José Manuel Gallegos to the assembly, because he had retained his Mexican citizenship and allegedly favored the Taos Revolt.

This movement was followed by a contentious word battle over the drawing of the border the Treaty of Guadalupe Hidalgo mandated; a joint boundary commission was appointed to draw the boundary between the United States and Mexico. After a bumpy start, John Russell Bartlett and the Mexican commissioners met in El Paso, Texas, to resolve the location of the southern boundary of New Mexico. Several serious discrepancies were found in the official Disturnell Treaty map used by the framers of the Treaty of Guadalupe Hidalgo when they set the boundaries. Bartlett and the Mexican Commissioner General Pedro García Conde reached a compromise in the spring of 1851. Immediately after the compromise, federal, state, and local representatives from New Mexico and the rest of the country claimed that Bartlett had sold them out by giving "their" land to Mexico. The statement angered Mexican authorities in the neighboring Mexican state of Chihuahua who charged that the United States was attempting to goad Mexico into another war in order to seize more territory. The rhetoric got so heated that Mexican troops were put on alert. The dispute was not settled until the United States pressured Mexico into signing the Gadsden Treaty of 1853.[33]

The Transition

According to Rubén Sálaz, in 1846 some 6,000 persons, about 10 percent of New Mexican families, lived on small land claims without titles. An estimated 3,000 persons, or 1 out of every 26 New Mexicans, were small farmers. The overwhelming majority resided on community grants where they owned their private residential and agricultural lands and shared the common lands. Thus, most New Mexicans followed a tradition where water, pasture, and forests were communal. The new order was different: water and open space such as forests and pastures were private property whose value was determined by the marketplace.[34]

Compared with most western states, New Mexico's population was dense. Many New Mexicans favored statehood because it would allow them to vote for the governor and judges. A small percentage, mostly New Mexican elites, favored a territorial form of government because they could circumvent electoral democracy and directly lobby and influence the selection of public officials. The president of the United States would appoint the governor, and the governor would in turn appoint the courts and many territorial officeholders. The president would designate the headland surveyor. Hence, the electoral power of New Mexicans would be limited to voting for the territorial assembly and local offices.

U.S. authorities justified the heavy military presence after the Taos revolt, claiming that there were tensions with the Indians as well as internal discord. Some 10,000 Navajo, 2,000 Utes, and 5,000 Apaches lived in the territory, and increased encroachments by white settlers made them restless. In reality, the military forts enriched local merchants, freighters, cattle owners, and elites and accelerated mercantile capitalism.

During the 1850s the number of horses and mules increased from 13,733 to 21,357; heads of cattle from 32,977 to 88,729; and sheep from 377,271 to 830,116. The California Gold Rush increased demand for beef, wool, and transportation animals. Wagons and mules transported freight, making the cost high; freighters charged between 9 and 10 cents a pound to ship goods to St. Louis or Chihuahua. Trade fairs were still popular throughout the territory. The profits from this trade encouraged the ricos to expand their holdings, putting tremendous stress on the Pueblos and the villagers, as cattle and sheep owners encroached on their land, pushing many villagers out of their river valleys. In the 1860s, settlers from the northern villages moved from the Rio Arriba area to the northwest and from the Chama Valley to the San Juan area. By the 1870s, wealthy and powerful cattlemen expanded their holdings in Rio Arriba, squeezing out the small farmers. The new order reduced small farmers to using sheep as their only medium of exchange.[35]

The Illusion of Inclusion

On June 2, 1851, the Hispano elite controlled the first New Mexican territorial assembly, and the legislature published the proceedings in Spanish and English. Rio Abajo hacendados, land speculators, the Catholic Church hierarchy, and merchants dominated the assembly. In 1850, 25,085 adults could not read or write, with that number increasing to 32,785 a decade later. New Mexico did not address the problem and had only 17 public schools with 33 teachers throughout the territory. Although the territorial legislature mandated public education, it was up to local taxpayers to support the schools. Voters often did not approve the funding. Better-off New Mexicans who could afford an education went to Catholic boarding school. Later in the century, Protestant missionaries offered inexpensive education at mission schools, but the Catholic Church opposed these schools and made deals with legislators to keep control of education. Access to schooling depended not only on personal wealth but on color. Those of Mexican extraction fared worse than their white counterparts, and by 1913 only 7 of 87 students graduating from New Mexico's public schools were of Mexican origin.

Hispano elites cannot be absolved and their performance in the territorial legislature was horrific. According to Sarah Deutsch, "At the time of the Emancipation Proclamation there were some six hundred Indian slaves in the territory. The territorial legislature was not thinking only of Negroes when, in 1859, it passed an act 'for the protection of slave property in the territory.'"[36] Hispano legislators refused to abolish debt-peonage or Native American slavery until Congress did so in 1867. As mentioned, they did not fund public education, favoring a parochial school system, which almost exclusively served the rich. It was not until 1891 that the legislators approved an education bill, and this occurred because Congress was about to pass one. Moreover, statehood was inevitable, and compulsory education was a prerequisite for statehood.

Gringos and los Ricos

By the time of the Civil War (1861–1865), the ricos' alliance with Euro-American elites was sealed. The ricos controlled the New Mexican peasant and villager vote. Through the legislature, they could block policies that did not serve their interests. The arrangement continued until a more aggressive and educated breed of North American entered the territory after the Civil War. As with Texas, political machines dominated the economic and political life of New Mexico. These cabals used their political influence in Washington, D.C., to influence the appointment of the governor and friendly bureaucrats.[37] Aside from their control of the legislature, the ricos controlled municipalities throughout New Mexico. Nevertheless, the ultimate control was concentrated in the hands of the Santa Fe Ring, which manipulated territorial politics through a number of smaller satellite rings operating at the county levels. In the two decades that followed the Civil War, ring members grabbed an estimated 80 percent of the New Mexico land grants. (The U.S. government approved 48 of 212 grants before 1891. The 212 grants were but a fraction of the approximately 1,000 grants that had been granted by the Spanish and Mexican governments. Out of the 8.5 million acres confirmed, the Court of Private Claims reduced that amount to 2 million acres.) The excessive cost of litigation discouraged many Mexican grantees from filing their claims.

The power of the Santa Fe Ring rested in its monopoly of the territorial bureaucracy. Through its Washington connections, it influenced the appointment of the governor, who, in turn, influenced the appointment of judges, surveyors, and other officials. Money and influence help the ring centralize control of the territory. The new policies ignored the protections of the Treaty of Guadalupe Hidalgo by invalidating Spanish and Mexican land titles. At the direction of the ring, colonial bureaucrats confused land laws and titles to create an environment that legitimized the ring's plunder. Lawyers and speculators, through intimidation, bribery, and fraud, wielded enormous power and made huge profits.[38]

The losers were the people. In 1850 there were 1,578 Euro-Americans, and 50,000 by 1900. In 1850 the number of people of Mexican origin was about 55,000, increasing to just over 93,000 by 1900, while the Pueblo people increased from about 5,000 to just over 8,000.[39] The battle was in the "Communities [that] were located on running rivers or streams, often in mountain valleys. The valleys contained the best land for crop cultivation. Each individual family received a 'long-lot' of this agricultural land, near or on the river."[40] Monopolization and privatization of these resources would uproot the families.

How Was It Done?

As mentioned, the Santa Fe Ring took form after the Civil War through an alliance between elite New Mexicans and Euro-Americans. In 1848 private and communal land grants encompassed 15 million square acres. Congress established a surveyor's office with broad powers that put the burden on the grantees to prove ownership. The land could not be sold until titles were confirmed. By 1863 only 25 private and town grants and 17 Pueblo grants had been filed. The ring abused the political process to shift vast amounts of land to privatize the land. New Mexico was a territory, so the president of the United States could appoint a lackey as territorial governor. A small cabal controlled the police—local, state, and federal. Through violence, the ruling class enforced its schemes. The political oligarchy, with the support of the ricos, monopolized control of the legislature and passed laws favoring the cabal. The ring tightened its control through their banks, giving them access to capital. Meanwhile, merchants and bankers charged excessive interest rates, forcing New Mexicans to borrow money at excessive interest rates. They used their land as collateral, and foreclosures accelerated when the Mexican landowners were unable to meet payments.[41]

After the Civil War, the U.S. government subsidized corporate agriculturalists by supplying large quantities of water at government expense. Reclamation projects changed the balance of nature, greatly affecting the Rio Grande by reducing the supply of water in many areas and providing too much water in other places. The people were given no say in where the government would build dams. New Mexican farmers paid for "improvements" through taxes whether they wanted them or not; when they could not pay the increased taxes, their land was foreclosed. Mechanization gave farm corporations an edge in the production of cash crops such as cotton. Small farmers could not compete, because they did not have the capital to mechanize.

Finally, the federal government granted large concessions of land to railroad corporations and to some institutions of higher learning. Conservationists, concerned over industry's rape of timber and recreation land, pressed, at the turn of the century, to create national forests. The conservationists did not allow shepherds to graze their flocks on national forest lands without permits, and these permits over the years went increasingly to the large operators. New Mexicans lost 2 million acres of private land and 1.7 million acres of communal land. Since community and communal holdings were more common than individual grants, and they had less money, they were more vulnerable. More than 80 percent of the grant holders lost their lands. The slowness of litigation fell hardest on small farmers and herders, who did not have the means to survive the process. Historian Deena González writes that within "ten years of the signing of the treaty ending the war, ninety percent of New Mexicans had lost their lands."[42]

The Santa Fe Ring and the Land Grab

As mentioned, money drove the influence of the Santa Fe Ring. In the early stages of the occupation, some Mexicans competed in economic enterprises such as freighting. However, as time went by, access to capital became more crucial, and so did dependence on government contacts. The Santa Fe Ring, comprised mostly of lawyers, used government contacts to make a killing in real-estate deals. Thomas B. Catron, Stephen B. Elkins, and Le Baron Bradford Prince were mostly Republicans; but there was no shortage of Democrats or elite Mexicans. Most officeholders were in one way or another associated with the ring. This included Max Frost, editor of *The New Mexican*, the territory's most influential newspaper.

Catron, the ring's leader, arrived in New Mexico in the late 1860s, eventually becoming U.S. attorney general for the territory. Through litigation, purchases, and fraud, he acquired more than 1 million acres of land. Stephen Elkins, a lawyer and close friend of Catron, arrived in 1863. Eight years later, he was president of the First National Bank of Santa Fe, and represented the ring's interests in Washington. He became a delegate to the U.S. Congress, later serving as President Benjamin Harrison's secretary of war.[43] In 1884, Elkins was chairman of the executive committee of the National Republican Committee. Le Baron Bradford Prince was from New York, where he had engaged in machine politics. Through the influence of powerful friends in Washington, President Arthur offered him the governorship of New Mexico, but he declined and became the chief justice of New Mexico in 1879. Finally, he became the governor of the territory in the 1890s. The cabal accumulated ill-gotten profits by forming joint stock companies and private investment pools. The Santa Fe Ring was complemented by a host of individual speculators and numerous smaller rings who were active in land deals, railroads, mills, farming, small-scale manufacturing, and shipping.[44] The ring's most audacious caper was its takeover of the Maxwell Land Grant: Charles Beaubien and Guadalupe Miranda had received the grant in 1841. Fray Martínez, the leader of the Mexican clergy, objected to the grant because it was, according to Martínez, part of the Taos community grant, and he charged that the grant was being given to the North American clique that was becoming more numerous in New Mexico. Over the next few years, Beaubien, Indians, Mexican tenant farmers, Mexican villages, and Euro-American squatters contested parts of the Maxwell grant. In 1858, Lucien Maxwell, the son-in-law of Beaubien, bought out Miranda's share, as well as his father-in-law's interests in the land grant. Some years later, after the death of his father-in-law, Maxwell purchased other shares, for a total outlay of no more than $50,000. In 1869, Maxwell sold his grant to a British combine, which included members of the Santa Fe Ring, for $1.5 million. After the combine took control of the Maxwell Land Grant, it encountered problems with tenant farmers. Meanwhile, in 1866 gold was discovered on the property, attracting prospectors to the area. The title to the land became even murkier as the federal government claimed part of the grant for a reservation and parkland. Encouraged by these challenges, Mexican and Euro-American squatters occupied the land, believing it would become public domain. If it did, they would be entitled to between 20 and 50 acres of irrigated land. The government had not surveyed the grant; thus, the grant boundaries were in question.

Lucien Maxwell estimated the grant as measuring between 32,000 and 97,424 acres. However, by the time the ring reconfigured it, the grant encompassed 1,714,765 acres. This was despite the fact that the Mexican Colonization Act limited grants of this category to 22 leagues (97,000 acres). One of the consequences was that the altered Maxwell Grant threatened the land titles of residents of Colfax County, who prepared to defend their property. On September 14, 1875, T. J. Tolby, a Methodist minister and a leading opponent of the ring, was murdered. Vigilantes accused Cruz Vega, the Mexican constable of the Cimarron precinct, of the homicide; he denied any involvement but they lynched him anyway. The hanging was racially motivated, and the tensions set the stage for a bloody war between the Maxwell Land Grant Company and the white squatters. A natural alliance would have been between the white squatters and the Mexicanos. But because of the racism of the squatters, it did not happen, and Mexicans remained neutral during the decade of the 1870s.[45]

It was not until the 1880s that more New Mexicans began to contest the ownership of the Maxwell Land Grant. In 1881, when the squatters formed the Squatters Club to raise money for defense, only one New Mexican was a member. Slowly alliances were entered into, and by 1887 the Mexican and Euro-American squatters rode together. Meanwhile, the combine brought legal proceedings against the squatters. M. P. Pels, the company agent, promised cash settlements if they would leave. On July 23, 1888, 75 armed Mexicans and Euro-Americans prevented the sheriff and the company from evicting them. Jacinto Santistevan and his son Julian were among the resistance leaders. The unity was short lived, as divisions arose between the two races. The failure of the white farmers to support Mexican farmers when the company agent evicted them from Vermejo Park angered the Mexicans, who vowed never to help the gringos again.

On February 21, 1891, after the rebels killed a business agent, the company retaliated by raising a 23-man posse to track down the killers. Mexicans burned crops, cut fences, destroyed buildings, and slaughtered cattle. As the spring wore on, armed outbreaks became even more common. In responding to the stiff resistance, the company changed its tactics and began to give Mexicans preferential treatment, hoping to turn U.S. farmers against them. By 1893, litigation took its toll and Santistevan left the area. After this point, many farmers capitulated. A Dutch combine placed the management of the grant into the hands of the Maxwell Land and Railway Company.

Throughout the violence, the Santa Fe group shamelessly manipulated the legal system. The territorial legislature passed laws authorizing the courts to partition grants if even the smallest owner of the property requested a partition. This meant that the ring could buy out a minority holder and force the sale of the entire grant. The territorial legislature then passed a law in January 1876 that annexed Colfax County to Taos County. This development was significant since the Taos judges were controlled by the ring and, hence, they sided with the ring's interests in dispossessing small farmers. Because the ring controlled the appointment of the governor, the governor refused to intervene in the ring's wars or fraudulent deals. The appointment of John T. Elkins, brother of Stephen B. Elkins, to survey the Maxwell Grant put the final nail in the coffin. The Maxwell holdings included millions of acres in southern Colorado and northern New Mexico.[46]

What the land grabbers and their brokers did not steal, the state and federal governments did. Today, the federal government owns 34.9 percent of the land in New Mexico. The state government owns 12 percent, while federal Indian reservations own 6.8 percent. Thus the state and federal governments together own 53.7 percent of New Mexico, with the U.S. Forest Service controlling one-third of the state's land.[47] It is important to note that government control of public lands did not ensure public use or the public good. Special interests that had greater access to government and its resources consequently were able to monopolize New Mexico's wealth.

The Lincoln County War

World events affected happenings in New Mexico. For instance, in the 1870s the increased demand for beef and mutton in the United Kingdom and in the eastern United States led to the growth of the beef industry and intensified competition for the open range in New Mexico, leading to range wars and land speculation. The land grabs greatly affected the small subsistence farmer and sheepherder.

In the 1870s, the arrival of large numbers of Euro-Americans seeking to make a killing by running cattle on the open rangeland in places like Lincoln County pushed Mexicans off the land. The cowboys clashed with the Mexicans, who herded sheep on the range, and invented the fiction that sheep and cattle could not graze on the same land. Since the early 1870s, ring member Laurence Gustave Murphy had enjoyed a near-monopoly, supplying the government with beef for forts and reservations, and shutting out other cattlemen from the county. John H. Chisum, owner of the largest herds in the territory, challenged Murphy with the support of the local Mexican population, bringing on the Lincoln County War.[48]

The Murphy clan hired outlaws as rustlers to steal cattle for their beef-supply enterprise. Many Texans, renowned for their hatred of Mexicans, joined the Murphy gang. By January 27, 1874, the Sante Fe *New Mexican* editorialized that Lincoln County had exploded into an "unfortunate war between the Texans and the Mexicans."[49] The newspaper intentionally distracted the public's attention by focusing on racial conflicts instead of the economic causes of the conflict. The war broke down along racial and political lines. The Murphy group controlled Republican Party politics, while Chisum represented the Democrats.

Juan Patrón was the Mexican leader in Lincoln. North American outlaws had killed his father. Born in 1855 in La Placita, he attended parochial schools in New Mexico, eventually graduating from the University of Notre Dame in Indiana. Friends described him as honest, studious, and industrious. In 1878, as a delegate to the territorial House of Representatives, he was elected speaker by the deputies. He also served without pay as Lincoln's sole schoolteacher.

The Lincoln County War broke out in the spring of 1877 when Englishman John H. Tunstall opened a mercantile store that competed with the Murphy establishment. Alexander McSween, a lawyer, and John Chisum were Tunstall's principal allies. The Chisum–Tunstall group also opened a bank that competed with the First National Bank, controlled by Stephen Elkins and Catron. Most Mexicans joined Juan Patrón in backing the Tunstall group, and there were frequent shootouts. The ring brought in the Jesse Evans gang to do its dirty work, launching a reign of terror. Finally, the ring murdered Tunstall, whereupon the Englishman's supporters, among them the notorious William Bonnie, alias Billy the Kid, sought revenge. The ring attacked Patrón in the *New Mexican*, charging that he was leader of the county's lawless Mexican element. The truth be told, it was the ring that had hired ruthless gunslingers, spreading a reign of terror and committing multiple atrocities.[50]

Governor Samuel B. Axtell refused to intervene, but the murders of Reverend Tolby in Colfax and of Tunstall, a British subject, attracted national and international attention. On September 4, 1878, over the protests of Catron, Elkins, and other prominent ring members, U.S. President Rutherford B. Hayes appointed General Lew Wallace governor. Hayes gave Wallace a mandate to clean up the mess in Lincoln County. Upon arriving in New Mexico, Wallace formed a local militia, led by Juan Patrón, and restored peace in 1879.

Because of harassment, Patrón moved to Puerto de Luna, several hundred miles away from Lincoln County. While having a drink in a saloon with a friend, Patron was murdered by a cowboy named Mitch Maney. Although Maney was a penniless cowboy, one of the most high-powered legal firms in the territory represented him. Moreover, his prosecutor was none other than Thomas Catron. The result was a hung jury, and Maney was never retried.

Mexican shepherds and Texas cowboys continued to fight over land and water, but by the 1880s, the cattle raisers had eliminated the Mexican as a competitor. During the decade, the conflict degenerated into a race war. With railroads linking Lincoln County to national and international markets, time favored the Euro-Americans. During the same period, railroads made wool more accessible to the world market; soon nearly 3 million head of sheep roamed the territory, most belonging to Euro-Americans.[51]

Socialization

Historian Deena González writes, "Conquest and colonization impoverished most of the residents of Santa Fe and perhaps much of the New Mexican north. It disempowered women, who had previously exercised certain rights guaranteed by Spanish law. And it made most Spanish-Mexicans dependent on wages earned in jobs controlled by Euro-Americans."[52] The new merchant capitalists displayed racial and cultural prejudices toward the resident population throughout the territory—more evident in places like Santa Fe because of the large numbers of Euro-Americans. The first thing they noticed was the New Mexican woman's dark skin. One soldier wrote, "Instead of the black-eyed Spanish women, we found ourselves amongst a swarthy, copper-colored, half-Indian race."[53] Professor González reminds us that 75 percent of the female adult population (over the age of 15) labored as domestics, laundresses, or seamstresses in 1860. This number increased during the American "liberation." The already marginalized extended family networks, held together by rich and poor women alike, were destroyed. However, there was a difference between rich and poor, with women with powerful family ties being able to better negotiate their space.

Intermarriage took place between Euro-Americans and New Mexican elites. In the overall scheme, however, the number was relatively small if one considers there were only 239 Euro-Americans in Santa Fe compared with 4,000 New Mexicans.[54] As in Texas, intermarriage decreased with the passage of time and the arrival of white women.

The Americanization of the Catholic Church

The Catholic Church played a perplexing role, splitting into a Mexican and a Euro-American Catholic church. The leader of the Mexican clergy was Father Antonio José Martínez, known as "the priest of Taos." Born in Abiquiú in Rio Arriba County on January 7, 1793, Martínez had married, but his wife and daughter died and he then became a priest. In 1824, Martínez was pastor of parish in Taos, where after two years he established a seminary. Through his graduates, Martínez's ideas spread throughout New Mexico. From 1830 to 1836, Martínez served in the New Mexico's departmental assembly, and in 1835, he published a newspaper called *El Crepúsculo* (*The Dawn*). Martínez frequently criticized the Church for allowing priests to charge excessive fees. He also opposed the granting of large land grants, insisting that the land should go to the people. Under Euro-American rule he served in the legislature from 1851 to 1853.

In 1851, a new vicar general, Fray J. B. Lamy, arrived in New Mexico. French by birth, Lamy had worked in the Baltimore diocese and in the mid-1850s became a bishop. Lamy's partisans claim that Lamy revitalized religion in New Mexico by founding schools, building churches, and increasing the number of priests in his diocese from 10 to 37. Through his alliance with government officials, Lamy kept control of education. His critics allege that Lamy did this on the back of the poor, and they condemn him for his failure to speak out against the injustices suffered by the people.

Lamy did not respect the Mexican clergy. A product of post-revolutionary France, he looked upon liberalism as anti-Catholic. Lamy began almost immediately to pattern New Mexican churches after French models based on orthodoxy. The controversy over the separation of Church and state profoundly influenced him as did the debate over the infallibility of the Pope. To strengthen the New Mexican Church and insulate it from the challenge of the Protestant sects that by 1890 were 5 percent of the population, Lamy taxed the poor and collected church fees for baptism, marriage, and other rites, which is a criticism that could be directed at the institution itself. There also appears to be some sentiment that Mexican priests had been more lenient in their collection.[55]

Lamy purged the Holy Brotherhood of Penitentes, an association popular among the poor of northern New Mexico. (Indeed, confraternities were a part of the culture of the Spanish and then Mexican churches.) Descended from the Third Order of St. Francis of Assisi, it practiced public flagellation and, during Holy Week, imitated the ordeals of Christ. It was a secret society, to which prominent leaders such as Antonio José Martínez belonged. Establishment Mexicans like Miguel A. Otero disdained the Brotherhood, seeing it as backward and ignorant. Lamy and his successors persecuted members, denying them the sacraments.[56]

Soon after Lamy's arrival, a power struggle broke out between him and the Mexican clergy, many of whom were Martínez's former students. Critics attacked Martínez and his followers for not being celibate (which may or may not have been true). Defenders say that the real reason was the involvement of the Mexican clergy in temporal matters, especially their role as advocates for the people. Martínez avoided an open rift with Lamy, keeping quiet even when Lamy excommunicated Martínez's close friends. When Lamy sent a letter to all the parishes insisting that priests collect tithes and first fruits and instructing them to withhold the sacraments from those who did not comply, Martínez rebelled. Lamy then excommunicated Martínez.

Lamy set the pattern for church–state cooperation and the church's almost unconditional support of the state. Writing in his later years, Lamy wrote, "Our Mexican population has quite a sad future. Very few of them will be able to follow modern progress. They cannot be compared to the Americans in the way of intellectual liveliness, ordinary skills, and industry; they will thus be scorned and considered an inferior race."[57]

The New Mexican Diaspora

The Civil War brought an increased demand for cattle that further commercialized the economy. Within 25 years newcomers overcrowded New Mexico with the arrival of the railroad bringing big capital: railroads, lumber mills, coal mines, and commercial agriculture and stock enterprises. Wage-paying jobs momentarily gave Mexican males opportunity, but for many it changed their relationship to the land.

In most villages, each settler owned a small plot of lot of land, a house, and some farmland. Most holdings in Rio Arriba allowed villagers to use pastures and the forests in common. But in the new economy men became seasonal migrants or they migrated to the mines of southern Colorado. Meanwhile, women sometimes plowed, harrowed, hoed, harvested, and threshed. Women also herded and sheared sheep collectively. Subsistence farming was further marginalized, and seasonal wage labor became a necessity for families to survive.[58]

The merchants of northern New Mexico and southern Colorado were not as powerful as the hacendados of Rio Abajo or the cattlemen on the territorial ranges—nevertheless, they were wealthy. As time went by, more families could not survive solely on what they grew or raised. The villages became overcrowded, the land overused, and the pastures depleted. In Rio Arriba County, sheepmen had grazed 21 sheep per square mile; by 1900, this number increased to almost 120.[59]

"El Agua Es la Vida"

New Mexico's "acequia culture" is not unique—it is a product of the Spanish conquest, and as Denise Holladay Damico points out, part of the Spanish project of colonization in New Spain's far northern frontier. The acequia was often the only local form of government that villagers had daily contact with. This was the same whether the villagers lived in northern New Mexico, Chihuahua, or Sonora. Through Spanish custom they located communities along running rivers or streams, as well as in mountain valleys.

After plots were allocated the villagers dug the acequia to irrigate their agricultural lots. An intensification of the market economy began in the late eighteenth century. Forces such as mining provided markets. In the nineteenth century, the opening of the Santa Fe Trail in 1821 and the Treaty of Guadalupe Hidalgo in 1848 led to increased commercialization. In New Mexico the latter two events were a boon to locations such as Taos, resulting in competition for land that caused tensions between locals and incoming Euro-Americans. The tension drew a line under the interconnections between land and water disputes.

This same process was occurring in Chihuahua where most acequias had been dug in the nineteenth century. Fighting over water took various forms. Disputants often physically diverted the water into their ditch, or sabotaged their foe's canal. They often sued in order to resolve water conflicts. Frequently commercial farmers encroached on mission and Indian lands or bought out other villagers. The land was almost worthless without water and irrigated land had a much higher value. Disputes grew ugly during drought periods or when an upriver community diverted too much water. Litigation was expensive in New Mexico and Chihuahua, placing added burdens on the litigants, who were generally cash strapped. Meanwhile, the land grant grabs threatened the Pueblos and the villagers. In the late nineteenth century in northern Mexico and New Mexico, the arrival of the railroad heightened tensions as it added pressure to privatize land and water.

The railroad increased agricultural production and encroachment. In the 1880s, railroad tracks from Colorado were built south to Las Vegas and then Albuquerque. On November 26, 1884, the Atlantic and Pacific Railroad ran tracks through Acoma Pueblo, taking ownership of the land along those tracks. The corporation brought its lawyers along. In 1887 a new state law allowed the incorporation of for-profit companies privatizing the sale of water. The law explicitly linked the supplying of water and "colonization" and "improvement" of lands. Water was thus brought in via pipeline or canal. The railroads played an active role. In comparing documents from New Mexico, Chihuahua, and Sonora, the parallels are inescapable.[60]

The Marketplace

In the new market economy, the land base was inadequate to support the needs of the villagers; by the turn of the century, at least 50 percent of them had partido contracts. "The seasonal nature of agricultural, livestock, and even wage income in the area resulted in the extension of so much credit that some 70 to 80 percent of the trade was of this nature," forcing the small merchant out of the marketplace. In addition, New Mexicans were increasingly shut out of the grazing land, because either they could not afford grazing permits or they did not have the political connections to obtain them.

Women worked outside the home as midwives, took in boarders, and often contributed to the survival of the family through family gardens. "As the loss of land led to a decline in livestock, the garden grew in significance." Often the family sold the women's surplus *chili* for cash or goat's milk. (Chili was one of the principal cash crops.) "Picking the peppers from the plant, sorting, and stringing them supplied many of the women and some of the men living on small farms with a supplemental income."[61] The gardens freed the family from buying outside goods. However, the transformation changed the sphere of so-called women's work. The women had been involved in plastering their homes for years, but by the twentieth century, many were doing this work for other villagers. Women also made money by weaving and mattress making.[62]

New Mexico in Colorado

By 1881 cattle and sheep replaced the buffalo herds on Colorado's plains, and in that decade, steel was produced in Pueblo. The growth of coal mining in southern Colorado literally changed the landscape of Mexican pueblos there. Their plazas greatly resembled those in northern New Mexico in their social and economic function, but mining camps surrounded the Colorado villages. While over 11,000 New Mexicans migrated to southern Colorado in the first decade of the 1900s, thousands of working-class Europeans also moved to southern Colorado during this period, making the Mexicans a minority. Discrimination was rampant; for instance, in 1880, suffragist Susan B. Anthony blamed the failure of a tour in Colorado on the "Mexican greasers." Research on the Western Federation of Miners and its magazine, from its inception to about 1920, clearly shows the marginalization of Mexican miners by organizers and the rank and file.

In sum, depressions and droughts such as those that occurred in the early 1890s forced many marginal ranchers to migrate to Colorado in search of wage work. Migrancy affected the entire family—women, men, and children all suffered. However, for many northern New Mexicans, migrancy was a way of life where they were able to earn enough money to help their families subsist and then return home to plant or harvest their crops.[63]

In the next decade, the Dingley Tariff of 1897 intensified sugar beet production in northern Colorado, attracting New Mexican migrant farm labor. Again, it put additional burdens on the women and the family; since entire families worked as migrants, family farm plots became neglected. By the end of the century, whole villages worked outside the village as farm laborers, shepherds, or railroad workers. These workers and their families had to adjust to the new changes, along with discrimination on the job in form of wages.

The Resistance

San Miguel County is in northern New Mexico, a mountainous land with the town of Las Vegas at its center. The tract of land that came to be known as the Las Vegas Grant contained 500,000 acres of fine timber, agricultural, and grazing lands, the meadows in the area of Las Vegas being especially rich.

As early as 1821, the Spanish crown awarded grants to portions of this region to individuals; however, because of indigenous attacks, most of the grantees failed to settle on their lands. Yet by 1841, 131 families lived around Las Vegas. "On June 21, 1860, Congress confirmed 496,446 acres as belonging to the town of Las Vegas."[64] A large sector of the population of Las Vegas subsisted by grazing sheep and farming. According to Mexican law and traditions, the people held the land in common and it could not be sold.

After the Civil War, the arrival of Euro-Americans threatened this way of life. They came with a tradition of squatting on public domain land with little knowledge or respect for village lands or the open range. In the 1880s, merchants and farmers with capital began to buy tracts from New Mexicans even though, according to Mexican law, the settlers, as users of the land, did not have the right to sell the land if such a sale conflicted with communal interests.

At every level, Euro-Americans dominated the economy. By 1875 nearly all the businesses were owned by Euro-Americans. The arrival of the railroad concentrated wealth and within five years 84 percent of the merchants were Euro-American. Women of all colors were peripheral; Mexican women worked as waitresses and at menial jobs. The Euro-Americans of both sexes saw the Mexican women as backward, superstitious, morally lax, and poor due to their Catholic faith and sought to Americanize them. The town of Las Vegas looked like a brickyard to one Euro-American wife—composed of "mud-hovels" to another.[65]

Barbed Wire, Irrigation, and the Railroad

Land grabbers moved onto the land and fenced their claims, enclosing as many as 10,000 acres. The fencing denied Mexicans access to timber, water, and grazing lands. Mexicans resented the enclosure, and in 1887 Euro-Americans sued the villagers, in *Milhiser v. Padilla*, to test ownership. The court found that "the Las

Vegas Grant was a community grant and that the plaintiffs had no case. . . . However, the plaintiffs muted the finding by dropping their case on November 25, 1889, thus not allowing the judgment to be finalized." The favorable court decision did nothing to slow down fencing and other encroachments. Territorial authorities encouraged the encroachments by looking the other way as the rapidly increasing white population intensified the struggle for resources.[66]

The Village People Defend Their Land

The 1880s saw increased opposition to land encroachments and the enclosure movement. Mexicans suffered racially motivated lynching. In 1882, near Bloomfield, in the northeastern part of the territory, a mob lynched Sheriff Guadalupe Archuleta because he shot and killed a white man in the line of duty. That same year in Lincoln County a mob broke into the jail and kidnapped a Mexican accused of stealing horses; he was never found. A mob broke into a jail in northern New Mexico at Los Lunas and hanged Mexicans accused of murdering a saloon keeper.[67] The railroad intensified tensions, as private contractors stripped the timber from the mountainsides. Competition with North American workers strained an already bad economic situation; and inequalities in the pay gap between Euro-American and Mexican workers widened. By the middle of the decade, Mexicans organized the Association of the Brotherhood for the Protection of the Rights and Privileges of the People of New Mexico, whose stated purpose was to liberate New Mexico from corrupt politicians and monopolies—symbolized by the railroads and fences. A leading figure in the struggle against the encroachers, Juan José Herrera, formed *Las Gorras Blancas* (the White Caps) around 1887. Herrera served as a district organizer for the Knights of Labor, a national trade union founded in 1869 by garment workers. In response to the railroads and the inequality they produced, workers organized the Knights in San Miguel County in 1884; within three years, it had three assemblies in the city of Las Vegas, New Mexico. In 1887 the union formed the Las Vegas Grant Association to give legal aid to the townspeople so that they could defend themselves against land speculators.[68]

On November 1, 1889, "[a]rmed with rifles and pistols, draped in long black coats and slickers, their faces hidden behind white masks," 66 Mexican horsemen rode into Las Vegas. They converged on the jail, asking for Sheriff Lorenzo López, who represented conservatives within the town, and then rode on to the home of Miguel Salazar, the prosecuting attorney. The presence of the night riders climaxed a year of fence cutting, but this time they damaged no property. Authorities blamed "criminal" behavior on Las Gorras Blancas and indicted several Mexicans. On November 25, county officials brought 26 indictments against 47 suspects, among who were Juan José and Pablo Herrera.

The White Caps had public support and claimed a membership of 1,500. On December 16, the townspeople marched through the city to demand the release of suspected White Caps. On March 11, 1890, Las Gorras toured east Las Vegas, distributing copies of their platform, which in part read,

> Nuestra Plataforma
> *Our purpose is to protect the rights and interests of the people in general and especially those of the helpless classes.*
> *We want the Las Vegas Grant settled to the benefit of all concerned, and this we hold is the entire community within the Grant.*
> *We want no "land grabbers" or obstructionists of any sort to interfere. We will watch them.*
> *We are not down on lawyers as a class, but the usual knavery and unfair treatment of the people must be stopped.*
> *Our judiciary hereafter must understand that we will sustain it only when "justice" is its watchword.*[69]

Many Euro-Americans and establishment Mexicans condemned the platform as anti-American and radical. Miguel A. Otero described the White Caps as "a criminal organization."[70] *The Optic*, the town newspaper, portrayed them as a destructive influence in the community. Nevertheless, by 1890, the White Cap raids had spread to Santa Fe County.

Las Gorras continued cutting fences and destroying property; they attacked the railroad because of the high-handed manner in which it appropriated land for rights-of-way. Meanwhile, the government stepped up operations against the fence cutters. Governor Le Baron Prince threatened to send troops into the area if local authorities did not stop Las Gorras. He proposed that one or two companies of federal troops be stationed in San Miguel to protect railroad property and that detectives be hired to infiltrate Las Gorras. He was not able to carry out his plans because the secretary of the interior would not cooperate. When Prince finally visited Las Vegas, he learned, to his dismay that four-fifths of those citizens whom he met sympathized with Las Gorras.

Meanwhile, Terence Powderly, president of the Knights of Labor, became concerned about Las Gorras' militancy and the group's link to the union through the Herreras. Even local members worried about the infiltration of Las Gorras and "the large number of 'Mexican people' of the lower classes who were being admitted to their union."[71] The Knights also resented the night riders' meddling in labor politics—on April 3, 1890, for instance, Las Gorras posted wage rates in which they told the workers what to demand for cutting and hauling railroad ties. The previous month, 300 armed men had destroyed approximately 9,000 ties belonging to the Santa Fe Railway. Las Gorras harassed workers who did not support the rate standard. Ultimately, however, the railroad undercut Las Gorras by announcing that it would no longer purchase ties in San Miguel County. This reprisal cost the county $100,000 annually, worsening unemployment. Hungry workers blamed Las Gorras instead of the railroad. Powderly and the Knights' leadership disavowed any connection with White Cap leader Juan José Herrera.

The Herreras' involvement in the People's Party also annoyed the national Knights' leadership. The People's Party challenged the boss-ridden Republicans and attracted many disillusioned members of both parties. By 1890, many party loyalists boasted that most San Miguel voters supported their organization. The Herreras represented the militants, and Félix Martínez and Nestor Montoya, who published *La Voz del Pueblo*, led the moderates. Although not condoning fence cutting, *La Voz* did explain the reasons for it. When the party nominated Pablo Herrera for the territorial House of Representatives, the moderates charged that the Herreras were extremists.[72] However, mob violence was most often perpetuated by white vigilantes and continued into 1928 when a mob broke into a hospital and hanged Rafael Benavides in Farmington, New Mexico.

More Illusions of Inclusion

Political participation gives the illusion that change is possible through the ballot box. This illusion discouraged direct action, and the shift from more assertive tactics like fence cutting took place. Initially, the People's Party in 1890 swept the county elections, and the party's candidates won four seats in the Assembly. Yet, it was one thing to win elections, but another to pass reform legislation to regulate railroad rates or to protect the Las Vegas grant. Soon after his election, Assemblyman Pablo Herrera announced his disillusionment. Speaking before the legislature in February 1891, he said,

> *Gentlemen . . . I have served several years' time in the penitentiary but only sixty days in the legislature . . . I have watched the proceedings here carefully. I would like to say that the time I spent in the penitentiary was more enjoyable than the time I spent here. There is more honesty in . . . prison than . . . [in] the legislature. I would prefer another term in prison than another election in the house.*[73]

Pablo Herrera returned to San Miguel and attempted to revive Las Gorras Blancas. Meanwhile, Knights of Labor expelled him. Moderates isolated him and he became a fugitive after killing a man in Las Vegas. Felipe López, a deputy sheriff, eventually killed Herrera.

Meanwhile, Juan José Herrera was elected probate judge. He was supported by the poor, who distrusted the conservative and moderate factions, seeing them as *políticos*. During 1889 and 1890, under the leadership of Juan José, the White Caps effectively stemmed land speculation; however, after this point, like Pablo Herrera, Juan José put his energies into the People's Party, struggling to keep it from ripping itself apart. Cutting fences gave way to long-drawn-out litigation that often weakened the people's initial enthusiasm and hope. Government infiltration and provocateuring also took its toll. Pinkerton agent Charles A. Stiringo, the infamous Spanish-speaking spy, infiltrated the party ranks. Stiringo regularly reported on the activities of the Herreras. For these and other reasons, by 1896, the party faded.

By this time, Mexican representation in the legislature was limited to 26 families who served the interests of only 5 percent of Mexican Americans. Collusion served the ricos well, and their flocks went undertaxed while the poor stockowners paid their full share. This inequity contributed to alienation between ricos and *pobres*—nationalism went only so far.

In 1894, the United States Court of Private Land Claims ruled that the San Miguel claim was a community grant, but the court limited its decision to house lots and garden plots, excluding common pasturage. Although *los hombres pobres* continued to cut fences as late as 1926 (and later in other parts of New Mexico), they failed to stop the influx of Euro-Americans and capital that symbolized the changes taking place.[74]

The End of the Frontier

The Santa Fe Ring's heyday, years of government corruption, warfare, and political favoritism, lasted from 1865 to 1885. With the death of the Santa Fe Ring, machine politics did not end, however; the machine simply became more professional, with merchant capitalists becoming bankers and investing their profits in mining, cattle, and land. The arrival of the Atchison, Topeka & Santa Fe Railway in 1879 made possible the changes that ended New Mexico's isolation. Within two years, this railroad joined the Southern Pacific at Deming, New Mexico, to give the territory its first transcontinental link.

The Growth of Industrial Mining

Mining exploration took place in southwest New Mexico and eastern Arizona beginning in the 1870s. However, mining development was limited, since the ore had to be freighted out by mule. At this stage, merchant capitalists were financing mining, and its development attracted commercial farms to supply the new mining camps, and to establish a string of settlements in the Mesilla Valley and elsewhere in New Mexico. Former villages attracted a large army of migrant workers from Mexico. Southern New Mexico was at the crossroads of this activity, with miners from Chihuahua and points south also passing through the Mesilla Corridor en route to the mines of Arizona and the sugar beet fields and mines of Colorado. Towns such as Las Cruces, Silver City, and Gallup grew as the result of the mixture of mines and railroad links.

By the 1880s, these enterprises would expand beyond the capabilities of the merchant capitalists. Eastern and foreign investors who committed large amounts of capital to build railroad spurs and exploit the area's resources replaced them. A more capital-intense society replaced the monopoly of the merchants and their network of village stores, a "money-credit economy [that] forced Hispano farmers into increased dependency on the partido and on land for grazing the flocks." Also, the reduction of the nomadic tribes and the dispatch of Comanches to reservations further depressed the state of the subsistence farmer by eliminating a source of trade.[75]

Changes in Society

The territory's population jumped from 119,000 in 1880 to 195,000 in 1900. Property values rose from $41 million in the 1880s to $231 million by the start of the 1890s. In the decade of the 1880s, the number of sheep grew from 347,000 to over 1.5 million. By 1890, 210,000 head of cattle were raised in New Mexico, compared with 14,000 in 1870. The railroad made possible the mass marketing of the territory's resources. In this whirl of change, the influence of the Santa Fe Ring lessened as many young merchants and lawyers resented the monopoly and privileges of ring members. Hence, they challenged its power. At issue were the machine's control of the Mexican vote and the manipulation of elections. Yet, the ring's decline did not end violence, which flourished into the 1890s. Modernization turned many subsistence farmers into wage earners—a large number of whom worked on the railroads, in the mines, and on commercial farms. Industrialization promoted "urbanism, capital-intensive production, and a mass labor force of individual wage earners that rapidly overwhelmed local society, no matter how collectivized."[76]

During these years, there was a tightening of social and political controls. Although warfare still raged on the Maxwell Land Grant and in San Miguel County in the 1890s, by 1896 only Stonewall County remained subject to open rebellion. Improved transportation ended isolation and eased the quick deployment of various law enforcement agencies. For example, the governor's control of the militia helped frustrate the development of a militant trade union movement in the territory.

Meanwhile, New Mexicans organized their own *mutualistas*—mutual aid societies—in Las Vegas, Santa Fe, Española, Albuquerque, Roswell, and Las Cruces. Between 1885 and 1912, New Mexican railroad track workers founded eight branches of the Colorado *La Sociedad Protección Mutua de Trabajadores Unidos*. Like other mutualistas it developed insurance programs, but it was also used to mobilize Mexicans against the growing incidence of discrimination.[77] After the turn of the century, the *Alianza Hispano Americana* organized chapters throughout the territory.

Federal Encroachment

After the turn of the century, the federal government further stimulated large farming operations by the construction of dams. Small farmers who had been hanging on by their fingernails could not compete with large commercial farmers. And, even though agribusinesses represented a small portion of the population, they controlled more than half the territory's grazing land.[78] The 1900s also brought another wave of encroachers. The U.S. Congress, concerned that Mexicans owned most of the small independent farms, refused to admit New Mexico to statehood in 1903. This snub encouraged new schemes to dislodge the remaining villagers' access to land. Agribusiness wanted ownership of land held by the federal and territorial governments—that is, land in the public domain. Because they knew that conservationists would oppose the sale of such lands, the agribusinesses withdrew their opposition to homesteading under the guise that it would attract more North Americans. The intent was to give homesteaders access to the public lands, knowing that the lack of water would make survival impossible for them; in fact, large agribusiness interests already owned most of the land irrigated by federal water projects. When the homesteaders failed, the monopolists purchased their land.

In all, the federal government distributed 30 million acres to homesteaders—7 million in 1909 alone. The system affected New Mexican subsistence farmers, who had grazed small flocks of sheep on government land to supplement their farming. To survive, many New Mexicans had to run sheep on shares for larger companies; others had to look for day work; others migrated. These changes modified the gender division of labor, and women assumed additional responsibilities, irrigating their holdings and caring for the animals, while their husbands traveled to look for work at the mines, at the railroads, and in the cities.

Until the 1930s, various forms of machine politics and the Catholic Church mediated conflicts between North Americans and Mexicans. Appointments of "safe" Mexicans such as Miguel Otero as territorial governor in 1897 proved meaningless to the situation of Mexicanos, since he merely strengthened his own political machine. During Otero's administration, the spoils system sank to lower depths.[79]

Conclusion: The Decline of a Way of Life

The blatant opportunism of "Spanish American" brokers delayed the statehood of New Mexico. For them, statehood represented the end of their power as local bosses. According to them, statehood "meant Anglo-American rule, taxes, public schools, anti-Church policies, and the acquisition of their remaining lands."[80] The "Spanish American" elites also strongly opposed public education, rationalizing their opposition on religious grounds. They believed *Educar un muchacho es perder un buen pastor*—"To educate a boy is to lose a good shepherd"—and statehood would mean paying taxes to educate the poor. In terms of what this meant to the average villager in New Mexico, out of 109,505 inhabitants, 57,156 did not know how to read or write by the end of the territorial period and the overwhelming majority of these illiterate were Mexican. Of 44,000 children, only 12,000 Mexican youngsters attended schools.

The debate over statehood also raised the race issue. At the Constitutional Convention, Mexican-born Octaviano A. Larrazolo raised the issue of equality of Mexicans. Although some North Americans objected to using the race card, a coalition of Mexicans and Euro-Americans passed a measure making certain that Mexicans could vote, hold office, and could not be denied the right to sit on a jury because of "religion, race, language or Spanish languages"—giving the illusion of equality. However, the race question was far from resolved. New Mexico, despite the participation of Spanish American politicos in the system, continued to be one of the poorest states in the United States.[81]

Notes

1. Historical Maps of New Mexico, http://alabamamaps.ua .edu/historicalmaps/us_states/newmexico/index.html. Perry-Castañeda Library Map Collection: New Mexico Maps, University of Texas Austin, http://www.lib.utexas.edu/maps/ new_mexico.html. David J. Weber, *The Mexican Frontier, 1821–1846: The American Southwest under Mexico* (Albuquerque: University of New Mexico Press, 1982), 226–28.

2. Ralph Emerson, *The Leading Facts of New Mexican History*, Vol. I (Horn and Wallace, 1911), FN506, 474.

3. Robert Hixson Julyan, *The Place Names of New Mexico*, revised ed. (Albuquerque: University of New Mexico Press, 1996), 292. Raymond Ortiz and Lauren Reichelt, "The History of Rio Arriba," http://www.rio-arriba.org/places_to_see,_things_to_ do/local_history/index.html. Philip Colee, "Rio Abajo Population Movements: 1670–1750," *JSTOR:Ethnohistory*, 18, no. 4 (Autumn 1974): 353–60.

4. Luis Aboites, *Breve historia de Chihuahua* (México, D.F.: Fondo De Cultura Económica, 1994), 56–57. William B. Griffen, *Apaches at War and Peace: The Janos Presidio, 1750–1858* (Norman: University of Oklahoma Press, 1988), viii–ix, 11.

5. Donald R. Lavash, *A Journey Through New Mexico History* (Albuquerque, NM: Sunstone Press, Updated and Revised, 2006), 111. Weber, *Spanish Frontier*, 148–49. Luis Aboites, *Breve historia de Chihuahua* (México, D.F.: Fondo De Cultura Económica, 1994): 56–57.

6. Phillip B. Gonzales, "Struggle for Survival: The Hispanic Land Grants of New Mexico, 1848–2001," *Agricultural History* 77, no. 2 (Spring 2003): 296–97. Deena J. González, *Refusing the Favor: The Spanish-Mexican Women of Santa Fe, 1820–1880* (New York: Oxford University Press, 2001). Oakah L. Jones, *Los Paisanos: Spanish Settlers on the Northern Frontier of New Spain* (Norman: University of Oklahoma Press, 1996). Max L. Moorhead, *New Mexico's Royal Road: Trade and Travel on the Chihuahua Trail* (Norman: University of Oklahoma Press, 1995), 7, 40. "The Concept of Common Lands Defines Community Land Grants," U.S. Government Accountability Office, http://www.gao.gov/ guadalupe/commland.htm: "Land grant documents contain no direct reference to 'community land grants' nor do

Spanish and Mexican laws define or use this term. Scholars, land grant literature, and popular terminology use the phrase 'community land grants' to denote land grants that set aside common lands for the use of the entire community . . . Under Spanish and Mexican law, common lands set aside as part of an original grant belonged to the entire community and could not be sold." Tom Sharpe, "New Book Explores Spanish Conquest Brutality," *The New Mexican*, March 11, 2010, http://www.santafenewmexican.com/LocalNews/New-book-explores-Spanish-conquest-brutality#.UIrNEYbs9nU.

7. Denise Holladay Damico, "'El Agua Es La Vida' (Water Is Life): Water Conflict and Conquest in Nineteenth Century New Mexico" (PhD dissertation, Brandeis University, 2008), 8. Tracy Brown, "Tradition and Change in Eighteenth-Century Pueblo Indian Communities," *Journal of the Southwest* 46, no. 3 (Autumn 2004): 463–500.

8. Weber, *The Mexican Frontier, 1821–1846*, 102, 126, 130, 135–37. Richard L. Nostrand, *The Hispano Homeland* (Norman: University of Oklahoma Press, 1996), 20, 80, 302. U.S. Bureau of Census, Schedules of Seventh Census, 1850, showed Hispanos 54,394, Mexican Americans 394, Pueblo Indians 3,324, Nomads 164, Anglos 1,578, Homeland 59,830 in the Southwest. This was a huge undercount. Russell Steele Saxton, "Ethnocentrism in the Historical Literature of Territorial New Mexico" (PhD dissertation, University of New Mexico, 1980), 2, estimates 60,000 Hispanos, 9,000 Pueblos, 15,000 nomadic natives, and less than 2000 Euro-Americans.

9. Roxanne Dunbar Ortiz, *Roots of Resistance: Land Tenure in New Mexico, 1680–1980* (Los Angeles: Chicano Studies Research Center Publications, UCLA, 1980), 41, 62. Rodolfo F. Acuña, *Corridors of Migration: The Odyssey of Mexican Laborers, 1600–1933* (Tucson: University of Arizona Press, 2007), see Chapters 1 and 2 for similar water questions in Chihuahua, Mexico.

10. Kenneth M. Orona, *River of Culture, River of Power: Identity, Modernism, and Contest in the Middle Rio Grande Valley, 1848–1947* (New Haven, CT: Yale University, 1998), vii.

11. Orona, "River of Culture, River of Power," 55. Josiah Gregg, *Commerce of the Prairies: Life on the Great Plains in the 1830's and 1840's*, 2nd ed. (Crabtree, OR: The Narrative Press, 2001), 107.

12. Carlos Vélez-Ibáñez, *Border Visions: Mexican Cultures of the Southwest United States* (Tucson: University of Arizona Press, 1996), 58. Roxanne Amanda Dunbar, "Land Tenure in Northern New Mexico: An Historical Perspective" (PhD dissertation, UCLA, 1974), 146, 147. Bent married into the Jaramillo family. Kit Carson married into the same family. By 1831 there were Euro-American traders and trappers, tailors, carpenters, blacksmiths, shoemakers, gunsmiths, and other craftspeople in New Mexican towns. Charles Bent, The Mexico Office of the State Historian, http://www.newmexicohistory.org/filedetails.php?fileID=548.

13. González, *Refusing the Favor*, 87.

14. George B. Anderson, *History of New Mexico: Its Resources and People* (Los Angeles: Pacific States Publishing, 1907), 81. The population was probably closer to 6,000. Jones, *Los Paisanos*, 122. David A. Sandoval, "The American Invasion of New Mexico and Mexican Merchants," *Journal of Popular Culture* 35, no. 2 (Fall 2001): 61–70.

15. A Euro-American interpretation of Bent's Fort, http://www.youtube.com/watch?v=fEyF1VtV4a4. George William Beattie, "Reopening the Anza Road," *Pacific Historical Review* 2, no. 1 (March 1933), 52. Juan Bautista de Anza opened the Old Spanish Trail from Sonora to California in 1774. In 1829 Antonio Armijo with 60 men left Abiquiú, New Mexico, for California, arriving 86 days later. This opened the flood gates to other trade expeditions the following year. These openings continued and multiplied during the 1830s and 1840s. Many New Mexicans that settled in California left their footprints, such as Julian Chávez, for whom the famous Chavez Ravine was named. Old Spanish Trail, http://digital-desert.com/old-spanish-trail/.

16. Acuña, *Corridors of Migration*, 13–14, 22. See Jack D. Forbes, *Apache, Navaho and Spaniard* (Norman: University of Oklahoma Press, 1960), this is a classic. Apaches were also sold in Havana and Manila, and about 100,000 Filipinos were transported to Mexico.

17. Dunbar, "Land Tenure in Northern New Mexico," 141, 144. Ortiz, *Roots of Resistance*, 66. Camino Real de Tierra Adentro National Historic Trail, National Park Service, Department of the Interior, http://www.nps.gov/elca/. Marc Simmons, *New Mexico!*, 3rd ed. (Albuquerque: University of New Mexico, 2004), 132–38. Santa Fe Trail, http://www.youtube.com/watch?v=g8AnAy2DdK4.

18. Eastern and European capital was arriving even before the arrival of the railroad. Dunbar, "Land Tenure in Northern New Mexico," 141, 142, 144, 150. Ortiz, *Roots of Resistance*, 66. González, *Refusing the Favor*, 41, 115–16. Robert Luthe Duffus, *The Santa Fe Trail* (Albuquerque: University of New Mexico Press, 1972), 156. Stella M. Drumm, ed., *Down the Santa Fe Trail and into Mexico: The Diary of Susan Shelby Magoffin, 1846–1847* (Lincoln, NE: Bison Books, 1982); her husband was Samuel Magoffin, a veteran Santa Fe trader; she has graphic descriptions of the people along the trail.

19. Vicente M. Martínez, *The Progeny of Padre Martínez of Taos, Fundación Presbítero Antonio*. Damico, "El Agua Es La Vida," 35–39.

20. Ward Alan Minge, *Frontier Problems in New Mexico Preceding the Mexican War, 1840–1846* (Albuquerque: University of New Mexico Press, 1965), 41, 44, 304–6. Howard R. Lamar, *The Far Southwest, 1846–1912: A Territorial History* (New York: Norton, 1970), 53. Hubert Howe Bancroft, *History of Arizona and New Mexico, 1530–1888*, Vol. XVII (San Francisco, CA: The History Company, Publishers, 1889), 320–29. Benjamin M. Read, *Illustrated History of New Mexico* (New York: Arno Press, 1976), 407–8. Thomas M. Murray, *A Study of the Resolution of the Texas-New Mexico Boundary Conflict: The Compromise of 1850* (Master of Arts thesis, Waco, Texas: Baylor University, 1995), 31, 34–47. Ralph Emerson Twitchell, *The History of the Military Occupation of the Territory of New Mexico* (New York: Arno Press, 1976), 203–5.

21. Magoffin arrived in the region in 1828 and was married to María Gertrudes Váldez. He met with U.S. President Polk before the invasion, giving him a considerable amount of information about New Mexico. Stella M. Drumm, ed., *Down the Santa Fe Trail and into New Mexico* (New Haven, CT: Yale University Press, 1962), xxiv. William Aloysius Keleher, *Turmoil in New Mexico* (Santa Fe, NM: Rydal Press, 1951), 29–35. 63rd Congress, Senate, Doc. Number 608 (Washington, D.C.: Government Printing Office). John Taylor Hughes, *Doniphan's Expedition: Containing an Account of the Conquest of New Mexico* (Whitefish, MT: Kessinger Publishing, 2006).

22. Warren A. Beck, *New Mexico: A History of Four Centuries* (Norman: University of Oklahoma Press, 1962), 134. Lynn I. Perrigo, *The American Southwest* (New York: Holt, Rinehart and Winston, 1971), 164. Ralph Emerson Twitchell, *The Conquest of Santa Fe 1846* (Española, NM: Tate Gallery Publications, 1967), 52. Carolyn Zeleny, "Relations Between the Spanish-Americans and Anglo-Americans in New Mexico: A Study of Conflict and Accommodation in Dual Ethnic Situation" (PhD dissertation, Yale University, 1944), 137.

23. González, *Refusing the Favor*, 73. Alvin R. Sunseri, "New Mexico in the Aftermath of the Anglo-American Conquest" (PhD dissertation, Louisiana State University and Agricultural and Mechanical College, Baton Rouge, 1973), 131. Eric Foner on the Taos Revolt, http://www.youtube.com/watch?v=E9cX2W91fCk&playnext=1&list=PLOUTliemF1U4YXkM0sd4fBfmDJ7nBgw_z&feature=results_main.

24. Twitchell, *The History of the Military Occupation of the Territory of New Mexico*, 125. Lamar, *The Far Southwest, 1846–1912*, 70. There were also widespread acts of resistance in Arroyo. Fundación Presbítero Don Antonio José Martínez, Inc., http://padremartinez.org/index.php.

25. Dunbar, "Land Tenure in Northern New Mexico," 191. Twitchell, *The Conquest of Santa Fe*, 133. New Mexico Massacre: The Taos Rebellion, February 8, 2012, http://adamjamesjones.wordpress.com/2012/02/08/new-mexico-massacre-the-taos-revolt/.

26. Laura E. Gómez, *Manifest Destinies: The Making of the Mexican American Race* (New York: New York University Press, 2007), 15–16, 34, 35. According to Gómez, the six executions were criticized because the U.S. did not have political sovereignty. Bancroft, *History of Arizona and New Mexico*,

1530–1888, 436. Carey McWilliams, *North from Mexico* (New York: Greenwood Press, 1968), 118. Zeleny, "Relations between the Spanish-Americans and Anglo-Americans," 118. (Sister Mary) Loyola, *The American Occupation of New Mexico, 1821–1852* (New York: Arno Press, 1976), 71.

27. Sunseri, "New Mexico in the Aftermath of the Anglo-American Conquest," 143. Larry Dagwood Ball, "The Office of the United States Marshall in Arizona and the New Mexico Territory, 1851–1912" (PhD dissertation, University of Colorado, Boulder, 1970), 23.

28. According to Bancroft, *History of Arizona and New Mexico, 1530–1888*, 642, the U.S. Census of 1850 listed a population of 61,547, exclusive of the Indian population; in 1860 the figure was 80,853, of whom 3,859 were native to New Mexico. D. W. Meinig, *Southwest: Three Peoples in Geographical Change, 1600–1970* (New York: Oxford University Press, 1971), 31. Lamar, *The Far Southwest, 1846–1912*, 30. Gómez, *Manifest Destinies*, 25, 27.

29. Pem Davidson Buck, "Whither Whiteness? Empire, State, and the Re-Ordering of Whiteness," *Transforming Anthropology* 20, no. 2 (October 2012): 103, argues "Acting for elite interests by shedding blood and enforcing labor exploitation has historically whitened and may again whiten some who are seen as a threat to White supremacy and the racially defined mythical nation."

30. Nancie González, *The Spanish-Americans of New Mexico: A Heritage of Pride* (Albuquerque: University of New Mexico Press, 1967), 205. New Mexico's racial identification resembles that of other northern Mexican states. The 1793 census of Sonora found that out of 40,249 inhabitants, less than 0.3 percent was white, 42 percent mestizo, and 58 percent Indian. Acuña, *Corridors of Migration*, 70. However, despite Mexico being a mestizo and Indian nation (90 percent), 41.85 percent of Sonorans identified as white in 1921. In Chihuahua 36.33 percent identified as white in that census, although in 1810 most identified as Indian and mestizo with 10 percent identified as mulato. John P. Schmal, Indigenous Identity in the Mexican Census, Houston Institute for Culture, http://www.houstonculture.org/hispanic/census.html.

31. Samuel E. Sisneros, "Los Emigrantes Nuevomexicanos: The 1849 Repatriation to Guadalupe and San Ignacio, Chihuahua, Mexico" (Master's thesis, University of Texas at El Paso, 2001), 1.

32. Bancroft, *History of Arizona and New Mexico, 1530–1888*, 468, 472.

33. "Governor William Carr Lane's Manifesto Regarding the Drawing of the Boundary between Mexico and the United States, 1853," *New York Daily Times* (June 20, 1853), 3. Commissioner James Bartlett's Reply to William Carr Lane, 1853, "The Mesilla Valley," *New York Daily Times* (May 5, 1853), 6. John Disturnell to the *New York Daily Times* on the Drawing of the New-Mexican Boundary (May 6, 1853), *New York Daily Times* (May 7, 1853), 3. Acuña, *Corridors of Migration*, 32. Gadsden Purchase Treaty, December 30, 1853, The Avalon Project, Yale University Law School, http://avalon.law.yale.edu/19th_century/mx1853.asp. The vicinity of the Rio Grande and Southern Boundary of New Mexico as referred to by US Surveyor 1851, http://atlas.nmhum.org/pdfs/Gray1851NewMexico.pdf.

34. Rubén D Sálaz, Land Grant History, 1999, http://www.historynothype.com/landgrants.htm. Malcolm Ebright, *Land Grants and Lawsuits in Northern New Mexico* (Albuquerque: University of New Mexico Press, 1994), excellent synthesis of land grant process. Ruben Salaz Marquez, *New Mexico: A Brief Multi-History* (Albuquerque, NM: Cosmic House, 2007).

35. Bancroft, *History of Arizona and New Mexico, 1530–1888*, 632–33. Erna Fergusson, *New Mexico: A Pageant of Three Peoples*, 2nd ed. (Albuquerque: University of New Mexico Press, 1973), 316. Dunbar, "Land Tenure in Northern New Mexico," 227. González, *Refusing the Favor*, 30. Joseph Franklin Sexton, "New Mexico: Intellectual and Cultural Developments 1885–1825: Conflict Among Ideas and Institutions" (PhD dissertation, University of Oklahoma, Norman, 1982), 6. The period 1850–1880 was a transition as Euro-Americans constructed their hegemony. Susan A. Roberts, *New Mexico* (Albuquerque: University of New Mexico Press, 2006), 107–8.

36. Sarah Deutsch, *No Separate Refuge: Culture, Class, and Gender on an Anglo-Hispanic Frontier in the American Southwest, 1880–1940* (New York: Oxford University Press, 1987), 27–28, 66. Fergusson, *New Mexico*, 270. Roberts, *New Mexico*, 108–11. Benjamin M. Reed, *A History of Education in New Mexico* (Santa Fe: New Mexico Printing Co., 1911), 16–18, http://www.archive.org/stream/historyofeducati00reediala. Estevan Rael-Galvez. "Identifying Captivity and Capturing Identity: Narratives of American Indian Slavery in Colorado and New Mexico, 1776–1934." *American Quarterly* 55, no. 4 (2003): 817.

37. Robert Johnson Rosenbaum, "Mexicano Versus Americano: A Study of Hispanic-American Resistance to Anglo-American Control in New Mexico Territory, 1870–1900" (PhD dissertation, University of Texas, Arlington, 1972), 5. Meinig, *Southwest*, 63–64.

38. Dunbar, "Land Tenure in Northern New Mexico," 207. Deutsch, *No Separate Refuge*, 20. Ortiz, *Roots of Resistance*, 94. Robert J. Rosenbaum, *Mexicano Resistance in the Southwest* (Austin: University of Texas Press, 1981), 23. The import of the Treaty of Guadalupe Hidalgo can be surmised by reading the excluded Article X. See Treaty of Guadalupe Hidalgo, February 2, 1848. The Avalon Project at Yale Law School, http://avalon.law.yale.edu/19th_century/guadhida.asp. The Querétaro Protocol, May 26, 1848, Protocol of Querétaro in La Prensa de San Diego, http://laprensa-sandiego.org/archieve/september21/treaty.htm. President James K. Polk (1795–1849) on Article X of the Treaty of Guadalupe Hidalgo, February 22, 1848, U.S. Senate, 30th Cong., 1st Sess., Executive Order 68. *Congressional Record*; cited in Rodolfo F. Acuña and Guadalupe Compeán, eds., *Voices of the U.S. Latino Experience*, 3 Vols (Westport, CT: Greenwood, 2008), 113. It is difficult to conclude that there was no intention to deceive the Mexican negotiators.

39. Damico, "El agua es la vida," 10, 14, 17. Nostrand, *The Hispano Homeland*, 20.

40. Nostrand, Hispano Homeland, 11. Denise Holladay Damico' "El Agua Es la Vida" (Water Is Life): Water Conflict and Conquest in Nineteenth Century New Mexico (Waltham, Mass.: Brandeis University, PhD Dissertation, 2008), 14.

41. Gordon Morris Bakken, ed., *Law in Western United States* (Norman: University of Oklahoma Press, 2000), 534.

42. González, *Refusing the Favor*, 140. David J. Weber, ed., *Foreigners in Their Native Land: Historical Roots of the Mexican Americans* (Albuquerque: University of New Mexico Press, 1973), 157. González, *The Spanish-Americans of New Mexico*, 52–53.

43. McWilliams, *North from Mexico*, 122. Robert W. Larson, *New Mexico's Quest for Statehood, 1846–1912* (Albuquerque: University of New Mexico Press, 1968), 143. William A. Keleher, *The Maxwell Grant* (Santa Fe: Rydal Press, 1942), 152. Howard R. Lamar, *The Far Southwest, 1846–1919* (New Haven, CT: Yale University Press, 1966), 150. Miguel Antonio Otero, *The Real Billy the Kid: With New Light on the Lincoln County War* (Houston, TX: Arte Público Press, 1998), xxx–xxxiii, 45. Robert J. Torres, *Myth of the Hanging Tree: Stories of Crime and Punishment in Territorial New Mexico* (Albuquerque: University of New Mexico Press, 2008), 68–69, based heavily on the Catron Papers.

44. Herbert O. Brayer, *William Blackmore: The Spanish-Mexican Land Grants of New Mexico and Colorado, 1863–1878* (Denver, CO: Bradford-Robinson, 1949), reprinted in Carlos E. Cortés, ed., *Spanish and Mexican Land Grants* (New York: Arno Press, 1974), 173.

45. Keleher, *The Maxwell Grant*, 29, 150. Rosenbaum, "Mexicano Versus Americano," 42, 61, 64, 71, 75–79. Lamar, *The Far Southwest, 1846–1912*, 142. F. Stanley, *The Grant That Maxwell Bought* (Denver, CO: World Press, 1953), i. William H. Wroth, "Maxwell Land Grant," New Mexico Office of the State Historian, http://www.newmexicohistory.org/filedetails.php?fileID=512, has original documents and maps.

46. Rosenbaum, "Mexicano Versus Americano," 80, 86–93, 95–96, 98–99. Keleher, *The Maxwell Grant*, 109–10. Larson, *New Mexico's Quest for Statehood*, 138. Sexton, "New Mexico: Intellectual and Cultural," 67–68, 114–16. Maria Elaine Montoya, "Disposed People: Settler Resistance on the Maxwell Land Grant, 1860–1901" (PhD dissertation, Yale University, New Haven, 1993), 1, 11, 87, excellent synthesis.

47. Stan Steiner, *La Raza: The Mexican Americans* (New York: Harper & Row, 1969), 8.

48. Otero, *The Real Billy the Kid*, 43. Dunbar, "Land Tenure in Northern New Mexico," 221. Charles L. Kenner, *A History of New Mexican-Plains Indian Relations* (Norman: University of Oklahoma Press, 1969), 41. Brayer, *William Blackmore*, 244–45. Beck, *New Mexico*, 255, 260. Maurice G. Fulton, *History of the Lincoln County War*, in Robert N. Mullen, ed. (Tucson: University of Arizona Press, 1968), 8.

49. Rosenbaum, "Mexicano Versus Americano," 116.

50. Otero, *The Real Billy*, 5–6. Elego Baca, New Mexico, American Memory, Library of Congress, http://lcweb2.loc.gov/wpa/20040209.html.

51. Fulton, *History of the Lincoln County War*, 45–47, 291–92, 405–9. Rosenbaum, "Mexicano Versus Americano," 119, 340.

Perrigo, *The American Southwest*, 279. Fergusson, *New Mexico*, 275–76. Otero, *The Real Billy*, 61.

52. González, *Refusing the Favor*, 9. Carol Archer, "Surviving the Transition: Women's Property Rights and Inheritance in New Mexico, 1848–1912," Master of Arts thesis, University of Calgary, Alberta, 2006, 19, 30, makes the point that New Mexican women lost property rights under Euro-American law. A significant number of Euro-American males married Mexican women, acquiring property rights. Doña Ana County has the highest percentage of inter-marriages, 27.5 percent. Jason Pierce, "Making the White Man's West: Whiteness and the Creation of the American West" (PhD dissertation, University of Arkansas, Fayetteville, 2008), 2; Pierce makes the point that whiteness was narrowly defined since colonial times.

53. Janet Lecompte, "The Independent Women of Hispanic New Mexico, 1821–1846," *Western Historical Quarterly* 12, no. 1 (January 1981), quote on 18. The article gives a clear portrait of the women's lives.

54. González, *Refusing the Favor*, 41–55, 168, 215–16.

55. Pedro Sánchez, *Memorias Sobre la Vida del Presbitero Don Antonio José Antonio Martínez* (Santa Fe: Compania Impresora del Nuevo Mexicano, 1903), reprinted in David Weber, ed., *Northern Mexico on the Eve of the North American Invasion* (New York: Arno Press, 1976), 11. William A. Keleher, *Turmoil in New Mexico, 1846–1868* (Santa Fe, NM: Rydal Press, 1952), 132, n. 71. Keleher, *The Maxwell Grant*, 15, 133. Fergusson, *New Mexico*, 260–61. Zeleny, "Relations between the Spanish-Americans and Anglo-Americans," 257–58. Larson, *New Mexico's Quest for Statehood*, 82. Perrigo, *The American Southwest*, 219–20. Loyola, *The American Occupation of New Mexico, 1821–1852*, 35. Paul Horgan, *Lamy of Santa Fe: His Life and Times* (New York: Farrar, Straus & Giroux, 1975). For an excellent discussion of the Church in New Mexico, see González, *Refusing the Favor*, 64, 199–214. Ray John De Aragón, *Padre Martínez and Bishop Lamy* (Las Vegas, NV: Pan-American Publishing, 1978), 98. Shirley Jean Sands, "Religious Art: Reflectors of Change In the Catholic Church of New Mexico, 1830–1910," (PhD dissertation, Louisiana State University, Baton Rouge, 1999), 2–3, 48–49, 59, 175. The clash between the Mexican clergy was both with the Euro-American and the French; before the coming of the foreign church, New Mexico had been administered by the Bishop of Durango.

56. Alex M. Darley, *The Passionist of the Southwest or the Holy Brotherhood* (1893), reprinted in Carlos E. Cortés, ed., *The Penitentes of New Mexico* (New York: Arno Press, 1974), 5. Francis Leon Swadesh, *Los Primeros Pobladores* (Notre Dame: University of Notre Dame Press, 1974), 78. Miguel Antonio Otero, *Otero: An Autobiographical Trilogy*, Vol. 2 (New York: Arno Press, 1974), 46. Los Hermanos Penitentes, *Société Périllos*, http://www.perillos.com/penitentes.html (accessed April 30, 2009).

57. Quoted in De Aragón, *Padre Martínez and Bishop Lamy*, 105. Horgan, *Lamy of Santa Fe*, 229. On 353 Horgan makes the point that Martínez died one of the richest men in New Mexico.

58. Deutsch, *No Separate Refuge*, 13, 14. Marta Weigle, *Hispanic Villages of Northern New Mexico: A Reprint of Volume II of the 1935 Tewa Basin Study, with Supplementary Materials* (Santa Fe, NM: Lightning Tree, 1975), 35. González, *Refusing the Favor*, 80.

59. Deutsch, *No Separate Refuge*, 15–17, 21.

60. Damico, "El Agua Es La Vida," 12, 14, 20, 36–39, 90, 98, 106, 112, 118. Luis Aboites Aguilar, *La Irrigación Revolucionaria: Historia Del Sistema Nacional De Riego Del Río Conchos, Chihuahua, 1927–1938* (México, D.F.: Centro de Investigaciones y Estudios Superiores en Antropologia Social, 1987), 59. Rocio Castañeda González, *Irrigacion y reforma agraria: las comunidades de riego del valle de Santa Rosalía, Chihuahua 1920-1945* (México, D.F.: Centro de Investigaciones y Estudios Superiores en Antropologia Social, 1995), 21-22. Acuña, *Corridors of Migration*, Chapters 1 and 2. See extensive archival material in Rodolfo F. Acuña Archives, Special Collection, Oviatt Library, California State University Northridge.

61. Weigle, *Hispanic Villages of Northern New Mexico*, 229.

62. Weigle, *Hispanic Villages of Northern New Mexico*, 120, 151, 229. Deutsch, *No Separate Refuge*, 50–51, 101, 87–106.

63. Weigle, *Hispanic Villages of Northern New Mexico*, 151.

64. Deutsch, *No Separate Refuge*, 87–106.

65. Kate Horsley Parker, "'I Brought with Me Many Eastern Ways': Euro-American Income-Earning Women in New Mexico, 1850–1880" (PhD dissertation, University of New Mexico, Albuquerque, 1984), 10. Cheryl J. Foote, *Women of the New Mexico Frontier, 1846–1912*, 2nd ed. (Albuquerque: University of New Mexico Press, 2005), xx, 32, 74. Race, religious, and gender conflict separated these two worlds as much as class.

66. Rosenbaum, "Mexicano Versus Americano," 148, 198. William Aloysius Keleher, *The Fabulous Frontier* (Albuquerque: University of New Mexico Press, 1982), xxi, 6, 185, 280. *New Mexico: Its Resources and People Illustrated*, Vol. I (Los Angeles: Pacific States Publishing, 1907), 314.

67. William Carrigan and Clive Webb, *Forgotten Dead: Mob Violence Against Mexicans in the United States, 1848-1928* (New York: Oxford University Press, 2013), 69, 127. (Final Manuscript). The authors make the point that the Mexicans' majority in New Mexico put a firewall between them and vigilantes, and set it apart from the other former Mexican provinces.

68. Andrew Bancroft Schlesinger, "Las Gorras Blancas, 1889–1891," *Journal of Mexican American History* 1 (Spring 1971): 93, 44. Herrera, a native of New Mexico, had lived in Santa Fe and San Miguel counties until 1866, when he left the territory. Meeting the Knights in Colorado, he reputedly became acquainted in 1883 with the philosophy of Joseph Buchanan, founder of the anarchist Red International. Four years later Herrera returned to Las Vegas. Meanwhile, a rift occurred within the Knights between its president, Terence Powderly, and union militants. Juan José Herrera, joined by his two brothers, Pablo and Nicanor, identified with the militants. Robert W. Larson, "The Knights of Labor and Native Protest in New Mexico," in Robert Kern, ed., *Labor in New Mexico: Union, Strikes and Social History Since 1881* (Albuquerque: University of New Mexico Press, 1983), 4, 36. Rosenbaum, "Mexicano Versus Americano," 132–33, 139–40. Schlesinger, "Las Gorras Blancas, 1889–1891," 87–143. David Correia, "'Retribution Will Be Their Reward': New Mexico's Las Gorras Blancas and the Fight for the Las Vegas Land Grant Commons," *Radical History Review* no. 108 (Fall 2010): 49–72, well illustrated.

69. *The Optic*, March 12, 1890, quoted in Schlesinger, "Las Gorras Blancas," 107–8. Las Gorras Blancas, New Mexico Office of the State Historian, http://www.newmexicohistory.org/filedetails.php?fileID=375.

70. Otero, *Otero*, Vol. 2, 166.

71. Rosenbaum, "Mexicano Versus Americano," 156, 171, 200. Larson, "The Knights of Labor and Native Protest in New Mexico," 39.

72. Schlesinger, "Las Gorras Blancas," 121, 122. Rosenbaum, "Mexicano Versus Americano," 201, 225, 229, 235. Already a *jefe político* (political boss), San Miguel County Sheriff Lorenzo López joined because of a rift with his brother-in-law Eugenio Romero, the boss of San Miguel's Republican Party.

73. Schlesinger, "Las Gorras Blancas," 123.

74. Deutsch, *No Separate Refuge*, 29. Rosenbaum, "Mexicano Versus Americano," 247, 261, 324. Between 1891 and 1904, the Court of Private Land Claims heard cases involving 235,491,020 acres, allowing 2,051,526 acres to remain intact. Weber, *Foreigners in Their Native Land*, 157, writes, "In New Mexico, for example, more than 80 percent of the grant builders lost their land. There, since community grants and communal holdings were more common than individual grants, the slowness of litigation had its greatest impact on small farmers and herders." James W. Fraser, *A History of Hope When Americans Have Dared to Dream of a Better Future* (Basingstoke, England: Palgrave Macmillan, 2003), 60–65.

75. Fergusson, *New Mexico*, 298–314. William Taylor and Elliot West, "Patron Leadership at the Crossroads: Southern Colorado in the Late Nineteenth Century," in Norris Hundley, Jr., ed., *The Chicano* (Santa Barbara: Clio, 1975), 79. By 1900, the Rocky Mountain Timber Company merged with the Maxwell Land Grant Company. Dunbar, "Land Tenure in Northern New Mexico," 225–26. González, *Refusing the Favor*, 45.

76. Kern, *Labor in New Mexico*, 4. Dunbar, "Land Tenure in Northern New Mexico," 220. Lamar, *The Far Southwest, 1846-1912*, 172-201.

77. Deutsch, *No Separate Refuge*, 26. Michael Leon Trujillo, "The Land of Disenchantment: Transformation, Continuity, and Negation in the Greater Española Valley, New Mexico" (PhD dissertation, University of Texas at Austin, 2005), 5–6. "The Greater Española Valley is largely located within Rio Arriba County and is situated at the center of the Rio Arriba region of northern New Mexico and southern Colorado. This region has long maintained a concentrated and long-term resident Hispanic population."

78. Zeleny, "Relations between the Spanish-Americans and Anglo-Americans," 176–77.

79. Joan Jensen, "New Mexico Farm Women, 1900-1940." In Kern, ed., *Labor in New Mexico: Strikes, Unions and Social*

History since 1881 (Albuquerque: University of New Mexico Press, 1983), 63. Zeleny, "Relations between the Spanish-Americans and Anglo-Americans," 179, 187, 190, 192–93, 200–1, 216, 217.

80. Lamar, *The Far Southwest, 1846–1912*, 190.

81. Zeleny, "Relations between the Spanish-Americans and Anglo-Americans," 218–19. Octaviano Ambrosio Larrazolo (1859–1930) was born in El Valle de San Bartolome (now known as the Valle de Allende) in Chihuahua, Mexico, on December 7, 1859. J. B. Salpointe, Bishop of Arizona, a family friend, brought him to the United States in 1870 and he lived in Tucson, Arizona. When Salpointe became archbishop of Santa Fe in 1875, he took Larrazolo with him. Larrazolo served as Republican governor of New Mexico from 1919 to 1921. Larrazolo was a member of the New Mexico State House of Representatives in 1927 and a U.S. senator from New Mexico in 1928–1929. Larrazolo, an attorney, was known as the "Silver Tongued Orator of the Southwest." Ezequiel Cabeza de Baca (1864–1917) served as lieutenant governor of New Mexico in 1911 and as governor of New Mexico in 1917.

CHAPTER 6

Sonora Invaded: The Occupation of Arizona

LEARNING OBJECTIVES

- Discuss how the occupation of Arizona was the occupation of Sonora, Mexico.
- Analyze the economic motives behind the Gadsden Purchase.
- Show the importance of Tucson as a trade center.

- Explain the importance of Mexican labor to the copper mines and agriculture in Arizona,
- Interpret the role of the railroad in the industrialization of Arizona.
- Describe Mexican labor struggles for equality through mutualistas (mutual-aid societies).

The Treaty of Guadalupe Hidalgo (1848) ceded the northern part of Arizona to the United States; the southern region remained part of the Mexican state of Sonora—which had a population of over 100,000—until 1853 when it became part of the United States. For most of the remainder of the century, Arizona's historical ties with Sonora continued. The timeline helps organize the story and explain

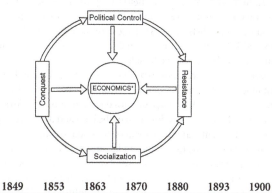

| 1821 | 1846 | 1848 | 1849 | 1853 | 1863 | 1870 | 1880 | 1893 | 1900 | 1902 | 1912 |

---

* In applying the above model, we must remember that each of the four states—Texas, New Mexico, Arizona, and California—had its own peculiarities, such as distance from Mexico, the size of its population, the number of Euro-Americans entering the territory, and the availability of natural resources. We also need to take into account the stages through which these societies evolved: subsistence farming, mercantile capitalism, and industrial capitalism.

how Arizona evolved from subsistence farming communities to mercantile capitalism and finally to industrial capitalism, and how these changes affected the Mexican people in that territory. The wheel presented on the previous page is intended to aid the reader in understanding the various causes and effects that shaped Chicano history during these stages of development.

In applying the wheel model, we must remember that each of the four states—Texas, New Mexico, Arizona, and California—had its own peculiarities, such as distance from Mexico, the size of its population, the number of Euro-Americans entering the territory, and the availability of natural resources. We also need to take into account the stages through which these societies evolved: subsistence farming, mercantile capitalism, and industrial capitalism.

It has become evident in reading the chapters on Texas and New Mexico that their histories and that of Arizona begin south of the border. As they became integrated with the rest of the Southwest through improved transportation, their worldview expanded. Unfortunately some Chicana/o historians take an exceptionalist view of history, and their place study becomes their Zion. Putting Arizona into a historical context, modern Sonora–Arizona was formed as miners from other provinces of New Spain rushed there, lured by mining bonanzas. As elsewhere in northern New Spain, they clashed with Sonoran natives, leading to the death of large numbers of indigenous people owing to warfare and disease. Although much of Sonora was arid and mountainous, it had more water resources than the other northern Mexican states. Sonora lay on the west side of the Sierra Madre Occidental, and the mountain captured the moisture of the winds blowing off the ocean, producing great running rivers such as the mighty Rio Yaquí[1] and other relatively smaller rivers such as the Mayo, Sonora, Gila, and Colorado. Availability of a constant source of water facilitated the concentration of populations along these rivers; bands grew into village settlements.

Before it became part of the United States, in two stages—in 1848 and 1853, respectively—Arizona made up the northern frontier of Sonora. Colonialism brought about some commonalities among the colonized and the colonizers; however, there were also differences. Even after a century of cohabitation many of the indigenous peoples did not perceive themselves as Mexicans or even *Sonorenses,* and, at the time of Mexican independence, they still saw themselves as separate Opata, Pima, Tohono O'odham, Seri, and Yaqui nations.[2]

A small class of rancheros eked out a precarious existence cultivating wheat and raising cattle, while a racial and social hierarchy controlled the mines and the settlements orbiting them. Sonoran notables differentiated themselves from the larger mixed-blood population and, much like the elites in other parts of northern Mexico, nurtured the myth of their racial purity. The colonial construct formed a colonial mentality in Sonora and in Arizona, which was common among more well-to-do Mexicans well into the twentieth century.[3]

Despite the myths about their racial purity, a quilt of mixed colored people refuted the pretension that Sonora was a criollo province. Other censuses substantiate this, though they vary greatly in terms of areas covered. For example, Gonzalo Aguirre Beltrán reports that the 1793 census of northern Sonora lists 128 Europeans, only two of whom were women. Euro-mestizo males numbered 4,216, and Euro-mestizo females, 5,899. The same census lists 1,630 Afro-mestizo males and 1,385 Afro-mestizo females, and 1,932 Indio-mestizo males and 1,870 Indio-mestizo females. The indigenous population outnumbered all others, with 12,569 native males and 10,620 native females.[4]

Like Nueva Vizcaya, the Sonorenses also practiced slavery; African and Indian slaves labored at the mines and haciendas. Spain inherited the practice of slavery from the Romans and sank to lower depths in their conquests in the Americas, Africa, and Asia. They imported large numbers of Africans to meet their insatiable demand for human labor, which made the exploitation of the land and its minerals profitable. Although the crown forbade the enslavement of Indians, the mine owners, hacendados, and other colonists used loopholes in the law to force the Indians to work in the mines, haciendas, and public projects. For instance, it was permissible to enslave Indians taken in open and just warfare, those who were cannibals, or those who renounced Jesus. Spanish slave-hunters invaded the Sonoran frontier and took slaves from northern Pima villages. The enslavement of the Apache was common practice since the seventeenth century. In 1734 a local pastor, Fray Joseph Manuel de Equia y Leronbe, of Nambe, an Indian village north of Santa Fe, wrote, "They claim that by selling Apache Indians into slavery they will be redeemed from their lives as infidels. What benefit is it to condemn them so that they do not live as infidels? Enslave them so that they do not have freedom?" Greed encouraged the enslavement of Indians in increasing numbers: it cost up to five times more to buy an African slave than an Indian slave. Because Indians were worth less money, they were expendable and were assigned to the most hazardous work.[5]

The Frontier

The Sonoran Desert, which includes southern Arizona, was inhabited for 10 millennia. Extensive canal irrigation took place in the Tucson area during the first millennium BC. However, it disappeared shortly before the Spaniards arrived in the New World. Hohokam occupation of the Phoenix Basin flourished between AD 500 and AD 1400; the area was irrigated by the Salt and Gila Rivers. It sustained large urban centers and trading systems and an infrastructure that supported 225 ball courts. The sudden disappearance of the Hohokam remains a mystery. Scholars speculate that the Pima and the Tohono O'odham, who to this day are excellent farmers, are descendants of the Hohokam.[6]

In the 1830s, a presidio stood guard over a tiny Tucson settlement, defending it from the raids of nomadic tribes. The population of 465 Mexicans and about 486 Apache Mansos were mostly farmers. With the independence of Mexico and the secularization of the missions, Sonoran elites began actively exploiting southeast Arizona and developing the area around Tucson, driving the Pima along the Santa Cruz River off their farms. Also, after independence from Spain, the Mexican government stepped up the parceling of large land grants, further usurping the Indian land and thus provoking them to fight to retain their custody over the river valleys. Earlier the Spanish state pacified the Apache by bribing them with goods. When the Mexican government discontinued this practice shortly after independence, the Apache were forced to maraud. By the 1830s the Apache nations and the Sonorans were at war once again, and in the 1840s the Apache drove the settlers off their land grants.[7]

The Gadsden Purchase

Large numbers of Euro-Americans became acquainted with the Mesilla, or southern Arizona, during the California Gold Rush of 1848–1850 when thousands of Euro-Americans and more than 10,000 Sonorans passed through it to get to the gold fields. They coveted the legendary mineral wealth of Sonora and hence worried about the growing influence of the French in Sonora and their attempts to establish French colonies there. Many Euro-American politicos urged Washington, D.C., to invoke the Monroe Doctrine and to take Sonora so the French could not get it. In 1853, President Franklin Pierce appointed James Gadsden—a soldier, diplomat, and railroad president—as U.S. minister to Mexico, with instructions to purchase as much of northern Mexico as possible. Gadsden proposed the purchase of five northern Mexican states and Baja California. When Mexican officials refused the deal, the United States sent 2,000 troops to the New Mexico border "to preserve order." Mexico would not sell even Sonora, so Gadsden settled for the Mesilla, threatening Mexican ministers that, if Mexico did not sell southern Arizona and parts of New Mexico, "we shall take it."[8]

In 1853, Mexico ceded more than 45,000 square miles to the United States, of which some 35,000 were in southern Arizona, for $10 million. The United States claimed that it wanted the land for a railroad route from El Paso to the California coast. Mexican sources, however, countered that what the United States really wanted was the port of Guaymas, Sonora.[9] This was a reasonable assumption, since vast deserts separated the Arizona mines from California ports, and Guaymas had one of the finest ports on the Pacific Coast. Nearby Sonora, Mexico, also had a pool of experienced miners and manual laborers as well as urban centers. Historian Hubert Howe Bancroft wrote, "the northern republic could afford to pay for a railroad route through a country said to be rich in mines." In 1854, Charles Poston and Sylvester Mowry operated mines in the newly acquired land with the backing of eastern capital; however, the military did not take possession of the Mesilla until two years later.[10]

The War with Sonora

The Apache raids were so relentless that Sonorans accused Euro-Americans of instigating the Apache to raid Sonora. The cynicism of Euro-Americans is manifested in Sylvester Mowry's address to the Geographical Society in New York on February 3, 1859:

> *The Apache Indian is preparing Sonora for the rule of a higher civilization than the Mexican.*
> *In the past half century the Mexican element has disappeared from that which is now called*

Arizona, before the devastating career of the Apache. It is every day retreating further south, leaving to us (when the time is ripe for our own possession) the territory without the population.[11]

Beyond a doubt Arizona miners and ranchers struck bargains with the Apaches, guaranteeing them sanctuary in return for not being raided; Poston, owner of the Sonora Exploring and Mining Company and the so-called "Father of Arizona," made such deals. In return for sanctuary and arms, the Apaches agreed not to steal from Poston, nor to kill his men. Moreover, Captain R. S. Ewell, the commanding officer at Fort Buchanan, was too busy working on his Patagonia mine to deal with military and civil matters.

The *Weekly Arizonian,* on April 28, 1859, strongly condemned as piracy the use of the Apache to annihilate Sonorans. Miner and soldier Herman Ehrenberg added, "If we hate Mexicans, or if we want to take their country, we want no bloodthirsty savages to do the work for us, or to injure them."[12] It was not altruism in Ehrenberg's part, he knew that Mexican labor and trade with Sonora were essential to the growth of Arizona, and condemned the policy of making separate treaties with the Apache.

Filibustering Expeditions into Sonora

Filibustering expeditions continued throughout the 1850s. Henry Crabb, a southerner and former member of the California legislature, in 1857 led about a hundred Californians into Sonora on what some Euro-American sources described as a peaceful colonizing expedition. The Mexicans ordered Crabb to leave the state. When he did not, the Sonorans ambushed his army and executed Crabb; they cut off his head and preserved it in alcohol. President James Buchanan condemned the Mexican "brutality" and attempted to use the incident as an excuse to invade Mexico.[13]

In the Senate, Sam Houston sponsored a resolution proposing that Mexico be made a protectorate of the United States. Two decades later, Poston confirmed that President Buchanan and his cabinet, prodded by powerful New York and New England capitalists, agreed to first occupy northern Sonora and afterward submit the matter to Congress. Thus, Buchanan in 1859 sent the USS *St. Mary* to Guaymas for the purpose of provoking a war. The pretext was Governor Ignacio Pesqueira's refusal to allow Charles P. Stone to survey public lands of Sonora. The Mexican government had signed a contract with the Jecker-Torre Company and a group of U.S. investors, giving them rights over one-third of the public lands they surveyed, with an option to buy another third of the surveyed lands. The company's agent, Stone, was obnoxious and arrogant, so Pesqueira refused to honor the agreement and ordered Stone out of the state. Stone then lobbied American authorities for government intervention.

Enter Captain William Porter of the *St. Mary* in 1859, who demanded that Pesqueira permit Stone to continue his survey. In November, Porter threatened to bombard Guaymas. Pesqueira responded that if one shell fell on Guaymas, he would not guarantee the safety of Euro-Americans' life or property in Sonora. The *St. Mary* left, but tensions continued as Buchanan stoked passions, claiming that Mexicans had expelled peaceful Euro-Americans, violating their personal and real property rights. He requested that Congress approve the occupation of Sonora as well as Chihuahua. However, sectional divisions and the impending Civil War prevented Buchanan from waging yet another unjust war.[14]

Mexicans in Early Arizona

Mining was the sole economic enterprise during the early period, and eastern companies invested considerable amounts of capital in silver mines. This investment was undoubtedly accompanied by lobbying of Washington, D.C., officials, to station soldiers in Arizona to protect the mines against the Apache. In 1859, the population of the Mesilla was estimated at 7,695 residents, 7,125 of whom were Mexicans. Approximately 5,000–10,000 Pima and Tohono O'odham lived in the Mesilla.

In 1860, just over 70 percent of Tucson's population was Mexican. Most of the freight from and to Tucson traveled through Guaymas, Sonora. The trip took 16 days and it cost about $80 a ton to transport cargo from and to San Francisco by ship. Over land, it took four months and cost $350–$400 a ton.[15] Consequently there was brisk trade between Guaymas and San Francisco. During the 1850s and 1860s,

Arizona remained in the Sonoran orbit, using Mexican pesos as its currency. During this period, political turmoil in Sonora both weakened and strengthened the ties between Mexico and the United States. Events such as the French Intervention (1861–1865), which saw France invade Mexico and compel an Austrian emperor (1864–1867) on the country, brought about a civil war that discouraged repatriation to Sonora. In turn, political refugees from Mexico poured into Tucson.[16]

The U.S. Congress separated Arizona from New Mexico, establishing the Arizona territory in 1863.[17] As in Texas and New Mexico, a political elite controlled government patronage. The new territorial government replaced the Santa Fe appointees who ran Arizona until that time, with its own white cronies. During the Civil War most Euro-Americans in the territory harbored pro-Southern sympathies, and Arizona became a Confederate state in March 1861. This changed in June 1862 when the California Volunteers, under Major General James Henry Carelton, drove the Confederate forces out of Arizona. To defend Arizona from possible sedition and from the Apache, and to ward off the possibility of a French intervention in Sonora, the U.S. government dispatched additional federal troops to the territory. Consequently, the North American population in Arizona increased, with Euro-American farmers settling along the rivers in the center of the territory, concentrated in the Santa Cruz Valley (the location of Tucson and Tubac), the lower reaches of the Gila and Colorado Rivers, and central Arizona.[18]

Territorial status also brought public education to Arizona. In 1863 the Arizona legislature allocated $500 for Tucson public schools with the stipulation that English would be part of the curriculum. Americanization was very much on the mind of the legislators. Augustus Britcha was the town's first school teacher. However, owing to a lack of funds, the establishment of the public school got off to a shaky start. In 1870 the sisters of St. Joseph established a school for girls; San Agustín remained the school for boys. In 1872 the Arizona territorial legislature enacted the first public school law, and by the end of the 1870s with the moral and financial support of the Mexican community, public school education had become a reality. Nevertheless, the Mexican population preferred parochial schools because they allowed the teaching of Spanish and religion. Moreover, many opposed coeducation, which was the norm in the public schools.[19]

The War of the Races

Arizona was a lawless and violent place. At times, a war of races seemed imminent. Aware of the racism, Mexican authorities often refused to extradite alleged criminals. A case in point was the Mission Camp shootings. On December 24, 1870, Mexicans killed three Euro-Americans, Charles Reed, James Little, and Thomas Oliver, and wounded Reed's wife in a dispute over the alleged theft of furniture and five horses. After the shooting, one of the suspects fled into Sonora, and Arizona authorities demanded his extradition. The suspect and his cohorts claimed that the employer had severely beaten one of them and they had acted in self-defense. On the U.S. side, vigilantes rode to the ranch of Francisco Gándara (brother of the former governor of Sonora), shot him in front of his wife and children, and stole his valuables. Without proof, Gándara was accused of stealing a mule and killing a Euro-American.[20]

The murder of Gándara was not an aberration. William Carrigan and Clive Webb list seven victims of mob violence before the shooting of Gándara, whose murder they did not list (proving that there were probably many more). Carrigan and Webb write that on May 9, 1859, four Mexicans were shot and killed in the Sonoita Valley. Euro-Americans were trying to run Mexicans out of the valley using the murder of a white man as a pretext. On August 3, 1859, Rafael Polaco was hanged in Tucson. On October 15 of the same year an unknown Mexican was shot and his ears were cut off near Tubac, and Mateo García was hanged in Arizona City. During the same decade that Gándara was killed, other Mexicans fell to mob violence: Ramón Cordova, hanged, Phoenix, 1872; Domingo García, clubbed to death, near Tucson, 1873, Mariano Tisnado, hanged, Phoenix, 1873; vigilantes hanged nine Mexicans, Phoenix, 1873; that same month two other unknown Mexicans were hanged; the next month Leonard Cordova, Clemente López, and Jesús Saguaripa were hanged in Tucson. On the 31st of the month Lúcas Lugas was shot in the back of the head by a posse at Kenyon Station; and in early September a mob hanged Manuel Subiate in Yuma City. What was more remarkable was that at the time Mexicans were in the majority in the territory.[21]

Racial tensions worsened with the arrival of the so-called "cowboys," which generally meant Texans who fanned the antagonism between Mexicans and Euro-Americans. The town of Tombstone harbored the worst of the Texas outlaws, and racism thrived, as owners of businesses and mines would not hire Mexicans for fear of inciting the cowboys who controlled the town. Using Tombstone, which was founded in 1879, as a base, the cowboys formed gangs that raided defenseless Mexican villages on the other side of the border. The Texans showed little respect for women or children.[22] Racial harmony surely would have deteriorated beyond repair if it were not for the Euro-Americans' fear of the Apache, who continued to threaten Arizona settlements during the 1870s. This vulnerability often necessitated cooperation with the Mexican elites.

The Race Question

Among the Mexican elites the question of race was complex. Poor whites generalized racism, whereas elite whites were more selective in their prejudices, depending on their requirement for marital relations, defense, and/or business contacts. Sonora was right next door, and trade was essential to their prosperity. The Mexican elites did not take advantage of this vulnerability and permitted racism to run wild. Many of them were descendants of criollos who arrived in Sonora and Chihuahua during the eighteenth century, and they considered themselves superior to poor whites and the darker-skinned Mexicans. Moreover, many prized their contacts with white power brokers. As in New Mexico, a number of Mexicans in Arizona prospered under U.S. colonialism.

Many Mexicans, returning from California diggings, realized that wealth was not only in mining but in providing services. Businessmen arrived from Sonora and from El Paso and Santa Cruz, which had become major trading centers. Some started up small mercantile businesses; others freighted ores and other goods. For instance, Felipe Amabisca and Antonio Contreras reached Arizona City in 1858 and opened a mercantile store and a freighting business. Esteván Ochoa, originally from Chihuahua, educated in Independence, Missouri, and formerly from New Mexico's Mesilla, moved to Tucson and started a freighting business with Pinckney Randolph Tully. M. G. Samaniego, born in Sonora and raised in Chihuahua, had successful businesses in Chihuahua and the Mesilla before arriving in Tucson. Samaniego was a graduate of St. Louis University. He was conservative, and sympathized with Confederates during the Civil War. These men had the necessary educational and financial capital to succeed. As in New Mexico, a clique consisting of Euro-Americans and their Mexican allies ran the territorial government after the Civil War. Federal appointees in Tucson, along with business leaders and voters, lobbied Congress for appropriations to subsidize military operations, highways, Indian reservations, and the railroad. Freighters like Tully and Ochoa profited handsomely from government contracts, which they got through their political acquaintances.[23] By contrast, an overwhelming number of Mexicans labored for subsistence wages.

Marrying Up!

How Euro-Americans treated or thought of Mexican women greatly varied and depended on the hue of their skin and class. Euro-American suitors often described them as independent and skilled in mounting horses; they occasionally described higher-class Sonoran women as intelligent and white. Not much was written about the poor women. What we know is that all classes migrated to Arizona in family units. Even with its harshness, the frontier gave Mexican women better access to traditionally male-dominated occupations. The better off among them inherited land and merchant houses from their fathers or husbands. The advantage for the rich Mexican was that a white son-in-law offered a measure of protection. Nevertheless, not all the marriages were between prominent Mexican women and white males. According to Salvador Acosta, "working-class Mexican women accounted for a large percentage of the wives of white men in nineteenth-century Tucson, most of whom were also of working-class origins." Poor women did not take capital to their unions but they did much more, performing the menial chores, caring for the animals, working on farms, and contributing to the defense of the community. In cases of interracial relationships, poor women lacked the protection of a powerful family, however.[24] The 1860 Arizona census shows that women in Tucson were concentrated in jobs such as seamstress or washerwoman, work that could be done from home. Mexican males worked in blue-collar occupations; nearly half of them were unskilled. Indeed, Mexicans made up 58 percent of Tucson's laborers, and only seven Mexicans out of a total Mexican population of 653 persons worked as merchants, traders, or shopkeepers. Tucson listed 168 Euro-Americans, 160 of whom were male. That same census listed 1,716 Mexicans and 871 non-Mexicans in southern Arizona.

By the 1870s, 62 percent of marriages involving whites in Pima County (where Tucson was located) were between Euro-American males and Mexican females. According to historian Salvador Acosta, Mexicans were technically white so the territory's anti-miscegenation laws did not legally apply to them, but the interpretation was at the convenience of white colonists. There were marriages between Mexican and other races only until there were sufficient white women available for the white male population. Acosta lists the wedding between Emmett Woodley, a black man, and Leonicia Terrazas that although frowned upon by the Church was performed at Saint Augustine Catholic Church on March 23, 1872. Technically Mexicans were white when convenient for society.[25] This ambiguous status worked to the advantage of the white population because without Mexicans the territory would only have 600 white residents. Arizona's first legislature (1864) followed the lead of other western states and passed anti-miscegenation laws that remained in effect to 1962. Mexican women accounted for large percentages of all marriages for white, black, and Chinese men. Indeed, Arizona was one of the first legislatures to adopt strict definitions of whiteness.[26]

Between 1872 and 1899, intermarriage between white men and Mexican females remained high, at 148 of 784, or 19 percent of all marriages; during the same period only six marriages involved Mexican men and Euro-American women. Acosta surmises that "Between 1860 and 1900, Mexican women accounted for 30 percent of all unions for white men. The percentages break down as follows: 67 percent in1860, 91 percent in 1864, 79 percent in 1870, 40 percent in 1880, and 16 percent in 1900." Intermarriages among people of mixed ancestry almost always had Euro-American surnames. After this point unions between Mexican males and white women became more widespread, although the frequency of intermarriages overall did not approach those of the nineteenth century. In 1946, only 3 percent of the marriages took place between Euro-American men and Mexican women, and only 1 percent, between Mexican men and white females.[27]

Intermarriage provided the opportunity for the newcomers to inherit property from a Mexican father-in-law or to go into business with a wife's family. Mexican women also held the key to participation in the social life of the pueblo and access to extended families. As time went by intermarriage became less advantageous: the railroad ended Arizona's isolation and Euro-American women arrived in larger numbers in the 1800s, making Mexican women less attractive to the gringos. The railroad also ended the Apache threat by accelerating the transportation of troops and dramatically increasing the territory's population.[28]

Although Mexican women mainly were housewives or worked as domestics, and some even in *cantinas* (bars), a few of them also operated businesses and subsistence farms. For instance, Eulalia Elías (1788–1860) ran the first major cattle ranch in Arizona. (She was admitted to the Arizona Women's Hall of Fame in the 1980s.) Though noteworthy, it was not surprising because Eulalia belonged to a wealthy and powerful founding family. Such opportunities were not open to poor Mexicans of either gender. The highest job a Mexican woman could aspire to was that of a schoolteacher, as in the case of Rosa Ortiz, who in the 1870s ran a Mexican private school where the medium of learning was Spanish.[29]

The Alliance of Elites

By the 1870s, Tucson and the rest of Arizona were starting to become culturally "American." The population of Tucson had mushroomed to 8,007 residents, including a large number of Euro-Americans. Most new "American" immigrants settled in the northern part of the territory, with the state capital moving from Tucson to Prescott in 1877. A year later Arizona's population had grown to 40,000. The number of elected Mexican officials declined with the changing demographics, and fewer Spanish surnames appeared even in the social columns of Tucson English-language newspapers. Still, the Mexican population kept a vibrant social and cultural presence in the pueblo. Spanish-language newspapers such as *Las Dos Repúblicas*,

El Fronterizo, and, later, *El Tucsonense,* which began publishing in the mid-1870s, covered local news as well as that of Sonora and the rest of Latin America. *El Tucsonense* vigorously protested the negative stereotypes of Mexicans and championed their rights.

By the late 1870s, upward social and economic mobility among Mexicans was even slower as businesses became capital-intensive enterprises and as Mexicans' access to available capital became less and less probable. For all intents and purposes, they were excluded from Tucson's historical past. For example, in 1884 when Samaniego became a member of the Society of Arizona Pioneers, consisting of persons who came to Arizona before 1870, fewer than 10 percent of its members were Mexican American.[30]

The War on the Apache

The cooperation among the races in fighting the Apache was not always admirable. For example, in 1871, a group comprising 6 Euro-Americans, 48 Mexicans, and 94 Tohono O'odhams attacked a defenseless Apache camp near Camp Grant, massacring more than 100 Apache women and children. Army officials blamed it on freighters and government contractors, who allegedly provoked the incident to keep the forts stocked. Arizona historian Thomas Sheridan argues that this is an oversimplification, since passions ran deep and the Apache had warred with Tohono O'odhams and Mexicans for decades. "Both sides murdered adults and carried off children whenever they found them. Both sought vengeance for their dead. . . . Bloody as it was, the Camp Grant Massacre was no aberration. On the contrary, it was," according to Sheridan, "the culmination of two centuries of conflict on the Arizona frontier." Though this may be partly true, to excuse the massacre is to ignore the impact of the Euro-American and Spanish colonialism that abetted this kind of behavior. The military and the so-called citizens' militias pursued the Apache throughout the 1870s, capturing and shipping hundreds to Florida and the other so-called reservations. The Apaches were not the only natives to suffer. Colonists also relentlessly pursued the Navajo in Arizona and New Mexico.[31]

The Fate of the "Friendly Indian"

Before the 1870s, the Pima and the Tohono O'odhams, who were generally considered "friendly Indians," did much of the farming in Arizona. The Homestead Act of 1862 encouraged the in-migration of white colonists, intensifying competition for land and water. Euro-American farmers trickled into Arizona in the 1860s, but by the 1870s, irrigation projects were initiated in the Salt River Valley. By the middle of the decade, Euro-American farmers were cultivating hay and cotton. The development of commercial agriculture worsened mutual relations among the Mexicans, the natives, and Euro-Americans.

The end of the Apache threat opened up more space for settlers and encouraged further encroachment on Pima land. By the 1870s, the Pima, former allies of the Spanish colonists, who fed Euro-American and Mexican Argonauts during the California Gold Rush, were producing 3 million pounds of wheat a year. A decade earlier, Euro-American and Mexican farmers had dug irrigation canals upriver from the Pima around Florence, diverting water. When the Pima complained in 1873 to Washington officials, authorities suggested that they move to Indian Territory in Oklahoma. Over time, the Pima's lands were almost bled dry; eventually, they were reduced to a small ration of water.[32]

The Land-Grant Grab

As elsewhere in the Southwest, Mexicans in Arizona fought the land-grant battle, although on a smaller scale. Congress in 1870 authorized the surveyor general of Arizona "to ascertain and report" upon claims. The surveys were purposely slow, dragging into the 1880s and thus encouraging squatters to occupy the land. The nonfeasance and, in some cases, the malfeasance of the courts encouraged the filing of fraudulent claims and schemes to invalidate Mexican titles. The law gave landowners little or no protection against squatters. They could not work their land and thus were prevented from paying taxes, which resulted in further loss of land.[33] The railroad land grants took a healthy bite. New Mexico and Arizona Land Co. acquired land and uranium ore deposits throughout Arizona, Texas, New Mexico, and Colorado.[34]

The Transformation of Arizona

From the beginning of the U.S. occupation, the federal government promoted the cattle trade. However, the number of cattle remained low because of Apache raids, and most cattle raisers were small operators. The railroads and the1877 Desert Land Act changed this, and accelerated Arizona's transformation from commercial to industrial capitalism. Mining also stimulated cattle and farming enterprises, attracting large numbers of Texas cowboys, who, according to Professor Raquel Rubio Goldsmith, brought in "their English language and dislike of Mexicans." The *New York Times* announced the availability of homestead land in Arizona, writing on June 4, 1880, "This Territory is largely populated by ignorant and non-English speaking Mexicans and 'greasers,' and has been much harried by Indian wars." The *Times* wrote that the main attraction was mining and livestock grazing and that there was no reason to fear the Indians any longer.[35]

Cattlemen took the cue and flocked to Arizona during the 1880s, overgrazing the range and causing ecological damage. Commercial sheep raising, mainly run by non-Indians, also increased, with the number of commercially raised sheep growing from 76,524 in 1880 to 698,404 in 1890. Stock raising also furthered Arizona's dependence on national and international markets. The dependence led to hardships during times of economic fluctuation and in the years of El Niño weather patterns in which floods, droughts, and abnormal weather conditions result from an abnormal warming of surface ocean waters in the eastern tropical Pacific. The last decades of the nineteenth century saw rapid agricultural and commercial expansion.

From Adobe to Copper

Tucson continued to be a center of Mexican activity. In 1879 the *New York Times* described Tucson as having some 10,000 souls "living in the low adobe houses, lining irregular and narrow streets, deserted in the heat of the day," and coming to life during the evening hours. The *Times* referred to the Mexicans as "greasers," saying that few Americans lived there and "fewer" were blessed with wives of their color. According to the *Times*, "jealous" Mexicans stood guard over their female property.

During the first years of Euro-American occupation, travelers stopped in Tucson en route to California, and it was the overland gateway to Sonora and California. Trade with Sonora increased, and Tucson was the center of that trade. Tucson merchants catered to the military posts, the mines, and the farms in its area. However, the importance of Tucson dimmed as irrigation projects opened large agricultural areas north of the Gila River, and the links to California eclipsed those to Guaymas. Government contractors used the road through Yuma to ship their army supplies. This road took a more northern route, following the Gila River, and almost completely bypassed Tucson. This trade contributed to the growth of Pumpkinville, population 300, which became Phoenix in 1871. Its population began to increase owing to the growth of commercial agriculture in the Salt River Valley. Population changes enhanced the political influence of Phoenix at the expense of Tucson. This switch affected the fortunes of the Mexican elite centered in Tucson and marked the decline of the popularity of Mexican peso, the "doby dollar" ("adobe dollar"), as a medium of exchange.[36]

The decline of the Tucson elite did not reduce the presence of Mexicans; nor did it mean that Tucson was no longer a commercial center. In the 1880s, railroads bound Sonora to the United States. Nogales was the main port of entry from Sonora. However, Nogales did not share the distinctiveness or historical importance of El Paso. Tucson, which was 70 miles north of La Línea, was older than Nogales and remained the commercial center of the Sonora–Arizona border area; it became a hub city for the copper mines of northern Sonora and eastern Arizona. As the city grew, Mexican laborers were attracted to Tucson, while Sonoran notables sent their sons and daughters there for schooling. Members of the more prominent families lived in more prosperous northern Tucson, while laborers lived clustered in the southern part of the city, close to the old plaza, and isolated from whites.

Spanish-language newspapers regularly reported the separate literary and social life of Mexicans. Mexicans celebrated *las fiestas patrias* and San Juan's Day (St. John the Baptist) on June 24—dancing, picnicking, and swimming in the Santa Cruz River. Many traveled to Magdalena, Sonora, for the feast of

San Francisco in early October. Tucson's Mexican population also patronized traveling Sonoran troupes. Culturally, Mexicans and Euro-Americans grew even further apart as the twentieth century approached.[37]

Border Conflicts

As the territory's population grew, polarization between the two races increased. The arrival of new colonials, mostly farmers, from Utah, Colorado, and points east worsened racial discrimination. The new settlers were "peace-loving and God-fearing" people who were also racist, rationalizing that the Mexicans were the intruders. Even the saloons were separate and unequal; in 1880, for instance, Jesús Carrillo entered the Tip Top saloon in Prescott, only to be beaten up by white miners, who put a noose around his neck and dragged him around town. Few women lived in the mining camps, and the majority who did were Mexican. They were the targets of stereotypes and sexual harassment. This tension was a sign of what was happening at the border, where cattle rustling and murders raged on both sides; fights often broke out over women. Tombstone remained a hot spot as drunken white laborers publicly tried to take women away from their Mexican partners. Conflict between Euro-Americans and Mexican authorities did not abate during this decade even as commercial relations increased between the two peoples.[38]

The Pull Factors

Copper mining attracted huge numbers of skilled and nonskilled laborers from Mexico, beginning in the 1880s. Up to this point the maximum in-migration was from Sonora, but with the growth of copper mining, larger numbers arrived from New Mexico, Chihuahua, and other Mexican states. Mexicans in these states had a tradition of working plots of land and, in the off-season, working in nearby mines for cash and goods. Reminiscent of the colonial period, large numbers of people were lured by mining bonanzas. Mining generated ripples of economic activity, such as the agriculture and livestock operations that fed the mines.

The first mine owners of eastern Arizona were merchants and prospectors from the Las Cruces and Silver City areas, who then recruited Mexican miners and their families from El Paso.[39] Many Mexican miners had previously been small farmers who worked seasonally in mining. Besides the recruits from El Paso–Juárez, Mexican workers migrated to eastern Arizona from New Mexico and Sonora. By the turn of the century, these two corridors were deeply rutted, as thousands of workers traveled back and forth across the border from and to the mines.

The Industrialization of Arizona

The Southern Pacific railroad reached Tucson in 1880, and 10 years later the territory had 1,000 miles of line, in addition to 700 miles of canals. Arizona, like the rest of the Southwest, was underdeveloped before the introduction of the railroad, which made possible the large-scale exploitation of the territory's resources. Improved transportation brought industrialization and more Euro-Americans and, along with them, eastern and foreign capital. The railroad incorporated Arizona into the rest of the country, dramatically transforming its economy. The Southern Pacific, for example, could haul goods from Yuma to Tucson for $1^1/_2$ cents a pound and in one day, whereas freighters charged $5^1/_2$–14 cents per pound, and took up to 20 days to deliver their cargo. The railroad ushered in the era of the "Three C's"—cattle, copper, and cotton—and a changing Mexican identity, as fewer Mexicans controlled production.[40]

The Importance of Mining

Mining was important even before the arrival of the railroad. Mexicans worked as prospectors and laborers in camps around the Gila and Colorado Rivers. Mexican miners were usually the first to enter the camps and remained even after the camps were abandoned. They made possible the mining strikes at Black Canyon, Bradshaw District, and Walnut Grove. Despite intense discrimination, Mexicans endured and pushed the frontier back.

The Walker diggings at Lynx Creek typify Euro-American–Mexican clashes in these camps. In 1863–1864, the town of Walker passed a law that "no Mexicans shall have the right to buy, take up, or preempt a claim on this river [the Hassayampa] or in this district for the term of six months." Although the town did not allow Mexicans to own claims, the townspeople did permit them to work for wages. The white miners nicknamed Walker "Greaserville."[41]

Although gold and silver were important, copper was the territory's most valuable asset; by the turn of the century Arizona was a major producer of ore, and would attract large armies of Mexican workers. Development began in the 1870s when merchant capitalists funded mining enterprises. Arizona in the early twentieth century would become the second largest and then the largest copper producer in the world. Clifton-Morenci-Metcalf, the Copper Queen of Bisbee, and the copper mining camps of Jerome, Globe, and Miami became the sites of legendary mining companies built by the blood and sweat of Mexicans. Monopolization grew and, by the end of the 1880s, large Scottish combines, along with eastern capital, controlled Arizona copper. Railroads linked Arizona mines with the copper mines of Cananea and Nacozari, Sonora, and the smelters of El Paso. (These enterprises attracted thousands of Mexican laborers.) The copper mining industry fueled a second American industrial revolution, as copper wiring was the mainstay of electricity distribution, motors, and other products needed by the growing nation. The mammoth copper production industry required massive amounts of labor, which in Arizona meant Mexicans.[42]

The Expansion of Capital

Arizona's population expanded rapidly and the number of people engaging in commercial enterprises jumped from 591 in 1870 to 3,252 in 1880. A decade before, Arizona had no banks—merchants provided banking services, and thus the territory had a weak financial infrastructure. The Bank of Arizona was chartered in Prescott in 1877 to serve 3,000 miners in the nearby Bradshaw Mountains. As the Arizona market expanded, San Francisco and New York bankers came into the territory and established monopolies. As mentioned, copper was king in Arizona; demands of emerging technology prompted its prominence. Nikola Tesla, a former employee of Thomas Edison, developed the alternating current (AC) system of electricity in 1887. This system made possible long-distance transmission of electricity, which used copper as the conductor. The rights were bought by George Westinghouse, a major competitor of Edison. The most efficient conduit for the AC was copper.[43]

The railroads, new technology, and engineering drove the mining boom in the 1880s. Telegraph and electrical wires required copper, and the copper mines of southern Arizona lured investors from San Francisco and the eastern United States, as well as attracting foreign capital. In 1880 the Copper Queen Mining Company, financed by California capitalists and Louis Zeckendorf, was founded in Bisbee; the mine was later passed to the Phelps–Dodge Company, which became the largest copper producer in the territory.

New industries received more federal protection, which meant more army forts, which in turn meant more government contracts. The army herded Native Americans onto reservations, bringing even more government contracts to the territory. The demand for large quantities of wood for the mineshafts spread the economic boom to northern Arizona. In all, the territory's population increased from 40,000 in 1880 to 90,000 seven years later, with Euro-Americans outnumbering Mexicans. Arizona was booming as the market value of property increased to $26 million.[44]

The 1890s: The De-skilling of Mine Work

In the 1890s, Sonoran workers continued to meet most of Arizona's labor needs—the Mexicans continued to endure racism. High-grade copper mines were depleted by the 1890s. As a consequence, the mode of production changed, and technology made possible the mining of lower-grade ores of copper. The de-skilled mining required massive of amounts of dirt to be taken out of the earth from which the ore had to be concentrated, leached out, and refined.[45] This form of production required armies of miners with picks and shovels. The need for nonskilled labor led to the importation of large numbers of Mexican workers from Chihuahua and points south via El Paso and New Mexico.

The arrival of the railroad opened up opportunities beyond the low-wage work for just a few Mexicans, specifically those with access to capital. For the most part, small Mexican businesses could not compete. Even the merchant capitalists who initially financed the copper mines often could not afford upgrades necessitated by the new technology. For example, in the early 1880s, the Longfellow Mining Company built a 36-inch narrow-gauge railway between Clifton, Arizona, and Lordsburg, New Mexico, at a cost of $1,542,275 for 71 miles—a fortune at the time.[46] Mine owners also had to construct dozens of small inclines and spurs in the Clifton-Morenci-Metcalf area alone.

The burro- and horse-drawn mills and hand pulverization processes gave way to larger and more sophisticated smelters and concentrators for processing the ore. Mechanization quickly restructured the industry, as unskilled miners replaced the skilled hard-rock miners, who blamed Mexicans for the changes. Even in good times, workers were vulnerable, with frequent economic depressions wreaking havoc. There were no economic safety nets, and unemployment too often meant starvation for families. Worsening the plight of the miners was the lack of workers' compensation if they were injured on the job. Adding to this stress, the mine managers used the racial tensions between the Mexican and the Euro-American miners to divide and conquer, promoting segregated communities and even segregated dressing areas for miners. At home, the workers lived in hovels with their wives, who were expended physically with washing their work clothes. Mexican hovels lacked plumbing, and the women had to walk miles for water, which they hauled back to their homes and heated.

The Impact of Industrialization on Mexicans

In 1870, Arizona numbered 9,658 persons; 30 years later, the population grew to 122,931, of which 14,171 Mexicans were born in Mexico and 29,000 in the United States. In 1880, Tucson had 7,007 residents; 4,469 were of Mexican origin. Tucson, however, grew only marginally in the next 20 years, to a town of 7,531; its Mexican population fell to 4,122. Tucson no longer housed the largest concentration of Mexicans; this status shifted to the mining towns and to commercial-agriculture areas along the uppermost western part of the Gila River. But despite this shift, Tucson continued as the organizational and social capital of Mexicans in the territory, largely because the Mexican population in the mining camps was highly transitory. Tucson was the gateway to Sonora, where many of the miners had homes. Miners from camps throughout Arizona would also travel to Tucson for shopping and fiestas.[47]

Mutual-Aid Societies

Mexicans formed organizations throughout the 1860s and 1870s. With the growing alienation of Mexican workers, the decline of labor guilds, and the isolation of the Mexican population, new forms of self-help societies and fraternal organizations sprang up among the workers and the middle class. *Mutualistas*, or mutual-aid societies, were among the most popular self-help groups. Mexican immigrants were familiar with such organizations, which had sprung up during Mexico's economic transformation of the late nineteenth century when workers and skilled tradesmen struggled to cope. Further, as part of the state-building process, *juntas patrióticas* were formed on both sides of the border to celebrate Mexican heroes and historical events. These organizations became more nationalistic during the French Intervention, and they often lobbied for the liberal cause in the United States. (The reverse is also true: conservatives vied with liberals for the hearts and minds of the populace.)

As with the Irish experience, these societies and organizations helped Mexican workers integrate into the existing immigrant community. When migrating to different camps, the miner found support in local chapters of the *mutualista* he or she belonged to. This sense of *mutualismo* often grew out of shared race, religion, national origin, or some combination of these. A sense of unity and ethnicity, and the desire to share in and strengthen that sense, was at the heart of mutual-aid efforts and fraternal associations. The *mutualistas* differed according to the work environment; in the mines, for example, they often served as forums for labor activities. Socialists, for the most part, criticized *mutualistas,* alleging that they relieved capitalism of the duty of paying for the social costs of production.[48]

On January 14, 1894, *Tucsonenses* formed *La Alianza Hispano Americana* in response to the anti-immigrant assaults, worsened by the Depression of 1893. The American Protective Association that harbored white nativists had an aggressive anti-Mexican agenda. Ignacio Calvillo, a founder of *La Alianza,* remembered, "In those days the English and Spanish-speaking had a hard time getting along. The element opposed to the Spanish-American people in the Southwest had organized itself into the American Protective Association." *La Alianza,* initially a local organization, expanded, and in 1897 held its first national convention. By 1910, it grew to more than 3,000 members and had chapters in Arizona, Texas, New Mexico, California, and Mexico. *La Alianza* was popular in the mining camps of Arizona. Its prime mover was Carlos I. Velasco, who had been a member of the Sonoran legislature (ca. 1869) before he immigrated to Arizona. He worked as a clerk in a store in 1870. Starting in 1878, Velasco was editor of the Tucson newspaper *El Fronterizo,* and he was a founding member of *La Alianza* and its Supreme President during 1894–1896.[49]

The Mexican Middle Class

Tucson's Mexican middle class represented the interests of its class and culture. Many of them were the descendants of the criollo notables who founded Sonora, joined by a smattering of Mexicans from Border States such as Chihuahua. Family connections and pretensions were important socially and economically, as Féderico José María Ronstadt recalled. At the age of 14, Ronstadt went to Tucson from Magdalena, Sonora, to serve as an apprentice to his mother's brother-in-law, and lived with his aunt. Ronstadt was related to many of the old families of Sonora that maintained links with elites in Tucson.[50]

Settled families supported other family members who immigrated later, helping them in business and quickly integrating them into the social life of their circle of clubs. As a class they were anything but liberal; on the contrary, most were quite conservative and their organizations more often opposed organized labor. As early as 1878, the Spanish-language newspaper *Las Dos Repúblicas* condemned workers' societies, alleging that they were made up of "idle and depraved people" who wanted "a repetition of the 1792 Revolution in France."[51]

Although segregated housing and commercial enterprises became more common and racial slurs more frequent, few middle-class leaders made the connection between the racism they were experiencing and the exploitation of Mexican and other workers. The reality was that they considered themselves white and superior to Euro-Americans and they were thus somewhat surprised and offended that they would be considered "colored."

Small Favors to Women

Women played a subservient role in Tucson society; changes were, however, taking place. Women headed a quarter of the households in 1880; this number climbed to a third by 1900. Widows headed most of these households. In some cases, female roles were adapted to the demands of the workplace. For example, after the turn of the century in Douglas, where U.S. stores relied on trade from northern Sonora for survival, "young women who could speak both Spanish and English were critical intermediaries. Women [however] were restricted to clerk positions, but there was little open discrimination because they were in demand. . . . Mexican American women with less education or English worked as maids and cooks."[52]

The Emergence of Trade Unions

In 1871, Arizona produced only 1 percent of copper produced nationwide; by 1885, its share had risen to 15 percent. As mentioned, during the early decades, hard-rock miners did most of the mining. But the deskilling of the industry caused the number of workers to multiply by leaps and bounds. Laborers organized to meet the challenges posed by the giant corporations that controlled the mines. However, these unions were racist and excluded Mexicans from the brotherhoods. Even the Western Federation of Miners (WFM), a union supposedly led by radicals, did not recruit Mexicans in Arizona because of the hostility of white miners toward them. They branded Mexican workers as "cheap labor" and moved to exclude them from the camps.

The WFM encouraged the designation of Globe as a white man's camp and Clifton-Morenci-Metcalf as Mexican camps where wages and housing were dismal. The WFM led the struggle to limit the number of Mexicans living in the mining camps. The lack of working-class unity and the assumed superiority of white miners allowed employers to continue a double-wage standard that paid Mexicans lower wages than were paid to Euro-Americans. Mexicans, in turn, resented getting paid less for the same work and the other forms of discrimination that went with it—segregated housing, facilities, and so on. In 1901, the Arizona Legislature created the Arizona Rangers, who closely resembled the Texas Rangers, to keep Mexicans in their place. Although politicos claimed that the Rangers were formed to stop cattle rustling, they were more often used as strikebreakers.[53]

It's the Water

Commercial farming lagged a decade or two behind mining. Like mining, it grew from small to huge, with absentee owners and managers running the operations. As mentioned, commercial farmers and ranchers drove out small farmers by diverting waterways and gaining a monopoly over the water resources. Small Mexican farmers operated near the mining camps, but with time they became an endangered species. Water was at a premium in Arizona, and irrigation cost money. The lack of capital drove many Mexican, Native American and small white farmers out of farming. Meanwhile, farming became agribusiness, and the greening of the Salt River and Imperial Valleys attracted large armies of Mexican workers and their families to Arizona's and eastern California's deserts. As a consequence of the Reclamation Act of 1902, western Arizona desert farmers in the Salt River Valley received federal assistance to construct irrigation projects that included large dams on the Salt River and later on the Verde River.[54]

Under the Federal Reclamation Act, the Roosevelt Dam was constructed between 1905 and 1911, which eventually had the potential of irrigating fields in the desert for about two years "even if no rain" fell. The Roosevelt Dam made possible the setting up of huge cotton plantations. Although the Reclamation Act was supposed to create a class of small farmers, big planters monopolized the land, and some 1,000 Euro-American families acquired 200,000 acres of well-watered land. The expansion of the plantation farms drove the growth of Phoenix and pointed the way for the damming of the Colorado River.[55]

Phoenix's Mexican community had lived there since the beginning of the town's existence. In 1870 the valley had 240 residents, 124 of them Mexican. Many of the workers employed on irrigation projects or the Phoenix town site were laid-off miners or laborers who alternated between mining and agriculture. According to Bradford Luckingham, "The labor and expertise of Mexicans proved essential to the success of early irrigation operations in the valley."[56]

As elsewhere in the Southwest, development depended on railroads that linked the fields to a core city. The railroads also brought in more Mexicans to work in the fields and in other industries. The Southern Pacific was a major player, acquiring land not far from Phoenix, which became the territorial capital, attracting equipment, investors, and Mexicans. Massive water projects not only expanded commercial farming but also generated energy. Pacific Gas and Electric, a Phoenix–Los Angeles Corporation, held a monopoly on hydroelectric power generation. The government had spent $61 million reclaiming the land, which farmers claimed would be repaid—but never was.[57]

Los Angeles capitalists flocked to the Salt River area, which was as important to Los Angeles as was the Imperial Valley. In the Phoenix area, L.A. capitalists speculated heavily in real estate and farming. Arizona tourists also spent $1 million to $2 million annually in Los Angeles. By 1912, the reclaimed land was producing and marketing more than 450 bales of Egyptian cotton annually, which in reality was the newly developed Pima cotton. (Pima was an extra-long staple and was grown in the Southwest United States starting about 1910.) The longer staple length made Pima a premium cotton fiber and ideal for tire building. The dramatic jump in the production of cotton meant a need for more seasonal workers, who were drawn from the mines, Sonora, and deeper interiors of Mexico. The growth of population also meant more pick-and-shovel work, which meant more Mexicans.[58]

In 1915, the completion of the Roosevelt reservoir gave added life to Salt River Valley. Wheat, cantaloupe, and watermelon crops were taking off, keeping many pickers and their families in the area year round. That year, six carloads of Thompson seedless grapes were shipped east. In 1916, cotton prices increased by 10 cents, reaching 40 cents a pound, and planters made a $70-an-acre profit. Meanwhile, as tire production multiplied, there was an increasing demand for Pima cotton. By 1918, Texans had come to Arizona to lease land and to pick cotton, and their arrival generally meant an increase of racial discrimination toward the Mexicans.[59]

Conclusion: The Industrialization of Arizona

In less than 50 years, Arizona moved from an economy of subsistence farming, passing through mercantile capitalism, to become one of the most industrialized provinces in the United States. This transformation was made possible by the iron horse and the pounding of the Chiricahua Apache into submission and herding them into concentration camps called reservations. The mining boom created cities, and racism in the mining camps sowed the seeds of nationalism among Mexicans, who played a different role in each of the cycles of transformation. The political process was used to control the populace, as wealth was concentrated in the hands of a few elites and absentee owners of mines and farms. Mexican elites maintained somewhat cordial relations with the ruling Euro-American elite, but this status changed as personal relationships gave way to the establishment of a managerial class with access to large amounts of capital. The gap between the rich and the poor, the white and the Mexicans, became insurmountable.

Through each of the cycles, racism remained unabated in regard to the working class, and it spread toward the middle-class Mexicans as the province became more American. Mining attracted investment and enterprises that grew in size as Arizona became more industrialized. Ventures such as cattle raising and agribusiness generated surpluses, which were exported to other regions. By the 1890s, massive numbers of Mexican workers were migrating not only to the mines of Arizona but also to industrialized farms, the irrigation of which at the moment was being financed by private and public capital. Newspapers referred to the lower valleys of the Gila and Salt River Valleys as the "garden of Arizona." In the 1890s, there were an estimated 400,000 arable acres in the Arizona Territory, and these engendered a further pull of Mexicans into Arizona.[60]

Tucson continued to be a Sonoran pueblo. Migration from Sonora was continuous and, with the building of the railroad from Guaymas to Nogales, the south–north flow increased. It was easier to travel from Hermosillo to Tucson and on to New York than it was to go to Mexico City. The economy and family ties bonded the people on both sides of the border. Euro-American capitalists invested huge amounts of capital not only in mining but also in Sonoran agriculture.[61] Mexicans from states other than the Border States of Sonora and Chihuahua began to migrate to Arizona in larger numbers, and, although Tucson was still largely Sonorense, the surrounding mines were beginning to incorporate the workers from the interior of Mexico.

Notes

1. Yaqui River, http://www.youtube.com/watch?v=lPnaQP7jJpk. Rio Yaqui - vida y muerte, http://www.youtube.com/watch?v=K0JAWRGVyyk.

2. Arizona Native Americans, http://jeff.scott.tripod.com/natives.html. Antonio Campa Soza Arizona Pictorial Biography has digital maps. See http://parentseyes.arizona.edu/booksbyedwardsoza/azpictorialbiography/foreword.htm.

3. Henry F. Dobyns, *Spanish Colonial Tucson: A Demographic History* (Tucson: University of Arizona Press, 1976). Thomas E. Sheridan, *Los Tucsonenses: The Mexican Community in Tucson, 1854–1941* (Tucson: University of Arizona Press, 1986). Miguel Tinker Salas, *In the Shadow of the Eagles: Sonora*

and the Transformation of the Border During the Porfiriato (Berkeley: University of California Press, 1997), 4, 7, 27.

4. Robert H. Jackson, *Indian Population Decline: The Missions of Northwestern New Spain, 1687–1840* (Albuquerque: University of New Mexico Press, 1994), 195, fn 48, says it is difficult to establish with precision the racial–ethnic origins of the Sonoran population. Parish priests, as with Chihuahua, exercised a wide discretion. Moreover, the parish rolls of selected northern Sonora Parish Polls in the years 1796–1814 show that it was quite common to see the listing of coyote, mulato, pardo, and mestizo. Gonzalo Aguirre Beltrán, *La población negra de México* (México, DF: Colección Firme, 1972), 228, 234–37. Horacio

Sobarzo, *Vocabulario Sonorense* (México, DF: Editorial Porrua, S/S., 1966), 153. Oakah L. Jones, *Los Paisanos: Spanish Settlers on the Northern Frontier of New Spain* (Norman: University of Oklahoma Press, 1996), 184, infers different figures: A census in the early nineteenth century reported a population of 135,385, which included 38,640 Spaniards, 35,766 mixed-bloods, and 60,855 village-dwelling Christianized Indians. Both figures seem exaggerated, especially the Spaniard category.

5. Henry F. Dobyns, "Tubac Through Four Centuries: An Historical Resume and Analysis," The Arizona State Parks Board (March 15, 1959), Through Our Parent's Eyes, Chapters 4, http://parentseyes.arizona.edu/tubac/ (accessed October 27, 2009). Rodolfo F. Acuña, *Corridors of Migration: The Odyssey of Mexican Laborers, 1600-1933* (Tucson: University of Arizona, 2007), 2, 4–5, 7, 13–14, 17–34. "Comment on Indian Slavery," New Mexico Office of the State Historian, http://www.new-mexicohistory.org/searchbytime.php?CategoryLevel_1=127& CategoryLevel_2=134; also in the Archivo General de la Nacion (Mexico City, Mexico), Inquisicion 1734, 854.

6. Robert C. Hunt, David Guillet, David R. Abbott, James Bayman, Paul Fish, Suzanne Fish, Keith Kintigh, and James A. Neely, "Plausible Ethnographic Analogies for the Social Organization of Hohokam Canal Irrigation," *American Antiquity* 70, no. 3 (July 2005): 433. Donald M. Bahr, "Who Were the Hohokam? The Evidence from Pima-Papago Myths," *Ethnohistory* 18, no. 3 (Summer 1971), 246. Julian D. Hayden, "Of Hohokam Origins and Other Matters," *American Antiquity* 35, no. 1 (January 1970): 87. Prehistoric and Hohokam history in Tucson Area, http://tucsonarizonahistory.tripod.com/hokoham_p1.htm.

7. Thomas E. Sheridan, *Arizona: A History* (Tucson: University of Arizona Press, 1995), 47. Sheridan, *Los Tucsonenses*, 17. See Ramón Eduardo Ruiz, *On the Rim of Mexico: Encounters of the Rich and Poor* (Boulder, CO: Westview Press, 1998). Archaeological and Historical Research at Presidio San Agustín del Tucson, Center for Desert Archaeology, http://www .cdarc.org/pages/what/past/rio_nuevo/arch/tp/presidio.php. Apache Camp, http://www.sonofthesouth.net/american-indians/apache-camp.htm.

8. Jack A. Dabbs, *The French Army in Mexico, 1861-1867* (The Hague: Mouton, 1963), 14, 65, 241, 283. Don Francisco Xavier de Gamboa, *Commentaries on the Mining Ordinances of Spain*, Vol. 2, trans. Richard Heathfield (London: Longman, Rees, Orme, Brown, and Green, 1830), 333. "The French in Sonora and Dominica—The Monroe Declaration," *New York Daily Times* (December 16, 1852). "Sonora; History of the Late French Expedition," *New York Daily Times* (January 14, 1853). Sheridan, *Los Tucsonenses*, 29. John Hosmer and the Ninth and Tenth Grade Classes of Green Fields County Day School and University High School, Tucson, eds., "From the Santa Cruz to the Gila in 1850: An Excerpt from the Overland Journal of William Huff," *Journal of Arizona History* 32, no. 1 (Spring 1991): 41–110. J. Fred Rippy, "A Ray of Light on the Gadsden Treaty," *Southwestern Historical Quarterly* 24 (January 1921): 241. Gadsden Purchase Treaty: December 30, 1853, Avalon Project, Yale University, http://avalon.law. yale.edu/19th_century/mx1853.asp. Desert Diar, History/

Gadsden Purchase, http://museum2.utep.edu/archive/history/DDgadsden.htm. Richard Cavendish, "The Gadsden Purchase," *History Today* 53, no. 12 (December 2003): 55–56.

9. Vista panorámica de Guaymas y la bahía, Guaymas, Sonora, http://www.esmexico.com/antiguas/?seccion=2&cat=Sonora &subcat=Guaymas&clave=MX12182401749055&pagina=1.

10. James Neff Garber, *The Gadsden Treaty* (Gloucester, MA: Peter Smith, 1959). Hubert Howe Bancroft, *History of Arizona and New Mexico, 1530-1888,* Vol. XVII (San Francisco, CA: The History Company, Publishers, 1889), 493, 496, 498, 579. Howard R. Lamar, *The Far Southwest, 1846-1912: A Territorial History* (New York: Norton, 1970), 417–18. John B. Brebner, *Explorers of North America, 1492-1806* (Cleveland, OH: World Publishing, 1966), 407. Francisco R. Almada, *Diccionario de historia, geografía y biografía sonorenses* (Chihuahua: n.p., 1952), 140–44. Fernando Pesqueira, "Documentos Para la Historia de Sonora," 2d series, Vol. 3, Manuscript in the University of Sonora Library, Hermosillo, Sonora. Within Sonora, there was harsh and bitter criticism of the loss of the state's patrimony. Charles D. Poston, Arizona Pioneer, http:// www.discoverseaz.com/History/Poston.html.

11. Sylvester Mowry, *Arizona and Sonora* (New York: Harper & Row, 1864), 35. Laureano Calvo Berber, *Nociones de Historia de Sonora* (México, DF: Libería de Manuel Porrúa, 1958), 50. "The Mowry Mine, originally the Patagonia Mine," http:// www.discoverseaz.com/History/Mowry_Mine.html.

12. Charles D. Poston, "Building a State in Apache Land," *Overland Monthly* 24 (August 1894): 204. G. Hamlin, ed., *The Making of a Soldier: Letters of General B. S. Ewell* (Richmond, VA: Whittel & Shepperson, 1935). Clement W. Eaton, "Frontier Life in Southern Arizona, 1858-1861," *Southwestern Historical Quarterly* 36 (January 1933). Quoted in Joseph F. Park, "The History of Mexican Labor in Arizona During the Territorial Period" (M.A. thesis, University of Arizona, 1961), 20. Newspapers are important in documenting history. See Arizona Newspaper Project, Arizona State Library Archives and Public Records, http://adnp.azlibrary.gov/cdm4/colln_dir.php.

13. Diana Lindsay, ed., "Henry A. Crabb, Filibuster, and the *San Diego Herald*," *Journal of San Diego History* 19, no. 1 (Winter 1973), http://www.sandiegohistory.org/journal/73winter/ crabb.htm. Rufus Kay Wyllys, "Henry A. Crabb: A Tragedy of the Sonora Frontier," *Arizona and the West* 9, no. 2 (June 1940): 183–194, a seminal article.

14. "Invasion of Sonora," *New York Daily Times* (May 21, 1857). Bancroft, *History of Arizona and New Mexico, 1530-1888*, 503. *Arizona Weekly Star*, quoted in Park, "The History of Mexican Labor," 29. Stone to Lewis Cass, Guaymas, December 23, 1858, dispatches from U.S. consuls in Guaymas. "From Arizona, Indian Dependations—Outrages by Mexicans— Business," *New York Times* (September 9, 1859). "From Arizona: Mexican and American Affairs on the Frontier," *New York Times* (November 26, 1859). "The Stone Land Grant," *New York Times* (January 13, 1860). Edward Conner to Cass, Mazatlán, México, May 26, 1859, dispatches from U.S. consuls in Mazatlán, México, GRDS, RG 59. *La Estrella de Occidente* (November 18, 1859). Alden to Cass, Guaymas, November 18,

21, 1859. Thomas Robinson to Alden, Guaymas, November 20, 1859, dispatches from U.S. consuls in Guaymas. Rodolfo F. Acuña, "Ignacio Pesqueira: Sonoran Caudillo," *Arizona and the West* 12, no. 2 (Summer 1970): 152–54. Rodolfo F. Acuña, *Sonoran Strongman: Ignacio Pesqueira and His Times* (Tucson: University of Arizona Press, 1974), 52–64.

15. *Cuentos de Nuestros Padres*, Stories of Our Fathers, Our Mexican American Community, University of Arizona, http://parentseyes.arizona.edu/community_mexBio.php.

16. "Arizona and Sonora—no. iv, Silver Mines," *New York Times* (January 11, 1859). "Arizona and Sonora—no. vii; The Apaches—Military Garrisons and Indian Agencies—Petition from Citizens of Arizona—Mistaken Action of the Government—The Military Becoming Interested in Mines," *New York Times* (January 26, 1859). Ed Dunbar, "Arizona and Sonora—no. ix; Population of Arizona—Fort Yuma—Cost of Transportation in Arizona—Cost of Transportation in Sonora—Difference in Favor of Sonora—Military—Difficulties and Dangers Attending Settlers—Murders by Apaches—Abandoned Trading Posts," *New York Times* (February 10, 1859). William Henry Robinson, *The Story of Arizona* (Phoenix: Berryhill Company, 1919), 244. French intervention and the Second Mexican Empire 1864–1867, MexicanHistory.org, http://mexicanhistory.org/French.htm.

17. An Act to provide temporary government for the Territory of Arizona, 1863, http://www.archives.gov/legislative/features/nm-az-statehood/hr357.html.

18. Edited by Konrad F. Schreier, Jr. "The California Column in the Civil War, Hazen's Civil War Diary," *Journal of San Diego History* 26, no. 2 (Spring 1976), http://www.sandiegohistory.org/journal/76spring/civilwar.htm. The Civil War in Arizona/New Mexico Territory, http://www.discoverseaz.com/History/Civil_War.html. 1864 federal census for the First Judicial District, Arizona Territory, http://www.rootsweb.ancestry.com/~cenfiles/az/1864/jd1/dist1-pt03.txt. The various censuses to 1940 can be obtained through www.ancestry.com.

19. Elise DuBord, "Mexican Elites and Language Policy in Tucson's First Public Schools," *Divergencias: Revistas de estudios lingüísticos y literarios* 1 (otoño 2003): 3–17. Laura K Munoz, "Desert dreams: Mexican American education in Arizona, 1870–1930," (PhD dissertation, Arizona State University, Tempe, 2006), 1–2, 24. She makes the point that Mexican parents were active throughout the territory in the education of their children, citing the work in Apache County.

20. Bancroft, *History of Arizona and New Mexico, 1530–1888*, 503, 575. Editorial, *La Estrella e Occidente* (April 12, 1872). "La Prensa de Arizona y los Horrores Perpetados en el Río Gila," *La Estrella de Occidente* (March 22, 1872). "Asesinator en el Gila," *La Estrella de Occidente* (March 22, 1872). "Trouble Ahead," *Arizona Citizen* (June 24, 1871). "Mexican Raids in Arizona; Recent Outrages Several Families Murdered Correspondence Between the Governor of Arizona and the State Department," *New York Times* (February 5, 1872). Tinker Salas, *In the Shadow of the Eagles*.

21. William Carrigan and Cleve Webb, *Forgotten Dead: Mob Violence Against Mexicans In the United States, 1848–1928* (New York: Oxford University Press), Appendix A, 319–43.

22. Douglas D. Martin, *Tombstone's Epitaph* (Albuquerque: University of New Mexico Press, 1951), 139–65.

23. Sheridan, *Los Tucsoneses*, 2, 41–54, 108. Manuel G. Gonzales, "Mariano G. Samaniego," *Arizona Journal of Arizona History* 31, no. 2 (Summer 1990): 141–60. Manuel G. Gonzales, *Mexicanos: A History of Mexicans in the United States* (Bloomington: Indiana University Press, 1999), 94–96.

24. Tinker Salas, *In the Shadow of Eagles*, 27–28, 63, 191–92, points out that in the 1890 census, women in Sonora controlled 31 commercial establishments, including several saloons and bordellos. Women played a prominent role in mining camps. Katherine A. Benton, "What About Women in the White Man's Camp?: Gender, Nation, and the Redefinition of Race in Cochise County, Arizona, 1853–1941" (PhD dissertation, University of Wisconsin, 2002), 33, puts forth that the status of women depended a great deal on the hue of their skin, their family backup, and where they lived. Tucson had a support network and ties to Sonoran families, whereas in the mining camps all Mexican women were vulnerable and subject to prejudices.

25. Salvador Acosta, "Crossing Borders, Erasing Boundaries: Interethnic Marriages in Tucson, 1854–1930" (PhD dissertation, University of Arizona, Tucson, 2010), 12–13. Acosta's dissertation improved many of my previous citations.

26. Ibid., 40, 42, 44. The 1865 Arizona legislature called "for the removal of friendly Indians and the pacification and even extermination of tribes."

27. Ibid., 20, 31, 181. Marriages between Mexicans and Chinese were also common.

28. Sheridan, *Los Tucsonenses*, 38–39, 47. Jay J. Wagoner, *Arizona Territory 1863–1912: A Political History* (Tucson: University of Arizona Press, 1970), 70. Sheridan, *Arizona*, 109. Kay Lysen Briegel, "Alianza Hispano-Americana, 1894–1965: A Mexican American Fraternal Insurance Society" (PhD dissertation, University of Southern California, 1974), 27. Marcy Gail Goldstein, "Americanization and Mexicanization: The Mexican Elite and Anglo-Americans in the Gadsden Purchase Lands, 1853–1880" (PhD dissertation, Case Western Reserve University, 1977). Carlos G. Vélez-Ibáñez, *Border Visions: Mexican Cultures of the Southwest United States* (Tucson: University of Arizona Press, 1996), 13–19, 95. Harry T. Getty, "Interethnic Relationships in the Community of Tucson" (PhD dissertation, University of Chicago, 1950), 10, 20, 48, 177, 208–9. "Arizona's miscegenation law (1864–1962) prohibited the marriages of whites with blacks, Chinese, and Indians—and eventually those with Asian Indians and Filipinos. Mexicans, legally white, could intermarry with whites, but the anti-Mexican rhetoric of manifest destiny suggests that these unions represented social transgressions."

29. Eulalia Elías 1788–1865, Arizona Women's Hall of Fame, Arizona State Library, Archives and Public Records Carnegie Center, http://www.lib.az.us/awhof/women/elias.cfm.

30. Gonzales, "Mariano G. Samaniego," 152. Pioneer Families of the Presidio De San Agustin, Tucson's Origins, Center for Desert Archaeology, http://www.cdarc.org/pages/what/past/rio_nuevo/people/families.php. Excellent site that includes biographies of original families.

31. Sheridan, *Arizona*, 98 [quote], 79–81. Report of Lt. Royal E. Whitman, "The Camp Grant Massacre; Lieut. Whitman's Report a Fearful Tale—Women and Children Butchered," *New York Times*, July 20, 1871, http://query.nytimes.com/gst/abstract.html?res=9A04E0D7103EEE34BC4851DFB166838A669FDE. Sheridan, *Los Tucsonenses*, 69–70. In a very interesting article, "Inter-Ethnic Fighting in Arizona: Counting the Cost of Conquest," *Journal of Arizona History* 35, no. 2 (Summer 1994): 163–89, Henry F. Dobyns estimated that 6,443 persons were killed in Arizona's interethnic conflict between 1680 and 1890, 89.4 percent of whom (5,759) were Native Americans.

32. Sheridan, *Arizona*, 98. See Allen Broussard, "Law, Order, and Water Policy on the Arizona Frontier," *Journal of Arizona History* 34, no. 2 (Summer 1993): 155–76. Peter L. Reich, "The 'Hispanic' Roots of Prior Appropriation in Arizona," *Arizona State Law Journal* 27, no. 2 (Summer 1995): 649–62.

33. Wagoner, *Arizona Territory 1863–1912*, 164. Bancroft, *History of Arizona and New Mexico, 1530–1888*, 599–600. "Claim for 50,000,000 Acres," *New York Times* (July 2, 1897), 1. There were cases of fraud: The Baron of Arizona, http://www.miningswindles.com/html/the_baron_of_arizona.html. James H. McClintock, *Arizona: Prehistoric, Aboriginal Pioneer, Modern: The Nation's Youngest Commonwealth Within a Land of Ancient Culture*, Vol. 2 (Chicago: S. J. Clarke Publishing, 1916), 529–37.

34. Stephanie Balzer, "N.M.-Arizona Land Acquires RRH Financial." *The Business Journal* (1997): 4.

35. Raquel Rubio Goldsmith, "Hispanics in Arizona and Their Experiences with the Humanities," in F. Arturo Francisco Rosales and David William Foster, eds., *Hispanics and the Humanities in the Southwest: A Directory of Resources* (Tempe: Center for Latin American Studies, Arizona State University, 1983), 14. Sheridan, *Arizona*, 137. "Farms in the Great West; Opportunities for Settlers upon the Public Lands," *New York Times* (June 4, 1880). "The Indians in Arizona; Settlers and Miners Have Little Reason to Fear Them," *New York Times* (June 4, 1880).

36. "Tucson's Valuable Site; a Typical Mexican Town in Arizona. Dreary by Day and Full of Excitement at Night; The Business of Which It Is the Centre; The Rivalry of the Southern Pacific and the Atchison, Topeka, and Santa Fe Roads," *New York Times* (July 13, 1879). C. L. Sonnichsen, *Tucson: The Life and Times of an American City* (Norman: University of Oklahoma Press, 1982), 91. Lamar, *The Far Southwest*, 453–54. Linda Gordon, *The Great Arizona Orphan Abduction* (Cambridge, MA: Harvard University Press, 1999), 23. "El Ferrocaril de Guaymas," *El Fronterizo* (February 8, 1880). *El Fronterizo* (February 22, 1880).

37. Patricia Preciado Martin, *Images and Conversations: Mexican Americans Recall a Southwestern Past* (Tucson: University of Arizona Press, 1983). Also see Heather S. Hatch, "Fiestas Patrias and Uncle Sam: A Photographic Glimpse of Arizona Patriotism," *Journal of Arizona History* 35, no. 4 (Winter 1994): 427–35.

38. Sheridan, *Arizona*, 151. "War on the Borders. Mexicans Massacre Five Americans in Arizona," *New York Times* (August 19, 1881). "Riddled with Bullets," *New York Times* (March 24, 1882). "Mexican Killed at Tombstone," "Mexicans and Americans Fighting," *New York Times* (May 25, 1882). "Feeling Against the Mexican," *New York Times* (February 23, 1886). "Dangerous Mexican Soldiers," *New York Times* (March 18, 1887). "Warning to Mexican Officers," *New York Times* (May 12, 1888).

39. The 1870 U.S. Federal Census, Apache Press, Pima Territory, found at www.Ancestry.com. The 1870 Census is important; it lists the state in Mexico that the workers came from. The first two listed on the census were Joaquin Salazar, 27, laborer, Sonora M593_46 Page: 10 Image: 19 Year: 1870 and Tomas Quiros, 26, Laborer, Sonora Tucson Roll: M593_46 Page: 10 Image: 19 Year: 1870. In the 1880 U.S. Census the following Subias were listed: Luis Subia, 25, Clifton Copper Mine, Apache, Arizona, single. (U.S. Census, 1880; Census Place: Clifton Copper Mine, Apache, Arizona; Roll: T9_36; Family History Film: 1254036; Page: 9B; Enumeration District: 35; Image: 0025; Delfina Subia, 38, Faustina Subia, 38, Francisco Subia, 35, from El Paso and all single.

40. Lamar, *The Far Southwest*, 475. Sheridan, *Arizona*, 104. Jacqueline Jo Ann Taylor, "Ethnic Identity and Upward Mobility of Mexican Americans in Tucson" (PhD dissertation, University of Arizona, 1973), 16.

41. Robert L. Sprude in "The Walker-Weaver Digging and the Mexican Placero, 1863–1864," *Journal of the West* (October 1975): 64–74.

42. See Acuña, *Corridors of Migration*. James Colquhoun, "The Early History of the Clifton-Morenci District," reprinted in Carlos E. Cortés, ed., *The Mexican Experience in Arizona* (New York: Arno Press, 1976). Mining ~ Minería, Chicana/o Collection, Arizona State University Library, http://www.asu.edu/lib/archives/website/mining.htm.

43. Bancroft, *History of Arizona and New Mexico, 1530–1888*, 602. Lamar, *The Far Southwest*, 454. Larry Schweikart, *History of Banking in Arizona* (Tucson: University of Arizona Press, 1982), 1. Sheridan, *Arizona*, 49, 123. Frank J. Tuck, "Fifty Years of Mining in the State of Arizona, 1912–1962" M 91, Arisona Historical Society. Mining in Arizona, http://jeff.scott.tripod.com/miningaz.html. Nikola Tesla, http://en.wikipedia.org/wiki/Nikola_Tesla.

44. Lamar, *The Far Southwest*, 475. David J. Weber, ed., *Foreigners in Their Native Land* (Albuquerque: University of New Mexico Press, 1973), 211.

45. "Morenci Copper Mine, Arizona, USA," MiningTechnology.com, http://www.mining-technology.com/projects/morenci/. "A History of Mining in AZ," http://www.azmining.com/mining-in-az/mining-history-.

46. Ramón Eduardo Ruiz, *The People of Sonora and Yankee Capitalists* (Tucson: University of Arizona Press, 1988). Mark C. Vinson, "Vanished Clifton-Morenci: An Architect's Perspective," *Journal of Arizona History* 33, no. 2 (Summer 1992): 183–206. It has excellent descriptions and photos of Clifton-Morenci.

47. Sheridan, *Los Tucsonenses*, 3.

48. Sheridan, *Los Tucsonenses*, 103–9. Josiah Heyman, "Oral History of the Mexican American Community of Douglas,

Arizona, 1901–1942," *Journal of the Southwest* 35, no. 2 (Summer 1993): 197–201. David T. Beito, "Poor Before Welfare: Fraternal Societies and Mutual Aid Societies Kept the Poor Afloat Long Before the Welfare State," *National Review* 48, no. 8 (May 6, 1996): 42ff. For the People: Mutual Aid Societies/Para la Gente: Sociedades de Ayuda Mútua, http://www.asu.edu/lib/archives/website/organiza.htm (accessed October 27, 2009).

49. Briegel, "Alianza Hispano-Americana, 1894–1965," 34–38, 51, 64. Manuel Servín, "The Role of Mexican Americans in the Development of Early Arizona," in Manuel Servín, ed., *An Awakening Minority: The Mexican American*, 2nd ed. (Beverly Hills, CA: Glencoe Press, 1974), 28. Sheridan, *Los Tucsonenses*, 111–30. Carlos Y. Velasco, 1842–1914, Arizona Memory Project, http://azmemory.lib.az.us/cdm4/item_viewer.php?CISOROOT=/ahstuc&CISOPTR=112&CISOBOX=1&REC=3.

50. Edward F. Ronstadt, *Borderman: The Memoirs of Federico José María Ronstadt* (Tucson: University of Arizona Press, 1993), http://parentseyes.arizona.edu/borderman/index.html. Sheridan, *Los Tucsonenses*, 94–95. Ronstadt was born in Las Delicias, Sonora, in 1868. After working as a carriage maker apprentice, Ronstadt worked for Southern Pacific as a blacksmith. Eventually, he started his own carriage business. His father was a German engineer. The importance of these family connections cannot be underestimated.

51. Sheridan, *Los Tucsonenses*, 85.

52. Heyman, "Oral History of the Mexican American Community of Douglas, Arizona, 1901–1942," 192.

53. James W. Byrkit, *Forging the Copper Collar: Arizona's Labor-Management War of 1901–1921* (Tucson: University of Arizona Press, 1982), 26. For a history of the WFM, see Philip J. Mellinger, *Race and Labor in Western Copper: The Fight for Equality, 1896–1918* (Tucson: University of Arizona Press, 1995), 17–32. Carl M. Rathbun, "Keeping the Peace Along the Mexican Border," *Harper's Weekly* 50 (November 17, 1906): 16–32.

54. Adam M. Sowards, "Reclamation, Ranching, and Reservation: Environmental, Cultural, and Governmental Rivalries in Transitional Arizona," *Journal of the Southwest* 40, no. 3 (Autumn 1998): 333.

55. Bradford Luckingham, *Minorities in Phoenix: A Profile of Mexican American, Chinese American, and African American Communities, 1860–1992* (Tucson: University of Arizona Press, 1994). Bradford Luckingham, *Phoenix: The History of a Southwestern Metropolis*, reissue ed. (Tucson: University of Arizona Press, 1995), 8. "The Great Roosevelt Dam," *Los Angeles Times* (May 6, 1906). Robert Conway Stevens,

"A History of Chandler, Arizona," *Social Science Bulletin No. 25, University of Arizona Bulletin Series* XXV, no. 4 (October 1954): 5–7, 14, 20–25. Sowards, "A 'Wasteland' Transformed: Reclamation," 301. David Brown, "Early Inhabitants and Their Canals Pave Way for Newcomers," *Arizona History* 65, no. 1 (January 2003): 14. Paul S. Taylor, "Mexicans North of the Rio Grande," *The Survey* LXVI, no. 3 (May 1, 1931): 135–36. Peter W. van der Pas, ed., "The Imperial Valley in 1904: An Account by Hugo de Vries," *Journal of San Diego History* 22, no. 1 (Winter 1976), http://www.sandiegohistory.org/journal/76winter/imperial.htm. "Government Is Buying Canals; Which Pass into Control of Reclamation Service," *Los Angeles Times* (February 28, 1907). "Indians Thirsty for Revenge," *Los Angeles Times* (May 16, 1906). The bulk of the labor was done by Native Americans.

56. Luckingham, *Minorities in Phoenix*, 17. Interviewer: Scott Solliday. Narrator: Joe Soto. Tempe Oral History, Barrios Oral History Project. Date of Interview: January 25, 1994. Number: OH-139.

57. "Railroad Yards in Expansion; Southern Pacific Buys Land near Phoenix," *Los Angeles Times* (September 24, 1907). "Land Hold-up Big by Yuma; Scores of Entries Now in Abeyance There," *Los Angeles Times* (October 4, 1907). "Follow after Aztecs"; "The Government's Irrigation Ditches in Arizona Follow Prehistoric Canals," *Los Angeles Times* (December 25, 1907). Railroads of Arizona (2002), http://www.azrymuseum.org/Information/Arizona_Railroad_Map_2002.pdf.

58. "Angelenos Are Heavy Buyers of Lots in Parker Townsite," *Los Angeles Times* (May 17, 1910). "Phoenix Has Boom, Epoch," *Los Angeles Times* (October 8, 1909). "Los Angeles Pledges a Hundred Thousand," *Los Angeles Times* (September 18, 1912). "Cotton Crop Is Marketed," *Los Angeles Times* (November 29, 1912). "Settlers Push Verde Project," *Los Angeles Times* (September 12, 1913). "Valley Cotton of High Grade," *Los Angeles Times* (November 27, 1913). "Cotton Harvest in Full Swing," *Los Angeles Times* (October 11, 1914).

59. "Happenings on the Pacific Slope," *Los Angeles Times* (August 1, 1915). "Cotton Prices up One Dime," *Los Angeles Times* (October 31, 1916). "Arizona Cotton Brings Top Price," *Los Angeles Times* (March 26, 1917). "Arizona Cotton Crop Big of Good Quality," *Los Angeles Times* (November 1, 1918).

60. "The Mexican Land Claims," *New York Times* (September 19, 1890). "The Wealth of Arizona; Early Explorations and the Present Rich Mines," *New York Times* (December 22, 1890).

61. Sterling Evans, "Yaquis vs. Yanquis: An Environmental and Historical Comparison of Coping with Aridity in Southern Sonora," *Journal of the Southwest* 40, no. 3 (Autumn 1998): 363.

CHAPTER 7

California Lost: Image and Reality

LEARNING OBJECTIVES

- Tell the story of Spanish and Mexican colonization of California.

- Discuss why Yankee merchants were attracted to California.

- Explain how Americans infiltrated and invaded California.

- Discuss the role of the Gold Rush in marginalizing Mexican and other foreign miners.

- Interpret how the laws perpetuated racism toward Mexicans.

- Analyze the role of the social bandit in California.

- Describe how Mexicans became a minority of minorities in California.

In applying the wheel to California the economics-centered wheel spins like a slot machine, largely due to the 1849 Gold Rush and the early infusion of huge amounts of capital and numbers of people. Almost overnight, California went from a mercantile economy to a highly capitalized society, heavily dependent

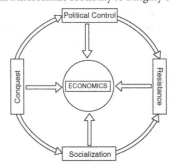

| 1769 | 1821 | 1836 | 1841 | 1848 | 1849 | 1850 | 1860 | 1870 | 1880 | 1890 | 1900 |

on state and national markets. Major settlements developed along the coast on the backs of the missions, presidios, and an occasional pueblo. The pattern resembled that of northern Mexico, where mines gave birth to river valley communities of missions, haciendas, and ranchos, a difference was that in California the mines came last. So embedded was the old in California that the names of towns and places today tell the reader that the Euro-American was not the first to arrive.

The Myth That Has Become Legend

John Steven McGroarty in his book *Mission Memories* (1929) wrote,

> *California was the happiest land the world had ever known. There was peace and plenty, and hospitality became a religion. Song and laughter filled the sunny mornings. There was feasting and music, the strum of guitars and the click of castanets under the low hanging mofons . . . Nothing like it ever existed before, nor has any approach to it existed since.*[1]

The myth of California as the "American apotheosis" was popularized by the play *Ramona*—ironically, based on a novel by Helen Hunt Jackson that was intended to be critical of the treatment of the Californian Indian.[2] The myth created an illusion, a disconnect between image and reality, which Don Mitchell shows in his description of the Joads reaching the crest of the Tehachapi Pass and looking down at the California Eden.[3] In this instance the landscape is a metaphor for how people saw the California Eden: the romantic story of how the Spaniards brought civilization to California and with it salvation and an idyllic life. However, as the Joads get closer they see the suffering of the workers. They see what Carey McWilliams in his classic *North from Mexico* calls a "Fantasy Heritage."[4]

The reality is that, before the arrival of the Spaniards, California was one of the most heavily populated areas in what is today known as the United States. A half million indigenous people lived in what became the Golden State, with the major tribes including the Chumash, Paiute, and Shasta. The Spanish colonization was a continuation of Baja California, which the Jesuits missionized beginning in 1697. By 1769 the Franciscans moved to conquer Alta California. The first colonists were Africans, Indians, and mestizos and mixed-race people called castas. The full-blooded Spaniards were an exception—Baja and, later, Alta California were on the frontier of Sonora, and the Spaniards preferred urban areas, especially those where they could get rich fast, such as mining districts.

California was a refuge for the unwanted. In the interior of New Spain, California was known as a convict colony. Fray Junípero Serra complained that Spanish authorities used California as a dumping ground. As late as 1829, the Mexican government shipped a load of convicts to California—an act that was condemned by the Californios, who by this time had pretensions of being *hidalgos,* or minor nobility.[5]

The presidios (forts) supported the missions' expansion, and soldiers regularly hunted down runaway natives. The natives tired of mistreatment by the colonists, missionaries, and soldiers, and in 1785 the Indians at Mission San Gabriel near present-day Los Angeles rebelled, incited by Toypurina, an unbaptized Indian woman, and Nicolás José, a mission Indian, both of whom had grievances against the Franciscan friars and the mission as a whole. Mission San Gabriel was the jewel of the mission system; it was one of the largest in the string of 21 missions, and some called it the breadbasket of the colony. The mission flourished and by 1785, its missionaries had baptized well over 1,200 Indians. Toypurina became the symbol of Gabrielino resistance, although there is good evidence that she was made the scapegoat.[6]

In 1812, rebels killed Padre Andrés Quintana at Mission Santa Cruz. The so-called homicide had been caused by beatings of the Indians. After the death of Father Quintana, Padre Ramón Olbés became more oppressive. On one occasion when an Indian woman could not conceive, Olbés tried to examine her vagina; the infuriated woman bit Olbés. She was given 50 lashes and was shackled and ordered to walk around holding a wooden doll.[7] The cumulative indignities led to the great Chumash uprising of 1824, which encompassed Santa Inés, La Purisima Concepción, and Santa Barbara Missions. The Chumash disarmed the soldiers and forced them to retreat to the presidio. The revolt was triggered by the unfair punishment meted out to a mission Indian, the injustice of which outraged his friends. When the soldiers attacked in force, the rebels abandoned Santa Barbara and retreated to the hills. The rebellion came to an end when Spanish authorities unconditionally pardoned the rebels. It was the largest organized revolt in the history of the California missions and was put down by brutal military campaigns. Throughout the Spanish and Mexican Periods, Indian women not only took part in revolts, but, as in the interior of Mexico and elsewhere in Spanish America, they used the Spanish legal system to challenge cruel friars, abusive soldiers, and despotic officials.[8]

Smallpox, syphilis, diphtheria, chicken pox, and measles caused suffering and death among those living near the Spanish centers of population. Excessive backbreaking labor and poor nutrition increased the natives' susceptibility to disease. As much as 60 percent of the mission Indians died of European diseases. The epidemics eroded whatever little faith Native Americans had in the new order, and many Indians escaped and returned to their native shamans. Further, the Indians were sexually abused by soldiers and, in some cases, by priests.[9] The reality beneath the image of the missions was that life had changed for the indigenous people—it was for the worse.[10]

Mexican Period

In 1821 California became part of the Mexican republic, and the province was opened to outside trade. Mexico's liberalization of trade and immigration regulations encouraged foreigners to enter and live in California. Mercantile capitalism transformed missions into thriving enterprises—the envy of the growing ranchos that pushed for the missions' privatization. Improved transportation and increasing opportunities attracted hundreds of non-Mexicans who arrived and stayed; and, as in Texas and New Mexico, the white newcomers were a Trojan horse opening the door for the later U.S. invasion of California.[11]

By 1823, Alta California had been reduced to about 21 missions and their satellite presidios, pueblos, and ranchos. The Indian was a class apart—in every sense of the word a colonized people. The Franciscan missions forced a religious and sexual discipline that wiped out the Indian culture, which included sexuality, intimacy, and biological and social reproduction. The mission friars defended their intrusion by saying that the Indian was being given the privilege of the Spanish culture, the protection of its laws, and salvation through Jesus Christ. The consequence was that the Indian was thought of as a chattel who was culturally and racially inferior.

Brian McCormack makes the point that "marriage and sexual exchange in most areas served as the predominant vehicles through which Native individuals, households, and villages were drawn into a wider web of social relations. Through marriage, new households were created and ties of cooperation and dependency were cemented; Native men and women, and the communities of which they were a part, fashioned new familial . . . ties and networks and cooperative bonds." In this system, levels of violence and homicide were high, and sexism was the norm.[12]

The Class Gap

The missions thrived during the 1820s—so much so that by 1827 the missions had 210,000 branded cattle, and an estimated 100,000 unbranded cows. This wealth did not go unnoticed by the small emerging ranchero class, who would most benefit from the secularization of the missions in 1834.[13] The rancheros were slaughtering 60,000 cows annually, and selling 30,000–40,000 hides at two pesos apiece, a system that was maintained by Indian labor. This growth coincided with the industrial revolutions in England and other parts of Europe, as well as in the United States; they were the main markets for cattle products such as leather (for footwear) and tallow (for candles).

Consequent to secularization, restraints on the use of native labor lessened and encroachment on their land increased. Theoretically, Native Americans owned half the secularized property. But the native Californians never received its bounties. Secularization forced the natives to work for wages as *vaqueros* (cowboys) in the expanding rancho system or as laborers in pueblos (towns). It hardly made the Indians free and/or independent. It was a system in which lower-class mestizos and mulatos competed with the natives in this labor pool.[14] Secularization also meant the abandonment of the presidios. Few *hacendados* (large landowners) had enough money to support a small standing army and pay soldiers.

Mercantile capitalism widened the gap between landholders and the landless. Meanwhile, the Californios justified their privileged status, invoking theories of their racial superiority. According to them, the natives were not intelligent enough to develop the land. Like most nineteenth-century liberals, Californios favored local control over government, and they believed that they had the right to control the native labor. Violence remained an integral part of the system, provoking Native American revolts throughout the Mexican Period.[15]

Meanwhile, the secularization of the missions uprooted the mission Indians, disorienting them and thus increasing their vulnerability to exploitation. Landless, and also wracked by disease and afflicted by alcoholism, many former mission natives wandered the countryside. At will the Californios treated them as wards of the government.[16]

Secularization also impacted pueblos such as Los Angeles since they were forced to absorb large numbers of dispossessed natives. "[P]ueblos thus began to see homeless Indians, hungry, cold, and begging—no longer subservient to the missionaries."[17] The pueblos became the centers for artisan workers and day laborers, as well as merchants. But ultimately the large influx of Native American labor flooded the pueblos' infrastructure. In 1836, the census reported 252 natives in Los Angeles; eight years later, there were 650. Many Indians had no other choice but to join the military. As early as the late 1810s, natives served in the cavalry against their own people. Militarization of the natives further divided the indigenous population.[18]

The secularization of the missions was part of the transformation to capitalism; ironically, the pretext of the rancheros for ending the mission system was that missionaries enslaved the natives.[19] After secularization the land passed to private ranch owners who conveniently overlooked that Native Americans legally owned half of the secularized property.[20] Secularization also meant the abandonment of the presidios, which left the Spanish settlements vulnerable to attacks. Of the new hacendados, only Mariano Vallejo had enough money to afford a small standing army and pay soldiers to control Indian workers.

California experienced other changes during the 1830s. Californio rancheros no longer produced solely for local consumption, but entered the mercantile capitalist cycle and assumed the right to define their own legitimacy. They controlled California government, and as University of California Santa Cruz Historian Lisbeth Haas writes, "Californios used Spanish colonial ideas to define their territorial government's right to control the land of mission Indians."[21]

With the secularization of the missions the hide and tallow trade passed to a small group of rancheros. Ranchos and haciendas were carved out of former mission holdings along the coast. Landless, the Indians either wandered the countryside or were forcibly tied to the land. They had few options since their institutions had been destroyed and the missions system was also torn down.[22] Meanwhile, the surviving missionaries "leased out" former mission natives to rancheros, reinforcing the notion that native people could be rented out.[23]

Not all Californios treated the natives badly or approved of forced labor; generational differences existed among the Californios. For instance, the second generation of Californios considered themselves entitled as the native sons of California—in their minds, they were the real proprietors of the land, with more right to the land than even the indigenous people. To them, Mexican immigrants who came to California during the Mexican Period were foreigners—a mind-set that was deepened by a paranoia that Mexicans from the interior were coming to California to steal what belonged to the native sons.

The truth be told, most Californios did not come from elite Mexican families—very few were criollos. For example, Pío de Jesús Pico belonged to a mixed race of Spanish, African, Italian, and Native American races. His parents migrated to the San Gabriel Mission from Sinaloa with the famous overland Juan Bautista de Anza expedition of 1775.[24] Pico was born in the San Gabriel Mission in 1801. He lived a conspicuous life style and squandered wealth appropriate to an hidalgo. Pico became governor in 1832 and again in 1845, something that would have been improbable anywhere else in New Spain. His upward mobility was based not on democratic ideals or merit but rather on illusions of superiority. Even his race was an illusion, and his racial purity was maintained through family ties among Californios who were also largely of mixed race. Race mattered little because of their wealth, family connections, and political power.[25]

Women in the Transformation of California

When the colonization began, mission fathers relied on native women from Baja California, Sonora, and Sinaloa to socialize Californian native women. Life was harsh for native Californian women. The missionaries selected the highest-ranking native women as brides for Spanish-Mexican male colonists to forge a mestizo culture, a culture closer to the criollo ideal. Through women, the priests passed on religious tradition and the custom of protecting their daughters' chastity until marriage. Some women did achieve a measure of power, or better still, influence. In the 1830s, Doña Apolinaria Lorenzana claimed and administered but lost Rancho Santa Clara de Jamacha.[26] Her mother brought to Alta California, but then abandoned her after the mother's marriage. Apolinaria taught herself to read, and managed a school on an estate where she taught girls reading, catechism, and sewing. She later worked as a curandera (healer). Like Fermina Espinosa, owner of the Santa Rita Rancho, Lorenzana rode horses and roped steers. Women could inherit ranchos and other property; they also worked as shopkeepers and midwives. Take the case of Juana Briones de Miranda, born in 1802 in what is now Santa Cruz. Juana was of mixed Spanish, African, and Indian ancestry. Despite a brutal marriage, she bought property in what is today San Francisco, built a cattle ranch and a dairy business in the San José area, and defended her property before the U.S. Land Commission Hearings. Even with these exceptions, Californio families were patriarchal; according to Antonia Castañeda, sexual violence, rape and incest, and family violence were common.[27]

However, Mexican women were better off legally than their Euro-American counterparts. They could own property and use the courts to defend their property interests. The status of women in Spanish and, later, in Mexican California differed subtly from that in other parts of Mexico. It was isolated and provincial unlike, for example, mining centers where gender and class lines often broke down. In California groundbreaking work is being done by scholars such as Castañeda and Virginia Marie Bouvier, who are discovering the footprints that piece together the tribulations of native and mixed-blood women in California. They have opened a treasure trove of documents such as testimonies of women like Eulalia Pérez, a caretaker of Missión San Gabriel Arcángel and owner of Rancho del Rincón de San Pascual in the present-day Los Angeles area.[28]

The Bear Flag

During the Mexican Period, Euro-Americans arrived mostly by sea. Those who stayed formed strong ties with the Mexican rancheros and hacendados, often intermarrying. By 1841, the few foreigners in California consisted of ex-sailors, commercial agents, and businessmen, many of who assimilated into Mexican society. Then between 1843 and 1846, about 1,500 Euro-Americans arrived in California, traveling overland from the Midwest with their wives and families. The new wave of immigrants mixed with the natives to a lesser extent than did their predecessors, resulting in less intermarriage. The newcomers settled in the inland areas—uninhabited, according to them, since only natives lived there. Some Euro-Americans migrated west after they had gone bankrupt and lost their lands in the depression of 1819 and the Panic of 1837. As in Texas filibusters migrated to California after 1819.

John C. Fremont and the Bear Flag

John C. Fremont's third expedition stands out in the rush to California. The expedition left St. Louis in May 1845, reaching California at the end of May; Fremont immediately marched to Monterey to purchase supplies. There, he met with Thomas O. Larkin, a prominent merchant who had arrived in California in 1832 and served as the U.S. consul. Larkin's letters to the U.S. State Department had supplied the government with critical information about California. The Mexican governor gave Fremont permission to camp as long as he stayed away from coastal settlements. More Euro-American reinforcements soon arrived and in March 1846, Fremont raised the U.S. flag at Hawk's Peak, about 25 miles from Monterey. Fremont was ordered to leave California right away. Just as the expedition was about to depart,

Marine Lieutenant Archibald H. Gillespie reached Fremont and delivered personal letters to him, along with verbal instructions from President James K. Polk.[29] The communiqué instructed Fremont that war with Mexico was imminent, encouraging him to return to the Sacramento Valley. Euro-Americans rallied to Fremont's Bear Flag and declared war on Mexico. Their merchants convinced some Mexican ranch owners that joining the invasion was in their best interest; the poor, on the other hand, remained loyal and resented the gringos. Meanwhile, the behavior of the "Bear Flaggers" alienated their few friends. In June 1846, Fremont's soldiers took Mexican general Mariano Vallejo prisoner at his ranch in Sonoma. Vallejo and his brother were sent to Sutter's Fort and harassed, even though Vallejo was sympathetic to Euro-Americans. Fremont further estranged rich merchants and landowners by initiating a policy of forced loans and confiscation of land and property.[30]

Bear Flaggers rustled cattle and horses, looted homes, and wounded and murdered innocent people. On one occasion, a scouting party under Kit Carson's command came upon José de los Reyes Berreyesa and his twin nephews, Francisco and Ramón de Haro. The men were unarmed, but the Euro-Americans shot them anyway. They killed Ramón, and his brother Francisco "threw himself upon his brother's body." One of the assassins then shouted, "Kill the other son of a bitch!" Upon seeing his two nephews murdered, the old man—José—called out to the Euro-Americans, "Is it possible that you kill these young men for no reason at all? It is better that you kill me who am old too!" The Bear Flaggers obliged by killing him as well.[31] The Berreyesa murders served no military purpose, they were extra-legal, and their assassinations ushered in a period of the wanton murder of Mexicans, mostly by lynching. William Carrigan and Cleve Webb confirm that at least 143 were victims of lethal mob violence. California ranked second to Texas, which had 232 victims.[32]

U.S. Invasion of California

In July, Commodore John Drake Sloat landed 250 Marines at Monterey and raised the U.S. flag. Later, Commodore Robert F. Stockton, a known expansionist, replaced Sloat. Fremont, promoted to the rank of major, was placed in command of the California Battalion of Volunteers. Naval forces entered Los Angeles harbor, with Captain Archibald Gillespie in charge of occupying the area. Meanwhile, José María Flores led the resistance in Los Angeles. Although the Californios were poorly armed, they defeated Gillespie and forced him to surrender. During the battle, large numbers of Angelenos cheered Flores's men.

Colonel Stephen Kearny, leader of the Army of the West, arrived from New Mexico. On December 5, 1846, a force of 65 Mexicans met the invading army at San Pasqual Pass, northeast of San Diego. Led by Andrés Pico, the Mexicans killed 18 Euro-Americans and wounded Kearny and many of his men; the Mexicans suffered no losses. A well-armed cavalry soon arrived, overwhelming the Mexican defenders. Kearny's army entered Los Angeles on January 10, 1847, and Andrés Pico surrendered at the Cahuenga Pass and signed the Treaty of Cahuenga.[33]

Gold Transforms California

The end of the old order came with the Gold Rush of 1849. The world knew for some time that there was gold in California. Six years before the crucial discovery at Sutter's Mill, Francisco López found gold in Placerita Canyon, just north of the San Fernando Valley.[34] From 1842 to 1847, Mexican miners culled some 1,300 pounds of gold from the site. On January 24, 1848, James Wilson Marshall found gold on John Sutter's property. Thousands of outsiders flooded into California, overwhelming the Mexican population, and ending any hope they might have had of participating in the governance of California.[35]

The Gold Rush, in the northern part of the state, instantly turned Mexicans into a minority there. Chileans, Peruvians, and other Latin Americans joined them on the northern riverbanks. In 1848, about 1,300 Mexicans and 4,000 Yankees worked in the gold fields, and the two races got along moderately well. By mid-1849, nearly 100,000 miners panned for gold—80,000 were white, 8,000 were Mexicans, 5,000 were South Americans, and several thousands were Europeans.[36]

The Gold Rush Creates a Template

The gold rush set a template for North American–Mexican relations. Within a few years of the arrival of the miners, houses of prostitution flourished and were restricted to the nonwhite residential areas. Although the overwhelming majority of northern California's inhabitants were white, three-quarters of the prostitutes were nonwhite. The 1850 census showed that 50 percent of California residents worked in gold mining; in 1852, a peak year, gold mines produced $80 million. According to the 1860 census, 38 percent of Californians still worked in gold mining. By 1865, Californians had mined three-quarters of a billion dollars in gold. The increasingly large amounts of capital demanded for gold mining further concentrated wealth in the hands of a few, solidifying the monopolization of California politics by the elite: gold belonged to those who could afford to finance the stamp mills, smelters, and foundries.

Gold mining introduced the banking system to California. Saloon keepers, freight express and stage operators, and mercantile capitalists—especially those who owned wholesale and retail warehouses—were the first bankers. Merchants bought and sold gold, transporting the bullion to the East or holding the ore for safekeeping, and charging 5 percent per month for their services. In 1854, some investors founded the Bank of California; by the following year, 19 banks and 9 insurance companies operated in California. The accumulation of capital enabled bankers to expand their operations. California financiers invested heavily in the Virginia City, Nevada, Comstock Strike of 1859. The new capitalist class also bankrolled iron works, flour mills, and sugar beet refineries; San Francisco capitalists underwrote ventures throughout the Southwest. By 1862, capitalists founded the San Francisco Stock Exchange Board, facilitating even more rapid growth of the economy.[37]

Complicity of the Californios

By 1849, California's population grew to more than 200,000 people—100,000 of whom were Californian Indians, and 13,000 Mexicans. The Californios' new social order rejected their Mexicanness and cultivated the pretensions of the *don*.[38] The large white population guaranteed the territory statehood, and a constitutional convention was held in August of that year at Monterey. Eight of the 48 delegates to the convention were Californios, who had the opportunity to vote as a bloc. However, the Californios failed to protect the interests of Mexicans, believing that they would share in the governance and bounties of the new order. After all, Californios considered themselves different from the *cholo* masses (pejorative term for low-caste Mexicans); they rationalized that they had more in common with those with a lighter skin hue. Instead of voting as a bloc, Californios voted individually for their own immediate self-interests. For example, of the eight Spanish-speaking delegates, only José A. Carrillo voted for the free admission of Negroes into California. Carrillo, however, cast his vote out of political opportunism, because he felt this stance would better California's chances for early statehood. A criticism is that Mexican delegates more interested in having fun than in the task at hand were largely silent during the proceedings while many white delegates who were in large part lawyers dominated the proceedings.[39]

The Californios could have voted to split the territory into north and south, giving Mexicans control of the southern half. Again, Californios voted for their self-interest; many delegates belonged to the propertied class and believed that taxes would be imposed on northern commerce rather than on land. Californios won some minor victories: suffrage was not limited to white males; the state would print laws in Spanish and English; and so on. On the other hand, Californios accepted the California Bear, the symbol of the conquest, as the state symbol. Tragically, "the constitution was the only document of importance in whose drafting the Mexican Californians shared."[40]

Even more disturbing is that the Mexican delegates did not protect the Indians. They abetted the belief that the Indians were brutish and only partially civilized. Less than a year after the delegates voted to make California a "free state," the legislature passed the California 1850 Act for the Government and Protection of Indians. Commercial agriculturists led the fight for its passage; this class was comprised of Euro-Americans and Californios who owned California's Spanish and Mexican rancho grants. The Act effectively kept intact the Mexican rancho labor system, making the Indians peons. Michael Magliari in an excellent article dissects the 1850 California Indian Act, writing that Section 3

> *allowed employers to obtain custody of Native American children and to keep them until they reached the age of majority, which the law defined as eighteen years for males and fifteen for females. The section led to a flourishing trade in Indian children kidnapped from their parents or seized as the spoils of war by California militiamen who campaigned throughout the state during the 1850s and 1860s.*

Section 3 made Indian minors indentured servants under the guise of "apprenticeship." Those determined by the courts to be vagrants could be put in apprenticeships in which they worked without pay. The Indian Act sanctioned Indian convict leasing and indentured servitude, and the hunting down of those attempting to escape.[41]

Legalized Theft: The Foreign Miners' Tax

Gold encouraged a get-rich-quick mentality. Most Argonauts wanted to strike it rich and go home; few planned to remain in California. For many speculators, however, hopes for instant fortune failed to materialize. The frustration of shattered dreams drove men to invent rationalizations and find scapegoats. Mexicans became the scapegoats for Euro-American miners' failures, and Euro-American merchants resented the success of Mexican peddlers and mule dealers. General Persifor F. Smith in 1849 published a circular labeling noncitizens trespassers and advocating fines and imprisonment for trespassers.

White miners applauded the Smith "doctrine" because they believed that if they allowed foreigners to mine, these outsiders would take all the gold out of the United States and strengthen another nation at the expense of Euro-America. The Mexican minister to Washington, D.C., referring to the Treaty of Guadalupe Hidalgo, sent an official protest condemning violent treatment of Mexicans in California.

Opportunist politicos took cheap shots; in Sacramento G. B. Tingley warned of a foreign invasion, describing Mexicans as "devoid of intelligence." Thomas Jefferson Green—a Texan, hater of Mexicans, expansionist, and white supremacist—proposed a compromise bill: foreigners would be taxed $20 per month. The legislators rationalized that taxing foreigners would prevent violence. That is, if foreigners paid for the right to mine, they would be more acceptable to white miners. On April 13, 1850, the California state legislature passed its first foreign miners' tax. Legislators repealed the tax less than a year after it had passed, not because the legislators cared about Mexicans or other foreigners, but because the merchants pressured Sacramento. Still the racist rhetoric about the Mexican and Chinese stealing their gold persisted among the whites. Coya Brownrrig writes: "Significantly, the lynching of Hispanos was tied to a larger pattern of displacement from land and economic resources. Lynchings punished not only individual Hispanos but were often accompanied by attacks on Hispanos en masse, as the discourse of Hispano criminality combined with the urgency of an immediate and local threat was used to justify the rounding up and running out of all local Hispanos, whose land, property, or mining claims would then be appropriated by Anglo residents." According to historians Carrigan and Webb, "Gold Rush California was critically important in the national dissemination of this defense of vigilantism," and its justification. The Gold Rush was also why California led the nation in mob violence during the 1850s, and according to scholars set the template for today's violence against immigrants.[42]

Decline of the Californios

Even before the Gold Rush ended, the Yankees turned their attention to securing more land for themselves. In 1851 the U.S. Congress passed a law that encouraged squatters to challenge Spanish and Mexican land grants by requiring all owners to prove title and establishing a land court. The California Land Act of 1851 clearly violated the Treaty of Guadalupe Hidalgo. Euro-Americans, believing that they had special privileges by right of conquest, thought it "undemocratic" for 200 Mexican families to own 14 million acres of land, even though the Treaty of Guadalupe Hidalgo and its Statement of Protocol clearly gave Mexicans specific guarantees as to these grants. The author of the law, Senator William Gwinn, later admitted that the law was designed to encourage squatters to invade Mexican ranchos and force owners off their land.[43]

The California Land Act established a Board of Land Commissioners to review claims. Judgments could be appealed to the U.S. district court and even the Supreme Court. The process was costly—of 813 claims, 549 were appealed as many as six times each. Litigation dragged on. The delay encouraged Euro-Americans to move onto ranches with legal title and squat on them. They were given a legal footing equal to that of the landowners, who had the burden of proof and had to pay exorbitant legal fees to defend titles to land that was already theirs. Judges, juries, and land commissioners were biased and easily bribed. Hearings were held in English, which put Spanish-speaking grantees at an additional disadvantage. The result was that the commission heard 813 cases and approved only 520 of the grantees' claims, rejecting 273, with 20 not making it through the process.[44]

The Locusts

In 1858, 200 squatters and 1,000 "gun-carrying settlers" ambushed surveyors and held landowner Domingo Peralta hostage. Another landowner, Salvador Vallejo, rather than lose everything, sold his Napa ranch for $160,000; he had paid $80,000 in legal fees to secure its title. By 1853, squatters had moved onto every rancho around San Francisco.[45] The Land Act cast doubt on the legality of Mexican land titles. It sent a message to land-hungry Euro-Americans that there was a chance the Californios did not own the land, that their land was part of the public domain, which gave Euro-Americans a right to homestead it. They knew that local authorities would not or could not do anything about it. Hence, they invaded and swarmed the land like locusts, harassing and intimidating many landowners. Simultaneously, claimants insidiously bled the Californios by pressing expensive litigation that challenged their grants in federal court.

Taxation without Representation

Forced out of northern California, Mexicans retained influence only in the southern half of the state, which was cattle country and highly vulnerable to swings of the economy and the natural environment. The rancheros experienced a brief boom in the early 1850s, when they drove 55,000 head of cattle to San Francisco annually at $50–$60 a head; but by 1855, the price of cattle had fallen. In 1850, the state legislature initiated a tax on land, shifting the tax burden from northern to southern California. In 1852, six southern California cattle counties had a population of 6,000 (mostly Mexican) and paid $42,000 in property taxes and $4,000 in poll taxes.

By contrast, northern California—with 120,000 persons—paid only $21,000 in property taxes and $3,500 in poll taxes. Simultaneously, rancheros had to pay county taxes, road tolls, and other special taxes. Between 1850 and 1856, the tax rate doubled on land, while mines were exempted. All in all, rancheros were unable to cope with fluctuations in the economy and pay taxes. Californios, inexperienced in the new economic order, speculated and heavily mortgaged their property during the early 1850s. Thus, when the price of cattle fell they could not meet their mortgage payments.

Some historians speculate that the size of Spanish-Mexican land grants determined the gigantic size of California's agribusiness holdings; however, this isn't so. From the beginning of their conquests, capitalists played the game of monopoly, and the results would most likely have been the same whether or not there had been large ranchos and haciendas. The Southern Pacific Railroad alone accumulated 11,588,000 acres—an area equivalent to one-fifth of privately owned land today in California, and larger than the 8,850,000 acres once owned by the Californios.

Historian Lisbeth Haas points out that in Santa Ana and San Juan in 1860, Californios owned 62 percent of the land; 10 years later, that figure had dropped to 11 percent. Mexicans owned 6 percent in 1860, and 1 percent in 1870; Native Americans owned 1 percent in 1860 and 10 years later zero. According to Richard Griswold del Castillo, only 3 percent of the 10,000 Mexican Californios owned large ranchos while 61 percent owned small parcels of land worth more than $100 in 1850. Ten years later the proportion fell to 29 percent and by 1870 it was only 21 percent. The Indian population of California fell from 150,000 in 1845 to less than

30,000 in 1870. By contrast, the European share of the population went up from 25 to 51 percent, and the Euro-Americans owning land went from 6 to 36 percent. The pattern of white monopolization was similar throughout California economic recessions that encouraged the growth of the Know Nothing Party throughout the nation. The Homestead Act was the culmination and justification for the squatter movement.[46]

Marrying White

Intermarriage with daughters of the ricos was profitable for the newcomer; for the ricos it was a way to preserve their power. Horace Bell describes white males in such marriages as "matrimonial sharks" marrying "unsophisticated pastoral provincials." He wrote, "Marrying a daughter of one of the big landowners was in some respects a quicker way to clean her family of its assets than to lend money to the 'old man.'"[47]

Dara Orenstein put it best,

Whites benefited from marrying Mexicans. White-Mexican marriages facilitated the exchange of property from an elite in "decline" to its successor elite, typically uniting white male settlers with Mexican women from established families. While historians have debated the frequency of these marriages, and feminist historians have read them as complex emotional affairs rather than simply as economic transfers, most agree they greatly determined California's distribution of wealth. In addition, by pitting "Spanish Californios" against "dirty" and "law-less" cholos and by fueling the racialization of class differences among Mexicans, these marriages enabled white settlers to avert mutiny in a society in which whites were vastly outnumbered. What is more, these marriages even aided settlers discursively.[48]

Stephen C. Foster married Don Antonio María Lugo's daughter, who was a widow and a wealthy woman in her own right, based on interests in her father's holdings. Two granddaughters of Antonio Lugo, who were the daughters of Isaac Williams, married Euro-Americans. One of them, John Rains, inherited the Chino Ranch. All of the granddaughters of General Mariano Vallejo of Sonoma married Euro-Americans; Vallejo had obviously forgotten that "his liberators" once called him a greaser. According to Bell, "Mostly the native daughters married good looking and outwardly virile but really lazy, worthless, dissolute vagabond Americans whose object of marriage was to get rich without work."[49] Many of them brought the women they married to ruin.

As in other southwestern states, there is little to suggest that any significant number of Mexican men, whether rich or poor, married white women. There was a scarcity of white women, and the old game of supply and demand ruled. Thus, the conquerors monopolized the available supply of women, whom they reduced to commodities. As Bell explained, the heads of Mexican families often "felt that the future was in the hands of the invading race" and that the marriage of the daughter to a gringo was a form of protection. Bell also thought "the girls felt that they acquired prestige by marrying into the dominant race." To marry a gringo was to be accepted as white; to marry a gringo was to associate oneself with privilege, and it went a long way in feeding the Californios' sense of inferiority.[50]

Legalizing Racism

While the degree of racism differed across class lines, los ricos were not spared even if they married gringos. Most Californios were not pure-blooded Castilians, but descendants of the frontier people, who were mixtures of Indian, African American, and Spanish. As more Euro-Americans poured into the territory, racism increased, and to the new majority a greaser was a greaser. Most had not read the Treaty of Guadalupe Hidalgo, nor did they care to.

For instance, Section 394 of the Civil Practice Act of 1850 prohibited Chinese and Native Americans from testifying against whites. In *People v. Hall* (1854), a judge reversed the conviction of George Hall because it was based on the testimony of a Chinese. The courts also applied this section to Mexicans.[51] In 1855 the state legislature refused to provide funds for translation of state laws into Spanish despite the Treaty of Guadalupe Hidalgo and the state constitution. That same year the legislature passed the Greaser Act, which defined vagrants as "all persons who [were] commonly known as 'Greasers' or the issue of Spanish or Indian blood."

In April 1857 in *People v. Elyea*, a court denied Manuel Domínguez, a signer of the first California constitution, a wealthy landowner, and a county supervisor, the right to testify because of his Native American blood.[52]

Legitimization of Violence

The term *vigilante* comes from groups known as the Committees of Vigilance. Such groups were common in the days following the California Gold Rush.[53] Some historical accounts have romanticized the vigilantes as local citizens banded together to fight crime, bringing down the crime rate in places like San Francisco. However, vigilantes played out the biases of their participants. On June 15, 1849, a "benevolent, self-protective and relief society" called *the Hounds* attacked a Chilean barrio in San Francisco. The drunken mob killed one woman, raped two more, looted, and plundered. On July 10, 1850, four Yaqui were charged with the murder of four Euro-Americans near Sonora, California.[54] Justice of the Peace R. C. Barry believed that the men were innocent and attempted to forestall violence, but the mob hanged the four men. In 1851, when the state passed the foreign miners' tax, Antonio Coronel, a schoolteacher, came upon a mob that was about to lynch five foreigners accused of stealing 5 pounds of gold. Although Coronel offered to pay them the cost of the gold for the release of the prisoners, the miners refused. They then whipped three of the men and hanged the other two.

Public whipping and branding were common, and it did not matter if the victims were citizens or not. Spanish-speakers were lumped together as "interlopers" and "greasers." Historians have portrayed vigilantism as an expression of democracy in action. In other words, the mob championed law and order, which meant taking "an eye for an eye." Accordingly, Mexicans had a criminal nature that had to be controlled, and to North Americans every Mexican was a potential outlaw. They used outlaw activity as an excuse to rob and murder peaceful Mexicans.

It is estimated that 547 Mexicans were the victims of mobs in the United States between 1848 and 1928. Many of these were not hanged by vigilance committees but were summarily executed by mobs. As mentioned above, the foreign miners' tax fueled ethnic conflict and at least 143 Mexicans were victims in California between 1848 and 1860. These summary executions continued throughout the century.[55]

The Mexican Prostitute

The most flagrant act of vigilantism happened at Downieville in 1851, when, after a kangaroo trial, a mob lynched a Mexican woman they called Juanita.[56] Only 26 years old, she was the *first* woman hanged in California. Popular lore held that Juanita (AKA Josefa Segovia) was a prostitute who lived with a gambler, Manuel José Loaiza. (Her real name was Josefa, and she was married to Loaiza.) On July 4, 1851, in a drunken rage, Fred Cannon, a miner, intentionally broke down the door of Josefa's home and tried to elicit sexual favors from her. She chased him off and the next day when Josefa and her husband demanded that Cannon pay for the broken door, he became belligerent and called her a whore. Standing in the doorway, Josefa challenged, "This is no place to call me bad names, come into my house and call me that." As Cannon forcibly entered the house, still calling her vile names, Josefa avenged her honor by killing him with a knife.[57]

Although the miners wanted to lynch Josefa and José on the spot, they held a kangaroo trial. With Cannon's body on display in a tent, dressed in a red flannel shirt, unbuttoned to display the wound, Josefa was convicted. It did not matter that she was pregnant. She was hanged from a bridge, while over 2,000 men lined the river to watch. After this incident, lynching became commonplace in California. Among Mexicans Euro-American democracy came to be known as "*Linchocracia*" (Lynchocracy). In 1875, José María Loaiza filed a claim for Josefa's lynching and his banishment by a mob in 1852 in Downieville, California. The commissioner dismissed the claim.[58]

The American Delusion, The Lugos Trial

For early merchants such as Abel Stearns, racism was a matter of grape picking: they would select which Mexicans were acceptable and which were not. Stearns married Arcadia Bandini, member of an elite rancher family and said to be the most beautiful woman in of all California.[59] However, tensions became common as lower-class white Americans became numerous. To them a greaser was a greaser, and they did not distinguish between rich and poor Mexicans. It was this generalization that bothered the Californio elite who fashioned themselves as white or near white. As the Californios lost their land and their political clout, fewer Euro-Americans bothered to make distinctions.

Mexicans still retained absolute majorities in the southern counties. For a time, they were able to hold on to local offices, but the massive increase of Euro-American population was nudging them out of offices statewide. By 1851, all California-born Mexicans were excluded from the State Senate; by the 1860s, only a few Mexicans remained in the Assembly; and by the 1880s, few people with Spanish surnames could be found in public offices. During these years, Mexican bosses such as Tomás Sánchez and Antonio Coronel delivered the Mexican vote in Los Angeles. However, there were chasms within the Mexican community itself—especially between the Californios and the new arrivals from Sonora and Mexico. The so-called elite pejoratively referred to the new arrivals as "cholos." Ex-Mexican governor Juan Bautista Alvarado called Indians "backward," saying they were indolent, ignorant, and lazy people.

Racial tensions polarized the Mexican and Euro-American communities. This was true especially in Los Angeles, where, although the Mexican elite actively cooperated with the new order, they often became victims of mob violence. A celebrated case involved the Lugo brothers—Francisco, 16, and Benito, 18— accused of killing a white man and his Native American companion. The brothers were the grandsons of Antonio María Lugo, head of one of the richest and most powerful California families. Joseph Lancaster Brent, a Los Angeles attorney with strong Southern sympathies, who later served as a general in the Confederate army, defended the Lugos. Brent cultivated alliances with the ranchero elite. A Catholic from Maryland, he won over many wealthy Mexican families and in the process made a fortune representing them in court.

In January 1851, the Lugos were charged with murdering Patrick McSwiggin and his Creek Indian companion. At the time, only about 75 "Americans" lived permanently in Los Angeles, and they were in perpetual fear of a Californio revolt. Hearing about the murders, they began to arm themselves. Allegedly there was an eyewitness to the shooting, but *vaqueros* (cowboys) riding with the Lugos contradicted his testimony; they swore that the brothers had never left the camp and that the murders were not committed by them.

During the trial, Captain John "Red" Irving and about 25 men approached Brent and demanded $10,000 to ensure the safety of the Lugos. When the family refused the offer, Irving vowed to kill the brothers. With the help of Brent, about 60 armed Californios showed up, followed by U.S. troops, whose presence prevented a confrontation. The Californios escorted the Lugos to the judge, who released them on bail; further, they escorted the Lugos to their ranch.

A month later, Red Irving and his men set out for the Lugo ranch to kill the brothers. Cahuilla Indian allies of the Lugos set a trap and killed all the gang members except one. The court finally dismissed the case in October 1852. Rumor had it that Brent collected a fee of $20,000, a measure of the price paid for justice. This was one of the few instances where the Californios showed unity, and it was based on class rather than race.[60]

The Disillusionment

At the beginning of the U.S. occupation some Mexicans were optimistic about their future. Disillusionment soon set in, and many chose to repatriate to Mexico. Many of those who remained saw their status decline and injustices proliferate. A division occurred between the Californios along ideological lines, with the more conservative aligning themselves with Euro-Americans who were often proslavery. The more progressive Californios were critical of the system and opposed southern racism. The latter maintained contact with Latin America and supported the social and political movements in those countries. They were also critical of the fate suffered by Mexicans in California. This minority within a minority did not have the resources of the Picos and other Californios, who often squandered their fortunes and generally refused to fund liberal causes. In turn, the progressives started small newspapers which often had short runs because they lacked financial support. For example, the *Clamor Público* in Los Angeles had a run of four years and its readership was about 100.[61]

El Clamor Público

At the age of 18, Francisco Ramírez, a former compositor of the Spanish page of the *Los Angeles Star*, began to publish *El Clamor Público* in Los Angeles in 1855. Four years later, the newspaper went out of business because of lack of funds. Ramírez then migrated to Sonora, where he edited the state newspaper. After a short period, he returned to California and held jobs as a printer, as postmaster, and as the official translator for the state. He tried a comeback in 1872 as editor of *La Crónica* in Los Angeles. Ramírez had very little formal schooling and, like many Californios and literate people throughout the world, was home-schooled. His grandfather was from Tepic and had migrated to the Mission Santa Barbara. The family moved to Los Angeles in the late 1820s, where Francisco was born.

Ramírez incorporated the best of Latin American newspapers in *El Clamor*. Not only did he report the news but also printed poetry, essays, and short stories of the time. Along with *La Crónica*, *El Eco del Pacífico*, *El Nuevo Mundo de San Francisco*, and others, *El Clamor* reflected the intellectual curiosity and intellectual life of Spanish-speaking Californians and the liberal-rationalist thought of the mid-nineteenth century. Many of its contributors were local. Ramírez's dialectic exposed the barbarity of Anglo-Saxons who had come to California to civilize the Mexican.[62]

Professor José Luis Benavides makes the point that many Spanish-language newspapers, such as the *Santa Barbara Gazette* (1855–1858), acted as agents of social control. Californios—or, to be more specific, California-born Mexicans along with recently arrived Mexicans—composed 95 percent of the population of the Los Angeles area. Euro-Americans established the *Gazette* with a Spanish-language section, *La Gaceta*, that promoted a Euro-American worldview; it was a translation of what the 5 percent wanted to hear. *La Gaceta* lasted six months. On the other hand, *El Clamor* rose above translation and reported the interests of the larger audience. Ramírez's editorials reflected the Mexicanos' disappointments with Euro-American justice.

On June 19, 1855, a Ramírez newspaper editorial called for justice within the system and the recognition by California's Mexicans that the state was now part of the United States. Ramírez asked the Californios for financial support, writing that a free press was their best guarantee of liberty in the new order.[63] However, Ramírez's editorials soon became less moderate and more strident. About the filibuster William Walker,[64] Ramírez wrote, "World history tells us that the Anglo-Saxons were in the beginning thieves and pirates, the same as other nations in their infancy ... [but] the pirate instinct of old Anglo-Saxons is still active."[65] Through the newspaper's four-year run, Walker was the prototype of the other "pirates," the politicians and filibusters who had designs on Mexico or Latin America. In September 1855 Ramírez reprinted an article that began "Who is the foreigner in California?" and continued, "The North Americans pretend to give us lessons in humanity and to bring to our people the doctrine of salvation so we can govern ourselves, to respect the laws and conserve order. Are these the ones who treat us worse than slaves?"[66] As early as October 1855, Ramírez had encouraged Mexicans and Chileans to join Jesús Isla's *Junta Colonizadora de Sonora* and return to Mexico. Ramírez editorialized, "California has fallen into the hands of the ambitious sons of North America who will not stop until they have satisfied their passions, by driving the first occupants of the land out of the country, vilifying their religion and disfiguring their customs."[67]

A reader objected to Ramírez's "return to Mexico" campaign, writing, "California has always been the asylum of Sonorans, and the place where they have found good wages, hospitality, and happiness." Ramírez caustically responded that the letter did not merit comment and asked, "Are the Californios as happy today as when they belonged to the Republic of Mexico, in spite of all of its revolutions and changes in government?"[68]

What distinguished *El Clamor* was its coverage of lynchings. On March 28, 1857, *El Clamor Público* reprinted a *San Francisco Daily Herald* letter by José S. Berreyesa, who recounted the Bear Flaggers' assassination of the elder Berreyesa and his two nephews. It went on to report that in July 1854 the body of a Euro-American was found on the San Vicente ranch, which belonged to the Berreyesa family. Suspecting that Encarnación Berreyesa had murdered the man, Euro-Americans dragged him out of the house as his wife and children looked on and suspended him from a tree. When Encarnación did not confess to the killings, vigilantes left him half dead and instead hanged his brother Nemesio. Encarnación was later charged with the murder of a Euro-American in Santa Clara and lynched by the vigilantes.[69] After six years of such assassinations, the Californios began arming themselves to protect their families. Soon after, on July 26, 1856, Francisco Ramírez wrote in *El Clamor Público* that conditions for Californios had never been as bad.

Ramírez continued to speak out against the indiscriminate murder of Mexicanos. The murder of Antonio Ruiz was the straw that broke the camel's back. Deputy Marshal William W. Jenkins, a deputy sheriff, alleged that Antonio Ruiz interfered with him when he tried to take repossession of a guitar in payment of a debt. An argument ensued between the deputy and Ruiz and the sheriff shot Ruiz, a respected member of the community. Friends streamed by Ruiz's deathbed to bid him a tearful goodbye. The defense badgered the witnesses to Ruiz's death. It took the all-white jury only 15 minutes to reach a verdict of not guilty. Soon afterward, Jenkins returned to the task of maintaining "law and order" in Los Angeles. The murder of Antonio Ruiz divided Mexicans across class lines, with the lower classes harboring deep-seated grievances against Euro-Americans.[70]

Class Divisions

Many of los ricos pandered to the white minority that included people who were often among the worst of U.S. society. A case in point was their support of the El Monte gang who were located in El Monte, California, located east of the Los Angeles plaza. El Monte was infested by Texans, some of whom were former Rangers. The El Monte crowd postured as defenders of white supremacy.

During 1856 and 1857, the El Monte boys used the pretext of the Juan Flores gang to commit atrocities against the Mexican community. Twenty-one-year-old Juan Flores had escaped from San Quentin Prison and formed a band of almost 50 Mexicanos, including Pancho Daniel. In a shootout, the rebels killed the sheriff. Rumors spread that Flores intended to kill all whites.

Without any legal authority or evidence, the El Monte gang arrested Diego Navarro, who was seen riding away from the gun battle. Navarro admitted that he saw the gunfight, but took off knowing that all Mexicans would be suspect. The mob threw hot tar on Navarro's family home and broke into the house. They dragged him out and executed him, along with two other Mexicans accused of being members of the Flores gang.

Many ricos backed the gringos in hunting down the rebels; *los de abajo* (the underdogs) supported Flores. In a January 31, 1857, editorial even the normally progressive Ramírez called for Californios to help enforce the laws. He praised Tomás Sánchez, the Democratic Party *cacique* (boss), and Andrés Pico for riding with the El Monte gringos.

The El Monte gang captured Flores and Daniel, who soon escaped. To make sure this did not happen again, they hanged their next nine captives immediately. Meanwhile, Andrés Pico and California Native Americans tracked Flores. Pico caught up with two members of the Flores gang and hanged them. Operating independently, the Pico posse and the El Monte people broke into houses in the middle of the night and herded suspects to jail. Fifty-two men were crammed into the jails. All except Daniel were captured. A kangaroo court convicted Flores on February 14, 1857, and he was hanged.[71] *El Clamor Público* praised Andrés Pico in a February 7 editorial saying that the Californios had vindicated the Californios' honor. Not everyone shared Ramírez's enthusiasm, though, and as Leonard Pitt notes, "Sánchez and Pico, who gladly rode with Texans to track down 'their own kind,' thereby won the gringos' everlasting gratitude." They were rewarded: Sánchez became a sheriff, and Pico became a brigadier in the California militia and was elected to the State Assembly. Many Mexicanos did not share the enthusiasm of *El Clamor Público* and the ricos, and condemned their participation in suppressing the Flores–Daniel rebellion. The poor could not ignore the racial and ethnic divide between "American" citizens.[72]

It is ironic that Ramírez supported this charade, since the Picos and other Californios did not financially support his newspaper. Sánchez and others supported the Democrats, who were, among other things, proslavery. Ramírez acquiesced in the hanging of Flores; but when Daniel was caught and lynched he called the execution "barbaric and diabolic" and wrote,

> *And you, imbecile Californios! You are to blame for the lamentations that we are witnessing. We are tired of saying: open your eyes, and it is time that we demand our rights and interests. It is with shame that we say, and difficult to confess it: you are the sarcasm of humanity!*

Ramírez scolded readers for not voting and for putting up with indignities, calling them "cowards and stupid." Ramírez warned Californios that until they cared, they could never cast off the "yoke of slavery."[73]

However, we should be cautious in criticizing Ramírez's fluctuating sympathies. Paul Bryan Gray calls him "a brilliant and astonishingly precocious 18-year-old named Francisco P. Ramírez who presented his journal as a champion of the Mexican people," and says that "Ramírez had embraced the principles of nineteenth century liberalism, especially the variety encountered in Mexico. He probably read the work of Mexicans like José María Luis Mora, Ignacio Ramírez 'El Nigromante,' and other ideologues of the liberal movement headed by Benito Juárez."[74] Gray also takes the Picos and other elites to task for not financially supporting Ramírez.

Most of Gray's observations are accurate. However, some statements must be qualified; for example, the word liberal did not mean what it does today. The so-called liberals worshiped the marketplace; they were not champions of the people, and in Mexico they pushed immigration policies that would have Europeanized Mexico. It was also the liberals who harbored the deepest anti–Native American biases. They encroached on Indian land, and launched wars against the Yaqui and others. As for lack of support from the Picos and company, why should they have been expected to support Ramírez? Surely, his progressive white buddies did not support him. The truth was that most of the wealthy Californios were Democrats in the pro-slavery tradition. Andrés Pico was a financial backer of the newspaper *Southern Californian*, started in July 1854 by C. N. Richards and William Butts. Pico sank $10,000 into the company, which he sold to Colonel J. J. Warner in 1856. By 1855, Andrés and his brother Pío Pico owned 532,000 acres of land between them. But they had no interest in democracy or equality—they were more interested in lavish life styles. They had frequent guests and provided them with trayfuls of coins, so the guests would not have to spend their own money. It is not surprising that visitors often stayed for weeks at a time.[75]

These comments do not minimize Ramírez's contributions. However, he should be placed in the context of Professor Benavides's excellent treatise on *El Clamor Público*. Ramírez had, in fact, challenged the ideology of white supremacy in pointing out injustices committed against blacks and Chinese. Furthermore, he opposed slavery and efforts to exclude free African Americans. As Benavides points out, *El Clamor* also "reproduced stereotypes about Blacks and Indians, did not defend the rights of Indians to equal treatment, and justified the mass killings of Indians as a 'war.'" Despite his progressive pretensions, Ramírez still found "insulting" comments that put Mexicans, blacks, and Indians on equal footing.[76]

Social Banditry

Hollywood has made at least four movies based on the life and times of Joaquin Murieta.[77] Both Chileans and Mexicans claim Murieta, who is undoubtedly the best-known so-called bandit in California history. Despite the myths, considerable documentation attests that Murieta and his family came to California during the Gold Rush from Villa San Rafael de los Alamitos in Sonora, Mexico. Land-claim-jumpers twice invaded his land, and lynched his older brother. The gang raped his wife, and left Joaquin for dead. Unable to get justice from the system, Murieta sought his own justice and stole from the gringo. He became so notorious that at least 41 Mexican bandits were identified as Joaquin Murieta. In 1853, the California legislature hired Captain Harry Love, a former Texas Ranger, to hunt down Joaquin. Love allegedly caught and killed Murieta and his band. The unresolved question is, was it really Murieta?

I Am Joaquin!

Joaquin Murieta (the way his name is spelled varies according to source) has fascinated Hollywood. No less than the great Chilean poet Pablo Neruda (1904–1973) claims Joaquin as a Chilean. The legendary movie *Zorro* was fashioned on his times. The story is simple. Murieta was attacked by Euro-Americans who raped his wife and killed his family members. Jill L. Cossley-Batt, describing the death of Murieta, wrote,

> *The bandits were armed exclusively with six-shooters, whereas the Rangers, being fitted out with rifles, revolvers, and shot-guns, had the advantage, and soon made short work of the swarthy*

desperadoes. Twelve were killed outright and two were taken prisoners. The Rangers were unin-jured, but Captain Love had experienced a "close shave."[78]

In order to prove that they killed Joaquin, Love severed Murieta's head and his associate Three Fingered Jack's hand was cut off and pickled in vinegar.

Horace Bell, a Los Angeles attorney who rode in a posse looking for Joaquin, wrote in his autobiography that although he chased Murieta and other so-called Mexican bandits, he attributed much of the tension to white American racism and mistreatment of Mexicans.

His acts were so bold and daring, and attended with such remarkable success, that he drew to him all the Mexican outlaws, cut-throats and thieves that infested the country extending from San Diego to Stockton. No one will deny the assertion that Joaquín in his organizations, and the successful ramifications of his various bands, his eluding capture, the secret intelligence conveyed from points remote from each other, manifested a degree of executive ability and genius that well fitted him for a more honorable position than that of chief of a band of robbers. In any country in America except the United States, the bold defiance of the power of the government, a half year's successful resistance, a continuous conflict with the military and civil authorities and the armed populace—the writer repeats that in any other country in America other than the United States—the operations of Joaquín Murietta would have been dignified by the title. . . . there is little doubt in the writer's mind that Joaquin's aims were higher than that of mere revenge and pillage. Educated in the school of revolution in his own country, where the line of demarcation between rebel and robber, pillager and patriot, was dimly defined, it is easy to perceive that Joaquín felt himself to be more the champion of his countrymen than an outlaw and an enemy to the human race.[79]

The Social Bandit

When people cannot earn a living within the system or when they are degraded, they strike out. Rebellion against the system can take the form of organized resistance, as in the case of Juan Cortina in Texas, or it can express itself in bandit activity.

Tiburcio Vásquez was born in Monterey on August 11, 1835. His parents were of a good reputation, and Vásquez had an above-average education for the times. Vásquez never married. In about 1852 during a fiesta he was involved in the shooting of a constable and fled to the hills.[80] At the end of his career, Vásquez explained the incident and his reasons for turning *bandido*:

My career grew out of the circumstances by which I was surrounded. As I grew to manhood I was in the habit of attending balls and parties given by the native Californians, into which the Americans, then beginning to become numerous, would force themselves and shove the native born men aside, monopolizing the dance and the women. This was about 1852. A spirit of hatred and revenge took possession of me. I had numerous fights in defense of my countrymen. The officers were continually in pursuit of me. I believed we were unjustly and wrongfully deprived of the social rights that belonged to us.[81]

By the middle of the 1850s California "was experiencing an economic depression. Money was short, the great flood of gold was nearly played out, land and cattle prices were down, and banditry was rampant."[82] Vásquez attracted a large following and his popularity grew among the poor. While the ricos were afraid that he wanted to incite an uprising or revolution against the "Yankee invaders" of California, the rural poor supported and shielded him.[83] The *Los Angeles Express* of May 16, 1874, quotes Vásquez as claiming, "Given $60,000 I would be able to recruit enough arms and men to revolutionize Southern California."

In the fall of 1871 Vásquez and his men robbed the Visalia stage. His reputation as a *desperado* grew, and soon he was being blamed for crimes that he had not committed. The magnitude of the manhunts increased. Authorities offered money to informers in an effort to locate Vásquez. Throughout 1871, Vásquez not only evaded arrest but also continued his activities. The Mexican populace aided him, for "to some, Vásquez must have seemed a hero dealing out his own particular brand of justice. Certainly his reputation was growing fast."[84]

On August 16, 1873, Vásquez and his men robbed Snyder's store in Tres Pinos of $1,200. This daring raid escalated him to statewide prominence. Newspapers sensationalized Vásquez's raids and wanted posters circulated. Vásquez prudently shifted activities to southern California.

During the next year the newspapers played up his exploits, and Sheriff Harry Morse quickened the chase, covering 2,720 miles in 61 days searching for Vásquez. Authorities learned that Vásquez was hiding out at the ranch of George Allen, better known as Greek George, and surrounded the ranch. Vásquez was captured. An all-Euro-American jury found him guilty, and he was sentenced to hang.

George A. Beers, a special correspondent for the *San Francisco Chronicle*, offered a partial explanation of why Vásquez captured the imagination of the Mexican populace:

> *Vásquez turned to the life of a bandido because of the bitter animosity then existing, and which still exists, between the white settlers and the native or Mexican portion of the population. The native Californians, especially the lower classes, never took kindly to the stars and stripes. Their youth were taught from the very cradle to look upon the American government as that of a foreign nation.*
>
> *This feeling was greatly intensified by the rough, brutal conduct of the worst class of American settlers, who never missed an opportunity to openly exhibit their contempt for the native Californian or Mexican population—designating them as "d—d Greasers," and treating them like dogs. Add to this the fact that these helpless people were cheated out of their lands and possessions by every subterfuge—in many instances their property being actually wrested from them by force, and their women debauched whenever practicable—and we can understand very clearly some of the causes which have given to Joaquin (Murietta), Vasquez, and others of their stripe, the power to call around them at any time all the followers they required, and which secured to them aid and comfort from the Mexican settlers everywhere.[85]*

Vásquez's execution deepened racial tensions. Two weeks after the hanging, a man named Romo killed two Euro-Americans who had participated in Vásquez's capture; Romo was captured and lynched. Groups of Mexicanos met secretly, and the ricos feared a race war that would include them. Tiburcio Vásquez's death ended the era of intense Mexican rebellion.

Mexicans in a Changing Society

Natural disasters of the 1860s accelerated the decline of Mexicano elite. In 1862, a flood devastated California ranches. Two years of drought, the loss of most of southern California's large cattle herds, and falling cattle prices forced ranch owners to mortgage their property at outlandish interest rates, resulting in foreclosures. With the loss of land came the loss of political power, and Mexicans without money were just greasers. Piece by piece, they sold their land to pay mortgages. Within a decade, the Californios were relatively landless in California.

Meanwhile, the Mexican community was growing throughout California. They formed enclaves called *barrios* or *colonias* throughout the state. The French Intervention (1861–1868) in Mexico brought exiles to California, who were recruited by the various factions. David Hayes-Bautista and his team of researchers are currently documenting the California *Juntas Patrióticas*, patriotic committees that often worked with the Mexican consulate, which flourished during this period (and still do). The French Intervention sharpened Mexican nationalism and the importance of holidays such as the Cinco de Mayo.

Through the presence of the recent exiles, areas of support for Benito Juárez and the liberal cause can be documented; their absence in certain regions suggests the existence of conservative strongholds such as Santa Bárbara and San Diego. The nationalism of the newcomers further separated the Californios and the masses.[86]

Mexicans attempted to deal with these problems within their own community. They formed self-help associations—such as *La Sociedad Hispanoamericana de Beneficio Mutua*, founded in Los Angeles in 1875—to raise money for hospitals and charitable causes such as the Sisters of Charity hospital for indigents, founded in 1887.[87] Organizations in these years reflected the Mexicans' isolation and hence they became increasingly nationalistic, celebrating the Mexican patriotic holidays (such as the Mexican Independence Day on September 16 and the Battle of Puebla on May 5 commemorating the Mexicans' defeat of the French Army in the 1860s) and sponsoring parades, speeches, and other festivities.

The transcontinental railroad completed its link to California in 1869, and over the next decade the railroad spread throughout the state. As elsewhere in the Southwest, the "iron horse" was transforming social relations. It ended the isolation of southern California, accelerating its eventual transformation into a region of large-scale agriculture. The railroad brought 70,000 newcomers a year to California, and the Mexican isolation of the 1850s and 1860s abruptly ended. After the arrival of large numbers of Euro-Americans, Mexicans played the role of a small and politically insignificant minority. Southern California had entered the era of industrialized capitalism: the Panic of 1873 put the lid on the coffin, and the arrival of the Southern Pacific Railroad in 1876 drove in the nails.[88]

Becoming a Minority

The Mexican population of Los Angeles had increased only slightly from 1,331 in 1850 to 2,231 in 1880, whereas the Euro-American population rose from under 300 to some 8,000 during this same period. By 1890, the city's population had grown to 50,395 (the county's, to 101,454); again the Mexican population had increased only slightly. Los Angeles underwent other changes as well. In 1850, it had one factory employing two men; in 1880, it had 172 factories and 700 workers. Total property values in this period increased from $2,282,949 to $20,916,835. The white population grew from 18 percent of the total population in 1850 to 80 percent in 1880.

The 1880s transformed Los Angeles into a modern city. However, Mexicans were not part of this new prosperity; their status changed little. For instance, 65 percent of Mexicans were employed as manual laborers, in contrast to the 26 percent of Euro-Americans employed as laborers. The economic order froze Mexicans into a lower class, and occupational mobility was limited among all workers; race and a historical tradition of oppression caused continued subjugation.

Though the isolation of Los Angeles was ending, segregation of Mexicans became more common. In southern California, Euro-Americans became the majority in the 1870s. By 1873, the participation of Mexicans on juries became less frequent, as did their involvement in any other activity of governance. Mexican political bosses declined in power; by the 1880s, they had little to broker. Consequently, city officials ignored problems of health and urbanization in the barrios (known as "Sonoratown").[89] Between 1877 and 1888, infant mortality among Mexicans was double that of Euro-Americans; the death rate among Mexicans between ages 5 and 20 was also double, with smallpox being a leading killer. The cost of medical care was prohibitive; doctors charged for house calls according to how far away the patient lived. Since most doctors did not live close to the Mexican colonias, the usual fee was $10—a week's salary for most Mexicans.[90]

The Church's Role

The Catholic Church methodically destroyed any nationalist movement among the Mexican populace. Soon after the Euro-American takeover, New York Bishop John Hughes contacted José Noriega de la Guerra seeking his advice on whom he should support to be the next Bishop of California. De La Guerra advised that it should be a Spanish-born bishop since most of the Californios were Spanish, advice that Hughes followed.[91] In 1850, Fr. Joseph Sadoc Alemany was appointed Archbishop of San Francisco, the first archbishop in California. Alemany was a Catalán and a member of the Order of St. Dominic. Evidence suggests that he did not confront the impoverished state of the masses of Mexicans and the natives. His passion was to recover control of the Pious Fund (a large fund collected during the Spanish colonial period for the benefit of the missions). That Alemany was a Dominican friar was significant: the order was at the forefront of Catholic orthodoxy and a leader in the opposition to the separation of church and state. The Spanish province of Catalán was a battleground, and the scene of violent clashes, in this controversy. As such, Alemany probably sided with the church party in Mexico and opposed liberalism, which the Dominicans and the church saw as the Antichrist.[92]

In 1853 Vincentian Father Taddeus Amat was appointed Bishop of Monterey, which later became part of the Diocese of Monterey–Los Angeles. Like Alemany, he too was a Catalán. Amat summed up the priority of the church in 1870, stating that the church was "the main support of society and order, which imperatively demands respect for legitimate authority and subjugation to legitimate law."[93] The construction of new churches further segregated the Mexican poor. St. Viviana's Cathedral, built in 1876, served a Euro-American parish, as did St. Vincent's (1886), St. Andrew's (1886), and Sacred Heart (1887). St. Joseph's, built in 1888, also catered to Euro-Americans. The construction of the churches in the 1880s coincided with the en masse arrival of thousands of Euro-Americans, who found sanctuary for their racism in these segregated houses of worship. The Mexicans continued to attend the *placita* (the plaza church).[94]

Labor

Unlike the situation in Arizona, Mexican labor did not dominate the labor force in California during the nineteenth century. The laborers of choice were Chinese immigrants (supplemented by indigenous Californians); for a period, the Chinese outnumbered Mexicans in the state. The new order, like the old order, treated Native Americans shamefully. They continued to be captured, sold, and raped. In 1886, the California Supreme Court, in *Thompson v. Doaksum*, ruled that land held by indigenous people during the Mexican Period and not claimed by the Land Law of 1851 was public domain. In *Botiller v. Dominguez* (1889), the highest court in the land ruled that indigenous claims by title or occupancy were invalid if they had not been legally confirmed previously. These laws were intended to legally segregate and enslave Native Americans. California vagrancy law allowed the jail keepers to sell the labor of Indians to private contractors who would in turn pay their fines. From 1852 to 1867, Mexicans and Euro-Americans were involved in slave trafficking, kidnapping, and selling more than 4,000 Native American children to Mexican rancheros and Euro-American colonists.[95]

The Exclusion of the Other

The demand for Mexican labor was directly related to the decline in population of Chinese workers and Indians. For example, the Chinese Exclusion Act of 1882 almost entirely stopped Chinese immigration to the United States. This, along with the dying off of the California natives, created a shortage of manual laborers and a demand for Mexican workers. Mexicans moved from pastoral occupations to menial-wage work. They took jobs at the lowest rung of the ladder. Increasingly, they became wage earners, driven from subsistence farming by the sale of common lands. At the same time, thousands of Mexicans migrated to California from Mexico and elsewhere in the Southwest.

Much of this labor was segregated. For example, 13 miles south of San Jose, the Almaden mercury mines, active since the Mexican Period, employed mostly Mexicans. Fifteen hundred miners worked at the Quicksilver Mine Company.[96] Using ancient methods, they hauled ore out of the underground mines with 200-pound sacks strapped to their foreheads and resting on their backs. Miners produced 220,000 pounds of ore per month. The company kept tight control of its workers. It segregated them not only by race, but also by occupation. The Cornish miners, for example, lived separately from the Mexican miners, who were condemned to a distinctively lower standard of living, and neither Mexican workers nor their families were allowed contact with English adults or children, who attended separate schools and churches.[97]

Colonias

An interesting account of the various colonias along the Southern Pacific rail route in northern California appeared in the San Francisco *El Cronista* in April 1885. In "Ferrocarril del Sur," Sóstenes Betancourt talks about the nationalism of the Mexican people and their genuine love for the homeland, of merchants such as Estolano F. Larios of Tres Pinos, and about the presence of Mexican ranchers. One gets a definite sense of community in Tres Pinos, which had a population of 250, 50 of whom were Mexicans. Throughout his trip, Betancourt came across Argentines and Chileans who had integrated into the Mexican population.

Betancourt speaks of the miracles attributed to Joaquin Murieta's alleged wife, Mariana. In the valleys, Betancourt recounts, people spoke of the adventures of the legendary Joaquin Murieta as if they were still happening. Mariana, who had disappeared, returned to the *valle de Santa Cruz* in the company of a Frenchman and several assistants to preach about the sainthood of Franciscan Padre Magín Catalán, known as "the holy man of Santa Clara," the first missionary of the mission of that name. They claimed they were sent by *el santo padre Magín,* and on his behalf met with thousands of persons, who could "communicate" with the saint through Mariana. Apparently, the cult collected large sums of money. Mariana and her cabal then disappeared once more, with about $8,000. Betancourt suggests that millenarian motives inspired the people's fascination for Mariana who they believed would liberate them.[98]

Conclusion: The Decline and Return of the Mexican

Between 1880 and 1920 California built an agricultural empire, mostly utilizing Chinese labor, whose dominance helped in the transition from peonage. The Southern Pacific Railroad alone owned more land than all the rancheros combined. It was the state's largest employer. The company advertised throughout the East and Europe for buyers of its land. It even established an employment agency for the new settlers. Industrial growth meant a heavy demand for cheap labor. By the 1890s, agriculture had become intensive, and California was becoming a major exporter of grains, fruits, and vegetables.[99] After the Chinese Exclusion Act (1882), other groups filled the vacuum. Meanwhile, the reclamation programs of the early 1900s caused a revolution in agriculture that forced California capitalists to look to the most logical and available source of labor—Mexico. The discovery of oil and the opening of the Panama Canal brought about further changes in the 1900s. The isolation of California and Los Angeles had completely ended. Beginning in the 1880s, Los Angeles was in the firm grip of the ruling elite, led by the *Los Angeles Times* and a cabal of white land speculators, bankers, and developers who ran the city and county for personal gain.

Discrimination toward Mexicans in the wage-labor market increased; a dual-wage system persisted, with Mexicans and Chinese paid less compared to Euro-Americans. This arbitrary treatment of Mexicans often led to confrontations. In 1889, for instance, Modesta Avila was hauled before the Orange County Superior Court, accused of placing a sign on the tracks of the Santa Fe Railroad that read, "This land belongs to me. And if the railroad wants to run here, they will have to pay me ten thousand dollars." Avila posted the sign some 15 feet from the doorstep of her home on the former San Juan Capistrano Mission. Local authorities had told Avila not to do this, to which she replied, "If they pay me for my land, they can go by." Avila was sentenced to three years in jail and died in San Quentin; she was in her mid-20s at the time of her death.[100]

In another example of the inequality suffered by Mexican laborers, a mob in August 1892 broke into the Santa Ana jail and hanged Francisco Torres, a native of Colima, Mexico. Torres worked at the Modjeska Ranch for a wage of $9 for a six-day week. The ranch foreman, William McKelvey, withheld money for a road poll tax from Torres's wages, but not from any of the other workers' pay. Torres refused his wages, demanding full payment, and in the ensuing argument, Torres killed McKelvey, with a knife, in self-defense. Torres stated that he did not have a gun and that he had taken a club away from the larger man; then, fearing that the foreman would use his gun, he stabbed him.

Before Torres could be tried, a mob broke into the jail and executed him, hanging a sign around his neck that read, "Change of venue." The *Santa Ana Standard* wrote that Torres was of a low type of Mexican race, emphasizing his Indian features. By contrast, *Las Dos Repúblicas* wrote that Torres was only guilty of being a Mexican. The execution went unpunished.[101]

By 1900, the railroad had fully integrated California into the nation's marketplace. California had made the complete transition from a Mexican province to a North American state. Its population, overwhelmingly white in color and culture, numbered 1.5 million. By then, the native Californian population had dropped to about 15,000; Mexicans numbered between 10,000 and 17,000. The African American population numbered 11,045. The unprecedented economic transformation of the next century would dramatically change these proportions.[102]

Notes

1. John Steven McGroarty, *Mission Memories* (Los Angeles, CA: Neuner Corporation, 1929), 7. Also quoted in Lisa Riggin-Walden, "Spanish Missions: The Death and Resurrection of a California Institution" (PhD dissertation, University of California Riverside, 2006), 1.

2. Helen Hunt Jackson, *Ramona* (Boston: Little, Brown, 1900). The novel tells the tragic love story of a mestiza (unknown to her) falling in love with an Indian male. It exposed the brutal treatment of the Californian Indian. The novel was romanticized in a play called *Ramona* that created the myth of "American apotheosis." Janice Albert, "Helen Hunt Jackson (1830–1885)," California Teachers of English, http://www.cateweb.org/CA_Authors/Jackson.html.

3. Don Mitchell, *The Lie of the Land: Migrant Workers and the California Landscape* (St. Paul: University of Minnesota Press, 1996), 9, 13.

4. Carey McWilliams, *North from Mexico: The Spanish-Speaking People of the United States* (New York: J. B. Lippincott, 1948), 35. It can also explain how the Dreamers who want to become Americans look at the United States.

5. Douglas Monroy, *Thrown Among Strangers: The Making of Mexican Culture in Frontier California* (Berkeley: University of California Press, 1990), 101. Gabriel Gutiérrez, "Bell Towers, Crucifixes, and Cañones Violentos: State and Identity Formation in Pre-industrial Alta California" (PhD dissertation, University of California, Santa Barbara, 1997), 63–72. The Royal Presidio of San Diego 1769–1835, California History and Culture Conservancy, http://historyandculture.com/chcc/presidio1.html. Greg Pabst, "To Have But Not to Hold: The Bernals of Early San Francisco and Their Lost Corner of the City," http://gregnoevly.home.mindspring.com/Bernal.html. See map of Sonora and California.

6. Steven W. Hackel, "Sources of Rebellion: Indian Testimony and the Mission San Gabriel Uprising of 1785," *Ethnohistory* 50, no. 4 (Fall 2003): 643–49, 651, 655, 657. The Holy Woman Toypurina Attempts to Liberate the "Indios" at San Gabriel Mission, http://www.suppressedhistories.net/articles/toypurina.html. Edward D. Castillo, "An Indian Account of the Decline and Collapse of Mexico's Hegemony over the Missionized Indians of California," *American Indian Quarterly* 13, no. 4 (Autumn 1989): 393. Duke Helfand, "Tragic Side of Mission Era Being Told; Education: Lessons Now Acknowledge the Role That Franciscans Played in Demise of Indians. Series . . ." *Los Angeles Times*, September 2, 1997, A, 1:3. Sandy Banks, "Native Americans Resurrect Heritage; Ancestry: The Missions' Assimilation of Tribes into Spanish Culture Left Many with No Knowledge of their Roots," *Los Angeles Times* [Valley Edition], September 3, 1997, 1.

7. Castillo, "An Indian Account," 393. Kent G. Lightfoot, *Indians, Missionaries, and Merchants: The Legacy of Colonial Encounters on the California Frontiers* (Berkeley: University of California Press, 2004), 89–90. James A. Sandos, *Converting California: Indians and Franciscans in the Missions* (New Haven, CT: Yale University Press, 2004), 125.

8. Rose Marie Beebe and Robert M. Senkewicz, "The End of the 1824 Chumash Revolt in Alta California: Father Vicente Sarría's Account," *The Americas* 53, no. 2 (October 1996): 273–75. Thomas Blackburn, "The Chumash Revolt of 1824: A Native Account," *Journal of California Anthropology* 2, no. 2 (1975): 223–27, http://repositories.cdlib.org/cgi/viewcontent.cgi?article=1079&context=ucmercedlibrary/jca. Brian T. McCormack, "Conjugal Violence, Sex, Sin, and Murder in the Mission Communities of Alta California," *Journal of the History of Sexuality* 16, no. 3 (September 2007): 410. Rose Marie Beebe and Robert M. Senkewicz, "The End of the 1824 Chumash Revolt in Alta California: Father Vicente Sarría's Account," *The Americas* 53, no. 2 (October, 1996): 273–283. P. Nabokov, "Reconstituting the Chumash: A Review Essay." *American Indian Quarterly* 13, no. 4 (1989): 535–43.

9. Quincy Newell, "'The Indians Generally Love Their Wives and Children': Native American Marriage and Sexual Practices in Missions San Francisco, Santa Clara, and San Jose," *Catholic Historical Review* 91, no. 1 (January 2005): 60–82ff. Sandos, *Converting California*, 182–84. Efforts to canonize Serra unleashed a torrent of criticism from those claiming that the mission Indians had been abused. California Genocide, Indian Country Diaries, http://www.pbs.org/indiancountry/history/calif.html. Diana G. Tumminia, "California Indian Memorial," http://www.csus.edu/indiv/t/tumminia/MEMORIAL.HTM. This is a virtual memorial to all the California Indians who died in the many years of genocide. Monroy, *Thrown Among Strangers*, 81. There was always tension between the missionaries and the soldiers. The latter brought syphilis to the natives; James A. Sandos, "Between Cucifix and

Lance: Indian-White Relations in California, 1769–1848," in Ramón Gutiérrez and Richard L. Orsi, eds., *Contested Eden: California Before the Gold Rush* (Berkeley: University of California Press, 1998), 196–229. Sandos makes an educated assumption that many natives died as a result of syphilis. However, death by syphilis is almost impossible to diagnose.

10. Erika Pérez, "Colonial Intimacies: Interethnic Kinship, Sexuality, and Marriage in Southern California, 1769–1885" (PhD dissertation, University of California, Los Angeles, 2010), 3, 18–20, 28–32, 34–41, 290. Pérez builds her narrative around excellent use of oral testimonies. She analyzes how the compadrazgo and the confessional served as instruments of social control, and reaches the conclusion that because of compadrazgo southern Indians survived.

11. M. Kat Anderson, Michael G. Barbour, and Valerie Whitworth, "A World of Balance and Plenty: Land, Plants, Animals, and Humans in a Pre-European California," in Gutiérrez and Orsi, eds., *Contested Eden*, 12–47. Monroy, *Thrown Among Strangers*, 101. Doyce B. Nunis, Jr., "Alta California's Trojan Horse: Foreign Immigration," in Gutiérrez and Orsi, eds., *Contested Eden*, 299–330. David J. Weber, *The Mexican Frontier, 1821–1846: The American Southwest Under Mexico* (Albuquerque: University of New Mexico Press, 1982), 136.

12. McCormack, "Conjugal Violence, Sex, Sin, and Murder in the Mission Communities of Alta California," 391–415.

13. Monroy, *Thrown Among Strangers*, 66–67. Gabriel Gutiérrez, "Bell Towers," 62.

14. Steven W. Hackel, "Land, Labor, and Production," *California History* 76 (Summer and Fall, 1997): 134. Rosaura Sánchez, *Telling Identities: The Californio Testimonios* (St. Paul: University of Minnesota Press, 1995), 82–83, 86. José Bandini, *A Description of California in 1828* (Berkeley, CA: Friends of the Bancroft Library, 1951), vi, 11. Don Thomas Coulter, *Notes on Upper California: A Journey from Monterey to the Colorado River in 1832* (Los Angeles: Glen Dawson, 1951), 23. Robert F. Heizer and Allan F. Almquist, *The Other Californians* (Berkeley: University of California Press, 1971), 120.

15. Cris Pérez, "Extracts from Grants of Land in California Made by Spanish or Mexican Authorities," Ranchos of California, University of California Berkeley Library, http://www.lib.berkeley.edu/EART/rancho.html. William H. Dusenberry, *The Mexican Mesta: The Administration of Ranching in Colonial Mexico* (Urbana: University of Illinois Press, 1963), 181.

16. Lisbeth Haas, *Conquests and Historical Identities in California, 1769–1936* (Berkeley: University of California Press, 1996), 42, 58. Michael J. González, "'The Child of the Wilderness Weeps for the Father of Our Country': The Indian and the Politics of Church and State in Provincial California," in Gutiérrez and Orsi, eds., *Contested Eden*, 147–72. Monroy, *Thrown Among Strangers*, 59, 127.

17. Sánchez, *Telling Identities*, 168.

18. Hackel, "Land, Labor, and Production," 135–36. Sánchez, *Telling Identities*, 168. Gutiérrez, "Bell Towers," 152–58. Heather Valdez Singleton, "Surviving Urbanization: The Gabrieleño, 1850–1928," *Wicazo Sa Review* 19, no. 2 (2004): 49–50.

19. Hackel, "Land, Labor, and Production," 134. For the ideological transformation that took place during the Mexican Period, see Gutiérrez, "Bell Towers," 60–62.

20. José Bandini, *A Description of California in 1828* (Berkeley, CA: Friends of the Bancroft Library 1951), reprinted in Carlos E. Cortés, ed., *Mexican California* (New York: Arno Press, 1976), vi, 11; Don Thomas Coulter, *Notes on Upper California: A Journey from Monterey to the Colorado River in 1832* (Los Angeles: Glen Dawson, 1951), 23. Heizer and Almquist, *The Other Californians*, 120.

21. Haas, *Conquests and Historical Identities*, 3–4, 81.

22. Monroy, *Thrown Among Strangers*, 127; aside from disease and alcoholism, the natives were disoriented by the loss of population and the destruction of their family network.

23. Sánchez, *Telling Identities*, 161.

24. Juan Bautista de Anza, National Park Service, http://www.nps.gov/juba/index.htm. Welcome to Web de Anza, http://anza.uoregon.edu/.

25. Carlos Manuel Salomon, "California Son: The Life of Pio Pico" (PhD dissertation, University of New Mexico, Albuquerque, 2002), v, 5, 10, 24, 25. Pico was involved in over 100 legal cases. In the final one, *Pico v. Cohn*, his struggle to save Rancho Margarita finally broke him. The author could have been more critical. Pico's father was listed as Spanish but the family was listed as mulato as was his mother. Salomon does an excellent job of tracing connections between Californio families.

26. Apolinaria Lorenzana memorias: Sta. Barbara, Calif.: ms., 1878 Mar., Online Archive of California, http://content.cdlib.org/ark:/13030/hb9j49p4ms/?&brand=oac.

27. Virginia Marie Bouvier, *Women and the Conquest of California, 1542–1840: Codes of Silence* (Tucson: University of Arizona Press, 2001), 85. Sánchez, *Telling Identities*, 15. Antonia I. Castañeda, "Engendering the History of Alta California, 1769–1848: Gender, Sexuality, and the Family" in Gutiérrez and Orsi, eds., *Contested Eden*, 251. Jeanne Farr McDonnell, *Juana Briones of Nineteenth-Century California* (Tucson: University of Arizona Press, 2008). Juana Briones Heritage, http://www.brioneshouse.org/juanas_life.htm.

28. Rodolfo F. Acuña, *Corridors of Migration: The Odyssey of Mexican Laborers, 1600–1933* (Tucson: University of Arizona Press, 2008), 12–14. See Cheryl English Martin, *Governance and Society in Colonial Mexico: Chihuahua in the Eighteenth Century* (Stanford, CA: Stanford University Press, 1996), for excellent accounts of women fighting back in Colonial Chihuahua. For Testimony of Eulalia Pérez see Nancy F. Cott, Jeanne Boydson, Ann Braude, Lori D. Ginzberg, Molly Ladd-Taylor, eds., *Root of Bitterness: Documents of the Social History of American Women* (Boston: Northeastern, 1996), 185–92. Eulalia Pérez de Guillén Mariné (1766–1878), http://en.wikipedia.org/wiki/Eulalia_P%C3%A9rez_de_Guill%C3%A9n_Marin%C3%A9.

29. Josiah Royce, *California* (Santa Barbara, CA: Peregrine Publishers, Inc., 1970), 31–32. Leonard Pitt, *The Decline of the Californios* (Berkeley and Los Angeles: University of California Press, 1966), 26. George Winston Smith and Charles Judah, *Chronicles of the Gringos* (Albuquerque: University of New Mexico Press,

1968), 141, 149. John Bidwell (Pioneer of '41), "Frémont in the Conquest of California," Virtual Museum of the City of San Francisco, http://www.sfmuseum.org/hist6/fremont.html.

30. Oscar Lewis, ed., *California in 1846* (San Francisco, CA: Grab-horn Press, 1934); reprinted in Carlos E. Cortés, ed., *Mexicans in the U.S. Conquest of California* (New York: Arno Press, 1976), 31. Pitt, *Decline of Californios*, 27. Richard Griswold del Castillo, "La Raza Hispano-Americana: The Emergence of an Urban Culture Among the Spanish Speaking of Los Angeles, 1850–1880" (PhD dissertation, University of California at Los Angeles, 1974), 49. Genaro M. Padilla, *My History, Not Yours: The Formation of Mexican American Autobiography* (Madison: University of Wisconsin Press, 1993), 42–73, 77–108.

31. Pitt, *Decline of Californios*, 30.

32. William D. Carrigan and Clive Webb, *Forgotten Dead: Mob Violence Against Mexicans in the United States, 1848–1928* (New York: Oxford University Press, 2013), 332–57, Table 10.1.

33. Walter Colton, *Three Years in California* (New York: A.S. Barnes, 1850), 2. Mark J. Denger, "The Mexican War and California: The Treaty of Campo de Cahuenga," California State Military Department, The California State Military Museum, A United States Army Museum Activity, Preserving California's Military Heritage, http://www.militarymuseum.org/Cahuenga.html (accessed October 21, 2009). Hubert Howe Bancroft, *History California Vol V. 1846–1848* (San Francisco, CA: The History Company, Publishers, 1890), 422–24.

34. Leon Worden, "California's REAL First Gold," *COINage mag-azine* (October 2005), http://www.scvhistory.com/scvhistory/signal/coins/worden-coinage1005.htm.

35. Donald J. Pisani, "Squatter Law in California, 1850–1858," *Western Historical Quarterly* 25, no. 3 (Autumn 1994): 278; prior to the finding of gold the Mexican governor had award-ed Sutter 49,000 acres of land. Sutter had a made-up title but in California was treated as royalty.

36. Tomás Almaguer, *Racial Fault Lines: The Historical Origins of White Supremacy in California* (Berkeley: University of California Press, 1994), 26–27. By 1860 there were 146,528 foreign-born in California: 34,935 were Chinese, 33,247 Irish, 21,646 German, 12,227 English, and only 9,150 Mexican-born immigrants. Heizer and Almquist, *The Other Californians*, 144. Gold Fever! http://www.museumca.org/goldrush/fever01.html.

37. Katherine H. Chandler, "San Francisco at Statehood," Virtual Museum of the City of San Francisco, http://www.sfmuseum.com/hist5/oldsf.html.

38. David S. Torres-Rouff, "Making Los Angeles: Race, Space, and Municipal Power, 1822–1890" (PhD dissertation, University of California, Santa Barbara, 2006), 73.

39. California Constitutional Convention of 1849, http://www.militarymuseum.org/Constitution.htm. Susan PatriciaTay-lor, "Pride versus Prejudice: The Disparate Delegates to the California Constitution Convention of 1849, and the Moder-ate Constitution That They Fashioned" (Master of Arts thesis, California State University, Dominguez Hills, 2010), 4.

40. Almaguer, *Racial Fault Lines*, 9. Heizer and Almquist, *The Other Californians*, 149. Stephen Clark Foster, "El Quachero: How I Want to Help Make the Constitution of California—Stirring Historical Incidents," in Carlos E. Cortés, ed., *Mexicans in California After the U.S. Conquest* (New York: Arno Press, 1976). Foster was a delegate to the Constitutional Convention of 1849. John Ross Browne, *Report of the Debates in the Conven-tion of California on the Formation of the State Constitution, in Sept. & Oct. 1849* (Manchester, NH: Ayer, 1973).

41. Michael Magliari, "Free Soil, Unfree Labor: Cave Johnson Couts and the Binding of Indian Workers in California, 1850–1867," *Pacific Historical Review* 73, no. 3 (August 2004): 349, 351, 352–57. A History of American Indians in California: 1849–1879, National Park Service, http://www.nps.gov/history/history/online_books/5views/5views1c.htm. Michael Woodiwiss, *Organized Crime and American Power: A History* (Toronto: University of Toronto Press, 2001), 50–51. James J Rawls, *Indians of California: The Changing Image* (Norman: University of Oklahoma Press, 1986), 20–21. David J. Weber, *The Mexican Frontier, 1821–1846* (Albuquerque: University of New Mexico, 1982), 211–12. Albert L. Hurtado, *Indian Sur-vival on the California Frontier* (New Haven, CT: Yale Univer-sity Press, 1990), 3–4. An Act for the Government and Protec-tion of Indians, Chapter 133, Statutes of California (April 22, 1850), http://www.indiancanyon.org/ACTof1850.html.

42. Heizer and Almquist, *The Other Californians*, 143, 144, 155. Leonard Pitt, "The Foreign Miner's Tax of 1850: A Study of Nativism and Anti-Nativism in Gold Rush California" (Mas-ter's thesis, University of California at Los Angeles, 1955), 9. David J. Weber, ed., *Foreigners in Their Native Land* (Albuquerque: University of New Mexico Press, 1973), 151. Richard Morefield, "Mexicans in the California Mines, 1848–1853," *California Historical Quarterly* 24 (March 1956): 38, 43. *Daily Pacific News* (October 19, 1850). Carrigan and Webb, *Forgotten Dead*, 35. Coya Brownrigg, "A Changing Lynchocracy: Lynching and the Performance of American Identity in Gold Rush California, 1848–1858" (PhD dis-sertation, University of Illinois, Evanston, 2010), 4, 10, 17. "I argue that the lynching of Hispanos provides an important site from which to examine the role of public violence in con-structing racial and national identities, an intervention that is particularly urgent given the contemporary resurgence of antiimmigrant" activity.

43. Van Hastings Garner, "The Treaty of Guadalupe Hidalgo and the California Indians," *Indian Historian* (1976): 10–13. Natalia Molina, "'In a Race All Their Own': The Quest to Make Mexicans Ineligible for U.S. Citizenship," *Pacific His-torical Review* 79, no. 2 (May 2010): 167–201.

44. Charles Hughes, "The Decline of the Californios: The Case of San Diego, 1846–1856," in Cortés, ed., *Mexicans in California*, 17. Haas, *Conquests and Historical Identities*, 58–60, 63, 64. Mario T. García, "Merchants and Dons: San Diego's Attempt at Modernization, 1850–1860," in Cortés, *Mexicans in Cali-fornia*, 70. Pitt, in *Decline of the Californios*, 118, states that 813 titles were reviewed and 3 rejected. Walton Bean, *Cali-fornia*, 2d ed. (New York: McGraw-Hill, 1973), 157, says that more than 800 cases were heard, of which 604 were confirmed and 209 rejected.

45. Hughes, *The Case of San Diego*, 17. Heizer and Almquist, *The Other Californians*, 150. Pisani, "Squatter Law in California, 1850–1858," 277–310.

46. Haas, *Conquests and Historical Identities*, 67. Richard Griswold del Castillo, *Los Angeles Barrio, 1850-1890: A Social History* (Berkeley: University of California Press, 1979), 31, 46–51. Griswold del Castillo, "La Raza Hispano-Americana," 76. John W. Caughey, *California: A Remarkable State's Life History*, 3d ed. (Englewood Cliffs, NJ: Prentice-Hall, 1970), 219. Hughes, *The Case of San Diego*, 18. Pisani, "Squatter Law in California, 1850–1858," 280, 287, 295. Squatters were like locusts and Sutter wanted the governor to send the militia to Sacramento.

47. Horace Bell, *On the Old West Coast* (New York: Morrow, 1930), 255–57. Haas, *Conquests and Historical Identities*, 73–75. Monroy, *Thrown Among Strangers*, 159. Salomon, "California Son," 25.

48. Dara Orenstein, "Void for Vagueness: Mexicans and the Collapse of Miscegenation Law in California," *Pacific Historical Review* 74, no. 3 (August 2005): 376.

49. Bell, *On the Old West Coast*, 255–57.

50. Bell, *On the Old West Coast*, 255–57. Almaguer, *Racial Fault Lines*, 58.

51. *People v. Hall* (1854), http://www.cetel.org/1854_hall.html (accessed October 21, 2009). David S. Goldstein and Audrey B. Thacker, eds., *Complicating Constructions: Race, Ethnicity, and Hybridity in American Texts* (Seattle: University of Washington Press, 2008), 6–7.

52. Heizer and Almquist, *The Other Californians*, 128–29, 131, 151. Almaguer, *Racial Fault Lines*, 13. Stephen B. Oates, *The Approaching Fury: Voices of the Storm, 1820-1861* (New York: Harper Collins, 1998).

53. Mary Floyd Williams, *Committee of Vigilance of 1851: A Study of Social Control on the California Frontier in the Days of the Gold Rush* (Berkeley: University of California Press, 1921).

54. Clare V. McKanna, "Enclaves of Violence in Nineteenth-Century California," *Pacific Historical Review* 73, no. 3 (August 2004): 402–3. Sonora became an "instant city" in 1850 with a population of 4,000, while Columbia exploded to 8,151. These gold camps were 95 percent male from Chile, Peru, Mexico, Australia, France, China, and the United States. Alcohol played a huge role in homicides; 65 percent of the killers and 59.5 percent of the victims had been drinking.

55. Pitt, *Decline of Californios*, 50–53, 61–63. William D. Carrigan and Clive Webb, "The Lynching of Persons of Mexican Origin or Descent in the United States, 1848 to 1928," *Journal of Social History* 37, no. 2 (2003): 415. Coya Paz Brownrigg, "Linchocracia: Performing 'America' in *El Clamor Público*," *California History* 84, no. 2 (Winter 2006–2007): 40–53. See also Coya Paz Brownrigg, "Linchocracia: Performing 'America'" (paper presented at the conference "*El Clamor Público*: 150 years of Latino Newspapers in Southern California," Huntington-USC Institute on California and the West, October 28, 2005). *El Clamor Público* Collection 1855–1859, University of Southern California Digital Library, http://digitallibrary.usc.edu/cdm/landingpage/collection/p15799coll70.

56. There was a tendency to stereotype all Mexican women as "Rosa," "María," or "Juanita."

57. Maythee Rojas, "Re-Membering Josefa: Reading the Mexican Female Body in California Gold Rush Chronicles," *Women's Studies Quarterly* 35, no. ½ (Spring /Summer 2007): 126–148.

58. William B. Secrest, *Juanita: The Only Woman Lynched in the Gold Rush Days* (Fresno, CA: Sage-West, 1967), 8–29. Readings on the Internet can greatly enrich our knowledge of Mexican Americans in California. Roberto Carrillo Gantz, who is a vocational instructor for Sacramento County Regional Occupational Program (ROP) and a historian and a screenwriter, has done quite a bit of research on the subject. Moved by a PBS TV program about the California Gold Rush and about the lynching of Josefa, he went to the California State Library in Sacramento, researching the injustice for a screenplay. While browsing microfiche on the U.S. Mexican Claims Commission, he came across a claim made by Josefa's husband, José María Loaiza, filed against the U.S. government for "the lynching of his wife and the banishment of himself by a mob . . . July 4, 1852 . . . Downieville, California." [The date was inaccurate but further research verified that it was Josefa's husband.] Josefa and José María Loaiza were from Sonora. "Schedule of Mexican Claims against the United States," Senate Executive Document 31, 44th Congress 2nd Session. Docket Number 904. The claim was made on June 11, 1875; it was dismissed by the commissioner. *El Clámor Público* (4 and 16 April 1857). Ken Gonzales-Day, *Lynching in the West: 1850–1935* (Durham, NC: Duke University Press, 2006), 185–89. Alton Pryor, *Fascinating Women in California History* (Roseville, CA: Stagecoach Publishers, 2003), 43–46. Lynch Law of the Mother Lode, http://www.genealogyimagesofhistory.com/images/Lynchlaw.jpg.

59. Torres-Rouff, "Making Los Angeles," 82, 87. By 1840 racial categories hardened with the Californios casting themselves as white. Portrait of a drawing of Abel Stearns, ca. 1840–1860, USC Digital Archive, http://digarc.usc.edu/search/controller/view/chs-m15210.html.

60. W. W. Robinson, *People Versus Lugo: Story of a Famous Los Angeles Murder Case and Its Aftermath* (Los Angeles: Dawson's Book Shop, 1962), 6. Joseph Lancaster Brent, *The Lugo Case: A Personal Experience* (New Orleans, LA: Searcy & Pfaff, 1926), 4, 17, 19–23, reprinted in Cortés, *Mexicans in California*, 12–13. Robinson, *People Versus Lugo*, 1–5, 10–11, 17–18, 21–22, 26–27, 33–37, 40. Paul Bryan Gray, "Biographical Sketch of Francisco Ramírez" (paper presented at the conference *El Clamor Público*, October 28, 2005).

61. Nicolás Kanellos, "*El Clamor Público* and Its Place in American Journalism" (keynote speech given at the conference *El Clamor Público*, October 28, 2005). *El Clamor Público* has been digitized for home viewing. University of Southern California Library, http://digitallibrary.usc.edu/cdm/landingpage/collection/p15799coll70.

62. José Luis Benavides, "Caught in the Middle: How *El Clamor Público* Portrayed Communities of Color" (paper presented at the conference *El Clamor Público*, October 28, 2005). Armando Miguélez, "La trémula luz del relámpago: Lenguaje

metafórico en *El Clamor Público*" (*trabajo presentado en la conferencia El Clamor Público*, October 28, 2005). Pitt, *Decline of Californios*, Chapter 17. Paul Bryan Gray, "A Biographical Sketch of Francisco Ramírez" (paper presented at the conference *El Clamor Público*, October 28, 2005).

63. *El Clamor Público* (June 19, 1855).

64. William Walker, http://en.wikipedia.org/wiki/William_Walker_%28filibuster%29.

65. See Monroy, *Thrown Among Strangers*, 219–22, for general treatment. Quote in *El Clamor Público* (August 20, 1855).

66. *El Clamor Público* (September 18, 1855).

67. *El Clamor Público* (August 20, 1855).

68. *El Clamor Público* (May 10, 1856). *El Clamor Público* (May 17, 1856).

69. Brownrigg, "A Changing Lynchocracy," 11–12.

70. Veronica Torrejon, "A 'Mexican Window' into the City's Past; Los Angeles' First Spanish-Language Newspaper, *El Clamor Publico*, Was Founded 150 Years Ago by an 18-Year-Old Printer." Center for Law in the Public Interest, June 23, 2005, http://www.cityprojectca.org/blog/archives/115.

71. Bell, *Old West Coast*, 72. Hubert Howe Bancroft, *Popular Tribunals*, Vol. 1 (San Francisco, CA: History Company, 1887), 501–3.

72. Pitt, *Decline of Californios*, 174.

73. *El Clamor Público* (December 18, 1858).

74. Paul Bryan Gray, "A Biographical Sketch of Francisco Ramírez" (paper presented at the conference *El Clamor Público*, October 28, 2005).

75. J. M. Scanland. "The Newspapers of Los Angeles; Their Trials and Tragedies," *Los Angeles Times* (September 4, 1932).

76. Benavides, "Caught in the Middle." *El Clamor Público* (November 14, 1857).

77. Joaquin Murrieta http://www.youtube.com/watch?v=gyLasgzfd0.

78. Cossley-Batt, *The Last of the California Rangers* (New York: Funk & Wagnalls, 1928). http://www.yosemite.ca.us/library/california_rangers/joaquin_murieta.html. A descendant of Joaquin states that he died in Sonora, Mexico. Interview with Antonio Rivera Murieta, Phoenix AZ (December 15, 2001) from David Bacon, *Communities Without Borders* (Ithaca, NY: Cornell/ILR Press, 2006), http://dbacon.igc.org/TWC/mm02_Murrieta.htm. Joaquin Murrieta—Patriot or Desperado? California Legends, http://www.legendsofamerica.com/CA-Murieta.html. Through the tireless work of Alfredo Figueroa, a composer and Chicano activist from Blythe, California, we know that the California Rangers got the wrong man, and the real Joaquin Murieta died of old age in Sonora, Mexico.

79. Major Horace Bell, *Reminiscences of a Ranger; or, Early Times in Southern California* (Los Angeles: Yarnell, Caystile & Mathes, Printers, 1881), 23–29, 72, 108. http://memory.loc.gov/cgi-bin/query/r?ammem/calbk:%20@field%28DOCID+@lit%28calbk103%29%29.

80. Ernest May, "Tiburcio Vásquez," *Historical Society of Southern California Quarterly* 24 (1947): 123–24, places the time of the shootout in the spring of 1851. Griswold del Castillo, "La

Raza Hispano-Americana," 198, states that Vásquez began his career by escaping from a lynch mob. Monroy, *Thrown Among Strangers*, 215–19.

81. Interview of Tiburcio Vasquez, *The Los Angeles Star* (May 16, 1874). Robert Greenwood, *The California Outlaw: Tiburcio Vásquez* (Los Gatos, CA: Talisman Press, 1960), 12.

82. Heizer and Almquist, *The Other Californians*, 150–51.

83. May, "Tiburcio Vásquez," 124. Greenwood, *The California Outlaw*, 13. Griswold del Castillo, "La Raza Hispano-Americana," 199. Cecile Page Vargo, "El Bandito, Vasquez," Explore Historic California, http://www.explorehistoricalif.com/bandito2.html.

84. Greenwood, *The California Outlaw*, 23–24. Griswold del Castillo, *Los Angeles Barrio*, 114–15. *La Crónica* (May 2, 1874).

85. Greenwood, *The California Outlaw*, 75. Will H. Thrall, "The Haunts and Hideouts of Tiburcio Vasquez," *Historical Society of Southern California The Quarterly XXX*, no. 2 (June 1948), http://www.scvhistory.com/scvhistory/vasquez-thrall.htm. High school students in Acton, California, named their high school after Tiburcio Vásquez.

86. David E. Hayes-Bautista et al., "Empowerment, Expansion, and Engagement: Las Juntas Patrioticas in California, 1848–1869," *California History* 85, no. 1 (Winter 2007): 4–23.

87. David E. Hayes-Bautista, "The Latino Social Context of El Clamor Público: Indications from las Juntas Patrióticas" (paper presented at the conference *El Clamor Público*, October 28, 2005). Griswold del Castillo, "La Raza Hispano-Americana," 227. Griswold del Castillo, "Health and the Mexican Americans in Los Angeles, 1850–1867," *Journal of Mexican History* 4 (1974): 22.

88. Monroy, *Thrown Among Strangers*, 234–37. Albert Michael Camarillo, "The Making of a Chicano Community: A History of the Chicanos in Santa Barbara, California, 1850–1930" (PhD dissertation, University of California at Los Angeles, 1975), 116.

89. Birdseye View of Sonora Town from Fort Hill, Los Angeles, ca. 1885, USC Digital Archive, http://digarc.usc.edu/search/controller/view/chs-m4932.html. Historic Buildings and Sites, El Pueblo de Los Angeles, http://www.lasangelitas.org/buildings.htm.

90. Richard Griswold del Castillo, "Health and the Mexican Americans," 22. Caughey, *California*, 349–50.

91. Roberto Ramon Lint Sagarena, "Inheriting the Land: Defining Place in Southern California from the Mexican American War to the Plan Espiritual de Aztlán" (PhD dissertation, Princeton University, 2000), 38–39, 47.

92. Holy Cross Cemetery/Archbishop Joseph Sadoc Alemany, O.P., http://www.nps.gov/history/history/online_books/5views/5views5h41.htm.

93. Quoted in Griswold del Castillo, "La Raza Hispano-Americana," 271.

94. Monroy, *Thrown Among Strangers*, 165.

95. Almaguer, *Racial Fault Lines*, 120, 133, 149. *Thompson v. Doaksum*, No. 9546, Supreme Court of California, 68 Cal. 593, 10 P. 199 (1886) Cal. LEXIS 498, February 25, 1886. *Botiller v. Dominguez*, No. 1370, Supreme Court of the United States, 130 U.S. 238, 9 S. Ct. 525, 32 L. Ed. 926 (1889) U.S. LEXIS

1744. Submitted January 7, 1889; Decided April 1, 1889. Monroy, *Thrown Among Strangers*, 190–94.

96. The Legacy of the Mercury Mines, http://oaklandmuseumof-california.com/creeks/z-mercurymines.html.

97. Albert Michael Camarillo, *Chicanos in California* (San Francisco, CA: Boyd & Foster, 1984), 24–25.

98. Sóstenes Betancourt, "Ferrocarril del Sur (Sección del Norte) (Impresiones de viaje)," *El Cronista*, San Francisco, año II, no. 62, sábado, abril 18, 1885, furnished by Armando Miguelez. Stephen J. Pitti, *The Devil in Silicon Valley: Northern California, Race and Mexican Americans* (Princeton: Princeton University Press, 2003) is an excellent history of the evolution of San José, Santa Clara, and northern California enclaves.

99. Caughey, *California*, 344–45. Almaguer, *Racial Fault Lines*, 75–104, describes the transformation of Ventura County agriculture, showing how the small-scale farmer was driven out of the market. Keith William Cox, "Conflicts of Interest: Race, Class, Mexicanidad and the Negotiation of Rule in U.S. Occupied Mexico, 1846–1848" (PhD dissertation, University of California Riverside, 2007), 40.

100. Quoted in Haas, *Conquests and Historical Identities*, 1. "First Felon Was Railroaded—Story of Modesta Avila," Capistrano, http://www.sanjuancapistrano.net/history/avila.html.

101. Jean F. Riss, "The Lynching of Francisco Torres," *Journal of Mexican American History* (Spring 1972): 90–111. Griswold del Castillo, "La Raza Hispano-Americana," 193. Also see Richard Griswold del Castillo, "Myth and Reality: Chicano Economic Mobility in Los Angeles, 1850–1890," *Aztlán* 6, no. 2 (Summer 1975): 151–71. "Torres Taken," *Los Angeles Times* (August 11, 1892). "Lynch Law at Santa Ana," *Los Angeles Times* (August 21, 1892), 14. Larry Welborn, "Searching for the Most Notorious Criminal Case in Orange County History," *Orange County Register*, October 31, 2009, http://www.ocregister.com/articles/gibson-217191-county-case.html.

102. Almaguer, *Racial Fault Lines*, 29.

Empire

The scenarios of the wars with Mexico (1847) and Spain (1898) were similar—on both occasions Euro-Americans denied that the United States was the aggressor or harbored imperialist designs. It was claimed that the United States was not like western Europe, which controlled most of the Third World. The war with Mexico pushed the borders south, crossing people, rivers, and other resources. The war cost Mexico more than 500,000 square miles of territory, the lives of over 25,000 with many more wounded, and valuable rivers and resources. The 1898 Treaty of Paris gave Cuba and Puerto Rico independence from Spain, and took the victory away from the *independistas*.

Consequent to both wars, the U.S. worldview expanded. Prior to 1848, U.S. foreign policy in the Caribbean focused on Cuba. Cuba was the largest island in the Caribbean, only 90 miles from Florida, and coveted by slave states. After the Mexican War, American aims expanded to the entire Caribbean and the Isthmus of Panama, which Americans saw as vital to their security. Using the Monroe Doctrine as its divine inspiration, the U.S. Navy and filibusters infringed on the Caribbean and Central America.

Cubans and Puerto Ricans had fought for five decades to break the ties of Spanish imperialism. People from other Latin American countries also participated in these wars. Manuel de Quesada, a Cuban patriot born in Puerto Rico, was forced to immigrate to Mexico in 1853.[1] There he joined the ranks of Mexican President Benito Juárez and fought against the French from 1861 to 1868. He was made a brigadier general and the governor of Coahuila and Durango, Mexico. Quesada led the first popular Cuban insurrection before he died in 1886. Quesada—like many of the precursors of the Cuban and Puerto Rican independence—entreated the United States for support that was not forthcoming.[2]

In 1898 the United States supported the Cuban independence movement. In a short time, it signed the Treaty of Paris (1898) with Spain. The liberation fighters were not included in the negotiations.[3] The treaty sanctioned the U.S. occupation of Cuba and enabled the Platt Amendment (1902) that gave the United States the right to intervene militarily in Cuba, and it leased Guantanamo Bay to the United States for a naval base in perpetuity. Spain ceded to the United States the island of Puerto Rico and other West Indies islands and the island of Guam in the Marianas or Ladrones. This began the American occupation of the Philippines. Soon afterwards the U.S. built its canal in Panama followed by a century of armed intervention.[4]

Just as the occupation of Mexican lands fulfilled the prophecy of Manifest Destiny, the Spanish–American War boosted the feelings of U.S. entitlement at home and abroad. It kindled a debate as to whether the United States should strive to be an imperial power.[5] The U.S. senator from Indiana Albert Beveridge was a fervent advocate of Euro-American imperialism, which meant U.S. control of territories outside its borders. Beveridge argued that the United States should be an imperial power, the Philippines was theirs forever: it was "territory belonging to the United States," adding:

> It is a noble land that God has given us; a land that can feed and clothe the world; a land whose coastlines would inclose [sic] half the countries of Europe; a land set like a sentinel between the two imperial oceans of the globe, a greater England with a nobler destiny. . . . We cannot fly from our world duties; it is ours to execute the purpose of a fate that has driven us to be greater than our small intentions. We cannot retreat from any soil where Providence has unfurled our banner; it is ours to save that soil for liberty and civilization.[6]

The next year, Rudyard Kipling, a British novelist and poet, wrote "The White Man's Burden: The United States and the Philippine Islands":

> THE WHITE MAN'S BURDEN
>
> Take up the White Man's burden—
> Send forth the best ye breed—
> Go send your sons to exile
> To serve your captives' need
> To wait in heavy harness
> On fluttered folk and wild—
> Your new-caught, sullen peoples,
> Half devil and half child . . .[7]

This sense of "burden" gave Americans the feeling that they were taking care of their little brown brothers, justifying frequent intervention into the affairs of Latin America. They were doing it for their Little Brown Brothers' own good.[8]

In the worldview of the United States, the Caribbean and Central America were inseparable. The Panama Canal was the linchpin. The completion of the 51-mile canal linking the two oceans was essential to the security of the United States. Accordingly the canal was a natural extension of the United States. The heavy-handedness of the United States in building the canal caused bitterness and resentment that has lasted to this day. It unified Latin America in the hatred and distrust of the Colossus of the North.

Notes

1. M. Quesada, *Address of Cuba to the United States* (New York: Comes, Lawrence & Co., Stationers and Printers, 1873), 1–40. Library of Congress, http://memory.loc.gov/cgi-bin/query/r?ammem/murray:@field(DOCID+@lit(lcrbmrpt2502div2)).

2. Rodolfo F. Acuña and Guadalupe Compeán, eds., *Voices of the U.S. Latino Experience* (Santa Barbara: ABC-CLIO E-Book, 2008), 275–306, documents events leading up to the Spanish–American War.

3. The World of 1898: The Spanish American War, Hispanic Division of Library of Congress, http://www.loc.gov/rr/hispanic/1898/intro.html. Treaty of Paris, Text of the Treaty Ending the Spanish–American War, Home of Heroes, http://www.homeofheroes.com/wallofhonor/spanish_am/18_treaty.html.

4. Acuña and Compeán, eds., *Voices of U.S. Latino*, 307–336.

5. The Age of Imperialism, An Online History of the United States, Small Planet Communications, http://www.smplanet.com/imperialism/toc.html.

6. Albert Beveridge: The March of the Flag, Fordham University's Online Modern History Sourcebook, http://www.fordham.edu/halsall/mod/1898beveridge.html.

7. Rudyard Kipling, "The White Man's Burden," *McClure's Magazine* 12 (February 1899), available at http://www.fordham.edu/halsall/mod/Kipling.html.

8. U.S. Interventions in Latin America, http://www.zompist.com/latam.html.

CHAPTER 8

Immigration, Labor, and Generational Change

LEARNING OBJECTIVES

- Show how the railroad industrialized the United States and Mexico.

- Explain the concepts of push, pull, and nativism in the diaspora of Mexicans north.

- Describe how the numerous immigration laws increased the pull of Mexicans into the United States.

- Analyze the importance of the events leading up to and following the Mexican Revolution of 1910.

- Discuss how the Mexicans' move from rural to urban life changed their issues and organizations.

- Tell why World War I was a watershed in the formation of Mexican American identity.

The wheel diagram opening each of the last three chapters illustrates a theory that explains how economics, conquest, political control, resistance, and socialization are interrelated. This chapter does not advance a theory per se; instead, it encourages the reader to get into the habit of thinking about the past by focusing on timelines that are filled in by story boards. The objective is to prod the reader to think like a scientist and explore ideas in a systematic way. Although there is no unique way of thinking about history, timelines are helpful tools in charting out how and why events happened. Looking back often helps the historian, and the curious reader, see a relationship between events.

In this chapter we will be covering the first two decades of the twentieth century. Note that I begin the timeline in 1880, the year that marked the arrival of the railroad in most of the Southwest; 1882 is the year when the Chinese Exclusion act was passed; and 1898 is when the Spanish–American War ended. How did these events contribute to the developments in the 1900–1920 time period?

1880	1882	1898	1900	1903	1907	1910	1913	1917	1920

Overview

By the 1880s, the railroad had facilitated the expansion of trade in both Mexico and the United States. As communal lands and open-range ranching in Mexico gave way to the expansion of mining and commercial agriculture, large numbers of Mexican farmers were displaced. A substantial number of Mexicans migrated to the United States even before the first two decades of the twentieth century began. The railroad facilitated the movement of thousands more.[1] The railroad linked the interior to U.S. markets as well as to the mines of northern Mexico. Commercial agriculture in Mexico created *push factors* that uprooted thousands of Mexican laborers and their families. Initially they migrated to urban centers near their villages; then some went to work on railroads; some sought employment in the mines of northern Mexico; and others fled to the Southwest. They went north because of *pull factors*—simply put, because there were jobs in the north that attracted them. The railroads had integrated and industrialized the U.S. economy and created jobs at the bottom level of the market.[2] Mexicans met these needs as they filled low-end jobs in factories, mines, railroads, farms, and ranches.

Migration of Mexicans to the United States was foreseeable. The two nations' counties shared a 2,000-mile border, with parts of the United States only 700 miles away from Mexico's interior. Early immigrants came mainly from the Border States; but, by the turn of the century, the railroad had shrunk distances between the interior and northern reaches of Mexico, and people from the interior migrated in larger numbers. Not all Mexicans were uprooted peasants: many political refugees fled the dictatorship of Porfirio Díaz; some were skilled workers; others came for short periods and returned; and still others were pushed north because of natural disasters such as droughts.[3]

This migration was hastened by the privatization of the land and resources of the country that favored the rich and foreign investors. Fifteen thousand miles of railroad were built during the *Porfiriato*; most lines ran north and south, with spur tracks providing better access to local and regional markets. Mines attracted armies of Mexican workers to northern Mexican states as well as to Arizona, New Mexico, and Colorado. The dramatic expansion of commercial agriculture and the cities generated a demand for tens of thousands of laborers.

Another push factor was population growth. In the 1840s, Mexico's population was about 7 million; it reached 9.5 million in 1875, and 12.6 million by 1895. At the end of the *Porfiriato* in 1910, the census counted more than 15 million inhabitants. Small family farms could no longer support the larger numbers of people, most of whom eventually moved to the cities to find supplemental or permanent employment.[4] By 1910 Mexico had 22 cities with populations of 20,000–50,000; 5 cities with populations of 50,000–100,000; and 2 cities with populations of more than 100,000. Mexico had a small industrial proletariat class, with 16.3 percent of its labor force working in manufacturing (68 percent worked in agriculture).[5]

The post–Civil War period (1861–1865) saw an unprecedented industrial growth in the United States, which up to this point was mostly a nation of farms and small towns. Factories and urban centers came to dominate the eastern seaboard as European immigrants flocked to them for jobs. The railroad system expanded and accelerated the commercialization of the West, where machines replaced animals. The construction of railroads created a demand for iron and steel, a demand for rails and locomotives, a demand for capital, a demand for workers, and a demand for food. The arrival of more immigrants evoked angst among the Euro-American population, which cried for limiting immigration. The passage of the Chinese Exclusion Acts of 1882, 1892, and 1902 and the Gentlemen's Agreements with Japan of 1900 and 1907 first reduced and then eliminated the number of Chinese and Japanese immigrating to the United States, increasing the pull of Mexican workers. California, which had depended on Native American and then Chinese labor, could not get enough Native Americans by 1900; their numbers fell to just 17,500. With the decline in the number of Chinese and Native American workers available, the solution was to hire more Mexicans.

Railroad networks that knitted the two countries together facilitated the increased interaction resulting from industrial development in Mexico and the United States. Workers from the interior of Mexico were pulled toward large commercial farming areas such as the Laguna in the northern Mexican states of Durango and Coahuila. Once the harvest was over, many of these workers migrated to other agricultural areas in Mexico and the United States, literally following the crops. Others migrated to the mines and the cities of northern Mexico and the United States. In other words, the border was a revolving door, with Mexican labor moving into and out of the United States, and in the process developing the Euro-American Southwest.[6]

More than a million Mexicans arrived in the United States during this 20-year period (1900–1920). As the number of European immigrants decreased, the Mexican population in the United States grew. The 1900 census showed an estimated 330,000 U.S.-born Mexicans—more than three times the Mexican-born population in the United States. California had 8,086 Mexican-born residents and about 33,000 U.S.-born Mexicans; in Arizona the corresponding numbers were 14,171 and 29,000. New Mexico's population only numbered 6,649 Mexican immigrants compared with 122,000 U.S.-born Mexicans. Texas had the largest numbers by far, with 71,062 immigrants and 131,000 U.S.-born Mexicans. Colorado had the fewest— 274 immigrants and 15,000 U.S.-born Mexicans.[7]

By the 1920s, Mexicans accounted for more than 10 percent of all immigrants in the United States; however, a majority of Mexicans in the United States were born there. Visibility triggered a virulent strain of racist nativism, a mixture of racism and xenophobia, toward Mexicans.[8] Differences also arose among the immigrants according to where they settled and what work they did. The wave in which they arrived spelled further differences. For example, middle-class Mexicans arriving before the Mexican Revolution were more apt to be liberal and differed from the post-1910-era exiles, who were often conservative politically. There were also variations within generations. For example, many rural migrants continued to use Spanish as their primary language whereas Mexicans in urban areas tended to adopt English more quickly, especially the second generation.

Ideas Cross Borders

In 1910 the U.S. consul in Mexico, Luther E. Ellsworth, who sometimes spied for the government of Mexican dictator Porfirio Díaz, wrote:

> *I have the honor to report increasing activity of the very intelligent class of Mexican exiles in the Cities and Towns along the Mexican-American Border line, between the Gulf and the Pacific Ocean . . . [They] are busily engaged [in] writing and publishing inflammatory articles intended to educate up to date, in new revolutionary ideas, the thousands of Mexicans now on the American side of the Border line, and as many as possible of those on the Mexican side.[9]*

A significant number of the Mexican migrants were political refugees. Once in the United States, they organized and rallied support for the struggle to overthrow Díaz, whom they accused of subverting the Constitution of 1857. They established newspapers and became involved in civic and labor organizing.

Throughout the nineteenth century, many Mexicans read the works of European thinkers in an effort to understand government, democracy, and modernization. Because of the dramatic transformations that took place, disparate ideologies emerged to explain the changes in the new industrial society and the disorder caused by it. The anarchist philosophy of Joseph Proudhon and Mikhail Bakunin was among the most popular among Mexicans, partially because they were more available in Spanish and Italian than were Marxist writings. Urbanization led to the formation of *mutualistas* (mutual-aid societies) that were used to organize workers for self-help and even strikes. In 1879, Carmen Huerta, a Mexicana, was elected president of the anarchist *El Gran Círculo de Obreros de México* (The Great Center of the Workers of Mexico).[10] "These organizations espoused mutual aid, workers' defense, and a wide range of radical and conservative ideologies."[11]

Mexican workers' resentment increased during the *Porfiriato* as the foreign presence in Mexico multiplied. U.S. investment was ubiquitous, and white U.S. workers enjoyed privileges and wages denied to Mexicans. Díaz jailed the dissidents, forcing many of them to go into exile, where they planned revolts against the regime.[12] One of the first worker actions was on September 26, 1881, when a Mexican Central

Railroad foreman cut workers' wages by one-quarter, from 2 pesos to 1.50 pesos. The workers went on strike; but, like most of the strikes of the period, it was short lived. The first miners' strike occurred in Pinos Altos, in the Municipio de Ocampo, Chihuahua, on January 21, 1883. The British Mining Company *Compañía Minera de Pinos Altos* required that miners spend half their wages at the company store; the workers refused and occupied the company store in protest. Local authorities sided with the management, deputizing a dozen men to put down the strike. When the mine manager attempted to address the workers, he was shot and killed, whereupon the township president arrived with 25 men and put the mining camp under martial law. He arrested the strike leaders and executed Blas Venegas, Cruz Baca, Ramón Mena, Francisco Campos, and Juan Valenzuela. All of this happened three years before the famous Haymarket Square Riot in Chicago on May 4, 1886 (which the Labor Day on May 1 commemorates), in which seven policemen and four protestors were killed and four anarchists later executed.[13]

Internal opposition to Díaz crystallized in 1906 as strikes took place in mining, railroad, and textile industries. In July 1906, mechanics on the Mexican Central Railroad in Chihuahua struck the line. Workers shut down repair shops from the border to Mexico City, and by mid-August, the spreading strike involved 1,500 mechanics and 3,000 other railroad employees. Díaz ordered the workers to return their job and backed his order with a show of force. The modernization of communication helped spread the word of worker discontent to urban centers and rural areas on both sides of La Línea, the Rio Bravo.[14]

Justice Knows No Borders

Radicals such as Catarino Garza, Victor Ochoa, and Lauro Aguirre[15] planned and carried out unsuccessful revolutionary activities before the turn of the century. El Paso was a gathering point for revolutionaries; Teresa Urrea, also called "*La Santa de Cabora,*" made it her base of operation for a time. A millenarian figure, Teresa empowered the disenfranchised villagers of Chihuahua where the Indians prayed for deliverance from the Díaz dictatorship. The next significant wave of revolutionaries arrived after the turn of the century and was led by the followers of Ricardo Flores Magón, who spent more than 20 years in the United States, leading the *Partido Liberal Mexicano* (PLM) and writing not only about tyranny in Mexico but also about economic, political, and social discrimination suffered by Mexicans in "Utopia"—the United States.

Born in Oaxaca in 1873, Ricardo Flores Magón and his colleagues (known as *magonistas*) crossed the border in 1904 and started a newspaper, *Regeneración,* to educate Mexicans and Euro-Americans about conditions in Mexico and the United States. While here, they planned and carried out invasions of Mexican territory.[16] Along with Librado Rivera and Antonio I. Villarreal, Ricardo was arrested in August 1907 and held in the Los Angeles County Jail for several months. They were then transferred to Tombstone, Arizona, where they were found guilty of conspiracy to violate the neutrality laws and sentenced to 18 months in the territorial prison. In March 1918, the PLM issued a manifesto calling for a world anarchist revolution. The courts sentenced Flores Magón to 20 years in prison, and his comrade Librado Rivera to 15 years, for violation of U.S. neutrality acts. In November 1922, before his release, Flores Magón mysteriously died in his cell—he was murdered.[17]

Mexican women, seeing the injustices of the system, began to criticize them. In 1870, Mexican poet and educator Rita Cetina Gutiérrez formed a group, mostly of schoolteachers, called *La Siempreviva* in Mérida, Yucatán; their focus was educating the poor and establishing a secondary school for girls. The group published a newspaper and was a strong supporter of women's rights, advocating collective action. Yucatán became the center for feminist activity, and later a feminist league was named after Rita Cetina Gutiérrez. Three years later, women textile workers in the Federal District organized *Las Hijas de Anáhuac.* These groups set the stage for the establishment of a sizable number of feminist groups and newspapers that later shared the goals of groups such as the PLM. Their members saw revolution as a vehicle for social change. Middle- and upper-class women became writers and journalists; they organized feminist and women's magazines and newspapers in which they argued for reform and gender equality. Meanwhile, as more women became professionals, their readership expanded.[18]

Feminist ideas evolved into a body of feminist thought as the critiques of the Porfirian society matured. In 1904, Dolores Correa de Zapata, a schoolteacher; Laura Méndez de Cuenca; and Murgía Manteana brought out the feminist magazine *La Mujer Mexicana*, which was published monthly until 1908. María Sándoval de Zarco, who became Mexico's first female attorney in 1889, and Dr. Columba Rivera, its second female practicing physician, wrote for the magazine. In Laredo, Texas, Sara Estela Ramírez (1881–1910) edited *La Corregidora* and *Aurora*. A friend and supporter of Flores Magón, Ramírez worked for the Federal Labor Union and *La Sociedad de Obreros, Igualdad y Progreso,* a mutual-aid society formed in the mid-1880s. Another activist, Juana Gutiérrez de Méndoza, writing for *El Diario del Hogar*, as early as the 1890s criticized mining conditions. She served three months in jail for her anti-Díaz activities. By 1901, she published *Vésper: Justicia y Libertad* (justice and liberty) and soon broke with Ricardo Flores Magón over what she termed "matters of principle." Juana died in Mexico City in 1942, poor and forgotten.[19] Teresa Villarreal founded *El Obrero* in San Antonio, Texas, before 1910. It targeted the proletariat—both men and women. From 1913 to 1915, Blanca de Moncaleano published *Pluma Roja* in Los Angeles, which, according to Clara Lomas, "*placed* the emancipation of women at the center of its anarchist agenda, adding a new dimension to the politics of the revolutionary struggle." [20]

Industrial Bonanzas

During the colonial era bonanzas drove the northward movement: silver and gold strikes that attracted huge numbers of workers who hoped to strike it rich. There would be periods of expansion, and then contraction, as the workers moved on to yet another bonanza, with the hope of bettering their lives. Industrialization functions much the same way; it creates gigantic pools of jobs that attract huge numbers of Mexican laborers. Copper was at the center of one of these bonanza phenomena.

After the U.S. Civil War (1861–1865), transportation costs dropped dramatically, which encouraged the investment of capital to exploit copper. Copper was the best and the least expensive conductor used in long-distance transmission of electricity. Railroads rendered giant copper camps profitable; and the "electric age" created an insatiable market for copper. The prime attraction of Arizona was its copper mines that employed tens of thousands of laborers. The copper mines of Clifton, Globe, Bisbee, and Jerome were all opened in the 1870s and 1880s. (See Chapter 6.) These four districts in time would each produce more than 5 billion pounds of copper; and Arizona would become a global leader in the production of copper. Simultaneously, Euro-American copper barons exploited the great Mexican copper mines of Cananea, Nacozari, and other parts of Sonora.[21]

Workers Find Their Voice

On January 19, 1903, the Arizona legislature passed a law prohibiting miners from working more than eight hours per day underground. The eight-hour law was a major victory for union men. However, its true purpose was to eliminate foreign-born Mexicans, who had to work 10–12 hours a day to make ends meet with their lower wage scale. The cut in hours meant that Mexican miners would take less money home because mine owners cut workers' daily wages at Clifton-Morenci-Metcalf by 10 percent. On the morning of June 3, miners responded by walking off the job, shutting down the smelters and mills, and beginning what Jeanne Parks Ringgold, granddaughter of then-sheriff Jim Parks of Clifton, called the "bloodiest battle in the history of mining in Arizona." Around 1,200–1,500 miners participated, of whom 80–90 percent were Mexican, who were frustrated by the mine owners stonewalling them. Consequently the miners armed themselves and took control of the mines, and shut them down.[22]

The *Bisbee Daily Review* of June 3, 1903, wrote, "The Mexicans belong to numerous societies and through these they can exert some sort of organization to stand together." At first, there was cooperation among the ethnic groups. Abraham Salcido, the president of a *mutualista;* Frank Colombo, an Italian; Weneslado H. Laustaunau, a Mexican miner; and A. C. Cruz, another Mexican worker, led the strike. Two days later, the *Bisbee Daily Review* observed, "the strike is now composed almost entirely of Mexicans. Quite a number of Americans have left." Among the demands of the strikers were free hospitalization, paid life insurance for miners, locker rooms, fair prices at the company store, hiring only of men who were members of the society, and protection against being fired without cause.[23] The governor ordered the Arizona Rangers into Clifton-Morenci, and on June 9, 1903, workers staged a demonstration of solidarity. In direct defiance of the Rangers, 2,000 Mexicans marched through the streets of Morenci in torrential rains. A clash seemed imminent, but the storm dispersed the strikers, and floods drowned almost 50 people and damaged some $100,000 worth of property.

Mine owners sent Mexican consul Arturo Elías, an official of Porfirio Díaz, "to talk some sense to the Mexicans." Workers accused Elías of selling them out to the owners.[24] Meanwhile, Salcido, Colombo, Laustaunau, and Cruz were convicted for inciting a riot. Authorities sentenced them to Yuma State Penitentiary, where Laustaunau died (some believe murdered). The mining camps of the region would remain areas of discontent from which revolutionary leaders would recruit supporters in large numbers.

Upon his release from prison in 1906, Salcido gave a fiery speech before 2,000 people in Metcalf, denouncing Mexican President Porfirio Díaz and calling him a "traitor," "tyrant," and "thief." Pressured by U.S. authorities and the Mexican consul, Salcido was kicked out of the area and he went to the border town of Douglas, where he became involved with the PLM. U.S. authorities arrested Salcido and others in September 1906 for a conspiracy to invade Mexico. Salcido was deported and sent to the dreaded San Juan de Ulúa prison near Veracruz, Mexico.[25]

A distinguishing feature of this strike and other strikes of the decade is that the workers organized them through their *mutualistas*. These associations varied greatly in their political ideology, ranging from apolitical to reformist to radical. Mutual-aid societies met the immigrants' need for "fellowship, security, and recreation" and were a form of collective and voluntary self-help and self-defense. Their motto—*Patria, Unión y Beneficencia* (country, unity, and benevolence)—became a common unifying symbol throughout the Southwest and eventually throughout the Midwest as well. Shut out of mainstream unions, Mexicans often used *mutualistas* as a front for union activities.[26]

Meanwhile, in May 1906, Mexican workers in Cananea, Sonora, demanded that the Consolidated Copper Company treat them the same way as it did white miners. Euro-Americans worked eight hours while Mexicans labored for 10–12 hours—at half the Euro-American wage scale. On the evening of May 31, Mexican workers walked off the Oversight mine, demanding 5 pesos for an eight-hour day. Sonoran governor Rafael Izábal ordered the state militia to support mine owner Colonel William C. Greene. Tempers rose, and a company employee killed three demonstrators. Mexican workers responded by burning the lumberyard. Arizona Rangers crossed the international line into Mexico to help Greene; Mexican federal troops poured into Cananea. The military commander issued an ultimatum to miners—either go back to work or get drafted into the army and go fight the Yaqui Indians.[27]

The Nurturing of Ideas

Even to this day, the residents of Clifton and Morenci, former mining districts, remember that Teresa Urrea once lived and died in Clifton. *La Santa de Cabora,* as Teresa was known, was one of many Mexican immigrants who contributed to the making of the Mexican Revolution of 1910. After the Yaqui of Sonora revolted in the 1890s, invoking her name as their patron, Mexican authorities targeted her. Teresa fled to the United States with her father Tomás and the revolutionary journalist Lauro Aguirre. Fleeing to Via Nogales and then to El Paso, Teresa finally settled in Clifton. While evidence does not directly link Teresa to revolutionary cells, it does imply the involvement of her father and stepmother. The home of her stepmother, Gabriela Cantúa, was used as the headquarters of the PLM, and Mexican consular records suggest that Cantúa was under constant surveillance in the years before the 1910 Mexican Revolution. The great revolutionary Práxedis Guerrero, who was a member of the PLM's junta, also lived and organized miners in the Clifton-Morenci-Metcalf mining camps.[28]

"Mexicans are Not Fit to Raise White Babies"

Life experiences nurtured memories of racism. In October 1904, some 16 months after the 1903 mining strike, 3 nuns, 4 nurses, and 40 Irish orphans from New York City arrived in the Arizona mining town of Clifton for placement in respectable Catholic homes. Father Constant Mandin, the local priest, requested the orphans, and closely screened the adoptive parents. The priest spoke little English and limited Spanish.[29] Upon hearing that Mexicans were adopting white babies, a posse of white males armed with Winchester rifles marched to the Mexican quarter of North Clifton, to "rescue" the 40 blond babies. White men with guns banged the doors of the Mexican homes with the butts of their rifles and seized the white orphans. The so-called posse rounded up 16 of the foundlings and abducted them to the local church. The posse, incited by their wives, threatened the priest, the nuns, and their agent, and forced them to relinquish control of some of the children to white foster families, who were neither Catholic nor screened.

At the trial, the potential Mexican adoptive mothers were portrayed as prostitutes. In fact, they were married and were of good reputation. White women testified that they felt it was their duty to save the children from the Mexicans. The court accepted the narrative of the abductors that the Mexicans were

> wholly unfit to be entrusted with them; that they were, with possibly one or two exceptions, of the lowest class of half-breed Mexican Indians; that they were impecunious, illiterate, unacquainted with the English language, vicious, and, in several instances, prostitutes and persons of notoriously bad character; that their homes were of the crudest sort, being for the most part built of adobe, with dirt floors and roofs; that many of them had children of their own, whom they were unable properly to support.

Charles E. Mills, the superintendent of Phelps–Dodge, which employed the Mexicans and owned the housing, sided with the vigilantes, claiming that the homes were unfit for white children. In the end, the law found that Mexicans were unfit to raise white children.[30]

The Mexican Diaspora

Because three-quarters of the Mexican–U.S. border is in Texas, many incoming Mexicans first settled there. However, changes were occurring and in 1908 Victor Clark, in a U.S. government study titled *Report of the Immigration Commission*, stated, "As recently as 1900, immigrant Mexicans were seldom found more than one hundred miles from the border. Now they are working as unskilled laborers and as section hands as far east as Chicago and as far north as Iowa, Wyoming, and San Francisco."

Mexican laborers and their families migrated in response to bonanzas, sources of job opportunities, other than mining. The industrialization of agriculture and the growth of cities demanded huge amounts of labor. The expansion and contraction of these industries constantly attracted and uprooted these armies of workers who were in search of stability and control over their lives. Clark estimated that before 1908 about 60,000 entered the United States annually, with most Mexicans remaining for only a brief period. Officially, 103,000 immigrants had entered the United States by 1900, but the actual number was probably much higher. Likewise, the official figure of 222,000 for 1910 is probably too low; experts estimate that the number may have been as high as 500,000.[31]

The Mexican diaspora was accelerated by U.S. policies such as the Dingley Tariff of 1897 that raised the tax on imported sugar, dramatically expanding the cultivation of sugar beets in the Southwest and Midwest, and in turn increasing the demand for migrant workers. The number of sugar beet companies in Colorado, Kansas, and California quadrupled between 1900 and 1907. Firms such as the Holly Sugar Company and the American Sugar Beet Company recruited and transported large numbers of Mexicans to farms throughout the Southwest, Northwest, and Midwest. By 1912, a Mexican colonia formed on the west side of St. Paul, Minnesota, where Mexican beet workers migrated during winter.[32] In Colorado in 1909 the Great Western Company alone employed 2,600 Mexican beet workers and the number was going up.

Meanwhile, throughout the Rio Grande Valley Mexican workers cleared brush and planted cotton and winter vegetables. The open range disappeared, and wire fencing sectioned off the land. At the turn of the century, the population of south Texas was 79,934; the 1920 Census counted 159,822; and in 1930, the number was 322,845. During the same period, the population of the Winter Garden area of Texas grew from 8,401 to 36,816. These numbers show that "Texas Mexican and Anglo frontier settlers were overrun by *fuereños* (outsiders) from the interior [of Mexico] and newcomers from the Midwest and South." However, because of the heavy demand for labor, "South Texas remained basically Mexican"—with Mexicans moving out and other Mexicans moving in.[33]

Texas growers encouraged this heavy migration of Mexicans, knowing that the development of the area depended on Mexican labor. The continual migration changed long-established Mexican communities within south Texas, such as Corpus Christi, Laredo, and Brownsville, where recently arrived Mexicans outnumbered the older Texas Mexican residents. Outside south Texas, cities such as Austin, Houston, Dallas, and Lubbock also saw the formation of Mexican enclaves. At the turn of the nineteenth century, Houston had only a few hundred Mexicans; 30 years later, that number had climbed to more than 15,000. Cotton was the main cash crop and the *pull factor* that attracted Mexicans until the late 1920s, after which spinach and other vegetables acquired a greater share of the market. Mexicans moved from ranchos to colonias, where contractors recruited them to work as farmhands in California, Colorado, and Michigan.[34]

Agribusiness also increased the number of Mexicans in Arizona and California. The transformation in California began in the 1890s, and it accelerated in the first decade of the twentieth century with the huge reclamation projects in western Arizona and in the Imperial Valley of California. By the beginning of the twentieth century, the value of intensive crops in California rose to $52 million—up from a mere $2.8 million 20 years earlier. In 1907 the *California Fruit Grower* magazine noted that Mexicans were "plentiful, generally peaceable, and are satisfied with very low social conditions."[35] The next year, farmers reaped the first commercial cotton harvest in the Imperial Valley of California. From 1907 to 1920, orange and lemon production in California quadrupled; between 1917 and 1922, cantaloupe production doubled, grapes tripled, and lettuce quadrupled. Such unprecedented production intensified the demand for Mexican labor in California agriculture, which became nothing short of a bonanza for them.[36]

Early Mexican American Struggles to Control the Work Place

As mentioned, the first wave of Mexicans coming to the United States before the turn of the nineteenth century mostly worked on the railroads, on farms, and in mines. Some also migrated to commercial centers such as Tucson, San Antonio, and then Los Angeles. Although they had greater opportunities than those in the migrant stream, economic and social mobility was limited by a racist ceiling that assumed they were unequal and deserved less pay than white people. As a white mechanic conceded,

> *They will never pay a Mexican what he's really worth compared with a white man. I know a Mexican that's the best blacksmith I ever knew. He has made some of the best tools I ever used. But they pay him $1.50 a day as a helper, working under an American blacksmith who gets $7 a day.*[37]

As a consequence there was a wave of strikes; Mexican workers demanded democracy in the workplace. In 1901, 200 Mexican construction workers went on a strike at the El Paso Electric Street Car Company demanding higher wages and better work conditions. In 1907, 150 workers at another El Paso smelter struck. Throughout the decade, and into the next, there were many incidents of smelter workers organizing and striking to better their lives. The concentration of workers at the various smelters, refineries, and railroads would draw labor organizations such as the Western Federation of Miners (WFM) and the Industrial Workers of the World (IWW) to the Gateway City that had a history of labor militancy.[38]

Meanwhile, in 1903 in California, Japanese and Mexican workers in Oxnard protested the practices of the Western Agricultural Contracting Company (WACC), which was withholding some of the workers' salaries until the end of the contract; 500 Japanese and 200 Mexican members of the Japanese–Mexican Labor Association (JMLA) called a strike. On March 23, two Mexican and two Japanese laborers were wounded, and 21-year-old Luis Vásquez was killed. The WACC conceded to most of the laborers' demands.

After the strike, the workers formed the Sugar Beet and Farm Laborers Union of Oxnard and petitioned the American Federation of Labor (AFL) for affiliation. Samuel Gompers, president of the AFL, turned down the request and denied affiliation unless the membership guaranteed that Chinese and Japanese workers would not be admitted. Mexican workers refused to abandon their Japanese comrades. They issued a statement in a letter to the AFL president:

> *We refuse any other kind of charter, except one which will wipe out race prejudices and recognize our fellow workers as being as good as ourselves. I am ordered by the Mexican union to write this letter to you and they fully approve its words.*[39]

That same year, Mexican workers at the Johnston Fruit Company in Santa Barbara, California, struck for higher wages and shorter hours. Lemon pickers and graders demanded the lowering of the 10-hour workday to 9 hours. The demand came at the height of the season, and workers got their 9-hour day and overtime.[40]

In the spring of 1903 Mexican workers of Henry E. Huntington's Pacific Electric railway went on strike. Huntington was Los Angeles's largest employer and developed a "no concession to labor" policy, based on his experiences during the Pullman Strike in 1894. Mexican track workers had formed *La Unión Federal Mexicana* (the Mexican Federal Union), with A. N. Nieto serving as executive secretary. It had 900 members and a bank account of $600, and was headquartered in Sonoratown (as the Mexican barrio in Los Angeles was called). Mexicans demanded a raise from 17.5¢ an hour to 20¢ an hour, 30¢ an hour for evenings, and 40¢ an hour for Sundays. The Los Angeles Merchants and Manufacturers Association and the Citizens' Alliance joined with Huntington to fight trade unions and to keep Los Angeles an open-shop city. "The PE retaliated by firing the strikers and replacing them with Japanese, black, and white laborers whom it paid twenty-two and a half cents per hour. Again, Huntington received police protection for strikebreakers. The strike quickly collapsed." Although these organizational efforts failed, the results did not mitigate worker discontent, and another unsuccessful strike against the railway company took place in 1910.[41]

Forging a Community

An important part of forming a community is concentrating enough people so they can fight for rights, such as an education for one's children. Without an education, a people are frozen into the lower castes. Segregated schools were an important vehicle for whites to maintain control of the system. The pretexts for excluding Mexicans from white schools were that Mexicans were ill-clad, unclean, and immoral; interracial contact would lead to other relationships; Mexican children were not intelligent and learned more slowly; and so forth. In San Angelo, Texas, a community of about 10,000 inhabitants including about 1,500 Mexicans, about 200 Mexican children attended segregated schools staffed by ill-equipped white teachers.

In 1910, San Angelo built new buildings for white children, and the school board assigned the old buildings to Mexicans. Mexican parents boycotted the school—they wanted their children to share the new buildings with the white children or at least have all the buildings on the same grounds. The board refused to meet their demands. During the boycott, many parents sent their children to the Immaculate Conception Academy, a Catholic school that segregated Mexican students into a "Mexican room"; the Catholic school also refused their request to integrate. In 1912 the Presbyterian Church set up a Mexicans-only mission school, which taught writing English and Spanish languages, and other subjects such as mathematics, geography, and physiology. The boycott continued for several years till attrition ended it around 1915.[42]

Euro-American xenophobia and racial attitudes that were part of American culture plagued each new wave of Mexican immigrants. For example, a 1910 *Report of the Immigration Commission* stated that Mexicans were the lowest paid of any laborers and that the majority worked as transient and migratory labor, did not settle, and returned to Mexico after only a few months. The report professed that this was due to the fact that "The assimilative qualities of the Mexicans are slight because of the backward educational facilities in their native land and a constitutional prejudice on the part of the peons toward school attendance." According to the report, Mexicans regarded public relief as a "pension"; the only saving grace was that they would return to Mexico within a few months.[43] Meanwhile, the Mexican Revolution, which began in the same year the Immigration Report was issued, brought one of the largest shifts of population between the two countries, and the abruptly increased presence of brown-skinned people in the United States encouraged even more exaggerated stereotypes.

The Mexican Revolution

By 1910, the population of Mexico reached 15.16 million, and at least 382,002 persons of Mexican nativity lived in the United States. (This figure does not include U.S.-born Mexicans.)[44] The Mexican Revolution (1910–1920), which began that year, had a huge impact on the area along the 2,000 miles of U.S.–Mexican border that separated four U.S. and six Mexican states. The Revolution produced hundreds of icons: Francisco Madero, Ricardo Flores Magón, Pancho Villa, Emiliano Zapata, and Las Adelitas—Mexican women who risked their lives along with Mexican soldiers in the violent civil war.[45]

The Revolution struck an irrational fear into many Euro-Americans, who panicked and committed violent acts of racism. For example, in Rock Springs, Texas, in November 1910, a mob killed Antonio Rodríguez, 20, while he awaited trial. Vigilantes dragged Rodríguez out of his cell, tied him to a stake, and burned him alive. Rodríguez's murder so enraged Mexicans south of the Rio Bravo that citizens throughout Mexico revolted against Díaz—days before November 20, 1910, when the Mexican Revolution supposedly began. The following June, Antonio Gómez, 14, was asked to leave a place of business in Thorndale, Texas. When Gómez refused, a fight broke out; Gómez was jailed for killing a Texas-born German. An enraged mob, after dragging Gómez from the jail and killing him, dragged his body around town tied to the back of a buggy.[46]

In July 1911, local authorities arrested León Cárdenas Martínez, age 15, for the murder of Emma Brown in Saragosa, Texas. Cárdenas Martínez signed a confession after local police held a carbine to his head. The judge sentenced Cárdenas to death; later the courts reduced the sentence to 30 years in jail. The townspeople then broke up Cárdenas's support meetings, chased his lawyer and the Cárdenas family out of town, and lynched the prisoner.[47]

Bullets across the Border

Some of the heaviest fighting along the U.S.–Mexican border took place in Chihuahua and to a lesser extent in Sonora. These were two highly industrialized states with customhouses, which made them attractive to the rebels and the federales. Sonora had giant copper mining centers in its northeastern region, only 25 miles from Douglas, Arizona, and connected through a railroad system. Even a decade before the 1910 Revolution, rebels from the various factions of the revolution recruited heavily in Arizona mining camps. Miners as a rule owned rifles and ammunition. Because of living at close quarters and because of the nature of their work, miners were more militant than other workers. Further, the frequent economic recessions and depressions made them restless and willing recruits for the various factions. Tensions built up as U.S. troops, marshals, and officers of every description massed on the border as fighting broke out close to La Línea. When Sonoran rebels in March 1911 captured El Tigre Mining Camp and secured over 100 high-powered rifles, U.S. authorities expressed alarm.[48]

The *Porfiriato* had changed Chihuahua's population as it pushed people north. As Luis Aboites points out, "Part of this population was originally from Durango, Zacatecas and other places in the interior of the nation, and were attracted by the high salaries that were paid in Chihuahua."[49] The commercialization of agriculture and the construction of water projects increased the number of ranchos and attracted workers from within and outside the state. In the districts of Guerrero and Benito Juárez (Cusihuiriáchic) alone, the number of ranches increased from 79 in 1893 to 297 by 1908. The serranos were isolated and resembled the villagers of Rio Arriba in New Mexico, while places like Camargo were way stations for the south to north migration. Chihuahua was more industrialized than other states; according to Michael Meyer, it had "a relatively large middle class of merchants, artisans, coachmen, railroad men, and clerks," which socialized migrants and residents alike. At the same time, it was more provincial and resented the gringos as well as encroachments by the federal government. During the first two years of the Revolution, the serrano villagers and other Chihuahuense guerrilleros helped overthrow Díaz and then Victoriano Huerta. However, there was factionalism within the ranks of the revolutionists, which led to the Pascual Orozco revolt.[50]

Hysteria across the Border

After 1913, Francisco "Pancho" Villa emerged as the most popular leader in Chihuahua and throughout much of Mexico. The Mexican Revolution was a milestone in the lives of Mexicans and pivotal in forming the stereotype of the Mexican as a bandit. From the start, the North American press whipped up anti-Mexican sentiments, contributing to intensified discrimination against Mexican immigrants and perpetuating many negative images of Mexicans.

From the beginning of the conflict, in 1910, U.S. corporations, individuals doing business in Mexico, and the Catholic Church called for military intervention. Many business leaders had supported Porfirio Díaz because he pandered to their interests. Twice, the United States violated Mexican sovereignty. First was when it bombarded Veracruz in March 1914, claiming more than 300 Mexican lives. Supposedly, the United States was stopping a shipment of German arms to the *huertistas*—followers of the reactionary Mexican president Victoriano Huerta. The second violation of Mexican sovereignty occurred when, from March 16, 1916, to February 14, 1917, Brigadier General John J. "Black Jack" Pershing and an expeditionary force of more than 14,000 regular army troops chased Pancho Villa, who had begun his career as a bandit, but became a revolutionary icon; the chase cost over $100 million.

President Woodrow Wilson mobilized another 140,000-troop army, while National Guard troops patrolled the nearly 2,000-mile border between Mexico and the United States. The size of the force was huge, if we consider that the U.S. population at the time was only 91,641,195. The total number of military personnel mobilized for this attack approached the population of Arizona, which then was 204,354 (New Mexico, 327,299; California, 2.3 million; and Texas, 3.8 million). The size of the army was larger than the population of either Nevada (81,875) or Wyoming (145,965). This mobilization certainly prepared the people for a war with Mexico and conditioned the soldiers and their families to fear and hate Mexicans. The Hearst newspapers and the Chandlers, who ran the *Los Angeles Times*, were especially strident during this period, spreading the myth that U.S. Mexicans were on the verge of revolution and blaming organizations like the PLM. A general revival of industrial activity throughout the Southwest created a demand for unskilled labor and the nativism began to subside.[51]

The Villa hysteria found fertile ground in places like Los Angeles, where the Mexican population swelled after 1910. On November 18, 1913, the Los Angeles police assigned several officers to investigate a subversive plot by Mexican "reds" and *cholos* (half-breeds). According to the *Los Angeles Times*, at least 10 percent of the city's 35,000 Mexicans were "known to the police to be rabid sympathizers of the outlaw [Pancho] Villa." Two days after Villa's raid on Columbus, New Mexico, in March 1916, Los Angeles County supervisors requested federal action to deport "*cholos* likely to become public charges." When 200 Mexican laborers for the Pacific Sewer Pipe Company went on strike in 1918, authorities labeled the strike "German-made" to further stigmatize Mexicans by aligning them with the United States' arch enemy.[52]

In Defense of the Community

The U.S. Mexican community responded by organizing themselves. Nicasio Idar, publisher of the Texas-based *La Crónica* newspaper, condemned the Cárdenas murder.[53] Idar and others convened *El Primer Congreso Mexicanista* (the First Mexican Congress) on September 11, 1911, to discuss deteriorating Texas-Mexican economic conditions; the loss of Mexican culture and Spanish language; widespread social discrimination; educational discrimination; and lynching. Men and women attended workshops and discussed issues. Delegates also protested the insult to State Representative J. T. Canales, whom a white politico had called "the greaser from Brownsville." The Congreso created *La Liga Femenil Mexicanista* (the Mexican

Feminist League); its first president was Jovita Idar. The women's contingent was largely composed of schoolteachers, who raised educational issues.[54]

La Agrupación Protectora Mexicana (Mexican Protective Association) was founded in 1911 in San Antonio; its avowed purpose was to defend the human rights of Mexicans. Although *La Agrupación* supported union organizing, it focused more on police brutality and lynchings. For example, *La Agrupación's* members campaigned for the release of prisoner Gregorio Cortez. *La Agrupación* functioned until 1914, before internecine strife split the organization. The *Alianza Hispano Americana* was another influential Mexican organization, which had expanded dramatically since its founding in the 1890s and focused on defending community rights throughout Arizona and the southwest.[55]

La Liga Protectora Latina was organized for the protection of the rights of the foreign-born. It opposed the Arizona Claypool–Kinney Bill, which would force the mines to employ 80 percent U.S. citizens. It had chapters in Phoenix and other mining towns throughout the state, the Southwest, and even Mexico. Much of its leadership came from the middle class and belonged to the *Alianza Hispano Americana* and other patriotic societies and *mutualistas.* Besides sponsoring social activities, the leaders of these organizations were very much involved in politics.

Much of the leadership was middle class, and many arrived after 1910. In general, they were supporters of Porfirio Díaz and opposed the Mexican Revolution. Articles from *El Tucsonense* during the 1910s make it obvious that the newspaper's leadership supported U.S. policy toward Mexico and Republican candidates. They maintained good relations with corporate leaders such as those of Southern Pacific and Phelps–Dodge. For the most part, they were nationalistic, conservative, and anti–labor union. However, they did fight against racism and nativist immigration laws.

In perspective, middle-class Mexican organizations derived some antiunion sentiment from the refusal of the unions to admit Mexicans or promote their interests. For example, "As early as 1904, Bernabé Brichta spoke out against the Locomotive Stokers Union, the Locomotive Engineers Union, and the Machinist Union because they refused to admit Mexicans, Blacks, or Chinese as members."[56] The railroad, arguably Tucson's most important industry, reserved its skilled trades for Euro-Americans. Brichta demanded an end to the unions' discrimination against Mexicans, but he also argued that they should not lump Mexicans with African Americans and Chinese. The antiunion stance of the Mexican middle class was such that the *Tucsonense* failed to support strikes even when Mexican workers were involved. According to Carlos Vélez-Ibañez, "proving and gaining class legitimacy was a major effort" among this class, in which one's family name and color still played a major role.[57]

The extent of the pro-immigrant struggle, warts and all, forged an impressive organizational network of middle-class Mexicans in the United States. In 1914 at Phoenix, Mexican middle-class leadership formed *La Liga.* By May 1915, *La Liga's* Tempe lodge, with 80 members, had established a bureau to provide employment referral and financial assistance. *La Liga* also supported striking miners at Ray, Arizona, which appears to have been an aberration: It was more involved with the education and protection of Mexicans' political and social rights. By 1917, it had 30 lodges; through political and legal action it sought to protect the rights of Mexicans, increase mutual aid for *Liga* members, and improve education. Despite its support for the miners themselves, *La Liga's* leadership resented labor's militancy and often opposed the union leadership during strikes. The opposition of some members stemmed from nationalism and class interests.

To this end, *La Liga* cultivated strong ties to the Republican Party. The leadership courted the Republicans because the Democrats favored the unions and pushed a nativist agenda. Elite leaders of *La Liga* believed that they could get political concessions because its members were well educated and, hence, would be listened to. To that end, it held a series of meetings with Republican Governor Tom Campbell, calling for night classes, especially in mining areas. Although Campbell was antilabor, *La Liga* supported his candidacy because Democrats were attempting to revive the 80 percent bill.

At its third annual convention, *La Liga* members established a commission headed by Amado Cota Robles to lobby the state legislature for bilingual education at the primary level. Under Cota Robles's leadership, *La Liga* initiated night classes in Spanish language, arithmetic, geometry, geography, and Mexican history. Emphasis was placed on learning English and on reading. By 1919, the organization had 3,752 members and lodges in Arizona, California, New Mexico, and Philadelphia, and the group began the publication of a journal,

La Justicia. However, in 1920 the organization started to decline. When *La Liga* raised the membership subscription to a $3 initiation fee and $1.25 a month, poor members protested, and a division developed along class lines. The isolation of the Mexicans in Arizona—and in other areas of the United States—would continue.[58]

A Changing Society

In 1900, most Mexicans worked in agriculture and were the least urbanized immigrant group in the United States. By 1920, however, 47 percent of the Mexicans who were born in Mexico lived in urban areas; the percentage would have probably been higher if U.S.-born Mexicans were included in the count. Many second-generation Mexicans, along with political refugees, became merchants or took middle-level jobs.[59] What happened during the 20 in-between years? Mexicans adapted to the Euro-American society in stages. Each generation included U.S.-born children, some of whom took immigrant spouses and others took U.S.-born spouses. There were subtle differences between the disparate generations, as well as within generations depending on the hue of their skin and where they lived.

Racism was always more severe in Texas, a former Confederate state, than in other southwestern states; along with this, an influx of midwesterners into Texas worsened racial tensions. The white newcomers often resented Mexicans because they saw the Mexicans as the base of the political machines that ran south Texas, and thus as a part of the political problem. By the 1910s, Mexicans were caught in the middle of these contending groups; the midwestern faction was winning out and overthrowing old political bosses. In theory, this was a victory for democracy; in reality, the decline of the political machines removed arrangements that had cushioned racism toward Mexicans. The new political order came with new ways of excluding Mexicans, such as the "White Man's Primary," which was instituted to prevent Mexicans from voting in primaries and to ensure the control of the white farmer. The decline of the bosses marked the beginning of an era that saw not only the transformation of the economy of south Texas but also the increased migrancy of Mexican laborers.[60]

Mexican Workers under Siege

Labor organization was rare in rural areas; it was far more common in urban settings and in the mining camps. Given the discriminatory exclusion of Mexicans from trade unions, throughout the 1910s *mutualistas* continued to be their most popular form of association. Occasionally, organizations such as the IWW were active in organizing casual workers in mining and agriculture. The Wobblies, as they were called, included people of color within their "one big union." One of the most dramatic strikes involving the IWW was the Wheatland Riot of August 3, 1913, at the Ralph Durst Ranch in Wheatland, California. A crisis developed when a hops grower advertised for 1,000 picking jobs and some 2,800 people showed up. Working and living conditions at the ranch were horrendous, and wages were less than those advertised. Tempers soared and the workers struck. The state actively intervened on the side of the growers to rid the fields of the IWW militants, resulting in the killing of four men and the wounding of a dozen others.[61]

Another travesty of justice was the Ludlow Massacre of 1913 in Ludlow, Colorado, where the Colorado Fuel and Iron Company—substantially owned by the Rockefellers, John D. Sr. and John Jr.—evicted miners from company housing. As the cold winter approached, tensions grew, and the governor ordered the National Guard into the area. Baldwin–Felts Detective Agency, which was assigned the job, hunted down and killed the strike leaders. On April 20, 1914, the Guard occupied a hill overlooking the camp, mounted a machine gun, and exploded two bombs into the camp. The miners armed themselves, and the Guard attacked the tent colony. Initially, 18 were killed, including 9 Mexicans, 5 of whom were children. In total, 50 workers and their family members were killed.[62]

As dramatic as these events were, the killing fields of Arizona ranked far higher in the annals of labor history; yet little has been written about them. Virtual wars raged between Mexican and Euro-American miners, largely mediated by owners. Ray, Arizona, was clustered in the mountains alongside the colonias of Sonora and Barcelona, about 80 miles southeast of Phoenix; the Ray Consolidated Copper Company owned all of the area's mining operations. Mexican workers and their families migrated there in large numbers, and by 1907, they established the colonia of Sonora, which grew to a population of about 5,000 in 1914–1915. "Barcelona," a Spanish colonia, developed next to Sonora and had about 1,000 residents. Ray itself had 1,000 residents, mostly Anglo and Irish.[63] Ray Consolidated employed 1,400 men, most of whom were Mexican nationals segregated by race, not only physically, but also by a dual wage system.

The Western Federation of Miners (WFM) abetted Ray Consolidated's racial policies by not organizing across racial lines. Ray became a hotbed of Mexican activism, and revolutionary organizers constantly visited it, looking for volunteers, arms, and money. The Arizona Alien Labor Law, requiring companies to employ at least 80 percent Euro-American labor, increased tensions between Mexican and Euro-American miners. Violence broke out in the summer of 1914 when Euro-Americans chased Peter Smith, a half-breed Mexican, after he allegedly stole a horse in Ray and took to the hills. Smith and two (or more) of his companions ambushed the posse.[64] In retaliation, someone stabbed a Mexican boss of an all-Mexican mine crew to death while he was asleep. Several more shootings occurred, and a race war followed.

Regeneración reported on "A War of Races in Arizona." According to the PLM newspaper, white scabs attacked 19 Mexican workers in Ray, Arizona. Sheriff Brown was killed, along with two Mexicans, in the Canyon of the Devil near Ray. That night a second confrontation took place and another Mexican was killed. Masses of whites, descending into the Mexican barrio, entered Mexican homes and committed atrocities. They went into the hills looking for Mexicans. "The American working class is the most mentally retarded class," wrote *Regeneración*, "not knowing its interests as workers." The *Los Angeles Times* on August 20, 1914, also wrote, "Race War in Arizona—Death List Is Sixteen." Four Euro-Americans and 12 Mexicans had been killed in the bloody riot.[65] Thus began the reign of terror, which was abetted by the management of Ray Consolidated.

Meanwhile, the WFM was beginning to reconsider its policy of excluding Mexicans, because of competition from the IWW. By 1914, the copper barons had escalated their campaign of intimidation, subversion, libel, and slander against labor. A core of Mexican union leaders had emerged, with the backing of a minority of Euro-American organizers who wanted to include Mexicans as members. Through this cooperation, in 1915 the union launched a strike at the Clifton-Morenci-Metcalf mining camps, which drew a bevy of inclusionist WFM and Mexican organizers, such as Lazaro Gutiérrez de Lara. The strike lasted five months. Although it was a bitter one, violence was averted because of the intervention of Arizona Governor George W. P. Hunt and local Sheriff James Cash, who were determined to prevent another Ludlow Massacre. The workers won some concessions, although management did not recognize the WFM. Strikes continued to take place at the Miami, Globe, Ray, Ajo, Jerome, and Warren mines, where Mexican miners were at the vanguard.

After this point, led by Phelps–Dodge's Walter Douglas, mine owners took the offensive and effectively agitated nativist sentiments among Euro-Americans. Unfounded fears that Mexican outlaw Pancho Villa would invade the United States were used to justify the firing of some 1,200 Mexican miners at Ajo in 1916, when workers requested a raise and a grievance redressal committee.[66] In 1917, Locals 80, 84, and 86 in Clifton-Morenci-Metcalf had a membership of some 5,000 Mexican miners. Yet, the copper barons purposely threw down the gauntlet and refused to give workers any meaningful concessions—in fact, they refused to negotiate. Any opposition was labeled anti-American. By this time, there were 14,000 Mexican miners in Arizona alone. Conditions were horrible: in the neighboring state of New Mexico, in the town of Dawson alone, 600 miners died in the mine disasters of 1913, 1920, and 1923. Despite these desperate conditions, AFL President Samuel Gompers chose not to organize Mexican miners. He became increasingly paranoid about Mexicans filtering into the urban factories and competing with white workers.[67]

By 1917, the war between the workers and the copper barons came to a head. On June 24, the union struck at Bisbee and Jerome, where a large number of Mexican miners worked. The Cochise County sheriff immediately labeled the strike as subversive and announced intentions to deport any members of the IWW. With the aid of a vigilante committee, a posse deported 67 miners from Jerome and some 1,200 from Bisbee. The sheriff seized the telegraph and telephone office, and did not permit news dispatches. Local authorities, along with racist nativists, loaded strikers into boxcars and shipped them to the outskirts of Columbus, New Mexico, where state police authorities dumped them in the open desert without food or water. Because President Woodrow Wilson had strong ties to Phelps–Dodge, no one was punished for the gross constitutional violations. A presidential commission was sent out to study the problem, but in the end the copper barons had their way. They purged the mines of militant Mexicans and repatriated thousands, with thousands more going into agriculture, to the cities, or to the ranks of the Mexican Revolution.[68]

The "Amazon" Protest: Story of Carmelita Torres

The era was replete with examples of the oppression of Mexican workers and their families. There is the story of the exceptional heroism of Carmelita Torres, age 17, a maid, who in 1917 refused to take a gasoline bath when she entered the United States from Ciudad Juárez. In El Paso, Texas, and elsewhere along the border, Mexicans were routinely forced to undergo strip searches and were fumigated with toxic gases. The excuse for administering baths was that Mexicans spread typhoid or that Mexicans had lice or that they were bringing diseases into the country. The soldiers would stare at the disrobed women as they took the DDT baths. The previous year, Mexican prisoners in El Paso were given a bath in gasoline and were burned to death when a fire broke out and ignited the gas. Carmelita, tired of suffering this indignity, persuaded the other passengers on a trolley not to take it. Thirty trolley passengers joined the protest, touching off two days of uprisings. The *El Paso Times* labeled the women "the Amazons." An hour later more than 200 Mexican women blocked traffic entering the city, lying in front of the tracks. Within four hours "several thousand" joined the demonstration. Troops from Fort Bliss were joined by the *Carrancista el escuadrón de la muerte* (the death squad). When José María Sánchez shouted "Viva Villa!" he was escorted to the Juárez cemetery and shot. The resistance lasted for several days—shots were fired—and the Mexican women were driven back across the bridge.[69]

The Hysteria: The Plan of San Diego

The harshness of this repression of Mexicans on the U.S. side of the border produced a variety of reactions. For example, in 1915, Texas authorities used the "Plan of San Diego" as an excuse to step up a reign of terror along the border. The plan, found on the person of rebel leader Basilio Ramos, called for a general uprising of Mexicans and other minorities starting February 20. The supporters were to execute all white males over age 16—blacks, Asians, and Native Americans were to be spared. The Southwest was to become a Chicano nation, and blacks and Native Americans were to form independent countries. Most Mexicans found the plan extreme and as taking the focus away from legitimate grievances. For example, Flores Magón, in *Regeneración*, never acknowledged or supported the plan, except for stating once that Texas authorities wanted "to make it appear as if the Mexican uprising in that section of the United States is part of the Plan of San Diego" in order to justify its reign of terror.

Clearly, the most problematic part of the plan was the call for the murder of all white males over 16. The statement, simply put, confused or blurred the legitimate reasons for an uprising. At first, officials did not take the plan seriously, viewing rebels' raids as banditry and rustling. But by July 1915, the rebels issued their plan, which was followed by a series of raids in the lower Rio Grande Valley. The supporters of the plan seemed to be either *huertistas,* followers of Huerta, or *carrancistas,* followers of the Mexican President Venustiano Carranza; most of them had their roots in the United States. For instance, Luis de la Rosa was a former deputy sheriff in Cameron County and was in command. Ancieta Pizaña, second in command, was a *carrancista.* In all, they had a force of 50 men. Between July 1915 and July 1916, this small band of rebels carried out a total of 30 raids into Texas.[70]

The Euro-Americans' angst over what they perceived as revolutionary incitement led to the killing of hundreds of Mexicans. In the end, U.S. authorities admitted shooting, hanging, or beating to death 300 "suspected" Mexicans, while the rebels killed 21 Euro-Americans during this period. George Marvin wrote in *World's Work* magazine in 1917 that it was "open season" on Mexicans. Walter Prescott Webb justified the "Reign of Terror" by putting the blame on the Mexican Revolution and the border incidents, and on Pancho Villa, or the San Diego Plan, and/or the Germans, or Prohibition.[71]

World War I: The Shift

Meanwhile, World War I produced a labor shortage, and the U.S. government, fearing that Mexicans would flee the country, enlisted Catholic bishops to assure Mexicans that they would not be drafted. Further contributing to the labor shortage, the Literacy Law of the Immigration Act of 1917 severely restricted the number of Europeans allowed into the country, and it also slowed down the flow of Mexicans. However, profit motive trumped racism in this instance, and soon afterward, to ease the labor crisis, U.S. officials allowed exemptions for illiterate contract workers from Mexico entering the United States, but required that they pay an $8 head tax, which was later waived owing to pressure from U.S. farmers.

Despite the United States' entry into World War I, it had markedly relaxed efforts to control immigration. Evidently profit trumped border security and the military turned the other way as thousands of Mexicans flowed freely across the river. In the four years the exemptions were in force (1917–1921), 72,862 Mexicans entered the United States with documents, and hundreds of thousands more crossed the border without documents.[72]

Meanwhile, World War I intensified industrialization and urbanization in California. The war industries attracted many Mexicans and African Americans, and the large numbers of Mexicans settling in Los Angeles created new social and economic pressures. Mexicans' choices as to where they would settle were determined by such factors as language and availability of transportation. For example, in Los Angeles the largest concentration of Mexicans was in and around the Central Plaza district, where 40.1 percent of the Mexican workers surveyed worked for the Southern Pacific Railroad. In an area of less than 5,000 square feet of living space, 20 needy families were forced to live in dilapidated house courts. By 1919, Mexicans comprised 5 percent of Los Angeles's population of over a million. Twenty-eight percent of Mexicans lived in houses with no sinks, 32 percent had no lavatories, and 79 percent had no baths. The infant mortality rate for Euro-Americans was 54 out of 1,000; the rate for Mexicans was 152 out of 1,000. In 1914, Mexicans constituted 11.1 percent of the deaths in Los Angeles. "Americans" blamed the blight around the Central Plaza on the Mexicans, saying that these foreigners contributed to a rapid disintegration of traditional "American values."[73]

Shifts in Political Consciousness

World War I represented a crucial juncture in the assimilation of Mexicans.[74] The longer the Mexicans remained in the United States, the more entitled they felt to constitutional guarantees. This attitude became more noticeable with each succeeding generation. Accordingly, many Mexicans in the United States were beginning to feel more American, and the war accelerated their assimilation. On the other hand, the war also reinforced existing inequalities. Some Tejanos (Mexicans born in Texas) and Mexicans did not know how to read or write English and were supposedly exempt, yet local boards drafted them into the army; Mexicans, or other poor people, were often the only ones called upon to serve.

Mexican casualties were high. Unacknowledged acts of bravery burned in the memories of many veterans such as J. Luz Sáenz, who recorded his recollections in his book *Los méxico-americanos en la gran guerra y su contingente en pró de la democracia, la humanidad y justicia*.[75] Marcelino Serna, a Mexican immigrant from El Paso, single-handedly captured 24 German prisoners and prevented another soldier from shooting them. He was awarded the Distinguished Service Cross, two Purple Hearts, France's Croix de Guerre and Military Medal, Italy's Cross of Merit, and Britain's Medal of Bravery. Serna probably did not receive the Medal of Honor because he could not read or write English. The military also discriminated against Mexican American soldiers in other ways. El Paso veterans, most of whom were Mexican immigrants, complained that they were gassed in France but received no government disability benefits.[76] Sáenz himself, who had university training and taught for eight years in Texas schools, and who later was a leader of the League of United Latin American Citizens, was denied officer training.

Mexican Responses to Industrial Transformation

In the spring of 1917, several farm strikes hit the Corona, Riverside, Colton, Redlands, and San Bernardino areas of California. The cost of living had zoomed because of World War I, but the workers' wages remained the same. On March 5, Mexican workers went on strike at the Corona Lemon Company. White workers refused to join the action, and local authorities arrested Juan Peña and other leaders on unspecified charges. On March 27, 300 Mexican and Japanese orange pickers in Riverside, California, joined the strike, which the growers violently suppressed by importing large numbers of strikebreakers from El Paso. Significantly, many of the participants had worked in mining and had previously experienced labor strife.[77]

European immigration had slowed, and Mexican workers began to filter in greater numbers into the Midwest. During the 1919 steel strike in the Chicago-Calumet area, the steel companies imported Mexicans, who worked under guard. Throughout the history of the U.S. labor movement, labor leaders have accused the most recently arrived immigrants of being strikebreakers. This is true whether they were Mexican, Polish, Italian, or any other nationality. Mexicans employed in the steel industry before the strike supported collective bargaining efforts. However, white workers stereotyped Mexicans as scabs when in reality they were a minority of the strikebreakers. A report by Homestead Steel Works, Howard Axle Works, and Carrie Furnaces on October 8, 1919, showed that out of the 14,687 employed by these mills, only 130 were Mexican—that is, Mexicans comprised less than 1 percent of the workforce.[78]

Meanwhile, sugar beet companies relentlessly hunted for Mexican labor. By 1919, 98 U.S. factories produced almost 1 million tons of sugar annually. Leading sugar beet–producing states were Michigan, Ohio, and Wisconsin in the Midwest; Colorado, Utah, and Idaho in the mountain region; and California in the Far West. A constant increase in production and, in turn, a heavy reliance on Mexican labor prompted farm journals in 1920 to refer to the sugar crop as a "Mexican Harvest."[79]

Urbanization of Mexicans in general opened up significant space for women workers of all colors. Hearings conducted in El Paso in November 1919 by the Texas Industrial Welfare Commission found that Mexican women were "the lowest-paid and most vulnerable workers in the city." El Paso laundries employed large numbers of Mexicanas at unskilled jobs, whereas Euro-American women took the skilled jobs. Mexicanas earned $8 a week compared to $16.55 earned by Euro-American women. The work areas were segregated. In department stores Euro-American women generally worked on the main floor, whereas Mexicanas worked in the rear or basement. Euro-Americans earned as high as $40 a week compared to Mexican clerks, who were paid $10–$20 a week. Mexicanas also comprised the overwhelming majority of workers in the El Paso garment industry. White women workers in a union shop were reported to average between $18 and $20 a week for piecework, although the owner of one factory conceded that Mexicanas working there averaged $9.50. The pretext for the double standard was that Mexicans had fewer needs than did whites and thus required less money.[80]

Mexican women workers at El Paso's Acme Laundry called for a strike because the laundry had fired two workers for union activity. Almost 500 women walked out of six other laundries. The Central Labor Union (CLU) leadership undermined worker solidarity by assigning the Mexican women to the minor role of dissuading scabs from breaking the picket line. The CLU portrayed the Mexican woman as passive. However, the women strikers soon broke the stereotype as they poised themselves at the international bridge to prevent the entry of scabs. The newspapers, too, depicted a negative image of the emotional Mexican. The CLU became increasingly conservative, with many of its members entering into an alliance with a Ku Klux Klan–dominated, good-government movement. In the end, the union deserted the Mexican women. However, the experience enhanced their political consciousness, and it advanced the notion of equality between Mexican women and white women in the workplace.[81]

The Failure of American Brotherhood

It was not as if organized labor were not conscious of the necessity or justice of including Mexicans. The Arizona mining strikes proved that Mexicans wanted to be part of labor solidarity, and their unity often exceeded that of white workers. However, Samuel Gompers (and also the AFL) played contradicting roles:

while they advocated "Pan-Americanism" and paid lip service to organizing Mexicans, they allowed racism among the rank and file locals that excluded Mexicans. For example, the 1916 AFL Constitution stated that unions should organize Mexicans in the United States and assist in the organization of workers in Mexico. In Los Angeles alone there were 15,000 Mexican workers, and there were thousands more in mining communities in Arizona and Colorado. But the locals were free to discriminate against Mexicans and push legislation that excluded them from the country. At heart, Gompers feared Mexicans would move to the cities and there take jobs held by whites. On the other hand, white workers were just plain racist.

At the first Pan-American Conference in 1918, a debate broke out between Mexican and Euro-American delegates, as the former demanded full union membership and accused Euro-Americans of generally discriminating against Mexicans. They also attacked U.S. border authorities for their harsh treatment of the Mexicans. Even after his experiences as an organizer in the 1917 mining strikes, H. S. McCluskey of the Mine, Mill & Smelter Workers (UMM&S) Union attacked Mexican immigrant workers for their failure to organize or support AFL unions, thus perpetuating a myth. In McCluskey's case it was not a matter of not knowing better. The Mexican representatives reacted immediately, reminding McCluskey of the AFL's attitude toward Mexican workers. A delegate admitted that there was some truth in what McCluskey had said; but he objected to the racism of political candidates and pointed out that a certain candidate for the post of the governor of Arizona had called for death penalty for "Mexicans and niggers." In the 1920s, as the country became more nativist, calls for exclusion and deportation of Mexicans heightened, with American labor rewriting history.[82]

The Westward Movement of King Cotton

As early as 1913, the PLM was tracking the movement of Mexican workers onto cotton plantations. Cotton was important because it attracted huge armies of pickers and their families, determining where Mexicans settled. Between 1918 and 1921, the Arizona Cotton Growers Association imported more than 30,000 Mexicans at a cost of $300,000. Because of the proximity to the border, Arizona cotton growers had an ample supply of pickers. In 1916, only 7,600 acres were dedicated to cotton in Arizona; a decade later, cotton was produced on 210,000 acres, of which 186,000 acres were in the Salt River Valley. On November 3, 1919, the *Los Angeles Times* reported, "Flood of Mexican Aliens a Problem," pointing out that the Mexican pickers came with their families and picked as a unit. In 1919, a projected $20 million Goodyear Tire and Rubber Company factory was announced for Los Angeles. The Goodyear Company had ranches in Arizona, which supplied cotton to the factory; but they bought additional cotton from other ranches as well.[83]

Meanwhile, the production of cotton in the Imperial Valley expanded and spread to the San Joaquin Valley. The cultivation of cotton and other crops formed a land bridge to Los Angeles, from where Mexican workers followed the crops north, south, east, and west. Many of the Mexican workers' families remained in Los Angeles. The buildup of the Mexican population was made possible by irrigated farming and the land reclamation projects of the early twentieth century, which resulted in the construction of massive dams and the cultivation of hundreds of thousands of acres of land.

Similar developments were taking place in Texas, which had become a leading agricultural state. Cotton was important in driving the demand for Mexican labor. San Antonio, like Los Angeles, stood as a distribution center for Mexican labor and a favored destination for Mexican families. The Lone Star State was a reserve labor pool for the Midwest, where Mexican agricultural workers were replacing European immigrants as the 1917 Literacy Act excluded them.

Conclusion: Mexicans in the City, The Backlash

The timeline at the beginning of the chapter is intended to help the reader understand the relationships between events. Remember, a cause is something that makes something else happen; an effect is what happens because of the cause. For example, Mexicans came into the United States in large numbers, not because they enjoyed the company of white Americans, but because they were uprooted. The expansion of railroads that linked Mexico and the United States was a major factor in the modernization of Mexico. Thus, the uprooting did not cause the building of the railroad; it was the other way around. The timeline helps plot causes and effects, and it is up to the reader to relate them.

Where Mexicans moved to is also related to causes and effects. Railroads, farming, construction work, and mining all pulled Mexicans to the United States. The presence of large numbers of Mexicans caused irrational responses on the part of many Euro-Americans, responses that generated their own effects. What were the effects of this irrationality? Thus, in studying the history of Chicanos during this period it will be necessary for the reader to understand the definition of racism and identify its causes and effects.

Just as Mexican immigration to the United States did not happen by accident, neither did the Mexican Revolution occur in a vacuum. Mexicans did not wake up one day and decide to overthrow Porfirio Díaz. What caused the revolution and what was its effect?

The cause-and-effect relationship of events in this chapter tends to be more complex than that of the nineteenth-century history of Chicanos. The immediate difference is that there were more people. Where they lived was also significant, that is, the city or the countryside. In many cases, they were the minority and interacting with people who considered them foreigners and intruders. As we mentioned at the outset, immigrants have never been welcomed to participate in social life and were expected to stay at the bottom of the economic ladder. Further, generational differences occurred within families. At first, the Mexican community was overwhelmingly Mexico-born, whereas by 1920 the second generation was outnumbering the first. This is important. Look at your own life. How do you differ from your parents and grandparents?

Notes

1. Jaime Gilbert Jue, "Interrregional Trade and Market Integration: California and the Transcontinental Railroad, 1860–1900" (PhD dissertation, University of California, Berkeley, 1999), 5. The railroad contributes to the integration of markets.

2. Teresa M. Van Hoy, "La Marcha Violenta? Railroads and Land in 19th-Century Mexico," *Bulletin of Latin American Research* 19, no. 1 (January 2000): 32–33, the 1882 law allowed the expropriation of land for public works. The purpose of the law was to force and facilitate railroad development. Disastrous for Indian tribes such as the Yaqui. Also see John Coatsworth, "Indispensable Railroads in a Backward Economy: The Case of Mexico," *Journal of Economic History* 39, no. 4 (1979): 939–60.

3. Rodolfo F. Acuña, *Corridors of Migration: The Odyssey of Mexican Laborers, 1600–1933* (Tucson: University of Arizona, 2007).

4. George J. Sánchez, *Becoming Mexican American: Ethnicity, Culture, and Identity in Chicano Los Angeles, 1900–1945* (New York: Oxford University Press, 1993), 41. James D. Cockcroft, *Intellectual Precursors of the Mexican Revolution, 1900–1913* (Austin: University of Texas Press, 1968), 14. Charles C. Cumberland, *Mexico: The Struggle for Modernity* (New York: Oxford University Press, 1968), 216. James Cockcroft, *Mexico* (New York: Monthly Review Press, 1983), 81. Lawrence Anthony Cardoso, "Mexican Emigration to the United States, 1900–1930: An Analysis of Socio-Economic Causes" (PhD dissertation, University of Connecticut, 1974), 23, 34–35, 43–59. John Mason Hart, *Empire and Revolution: The Americans in Mexico Since the Civil War* (Berkeley: University of California Press, 2002), 122.

5. Eric Wolf, *Sons of the Shaking Earth* (Chicago: University of Chicago Press, 1959), 247. Rodney D. Anderson, *Outcasts in Their Own Land: Mexican Workers, 1906–1911* (De Kalb: Northern Illinois Press, 1978), 38, 43. Hudson Stroude, *Timeless Mexico* (New York: Harcourt Brace Jovanovich, 1944), 210.

6. Emilio Zamora, *The World of the Mexican Worker in Texas* (College Station: Texas A&M University Press, 1993), 15–16, 19. George C. Kiser, "Mexican American Labor Before World War II," *Journal of Mexican American History* (Spring 1972): 123. Tomás Almaguer, *Racial Fault Lines: The Historical Origins of White Supremacy in California* (Berkeley: University of California Press, 1994), 29. Mario T. García, *Desert Immigrants: The Mexicans of El Paso, 1880–1920* (New Haven, CT: Yale University Press, 1981), 17–19.

7. Neil Foley, *The White Scourge: Mexicans, Blacks, and Poor Whites in Texas Cotton Culture* (Berkeley: University of California Press, 1997), 118–40. Matt S. Meier and Feliciano Rivera, *Dictionary of Mexican American History* (Westport, CT: Greenwood Press, 1981), 287. David G. Gutierrez, *Walls and Mirrors: Mexican Americans, Mexican Immigrants, and the Politics of Ethnicity* (Berkeley: University of California Press, 1995), 44–48. Frank D. Bean and Marta Tienda, *The Hispanic Population of the United States* (New York: Russell Sage Foundation, 1988), 16–20.

8. John Higham, *Strangers in the Land: Patterns of American Nativism, 1860–1925* (New Brunswick, NJ: Rutgers University Press, 2002).

9. Luther E. Ellsworth, "Informe al Secretario de Estado, Fechado el 12 de Octubre de 1910 en Ciudad Porfirio Díaz, México,"

in Gene Z. Hanrahan, ed., *Documents on the Mexican Revolution* (Salisbury, NC: Documentary Publications, 1976) quoted in Clara Lomas, "Transborder Discourse: The Articulation of Gender in the Borderlands in the Early Twentieth Century," *Frontiers* 24, nos. 2&3 (2003): 52.

10. Manuel Díaz Ramírez, *Apuntes Sobre El Movimiento Obrero Campesino de México* (México, DF: Ediciones de Cultura Popular, 1974), 66, 67–68, 70, 83. John Mason Hart, *Anarchism and the Mexican Working Class* (Austin: University of Texas Press, 1978), 32–41. Anderson, *Outcasts in Their Own Land*, 81. Los obreros en México, 1875–1925, http://www.monografias.com/trabajos10/obre/obre.shtml.

11. Cockcroft, *Mexico*, 82.

12. Michael J. Gonzales, *The Mexican Revolution, 1910–1940* (Albuquerque: University of New Mexico Press, 2002), 5–26. David W. Walker, "Porfirian Labor Politics: Working Class Organizations in Mexico City and Porfirio Díaz, 1876–1902," *The Americas* 37, no. 3 (January 1981): 257–89.

13. Luis Aboites Aguilar, *Breve Historia de Chihuahua* (Mexico, DF: Fondo de Cultura Economica, 1994), 117. Francisco R. Almada, *Resumén de historia del estado de Chihuahua* (Mexico City: Libros Mexicanos, 1955), 330. "Huelga de Pinos Altos, 1883," 1–11, in Manuel González Ramírez, AGN v. 4. Anderson, *Outcasts in Their Own Land*, 87–88. Francisco R. Almada, *Diccionario de historia, geografía y biografía chihuahuenses*, 2d Edicion (Ciudad Juarez: Universidad de Chihuahua, 1968), 257. Acuña, *Corridors of Migration*. 40. "The Dramas of Haymarket," Chicago Historical Society, http://www.chicagohistory.org/dramas/.

14. Aboites Aguilar, *Breve Historia*, 117. Francisco R. Almada, *Resumén del estado de Chihuahua* (Mexico, DF: Libros Mexicanos, 1955), 330. Manuel Díaz Ramírez, *Apuntes Sobre El Movimiento Obrero y Campesinos de México*, 66, 67–68, 70, 83. Douglas Kevin Bryson, "Chihuahua, the United States and the origins of a revolution" (PhD dissertation, University of Houston, 2006), 112. By 1902 U.S. capital had invested a half billion dollars in Mexican railroads.

15. Garza, Catarino Erasmo (1859–1895), The Handbook of Texas Online, http://www.tshaonline.org/handbook/online/articles/GG/fga38.html. Victor Ochoa, http://www.smithsonianeducation.org/scitech/impacto/graphic/victor/index.html. "Mexican Revolutionists Caught"; "Aguirre and Chapa Had Planned to Start a Paper Urging the People to Revolt Against Government," *New York Times* (March 12, 1896), 1, http://query.nytimes.com/mem/archive-free/pdf?res=9E01E5DC12 3EE333A25751C1A9659C94679ED7CF.

16. Juan Gómez-Quiñones, *Sembradores: Ricardo Flores Magón y el Partido Liberal Mexicano: A Eulogy and Critique* (Los Angeles, CA: Aztlán, 1973), 23. Cockcroft, *Intellectual Precursors*, 124. Zamora, *The World of the Mexican Worker*, 133–61. Teresa Urrea Slide Show, http://vimeo.com/41589009. Ricardo Flores Magón, http://flag.blackened.net/revolt/ws98/ws53_magon.html.

17. Cockcroft, *Intellectual Precursors*, 231. Ricardo Flores Magón, History, http://dwardmac.pitzer.edu/Anarchist_Archives/bright/magon/history/index.html.

18. Julia Tuñón Pablos, *Women in Mexico: A Past Unveiled* (Austin: University of Texas Press, 1999), 80–81. Francesca Miller, *Latin American Women and the Search for Social Justice* (Lebanon, NH: University Press of New England, 1991), 71–72. Asunción Lavrin, *Latin American Women Historical Perspectives* (Westport, CT: Greenwood Press, 1978), 291–92. Marysa Navarro, Virginia Sánchez Korrol, and Kecia Ali, *Women in Latin America and the Caribbean: Restoring Women to History* (Indianapolis: University of Indiana, 1999), 87, 91. Mtra. Ma. de Lourdes Alvarado. (CESU-UNAM) Con la colaboración de Elizabeth Becerril Guzmán. Mujeres y educación superior en el México del siglo XIX, http://biblioweb.tic.unam.mx/diccionario/htm/articulos/sec_10.htm.

19. Sara Estela Ramírez, *Handbook of Texas Online*, http://www.tshaonline.org/handbook/online/articles/RR/fra60.html. Juana Belén Gutiérrez de Méndoza, http://www.immortaltechnique.co.uk/Thread-Anarchists-Juana-Bel%C3%A9n-Guti%C3%A9rrez-de-Mendoza. Shirlene Soto, *Emergence of the Modern Mexican Woman: Her Participation in Revolution and Struggle for Equality, 1910–1940* (Denver, CO: Arden Press, 1990), 11–12, 15, 21–23. Emma M. Pérez, "'A La Mujer': A Critique of the Parido Liberal Mexicano's Gender Ideology on Women," in Adelaida R. Del Castillo, ed., *Between Borders: Essays on Mexicana/Chicana History* (Los Angeles, CA: Floricanto Press, 1990), 459–82, 459, 461. Gómez-Quiñones, *Sembradores*, 46. *Regeneración* (January 14, 1911). Emilio Zamora, "Chicano Socialist Labor Activity in Texas, 1900–1920," *Aztlán* 6, no. 2 (Summer 1975): 235. Lucy Eldine Gonzales from Johnson County, Texas, was married to Albert Parsons, who was executed by the state of Illinois as an alleged conspirator in the Haymarket Riot of 1886. Gonzales, an avowed anarchist, published newspapers, pamphlets, and books; traveled and lectured extensively; and led many demonstrations for worker equality. In the 1870s Gonzales was a charter member of the Chicago Working Women's Union, and in 1905 she was among the founding members of the Industrial Workers of the World (IWW). Carolyn Asbaugh, *Lucy Parsons: American Revolutionary* (Chicago: Herr, 1976), 267–68.

20. Lomas, "Transborder Discourse," 54. Daniel Levy and Gabriel Székely, *México: Paradoxes of Stability and Change* (Boulder, CO: Westview Press, 1987), 26–27. Tereza Jandura, "Revolutionary Mexican Women," University of Arizona, http://www.ic.arizona.edu/ic/mcbride/ws200/mex-jand.htm. Elena Poniatowska and David Dorado Romo, *Las Soldaderas: Women of the Mexican Revolution* (El Paso, TX: Cinco Puntos Press, 2006).

21. Richard A. Bideaux and Terry C. Wallace, "Arizona Copper," *Rocks & Minerals* 72 (January/February 1997): 10–26. A dispute exists as to whether copper or gold was the first metal used by man. Copper has played an important role in human society for at least 7,500 years. Charles S. Sargent, "Copper Star of the Arizona Urban Firmament," in Carlos A. Schwantes, ed., *Bisbee: Urban Outpost on the Frontier* (Tucson: University of Arizona Press, 1992), 30–31. By 1880,

copper was mined by Globe, which brought stress to the San Carlos Indian Reservation. Clifton and Morenci had been removed from the reservation jurisdiction earlier. George H. Hildebrand and Garth L. Mangum, *Capital and Labor in American Copper, 1845–1990: Linkages Between Product and Labor Markets* (Cambridge, MA: Harvard University Press, 1991), 1, 30, 43, 50. In 1906, open-pit mining was pioneered at Bingham Canyon in Utah. Carlos A. Schwantes, "Introduction," in Schwantes, ed., *Bisbee*, 21.

22. Joseph F. Park, "The 1903 'Mexican Affair' at Clifton," *Journal of Arizona History* 18 (Summer 1977): 119–48, http://www.library.arizona.edu/exhibits/bisbee/docs/jahpark.html. Mining, http://www.asu.edu/lib/archives/website/mining.htm.

23. Acuña, *Corridors of Migration*, 112–18. Jay J. Wagoner, *Arizona Territory 1863–1912: A Political History* (Tucson: University of Arizona Press, 1970), 386. *Bisbee Daily Review* (June 5, 1903), quoted in Park, "Mexican Affair," 257. Ghosts of the Yuma Territorial Prison, Ghosts of the Prairie, History & Hauntings of America, Haunted Arizona, http://www.prairieghosts.com/yuma.html. Yuma Territorial Prison Cemetery, Yuma, Yuma County, Arizona, http://www.interment.net/data/us/az/yuma/prison/prison.htm.

24. Acuña, *Corridors of Migration*, 116.

25. James H. McClintock, *Arizona: The Youngest State*, Vol. 2 (Chicago: Clarke, 1916), 424. Park, "Mexican Affair," 258. Philip J. Mellinger, *Race and Labor in Western Copper: The Fight for Equality, 1896–1918* (Tucson: University of Arizona Press, 1995), 55. Acuña, *Corridors of Migration*, 130–33.

26. Carl Wittke, *We Built America*, rev. ed. (Cleveland, OH: Case Western Reserve University, 1967), 466. Kaye Lyon Briegel, "Alianza Hispano-Americana, 1894–1965: A Mexican Fraternal Insurance Society" (PhD dissertation, University of Southern California, 1974), 12–15. Victor S. Clark, *Mexican Labor in the United States*, U.S. Department of Commerce Bulletin no. 78 (Washington, D.C.: Government Printing Office, 1908), 485, 492–93. Kiser, "Mexican American Labor," 125, 492–93. Zamora, "Chicano Socialist Labor," 221. Manuel G. Gonzales, *Mexicanos: A History of Mexicans in the United States* (Indianapolis: University of Indiana Press, 1999), 151. *Sociedades Mutualistas*, Handbook of Texas Online, http://www.tshaonline.org/handbook/online/articles/SS/ves1.html.

27. Hart, *Anarchism*, 32–41. Anderson, *Outcasts*, 8, 88, 92. Cockcroft, *Intellectual Precursors*, 82. Juan Gómez-Quiñones, "The First Steps: Chicano Labor Conflict and Organizing, 1900–1920," *Aztlán* 3, no. 1 (1973): 18, 20. Charles C. Cumberland, *Mexican Revolution: Genesis Under Madero* (Austin: University of Texas Press, 1952), 16. Laureano Clavo Berber, *Nociones de Historia de Sonora* (México, DF: Publicaciones del Gobierno del Estado de Sonora, 1958), 277. Antonio G. Rivera, *La Revolución en Sonora* (México, DF: n.p., 1969), 139, 159. "Cananea: A Century of Internationalist Class Struggle," *The Internationalist*, http://www.internationalist.org/cananeastrike1906.html. Samuel Truett, *Fugitive Landscapes: The Forgotten History of the U.S.-Mexico Borderlands* (New Haven, CT: Yale University Press, 2006), 157. Acuña, *Corridors of Migration*, 124–32.

28. Acuña, *Corridors of Migration*, 109, 112, 137. The Urreas as well as Abrán Salcido and others can be traced through the 1900 and 1910 censuses. See www.ancestry.com.

29. Linda Gordon, *The Great Arizona Orphan Abduction* (Cambridge, MA: Harvard University Press, 1999), 1–2.

30. Gordon, *The Great Arizona Orphan Abduction*, 37–43, 118, 119–20, 154, 200–205. *New York Foundling Hospital v. William Norton*, in the Custody of John C. Gatti, Respondent Criminal No. 209, Supreme Court of Arizona, 9 Ariz. 105 (1905); 1905 Ariz. LEXIS 83, January 21, 1905, Filed. *New York Foundling Hospital v. Gatti*. No. 21. Supreme Court of the United States. 203 U.S. 429, 27 S. Ct. 53, 51 L. Ed. 254 (1906); 1906 U.S. LEXIS 1906. Argued April 26, 1906. Decided December 3, 1906. Acuña, *Corridors of Migration*, 119–24. As with other parts of *Corridors*, I traced the orphans through the *New York Times* and *Los Angeles Times*; this established a template. The censuses were also invaluable. Margaret Regan, "The Irish Orphan Abduction: A Tale of Race, Religion and Lawlessness in Turn-of-the-Century Southern Arizona," *Tucson Weekly* (March 15, 2007), http://www.tucsonweekly.com/tucson/the-irish-orphan-abduction/Content?oid=1087070.

31. Clark, *Mexican Labor in the United States*. Paul S. Taylor, *An American-Mexican Frontier: Nueces County, Texas* (New York: Russell and Russell, 1971), 173. Larry García y Griego, "*Los Primeros Pasos al Norte*: Mexican Migration to the United States" (Bachelor's thesis, Princeton University, 1973). Jorge A. Bustamante, "Mexican Immigration and the Social Relations of Capitalism" (PhD dissertation, University of Notre Dame, Indiana, 1975), 50. Cardoso, "Mexican Emigration," 60.

32. Robert N. McLean and Charles A. Thomson, Spanish and Mexicans in Colorado: A Survey of the Spanish Americans and Mexicans in the State of Colorado (New York: Board of National Missions of the Presbyterian Church in the U.S.A., 1924), 34. Dennis Nodín Valdés, Mexicans in Minnesota (Minneapolis: Minnesota Historical Society Press, 2005), 1–5. Beet Sugar Industry, Local History Archive, Fort Collins Colorado, http://library.ci.fort-collins.co.us/local_history/topics/Ethnic/mex-beet.htm, http://history.fcgov.com/cdm4/item_viewer.php?CISOROOT=/wp2&CISOPTR=72&CISOBOX=1&REC=1.

33. David Montejano, *Anglos and Mexicans in the Making of Texas, 1836–1986* (Austin: University of Texas Press, 1987), 104, 109–10. Camilo Amado Martinez, Jr., "The Mexican and Mexican-American Laborers in the Lower Rio Grande Valley of Texas, 1870–1930" (PhD dissertation, Texas A&M. University, 1987), 31: sugar was also grown in the valley.

34. Zamora, *The World of the Mexican Worker*, 12. Taylor, *An American-Mexican Frontier*, 85–89, 131. Montejano, *Anglos and Mexicans*, 20, 24, 31. Douglas E. Foley, Clarice Mora, Donald E. Post, and Ignacio Lozano, *From Peones to Politicos: Ethnic Relations in a South Texas Town, 1900–1977* (Austin:

University of Texas Press, Center for Mexican American Studies, 1977), 6–7, 70–71, 85.

35. Almaguer, *Racial Fault Lines*, 90–104.

36. Gilbert G. González, *Labor and Community: Mexican Citrus Worker Villages in a Southern California County, 1900-1950* (Urbana: University of Illinois Press, 1994), 20. Mark Reisler, "Passing Through Our Egypt: Mexican Labor in the United States, 1900-1940" (PhD dissertation, Cornell University, 1974), 8–9, 13, 15.

37. Clark, *Mexican Labor in the United States*, 494, 507, 511. Sánchez, *Becoming Mexican American*, 71.

38. García, *Desert Immigrants*, 107. Acuña, *Corridors of Migration*, 176.

39. Quoted in Almaguer, *Racial Fault Lines,* 202.

40. Oxnard, California Japantowns, http://www.californiajapantowns.org/oxnard.html. Gómez-Quiñones, "The First Steps," 26. Sam Kushner, *Long Road to Delano* (New York: International Publishers, 1975), 20. Almaguer, *Racial Fault Lines*, 200. Alberto M. Camarillo, "Chicano Urban History: A Study of Compton's Barrio, 1936-1970," *Aztlán* 2, no. 2 (Fall 1971): 79–106. Also see Alberto Camarillo, *Chicano in a Changing Society: From Mexican Pueblos to American Barrios in Santa Barbara and Southern California, 1848-1930* (Cambridge: Harvard University Press, 1979). "A Foretaste of the Orient": John Murray Criticizes the AFL, http://historymatters.gmu.edu/d/5564/. A History of Mexican Americans in California: Historic Sites, http://www.nps.gov/history/history/online_books/5views/5views5h21.htm.

41. Quoted in William B. Friedricks, *Henry E. Huntington and the Creation of Southern California,* E-book Format (Columbus: Ohio State University Press, 1992), 140, http://www.ohiostate-press.org/Books/Complete%20PDFs/Friedricks%20Henry/Friedricks%20Henry.htm. Charles Wollenberg, "Working on *El Traque*," in Norris Hundley, Jr., ed., *The Chicano* (Santa Barbara, CA: Clio Books, 1975), 96–98, 102–05. Louis B. Perry and Richard S. Perry, *A History of the Los Angeles Labor Movement, 1911-1941* (Los Angeles: University of California Press, 1963), 71. Picture Gallery of Los Angeles History, http://www.lanopalera.net/LAHistory/LAHistoryGally.html.

42. B. A. Hodges, *A History of the Mexican Mission Work* (1931), reprinted in Carlos E. Cortés, ed., *Church Views of the Mexican American* (New York: Arno Press, 1974), 5–7. Arnoldo De León, "Blowout 1910 Style: A Chicano School Boycott in West Texas," *Texana* 12, no. 2 (November 1974): 124, 129.

43. U.S. Congress, *Report of the Immigration Commission*, 61st Cong., 3d Sess. (1910–1911), I: 682–91 quoted in Job West Neal, "The Policy of the United States Toward Immigration from Mexico" (Master's thesis, University of Texas at Austin, 1941), 58–59. U.S. Department of Labor, "Report of the Commissioner General of Immigration," *Report of the Department of Labor* (Washington, D.C.: Government Printing Office, 1913), 337.

44. Elizabeth Broadbent, "The Distribution of Mexican Population in the U.S." (PhD dissertation, University of Chicago, 1941), 3, 33. Clark, *Mexican Labor in the United States*, 471, 496.

45. Robert McCaan, "Missing Millions: The Human Cost of the Mexican Revolution," University of Minnesota Population Center (2001), http://www.hist.umn.edu/~rmccaa/missmill/index.htm. John Hardman, "Postcards of the Mexican Revolution," Mex Rev PC, http://www.netdotcom.com/revmexpc/default.htm. Mexican Revolution Photos, Fotki, http://public.fotki.com/Mudhooks/my_stuff/illustrations/propaganda_posters/mexican_war_photos/. Diana Suet and Raquel Macias, "Soldaderas Played Important Roles in Revolution," Borderlands: El Paso Community College, http://epcc.libguides.com/content.php?pid=309255&sid=2604389.

46. Blancos, blancos, *Regeneracion* (November 19, 1910). Impundidad Para Los Linchadores, *Regeneración* (December 24, 1910). *Regeneración* (August 5, 1911). "La Víctima de los 'Civilizados,'" *Regeneración* (August 26, 1911). Ricardo Flores Magón, "A Salvar a un Inocente," *Regeneración* (September 9, 1911). "En defensa de los Mexicanos," *Regeneración* (August 17, 1912). "Draws Lesson from Lynching," *Los Angeles Times* (November 16, 1910). *Graham Guardian* (November 18, 1910). "Americans Protest Against Insult," *Copper Era* (November 18, 1910). W. Dirk Raat, *Revoltosos: Mexico's Rebels in the United States, 1903-1923* (College Station: Texas A&M Press, 1981), 28. Florence C. Lister and Robert H. Lister, *Chihuahua: Storehouse of Storms* (Albuquerque: University of New Mexico Press, 1966), 212.

47. RFM, "La Barbarie En Los Estados Unidos," *Regeneración* (August 5, 1911). "La Víctima de los Civilizados," *Regeneración* (August 26, 1911); Ricardo Flores Magón, "A Salvar a un Inocente," *Regeneración* (September 9, 1911); RFM, "Quemaron vivo a un hombre," *Regeneración* (December 9, 1911).

48. Acuña, *Corridors of Migration*, 142–54. Luther T. Ellsworth, American Consul, San Antonio, to Secretary of State (March 4, 1911), in Hanrahan, ed., *Documents on the Mexican Revolution,* Vol. I, pt 1, 203–208. Luther T. Ellsworth, Eagle Pass, Texas, to Secretary of State (December 23, 1910), in Hanrahan, ed., *Documents on the Mexican Revolution,* Vol. I, pt. 1, 100. Ellsworth to Secretary of State (February 18, 1911) in Hanrahan, ed., *Documents on the Mexican Revolution,* Vol. I, pt 1, 165. Linda B. Hall and Don M. Coerver, *Revolution on the Border: The United States and Mexico, 1910-1920* (Albuquerque: University of New Mexico Press, 1988), 16–27. "Sonora Mines Again Active," *Copper Era* (January 13, 1910).

49. Aboites Aguilar, *Breve Historia*, 121. D. W. Meinig, *The Shaping of America: A Geographical Perspective on 500 Years of History* (New Haven, CT: Yale University Press, 2000), 153–55. See map on page 154.

50. Michael C. Meyer, *Mexican Rebel: Pascual Orozco and the Mexican Revolution, 1910-1915* (Lincoln: University of Nebraska Press, 1967), 9, 19. Mark Wasserman, *Capitalists, Caciques, and Revolution: Native Elite and Foreign Enterprise in Chihuahua, Mexico, 1854-1911* (Chapel Hill: University or North Carolina Press, 1984), 144.

51. Ricardo Romo, "Responses to Mexican Immigration, 1910–1930," *Aztlán* 6, no. 2 (Summer 1975), 109, 116, 117–18, 122. United States Historical Census Data Browser, http://fisher.lib.virginia.edu/census (accessed October 22, 2009). John S. D. Eisenhower, *Intervention! The United States and the Mexican Revolution: 1913–1917* (Baltimore, MD: Johns Hopkins University Press 1995), 103, 105, 231. Hall and Coerver, *Revolution on the Border,* 57–77. *Regeneración* (February 4 and 18, 1911).

52. Ricardo Romo, *East Los Angeles: A History of a Barrio* (Austin: University of Texas, 1983), 103, 108. U.S. Department of Labor, "Report of the Commissioner General of Immigration," 397.

53. Idar, Nicasio (1855–1914), *Handbook of Texas Online,* http://www.tshaonline.org/handbook/online/articles/II/fid2.html.

54. Jovita Idar, Journalist and Activist, 1885–1946, University of Texas Austin, http://www.utexas.edu/gtw/idar.php (accessed October 22, 2009). Zamora, *The World of the Mexican Worker,* 61–65, 98. Vicki Ruiz, *From Out of the Shadows: Mexican Women in Twentieth Century America* (New York: Oxford University Press, 1998), 99. José E. Limón, "*El Primer Congreso Mexicanista de 1911:* A Precursor to Contemporary Chicanismo," *Aztlán* 5, nos. 1–2 (Spring and Fall 1974): 80, 88, 89. Teresa Palomo Acosta, *El Primer Congreso Mexicanista,* Handbook of Texas Online, http://www.tshaonline.org/handbook/online/articles/CC/vecyk.html. Benjamin Heber Johnson, *Revolution in Texas: How a Forgotten Rebellion and Its Bloody Suppression Turned Mexicans into Americans* (New Haven, CT: Yale University Press, 2005), 52–53, 85–88.

55. F. Arturo Rosales, *Dictionary of Latino Civil Rights History* (Houston, TX: Arte Publico Press, 2007), 4. *Sociedades Mutualistas,* Handbook of Texas Online, http://www.tshaonline.org/handbook/online/articles/SS/ves1.html.

56. Thomas E. Sheridan, *Tucsonense: The Mexican Community in Tucson 1854–1941* (Tucson: University of Arizona, 1986), 179.

57. Carlos G. Vélez-Ibañez, *Border Visions: Mexican Cultures of the Southwest United States* (Tucson: University of Arizona, 1996), 69.

58. James D. McBride, "The *Liga Protectora Latina:* A Mexican American Benevolent Society in Arizona," *Journal of the West* 14, no. 4 (October 1975): 83, 85–87. Organizations ~ Organizaciones, Arizona State University Library, http://www.asu.edu/lib/archives/website/organiza.htm. Eric V. Meeks, *Border Citizens: The Making of Indians, Mexicans, and Anglos in Arizona* (Austin: University of Texas, 2007), 93–96.

59. Leo Grebler, Joan W. Moore, and Ralph C. Guzmán, *The Mexican-American People: The Nation's Second Largest Minority* (New York: Free Press, 1970), 84. Zamora, *The World of the Mexican Worker,* 21. New Mexico and Arizona had the largest concentration of foreign-born, with many working in the mines.

60. Montejano, *Anglos and Mexicans,* 131–33, 143–46, 162. Zamora, *The World of the Mexican Worker,* 40.

61. Don Mitchell, *The Lie of the Land: Migrant Workers and the California Landscape* (Minneapolis: University of Minnesota Press, 1996), 40. Philip Taft, *Labor Politics American Style: California Federation of Labor* (Cambridge: Harvard University, 1968), 38–39. Labor—and a Whole Lot More: The Legacy of Wheatland, http://www.dickmeister.com/id113.html. 1913: Wheatland Hop Riot, libcom.org, http://libcom.org/history/1913-wheatland-hop-riot.

62. Samuel Yellen, *American Labor Struggles* (New York: Russell, 1936), 205–6. Walter Fink, *The Ludlow Massacre* (Denver, CO: Williamson-Haffner, printers, 1914) and George West, *Report on the Colorado Strike* (Washington, D.C.: U.S. Commission on Industrial Relations, 1915), reprinted in Leon Stein and Philip Taft, eds., *Massacre at Ludlow: Four Reports* (New York: Arno Press, 1971), 15–16, 31. Carey McWilliams, *Factories in Fields: The Story of Migratory Labor in California* (Santa Barbara, CA, and Salt Lake City, UT: Peregrine Publishers, 1971), 89. Stuart Jamieson, *Labor Unionism in American Agriculture* (New York: Arno Press, 1976), 236–39. Colorado Coal Field War Project, http://www.du.edu/ludlow/index.html. "The Ludlow Massacre," American Experience, PBS, http://www.pbs.org/wgbh/amex/rockefellers/sfeature/sf_8.html.

63. Acuña, *Corridors of Migration,* 177–78. "Western Miners Threaten to Tie Up Smelters," *Copper Era* (June 13, 1913). "Mining Men Have Meeting and Organize," *Copper Era* (March 19, 1914). Andrea Yvette Huginnie, " 'Strikitos': race, class, and work in the Arizona copper industry, 1870–1920" (PhD dissertation, Yale University, 1991), 109, 172. Wilma Gray Sain, "A History of the Miami area, Arizona" (Master's thesis, University of Arizona, Tucson, 1944), 134.

64. Acuña, *Corridors of Migration,* 179–83. James R. Kluger, *The Clifton-Morenci Strike; Labor Difficulty in Arizona, 1915–1916* (Tucson: University of Arizona Press, 1970), 26. "Eighty Per Cent Law Changes," *Copper Era* (July 31, 1914). "The Flag and Eighty Per Cent," *Copper Era* (September 4, 1914). "Eighty Per Cent Case Before Court" *Copper Era* (October 22, 1915). "80 Per Cent Law Invalid Says Court," *Copper Era* (November 5, 1915). "Conflict with Personal Liberties and Treaties," *Graham Guardian* (January 8, 1915). "80 Percent Law Declared Unconstitutional by Federal Tribunal in San Francisco," *The Miners Magazine* (November 6, 1913), 10. "The Convention of the Arizona States Federation of Labor" second annual convention at Bisbee on October 27 endorsed 80-percent-American goal. "Foreigners To Be Barred Out," *Los Angeles Times* (February 20, 1912). The Western Federation of Miners, http://www.law.umkc.edu/faculty/projects/ftrials/haywood/HAY_WFM.HTM.

65. "Guerra de razas en Arizona," *Regeneración* (August 22, 1914). "Race War in Arizona; Death List Is Sixteen," *Los Angeles Times* (August 20, 1914).

66. Michael E. Parrish, *Mexican Workers, Progressives and Copper: The Failure of Industrial Democracy in Arizona During the Wilson Years* (La Jolla, CA: Chicano Research Publication, 1979), 32. To follow the events that were happening in Sonora and Mexico, see Acuña, *Corridors of Migration,* 150–69.

67. Robert Kern, ed., *Labor in New Mexico: Unions, Strikes, and Social History Since 1881* (Albuquerque: University of New

Mexico Press, 1983), 6–7. R. Romo, "Responses to Mexican Immigration," 186–87.

68. Ralph Guzmán, *The Political Socialization of the Mexican American People* (New York: Arno Press, 1976), 65–66. Acuña, *Corridors of Migration*, 199–209. The Bisbee Deportation of 1917, The University of Arizona Web Exhibit, http://www.library.arizona.edu/exhibits/bisbee/. Report of the Bisbee Deportations, University of Arizona Web Exhibit, http://www.library.arizona.edu/exhibits/bisbee/primarysources/reports/president/index.php.

69. *Los Angeles Times* (January 31, 1917), I5. *Los Angeles Times* (January 29, 1917), I1. Indignity on the Border, http://www.youtube.com/watch?v=3Nz-253RaQo. Community, "Indignity on the Border," http://forchicanachicanostudies.wikispaces.com/Community. David Dorado Romo, *Ringside Seat to a Revolution, An Underground Cultural History of El Paso and Juarez: 1893–1923* (El Paso, TX: Cinco Puntos Press, 2005), 223–27. "'Viva Villa' Shouted in Riots at Juarez," *Los Angeles Times* (January 29, 1917). "Mexicans Given Baths," *Los Angeles Times* (January 31, 1917). The practice was continued until a "compromise" was reached in the late 1950s whereby Mexicans got the bath in Juárez, where they received a certificate. Allen Morrison, "The Tramways of Ciudad Juárez," http://www.tramz.com/mx/cj/cj.html.

70. Montejano, *Anglos and Mexicans*, 125. William M. Hager, "The Plan of San Diego: Unrest on the Texas Border in 1915," *Arizona and the West* 5, no. 4 (Winter 1963): 330–36. Walter Prescott Webb, *The Texas Rangers*, 2d ed. (Austin: University of Texas Press, 1965), 478–79, 484–85. Juan Gómez-Quiñones, "*Plan de San Diego* Reviewed," *Aztlán* 1, no. 1 (Spring 1970): 125–26. Charles C. Cumberland, "Border Raids in the Lower Rio Grande Valley—1915," *Southwestern Historical Quarterly* 57 (January 1954): 290–94. *Regeneración* (October 2, 1915). Don M. Coerver and Linda B. Hall, *Texas and the Mexican Revolution: A Study in State and National Policy, 1910–1920* (San Antonio, TX: Trinity University Press, 1984), 85–108. "Mexico Repudiates Plan of San Diego "*New York Times*, http://query.nytimes.com/gst/abstract.html?res=9C06E2D61F30E033A25750C1A9649D946896D6CF. Plan of San Diego, Handbook of Texas Online, http://www.tshaonline.org/handbook/online/articles/PP/ngp4.html.

71. Johnson, *Revolution in Texas*, 79–85. Edwin Larry Dickens, "The Political Role of Mexican-Americans in San Antonio" (PhD dissertation, Texas Tech University, 1969), 38. George Marvin, "The Quick and the Dead on the Border," *The World's Word* (January 1917): 295. Webb, *The Texas Rangers*, 474, 475, 478. The 1919 Ranger Investigation Reports, http://www.tsl.state.tx.us/treasures/law/index.html. Transcripts of the three-volume investigation can be downloaded.

72. Cardoso, "Mexican Emigration," 83–87. Neal, "The Policy," 81, 100. Mark Reisler, *By the Sweat of Their Brow: Mexican Immigrant Labor in the United States, 1900–1940* (Westport, CT: Greenwood Press, 1976), 38.

73. Ricardo Romo, "Mexican Workers in the City: Los Angeles, 1915–1930" (PhD dissertation, University of California at Los Angeles, 1975), 56–57, 81–83, 104, 106–7, 109–11, 123. R. Romo, *East Los Angeles*, 76–78. Sánchez, *Becoming Mexican American*, 81. William David Estrada, *The Los Angeles Plaza Sacred and Contested Space* (Austin: University of Texas Press, 2008), 133–59.

74. Carole E. Christian, "Joining the American Mainstream: Texas's Mexican Americans During World War I," *Southwestern Historical Quarterly* 92, no. 4 (April 1, 1989): 559–95. Lee Stacy, ed., *Mexico and the United States* (Tarrytown, NY: Marshall Cavendish, 2003), 409.

75. A classic work on World War I and the Mexican American presence is J. Luz Sáenz, *Los méxico-americanos en la gran guerra y su contingente en pró de la democracia, la humanidad y justicia* (San Antonio, TX: Artes Gráficas, 1933). Johnson, *Revolution in Texas*, 60–62.

76. Elena Gómez, "Marcelino Serna Became World War I Hero," *Borderlands*: El Paso Community College, http://epcc.libguides.com/content.php?pid=309255&sid=2603468. Congressional Medal of Honor Award Private Marcelino Serna U.S. Army WW I, League of United Latin American Citizens, http://www.lulac.net/advocacy/resolutions/2007/mil3.html. Julie Leininger Prycior, "*La Raza* organizes: Mexican American Life in San Antonio, 1915–1930. As Reflected in *Mutualista* Activities" (PhD dissertation, University of Notre Dame, 1979), 83, 97–98, 105.

77. Jeffrey M. Garcilazo, "Mexican Strike Activity in the Riverside and San Bernardino Areas, 1917" (paper presented at the Annual National Association for Chicano Studies Conference, West Sacramento, California, March 23, 1985).

78. Paul S. Taylor, *Mexican Labor in the United States*, Vol. 2 (New York: Arno Press, 1970), 114–17. R. Romo, "Responses to Mexican Immigration," 187–90.

79. McLean and Thomson, *Spanish and Mexicans in Colorado*, 29–30, 34. Ruben Donato, *Mexicans and Hispanos in Colorado Schools and Communities, 1920–1960* (Albany: State University of New York Press, 2007), 65–75.

80. Mario T. García, "Racial Dualism in the El Paso Labor Market, 1880–1920," *Aztlán* 6, no. 2 (Summer 1975): 197–218. Mario T. García, "Obreros: The Mexican Workers of El Paso, 1900–1920" (PhD dissertation, University of California at San Diego, 1975), 199, 201–5. Teresa Palomo Acosta and Ruthe Winegarten, Las Tejanas: 300 Years of History (Austin: University of Texas, 2003), 131–34.

81. Irene Ledesma, "Texas Newspapers and Chicana Workers' Activism, 1919–1974," *Western Historical Quarterly* 26, no. 3 (Fall 1995): 309–31.

82. William Clark Roberts, *American Federation of Labor: History, Encyclopedia, Reference Book*, Vol. 1 (Washington, DC: American Federation of Labor, 1919–1960), 447–53. "I.W.W. Activities in Arizona," *The Miners' Magazine*, newspaper format (March 1917). *Pan-American Labor Press* (November 13, 1918). Pan American Federation of Labor, Record Group 63, Records of the Committee on Public Information, Selected Items to the American Federation of Labor—GSA, National Archives and Records Service, Washington, 1959, John Murray Collection. Sinclair Snow, "Samuel Gompers and the Pan-American

Federation of Labor" (PhD dissertation, University of Virginia, 1960), 1–3, 162, 164–66. Charles Toth, "Bulwark for Freedom: Samuel Gompers' Pan American Federation of Labor," *Separata de la Revista/Review Interamericana* IX, no. 3 (Fall 1979): 460, 461. The Punitive Expedition played a role in the decision to establish the PAFL. A letter from Antonio I. Villarreal, Pan American Labor Press/Obrero Pan-Americano, September 18, 1918. "Border Mexicans Treated Badly by Americans Safe," *Pan-American Labor Press* (San Antonio, October 2, 1918). "Latins Ask Gompers Why A.F.L. Harpoons Their Workers," *New York Call* (July 8, 1919). "Pan Am Feels Weight of Rule by Gompers, Re-elects Him," *New York Call* (July 10, 1919).

83. "Twenty-million-dollar Tire Factory Coming to Los Angeles Soon," *Los Angeles Times* (June 29, 1919).

CHAPTER 9

The 1920s: The Effects of World War I

LEARNING OBJECTIVES

- Discuss the organizational changes in the Mexican American population in the aftermath of World War I.

- Explain the reasoning behind the National Origins and the Immigration Acts of 1921 and 1924.

- Analyze the debates leading to the passage of the Immigration Acts vis-à-vis putting Mexicans on a quota.

- Describe the various aspects of Americanization.

- Debate the causes of the differences between Mexican-born Mexicans and Mexican Americans.

- Consider how the formation of the League of United Latin American Citizens was a watershed in the history of Mexican Americans.

Why 1798? In that year Congress passed the Alien and Sedition Acts, which were directed at enemy aliens and radical ideas.[1] The year 1898 marked the end of the Spanish–American War and the popularization of the Euro-American notion of empire; and 1910 witnessed the Mexican Revolution, which challenged U.S. economic and political hegemony in Mexico. The rise of the Bolsheviks in October 1917 exacerbated Euro-American xenophobia. The following year the United States sent large numbers of troops into World War I, and many second-generation Mexican Americans became involved in the armed forces.[2] The Russian Revolution drove many Americans to irrational heights with many white Americans linking Communism to the immigration of millions of Europeans. They feared losing control of *their* nation. Nativists offered nationalism as a remedy to cure the foreign disease.

At the start of the 1920s, the U.S.-Mexican workforce was "nearly equally divided between those who worked in agriculture (40 percent) and those who did not (45 percent), including manufacturing (26 percent) and transportation (19 percent)."[3] By the end of the decade, 51 percent of the Mexican population lived in urban areas (which was a percentage close to that for the U.S. population at large, 56 percent

1798	1898	1910	1917	1918	1921	1924	1928	1929

of which lived in cities). The increased visibility of Mexicans in southwestern cities set off racist nativism among Euro-Americans. At the same time, differences emerged within the Mexican community based on generations, classes, birthplaces, and assimilation patterns; these differences impacted how Mexicans responded to the majority society.[4]

The growth of the Mexican-origin population and their move to cities put them in harm's way, and in clear view of the nativists. As in all postwar periods, American capital moved to gain more control of the nation's resources. Capital pushed the economic philosophy of laissez-faire ("leave it alone") and the myth that the markets always know best. Accordingly, government should not regulate or otherwise interfere with businesses. The outcome was that lawmakers slashed government regulation and anti-trust enforcement. These policies were intertwined with the nationalism of the times. In the previous decade, big business used the Red Scare to attack and destroy the unions, and to brand members radicals. During the 1920s, many business leaders continued the line that to criticize business was un-American; they promoted class warfare and restrained progress. To hide their greed, they made immigrants the scapegoats, and pushed the rhetoric of total assimilation, creating social tensions that distracted Euro-Americans from the reality of growing economic, political, and social inequality. They were incredibly successful until everything tumbled down in 1929.

Americanization: A Study of Extremes

Between 1900 and 1910, almost 1 million immigrants entered the United States annually. The new immigrants differed from the earlier arrivals from the British Isles and northern Europe, who had dominated immigration and maintained a steady flow before and through the Civil War years (1861–1865). Most of the newcomers were southern and central Europeans, who were physically and culturally different. The older WASP (white Anglo-Saxon Protestant) population, who considered themselves the "real Americans," panicked and initiated a campaign based on fear to put a brake on immigration. Simultaneously, the xenophobes set out to Americanize those who were already in the country. In the Southwest, the post–World War I era ushered in intense campaigns to "Americanize" Mexican families. Euro-Americans established English-only schools and tried to alter the family life patterns and dietary and health habits of the Mexican community.[5]

As early as 1892, Mexican children (i.e., all children of Mexican descent) were denied entrance to white schools in towns such as Corpus Christi, Texas. In 1919 the Santa Ana, California, school district solicited an opinion from the state attorney general on whether segregating Mexicans to meet their "special needs" was permissible. The growing xenophobia of the 1920s saw many public school districts require students to recite the Pledge of Allegiance to the flag. The words "my flag" were replaced with "the flag of the United States" supposedly to prevent immigrants and others from swearing allegiance to a foreign flag while facing the American flag. The American Legion and the Daughters of the American Revolution pushed the new wording at the first National Flag Conference in Washington, D.C., on June 14, 1923.[6] Americanization programs encouraged the de facto segregation of Mexican children. The reasoning was that Mexicans were "dirty, shiftless, lazy, irresponsible, unambitious, thriftless, fatalistic, selfish, promiscuous, and prone to drinking, violence, and criminal behavior"; the nativists saw it as their mission to cure these evils by indoctrinating Mexican children, making sure that they had an appreciation of the institutions of this country. The continuing popularity and use of Spanish language was considered a "very real educational barrier" to the Americanization of children. The Los Angeles City schools offered adult sessions in evening school and at industrial work sites, day classes for mothers, and naturalization classes.[7]

From 1915 to 1929, the home teacher—usually a single, middle-class, WASP woman—was a tool for Americanization efforts aimed at the Mexican family: teach Mexican women to speak English; learn the "American way." When women did not respond, they blamed it on the patriarchal Mexican family. Religious missions and grower exchanges (or associations) also promoted campaigns to Americanize workers.

IQ testing played a major role in justifying programs that trained Mexicans for subordinate roles in American society. The IQ test was the alleged reason of American educators for not educating Mexicans; the test proved to them that intellectual performance was biologically determined and proved that Mexicans were not capable of learning. Why waste tax money in trying to educate them? Mexican American educators such as Dr. George I. Sánchez, then a young graduate student, countered this pseudoscience by emphasizing that environmental factors were extremely influential in determining test results. Sánchez exploded the myth popularized by U.S. social scientists that the reason Mexicans were not assimilating quickly was a lack of intelligence. The standardized tests were in English and dealt with things strangely "Anglo" to Mexicans. Sánchez throughout his life battled against standardized tests, segregation based on not being proficient in English, and other forms of racism.[8]

Racial stereotypes allowed school boards to track Mexican students into vocational education programs. School districts rationalized that intellectually weaker students should be removed from the "normal" student population and tracked separately. Hence, a high percentage of Mexican students ended up in classes for slow learners or the mentally retarded; racist school boards abused these programs.

Before the 1920s, Mexican children were not universally segregated. However, segregation became widespread during the 1920s, aided by the "No Spanish Rule"—the rule prohibiting Mexican children from speaking Spanish in school. By the end of the decade about half of Mexican students were attending segregated schools. In Texas, the number of special Mexican school districts doubled from 20 in 1922 to 40 in 1932. School authorities required Mexicans to attend Mexican schools, while not restricting white children by neighborhood or even by county.

As the heavy influx of Mexican children continued, strategies to isolate the youngsters became more popular. By 1928, Mexicans comprised 13 percent of the Texas school population (African Americans made up 16.8 percent). In 1920, 11,000 Mexican students attended San Antonio elementary schools, with only 250 enrolled in high school. In 1928, in the entire state of Texas, only 250 Mexicans attended college. The excuse was that Mexican Americans were slow learners. This was confuted by the fact that in 1925, Mexican students in San Antonio scored 70 percent higher on IQ tests administered in Spanish than on tests given in English. Meanwhile, the district profited from Mexican schools because it spent less on educating Mexican students. It did not care if Mexicans dropped out of school because it could then spend more on the education of white students. One of the first successful legal challenges was brought in Tempe, Arizona, an eastern suburb of Phoenix, in 1925; a Mexican American rancher named Adolpho "Babe" Romo, Sr., successfully sued the Tempe Elementary School District for denying admission to his four children in the newly opened Tenth Street School. Because the suit was not a class action suit, the impact was limited, and only Romo's children were admitted to the white school.[9]

Protestant Churches and Americanization of the Mexican

The Catholic Church often interpreted Americanization as being synonymous with Protestantism and resisted the Americanization programs because Church leaders saw Mexicans as exclusively Catholic—though, generally, as unequal members. While most Protestant churches considered Mexicans primitive, there were exceptions. For instance, some Protestant churches recruited Spanish-speaking ministers, many of whom were Latinos and Mexicans. This was a tradition that dated back to the Protestant missionary work in the nineteenth century in Mexico. One of the most popular methods of converting Mexicans was through youth programs such as the Young Men's Christian Association (YMCA) that conducted surveys and published valuable studies on Mexican American communities.

The Reverend Robert N. McLean, an associate director of the Presbyterian Board of Missions in the United States, was from a family of ministers. The U.S. Presbyterian Church was heavily invested in missionary work worldwide, especially in countries such as China, Ireland, Puerto Rico, and Mexico. Mexicans in the United States were seen as an extension of those in Mexico, where many Mexican ministers were trained and schools established. McLean belonged to the more progressive arm of the Presbyterian Church that often advocated for the material well-being of Mexicans; church people like McLean were among the few pro-immigrant voices of the period.[10]

The work of the Protestant churches cannot be overstated. There were 60 Mexican Protestant churches in Texas as well as a network in Mexico. The Methodist Episcopal denomination established the Frances Pauw Industrial School for Girls in Los Angeles, the Harwood Industrial School for Girls in

Albuquerque, another school for girls in Tucson, and a settlement house in El Paso. The jewel in the crown was the Spanish American Institute, which was a boarding house and school for boys. The Institute, opened in 1913, was shut down in 1971 due to a lack of funds and stricter immigration laws. It focused on vocational education, and, according to McLean, these boys were the bridge between the churches in Latin America, Mexico, and the United States since some students were recruited from families in Mexico. Many of the leaders of the Mexican American Movement in the 1930s and 1940s were educated at this school located in Gardena, California.[11]

Catholic Churches React to Americanization

The response of the Catholic Church depended on what proportion of a diocese was Mexican. In San Antonio, the parishioners were overwhelmingly Mexican, but this was not so in Los Angeles. Wherever Mexicans were not the majority, non-Mexican parishioners often opposed programs for the integration of Mexican American families. For instance, the Protestant challenge to traditional Catholicism nudged Los Angeles Bishop John J. Cantwell to organize—with some opposition from within—the Immigrant Welfare Department within Associated Catholic Charities. He then appointed Father Robert E. Lucey, who had been born in Los Angeles, as the head of the diocesan Bureau of Catholic Charities. Lucey later became Archbishop of San Antonio. In Los Angeles, Lucey launched a major campaign to include Mexicans in Church affairs, and even established a free health clinic within the Santa Rita Settlement House. The Church distributed religious books written in Spanish to Mexican Catholics, and organized Confraternity of Christian Doctrine (CCD) to serve youngsters from public schools. Fearing opposition from white parishioners, Cantwell hid the costs of these programs. *The Tidings*, the official diocesan newspaper, insisted that the Catholic Church should not promote social justice.[12]

Nationalism versus Americanization

Racist nativism generalized all social and economic classes of Mexicans. In defense of their culture Mexican Americans reacted organizationally. Mexican consulates sponsored honorary societies, which were intended to foster, among other things, nationalism. In California they established *escuelitas* (private schools) throughout the state. However, these efforts proved grossly inadequate to serve the increasing numbers of immigrants; for instance, in Los Angeles the escuelitas served only 200 students out of an estimated total of 80,000 Mexican and Mexican American children.[13] In Texas and Arizona, too, the immigrant population became more nationalistic and moved to preserve their Mexican identity by forming *escuelitas*. In Phoenix, the Mexican consul in 1923 set up literacy classes for Mexican children. Five years later the Mexican Ministry of Education sent representatives to help set up *escuelitas* whose aim was to disprove the popular notion that Mexicans were backward peasants and had to Americanize to learn. Meanwhile, a subtle division was taking shape between first and second generations.[14]

Mexicans and Mexican Americans

David G. Gutiérrez, in *Walls and Mirrors,* argues that the massive migration of Mexicans in the 1920s resulted in increased tensions between Mexican Americans and the new arrivals. This follows a pattern similar to the tensions between northern and southern Italians, between German Jews and Slavic Jews, and between the long-time settlers and the recent arrivals from Europe. Like European newcomers, Mexican newcomers competed for space with Mexican Americans, some of whose families had lived in the United States for generations. On the positive side, the large presence of Mexican-born immigrants reinforced Mexican culture and the Spanish language, and affected the cultural identity of those born in the United States. Most recent Mexican immigrants were poor, and from the interior of Mexico. They tended to be darker than Mexicans from the Border States, who once made up the bulk of the arrivals from Mexico. Class differences within the Mexican-origin community in the United States also splintered it into middle-class immigrant and middle-class Mexican American groups, and then into rich and poor. Not only Mexican Americans took on airs, but many Mexican political refugees fleeing the Mexican Revolution in 1913 considered themselves culturally and even racially superior to poor Mexican immigrants as well as middle-class Mexican Americans.[15]

The massive influx of Mexican immigrants posed a challenge to working-class Mexican Americans by competing with them in the labor market. There was also resentment among middle-class Mexican Americans toward better-off Mexicans that was also predictable since it was the sector most affected by competition from the incoming Mexican middle class; as small as it was, the Mexican middle class was better educated than the Mexican American middle class. Moreover, conditioned by history, the Mexican American middle class was very conscious of the darker hue of the recently arrived working class; on the other hand, the pretensions of newly arrived middle- and upper-class Mexican political refugees made them uneasy. The Mexican elites' disdain for the *pocho*[16] (a pejorative term for Mexican Americans who have become Americanized) and the perceived inferiority of "American" culture also unsettled many Mexican Americans. Despite these tensions, with time they adjusted to each other. Euro-American racism played an important role in this adjustment as well as in defining the community, since most outsiders did not make distinctions between the Mexican-born and the Mexican American—they considered them all "greasers."[17]

The divide between the two groups varied not only from class to class, but also from region to region and from state to state. For example, the old California Mexican families—the Californios—did not play as important a role as the old families did in Texas. The Californios exhibited biases toward the Mexicans and did not relate to them politically, socially, or culturally. By the 1920s, the size of the immigrant population eclipsed that of the Californio and the rest of the resident Mexican American community. In Arizona, relations between Mexican Americans and Mexican nationals appeared to be more cordial, given the interaction and constant communication between that state and neighboring Sonora. Mexican and Mexican American businessmen were often related, even though twice removed.[18]

In New Mexico, Mexican immigrants were concentrated in the southern parts, especially in the mining districts. The bulk of the older Spanish-speaking New Mexican population lived in the north, where some of the New Mexicans voiced prejudices toward the *surrumatos* (a pejorative term meaning "southerner" or "Mexican"). A sizable out-migration of *manitos*—as other Mexicans knew New Mexicans, because they used the word *hermanito* (little brother)—took place during this decade. As early as 1870, *manitos* could be found in the mining camps of Arizona, where they were categorized simply as Mexicans. This population played an important role in the fight for equality, as its members were often the civil rights leaders.

Texas had a diverse Mexican-origin population, with a larger proportion of second- and third-generation Mexican Americans than in any other state but New Mexico. In Texas—a huge state—the Mexican-origin population differed greatly from region to region. Tensions seemed most intense in cities, where heavy immigration strained the infrastructure the most. The upper-middle-class and elite *Tejanos* (a popular name for Mexican Texans) consisted largely of professionals, schoolteachers, small shopkeepers, and artisans. Their organization and social life was separate from those of the working-class Tejano. The middle class was important in the development of the civil rights discourse of the time, which emphasized politics of inclusion as American citizens.[19]

The Influence of World War I on Becoming Mexican American

Returning from World War I, many of the Mexican American veterans became more involved in politics. In Texas, which had the largest Mexican American population, this experience paved the way for new organizations that differed from the older mutual-aid societies. Many new organizations were more concerned with members acquiring U.S. citizenship and becoming Mexican American than they were with maintaining the Mexican culture. Emerging after World War I were new leaders such as

J. Luz Sáenz, a World War I veteran who in the early 1930s wrote *Los México-Americanos en la Gran Guerra* (Mexican Americans in the Great War). As a rule, the *veteranos* (veterans) pursued their political rights more aggressively than did the first generation, because they felt entitled as veterans. This is not to say that the *mutualistas* disappeared, or that Mexican and Mexican American veterans did not belong to *mutualistas*, but merely that the issues addressed by the new organizations, as well as those by the *mutualistas*, changed. For example, after the war the mutual-aid societies petitioned President Woodrow Wilson to do something about the negative stereotyping of Mexicans in the movies; and in 1922–1923, Mexicans protested what they called the Ku Klux Klan–Texas Ranger alliance.[20]

By the 1920s, many Mexican Americans came to accept that they would not be returning to Mexico and began to distinguish between Tejanos and Mexicans. Today, some Mexican Americans still smart over the fact that David Barkley, the first person of Mexican descent to win a Congressional Medal of Honor, enlisted in the U.S. Army using his Anglo father's name to avoid being segregated. Born in Laredo, Texas, and raised by his mother Antonia Cantú, David Barkley died in action in 1918 during World War I and was posthumously awarded the Medal of Honor; it was not until 71 years later that his Mexican lineage became known. Although not all Mexican Americans were war veterans, the veterans' presence influenced the development of a community identity. They contributed to a growing sense that Mexican Americans were citizens and equals.[21]

The intergroup differences between Mexicans and Mexican Americans became noticeable during these years. For example, the *Hijos de México* (Sons of Mexico), organized in San Antonio in 1897, admitted only Mexican citizens and promoted Mexican culture. The association disbanded in 1914, but reorganized nine years later. In 1921, Professor Sáenz, along with Santiago Tafolla (a lawyer) and other Mexican American World War I veterans and professionals, formed *La Orden de Hijos de América* (the Order of the Sons of America). This was a transitional organization that did not insist on U.S. citizenship as a membership requirement; it did, however, emphasize the betterment of the Mexican American in the United States. Within two years, *Los Hijos de América* had 250 members and three branches in south Texas.

By 1922, *Los Hijos de América* split, and a dissident group, *Los Hijos de Texas* (the Sons of Texas), was formed. Led by police officer Feliciano G. Flores and attorney Alonso S. Perales, the society worked for the interests of Americans of Mexican extraction. In 1927, they formed *La Orden de Caballeros* (the Order of Knights). Some of the leaders of these groups also held offices in the various *mutualistas*, and *Los Hijos de América* was a member of the San Antonio Alliance of Mutualista Societies. However, leaders such as Perales and Sáenz never joined *mutualistas*, and they typified the post–World War I leadership among Mexican Americans.[22]

The League of United Latin American Citizens

The progression to an exclusively Mexican American organization was completed with the formation of the League of United Latin American Citizens (LULAC). For many years, Tejanos discussed the need for a statewide organization that had the potential to become national. In 1927 Alonso Perales called together leaders of various organizations from south Texas to explore the possibility of merging into a single organization. Two years later, on February 17, 1929, in Corpus Christi, *Los Caballeros de América* of San Antonio, *Los Hijos de América* of Corpus Christi, and the League of Latin American Citizens of South Texas merged to form LULAC.[23] The founding members represented both the educated elite and the lower and middle class. Fluent in English and highly urbanized, they worked on civil rights issues such as the betterment of schools and voter registration drives, much in the same tradition as other racial and ethnic groups. For them, political and social equality was synonymous with being American. They wanted economic, social, and racial equality, although women did not become voting members until 1933. The formation of LULAC marked a milestone in Chicano civil rights history.[24]

LULAC also represented a new direction in the organizational history of persons of Mexican origin in the United States. Before LULAC was formed, many issues of the Mexican and Mexican American community emanated from south of the Rio Grande, and not from the United States. For instance, the community was concerned with the Mexican Revolution and whether or not the United States would intervene.

Now, community leaders acted on their own behalf as Americans struggling against discrimination and inequality. With the formation of LULAC, the leadership demanded their rights as U.S. citizens. The formation of LULAC also represented a symbolic break with the Mexican consular leadership.

This change was mirrored in the readership of Spanish-language newspapers that mostly catered to immigrants. During the nineteenth century, 136 Spanish-language newspapers were published in the Southwest, 38 of them in Texas. Spanish-language newspapers ranked third among the foreign-language media in the United States at the close of the nineteenth century. The readership multiplied as immigrants streamed into the Southwest.

In Texas, Spanish-language newspapers addressing Mexican American issues increased after the war. They represented a separate worldview, different than that of the immigrant press. *La Prensa* of San Antonio catered to the Mexican exiles, and *Evolución* and *El Demócrata* of Laredo catered to the local crowd. During World War I, *La Prensa* often covered the war from a French point of view, translating French coverage of the war into Spanish. It was preoccupied with pride in Mexican nationality. *Evolución* urged its readers to be patriotic Americans. It gave a pro-American coverage of the war. "For *La Prensa*, these dough boys exemplify the fighting ideals of *la raza*; in contrast, *La Evolución* presents Mexican American servicemen as patriotic American citizens."[25]

The self-identity of the new immigrants sometimes varied from the attitudes of the Mexican Americans. Often it was based on the latter's jealousy and/or the snobbery of the Mexican intelligentsia. This division at times was reflected in the content of the newspapers. *La Prensa* betrayed the elitist notion of a Spanish cultural heritage, while other Mexican papers downplayed the Spanish past and exalted the Mexicans' indigenous past.[26]

LULAC expressed the view of the new Mexican American generation when it excluded noncitizens. This exclusion has been labeled by critics as racist and anti-Mexican. But in fairness to LULAC founders, they were expressing the common sense of the civil rights movement of the time. Many of its goals and political strategies paralleled those of the National Association for the Advancement of Colored People (NAACP). W. E. B. DuBois, an NAACP founder, constantly spoke and wrote about an "educated elite" that, according to him, "would lead the masses with appropriate goals and lift them to civilization." Most labor organizations in the 1920s also believed this, and most civil rights leaders belonged to the middle or upper class.[27]

Although LULAC leadership stated that it did not want to offend Mexican nationals, it did distinguish between "Americans of Latin extraction" and the "peon class." Alonso S. Perales, who in 1928 served in a Department of State diplomatic post in Nicaragua, was a prime proponent of Americanization. Writing to a fellow Tejano leader about the poverty and the "filthy and backward towns and cities" in Nicaragua, Perales asked what Mexican Americans were going to do about similar situations back home: "Are we going to continue our backward state of the past, or are we going to get out of the rut, forge ahead and keep abreast of the hardworking Anglo-Saxon?"[28]

LULAC leader Judge J. T. Canales also played a key role in the exclusion of Mexican nationals. His rationale was that Mexicans were not skillful enough to work in the political arena, and, therefore, only American citizens of Mexican origin should form the new organization. According to the Spanish-language newspaper *El Comercio*, Canales said, "This organization should be integrated by Mexican Americans exclusively, since Mexicans from MEXICO are a PITIFUL LOT who come to this country in great caravans to retard the Mexican Americans' work for unity that should be at the Anglo-Saxon's level."[29]

The Move to the Cities

Mexican immigrants lived in large cities and small villages; many worked seasonally in agriculture and on railroad crews; others sought stable situations in the face of major adjustments in the United States. The first wave of Mexican immigrants was largely composed of single males. Mexican immigrants in general were apt to return home at some point—either to bring their wives and families or, in the case of single Mexican males, to marry Mexican-born females and return to the States with them. The influx of women expedited the forging of a community in the United States—that is, the bonding of Mexicans with others of the same race within a specific space. The early arrival of the family distinguished Mexicans from the European immigrant communities, where the ratio of men to women was always much higher.

By 1920, 50 percent of all Mexican immigrants were comprised of women and children.[30] The presence of women and children generally suggested permanency, and many communities formed within the existing Mexican American enclaves. Formation of community had both positive and negative fallouts: the presence of their families often made workers more vulnerable and discouraged militant behavior that might put their families at risk.

San Antonio's West Side

By 1920, San Antonio grew to 161,379 residents, of whom about 60,000 were of Mexican origin. At the end of the decade about 70,000 of the city's 232,542 residents were of Mexican extraction. Some of these were Mexican religious refugees, i.e., those fleeing the so-called religious persecution in Mexico. (The 1920s was at the height of the *Cristero* movement. The Catholic Church, mainly in the Mexican state of Jalisco, resisted the reforms of the 1917 Mexican Constitution and a civil war broke out. The militant supporters of the Church were called the cristeros.) Many of the new Mexican immigrant arrivals of this decade were middle and upper class, in contrast to the resident Mexican population of San Antonio that mostly worked as laborers by 1926. A few businessmen owned small stores and butcher shops; only 21 percent were skilled workers. Opportunities for women were limited; they usually filled lower-status jobs and only occasionally worked in Mexican-run businesses as clerks. As with their male counterparts, women's skin color determined their level of equality. Despite this the social network of Mexican women widened during the decade.[31]

This movement to the cities came not without a cost. The existing housing and the labor market could not absorb the flood of Mexicans into San Antonio. Two-thirds of the Mexicans lived in shacks on the West Side, hovels that filled the empty spaces between the warehouses and the rails, and were surrounded by a red-light district. Crowded courts—a series of one- and two-room units sharing a common toilet and a water spigot—barely met the housing needs of the poor. Mexicans also lived in long one-story *corrales* extending 100 yards with overcrowded stalls resembling stables. The workers put up with these unsanitary living conditions and all other miseries to earn a wage of 90¢ to $1.25 a week. The blight worsened with the heavy influx of farmworkers during the off-season.[32]

Powerless and too poor to pay the poll tax, Mexican Americans voted when different interest groups or political parties paid the tab. The Commission Ring, as they called it, ran the city for the interests of elites, giving free land to the military to attract bases. In the 1920s, the $38 million spent annually by military personnel in San Antonio contributed to the merchants' prosperity. However, because the trading installations were not taxed, little money was available for civic improvements. There were few recreation clubs to serve the poor Mexicans, who congregated at Milam Park, waiting to be picked up for day labor—both within the city and as migrant workers.

Despite these difficulties, San Antonio's Mexican population was stable and self-help organizations flourished. Between 1915 and 1930, 10,000 Mexicans joined 19 *mutualistas* and 6 *mutualista* labor unions in San Antonio; the largest was *La Sociedad de la Unión*, with more than 1,100 members in 1920. At least one *mutualista* was headed by a woman, Luisa M. De González. *Mutualistas* appealed more to families than to young single males or females. The 1920s also brought an expansion of the social life of the West Side. The wealthy Mexicans frequented separate social clubs and, as a rule, did not join the *mutualistas*.[33]

As mentioned, the Mexican community supported the numerous Spanish-language newspapers. The most popular was the Spanish-language daily *La Prensa* that covered a variety of events; Beatriz Blanca de Hinojosa, the wife of the editor, wrote a regular column. Along with Aurora Herrera de Nobregas of *La Epoca*, Blanca de Hinojosa advocated the end of the double standard for women. Although some Mexican women expressed feminist ideas, the majority did not. An exception, *Prensa* columnist Arianda, wrote that feminism was simply the "realization that women are not inferior to men." She implored women to become active against alcoholism, militarism, child labor, and the "degradation of women." María Luisa Garza, editor of *La Epoca*, attended the 1922 Pan American Women's Conference in Baltimore. She later resigned to found *Alma Femenina*.

The status of women in the *mutualistas* varied; most groups admitted women and allowed them to hold office. Contrary to popular myth, not all Mexican women remained at home; 16 percent of Mexican women worked outside the home, compared to 17 percent of all women in Texas. More Mexican than Mexican Texan women were wage earners.[34]

Mutualistas often defended compatriots alleged to have committed crimes, raising funds and petitioning authorities on their behalf. In response to the courts sentencing Agustín Sánchez to death for murder, Mexicans in San Antonio formed a committee to seek a stay of execution, convinced that he had acted in self-defense. As a rule, *mutualistas* did not allow any political discussions at their meetings. However, members rationalized that the protection of their civil rights was not a political issue so it was proper to discuss them. They regularly allowed groups such as *La Liga Pro-Mexicana* (1927), a civil rights organization, to use their facilities for free; they also lent the facilities to labor associations. San Antonio *mutualistas* avoided radical organizations such as the Industrial Workers of the World (IWW). Class differences among mutualista members slowed solidarity among the members and among groups. Even so, members closed ranks in the face of discrimination. Most Mexicans were absorbed with their own economic survival. For the most part, the *mutualistas* maintained close ties with the Mexican consul, who frequently attended their functions.[35]

Los Angeles: "Where Only the Weeds Grow"

In the 1920s Los Angeles surpassed San Antonio as the U.S. city with the largest Mexican population. The Guadalajara–Nogales–Los Angeles railroad line, completed in 1927, facilitated the movement of Mexicans to the West Coast. The expansion of Los Angeles led Ignacio Lozano, the publisher of *La Prensa*, to move west where he founded *La Opinión*. Los Angeles was surpassing San Antonio as the new Mexican mecca in the United Sates.[36]

Los Angeles was far from homogeneous. It housed an economically and socially diverse Mexican-origin population. In 1917 in Los Angeles, 91.5 percent of Mexicans held blue-collar jobs, compared with 53 percent of the white population; 68 percent were engaged in manual labor such as pick-and-shovel work, compared with 6 percent of the white Angelenos.[37] As in San Antonio, a sizable number of middle-class refugees moved to Los Angeles; Mexican Angelenos differed from those in the Alamo City because not all Mexicans lived on the Eastside, and a number of them lived in racially integrated neighborhoods. The social life of many middle-class Mexicans differed from that of the barrio dweller; in fact, there was often minimal contact among the disparate social classes. Events such as *bailes blanco y negro* (black and white dances) did not refer to race, but to a dance in which men wore black tuxedos and women wore white gowns.[38]

Mexican landowners, bankers, and business and professional men gathered at the *Centro Hispano Americano* in West Adams, where they held weekly formal balls. According to the *Los Angeles Times*, "the Mexican señorita" was changing for the better and becoming "the modern girl" who spoke perfect English and benefited from the "independent qualities borrowed from the American girl." Pretentious Mexicans also gathered at Café Cuba on Main Street. Immigrants, day laborers, truck drivers, and railroad trackwalkers frequented the plaza. According to Historian Robin Scott, upper-class Mexicans in Los Angeles "extolled virtues of Mexican culture and heritage."[39]

The Mexican working class joined a polyglot of races in Sonoratown (near the *plaza*—town square—that served as a sort of community center for single males). Because of Sonoratown's proximity to the Civic Center, the land was much sought after as population density increased and city government grew. As the value of this downtown land escalated, government buildings impinged on Mexican living space, and eventually Sonoratown was bulldozed. As a result, much of the plaza population moved east of the Los Angeles River.[40]

By the late 1920s, five "little Mexicos" formed in Belvedere Park, Maravilla Park, Boyle Heights, Palo Verde, and Lincoln Heights—with fierce competition between the Protestant and Catholic churches for their souls. The urban poor in Los Angeles, as in San Antonio and other urban centers, put up with atrocious living conditions. Los Angeles's downtown white elite controlled city and county government and promoted an unregulated land boom that attracted industry and developed the agricultural resources of the region. It also brought in hundreds of thousands of Euro-Americans, crowding the Mexican population who lived in makeshift housing around the plaza. In 1912, a contemporary observer described the Sonoratown as a place populated by shacks, tents, and "nondescript barn-tenements of one and two rooms" often jammed with two or more families. The families occupying the housing shared the same toilet and water faucet in the rear of the courtyard. The city tore down many housing courts between 1906 and 1913, when the city council gave the Los Angeles Housing Commission the power of eminent domain.[41]

In the early 1920s, many Mexicans moved to the Belvedere–Maravilla area, about 4 miles east of the Civic Center, in the unincorporated portion of the county. About 30,000 Mexicans lived there by the end of the 1920s; in fact, Maravilla Park was almost 100 percent Mexican. Mexicans also occupied the crevices of Boyle Heights—once the home of a fashionable "American" community—between Sonoratown and Belvedere–Maravilla.[42]

Considerable intermarriage took place between Mexican immigrants, Mexican Americans, and Euro-Americans despite racial tensions,. Historian George J. Sánchez says that four-fifths of the Mexican immigrants who intermarried arrived before the age of 20. "Immigrants born in Mexico City were particularly likely to intermarry. In fact, the sample revealed that more immigrants from the Mexican capital married Anglo Americans in Los Angeles (38%) than married other Mexican immigrants (24%)." Intermarried couples were more likely to live outside the barrio. The number of children per family also varied according to class among families of Mexican descent: Mexican immigrant families averaged 3.17 children; Mexican/Mexican American, 2.71; and Mexican/Anglo, 1.3.[43]

The city also changed traditional husband–wife relations. Although it was uncommon, many Mexican women were working outside the home. The practical reason behind this trend was that during the 1920s many skilled workmen could afford housing in places like Brooklyn Heights or Lincoln Heights, but only with the added income of their wives, or in some cases with families pooling their resources. Significantly, Mexican-born women were more likely to be employed than were U.S.-born Chicanas. It was also common for a woman to work outside the home to make up for her husband's lost job or to improve the family's living conditions.

Poor housing and sanitation contributed to health problems. In Los Angeles, infant mortality among Mexicans was two-and-a-half times higher than that among Euro-Americans. Although Mexicans comprised one-tenth of the population, they made up one-fourth of the tuberculosis (TB) cases at city clinics. TB was one of the most dreaded diseases of the time. In 1924–1925, even though the city had exterminated over hundred thousand rats in the downtown barrio, plague hit Sonoratown. Thirty Mexicans died of pneumonic plague and five of bubonic plague.

The organizational life of Mexicans in Los Angeles resembled that of San Antonio, but it also differed. *Mutualistas*, as in San Antonio, met the immigrant families' "basic needs," such as maintaining their culture and when possible defending their civil rights. However, the *mutualistas* did not play the central role they did in San Antonio, partly because the Mexican-origin population of Los Angeles was widely scattered; also, proportionately San Antonio had a larger Mexican American population than did Los Angeles. The Mexican consul in Los Angeles played an influential role in establishing *mutualista*-like organizations, such as *La Cruz Azul* (the Blue Cross) for women and *La Comisión Honorífica* (the Honor Commission) for men. These organizations were engaged in charitable work under the consul's auspices.[44]

Many women's organizations were active during the 1920s. A group called *La Sociedad de Madres Mexicanas* was organized in Los Angeles in 1926 to help raise funds for the civil or criminal defense of Mexicans. *Las Madres* (The Mothers), or *Madrecitas* (Little Mothers), as they were called, supported cases that others ignored. One of their most noteworthy was that of Juan Reyna of Los Angeles. Police officers had called him a "dirty Mexican" and "you filthy Mexican" while dragging him off to jail. The officers' anger was provoked because Reyna disarmed them in a scuffle, shot and killed one officer, and wounded another before being subdued. Reyna was unrepentant and said he wished he'd killed all three for their racist insults. Reyna went through sensational trials, which the Mexican public attended, before he mysteriously died in prison. *Corridos* (folk ballads) immortalized him as a defender of his dignity.[45]

Another case was that of Aurelio Pompa, a Mexican immigrant, convicted in 1923 for killing a Euro-American in self-defense. Pompa's boss berated him daily and called him a dirty Mexican. When he was badly beaten up by his boss, an enraged Pompa went home to fetch a gun and returned to shoot the man. The defense committee hired Mexican American attorney Frank Domínguez to defend Pompa. *Mutualistas,* including *La Sociedad Melchor Ocampo* and other civic groups, supported Pompa, and they pressured the Mexican consul for support. Juan de Heras, editor of *El Heraldo,* led the movement to free Pompa. Supporters handed a petition with 12,915 signatures to Governor F. W. Richardson. Mexican President Alvaro Obregón, too, petitioned Richardson to save Pompa's life. Despite public pressure, however, the state executed Pompa. Years later, and throughout the author's childhood, his father and grandfather would tell and retell the story of Aurelio Pompa, whose body was repatriated to his native place in Sonora. As the story went, the train taking the coffin to its destination stopped in Los Angeles for several hours as thousands of Mexicans held vigil.[46]

A measure of Mexicans' Americanization was discernible as Mexicans became mass consumers. The automobile changed adolescents and youth overall. It enabled them to leave the confines of the barrio and to visit the downtown commercial center, and indulge in window-shopping, which became a favorite pastime. Youth became more fashion-conscious, going in for the latest in dresses. Euro-American entertainment had a tremendous impact—especially the motion pictures. One-third of the Mexican households owned a radio, which exposed them to American pop music. However, Spanish-language entertainment remained popular, and it had its place alongside Euro-American movies and music.[47]

Carpas (tent theaters) were the main entertainment providers throughout the nineteenth and into the twentieth century. Many troupes came from Mexico City, enacting classic as well as popular plays. These theaters kept alive the oral traditions of the people. Immigrants and the native-born were seated according to their class, with admission prices determining the seating arrangement of the audience. The *Teatro Calderón* and the *Teatro Progreso* were the most popular theaters in the Los Angeles area. There were smaller theaters as well, which were less expensive. The *California–El Teatro Digno de la Raza* was one of the 15 theaters that operated in or around Los Angeles. Plays were often based on current events—like the lynching of Francisco Torres in Santa Ana in 1891.[48] These theaters kept alive the cultural consciousness of the Spanish-speaking community. As a small child in the 1930s, the author sometimes accompanied his grandmother, and at other times his parents, to the California, the Orpheum, and the Million Dollar movie houses, where the *variedades* (variety shows) and the movies played side by side. Popcorn and ice cream vendors, tacos, hot dogs, and drinks also competed with the *variedades* and the movies for attention.

Mexicans in the Midwest and Points East

By the late 1920s, an estimated 58,000 Mexicans, comprising 4 percent of the Mexican population in the United States, lived in the Midwest. Chicago was the midwestern Mexican capital because it was a wintering quarter with service industries, stockyards, and factories. The 1910 Census showed 672 Mexicans in Illinois; 10 years later 1,224 Mexicans lived in Chicago alone and, by the end of the decade, almost 20,000 resided in the Windy City. Eighty-two percent of Mexicans in Chicago worked unskilled jobs.[49]

The bitter cold in winter made life in Chicago more severe than in the Southwest. As in other cities, in Chicago Mexicans clustered in barrios close to their workplace. They suffered the litany of abuses experienced by the poor, by now familiar to the reader: overcrowded housing, low-paying jobs, inadequate schooling, police harassment, and little hope for the future. Racism, too, was a problem to contend with: For instance, competing for limited housing, Mexicans paid $27 a month in rent; an Irish family paid $21 for the same accommodation. Socially, Euro-American Chicagoans segregated Mexicans. In East Chicago, two theater owners limited Mexicans to the African American section; and in Gary, Indiana, a section of the municipal cemetery was reserved for Mexicans. In addition, as elsewhere, the criminal justice system had little sympathy for Mexicans. In the mid-20s, at least seven Mexicans were being tried for murder in the first degree in the Midwest where the arrest rate was higher than in the Southwest. It is significant that California with a much larger Mexican population had four sentenced to die in San Quentin in 1926. One response was from the *mutualistas,* which, as in the Southwest, petitioned the help of the Mexican consul.[50]

In Davenport, Iowa, *El Trabajo* documented the networking and unity among Midwestern Mexicans. The paper reported support for José Ortiz Esquivel of Illinois, sentenced to die on June 12, 1925, for murdering his sweetheart. The Mexican community raised donations and successfully moved the court to postpone the execution date to June 24. Ortiz would have been the first man in Illinois in 15 years to be executed. *El Trabajo* implored its readers to fight against the double standard of justice for Mexicans and Euro-Americans. The newspaper equated the Ortiz case with Mexican deaths in the Southwest. Apparently, efforts of the Midwestern Mexican community were successful; the Illinois Supreme Court granted Ortiz a fresh trial.[51]

Midwestern Mexicans were nationalistic. When Euro-Americans complained that the rights of U.S. citizens were being violated in Mexico, *El Correo Mexicano,* a Chicago newspaper, on September 30, 1926, replied, "The *Chicago Tribune* and other North American papers, like the *Boston Transcript,* should not be scandalized when an American citizen in Mexico is attacked, not by the authorities, as here, but by bandits and highwaymen."[52] Pointing out that police in Chicago and other cities victimized Mexicans on a daily basis, the *Correo* ridiculed Euro-Americans for calling for immediate justice in Mexico.

In Chicago, police regularly arrested Mexicans for disorderly conduct; in 1928–1929 this charge consisted of almost 79 percent of all misdemeanor offenses. Another common booking in Chicago and in the rural Midwest was vagrancy. Polish police officers were especially brutal toward Mexicans and Mexican Americans. They looked upon Mexicans as competitors. A desk sergeant in 1925 readily admitted that he hated Mexicans, and that he had told officers at another station not to take chances with Mexicans: "[they] are quick on the knife and are hot tempered."[53] Many arrests used "dragnet" methods—that is, police made sweeps of streets and places like pool halls, arresting Mexicans for carrying a jackknife or on the usual charge of disorderly conduct. Poverty among Mexicans made getting justice difficult, if not impossible, since over three-quarters "did not have the money to hire a lawyer to defend them when they found themselves in trouble."[54] The quality of the defense attorney—when they could hire one—was generally poor, and the inability to speak English handicapped the defendant even further.

Settlement houses such as Chicago's Hull House were popular centers where Mexican families sought help in the form of educational and recreational services. These houses served as intermediaries between Mexicans and the municipal apparatus, including police, public health, and welfare agencies. Protestant missionaries made inroads among Chicago Mexicans; by the early 1930s, 23 percent of the active churchgoing Mexicans in the city were Protestants. The success of Protestants at converting Mexicans can be attributed to their offering of social services, legal aid, medical assistance, classes in English, and other forms of aid. The Masons also sponsored three Mexican lodges. In addition, Mexican Americans established societies to aid their poor. In 1924 in St. Paul, Minnesota, Luis Garzán and friends formed the *Anahuac* Society to sponsor dances to raise money for the needy.[55]

Though church attendance among Catholic Mexicans was low, it is impossible to overestimate the importance of the Catholic Church for Mexicans. For instance, in South Chicago the congregating center for Mexican Catholics was Our Lady of Guadalupe Chapel, built for Mexican workers by the Inland Steel Company. Apart from providing religious space, the Catholic Church gave Mexicans important social space. The Church was especially important to Mexican families. However, many Catholic parishes were racist and discouraged Mexicans from attending their services. In the Back of the Yards section in Chicago (close to the railroad and stockyards), Poles and Irish—adamantly anti-Mexican—discouraged Mexicans from attending their churches. In 1928 in the Near West Side of Chicago (not too far from Back of the Yards), after the parishioners excluded Mexicans from Polish and Slavic Catholic parishes, Mexicans took over the Italian parish of St. Francis and made it the center for Mexican Catholics. The Church's importance grew during this decade as more married couples put down roots in Chicago.[56]

Life for Mexican women was difficult in the Midwest. They were a minority within a minority, and their employment opportunities outside the home were limited due to the surplus of female labor and by Mexican custom. In 1924, Mexicanas made up less than a third of the Mexican population; 11 years later, they comprised more than 50 percent, which suggests the formation of more permanent communities. During the 1920s, Mexican women in Chicago and other cities of the Midwest often relied heavily on their own institutions, such as midwives to deliver children. Mexican women supplemented their family's income with most working as domestics; a large number also took in lodgers. The cold winters were an added burden: warm clothing and heating were expensive, and respiratory diseases were common. Life was precarious at best: that there were few women made them targets for unwanted sexual advances, and they were vulnerable to abuse. They lacked support networks that cushioned the effects of spousal abuse and alcoholism, which were much too common within immigrant communities.

As in San Antonio and Los Angeles, in Chicago the *mutualistas* were a vehicle for self-help and cultural enrichment. Mexican workers in South Chicago formed *La Sociedad Mutualista de Obreros Libres Mexicanos* (Mutual Aid Society of Independent Mexican Workers), which, among other things, funded a Mexican band to play popular Mexican music. In cities like Chicago, Mexican workers were also exposed to more militant forms of trade union organizing. As with the Irish, the Church hierarchy opposed militant unionism for Mexicans. The U.S. Catholic Church, conditioned by the *cristero* (Followers of Christ, or Christ Firsters) revolt in Mexico during the 1920s, became even more conservative. (The cristeros were militant Catholics who refused to accept the Mexican government's attempts to end the Catholic Church's special privileges.)

Mexicans also moved to Detroit as early as 1918, when Henry Ford imported them to work in his Ford auto plants. Attracted by employment opportunities, more than 16,000 Mexicans migrated to that city during the 1920s. In 1923, Bethlehem Steel imported 948 Mexicans to Pennsylvania to work in its mills. To help the impoverished and the ill, Mexicans organized three beneficent associations in their small steel colony. In 1927, they founded *La Unión Protectora* (the Protective Union), which was later disbanded because Mexicans believed that noncitizens were not permitted to organize a union. They organized *La Sociedad Azteca Mexicana* (the Mexican Aztec Society) the next year; by 1930, it had 130 members. The organization also owned and operated a community hall.[57]

Mexican Labor in the 1920s

Where Mexicans moved and what type of work they did was determined by the economic and political changes of previous years. For example, improved transportation brought the increased industrialization of the Southwest—and, in turn, the growth of the region's cities and the mega growth of commercial agriculture. The Literacy Act of 1917 slowed European immigration, as did World War I, thus increasing the dependence on Mexican labor as demand for pick-and-shovel work grew.

Although many were moving to the cities, agriculture was still a major employer of Mexicans. The increased demand for Mexican labor also encouraged Mexican Americans from New Mexico, Texas, and elsewhere in the Southwest to migrate to other parts of the United States for agricultural and nonagricultural work. During the nineteenth and early twentieth centuries, Mexicans frequently settled in enclaves that had previously housed large numbers of European immigrants. This often led to clashes with the European ethnic groups, who considered them competitors in the workplace and housing market. The city, however, offered positive experiences. Older workers socialized the more recent arrivals and in a sense contributed to building their political vocabulary. In fact, Mexican immigrants often participated in workers' strike actions. Cities also provided Mexican-origin children more opportunity to attend school.

With the spread of factory farms and the mega production of crops such as cotton, demand for migrant labor soared; between 1918 and 1921, the Arizona Cotton Growers Association (ACGA) imported over 30,000 Mexicans. Meanwhile, mine owners displaced many Mexican miners, some of whom then became farmworkers. The displaced miners brought with them collective memories of the militant mining strikes that occurred during the first two decades of the century.

Although highly industrialized, the factory farms resembled the old haciendas, where forced-labor systems such as the *repartimiento* would deliver Native Mexicans to the *mayordomo*. Under the new system, contractors delivered Mexicans to the growers. Abuse was rampant. In 1919, *La Liga Protectora Latina* of Arizona filed charges of bullying and abuse of Mexican workers against Rafael Estrada, a labor contractor for cotton growers in Arizona. The Arizona Federation of Labor organized cotton pickers in the Salt River Valley. Growers combatted these organizational drives by deporting Mexicans as soon as they complained of low wages and breaches of contract. This caused hardships: Apolino Cruz was picked up for deportation, and his 8-year-old son was left on a ditch bank. Friends later took the boy to Tempe, and the ACGA sent him unescorted to Mexico.[58]

The farming operations were huge. In the Salt River Valley temperatures often reached well above 100 degrees. Some 12,000–15,000 Mexicans could be found, housed in tents. This population was larger than that of the mining camps—and had even worse facilities. Mexican workers were often deported before they were paid. The U.S. Justice Department and local authorities routinely sided with the ACGA in these employer–worker disputes. The Arizona State Federation of Labor attempted mostly in Maricopa County to organize farmworkers but with limited success. Despite the barriers, by 1921 the federation had formed 14 federal unions, averaging 300–400 members per local. But with the recession of 1920–1921, the bottom fell out of the market and thousands of Mexicans were stranded in the desert. With no job market, within a year the locals fell apart.[59]

Importance of the Sugar Beet Industry

Reclamation projects stimulated the growth of sugar beet and cotton production. These crops, valued at $28,043,322 in 1928, represented 34.6 percent of all crops produced by the four reclamation projects in the Southwest; Mexicans comprised 65 percent of the common labor in these areas. Most of the beet workers came by way of Texas, spreading out to the rest of the southwestern fields and then throughout the Midwest. The seasonal nature of the work encouraged dispersion as well as urbanization, as many workers migrated to cities in search of work or shelter during the winter months.[60] Labor contractors, who further depressed the already low wages by oversupplying growers with workers, furnished most Mexican labor.

There was a division of labor. Whites planted, irrigated, and cultivated, while Mexicans did the heavier work of weeding, hoeing, thinning, and topping. Company stores charged workers exorbitant prices. Beet workers formed small *mutualistas* to help cope with these inequalities. Best known among them was *La Sociedad de Obreros Libres* (Free Workers Society) of Gilcrest, Colorado. A chapter of the *Alianza Hispano-Americana* (Hispano-American Alliance) was organized in the beet fields around Brighton, Colorado, and Cheyenne, Wyoming. The IWW also formed the Agricultural Workers Industrial Union Local 110, but it had limited success because Colorado authorities intimidated workers, and state troopers were deployed in the fields to discourage strike activity. Beet workers demanded improved housing, clean drinking water, sanitary facilities, and payment of wages at a guaranteed rate. Although management responded that the demands were reasonable, they did nothing. The local Knights of Columbus subverted workers' efforts by labeling their actions as "red socialist menace." These strike actions added to the political vocabulary of Mexican workers, who retold these experiences to others, raising workers' political consciousness.

Colorado refined one-fourth of all sugar processed in the United States. Until World War I, east-central European immigrants did most of the manual labor associated with sugar beet production; however, the 1921 and 1924 immigration acts limited access to European labor. The Great Western Sugar Company of northern Colorado relentlessly recruited labor and, after the passage of the 1917 Literacy Act, the company saw Mexican labor as essential to its prosperity. The New Mexican villages had contributed workers to Colorado since the turn of the century and they served as a reserve labor pool for the sugar companies, which were able to cut their labor costs because of the companies' proximity to New Mexico. Employment agents recruited Mexicans (and New Mexicans) to do the backbreaking work. The railroads, too, hired Mexicans; an estimated 5,000 Mexicans worked on the maintenance crews within the state of Colorado. Mines and other industries requiring cheap labor also hired Mexicans.[61]

In Colorado, Mexicans often lived in small, isolated clusters of two to eight families. Some moved to the cities, where the increased numbers of Mexicans triggered nativism—for instance, the Ku Klux Klan was active in Walsenburg.[62] As the Mexican and New Mexican communities became more socialized by the workplace, they struggled to improve their quality of life by campaigning for equal treatment of Mexicans. By 1925, almost two-thirds of the Chicano children were three years behind white students in grade level. The Mexican and New Mexican community protested school segregation, but with little success. In 1927, Mexicans filed a civil rights case against restaurant proprietors in Greeley for denying them service. In the same year Chicanos called successful boycotts in Greeley and Johnstown, demanding that pejorative window signs be taken down. "White Trade Only" signs were common, and Euro-Americans spoke about the "Mexican invasion." The Mexicans fought back and protested against increased Ku Klux Klan activity.

For women in Colorado, the loss of the family network they enjoyed in New Mexico resulted in a life of isolation and loneliness. Villagers often migrated to southern Colorado, seeking seasonal employment there and returning home in time to harvest their crops. The histories of these two states are intertwined, and the migration affected the lives of the manitos that often came to Colorado and left behind their families. Back home, the New Mexican women commonly maintained their homes and a small garden, and took care of their farms as well. In great part, however, the New Mexican families could not withstand competition from commercial farmers and stock raisers, and many New Mexicans were forced to sell or lose their holdings. Thus, families soon followed their menfolk to Colorado, where they were employed primarily in the sugar beet industry, mining, and railroad work. Over half of the newly arrived women went to work in the beet fields.[63]

Mexicans in the Northwest

The Mexican community also grew in Utah, where they worked for the railroads, in mines, and on farms. At the beginning of the 1920s, 1,200 Mexicans lived in Utah; 10 years later the number grew to more than 4,000. Juan Ramón Martínez, a native of New Mexico, founded the Provisional Lamanite Branch of the Church of the Latter-Day Saints (Mormons) in 1921. The mid-1920s saw the formation of the usual *mutualistas*, along with Mexican protective associations such as *La Cruz Azul* (the Blue Cross, a Mexican government self-help group). Mexicans also regularly celebrated *Cinco de Mayo* (Fifth of May) and other Mexican holidays. By 1930, Mexicans had established Our Lady of Guadalupe Church as a mission in Utah.

Small numbers of Mexicans also lived in Idaho, Washington, and Oregon in the 1920s. Mexicans had individually moved to these states before World War I. After the war, sugar beet companies imported Mexicans to Idaho. By the 1920s decade, families made up a significant portion of the immigration; men, however, still comprised 65–70 percent of immigrants—even though women may have joined the males by entering without documents to avoid crossing fees. By the late 1920s, increasing numbers of Mexicans worked on railroad maintenance crews in the region. As agriculture became more labor intensive, the industry also attracted more Mexicans to Oregon and Washington.[64]

Mexican Workers in Texas

Differentials in pay rates played a big part in geographic dispersion. For instance, in Texas a cotton picker averaged $1.75 a day; in Arizona, $2.75; in California, $3.25; and—ironically, considering they were former slave states—in Arkansas, Louisiana, and Mississippi, $4. One reason Texas growers kept wages low was their belief that lower wages would limit the resources of Mexicans, making it more difficult for them to leave. Texas growers shared the obsession of California and Arizona growers with creating and controlling a large surplus labor pool. Texas relied heavily on migrant labor, much of which it recruited directly from Mexico.[65]

Because Texas Mexicans were mostly landless and dependent on wages, they were especially vulnerable to exploitation. A form of debt peonage existed: local sheriffs arrested Mexicans by enforcing vagrancy laws and then contracted the arrested workers to local farmers. Law enforcement officials deceived Mexicans into believing that they would face imprisonment if they left without paying commissary debts. Cotton growers also tried to hold on to Mexican workers by restraining the recruitment drives of northern sugar beet companies. Labor contractors from Michigan and northern Ohio alone hired about 10,000 Texas Mexicans each year. The Texas legislature passed a law, in effect until the 1940s, that limited the ability of labor contractors to recruit Mexican workers in the Lone Star State.[66]

Mexican Workers in the Midwest

Better pay and opportunities made migration from Texas into the Midwest attractive. Labor contractors, who distributed workers to various industries and farms, recruited many of the migrants to this region. Initially, many of the Mexicans worked on the railroads and farms before jumping off into the cities. The railroads paid Mexicans the lowest industrial salaries: 35¢–39¢ an hour. In the 1920s, Mexicans comprised 40 percent of the total railroad maintenance crews of Chicago. Packing houses paid workers 45¢–47¢ an hour, while in steel factories they earned 45¢–50¢ an hour for 8-hour or 44¢ an hour for 10-hour workdays. These salaries were much higher than those in the Southwest and in agriculture in general, but more important was the year-round employment offered in the city. However, even with higher pay, two-thirds of Mexicans in Chicago earned less than $100 a month, which was considered below the poverty line.

Not one steel plant in the Midwest employed a supervisor of Mexican extraction. Rank-and-file Euro-American workers openly practiced racism toward Mexican workers. Unions excluded Chicanos from building trades, which generally required citizenship for union membership. The American Federation of Railroad Workers did not have a single Mexican tradesman. Organized labor continued to stereotype Mexicans as wage cutters. Other ethnic groups as well were antagonistic toward Mexicans. Factory tensions carried over into the streets, and many neighborhoods would not rent houses to Mexicans.

The Mexican population suffered a temporary setback in 1920–1921; as in the Southwest, many Mexicans were repatriated as a consequence of a deep economic recession. The situation improved as the railroads and steel mills employed more Mexican workers. As agriculture recovered, the number of Mexican farmworkers swelled the population during the picking season. The labor bonanza of the sugar beet industry drew thousands of migrants. In Ohio, Indiana, Michigan, Wisconsin, and Illinois, the Mexican community grew from 7,583 in 1920 to 58,317 ten years later. By the end of the decade, Midwest Mexicans were more urbanized (from just under 70 percent to some 88 percent). Nationwide, by 1930, 40.5 percent of the Mexican males were employed in agriculture, 26 percent in manufacturing, and 16.3 percent in transportation.[67]

The Growth of California Agribusiness

California housed "farm factories"; its climate allowed year-round production. In many places, the federal government made available water at below-cost levels, facilitating the irrigation of vast areas, and the state could boast of 118 distinct types of farms producing 214 different agricultural products. Growers created exchanges that recruited an oversupply of labor and concentrated production and distribution. They formed organizations such as the Valley Fruit Growers of San Joaquin County, the Sun-Maid Raisin Growers Association (which included 75–90 percent of the raisin farmers), the Western Growers Protective Association, and the California Growers Exchange, to name just a few. The San Joaquin Valley Agriculture Labor Bureau was founded in 1925. The organization consisted of six county farm bureaus, six county Chambers of Commerce, and countless raisin, fresh fruit, and cotton operations. Its job was to maximize profit by developing a pool of surplus labor that could be hired at the lowest possible rate.

Mechanization displaced many year-round farmworkers and increased the dependence on temporary migrant labor (read *Mexicans*), since more production meant a demand for larger labor pools at harvest time. U.S. farms were mechanizing at an unprecedented rate. Furthermore, mechanization made it possible to cultivate more land. From 1920 to 1930, the number of Mexicans in agriculture tripled, increasing from 121,176 to 368,013. Also, as machines displaced animals, growers could turn land used for feed to cash crops, further increasing the demand for labor.[68]

The Formation of Mexican Unions

In 1928, as Paul S. Taylor describes it,

> *One-third of Imperial Valley is Mexican. Changing rapidly from desert in 1900 to an area of intensive agriculture, the valley has met its expanding labor needs largely with immigrants from*

across our southern border. … In this valley, a world to itself, isolated, yet an integral part of the agricultural Southwest, the Mexican is now inextricably a part of the social and economic life of the community.[69]

The earliest Mexican workers came as track laborers. By 1910, there were Mexican colonies in the Imperial Valley and El Centro areas of southern California. As the demand for workers in cantaloupe, lettuce, and cotton grew, so did the demand for Mexicans. Meanwhile, driven largely by cotton, the influx of southern whites and blacks continued. By 1916, this "southern help" was migrating to the San Joaquin Valley, which coincided with the growth of cotton production there. Growers turned more seriously to Mexico after 1917, when sugar beet growers recruited large numbers of Mexicans. By the turn of the decade, Mexicans became the dominant workforce, their concentration depending on the crops. At harvest time, Mexicans composed 90 percent of field workers in the Imperial Valley.

The presence of the corporate farms led to the development of gigantic labor pools, which allowed many workers to stay in the same place for longer than was possible earlier, and often to become permanent residents. The involvement of Mexicans in mining before World War I expanded the corps of proletariat workers. Thousands of Mexican miners in Arizona alone, where Mexicans comprised nearly half of the miners in the state, had participated in the intense strikes of the 1910s. These strikes gave organizational experience to a core of Mexican workers who continued to organize in mining and other industries. The Mexican Revolution and the formation of national labor organizations such as *La Confederación Regional Obrera Mexicana* (CROM; Federation of Regional Mexican Workers) also offered some direction. Despite this proven interest by Mexicans in collectively confronting capitalist inequities, American labor unions progressed little on the Mexican question, especially regarding Mexican immigrants.[70]

This is not to say that the American Federation of Labor (AFL) was oblivious to the needs of Mexican workers. In 1927, it sent Clemente N. Idar to organize beet workers. In the next two-and-a-half years, Idar traveled Colorado, Nebraska, and Wyoming. In 1929, he was able to put together a labor front consisting of the AFL, the IWW, the communists, and the various Mexican unions. Under Idar's leadership, the Beet Workers Association stayed together. However, when Idar took ill and had to leave, the association fell apart.[71]

California farmworkers' organizing efforts faced overwhelming opposition by agribusiness owners. Undoubtedly, many small Mexican labor unions existed; however, they were short lived because of the Mexicans' vulnerability to deportation and the willingness of U.S. capitalists to do anything to disorganize labor—for example, making even membership in the IWW illegal. In times of labor tensions, agribusiness used immigration authorities to comb Mexican *colonias:* Mexicans were vulnerable because some 80 percent had no documents. The most powerful growers' association, the American Farm Bureau Federation (AFBF), united farmers nationally. It also had local and state chapters that were linked to chambers of commerce; the American Legion; the National Association of Manufacturers; and local, state, and federal elected officials and law enforcement.[72]

Like the industry associations, labor contractors, who managed work crews, also controlled the lives of workers. Growers paid the contractors, who in turn paid workers after subtracting their fee from each worker's earnings. Contractors withheld the first week's wages until the end of the harvest. Many workers complained that contractors often absconded with their money.[73]

In November 1927 the Federation of Mexican Societies, mostly *mutualistas*, met in Los Angeles with the express purpose of encouraging members to support trade unionism by financing their organizational efforts. In March, they formed *La Confederación de Uniónes de Campesinos y Obreros Mexicanos* (CUCOM; Federation of Mexican Workers Unions). Meanwhile, with the assistance of the Mexican consul, *mutualista* leaders formed *La Unión de Trabajadores del Valle Imperial* (the Imperial Valley Workers' Union).

In early May, the newly formed union sent cantaloupe growers and the chambers of commerce in Brawley and El Centro letters requesting that wages be increased to 15¢ per standard crate of cantaloupes, or 75¢ an hour; that growers supply free picking sacks and ice; and that growers, not the contractors, be responsible for paying workers' wages. The growers refused. On May 7 workers at the Sears Brothers Ranch walked out. Soon, 2,000–3,000 workers joined the strike. On May 10, Sheriff Charles L. Gillett shut down the union's offices, outlawed all future strikes, and arrested more than 60 union activists. Local newspapers, public opinion, and local politicos supported the get-tough tactics of Sheriff Gillett.[74]

Greasers Go Home

As mentioned above, in early 1921 the bottom fell out of the economy and a depression caused heavy unemployment. Sarah Deutsch estimates that some 150,000 Mexicans were repatriated during the crisis. Although as a matter of policy the Mexican government welcomed back repatriates, the sudden return of so many to the homeland caught the government off guard. In essence, the Mexican government could not afford the expense of the repatriation.[75] Mexico was offended by the affront to its citizens and the obvious callousness with which deportations were carried out—an insult to the nation's revolutionary nationalism. Literally, many Mexicans were cheated out of their wages and dumped across the border. *El Universal* of Mexico City on March 5, 1921, reported, "When they arrived at Phoenix a party of Mexican workers were taken to Tempe and introduced to a concentration camp that looks like a dung-heap." According to this source, the men were chained and put into work gangs. Similar abuses were reported in Kansas City, Chicago, and Colorado.[76]

In Fort Worth, Texas, 90 percent of 12,000 Mexicans became unemployed; whites threatened to burn the Mexicans' homes and rid the city of "cheap Mexican labor." Police authorities escorted truckloads of Mexicans to Texas chain gangs. In Ranger, Texas, terrorists dragged 100 Mexican men, women, and children from their tents and makeshift homes, beat them up, and ordered them to clear out of town. In Chicago, employment of Mexicans shrank by two-thirds between 1920 and 1921; police made frequent raids and strictly enforced vagrancy laws in the Windy City. Chicago Mayor William Hall Thompson allocated funds to ship several hundred families back to the border. A *Denver Post* headline claimed, "Denver Safety Is Menaced by 3,500 Starving Mexicans"; authorities shipped Mexican workers en masse from the Denver area to the border. Although U.S. corporations and farmers had recruited these workers to the United States in the first place, they and the U.S. government did little to relieve their suffering. The Mexican government, by contrast, spent $2.5 million to aid stranded Mexicans.[77] Many workers would have starved to death had it not been for the financial assistance sanctioned by Mexican President Alvaro Obregón.

Keeping America Blond and White

Euro-Americans wanted to keep America "American" by ensuring a Nordic look. After years of debate over keeping the United States an Aryan nation, Congress passed the Emergency Quota Act of 1921, which limited the annual number of immigrants who could be admitted from any country to 3 percent of the number of persons from that country living in the United States in 1910. The total number to be admitted under the 1921 quota was 357,802 people. Of that number, just over half was allocated for northern and western Europeans and the remainder for eastern and southern Europeans. The Immigration Act of 1924, also known as the National Origins Act or the Johnson–Reed Act, then limited the number of immigrants who could be admitted from any country to 2 percent of the number of persons from that country who were already living in the United States in 1890. The law was aimed at further restricting southern and eastern Europeans, limiting their number to 164,000 annually, as well as East Asians and Asian Indians, who were excluded entirely. President Calvin Coolidge, when signing the bill into law, said, "America must be kept American," and the law ushered in generations of racial engineering. The quotas drastically reduced the flow of immigrants from southeastern Europe, since they were a relatively small percentage of new arrivals in the United States in the late 1800s. However, the act set no limits on immigrants from Latin America; their presence was necessary to the functioning of the Southwest's economy.

The act started a battle between the restrictionists, who wanted to keep the country WASP (white Anglo-Saxon Protestant) and felt that too many foreigners would subvert the "American way of life," and the capitalists, who set aside prejudices toward Mexicans because they needed cheap labor. Many of the growers recalled that the 1917 act had initially restricted the flow of Mexican immigrants, creating a severe labor shortage that hurt them financially; thus, the western growers opposed any restrictions on the free flow of Mexicans into the United States. By 1923, the economy had sufficiently recovered to again entice Mexican workers to the United States in large numbers. How many of these were undocumented is difficult to estimate.

In 1924, Congress debated putting Mexicans on the quota. Albert Johnson of Washington, chair of the House Immigration and Naturalization Committee and sponsor of the bill, bluntly stated that the committee did not restrict Mexicans because it did not want to hinder the passage of the 1924 Immigration Act. Johnson promised that the committee would sponsor another bill to create a border patrol to enforce existing laws, and he claimed that a quota alone would not be effective. Antirestrictionists responded that enforcing such a quota would be difficult, that Mexicans stayed only temporarily anyway, that they did the work white men would not, and that an economic burden would result. In order to compensate, border officials strictly applied the $8 head tax, in addition to the $10 visa fee. However, Mexicans continued to enter the States with and without documents. Meanwhile, Johnson's committee began hearings on the Mexican problem.[78]

In 1926, the commissioner wrote that 855,898 Mexicans had entered with documents and predicted, "It is safe to say that over a million Mexicans are in the United States at the present time [including undocumented], and under present laws this number may be added to practically without limit."[79] Congressman John Box introduced a bill that would apply quota provisions to the whole of the Western Hemisphere. Representative Robert L. Bacon (New York) sought to limit the extension of the quota system only to Mexico. Western representatives opposed any attempt to restrict Mexicans. S. Parker Frieselle of California stated that while he did not want Mexicans to become part of the race stock of California, Mexican labor was necessary, and for him there was simply no other alternative available.[80]

Meanwhile, Secretary of Labor James J. Davis called for a quota for the Western Hemisphere. Secretary Davis arranged meetings with Samuel Gompers, head of the AFL, to plan a strategy to remove the Mexican "menace." Representative Martin Madden of Chicago, Chairman of the House Appropriations Committee, stated,

> The bill opens the doors for perhaps the worst element that comes into the United States—the Mexican peon. . . . [It] opens the door wide and unrestricted to the most undesirable people who come under the flag.[81]

In the Senate, Frank B. Willis of Ohio echoed restrictionist sentiment: "Many of [them] . . . now coming in are, unfortunately, practically without education, and largely without experience in self-government, and in most cases not at all qualified for present citizenship or for assimilation into this country." Senator Matthew M. Neeley of West Virginia charged, "On the basis of merit, Mexico is the last country we should grant a special favor or extend a peculiar privilege. ... The immigrants from many of the countries of Europe have more in common with us than the Mexicanos have."[82] On the other hand, Representative John Nance Garner of Texas emphasized that Mexicans did not pose a problem because they returned home after every picking season:

> All they want is a month's labor in the United States, and that is enough to support them in Mexico for six months. ... In our country they do not cause any trouble, unless they stay there a long time and become Americanized; but they are a docile people. They can be imposed on; the sheriff can go out and make them do anything.[83]

Congressman John Calvin Box (D-Texas) candidly accused opponents of his bill of attempting to attract "floating Mexican *peons*" in order to exploit them, underscoring, "They are objectionable as citizens and as residents."[84] During committee hearings, Box asked a farmer whether what he really wanted was a subservient class of Mexican workers "who do not want to own land, who can be directed by men in the upper stratum of society." The farmer answered, "I believe that is about it." Box then asked, "Now, do you believe that is good Americanism?" The farmer replied, "I think it is necessary Americanism to preserve Americanism."[85] The quota act had drastically reduced the available labor pool, and agricultural and industrial interests committed themselves to keeping the Mexican unrestricted.

In 1928, a clear split developed between the Department of Labor, which favored putting Mexicans on a quota system, and the Department of State, which opposed it. The State Department knew that it would seriously weaken its negotiations with Latin America and endanger trade treaties and privileges that furthered U.S. interests. Latin Americans were sensitive to American racism. The State Department joined southwestern industrialists to kill restrictionist proposals. However, many congressmen were not satisfied and pushed for quantitative restrictions. Euro-American labor supported the restrictionists, asking, "Do you want a mongrel population, consisting largely of Mexicans?"[86]

Conclusion: Moving to the City

Subtle changes had taken place during the decade. In the 1920 U.S. Census, Mexicans had been listed as white; 10 years later, census takers listed the race for the same person as Mexican, which, according to the standards of the times, demarcated Mexicans even more from Euro-Americans. This loss in status would not go unnoticed by Mexican Americans. Other subtle changes occurred, such as listing the same person as "Pedro" in 1920 and "Pete" in 1930, and changing "Francisco" to "Frank" and "Miguel" to "Mike." Such changes, though not universal, were frequent enough to be noted.

Americanization was having an impact on the second generation; more students were confused about their identity. All in all, however, it was the city and its bright lights and material symbols that caused the greatest changes. Like the ceremonial and trade centers of pre-Columbian times, the urban centers integrated the surrounding enclaves. Increasingly Mexicans, like other residents of the country, traveled to the downtown areas where many would seek out an escape from the drudgery of work. It was not only the radio, the music, and the silent films that intruded into their lives, subtly Americanizing them; downtown was a place where even the penniless could walk and admire the window displays of the department stores that featured material goods such as clothing and household items. The subliminal message was that the goods were available to anyone, *if* they became American.

Notes

1. The Alien and Sedition Acts of 1798 from Folwell's "Laws of the U.S.," Archiving Early America, http://www.earlyamerica.com/earlyamerica/milestones/sedition/.

2. The Russian Revolution, http://www.barnsdle.demon.co.uk/russ/rusrev.html,http://www.youtube.com/watch?v=-2WrBC-3Qlk.

3. [Quote] Irving Bernstein, *History of the American Worker 1920–1933: The Lean Years* (Boston: Houghton-Mifflin, 1960), 47–50. Gilbert G. González, *Chicano Education in the Era of Segregation* (Philadelphia, PA: Balch Institute Press, 1990), 19. Juan Gómez-Quiñones, *Mexican American Labor 1790–1990* (Albuquerque: University of New Mexico Press, 1994), 101.

4. Chapter VII, War and Repression 1900–1930, Social Work History Station, http://www.socialworkhistorystation.org/US/chapters/CHAPTER%207.htm. Historical Census Statistics on the Foreign-Born Population of the United States: 1850 to 1990, http://www.census.gov/population/www/documentation/twps0029/twps0029.html. Trinidad Gonzales, "The World of Mexico Texanos, Mexicanos and Mexico Americanos: Transnational and National Identities in the Lower Rio Grande River Valley, During the Last Phase of United States Colonization, 1900–1930" (PhD dissertation, University of Houston, 2008), does a good job tracing generational changes in this small confined area.

5. George J. Sánchez, *Becoming Mexican American: Ethnicity, Culture and Identity in Chicano Los Angeles,* *1900–1945* (New York: Oxford University Press, 1993), 91, 97, 99, 101, 102, 155. Frederick C. Millett, Americanization, http://uscourse.wikispaces.com/How+the+USA+influences+the+world. The model for Americanization was the earlier efforts to remake the Native American. See Americanization (of Native Americans), BookRags.Com, http://www.bookrags.com/studyguide-native-roots/chapanal005.html. Theodore Roosevelt, "True Americanism," *The Forum* (April 1894), http://www.theodore-roosevelt.com/images/research/speeches/trta.pdf. Rodolfo F. Acuña and Guadalupe Compeán, eds., *Voices of the U.S. Latino Experience*, Vol. 2, (Westport, CT: Greenwood, 2008), 468–75. M. Glancy, "Temporary American Citizens? British Audiences, Hollywood Films and the Threat of Americanization in the 1920s," *Historical Journal of Film Radio and Television* 26, no. 4 (2006): 461–84.

6. R. G. Price, "Fascism Part II: The Rise of American Fascism" (May 15, 2004), http://rationalrevolution.net/articles/rise_of_american_fascism.htm. The article points out the extremes that the Americanization programs went to.

7. G. González, *Chicano Education in the Era of Segregation,* 13, 20–21, 36, 41, 46, 67, 77. Gilbert G. González, "Chicano Education History: A Legacy of Inequality," *Humboldt Journal of Social Relations* 22, no. 1 (1996): 43–56. Gilbert G. González, *Labor and Community, Mexican Citrus Worker Villages in a Southern California County, 1900–1950* (Urbana: University of Illinois Press, 1994), 99–134.

8. Sánchez, George Isidore (1906–1972), Handbook of Texas Online, http://www.tshaonline.org/handbook/online/articles/SS/fsa20.html. George Isidore Sánchez Papers, http://www.lib.utexas.edu/photodraw/sanchez/.

9. Richard R. Valencia, *Chicano Students and the Courts: The Mexican American Legal Struggle for Educational Equality* (New York: New York University Press, 2008), 14–15. Meyer Weinberg, *A Chance to Learn: A History of Race and Education in the United States* (New York: Cambridge University Press, 1977), 145–65. An excellent article on the abuse of testing is Miroslava Chávez-García, "Intelligence Testing at Whittier School, 1890–1920," *Pacific Historical Review* 76, no. 2 (May 2007): 193–228. Laura K. Muñoz, "Separate But Equal? A Case Study of *Romo v. Laird* and Mexican American Education," http://www.slideshare.net/greenje/mexican-americans-presentation.

10. Sánchez, *Becoming Mexican American*, 255. Ernestine M. Alvarado, "A Plea for Mutual Understanding between Mexican Immigrants and Native Americans," 1920 annual session of the National Conference of Social Work (1920), 264–66 (Protestant sponsored). Lina E. Bresette, *Mexicans in the United States: A Report of a Brief Survey* (Washington, DC: Social Action Department, National Catholic Welfare Conference, 1929), iii, 16, 17, 19. Robert N. McLean and Charles A. Thompson, *Spanish and Mexican in Colorado: A Survey of the Spanish Americans and Mexicans in the State of Colorado* (New York: Board of National Missions, Presbyterian Church in the U.S.A., 1924), vii–x, reprinted in Carlos E. Cortés, ed., *Church Views of the Mexican American* (New York: Arno Press, 1974), ix, x, 17. Ernesto Galarza, "Life in the United States for Mexican People: Out of the Experience of a Mexican," Proceedings of the National Conference of Social Work, 56th Annual Session, University of Chicago Press, 1929, excepts in Digital History, http://www.digitalhistory.uh.edu/disp_textbook.cfm?smtID=3&psid=592. Paul Barton, *Hispanic Methodists, Presbyterians, and Baptists in Texas* (Austin: University of Texas Press, 2006), 12–14, 47 points out that members of Pancho Villa's family attended the Baptist Church in San Antonio.

11. Robert McLean and Grace Petrie Williams, *Old Spain in New America* (New York: Council of Women for Home Missions, 1916), 155–56. Guadalupe San Miguel, Jr., "Culture and Education in the American Southwest: Towards an Explanation of Chicano School Attendance," *Journal of American Ethnic History* 7, no.2 (Spring, 1988): 6, 9. "Spanish American Institute, 1913–1971 Service to Boys," Distributed as pamphlet on May 30, 1971, Courtesy of Professor Everto Ruiz, California State University, Northridge.

12. Sánchez, *Becoming Mexican American*, 151–69. Anthony M. Stevens-Arroyo, "Pious Colonialism: Assessing the Church Paradigm for Chicano Identity," in Gastón Espinosa and Mario T. García, eds., *Mexican American Religions: Spirituality, Activism, and Culture* (Durham, NC: Duke University Press, 2008), 71–75. Lucey, Robert Emmet (1891–1977), Handbook of Texas Online, http://www.tshaonline.org/handbook/online/articles/LL/flu14.html.

13. Sánchez, *Becoming Mexican American,* 114–20. Unfortunately, much of the curriculum was nationalist in content, and the method followed had the positivist bent of the porfiriato and continued with a *científico* (scientist) positivist view of Mexico. Bilingual Education. Handbook of Texas Online, http://www.tshaonline.org/handbook/online/articles/BB/khb2.html. Francisco Arturo Rosales, *Chicano!: The History of the Mexican American Civil Rights Movement*, Revised ed. (Houston, TX: Arte Público Press, 1997), 81.

14. Lee Stacy, *Mexico and the United States* (Tarrytown, NY: Marshall Cavendish Corporation, 2002), 48–49.

15. David G. Gutiérrez, *Walls and Mirrors: Mexican Americans, Mexican Immigrants and the Politics of Ethnicity* (Berkeley: University of California Press, 1995). Many of the political exiles had been supporters of Porfirio Díaz; they allied themselves with the Catholic Church and lobbied for U.S. intervention in Mexico. The Cristero Movement in central-western Mexico (1926–1929) motivated yet another migration to *el norte*. Many of its adherents came to the United States and carried on anti-Mexican government activities there. A Growing Community, Immigration, The Library of Congress, http://www.loc.gov/teachers/classroommaterials/presentationsandactivities/presentations/immigration/alt/mexican4.html. Cristero Rebellion (1926–1929), Latin American Studies, www.latinamericanstudies.org/cristero.htm.

16. *Pocho* literally means "Mexican Americans who do not speak Spanish, or mix it with English." Also refers to those who have adopted Euro-American customs and dress.

17. Steven Bender, *Greasers and Gringos: Latinos, Law, and the American Imagination* (New York: New York University Press, 2003), xiii–xiv. Arnoldo De León, *They Called Them Greasers: Anglo Attitudes Toward Mexicans in Texas, 1821–1900* (Austin: University of Texas Press, 1983), Preface.

18. Lisbeth Haas, *Conquests and Historical Identities in California, 1769–1936* (Berkeley: University of California Press, 1995), 118–20, 124. Thomas E. Sheridan, *Los Tucsonenses: The Mexican Community in Tucson, 1854–1941* (Tucson: University of Arizona Press, 1986).

19. Cynthia E. Orozco, "The Origins of the League of United Latin American Citizens (LULAC) and the Mexican American Civil Rights Movement in Texas with an Analysis of Women's Political Participation in a Gendered Context, 1910–1929" (PhD dissertation, University of California, Los Angeles, 1992). Cynthia E. Orozco, *No Mexicans, Women, or Dogs Allowed: The Rise of the Mexican American Civil Rights Movement* (Austin: University of Texas at Austin, 2009).

20. Julie Leininger Pycior, "*La Raza* Organizes: Mexican American Life in San Antonio, 1915–1930, as Reflected in Mutualista Activities" (PhD dissertation, University of Notre Dame, 1979), 83, 97–98, 105. José de la Luz Sáenz Papers, 1908–1998, Texas Archival Resources Online, http://www.lib.utexas.edu/taro/utlac/00072/lac-00072.html. J. Luz Sáenz, *Los mexico-americanos en la Gran Guerra: y su contingente en pró de la democracia, la humanidad y la justicia* (San Antonio, TX: Artes Gráficas, 1933). Benjamin Heber Johnson, *Revolution in Texas: How a Forgotten Rebellion and Its Bloody*

Suppression Turned Mexicans into Americans (New Haven: Yale University Press, 2005), 178–82.

21. Orozco, "LULAC," 27–32, 123–24, 131. Guide to the Collections of the League of United Latin American Citizens (LULAC) Archives, http://www.lib.utexas.edu/benson/lulac/lulacindex.html. David Bennes Barkley, Texas State Cemetery, http://www.cemetery.state.tx.us/pub/user_form.asp?step=1&pers_id=11240. Hispanic-American Medal of Honor Recipients, http://www.buffalosoldier.net/Hispanic-AmericanMedalofHonorRecipients.htm.

22. Alonso S. Perales, "Defending Mexican Americans," in Josh Gottheimer, ed., *Ripples of Hope: Great American Civil Rights Speeches* (New York: Basic Civitas Books, 2003), 160–62. Perales, Alonso S. (1898–1960), Handbook of Texas Online, http://www.tshaonline.org/handbook/online/articles/PP/fpe56.html. Order Sons of America (Council 5) Records, 1927, Abstract Minutes and financial records from 1927 for the Alice, Texas, organization that was a precursor of the League of United Latin American Citizens (LULAC). Accession No. BENSON-MS ORDER SONS OF AMERICA, Texas Archival Resources, http://www.lib.utexas.edu/taro/utlac/00246/lac-00246.html. Latino Civil Rights Timeline, 1903 to 2006, Teaching Tolerance, Southern Poverty Law Center, http://www.tolerance.org/latino-civil-rights-timeline.

23. Adela Sloss Vento, *Alonso S. Perales: His Struggle for the Rights of Mexican-Americans* (San Antonio, TX: Artes Gráficas, 1977), vii. Alonso S. Perales (1898–1960), "In Defense of My People," University of Houston Libraries, http://info.lib.uh.edu/about/campus-libraries-collections/special-collections/library-exhibits/defense-my-people-alonso-s-p. Alonso S. Perales Papers, 1898–1991, University of Houston Libraries, Overview, http://archon.lib.uh.edu/?p=collections/findingaid&id=436&q=&rootcontentid=96841.

24. Cynthia E. Orozco, *No Mexicans, Women, or Dogs Allowed: The Rise of the Mexican American Civil Rights Movement* (University of Texas Press, 2009).

25. Carole E. Christian, "Joining the American Mainstream: Texas's Mexican Americans During World War I," *Southwestern Historical Quarterly* 92, no. 4 (April 1, 1989): 559–95. Roberto R. Treviño, "Prensa y patria: The Spanish-Language Press and the Biculturation of the Tejano Middle Class, 1920–1940," *Western Historical Quarterly* 22, no. 4 (November 1, 1991): 451–72. *La Prensa*, Handbook of Texas Online, http://www.tshaonline.org/handbook/online/articles/LL/eel3.html. John Maynard, "First Spanish-Language Newspaper Founded 200 Years Ago," Newseum, Washington DC, September 15, 2008, http://www.newseum.org/news/2008/09/first-spanish-language-newspaper-founded-200-years-ago.html. Nicolás Kanellos, "A Brief History of Hispanic Periodicals in the United States," Hispanic Periodicals,http://docs.newsbank.com/bibs/KanellosNicolas/Hispanic_history.pdf.

26. Treviño, "Prensa y patria," 453, 457.

27. Gutiérrez, *Walls and Mirrors,* 77. Orozco, "LULAC," 302. Rutledge M. Dennis, "Du Bois and the Role of the Educated Elite," *Journal of Negro Education* 46, no. 4 (Autumn 1977): 388–402.

28. Quoted in Gutiérrez, *Walls and Mirrors,* 81–83.

29. Quoted in Orozco, "LULAC," 232–33. Lupe S. Salinas, "Legally White, Socially Brown: Alonso S. Perales and His Crusade for Justice for La Raza," University of Houston, http://www.latinoteca.com/recovery/recovery-content/papers-perales-conference/LegallyWhiteSociallyBrown_Salinas.pdf. Despite the damaging quote, Canales was a trailblazer in the civil rights history of Texas and tireless in his crusade against the Texas Rangers. Also see Joseph Orbock Medina, "Trials of Unity: Rethinking the Mexican American Generation in Texas, 1948–1955," University of California at Berkeley, November 2011, http://www.latinoteca.com/recovery/recovery-content/papers-perales-conference/TrialsofUnityOrbockMedinaspaper.pdf.

30. Sánchez, *Becoming Mexican American,* 131–33. Neil Foley, *The White Scourge: Mexicans, Blacks, and Poor Whites in Texas Cotton Culture* (Berkeley: University of California Press, 1997), 43.

31. Emilio Zamora, *The World of Mexican Workers in Texas* (College Station: Texas A&M Press, 1993), 24–28. 1920 United States Federal Census, www.ancestry.com. http://content.ancestry.com/Browse/list.aspx?dbid=6061&path=texas.Bexar.San+Antonio+Ward+1. Adriana Ayala, "Negotiating Race Relations Through Activism: Women Activists and Women's Organizations in San Antonio, Texas during the 1920s" (PhD dissertation, University of Texas at Austin, 2005), iii, Mexican women active in varied organizations such as the Cruz Azul, Young Women's Christian Association (YWCA), the Pan American Round Table of San Antonio, the San Antonio Mission Home and Training School, the Mexican Christian Institute, the House of Neighborly Service, the Wesley Community Center, and the Catholic Community Center.

32. Prycior, "*La Raza* Organizes," 15–17. Frances Jerome Woods, *Mexican Ethnic Leadership in San Antonio* (Washington, DC: Catholic University Press, 1949), 20. Emilio Zamora, "Mexican Labor Activity in South Texas, 1900–1920" (PhD dissertation, University of Texas, Austin, 1983), 160. Julia Kirk Blackwelder, *Women of the Depression: Caste and Culture in San Antonio, 1929–1939* (College Station: Texas A&M Press, 1984), 18. George Isidro Sánchez Papers, Digitalized Photos, http://www.lib.utexas.edu/photodraw/sanchez/. For digital photos see University of Texas at San Antonio, http://digital.utsa.edu/cdm/search/searchterm/gebhardt!Box%2003,%20folder%2005/field/all!all/mode/all!exact/conn/or!or/cosuppress/. Also browse the Library of Congress, http://www.loc.gov/pictures/.

33. Orozco, "LULAC," 156. *Mutualistas* thrived throughout the Southwest and Midwest. For a more complete background, see James B. Lane and Edward J. Escobar, eds., *Forging a Community: The Latino Experience in Northwest Indiana, 1919–1975* (Chicago, IL: Cattails Press, 1987). The largest association, La Unión, had 1,540 members, mostly skilled workers and some *jornaleros* (day laborers). *Mutualistas* operated as insurance groups, giving funeral benefits to members and a stipend to widows. They paid 25¢ a month to widows and $1 when a member died. These *mutualistas*

interacted with each other and comprised an informal network that spoke for the community. For *mutualista* activity in Texas, see Zamora, *The World of Mexican Workers in Texas,* 71–81. David Montejano, *Anglos and Mexicans in the Making of Texas, 1836–1986* (Austin: University of Texas Press, 1987), 204.

34. Kathleen González, "The Mexican Family in San Antonio" (Master's thesis, University of Texas at Austin, 1928), 5–6. Prycior, *"La Raza* Organizes," 77. Orozco, "LULAC," 41–46.

35. Sánchez, *Becoming Mexican American,* 69–70.

36. Drawn Southern Pacific Railway Advertisement with the Heading, "The West Coast of Mexico," ca. 1930, http://digarc.usc.edu/search/controller/view/chs-m12027.html.

37. The title of this section is taken from Guadalupe Compeán, "Where Only the Weeds Grow: An Ecological Study of Mexican Housing in Boyle Heights, 1910–1940" (Unpublished paper, School of Architecture and Urban Planning, University of California Los Angeles, December 1984). Ricardo Romo, *East Los Angeles: History of a Barrio* (Austin: University of Texas Press, 1983), 102. Pedro Castillo, "The Making of a Mexican Barrio: Los Angeles, 1890–1920" (PhD dissertation, University of California Santa Barbara, 1979).

38. Group photo of the Circulo Cosmopolita, 1st Anniversary, Los Angeles Public Library, See Two Los Angeles', http://forchicanachicanostudies.wikispaces.com/Community.

39. "Mexican Señoritas Now Adorn Local Society," *Los Angeles Times* (October 22, 1922). "Sonoratown, Backwater in Swirling Life of City," *Los Angeles Times* (September 9, 1923). Robin Fitzgerald Scott, "The Mexican-American in the Los Angeles Area, 1920–1950: From Acquiescence to Activity" (PhD dissertation, University of Southern California, 1971), 32–33.

40. Sonora Town, University of Southern California Digital, http://digitallibrary.usc.edu/search/controller/simplesearch.htm, http://digitallibrary.usc.edu/search/controller/view/chs-m4929.html?x=1352074189141; follow the link, and on the Search Bar type in "Sonora Town."

41. Cloyd V. Gustavson, "An Ecological Analysis of the Hollenbeck Area of Los Angeles" (Master's thesis, University of Southern California, 1940), 43. Elizabeth Fuller, "The Mexican Housing Problem in Los Angeles," in Carlos E. Cortés, ed., *Perspectives on Mexican-American Life* (New York: Arno Press, 1974), 6. In her 1920 study Elizabeth Fuller found that 92 percent of the homes she visited did not have gas, and 72 percent had no electricity. Los Angeles at Work 1920–1939, Belvedere, USC Library DIGITAL Archive, http://digitallibrary.usc.edu/search/controller/simplesearch.htm. View from Boyle Heights of a bridge leading into Los Angeles, ca. 1930–1939, USC Library DIGITAL Archive, http://digarc.usc.edu/search/controller/view/chs-m2875.html.

42. View of Whittier Boulevard in Whittier, showing a milk truck, ca. 1924, USC Library DIGITAL Archive, http://digarc.usc.edu/search/controller/view/chs-m6804.html?x=1242327858186 (accessed November 3, 2009).

43. Sánchez, *Becoming Mexican American,* 138–39, 147–48. Kevin Starr, *Material Dreams: Southern California through the 1920s* (New York: Oxford University Press, 1990), 147–49. William Deverell, "My America or Yours? Americanization and the Battle for the Youth of Los Angeles," in Tom Sitton and William Deverell, eds., *Metropolis in the Making: Los Angeles in the 1920s* (Berkeley: University of California Press, 2001), 277–99. Edward J. Escobar, *Race, Police, and the Making of a Political Identity: Mexican Americans and the Los Angeles Police Department, 1900–1945* (Berkeley: University of California Press, 1999), 78–81.

44. Cynthia Orozco, "Comisión Honorífica Mexicana," *The Handbook of Texas Online,* http://www.tshaonline.org/handbook/online/articles/CC/pqc1.html.

45. Francisco E. Balderama and Raymond Rodríguez, *Decade of Betrayal: Mexican Repatriation in the 1930s* (Albuquerque: University of New Mexico Press, 1995), 42–43. Emma Pérez, *The Decolonial Imaginary: Writing Chicanas into History* (Bloomington: University of Indiana Press, 1999), 97–98. "Latinas," Area Studies Collection, Library of Congress, http://memory.loc.gov/ammem/awhhtml/awas12/latinas.html.

46. Francisco Arturo Rosales, *Testimonio: A Documentary History of the Mexican-American Struggle for Civil Rights* (Houston, TX: Arte Publico Press, 2000), 123–25. Stuart Banner, *The Death Penalty: An American History* (Cambridge: Harvard University Press, 2002), 173. Newspaper Archives—248 Aurelio Pompa Documents, Genealogy Bank, http://www.genealogybank.com/gbnk/newspapers/?sort=_rank_%3AD&lname=pompa+&fname=aurelio&kwinc=&kwexc=&formDate=&processingtime=&group.

47. Sánchez, *Becoming Mexican American,* 171–87. Mark Reisler, "Always the Laborer, Never the Citizen: Anglo Perceptions of the Mexican Immigrant During the 1920s," in David G. Gutiérrez, ed., *Between Two Worlds: Mexican Immigrants in the United States* (Lanham, MD: Rowan & Littlefield, 1977), 23.

48. Haas, *Conquests,* 138–64. Nicolas Kanellos, *Hispanic Literature of the United States: A Comprehensive Reference* (Westport, CT: Greenwood Press, 2003), 252–58. Yolanda Broyles-González, *El Teatro Campesino Theater in the Chicano Movement* (Austin: University of Texas, 1994), 52. Las Carpas, Latinos in 60 Seconds, Public Broadcast System, http://video.pbs.org/program/1247309894/.

49. Juan R. García, *Mexicans in the Midwest, 1900–1932* (Tucson: University of Arizona Press, 1996). Zaragosa Vargas, *Proletarians of the North: A History of Mexican Industrial Workers in Detroit and the Midwest, 1917–1933* (Berkeley: University of California Press, 1993). Dennis Váldes, *Al Norte: Agricultural Workers in the Great Lakes Region* (Austin: University of Texas Press, 1991). Mark Reisler, *By the Sweat of Their Brow: Mexican Immigrant Labor in the United States, 1900–1921* (Westport, CT: Greenwood Press, 1976), 99–102. Ricardo Parra, "Latinos in the Midwest: Civil Rights and Community Organization," in Gilberto Cardenas, ed., *La Causa: Civil Rights, Social Justice and the Struggle for Equality in the Midwest* (Houston, TX: Arte Público Press, 2004), 4–6. Gabriela F. Arredondo, "Mexicanas in Chicago," Northern Illinois University, http://www.lib.niu.edu/2003/iht1020357.html.

50. Paul S. Taylor, "Crime and the Foreign Born: The Problem of the Mexican," in Carlos E. Cortés, ed., *The Mexican-American and the Law* (New York: Arno Press, 1974), 232. Rosales, *Chicano,* 66. Rosales, *Testimonios,* 105.

51. *El Trabajo* (April 18, May 16 and 23, June 11, 14, and 26, and July 31, 1925).

52. Quoted in Taylor, "Crime and the Foreign Born," 232.

53. Paul Livingston Warnshuis, "Crime and Criminal Justice Among Mexicans of Illinois," in Cortés, ed., *The Mexican-American and the Law,* 282–84.

54. Ibid.

55. Gabriela F. Arredondo, "Mexicanas in Chicago," http://www.lib.niu.edu/2003/iht1020357.html. Louise A. Kerr, "Mexicans in Chicago," http://www.lib.niu.edu/1999/iht629962.html.

56. Our Lady of Guadalupe Church (Chicago), http://www.neiu.edu/~reseller/cultinstp15.htm.

57. Warnshuis, "Crime and Criminal Justice," in Cortés, ed., *The Mexican-American and the Law,* 282–84, 287, 320. Louise Año Nuevo Kerr, "The Chicano Experience in Chicago: 1920-1970" (PhD dissertation, University of Illinois at Chicago Circle, 1976), 36, 39, 47, 49, 50, 52, 53. Reisler, *By the Sweat of Their Brow,* 141–42. John R. Scotford, *Within These Borders* (New York: Friendship Press, 1953), 105. John J. Betancur, "The Settlement Experience of Latinos in Chicago: Segregation, Speculation, and the Ecology Model," *Social Forces* 74, no. 4 (June 1996), 1299–324. Anita Edgar Jones, "Mexican Colonies in Chicago," *Social Service Review* 2, no. 4 (December 1928), 579–97.

58. Herbert B. Peterson, "Twentieth-Century Search for Cibola: Post World War I Mexican Labor Exploitation in Arizona," in Manuel Servín, ed., *An Awakening Minority: The Mexican American,* 2d ed. (Beverly Hills, CA: Glencoe Press, 1974), 117, 119–21. Carey McWilliams, *Ill Fares the Land: Migrants and Migratory Labor in the United States* (New York: Arno Press, 1976), 79. The Chicana Chicano Experience in Agriculture, http://www.asu.edu/lib/archives/website/agricult.htm. For the People: Mutual Aid Societies/Para la Gente: Sociedades de Ayuda Mútua, http://www.asu.edu/lib/archives/website/organiza.htm. Arizona Cotton Growers Association Collection, Arizona Historical Foundation, http://www.ahfweb.org/download/Cotton_MSS_30.pdf.

59. Peterson, "Twentieth-Century Search for Cibola," 117, 119–21. Rodolfo F. Acuña, *Corridors of Migration: The Odyssey of Mexican Laborers, 1600-1933* (Tucson: University of Arizona Press, 2007), 215–19.

60. Reisler, *By the Sweat of Their Brow,* 102. George Hinman, "Report of the Commission on International and Interracial Factors in the Problems of Mexicans in the United States," National Conference Concerning Mexican and Spanish Americans in the United States (Austin: University of Texas, 1926), 14, 27, 29. Paul S. Taylor, *Mexican Labor in the United States: Chicago and the Calumet Region* (Berkeley: University of California Press, 1932), 2, 111–12, 119–20, 222, 229. Immigration Committee, "Mexican Immigration," Chamber of Commerce of the United States, Washington, DC, July 1930 (draft in the Bancroft Library), 21, 27. Selden C. Menefee, "Mexican Migratory Workers of South Texas," reprinted in Carlos E. Cortés, ed., *Mexican Labor in the United States* (Washington, DC: Works Progress Administration, 1941), 17–26, 41. Ruben Donato, *Mexicans and Hispanos in Colorado Schools and Communities, 1920-1960* (Albany: State University of New York Press, 2007), 65–75. Sidney Mintz, "Beet Sugar Industry," Fort Collins, Colorado, Local History Archive, http://library.ci.fort-collins.co.us/local_history/topics/Ethnic/mex-beet.htm. Spreckels' "Little Tijuana" A History of Mexican Americans in California: Historic Sites, http://www.nps.gov/history/history/online_books/5views/5views5h88.htm.

61. Sara Deutsch, *No Separate Refuge: Culture, Class, and Gender on an Anglo-Hispanic Frontier in the American Southwest, 1880-1940* (New York: Oxford University Press, 1987), 137. Late 1910s Sugar Beets and Migrant Labor, http://events.mnhs.org/timepieces/Preview.cfm?EventID=216.

62. McLean and Thomson, *Spanish and Mexicans in Colorado,* in Cortés, ed., *Church Views,* ix, x, 17. Frederic J. Athearn, "Hard Times: 1920-1940," *Land of Contrast: A History of Southeast Colorado,* Cultural Resources Series, Number 17 (Colorado: Bureau of Land Management, Colorado, 1985), Chapter 11, http://www.nps.gov/history/history/online_books/blm/co/17/chap12.htm.

63. Deutsch, *No Separate Refuge,* 107–61. In 1920 there were 11,037 Mexican-born residents in Colorado and 10,272 in New Mexico. Barbara Hawthorne, Mexican American Cultural History, http://history.fcgov.com/archive/ethnic/Mexican.php.

64. Paul Morgan and Vince Mayer, "The Spanish-Speaking Population of Utah: From 1900 to 1935," Working Papers Toward a History of the Spanish-Speaking People of Utah (American West Center, Mexican-American Documentation Project, University of Utah, 1973), 32–34, 41, 46–47, 50–52. Pierrete Hondagneu-Sotelo, *Gendered Transitions: Mexican Experiences of Immigration* (Berkeley: University of California Press, 1994), 21–22. Erasmo Gamboa, "Chicanos in the Northwest: An Historical Perspective," *El Grito* 6, no. 4 (Summer 1973): 58–59, 60–62. Richard W. Slatta, "Chicanos in the Pacific Northwest: An Historical Overview of Oregon's Chicanos," *Aztlán* 6, no. 3 (Fall 1975): 328–29. Erasmo Gamboa, *Mexican Labor and World War II: Braceros in the Pacific Northwest, 1942-1947* (Seattle: University of Washington Press, 1999), 8, 27. *Mexican Americans in the Columbia Basin: Historical Overview,* http://www.vancouver.wsu.edu/crbeha/ma/ma.htm#intro. Carlos Arnaldo Schwantes, *The Pacific Northwest: An Interpretive History,* Revised and Enlarged ed. (Omaha: University of Nebraska Press, 1996), 228–32. Jerry García, "History of Latinos in the Northwest," Latino Hispanic Assessment Report, State of Washington, 2009-2010, http://www.k12.wa.us/CISL/pubdocs/historylatinopacificnorthwest.pdf.

65. Montejano, *Anglos and Mexicans,* 159, 207–11. Sana Loue and Beth E. Quill, eds., *Handbook of Rural Health* (New York: Springer, 2001), 104.

66. Montejano, *Anglos and Mexicans,* 164, 204, 207, 213. Paul S. Taylor, *An American-Mexican Frontier* (New York: Russell & Russell, 1971), 150. George Otis Coalson, *The Development of the Migratory Farm Labor System in Texas, 1900-1954* (San Francisco, CA: R and E Research Associates, 1977), 26. McWilliams, *Ill Fares the Land,* 264.

67. Daniel Rothenberg, *With These Hands: The Hidden World of Migrant Farmworkers Today* (Berkeley: University of California, 2000), 10, 274. Richard L. Nostrand, *Hispano Homeland* (Norman: University of Oklahoma, 1996), 164. Louise Año Nuevo Kerr, "Chicano Settlements in Chicago," in Manuel G. Gonzales and Cynthia M. Gonzales, eds., *En Aquel Entonces: Readings in Mexican-American History* (Bloomington: University of Indiana, 2000), 109-16. Zaragosa Vargas, "Armies in the Fields and Factories: The Mexican Working Classes in the Midwest in the 1920s," *Mexican Studies/Estudios Mexicanos* 7, no. 1 (Winter 1991): 47-71. Taylor, *Mexican Labor in the United States,* 50, 73-77, 98. Vargas, *Proletarians of the North,* 10, 59, 90. Dionicio Nodín Valdés, *Barrios Norteños: St. Paul and Midwestern Mexican Communities in the Twentieth Century* (Austin: University of Texas, 2000), 25, 32, 102.

68. Royce D. Delmatier, Clarence F. McIntosh, and Earl G. Waters, eds., *The Rumble of California Politics, 1848-1970* (New York: Wiley, 1970), 212, 216-17. Carey McWilliams, *Factories in Fields: The Story of Migratory Labor in California* (Santa Barbara and Salt Lake City: Peregrine Publishers, 1971), 185, 188. Stuart Jamieson, *Labor Unionism in American Agriculture* (New York: Arno Press, 1976), 71-72. Reisler, *By the Sweat of Their Brow,* 77-78. Revolution to Depression: 1900-1940, Five Views: An Ethnic Historic Site Survey for California, http://www.nps.gov/history/history/online_books/5views/5views5c.htm.

69. Paul S. Taylor, "Mexican Labor in the United States: Imperial Valley," in *Mexican Labor in the United States* (New York: Arno Press, 1970), 2, 7-8, 17. Mark Reisler, "Mexican Unionization in California Agriculture, 1927-1936: A History of Mexican Americans in California," *Labor History* 14, no. 4 (Autumn 1973): 562-79.

70. Sinclair Snow, "Samuel Gompers and the Pan-American Federation of Labor" (PhD dissertation, University of Virginia, 1960), 203. Gilbert G. González, "Company Unions, the Mexican Consulate, and the Imperial Valley Agricultural Strikes, 1928-1934," *Western Historical Quarterly* 27, no. 1 (Spring 1996): 53-73.

71. Coalson, *The Development of the Migratory Farm Labor,* 36. Reisler, *By the Sweat of Their Brow,* 88. Mark Erenberg, "A Study of the Political Relocation of Texas-Mexican Migratory Farm Workers to Wisconsin" (PhD dissertation, University of Wisconsin, 1969), 11. Immigration Committee, "Mexican Immigration," 11. McWilliams, *Factories in Fields,* 89. Kay Lysen Briegel, "Alianza Hispano-Americana, 1894-1965: A Mexican American Fraternal Insurance Society" (PhD dissertation, University of Southern California, 1974), 94. Taylor, *Mexican Labor in the United States,* 184. Manuel Gamio, *Mexican Immigration to the United States: A Study of Human Migration and Adjustment* (New York: Dover Publications, 1971), 86. Jamieson, *Labor Unionism,* 236-39.

72. Clark A. Chambers, *California Farm Organizations* (Berkeley: University of California Press, 1952), 22. Grant McConnell, *The Decline of Agrarian Democracy* (Berkeley: University of California Press, 1957), 160. Devra Weber, *Dark Sweat, White Gold: California Farm Workers, Cotton, and the New Deal* (Berkeley: University of California, 1994), 18-24, 84. Acuña, *Corridors of Migration,* 226. "We Have Fed You All for a Thousand Years," http://www.farmworkers.org/strugcal.html.

73. Jamieson, *Labor Unionism,* 75-76. Report of Governor C. C. Young's Fact Finding Committee in California, October 1930, Reprint (San Francisco: R&E Research Associates, 1970), 123, 126. George T. Edson, "Mexicans in the Beet Fields of Northeastern Colorado," August 27, 1924, in the Bancroft Library (Berkeley, CA), 5-10. Norman Lowenstein, "Strikes and Strike Tactics in California Agriculture" (Master's thesis, University of California, Berkeley, 1940), 25. Scott, "The Mexican-American," 25-26. Charles Wollenberg, "Huelga, 1928 Style: The Imperial Valley Cantaloupe Worker's Strike," *Pacific Historical Review* 38 (February 1969): 48. G. González, "Company Unions," 53-73.

74. G. González, in "Company Unions," 54, points out that the consul's role was generally to intervene in favor of management. Attempts were made as early as 1917 to organize Imperial Valley farmworkers.

75. Jaime Aguila, "Mexican/U.S. Immigration Policy prior to the Great Depression," *Diplomatic History* 31, no. 2 (2007): 216. He quotes Moisés González Navarro, *Los Extranjeros en México y los Mexicanos en el Extranjero, 1821-1970* (Mexico City: Colegio de México, Centro de Estudios Históricos, 1994), III: 242. "During his first eighteen months in office, he [Mexican President Alvaro Obregón] helped repatriate over 150,000 Mexicans." Obregón, a native son of the northern state of Sonora, which borders Arizona, acted out of personal concern for his compatriots abroad. Obregón wrote: "With wagons full of people, like cattle cars, which the enganchadores [smugglers] come to steal from our nation, taking advantage of this economic urgency for those unemployed, and I have seen many of those men return a few days later to the international boundary, begging for a plate of food, and for a ticket to return to their home."

76. Deutsch, *No Separate Refuge,* 124-25. Balderama and Rodríguez, *Decade of Betrayal,* 129-32. *El Universal* quoted in Peterson, "Twentieth-Century Search for Cibola," 127-28.

77. Lawrence A. Cardoso, *Mexican Emigration to the United States, 1897-1931: Socio-Economic Patterns* (Tucson: University of Arizona Press, 1980), 97. Reisler, *By the Sweat of Their Brow,* 39, 50-51, 53. Morgan and Mayer, "Spanish-Speaking Population," 8, 39.

78. Job West Neal, "The Policy of the United States toward Immigration from Mexico" (Master's thesis, University of Texas at Austin, 1941), 106-13.

79. U.S. Department of Labor, *Annual Report of the Commissioner General of Immigration* (Washington, DC: Government Printing Office, 1926), 10. "Naturalization Bill Alters Women's Status," *New York Times* (January 6, 1921), 6.

Immigration Act, 1921, Historical Documents, http://www
.u-s-history.com/pages/h1398.html. The 1921 Act, http://www.
memoriesfromhamblin.org/actof1921.html. The National
Origins Immigration Act of 1924, *The Statutes at Large of the
United States of America, from December 1923 to March 1925,*
Vol. XLII, Part 1 (Washington, DC: Government Printing Office, 1925), 153–69. The 1924 Act, http://www-personal.umd.
umich.edu/~ppennock/doc-immigAct.htm.

80. U.S. Congress, House Committee on Immigration and
Naturalization, Seasonal Agricultural Laborers from Mexico:
Hearing No. 69.1.7 on H.R. 6741, H.R. 7559, H.R. 9036, 69th
Cong., 1st Sess. (1926), 24. Who Was Shut Out?: Immigration
Quotas, 1925–1927, History Matters, http://historymatters.
gmu.edu/d/5078. Maldwyn Allen Jones, *American
Immigration,* 2d ed. (Chicago: University of Chicago Press,

1992), 237–39. "National Origins," *Time Magazine* (Monday,
March 11, 1929), http://www.time.com/time/magazine/
article/0,9171,846255,00.html.

81. [quote] Neal, "The Policy," 106, 107–8. U.S. Department
of Labor, *Annual Report of the Commissioner General of
Immigration* (Washington, D.C.: Government Printing
Office, 1923), 16. Reisler, *By the Sweat of Their Brow,* 55, 66–69 .

82. Quoted in Neal, "The Policy," 112, 113.

83. U.S. Congress, 190.

84. Ibid., 325.

85. Ibid., 112.

86. Quoted in Robert J. Lipshultz, "American Attitudes Toward Mexican Immigration, 1924–1952" (Master's thesis,
University of Chicago, 1962), 61.

CHAPTER 10

Mexican American Communities in the Making: The Depression Years

---

LEARNING OBJECTIVES

- Debate the causes of the Great Depression.

- Examine the repatriation of Mexicans and its impact on the community.

- Discuss how and why Mexican women were especially militant during this decade.

- Argue whether the New Deal was or was not racist toward Mexicans.

- Compare the disparate strikes that Mexicans/Mexican Americans were involved in and how they differed from those during the first two decades of the century.

- Appraise the generational organizational changes within the Mexican-origin community.

Most Mexican-origin people in the United States live in places that were once part of their homeland. This is important and must be taken into account when comparing them with other immigrants. In this context, the saying "the borders crossed us" takes on a special meaning. After studying the below timeline, look at a map of the 2,000-mile border between the two countries. Parts of Texas are further south and closer to Mexico City than are Tijuana, Hermosillo, or Chihuahua City. Then look at the names of towns and cities on the U.S. side of the border and compare them with those on the eastern seaboard.[1]

The Great Depression was a massive global economic crisis that took place from 1929 to about 1941. This decade took a toll on the Mexican-origin population as they became targets for nativists who blamed them for unemployment and demanded their deportation; this defied logic since the causes of the Great Depression were far too complex for the Mexicans, or any group other than Wall Street, to be at fault. The causes can be traced to World War I, when federal spending grew at a rate three times the growth rate of tax collections. The government cut back spending in 1920 to balance the budget, and a severe recession resulted. The nation rebounded and a decade of uncontrolled growth took place; mergers, takeovers, and cutthroat business practices went unregulated. By 1929, the richest 1 percent of the population owned 40 percent of the nation's wealth, while the bottom 93 percent experienced a 4 percent drop in per capita income.[2]

| 1929 | 1930 | 1931 | 1932 | 1933 | 1934 | 1935 | 1936 | 1937 | 1938 | 1939 | 1940 | 1941 |

Between 1929 and 1932, more than 13 million workers lost their jobs. As with the 1921 recession, nativists made the foreign-born scapegoats. The so-called repatriation programs sprang up throughout the country, and the thin line between deportation and repatriation was crossed. Deportation is forced, while repatriation is supposedly voluntary. Before the 1930s, large numbers of Mexicans had been repatriated from Texas, New Mexico, Arizona, and elsewhere in the United States. What distinguished the 1930s repatriation was its massiveness, and the fact that it was done under the pretext of the Depression. The number of Mexicans deported or shoved out has been estimated to be between 600,000 and a million. This reduction in population affected the Mexican community for generations to come.[3]

During the 1930s, massive unemployment due to job loss in the Southwest accelerated the migration of larger numbers of Mexicans to the Midwest and elsewhere in search of seasonal farm work. By 1930 there was a sizable Mexican population in places such as Chicago, Detroit, Gary, and other industrial centers. Steel and auto factories actively recruited Mexican workers after the passage of the 1917 Literacy Act that initially was limited to agricultural workers but was extended to the railroads and then to other industries. Their agricultural migration often deprived farmworker children the opportunity to attend school or learn English. However, newer opportunities opened for many Mexicans and Mexican Americans who resettled in cities. Greater numbers of Mexican women and men joined the workforce, unions, and other organizations. City life benefited many of the migrants, who gained experience from the increased social interaction and access to public education.[4]

President Roosevelt's New Deal offered little help to Mexican nationals in the United States. The form of assistance was a mixed bag: generally noncitizens were barred from receiving public assistance. However, some Mexicans along with Mexican Americans benefited from programs such as the Farm Security Administration that established camps for migrant farmworkers in California and elsewhere. Mexican Americans participated in the Civilian Conservation Corps (CCC) and Works Progress Administration (WPA) that provided relief jobs to unemployed Mexican Americans. But access was not even and many Mexican Americans, although citizens, did not qualify for relief assistance because either they did not meet residency requirements or they were farmworkers who, as a class, were excluded from New Deal programs such as workers' compensation, Social Security, and the National Labor Relations Act.[5]

The Great Depression: *La Crisis*

The Depression—or *La Crisis* (the Crisis), as many Mexicans called the Depression—profoundly affected Mexicans on the Euro-American side of *La Línea*. By then the Mexican-origin population in the United States numbered from 2 to 3 million—probably higher. The younger-generation Mexican Americans, mostly U.S. citizens, differed from the older population, which was mostly Mexican-born. Mexicans as a whole were vulnerable; they worked at menial jobs that the Depression hit the hardest. The 1930 Census showed that 56.6 percent of the 1,422,533 Mexicans listed were native-born U.S. citizens. Migration to the cities quickened during the next 10 years, as opportunities in agriculture dried up, with farmers preferring to hire white over brown in California. In Texas, conditions worsened with the state legislature refusing to appropriate general revenue funds for relief or allow bonds to raise revenue for local relief agencies. Moreover, the gap between city and rural wages widened.[6] Nationally, unemployment rose to the 15 million mark by 1933, the same year in which unemployment for all workers peaked at 41.6 percent in Los Angeles.[7]

Unemployed white "Americans" began to look for any kind of work, even "Mexican work," which they once shunned. Some felt that Mexicans were taking away their job opportunities—and, with this notion, they revived the racism of the 1920s, when nativists feared the loss of their America to foreigners. With the backdrop of this jingoism, the California legislature passed the 1931 Alien Labor Law, which forbade contractors from hiring alien workers for highway construction, school and government office buildings, and other public projects.[8] The so-called Americans used the pretext of taking care of their own people to displace Mexicans from the labor market.

That same year, Assemblyman George R. Bliss of Carpinteria, California, introduced a bill that would have legalized the segregation of Mexican and Mexican American students. As a Carpinteria school board member, Bliss successfully segregated Mexican children, labeling their school an "Indian School." Under the California School Code, school districts were given "The power to establish separate school for Indian children and children of Chinese, Japanese, and Mongolian ancestry." The Bliss Bill was defeated, but it raised the issue of disparate treatment of minorities. Indian, Chinese, and Japanese children were already segregated; however, similar categorization of Mexicans was problematic as they were classified as white largely based on the Treaty of Guadalupe Hidalgo. The 1930 Census shifted the battlefield by classifying Mexicans as a separate race. This shift had been taking place throughout the twenties as "Mexican Schools" had proliferated under the pretext of Americanization. Mexico City's *Excelsior* blasted the Bliss Bill, writing, "The measure which it is intended to carry into effect with respect to Mexican children is degrading, ignoble and devoid of justice, and it has raised waves of indignation." The newspaper concluded that the bill victimized Mexican children.[9]

Taking a clue from Bliss, in January 1931, Jerome T. Green, principal of the Lemon Grove Grammar School, on instructions from the school trustees, announced that Mexican children would have to attend a newly constructed school that Mexicans labeled the barnyard. The parents led a boycott and filed a suit—*Roberto Alvarez v. the Board of Trustees of the Lemon Grove School District.* The board had been encouraged by attempted legislation such as the Bliss Bill. Moreover, during the 1920s, segregation of Mexican children had been institutionalized. As Roberto Alvárez underscores, "The segregation of Mexican-American children became widespread in California and Texas. In 1928, the enrollment of sixty-four schools in eight California counties was 90–100% Mexican-American." However, San Diego Judge Claude Chambers found for the plaintiffs and ordered that the Mexican students be reinstated.[10]

Meanwhile, urban centers throughout the Southwest and Midwest attracted Mexicans and Mexican Americans. Because only 27,900 Mexicans entered the United States with permanent visas in the 1930s, most of the migration was interstate, primarily to California, where Los Angeles's population tripled between 1920 and 1930 and continued to grow after that.[11] City life greatly affected the Mexican-origin community. In addition, the shipment of at least 600,000 Mexicans back to Mexico dramatically changed the life of the Mexican community in the United States.

Stresses and Strains During *La Crisis*

Although Los Angeles experienced bad times, it was nevertheless a place of relative opportunity. For instance, after *La Crisis* hit Tucson, a railroad hub, the Southern Pacific railroad transferred its jobs to El Paso, Los Angeles, and Phoenix.[12] Apart from economic reasons, availability of medical care pulled Mexicans to Los Angeles where they competed with those at the bottom. In Los Angeles, Mexicans proportionately suffered the highest incidence of tuberculosis, more than twice the proportion for African Americans and five times that of Euro-Americans. Since the mid-1920s, the Los Angeles County Department of Health and its director, John L. Pomeroy, had used these statistics to clamor for restricting Mexicans from entering the United States. Under the guise of preventing the spread of TB, this department played a major role in their deportation. Generally Mexicans were treated at segregated medical facilities. Pomeroy justified the segregation, claiming Mexicans' and whites' needs and demands differed. Throughout this period, the department played on the whites' fears and prejudices. But given that Los Angeles was one of the largest cities in the country, medical care was, for the most part, better than it was elsewhere.[13]

Life was harder for Mexican Americans in other parts of the Southwest. In Tucson, the outmigration of industries and the inmigration of displaced miners and farmworkers worsened conditions. Historian Thomas Sheridan tells the story of Teresa García Coronado, who, along with her husband, fled the Mexican Revolution. Her husband labored in the mines of Arizona, and when he lost his job during the Depression, the family migrated to the cotton fields. Teresa's daughter, Concepción, was stricken with an unknown disease, and her husband stole eggs from neighbors' barns to feed his sick daughter. Teresa pulled the family through hard times by scavenging from garbage dumps.[14]

Life During the Great Depression

Not all Mexicans suffered equally during *La Crisis*, but families, like Teresa's, pulled together to survive. In the Mexican community both the nuclear and the extended families played large roles in surviving the Great Depression. It was common for three and even four generations to live together as a household.

During this time, regional tensions persisted within the Mexican American community. Intermingling of families in the colonias lessened the friction between native-born and immigrants, but some divides still persisted. For example, some northern Mexicans considered themselves superior to Mexicans from the interior because of their lighter complexion; New Mexicans were generally lighter skinned and believed that they were more "Spanish" than Mexican. Despite these differences, the Mexican community as a whole shared many characteristics, including the Spanish language, more or less similar skin color, and, for the most part, Catholicism. Changes were taking place: numerous Protestant churches thrived, even deep in the heart of the West Side of San Antonio and in East Los Angeles. Many Mexicans turned to the Protestant churches for assistance during *La Crisis* and, upon receiving help, joined them.[15] Catholics not too fondly called Protestants *aleluyas* (amens).

Tradition and cultural involvement helped families weather the economic turmoil. Sunday was always a big day when everyone dressed up for mass, wearing his or her Sunday best. Afterward, there was the Sunday meal—at home, or at the home of a friend or a relative. Those who traveled never worried about where to spend vacations; there were always friends or relatives who would add more water to the *frijoles* (beans) when the guests got there.

Popularity of movies was on the rise in most Mexican *barrios*. The *corridos* (ballads) and the *rancheras* (ranch music) gave way to a nightclub dance craze, with live bands playing Latin American music.[16] Going down to the local theater to see a *variedad* (variety show) was a treat for many families. Mexicans loved sports, and boxing remained a favorite. In Los Angeles, many Mexican fans compared the new boxers with the all-time favorite Bert Colima. They also played baseball and handball. The YMCA sponsored leagues, as did the Catholic Church. The Church organized the Catholic Youth Organization (CYO) in response to the Protestant challenge.[17]

In Texas, there was the Mexican Baseball League, sponsored by businesses, which toured the Rio Grande Valley. In southern California there were many Mexican baseball clubs that José Alamillo points out were often used by employers to Americanize and control Mexican workers. However, the popularity went beyond this and resulted in community-based semi-pro teams, "the Corona Athletics Baseball Club, which boasted a lineup of Mexican American male ballplayers that claimed several championship pennants and earned a reputation for producing major league players. In the face of racial discrimination and limited economic opportunities that afflicted the Mexican population in this agricultural-industrial town, baseball took on a symbolic and real social significance." Alamillo adds, "Mexican Americans used baseball clubs to promote ethnic consciousness, build community solidarity, display masculine behavior, and sharpen their organizing and leadership skills." However, the popularity of baseball spread beyond the male universe and Mexican women's clubs were formed. "Some examples of team names included: 'Los Tomboys' (Orange, CA), 'Las Debs' (Corona, CA), and 'Mexico Libre' and 'Four Star Eagles' (Los Angeles, CA)."[18]

The second generation, which often preferred Euro-American forms of entertainment, was English-speaking. The younger generation created a hybrid culture and "their tastes redefined the community's cultural practices and future directions of cultural adaptation."[19] The cultural assimilation of Mexican American youth, however, did little to prevent ongoing racism. The city's white nativists, the English-only crowd, harassed local radio stations about running Spanish-language programs. They, along with District Attorney Buron Fitts, insisted that Mexicans should listen only to English on radio. Thus it forced stations to move much of the Spanish-language broadcasting to the Mexican side of the border.[20]

Los Angeles offered better employment opportunities than did the rural areas that had higher unemployment. In large numbers, Mexicans moved out of highly seasonal agriculture and railroad work and into the factories in the city. Whereas the agriculture industry employed a majority of Mexicans through the 1920s, by 1930, only 45 percent of Mexican males worked in agriculture; 24 percent worked in manufacturing, 13 percent in transportation, and only 1 percent were professionals. Of Mexican females working outside the home, 38 percent were in the service sector, 25 percent worked in blue-collar occupations, 21 percent in agriculture, and 10 percent in clerical or sales; only 3 percent were professionals.[21]

The 1930 Census showed that 18.6 percent of Mexicans in Los Angeles owned homes. In places such as Belvedere, the rate was even higher, with 44.8 percent owning homes. Although home ownership did not necessarily mean moving up the economic ladder, it did suggest a degree of permanency. It seems as if the dream of every Mexican was to own a home, and even a second one for retirement. This gave the homeowners and their children a sense of stability. Land has always been important to Mexicans. The author remembers his grandfather putting dirt in his mouth and tasting it, saying that he felt that the land on which the family lived was theirs (and the bank's).

Many Mexicans owned homes in the city, alternating between factory work and agriculture. They often fared better in agriculture than in the factory where the father was the sole breadwinner, whereas in farming all family members joined in. Urban-based migrant families followed the crops and returned to their homes when the harvests ended. Permanency came at a cost to women; they often worked to supplement the family income to buy a home or a car. Older children also worked and contributed a portion of their salaries to the family kitty. Studies show that women worked at seasonal industries such as fruit packaging and food processing. In Los Angeles, food processing and packaging employed more Mexican women than did any other local industry. By 1930, some 25 percent of Mexican (and Mexican American) women were in some kind of industrial employment.[22]

The workplace socialized Mexican women, and the mere act of drawing pay lessened their dependence—they no longer relied on "his" money. As in earlier decades, sometimes a family would take in boarders, often members of the extended family. Historian Juan R. García writes that in the Midwest, "Like their mothers, working daughters were subjected to exploitative wage practices. Although they required sons to contribute only part of their paychecks to their families, daughters had to give all of their earnings to their parents," adding that "Despite the long hours, unhealthy conditions, and poor wages, many young women preferred working to staying at home [where they also worked]."[23]

Self-help groups for women flourished during the Depression. María Olazábal in 1931 organized the Cooperative Society of Unemployed Mexican Ladies. Olazábal had experienced hardships, such as the gas and electric companies shutting off power in her home in East Los Angeles. Members of the cooperative sold tamales at cost to the unemployed, being careful not to hurt their feelings—for only the most desperate would take any kind of charity. Although many Mexican families teetered on the brink of starvation, they considered taking welfare shameful.

As in Los Angeles and the rest of the Southwest, self-help played a big role in Tucson's survival. The Club Latino, formed in the spring of 1930, held dances and donated the funds to the Ochoa School for providing free lunch to students. Dora Munguía formed a chapter of the Mexican Blue Cross. Mexican organizations also fought discrimination; when S. H. Kress & Co. dismissed several Mexican female employees on racial grounds and replaced them with Euro-Americans, the Mexican community organizations pressured Kress to get the Mexicanas reinstated.[24]

Family culture was not always positive. Older children often missed school to care for younger ones and acted as official interpreters for their parents. The Mexican school persisted through the decade. The quality of Mexican schools was universally poor, with schools described as "barns" or "chicken coops." In California, Mexican schoolteachers were a rarity. In response to pressure by a local YMCA administrator, the Placentia Board of Education hired Bert Valádez as a teacher in 1937. A year afterward, the board hired Mary Ann González. The Fullerton Union High School in 1932 voted to end the Department of Americanization.[25]

Popular culture and movies influenced Mexican youth. As "outsiders," many related to *Mafiosi* as cult heroes, since they were immigrants with power. Movies such as the *Dead-End Kids* glorified gangs, as did their young actors, and their defiance must have impressed disempowered youth.[26] By the 1930s, there were distinctive *barrios* (neighborhoods) across the Southwest. Sociologist Joan W. Moore describes the Macy Street and Dogtown *barrios* that established distinct identities as well as local industry. These were poor areas. Often the father's inability to provide for the family eroded the children's respect for him, and Chicano gangs based on territoriality began to emerge with the decline of parental authority. One of the first gangs in Los Angeles was from Maravilla, a *barrio* that included the poorest of the poor.

Many families still used the *barrio* as a base while filling the demand for agricultural labor throughout the region; most spoke Spanish. Mexicans were overrepresented in *las escuelas de burro* (schools that segregate low-achievement students), where schoolwork was easy and students could coast. "By the end of the 1930s some children were learning how to 'qualify' for these schools—how to flunk tests and act dumb to Anglo teachers."[27] El Hoyo Maravilla gang—like other Maravilla gangs—evolved in the 1930s out of this environment. Racism, the Depression, and the social circumstances of Mexicans all formed their gang identities.[28]

The Importance of Being San Antonio

San Antonio was a reception depot where people would stop off, recover, and move on or settle in. Geography favored San Antonio, which was not far from population centers of Mexico and south Texas. Mexicans lived for the most part on San Antonio's West Side. Many houses were floorless shacks without plumbing, sewer connections, or electricity. San Antonio had a more diversified economy than that of places like Tucson or Santa Fe. Besides having military bases, it had dozens of smaller industries and served as a major center for farm-labor recruiting. Many newcomers arrived with little or no urban-life experience. City agencies refused them relief, and only a few churches and a small number of middle- and upper-class Mexican organizations provided some help, handing out food and clothing. Within the Mexican community, there were the usual divisions between Mexico- and U.S.-born Mexicans. Other than a few elite Mexican-born families, U.S.-born Mexicans generally fared better than the new immigrants, who often occupied the bottommost rung of the economic and social ladder.[29]

With the exception of Father Carmelo Tranchese, an Italian-born Jesuit priest whom the Church assigned to Our Lady of Guadalupe Church in 1932, the Catholic Church was largely uninvolved. Fr. Tranchese supported workers' causes and promoted social justice.[30] He endorsed the West Side School Improvement League, which advocated reform of the public schools. Tranchese lobbied for federally funded public housing projects on the West Side, and was surprised at the resistance of the Mexican middle class to the project. In 1935, Tranchese started *La Voz de la Parroquia* (The Parish Voice). Two years later, the archbishop took over *La Voz*, making it less political.

Although competition from Protestants forced the Catholic Church to make concessions, such as recruiting bilingual clergy, Mexican parishes lagged behind Euro-American parishes, which sometimes incorporated programs to attract the foreign-born. However, changes were taking place gradually, and by the mid-1930s, some parishes on the North Side, such as Our Lady of Sorrows, preached sermons in both English and Spanish.

San Antonio was the only major city in the United States that refused to provide public aid to starving residents. Thus, the charitable programs of the Catholic and Protestant Churches became essential. State and federal agencies doled out whatever little welfare there was, although the WPA and other federal programs routinely excluded noncitizens. Consequently, San Antonio had a large labor pool of Mexicans who were willing to work for almost nothing.[31]

Death and disease stalked the West Side throughout the 1930s. Tuberculosis rates continued to be five times as high for Mexicans compared to whites, and infant mortality rates also were much higher. Desperate people sought desperate solutions to the inadequacy of health care for the Mexican community; for example, in 1938, 28-year-old Antonia Mena, a married woman, was found dead in the living room of an abortionist.[32]

Nativist Deportations of the 1930s

As in every economic downturn in U.S. history, the ugly head of racist nativism revealed itself, this time with added intensity. The deportation and repatriation programs sent at least one-third of the Mexican community in the United States back to Mexico. The usual excuse for deportation was illegal entry into the country. Especially insidious was the emptying of prisons: giving prisoners reprieves or commuting sentences in return for voluntary "repatriation."[33]

The hysteria over uncontrolled Mexican migration had been drummed up since the 1920s. President Herbert Hoover carried on with the policies of the Calvin Coolidge administration to control immigration. The U.S. consulate in Mexico City restricted visas; in 1924 Congress had passed the Labor Appropriation Act, officially establishing the U.S. Border Patrol supposedly to secure the border between inspection stations. With politicos and the press inflaming anti-Mexican fears, most Euro-Americans felt that the government did not go far enough in deporting Mexicans.

The Depression took this racist nativism to a new high, provoked by the press, the public, and organizations—from the American Federation of Labor (AFL) to the American Legion to the American Eugenics Society. Representative John Box (D-Texas) dug out his failed bill, which was originally intended to remove the exemption of Mexicans from immigration quota laws on racial grounds. His racist agenda was backed by so-called authorities such as eugenics professor Roy L. Garis of Vanderbilt University, who attested to the Mexicans' moral and physical inferiority. When, in May 1930, the Senate passed the Mexican-quota bill by a voice vote of 51–16, the presence of racism was clear. The bill was referred to the House, where it was placed on the calendar. But by August 1930 the bill was moot; the Depression had reduced the number of Mexicans entering the country to a few hundred, giving western growers the space to forestall a vote.[34]

Until recently, the best estimate was that 500,000–600,000 Mexicans and their U.S.-born children were deported between 1929 and 1939. Some scholars have revised these figures upward to as high as 2 million, of which U.S.-born children comprised 60–75 percent. Although the repatriation was mostly local, politicos took their cue from President Herbert Hoover, who blamed the undocumented workers for the Depression. Secretary of Labor William N. Doak bellowed, "My conviction is that by strict limitation and a wise selection of immigration, we can make America stronger in every way, hastening the day when our population shall be more homogeneous." On January 6, 1931, Doak requested that Congress appropriate funds for the deportation of illegal Mexicans from the United States; he alleged that an investigation had revealed that 400,000 aliens had evaded immigration laws. The California Senate proposed a bill to prohibit "illegal aliens from engaging in business or seeking employment, and making it a misdemeanor to have such an alien as a partner."[35]

Los Angeles papers ran inflammatory headlines such as "U.S. and City Join in Drive on L.A. Aliens." According to them, the alien was responsible for shootings, fights, and rapes. The strategy was to scare Mexicans out of the city, and local authorities conducted a well-orchestrated campaign of intimidation and fear. C. P. Visel, the Los Angeles local coordinator for unemployment relief, telegraphed Washington that conditions in Los Angeles were desperate and that local citizens needed the jobs the undocumented Mexicans were taking. Visel circulated leaflets that did not differentiate between legal and illegal Mexicans. Visel warned, "20,000 deportable aliens [are] in the Los Angeles area."

Meanwhile, in nearby Pacoima and San Fernando, federal immigration agents went door to door demanding the residents' proper identification. At 3 p.m. on February 26, 1931, aided by a dozen police, immigration authorities surrounded the Los Angeles plaza, detaining more than 400 people for over an hour, and arresting 11 Mexicans and 9 Chinese. Authorities pressured even the naturalized U.S. citizens to repatriate.[36] Meanwhile, the California Department of Unemployment pressured Mexican clients to return to Mexico. Carey McWilliams posits that the repatriation was largely motivated by money: "It cost the County of Los Angeles $77,249.29 to repatriate one train load, but the savings in relief amounted to $347,468.41"—a net savings of $270,219.12.[37]

The states of Illinois, Michigan, Indiana, and Ohio also pressured Mexicans to leave, withdrawing food rations and making them feel unwelcome. As in the Southwest, local authorities became less zealous when they learned that funds from the Reconstruction Finance Corporation (RFC) could no longer be used for the transportation of repatriates. The *Excelsior* (a Mexico City newspaper), on May 11, 1931, called U.S. behavior "shameful from the legal and humanitarian point of view."[38]

Repatriation Texas-Style

The Texas repatriation program was harsher than that in the other states. Authorities often did not permit deportees to sell their property or collect their wages first; counties shipped the healthy and the sick alike;

and families were often separated. The program began in the Lower Rio Grande Valley and fanned out. Most of the repatriates were from the Lower Valley and were employed as laborers on large truck farms; some worked in packing plants and other agribusinesses. The next wave of repatriates was from south Texas, where Mexicans worked on cotton plantations as tenant farmers and laborers. Then came those from rural communities and small towns throughout central Texas, and, last, the Mexicans from southwest Texas, where they worked as cattlemen, sheepherders, and farmworkers.[39]

One of the stories of abominable abuses that took place in Texas was that of Mrs. Angeles Hernández de Sánchez, who had lived in the United States for 14 years. In 1931, after she returned from a long visit to Chihuahua, authorities detained her for "medical reasons" and proof of residence. Although an examination had proved that Hernández de Sánchez did not have venereal disease, the doctor stated that he suspected she had syphilis. The Department of Labor ordered Mrs. Hernández and her children deported. After working in Juárez as a servant, she again applied for reentry in 1938, but authorities denied her petition because they had deported her. The fate of Hernández and her two U.S.-born children is unknown.[40]

In July 1931, federal judge F. M. Kennerly heard the evidence in 83 cases, 70 of which violated immigration statutes. In one six-hour session, Kennerly found all of the immigration defendants guilty. The court deported 49 of them and jailed the rest. In Laredo that same year, the same judge heard 98 cases in three hours and convicted all the defendants, deporting 72 and jailing 26. Sixty percent of the Mexican residents of Austin were reportedly returned to Mexico by January 1931.[41]

The Fate of the Deportee in Mexico

Often, deportee women were forced to travel to the homeland alone with small children. Adela S. Delgado traveled from Pueblo, Colorado, to the environs of Chihuahua City, Chihuahua, in an old Dodge, with three daughters, ages 13, 12, and 9. Many women rode in packed trucks to remote parts of Mexico from where they walked to reach their villages. Apart from petty jealousies caused by the illusion that the Mexican government gave preferential treatment to the newly arrived *repatriados*, the returnees suffered from culture shock. It was especially difficult for women to adjust. They did not have the spatial freedom they enjoyed in the United States, and many villages lacked material amenities such as plumbing and inside stoves. In addition, the Mexican government did not have the resources to make good on its promises of free land to the repatriates. In 1932, the repatriates formed *La Unión de Repatriados Mexicanos* (the Union of Mexican Repatriates) to pressure the Mexican government to live up to its promises. The *Unión* sent word back to the United States about the Mexican government's noncompliance, and it publicized the repatriates' destitute condition. These reports dampened the enthusiasm of many Mexicans for returning home.[42]

The repatriates were not the only losers; the Mexican American community as a whole suffered losses because of their departure. Some of the repatriates might have lived in poverty, yet their contribution to the *barrio* economy had been significant. Their exodus worried merchants, who feared a negative impact on their business. Indeed, many merchants went broke because of the loss of capital and loss of human resources. Banks also suffered as Mexican clients, in anticipation of being repatriated, withdrew funds. In Los Angeles alone, bank deposits were depleted by more than $7 million.[43]

Factories in the Fields

As the Depression took its course, labor surpluses and the migrant pool in California expanded from 119,800 in 1920 to 190,000 in 1930 and to nearly 350,000 in 1939. By the mid-1930s, Euro-Americans outnumbered Mexicans in the California fields. Meanwhile, crop prices fell by more than 50 percent while electricity, water, fertilizer, and transportation costs remained the same. Growers sought to make up the difference by lowering workers' wages by more than 50 percent, making it almost impossible for farmworkers to survive. These difficulties contributed to labor unrest throughout the 1930s.

The situations for California and Arizona farms were different from other states. Carey McWilliams wrote that "farming [in California] has always resembled mining. The soil is really mined, not farmed."

The concentration of farmland had accelerated during the 1920s, with rapid expansion in labor-intensive crops like cotton, fruit, nuts, and vegetables, so that, to the farmer, a large supply of labor meant economic progress. Employer–employee relations became more distant, resembling urban industrial relations. Industrialization of agriculture forged a class system similar to that in the urban areas, with a political, economic, and social chasm between growers at the top and migrant labor at the bottom.[44]

Texas Farms

In 1930, 35 percent of Mexicans in Texas worked as farm laborers and 15 percent as tenant farmers. Because Texas farms underwent dramatic changes and were depressed throughout the 1920s, the condition of these workers worsened during the 1930s. The Texas farm economy was still to a large degree geared to a single crop—cotton—although the number of truck farms was rapidly increasing. The Depression hit cotton production especially hard. The New Deal and state laws took acreage out of production, worsening conditions for tenants and fieldworkers. Between 1929 and 1940, Texas cotton acreage decreased by 60 percent. Technological innovations, such as increased use of tractors and cotton sleds, also reduced the need for labor. Natural disasters—droughts, hurricanes, and floods—took their toll and devastated thousands of other tenants and farmworkers. In 1930, the number of sharecroppers was 205,122; it declined to 76,468 in 1935 and reached a low of 39,821 in 1940.[45]

Renting Mexicans

Agriculture, mining, railroads, and other industries, including construction companies and the garment trade, used labor contractors. The contractors, usually Mexican Americans or Mexicans, spoke English and could talk and deal with both the growers and the workers. Many of the 66,100 Mexicans who annually left Texas for other parts of the country worked through contractors, who found them jobs and arranged transportation to the farms. Contractors recruited most of the 3,000–4,000 workers who migrated each year to sugar beet fields in Minnesota, Kansas, and Missouri. Another 10,000 migrated to the sugar beet fields of Michigan and northern Ohio, where contractors recruited 85 percent of the labor force—some 57 percent of whom were from Texas.[46]

Some labor contractors did well. For example, Frank Cortez of San Antonio was able to accumulate several stores, cafes, and a funeral parlor. Cortez shipped 6,000 workers annually to Michigan at $1 a head. Growers advanced Cortez this fee, which they later withdrew from the workers' pay. Cortez had no overhead costs, recruiting right outside his funeral parlor. He sent workers to the Midwest by railroad, truck, and passenger cars; frequently, 60–65 Mexicans were crammed into a truck. Passengers often had to stand all the way, stopping "a few times for bowel evacuation and eating" or for gas and oil. Upon delivery, growers paid Cortez's agent $10 for each worker.

Most labor contractors did not transport the volumes that Cortez did. Many traveled with their crews, acting as "straw bosses" (crew leaders). Some Mexican workers would work for as many as three employers a day. Employers and contractors charged workers for everything from cigarettes to transportation. Employers often paid contractors directly, and contractors, in turn, paid workers. In the sugar beet industry, contractors recruited workers, handled their wages, and ran camps. Pickers sometimes received pay in tickets that they redeemed at local stores for a discount. To employers, contractors were indispensable, since contractors delivered a crew on the day promised. The system was wrought with abuses such as child labor, short weighing of the pickers' crops, and gross violations of human rights.[47]

The Farmworkers' Revolt

In California, farmwork wages plummeted from 35¢–50¢ an hour in 1931 to 15¢–16¢ an hour by mid-1933. Restlessness increased among workers, and, because agribusiness attracted large armies of pickers, a series of huge strikes resulted throughout the state. The center of unrest was the Imperial Valley, which experienced a strike in 1928 and where there were a core of activists and unresolved issues. In January 1933, 5,000 Imperial Valley workers, led by the Mexican Mutual Aid Association, struck. Growers quickly settled with white packers and trimmers, most of who resided in the area. They did not settle with harvesters, however, and workers prepared to strike the planters, who were vulnerable during the spring cantaloupe harvest. But an internecine conflict between radicals and moderates weakened the Mexican union, as did the Mexican consul's conspiring with the Western Growers Protective Association and immigration authorities.

A power struggle also broke out between the Mexican union and the Agricultural Workers Industrial League (AWIL). The latter was led by the Communist Party, which had abandoned its "boring from within" strategy and formed the Trade Union Unity League (TUUL) to organize workers. Although Communist organizers initially joined the efforts of the Mexican union, soon afterward Communist Party organizers accused the Mexican leadership of selling out and/or being reformist. Mexican merchants and tradespeople who controlled the *mutualistas* felt threatened by the radical solutions of pushy gringos. These divisions weakened worker solidarity. The presence of Communist organizers in the Valley granted Sheriff Charles L. Gillett license to conduct wholesale raids—he made 103 arrests in April 1933 alone. Meanwhile, the district attorney brought indictments against eight union leaders for criminal syndicalism. Convicted by the court, the defendants received sentences of 2–28 years.[48]

California Mexicans took part in strikes throughout 1930, 1931, and 1932. In July 1931, the AWIL changed its name to the Cannery and Agricultural Workers Industrial Union (C&AWIU). Failure of Mexican unions to gain concessions from employers opened the field for the Communist union. In its first years, the C&AWIU generally joined the strikes after they had started. It was not until November 1932, at Vacaville, California, that the union led strike activity. In 1933 there were 37 strikes involving some 47,575 farmworkers in California. The C&AWIU participated in 25 of these strikes, which involved 32,800 workers. Most of the strikes resulted in partial victories.[49]

The El Monte Strike

The Los Angeles area's mix of agricultural and industrial production encouraged the movement of workers to the city. In the mid-1930s, there were 13,549 farms in the county, with 619,769 acres of land devoted to agriculture. Farming was a $76 million industry in Los Angeles, surpassing the $23 million produced in the Imperial Valley. Thousands of Mexican workers either passed through Los Angeles or lived there during the off-season with their families. Farm labor strikes in the county provoked militancy among urban workers, and vice versa.[50]

El Monte, a town of 4,000 in the eastern half of the county, served as a trade area and housed 12,000 residents—75 percent were Euro-Americans, 20 percent Mexicans, and 5 percent Japanese. The Chicano *barrio*, known as Hicks' Camp, was a shack town located across a dry river gulch from El Monte proper. Many of its 1,100 Mexicans were migratory workers, forming the bulk of the town's cheap labor force and earning an average of 15¢–20¢ an hour.

In May 1933, Mexican, Japanese, and Euro-American workers of El Monte demanded higher wages in advance of the berry harvesting season. When management refused, the Mexican workers formed a strike committee. The strike began on June 1, and shortly afterward, the C&AWIU joined in, at first cooperating with the Mexican union. The growers were vulnerable, since the berries were highly perishable. The sheriff initially left the strikers alone, but his pressure on the strikers increased as the harvest season slipped by.

The Los Angeles Chamber of Commerce was concerned about the prolonging strike and contacted the U.S. Department of Labor to urge the growers to compromise. They offered the strikers a slight pay raise, which they rejected. After this point, the strike grew ugly; growers portrayed strike leaders as outside agitators and red-baited them (indiscriminately calling anyone on the left of the political spectrum a Communist, with the intention of discrediting him or her). The split between the faction led by the Mexican consul and that led by the C&AWIU weakened worker solidarity. The Mexican vice-consul cooperated with police authorities in an effort to purge Communist leaders, who had gained a substantial following among the strikers. By the time the growers finally made an offer, the peak of the harvest season had passed; the growers proposed a rate even lower than that originally rejected by the union—and the union, again, turned it down. The El Monte strike failed miserably.[51]

The Tagus Ranch

After the El Monte berry strike, worker militancy increased as strike veterans exported their militancy to other parts of California. In this charged atmosphere, the C&AWIU became more attractive to the rank and file. A series of strikes launched in August 1933 infused the "workers with a tremendous unifying spirit."[52] The most important of the August strikes, directed primarily at the California Packing Corporation, took place at the Tagus Ranch in the San Joaquín Valley. C&AWIU organizer Pat Chambers led the strike, which encompassed seven counties.

Deputies and ranch guards declared war, as growers armed themselves and conducted raids on union headquarters, resulting in mass arrests and deportations of strikers. During the strike, union organizers noticed the vulnerability of strikers who resided on company property; they devised new strategies, such as setting up private camps and roving pickets. They tried to divide the small farmers from the large planters, signing separate contracts, but met with limited success. After the bitter strike, strikers got a 25¢-an-hour settlement. The Tagus victory motivated pickers in other counties to rally for the 25¢ rate. This partial victory fueled worker militancy, but growers were also bitter and more resolved to destroy the worker movement once and for all. Thus, the Tagus Ranch strike set the stage for the San Joaquín cotton strike of October 1933.[53]

The San Joaquín Valley Cotton Strike

In the spring of 1933, San Joaquín cotton growers signed contracts with ginning and banking companies such as the Bank of America, the San Joaquín Ginning Company, and the local ginning operations of the Anderson Clayton Company. The contracts set the price of picked cotton at 40¢ per hundredweight (cwt.). The workers wanted $1 per cwt. The strike, which began on October 2, involved 10,000–12,000 workers—18,000 by some accounts. Eighty percent were Mexican; many were women.[54]

Business leaders, newspapers, chambers of commerce, farm bureaus, elected officials, and local city and county police authorities all supported the growers. The sheriffs arrested strikers, putting workers in bullpens. Cotton growers pressured authorities to cut relief payments of Los Angeles residents to swell the labor force and pressure strikers to work in the fields. Growers even mobilized local schoolchildren, declaring school holidays and pouring them into the fields. Meanwhile, federal authorities backed the growers and ordered the deportation of strikers charged with picketing.[55]

As expected, on October 4, growers began evicting strikers and their families. Union organizers had rented five campsites at Corcoran, McFarland, Porterville, Tulare, and Wasco. Strikers and their families moved into the camps. Each camp was given complete autonomy, and this self-control contributed to a spirit of unity and class consciousness among Mexicans. Mexican wives had their own networks that did much of the organizing within these communities; they knew each other from other camps or through kinship. Union organizers made it clear that if any of the camp committees voted to break the strike, they would end strike activities—the strike's success depended on the unity among the strikers in the camps. Therefore, it was essential for the strikers to maintain top security, and for organizers to keep grower propaganda from reaching the camps.[56]

The Corcoran camp housed 3,780 strikers, who outnumbered the 2,000 townspeople. An elected committee laid out streets, arranged toilet facilities, maintained sanitation and clean drinking water, settled disputes, and guarded the camp. Barbed wire enclosed the camp, and strike leaders posted guards at the entrance and exit. The camp committee established a tent school for about 70 children and an assembly space for meetings presided over by the mayor of the camp, Lino Sánchez. Strikers also held nightly performances that the residents dubbed an "Aztec Circus."[57]

The tendency of Mexicans to migrate in larger groupings gave them wider social networks than most Euro-American farm migrants enjoyed. According to Devra Weber, "Because women migrated with their families, they had sisters, mothers, aunts, cousins and friends from their home areas to rely on. Women who migrated without other women and were not yet part of ranch life often felt isolated." These networks reinforced solidarity among the Mexicans. Women had common experiences, of migrating and shouldering more than their share of responsibilities. Some stayed in the camps and cared for children; others joined the men on the picket lines. During the strike, besides running the camps, which were the backbone of the strike, women played the role of agitators, pushing the strikers and taunting the enemy.[58]

Violence broke the strike on October 10. At Pixley, an unarmed gathering of strikers were listening to Pat Chambers speak, when a dozen cars surrounded the group and opened fire; the strikers scurried back to the union hall. Two strikers were killed and 11 wounded. The assassinated strikers included Dolores Hernández, 52, and Defino D'Avila, 55. It was evident that the California Highway Patrol (CHP) was in collusion with the growers. B. H. Olivas of Madera stated that "ranchers told our patrolmen that beginning today they would beat to hell every striker who so much as laid a hand on the fences on their properties."[59] Meanwhile, the justice system tried eight ranchers for the murders and acquitted them.

Almost simultaneously, on the morning of October 10, in nearby Arvin, growers and picketers were engaged in an exchange of words—30 armed guards and about 200 picketers faced each other. About three o'clock, fighting broke out and a prominent grower shot into the crowd, killing Pedro Subia, age 57, and wounding several strikers. Witnesses testified that all the shots came from the growers' side and that the strikers did not have guns. Eyewitnesses also identified the man who shot Subia, but authorities refused to charge the killer. Instead, they booked seven picketers for Subia's murder.

After the shootings, growers became even more aggressive. With the complicity of local authorities, they implemented a strategy to starve out hungry strikers and their families. But when the state temporarily offered relief, even though the strikers were desperate, many refused to sign the return-to-work forms in exchange for relief, or to accept milk for their children upon condition that they sign waivers. At least nine infants died of malnutrition at the Corcoran camp alone. Top San Joaquín Valley industrialists such as J. G. Boswell encouraged the lawless behavior. Clarence "Cockeye" Salyer, one of the largest plantation owners in the valley, told his son Fred after the Pixley shooting that he had come home with his "hands covered with blood." Fred helped his father melt down the Colt 38 Special with which, he said, he had fired at the strikers. Clarence was not sure whether his bullet killed Dolores Hernández, but he was not taking any chances.[60]

The growers eventually settled the strike because of state intervention. In effect, the federal government promised the growers money to settle, rewarding their vigilantism. On October 23, the governor's fact-finding committee recommended a compromise, raising the rate for cotton to 75¢ per cwt. The committee also found gross violations of human rights. Growers agreed to the terms, but many workers held out for 80¢. The governor then ordered a halt to relief payments, which the workers had just begun drawing to avoid starvation.[61]

The Imperial Valley, 1934

The C&AWIU moved to capitalize on worker goodwill gained in the 1933 strikes. In December, the union once again entered the Imperial Valley, calling for more militant tactics. Many Mexicans joined the C&AWIU; others retained their membership in the Mexican union. By January 1934 the Imperial Valley labor conflicts had broken out once more, and they remained in the news throughout 1934–1935 as farmworkers demanded higher wages and toilets in the fields. In January, the C&AWIU sent two well-known Communist organizers, Dorothy Ray Healy and Stanley Hancock, to the Valley. While, according to Pat Chambers, the presence of Healy and Hancock generated excitement, it also drew time away from organizing efforts since Healy and Hancock had to hide from the police and were constantly on the move.

On January 12, 1934, gun-wielding police attacked a union meeting and killed two people, one of them a child. Vigilantes assaulted and tear-gassed the strikers at will, and, on January 23, they kidnapped American Civil Liberties Union (ACLU) lawyer H. L. Wirin. On February 19, local law enforcement officers literally crushed the strike by burning the workers' shacks and evicting all 2,000 of them. By then, even state authorities were shocked at the blatant disregard for human life; they forced the growers to arbitrate the pea strike at the northern end of the Imperial Valley.

Meanwhile, divisions among the workers widened. Mexican consul Joaquín Terrazas helped form *La Asociación Mexicana del Valle Imperial* (the Mexican Association of the Imperial Valley). The C&AWIU immediately branded the association a "company union." Initially, during the cantaloupe strike of April

1934, the Mexican union worked alongside the C&AWIU; but the C&AWIU soon seized control of the strike and its membership reached 1,806. Although both groups claimed limited victories, the growers kept control of the Imperial Valley. On March 28, 1934, California growers, the California Chamber of Commerce, and the Farm Bureau formed the Associated Farmers of California, which hired the Pinkerton Detective Agency to spy on union organizers. The Associated Farmers also sent photos of labor agitators to Frank J. Palomares of the San Joaquín Labor Bureau (SJLB), an organization funded by growers, sugar companies, oil companies, railroads, and utilities.[62]

On July 20, 1934, police raided Communist headquarters in Sacramento and, based on numerous confiscated pamphlets and papers, indicted 17 alleged Communists, and prosecuted 15, on charges of criminal syndicalism. The state convicted 8 of the 15, among who were Pat Chambers and Caroline Decker, who spent two years in jail before a higher court overturned their sentences. These arrests and convictions ended the four-year career of the C&AWIU.[63]

CUCOM and Mexican Strikes

Consequent to the collapse of the C&AWIU, Mexican workers formed many independent unions; some of its organizers shifted to *La Confederación de Uniónes de Campesinos y Obreros Mexicanos* (CUCOM). Mexicans took the leadership in 6 of the 18 strikes during 1935. As Mexican workers became more politically conscious following each strike, the number of union members grew.

In January 1936, CUCOM helped organize the Federation of Agricultural Workers of America, which included 11 multiracial locals of Filipinos, Japanese, and other nationalities. During the spring of 1936 in Los Angeles County, CUCOM led a walkout of 2,600 celery workers. The Los Angeles "red squads" tear-gassed parades and picket lines, beating and arresting union members.[64] A favorite grower tactic in breaking a strike was to pressure various California counties to withdraw relief, making places like Los Angeles their personal reserve labor pools.

In Orange County, 2,500–3,000 citrus-fruit pickers and packers went on strike on June 15, 1936. Workers averaged 22¢ an hour; they demanded an increase to 27.5¢, transportation, and union recognition. The activism in the county dated from the time of the *Confederación de Uniónes Mexicanas* (the Federation of Mexican Unions, 1928), which had 15 Orange County locals. One year earlier, vegetable workers organized a major walkout that set the stage for the citrus strike. Community members, the Mexican consul, and union leaders led the strike. On the other side, led by the Associated Farmers, growers recruited 400 special guards. The CHP harassed picketers along roads, and police authorities arrested some 200, herding them into stockades. Local newspapers described the situation as a civil war and blamed the Communists. The strike failed when growers would not concede to a single strike demand and state and grower violence increased.[65]

The Congress of Industrial Organizations

The National Labor Relations Act (1935) encouraged labor to expand and organize. The passage of the so-called Wagner Act coincided with actions by John L. Lewis of the United Mine Workers and other union leaders in establishing a committee of industrial unions to launch a vast organizing campaign. When the craft-oriented AFL refused to support the Committee of Industrial Organizations, led by Lewis, industrial unionists broke with the AFL and formed the Congress of Industrial Organizations (CIO) in 1937. The CIO was more receptive to organizing farmworkers and including people of color within the various locals. Similar to the Industrial Workers of the World (IWW) in the 1910s, the CIO put pressure on the AFL to organize Mexicans and African Americans. The CIO was a training ground for many militant Chicano organizers in the Southwest and in the Chicago area.[66]

Mexican-origin migrants and white migrants competed with each other in many places, such as the Yakima Valley in Washington State; they traveled south during the winter months to work and live in California, Texas, Arizona, Florida, or other states. The National Labor Relations Act (the Wagner Act), which guaranteed urban workers the right to organize, to engage in collective bargaining, and to strike, pointedly excluded farmworkers, making conditions even more desperate for them. Consequently, during 1937 and 1938, conditions in agriculture in the Southwest verged on class warfare.

By the second half of the decade, urban unions paid more attention to the plight of workers, fearing that conditions in the countryside might endanger their gains in the cities. Simultaneously, Mexican and Filipino unions realized that they were too small and isolated. Thus, during 1936 and 1937, CUCOM negotiated with other ethnic labor unions to form alliances. In July 1937, CUCOM sent delegates to Denver and joined the newly formed United Cannery, Agricultural, Packing, and Allied Workers of America (UCAPAWA), which promised to organize immigrant workers. UCAPAWA hired charismatic Latino leaders such as Luisa Moreno, who was the first Latina to serve on the executive committee of UCAPAWA. Born a wealthy Guatemalan, Moreno gave up her inheritance. Working in New York's garment industry before joining UCAPAWA, Moreno organized for the AFL. Historian David Gutiérrez writes, "UCAPAWA's immediate influence in the agricultural labor force was short-lived, however, due to the union's decision in 1938 to focus its energies on organizing packing-shed and cannery workers rather than workers in the fields."[67]

As the militancy among Mexicans increased, the planters used ever more repressive tactics to break them. Mexican locals and independent unions agitated throughout the 1930s. Growers and local authorities viciously attacked the strikes, and they were determined to drive the Mexican workers from the fields: "Okies" (from Oklahoma) and "Arkies" (from Arkansas) were employed in large numbers to replace the strikers. By the end of the decade, Mexican farmworkers were a lesser presence in the agricultural workforce.

The Arizona farm struggle resembled California with ownership and control of land more concentrated in the hands of the few. During the Depression years, Arizona became a highway for Dust Bowl refugees en route to California, with over 100,000 crossing the Arizona border in 1937 alone. During the 1920s and 1930s the AFL organized there, making early gains among cotton pickers. Organizational efforts met the same fate as they did in California, and the independent unions there eventually consolidated into the UCAPAWA.[68]

Rural Workers in the Lone Star State

We can assume that Texas was more difficult to organize than California: Agribusiness was not as large and it was more dispersed. Thus, workers were not as concentrated and were more difficult to reach. The Rio Grande Valley and San Antonio literally dipped deep into the heart of Mexico, and the distance from Laredo to Mexico City is about 698 miles versus 2,000 miles for Los Angeles. There was always a sizable presence of Mexicans in Texas, and even during the Depression years, it was only a matter of walking across the border. The better-paying fields of the Midwest offered a safety net for many Tex-Mexicans who owned or rented homes in the Valley. In addition, the progressive cores in Texas were not nearly as large or as strong as those in other states; for example, throughout the bloody agricultural strikes in California, white students from Stanford and Berkeley made their pilgrimage from San Francisco to support the strikers. Lastly, Texas was more rural and it could get away with an incredible amount of institutional violence.

The sheer size of Texas formed a large obstacle to union organizing of farmworkers. Eighty-five percent of the state's migrant labor force was Mexican; thus, it was easier to demonize and isolate it. Nevertheless, in 1933 in Laredo, Texas, Mexicans began yet another independent union, *La Asociación de Jornaleros* (Association of Laborers), which included hat makers, painters, carpenters, construction workers, miners, and farm laborers. The next year, agent provocateurs disrupted union activity, and in the spring of 1935 near Laredo, the union led a strike of more than 1,200 onion workers. The strike failed, partly because of the organizers' inexperience and partly because of harassment by Texas Rangers, who arrested 56 strikers. The union had refused to sign with individual growers and had held out for an industry-wide contract, but its members were persuaded to return to work by a federal mediation agreement. Growers, however, broke the agreement when the federal mediators left. Meanwhile, in west Texas about 750 members of the Sheep Shearers Union (SSU) agitated, making certain demands, for which 42 SSU members were arrested.

Throughout the 1930s, the Southern Tenant Farmers' Union (STFU), founded in Arkansas by 27 white and African American sharecroppers, organized in Texas. Although Mexicans were heavily involved in cotton, no major cotton strike happened in Texas during this decade. Tenants increasingly fled to the cities or to the migrant trail. The STFU organized 328 locals and more than 16,000 members in Arkansas, but only 8 locals with fewer than 500 members in Texas. Meanwhile, wages remained pegged at 40¢ per cwt. of cotton. In 1937, Mexican cotton pickers from the Laguna district in Mexico attended the STFU conference in Muskogee, Oklahoma. Still, the STFU was unsuccessful at building a biracial movement in Texas. Part of the problem was that the STFU did not view sharecroppers and farmworkers as industrial workers, which discouraged a permanent alliance with UCAPAWA. In addition, the STFU leadership was reluctant to work with the UCAPAWA because there were prominent Communists within the newly formed industrial union.

In January 1937, the Texas Federation of Labor formed the Texas Agriculture Organizing Committee (TAOC), which participated in a series of small strikes in late June and early July. However, growers and state authorities countered the TAOC's efforts by controlling the labor pool. The Texas State Employment Service, formed in 1935, recruited workers for the different crops; in 1939 alone, the service placed 550,047 farmworkers. Texas's surplus labor pool was simply too large to allow for effective organization. In the summer of 1937, UCAPAWA absorbed the committee, and it eventually recruited 5,000 dues-paying members.[69]

Colorado and the Manitos

The magnitude of the Colorado sugar beet operations attracted large numbers of Mexican beet laborers. It also attracted Communist organizers who formed AWIL locals in Greeley, Fort Lupton, Fort Collins, and Denver. In February 1932, various factions formed the United Front Committee of Agricultural Workers Unions, which became active in Colorado, Nebraska, and Wyoming. In May, the United Front called a strike, which the Great Western Sugar Company easily broke with cooperation from public agencies and law enforcement officials. The more radical factions blamed the Front's failure on "conservative" or "reformist organizations" such as the Spanish-American Citizens Association of Fort Collins; but the fact was that the strike was poorly planned. Mass arrests and the deportation of militant Mexican members marked the end of the United Front. Mexican workers formed the Spanish-Speaking Workers' League in Denver as a vehicle to hold more radical workers together after the 1932 strike.[70]

Mexican workers also joined TUUL (a federation of Communist trade unions) and "unemployed councils" of beet workers to agitate for adequate relief; the groups later merged with the Colorado State Federation of Labor (CFL). Membership in the council was free, but when members found jobs, they had to forfeit their cards. The CFL reportedly had 25,000 unemployed members. A few of the councils struck against work relief projects to improve conditions and also took part in small agricultural strikes.[71]

The Beet Workers Association claimed a membership of 35,000 in Colorado, Wyoming, Nebraska, and Montana. The Jones–Costigan Act of 1934 protected the growers, giving them subsidies averaging $17.15 per acre, if they did not use child labor. It also guaranteed workers a livable wage based on which workers demanded $23 an acre. However, the U.S. Department of Agriculture in Colorado set a rate of $19.50 per acre for northern Colorado and $17.50 for the southern section. This drove Mexicans and others to unite and form the Agriculture Workers Union (AWU). The next year 500 members struck near Blissfield and won a raise and union recognition. The next year, however, the U.S. Supreme Court declared the Jones–Costigan Act unconstitutional, and growers again employed child labor and imported WPA workers from the cities to break the union. In this war against labor, local authorities deputized more than 400 vigilantes.

The Sugar Act of 1937 subsidized farmers and authorized the secretary of agriculture to set a minimum wage for beet workers. The Sugar Act was the only labor legislation that directly benefited Mexican farm labor during the decade. In the 1920s, 7,000–10,000 Mexicans from New Mexico migrated to Colorado annually; by the early 1930s, the number had dwindled to only 2,000. Colorado authorities repatriated some 20,000 Mexicans between 1930 and 1935. Returning to New Mexico was not a homecoming. The infrastructures of Mexican villages were flooded, and were not capable of absorbing or caring for the needs of their prodigal sons and daughters. The return of so many compatriots worsened conditions, and the small villages were further impacted by the 1931–1932 drought and their time-tested gardens or their small flocks could save [the village farmers][72]

Away from their ancestral lands, New Mexicans in Colorado suffered intense racism. The Ku Klux Klan paraded in sugar beet towns, distributing handbills reading, "All Mexicans and all other aliens to leave the state of Colorado at once by orders of Colorado state vigilantes." The so-called "Americans" also resented Mexicans getting any type of federal relief, including work projects employment. They chided the Mexicans because they could not even "speak American." Life in Colorado was even more unequal than in New Mexico, where women continued to hold a wide variety of positions and authority. As women moved away from the villages, they lost their base of power.[73]

The City

As mentioned, Los Angeles offered opportunities for politicizing the entire family—opportunities that were not available to people on the move. Besides giving Mexican families more permanency, the city gave them opportunities for education and interaction with others. The Depression added to this politicization; it challenged Mexican cultural patterns, for more women had to work outside the home. In turn, factories offered more opportunities for socialization: earning paychecks, interacting with other women, and the sharing of grievances—all empowered women.

Mexican Women Garment Workers in Los Angeles

By the 1930s a majority of the garment factory labor pool of the Southwest was comprised of Mexican women. Los Angeles had an estimated 150 dress factories that employed about 2,000 workers. Seventy-five percent were Mexican females; the rest were Italians, Russians, Jews, and Euro-Americans. The Depression rendered these poorly paid workers even more vulnerable. In the summer of 1933, the Los Angeles garment industry began to revive its production, and the demand for workers increased. Employers, wanting to maximize their profits, hired Mexican women at substandard wages.

The National Recovery Act (NRA) code stipulated a pay rate of $15 a week for garment workers; however, employers violated the code and paid 40 percent of the women less than $5 a week. If women protested, they lost their jobs, or worse, were deported. Rose Pesotta, a union organizer for the International Ladies' Garment Workers Union (ILGWU), was an anarchist and a Jewish immigrant who broke with the conventional wisdom of her union that Mexican women could not be organized. Pesotta realized that the women were vulnerable: they were the victims of racism, many had unemployed husbands at home and many were the sole providers of their families. "Poorly paid and hard driven, many of these agricultural workers, seeking to leave their thankless labors, naturally gravitated to the principal California cities, where compatriots had preceded them. Thus hundreds of Mexican women and girls, traditionally skillful with needle and eager to get away from family domination, had found their way into the garment industry in Los Angeles." Pesotta further elaborates that they lived on the outskirts of towns, "at the end of the car-lines, in rickety old shacks, unpainted, unheated, usually without baths and with outside toilets," adding that "We get them … because we are the only *Americanos* who take them in as equals. They may well become the backbone of our union on the West Coast."[74] In 1933, the ILGWU began to recruit heavily among these Mexican women, who had nothing to lose. Pesotta recognized that these disenfranchised women were vital to the union on the West Coast.

On October 12, 1933, the new members of ILGWU—without any previous organization experience—effectuated a closedown of the Los Angeles dress industry. When the local radio station stopped broadcasting ILGWU news, they used Tijuana's *El Eco de México*, which broadcast union messages to Los Angeles. Strikers defied a court injunction prohibiting picketing by assembling 1,000 people in front of the Paramount Dress Company. Captain William Hynes and the "red squad" were powerless to disperse such a large gathering. Even so, the police harassed the picketers, forcing them to march two abreast, and forbidding them to holler "Scab!" Police arrested five strikers for disorderly conduct.

As their organizational experiences expanded their political vocabulary, the Mexican workers demanded more power in the union, arguing that although Mexicans composed most of Local 96, only 6 of the 19 union board members were Mexican. By 1936, the ILGWU had signed contracts for 2,650 workers in 56 firms. The contracts portrayed the gender bias of the day, paying women $28 weekly and men, $35. The next year, the local became part of the CIO and its membership climbed to 3,000.[75]

San Antonio Mexicana Workers

San Antonio's garment industry employed 6,000–7,000 persons—mostly piecework Mexican laborers. The city's pecan-shelling industry hired 12,000–15,000 Mexicans during peak season. Gender inequality in the workplace was common: employers paid women even less than the rates paid to Mexican males, who were not paid on par with their white colleagues. The pretext was that women did not need much money since they were more apt to be single and live with their parents. White women monopolized the white-collar clerical and sales occupations; 91 percent of African American women worked as domestics or in service jobs. Seventy-nine percent of Mexican women worked in industrial occupations.

In August 1933, a hundred cigar rollers and tobacco strippers walked out of the Finck Cigar Company after the employer announced that workers would be fined three good cigars' worth of wages for every bad one. Led by Mrs. W. H. Ernst, a Mexican woman, Mexicanas organized an independent union. As expected, authorities cracked down, arresting Mrs. Ernst. Federal and local authorities sided with Finck and the NRA's board signed an agreement with him, giving strippers 17.5¢ an hour and rollers 22.5¢, well below the 30¢ minimum set by the NRA. Even so, Finck blatantly violated the agreement, firing all union leaders. Again, in early 1934, the Mexicanas briefly walked out, this time affiliating with the San Antonio Trades Council. The NRA's regional board found working conditions at Finck's intolerable—that is, leaky pipes, unsanitary grounds, and inadequate toilet facilities. When the regional board ruled in favor of the workers, Finck appealed the findings, and retaliated by red-baiting the union and raising penalties for bad cigars to four to one.

The following year, members walked out again. The strike grew ugly as strikers attacked scabs, tearing off their clothes. Police Chief Owen Kilday again arrested Mrs. Ernst, and mass arrests followed. Supported by elected officials and the Chamber of Commerce, Finck imported replacement workers from Mexico and broke the strike.[76]

San Antonio was a major garment manufacturing center. Garment workers earned $3–$5 a week (6¢–11¢ an hour) and worked 45 hours a week. In March 1934, the ILGWU chartered two locals in the city: the Infants and Children's Wear Workers Union Local 180 and the Ladies' Garment Workers Union Local 123. The ILGWU called a strike at the A. B. Frank plant in 1936; workers closed down the plant. After six months of being picketed by Local 123, the Dorothy Frocks Company, a clothing manufacturer, moved to Dallas, where a local continued the strike until the company signed a contract in November 1936.[77]

As mentioned, the bitter Dorothy Frocks strike in San Antonio lasted six months. In 1936, during President Franklin Delano Roosevelt's car caravan through the city, some 50 strikers publicly disrobed company scabs. Chief Kilday conducted mass arrests, citing strikers for unlawful assembly and obstructing the sidewalk. In the spring of 1937, Local 180 called a strike against the Shirlee Frock Company. With a judge limiting picketing to no more than three persons and prohibiting the displaying of banners, Kilday arrested 50 picketers. But the strike was successful; employers were forced to recognize the ILGWU and workers received the minimum wage of 20¢ an hour.

However, the ILGWU enjoyed limited success in other Texas cities. Some blame must be assigned to the national leadership of the union, which never attempted to hire or develop Mexican organizers. The union hired Rebecca Taylor, a white woman, as the educational director of its San Antonio office. Taylor, a schoolteacher, took the job because union organizing paid better than teaching. Taylor's sole qualifications were that she spoke Spanish and had a college degree. Taylor was born in Mexico to a middle-class Arkansas–Oklahoma–Texas religious colony established in the 1890s, which revolutionaries later broke up. During Taylor's tenure with the union, she opposed anything involving radicalism and militancy, including the more progressive Chicano leadership that surfaced during the pecan shellers' strike of 1938. In the 1950s, Taylor quit the union and went to work for Tex-Son, one of the ILGWU's principal adversaries.[78]

La Pasionaria, the Pecan Shellers' Strike, and San Antonio

The pecan industry of San Antonio employed 5,000–12,000 Mexicans. Gustave Duerler, a Swiss candy manufacturer, began the industry during the Civil War. He bought pecans from the Native Americans and hired Mexicans to crack open the pecans and extract the meat. By the 1880s, Duerler was shipping pecans east. In 1914, Duerler mechanized the cracking phase of his operation, but continued to use Mexican women to extract the meat by hand. In 1926, he formed the Southern Pecan Shelling Company. Ten years later, the shelling company's gross annual revenue climbed to $3 million. The company then demechanized because hiring Chicanos was cheaper than buying and maintaining machines.[79]

The pecan industry used agribusiness employment practices. Contractors furnished crackers and pickers. Often, contractors employed workers to shell pecans in their own homes. Frequently, as many as 100 pickers were packed into unventilated rooms without toilets or running water. The shellers averaged less than $2 per week in 1934. The rate increased only slightly by 1936. Management justified the low wages, saying that the workers ate pecans while on the job. The owners claimed that the workers were satisfied because they had a warm place to work in company of their friends. Moreover, they said, the shellers would not work the required hours if the shelling company paid them more; they would earn 75¢ and go home, whether it was 3 p.m. or 6 p.m. Their justification for lower wages even went to the extent that if Mexicans earned more, they would just spend their wages "on tequila and on worthless trinkets in the dime stores."

In 1933, the Mexicanas, led by labor organizer Emma Tenayuca, formed the largest of the pecan workers' unions, which claimed a membership of 4,000 by 1936. When the management cut rates by 1¢ a pound, thousands of shellers walked off their jobs at the peak of the pecan-shelling season on February 1, 1938. Workers walked out of 130 plants throughout the West Side, affiliating with the CIO's UCAPAWA. Local law authorities backed the management and arrested more than 1,000 picketers on various charges, including blocking sidewalks, disturbing the peace, and unlawful assembly. City officials invoked an obscure city ordinance to prevent sign-carrying picketers from using public space.

Before completing high school, Emma Tenayuca walked the picket lines for cigar strikers at the Finck Cigar Company. Tenayuca had been an organizer for the Workers Alliance, and had led demonstrations attracting tens of thousands of participants. San Antonians called upon the fiery labor organizer Emma Tenayuca (also called *La Pasionaria*, Passion Flower, like the equally passionate Dolores Ibárruri, who was a leader of the Spanish Civil War that was taking place about the same time). Police Chief Kilday made Tenayuca his favorite scapegoat.[80]

At the start of the strike, *La Prensa* supported Tenayuca. Almost immediately, a power struggle over control of the strike developed between Tenayuca and the UCAPAWA leaders. Tenayuca was apparently forced, on the second day of the strike, to resign her leadership role to counteract charges of Communist influence. However, the workers voted Tenayuca the honorary strike leader.[81]

Tenayuca left San Antonio in 1939. Along with her husband, Homer Brooks, Tenayuca wrote one of the few works about the Mexican question in the Southwest, which was published by the Communist Party. The thesis was that society should respect the Mexicans' cultural integrity, shifting the responsibility of assimilation from the immigrant to the majority society. The treatise argued that Mexicans were part of the U.S. working class and should struggle within the American nation instead of within the Mexican (Mexico's) working class. Tenayuca later broke with the party because of its paternalism.

On August 25, 1938, Tenayuca planned a rally at the municipal auditorium. At 8 p.m., some 6,000–7,000 people, including ranchers, veterans, housewives, and schoolchildren, collected outside the auditorium and screamed at the small group inside the venue. The rednecks yelled, "Kill the dirty reds!" and broke into the auditorium while the audience skirted out of the hall. At that point, Tenayuca quit political work. We can only speculate on her reasons: nervous exhaustion, conflicts within the party, the chauvinism of many of its white members, and, to a degree, her removal as head of the pecan shellers' struggle.[82]

The Mexican Chamber of Commerce and the League of United Latin American Citizens (LULAC), as well as the Catholic Church, refused to support the pecan strike. These groups rarely opposed the Kilday machine, and the archbishop went as far as to congratulate the police for rooting out "Communistic influences." His Eminence did urge pecan owners to pay higher wages, because in his view lower wages bred Communism. Although federal authorities and the governor criticized Kilday's tactics, the chief flagrantly violated worker rights and closed down a soup kitchen that was dispensing free food to strikers, alleging that it violated city health ordinances.

After a prolonged struggle that lasted 37 days, the shellers won the dispute—"sort of." The shellers agreed to submit their grievances to arbitration. The board recognized Local 172 as the sole bargaining agent; it required owners to comply with the Fair Labor Standards Act, which Congress had passed on June 25, 1938, and pay the minimum wage of 25¢ an hour. The victory was short lived, however: owners replaced workers with machines. In 1938, the average income of the 521 pecan shellers' families in San Antonio, averaging 4.6 persons per family, was $251. This sum included earnings from work and the value of food and other commodities received from charities.[83]

Unionization in Los Angeles

The growth of industry in Los Angeles expanded the ranks of the Mexican proletariat in the city. Even before World War II, heavy industry began to move to Los Angeles. Eastern corporations, enticed by cheap land, reduced fuel costs, and cheap labor, looked west. Corporations also looked to the huge local markets for automobile-related products. Ford (1930), Willys-Overland (1929), Chrysler (1931), and General Motors (1936) all established plants in Los Angeles. Goodyear, Goodrich, Firestone, and U.S. Rubber soon followed. In 1936, Los Angeles ranked second only to Detroit in auto assembly and second only to Akron in tire and rubber manufacturing. The budding aircraft industry also housed itself in Los Angeles.[84]

Officially, just less than 100,000 Mexicans lived in the city and 167,024 in the county in 1930; unofficially, there were many more. Mexicans were the largest minority, followed by 46,000 African Americans and 35,000 Japanese. Mexicans, concentrated in limited industries, made up most of the casual labor in construction, dominating the hod-carriers' (laborers') unions. The CIO's secession from the AFL created increased competition between the two internationals—and suddenly Mexicans became attractive brothers and, in some cases, sisters. By 1940, the United Brick and Clay Workers Union, part of the AFL, had 2,000 Mexican members. The CIO had organized 15,000 Mexican workers in Los Angeles by the early 1940s.

The International Longshore and Warehouse Union (ILWU), founded on August 11, 1937, joined the CIO. Local 1–26 broke away from the AFL and became affiliated to the ILWU. The local had about 600 members then; one year after the affiliation to the CIO, membership increased to 1,300. Volunteer recruiters Bert Corona, William Trujillo, and other Chicanos conducted drives to enlist workers in the drug warehouse industry and in milling, paper, and hardware. By 1939, Local 1–26 had about 1,500 members. Similar organizing was done in other industries—furniture, garment, rubber, and automotive—which were multiracial and included a large contingent of women. Often the CIO and AFL fought for control of locals or set up parallel organizations. Chicanos were involved on both sides, divided by the industrial–craft debate. Meanwhile, the CIO attracted larger numbers of Mexican-origin workers than did the AFL, because of its nondiscrimination policies.[85]

Labor in the Midwest: Chicago

In Chicago in the 1930s, 66 percent of the Mexican population was unskilled versus 53 percent for African Americans, 35 percent for foreign-born whites, and 33 percent for native whites. These figures were significant, because in 1935, 83 percent of Chicagoans on relief were unskilled workers. Mexicans had a lower median level of education (in number of years) than the other groups: 3.2 years versus a median of 4.7 for African Americans and 5.3 for European whites. More than 30 percent of the Mexican workforce was unemployed; access to employment and relief was contingent on citizenship. Nativism increased and authorities even pressured Mexicans to produce documents proving legal residence or a willingness to become naturalized citizens.

During that period, to counter the effects of the Depression, Mexicans actively joined a variety of labor clubs, unions, and workers' organizations, for both the employed and the unemployed, much as they had in Los Angeles and San Antonio. *Mutualistas*, working with the goal of providing economic and social support for their members, remained the organizational form of choice. However, political ideology—both radical and conservative—also influenced their choice of membership. A chapter of *El Frente Popular Mexicano* (The Mexican Popular Front) sponsored meetings, discussions, and lectures; *El Frente*, led by Refugio Martínez, was housed at the University of Chicago Settlement House in the Back of the Yards neighborhood.[86] It defended Mexican workers, but also championed other causes such as protesting the despotism of Spain's fascist leader Francisco Franco. Another organization was *El Ideal Católico Mexicano* (the Mexican Catholic Ideal) formed in 1935 to counteract the radical appeal of *El Frente* and to crusade against Marxist ideas.[87]

Group membership also depended on locale and occupation. For example, the *Sociedad de Obreros Libres Mexicanos de Sud Chicago* (Society of Free Mexican Workers of South Chicago) consisted of steel and foundry workers of the South Chicago steel mills. Chicanos also participated in the Illinois Workers Alliance, which attracted a multiethnic membership of both employed and unemployed workers. As early as 1933 the Alliance had two locals with 50 Mexican members.

Unions such as the Brotherhood of Railroad and Maintenance Workers discriminated against Mexicans. However, after the passage of the Wagner Act (1935) and the split between the AFL and CIO, steel and meatpacking industrial unions increasingly opened their membership to Mexicans. In four months during 1936, the Steel Workers Organizing Committee (SWOC) recruited 150–200 Mexican workers, who were particularly active in Local 65 at U.S. Steel South Works in Chicago. By 1936, although they composed only 5 percent of the South Works employees, Mexicans comprised 11 percent of the union membership; furthermore, only 54 percent of the general membership voted, versus 88 percent of the Chicano membership. Following U.S. Steel's recognition of the union, workers elected Alfredo Avila to the first executive board.[88]

In 1937, Mexicans and their families joined other workers in striking the Republic Steel Company, the Youngstown Sheet and Tube Company, and several other steel mills. It was called the "Little Steel Strike" because these were the smaller of the steel corporations. Republic Steel refused to follow the lead of U.S. Steel (big steel) by signing a union contract. The Steel Workers Organizing Committee (SWOC) of the CIO called the strike. On Memorial Day 1937, thousands of steel workers and their families rallied in front of the Republic Steel mill in South Chicago. Amid the demonstrators were Max Guzmán and [Mrs.] Guadalupe (Lupe) Marshall, who were among a contingent of Mexican strikers. Many Mexican women had their children with them. Unexpectedly, Republic Steel representatives attacked the demonstrators, and police shot and killed 10 demonstrators.[89]

The Mexican American Miners' Revolt

During the first two decades of the twentieth century, open warfare raged in western mines. In Arizona, with the mass deportation of Mexican miners, the copper barons eliminated the trade union movement by the early 1920s. In the 1930s, these unions began to rebuild through militant worker struggles in which Mexicans played a leading role. The industry players remained the same: Phelps–Dodge, Anaconda, American Smelting and Refining (AS&R), and Nevada Consolidated. Mexicans composed 50–60 percent of the Southwest's industrial mine labor. Segregated, the Mexicans worked substandard jobs and were paid less in comparison with white miners. In Arizona, the mine owners controlled the state government as well as the company towns where workers lived. Slowly, as World War II heated up in Europe, the demand for copper and other ores heightened.

Meanwhile, during the Depression, production continued in Gallup, New Mexico, but owners reduced the force of 2,000 miners to a two- to three-day workweek. As in other parts of the country, the United Mine Workers of America (UMWA) and the Communist-led National Miners Union (NMU) fought for the hearts and minds of the workers. The NMU unsuccessfully led strikes in Pennsylvania and Ohio, as well as the bloody Harlan County, Kentucky, strikes of 1931 and 1932.

Dissatisfied with the UMWA, the largely Mexican workforce turned to the NMU, which was more militant and preached interracial solidarity. As a strike commenced in 1933, the governor mobilized the National Guard, placing McKinley County under martial law. Management red-baited the NMU and made racial slurs against the Mexicans. The controversy was mediated in favor of the owners, and, despite promises to the contrary, management retaliated against union members. In response, the Communist Party organized an Unemployed Council and a chapter of the International Labor Defense (ILD).

Without notice, the Gallup American Mining Co. sold its *Chihuahuita* property—where many of the blacklisted miners lived—to State Senator Clarence F. Vogel, who told the workers to buy the land on his terms or get out. The first evictions began in April 1935, with authorities targeting the home of Victor Campos. Workers defied the notice by returning Campos's furnishings to the house. Complaints were filed against Campos and other activists. The Unemployed Council immediately organized supporters who picketed the justice's office. An altercation erupted and deputies fired a tear gas bomb on the demonstrators, resulting in the death of the sheriff and two miners.

Led by the American Legion and the Veterans of Foreign Wars, vigilantes rounded up the so-called radicals. Fourteen miners and supporters were charged with first-degree murder. Authorities handed at least five of the seven acquitted defendants to immigration authorities. Juan Ochoa, Manuel Avitia, and Leandro Velarde were found guilty of second-degree murder. The judge delivered a speech on Communism and Bolshevism before sentencing the defendants to 46–60 years. The court of appeals reversed the Velarde conviction; in 1939, the governor pardoned Ochoa and Avitia.[90]

The coming of World War II increased demand for minerals, while open-pit mining transformed copper production. In eastern Arizona, an open pit swallowed the entire town of Metcalf. Militancy flourished with the return of prosperity and the corresponding rise in demand for cheap labor. At Silver City, New Mexico, resentful of social and economic conditions, miners began to organize. In Laredo, Texas, smelter workers, led by Juan Peña, rebuilt their union. Urban centers such as El Paso also saw the revival of AS&R Company and the revitalization of the workers' movement. One outspoken worker, Nicaraguan Humberto Silex, complained about the racism that kept Latinos as assistants. The managers made an example of Silex and fired him. The National Labor Relations Board (NLRB) later ruled that Silex and 40 members of the blacklisted Bisbee Miners Union had been discriminated against.

During World War II, rebuilding of unions continued. The Phelps–Dodge and AS&R refineries in Douglas–Bisbee and Laredo were unionized. In Morenci, the United Mine, Mill & Smelter Workers' (UMM&SW) union—known as Mine-Mill—represented 2,000 workers, most of them Mexican. By the war's end, Mine-Mill represented three-quarters of the copper production workers in the Southwest, with 3,000 members along the border alone. Unlike the Western Federation of Labor, Mine-Mill espoused a policy of ethnic and racial equality, and was destined to be the most progressive trade union in the Mexican American community.

In 1937, an SWOC local was formed in Los Angeles; within two years, the union established itself. At Utility Steel, workers elected a Chicano as lodge president, while the committee made gains at Bethlehem Steel and Continental Can. During these drives, a clear division existed between skilled and nonskilled Mexican workers. Mine-Mill, active in southern California, unionized in the foundries, smelters, and extraction plants. During World War II, as Chicanos trickled into these industries, white workers drifted to the war plants.[91]

The Mexican-Origin Community

The Texas-Mexican experience differed from that in California only in degree. Chicanos generally suffered more from segregation and racial barriers in the Lone Star State. It was a southern state with all the social, political, and intellectual limitations of the Confederate belt. Racism inculcated cohesiveness among Tejanos—or Tex-Mexicans, as they often called themselves. Without a doubt, the League of United Latin

American Citizens (LULAC) was the premier Tejano organization of this period. Although LULAC at first failed to incorporate women, it eventually bred women activists. Women generally shared the goals of the organization, and formed the LULAC Ladies' Councils in 1934. In almost every chapter there were women leaders—many either held college degrees or worked in white-collar occupations. In 1937, Alicía Dickerson Montemayor of Laredo served as the first Chicana elected to the office of second vice-president general of LULAC.

LULAC also produced intellectuals such as professors George I. Sánchez, Arthur L. Campa, and Carlos Castañeda. The various councils were vigilant in the protection of civil rights, and although later some Chicano scholars would criticize the intellectuals for ideological flaws, it is striking that Chicano intellectuals were involved at a time political repression was at its height, and they suffered discrimination for their involvement. For instance, during the 1930s, when Euro-American educators and social scientists perpetuated myths about the nonachieving Mexicans, educators George I. Sánchez and H. T. Manuel attacked culturally biased IQ tests. Sánchez and other Mexican American educators emphasized the role of environment in education, raising the issue of identity—that Mexican Americans were robbed of their historical heritage by Euro-American scholars, who dominated the analysis and interpretation of history. These early pioneers called for bilingual education and an end to de jure and de facto segregation.[92]

LULAC was at the forefront of the fight to desegregate the schools, and its leadership posited that "separate but equal" was a lie and segregation meant inequality. By 1930, 90 percent of south Texas schools were segregated—an essential feature in the organizing and disciplining of workers. Segregation produced a culture of "race-thinking which was in great part socially constructed by land developers and their model towns." San Antonio school districts in the early 1930s had 12,334 students in Mexican schools and 12,224 in non-Mexican schools; however, Mexicans had 11 schools as against Euro-Americans' 28. The disparity was even wider: despite Mexican and Euro-American schoolchildren being nearly equal in number, Mexican schools occupied 23 acres in total versus 82 acres for Euro-American schools; 286 teachers were employed versus 339 white teachers; and the school board spent $24.50 a year per Mexican student versus $35.96 per white.[93]

In the mid-1930s, LULAC took on public leadership by forming *La Liga Pro-Defensa Escolar* (the School Improvement League), which eventually represented 70 organizations with 75,000 members. Aware that being white carried privileges, in 1936, the San Angelo, Texas, LULAC council successfully sued the Social Security Administration regarding a requirement that Mexicans designate themselves as "Mexican" and not "white." While LULAC and middle-class leaders sought equal access to public institutions, members did not want to use LULAC as a political organization. The LULAC constitution stipulated that it remain nonpolitical. Members, however, did use fronts such as the *Club Democrático* and the League of Loyal Americans for their political activities. They believed they could achieve their goal—which was to become capitalists—in a dignified manner, like "decent" people. Their method was to work within the system and not in the streets.

LULAC wanted to improve the status of Mexican American through the strengthening of the family, church, education, and voting rights. Members represented a new generation that wanted to do it in their own way. Throughout the 1930s, they fought for better education and for equality. LULAC members, along with other members of the Mexican American middle class, the Mexican Chamber of Commerce, and the Catholic Church, were disturbed and often outraged by militants, whom they viewed as encroaching on their turf. LULAC members believed that they earned the right to represent the Mexican community, and that radicalism threatened their interests. This is not to suggest, however, that the Mexican American middle class was politically homogeneous.[94]

The Los Angeles Community

The Mexican community in Los Angeles continued to grow. Mexicans formed numerous enclaves throughout the city in what historian Ernesto Galarza called "doughnut communities"—the Mexican *barrio* was the hole and the Euro-American neighborhoods formed the dough. Not all Mexicans were poor, though. Better-off Mexicans often lived in affluent districts such as West Adams, Los Feliz, and

San Marino. They sponsored social functions such as the *Baile Blanco y Negro* (a white-gown, black-tie dance).

Activities of the lower middle class and the poor differed from those of the upwardly mobile middle class. A few joined the Young Democrats; some participated in the Unemployed Councils and the Worker Alliance. In 1930, the Federation of Spanish-Speaking Voters attempted to unite all Mexican societies, and some scholars speculate that it was the first political group to organize in Los Angeles. Meanwhile, the Young Men's Christian Association (YMCA) worked among Mexicans, as did the Catholic Church, which was conscious of the inroads made by the Protestant competition. To attract youth, the Catholic Church formed the CYO and the Catholic settlement houses.

The Communist Party continued to be active among Chicanos in Los Angeles. Reportedly, 10 percent of their local recruits were Mexican in 1936–1937. It formed *La Nueva Vida Club* (The New Life), and its *No Pasarán* (They Shall Not Pass) branch of the Young Communist League (YCL) publicized the Spanish Civil War. The Workers Alliance, which included capable organizers such as Lupe Méndoza and Guillermo Taylor, reached out to WPA workers and people on relief. The Workers Alliance had close ties to UCAPAWA, through which Luisa Moreno and Frank López had organized Chicanos.[95]

The Mexican American Movement

The Mexican American Movement (MAM) was an outgrowth of the YMCA's Older Boys' Conference in San Pedro in 1934. It sponsored annual conferences that later took the name Mexican Youth Congress. Through the years, the functions of the Youth Conference broadened, and it formed a steering committee. In 1938, MAM started a newspaper, *The Mexican Voice*. The next year, MAM set up a leadership institute and held its first regional conference at Santa Barbara. By the beginning of the next decade, MAM had sponsored a Mexican American Girls' Conference and a Mexican American Teachers' Association, and had established contacts with similar organizations in Arizona and Texas.

MAM's mission was to promote Chicano leadership in education, social work, business, and other professions. Its credo was "Progress Through Education"; its members—which included both men and women—struggled for better schools and family relations, fighting against discrimination and juvenile delinquency. Critics charge that MAM favored assimilation and—like its benefactor, the YMCA—favored Americanization. It probably did. However, we should remember that the YMCA also played a role in politically stimulating and educating Ernesto Galarza—the premier Chicano activist-scholar of the time. MAM members also criticized Mexicans who attempted to pass as Spanish. Leaders generally spoke about building pride in their race. On the other hand, MAM leaders told their members to think of themselves as American first and Mexican second.

Judging the organization by today's standards would be simplistic. Mexicans of Protestant backgrounds were over-represented among MAM leaders, and their interpretation of Americanization differed from that of many Euro-American missionaries, although they adopted aspects of the "Protestant ethic." They fought against the "Mexican school" and segregation. World War II curtailed some of MAM's activities, but it survived until about 1949. The *Mexican Voice* became the *Forward* in 1945 and reported on its members' progress in the armed forces.[96]

El Congreso de los Pueblos de Habla Español

In 1938, *El Congreso de los Pueblos de Habla Español* (the Congress of Spanish-Speaking People) of California held the first Conference of Spanish-Speaking Peoples in Los Angeles. It scheduled the First National Congress for March 1939 in Albuquerque. Because of red-baiting, organizers moved *El Congreso* to Los Angeles, and George I. Sánchez and Arthur L. Campa, professors at the University of New Mexico, were forced to resign. The principal organizers of the national congress were Luisa Moreno, a national organizer and later vice president for UCAPAWA; Josefina Fierro de Bright, its 18-year-old executive secretary; and Eduardo Quevedo, its first president and founder of the New Mexico–Arizona Club. Moreno traveled throughout the United States and generated considerable interest in the conference later held in Los Angeles.

Fierro de Bright's mother had been a partisan of Ricardo Flores Magón, and Fierro had come to Los Angeles to attend the University of California at Los Angeles. While singing in a nightclub, Fierro met John Bright, a Hollywood screenwriter, whom she later married. Through Fierro de Bright, *El Congreso* raised money from movie stars and other organizations. Eduardo Quevedo was an old-line politico, who later became active in the Sleepy Lagoon case (see Chapter 11). Quevedo was the moving force behind the Mexican American Political Association in 1959.

Representatives came to the First National Conference from all over the United States: Spanish and Cuban cigar makers from Tampa, Florida; Puerto Ricans from Harlem, New York; steelworkers from Pennsylvania, Illinois, and Indiana; meat packers, miners, and farmworkers from many localities; and elected officials from New Mexico. Delegates included workers, politicians, educators, and youth.

El Congreso proposed organizing workers and publishing a newspaper and a newsletter. It set legislative priorities and took stands against oppressive laws, immigration officials, vigilantes, and police brutality. Members pushed the right of farmworkers to organize and demanded the extension of the benefits of the National Labor Relations Act to farmworkers. *El Congreso* claimed a membership of more than 6,000 during 1938–1940.[97] Neither *El Congreso* nor the Chicano community had many friends in the media or in positions of power. Newspapers and local elected officials labeled it a "subversive gathering." Because of its radical stands, *El Congreso* opened itself to intense red-baiting, and the FBI harassed its members. After 1940, its effectiveness waned rapidly, though it continued to function in the post–World War II period.

El Congreso was important because it provided a forum for activists such as Luisa Moreno. On March 3, 1940, Moreno addressed a Panel on Deportation and Right of Asylum of the Fourth Annual Conference of the American Committee for the Protection of the Foreign Born, in Washington, D.C. She entitled her speech "Caravan of Sorrow":

> *Long before the "Grapes of Wrath" had ripened in California's vineyards a people lived on highways, under trees or tents, in shacks or railroad sections, picking crops—cotton, fruits, vegetables, cultivating sugar beets, building railroads and dams, making barren land fertile for new crops and greater riches.[98]*

Moreno continued that Mexicans had been brought "by the fruit exchanges, railroad companies and cotton interests in great need of underpaid labor during the early postwar period." She condemned the repatriations and the sufferings caused by them, charging that "today the Latin Americans of the United States are alarmed by an 'antialien' drive." Moreno concluded,

> *These people are not aliens. They have contributed their endurance, sacrificed youth and labor to the Southwest. Indirectly, they have paid more taxes than all the stockholders of California's industrialized agriculture, the sugar companies and the large cotton interests, that operate or have operated with the labor of Mexican workers.*

Moreno put *El Congreso de Los Pueblos de Habla Español* on record as opposing antialien legislation.

Fighting Segregation

During the 1930s, the segregation of schools and public facilities was a major issue. Newspapers such as *El Espectador*, published by Ignacio López in Upland, California, played a role in fighting segregation. In February 1939, two Chicanos entered a movie theater and looked for seats near the center. They were told that Mexicans sat in the first 15 rows. The youths went to López, who wrote a stinging editorial calling for a mass meeting, which more than a hundred community folk attended. The Mexican community boycotted the theater, forcing it to change its policy. López also exposed the fact that Chaffey Junior College segregated its swimming pool facilities during the summer. Chicanos could use the pool only on Mondays. Another boycott was called for, and the college reversed its policy. Shortly afterward, Mexicans sued the City of San Bernardino, and the court enjoined the city from excluding Mexicans from its pools.[99]

In an editorial entitled *Quién Es El Culpable?* (Who Is to Blame?), López reprimanded the Mexican American community for permitting segregation. He crusaded against police brutality and housing segregation, and emphasized the need for political integration. López's father was a Protestant minister; he was also a Protestant, as were Bert Corona, Ernesto Galarza, and George I. Sánchez. How much this Protestantism affected their strategies is open to study.[100]

The Manitos

Many New Mexican *Hispanos* were under the illusion that they were players in the state's political and social life. But even after World War II, out of 1,093 entries, *Who's Who in New Mexico* listed only 57 Mexicans. In eastern New Mexico, authorities barred Mexicans from "better" barbershops, cafes, hotels, and recreation centers. In Roswell, Mexicans could not use the public pool. In the late 1930s, the illiteracy rate in counties in which Mexicans were the majority was 16.6 percent, versus 3.1 percent in predominantly white counties. During the 1930s, white city councils segregated the public schools, and Mexican schools were obviously inferior to all-white schools. For instance, the percentage of public school teachers with degrees in Euro-American counties was 82.2, versus 46.6 in Mexican counties.

New Mexicans point to the fact that Congressman Dennis Chávez was elected to Congress at a time when there were no Chicano representatives in other states. However, in New Mexico, the Chicano population was proportionately larger and more concentrated than in other states. Chávez was appointed to the Senate after U.S. Senator Bronson Cutting was killed in an airplane accident. However, this appointment did not translate itself into power for the people. Concha Ortiz y Pino from Galisteo, New Mexico, was elected to the state legislature in 1936. Her voting record was spotty; she voted against the ratification of a constitutional amendment that prohibited child labor and regulated the number of hours women could work. Ortiz y Pino also condemned the welfare offices. Yet she introduced the first bill allowing women to serve on jury panels, which in the eyes of some historians absolves her.

Jesús Pallares migrated to the United States as a teenager. Pallares had worked as a miner in Gallup and Madrid, New Mexico. Fired and blacklisted for union activities, in 1934 Pallares became an organizer for *La Liga Obrera de Habla Española* (the League of Spanish-Speaking Workers). A year later, the *Liga* had 8,000 members, who militantly defended the rights of the poor. With the cooperation of the liberal U.S. Secretary of Labor Frances Perkins, state authorities had Pallares deported.

Another New Mexican activist from this period was Isabel Malagram Gonzales, who worked in New Mexico and Colorado. In the late 1920s, Gonzales led a strike of pea workers, and in 1930, she moved to Denver, where she worked for the Colorado Tuberculosis Society. In the 1940s she wrote for *Challenge*, a progressive newspaper, was active in politics, and ran for the city council. In 1946, the War Food Administration denied Gonzales the right to testify before it. In the late 1940s, she worked as a political activist in northern New Mexico. She died in Denver in 1949.[101]

Move to the Windy City: Chicago

By the late 1930s, more women and children lived in the *barrios* of Chicago compared to their numbers in the previous decade, an indication that Mexicans were forging communities. In addition, fewer Mexican families shared apartments, and the "boardinghouse" was disappearing. Official attitudes were slow to change, and state relief agencies still counted Chicanos as foreign-born. Chicanos concentrated in South Chicago, the Near West Side, and Back of the Yards, with each community evolving its own individual character. According to historian Louise Kerr, the Chicano Chicagoans were "less concerned with politics than with jobs, relief, education, and accommodation to the urban environment." They joined a variety of clubs, unions, and workers' associations to meet these needs. Local Spanish-language newspapers such as *La Defensa del Ideal Católico Mexicano* (the Defense of the Mexican Catholic Ideal), *La Voz de México* (the Voice of Mexico), and *La Alianza* (The Alliance) delineated community issues and divisions.

The pool hall, no longer the center of activity, gave ground to U.S. sports such as basketball. Mexican club teams, such as Los Aztecas, Los Mexicanos, and Los Reyes, played in leagues. As in other immigrant groups, youth gangs emerged in the Chicano community. According to Kerr, "social workers felt that participation in youth gangs was a form of adaptation to the local community," a form of assimilation "learned" by Mexican youths "from the Italians and Poles who preceded them." There was an increase in Mexican-run small businesses, and school attendance by Mexican youth improved. English classes for adults also became more popular.

Hull House on the Near West Side met the needs of Chicanos. But, as Hull House devoted more time to research, its advocacy role suffered. In the late 1930s, Frank Pax organized the Mexican Youth Party, which met at Hull House. Some Mexicans preferred the smaller Mexican Social Center, established in the early 1930s. In South Chicago, some Chicanos went to the Byrd Memorial Center staffed by the Congregational Church, whose employees looked on Mexicans as backward and undependable. Meanwhile, many Catholic parishes prohibited Chicanos from belonging to their communities.

Through the work of its long-time director Mary McDowell, the University of Chicago Settlement House (in Back of the Yards) had involvement with the Mexican community at a more personal level. McDowell worked toward interethnic cooperation and actively trained women to take leadership roles under the auspices of the Mexican Mothers' Club. The groups established by McDowell continued to function after her death. In 1937, the Mexican Mothers' Club sponsored a series of discussions on local Chicago issues, and interethnic cooperation remained better in this area than in other sections of the city.[102]

Conclusion: The Survivors

As the U.S. Mexican community approached the 1940s, the Mexican-origin population was becoming more visible. In the *Los Angeles Times* of October 15, 1939, Timothy G. Turner published an article titled, "Unique Fusion of Races Taking Place in El Paso; Anglo-Saxons, Americans and Indo-Spanish Mexicans Double Population in 25 Years." Turner reported that the U.S. population doubled in El Paso during the previous 25 years; two-thirds of the increase was Mexican in race and culture. This migration expanded the Mexican American middle class, but, according to Turner, the migration of poor Mexicans depressed wages. Turner suggested that it was not the presence of poor Mexicans that annoyed white Texans but the increase of the middle-class Mexican population. Attempting to be generous, Turner wrote, "There is a biologically inferior Mexican stock, no doubt, but many of the newcomers here [in El Paso] are of good northern Mexican ranch stock, light mestizos (that is Spanish Indian blood), and here they have had a break." The problem, he thought, was as Mexicans moved into the white-collar occupations that white people thought belonged to them, there was friction. The interaction described by Turner was played out throughout the Southwest and Midwest. It was emblematic of a greater problem. As long as Mexicans remained in their places and out of sight, most Euro-Americans could ignore them. However, when Mexicans moved up and took something they believed belonged to them, it was time for them to go.[103]

Notes

1. "U.S.-Mexican Border," *Business Week* (May 12, 1997), http://www.businessweek.com/1997/19/b35263.htm. "Mexico," WorldAtlas.com, http://www.graphicmaps.com/webimage/countrys/namerica/mx.htm.

2. The Crash of 1929, American Experience, Public Broadcasting System, http://www.pbs.org/wgbh/americanexperience/crash/. Photographs of the Great Depression, About.com: 20th Century History, http://history1900s.about.com/library/

photos/blyindexdepression.htm. The Great Depression, 42 explore, http://www.42explore2.com/depresn.htm.

3. Picture this: Depression Era: 1930s, Oakland Museum of California, http://www.museumca.org/picturethis/3_2.html.

4. "East Grand Forks, Minnesota Mexicans," Office of War Information Photograph Collection (Library of Congress), 1937, http://www.loc.gov/pictures/search/?q=mexican%20workers%20minnesota. Bruce Johansen and Roberto Maestas,

El Pueblo: The Gallegos Family's American Journey, 1503–1980 (New York: Monthly Review Press, 1983), 72, 74, 75, 78, 80. Leonardo Macias, "Mexican Immigration and Repatriation during the Great Depression" (Master of Arts thesis, Arizona State University, Tempe, 1992), 11–14. Jaime Aguila, "Mexican/U.S. Immigration Policy prior to the Great Depression," *Diplomatic History* 31, no. 2 (2007): 213.

5. "Mexican-Americans," Franklin Delano Roosevelt Front Page, Miller Center, University of Virginia, http://millercenter.org/president/fdroosevelt/essays/biography/8. Phyllis McKenzie, *The Mexican Texans* (College Station: Texas A&M University Press, 2004), 84. Ned Duran, "Conversations with Ed Duran," transcript of an oral history interview conducted on November 5, 2002, by David Washburn; Regional Oral History Office, Bancroft Library, University of California, Berkeley, 2002, in Rodolfo F. Acuña and Guadalupe Compeán, eds., *Voices of the U.S. Latino Experience*, Vol. 2 (Westport, CT: Greenwood Books, 2008), 563–68.

6. Clara E. Rodriguez, *Changing Race: Latinos, the Census and the History of Ethnicity* (New York: New York University Press, 2000), 101–4. Leo Grebler, Joan W. Moore, and Ralph C. Guzmán, *The Mexican-American People: The Nation's Second Largest Majority* (New York: Free Press, 1970), 84. Elizabeth Broadbent, "The Distribution of Mexican Population in the U.S." (PhD dissertation, University of Chicago, 1941), 33. David Hendricks and Amy Patterson, "Genealogy Notes: The 1930 Census in Perspective," *Prologue Magazine* 34, no. 2 (Summer 2002), The National Archives, http://www.archives.gov/publications/prologue/2002/summer/.

7. David G. Gutierrez. *Walls and Mirrors: Mexican Americans, Mexican Immigrants, and the Politics of Ethnicity* (Berkeley: University of California, 1995), 71–74. Macias, "Mexican Immigration and Repatriation," 29.

8. George J. Sánchez, *Becoming Mexican American: Ethnicity, Culture and Identity in Chicano Los Angeles, 1900–1945* (New York: Oxford University Press, 1993), 211. Mario T. García, *Mexican Americans: Leadership, Ideology, & Identity, 1930–1960* (New Haven, CT: Yale University Press, 1989), 15.

9. "New Protests on Bliss Bill," *Los Angeles Times* (April 5, 1933). Guadalupe T. Luna, "Beyond/Between Colors: On the Complexities of Race: The Treaty of Guadalupe Hidalgo and *Dred Scott v. Sandford*," *University of Miami Law Review* 53 (July 1999): 691–716. "Teacher Raps Race Division," *Los Angeles Times* (April 6, 1931). "'Excelsior' Fiercely Attacks Bliss Bill," *Los Angeles Times* (April 5, 1931). Sánchez, *Becoming Mexican American*, 211–12. Paula Rothenberg, *White Privilege* 3d ed. (New York: Worth Publishers, 2007), 60–62.

10. Robert R. Alvárez, Jr., "The Lemon Grove Incident: The Nation's First Successful Desegregation Court Case," *Journal of San Diego History* 32, no. 2 (Spring 1986), http://www.sandiegohistory.org/journal/86spring/lemongrove.htm. The documentary, http://www.youtube.com/watch?v=Uu9dxMMLGyU. E. Michael Madrid, "The Unheralded History of the Lemon Grove Desegregation Case," *Multicultural Education* 15, no. 3 (30 November 2007): 15–19.

11. Vicki L. Ruiz, *Cannery Women, Cannery Lives: Mexican Women, Unionization, and the California Food Processing Industry, 1930–1950* (Albuquerque: University of New Mexico Press, 1987), 5.

12. Macias, "Mexican Immigration and Repatriation," 15–16. Mercedes Carreras de Velasco, *Los Mexicanos Que Devolvió La Crisis: 1929–1932* (Tlatelolco, México, DF: Secretaria de Belaciones Exteriores, 1974), 121.

13. Emily K. Abel, "Only the Best Class of Immigration: Public Health Policy Toward Mexicans and Filipinos in Los Angeles, 1910–1940: Public Health Then and Now," *American Journal of Public Health* 94, no. 6 (June 2004): 933–36. Thomas E. Sheridan, *Los Tucsonenses: The Mexican Community in Tucson, 1854–1941* (Tucson: University of Arizona Press, 1986), 208. Richard A. García, *Rise of the Mexican American Middle Class: San Antonio, 1929–1941* (College Station: Texas A&M University Press, 1991), 39, 223–33.

14. Sheridan, *Los Tucsonenses*, 211–12. Francisco E. Balderama and Raymond Rodríguez, *Decade of Betrayal: Mexican Repatriation in the 1930s* (Albuquerque: University of New Mexico Press, 1995). For excellent oral interviews of miners and families in Morenci, Arizona, see Elena Diaz Bjorkist, "In the Shadow of the Smokestack: An Oral History of Mexican Americans in Morenci, Arizona." Unfortunately the site is defunct; write to the author for transcripts of interviews. See Elena Diaz Bjorkist, *Suffer Smoke* (Houston: Arte Público Press, 1996). Thomas E. Sheridan, "La Crisis," in Oscar J. Martínez, ed., *U.S.-Mexico Borderlands: Historical and Contemporary Perspectives* (Lanham, MD: Rowan & Littlefied, 1996), 162–68. Macias, "Mexican Immigration and Repatriation," 35.

15. Gloria E. Miranda, "The Mexican Immigrant Family: Economic and Cultural Survival in Los Angeles, 1900–1945," in Norman M. Klein and Martin Schiesl, eds., *20th Century Los Angeles: Power, Promotion, and Social Conflict* (Claremont, CA: Regina Books, 1990), 42. R. García, *San Antonio*, 156–63.

16. The radio was popular. A favorite in Los Angeles was Pedro J. González & Los Madrugadores, *Los Hermanos Sanchez y Linares, Chicho y Chencho: 1931–1937*, http://music.yahoo.com/madrugadores/albums/hermanos-sanchez-y-linares-chicho-y-chencho-1931-1937–28392112. Written by the late California State Senator Jack B. Tenney, the state's anti-Communist crusader and a bigot, *Mexicali Rose* was a classic played throughout the 1920s and 1930s. A movie starring Barbara Stanwyck came out in 1929. Gene Autry, The Singing Cowboy Mexicali Rose, http://www.youtube.com/watch?v=TjoQAaBcXpo&feature=related.

17. Gilbert G. González, *Labor and Community: Mexican Citrus Worker Villages in a Southern California County, 1900–1950* (Urbana: University of Illinois Press, 1994), 95. R. García, *San Antonio*, 93. M. García, *Mexican Americans*, 25. Bert Colima, Archive Photo, ca. 1924, BoxingTreasures.com, http://www.boxingtreasures.com/becoarphc192.html.

18. José M. Alamillo, "Peloteros in Paradise: Mexican American Baseball and Oppositional Politics in Southern California, 1930–1950," *Western Historical Quarterly* 34, no. 2 (Summer 2003): 192–95. Noe Torres, Baseball's First Mexican-American

Star, The Amazing Story of Leo Najo. Ghost Leagues of South Texas (Roswellbooks.com, 2008).

19. Quote by Sánchez, *Becoming Mexican American*, 186.

20. Sánchez, *Becoming Mexican American*, 185.

21. Sánchez, *Becoming Mexican American*, 186. Vicki L. Ruiz, *From Out of the Shadows: Mexican Women in Twentieth-Century America* (New York: Oxford University Press, 1998), 9. Karen Anderson, *Changing Woman: A History of Racial Ethnic Women in Modern America* (Cambridge, MA: Oxford University Press, 1997), 102–14. Christopher Tudico, "Before We Were Chicanas/os: The Mexican American Experience in California Higher Education, 1848–1945" (PhD dissertation, University of Pennsylvania, 2010).

22. Sánchez, *Becoming Mexican American*, 198, 200–2. Miranda, "Mexican Immigrant Family," 44. Ruiz, *Cannery Women*, 9, 14. For context, see Latinas, Area Studies Collections, http://memory.loc.gov/ammem/awhhtml/awas12/latinas.html.

23. Juan R. García, *Mexicans in the Midwest, 1900–1932* (Tucson: University of Arizona, 1996), 92–93. Ruth Hutchinson Crocker, "Gary Mexicans and 'Christian Americanization': A Study in Cultural Conflict," in James B. Lane and Edward J. Escobar, eds., *Forging a Community: The Latino Experience in Northwest Indiana, 1919–1975* (Chicago, IL: Cattails Press, 1987). Also in Lane and Escobar, see Juan R. García, "El Círculo de Obreros Católicos, San José, 1925–1930," 115–34, for a view of the organization life of this area south of Chicago.

24. Sánchez, *Becoming Mexican American*, 209, 213. Sheridan, *Los Tucsonenses*, 216.

25. G. González, *Labor and Community*, 103–4, 107, 134.

26. Dead End 1937 pt2, http://www.youtube.com/watch?v=RD4v5 Sxoy3Y&playnext=1&list=PL50403B555CFD0546&feature=res ults_main. Organized crime in Los Angeles in1930s, http://www .youtube.com/watch?v=UOv5PWKPUh8&feature=related.

27. Joan W. Moore, *Homeboys: Gangs, Drugs, and Prison in the Barrios of Los Angeles* (Philadelphia, PA: Temple University Press, 1978), 56–57. See Mario T. García, *Memories of Chicano History: The Life and Narrative of Bert Corona* (Berkeley: University of California Press, 1995), 103–5, on gangs. Miranda, "Mexican Immigrant Family," 56.

28. Gangster movies were often a "poor boy makes good" rendition of life. The gangster gets the car and the blonde. Scarface [1932] Part[1], http://www.youtube.com/ watch?v=tutdm85GekM. Also Bordertown—Original Trailer 1935, http://www.tcm.com/mediaroom/video/34920/Border-town-Re-issue-Trailer-.html.

29. R. García, *San Antonio*, 29, 35–36, 39. Julia Kirk Blackwelder, *Women of the Depression: Caste and Culture in San Antonio, 1929–1939* (College Station: Texas A&M Press, 1984), 9. "Mexican lunch wagon serving tortillas and fried beans to worker," Security Administration—Office of War Information Photograph Collection (Library of Congress), 1939, http://memory.loc.gov/ammem/browse/index.html; to view this photograph follow the link and in the Search Bar type in the title reproduced above in quotes.

30. Tranchese, Carmelo Antonio (1880–1956), http://www.tsha-online.org/handbook/online/articles/TT/ftr20.html.

31. R. García, *San Antonio*, 165. David A. Badillo, "Between Alienation and Ethnicity: The Evolution of Mexican-American Catholicism in San Antonio, 1910–1940," *Journal of American Ethnic History* 16, no. 4 (Summer 1997): 62ff.

32. Collage: Chicanas/os Struggle, Community, http://forchi-canachicanostudies.wikispaces.com/Community.

33. Mexican Repatriation: A Generation Between Two Borders, http://public.csusm.edu/frame004/images.html. Rosa Prieto, Veronica Smith, Rosa Moreno, Jonatán Jaimes, Adri Alatorre, and Ruth Vise, "Mexican Repatriation in 1930s Is Little Known Story," *Borderlands*, El Paso Community College, http://epcc.libguides.com/content.php?pid=309255&sid=2573137. Michigan Repatriation, http://www.umich.edu/~ac213/stu-dent_projects07/repatriados/history/detroithist.html.

34. Sánchez, *Becoming Mexican American*, 184. Camille Guérin-Gonzales, *Mexican Workers & American Dreams: Immigration, Repatriation, and California Farm Labor, 1900–1939* (New Brunswick, NJ: Rutgers University Press, 1994). Balderama and Rodríguez, *Decade of Betrayal*, 50–51. George C. Kiser and Martha Woody Kiser, eds., *Mexican Workers in the United States: Historical and Political Perspectives* (Albuquerque: University of New Mexico Press, 1979), 47. Job West Neal, "The Policy of the United States Toward Immigration from Mexico" (Master's thesis, University of Texas at Austin, 1941), 172, 194. U.S. Congress, House Committee on Immigration and Naturalization, *Western Hemisphere Immigration, H.R. 8523, H.R. 8530, H.R. 8702*, 71st Cong., 2d Sess. (1930), 436. James Hoffman Batten, "New Features of Mexican Immigration" (address before the National Conference of Social Work, Boston, June 9, 1930), 960.

35. Balderama and Rodríguez's *Decade of Betrayal* is the best book available on the topic. R. Reynolds McKay, "Texas Mexican Repatriation During the Great Depression" (PhD dissertation, University of Oklahoma, 1982), 556. M. García, *Bert Corona*, 59–61. Ronald W. López, "Los Repatriados" (Seminar paper, History Department, University of California at Los Angeles, 1968), 63. Gregory Ochoa, "Some Aspects of the Repatriation of Mexican Aliens in Los Angeles County, 1931–1938" (Seminar paper, History Department, San Fernando Valley State College, 1966). Clements Papers, Special Collections Library, University of California at Los Angeles. Abraham Hoffman, *Unwanted Mexican Americans in the Great Depression* (Tucson: University of Arizona Press, 1974). Peter Neal Kirstein, "Anglo over Bracero: A History of the Mexican Worker in the United States from Roosevelt to Nixon" (PhD dissertation, Saint Louis University, 1973). Abraham Hoffman, "Stimulus to Repatriation: The 1931 Federal Deportation Drive and the Los Angeles Mexican Community," in Norris Hundley, ed., *The Chicano* (Santa Barbara, CA: Clio, 1975), 110.

36. Quoted in Hoffman, *Unwanted Mexican Americans*, 52, 55, 113, 116, 118. López, "Los Repatriados," 43, 55, 58. Balderama and Rodríguez, *Decade of Betrayal*, 55–57, 63. Emory S. Bogardus, "Repatriation and Readjustment," in Manuel Servín, ed., *The Mexican-Americans: An Awakening Minority* (Beverly Hills, CA: Glencoe Press, 1970), 92–93. Norman D. Humphrey, "Mexican Repatriation from

Michigan: Public Assistance in Historical Perspective," *Social Service Review* 15 (September 1941): 505.

37. Carey McWilliams, *North from Mexico* (New York: Greenwood Press, 1968), 193. Robert N. McLean, "Good-bye Vincente," *Survey* 66 (May 1931): 195.

38. Hoffman, *Unwanted Mexican Americans*, 120. Neil Betten and Raymond A. Mohl, "From Discrimination to Repatriation: Mexican Life in Gary, Indiana, During the Great Depression," in Hundley, *The Chicano*, 125, 138, 139. George Kiser and David Silverman, "The Mexican Repatriation During the Great Depression," *Journal of Mexican American History* 3 (1973): 153. Ochoa, "Some Aspects of the Repatriation," 65–66. Kiser and Kiser, *Mexican Workers*, 36–37.

39. McKay, "Texas Mexican Repatriation," 17, 19. "Mexican Americans and Repatriation," *Handbook of Texas Online*, http://www.tshaonline.org/handbook/online/articles/MM/pqmyk.html. Edna Ewing Kelley, "The Mexicans Go Home," *Southwest Review* XVII, no. 3 (April 1932): 303–11.

40. McKay, "Texas Mexican Repatriation," 98–100.

41. Ibid., 131, 289–90. Repatriation in San Antonio, http://colfa.utsa.edu/users/jreynolds/Ybarra/part5.htm.

42. Aguila, "Mexican/U.S. Immigration Policy," 209–210, makes the point that Chicano historians have demonized the Mexican consul during this period. He states, "the Mexican government has simultaneously assumed a significant interest in aiding its compatriots who emigrate northward, worked at preventing their departure, and staged ad hoc repatriation drives as the only sure method to protect them from abuses abroad." Recent authors also make this point. The Mexican government had historically been for repatriation. Officially it sought to protect its citizens abroad. However, according to Aguila its effectiveness had been compromised since 1917 by conflicting U.S. immigration policies.

43. Balderama and Rodríguez, *Decade of Betrayal*, 107–9, 117. Valerie Orleans, "1930s Mexican Deportation," March 17, 2005, http://calstate.fullerton.edu/news/2005/valenciana.html. Susan Valot, Locals Recall 1930s Mexican Repatriation, 89.3 KPCC, May 16, 2007, http://origin-www.scpr.org/news/stories/2007/05/16/08_mexican_repatriation.html. Ben Fox, "Mexican Deportees Seek to Correct Old Wrongs . . ." *Orange County Register,* September 12, 2004, http://www.highbeam.com/doc/1P1-99048145.html.

44. Carey McWilliams, *California: The Great Exception* (Berkeley: University of California, 1999), 136. Stuart Jamieson, *Labor Unionism in American Agriculture* (New York: Arno Press, 1976), 7. Ernesto Galarza, *Farmworkers and Agribusiness in California, 1947-1960* (Notre Dame: University of Notre Dame Press, 1977), 25. Ronald B. Taylor, *Chavez and the Farm Workers* (Boston: Beacon Press, 1975), 39. Ellen L. Halcomb, "Efforts to Organize the Migrant Workers by the Cannery and Agricultural Workers Industrial Union in the 1930's" (Master's thesis, Chico State College, 1963), 1–2. Walter Goldschmidt, *As You Sow* (New York: Harcourt Brace Jovanovich, 1947), 248. Don Mitchell, *The Lie of the Land: Migrant Workers and the California Landscape* (Minneapolis: University of Minnesota Press, 1996), 110.

45. Neil Foley, *The White Scourge: Mexicans, Blacks, and Poor Whites in Texas Cotton Culture* (Berkeley: University of California Press, 1997), 65. Foley points out that the percentage of tenancy in Texas was 60.9 in 1930, falling to 48.9 in 1940. Daniel D. Arreola, *Tejano South Texas: A Mexican American Cultural Province* (Austin: University of Texas Press, 2002), 50–53. "Mexican carrot worker with son, Edinburg, Texas," Farm Security Administration—Office of War Information Photograph Collection (Library of Congress), 1939, http://www.loc.gov/index.html; to view this picture, follow the link and in the Search Bar type in the title reproduced above in quotes. "Mexican women leaving truck which brought them to the spinach field, La Pryor, Texas," Farm Security Administration—Office of War Information Photograph Collection (Library of Congress), 1939, http://totallyfreeimages.com/417571/Mexican-women-leaving-truck-which-brought-them-to-the-spinach-fi.

46. "Housing for Mexican sugar beet workers. Saginaw Farms, Michigan," Farm Security Administration—Office of War Information Photograph Collection (Library of Congress), 1941, http://www.ancientfaces.com/photo/housing-for-mexican-sugar-beet-workers-saginaw-far/760494.

47. Philip S. Foner, *History of the Labor Movement, Vol. 10: The TUEL, 1925-1929* (New York: International Publishers, 1991), 240–42. David Montejano, *Anglos and Mexicans in the Making of Texas, 1836-1986* (Austin: University of Texas Press, 1987), 9, 162–78. Lloyd Horace Fisher, *The Harvest Labor Market in California* (Cambridge: Harvard University Press, 1953), 22, 42. Carey McWilliams, *Ill Fares the Land: Migrants and Migratory Labor in the United States* (New York: Arno Press, 1976), 141, 257, 259–60, 264–66. George O. Coalson, *The Development of the Migratory Farm Labor System in Texas, 1900-1954* (San Francisco, CA: R&E Research Associates, 1977), 28. Mary G. Luck, "Labor Contractors," in Emily H. Huntington, ed., *Doors to Jobs* (Berkeley: University of California Press, 1942), 314, 317, 338–42. "Mexican labor contractor in center with two carrot workers eating "second breakfast" near Santa Maria, Texas," Farm Security Administration—Office of War Information Photograph Collection (Library of Congress), 1939, http://www.loc.gov/pictures/item/fsa1997024941/PP/. Ralph F. Grajeda, "Mexicans in Nebraska," Nebraska State Historical Society, http://www.nebraskahistory.org/lib-arch/whadoin/mexampub/mexicans.htm.

48. Sam Kushner, *Long Road to Delano* (New York: International Publishers, 1975), 58. Jamieson, *Labor Unionism*, 80–81, 83. Gilbert G. González, "Company Unions, the Mexican Consulate, and the Imperial Valley Agricultural Strikes, 1928-1934," *Western Historical Quarterly* 27, no. 1 (Spring 1996): 53–73. "Strike Agitators Named," *Los Angeles Times* (May 1, 1930). Sixteen leaders were taken in relation to Imperial Valley cantaloupe strike. "El Centro Convicts Nine Reds," *Los Angeles Times* (June 14, 1930). Emilio Alonzo was also listed as an inmate in the 1930 Census, Year: 1930; Census Place: El Centro, Imperial, California; Roll: 119; Enumeration District: 23; Image: 307.0. He was born in Mexico and was 24 years of age.

Interviews on the C&AWIU in the 1930s, Phonotape 49:3, 3056 C1, Bancroft Library, George Ewart, Interviewer, "Interviews on the organization of the Cannery and Agricultural Workers' Industrial Union in California in the 1930s."

49. Pat Chambers, Interview, California State University at Northridge (April 14, 1978). Jamieson, *Labor Unionism*, 83, 84–85. Kushner, *Long Road*, 28, 63. Joan London and Henry Anderson, *So Shall Ye Reap* (New York: Crowell, 1971), 28, 29. Devra Anne Weber, "The Organizing of Mexicano Agricultural Workers: Imperial Valley and Los Angeles, 1928–1934: An Oral History Approach," *Aztlán* 3, no. 2 (1972): 321. "Syndicalism and 'Sedition' Laws in 35 States and in Philippine Islands Must Be Smashed!" in the Paul S. Taylor Collection of the Bancroft Library. See Mitchell, *The Lie of the Land*, 124–29. "What were the Imperial Valley Strikes?" Chapter 7: La Lucha: The Beginnings of the Struggle, 1920–1930s, *San Diego Mexican & Chicano History*, http://www-rohan.sdsu.edu/dept/mas/chicanohistory/chapter07/c07s01.html.

50. Stephanie Lewthwaite, "Race, Paternalism, and 'California Pastoral': Rural Rehabilitation and Mexican Labor in Greater Los Angeles," *Agricultural History* 81, no. 1 (2007): 1–35.

51. Douglas Monroy, *Thrown Among Strangers: The Making of Mexican Culture in Frontier California* (Berkeley: University of California Press, 1990), 65. Selden C. Menefee and Orin C. Cassmore, *The Pecan Shellers of San Antonio: The Problem of Underpaid and Unemployed Mexican Labor* (Washington D.C.: Works Progress Administration, 1940), reprinted in Carlos E. Cortés, ed., *Mexican Labor in the United States* (New York: Arno Press, 1974), 24. See Don Mitchell, "The Disintegration of Landscape: The Workers' Revolt of 1933," in Mitchell, *The Lie of the Land*, 130–55. Sánchez, *Becoming Mexican American*, 236–38. Rodolfo F. Acuña, *Corridors of Migration: The Odyssey of Mexican Laborers, 1600–1933* (Tucson, University of Arizona Press: 2007), 226, 231–32.

52. Halcomb, "Efforts to Organize," 9.

53. Ibid., 9. Jamieson, *Labor Unionism*, 94, 95–96. Pat Chambers, Interview, April 13, 1978. Guérin-Gonzáles, *Mexican Workers*, 119–22. "Fruit Peace Hopes Rise," *Los Angeles Times* (August 17, 1933). "Strike Set May Be State-Wide," *Los Angeles Times* (August 19, 1933). "Ranch-Strike Injunction Case May Be Called Off," *Los Angeles Times* (August 22, 1933). "Fruit Workers Talk of Strike," *Los Angeles Times* (August 25, 1933). *Visalia Times Delta* (September 16, 1933). "Twenty Thousand California Legionnaires Will Parade at Pasadena Today," *Los Angeles Times* (August 14, 1933). "Strike Plot Laid to Reds," *Los Angeles Times* (August 17, 1933). Acuña, *Corridors of Migration*, 233–36.

54. Mitchell, *Lie of the Land*, 113–15. Clark A. Chambers, *California Farm Organizations* (Berkeley: University of California Press, 1952), 18, 66. Hearings Before a Subcommittee on Education and Labor, U.S. Senate, 76th Cong. (Washington, DC: Government Printing Office, 1940), part 51, 18579 (hereafter called *La Follette Hearings*). Paul S. Taylor and Clark Kerr, "San Joaquín Valley Strike, 1933. Violations of Free Speech and Rights of Labor," Hearings before a Subcommittee on Education and Labor, U.S. Senate, 77th Cong., pursuant to S. Res. 266, 74th Cong., part 54, *Agricultural Labor in California* (Washington, DC: Government Printing Office, 1940), 19947, 19949. *The Bakersfield Californian* (October 25, 1933) stated that the Southern California Edison Company registered a profit of $8,498,703 in the first nine months of 1933. Porter M. Chaffee, "A History of the Cannery and Agricultural Workers Industrial Workers Union," Unpublished Manuscript, Federal Writers Project Collection, Bancroft Library, University of California, Berkeley, Carton 35 (1938), 8. Pat Chambers, Interview (April 13, 1978). Jamieson, *Labor Unionism*, 101. Acuña, *Corridors of Migration*, 237–73.

55. *Visalia Times Delta* (September 19, 1933). Taylor and Kerr, "San Joaquin Valley Strike," 19992. "Caravan of striking cotton pickers south of Tulare, California," Farm Security Administration—Office of War Information Photograph Collection, 1933, http://www.ancientfaces.com/photo/caravan-of-striking-cotton-pickers-south-of-tulare/725860 also in http://www.loc.gov.

56. John W. Webb, *Transient Unemployed*, Monograph III (Washington, DC: Works Progress Administration, Division of Social Research, 1935), 1–5. Caroline Decker, Interview, August 8, 1973. Halcomb, "Efforts to Organize," 5. Jamieson, *Labor Unionism*, 102–4.

57. "Camp site of striking Mexican workers. Corcoran, California," Farm Security Administration—Office of War Information Photograph Collection, 1933, http://www.ancientfaces.com/photo/camp-site-of-striking-mexican-workers-corcoran-cal/1008762. Also see http://www.loc.gov.

58. Devra Anne Weber, *Dark Sweat, White Gold: California Farm Workers, Cotton, and the New Deal* (Berkeley: University of California Press, 1994), 11, 66, 94–95.

59. *Bakersfield Californian* (October 9, 1933). Taylor and Kerr, "San Joaquin Valley Strike," 19963. Chaffee, "A History of the Cannery," 49. O. W. Bryan, a local hardware store owner at the time of the strike, was interviewed on June 22, 1973. R. Taylor, *Chavez and the Farm Workers*, 54. Dr. Ira Cross to Raymond Cato, head of the CHP, Interview, February 20, 1934, Taylor Collection, Bancroft Library. *Pixley Enterprise* (January 12, 1934; February 2, 1934). *Visalia Times-Delta* (October 11, 1933). Acuña, *Corridors of Migration*, 245–47.

60. Mark Arax and Rick Wartzman, *The King of California: J. G. Boswell and the Making of a Secret American Empire* (New York: Public Affairs, 2003), 153–54. Taylor and Kerr, "San Joaquin Valley Strike," 19958, 19975–76, 19981, 19984. Pat Chambers, Interviews August 24, 1973; October 4, 1973; November 6, 1973. Halcomb in "Efforts to Organize," 75–76, reports 12 dead, 4 hurt, 113 jailed, and 9 children dead of malnutrition in the cotton camps. According to "Report on Cotton Strikers, Kings County," in the Taylor Collection, relief did not start until October 14, 1933. Chaffee, "A History of the Cannery," 35, 49.

61. In an interview with Paul Taylor on November 17, 1933, Taylor Collection, Bancroft Library, Kern County undersheriff Tom Carter stated that growers were well prepared for the strike. They had two machine guns and had bought $1,000 worth of tear gas. *Bakersfield Californian* (October 11, 1933).

Pedro Subia, 4717, Coroner's Inquest, County of Kern, State of California, October 14, 1933. Wofford B. Camp, *Cotton, Irrigation and the AAA: An Interview Conducted by Willa Lug Baum,* Regional Oral History Office, University of California, Bancroft Library, Berkeley (1971), 21. Louis Block, California State Emergency Relief Administration, C-R, f.4, Taylor Collection, Bancroft Library. Local authorities called for the state to send 1,000 CHP officers to Corcoran. The local sheriffs disbanded the camps. Corcoran was the last camp to disband. The growers burned the camp after the strikers left. The *Bakersfield Californian* (October 28, 1933) blared, "Growers to Import 1000 L.A. Workers." On January 13, 1934, the *Bakersfield Californian* reported "Cotton Men's Income Twice That of 1932." On February 6, it reported that the Agricultural Adjustment Agency paid Kern County growers $1,015,000 for plowing under 20–40 percent of their crop.

62. Norman Lowenstein, "Strikes and Strike Tactics in California Agriculture: A History" (Master's thesis, University of California at Berkeley, 1940), 94. Jamieson, *Labor Unionism,* 106–8. *La Follette Hearings,* part 55, 20140, 20180. Weber, *Dark Sweat,* 321, 323. Guillermo Martínez, Interview, Los Angeles, June 23, 1978. Pat Chambers, Interview, June 26, 1978. In February 1934, David Martínez, R. Salazar, and F. Bustamante were sentenced to eight months for disturbing the peace. Chaffee, "A History of the Cannery," section entitled "Imperial Valley in 1934," 34. See also Jamieson, *Labor Unionism,* 108–9. See C. B. Hutchison, W. C. Jacobson, and John Phillips, *Imperial Valley Farm Situation,* Report of the Special Investigating Committee Appointed at the Request of the California State Board of Agriculture, the California Farm Bureau Federation and the Agricultural Department of the California State Chamber of Commerce (April 16, 1934), 19, 24. The Agricultural Labor Bureau of the San Joaquin Valley was established in 1926 by the Farm Bureau Federation and the Chamber of Commerce. Palomares, along with the growers, fixed wages. See Mitchell, "Disintegration," 115. Herbert Klein and Carey McWilliams, "Cold Terror in California," *The Nation* 141, no. 3655 (July 24, 1934): 97, http://newdeal.feri.org/nation/na3497.htm.

63. Robert Justin Goldstein, *Political Repression in Modern America: From 1870 to 1976* (Urbana: University of Illinois Press, 2001), 222–23. McWilliams, *California,* 148–49. Anne Loftis, *Witnesses to the Struggle: Imaging the 1930s California Labor Movement* (Las Vegas: University of Nevada Press, 1998), 17–26.

64. Jamieson, *Labor Unionism,* 119, 122–25, 128–34. Weber, *Dark Sweat,* 330–31. Lowenstein, "Strikes and Strike Tactics," 29. Theodore Johns, "Field Workers in California Cotton" (Master's thesis, University of California at Berkeley, 1948), 86–92. Lucas Lucio was the leader of the *Comisión.* Most Mexican unions could not afford to affiliate with the AFL in this period.

65. Jamieson, *Labor Unionism,* 126–27. G. González, *Labor and Community,* 135–60. Lisbeth Haas, *Conquests and Historical Identities in California, 1769-1936* (Berkeley: University of California Press, 1995), 206–8.

66. Gutiérrez, *Walls and Mirrors,* 147–48.

67. Ibid., 110. Victoria Cepeda, "Latino Civil Rights Figures: Luisa Moreno." NewsTaco, http://www.newstaco.com/2011/08/11/latino-civil-rights-figures-luisa-moreno/. Heidi Moore, *Luisa Moreno* (London: Heinemann Educational Books, 2005). Luisa Moreno, http://www.youtube.com/watch?v=7upHqNX6654.

68. Ronald B. Taylor, *Sweatshops in the Sun: Child Labor on the Farms* (Boston: Beacon Press, 1973), 6–7. Peter Mattiessen, *Sal Si Puedes: César Chávez and the New American Revolution* (New York: Random House, 1969), 9. Carey McWilliams, *Factories in the Fields: The Story of Migratory Labor in California* (Santa Barbara and Salt Lake City: Peregrine Publishers, 1971), 196. Ruiz, *Cannery Women,* 43, 45, 53–55. Vicky L. Ruiz, "UCAPAWA, Chicanas, and the California Food Processing Industry, 1937-1950" (PhD dissertation, Stanford University, 1982), 127.

69. Foley, *White Scourge,* 183–201. Jamieson, *Labor Unionism,* 57, 270–73, 275–78. Selden C. Menefee, "Mexican Migratory Workers of South Texas" (Washington, DC: Works Progress Administration, 1941), reprinted in Carlos E. Cortés, ed., *Mexican Labor,* 52.

70. Coalson, in *Migratory Farm Labor System,* 40–42, reviews labor conditions in the sugar beet industry in Michigan, Ohio, and Wisconsin. McWilliams, in *Ill Fares the Land,* 257–58, states that 66,100 Mexicans left Texas annually for seasonal work. Many went to the beet fields. Jamieson, *Labor Unionism,* 233–35, 238–41.

71. Sarah Deutsch, *No Separate Refuge: Culture, Class, and Gender on the Anglo-Hispanic Frontier in the American Southwest, 1880-1940* (New York: Oxford University Press, 1987), 163–64.

72. Jamieson, *Labor Unionism,* 242–55. Menefee, "Mexican Migratory Workers," 24. Mark Reisler, *By the Sweat of Their Brow: Mexican Immigrant Labor in the United States, 1900-1940* (Westport, CT: Greenwood Press, 1976), 248–49; McWilliams, *Ill Fares the Land,* 125; Pauline Kibbe, *Latin Americans in Texas* (New York: Arno Press, 1974), 201.

73. Deutsch, *No Separate Refuge,* 174–75, 205. "[Mrs. Juan Valdes]," American Life Histories: Manuscripts from the Federal Writers' Project, 1936–1940, 1939, Library of Congress, http://newmexicowanderings.com/launio11.htm.

74. Rose Pesotta, *Bread upon the Water* (New York: Dodd, Mead, 1944), 19, 22, 23, 27–28, 40, 43, 50, 54–59. See Rose Pesotta, Anarchist Library, http://theanarchistlibrary.org/library/rose-pesotta-bread-upon-the-waters.

75. Sánchez, *Becoming Mexican American,* 227–41. John Lasslett and Mary Tyler, *The ILGWU in Los Angeles, 1907-1988* (Inglewood, CA: Ten Star Press, 1989), 26–44. Pesotta, in *Bread upon the Water,* 75, states that Mary Gonzáles and Beatrice López were union organizers in the sweatshops of San Francisco's Chinatown.

76. Blackwelder, *Women of the Depression,* 31–32, 76–77, 131–35.

77. International Ladies' Garment Workers' Union, *Handbook of Texas Online,* http://www.tshaonline.org/handbook/online/articles/II/oci2.html.

78. R. García, *San Antonio*, 62. George N. Green, "The ILGWU in Texas, 1930–1970," *Journal of Mexican American History* 1, no. 2 (Spring 1971): 144–45, 154, 158. Martha Cotera, *Profile of the Mexican American Woman* (Austin, TX: National Educational Laboratory Publishers, 1976), 86–87.

79. "Mexican women pecan shellers at work. Union plant. San Antonio, Texas", Security Administration—Office of War Information Photograph Collection (Library of Congress), 1939, http://www.ancientfaces.com/photo/mexican-women-pecan-shellers-at-work-union-plant-s/740401.

80. Altar for Emma Tenayuca, Houston Institute for Culture, http://www.houstonculture.org/mexico/altaremma.html. Development of Labor Unions in San Antonio, 1930s: Emma Tenayuca, Birth: December 21, 1916, Institute of Texas Cultures, http://www.teachingtexas.org/node/827.

81. Harold Arthur Shapiro, "Workers of San Antonio, Texas, 1900–1940" (PhD dissertation, University of Texas, 1952), 117, 119, 125, 126. Kenneth Walker, "The Pecan Shellers of San Antonio and Mechanization," *Southwestern Historical Quarterly* 69 (July 1965): 44–58. R. García, *San Antonio*, 62–64. Menefee and Cassmore, *Pecan Shellers*, 4–5. Green Peyton, *San Antonio: City in the Sun* (New York: McGraw-Hill, 1946), 169. Ruiz, *Out of the Shadows*, 80; three of the shellers at the bargain table in 1942 were officers in UCAPAWA Local No. 172: Lydia Domínguez, president, Margarita Rendón, vice-president, and Maizie Támez, secretary treasurer. Blackwelder, *Women of the Depression*, 145–53. Roberto Calderón and Emilio Zamora, "Manuela Solis and Emma Tenayuca: A Tribute," in *Between Borders: Essays on Mexicana/Chicana History* (Encino, CA: Floricanto Press, 1990), 269–79. Irene Ledesma, "Texas Newspapers and Chicana Workers' Activism, 1919–1974," *Western Historical Quarterly* 26, no. 3 (Fall 1995): 317–21. Zaragosa Vargas, "Tejana Radical: Emma Tenayuca and the San Antonio Labor Movement during the Great Depression," *Pacific Historical Review* 66, no. 4 (November 1997): 553–80.

82. Gabriela González, "Carolina Munguia and Emma Tenayuca: The Politics of Benevolence and Radical Reform," *Frontiers: Journal of Women Studies* 24, nos. 2 & 3, (2003), https://muse.jhu.edu/login?auth=0&type=summary&url=/journals/frontiers/v024/24.2gonzalez_g.html. Allan Turner, "A Night That Changed San Antonio/Woman Recalls Leading Labor Riot in 1939," *Houston Chronicle,* 2 Star ed. (December 14, 1986) reports that the incident happened in 1939.

83. Emma Tenayuca and Homer Brooks, "The Mexican Question in the Southwest," *Communist* 18 (May 1939): 257–68. Gutiérrez, *Walls and Mirrors*, 107–9. Peyton, *City in the Sun*, 172–74. Shapiro, "Workers of San Antonio," 130–32. Menefee and Cassmore, *Pecan Shellers*, 24. Audrey Granneberg, "Maury Maverick's San Antonio," *Survey Graphic* 28, no. 7 (July 1939): 421, http://newdeal.feri.org/survey/39a07.htm.

84. Robert M. Fogelson, *The Fragmented Metropolis: Los Angeles, 1850–1930* (Berkeley: University of California Press, 1993), 132–34.

85. Luis Leobardo Arroyo, "Chicano Participation in Organized Labor: CIO in Los Angeles, 1938–1950: An Extended Research Note," *Aztlán* 6, no. 2 (Summer 1975): 277. Monroy, *Thrown Among Strangers*, 70, 99.

86. Kathryn Close, "Back of the Yards: Packingtown's Latest Drama: Civic Unity," *Survey Graphic* 29, no. 12 (December 1, 1940), 612, http://newdeal.feri.org/search_details.cfm?link=http://newdeal.feri.org/survey/40c22.htm, describes beginnings of Saul Alinsky's organizing that would influence future generations of Mexican Americans. Dominic A. Pacyga, *Polish Immigrants and Industrial Chicago: Workers on the South Side, 1880–1922* (Chicago: University of Chicago Press, 2003), 159.

87. Gabriela F. Arredondo, Mexicanas in Chicago, Illinois Periodicals Online, Northern Illinois University Libraries, http://www.lib.niu.edu/2003/iht1020357.html. Louise A. N. Kerr, Mexicans in Chicago, http://www.lib.niu.edu/1999/iht629962.html (accessed November 3, 2009). Lizabeth Cohen, *Making a New Deal: Industrial Workers in Chicago, 1919–1939* (Cambridge: Cambridge University Press, 1991), 337–38. "[Jesse Perez], Chicago," American Life Histories: Manuscripts from the Federal Writers' Project, 1936–1940, 1939, http://memory.loc.gov/ammem/index.html. "Another Case of Racial Prejudice," *Chicago Defender* (October 17, 1936), 16.

88. Louise Kerr, "The Chicano Experience in Chicago, 1920–1970" (PhD dissertation, University of Illinois at Chicago Circle, 1976), 69–70, 72–78. The Chicago Mexican population had fallen from 20,000 in 1930 to 14,000 in 1933 and to 12,500 in 1934. See also Francisco A. Rosales and Daniel T. Simon, "Chicano Steelworkers and Unionism in the Midwest, 1919–1945," *Aztlán* 6 (Summer 1975): 267. Zaragosa Vargas, *Labor Rights Are Civil Rights: Mexican American Workers in Twentieth-Century America* (Princeton, NJ: Princeton University Press, 2005), 271–72.

89. U.S. Congress, Senate, Committee on Education and Labor, *Violations of Free Speech and Rights of Labor: Hearings Before a Subcommittee of the Committee on Education and Labor…* 75th Cong., 1st session, June 30–July 2, 1937, Part 14, "The Chicago Memorial Day Incident," pp. 4941–4949. In F. Arturo Rosales, ed, *Testimonio: A Documentary History of the Mexican American Struggle for Civil Rights.* (Houston, TX: Arte Público Press—University of Houston, 2000), 249–56. Little Steel Strike of 1937, Ohio History Central, http://www.ohiohistorycentral.org/entry.php?rec=513. Memorial Day massacre of 1937, http://en.wikipedia.org/wiki/Memorial_Day_massacre_of_1937.

90. Irving Bernstein, *History of the American Workers 1920–1933: The Lean Years* (Boston: Houghton-Mifflin, 1960). Harry R. Rubenstein, "Political Regression in New Mexico: The Destruction of the National Miners' Union in Gallup," in Robert Kern, ed., *Labor in New Mexico: Unions, Strikers, and Social History Since 1881* (Albuquerque: University of New Mexico Press, 1983), 93–95. See *State v. Ochoa et al.,* 41 N.M. 589; 72 2d 609; 1937 N.M. Lexis 70. Francisco A. Rosales, *Chicano! The History of the Mexican American Civil Rights Movement*, 2d Revised ed. (Houston, TX: Arte Público Press, 1997), 122.

91. D. W. Dinwoodie, "The Rise of the Mine-Mill Union in Southwestern Copper," in James C. Foster, ed., *American*

Labor in the Southwest (Tucson: University of Arizona Press, 1982), 46–48. Monroy, *Thrown Among Strangers*, 126–31. Texas State Industrial Union Council, *Handbook of Texas Online*, http://www.tshaonline.org/handbook/online/articles/octbg.

92. George I. Sánchez Charter School, http://www.aama.org/Sanchez-Charter-High-School/. Carlos K. Blanton, "George I. Sánchez, Ideology, and Whiteness in the Making of the Mexican American Civil Rights Movement, 1930–1960," *Journal of Southern History* 72, no. 3 (August 2006), 569–604.

93. M. García, *Mexican American*, 66–67.

94. League of United Latin American Citizens. *Handbook of Texas Online*, http://www.tshaonline.org/handbook/online/articles/LL/wel1.html. Gutiérrez, *Walls and Mirrors*, 87, 89–90. M. García, *Mexican Americans*, 3, 26–40, 62–83, 175–203, 232–51, 273–90. R. García, *San Antonio*, 278. Montejano, *Anglos and Mexicans*, 160–61. Daniel D. Arreola, "Mexican Origins of South Texas Mexican Americans, 1930," *Journal of Historical Geography* 19, no. 1 (January 1993): 48–63. Peyton, *City in the Sun*, 156–59.

95. Robin Fitzgerald Scott, "The Mexican-American in the Los Angeles Area, 1920–1950: From Acquiescence to Activity" (PhD dissertation, University of Southern California, 1971), 148–49. Monroy, *Thrown Among Strangers*, 109, 195–96.

96. Ruiz, *Out of the Shadows*, 36–50. M. García, *Bert Corona*, 30. Carlos Muñoz, Jr., *Youth, Identity, Power: The Chicano Movement* (London: Verso, 1989), 25. On March 6, 1979, Manuel Banda stated that Tom García, 33, the secretary of the YMCA, had the idea for the MAM. For more data on the MAM, see "Mexican-American Movement: Its Origins and Personnel," in the Angel Cano papers at California State University, Northridge/Chicano Studies, July 12, 1944, 3–4. (This collection is referred to hereafter as the Cano papers.) In CSUN Library, http://digital-library.csun.edu/LatArch/. See also Albert R. Lozano, "Progress Through Education," Cano papers. *Forward* (October 28, 1945 and February 24, 1949). "Félix Gutiérrez, Prominent Youth Worker, Dies at 37," *Lincoln Heights Bulletin-News* (December 1, 1955). *Forum News Bulletin* (August 7, 1949). José Rodríguez, "The Value of Education," *The Mexican Voice* (July 1938), quoted in C. Muñoz, *Youth, Identity, and Power*, 31. Rebecca Muñoz, "Horizons," *The Mexican Voice* (July 1939), quoted in C. Muñoz, *Youth, Identity, Power*, 34. C. Muñoz, *Youth, Identity, Power*, 19–42. "Supreme Council of the Mexican American Movement Papers" in Latino Archives collection, California State Northridge Urban Archives, http://digital-library.csun.edu/LatArch/.

97. Kevin Allen Leonard, *The Battle for Los Angeles: Racial Ideology and World War II* (Albuquerque: University of New Mexico Press, 2006), 27–28. Ruiz, *Cannery Women*, 99. M. García, *Mexican Americans*, 145–74. M. García, in *Mexican Americans*, 157, suggests that Quevedo might have been cooperating with the FBI during the time that he served as an officer in the Congress. Miguel Tirado, "Mexican American Community Political Organization: The Key to Chicano Political Power," in F. Chris García, ed., *La Causa Politica: A Chicano Politics Reader* (Notre Dame, IN: University of Notre Dame Press, 1974). F. Chris García, "Manitos and Chicanos in New Mexico Politics," in F. C. García, ed., *La Causa Politica*. Scott, "The Mexican-American," 147, 149. Gutiérrez, *Walls and Mirrors*, 111–14.

98. Luisa Moreno, "Non-citizen Americans of the Southwest: Caravan of Sorrow," Cano papers, California Sate University at Northridge, March 3, 1940, Quoted in M. García, *Mexican Americans*, 164. M. García, *Bert Corona*, 108–26.

99. Agustín Gurza, "Remembering El Espectador," *LatinoLA*, June 17, 2009, http://latinola.com/story.php?story=7568 (accessed November 3, 2009). Kaye Lyon Briegel, "*Alianza Hispano-Americana* and Some Mexican-American Civil Rights Cases in the 1950s," in Manuel Servín, ed., *An Awakening Minority: The Mexican-Americans*, 2d ed. (Beverly Hills, CA: Glencoe Press, 1974), 176. M. García, *Mexican Americans*, 84–112. M. García, *Bert Corona*, 32. Richard Griswold de Castillo, ed., *World War II and Mexican American Civil Rights* (Austin: University of Texas Press, 2008), 87–89. Rosales, *Chicano!*, 99.

100. Mexican ministers were sent to the United States to work with not only Mexicans but also Puerto Ricans. Alberto Báez, a New York Methodist minister, worked with Puerto Ricans. He wrote to President Roosevelt about the needs of the Puerto Rican people and the role that English played. Alberto Báez, the grandfather of folk singer Joan Báez, was from Monterrey, Mexico, and had worked with Puerto Ricans for almost 20 years. Letter from Pastor Alberto Báez to President Franklin D. Roosevelt's Administration, Franklin Delano Roosevelt Library, President's Personal File, Entry 21, Box 22, October 11, 1935. http://newdeal.feri.org/clergy/cl013.htm.

101. John R. Chávez, *The Lost Land: The Chicano Image of the Southwest* (Albuquerque: University of New Mexico Press, 1984), 97–98. Ruiz, *Out of the Shadows*, 93–94. D. H. Dinwoodie, "Deportation: The Immigration Service and the Chicano Labor Movement in the 1930s," in Antonio Rios Bustamante, ed., *Immigration and Public Policy: Human Rights for Undocumented Workers and Their Families* (Los Angeles, CA: Chicano Studies Center Publications, 1977), 163–74. Philip Stevenson, "Deporting Jesús," *The Nation* 143 (July 18, 1936): 67–69. Deutsch, *No Separate Refuge*, 173. Cotera, *Mexican American Woman*, 93–96.

102. Kerr, "Chicano Experience in Chicago," 69–74, 76–80, 83, 95–96, 99, 101–4. David Maciel, *El Mexico olvidado: La historia del pueblo chicano* (El Paso: University of Texas at El Paso, 1996), 372–75.

103. William S. Taylor, "Some Observations of Marginal Man in the United States," *Journal of Negro Education* 9, no. 4 (October 1940): 606–8.

CHAPTER 11

World War II: The Betrayal of Promises

LEARNING OBJECTIVES

- Discuss why many Mexican Americans were at first reluctant to fight in the war.

- Explore the events surrounding the Sleepy Lagoon trial and the zoot-suit riots.

- Explain the role of Chicanas and Chicanos during World War II.

- Analyze how the war changed the Mexican American community.

- Tell how the war changed Mexican Americans and conditioned their organizational response to the Cold War politics that followed the war.

As with other timelines, the years mark major events within the decade. In the 1940s, World War II dominates the narrative of the period. However, for any war, the causes may have happened before the decade itself. For example, many Americans believe World War II began in 1941 when Japan attacked Pearl Harbor. Was this the cause of the war? The year 1939 marks the start of the war in Europe, but did the war begin then? Or was it in 1919 when the punitive terms of the Treaty of Versailles led to the rise of Adolph Hitler? The causes of any major happening, including World War II, are more complex than can be attributed to a single episode, and the multiple causes almost always begin way before the decade in question. Like any other event, World War II was the culmination of a chain of events, and considering them builds an understanding of the war itself and its impact on the present.

Mexican Americans

At the start of World War II, some 60 percent of Mexican Americans lived in cities; 10 years later 70 percent did. The war years dramatically accelerated this rapid urbanization, greatly affecting the identity of the Mexican-origin population. Because of pressure from Mexican American organizations, the U.S. Census

1939	1940	1941	1942	1943	1945	1946	1947	1948	1949

again listed Mexicans as "white" in 1940 as it had in 1920, that is, unless they looked Indian or of another color. The Census counted 132,165,129 residents in the United States, of which, according to the best estimate, 5.6 percent were Latinos, composed overwhelmingly of people of Mexican origin. Most Mexicans lived in the Southwest; however, some were moving to the Midwest and Pacific Northwest. Repatriation and deportation of 600,000 to 1 million Mexicans tipped the balance to the second and third generations of Mexicans. A slowing down of Mexican immigration to the United States during the Depression years affected this trend. Nowhere was this change more noticeable than in the Midwestern states of Indiana, Illinois, and Michigan, which saw a decline of 72 percent, 52 percent, and 62 percent, respectively, in the Mexican population— California, Texas, Arizona, and New Mexico lost 33 percent, 40 percent, 49 percent, and 45 percent, respectively during the Great Depression.[1]

As with all wars, the poor paid a disproportionate cost. According to Robin Scott, 375,000–500,000 Mexicans, a high proportion of Mexican American males, served in the armed forces. In Los Angeles, Mexicans composed an estimated one-tenth of the population, yet accounted for one-fifth of the war casualties.[2] World War II accelerated the reformation of the Mexican family system. More women worked outside the home, and the departure of soldier fathers and husbands made them more independent. As always, not all the changes were entirely positive. The removal of male role models encouraged youth vagrancy, which—when mixed with poverty—led to a lessening of Mexican social control; these changes and the pressures of urban life would give rise to a proliferation of gangs, a made-in-the-USA institution. Within this racially charged environment, most Mexican Americans wanted to retain their identity as Mexicans in origin—a gut-level response to the racism of the white-dominated society that physically isolated the group.[3]

World War II and the Mexican

Steven Spielberg made the film *Saving Private Ryan* in 1998, and Tom Brokaw published his book *The Greatest Generation* that same year. Ken Burns in 2007 produced an award-winning documentary, "The War." What these works shared was that they ignored the Mexican American soldier. This is despite the fact that the ratio of Mexicans among buck privates serving in combat was one of the highest. Raúl Morín, in *Among the Valiant*, wrote that 25 percent of the U.S. military personnel on the infamous Bataan "Death March" were Mexican Americans. Forced to march 85 miles, 6,000 of the 16,000 soldiers perished. Twelve Mexican Americans won Medals of Honor during World War II; proportionately, this number was higher than that for any other ethnic group. For example, José M. López of Brownsville, Texas, received the Medal of Honor for bravely holding off the advancing Germans until his company was able to retreat.[4]

Many Los Angeles Mexicans were ambivalent when they heard that the United States declared war on Japan on December 8, 1941: "*Ya estuvo* (This is it)," said one, "Now we can look for the authorities to round up all the Mexicans and deport them to Mexico—bad security risks." At first, some Mexican Americans dissociated themselves, saying that their loyalty was to Mexico, not to the United States, but in the end they went into the service. Many Mexican Americans had witnessed the repatriation and the discrimination and second-class citizenship experienced by the community and were bitter.[5]

This was a generation, however, that intuitively wanted to prove itself. The song "*Soldado Raso*," by Felipe V. Leal, is a haunting memory of those feelings: The narrator in the song poignantly relates how he and his fellow soldiers journey to the front lines, leaving behind sorrowful mothers and sweethearts. The song goes on to say that the *soldado raso* (buck private), in leaving his mother, begs the Virgin of Guadalupe to take care of her while he is away. The *soldado* goes off to defend his country, proudly saying that his race "knows how to die anywhere."[6]

Many of the Mexican American soldiers were 17–21 years old, and some were even younger—like the author's cousin Rubén Villa, who lied about his age and enlisted in the Navy at 16. Apart from the soldiers' machismo of having to prove themselves, the statement that their race "knows how to die anywhere" represents the injustice of sending people with unequal rights and opportunities to war. Educational status, economic status, race, and gender all play a role in determining equality. (During the Vietnam War, Luis Valdez constructed a one-act play, protesting the war, around Leal's song.)

246 Chapter 11 • World War II: The Betrayal of Promises

The Case of Guy Gabaldón

Guy Gabaldón, serving in the western Pacific, captured hundreds of Japanese prisoners. His Navy Cross citation reads, "Working alone in front of the lines, he daringly entered enemy caves, pillboxes, buildings and jungle brush, frequently in the face of hostile fire, and succeeded in not only obtaining vital military information but in capturing well over 1,000 civilians and troops." Gabaldón learned the Japanese language as a child in East Los Angeles, where two Japanese American brothers had befriended him. Gabaldón often visited their home and eventually moved in with them. When he turned 17, he joined the Marine Corps. After the war, Gabaldón harbored resentment toward the U.S. Marines' decision to award him the Silver Star instead of the Medal of Honor. The Navy upgraded his citation to the Navy Cross after the release of the film *Hell to Eternity* (1960), which documented Guy's war experiences. The movie, however, did not mention that Gabaldón was a Mexican, and a blond, blue-eyed actor played his character.[7]

Gabaldón accused the Marines of racism toward Mexican Americans, pointing out that he captured more prisoners than the legendary Sergeant Alvin York, who received the Medal of Honor after killing 25 German soldiers and capturing 132 in France in 1918. He ridiculed the Corps' response that another recipient of the Medal was Hispanic: "Although the man indeed deserved the medal, the Marine's father was of Portuguese descent and his mother was Hawaiian."[8]

The Story of Company E: The All-Mexican Unit

Raúl Morín, the author of *Among the Valiant*, was semiliterate and had little research skill; nevertheless, he wanted to tell the neglected story of the Mexican American military contribution to World War II. One of his most dramatic stories was that of Company E of the 2nd Battalion, 141st Infantry Regiment of the 36th Infantry Division, which consisted of men from El Paso, Texas, that had belonged to an infantry company of the Texas National Guard formed in El Paso. Company E was an all-Chicano company that had a high esprit-de-corps and during basic training had been selected to receive Ranger training. Many of the members were related: it contained three brothers, Juan, Andres, and Antonio Saucedo. Many had attended Bowie High School.

Company E fought in North Africa and was part of the opening of the Italian campaign. When the company reached Italy's Rapido River near Monte Cassino monastery, 5th Army Commander General Mark Clark needed a diversionary attack to prevent the Germans from attacking the main Allied invasion forces landing at Anzio. Units of the 36th division took part, and in less than 48 hours, the division lost more than 1,700 men—more than half its number. After the Rapido River assault, Company E regrouped and received replacements to fill the badly depleted squads. The unit fought in the Cassino area and then fought at Anzio, helped liberate Rome from the Germans, and landed in southern France to take pressure off the Normandy landings (the backdrop of the movie *Saving Private Ryan*).[9]

Morín writes about the little-known incident that was a prelude to the Rapido massacre: the 5th Army command had ordered a platoon from Company E on a suicide mission to scout the Rapido Crossing. The patrol was led by Sergeant Gabriel Navarrete and was composed almost entirely of Mexican Americans. The Germans seriously wounded Navarrete and killed or captured most of his patrol. Navarrete, knowing that the company would lead the assault, reported his findings and pleaded that "his boys" not be again sent on the suicide mission. Navarrete closely identified with the men, who were mostly from El Paso barrios. The commander ordered the badly wounded Navarrete to the battalion hospital. Still, Navarrete insisted that Company E not be sent back across the river; he cautioned Battalion Commander Major Landley that if Landley sent Company E across, disaster was certain. Landley responded that the U.S. Army was not taking orders from an "incompetent" lieutenant "who was badly wounded and talked incoherently." Navarrete reportedly told Landley, "I will stand court martial as I am not worried for myself. But remember this, Major, if the plans are not changed and you sacrifice my E Company, you are going to answer to me personally; I will be looking for you and I will be armed." On January 21, 1944, Company E again spearheaded the crossing of the Rapido River. The crossing was a complete fiasco. Morín argues, among other things, that General Clark picked Company E, the all-Mexican company, for the most dangerous jobs.

When Navarrete learned of the disaster, he jumped from his cot and went gunning for the major. The high command immediately transferred the major out of the unit and ordered Navarrete—elevated to the rank of captain—back to the United States. "The Army brass tried to hush up the incident." Meanwhile, the army rewarded General Clark with another star, although the 36th Division Association objected. The involvement of Company E and the disaster was kept under wraps, and Navarrete was ordered to keep quiet. Navarrete, who earned a Distinguished Service Cross, a Bronze Star, and two Silver Stars, told the story to Morín. In a way, the story of Navarrete detracts from the extraordinary exploits of the all-Mexican Company E. However, his bravery or that of the rest of the men of Company E is not in doubt.[10]

Racism at Home and Abroad

Louis Téllez of Albuquerque was the only Mexican American in his platoon: "I'll never forget the first time I heard [a racial slur], it really hurt me. You can't do anything about it because you are all alone."[11] Leo Avila of Oakdale, California, a stateside instructor in the Army Air Corps B-29 Program, said, "I view the service and World War II, for me and many others, as the event that opened new doors. I was from a farm family. When I went into the Air Corps and I found I could compete with Anglo people effectively, even those with a couple of years of college, at some point along the way I realized I didn't want to go back to the farm."[12] Throughout the war, many white Americans treated Mexicans as second-class citizens. For example, Sergeant Macario García from Sugarland, Texas—a recipient of the Congressional Medal of Honor—could not buy a cup of coffee in a restaurant in Richmond, California. "An Anglo-American chased him out with a baseball bat."[13] And, the García incident was not an isolated occurrence.

A more subtle form of racism that persists to this day is the exclusion of Chicanos and Chicanas from the war narrative. Ken Burns's PBS documentary, *The War* (2007), leaves out the Chicano/a participation in World War II.[14] Movies have been made about Euro-American families with more than one family member in the war; however, this was pretty much the rule in Mexican American households. Rosaura Moralez from Anthony, New Mexico, prayed that her five boys return safely. She was fortunate that they did—even though the odds did not favor Raul, Armando, Catarino, Ricardo, and Esequiel Moralez's safe return, they all came back alive. Rita Sánchez tells the story of the five Sánchez brothers from Bernalillo, New Mexico. Four served in the armed forces, and the oldest Leo, 40, tried to enlist but was rejected because of age and medical reasons. Counting the Sánchez's extended family, dozens of kin served in the armed forces—they fought in Europe and in the Pacific. The Sánchez family was not as fortunate as the Moralez family, however; Severo was killed during heavy fighting on Leyte Island.

Lita De Los Santos remembers eight brothers who served in the war: Charlie, the eldest brother, was killed on Omaha Beach during the invasion of Normandy. Another brother was shot down over France—taken a prisoner of war in Germany. Another, Cano, served in Italy, where a piece of shrapnel got lodged in his heart. Ray was wounded in France, and Jesse and Pete were in combat in New Guinea and the Philippines, respectively. It is incredible that the so-called historians such as Ken Burns have missed these sacrifices.[15]

Chicanas in the Military

The song "*Soldado Raso*" dramatizes the mothers' role during the war. If a family had a serviceman in the family, they used to hang a blue star in their window. For every family member killed in the war, the household hung a flag with gold star. The sea of blue turned gold in the Mexican districts during the war. Sara Castro Vara had six sons who went into combat. Rudy Vara fought with General George Patton and was one of the first soldiers to help liberate the Nazi concentration camps. The Téllez family of Albuquerque sent six young men and two young women to the service. Such families were common in the Mexican American community.

Mexican women also joined the Women's Army Auxiliary Corps (WAAC) as well as the Navy Women's Service (WAVES) and Women's Air Force Service Pilots (WASP) units. Women went overseas as nurses and accepted other options that the war opened to them. For example, Anna Torres Vásquez of East Chicago, Indiana, volunteered for the WAAC, serving as an air-traffic controller at a Florida flight school. Rafaela Muñoz Esquivel from San Antonio was the second oldest in a family of 15 children; as a child, Rafaela had worked in the pecan-shelling industry in San Antonio. During World War II, she was an army nurse in the United States and then served in France, supporting the 82nd Airborne Division, and was stationed in Germany near Coblenz, about 5 miles from George Patton's 3rd Army. Three children in the Muñiz family served overseas during the war.[16]

A Profile of Courage

The courage to criticize popular causes, no matter how unjust they are, is difficult at the time the injustices are occurring. Ralph Lazo epitomized such a profile in courage. Lazo was raised among Asian Americans in the Temple–Beaudry neighborhood of Los Angeles, which included white, Jewish, Japanese, Filipino, Korean, Mexican, and Chinese residents. Ralph attended Central Junior High School and Belmont High School, where he interacted with friends of all races. He played basketball on a Filipino Community Church team and learned Japanese at his friends' homes; he also took Japanese language classes. His father, John Houston Lazo, a house painter and muralist, was a widower and raised Ralph and his sister, Virginia.

In February 1942, President Franklin D. Roosevelt signed Executive Order 9066, sending 110,000 Japanese Americans to internment (concentration) camps. Ralph Lazo, 16, whose sense of justice was offended, joined his Japanese American friends and went with them to the Manzanar internment camp. Lazo was the only non-Japanese in any of the internment camps. A local newspaper caustically wrote, "Mexican American passes for Japanese." Lazo's father, respecting his son's decision, made no effort to bring his son home. He graduated from Manzanar High School and was drafted in August 1944. Lazo served in the South Pacific, was among the troops that liberated the Philippines, and was awarded a Bronze Star for heroism in combat.

Lazo maintained close ties to the Japanese American community until his death in 1992. He was one of the 10 donors contributing $1,000 or more to the class action lawsuit against the U.S. government, which was made to financially compensate Japanese Americans who were interned. At a Manzanar High School reunion years later, his classmates paid tribute to Ralph, saying, "When 140 million Americans turned their backs on us and excluded us into remote, desolate prison camps, the separation was absolute—almost. Ralph Lazo's presence among us said, No, not everyone."[17]

Finding Scapegoats

Once the government removed the Japanese, Mexican Americans became the country's scapegoats of choice, especially as the American casualties of war (even though many of them were of Mexican origin) fueled public hatred against all foreigners. Despite the fact that most Mexican Americans were citizens, they were considered "aliens." Their color was their Star of David (the religious symbol Jews were forced to wear in Germany to identify them).

In Los Angeles during wartime, segregation was common, and many recreational facilities excluded Mexican Americans. They could not use public swimming pools in East Los Angeles and in other Southland communities. Often, Mexicans and blacks could swim only on Wednesdays—the day the county drained the water. In movie houses in places like San Fernando, Mexicans sat in the balcony.

A minority of Mexican youth between the ages of 13 and 17 were members of barrio clubs that carried the name of their neighborhoods—White Fence, Alpine Street, *El Hoyo*, Happy Valley. The fad among zoot-suiters, or *pachucos* as they were called, was to tattoo the left hand, between the thumb and index finger, with a small cross with three dots or dashes above it. When they dressed up, many *pachucos* wore the so-called zoot suit, popular among low-income youths. *Pachucos* not only spoke Spanish, but also used *Chuco* among their companions. *Chuco* was the barrio language—a mixture of Spanish, English, old Spanish, and words adapted by the border Mexicans. Many experts suggest that the language originated around El Paso among Mexicans, who brought it to Los Angeles in the 1930s.

Although similar gangs existed among Euro-American youth, Angelenos looked upon gangs as a Mexican problem, forgetting that urbanization was causing the gang phenomenon. The *Los Angeles Times*, not known for its analytic content, reinforced this stereotype and influenced the public with stories about "Mexican" hoodlums. Sociologist Joan Moore attributes the growth of gangs in Los Angeles to poverty and the lack of role models in the homes that resulted when the fathers and older brothers went off to the war. Other than the territorial nature of the gangs, their most distinctive feature was their individuality. Location and the class background of the gang members played a role. For example, during the war the White Fence gang emerged in Boyle Heights, around La Purissima Catholic Church. The Heights was a neighborhood of skilled workers from the brickyards, railroads, packinghouses, and other industries. Unlike Maravilla, Boyle Heights was racially integrated. In 1936, the Lorena Street School was only 22 percent Mexican; the Euclid Street School was 70 percent Mexican.[18]

Forgotten in this historical narrative has been the voice of Mexican American females who were ravaged by the press as well as by the public. Catherine Sue Ramírez has resurrected documents reviving painful memories of how Mexican girls were generalized as having all the negative stereotypes of the males and some more. The press characterized them as "girl hoodlums" and "Black Widows" who were infected with venereal disease. Young Mexican girls were offended, and they protested the allegations. Naturally, the press blamed the Mexican parent; the use of Spanish and their low standard of living were blamed and contrasted them to the self-perceived "wholesome" American way. Mexican women were at the same time portrayed as passive, as violent, and as having loose morals.[19]

The Sleepy Lagoon Trial

The name "Sleepy Lagoon" came from a popular melody played by bandleader Harry James. Unable to use public pools, Mexican youth used the name of the tune to romanticize a gravel pit where they frequently hung out. On the evening of August 1, 1942, members of the 38th Street Club in South Central Los Angeles were jumped by another gang. When the 38th Street members returned later with their friends, the rival gang was not there. Noticing a party in progress at the nearby Williams Ranch, the 38th Street gang crashed in, and a fight followed. The next morning José Díaz, a guest at the party, was found dead on a dirt road near the house. Authorities suspected members of the 38th Street Club beat him to death, and the police immediately jailed the entire gang. The press portrayed the Sleepy Lagoon defendants as Mexican hoodlums. Meanwhile, the police flagrantly violated the rights of the suspects, and authorities charged 22 members of the 38th Street boys with criminal conspiracy. Two others demanded a separate trial; the court dropped charges against them.[20]

Shortly after Díaz's death, a special committee of the grand jury accepted a report by Lieutenant Ed Durán Ayres, head of the Foreign Relations Bureau of the Los Angeles Sheriff's Department. The report justified the gross violation of human rights of the defendants. While admitting that there was discrimination against Mexicans in employment, education, schooling, recreation, and labor unions, it said that Mexicans were inherently criminal and violent. According to Ayres, Mexicans were Indians, who in turn were "Orientals," who in turn had an utter disregard for life. Therefore, Mexicans were genetically violent. The report concluded that Mexicans were descendants of the Aztecs, who, the report claimed, sacrificed 30,000 victims in a day.

Ayres allegedly wrote that Indians considered leniency a sign of weakness, pointing to the Mexican government's treatment of the Indians, which he maintained was quick and severe. Ayres urged that the courts imprison all gang members and give every Mexican youth over the age of 18 the option of working or enlisting in the armed forces. Mexicans, according to Ayres, could not change their spots; they had an innate need to use a knife and let blood. Alcohol and jealousy detonated that inborn cruelty.[21] The Ayres report, which represented official law enforcement views, goes a long way in explaining the events that subsequently took place around Sleepy Lagoon.

Henry Leyvas and the 38th Street gang were charged with Díaz's murder. Most of the defendants lived in what today is South Central Los Angeles, and many of them had attended McKinley Junior High and Jefferson High Schools—which were predominately African American. Their life experiences differed from those of Mexican Americans elsewhere in Los Angeles. The African American population was more aware of its rights, and influenced their Mexican neighbors. Mexican students saw African Americans challenge unjust teachers—"talk back" as they called it—and this attitude influenced many Mexican American students to question unfairness as well.

The Honorable Judge Charles W. Fricke permitted irregularities during the trial. The judge refused to allow the defendants to cut their hair or change their clothes for the duration of the proceedings. Fricke denied them the right to consult counsel—seating them in a separate section of the courtroom. Despite all these irregularities, the prosecution failed to prove that the 38th Street Club was a gang, that any criminal agreement or conspiracy existed, or that the accused murdered Díaz. In fact, witnesses testified that considerable drinking had occurred at the party *before* the 38th Street Club members arrived. If the conspiracy theory had been applied logically, all the defendants would have received the same sentences. However, when on January 12, 1943, the court passed its judicial punishments, three defendants were found guilty of first-degree murder; nine, of second-degree murder; and five, of assault; five were found not guilty.[22]

Under the leadership of LaRue McCormick, supporters formed the Sleepy Lagoon Defense Committee. Carey McWilliams, a noted journalist and lawyer, chaired the committee. The parents of the defendants raised funds by holding tamale sales and dances. Hollywood notables Anthony Quinn, Rita Hayworth, Orson Welles, and many other stars contributed money. African American leaders such as Carlotta Bass, editor of the *California Eagle* newspaper, condemned the injustice. She feared another Scottsboro case, in which nine black men, ages 14–21, were tried without competent counsel for the alleged rape of two white women in Alabama in March 1931. The Mexican community had been weakened by the recent repatriation and the disproportionate number of heads of households who had been inducted into the armed forces. Mainstream Mexican American organizations such as the League of United Latin American Citizens (LULAC) and the *mutualistas* were silent.[23]

Meanwhile, the press and police authorities harassed the committee, and red-baited McWilliams and the members of the Sleepy Lagoon committee. Police raided their meetings, and threatened to take away the First Unitarian Church of Los Angeles's tax exemption if it allowed meetings to be held there. The California Committee on Un-American Activities, headed by State Senator Jack Tenney, investigated the Sleepy Lagoon committee, charging that it was a Communist-front organization and that Carey McWilliams had "Communist leanings," because he opposed segregation and favored miscegenation. The FBI also viewed the committee as a Communist front, stating that it "opposed all types of discrimination against Mexicans."[24]

On October 4, 1944, the Second District Court of Appeals in a unanimous decision reversed the verdict of the lower court, holding that Judge Fricke conducted a biased trial and violated the constitutional rights of the defendants. The court also found no evidence of a conspiracy to commit murder or assaults with intent to commit murder, nor any evidence tying the defendants to José Díaz. The upper court held that Fricke erred by not allowing the defendants to challenge coerced statements made at the time of arrest; further, Fricke erred in refusing the defendants the right to consult with counsel. The Second Appellate Court found Fricke's conduct biased and unfair and found that he had admitted prejudicial evidence. Incredibly, the appellate court concluded that there was no evidence of racism. The defendants' sentences were reversed; however, they were not retried and, hence, did not have the opportunity to prove their innocence. The ordeal emotionally scarred the Sleepy Lagoon appellants and many returned to prison for other offenses.

Compounding the travesty was the imprisonment, without due process of law, of the female friends of the Sleepy Lagoon to the Ventura School for Girls, which according to Alice McGrath (a.k.a. Alice Greenfield in Luís Valdez's film *Zoot Suit*) had a worse reputation than San Quentin Prison did—San Quentin was a maximum-security facility that housed California's death row, lodging murderers and rapists. The Los Angeles Juvenile Court charged Bertha Aguilar, Dora Barrios, Lorena Encinas, Josephine Gonzales, Juanita Gonzales, Frances Silva, Lupe Ynostroza, and Betty Zeiss with rioting, and made them wards of the state under the Department of Institutions. The California Youth Authority persuaded the parents of five of the young ladies to commit their daughters. The judicial system had not convicted the girls of any crime; they were guilty by association. They remained institutionalized until the age of 21.[25]

Mutiny in the Streets of Los Angeles

In the spring of 1943, several minor altercations broke out in Los Angeles. In April, marines and sailors invaded the Mexican barrio and black ghetto in Oakland, assaulted the people, and "depantsed" zoot-suiters. Skirmishes continued through the month of May. The "sailor riots" began in earnest on June 3, 1943. Allegedly, Mexicans attacked a group of sailors for attempting to pick up some Chicanas. The details are vague; police did not try to get the Mexicans' side of the story, but took the sailors' report at face value. Fourteen off-duty police officers, led by a detective lieutenant, went looking for the "criminals." They found no evidence, but made certain that the press covered the story.

That same night, sailors went on a rampage—they broke into the Carmen Theater, tore zoot suits off customers, and beat up the youths. Police arrested the victims. Word spread that *pachucos* were fair game, and military personnel could assault Mexicans without fear of arrest. Sailors returned the next evening with some 200 allies. In 20 hired cabs, they cruised Whittier Boulevard, in the heart of the East Los Angeles barrio, jumping out of the cars to gang up on neighborhood youths. Police and the sheriff said they could not find the sailors. Finally, they arrested nine sailors but released them without filing charges. The press, portraying the sailors as heroes, slanted the news pieces and headlines so as to arouse racial hatred.

Sailors, encouraged by the press and the "responsible" elements of Los Angeles, assembled on the night of June 5 and marched four abreast down the streets, warning Mexicans to shed their zoot suits or face stripping by them. On that night and the next, servicemen broke into bars and other establishments and beat up Mexicans. Police continued to abet the lawlessness, arriving only after the servicemen left. Though sailors destroyed private property, law enforcement officials did little to enforce the law. When members of the Mexican community attempted to defend themselves, police arrested them.

Events climaxed on the evening of June 7, when thousands of soldiers, sailors, and civilians surged down Main Street and Broadway in search of *pachucos*. The mob crashed into bars and broke the legs off stools to use them as clubs. The press reported 500 zoot-suiters ready for battle. By that time, Filipinos and blacks also become targets. Mexicans, beaten up and their clothes ripped off, were left bleeding on the streets. The mob surged into movie theaters, turning on the lights, marching down the aisles, and pulling zoot-suit-clad youngsters out of their seats. Police arrested more than 600 Mexican youths without cause and labeled the arrests "preventive" action. Seventeen-year-old Enrico Herrera, after being beaten and arrested, spent 3 hours at a police station, where his mother found him, still naked and bleeding. A 12-year-old boy's jaw was broken. Through all this, Angelenos cheered the servicemen and their civilian allies.[26]

At the height of the turmoil, servicemen pulled a black man off a streetcar and gouged out his eye with a knife. Military authorities, realizing that the Los Angeles law enforcement agencies would not stop the brutality, intervened and declared downtown Los Angeles off limits for military personnel. Classified naval documents prove that the Navy believed it had a mutiny on its hands. The military shore patrols quashed the rioting—something the Los Angeles police refused to do.

For the next few days, police ordered mass arrests, even raiding a Catholic welfare center to arrest some of its occupants. The press and city officials agitated the residents. An editorial by Manchester Boddy in the June 9 *Los Angeles Daily News* urged the city to clamp down on the terrorists.[27] During the assaults, the *Los Angeles Daily News* and the *Los Angeles Times* cheered servicemen on, with headlines such as "Zoot Suit Chiefs Girding for War on Navy" and "Zoot Suiters Learn Lesson in Fight with Servicemen." Three other major newspapers ran similar headlines that poisoned the environment and generated a mass hysteria about zoot-suit violence. Radio broadcasts also inflamed the frenzy.

On June 16, 1943, the *Los Angeles Times* ran a story from Mexico City, with the headline "Mexican Government Expects Damages for Zoot Suit Riot Victims." The article stated, "the Mexican government took a mildly firm stand on the rights of its nationals, emphasizing its conviction that American justice would grant 'innocent victims' their proper retribution." Federal authorities expressed concern, and Mayor Fletcher Bowron assured Washington, D.C., that no racism was involved. Soon afterward, Bowron told the Los Angeles police to stop using "cream-puff techniques on the Mexican youths." Simultaneously he ordered the formation of a committee to "study the problem." City officials and the Los Angeles press became exceedingly touchy about charges of racism. When Eleanor Roosevelt commented in her nationally syndicated newspaper column that "longstanding discrimination against the Mexicans in the Southwest" caused the riots, the June 18 *Los Angeles Times* responded with the headline "Mrs. Roosevelt Blindly Stirs Race Discord." The article denied that racial discrimination had been a factor in the riots and charged that Mrs. Roosevelt's statement resembled propaganda used by the Communists; it stated that servicemen had looked for "costumes and not races." The article said that Angelenos were proud of their missions and Olvera Street, "a bit of old Mexico," and concluded, "We like Mexicans and think they like us."

Governor Earl Warren formed a committee to investigate the riots, to which he appointed Attorney General Robert W. Kenny; Catholic Bishop Joseph T. McGucken, who served as chair; Walter A. Gordon, Berkeley attorney; Leo Carrillo, screen actor; and Karl Holton, director of the California Youth Authority. The committee's report recommended punishment of all persons responsible for the riots—military and civilian alike. It took a slap at the press, recommending that newspapers limit the use of names and photos of juveniles. Finally, it called for better-educated and better-trained police officers to work with Spanish-speaking youth.[28]

Mexicanas Break Barriers

Throughout the Southwest and the entire nation, Mexican American women—like other Americans—supported the war effort, making sacrifices and writing to their boyfriends, husbands, and fathers in the armed forces. They formed support groups throughout the country. For example, in March 1944, Rosalio Ronquillo, a male, established a Tucson organization called the Spanish American Mothers and Wives Association. Unlike many other women's and men's organizations, the association was open to all women regardless of their socioeconomic class. Some 300 women—mothers, wives, daughters, sisters, and fiancées—as well as a handful of men, joined the organization. Rose Rodríguez edited its newsletter, *Chatter*, which the association sent to servicemen. Members also sold war bonds and raised money for a postwar veterans' center. Although women ran the organization, they made what seemed to be strategic concessions to males.[29]

Ronquillo acted as the association's permanent director. Women held the offices of president, vice president, treasurer, and secretary. The *Chatter* newsletter, originally called *Chismes*, was the lifeline to the male soldiers. Although a male chaired the organization, according to Julie A. Campbell, the structure of the association encouraged women to get out of the house, get involved in planning events, and be networked with other women. The organization also acted as a support group when the members' husbands or sons were wounded or killed in action. According to Campbell, by feeding the male ego, the women also got the support of leading businessmen, receiving economic assistance from merchants and a free-of-cost ride to meetings in *los buses de Laos* (buses of the Old Pueblo Transit Company, founded in 1924 by Roy Laos, Sr., primarily serving the Mexican community). The association also networked with other organizations for fund-raising or sponsoring events. Although the group planned to stay together after the war and raise money for a community social center, the association faded when the war ended.[30]

Elizabeth Rachel Escobedo gives a broader view, writing that many Chicanas were transformed by the Depression and that the war intensified a process that was already in progress—a process that was especially rapid among the second generation. The war gave them economic opportunities and weakened the institutions of social control. During the Depression, many had lived under fear of deportation, whereas with increased industrialization and war shortages, their labor was in demand, though temporarily. In many cases, the father and the older brothers were out of the house as were the restrictive husbands. Escobedo shows that even in the case of the female friends of the Sleepy Lagoon defendants, changes took place: when they were deprived of their civil rights at the Ventura Detention Facility, they would not conform and questioned. One authority commented about one of the young ladies, saying that she was "very clannish with Mexican girls and continues to speak Spanish in spite of repeated requests not to do so." Escobedo writes: "Ultimately the pachuca became both part and a symbol of the changing ethnic and gender landscape of World War II."[31]

One such case was that of Andrea Pérez, a municipal court clerk, and Sylvester Davis, an African American male, who met each other while working at Lockheed in Burbank, California. Owing to biases of both families, it was at first a clandestine relationship. After the war they applied for a marriage license; the County Clerk of Los Angeles turned them down, citing that Pérez had listed her race as "white," and Davis identified himself as "Negro." California law listed people of Mexican origin, unless it was convenient otherwise, as white. The denial was based on California Civil Code Section 60: "All marriages of white persons with Negroes, Mongolians, members of the Malay race, or mulattoes are illegal and void." Pérez petitioned the California Supreme Court for an original Writ of Mandate to compel the issuance of the license. Pérez and Davis were Catholics; they argued that the Church was willing to marry them, that the state's anti-miscegenation law infringed on their right to participate fully in the sacraments, and that they were being denied the fundamental right of marriage and thus were subjected to the violation of the Fourteenth Amendment. The California State Supreme Court sided with the plaintiffs in a narrow 4–3 decision, making California the first state in the twentieth century to hold an anti-miscegenation law unconstitutional. Pérez and Davis had a long and happy marriage; she later worked as an elementary schoolteacher in San Fernando, California.[32]

Rosita the Riveter[33]

Even before World War II, Mexican American women had begun to question the notion that a woman's place was in the home. During the war, Mexican American women played the traditional roles of volunteering, wrapping bandages, and writing letters, but ideas were still changing. Before the war, women—and certainly Mexican women—did not work for the Southern Pacific Railroad. However, because the war caused a labor crisis, the railroad began hiring women to do maintenance and even fire up locomotive engines. The "*Susanas del SP*" was the Mexican version of "Rosie the Riveter." Women also became miners in camps such as Morenci, Arizona, where they were often harassed and labeled "prostitutes." Other women went to work in the defense plants and did what was until then considered men's work.

Currently, the University of Texas at Austin runs an oral history project called "U.S. Latinos and Latinas & World War II," which is preserving some of this narrative. The collective stories of Chicanas in this project paint a mixed picture as to the impact the war had on the lives of Mexican women. For example, Josephine Ledesma—24, from Austin, Texas, and mother of a small child—was trained as an airplane mechanic. This training improved her earning power; before the war, Josephine had trouble finding a job in a department store. Despite contributing to a turnaround in women's economic status, the war did little to improve race relations. At the height of the war, Josephine and her husband were asked to leave a restaurant in Big Spring, Texas, because the proprietor would not serve Mexicans. "Big Spring was absolutely terrible with Mexican Americans and Blacks," stated Josephine.

The war improved the prospects of Henrietta López Rivas of San Antonio. At the age of 15, Henrietta, who grew up during the Great Depression, left school in the ninth grade, and headed north with her family as migrant farmworkers. They worked in the tomato and wheat fields of Ohio and Michigan. Upon returning to San Antonio, Henrietta took up cleaning jobs at houses and barnyards earning only $1.50 a week. In 1941, Henrietta found employment with the Civil Service Department as a Spanish-speaking interpreter; her income jumped from $1.50 a week to $90 a month. Later she was offered a better civil service job at Duncan (now Kelly) Air Force Base.

Elisa Rodríguez, 21, of Waco, eventually secured a job at Blackland Army Airfield and in the process developed strong opinions about her country and discrimination. While working at a local department store, Elisa attended night school and learned shorthand, typing, and other clerical skills. After graduation, she applied for a job at Blackland Army Airfield, which turned her down because she was a Mexican. After Elisa got a lawyer friend to call the company and remind the owner that the company received defense contracts, the boss said, "send her over." Having a defense contract meant that the employer had to follow federal antidiscrimination laws. Soon afterward, she got a job at Blackland, making about $2,000 a year; she was the only Latina at the base, and she routinely experienced discrimination. Eventually, Elisa became the equal employment opportunity coordinator. Nevertheless, she paid the price; she was never promoted.[34]

The Federal Fair Employment Practices Commission

The war raised questions of inequality. Executive Order 8802 expressly forbade discrimination of workers in defense industries. President Roosevelt established the Fair Employment Practices Commission (FEPC) in response to pressure from African American and Mexican American organizations and individuals. New Mexico Senator Dennis Chávez played a leadership role in the Senate subcommittee hearings on the FEPC, with the commission hearing cases from the Southwest to the Midwest and Pacific Northwest.[35]

However, the law is one thing and getting people to comply is another, as is apparent in the testimony of Los Angeles attorney Manuel Ruiz. Proving poverty and inequality was, and still is, an expensive proposition. Ruiz knew that discrimination existed, but there was a lack of data about Mexican Americans. Even the Census was deficient of hard data on U.S. Mexicans; and this had become more complicated with their designation as white. When Ruiz testified before the commission, he could not cite specific statistics proving discrimination toward Mexicans. Any reasonable person could go out the door and witness discrimination and inequality, but there were few studies that proved it. Indeed, outside Texas, few scholars researched the Mexican American population. The citing of data was critical to making a case for equal treatment. Without solid evidence, the FEPC could avoid enforcing the presidential executive order.[36]

Besides the interference of governors and local officials, the State Department also evaded the executive order by obstructing collection of data; when the FEPC planned hearings at El Paso, the State Department pressured the agency to call off the hearings. The State Department held that admitting that racism existed was bad for the U.S. image. The President participated in the charade, subordinating the FEPC to the War Manpower Commission (WMC). All in all, the administration had little respect for the concerns of U.S. Mexican leaders. Employees of the FEPC told historian Dr. Carlos E. Castañeda, a field investigator for the agency, that when the war "was over the Mexican American would be put in his place."[37]

Despite the lack of enforcement of nondiscrimination laws, Mexicans continued to organize miners through Congress of Industrial Organization (CIO) locals. CIO hearings showed that Mexican Americans were at the lowest end of the pay scale, and that white workers often refused to work alongside Mexicans; yet the copper barons refused even to acknowledge there was discrimination against Mexicans.

The FEPC hearings in Arizona confirmed what everyone else knew—that the copper barons in Arizona *did* discriminate against Mexicans. The Mine, Mill, and Smelter Workers Union supported a policy of nondiscrimination. However, mining companies such as Phelps–Dodge pretty much set the tone by officially condemning discrimination, while doing nothing to stop it. Complaints of discrimination toward Mexicans—registered by individual Mexican miners and by the union—kept rolling in. Castañeda's efforts to get the FEPC and other agencies to respond to discrimination were futile. Unable to decide whether to enforce the law or not, the Roosevelt administration did nothing. This charade cast doubt on the FEPC's and the government's commitment to equal employment.[38]

Few Mexicans were hired by defense factories, and even fewer rose to supervisory positions. Alonso S. Perales testified before the Senate Fair Employment Practices Act hearings in San Antonio in 1944 that Kelly Air Force Base in that city employed 10,000 people, and not one Mexican held a position above that of a laborer or mechanic's helper. According to Perales's testimony, 150 towns and cities in Texas had public facilities that refused to serve Mexicans—many of whom were servicemen.

At the same hearings Frank Paz, president of the Spanish-Speaking People's Council of Chicago, testified that 45,000 Mexicans worked in and around Chicago, mostly in railroads, steel mills, and packinghouses. The overwhelming majority worked as railroad section hands. The railroad companies refused to promote Mexican Americans. In fact, they were importing temporary workers (*braceros*) from Mexico to do skilled work as electricians, pipe fitters, steamfitters, millwrights, and so forth. According to Paz, between 1943 and 1945 the railroads imported 15,000 braceros. The Railroad Brotherhood, meanwhile, refused membership to Mexicans or blacks; consequently, Mexicans worked in track repair and maintenance, managed by Euro-American supervisors. The Operating Brotherhoods of the Southern Pacific did not knowingly admit Mexicans to their union until 1960—thus they were ineligible for skilled jobs and promotions.

Paz testified about the case of steelworker Ramón Martínez, a 20-year veteran, who was placed in charge of a section of workers because they spoke only Spanish. When he learned that he was being paid

$50 a month less than the other foremen, Martínez complained. The reasons given for the wage difference were that he was not a citizen and that he did not have a high school education. Martínez attended night school and received a diploma, but the railroad company still refused to pay him wages on par with other foremen.[39]

Castañeda testified that in Arizona, Mexicans comprised 8,000–10,000 of the 15,000–16,000 miners in the state, but the copper barons restricted them to menial labor categories. According to Castañeda, Mexicans throughout the United States were paid less than Euro-Americans for equal work. In California, in 1940, Mexicans numbered about 457,900 out of a total population of 6,907,387; Los Angeles had 315,000 Mexicans. As of the summer of 1942, only 5,000 Mexicans worked in the basic industries of that city. Further, Los Angeles County employed about 16,000 workers, only 400 of whom were Mexicans.[40] The war did not end racial barriers.

FBI records provide data on the underrepresentation of Mexican Americans in the defense economy. A confidential report of January 14, 1944, titled "Racial Conditions (Spanish-Mexican Activities in Los Angeles Field Division)," claimed that only a couple of thousand Mexican Americans worked in the Los Angeles war plants. The same account reported that the Los Angeles Police Department employed 22 Mexican American officers in a force of 2,547; the Los Angeles Sheriff's Department had 30 Spanish-surnamed deputies out of 821. The probation department employed three officers of Mexican extraction. Sadly, Mexicans were better represented in combat units, recruited to fight in a war presumably to ensure human rights abroad, something that they themselves were denied at home.[41]

Elizabeth Escobedo sheds more light on the topic. Though the FEPC brought to attention the question of equality and institutional racism, it did not resolve the contradictions. For instance, it did not address gender inequality in the workplace. After the war Mexican American women were driven out of the workplace, and the better-paying jobs went to returning white male veterans. Nevertheless, the reports show that the women during the war years were very active in using due process to protect their rights, which implies that they were the object of disparaging and rude remarks by fellow workers. According to Escobedo, FEPC complaints filed in the Los Angeles area by Mexican Americans far outnumbered those of all other national-origin groups; in December 1944 alone they filed some 93 cases. Employers admitted to hiring only lighter-skinned Mexicans. Escobedo has recorded a treasure trove of case studies such as that of Guadalupe Cordero who complained about Mexicans being replaced by inexperienced Euro-American "girls."[42]

Cold War Politics of Control

The post–World War II period ushered in the Cold War, which lasted into the early 1990s. In 1945, the United States controlled more than an estimated 40 percent of the world's wealth and power. In comparison, the British Empire, at its peak, was 25 percent. A global strategy for the war gave the United States a more global vision of the world, which continued during the postwar years, with the United States playing a decisive role in "military, political, and economic questions in all regions of the world." The preeminence of the United States gave the military and the citizenry the mind set of seeing the whole world as "our" oceans, "our" skies, "our" empire.[43] Most capitalists left behind the memories and the lessons of the Great Depression, forgetting that the New Deal saved their system, and that war made them richer by trillions of dollars. These capitalists felt that the "free world" needed a coherent ideology to successfully resist the Communists and waged a "Cold War" both internationally and nationally.

During the war, wages were frozen, though profits were unbridled. After the war, organized labor adopted a confrontational and militant posture; many industrialists blamed the unions—especially the CIO—for work stoppages. The captains of industry acted as if *they* had won the war and equated worker demands with Communism, and extended the Cold War to unions. Through the politicos to whose political campaigns they generously contributed, the industrialists pressured many locals to drop radical organizers, accusing them of being Communist or at best fellow travelers. Their main target was the CIO, which gave workers, among them Mexican Americans, control over the workplace.

In 1947, Congress passed the Taft–Hartley Act, which neutered the Wagner Act of 1935 and its National Labor Relations Board (NLRB). It gave the states authority to pass right-to-work laws. No longer did workers have to abide by the will of the majority of workers who wanted a union. It gave antiunion forces the power to petition for another election. Further, the U.S. president could enjoin a strike, if he thought the walkouts imperiled national security. It empowered the courts to fine strikers for alleged violations of the injunction and to establish a 60-day cooling-off period. It prohibited the use of union dues for political contributions and required all labor leaders to take a loyalty oath swearing that they were not Communists. If labor leaders refused to take the oath, the law denied their union the facilities of the NLRB. Thus, Taft–Hartley empowered employers and weakened the collective bargaining process.[44] Its purpose was to destroy labor unions and take control of government, and return to the Gilded Age, the late 1800s to the 1920s, when business leaders accumulated titanic fortunes.

These measures to control labor came at a time when Mexican Americans were just starting to make gains in industrial unions. Luisa Moreno, elected vice president of the United Cannery, Agricultural, Packing, and Allied Workers of America (UCAPAWA), was put in charge of organizing food processing in southern California. Mexican American women in increasing numbers became members of negotiating teams; more Latinas found their way in as shop stewards, and many became union officials as did their male counterparts. This increased involvement of Mexican Americans at the leadership level led to the organization of more Chicano workers and CIO locals. Following this growing influence of the CIO among Mexican American workers, the Teamsters, encouraged by the AFL, launched a jurisdictional fight with the Food, Tobacco, Agricultural, and Allied Workers of America (FTAAWA, formerly UCAPAWA).[45]

Red-baiting and thuggery characterized the Teamsters' campaign. The state and the Catholic Church joined the campaign to clean out the reds. The California Un-American Activities Committee (better known as the Tenney Committee) called hearings and smeared progressive unions, charging that the leadership was Communist. By 1947, Luisa Moreno retired to private life, and by the end of the decade, only three FTAAWA locals survived. The Loyalty Oath, Taft–Hartley, and mechanization all took their toll. Soon afterward, immigration authorities deported Moreno because of her activism.[46]

Josefina Fierro de Bright was also hounded by the state. Josefina became involved in social activism at the age of 18, while a student at UCLA; her mother and grandmother were Magonistas. She married screenwriter John Bright, a founder of the Screen Actors Guild, and soon became a community organizer, and by 1939 was an organizer for *El Congreso del Pueblo de Habla Española* (Spanish-speaking congress). Through her Hollywood contacts, she was able to raise money even for Mexican American causes. While active in *el Congreso,* she was involved in the defense of the Sleepy Lagoon defendants, and continued her association with Luisa Moreno. Under the leadership of Josefina, the *Congreso* attacked the Sinarquistas (The National Synarchist Union), a Mexican fascist group. She also criticized the schools for the treatment of Mexican children. In 1951 she unsuccessfully ran for Congress, supported by *la Asociacion Nacional Mexico-Americana*, which had been founded the year before to fight the deportation of foreign-born political activists; soon afterward she left for Mexico.[47]

The Communists are Coming

Although Mexican Americans earned their rights with their blood during the war, their patriotism—like that of Japanese Americans—was put into question. If they did not agree with the government and the excesses of capitalism, they were assumed to be disloyal. The G.I. Forum, LULAC, and most Mexican American organizations protested these charges. Yet, they were under suspicion. Political scientist José Angel Gutiérrez is pioneering research in police surveillance. Under the Freedom of Information Act, he obtained documents proving that the FBI had spied on LULAC and later on the G.I. Forum. In 1941, the FBI's Denver Office reported on the Antonio, Colorado, chapter of LULAC. Its officers included a county judge and a town marshal. The FBI also investigated respected leaders such as George I. Sánchez and Alonso Perales, reporting that Sánchez had earned the distrust of the Mexican community when he converted to Reformed Methodism.

In May 1946, the FBI infiltrated a Los Angeles meeting of LULAC. An informant claimed, without offering proof, that participants had a long history of Communist activity. Early in the 1950s, the FBI again investigated LULAC. It was suspect only because it had demanded racial integration.

FBI files show that it also conducted extensive surveillance of Los Angeles Mexican Americans during the Sleepy Lagoon case and the so-called Zoot Suit Riots. The bureau, highly critical of the Sleepy Lagoon Defense Committee, red-baited its members, singling out Eduardo Quevedo, chair of the Coordinating Council for Latin American Youth, and M. J. Avila, secretary of the Hollywood Bar Association. According to the FBI, local police authorities bent over backward to get along with Mexicans. The FBI also targeted the "Hispanic Movement" within the Catholic Church.[48]

Postwar Opportunities

Opportunities ended for most women after the war as the government promoted a policy of moving women out of the workforce so that they would have more babies. From 1946 to about 1963, the U.S. birthrate showed a marked upswing—a phenomenon that social scientists labeled the "Baby Boom." For many Mexican American males, the war had been a leveler—they had become leaders in combat. They had great expectations, but the dominant society was not ready to accept them as equals. Hence they became much more demanding and exercised their vote; how active they were depended on where they lived. For example, in Boyle Heights, California, Mexicans lived in proximity to Jewish Americans during an era when Jews were leading the fight against racism and for civil liberties. At the time, Boyle Heights still housed a sizable Jewish American community, and many of its more liberal members played a role in politicizing the Mexican American community. In 1948, many in the Boyle Heights community actively campaigned for the Independent Progressive Party (IPP), which supported Henry Wallace for president. The IPP recruited many Mexicans to its ranks.[49]

Though Euro-Americans throughout the country enjoyed unprecedented opportunity, the ability to take advantage of these openings depended on education and/or financial status. For instance, Californians received a windfall of federal and state monies such as the G.I. Bill and the development of the California State College System, which improved educational opportunity. In 1940 the white adults in California on average attained 9.8 years of schooling; the number rose to 11 by 1960. By contrast, blacks achieved 8.1 years in 1940, rising to 9.4 in 1960. Latinos had a median of 5.6 in 1940 and 7.7 in 1960. Euro-American college graduates increased from 7.2 percent in 1940 to 10.4 in 1960 and to 21.2 in 1980, whereas the number of black graduates grew from 2.6 percent in 1940 to 3.6 in 1960 and to 11.2 in 1980. The Latino graduates (mostly of Mexican origin) sputtered from 1.6 to 3.2 and to 5.4 percent in the respective years.[50]

In terms of education, Texas was a disaster: the median number of years of education for Mexican Americans was 3.5 in 1950—half that of California—compared with 10.3 for whites and 7.0 for nonwhites. Correspondingly in San Antonio, the median number of years was 4.5, half that of the general population of the city. Cities like Tucson, Arizona, mirrored California. "By 1940, nearly 75 percent of the Mexican work force was still in blue-collar occupations [in Tucson], compared with only 36 percent of Anglo workers," who comprised 96.5 percent of the white-collar and professional positions. Mexicans made up 54.5 percent of the unskilled labor, although they comprised only 30 percent of the city's workforce. In 1950, the median number of school years that Mexican Americans completed in the city was 6.5. Many returning Mexican American veterans felt that their community simply did not have the educational human capital to take advantage of the new opportunities.[51] On the upside, the number of Mexican Americans increased; the U.S. Census reported 1,077,000 Mexican-origin people (0.8 percent of the U.S. population) in 1940, 1,346,000 (0.9 percent) in 1950, 1,736,000 (1.0 percent) in 1960, 4,532,000 (2.2 percent) in 1970, and 8,740,000 (3.9 percent) in 1980.[52] However, these figures are flawed and reflect a serious undercount. After 1940, the Mexican-origin population became more engaged in correcting the Census Bureau, realizing that there is power in numbers, which determine government allocations, health studies, and political power.[53]

Toward a Civil Rights Agenda

The First Regional Conference on Education of the Spanish-Speaking People in the Southwest took place at the University of Texas at Austin on December 13–15, 1945. George I. Sánchez of the University of Texas and A. L. Campa of the University of New Mexico took an active part in the proceedings.

In 1946, Judge Paul J. McCormick, in the U.S. District Court in southern California, heard the *Méndez v. Westminster School District* case and ruled that the segregation of Mexican children was unconstitutional. Gonzalo, a Mexican American, and Felicitas Méndez, a Puerto Rican, took the leadership in filing the case. On April 14, 1947, the U.S. Court of Appeals for the Ninth Circuit affirmed the lower court decision, holding that Mexicans and other children were entitled to "the equal protection of the laws," and that neither language nor race could be used as a reason to segregate them. In response to the *Méndez* case, the Associated Farmers of Orange County launched a bitter red-baiting campaign of the Mexican communities and the leaders.[54]

On June 15, 1948, in another segregation case, Judge Ben H. Rice, Jr., U.S. District Court, Western District of Texas, found in *Delgado v. Bastrop Independent School District* that the school district violated the Fourteenth Amendment equal protection rights of the Mexican children. These two cases set precedents for the historic *Brown v. Board of Education* case in 1954. They also set a standard for the U.S. Supreme Court decision in *Hernandez v. Texas* (1954), which also held that the Fourteenth Amendment protected Mexican Americans. Yet the court also found that Mexican Americans did not constitute an identifiable ethnic minority.[55]

There was a considerable degree of cooperation between LULAC and the National Association for the Advancement of Colored People (NAACP) during the 1940s and 1950s. In November 1946, in Orange County, California, LULAC, with the assistance of Fred Ross (who later helped launch the Community Service Organization), initiated a campaign supporting Proposition 11 of the Fair Employment Practices Act, which prohibited employment discrimination. LULAC chapters went door to door registering people to vote. This organizational work was crucial in ensuring the civil rights that Mexican Americans and other Latinos take for granted today. The downside was that in 1947 the district attorney pressured LULAC to get rid of Ross, red-baiting him; Ross left for Los Angeles.[56]

The American G.I. Forum

Returning Mexican American veterans were denied many services because of their race. For instance, many American Legion and Veterans of Foreign Wars chapters refused to admit Mexicans as members. Recognizing the need, Dr. Hector Pérez García founded the American G.I. Forum in Corpus Christi, Texas. The Forum gained notoriety when a funeral home in Three Rivers, Texas, refused to hold services for Private Felix Longoria, who had died in the Philippines during World War II. This outrageous racist act attracted thousands of new members to the G.I. Forum, all demanding justice; the incident was very important in politicizing a new generation of activists. Senator Lyndon B. Johnson intervened and, with the cooperation of the Longoria family, had Longoria buried in Arlington National Cemetery with full honors.[57]

Forum members believed that Longoria should have been buried with full honors in his hometown, and the compromise of burying him in Arlington Cemetery was wrong. Tejanos vowed that never again would they accept second-class citizenship. Meanwhile, Texas officials claimed that they never denied Longoria a proper burial and accused the Forum of exploiting the issue. At hearings of the state Good Neighbor Commission, Dr. García and the Forum's attorney, Gus García, did a brilliant job of proving the Forum's case by presenting evidence of "Mexican" and "white" cemeteries and racist burial practices in Texas. However, the all-white commission found that there had been no discrimination. The blatant bias of the commissioners further strained race relations, and from that point on the Forum became more proactive. "Unlike LULAC, whose policy was not to involve itself directly in electoral politics, the Forum openly advocated getting out the vote and endorsing candidates."[58] The Forum did not limit membership to the middle class and those fluent in English, like LULAC did. It was not as accommodating to the feelings of Euro-Americans.[59]

Like most of the other Mexican American organizations of the time, the Forum stressed the importance of education. The G.I. Forum's motto was "Education is our freedom, and freedom should be everybody's business." This new aggressiveness of Mexican Americans in Texas and elsewhere signaled an increased intensity of involvement in civil rights (see Chapter 12).

Controlling Mexicans

During the 1940s in California, Mexican American Movement (MAM) membership dropped as it evolved from a student organization into a professional association. Mexican Americans after the war looked beyond single issues, and veterans became more involved in local politics. By the 1950s, Mexican Americans were also increasingly involved in national politics, as a response to the expanding powers of the federal government. Certainly, the fact that there was more opportunity in California to assimilate may also have played a role in the decreasing membership in MAM. A more probable explanation for the decline of MAM is that many of the 1930s' youth were now older and were veterans, and integrated themselves in national organizations such as LULAC, the G.I. Forum, and emerging organizations such as the Community Service Organization. Influenced by leaders such as Saul Alinsky and Fred Ross, more Mexican Americans began to think of community organizing as a path toward political power.[60]

These changes in Mexican Americans went unnoticed by the rest of the society, which continued to perceive them as foreigners who did not belong. Euro-Americans ignored the sacrifices made by Mexican Americans during World War II, which were disproportionate to their numbers. And although the Mexican American leadership continued to claim they were white in order to qualify for equal rights under the constitution, racism remained an issue. The war had not ended racism; the Mexican American youth were still targeted as scapegoats.

As large numbers of U.S. Mexicans moved into the cities, police harassment increased, as many police officers resented the use of Spanish language and what they perceived as the "cocky demeanor" of second-generation Mexican youth. Lupe Leyvas, the sister of Henry Leyvas, tells of an incident that marked a change in attitude. She and her family would sit on the porch of their South Central home, and every time a police car cruised the neighborhood, her mother would order everyone inside the house until one day Lupe rebelled and said, "Why should we go inside, we are not doing anything wrong."

The stigma of the *pachuco* carried over into the postwar era—law enforcement officers assumed that all Mexican youth were delinquents and wanted them to look down when spoken to. In July 1946, a sheriff's deputy in Monterey Park, California, shot Eugene Montenegro in the back; allegedly, the 13-year-old was seen coming out of a window and did not stop when the deputy ordered him to. Eugene was 5'3", unarmed, and an honors student at St. Alphonse parochial school. The press, covering the incident, portrayed Eugene's mother as irrational because she confronted the deputy who had mortally wounded her son.

In September 1947 Bruno Cano, a member of the United Furniture Workers of America Local 576, was brutally beaten by the police in East Los Angeles. Cano attempted to stop police from assaulting three Mexican youths at a tavern. Local 576, the Civil Rights Congress (CRC),[61] and the American Veterans Committee (Belvedere Chapter) protested Cano's beating. One of the officers, William Keyes, had a history of brutality; earlier in 1947, he shot two Mexicans in the back. Keyes faced no disciplinary action in either those shootings or Cano's beating.

In March 1948, Keyes and his partner E. R. Sánchez shot down 17-year-old Agustino Salcido. According to Keyes and Sánchez, Salcido offered to sell them stolen watches. Instead of taking Salcido to the police station, they escorted him to "an empty, locked building," and shot him. At the coroner's inquest, Keyes claimed that the unarmed Salcido had attempted to escape during interrogation. Witnesses contradicted Keyes, but the inquest exonerated him.[62]

The Los Angeles CIO Council and community organizations held a "people's trial" attended by nearly 600 Mexicans. Margo Albert (María Marguerita Guadalupe Teresa Estela Bolado), wife of actor Eddie Albert and a Mexican film star herself (she had acted in the film *Lost Horizon*), and the CRC played a leadership role. The mock trial found Keyes guilty; Keyes's notoriety also added to this, and pressure mounted on Judge Stanley Moffatt to accept the complaint. Meanwhile, Guillermo Gallegos, a witness to the shooting, was harassed and his life was threatened. Meanwhile, Judge Moffatt was red-baited by defense attorney Joseph Scott. The *Hollywood Citizen-News* accused Moffatt of being a Communist because he ran for Congress on the Henry Wallace ticket. The jury was deadlocked—seven for acquittal and five for conviction.[63]

In a new trial, Keyes appeared before a law-and-order judge. Keyes waived a jury trial and was acquitted because the judge found insufficient evidence to convict him. Yet the prosecution had proved that

Keyes and Sánchez had pumped bullets into Salcido, that Gallegos had seen him fire the gun at Salcido, and that Keyes's gun had killed Salcido. Between 1947 and 1956, the L.A. Community Service Organization conducted 35 investigations of police misconduct.[64] Enrique Buelna makes connections between the Salcido case, the *Amigos de Wallace* (Friends of [Henry] Wallace), and the pivotal role that the case had played in bringing together the activist community of the time. Besides the Salcido case, the battles over the FEPC, the Taft–Hartley fight, the Wallace Presidential Campaign in 1948, and the formation of *la Asociación Nacional México Americana* (ANMA) in 1949 gave rise to a new current of activism among Mexican Americans, which included activists such as the Luna sisters, Julia Mount and Celia Rodríguez, as well as Luis Moreno and Josefina Fierro de Bright, who was 28 at the time. Besides this radical core, returning veterans joined the Community Service Organization, which was pursuing political power.[65]

Texas housed an estimated 1 million Mexican Americans. During the postwar era, Mexican American organizations sponsored anti–poll tax drives, pressured local and state officials to investigate cases of police brutality, challenged segregation, and struggled to eliminate inequality in the education system. Mexican Americans would often challenge the refusal of local barbers to offer their services to them; many suffered savage beatings for this. LULAC and the G.I. Forum used the judicial process to effect changes, with the view of achieving equal protection under the law.

Alonso Perales documented dozens of cases of segregation and police malfeasance. In his book, titled *Are We Good Neighbors?* Perales presents his case. Affidavit after affidavit reveals the way white Texans viewed Mexicans—whether born in Mexico or the United States—as foreigners. This discrimination demoralized the U.S. Mexican community. The common notion was that the average Texan did not like Mexicans. For example, in February 1945, Reginaldo Romo was playing dice in a saloon, after-hours. August Zimmerman, a peace officer in Ugalde, pistol-whipped him. In San Angelo, Texas, Private Ben García Aguirre, 20, was beaten unconscious by about 15 Euro-Americans in September 1945. Authorities apprehended none of the assailants. In February 1946, Felipe Guarjado, Antonio Hinojosa, and Pascual Ortega were driving from San Antonio to Laredo. In Devine, Texas, they entered the Monte Carlos Inn, where Euro-Americans beat them and robbed them. They filed a complaint, but the justice of the peace instead filed charges against them. In another instance of police brutality, in March 1946, Sheriff E. E. Pond of Zavala County and two of his officers beat Manuel Delgado, 22. Delgado asked Pond not to push him, whereupon the sheriff ripped off his shirt. The other officers beat and arrested Delgado, whom the court fined $63.[66]

In Texas, when in trouble, call in the Texas Rangers. To this end, Colonel Homer Garrison, Jr., was appointed the new director of the Department of Public Safety, which gave a boost to the Texas Rangers. Garrison appointed Rangers as plainclothesmen, detectives, and Highway Patrol officers. In World War II, they rounded up "enemy aliens" to protect the "homeland." *Los Rinches* (a pejorative reference to Texas Rangers) was the symbol of Euro-American control—especially after World War II, when Mexicans and labor were kept in their place. The *Rinches* made certain that labor organizing did not take root in the Valley. Despite this obstacle, unionization continued in Texas; in 1953, the combined membership of the Texas State Federation of Labor (TSFL) and the CIO reached 375,000. However, the labor federations, faced with a rampantly conservative, if not reactionary, mind set, adjusted to management's agenda and surrendered much of their former militancy.

The war opened occupations outside agriculture to Mexicans. Indeed, after 1940 there was a rise in urban commercial interests and a massive relocation of Mexicans to the city. In the Fort Worth area, Mexicans moved into service jobs such as busboys, elevator operators, and the like. However, the better-paying corporations, such as Consolidated Fort Worth and North American Aircraft of Dallas, hired only a limited number of Mexican American workers. In the postwar era, the rapid unionization of industries helped Mexican workers little, since unions relied on the seniority system and few Mexicans qualified for membership in trade unions.

The Return of Farm Labor Militancy

On November 18, 1948, Bill Dredge wrote an article in the *Los Angeles Times* titled "Machines and Men Bringing in Cotton." San Joaquin Valley planters were starting to use robots to bring in the cotton.

Nevertheless, 100,000 persons were still needed to pick the cotton crop. Although Filipinos and other ethnics had been involved in this picking, by 1948 it was exclusively a Mexican affair. As important as the Mexicans were to the workforce, they were still considered "standby." Farmworkers had few opportunities, and agribusiness ruled. It was more successful in lobbying government for subsidies and exemptions from regulations protecting workers under the National Labor Relations Act than its urban counterparts.[67]

In the face of this awesome power structure, and despite agribusiness' ability to create huge labor pools, and the use of the *bracero* to depress wages and break strikes, farmworkers continued to organize. For instance, in October 1947, at the Di Giorgio Fruit Corporation at Arvin, California, workers picketed the Di Giorgio farm. The National Farm Labor Union (NFLU) Local 218 led the strike. Joseph Di Giorgio, founder of the corporation, refused the union's demands. *Fortune* magazine had dubbed him the "Kublai Khan of Kern County"; in 1946, Di Giorgio earned $18 million in sales. When Di Giorgio refused the union demands, the fight to stop production began.

As in the case of other agricultural strikes, local government, the Chambers of Commerce, the American Legion, the Boy Scouts, the Associated Farmers, the Farm Bureaus, and so on lined up in support of Di Giorgio. Hugh M. Burns of the California Senate Committee on Un-American Activities and the reactionary State Senator Jack Tenney held hearings investigating Communist involvement, but they failed to uncover any evidence. Through the media, Di Giorgio controlled the narrative. In November 1949 a subcommittee of the House Committee on Education and Labor held hearings at Bakersfield, California. Representative Cleveland M. Bailey (West Virginia) presided, and Representatives Richard M. Nixon (California) and Tom Steed (Oklahoma) joined him. The two other members of the subcommittee, Thurston B. Morton (Kentucky) and Leonard Irving (Missouri), did not attend the hearings. The proceedings took two days, hardly enough time to conduct an in-depth investigation. The Di Giorgio Corporation had filed a $2 million suit against the union and also against the Hollywood Film Council, claiming that the film *Poverty in the Land of Plenty,* produced in the spring of 1948, libeled Di Giorgio; he wanted the subcommittee to prove this charge. In the 1947 Arvin strike case, the subcommittee found nothing, so Congressman Bailey made no move to file an official report on the strike. Nor did he mention the controversy between the union and Di Giorgio in the report that the subcommittee eventually made to the committee.

In March 1949, Di Giorgio—still intent on an official condemnation of the union—commissioned Representative Thomas H. Werdel from Kern County to file a report, signed by Steed, Morton, and Nixon, in the appendix of the *Congressional Record.* The appendix serves no official function other than giving members of Congress a forum in which to publish material sent them by constituents. The report, "Agricultural Labor at Di Giorgio Farms, California," claimed that the strike was "solely one for the purpose of organization" and that workers had no grievances, for "wages, hours, working conditions, and living conditions have never been a real issue in the Di Giorgio strike," and concluded that *Poverty in the Land of Plenty* was libelous.

The phony report dealt a deathblow to the NFLU. The California Federation of Labor (CFL) leadership ordered Local 218 to settle the libel suit (the CFL would not pay defense costs) and demanded that the strike be ended. Di Giorgio agreed to settle the suit for $1 on the conditions that the NFLU plead guilty to the judgment, thus admitting libel; that they remove the film from circulation and recall all prints; that they reimburse the corporation for attorney fees; and that they call off the strike. Werdel, Steed, Morton, and Nixon all knew that the report had no official status and was, at best, an opinion. They knowingly deceived the public in order to break the strike.[68]

From this point on, the NFLU was powerless. Every time workers stopped production, growers used *braceros* and undocumented workers to break the strike. The departments of Labor, Agriculture, Justice, and State acted as the planters' personal agents. Even liberal Democratic administrations favored the growers, with little difference existing between Republican governor Goodwin Knight and Democratic governor Edmund G. Brown, Sr.

Renting Mexicans

After the United States placed Japanese American workers in concentration camps, there were two alternatives: simply open the border and allow Mexican workers to come into the United States unencumbered, or negotiate with Mexico for an agreed-upon number of Mexican *braceros*. The Mexican government, how-ever, would not permit this practice, insisting on a contract that protected the rights of its workers. In 1942, the two governments agreed to the Emergency Labor Program, under which both governments would supervise the recruitment of *braceros*. The program was literally an emergency program and—under the circumstances—no one complained.[69]

The contract stipulated that Mexican workers would not displace domestic workers, exempted *brace-ros* from military service, and obligated the U.S. government to prevent discrimination against these Mexi-can workers. The contract also regulated the transportation, housing, and wages of the *braceros*. Under this agreement, about 220,000 *braceros* were imported into the United States from 1942 to 1947.

At first, many farmers opposed the *bracero* agreement, preferring the World War I arrangement under which farmers recruited directly in Mexico with no government interference. Texas growers in par-ticular wanted the government to open the border. During the first year, only a handful of U.S. growers participated in the program. States like Texas had always had all the undocumented workers they needed, and they wanted to continue controlling the "free market." They did not want the federal government to regulate the Mexican workers' wages and housing. Growers especially disliked the 30¢ an hour minimum wage, charging that this was the first step in federal farm-labor legislation. Texas growers thus boycotted the program in 1942 and moved to avoid the agreement.

The executive branch did not receive congressional approval for the *bracero* program until 1943, when Congress passed Public Law 45. This law began the "administered migration" of Mexicans into the United States. Initially, the Farm Security Administration (FSA) oversaw the program; later, due to grower pressure, the president transferred supervisory responsibilities to the War Food Administration. Under sec-tion 5(g), the commissioner of immigration could lift the statutory limitations, if such an action was vital to the war effort. Almost immediately, farmers pressured the commissioner to use the escape clause, and to leave the border unilaterally open and unregulated.

Mexicans flooded into border areas, where farmers freely employed them. The Mexican government protested this violation of the agreement. However, Mexican authorities were persuaded to allow the work-ers who had already entered outside the contract agreement to remain for one year; but it was made clear that, in the future, Mexico would not tolerate uncontrolled migration.

In the summer of 1943, Texas growers finally agreed to recruit *braceros*. But the Mexican government refused to issue permits for Texas because of racism and brutal transgressions against Mexican workers. Governor Coke Stevenson, in an attempt to placate the Mexican government, induced the Texas legislature to pass the so-called Caucasian Race Resolution, which affirmed the rights of all Caucasians to equal treat-ment within Texas. Since most Texans did not consider Mexicans Caucasians, the law was not relevant. Governor Stevenson attempted to relieve tensions by publicly condemning racism. The Mexican govern-ment seemed on the verge of relenting when they learned of more racist incidents in Texas. On September 4, 1943, Stevenson established the Good Neighbor Commission of Texas, financed by federal funds, suppos-edly to end discrimination toward Mexicans through better understanding.

Not all *braceros* worked on farms; by August 1945, 67,704 *braceros* held jobs with U.S. railroads. The work was physically demanding and often hazardous. Records show deaths resulting from railroad accidents, sunstroke, heat prostration, and the like. Abuses of the contract agreement also were frequent. Employers did not pay many of the *braceros* their wages, or when paid, involuntary deductions were made—for example, for unsolicited meals. Some growers worked the *braceros* for 12 hours while paying them only for eight. In December 1943, the *braceros* went on strike at the Southern Pacific at Live Oaks, California, protesting the dismissal of three of their comrades.

From 1943 to 1947, Texas growers continued to press for the importation of more *braceros*; the Mexican government refused because there was no evidence of any decline in the Texas growers' mistreat-ment of them. Finally, in October 1947, the Mexican government relented and agreed to issue permits to Texas. Meanwhile, U.S. authorities had shipped some 46,972 braceros to Washington, Oregon, and Idaho during the first four years of the program. Mexican workers often were ill-prepared for the cold winters of the Yakima Valley and the Northwest; and, to add to their woes, managers at the prison-like camps did not speak Spanish. Food-poisoning incidents also broke out frequently. Townspeople, overtly racist, posted

"No Mexicans, White Trade Only" signs in beer parlors and pool halls. *Braceros* frequently revolted and, throughout World War II, their struggle to improve these conditions continued. By 1945, the demand for Mexican *braceros* decreased as Mexican Americans began infiltrating the Northwest from Texas.

Although labor shortages ceased after the war, the *bracero* program continued. The U.S. government functioned as a labor contractor at taxpayers' expense. It assured nativists that workers would return to Mexico once they finished picking the crops. Growers did not have to worry about labor disputes; government authorities, in collusion with the growers, had glutted the labor market with *braceros* to depress wages and to break strikes. Border patrol was often slackened, by the curtailing of government allocation of funds to the bureau to cut down on the number of border patrol officers. This was to ensure an open border for a constant flow of undocumented laborers into the United States.

When negotiations to renew the contract began, Mexico did not have the leverage it did during the war. Its economy was dependent on the money brought back into the country by the workers. The United States, now in a stronger negotiating position, pressured Mexico to continue the program on U.S. terms. The 1947 agreement allowed U.S. growers to recruit their own workers and did not require direct involvement of the U.S. government. The Mexican government bargained for recruitment from the interior and more guarantees for its citizens, but few of its demands were honored. Meanwhile, the U.S. government also permitted growers to hire undocumented workers and to certify them on the spot.

In October 1948, Mexican officials finally took a hard line, refusing to sign *bracero* contracts if Texas farmers did not pay workers $3 per hundredweight (cwt) for picked cotton as against the $2 per cwt offered by growers in other states. The Mexican government, still concerned about racism in Texas, continued to press for recruitment from the interior rather than at the border. Border recruitment compounded hardships on border towns, with workers frequently traveling thousands of miles and then not getting selected as *braceros*. (Border towns grew in population by more than 1,000 percent since 1920. Unemployment rates remained extremely high, and they continued to function as employment centers for U.S. industry.)

The Truman administration sided with the farmers. During a presidential whistle-stop tour in October 1948, El Paso farm agents, sugar company officials, and immigration agents apprised Truman of their problems with Mexican authorities. Shortly after Truman left, the Immigration and Naturalization Service (INS) allowed Mexicans to pour across the bridge into the United States, with or without Mexico's approval. Farmers waited with trucks, and a Great Western Sugar Company representative had a special train ready for the *braceros*. The unilateral opening of the border effectively destroyed Mexico's bargaining position. It could only accept official "regrets" from the United States and continue negotiations. A new agreement reaffirmed the growers' right to recruit *braceros* directly on either side of the border.

From January 23 to February 5, 1954, the United States again unilaterally opened the border. Short of shooting its own citizens, there was nothing Mexico could do to prevent the flood of workers that followed. Left with little choice, Mexico signed a contract favorable to the United States. The gunboat-like diplomacy of U.S. authorities flagrantly violated international law and caused bitter resentment in Latin America at the United States' reliance on the "big stick" and Mexico's obvious humiliation. Opening the border ended the labor shortage, while serving notice to Mexico that it should negotiate because the United States had the power to get all the workers it wanted from Mexico—agreement or no agreement. The United States would evidently act unilaterally, and it completely controlled the *bracero* program. In fact, many members of Congress suggested that the government abandon the pretense of the *bracero* program and simply open the border.

The steady decline of *braceros* beginning in the 1960s marks a convergence of several factors working against the program: resentment of the Mexican government, grievances of the *braceros*, increased opposition by domestic labor, and—probably most important—changes in agricultural labor-saving techniques and in the U.S. economy. It was clear that the farmers' claim that they could not find sufficient domestic labor was a pretext. The 1958 recession intensified organized labor's opposition to the *bracero* program, and the election of a Democratic president in 1960 moved the executive branch and Congress toward a pro-labor position. The AFL–CIO also put pressure on Democrats to end the *bracero* program. Congress and the administration, confronted with massive lobbying from labor as well as from Mexican organizations, allowed the *bracero* contract to lapse on December 31, 1964.[70]

Conclusion: The Sleeping Giant Snores

Historian Dennis Nodín Valdes writes, "Stimulated by World War II, corporate agriculture in the Midwest established an increasingly sophisticated mechanism to recruit, hire and employ workers to meet expanding production and offset the tighter labor market."[71] As a consequence, Texas Mexicans moved in larger numbers to the Midwest. Housing and medical care was primitive, and entire families, including children, worked. Many of the agricultural interests were huge. For instance, in 1950, Michigan Field Crops, Inc., organized during World War II, included as members 8,767 beet growers, 6,800 pickle growers, and an estimated 3,300 growers of miscellaneous crops. That year alone they imported 5,300 Texas Mexican farmworkers. The corridor leading from Texas had been worn even before the war, as contractors transported Mexicans laborers north. Once they got the hang of it, large numbers migrated on their own. The war did little to improve opportunity for Texas Mexicans in the Midwest, with many depending on seasonal work in cherries, cucumbers, tomatoes, and the familiar sugar beet. The grower associations used the reserve army of *braceros* to discipline domestic labor.

Concurrently Texas Mexicans migrated in larger numbers to the Pacific Northwest. The war helped forge the corridor to the Yakima Valley in southern Washington and other farm areas. It did not take long before there was a spillover to urban areas. By the 1940s Chicano communities in the Yakima Valley were formed, and by the end of the decade this region supported a Spanish-language radio station. Erasmo Gamboa points out that over 20 percent of the 220,640 *braceros* (46,954) shipped to the United States between 1943 and 1947 were sent to the Pacific Northwest (Washington, Idaho, and Oregon).[72] By contrast, by the late 1940s California received 8 percent of the *bracero* contract labor, and Texas, 56 percent. Many Texas Mexican workers were pushed out by cotton growers who abused the *bracero* program and created surplus labor. This led to a lowering of cotton wages in Texas by 11 percent, accelerating the Mexican-origin migration to the Midwest and the Northwest.[73]

Besides taking Mexicans north, labor contractors hauled workers throughout the state of Texas. They followed the migrant stream, picking cotton along the coast, throughout central Texas, and into west Texas. Many migrants, whether they went north or remained in Texas, returned for the winter to their base town where many owned small shacks. They would work at casual jobs until the trek began again. By the postwar era, these south Texas towns were interwoven by a network of contractors who furnished cheap labor to growers. Organized labor and Mexican American organizations in Texas frantically attempted to stop the manipulation of the *bracero* and undocumented worker by grower interests as the number of *braceros* contracted in Texas increased from 42,218 in 1949 to 158,704 five years later.[74] Thus, the escalation of the *bracero* program and World War II contributed to the dispersal of Mexican-origin laborers. By the late 1940s significant numbers were moving out of the Southwest. In all of these locations, Mexican Americans rooted communities that changed the cultural landscapes of their new homes.

Notes

1. Leo Grebler, Joan W. Moore, and Ralph C. Guzmán, *The Mexican-American People: The Nation's Second Largest Minority* (New York: Free Press, 1970), 206–18. U.S. Department of Commerce, Bureau of the Census, Fifteenth and Sixteenth Censuses of the United States: 1930–1940 Population. David Hendricks and Amy Patterson, "The 1930 Census in Perspective: The Historical Census," *Prologue Magazine* 34, no. 2 (Summer 2002), http://www.archives.gov/publications/prologue/2002/summer/1930-census-perspective.html. Clara E. Rodriguez, *Changing Race: Latinos, the Census and the History of Ethnicity* (New York: New York University Press, 2000), 101–4. Gloria Sandrino-Glasser, "Los Confundidos: Deconflating Latino'/Latinas Race and Ethnicity," in Kevin R. Johnson, ed., *Mixed Race America and the Law: A Reader* (New York: New York University Press, 2003), 221–22. Gerald D. Nash, *The American West Transformed: The Impact of the Second World War* (Lincoln: University of Nebraska Press, 1990), 107–11.

2. Raúl Morín, *Among the Valiant: Mexican Americans in WWII and Korea* (Alhambra, CA: Borden Publishing Co., 1966), 16. Robin Fitzgerald Scott, "The Mexican-American in the Los Angeles Area, 1920–1950: From Acquiescence to Activity" (PhD dissertation, University of Southern California, 1971), 156, 195, 256, 261. Thanks are due to Dr. Russell Bartley of

the history department at the University of Wisconsin/Milwaukee, who allowed me to review FBI files on the zoot-suit riots, 1943–1945, to which he received access under the Freedom of Information Act. FBI files provided to Russell Bartley, History Department, University of Wisconsin Milwaukee, under Freedom of Information Act; copies in Rodolfo F. Acuña Papers, Special Collections, California State University at Northridge.

3. David G. Gutiérrez, *Walls and Mirrors: Mexican Americans, Mexican Immigrants, and the Politics of Ethnicity* (Berkeley: University of California Press, 1995), 120–22. See U.S. Latino & Latina World War II, Oral History Project, University of Texas Austin, http://lib.utexas.edu/ww2latinos/ or http://lib.utexas.edu/ww2latinos/browse-index.html. It has the most extensive online collection of Mexican American and Latina/o veteran interviews.

4. Lynn Marie Getz, "Lost Momentum: World War II and the Education of Hispanos in New Mexico," in Maggie Rivas-Rodríguez, ed., *Mexican Americans and World War II* (Austin: University of Texas Press, 2005), 93, 108. Morín, *Among the Valiant*, 34–42, 166–71. Tom Brokaw, *The Greatest Generation* (New York: Random House, 1998). Refugio I. Rochin and Lionel Fernández, "U.S. Latino Patriots: From the American Revolution to Afghanistan, An Overview," Pew Hispanic Center, http://www.pewhispanic.org/files/reports/17.3.pdf. Ken Burns and Lynn Novick, *The War*, WETA and American Lives II Film Project, LLC, (Washington, DC: Public Broadcasting System, 2007), http://www.pbs.org/thewar/.

5. Morín, *Among the Valiant*, 15.

6. Pedro Infante—"El Soldado Raso" (Primera Grabación con Peerles), YouTube, http://www.youtube.com/watch?v=VtEWJlxXMdU. "me voy de soldado raso" http://www.youtube.com/watch?v=alYheabjEx8.

7. Rubén G. Rumbaut, "The Making of a People," in Marta Tienda and Faith Mitchell, *Hispanics and the Future of America* (Washington, DC: National Academic Press, 2003), 24, FN8, http://books.nap.edu/openbook.php?record_id=11539&page=16. The racism at the time cannot be minimized. Ted Williams's mother was Mexican American and he was raised with her family. In his autobiography, Ted Williams (2001) wrote that "if I had had my mother's name, there is no doubt I would have run into problems in those days, [with] the prejudices people had in Southern California." Williams was arguably baseball's greatest hitter. Ted Williams with John Underwood, *My Turn at Bat: The Story of My Life* (New York: Simon and Schuster, 1988), 28–30.

8. David Reyes, "California and the West; A Marine Who Wielded the Power of Persuasion; World War II: Effort Builds to Gain Medal of Honor for Storied Mexican American Veteran Who Talked More Than 1,000 Japanese into Surrendering," *Los Angeles Times* (August 31, 1998). Gabaldón also prevented some of his fellow soldiers from shooting the captured Japanese. Ruchika Joshi, "Guy Gabaldón," Oral History Project, U.S. Latino and Latina World War II, University of Texas, http://www.lib.utexas.edu/ww2latinos/

template-stories-indiv.html?work_urn=urn%3Autlol%3Awwlatin.034&work_title=Gabaldon%2C+Guy.

9. Jorge Rodriguez, "A History of El Paso's Company E in World War II" (Master of Arts thesis, University of Texas at El Paso, 2010), 1, 26, 41, 42, 50–55.

10. Morín, *Among the Valiant,* 67–74. Leigh E. Smith, Jr., "El Paso's Company E Survivors Remember Rapido River Assault," *Borderland: El Paso Community College* 13 (Spring 1995): 6–7. Leigh E. Smith Jr., "Company E Survivor Recalls Days as Prisoner of War," *EPCC Local History Project,* http://epcc.libguides.com/content.php?pid=309255&sid=2621916. Co. "E" Vets, June 4, 2008, http://elpasotimes.typepad.com/morgue/2008/06/co-e-vets.html. Rodriguez, "Company E," 45, 55–59, 60, 76, 82–96. This is the most complete account of Company E. "The following men of Company E were recommended for citations on September 12th [before El Rapido] for their actions in holding and repelling the German tank attacks: 1st Lt. James M. Humphries, 1st Sgt. Gabriel L. Navarrete, Sgt. Librado A. Gonzales, Sgt. Carlos Irrobali, Sgt. Jesus M. Lucio, Sgt. Rafael Q. Torres, Sgt. Marcelino Valadez, Staff Sgt. Enrique Ochotorena, Cpl. Santiago V. Jaramillo, Cpl. Benito G. Dominguez, Pvt. Abner C. Carrasco, Pvt. Tirso F. Carrillo, Pvt. Juan R. Padilla, Pvt. Miguel S. Garcia, Pvt. Alfredo P. Ruiz, Pvt. Salomon Santos, Pvt. Ramon G. Gutierrez, Pvt. Harold B. Beaver, Pvt. Juan Pruitt, Pvt. Manuel C. Gonzales."

11. Figueroa, "G.I. José," 22.

12. Ibid., 22.

13. Alonso Perales, ed., *Are We Good Neighbors?* (New York: Arno Press, 1974), 79.

14. Ken Burns's documentary on World War II drew nationwide protests from Latino groups because he distorted history by not acknowledging the presence of Mexican Americans and Puerto Ricans in WW II. Roberto Lovato, "Saving Private Ramos: Ken Burns' World War II Documentary Continues to Incite Latino Protest," *New America Media,* http://news.newamericamedia.org/news/view_article.html?article_id=74ce20bca4b84e4a5c35736d73a90d28.

15. Figueroa, "G.I. José," 22. Perales, *Are We Good Neighbors?* 79. Adrianna Alatorre, "Anthony Family Had Five Sons in World War II," *Borderlands,* El Paso Community College, http://epcc.libguides.com/content.php?pid=309255&sid=2559970. Rita Sanchez, "The Five Sanchez Brothers in World War II," in Rivas-Rodriguez, ed., *Mexican Americans & World War II,* 1–38. Brooke N. Miller, "Angelita De Los Santos," Latinos and Latinas & World War II, University of Texas, http://www.lib.utexas.edu/ww2latinos/template-stories-indiv.html?work_urn=urn%3Autlol%3Awwlatin.560&work_title=De+Los+Santos%2C+Lita. Richard Gonzales, "Latino War Vets Changed World at Home, Abroad," *National Public Radio* Weekend Edition—Sunday. http://www.npr.org/templates/story/story.php?storyId=14579935. World War II: Mexican Air Force Helped Liberate the Philippines, Historynet.com, http://www.historynet.com/world-war-ii-mexican-air-force-helped-liberate-the-philippines.htm. "Untold stories of Mexican-American WWII veterans,"

San Gabriel Valley Tribune, http://www.sgvtribune.com/mexicanveterans.

16. Figueroa, "G.I. José," 20. Joyce Valdez, "Stories Hispanic WWII Veterans Discuss Today's War Against Terrorism," *Hispanic Magazine* (March 3, 2002): 20–22. Joanne R. Sánchez, "Lifetime of Caring: War Nurse, Rafaela Muñiz Esquivel," *U.S. Latinos and Latinas & World War II* 3, no. 1 (Fall 2001), University of Texas at Austin; available at http://lib.utexas.edu/ww2latinos/template-stories-indiv.html?work_urn=urn%3Autlol%3Awwlatin.029&work_title=Esquivel%2C+Rafaela+Muniz. Roseanna Aytes, "Women Changed Wartime Work Patterns," *Borderlands*, El Paso Community College, http://epcc.libguides.com/content.php?pid=309255&sid=2621863. Chris Marín, Arizona Men and Women in Military, *BarrioZona* http://www.barriozona.com/Mexican-American_Men_and_Women_in_WWII.html.

17. Cecilia Rasmussen, "A Teenager's Courage Remembered," *Los Angeles Times*, Ventura County Edition (April 7, 1998). Janice Harumi Yen, "Who Was Ralph Lazo?" Nikkei for Civil Rights & Redress Education Committee, http://www.ncrr-la.org/news/7_6_03/2.html. NCRR and Visual Communications to premiere Stand Up for Justice at Day of Remembrance 2004, http://www.ncrr-la.org/news/stand_up_for_justice.html.

18. See Joan W. Moore, *Homeboys: Gangs, Drugs, and Prison in the Barrios of Los Angeles* (Philadelphia, PA: Temple University Press, 1978), 64. James Diego Vigil, *Barrio Gangs: Street Life and Identity in Southern California* (Austin: University of Texas Press, 1988), 9, 22, 33, 67, 93. Edward J. Escobar, *Race, Police, and the Making of a Political Identity: Mexican Americans and the Los Angeles Police Department, 1900–1945* (Berkeley: University of California Press, 1999), 181–82.

19. Catherine Sue Ramírez, "The Pachuca in Chicana/o Art, Literature and History: Reexamining Nation, Cultural Nationalism and Resistance" (PhD dissertation, University of California, Berkeley, 2000), 50, 96. Catherine Sue Ramírez, *The Woman in the Zoot Suit: Gender, Nationalism, and the Cultural Politics of Memory* (Durham, NC: Duke University Press, 2009). Elizabeth Rachel Escobedo, "Mexican American Home Front: The Politics of Gender, Culture, and Community in World War II Los Angeles" (PhD dissertation, University of Washington, 2004), 65, 71–72, 85, 97.

20. "Sleepy Lagoon," words and music by Jack Lawrence and Eric Coates, recorded by Harry James, 1940, http://www.youtube.com/watch?v=I1yQLPhEGGY&feature=related. Ismael Dieppa, "The Zoot-Suit Riots Revisited: The Role of Private Philanthropy in Youth Problems of Mexican-Americans" (DSW dissertation, University of Southern California, 1973), 14. Carey McWilliams Papers, Special Collections Library, University of California at Los Angeles. Ramírez, "The Pachuca in Chicana/o Art," 15–20. Escobedo, "Mexican American Home Front," 67–68.

21. Sheila Marie Contreras, *Blood Lines: Myth, Indigenism and Chicana/o Literature* (Austin: University of Texas Press, 2008), 75–76. Carey McWilliams, *North from Mexico* (New York: Greenwood Press, 1968), 233–35. Interestingly, Deputy Sheriff Ed Durán Ayres was also an amateur historian who wrote a series of articles for the *Civic Center Sun* (Los Angeles) on "The Background of the History of California." Some of these articles appeared in the April 18, April 25, May 16, May 30, June 6, July 4, and August 1, 1940, issues of the paper. The content of the articles seriously question whether Ayres wrote the Grand Jury Report. According to Guy Endore, the report was developed by the sheriffs, who signed Ayres's name. Kevin Allen Leonard, *The Battle for Los Angeles: Racial Ideology and World War II* (Albuquerque: University of New Mexico Press, 2006), 91–107. Luis Valdez's Zoot Suit (1982) should be seen on DVD. Video On Demand, Amazon.com.

22. George J. Sánchez, *Becoming Mexican American: Ethnicity, Culture and Identity in Chicano Los Angeles, 1900–1945* (New York: Oxford University Press, 1993), 251. Alice McGrath (1917–2009), American Experience, PBS, http://www.pbs.org/wgbh/amex/zoot/eng_peopleevents/p_mcgrath.html. Oxnard New FILM Alice McGrath interview, http://www.youtube.com/watch?v=96N-Y8RKYiE. Dear Alice Interview with Alice McGrath, Blip, http://blip.tv/el-teatro-campesino/dear-alice-an-interview-with-alice-mcgrath-3093765.

23. Mari Jo Buhle, Paul Buhle, and Dan Georgakas, eds., *Encyclopedia of the American Left* (Urbana: University of Illinois Press, 1992), 684–86. The Sleepy Lagoon Case Prepared by the Sleepy Lagoon Defense Committee (Formerly The Citizen's Committee for the Defense of Mexican-American Youth) (Los Angeles, CA: The Sleepy Lagoon Defense Committee, 1943), http://content.cdlib.org/view?docId=hb7779p4zc&brand=calisphere&doc.view=entire_text.

24. Conversations with Lupe Leyvas, sister of Henry Leyvas, over a period of 10 years (1988–1998). Confirmed in an interview on October 10, 1998. Her story, that of her family, and that of the other defendants' families remain untold. Anthony Quinn, *The Original Sin: A Self-Portrait by Anthony Quinn* (New York: Little, Brown & Company, 1972), 81–85. Scott, "The Mexican American," 223, 225. Citizen's Committee for the Defense of Mexican-American Youth, *The Sleepy Lagoon Case* (Los Angeles, 1942), 21. McWilliams, *North from Mexico*, 228–33. Mario García, *Mexican Americans, Leadership, Ideology, & Identity, 1930–1960* (New York: Yale University Press, 1989), 165–70. J. Sánchez, "Lifetime of Caring," 249. "Pachuco Crimes," Report of Joint Fact-Finding Committee on Un-American Activities in California, Senate Journal of April 16, 1945, 161–62, 171, 173–75, 181–83, in Rodolfo F. Acuña and Guadalupe Compeán, eds., *Voices of the U.S. Latino Experience*, 3 Vols. (Westport, CT: Greenwood Press, 2008), 694–99.

25. *The People v. Gus Zammora et al.*, 66 Cal. Ap. 2d 166; 152 2d 180; 1944 Cal. Ap. LEXIS 1170; October 4, 1944. "From Sleepy Lagoon to Zoot Suit: The Irreverent Path of Alice McGrath," video, 32 minutes (Santa Cruz, CA: Giges Productions, 1996). Alice McGrath was a CIO organizer who became executive secretary of the Sleepy Lagoon Defense Committee. One of the main characters in the play and movie Zoot Suit was patterned after her. Carlos Lozano, "Alice McGrath: 50 Years on

the Front Lines," *Los Angeles Times,* Ventura County Edition (February 22, 1998). Escobedo, "Mexican American Home Front," 67–68, 93–94. Ramírez, "The Pachuca in Chicana/o Art," 24–40. Nash, *American West,* 111–20.

26. Joseph Tovares, "American Experience: Zoot Suit Riots," *KCET-TV,* Los Angeles, February 10, 2002. Zoot Suit Documentary, http://www.pbs.org/wgbh/amex/zoot/eng_sfeature/sf_zoot_mx.html. McWilliams, *North from Mexico,* 244–54. Dieppa, "Zoot-Suit Riots," 9, 22–23. *Los Angeles Times* (June 7, 1943). *Time Magazine* (June 21, 1943). *PM* (June 10, 1943). S. I. Hayakawa, "Second Thoughts: The Zoot Suit War," *The Chicago Defender* (June 26, 1943), 15; this article appeared in a progressive African American newspaper. Hayakawa during the 1960s would become an ultra-conservative.

27. FBI Report, "Racial Conditions (Spanish-Mexican Activities in Los Angeles Field Division)" (Los Angeles, January 14, 1944). The *Eastside Journal* (Los Angeles, June 9, 1943), wrote an editorial defending the zoot-suiters; it pointed out that 112 had been hospitalized, 150 hurt, and 12 treated in the hospitals as outpatients. See also McWilliams, *North from Mexico,* 250–51. Ed Robbins, *PM* (June 9, 1943).

28. *Senate Journal* of April 16, 1945, containing Report of the Joint Fact-Finding Committee on Un-American Activities in California. State Senate of California, 161–62, 171, 173–75, 181–83. Acuña and Compeán, eds., *Voices of the U.S. Latino Experience,* 693–98. *Los Angeles Times* (June 10, 1943 and July 10, 1943). McGucken Report, California Legislature, Report and Recommendations of Citizens Committee on Civil Disturbances in Los Angeles (June 12, 1943), 1. Mauricio Mazón, *The Zoot-Suit Riots: The Psychology of Symbolic Annihilation* (Austin: University of Texas Press, 1988), 67–77.

29. Julie A. Campbell, "Madres y Esposas: Tucson's Spanish-American Mothers and Wives Association," *Journal of Arizona History* 31, no. 2 (Summer 1990): 161–82.

30. Ibid., 161–82. Christine Marin, La Asociacion Hispano-Americana de Madres y Esposas: Tucson's Mexican American Women in World War II, http://eric.ed.gov/?id=ED315253. Chris Lukinbeal, Daniel D. Arreola, and D. Drew Lucio, "Mexican Urban Colonias in the Salt River Valley of Arizona," *Geographical Review* (January 2012).

31. Escobedo, "Mexican American Home Front," 9, 11, 33, 93–94, 103.

32. *Andrea D. Perez et al.,* Petitioners, *v. W. G. Sharp,* as County Clerk, etc., Respondent. L.A. No. 20305. *Perez v. Sharp* 32 Cal.2d 711, 198 P.2d 17 (1948), http://www.multiracial.com/government/perez-v-sharp.html. The case would be cited in *Brown v. the Board of Education* (1954), http://sshl.ucsd.edu/brown/perez.htm. Derrick Z. Jackson, "Court's Ruling Opens New Era in Civil Rights," *Boston Globe* (November 21, 2003), http://www.commondreams.org/views03/1121-01.htm. Peggy Pascoe, "Miscegenation Law, Court Cases, and Ideologies of Race in Twentieth-Century America," in Werner Sollors, ed., *Interracialism: Black-White Intermarriage in American History, Literature, and Law* (Cambridge: Oxford University Press, 2000), 196–202.

33. "*Rosie the Riveter*: Real Women Workers in World War II," Journeys & Crossings, Library of Congress, http://www.loc.gov/rr/program/journey/rosie.html or http://www.youtube.com/watch?v=04VNBM1PqR8.

34. Carlos G. Vélez-Ibáñez, *Border Visions: Mexican Cultures of the Southwest United States* (Tucson: University of Arizona Press, 1996), 19. Hedda Garza, *Latinas: Hispanic Women in the United States* (New York: Franklin Watts, 1994), 74. Monica Rivera, "Josephine Kelly Ledesma Walker: A Woman Ahead of Her Time," *U.S. Latinos and Latinas & World War II* 3, no. 1 (Fall 2001), University of Texas at Austin; available at http://www.lib.utexas.edu/ww2latinos/template-stories-indiv.html?work_urn=urn%3Autlol%3Awwlatin.058&work_title=Ledesma+Walker%2C+Josephine+Kelly. Sherri Fauver, "Henrietta López Rivas—Kelly Air Force Base Her Proving Ground," *U.S. Latinos and Latinas & World War II* 1, no. 2 (Spring 2000); available at http://www.lib.utexas.edu/ww2latinos/template-stories-indiv.html?work_urn=urn%3Autlol%3Awwlatin.089&work_title=Rivas%2C+Henrietta++Lopez. Cheryl Smith, "Elisa Rodriguez: Wartime Civil Servant," *U.S. Latinos and Latinas & World War II* 1, no. 1 (Fall 1999); available at http://www.lib.utexas.edu/ww2latinos/template-stories-indiv.html?work_urn=urn%3Autlol%3Awwlatin.093&work_title=Rodriguez%2C+Maria+Elisa+Reyes. Richard Santillán, "Rosita and the Riveter: Midwest Mexican American Women During World War II, 1941–1945," *Perspectives in Mexican American Studies* 2 (1989): 115–46.

35. Carlos E. Castañeda, "Discrimination Against Mexican Americans in War Industries," Mexican American Voices, *Digital History,* University of Houston. Richard Griswold del Castillo, ed., *World War II and Mexican American Civil Rights* (Austin: University of Texas Press, 2008), 75–78. Robert Garland Landolt, *The Mexican-American Workers of San Antonio, Texas* (New York: Arno Press, 1976), 76–77, 88–117; Pauline R. Kibbe, *Latin Americans in Texas* (New York: Arno Press, 1974), 161–62; Charles Loomis and Nellie Loomis, "Skilled Spanish-American War Industry Workers from New Mexico," *Applied Anthropology* 2 (October–December 1942): 33.

36. Clete Daniel, *Chicano Workers and the Politics of Fairness: The FEPC in the Southwest, 1941–1945* (Austin: University of Texas Press, 1991), 8–9. Manuel Ruiz, Jr., "Closing Remarks," Making Public Employment: A Model of Equal Opportunity, A Report of the Proceedings of Regional Civil Rights Conference II. Sponsored by the U.S. Commission on Civil Rights in Boston, Massachusetts, September 22–24, 1974, 34–35. http://www.law.umaryland.edu/marshall/usccr/documents/cr12an72.pdf.

37. David Montejano, *Anglos and Mexicans in the Making of Texas, 1836–1986* (Austin: University of Texas Press, 1987), 270. Carlos E. Castañeda, September 8, 1944, on Bill 2048 to Prohibit Discrimination Because of Race, Creed, Color, National Origin or Ancestry, Fair Employment Practices Act Hearings, quote in Perales, ed., *Are We Good Neighbors?,* 92–104.

38. Vélez-Ibáñez, *Border Visions,* 117. Daniel, *Chicano Workers and the Politics of Fairness,* 77–105, 115. Matthew Gritter,

New School for Social Research, "Good Neighbors and Good Citizens: People of Mexican Origin and the FEPC1" (Under Review at Journal of Policy History), http://www.newschool.edu/uploadedFiles/NSSR/Departments_and_Faculty/Political_Science/Recent_Placements/GritterSample.pdf. Matthew Gritter, "Shaping Incorporation: People of Mexican Origin and Anti-Discrimination Policy" (Dissertation, New School for Social Research, New York, NY, 2010).

39. Statement of Frank Paz, President of the Spanish-Speaking People's Council of Chicago, quoted in Perales, ed., *Are We Good Neighbors?*, 111–14.

40. Perales, *Are We Good Neighbors?*, 93, 94, 112–13, 117, 121. Daniel, *Chicano Workers and the Politics of Fairness*, 1, 4–5, 42, 52–76, 64, 115. Emilio Zamora, "The Failed Promise of Wartime Opportunity for Mexicans in the Texas Oil Industry," *Southwestern Historical Quarterly* 95, no. 3 (January 1, 1992): 323–50, critiques the work of the FEPC in the booming oil industry in Texas.

41. FBI, "Racial Conditions (Spanish-Mexican Activities in Los Angeles Field Division)," A confidential report, January 14, 1944; available at Acuña Archives, CSUN Library.

42. Escobedo, "Mexican American Home Front," 14, 18, 125–36, 139, 153, 155.

43. Gary McLauchlan, "World War II and the Transformation of the U.S. State: The Wartime Foundations of U.S. Hegemony," *Sociological Inquiry* 67, no. 1 (Winter 1997): 1–2, 22.

44. Taft–Hartley Act—1947, http://www.historycentral.com/Documents/Tafthatley.html.

45. Luisa Moreno, http://www.youtube.com/watch?v=7up HqNX6654. Luisa Moreno Labor Studies Collection at Southern California Library, Allen Kerri, "The Legacy of Luisa Moreno," *The Hispanic Outlook in Higher Education. Paramus* 14, no. 18 (June 14, 2004): 22. G. Sánchez, *Becoming Mexican American*, 244–45, 249, 252.

46. Vicki L. Ruiz, *Cannery Women, Cannery Lives: Mexican Women, Unionization, and California Food Processing Industry, 1930-1950* (Albuquerque: University of New Mexico Press, 1987), 78–79, 83, 110–14. Patricia Zavella, *Women's Work & Chicano Families: Cannery Workers of the Santa Clara Valley* (Ithaca, NY: Cornell University, 1987), 49. Garza, *Latinas*, 79. David G. Gutiérrez, *Walls and Mirrors: Mexican Americans, Mexican Immigrants, and the Politics of Ethnicity* (Berkeley: University of California, 1995), 110–11. The Roots of the HUAC Committee, HistoryBlogger, http://thehistoryblogger.blogspot.com/2007/08/roots-of-huac-committee.html.

47. García, *Mexican Americans*, 145–74. Dolores Hayden, *The Power of Place: Urban Landscapes as Public History* (Boston: M.I.T. Press, 1997), 196–99. Francisco A. Rosales, *Chicano! The History of the Mexican American Civil Rights Movement*, 2d Revised ed. (Houston, TX: Arte Público Press, 1997), 123–24. Matt S. Meier and Margo Gutiérrez, *Encyclopedia of the Mexican American Civil Rights Movement* (Westport, CT: Greenwood Press, 2000), 82. Jeffrey M. Garcilazo, "McCarthyism, Mexican Americans, and the Los Angeles Committee for Protection of the Foreign-Born," *Western Historical Quarterly* 32, no. 3 (Autumn 2001): 278. Paul Buhle

and Dave Wagner, *Radical Hollywood: The Untold Story Behind America's Favorite Movies* (The New Press, 2002), 91. "Spanish Congress Hits War Job Discrimination," *Los Angeles Times* (May 24, 1942), A1. "Influences Behind Gang Wars Here to Be Studied," *Los Angeles Times* (December 14, 1942), A8. Escobedo, "Mexican American Home Front," 116. Josefina Fierro de Bright, 1920–1998, http://www.mhschool.com/ss/ca/eng/g4/u4/g4u4_bio2.html.

48. José Angel Gutiérrez, "Under Surveillance," *The Texas Observer Magazine* (January 9, 1987), 8–13. FBI Report (Los Angeles, June 16, 1943). FBI Report, "Racial Conditions" (January 14, 1944).

49. Enrique M. Buelna, "Resistance from the Margins: Mexican American Radical Activism in Los Angeles, 1930–1970" (PhD dissertation: University of California, Irvine, 2007). Rodolfo F. Acuña, *A Community Under Siege: A Chronicle of Chicanos East of the Los Angeles River, 1945-1975* (Los Angeles: Chicano Studies Research Center Publications, 1984), 21–106, 275–94, 407–50.

50. David E. Hayes-Bautista, Werner O. Schink, and Jorge Chapa, *The Burden of Support: Young Latinos in an Aging Society* (Stanford, CA: Stanford University Press, 1988), 15, 18–21. Mario García, *Memories of Chicano History: The Life and Narrative of Bert Corona* (Berkeley: University of California Press, 1994), 161–63. Katherine Underwood, "Pioneering Minority Representation: Edward Roybal and the Los Angeles City Council, 1949-1962," *Pacific Historical Review* 66, no. 3 (August 1, 1997), 399–425. John R. Chávez, *The Lost Land: The Chicano Image of the Southwest* (Albuquerque: University of New Mexico, 1984), 107–27.

51. Grebler et al., *The Mexican-American People,* 150, 154. Thomas E. Sheridan, *Los Tucsonenses: The Mexican Community in Tucson, 1854-1941* (Tucson: University of Arizona Press, 1986), 235–36. David A. Badillo, "From West San Antonio to East L.A.: Chicano Community Leadership Compare," Working Paper Series, No. 24 (April 1989), Stanford Center for Chicano Research.

52. U.S. Immigration and Naturalization Service. Historical Statistics of the United States, Part 1 (1975), U.S. Bureau of the Census, 1980 and 1990, and March Current Population Survey, 1995 and 1996. (1) These figures are based on CPS data that are adjusted for undercount and thus are not comparable to census figures. (2) Mexican-origin population calculated as a sum of the Mexican-born population and natives of Mexican parentage. See George J. Borjas and Lawrence F. Katz, "The Evolution of the Mexican-Born Workforce in the United States," Harvard University and National Bureau of Economic Research (April 2005), http://www.aeaweb.org/assa/2006/0108_1015_0302.pdf. Jeffrey Passel and D'Vera Cohn, "How Many Hispanics? Comparing Census Counts and Census Estimates," Pew Hispanic Center (March 15, 2011). One of the most accurate surveyors.

53. Miriam D. Rosenthal, "Striving for Perfection: A Brief History of Advances and Undercounts in the U.S. Census," *Government Information Quarterly* 30, no. 3 (July 2013): 217–318. Ray Hutchison, "Miscounting the Spanish Origin Population

in the United States: Corrections to the 1970 Census and their Implications," *International Migration* 22, no. 2 (April 1984): 73–89.

54. The 60th Anniversary of Mendez vs. Westminster, http://uprisingradio.org/home/?p=1896. Mendez v Westminister, http://mendezvwestminster.com/_wsn/page3.html.

55. *Delgado v. Bastrop ISD, Handbook of Texas Online,* http://www.tshaonline.org/handbook/online/articles/DD/jrd1.html.

56. Kibbe, *Latin Americans in Texas,* 212, 214–15. "First Regional Conference on the Education of Spanish-Speaking people in the Southwest—A Report" (March 1946). *Image* (Federation of Employed Latin American Descendants [FELAD], Vallejo, California), May 1976. J. Sánchez, "Lifetime of Caring," 9–11. Vélez-Ibáñez, *Border Visions,* 129. Gilbert G. González, *Labor and Community: Mexican Citrus Worker Villages in a Southern California County, 1900–1950* (Urbana: University of Illinois Press, 1994), 172–77. Steven H. Wilson, "Brown over Other White: Mexican Americans' Legal Arguments and Litigation Strategy in School Desegregation Lawsuits," *Law and History Review* 21, no.1 (Spring 2003): 145–194, http://www.historycooperative.org/journals/lhr/21.1/forum_wilson.html.

57. Henry A. J. Ramos, *The American G.I. Forum: In Pursuit of the Dream, 1948–1983* (Houston, TX: Arte Público Press, 1998), 23. Patrick J Carroll, *Felix Longoria's Wake: Bereavement, Racism, and the Rise of Mexican American Activism* (Austin: University of Texas, 2003). American G.I. Forum, http://www.pbs.org/kpbs/theborder/history/timeline/19.html. "A Class Apart," WGBH American Experience, http://www.pbs.org/wgbh/americanexperience/class/photoGallery/. Felix Z. Longoria: Private, United States Army, http://www.arlingtoncemetery.net/longoria.htm.

58. Rosales, *Chicano!,* 97.

59. Ramos, *The American G.I. Forum*, 23.

60. Mexican American Movement, Urban Archives, California State University at Northridge, http://library.csun.edu/Collections/SCA/UAC/SCMAM. Rosales, *Chicano!,* 99–102. G. Sánchez, *Becoming Mexican American,* 206–7, 257–61. Carlos Muñoz, *Youth, Identity, Power: The Chicano Movement*, Revised ed. (London: Verso, 2007), 35–44. Ohio Citizen Action, The Organizer's Tale, http://www.ohiocitizen.org/about/training/chavez.html. Saul Alinsky, community organizing and rules for radicals, http://www.infed.org/thinkers/alinsky.htm.

61. Lester Tate joins the Los Angeles Civil Rights Congress, January 1950, Los Angeles, University of Southern California Digital Collection, http://digarc.usc.edu/search/controller/view/scl-m0316.html. Gerald Horne, *Fire This Time: The Watts Uprising and the 1960s* (Charlottesville: University Press of Virginia, 1995), 7–9. Buelna, "Resistance from the Margins," 125, 132, 135, 190–91. Mexican Americans like Celia Rodríguez were very much involved in the Civil Rights Congress, which was a radical Black organization with ties to the Communist Party. It attracted activists such as Ralph Cuarón, who opened a storefront in Boyle Heights. In 1947, an affiliate was formed, the Mexican Civil Rights Committee, which became the Mexican American Civil Rights Congress.

This organization was involved in the Salcido case. Simultaneously, many of the activists were involved with the organizing committee of the Independent Progressive Party in 1947.

62. Acuña, *A Community Under Siege,* 25, 418–19. Buelna, "Resistance from the Margins," 105. John Sides, "'You Understand My Condition': The Civil Rights Congress in the Los Angeles African-American Community, 1946–1952," *Pacific Historical Review* 67, no. 2 (May 1998): 233–57. Tony Castro, *Chicano Power: The Emergence of Mexican-Americans* (New York: Saturday Review Press, 1974), 188. Miguel Tirado, "The Mexican-American Minority's Participation in Voluntary Political Associations" (PhD dissertation, Claremont Graduate School and University Center, 1970), 65. Luis Arroyo, "Chicano Participation in Organized Labor: The CIO in Los Angeles, 1938–1950, An Extended Research Note," *Aztlán* 6, no. 2 (Summer 1975): 297. *Eastside Sun* (Boyle Heights) (April 2, 1948). Keyes had shot four people in 18 months. See also Guy Endore, *Justice for Salcido* (Los Angeles: Civil Rights Congress of Los Angeles, 1948), 5–9, 13. Salcido was hit four times—in the head from ear to ear, twice in the back of the head, and in the arm.

63. Buelna, "Resistance from the Margins," 106, bases much of his dissertation on extensive interviews with Ralph Cuarón, one of the premier activists of the Post World War II era and through the 1960s. Like so many other activists, Cuarón's parents were originally from Chihuahua, settling of a time in the mining town of Morenci, Arizona, scene of many bitter copper strikes. Cuarón joined the Communist Party deeply touched by the Great Depression. Enrique Buelna calls the Justice for Salcido case a landmark civil rights case.

64. See Rodolfo Acuña, *Occupied America: A History of Chicanos,* 2d and 3d eds. (New York: Harper & Row, 1981 and 1988). *Eastside Sun* (April 9, 1948 and August 22, 1947). The Progressive Citizens of America, along with Councilman Christensen of the 9th Councilmanic District and Ed Elliot of the 44th Assembly District, requested the suspension of Keyes; *Eastside Sun* (April 23, 1948). The American Jewish Congress protested the admitted shooting of an unarmed Mexican. "AJC Requests Action in Salcido Killing," *Eastside Sun* (July 23, 1948). Endore, *Justice for Salcido,* 17, 19–21, 24, 29–30. "Community Teachers Support Civil Rights Congress," an article in the *Eastside Sun* (April 30, 1948), criticized the *Times* editorial, stating that Mexicans historically suffered police brutality. Grebler et al., *The Mexican-American People,* 533. Laura L. Cummings, "Cloth-Wrapped People, Trouble, and Power: Pachuco Culture in the Greater Southwest," *Journal of the Southwest* 45, no. 3 (Autumn 2003): 329–48. Arturo Madrid Barela, "In Search of the Authentic Pachuco—An Interpretive Essay, Part I," *Aztlan* 4, no. 1 (1973): 34–35.

65. Buelna, "Resistance from the Margins," 83, 105, 132, 135. "Amigos de Wallace" rally, 1948, Lincoln Park Stadium(?), Los Angeles, University of Southern California, Digital Archive, http://digarc.usc.edu/search/controller/view/scl-m0276. Selected Works of Henry A. Wallace, New Deal Network, Franklin and Eleanor Roosevelt Institute, http://newdeal.feri.org/wallace/index.htm.

66. Perales, *Are We Good Neighbors?*, 81, 165–66, 166–67, 173–74, 178–79, 283–96.

67. Bill Dredge, "Machines and Men Bringing in Cotton," *Los Angeles Times* (November 18, 1948). W. K. Barger and Ernesto M Reza, *The Farm Labor Movement in the Midwest: Social Change and Adaptation Among Migrant Farmworkers* (Austin: University of Texas Press, 1994), 21, map of migrant streams, http://www.illinoismigrant.org/farmwrk1.html. José Alamillo, 'El Otro Norte: Latinos and Latinas in the Pacific Northwest: The Latinization of the Pacific Northwest,' Latino's in Northwest Project, http://www.josealamillo.com/latinos%20northwest.htm. Mexican Americans in the Columbia Basin, Railroad and Migrant Workers, http://www.vancouver.wsu.edu/crbeha/ma/ma.htm#rail. Dennis Nodín Valdés, *Al Norte: Agricultural Workers in the Great Lakes Region, 1917 to 1970* (Austin: University of Texas Press, 1991).

68. Dennis Nodín Valdés, "Machine Politics in California Agriculture, 1945–1990s," *Pacific Historical Review* 63, no. 2 (May 1, 1994): 205. Ernesto Galarza, *Spiders in the House and Workers in the Field* (Notre Dame, IN: University of Notre Dame Press, 1970), 23–27, 35, 40–48, 64–66, 88, 153, 231–47, 288–97. John Phillip Carney, "Postwar Mexican Migration, 1945–1955, with Particular Reference to the Policies and Practices of the United States Concerning Its Control" (PhD dissertation, University of Southern California, 1957), 157. Ernesto Galarza, *Farmworkers and Agribusiness in California, 1947–1960* (Notre Dame: University of Notre Dame Press, 1977), 99, 100, 103. National Advisory Committee on Farm Labor, *Farm Labor Organizing, 1905–1967: A Brief History* (New York: National Advisory Committee on Farm Labor, 1967), 37. Sam Kushner, *Long Road to Delano* (New York: International Publishers, 1975), 82. D. Gutiérrez, *Walls and Mirrors*, 155–60. Rosales, *Chicano!*, 119–20. Ernesto Galarza Commemorative Lectures, Stanford University, http://www.stanford.edu/dept/csre/PUBL_galarza.htm.

69. Javier Flores Carrera y Jorge Alejandro Sosa Hernández, Alianza Nacional de Braceros, Centro de Tabajadores Agricolas, El Paso, Texas, Bracero 1 De 7 Documental Programa Bracero, a seven part series in Spanish. Excellent, http://www.youtube.com/watch?v=6l5fuTEpOeQ&feature=PlayList&p=D5DCDF858D4E313E&index=6. Ramón Rentería, "UTEP Works to Recover History of Braceros: Workers Helped Fill Void During WWII," *El Paso Times* (January 28, 2003). Braceros Resources in the OSU [Oregon State University] Libraries Collections, Photograph Collection, http://digitalcollections.library.oregonstate.edu/cdm4/client/bracero/related.php.

70. George O. Coalson, *The Development of the Migratory Farm Labor System in Texas: 1900–1954* (San Francisco, CA: R&E Research Associates, 1977), 67, 82, 94. Mark Reisler, *By the Sweat of Their Brow: Mexican Immigration to the United States, 1900–1940* (Westport, CT: Greenwood Press, 1976), 260. Ernesto Galarza, *Merchants of Labor* (Santa Barbara, CA: McNally & Lottin, 1964), 47. Richard B. Craig, *The Bracero Program* (Austin: University of Texas Press, 1971), 36, 54, 58–59, 104, 107, 109, 112, 119, 198. D. Gutiérrez, *Walls and Mirrors*, 143; according to D. Gutiérrez, 154–55, LULAC was among the foremost opponents of the *bracero* program and the use of undocumented labor. Henry Anderson, *The Bracero Program in California* (Berkeley: School of Public Health, University of California, July 1961), 146. Erasmo Gamboa, "Under the Thumb of Agriculture: Bracero and Mexican American Workers in the Pacific Northwest" (PhD dissertation, University of Washington, 1984), 24–26. Patricia Morgan, *Shame of a Nation* (Los Angeles: Committee for the Protection of Foreign Born, 1954), 28. Ernesto Galarza, *Tragedy at Chualar: El Crucero de las Treinta y dos Cruces* (Santa Barbara, CA: McNally & Loftin, 1977). The American Committee for the Protection of the Foreign Born, *Our Badge of Infamy*, A Petition to the United Nations on the Treatment of the Mexican Immigrant (April 1959), 24.

71. Nodín Valdés, *Al Norte*, 89–117, quote on 116.

72. Erasmo Gamboa, *Mexican Labor and World War II: Braceros in the Pacific Northwest, 1942–1947* (Seattle: University of Washington Press, 1999), viii.

73. Gregory W. Hill, *Texas-Mexican Migratory Agricultural Workers in Wisconsin*, Agricultural Experimental Station Stencil Bulletin 6 (Madison: University of Wisconsin, 1948), 5–6, 15–16, 18–20. Coalson, *The Development of the Migratory Farm Labor*, 110. Kibbe, *Latin Americans in Texas*, 199–200. Richard W. Slatta, "Chicanos in the Pacific Northwest: An Historical Overview of Chicanos," *Aztlán* 6, no. 3 (Fall 1975): 327. Erasmo Gamboa, "Chicanos in the Northwest: An Historical Perspective," *El Grito* 7, no. 4 (Summer 1973): 61–63. Everett Ross Clinchy, Jr., *Equality of Opportunity for Latin-Americans in Texas* (New York: Arno Press, 1974), 87.

74. Douglas E. Foley, Clarice Mota, Donald E. Post, and Ignacio Lozano, *From Peons to Politicos: Ethnic Relations in a South Texas Town, 1900–1977* (Austin: University of Texas, Center for Mexican American Studies, 1977), 75, 85–86, 89. Kibbe, *Latin Americans in Texas*, 153, 160–63, 169. Landolt, *The Mexican-American Workers*, 117. Coalson, *The Development of the Migratory Farm Labor*, 87–88, 100–2, 107.

CHAPTER 12

"Happy Days": Chicano Communities under Siege

LEARNING OBJECTIVES

- Discuss the chapter title "Chicano Communities under Siege."

- State the status of the Mexican American community in the 1950s.

- Describe nativism during the decade.

- Interpret the impact of the anti-communist movement and the Cold War on Mexican Americans.

- Explain the militarization of the U.S.–Mexican border.

- Show how U.S. policies and attitudes toward Latin America affected Mexican Americans.

In the first edition of *Occupied America* (1972) I wrote,

The 1950s presented an enigma. Many Anglo-Americans tend to associate the decade with President Dwight D. Eisenhower and, therefore, have concluded that it was a period of stability during which nothing much happened. To Chicanos, the 1950s represented a "decade of defense," a decade in which the proponents of reaction attempted to crush the rising aspirations for liberation by overtly intimidating them.[1]

For years, that statement that the 1950s was a "decade of defense" of civil liberties stuck in my throat. I could not answer some of the questions that my students asked. So to understand the decade better and test my hypothesis, I microfilmed the articles of the *Eastside Sun* and the *Belvedere Citizen* newspapers in Los Angeles covering 1933–1975. I then synthesized the articles on 5x8 cards, and I lined them up using a timeline similar to the below, and asked, "How do the articles and the dates interrelate? What were the causes and effects?" From this exercise I learned that the decade of the 1950s was extremely important: just like the 1920s, it was a decade when business interests tried to take control of government.

1949	1950	1951	1952	1953	1954	1955	1956	1957	1958	1959

As in the 1920s with a Republican president in power, the "military–industrial–congressional complex" set out to wipe out all the reforms and gains of the New Deal. The 1950s was a decade when the government's transportation and housing policies promoted bulldozing and destruction of minority communities, putting these communities under siege. The "economic royalists," as Franklin Roosevelt called them, used racism, nativism, and the Cold War to obfuscate class interests. Their surrogates in Congress led the attacks on New Deal programs using anti-communism as a smoke screen.

Mexican Americans

Mexicans and Mexican Americans continued to live primarily in the five southwestern states of Texas, New Mexico, Colorado, Arizona, and California in 1950. Officially, there were fewer than 3 million Spanish-surname residents in the region, 10.9 percent of all southwesterners. Over two-thirds of Mexican Americans lived in cities. In California, three-quarters of the Mexican-origin population lived in cities, and in Texas, slightly more than two-thirds.[2] The major urban centers were Los Angeles, El Paso, and San Antonio; however, large concentrations also lived in the Lower Rio Grande Valley, the Salt and Gila Valleys of Arizona, and Fresno County, California. Most were young, with a median age of 20.6, versus 31.6 for whites and 27.3 for nonwhites.[3]

In the Southwest, the median number of school years completed by Mexican Americans was 5.2, compared with 11.3 for Euro-Americans and 7.8 for nonwhites. In Texas, the median was 3.5; in Arizona, 6.0; in California, 7.8; in Colorado, 6.5; and in New Mexico, 6.1. The median was higher in the cities: for example, in Tucson the education median was 6.5 years; Los Angeles, 8.2; and Albuquerque, 7.7. Worse, in El Paso, it was 5.2 and in Lubbock, Texas, it was only 1.7. A rule of thumb was that the lower the median, the more segregated the schools were and the poorer the community.

The first- and second-generation Mexicans comprised a large percentage of the total Latino population. According to the 1950 U.S. Census, just less than 83 percent of the Latino population was native-born, with some 17 percent of all Spanish-surname persons born in Mexico or Latin America. Again, the figures varied from state to state, with New Mexico and Colorado having the highest native-born populations—87.2 percent and 83.2 percent, respectively—as well as the smallest born-in-Mexico population—3.9 and 4.2 percent, respectively. Throughout the decade, the birth rate among Mexican-origin people was 4.1 percent, versus 3.1 percent for Euro-Americans and 3.3 for the total population.

Mexicans based in the United States were a people on the move. Between 1955 and 1960, close to 60 percent of the interstate movers went to California; 17 percent went to Texas. During the decade of the 1950s, the percentage of Mexicans in Texas fell sharply from 45 percent to 36 percent; the corresponding percentage in California rose from 34 to 42. Arizona and New Mexico's Mexican population declined slightly, whereas Illinois picked up Mexican immigrants—nearly all went to the Chicago area. Mexicans developed regional differences: Tejanos, for example, wore boots and cowboy hats and spoke English with a Texas tang, saying "Y'all" and calling men "Sir!" Everyone seemed to want to move out of Texas during that time—the state was the principal exporter of Mexican workers to other regions. Still, many Mexican Americans who lived in the Midwest yearned for the sounds of the accordion—or the warmth of the sun. In Chicago, Mexicans lived in those brownstone houses that had no front lawns and always seemed cold. Perhaps because of their isolation, Midwestern Chicanos appeared to be more Mexican than Mexicans elsewhere—or than Tejanos, as the case may be. In New Mexico, New Mexicans said they were not Mexicans, but "Spanish Americans," and lived under the illusion that *they* were the founders of the state. Californians had no set identity—Californian Mexicans, it seemed, came from everywhere but California.

The layering of the generations was becoming very evident, and the baby boomers' generation was what others called *pochos*; that is, they did not speak Spanish well and seemed more assimilated than were earlier generations. However, there were exceptions, and these greatly depended on where people lived.[4]

The Cold War

By the end of 1949, reversals in the Cold War heightened American angst, and Communism was promoted as the country's number 1 enemy. Consequently, the 1950s saw the rise of McCarthyism and the simultaneous escalation of the Cold War, at home and abroad. Cold War anxieties agitated a red scare, which peaked from 1946 to 1952. Red hunters such as FBI director J. Edgar Hoover played on the Euro-American belief of a monolithic, worldwide conspiracy directed from Moscow. The presidential Loyalty Review Board continued its purges of "reds" in the unions, universities, and entertainment industry. A renewed military draft for the Korean War further ensnared the nation in the battle against Communism, while the 1940 Smith Act made it a criminal offense to advocate violent overthrow of the government or to be a member of a group devoted to such advocacy. Using the pretext of that act, the federal government prosecuted leaders of the Communist Party and the Socialist Workers Party, most of whom did not support such actions. By the early 1950s, Republican politicians such as Richard Nixon and Joseph McCarthy and Democrats such as Senator Pat McCarran played on this paranoia to boost their careers and advance their pro-business ideology.[5]

The Korean War: Historical Amnesia

It is ironic, if not tragic, that the Korean War has been called the "Forgotten War." Some 33,665 U.S. military personnel were killed in action and 3,275 died from nonhostile causes. Some 92,134 were wounded in action, and from June 25, 1950, to July 27, 1953, 1,789,000 served in the Korean theater. The Korean conflict began in June 1950 between the Democratic People's Republic of Korea (North Korea) and the Republic of Korea (South Korea). An estimated 3 million people lost their lives in this war, which was not officially called a war but a "conflict." The United States joined the war on the side of the South Koreans. The People's Republic of China (PRC), which had been established just two years earlier, eventually came to Communist North Korea's aid.

The North Korean forces overwhelmed the South Korean army; the latter had rushed four ill-equipped and ill-trained United Nations (UN) divisions into the battle. The UN forces were driven southward. Reinforcements led by General Douglas MacArthur turned the tide for the South Koreans. As the Allied forces advanced northward to the 38th parallel, which was the dividing line between North Korea and South Korea, China warned them of retaliatory action, fearing that the presence of UN forces in North Korea would be a threat to the security of China. The UN forces, however, ignored the warnings and crossed the 38th parallel into North Korea with the expressed purpose of "unifying" North and South Korea. In November 1950, China entered the war and approximately 180,000 Chinese troops drove the Allied troops southward. For the next two and a half years, both sides fought a bloody trench-and-guerrilla war. Many people feared the possibility of a global conflict. The heavy casualties and reports of South Korean atrocities made the war unpopular back home in the United States. Opposition to the war started slowly and then expanded, much like with the more recent war in Iraq. The war ended in July 1953, when the United States declared an armistice. The importance of the war globally was that it established a precedent for U.S. intervention to contain the so-called Communist expansion.

Six Mexican Americans won Medals of Honor during this conflict. Eugene A. Obregón, 20, from Los Angeles, had enlisted in the Marine Corps at the age of 17. The enemy killed him but not before he saved a fellow marine's life. Joseph C. Rodríguez was from San Bernardino, California. Rodolfo P. Hernández, from Colton, California, was in the 187th Airborne. Opposing troops killed Edward Gómez, 19, from Omaha, Nebraska, in battle. Ambrosio Guillén, 24, from La Junta, Colorado, was also killed in battle. Benito Martínez from Hancock, Texas, was posthumously awarded the Medal of Honor for his actions near Satae-ri in Korea.

According to anthropologist Carlos Vélez-Ibáñez, who served in Korea, "The disproportion of Mexicans fighting and dying in wars continued through Korea and Vietnam." Company E of the 13th Infantry

Battalion, U.S. Marine Corps Reserve of Tucson, Arizona, for example, was composed of 237 men, 80 percent of them Mexicans, when the company was called to active duty on July 31, 1950. Two months later, Company E landed as part of an invasion force in Inchon, Korea. The U.S. Marines had shipped these young Mexicans and others overseas with a scant two to three weeks of training, teaching them how to fire M-1 rifles and machine guns aboard ship and giving them only another two weeks of basic training in Japan. Ten of the 231 *Tucsonense* Chicanos who fought in Korea lost their lives.[6]

College deferments were available during most of the Korean War and sometimes led to draft avoidance. These deferments were beyond the reach of most Mexican Americans. The Educational Testing Service of Princeton, New Jersey, developed a nationwide Selective Service College Qualification Test for deferring draftees based on test scores. The Testing Service administered the test to college students and potential college students in the spring of 1951. It sent test scores to the students' local draft board along with their class standing. The draft maintained the armed forces throughout the Cold War. The Selective Service System drafted 1.5 million men during the Korean War; 1.3 million volunteered—mostly in the Navy and Air Force. Again, education was a litmus test for admission into the "safer" military branches. It was a vicious circle: U.S. Mexicans had to go into the army because of a lack of education and then they could not take advantage of the education stipends of the GI Bill, again because of a lack of education.[7]

Keeping America American

Post–World War II saw the Cold War that fueled a racist nativism, ushering in another kind of war that devastated the foreign born. [Labor activists such as Harry Bridges, later president of the International Longshoremen's and Warehousemen's Union, saw the danger and became in the American Committee for Protection of Foreign Born (ACPFB) that formed in 1933 to protect immigrants at that time. Bridges, who was accused of being a communist, had been a target of the xenophobes.] Organizers of the ACPFB had seen this danger during the Depression and formed in 1933 to protect immigrants at that time. Among those it defended were labor activists including Harry Bridges, later president of the International Longshoremen's and Warehousemen's Union. The Australian-born Bridges, who was accused of being a communist, had been a target of the xenophobes. After World War II, the ACPFB, along with the United Electrical, Radio, and Machine Workers Union, again led the struggle for the defense of the foreign born. Superpatriots labeled the ACPFB a Communist-led organization; however, there is evidence that most members were non-Communist. It had a record of fighting fascism, a fact that was recognized by Franklin Delano Roosevelt and other progressive-minded people. However, once the war ended, the forces of reactionism moved to smear its record with the charge that it was a Communist-front organization.[8]

The Los Angeles Committee for Protection of Foreign Born (LACPFB) was a defender of Mexican Americans and a foe of politically driven deportations of the late 1940s and 1950s.[9] Within the Mexican American community, the Civil Rights Congress (CRC), the Independent Progressive Party (IPP), the *Asociación Nacional México-Americana* (ANMA), and the Community Service Organization (CSO)[10] also struggled for the defense of the foreign-born throughout the 1950s.

The ACPFB predated McCarthyism, and Mexican American activists were part of this movement. For example, Isabel González of Denver, who was active in defending the rights of Mexican beet workers in the mid-1940s, served as ANMA's vice president. In 1947 she wrote *Step-Children of a Nation*. Aside from reporting on the oppression of U.S. Mexicans, she described the efforts of the Committee to Organize the Mexican People on behalf of Refugio Ramón Martínez of the United Packing Workers of America,[11] and Nicaraguan-born Humberto Silex of El Paso, former regional director of the International Union of Mine, Mill, and Smelter Workers of America.[12] They entered the country legally and had U.S.-born children, yet deportation proceedings were brought against both—based on political grounds.[13] Because Luisa Moreno refused to cooperate with the House of Un-American Activities Committee, her application for citizenship was denied and she was later deported.[14]

The Internal Security Act of 1950 and the McCarran–Walter Act of 1952 gave government broad powers, with which they could harass and deport foreign-born union activists. Francis E. Walter, chairman of the House Un-American Activities Committee, and Senator Pat McCarran from Nevada sponsored the 1950 McCarran Act to tighten immigration laws and to exclude those the reactionaries said were subversive elements. By the late 1940s, the problems of refugees and displaced persons created by World War II had encouraged many liberals to think about scrapping immigration quotas based on national origins. However, McCarran, who thought of himself as protector of the nation's racial purity, saw the admission of any number of foreigners as a threat.[15]

Title I of the McCarran Act established a Subversive Activities Control Board to investigate subversion in the United States. Title II authorized construction of concentration camps to intern suspected subversives without a trial or hearing if either the president or Congress declared a national emergency. Two years later, the government built six internment camps. Despite the draconian nature of the law, few groups protested it, and it was largely through efforts of the Japanese-American Citizens League that the courts abolished Title II in the 1970s.

Equally insidious was the 1952 McCarran–Walter Act. It made some reforms, but it also included a long list of grounds for the deportation or exclusion of aliens; for example, it allowed the denaturalization of naturalized citizens. It gave the Immigration and Naturalization Service (INS) the authority to interrogate so-called aliens suspected of being in the country "illegally." The immigration service could search boats, trains, cars, trucks, or planes and enter and search private lands within 25 miles of the border. The McCarran–Walter Act passed in 1952 over President Harry S. Truman's veto. The president opined that the law created a group of second-class citizens; it distinguished between native and naturalized citizens. Truman also objected to the revocation of the citizenship of naturalized citizens for political reasons.

The 1952 act eliminated the statutes of limitation for foreigners who had been members of a so-called subversive organization, and they could be deported even for minor technical violations. The Commission on Immigration and Naturalization, appointed by President Truman in 1952, criticized the act as unconstitutional because foreigners could be convicted of crimes after the fact—that is, crimes that were not crimes at the time they were committed. Indeed, the Internal Security and the McCarran–Walter Acts led to gross violations of human rights. The purpose was transparent—to bust unions and intimidate activists.

For example, Humberto Silex, who had faced deportation in 1946, again faced deportation proceedings in 1952. Silex organized Local 509 of the United Mine, Mill, and Smelter Workers Union of El Paso; management considered him a troublemaker. Silex had entered the country legally and served in the armed forces. Employed by the American Smelting and Refining Company, he helped organize the local union in 1938. In 1945 Silex got into a fistfight, for which he was arrested and fined $35; the following year, Silex faced deportation proceedings on grounds of "moral turpitude." Although Silex won the case, the court banned him from union organizing.

The LACPFB reported in 1954 that, of the Chicanos defended by the committee on deportation charges, seven lived in the country for more than seven years, three for more than 20 years, and three for more than 30 years; 17 had U.S.-born children and grandchildren; and 22 were trade unionists. For instance, Tobias Navarrette, 55, entered the United States in 1927. Married and with eight U.S.-born children, he had served in the armed forces. From 1936 to 1938, he was a member of the Workers Alliance. The INS alleged that he was also a member of the Communist Party. A paid informant who was himself facing deportation testified that he saw Navarrette at two Communist Party meetings and a rally. After a long struggle, Navarrette won his case and continued to work in Boyle Heights as a jeweler and watch repairer. He died in April 1964.

Many victims of the McCarran–Walter Act waited years for final resolution of their cases. After seven years, in a 5-4 decision, the U.S. Supreme Court absolved José Gastélum of charges that would have resulted in deportation. The LACPFB defended Gastélum. Organizations such as the American Civil Liberties Union (ACLU) committed resources to fighting these violations of human rights, and the Community Service Organization (CSO) in Los Angeles extended free legal services to anyone whose human rights were violated by immigration policies.[16]

Militarization of the Immigration and Naturalization Service

Several factors during the 1940s and 1950s contributed to the mass migration of Mexicans to the north. Improved transportation in Mexico eased flow from the interior. In 1940, all-weather roads covered about 2,000 miles; by 1950, the figure increased to just less than 15,000 miles. In addition, there were 15,000 miles of railroad lines. The population of Mexico grew by 2.7 percent per annum between 1940 and 1950, and by 3.1 percent per annum between 1950 and 1960. In 1950 there were 27 million Mexicans (in Mexico); ten years later, 35 million. Cotton production on the Mexican side of the border, especially around Matamoros, gave employment to workers from the interior. Like their counterparts in the United States, Mexican growers advertised for more workers than they needed; thus, many who had migrated from the interior but were unable to find employment continued their journey northward across the border to find work in the cotton fields of the Rio Grande Valley of Texas.

Furthermore, the INS intentionally left the border open to cross unimpeded. The INS rarely rounded up undocumented workers during harvest time, and it instructed its agents to withhold searches and deportations until after the picking season. A rule of thumb was that when sufficient numbers of *braceros* or domestic laborers worked cheaply enough, agents enforced the laws; when a labor shortage occurred, they opened the border's doors, disregarding both international and moral law. Finally, recessions such as that of 1949 resulted in massive roundups of undocumented workers. When the Korean War caused a labor shortage, the U.S. unilaterally opened the border; during the 1953–1955 recession that followed the war the U.S. unilaterally closed it. Newspapers called for the exclusion of the undocumented workers, whom they portrayed as dangerous, malicious, and subversive. Even liberal Democrats supported the border patrol, calling for fines on employers who hired these workers, as did the Mexican government and most Chicano organizations. This erratic U.S. policy brought hundreds of thousands of *braceros* into the country annually, then kicked them out when the economy slowed, turning the border into a revolving door.[17]

President Dwight Eisenhower's attorney general, Herbert Brownell, initially opposed additional appropriations for the border patrol. However, pressured by Ike, Brownell made a tour of the border, after which he called for increased appropriations for the border patrol as well as for tougher laws. At the urging of Eisenhower, Brownell became a hawk. His rhetoric, couched in military terms, grew hotter. Brownell reached a state of near-panic. He wanted to use the army to stem the "tide" by sending soldiers to the border, but army brass was cool to the idea. Ike then appointed Lieutenant General Joseph M. Swing to head the INS. His qualifications? He was a classmate of President Eisenhower at West Point, and participated on General John Pershing's punitive expedition against Pancho Villa in 1916. Swing upgraded the border patrol with new equipment and smart, forest-green uniforms. He then launched "Operation Wetback," a military-style campaign to kick the Mexicans out. He requested millions of dollars to build a 150-mile-long fence, and set a deportation quota for each target area.

According to its press releases, from 1953 to 1955, the INS deported more than a million Mexicans annually. Through newspapers and the heavy presence of INS officers in the *barrios*, it spread terror. Most mainstream Mexican American organizations favored controlling undocumented immigration. They bought into the rhetoric of national security. Avi Astor makes the point:

> Hispanic civic groups also partook in the use of securitizing rhetoric linking Mexican immigration to threats to internal security. The tenuousness of the relationship between Mexican Americans and Mexican immigrants has roots dating back to the nineteenth century. Up until the rise of the Chicano Movement and the civil rights struggles that took place during the 1960s and 1970s, the main strategy of Hispanic civic organizations was assimilationist. The goal was to become "white," rather than to gain acceptance as a national minority. Mexican Americans and long-term Mexican residents in the United States perceived the entry of poor Mexican peasants into the Southwest not only as a source of job competition, but also as a barrier to their full assimilation and acceptance in American society, as they were often poor, illiterate and unfamiliar with the cultural and linguistic norms of the United States.[18]

Existing Mexican American organizations had set the ideological framework for anti-immigrant campaigns of the 1950s.[19] However, there were those on the left in the community who were offended by the racist tone of INS propaganda and its violation of human rights. On October 15, 1953, Ralph Guzmán, a Chicano activist, wrote, "A few weeks ago Herbert Brownell, the U.S. Attorney General, wanted to shoot wetbacks crossing into the U.S., but farmers, fearing the loss of a cheap labor market because of G.I. bullets, complained bitterly and Brownell changes [sic] his mind." Guzmán's charge was well documented. In May 1954 William P. Allen, publisher of the *Laredo Times*, wrote to Eisenhower that Brownell had asked for the support of labor leaders at a May 11 dinner if he were to shoot the "wetbacks" down in cold blood.

ANMA, which was closely associated with progressive trade unions such as the Mine, Mill and Smelter Workers and cooperated with the IPP and the ACPFB, continuously condemned the INS raids. Meanwhile, Operation Wetback continued to spread fear and, for a time, supposedly ended the immigration flow. But improvements in the U.S. economy soon accelerated the northward movement of Mexicans.[20]

The abuse of human rights of the foreign-born was so blatant that on April 17, 1959, a group of progressive organizations and individuals presented a petition to the United Nations, charging that, in violation of the Universal Declaration of Human Rights, adopted in 1948, the U.S. government had mistreated Mexican immigrants. In the preface to the petition, San Antonio Archbishop Robert E. Lucey stated: "And so the poor bracero, compelled by force and fear, will endure any kind of injustice and exploitation to gain a few dollars that he needs so desperately." The report recalled the military-like sweeps of the mid-1950s, which kept Mexicans in "a state of permanent insecurity," subjecting them to "raids, arrests, and deportation drives."[21]

The Diaspora: An American Odyssey

As the Mexican centers of population in the Southwest swelled, Mexican migrants fanned out to the north, west, and east in search of other opportunities. Euro-Americans continued to consider Mexican Americans, especially migrants, as foreigners—even though 90 percent of the children were born in the United States. In the case of New Mexico and Colorado migrants, U.S. nativity went back as far as their great-grandparents. The story of the Gallegos family is typical. Originally from the New Mexican highlands, the family moved in the 1930s to the valley called Amalia, part of the Sangre de Cristo land grant of the 1870s. The family tried farming, working in sugar beets, but the white farming barons nudged them out.

During the 1950s, the Gallegos family worked on various farms from Colorado to Washington. Mechanization began with crops that needed the least care in handling, such as sugar beets and potatoes, crops in which Mexicans and Chicanos were concentrated. The Gallegos family went from place to place on recommendations of friends, finally settling in the Yakima Valley in Washington, one of the 10 most productive valleys in the United States.

The Gallegos family constantly suffered discrimination. In Odessa, Texas, Mexicans were not allowed in motels, and restaurants denied them service. In Prosser in the Yakima Valley, proprietors allowed Mexicans into the theater only on Sundays. During the week, Mexicans in the town ran the risk of being hassled by cops. As other Mexican families poured into the area from Colorado, the Midwest, and Texas, a sense of community began to form in the Yakima, although many still longed for home. This homesickness would change with the birth of offspring in the Yakima.[22]

The Cities

The 1950 U.S. Census still had a difficult time saying "Mexican-origin." Some 83 percent were native-born or naturalized American citizens. Some 16 percent were not born in the United States. Yet 55 percent still had one or both parents born in Mexico. A large portion of U.S. Mexicans lived outside the evolving *barrios* of El Paso, San Antonio, Los Angeles, and Chicago. Large numbers resided in Brownsville, Corpus Christi, Laredo, Albuquerque, Phoenix, San Diego, and San Francisco. Outside this Southwest belt, they resided in sizable numbers in Kansas City, Detroit, and Milwaukee. By 1960, for example, the vast migrations from the borderlands gave Illinois a Mexican population larger than Colorado's and New Mexico's combined.[23]

El Paso: In Search of a Home   By the 1950s, El Paso Mexicans no longer lived exclusively in Chihuahuita or its neighboring El Segundo Barrio, the oldest *barrios* in the city. The Alamito housing projects warehoused 2.3 percent of the south side neighborhood's housing. Landlords fought the construction of more public housing because federal grants brought stricter oversight in the form of more rigid housing codes. The El Segundo Barrio, or the "Second Ward," home to the poorest of the poor, deteriorated to the point that the military brass at Fort Bliss complained.[24]

The lack of decent housing continued to be a major problem. Only 5 percent of the families had showers; 3 percent had tubs. The average number of people per toilet was 71. A 1948 survey of South El Paso reported a population of 23,000. The area housed slightly more than 19 percent of the city's population, yet it registered just over 88 percent of its juvenile crime, 51 percent of its adult crime, and two-thirds of its infant mortality. Not surprisingly, poverty pushed up street crime. The El Paso press meanwhile blamed the victims and depicted Mexicans as murderers, drug users, and rapists. Conditions became so bad that, without the intervention of church agencies and local Mexican American organizations, the Second Ward would have self-destructed.

Between World War II and the Korean War, availability of low-interest federal housing loans to veterans accelerated movement to the suburbs. Federal funding also expedited highway construction. The Paisano Drive highway (1947), intended to improve transportation to the central city business district, displaced 750 families—6,000 residents of the Second Ward. The highway further isolated South El Paso, causing a "shanty" boom—with *jacales* (shacks) made of plywood, sheet metal, and cardboard replacing former homes.[25]

San Antonio   The 1950 U.S. Census showed that San Antonio Mexicans continued to suffer from a lack of education; less than half had gone beyond the fifth grade. Less than 10 percent finished high school, and less than 1 percent completed college. Their limited education checked the Mexicans' upward mobility during a time of prosperity for most Euro-Americans. The state's right-to-work law also hindered the Mexicans' advance in occupational status. Mexicans mostly belonged to pick-and-shovel unions—for instance, Mexicans comprised almost 100 percent of the hod carriers and 90 percent of the plasterers. They made up 6 percent of the electricians and just more than 10 percent of the cement masons. And San Antonio unions were weak; thus, wages were lower than in California, for example.

Many Mexicans still lived in floorless shacks without plumbing, sewage connections, or electricity. Open shallow wells—sources of water used for drinking and washing—were next to outside toilets. During World War II, San Antonio had had the distinction of having the highest tuberculosis death rate of any large city in the country—a distinction that San Antonio undoubtedly kept into the postwar era. After the war, with the return of thousands of Mexican American veterans, the conditions of overcrowded housing and unpaved streets and sidewalks only worsened.

The rapid economic growth brought about by the war and increased government spending in San Antonio attracted south Texans to the Alamo City. Highly segregated, Mexicans still lived mostly on the West Side. (Blacks resided on the East, lower- and middle-class whites on the South, and middle- and upper-class whites on the North Side.) Movement out of the *barrio* was still infrequent. The lack of unionization and the size of the reserve labor pool further depressed conditions. By design, San Antonio attracted only light industry, keeping heavy industry and unions out of the city. During the 1940s, civilian jobs at the military installations helped the city's total population grow from 253,854 to just less than 410,000. As in other U.S. cities, some San Antonians moved to the suburbs; the building of highways displaced the poorest residents. In turn, however, new housing meant jobs, as did the upswing in highway and airport construction.

The Mexican population in San Antonio climbed from 160,420 in 1950 to 243,627 (out of a total of 587,718) by the end of the decade. In 1959, San Antonio was second only to Los Angeles in the number of Mexicans. Its first and second generations increased from 30,299 to 75,590 in these same years. Over a quarter of the Mexican women worked outside the home, primarily in garment and electronic factories and as domestics and civil servants. Mexican employment in the military installations tripled during World War II, and by the 1950s, a small core of Mexicans had moved into supervisory and technical positions. Access to these jobs was often gained only by intervention of sympathetic elected officials. Opportunity generally remained unequal.[26]

Los Angeles   California's Mexican population of 760,453 in 1950 trailed that of Texas, which numbered over a million. Californian Chicanos were the most urbanized in the Southwest, making Los Angeles the favorite destination in California. Los Angeles differed structurally from San Antonio. The majority of Mexicans did not live in one section; instead, enclaves or *barrios* dotted the entire Los Angeles basin.

The G.I. Bill encouraged the suburbanization of the Mexican American middle class. Like other Angelenos, Mexicans followed the freeways. Much of the internal migration was toward the east from East Los Angeles, following Interstate 10 (the San Bernardino Freeway) to new communities like Pico-Rivera, La Puente, and Covina. Many Mexicans remained in outlying localities such as Wilmington, San Pedro, Venice, San Fernando, and Pacoima, many of which were once agricultural colonies. Overall, Mexicans were not as isolated in Los Angeles as they were in Texas. Mexican neighborhoods such as Boyle Heights were more polyglot ethnically and racially, with Japanese, Jews, Armenians, and others living close to each other. Intermarriage also increased dramatically after the war.[27]

Politically, Mexican Americans in Los Angeles mostly voted for Democrats and the party took them for granted. Politicos gerrymandered their districts, not so much to keep Mexicans powerless as to maintain their incumbents in office. Liberal incumbents benefited from this manipulation of electoral districts. Unlike the San Antonio elite, the Los Angeles ruling class did not need a traditional political machine to stay in office. It was white power all the way, and this group made huge profits by promoting the development of West Los Angeles and the San Fernando Valley.

From 1940 to 1960, the freeway system expanded dramatically, accelerating suburbanization and degrading city centers in the process. To revive the downtown area, the power elite formed the Greater Los Angeles Plans, Inc., which set three goals—to build a convention center, a sports arena, and a music center. This decision had far-reaching consequences for minorities and the poor, since these projects encroached on their living space. Until 1958, the downtown elite was entirely Republican; then the group expanded and supported "responsible" Democrats. Over the next few years, a committee of 25, based within the Chamber of Commerce, would informally plan and control the future of Los Angeles. Few of the elites even bothered to think about the thriving Mexican communities that would be displaced by "urban renewal."

Meanwhile, an important change took place in East Los Angeles that would impact succeeding generations of Mexican Americans. In January 1948, the new East Los Angeles College campus was opened near Atlantic Boulevard and Floral Avenue; and in 1956, the Los Angeles State College campus was opened on Los Angeles's East Side. The proximity of the two new campuses made higher education easier for working-class students who continue working to survive. Unlike UCLA, the new campuses were more accessible to the working student, and student fees ran less than $10 a semester. A new social awareness also became possible through forums sponsored by Los Angeles State.[28]

Chicago   World War II revived Mexican migration to Chicago. The repatriation of the 1930s had reduced the official number of Mexicans from 20,000 to 16,000. From 1943 to 1945, the railroads imported some 15,000 *braceros*. During the 1940s, the official Mexican population grew from 16,000 to 20,000 in the city and from 21,000 to 35,000 in the metropolitan area. In 1953, the INS estimated that 100,000 Mexicans lived in Chicago, of whom 15,000 were, according to the INS, "wetbacks."

Several Mexican *barrios* were located close to places of employment, in small pockets throughout the Chicago area. Until the 1960s, Mexicans shared space in these *barrios* with other ethnic groups. From the 1930s to the mid-1950s, Mexicans living in Back of the Yards belonged to the meatpackers' unions, which helped them assimilate. Work in the stockyards was stable, and wages were higher than in other industries. The Back of the Yards Neighborhood Council, organized in 1939 by social activist Saul Alinsky, depended on a network of Catholic Church groups.

Located on the south shore of Lake Michigan, South Chicago was untouched by urban renewal. As the number of Mexican steelworkers increased during the 1950s, they formed the Mexican Community Committee, which concerned itself with local issues. South Chicago Mexicans thrived economically in comparison to Mexican Americans in other sections of the city.

By the 1950s, the Mexican immigrant colonies in the communities of South Deering and South Chicago were magnets for new immigrants. Living near Serbian, Polish, Croatian, and other neighborhoods, Mexicans comprised roughly 24 percent of the foreign-born population in South Deering at this time. Still, a Chicago Commission on Human Relations report of the 1950s recognized the existence of inequality, and stated that Mexicans "carry the badge of color which places them as a minority group." Largely, they were unwelcome in the South Side. In turn, some Mexicans living in South Deering joined the racial hierarchy to violently resist the entry of African Americans into the community during the Trumbull Park riots. Some, feeling vulnerable to the massive deportation of Mexicans during 1953–1955, tried to prove themselves to the white establishment; others, remembering the violent history of their settlement there, refused to join the riots.

By the end of the decade, Mexicans were forming enclaves in other parts of Chicago as bulldozers uprooted older *barrios*. Gentrification displaced Mexicans in the Near Westside *barrio* of La Taylor during the decade, pushing them into the nearby Pilsen district.[29]

Seduced by the Game

Some people become involved in politics, believing that they can change things for the better, while others mistrust the political machine so much that they doubt individuals have the power to influence government policy. The Mexican American community walked the fine line between the believers and the doubters: on the one hand, they hoped that participation in the political process would bring their interests to the fore; on the other hand, they knew from past experience that the political machine had a tendency to disempower even its supporters in order to maintain the status quo.

For the Mexican American community, even though there were very few elected officials of Mexican origin, the Democratic Party was the party of choice. The aura of Franklin D. Roosevelt and the Civil Rights legislation of Harry Truman still lived in the 1950s. The high hopes of the New Deal and Fair Deal were dashed, however, by the radical postwar "turn to the right" of the political spectrum. Although organizations like LULAC and the American G.I. Forum continued to maintain that they were nonpartisan, most of the leadership and rank and file voted Democrat (when not blocked by the poll tax).[30]

New Mexico: The Illusion of It All

Most adult New Mexicans were eligible to vote and, as they made up almost half the state, they believed they had power. They did elect U.S. Senator Dennis Chávez, Jr., who supported the New Deal and the Fair Deal. Despite having more Mexican American elected officials than other states, New Mexico suffered from what the eminent Texas political scientist Rodolfo Rosales has called the "illusion of inclusion."

Drought, depression, and World War II had almost ended the New Mexican way of life. From 1940 to 1960, government had spent enormous sums of money to accelerate the industrialization of the state. Chain stores, national corporations, and large-scale finance institutions displaced merchant houses and speculative capital. In 1949, there were 1,362 farms operating in Taos; 10 years later, only 674 farms remained. Throughout the 1950s, the rural population declined. In 1947, the median per capita income in the seven northern counties was only $452.26, compared with $870.04 in the seven Euro-American counties.

Why was it that after 100 years of U.S. rule, New Mexicans lived in a "Third World" environment? By 1950, Mexican Americans comprised about half the population of New Mexico; just over 87 percent were U.S. born. Mexican Americans lived in seven northern counties, while Euro-Americans controlled eastern and southern New Mexico. Racism worsened after World War II when large numbers of white Texans arrived to work in the oil fields. "Little Texas" in the eastern half of the state harbored discrimination against Mexicans, barring them from the "better" barbershops, restaurants, hotels, and amusement centers. Mexicans attended separate schools and churches, and Mexican American war veterans could not even join the local American Legion Post.

Simply said, New Mexicans lacked education, a key factor in the new labor market. Illiteracy was 16.6 percent for Mexicans compared with 3.1 percent for others. Teachers in Mexican counties had less-than-adequate training: 46.2 percent held BAs, compared with 82.2 percent in the Euro-American counties. According to the 1950 U.S. Census, the median education for Mexicans was 6.1 years, compared with 11.8 for Euro-Americans. Ten years later, the figures were 7.4 and 12.2 years, respectively. In 1965, New Mexico had the highest percentage of draftees failing the intelligence exam of any southwestern state—25.4 percent. This was a population that was hardly prepared to compete in a technologically advanced society.[31]

Los Angeles Politics

From 1949 to 1962, Edward R. Roybal dominated the political history of Chicanos in Los Angeles. Roybal's rise is linked to the emergence of the Community Service Organization (CSO), California's most important Chicano association. CSO differed from LULAC in employing more strident tactics. The CSO used the strategies of the Industrial Areas Foundation (IAF) and its founder, Saul Alinsky. Many CSO leaders were middle class, and unlike LULAC professionals, they did not monopolize the leadership; leaders frequently came out of the labor movement. "By 1963 the CSO had established thirty-four chapters across the Southwest (primarily in California), with over 10,000 paid members."[32]

The roots of the CSO were in the small towns beyond East Los Angeles—in Chino, Ontario, and Pomona, where Ignacio López organized civic or unity leagues. In 1946, he formed the Pomona Unity League, and soon unity leagues sprang up in Chino, Ontario, and Redlands. Fred Ross of the American Council on Race Relations joined López. The leagues emphasized mass action, bloc voting, and neighborhood protests. Organizers held meetings in homes, churches, and public buildings. Their first order of business was to encourage Mexican Americans to run for political office, and get them elected to city councils.

Soon after, López and his organizers established unity leagues in San Bernardino and Riverside, California, where school discrimination was a primary issue. The leagues in turn influenced the IAF in the Back of the Yards area of South Chicago in the late 1940s. The IAF planned to work with Mexicans in the Los Angeles area. A group known as the Community Political Organization (CPO) formed in East Los Angeles about the same time. Not wanting to be confused with the Communist Party or with partisan politics, the CPO changed its name in 1947 to the Community Service Organization (CSO). The organization evolved from Chicano steelworkers and from volunteers in Roybal's unsuccessful bid for a Los Angeles City Council seat in 1947. The IAF moved to Los Angeles and merged efforts with the CSO.[33]

Although the CSO was supposedly not political, it registered 12,000 new voters. This increase in registered Chicano voters helped elect Roybal to the Los Angeles City Council in 1949—the first person of Mexican descent to serve on that body since 1881. After Roybal's victory, the CSO did not support another candidate for office. Instead, it concentrated on fighting housing discrimination, police brutality, and school segregation. In 1950 the CSO fielded 112 volunteer deputy registrars; within three months, 32,000 new Latino voters were registered. The CSO grew to 800 members in two years. By the early 1960s, it had 34 chapters with 10,000 dues-paying members. The CSO promoted understanding of local governance among taxpayers and urged them to press for better public services.

As a member of the City Council, Roybal had an outstanding career, confronting the Los Angeles power elite in defense of principle. The 1950 Census showed that the Los Angeles population was 81 percent white, 9 percent black, and 8 percent Latino/a. Roybal fought for a strong Fair Employment Practices Commission (FEPC) ordinance, opposed the registration of Communists, supported rent controls and public housing, and campaigned against urban renewal. He also criticized police brutality. However, Roybal had few allies on the City Council, where most of the members supported growth at the expense of minority areas. There was considerable bias on the council; on Roybal's first day on the job, the council president introduced him as the "Mexican Council member, elected by the Mexican people of his District."

Roybal's popularity went beyond the Mexican American community. His own district in 1950 was 34 percent Mexican American and 45 percent African American. Only some 16,000 registered voters out of 87,000 were Mexican Americans. In 1954, Roybal lost a campaign for lieutenant governor. Four years later, he ran for county supervisor, and won the election on the first ballot, only to lose after three dubitable recounts.

Many contemporary political observers still believe that what cost Roybal the election was his threatening the interests of the county's downtown power structure by exposing the Chávez Ravine giveaway to the Dodgers and the forced removal of the Bunker Hill residents (the area directly west of the Civic Center). Roybal submitted affidavits to the grand jury showing that supporters of his opponent had intimidated minority voters. Grace Montañez Davis, a volunteer campaign worker in the Roybal camp, sent 98 affidavits to the Federal Bureau of Investigation, the state FEPC, and the U.S. Civil Rights Commission.

That same year, Hank López also ran for lieutenant governor of California. Although the party swept the statewide elections, López lost. During the campaign, many Democrats refused to share the same platform with López.[34]

Many coordinating councils—the G.I. Forum, LULAC, and the Council for Mexican American Affairs (CMAA)—also emerged in Los Angeles. The CMAA, made up of select professionals, wanted to get the various groups together to coordinate Chicano political action. Mexican American groups expressed optimism, predicting the community's awakening and their achievement of political power. Nevertheless, Mexicans had few victories. They celebrated the appointment of Carlos Terán to the municipal court in 1958 with all the grandeur of a coronation.[35]

San Antonio

In Texas, the poll tax continued to frustrate voter registration drives. The leading Chicano politician was Henry B. González, whose parents were political refugees from Durango, Mexico, where they owned a mine. González was born in 1916; he graduated from St. Mary's Law School and then worked for a time as a juvenile officer. He was involved in civic affairs and ran unsuccessfully for state representative in 1950; a year later, he won a City Council seat. González, who did not belong to the LULAC clique, put together a grassroots campaign.

González often clashed with the Good Government League (GGL), established in the early fifties, which ran the city of San Antonio. Like Edward Roybal in Los Angeles, González championed Civil Rights causes. In 1956 he ran for the State Senate, winning by 282 votes. The campaign of Albert Peña, Jr., for county commissioner greatly helped González. The race issue resurfaced, with opponents frequently accusing González of being a leftist. In the State Senate, González championed liberal causes. In 1958, he unsuccessfully ran for governor.

A primary component in the politics of segregation, segregated schools continued to be the norm throughout Texas: in east Texas, legislators introduced a dozen bills in the 1956–1957 session to withhold funds from integrated schools and prohibit interracial sporting events. Nonetheless, some changes were taking place during the 1950s that would alter the political landscape of the late 1970s: an increasing number of legislative districts changed from rural to urban—which transformation favored those living in cities— and Mexican Americans who were now concentrated in cities developed a growing political awareness.[36] Veterans' organizations such as the Loyal American Democrats, the West Side Voters League, the Alamo Democrats, the School Improvement League, and the American G.I. Forum (AGIF) would challenge the old machines. The names of the new organizations were mostly in English, suggesting feelings of patriotism and a desire to assimilate. However, another explanation is that the political environment in Texas and the impact of McCarthyism might have coerced many Mexican Americans to adopt this sort of expression of Americanism to defuse racism and red-baiting, which were prevalent there.

El Paso

As in other cities, Chicanos in El Paso were politically more active during this decade. The illusion was that Chicanos could win if they ran politicos whom white people would accept. In 1957 Raymond Telles, a

Mexican American and a retired Korean War Air Force lieutenant colonel, ran for mayor of El Paso. The city elite opposed Telles though he took every opportunity to assure voters of his Americanism. Members of the El Paso business establishment openly said they did not believe that a Mexican was qualified to be mayor. Conservatives billed Telles's Euro-American opponent as the "candidate for all El Paso." Telles's victory shattered the myth that Mexicans would not turn out to vote—90 percent of eligible Mexicans voted.

Telles in many ways symbolized the times: He had "made it." Telles was educated in Catholic schools, and was a World War II veteran. El Pasoans had elected Telles as city clerk in 1948, and LULAC supported him throughout his career. Though he was well qualified to run for mayor in any case, one factor promoting his candidacy was his light skin. Given the logic of the times, this was rational, since most Euro-Americans and many Mexican Americans interpreted qualification as being white. To get Telles elected, LULAC and other organizations mobilized the voter base, which was the Mexican American community. Telles won by 2,754 votes—18,688 to 15,934. Voters reelected Telles in 1959, and he served four years as mayor. Despite generating high hopes, Telles's election brought little change. The 1960 Census showed little improvement in living conditions for Mexican Americans; 70 percent of the Southside housing remained deteriorated or dilapidated.[37]

Civil Rights

Organizationally, the Mexican Americans as a community evolved to the point that they became angrier at injustices directed at them and had the ability to respond. Some people will call this militancy, which after all is merely getting angry enough at an injustice to respond collectively. As the optimistic illusions of many Mexican Americans turned into skepticism, a sense of moral outrage developed and militancy increased. Inequality became more obvious to many as real wages fell 5 percent and corporate profits rose 69 percent during the so-called "Happy Days" of the 1950s. The gap between white people and people of color widened. This was in spite of the tax rate for the top bracket, those earning over $400,000, being 91 percent. (In 2003 it fell to 35 percent.)[38] In 1950, in California, a Latino male earned 69.5 percent of the wages of a Euro-American male counterpart; Latinas, correspondingly, earned 37.4 percent. Ten years later Latino males still earned 69.5 percent, and the rate for Latinas had fallen further to only 34.1 percent.[39] The power of labor declined as its leaders buckled under rightist pressure to clean out the left. Some of the expelled members had been the strongest advocates for increasing labor's inclusion of minorities. And in the mid-1950s, the CIO once again merged with the AFL, curtailing many of the CIO's community-oriented projects and lowering the admission of minorities. Still, a cadre of politicized Mexican Americans had developed within the middle and working classes despite efforts to repress them.

The "Salt of the Earth"

The so-called "Salt of the Earth" strike—pitting the 1,400 members (90 percent Mexican) of Local 890, International Union of Mine, Mill, and Smelter Workers, against Empire Zinc and Grant County—inspired a classic film by the same name that received worldwide acclaim but was banned in the United States. The film depicts the strike as well as the role of women in stopping production. The strike lasted 15 months, from October 1950 to January 1952; it was the longest strike in New Mexico's history. Although some of its leaders admittedly were Communists, the rank and file were more concerned about abusive working and living conditions than about ideology.[40]

The hysteria of the McCarthy period intimidated organized labor. The CIO buckled under political pressure and asked its union officers to sign affidavits that they were not Communists. Government did not even consider that the Communist Party's appeal to workers of color was a product of the racism that they were subject to; it rationalized that Communists were seducing Mexicans. Meanwhile, the Empire Zinc workers suffered indignities such as separate payroll lines, toilet facilities, and housing in the company town. Owners limited Mexicans to backbreaking mucking and underground mining jobs, while assigning whites to surface and craft jobs. Local 890 demanded payment for collar-to-collar work (i.e., compensation for all the time the miners spent underground), holiday pay, and the elimination of the no-strike clause in their contract. The miners did not consider these demands out of line, and Empire Zinc surprised the local when it refused to negotiate. Management obviously wanted to break the union.

Mexican Americans comprised 50 percent of Grant County. When the strike began, the county authorities demanded that the governor send the National Guard to the area. The strike itself developed into a typical management–labor dispute until a local judge issued an injunction that the workers stop picketing the mine. At that point, the women's auxiliary, formed in 1948, took over the lines because the injunction did not cover the women. A dramatic confrontation took place between the women and the deputies. At one point, deputies jailed 45 women, 17 children, and a 6-month-old baby. This event caught the attention of other unions and women's groups, who supported the auxiliary. Efforts to suppress the women led to frequent clashes between the women, the scabs, and the sheriff's deputies.

The governor intervened, siding with the management, and sent in state troopers, who enforced the injunction and prohibited the blocking of the road leading to the mine. The governor's action thwarted the use of women on the picket line, since the state penitentiary could house all the picketers. The strike halted, with the workers winning minimal gains. Empire Zinc was eager to settle because of wartime profits, but refused to drop charges against union leaders, many of whom eventually spent three months in jail and paid thousands of dollars in fines.[41]

Toward Equality

One of the main tactics on the civil rights front involved high-profile court cases that challenged the legality of de facto discrimination by public agencies, such as schools and police. A giant of these times was Texas attorney Gustavo C. García. Born in Laredo, García moved to San Antonio and graduated with a law degree from the University of Texas. During World War II, he served with the Judge Advocate Corps. In April 1947, he filed suit against school authorities in Cuero to force closure of the Mexican school there. Aided by Robert C. Eckhardt of Austin and A. L. Wirin of the Los Angeles Civil Liberties Union, García filed *Delgado v. Bastrop ISD* (1948). The case decision made illegal the segregation of children of Mexican descent in Texas. García played a leading role in revising the 1949 LULAC Constitution to permit non–Mexican Americans become members. He was also active in the Felix Longoria case (see Chapter 11) and advocated fair treatment for the *bracero*. As legal advisor to the American G.I. Forum, he worked to pass a general antidiscrimination bill in Texas and served on the first board of directors of the American Council of Spanish Speaking People and the Texas Council on Human Relations. García was an attorney in the *Hernandez v. State of Texas* case, which he argued before the Supreme Court. García died alone on a park bench in San Antonio in 1964.[42]

Mexican Americans in Texas applauded the landmark *Brown v. Board of Education* school desegregation decision.[43] A 1954 poll showed that Chicanos approved of integration in larger numbers than did African Americans or whites. Although 77 percent of all Mexicans surveyed supported integration of African Americans, only 62 percent of the African Americans themselves supported integration. In April 1955, Chicanos sued the schools of Carrizo Springs and Kingsville, Texas. In Kingsville, Austin Elementary had been segregated since 1914; it was known as the "Mexican Ward School," with a 100 percent Chicano student population. Of the 31 Chicano teachers in Kingsville, all but four taught in this all-Mexican school.

The Texas G.I. Forum also fought police brutality cases. On June 20, 1953, in Mercedes, the Forum brought enough pressure to force the resignation of Darrill F. Holmes, a policeman who intimidated George Sáenz and his wife at their grocery store; as a result of the police abuse, Sáenz was treated for a nervous condition. The Forum was also involved in the Jesse Ledesma case. On the afternoon of June 22, 1953, Austin police officer Bill Crow stopped Ledesma, who was suffering from insulin shock. Crow claimed Ledesma looked drunk and beat him up, inflicting a one-inch cut on the right side of his head and bruises on his legs, back, and shoulders.

On September 16, 1953, in Fort Worth, Texas, Officer Vernon Johnson shot Ernest L. García in the chest while delivering a court order for custody of a child. Johnson threatened members of the García family when they asked him if he had a warrant; the officer pulled a gun and pressed it against García's chest. Johnson claimed that he had shot Ernest because he was afraid the García family would mob him. The Forum lawyers handled the case and got Johnson indicted for aggravated assault.[44]

On May 3, 1954, the U.S. Supreme Court, in a unanimous decision, banned discrimination in jury selection. In Edna, Texas, an all-white jury found Peter Hernández guilty of the murder of Joe Espínosa and sentenced him to life imprisonment. The Court of Criminal Appeals turned down this case because, according to the court, Mexicans were white and therefore were not a class apart from the white population. Hernández appealed, and the U.S. Supreme Court found that for 25 years the Court of Criminal Appeals had treated Mexicans as a class apart, and that out of 6,000 citizens considered for jury duty, the panel had never selected a Mexican juror. The lower court again tried Peter Hernández; this time he pled guilty and the court sentenced him to 20 years.[45]

The Hernández case is a landmark civil rights case. While Black Americans were guaranteed the right to serve on juries by the Civil Rights Act of 1875, Mexican Americans had not won that right. The courts held that Mexicans were not guaranteed this right by the Fourteenth Amendment since they were legally white. However, the Mexican American attorneys argued that Mexican Americans were "a class apart"; they did not fit into the black–white Americans paradigm. The Supreme Court upheld the argument and ruled that as a "class apart" that had suffered historic discrimination, Mexican Americans were entitled to the protections of the Fourteenth Amendment.

California

In February 1950, Los Angeles county sheriffs raided a baby shower at the home of Natalia Gonzáles. Sheriffs had given the occupants three minutes to evacuate the premise. They arrested some 50 guests for charges ranging from disturbing the peace to resisting arrest. The Maravilla Chapter of the ANMA petitioned the county supervisors for relief. But the supervisors refused to intervene. Lieutenant Fimbres of the sheriff's foreign relations bureau whitewashed the incident. Virginia Ruiz, along with the ANMA, then formed the Maravilla Defense Committee.

On May 26, 1951, police raided a baptismal party at the home of Simon Fuentes. Officers had received a call complaining that the music was too loud. Police broke into the house without a warrant and assaulted the guests. They pushed an eight-months-pregnant woman and a disabled man to the floor. Police broke Frank Rodríguez's leg when he went to the aid of the disabled man. ANMA played an active role in this case as well. In the "Bloody Christmas" case, on December 24, 1951, approximately 50 Los Angeles police took seven young Mexicans out of their cells at the Lincoln Heights jail and brutally beat them. Police mauled Danny Rodella so badly that jailers had to send him to Los Angeles County General Hospital. Public outcries from the white, black, and brown communities forced the district attorney's office to bring charges against the officers. The courts indicted some of the officers and sentenced them to jail. According to historian Edward Escobar, "[Chief William] Parker and his allies in city government stifled external investigations into department matters, vilified LAPD critics, and even ignored perjury by officers. They thus helped create an organizational culture that valued LAPD independence above the rule of law and led to the LAPD's estrangement from Mexican American and other minority communities."[46]

On May 8, 1953, Los Angeles deputy sheriffs Lester Moll and Kenneth Stiler beat David Hidalgo, age 15; other deputies looked on as Hidalgo pleaded for mercy. Hidalgo's stepfather, Manuel Domínguez, pressed a civil suit against the Los Angeles County sheriff's department. *La Alianza Hispano-Americana* (the Hispano-American Alliance) supported his lawsuit. Two years later, the court awarded Domínguez damages of $1,000.

The *Alianza* handled the appeals in the murder and conspiracy conviction of Manuel Mata, Robert Márquez, and Ricardo Venegas, whom the state found guilty of murdering William D. Cluff in a fight in Los Angeles on December 6, 1953; Cluff intervened in a fight involving the three defendants and a marine. The defense introduced expert medical testimony that Cluff died of an enlarged heart, advanced arteriosclerosis of cerebral blood vessels, and arterial heart disease; he had not died of injuries inflicted during the fight. Los Angeles newspapers inflamed public rage, and the court convicted the three Mexican Americans. After a series of appeals, the defendants received a new trial.[47]

The CSO, along with the ACLU, assumed the leadership in police brutality cases in East Los Angeles. Chicano activist Ralph Guzmán wrote in the *Eastside Sun* on September 24, 1953, "It is no secret that for years law and order in the Eastside of Los Angeles County has been maintained through fear and brutal treatment." Los Angeles newspapers whipped up hysteria against Mexicans. Guzmán, again in the *Eastside Sun*, wrote on January 7, 1954, "It is becoming more and more difficult to walk through the streets of Los Angeles—and look Mexican!" On January 14, 1954, he continued, "Basically, Eugene Biscailuz's idea to curb kid gangs is the evening roundup, a well known western drive." Guzmán then vehemently castigated the Los Angeles press for its irresponsibility.

National Spanish-Speaking Council

Middle-class Mexican American organizations remained active during this period. Most preferred to follow the path set by the civil rights tradition, and to work within the mainstream. On May 18–19, 1951, leaders of many of these associations met in El Paso for the founding convention of the American Council of Spanish-Speaking People. George I. Sánchez chaired the convention. The *Alianza Hispano-Americana*, CSO, LULAC, the Texas G.I. Forum, and the Community Service Club of Colorado composed the core group. Chicano leaders such as Gus García, Tony Rios, Ignacio López, José Estrada, and Dennis Chávez, Jr., U.S. senator from New Mexico, attended the convention.

Tibo J. Chávez, the lieutenant governor of New Mexico, was elected president of the council, and George I. Sánchez served as its executive director. In 1952, the organization received a grant from the Robert Marshall Foundation to be used in promoting the civil rights of Chicanos. The council worked closely with the *Alianza* in desegregation cases. In 1952, for instance, in Arizona, these groups made challenges in Glendale, Douglas, Miami, and Winslow. In the case against Glendale and the Arizona Board of Education, the council challenged school segregation. The Glendale board refused to go to court, knowing that they would be forced to integrate.

In 1954, the *Alianza* initiated a suit against Winslow, Arizona, to open its swimming pool to Mexicans. Winslow officials settled the suit out of court. In 1955, the *Alianza* established a Civil Rights department and named Ralph Guzmán its director. In a desegregation case in El Centro, California, it collaborated with the NAACP. The El Centro School Board had assigned only black teachers to the two elementary schools that were predominantly Mexican and African American. El Centro had avoided desegregation by allowing white students to transfer to an adjoining district that was already overcrowded. A federal judge ruled that the plaintiffs must exhaust state courts before a federal court could hear the case. The Court of Appeals for the Ninth Circuit, however, reversed the lower court decision, holding that El Centro practiced segregation of students and staff. This cooperation between the *Alianza* and the NAACP was significant since the *Alianza* itself had excluded African Americans.[48]

The American Council of Spanish-Speaking People remained active for years, but like many other organizations, it perished when continued funding did not materialize. At that juncture in history, the Mexican American middle class was not large or prosperous enough to support such an ambitious project, and Euro-American foundations did not recognize the need. Older Mexican American associations continued to struggle through their own legal-aid programs.

The Struggle to Preserve the *Barrios*

Government transportation policy and federal loans accelerated the decay of the inner city. Thousands of miles of highways or freeways integrated the nation. At the same time, these programs helped segregate the United States, setting housing patterns that still exist in all metropolitan areas in the United States. Federal loan policy allowed federal administrators and the housing industry to work hand in hand with developers, separating the suburbs and inner cities. The highway policy gave the states hundreds of millions of dollars to link their disparate parts, and encouraged white middle-class workers to move to the suburbs: white flight did not occur by accident or by the invisible workings of the market. The Depression and industrialization had accelerated the Mexicans' move to the city, and housing and urban redevelopment policies enacted during the New Deal and postwar years encouraged the abandonment of inner cities by those who could afford to leave, reinforcing separation based on race and class.

The FHA Mortgage Guarantee and the G.I. Bill

The Federal Housing Administration's (FHA) mortgage-loan guarantees, established by the National Housing Act of 1934, and the Veterans Administration's (VA) loan guarantees of the Servicemen's Readjustment Act of 1944 (the G.I. Bill) created the suburban building boom that further encouraged segregation. The FHA was a major player in setting housing policy. For instance, between 1935 and 1974, the agency insured close to 11.5 million home mortgages. The money went mostly to mortgage insurance that backed the construction of new suburban housing. In this way, the FHA propelled the unprecedented flight of millions of Euro-Americans, who left the cities for the suburbs. In all, the FHA and VA programs insured about one-third of all homes purchased. Unfortunately, government administrators shared the real estate industry's view that racial segregation was closely linked to stability of neighborhoods and housing values. When the FHA issued its Underwriting Manual to banks in 1938, one of its guidelines for loan officers instructed them not to integrate new tracts. "A change in social or racial occupancy generally contributes to instability and a decline in values." Thus, government policy encouraged discrimination against Mexican Americans and African Americans who had limited options as to where they could buy.[49]

Urban Renewal: The Day of the Bulldozer

The 1949 Housing Act tied urban renewal to public housing, so that the worst slums were to be bulldozed for "a decent home and suitable living environment for every American family."[50] Politicians built their political careers on urban renewal, favoring clearance projects that protected downtown business districts from the slums. These policies of urban development perpetuated racial tension and shaped contemporary racist attitudes and stereotypes. Federally financed expressways ripped the urban core and furthered suburbanization. Minorities were prevented from buying homes in the suburbs, which created what is today's "underclass." All in all, the gap between people of color and Euro-Americans widened as low-cost housing gave homeowners tax breaks and inflation built home equity.

During the 1950s, urban renewal menaced Mexican Americans. By 1963, 609,000 people were uprooted nationwide, two-thirds of whom were minority group members. For Chicanos, Los Angeles was the prototype, and other cities mirrored its experiences. In Los Angeles, the Eastside *barrio* came under attack by urban-land grabbers engaged in freeway building, business enterprises, and urban renewal. Like other poor people throughout the United States, Mexicans had settled in the older sections near the center of the town. When freeway plans were proposed, planners considered poorer neighborhoods expendable. Government used the power of eminent domain to dislocate Chicanos so that money interests could reap large profits.

In the 1950s, the low-income housing stock decreased by 90 percent. By the fall of 1953, the San Bernardino, Santa Ana, and Long Beach freeways already scarred the Mexican area, and Chicanos protested the projected building of still another freeway through East Los Angeles. However, unlike the residents of Beverly Hills, Chicanos were not able to stop the bulldozers, and the $32 million Golden State Freeway wiped out another Mexican sector. In 1957, the Pomona Freeway displaced thousands of Chicanos in the Hollenbeck area. The history of freeways in Los Angeles is one of plunder, fraud, and utter disregard for the lives and welfare of people. Land developers knew just why and where they planned the routes; they conveniently bypassed the property of powerful corporate interests, such as the large Sears and Roebuck store and the *Los Angeles Times* facilities. Developers and politicians made millions.

The outcome was the erosion of the city's tax base. As a consequence, downtown developers and other elites pressured the federal government for relief, which they received through the Federal Housing Act of 1949. Over the years, the scope of the act broadened: under the public housing legislation of the New Deal, government could force a landowner to sell under the power of eminent domain if the condemned property was for public use; under urban renewal, land could also be taken for private use and to profit developers. Under the public housing program, municipalities bought and cleared the land and then sold it to developers at a loss. The federal government made up two-thirds of the loss. Often, developers bought the redeveloped property at 30 percent of cost.[51]

The Dodgers and Chávez Ravine

Because of the renewal process, Mexican neighborhoods were kept in a state of flux throughout the 1950s, as they became the targets of developers. In October 1957, the city removed Mexican homeowners from the Chávez Ravine neighborhood, near the center of Los Angeles, giving more than 300 acres of private land to Walter O'Malley, owner of the Dodgers baseball team. The Dodgers deal angered many Angelenos as well as residents of Chávez Ravine, who resisted physically. In one instance in 1959, the county sheriff's department forcibly removed the Aréchiga family. Councilman Ed Roybal condemned the action: "The eviction is the kind of thing you might expect in Nazi Germany or during the Spanish Inquisition." Supporters of the Aréchigas protested to the City Council. Victoria Augustian, a witness, pointed a finger at Council Member Rosalind Wyman, who, with Mayor Norris Poulson, supported the giveaway. Poulson was a puppet of the Chandler family, who owned the *Los Angeles Times*, which backed the land handover.[52]

Joseph Eli Kovner, publisher and editor of the *Eastside Sun*, exposed connections between the mayor's office and capitalist interests in Los Angeles, and urban renewal proposals in Watts, Pacoima, Canoga Park, Bunker Hill, and Boyle Heights (Watts is a black community and the other four are predominantly Mexican). Kovner cited a memo from the Sears Corporation to its executives, instructing them to support urban renewal because the company had an economic interest in protecting its investment. The presence of too many minorities in an area depressed land values and the trade was deprived of white middle-class customers. Urban renewal ensured construction of business sites and higher-rent apartments that inflated property values. On July 31, 1958, the *Eastside Sun* exposed the Boyle Heights Urban Renewal Committee's plot to remove 480 homes north of Brooklyn between McDonnell and Mednick and to displace more than 4,000 people.

Actions of the neorobber barons became so outlandish that De Witt McCann, an aide to Mayor Poulson's Urban Renewal Committee, resigned, stating, "I don't want to be responsible for taking one man's private property through the use of eminent domain and giving it over to another private individual for his private gain." Poulson and his associates had displaced thousands of poor, white senior citizens and Mexicans in Bunker Hill and turned over prime land in the downtown section of the city to private developers. Citizens of Bunker Hill lost their battle, but progressives derailed the scheme that eventually would have handed all of Boyle Heights, City Terrace, and Belvedere to private developers. Mayor Norris Poulson responded to the critics of urban renewal: "If you are not prepared to be part of this greatness, if you want Los Angeles to revert to pueblo status … then my best advice to you is to prepare to resettle elsewhere."

City officials, and especially the mayor, were guilty of criminal negligence. The Los Angeles Community Redevelopment Administration's board of directors ordered Gilbert Morris, superintendent of building and safety, not to enforce safety regulations in the Bunker Hill area. Improvements would raise the value of property and the officials wanted to keep costs down. Poulson also instructed the commissioner of the Board of Building and Safety not to issue building permits. Consequently, existing buildings deteriorated. The inevitable occurred when a four-story apartment building collapsed; fortunately, firefighters were able to save the 200 occupants. Councilman Ed Roybal accused Poulson of playing politics with human lives.[53]

Gentrification in the Midwest

Urban renewal followed a similar pattern in most cities in which Chicanos lived. The renewal process dispersed Mexicans throughout Detroit; many moved to the suburbs. As in other cities, a pattern of uprooting by speculators, industrialists, and land developers emerged, disrupting the phenomenon of community building that had been crucial to the security of Mexican Americans for so long. For instance, in the 1960s redevelopment plans wiped out and moved the Bagley Avenue Mexican business district to Vernor. The G.I.

Forum in Detroit defended the civil rights of displaced residents and lobbied to gain access for Mexicans to public institutions. Detroit Mexicans, fed up with the reactionary Catholic hierarchy that remained silent on these issues, refused to rebuild Nuestra Señora de Guadalupe Church and discouraged the formation of new Mexican Catholic groups.

In Chicago, freeways, the expansion of the university campus, and other renewal programs wiped out the Near West Side *barrio*. In 1947, the city of Chicago organized the Chicago Land Commission to supervise slum clearance and urban "removal." The flight of white families and industries from the city to the suburbs had begun and it cost city jobs. This loss of employment would greatly affect Mexican Americans.

Neighborhoods around the University of Chicago were also cleared and rebuilt during the late 1950s, as was a big part of the Lincoln Park neighborhood along North Avenue.[54] Later, the federal interstate highway program funded construction of five expressways that displaced 50,000 city dwellers. The civil rights movement of the late 1960s prevented most of the rest of Chicago from being gentrified. The targeted African Americans and other ethnics joined with white ethnic neighborhoods, like Taylor Street's Italian area, to revolt against urban renewal. In the early 1960s, however, developers bulldozed more than 800 houses and 200 businesses—most owned by citizens of Italian, Mexican, and Greek ancestry—to make way for what was then called the University of Illinois Chicago Circle Campus.

The aftershock of urban renewal would be felt in the 1960s, when accelerated redevelopment caused a major disruption of the dominant social order. It transformed downtowns and surrounding areas, contributing greatly to the decentralization of the city while centralizing commercial and political power in the hands of a few elites. The most obvious disruption for the poor was the destruction of sound, affordable housing without adequate replacement. Conditions in the inner city worsened as housing and services became overburdened. Unemployment and inflation resulted, and poverty increased—as did crime and neighborhood gang activity. Urban renewal, essentially, also killed public housing, which was labeled socialistic.[55]

Conclusion: Toward the Illusion of Civil Rights

With the Cuban Revolution that overthrew the U.S.-backed dictator Fulgencio Batista y Zaldívar in 1959, Fidel Castro became the symbol of Latin American resistance to American colonialism. That he had overthrown a dictator put in power by the United States during the 1930s was not lost on Latin America. For many younger Chicanos, attending universities, the study of Latin American history created an awareness of U.S. imperialism in the region. Also weighing on their minds was the 1954 overthrow of Guatemalan President Jacobo Arbenz, who was ousted in a *coup d'état* organized by the U.S. Central Intelligence Agency; he was replaced by Colonel Carlos Castillo Armas. The pretext was that U.S. Secretary of State John Foster Dulles considered Arbenz a Communist: Arbenz wanted to distribute to peasants land belonging to the United Fruit Co. (The Dulles family was heavily invested in this company.) This coup provoked a moral outrage among many Mexican Americans and Latinos, as U.S.-backed Guatemalan military dictators had slaughtered hundreds of thousands of peasants.[56]

At home, an excellent study prepared by the Historic Preservation Office of the City of Phoenix, Arizona, articulates what it calls the acculturation of Mexican Americans in the post–World War II years. It begins by making the point that World War II greatly impacted the Mexican community. Almost a half-million Mexican-origin people served in the armed forces, with several millions of family members suffering and vicariously relating with them. These soldiers fought not only as Americans but also as Mexicans—a fact they could not escape. Their deaths had a ripple effect on the family members. When the servicemen returned, their expectations were not met, and an expanded leadership that was nurtured by old-time activists both in mainstream and radical organizations formed or joined the struggle. Older *barrios* saw a sudden expansion and many moved to new neighborhoods—but they were acculturated, not assimilated.

Dramatic change occurred during World War II and the Korean War. The City of Phoenix study tells of Amadeo Suárez, a World War II veteran and professor at the American Institute of Foreign Trade, who in 1947 sought to buy a home in the white part of town but was prevented "due to the race restrictive deed, which stated, 'No lot or tract, or any part thereof, shall be leased, let, occupied, sold or transferred to anyone other than to members of the white or Caucasian race except those of Mexican or Spanish Ancestry,'" who were regularly discriminated against because they were considered nonwhite.[57]

During the World War many Mexican American women had taken white-collar and blue-collar jobs, but most still labored in the fields. Graciela Gil Olivárez was an exception; she became a radio disc jockey and a community leader, and, later, occupied an important government post in Washington, D.C. Born in 1928 in Phoenix and raised in the mining community of Barcelona, Arizona, she worked her way up, starting as a stenographer and translator at the KIFN Spanish-language radio; by 1952 she was Phoenix's first female disc jockey. She was involved in women's issues and soon went into counseling for the "Careers for Youth" program in Phoenix. During the 1960s Olivárez became State Director of the Office of Economic Opportunity for Arizona. She enrolled in the Notre Dame School of Law, and, in 1970, became the first woman to graduate from this school. In 1977, President Jimmy Carter appointed her Director of the Community Service Administration in Washington, D.C.

In 1952, Tempe, Arizona, attorney Ralph Estrada, on behalf of the *Alianza Hispano Americana*, founded in the 1890s, filed suit against the Tolleson School District to end segregation, as it violated the Fourteenth Amendment of the U.S. Constitution. School officials claimed that the separation was based on "language barriers." In 1955, the judge ruled the separation unconstitutional, which set off more cases against Arizona school districts.[58] All of these activities produced a measure of moral outrage—each victory, and even each defeat, politicized larger numbers of Mexican Americans.

Notes

1. Rodolfo Acuña, *Occupied America: The Chicano's Struggle Toward Liberation* (San Francisco, CA: Canfield Press, 1972), 210.

2. John P. Schmal, "The Tejano Struggle for Representation," The Hispanic Experience, Houston Institute for Culture, http://www.houstonculture.org/hispanic/tejano1.html. Also see http://www.houstonculture.org/hispanic/tejano2.html. Because of the size of the Mexican American population in Texas, and its longevity, it had a stronger organizational base at this time than California did.

3. An epic film on 1950s racism toward Mexican Americans in Texas is *Giant* (1956), director George Stevens's adaptation of the Edna Ferber novel about a great cattle ranch family in Texas starring Rock Hudson, James Dean, and Elizabeth Taylor; http://www.tcm.com/mediaroom/video/240954/Giant-Movie-Clip-Sarge-s-Place.html. Your school or public library should have a free copy. An epic book on the subject is Beatrice Griffith, *American Me* (Boston: Houghton Mifflin Co., 1948).

4. Leo Grebler, Joan W. Moore, and Ralph C. Guzman, *The Mexican-American People: The Nation's Second Largest Minority* (Glencoe, IL: Free Press, 1971), 105, 107, 112–13, 119, 121, 150, 154. Jorge Durand, Douglas Massey, and Chiara Capoferro, "The New Geography of Mexican Immigration," in Víctor Zúñiga and Rubén Hernández-León, eds., *New Destinations: Mexican Immigration in the United States* (New York: Russell Sage Foundation, 2005), 8.

5. Enrique Meza Buelna, "Resistance From the Margins: Mexican American Radical Activism in Los Angeles, 1930–1970"

(PhD dissertation, University of California, Irvine, 2007), 128, makes the succinct point that California state senator "Tenney was vehemently opposed to any legislation that attempted to outlaw discrimination, denouncing them as deliberate interference with employer rights and the free flow of trade." Senator Joseph McCarthy, Spartacus Educational, http://www.spartacus.schoolnet.co.uk/USAmccarthy.htm. Smith Act of 1940, http://en.wikipedia.org/wiki/Smith_Act. Smith Act Trials, http://www.english.illinois.edu/maps/poets/g_l/jerome/smithact.htm. Rick Kelly, "Anticommunism Run Amok: The Life of Senator Pat McCarran," (December 18, 2004), The World Socialist Web Site, http://www.wsws.org/articles/2004/dec2004/mcca-d18.shtml.

6. Carlos G. Vélez-Ibáñez, *Border Visions: Mexican Cultures of the Southwest United States* (Tucson: University of Arizona Press, 1996), 203–4.

7. Vélez-Ibáñez, *Border Visions*, 203–4. Carlos G. Vélez-Ibáñez, "Los Chavalones of E-Company: Extraordinary Men in Extraordinary Events," Address to the 40th Reunion of E Company, Tucson, Arizona, (July 28, 1990). "Selective Service/College Deferment," Korean War Educator, http://www.koreanwar-educator.org/topics/homefront/p_selective_service.htm. Hugh Deane, "Korea, China, and the United States: A Look Back (Cover Story)," *Monthly Review* 46, no. 9 (February 1995): 20ff. Raúl Morín, *Among the Valiant: Mexican Americans in WWII and Korea* (Alhambra, CA: Borden Publishing, 1966), 259–76. Kathy Gill, "Military Conscription, Recruiting and the Draft," *U.S. Politics: Current Events* (June 27, 2005), http://uspolitics.about.com/od/electionissues/a/

draft_2.htm Rodolfo Acuña, "Today's Hawks Conveniently Avoided Combat," *Miami Herald* (November 1, 2002).

8. K. Mason/K. Stallard, E. Uhl, 1983–1984, "Finding Aid for American Committee for Protection of Foreign Born," Records, 1926–1980s, Special Collections Library, Labadie Collection, University of Michigan, http://quod.lib.umich.edu/s/sclead/umich-scl-acpfb?rgn=main;view=text.

9. Los Angeles Committee for Protection of Foreign Born Records, 1938–1973, Online Archive of California, http://content.cdlib.org/view?docId=kt067nb6v8&chunk.id=scopecontent-1.7.4&brand=oac. Guide compiled by Martin Schipper, "Records of the Subversive Activities Control Board, 1950–1972," Part I: Communist Party USA, Part II: Communist-Action and Communist-Front Organizations, (A microfilm project of University Publications of America, 1988), http://cisupa.proquest.com/ksc_assets/catalog/10837.pdf .

10. Wendy Plotkin, Community Service Organization (CSO) History Project, http://comm-org.wisc.edu/papers96/alinsky/cso.html. Community Service Organization (CSO), members, California, Wayne State Labor Archives, http://www.reuther.wayne.edu/node/300. The Southern California Library: The People's Library, http://www.socallib.org/, is the most complete library of progressive documents of Los Angeles.

11. U.S. Supreme Court, *American Committee v. SACB*, 380 U.S. 503 (1965), Argued December 9, 1964, Decided April 26, 1965, http://supreme.justia.com/us/380/503/case.html.

12. Evelyn Barker, "Labor Activism During the Cold War: The Case of Humberto Silex," University of Texas at Arlington Library, http://www.uta.edu/library/k12/lessons/labor-files/labor-activism.pdf.

13. John W. Sherman, *A Communist Front at Mid-Century: The American Committee for Protection of Foreign Born, 1933–1959* (Westport, CT: Praeger Publishers, 2001). Jeffrey M. Garcilazo, "McCarthyism, Mexican Americans, and the Los Angeles Committee for Protection of the Foreign-born, 1950–1954," *Western Historical Quarterly* 32, no. 3 (Autumn 2001), 273–95. "President Lauds Tolerance Here; Foreign-born Group Urged to Be Vigilant Against Injustices," *Los Angeles Times* (March 3, 1940). Carey McWilliams, *North from Mexico: The Spanish-Speaking People of the United States.* New edition with Matt Meier (New York: Praeger, 1990), 23. Isabel González, *Step-Children of a Nation: The Status of Mexican-Americans* (New York: American Committee for Protection of Foreign Born, 1947). Rachel Ida Buff, "The Deportation Terror," *American Quarterly* 60, no. 3 (September 2008), 523–51.

14. Garcilazo, "McCarthyism," 274.

15. McCarran Act or Internal Security Act of 1950, http://www.writing.upenn.edu/~afilreis/50s/mccarran-act-intro.html. 1952 Immigration and Nationality Act, a.k.a. the McCarran–Walter Act, US immigration legislation online, University of Washington Bothell, http://library.uwb.edu/guides/USimmigration/1952_immigration_and_nationality_act.html.

16. Patricia Morgan, *Shame of a Nation* (Los Angeles Committee for Protection of Foreign Born, September 1954), 4, 39–47. Jethro K. Lieberman, *Are Americans Extinct?* (New York:

Walter, 1968), 106, 109. Rodolfo F. Acuña, *A Community Under Siege: A Chronicle of Chicanos East of the Los Angeles River, 1945–1975* (Los Angeles, CA: Chicano Studies Research Center Publications, 1984), 40. Steven R. Shapiro, "Commentary: Ideological Exclusions: Closing the Border to Political Dissidents," *Harvard Law Review* 100, no. 930 (February 1987). David G. Gutiérrez, *Walls and Mirrors: Mexican Americans, Mexican Immigrants, and the Politics of Ethnicity* (Berkeley: University of California Press, 1995), 172–78. U.S President's Commission on Immigration and Naturalization, *Whom We Shall Welcome* (New York: Da Capo Press, 1970), 196–98. See also Robert K. Murray, *Red Scare* (Minneapolis: University of Minnesota Press, 1955), 65. Grebler et al., *Mexican-American People*, 519. "Hope Mendoza Gets Immigration Job Appointment," *Eastside Sun* (Boyle Heights, June 4, 1953). Ralph Guzmán, "Front Line G.I. Faces Deportation," *Eastside Sun* (June 30, 1953). Louie Gilot, "Former ASARCO Labor Leader Dies at 99," *El Paso Times* (March 18, 2002). "Our Badge of Infamy, A Petition to the United Nations on the Treatment of the Mexican Immigrant," American Committee for the Protection of the Foreign Born (April 1959), 13–14, 36–38. "Nacional-Mexico Americano[sic] Fights Deportation Move," *Eastside Sun* (Boyle Heights, March 13, 1952). Joseph Eli Kovner, "The Tobias Navarrette Case," *Eastside Sun* (July 25, 1957). *Eastside Sun* (August 8 and August 29, 1957). George Mount, "Tobias Navarrette, E.L.A. Humanitarian, Is Dead," *Eastside Sun* (September 6, 1964). One of the best studies is Ralph Guzmán, *Roots Without Rights* (Los Angeles, CA: American Civil Liberties Union, Los Angeles Chapter, 1958). John F. Méndez, Editorial, *Eastside Sun* (May 2, 1957). Juan Ramón García, *Operation Wetback: The Mass Deportation of Mexican Undocumented Workers in 1954* (Westport, CT: Greenwood Press, 1980), 173–74. "Jose Gastelum Free of Mexico Deportation," *Eastside Sun* (Boyle Heights, June 20, 1963). "Deportation Is Meeting Topic," *Eastside Sun* (March 28, 1957).

17. John Dillin, "How Eisenhower Solved Illegal Border Crossings from Mexico," *Christian Science Monitor* (July 6, 2006), http://www.csmonitor.com/2006/0706/p09s01-coop.html. Pierre Tristam, "Operation Wetback: Illegal Immigration's Golden-Crisp Myth," *Daytona Beach News-Journal* (April 5, 2007). The Braceros, The Oregon Experience, Oregon Public Broadcasting, http://www.opb.org/programs/oregonexperiencearchive/braceros/.

18. Avi Astor, "Unauthorized Immigration, Securitization and the Making of Operation Wetback," Latino Studies 7, no. 1 (Spring 2009): 5–29: a link between immigration and communism was made. Ronald L. Mize, Jr., "Mexican Contract Workers and the U.S. Capitalist Agriculture Labor Process: The Formative Era, 1942–1964," *Rural Sociology* 71, no. 1 (2006): 85–108.

19. Carlos Kevin Blanton: "The Citizenship Sacrifice: Mexican Americans, the Saunders-Leonard Report, and the Politics of Immigration, 1951–1952," *Western Historical Quarterly* 40, no. 3 (Autumn 2009): 301. Garcilazo, "McCarthyism," 276–77.

20. Buelna, "Resistance from the Margins," 210. Kelly Lytle Hernández, "The Crimes and Consequences of Illegal Immigration: A Cross-Border Examination of Operation Wetback, 1943 to 1954," *Western Historical Quarterly* 37, no. 4 (Winter 2006): 430–34. Good account of deportees.

21. Saul Edmund Bronder, "Robert E. Lucey: A Texas Paradox" (PhD dissertation, Columbia University, New York, 1979), 138, 175. John Phillip Carney, "Postwar Mexican Migration: 1945–1955, with Particular Reference to the Policies and Practices of the United States Concerning Its Control" (PhD dissertation, University of Southern California, 1957), 20, 48, 127. Lyle Saunders and Olen E. Leonard, "The Wetback in the Lower Rio Grande Valley of Texas," reprinted in Carlos E. Cortés, ed., *Mexican Migration to the United States* (New York: Arno Press, 1976), 165. Art Liebson, "The Wetback Invasion," *Common Ground* 10 (Autumn 1949): 11–19. E. Idar, Jr., and Andrew C. McLellan, *What Price Wetbacks* (Austin: American G.I. Forum of Texas, Texas State Federation of Labor [AFL]), reprinted in Cortés, ed., *Mexican Migration,* 28–29. J. R. García, *Operation Wetback,* 172–74, 188–89, 192, 199, 206, 212, 225, 227–32, 235. Morgan, *Shame of a Nation,* 3. Lamar Babington Jones, "Mexican American Labor Problems in Texas" (PhD dissertation, University of Texas, 1965), 25–26. Acuña, *A Community Under Siege,* 30–36, 40–43, and accompanying *Belvedere Citizen* and *Eastside Sun* references. Gutiérrez, *Walls and Mirrors,* 155. John Dillin, "Clinton Promise to Curb Illegal Immigration Recalls Eisenhower's Border Crackdowns," *Christian Science Monitor* (August 25, 1993). Ralph Guzmán, "Ojinaga, Chihuahua and Wetbacks," *Eastside Sun* (October 15, 1953). "Our Badge of Infamy," iii–v.

22. Sarah Deutsch, *No Separate Refuge: Culture, Class, and Gender on an Anglo-Hispanic Frontier in the American Southwest, 1880–1940* (New York: Oxford University Press, 1987). Bruce Johansen and Roberto Maestas, *El Pueblo: The Gallegos Family's American Journey, 1503–1980* (New York: Monthly Review Press, 1983). Pauline R. Kibbe, *Latin Americans in Texas* (Albuquerque: University of New Mexico Press, 1946), 19, 91.

23. Gutiérrez, *Walls and Mirrors,* 162. Grebler et al., *The Mexican-American People,* 122.

24. "Paso del Sur," http://www.pasodelsur.com/historia/Intro.html. Chihuahuita began forming in the early 1800s as people from Ciudad Juárez moved across the river to build their homes. As the Mexican colonia expanded, Segundo Barrio formed as a distinct neighborhood, which eventually became the largest Mexican *barrio* in El Paso. There is an ongoing battle over the preservation of Segundo Barrio. I always wondered how it got the name Segundo Barrio until an old-timer told me recently, "Well, the first barrio is Juárez": it made sense. Eileen Welsome, "Eminent Disaster: A Cabal of Politicians and Profiteers Targets an El Paso Barrio," *The Texas Observer* (May 4, 2007), http://www.texasobserver.org/article.php?aid=2483.

25. Celeste Delgado, "Teens Rebel Against Authority," *Borderlands,* El Paso Community College, http://epcc.libguides.com/content.php?pid=309255&sid=2629727. Benjamin Márquez, "Power and Politics in a Chicano Barrio" (PhD dissertation, University of Wisconsin-Madison, 1983), 45–110.

26. Rodolfo Rosales, *The Illusion of Inclusion: The Untold Political Story of San Antonio* (Austin: University of Texas Press, 2000), 51. Everett Ross Clinchey, "Equality of Opportunity for Latin-Americans in Texas: A Study of the Economic, Social, and Educational Discrimination Against Latin-Americans in Texas, and the Efforts of the State Government on Their Behalf" (PhD dissertation, Columbia University, 1954). Robert Garland Landolt, "The Mexican American Workers of San Antonio, Texas" (PhD dissertation, University of Texas, Austin, 1965), 191–92. Edwin L. Dickens, "The Political Role of Mexican-Americans in San Antonio, Texas" (PhD dissertation, Texas Tech University, 1969), 44, 87–93, 140. Frances Jerome Woods, *Mexican Ethnic Leadership in San Antonio* (Washington, DC: Catholic University Press, 1949), 31–36. David R. Johnson, John A. Booth, and Richard J. Harris, eds., *The Politics of San Antonio: Community, Progress, and Power* (Lincoln: University of Nebraska Press, 1983), 19–23. Eugene Rodríguez, Jr., *Henry B. González: A Political Profile* (New York: Arno Press, 1976), 9. Grebler et al., *The Mexican-American People,* 54. Center for American History unveils Henry B. González Collection and Web site, University of Texas Austin (October 27, 2006), http://www.utexas.edu/news/2006/10/27/cah/.

27. Leland M. Roth, *American Architecture: A History,* 2d ed. (Boulder, CO: Westview Press, 2003), 460–61; in 1946, 2.15 million cars were built; by 1955, 7.5 million were being built annually; and 10 years later 9.3 million. Euro-Americans wanted to emulate the German autobahn system, and after the war the U.S. economy spurred by industry promoted this. In 1920, General Motors, Firestone Tire, Standard Oil of California, Phillips Petroleum, Mack, and the Federal Engineering Corporation organized a holding company, and bought up more than 100 electric systems in 45 cities. They then turned around and destroyed them, lobbying for more freeways. Los Angeles had two electric car systems, which were thus destroyed. Meanwhile, Los Angeles became a web of freeways that displaced tens of thousands of people. Federal funds were used to finance the system at a nine to one ratio. This was the plot of the motion picture *Who Framed Roger Rabbit?* Touchtone Films, 1988, http://www.youtube.com/watch?v=Smzs_0ZoheE&feature=related. The movie is about urban renewal and freeways in Los Angeles. The Mexicans are the toons—they work for peanuts.

28. Acuña, *A Community Under Siege,* 21–121. Jerry Gonzalez, "'A Place in the Sun': Mexican Americans, Race, and the Suburbanization of Los Angeles 1940–1980" (PhD dissertation, University of Southern California, Los Angeles, 2009).

29. Louise Año Nuevo Kerr, "The Chicano Experience in Chicago: 1920–1970" (PhD dissertation, University of Illinois at Chicago Circle, 1976), 116–210. Also see Howard Zinn, *A People's History of the United States* (New York: Colophon Books, 1980), 428. Richard O. Boyer and Herbert M. Morais, *Labor's Untold Story,* 3d ed. (New York: United Electrical, Radio and Machine Workers of America, 1974), 340. Peter

T Alter, "Mexicans and Serbs in Southeast Chicago: Racial Group Formation during the Twentieth Century," *Journal of the Illinois State Historical Society* (Winter 2001/2002), http://dig.lib.niu.edu/ISHS/ishs-2001winter/ishs-2001winter403.pdf.

30. Nicholas J. O'Shaughnessy, *Politics and Propaganda: Weapons of Mass Seduction* (Ann Arbor: University of Michigan Press, 2004). Gutiérrez, *Walls and Mirrors,* 162–67. Ellen Wight, "Making Mexican-ness in Pilsen: Perspectives on the Meaning of Cultural Production in City Space" (All Academic Research, January 17, 2006) can be downloaded at http://citation.allacademic.com/meta/p_mla_apa_research_citation/1/0/3/8/9/pages103892/p103892-3.php.

31. E. B. Fincher, *Spanish-Americans as a Factor in New Mexico* (New York: Arno Press, 1974), 27–49, 67–73, 94, 150–58. Rosales, *Illusion of Inclusion.* Grebler et al., *The Mexican-American People,* 150.

32. Carlos Conde, "Latino Kaleidoscope; Edward R. Roybal: The Angry Mexican-American," *Hispanic Outlook in Higher Education* 16, no. 8 (January 30, 2006): 8. I knew Roybal for the better part of 40 years. Shana Bernstein, "Interracial Activism in the Los Angeles Community Service Organization: Linking the World War II and Civil Rights Eras," *Pacific Historical Review* 80, no. 2 (May 2011): 231.

33. "Community Service Organization CSO Papers," Urban Archives, California State University Northridge, http://digital-library.csun.edu/cdm/singleitem/collection/LatinoArchives/id/236.

34. "Enrique Hank Lopez," *New York Times* (October 25, 1985), http://www.nytimes.com/1985/10/25/arts/enrique-hank-lopez.html.

35. Fincher, *Spanish-Americans as a Factor in New Mexico,* 27–49. Grebler et al., *The Mexican-American People,* 150. Mario T. García, *Mexican Americans: Leadership, Ideology, and Identity, 1930–1960* (New Haven, CT: Yale University Press, 1991), 88–112, 221, claims that Bert Corona insisted that CSO was formed to prevent "radicals" and "Communists" from organizing the Mexican communities. Mario T. García, *Memories of Chicano History: The Life and Narrative of Bert Corona* (Berkeley: University of California Press, 1995), 162–68. Acuña, *A Community Under Siege,* 27–29. Also see Raphael J. Sonenshein, *Politics in Black and White: Race and Power in Los Angeles* (Princeton, NJ: Princeton University Press, 1993), 31, 38, 41, 65. Kay Lyon Briegel, "*Alianza Hispano-Americana,* 1894–1965: A Mexican Fraternal Insurance Society" (PhD dissertation, University of Southern California, 1974), 175. George J. Sánchez, "Concerning Segregation of Spanish-Speaking Children in the Public Schools," Inter-American Education Papers (Austin: University of Texas, 1951), 13–19. Robin Fitzgerald Scott, "The Mexican American in the Los Angeles Area, 1920–1950: From Acquiescence to Activity" (PhD dissertation, University of Southern California, 1971), 293. Ralph C. Guzmán, *The Political Socialization of the Mexican American People* (New York: Arno Press, 1976), 138–39, 140, 141, 142. Katherine Underwood, "Pioneering Minority Representation: Edward Roybal and the Los Angeles City Council, 1949–1962," *Pacific Historical Review* 66, no. 3 (August 1, 1997): 399, 401, 403, 406, 415.

36. David Montejano, *Anglos and Mexicans in the Making of Texas, 1836–1986* (Austin: University of Texas Press, 1987), 276, 278. Rosales, *Illusion of Inclusion,* 13, 29, 42–43. Interview with Albert Peña, Jr., by José Angel Gutiérrez, July 2, 1996, Tejano Voices, University of Texas Arlington, http://library.uta.edu/tejanovoices/xml/CMAS_015.xml.

37. M. García, *Mexican Americans,* 113–41. Also see Mario T. García, *The Making of a Mexican American Mayor: Raymond L. Telles of El Paso* (El Paso: Texas Western, 1998). Márquez, "Power and Politics," 55–57, 72, 120–32. After the election, Democratic Party leaders abolished the primary for mayor. The party would now name its candidate, supposedly for saving the cost of running a primary. Telles, who had been chosen in a primary, supported the change because he incorrectly predicted it would improve the Mexican community's chances of electing a mayor.

38. "Are the Rich Really Different?" Economist.com, April 11, 2009, http://www.economist.com/blogs/freeexchange/2007/04/are_the_rich_really_different.cfm. This is significant because the rich argue that taxation stunts productivity.

39. David E. Hayes-Bautista, Werner O. Schrink, and Jorge Chapa, *The Burden of Support: Young Latinos in an Aging Society* (Stanford, CA: Stanford University Press, 1988), 58.

40. Salt of the Earth—Herbert Biberman (1954), [the entire movie] http://www.youtube.com/watch?v=aXTcDUxu22A. Michael Wilson, *Salt of the Earth,* Screenplay (New York: The Feminist Press at the City University of New York, 1977). Ellen R Baker, "Salt of the Earth': Women, the Mine, Mill and Smelter Workers' Union, and the Hollywood Blacklist in Grant County, New Mexico, 1941–1953" (PhD dissertation, University of Wisconsin-Madison, 1999), 179.

41. George J. Sánchez, *Becoming Mexican American: Ethnicity, Culture and Identity in Chicano Los Angeles, 1900–1945* (New York: Oxford University Press, 1993), 251. Jack Cargill, "Empire and Opposition: The 'Salt of the Earth' Strike," in Robert Kern, ed., *Labor in New Mexico: Unions, Strikes and Social History Since 1881* (Albuquerque: University of New Mexico Press, 1983), 179–240.

42. Best series on the *Hernandez v. State of Texas* case, *A Class Apart,* PBS Series, http://www.pbs.org/wgbh/americanexperience/films/class/player/. Best book on the case: Ignacio M. Garcia, *White But Not Equal: Mexican Americans, Jury Discrimination, and the Supreme Court* (Tucson: University of Arizona Press, 2008).

43. On May 17, 1954, the U.S. Supreme Court ruled unanimously that racial segregation in public schools violated the Fourteenth Amendment's equal protection clause, thus overturning *Plessy v. Ferguson* (1896) that permitted "separate but equal" public facilities. Meyer Weinberg, *Minority Students: Research Appraisal* (Washington, DC: U.S. Department of Health, Education and Welfare, 1977), 286–87. *G.I. Forum News Bulletin* (December 1953). "Edgar Taken to Federal Court on Segregation," *G.I. Forum News Bulletin* (April 1955). Carla M.

McCullough, "*Brown v. Board of Education* (1954): An Analysis of Policy Implementation, Outcomes, and Unintended Consequences" (Ed.D. dissertation: Loyola Marymount University, 2012).

44. *G.I. Forum News Bulletin* (January 1955). "Mercedes Policeman Who Menaced Family Resigns as Result of G.I. Forum Pressure," *G.I. Forum News Bulletin* (June 1953, September 1953, December 1953, May 1954, and February–March 1956). The G.I. Forum published numerous articles on police abuse throughout the Southwest.

45. *Hernandez v. Texas*, Civil Rights Story, http://forchicanachicanostudies.wikispaces.com/Reviews. "A Class Apart," Documentary on the Hernandez Case, http://www.pbs.org/wgbh/americanexperience/class/. Ignacio M. García, *White but Not Equal: Mexican Americans, Jury Discrimination, and the Supreme Court* (Tucson: University of Arizona Press, 2008). Clare Sheridan, "'Another White Race': Mexican Americans and the Paradox of Whiteness in Jury Selection," *Law and History Review* 21, no. 1 (Spring 2003), http://www.historycooperative.org/journals/lhr/21.1/forum_sheridan.html.

46. Edward J. Escobar, "Bloody Christmas and the Irony of Police Professionalism: The Los Angeles Police Department, Mexican Americans, and Police Reform in the 1950s," *Pacific Historical Review* 72, no. 2 (May 2003): 171.

47. Briegel, "*Alianza Hispano-Americana*," 183, 184. Armando Morales, "A Study of Mexican American Perceptions of Law Enforcement Policies and Practices in East Los Angeles" (DSW dissertation, University of Southern California, 1972), 41, 77. In August 1949, a "Committee of 21" was created in the Hollenbeck area to improve police–community relations. It held two meetings and then faded away (Morales, "A Study," 83–84). See also *Eastside Sun* (Boyle Heights, March 9, April 13, 20, 1951). "El Sereno Defense Group to Give Dance," *Eastside Sun* (July 12, 1951). Ralph Guzmán, *Eastside Sun* (December 29, 1953). *Eastside Sun* (Boyle Heights, September 17, 1953). *G.I. Forum News Bulletin* (February–March 1956).

48. Fincher, *Spanish-Americans as a Factor in New Mexico*, 95–97. *Eastside Sun* (Boyle Heights, February 16, April 20, July 20, 1950; August 7, September 4, 1952). "New Spanish Speaking Group Formed in Texas," *Eastside Sun* (May 31, 1951). See also *Eastside Sun* (August 11, November 29, 1951, September 11, 1952). Briegel, "*Alianza Hispano-Americana*," 179–83. *Eastside Sun* (Boyle Heights, February 10, 1955).

49. Dennis R. Judd, "Segregation Forever? Housing Discrimination," *The Nation* 253, no. 20 (December 9, 1991): 740 ff.

50. The reader is encouraged to analyze the coding in this quote. Was housing policy predicated on the goal of "a decent home and suitable living environment for every American family" or was this a pretext to spend hundreds of millions of dollars to satisfy the middle class and subsidize bankers and the construction industry?

51. Jacqueline Leavitt, "Urban Renewal Is Minority Renewal; Public Housing: Razing Units in Boyle Heights Reflects an Old Agenda," *Los Angeles Times* (October 11, 1996).

52. The History of Chavez Ravine, Independent Lens, PBS, http://www.pbs.org/independentlens/chavezravine/cr.html. Don Normark, *Chavez Ravine: 1949: A Los Angeles Story* (San Francisco, CA: Chronicle Books, 2003); wonderful photographs. Chavez Ravine & Segundo Barrio: Film Discussion, http://www.youtube.com/watch?v=MX1PDITprFA.

53. Acuña, *A Community Under Siege*, 58–61, 66–78; also accompanying references to the *Eastside Sun* and the *Belvedere Citizen*. Ronald William López, "The Battle for Chavez Ravine: Public Policy and Chicano Community Resistance in Post War Los Angeles, 1945–1962" (PhD dissertation, University of California, Berkeley, Fall 1999). Joseph Eli Kovner, "Route Would Slash Through Residential and Business Districts; Protests Mount," *Eastside Sun* (Boyle Heights, October 1, 1953). See also *Eastside Sun* (March 10, 1955; October 3, 17, and 24, 1957; February 27, December 30, 1958) and Joseph Eli Kovner, "The Arechiga Family Bodily Evicted from Home in Chavez Ravine," *Eastside Sun* (May 14, 1959). And see the Joseph Eli Kovner articles in the *Eastside Sun* (April 10, 17, 24; May 1, 8, 15; June 6, 12; July 3, 17, 24, 31, 1958). Joseph Eli Kovner, "Aide Quits in Bunker Hill Row," *Eastside Sun* (Boyle Heights October 9, 1958). *Eastside Sun* (December 4, 30, 1958). Joseph Eli Kovner, "'Resettle Elsewhere,' Says Mayor, 'If You Don't Want Urban Renewal,'" *Eastside Sun* (January 8, 1959). Joseph Eli Kovner, "Brazen Politics Endangers Lives to Lower Property Taxes," *Eastside Sun* (Boyle Heights, March 12, 1959). Bunker Hill cost the taxpayers $30 million to profit private individuals.

54. "Demographics of Chicago," http://en.wikipedia.org/wiki/Demographics_of_Chicago; follow the link and click on "1950 Ethnic Map of Chicago."

55. John McCarron, "Memory of Early Days Leaves Urban Renewal with Cross to Bear," *Chicago Tribune* (August 29, 1988). This section draws heavily from Dennis Nodín Valdes, *El Pueblo Mexicano en Detroit y Michigan: A Social History* (Detroit, MI: Wayne State University, 1982). Also see Manuel Castells, *The Urban Question: A Marxist Approach* (Cambridge, MA: MIT Press, 1979), 393–95. Lalo Guerrero: "Barrio Viejo," Cerritos College (1999), http://www.youtube.com/watch?v=vj-odkXy7hA, a nostalgic song on the destruction of Tucson's oldest *barrios*.

56. Central Intelligence Agency Document on Guatemala, 1954, Document 1, "CIA and Guatemala Assassination Proposals, 1952–1954," CIA and Assassinations: The Guatemala 1954 Documents, by Kate Doyle and Peter Kornbluh. National Security Archive Electronic Briefing Book No. 4, http://www.whale.to/b/doyle.html.

57. David R. Dean and Jean A. Reynolds, "Acculturation and the Roots of Social Change: 1940–1956," Hispanic Historic Property Survey, Historic Preservation Office, City of Phoenix (Athenaeum Public History Group, 2006), 73–75, 79–80, 85–86, 101–2, http://phoenix.gov/webcms/groups/internet/@inter/@dept/@dsd/documents/web_content/pdd_hp_pdf_00043.pdf.

58. Joe R. Romero et al., Plaintiffs, v. Guy Weakley et al., Defendants. R. J. Burleigh et al., Plaintiffs, v. Guy Weakley et al., Defendants. Nos. 1712-SD, 1713-SD. United States District Court for the Southern District of California, Southern Division. 131 F. Supp. 818; 1955 U.S. Dist. May 5, 1955. http://sshl.ucsd.edu/brown/romero.htm.

CHAPTER 13

Goodbye America: The Chicana/o in the 1960s

LEARNING OBJECTIVES

- Discuss how the Mexican American community had changed by the 1960s.

- Debate the differences in the Mexican American community vis-à-vis where they lived.

- Analyze what effect the baby boomers, rock and roll, the Civil Rights movement, and the Vietnam War had on Chicanas/os.

- Interpret the militancy of Chicanas/os and how it crystallized the grievances of the Mexican American community.

- List the major events of the 1960s relevant to the Chicana/o community in the order of their importance.

Historical decades are markers within a timeline that help the reader understand how a historical period fits into the development of nations or peoples. More often, however, successive decades merge into each other, as major events spill over from one decade into the next. In the above timeline, the year 1945 marks the end of World War II, an event that would have a huge impact on the 1960s. In turn, when trying to understand the "Sixties," it is important to recognize that it too will affect future generations and that the period did not end in 1969. As per the marker, some would generalize that this historical period actually ended in 1973 with the end of the Vietnam War. The decade of the Sixties is hugely important: the Mexican American identity reached a point where it was integrated into the political life of the nation. The Chicano population reached a critical mass in numbers, and because it was concentrated in cities, it could no longer be ignored. Numbers matter.

Breaking down the 1960s, one characteristic of the decade is the white baby boomers. The first wave of parents of the baby boomers were mostly born in the second half of the 1920s and the early 1930s. From 1946 to 1964, 76 million babies were born in the United States. The sheer magnitude of this group

1945   1959   1960   1961   1962   1963   1964   1965   1966   1967   1968   1969   1970   1973 profoundly affected the economy, politics, fashions, and music of the 1960s as well as their relations with Chicanos, who as a community were younger than other groups.[1] A significant number of this rock-and-roll generation supported integration and opposed the Vietnam War. Youth played a role in the "leveling" of society. For example, this progressive tendency of many youth resulted in support for the black Civil Rights movement, spread the antiwar campaign to university campuses, and affected the national conversation.[2]

The consciousness of the 1960s generation was shaped by World War II, which brought about the breakup of colonial empires. People in the Third World hoped to decolonize their countries and end their dependency on industrialized nations. The Western powers resisted this transformation of the world order, fearing that many of the new nations would be vulnerable to Communist control; hence, they opposed the liberation of nonwhite people. The Vietnam War resulted from the failure of the Western nations to live up to the promises of World War II—democracy for all—which made the movement to liberate the Third World inevitable and necessary. In turn, these liberation movements affected the black Civil Rights movement as well as liberal-minded people in the United States.[3]

World War II also heightened an awareness of civil rights and liberties among minorities. The bases of social movements were inequality and a moral outrage at the lack of fairness in the system. Organizations such as the National Association for the Advancement of Colored People (NAACP), the League of United Latin American Citizens (LULAC), and the *Alianza Hispano-Americana* had been active in obtaining these rights before WWII. During and after WWII, "civil rights" took on a new meaning.[4]

These currents were pulled together by rock and roll, which was symbolic of the period. Like the Civil Rights movement, it had its beginnings in the African American community after World War II, being influenced by blues tunes, gospel music, and jazz-influenced vocal music. It was adopted by the baby boomers of all colors, and set the rhythm for the Decade of Protest and innovation. While some connected with rock and roll took drugs, its appeal went far beyond drugs. It was a form of rebellion that pulled together youth of all races—often as a vehicle for political and cultural rebellion.[5]

The Early 1960s

Between 1950 and 1960 the Latino, or the Spanish-surnamed, population in the Southwest increased by 51 percent. Immigration from Mexico accounted for some of this growth, but much of the increase should be attributed to the U.S. Mexican population, whose fertility ran ahead of its Euro-American counterparts. The African American population of 18.9 million outnumbered the Mexican American population by almost five to one, and Latinos as a whole by slightly fewer than four to one. U.S. Mexicans were concentrated geographically, with Texas and California housing 82 percent of them.

The revolt of youth during the decade challenged the stability of the middle class and the ruling elite. As in the case of the Depression—when industrial trade unions opened space for minority workers—the Civil Rights, antiwar, and youth movements forged space for Chicanos and other Latinos within this opposition to the old order. Increasingly urban Chicanos would be influenced by the political language and expressions, for example, of African Americans—especially their emphasis on identity politics and their call for power.

Proving Your Poverty

Statistics are vital in proving the obvious—poverty and its causes. The Ford Foundation in the 1960s funded a million dollar grant to University of California economist Leo Grebler to study Mexican Americans in the 1960 Census.[6] That Census counted 3,464,999 Spanish-surnamed persons in the Southwest with a per capita income of $968, compared with $2,047 for white Americans and $1,044 for nonwhites. Of the Spanish-surnamed population, 29.7 percent lived in deteriorated housing versus 7.5 percent of Euro-Americans and 27.1 percent of other nonwhites. The Census further showed that the average size of the Spanish-surnamed family was 4.77 persons, compared with 3.39 for Euro-Americans and 4.54 for nonwhites. Unemployment, too, was higher among Chicanos than among whites. And the median school grade in the Southwest for

Spanish-surnamed persons over 14 years of age was 8.1, versus 12.0 for Euro-Americans and 9.7 for other nonwhites. The median school grade attained by Spanish-surnamed in Texas was 4.8. Although Chicanos were not as strictly segregated by the whites as were African Americans, most of them lived away from the white community. Social segregation still existed, and in places like Texas and eastern Oregon, "No Mexicans Allowed" signs were common.[7]

The Eyes of Texas: Poverty in San Antonio   Some places were more impacted by poverty than others. San Antonio, the second largest Mexican American city, had a Mexican population of 243,627—17.2 percent of the 1,417,810 Mexicanos in the Lone Star state. Some 30,299 were first generation; 75,950, second generation; and 137,738, third or later generations. As in El Paso and Corpus Christi, a substantial number of Mexicans in San Antonio worked as migrant workers. Unemployment for the Spanish-surnamed males was 7.7 percent, compared with 5.1 percent for males of all races; the unemployment of Chicanas was 7.9 percent, versus 4.7 percent for other females. Only 1.4 percent of the Chicanos had a college degree, and over three-quarters of Mexican youth were enrolled in vocational classes.

The average annual income of Mexican Americans was about $2,000 less than that of whites. Some 42 percent of Spanish-surnamed families earned wages below the poverty line of $3,000 per year, as compared with 16.2 percent for Euro-American families. In 1960, only Corpus Christi Mexicans had a lower median annual family income than San Antonio Mexicans—$2,974—who had a median of 4.5 years of education. In Houston, the Mexican families' median income was $4,339, and median school education 6.4 years. In south Texas as a region, Mexicans lived in even more depressing conditions.

In San Antonio, less than 10 percent of the workforce belonged to unions. Thus, few Mexicans were able to participate in apprenticeship programs in the city's craft unions; few could rise above the lowest ranks and become skilled tradesmen, who were in high demand and were better paid. Further, 85.4 percent and 90 percent of the hodcarriers and cement workers, respectively, were Mexicans. The city had 12 housing projects, and Mexicans made up 59.5 percent of the residents. Only 49.7 percent of the Mexican population lived in homes with plumbing, versus 94 percent for the whites.[8]

El Paso, the Gateway City   El Paso has historically been a port of entry—the home of the historic El Segundo Barrio.[9] In 1960 the median family income for El Paso Mexicans was $3,857; the median for education was 6.5 years. Mexicans were spread throughout the city, with older colonias such as Ysleta making up the core of the expanded *barrios*. El Segundo Barrio continued to house the poorest of the poor in dilapidated housing. In 1967 in El Paso, three children—Ismael, 8; Orlando, 7; and Leticia Rosales, 4— were burned to death in a fire caused by faulty electricity. Poverty projects, especially juvenile delinquency programs, brought together youth who formed the Mexican American Youth Association (MAYA), the most active Chicano organization in El Paso during the 1960s. Renters formed tenant unions to press for improvements in public housing. Militancy spilled over to the University of Texas at El Paso, where, by the end of the decade, Chicano students demanded the admission of more Chicanos and a Chicano studies program.[10]

City of the Angels   Los Angeles housed the largest Mexican American community in the United States by 1960.[11] Los Angeles County's Mexican population mushroomed during the 1960s, from 576,716 to 1,228,593—an increase of 113 percent. The white population decreased from 4,877,150 to 4,777,909—a 2 percent drop. In 1966, 76,619 white babies were born in Los Angeles, compared with 24,533 Latinos and 17,461 blacks. Eight years later, in 1974, 41,940 white babies, 45,113 Latino babies, and 16,173 black babies were born there. Toward the end of the decade, the San Francisco–Oakland area experienced a similar growth, as the Latino population increased to 362,900. This population growth, however, differed from that of Los Angeles; it included larger numbers of Central and South Americans and Puerto Ricans. Unemployment and poverty among Mexican Americans were high throughout the first half of the 1960s.

Residential segregation increased and consequently the schools were also more segregated. Mexicans made up more than 80 percent of the Boyle Heights–East Los Angeles area. Eastside schools had over-crowded classrooms, double sessions, a lack of Mexican American teachers, and high pushout (dropout) rates.[12] Local leaders, along with the press, complained about the rise in juvenile delinquency and crime. By contrast, the San Fernando Valley, then a white bedroom community where the white baby boomers went to school, received the bulk of the city's education and building funds. Even in the Valley Mexicans were segregated and lived in doughnut enclaves—they were the hole in the middle of the dough.[13]

Chicago: Reign of the Bulldozers   The Chicago story is gentrification. Mayor Richard Daley, land speculators, and developers made a bundle of money bulldozing neighborhoods. During the 1950s and 1960s, many Mexicans, displaced by expressways, the expansion of the Medical Center, and the University of Illinois at Chicago, moved a few blocks south and settled on 18th Street, in the Pilsen barrio. The Pilsen was the center of an international working class, where the 1886 strike at the McCormick Reaper had taken place. The last wave of ethnics to occupy the Pilsen, also known as *La Dieciocho* (the18th Street), was that of Mexicans, many of whom were newcomers from Guanajuato, Jalisco, and Michoacan. The Mexican community was fractured along lines of undocumented, citizenship, and language. The median age in the Pilsen district—22—was lower than in Back of the Yards and South Chicago, 24.5 and 26 years, respectively. The most stable Chicano community was the South Side, although Mexicans shared the area with other groups, including a significant number of Puerto Ricans.[14]

From 1950 to 1960, Chicago's Chicano population grew nearly fivefold—from 24,000 to 108,000—and congestion in the *barrios* worsened. Increasingly, new residents came not through Texas but directly from Mexico. The result was white flight: from 1940 to 1960, approximately 401,000 whites fled the city. In the 1950s, the white population in the south suburbs nearly doubled and segregation became even more acute for the ghetto poor of the inner city. More than a third of Mexicans lived in overcrowded housing, paying abnormally high rent. This underclass suffered only moderate levels of discrimination since most outside Pilsen lived in ethnic ghettos. Indeed, although an estimated 6,000 Chicanos worked in the steel mills after the War, there was not a single Chicano staff member in the union.[15]

Harvest of Shame: The Forgotten People

On November 25, 1960—the night after Thanksgiving—a one-hour television documentary, *Harvest of Shame,* was aired, narrated by Edward R. Murrow. Murrow began, "These are the forgotten people, the underprotected, the undereducated, the underclothed, the underfed." The documentary went on to tell the miserable plight of migrant workers, showing families working in blistering heat and living in run-down housing, enduring misery so that an affluent nation could be fed. Unlike their urban counterparts, migrants did not even receive Social Security benefits, since the government had exempted growers from paying into the fund. And over three-quarters of the children of migrants lived in conditions below the poverty line.[16]

The largest migrant stream, composed mostly of Mexican Americans, was from south Texas and included entire families. Some would travel only within the state, but many went into the Rocky Mountain, Great Plains, and Great Lakes states; the Northwest; and Florida. According to the documentary, "Along the routes, the Anglos are usually employed in tree crops, the Mexican Americans in stoop labor."[17]

In 1960, 16 percent of Spanish-surnamed males in the Southwest were farm laborers, compared with 2.1 percent of whites. In 1968, three-quarters of the Texas migrants worked in family groups. In south Texas, the average Mexican American family consisted of 6.5 members. In the 1960s (and even today), whole families—with small children often younger than 12 years of age—worked in the fields. The long work hours interfered with the education of the child workers, and few received more than primary education.

Another migrant stream, composed mostly of Mexican Americans, traveled within California and along the Pacific Coast, often intersecting with Tejano migrants. Wages had changed little since 1956, when the average daily wage for a migrant was $5.14 in Texas. In that same year, a single migrant averaged $781 per year, and family income (i.e., with small children working at stoop labor) approximated $2,240 per year.[18] Most migrants did not get paid for holidays, sick days, or overtime, and there were no retirement or disability plans, or medical coverage.[19]

Delusions of the Awakening of the Sleeping Giant

In January 1961, North Americans had high hopes that President John Fitzgerald Kennedy would get the country moving again. No group was more optimistic than Mexican Americans; they had played an active role in Kennedy's narrow victory in 1960. Without their vote, Kennedy would have lost Texas and the election.

Officially, the U.S. Census counted nearly 4 million Mexican Americans: 87 percent lived in the Southwest, and 85 percent were born in the United States. This number was up 2 percent from 1950. The feeling among many Mexican Americans was that they achieved the critical mass to force society to close the gaps in socioeconomic and political inequality through the ballot box. "Viva Kennedy" clubs almost gave JFK a victory in California and furnished a narrow win in Texas. Hence, the Mexican Americans felt that their vote had been crucial to Kennedy's election, and this gave them the illusion of power and acceptance in the world of gringo politics.[20]

San Antonio and Texas Politics

The Good Government League (GGL) controlled San Antonio politics, which consisted of a downtown elite of bankers, developers, merchants, and real estate brokers. Members of the GGL filled the San Antonio utility boards, and planning and zoning commissions as well. As a matter of policy, the city government made few civic improvements on the West Side. Mayor W. W. McAllister, hostile to improvements in minority areas, promoted private development efforts, such as the Hemisfair, the South Texas Medical Center, the University of Texas at San Antonio, and new industry. He kept taxes low by depriving minority communities of public services.

LULAC and the G.I. Forum were active in San Antonio and south Texas and challenged the GGL. The leaders in both LULAC and the Forum had strong ties to the Democratic Party establishment. Most Mexican Americans were Catholic and Democrats, and supported President Lyndon Baines Johnson (LBJ succeeded JFK following his 1963 assassination), who funneled patronage through the major Chicano organizations.

Many Mexicans splintered off into a more liberal faction led by George I. Sánchez and Mexican American labor leaders. They supported Ralph Yarborough's 1963 bid for governor, against LBJ's choice. The LBJ faction was composed of the old rural, conservative Mexican American leadership. LBJ nurtured his Mexican ties by referring to the Longoria case, his teaching in a Mexican school, his patronage to Mexicans, and his friendship with Mexican American leaders. He actively courted LULAC and the Forum in his unsuccessful 1960 bid for the presidency. However, most Mexican Americans had supported JFK, with liberals criticizing LBJ's anti–civil rights record.

The Viva Kennedy clubs and the candidacy of President John F. Kennedy stimulated political activity. Henry B. González was elected to the San Antonio City Council in 1951; by 1961 he was a congressman.[21] County Commissioner Albert Peña, Jr., and his aide Albert Fuentes organized Viva Kennedy clubs throughout Texas.[22] These clubs played a key role in electing Kennedy and in the formation of the Political Association of Spanish-speaking Organizations (PASO)[23] in 1961, which became an all-Texas affair. Peña and the Teamsters supported the Mexican American efforts to gain majority representation on nearby Crystal City's city council in 1963, with temporary success.

PASO split into liberal and conservative factions. Peña led the liberals; the G.I. Forum's Dr. Hector García, along with LULAC's Bonilla brothers, William and Tony, headed the conservatives. García and the Bonillas criticized PASO's role in the Crystal City takeover, claiming that the Teamsters had gained control of PASO. Dr. García walked out of PASO's 1963 convention, followed by members of LULAC. García, a staunch supporter of LBJ and Texas Governor John Connally, feared Mexican involvement with more liberal Democrats. Shortly afterward, LULAC and the Forum entered the poverty program network. The Crystal City takeover lasted only two years. Personality conflicts and factionalism tore the coalition apart.

Meanwhile, Mexican Americans were upset when Kennedy did not give them representation in office. They criticized the selection of conservative Reynaldo Garza, an old friend of LBJ, to the federal court.

To the south of San Antonio, at Crystal City, Texas—a small town of 10,000 in the Winter Garden region of southwest Texas—the majority was Mexican people. It was chosen by PASO for a get-out-the-Mexican-vote drive. PASO's slate of candidates for the city council was successful, electing Juan Cornejo, a local Teamsters Union business agent, along with four other Mexican Americans. Though the electoral coup only lasted two years, it lit a spark for later successes and was a training ground for leaders such as José Angel Gutiérrez, who later founded the Mexican American Youth Organization (MAYO) in 1967 and *La Raza Unida* Party in 1969. *Time* magazine ran an article that the sleeping giant had awakened, predicting that it was going to become a national power group. It described how the Texas Rangers stood by in case of trouble. The article went on:

> *In a way, the Crystal City Mexicans did stir up trouble for themselves. They control the town's government, but the Anglos control its economy. One council-seat winner got fired from his job in a hardware store. Another found his wages cut in half by his Anglo employer. But, mindful that Mexicans outnumber Anglos in South Texas, PASO looks upon the Crystal City election as a momentous triumph. Says Albert Fuentes, the PASO official who led the campaign: "We have done the impossible. If we can do it in Crystal City, we can do it all over Texas. We can awake the sleeping giant." On election day, the Mexicans have learned, all South Texans are equal.*[24]

In 1964, Mexican Americans elected Eligio (Kika) de la Garza to Congress.[25] Slowly, the playing field became less bumpy, and in 1966, the 24th Amendment abolished the poll tax. It renewed hope as Mexican Americans increasingly ran for office. In Mathis, in San Patricio County near Corpus Christi, Mexicans formed the Action Party in 1965, taking control of the municipal government. Their goal was to improve municipal services for Mexicans. In 1967, the Action Party won reelection.[26]

Los Angeles Politics

California did not have an organizational network comparable to that of Texas. The Mexican American Political Association (MAPA) formed in 1959, but like most Chicano organizations its membership was low. Many MAPA members were active in the liberal California Democratic Council (CDC), which supported the Civil Rights movement and promoted representation for African Americans but ignored Mexicans. Indeed, party leaders rationalized that gerrymandering Mexican districts would be beneficial for that community. Incumbents blatantly gerrymandered Mexican *barrios* throughout California. Reapportionments in 1961, 1965, and 1967 often purposely split the Mexican American population, i.e., in East Los Angeles, where the 40th, 45th, 48th, 50th, and 51st Assembly Districts cut into the area to pick up 20–30 percent of the Mexican American districts; the 52nd, 53rd, 65th, and 66th took smaller bites.[27]

In 1962, John Moreno and Phil Soto were elected to the California Assembly. Moreno failed to get reelected two years later, and Soto was voted out in 1966.[28] The election of Edward R. Roybal to the U.S. Congress, also in 1962, left a void in local politics. The Los Angeles City Council, despite community protests, appointed an African American—Gilbert Lindsay—to replace Roybal. The council reapportioned the districts, making the election of three blacks probable but a victory for a Mexican American impossible. Without local leadership, the Mexican community was vulnerable to the schemes of opportunistic politicians such as Councilwoman Rosalind Wyman.

Los Angeles dominated California politics. Although its Mexican population was the largest in the United States, Mexican Americans did not hold many political offices. The Democratic Party purposely allowed the voting registration of Mexican Americans to lapse. The only place Mexican Americans could win was in small compact districts such as judicial races. In 1963, Los Angeles Municipal Court Judge Leopold Sánchez stated that out of 5,000 judicial appointments made by Governor Edmund G. Brown, Sr., less than 30 were Chicanos. Mexican Americans were incensed when Brown implied a lack of qualified persons among them.[29]

Political Organizing in Chicago

The type of political involvement of Mexicans depended on where they lived in Chicago. For example, in South Chicago second-generation steelworkers took part in union affairs and local politics. By mid-decade, they formed the Tenth Ward Spanish-Speaking Democratic Organization. With the support of this Tenth Ward Organization and that of the steelworkers' union, John Chico openly challenged the Daley machine by running for office. Chico lost the election, and Daley withheld patronage, gerrymandering the Tenth into two separate wards to dilute Mexican voting power.[30]

During the decade, Pilsen, the only exclusively Mexican *barrio*, developed its own identity. Neighborhood organizations evolved to defend the space against gentrification. The new residents were poor and had problems such as gangs, crime, and high rates of school dropouts—yet there was a growing awareness of place among Chicanos. Increasingly, they identified with Chicano movement.

During the 1960s, the Little Village community (26th Street) integrated into Pilsen. Little Village Mexicans/Latinos were on the average economically better off than the Pilsen residents. During the time, there was not even the illusion of inclusion as the schools, the churches, and the Daley machine responded only to the older, better-established ethnics. By the end of the 1960s, however, Mexican institutions and agencies emerged in greater numbers: *El Centro de La Causa,* BASTA (Brotherhood Against Slavery to Addiction), Chicano Mental Health, the Mexican American Council on Education, the Brown Berets, and the Organization of Latin American Students. In response to this growing Mexican nationalism, Howell House changed its name to Casa Aztlán, the home of the Benito Juárez Health Clinic. Chicanos in Chicago readily adopted the nationalist symbols of their southwestern counterparts.[31]

The Building of a Civil Rights Coalition

John Kennedy, moved by demonstrations and urban and campus unrest, appealed to liberals and minorities by announcing his "New Frontier" initiative. It was more a statement of aspirations than a program. The assassination of Kennedy in November 1963 and the growing militancy among the black community changed the public mood. As a consequence, President Lyndon B. Johnson was able to skillfully push major civil rights legislation through Congress and launch his Great Society (the so-called War on Poverty). Like Kennedy and Franklin Roosevelt, Johnson relied heavily on eastern intellectuals to plan his national program, part of which was intended to placate the growing militancy among African Americans.[32]

Viva Johnson

Johnson's 1964 election campaign immediately built a Viva Johnson network. Hector García headed the Texas operation, and Bert Corona, the California campaign. Johnson brought back Vicente Ximenes, the ambassador to Ecuador, to head the national effort to garner the Mexican American vote. Ximenes actively recruited Mexican American women as volunteers and staff, calling them the "best source of grassroots campaign work." Few found their way into the higher levels of the organization, however. Some of these women, such as Fran Flores (California); Polly Baca (Colorado), head of the G.I. Forum Ladies Auxiliary; and Cleotilde García (Texas), although crucial to operations, were limited to advisory roles.

Not all Mexican American organizations worked under the Viva Johnson campaign. Labor leader César Chávez and the farmworkers worked independently to support Johnson. Herman Gallegos and the Community Service Organization (CSO) operated through the California State Democratic Committee. After the election, the Democratic Party again showed its lack of loyalty by dismantling the Viva Johnson network, much as it had dismantled Viva Kennedy.[33]

Building the Great Society

In 1964, LBJ went beyond JFK's New Frontier and, declaring a "War on Poverty," proposed the Economic Opportunity Act of 1964. The act laid the framework for the planning and coordination of the so-called war through the Office of Economic Opportunity (OEO).[34] Johnson's plan, labeled "The Great Society," dramatically escalated job-training programs, which were initiated by the Manpower Development and Training Act (MDTA) of 1962. New programs such as the Job Corps, Head Start, Upward Bound, and Volunteers in Service to America (VISTA) fell under the OEO. Congress allocated $1.6 billion annually to eliminate poverty—an amount that, considering the 30–40 million poor living in the United States, did not go very far.[35]

The War on Poverty strengthened LBJ's patronage network, and the G.I. Forum and LULAC were first in line for patronage funds. Congressman Henry B. González received his share of the patronage. Though Johnson practiced more inclusion of Mexican Americans, Chicanas did not fare well with him personally. According to historian Julie Leininger Prycior, supporters knew Johnson was antagonistic toward women; he refused to include them in meetings, saying, "Get those women out of here!" Nevertheless, there were exceptions. Cleotilde García established nursing programs in south Texas with OEO seed money; María Urquides of Arizona served on the National Advisory Council on Extension and Continuing Education; and Californian Henrietta Villaescusa acted as a liaison between the Department of Health, Education, and Welfare and local community groups.[36] Graciela Olivárez of Arizona worked her way up the OEO bureaucracy to become Arizona's acting OEO director, but she was bypassed for the permanent position. Olivárez was the first Chicana to organize on a national scale when Johnson appointed her to the Equal Employment Opportunity Commission (EEOC).[37]

The Albuquerque, New Mexico, Walkout

On March 28, 1966, the federal Equal Employment Opportunity Commission (EEOC) held a meeting in Albuquerque, New Mexico, to investigate Chicano employment problems. Fifty Chicanos, including Graciela Olivarez, walked out because, although the commission advocated equal employment, Mexicans were vastly underrepresented on the EEOC staff itself. When asked for a reason, EEOC Executive Director Herman Edelman blamed Mexican American organizations, stating that only 12 of the 300 complaints since 1965 had come from Mexican Americans. The dissidents formed the Mexican American Ad Hoc Committee in Equal Employment Opportunity. President Johnson met with *selected* MAPA, G.I. Forum, and LULAC leaders at the White House on May 26, 1966. Johnson seemingly seduced the invited guests by promising them a White House conference. In June 1967 he appointed Vicente Ximenes to the EEOC. Shortly afterward, LBJ named Ximenes head of the newly created Interagency Committee on Mexican American Affairs. This appointment mollified some middle-class activists whose goal was affirmative action.

LBJ did not keep his promise of holding a White House conference. The president feared that Chicanos would walk out and embarrass him politically. Instead, in October 1967 Johnson held cabinet committee hearings at El Paso, Texas. Johnson did not bother to invite the leading activists—César Chávez, Reies López Tijerina, or Rodolfo "Corky" Gonzales. The conference coincided with the celebration of the signing of the Chamizal Treaty regarding a disputed section of land on the Mexico–Texas border. (The Rio Grande had shifted over the years, leaving land formerly belonging to Mexico on the U.S. side. The treaty gave the disputed land back to Mexico. The Chamizal Treaty displaced 5,595 residents, mostly Mexican American, who had to move to the U.S. side.) At El Paso, Johnson bused *his* Mexicans to join the celebrations of the return of the Chamizal people to Mexico.

LULAC and G.I. Forum were the largest groups represented at the cabinet committee hearings. However, dissident activists boycotted and picketed the hearings. They called their group *La Raza Unida* (the United Race or People); Ernesto Galarza of San José, Corky Gonzales, and Reies López Tijerina played leading roles in this opposition. Representatives of 50 Chicano organizations met at San Antonio and pledged support to the idea of *La Raza Unida*; about 1,200 people attended.[38]

Bilingual Education

According to Congressman Edward R. Roybal, a California Democrat, Johnson pushed the concept of bilingual education. On a flight in Air Force One, LBJ recalled his teaching experience in a Mexican school—how smart the children were; but they could not speak English. They therefore lost valuable time learning to speak English. Indeed, bilingual education in the early days was a simple concept in which the Mexican American child would be bilingual–bicultural and learn to speak both languages. It was never meant to be for remediation, as Dr. George I. Sánchez so aptly put it. In Sánchez's view, it also included the teaching of Spanish language to Mexican Americans.[39]

In reality, the initiative for the first bilingual bill came from U.S. Senator from Texas Ralph Yarborough. Lupe Anguiano, who had joined the Department of Health, Education and Welfare after the pre-planning conference for the El Paso Hearings, and others also lobbied for bilingual education.[40] Anguiano became an advocate after witnessing the great number of schools in California labeling students "mentally retarded" because they did not know how to speak English. Schools through the Southwest banned the speaking of Spanish on school grounds. Anguiano and others prepped sponsors on the bill, which was introduced on January 17, 1967.

Meanwhile, the Office of Education offered Armando Rodríguez the job of heading up a Mexican American unit in which he would work with White House staffers to draw up a bill. Up to this point Lupe Anguiano had organized strategy in the House of Representatives, and she had lobbied for a Mexican American to head up the newly formed unit. However, Anguiano and Rodríguez clashed over policy, and by the end of the year, Anguiano quit and joined César Chávez.

Rodríguez veered from the course set out by Dr. Sánchez as he emphasized that the purpose of the bill was to teach Chicanos to speak English. His approach was that students should maintain Spanish while they became proficient in English. Nevertheless, there was consensus among Rodríguez, Anguiano, and Roybal that the bilingual education bill should not be included in the poverty bill; they feared that the program would be stigmatized. The bill passed 12 months later, with little support from White House aides. Indeed, much of the funding for the first bilingual program came from the Hearst Corporation.[41]

The Black–White Syndrome

Because of the War on Poverty, African Americans and other minorities competed for resources. Many Chicanos at the time believed that federal and state bureaucrats played off the two groups against each other—seeing life on a black and white TV. Undoubtedly, the intensity of the African American struggle and the size of its population forced Washington to pay more attention to the demands of blacks. During the mid-1960s, the black community exploded. Urban renewal in the 1950s had reduced the supply of low-rent housing, thus dislocating thousands of poor. Northern cities became tinderboxes. The black population of Los Angeles, small before World War II, zoomed in the postwar years. Freeways isolated that community, hiding poverty behind concrete walls. In places like Watts, the infrastructure was grossly inadequate to absorb newcomers. Unemployment hovered around 30 percent. As a consequence of the Civil Rights movement, President Johnson was able to push through the Voting Rights Act of 1965.[42]

In August 1965, the African Americans in Watts rebelled, leaving 35 dead and causing property damage of $200 million.[43] The governor sent 14,000 members of the National Guard to occupy Watts. Two years later, another rebellion hit Newark, New Jersey, leaving 26 dead. In 1969, 43 died in a rebellion in Detroit, where 8,000 guardsmen and 4,700 paratroopers occupied the battle zone. Because these incidents heightened middle-class fears, Congress passed legislation to control the political threat by keeping the rebellious African Americans in tow.

Substandard economic and social conditions similar to those of African Americans plagued *barrios* throughout the United States. The *barrios* did not explode with the same force as the black ghettos did. In the mid-1960s, some Chicanos offered naïve cultural explanations about why Mexicans did not riot; they pictured themselves as more peaceful than African Americans. According to Lorena Oropeza, the tendency of many established Mexican American leaders was to represent their community as worthy of society's attention "based upon the Mexican Americans' commendable behavior on the battlefield, but also—indicating increasing political participation—at the polls."[44] One explanation for the difference in the responses of the two communities to oppression is that the institutions of social control were stronger in the Mexican *barrios* than in ghettos like Watts. Mexicans had lived in colonias such as San Antonio for generations. In Los Angeles, Chicano communities, despite continuous population turnover, were more stable than the black areas. The Mexican family remained much more intact than families in Watts. A common language and a similar cultural background conveyed at least the facade of a community. Homeownership was also higher in Mexican American areas than in Watts.

The lack of a militant response by the Mexican American community made African Americans think that they were not making the same level of sacrifice as blacks were. Given the overwhelming presence of African Americans, Mexican Americans and other minorities had a difficult time convincing people that they too belonged to the Civil Rights movement. When the United Civil Rights Coalition was formed in Los Angeles in 1963, it refused to admit Mexican Americans. Chicanos had to wait until the *Cisneros v. Corpus Christi Independent School District* decision (1970) for the courts to classify Mexican Americans as an "identifiable ethnic minority with a pattern of discrimination."[45]

The Disillusion

Almost from the beginning, the War on Poverty ran into difficulties. City bosses saw community action programs, which purportedly organized the poor, as being subversive and, in effect, promoting rebellion. These political machines acted to gain local control of the federally administered poverty programs and their budgets. The War on Poverty also ran into problems because the Johnson administration siphoned off its money to finance the Vietnam War. Simply, the country could not afford two wars. Space, missile, and armament programs took precedence over people. North American society did not consider the ending of poverty a worthwhile goal. Euro-Americans increasingly wanted the poor to just go away. According to U.S. Senator Barry Goldwater, "The fact is that most people who have no skill have no education for the same reason—low intelligence or low ambition."[46]

Bureaucratic conflicts also weakened the War on Poverty. The Department of Labor refused to cooperate with OEO; social workers perceived it as a threat to the welfare bureaucracy and their hegemony among the poor. Local politicians claimed that OEO programs "fostered class struggle." Meanwhile, as government officials and others quickly gained control of the programs, the participation of the poor declined. By 1966, President Johnson began dismantling the OEO, with Head Start going to Health, Education, and Welfare, and the Job Corps, to the Department of Labor. He then substituted the "Model Cities" program for OEO. Johnson, faced with opposition within his own party over the war in Vietnam, announced that he would not seek reelection. The assassination of Robert Kennedy during the California primary also dealt a blow to Mexican American hope. The election of Richard Nixon in 1968 put the proverbial final nail in the coffin.

Impact of the War on Poverty

The impact of the War on Poverty on Chicanos was huge. A study of 60 OEO advisory boards in East Los Angeles—Boyle Heights–South Lincoln Heights, for instance—showed that 1,520 individuals, 71 percent of whom lived in these communities, served on the boards; two-thirds were women. Many Chicano activists of the 1960s developed a sense of political consciousness as a result of poverty programs, which advertised the demands and grievances of the poor and created an ideology that legitimized protest. Many minorities came to learn that they had the right to work in government and to petition it. Legal aid programs and Head Start, a public preschool system, also proved invaluable to the poor. The number of poor fell dramatically between 1965 and 1970 as Social Security, health, and welfare payments more than doubled. When the federal government cut the last of the War on Poverty programs in the 1980s, poverty escalated.[47]

Magnetization of the Border

A population boom in Mexico tossed millions into Mexico's labor pool, thus intensifying the push factors. In 1950, Mexico had a population of 25.8 million; it jumped to 34.9 million 10 years later and was rushing toward 50 million by the end of the 1960s. Driving this increase was the fertility rate of Mexican women.

The data are based on the percentage of growth for a particular year or years. For example, the Mexican population increased from an average of 1.75 percent in 1922–1939 to 2.25 percent in 1939–1946 and to 6.9 percent in the late 1950s. These data determine the rate at which the Mexican population is growing or has slipped.[48] Mexico during these years had the fastest-growing gross national product (GNP) in Latin America, but it did not offset this increase in population.

The termination of the *bracero* (guest worker) program in 1964 worsened Mexico's economic plight, drastically cutting remittances sent by the migrant workers to their families at home. Mexico's economy simply could not absorb its increasing population. Matters worsened with a decline of ruralism, caused in part by mechanization and the growing commercialization of Mexican farms, which displaced small farmers. Concurrently, the United States was going through good times, attracting underemployed and unemployed Mexican workers. The wartime economy, the Civil Rights movement, and the youth culture temporarily distracted the common Euro-American citizens so that the heavy migration of undocumented workers went largely unnoticed; and the nation's racist, nativist tendencies remained dormant.

In the United States, growers pressured the border patrol to keep the border porous, ensuring a continual flood of workers. In this context the phenomenon known as the "runaway shop" took form. Simply said, Mexico became the destination for North American multinational businesses to enjoy special privileges and exploit loopholes provided by law in the United States. The Customs Simplification Act of 1956 allowed the processing abroad of metal goods, which would then be returned to the United States for finishing. Congress broadened this provision in 1963 to include items such as apparel and toys. These runaway shops located along the border cut down on transportation and labor costs. Understandably, U.S. labor opposed these loopholes, but it lacked sufficient power to stop the flow of jobs out of the United States.

Mexico agreed to the Border Industrialization Program (BIP), waiving duties and regulations on the import of raw materials and relaxing restrictions on foreign capital within 12.5 miles of the border (this area has continuously been expanded); 100 percent of the finished products were to be exported out of the country and 90 percent of the labor force was to consist of Mexicans. In 1966, 20 BIP plants operated along the border; this number increased to 120 in 1970 and to 476 in 1976. The so-called *maquiladoras* (assembly plants) did create jobs (20,327 in 1970) but did not relieve Mexico's unemployment problem. Owners paid the BIP workforce, more than 70 percent of whom were women, minimum Mexican wages. North American employers gave no job security, and the *maquiladoras* could move at the owners' whim. Furthermore, the BIP left relatively little capital in Mexico. Like the *bracero* program, the border program increased Mexican dependence on the United States.[49]

The Immigration Act of 1965

Journalist Theodore White said that the 1965 Amendment to the Immigration Act "was noble, revolutionary— and probably the most thoughtless of the many acts of the Great Society."[50] The act changed immigration policy: the basis for admitting immigrants shifted from national origin to family preference; those already having family in the United States would be given higher quota preferences. At the time, legislators expected Europeans to be the main applicants; thus, there was no apparent problem.

The national-origin system of immigration of the 1920s shielded the United States from further onslaughts of Poles, Italians, Slavs, and eastern European Jews. From 1930 to 1960, about 80 percent of U.S. immigrants came from European countries or Canada. The 1965 act opened the country to other races and ethnic peoples, specifically Asians. (Improved conditions in western Europe made the United States less of an attraction to European peoples, and few applied.) During the first years of the act, not too many Euro-Americans were concerned, because those applying were highly educated Latin Americans and Asians. Liberals such as Senator Edward Kennedy sponsored the legislation because they wanted to correct the past injustice of excluding Asians from legal entry. Before the act there had been no quota for Latin Americans; however, the trade-off for taking the exclusion of Asians off the books was the placing of Latin Americans and Canadians on a quota system. The law specified that 170,000 immigrants from the Eastern Hemisphere and 120,000 from the Western could enter annually. Until the act, Mexico was the principal source of Latin American immigration; the new law put a cap of 40,000 from any one nation.[51]

Mexican American Reaction to Nativism

During the 1950s Mexican American organizations had supported restricting undocumented workers and had encouraged the government to exclude undocumented Mexicans. Organizations such as the American G.I. Forum and LULAC gave the federal government almost unconditional support. Trade unions supporting this restrictionist policy rationalized that the exclusion of the Mexican national was necessary to cut unfair labor competition with Mexican American and other U.S.-based workers. Even so, Mexican American organizations had become distressed about the gross human rights abuses, and pro-foreign-born groups concerned with human rights flourished among Latinos. Immigration, however, was not a priority issue among Mexican Americans in 1965.

Yet the cumulative experiences of old-time activists made some wary about the renewal of racist nativism. *La Hermandad Mexicana Nacional* (the Mexican National Brotherhood), based out of the San Diego area and established in 1951, reflected the tradition of the American Committee for Protection of Foreign Born. During the 1960s, Hermandad joined hands with Bert Corona, then the driving force behind MAPA. Corona correctly assumed that, with the passage of the 1965 Immigration Act, there would be a recurrence of the nativism of the 1950s. With Soledad "Cole" Alatorre, an L.A. labor organizer, and Juan Mariscal and Estella García, among others, Corona opened a Hermandad office in Los Angeles to protect the constitutional rights of workers without papers. Hermandad functioned like a *mutualista* of old, offering self-help services. It then opened additional centers known as *Centro de Acción Social Autónoma* (CASA). At the height of its influence, CASA had 4,000 members. Both Corona and Alatorre were also very active in other aspects of the Chicano political life of the time, and their influence would be felt through the next three decades. In fact, CASA created the progressive template for the protection of the foreign-born.[52]

The Road to Delano

For many, César Chávez began the Chicano movement. Chávez and the farmworkers gave Chicanos a cause, symbols, and a national space to claim their presence in the country's Civil Rights movement.[53] On September 8, 1965, the Filipinos in the Agricultural Workers Organizing Committee (AWOC) struck the grape growers of the Delano area in the San Joaquín Valley. The Di Giorgio Corporation led the growers. On September 16, the National Farm Workers Association (NFWA) voted to join the Filipinos. The end of the *bracero* program in late 1964 had significantly strengthened the union's position. The strike itself dragged on for years, during which time its dramatic events and the brutality of many of the growers attracted millions of non-Chicano supporters. Chávez's strategy was to maintain the union's moral authority by employing civil disobedience and fasts to call attention to the *causa* (cause), following the example of Mohandas Gandhi and the Rev. Martin Luther King, Jr. The strategy of civil disobedience was to actively refuse to obey unjust laws and injunctions. César frequently went to jail and would fast in order to rally his supporters.[54]

Born in Yuma, Arizona, in 1927, César Chávez spent his childhood as a migrant worker. In the 1940s, he moved to San José, California, where he married Helen Fabela. In San José, Chávez met Father Donald McDonnell, who tutored him in *Rerum Novarum*, Pope Leo XIII's encyclical supporting labor unions and social justice. Chávez met Fred Ross of the CSO and became an organizer for the CSO, learning grassroots organizing methods. He went on to become the general director of the national CSO, but in 1962, he resigned and moved to Delano, where he organized the NFWA.[55]

Chávez carefully selected a loyal cadre of proven organizers, such as Dolores Huerta and Gil Padilla, whom he had met in the CSO. Huerta was born Dolores Fernández in a mining town in New Mexico in 1930. She was a third-generation Mexican American, and her father was a miner and seasonal beet worker. When her parents divorced, Huerta's mother and siblings moved to Stockton, California, where her mother worked night shift in a cannery. Huerta was also a CSO organizer; it was there that she met César Chávez, whom she joined in forming the NFWA.[56]

By the middle of 1964, the NFWA was self-supporting; a year later, the union had some 1,700 members. Volunteers, fresh from civil rights activities in the South, joined the NFWA at Delano. Protestant groups inspired by the Civil Rights movement championed the workers' cause. A small number of Catholic priests, influenced by the Second Vatican Council, joined Chávez.[57] Euro-American labor belatedly joined the cause. In Chávez's favor was the growing number of Chicano workers living in the United States. The changing times allowed Chávez to make the farmworkers' movement a crusade.

The most effective strategy was the boycott. The NFWA urged supporters not to buy Schenley products or Di Giorgio grapes. The first breakthrough came in 1966 when the Schenley Corporation signed a contract with the union. The next opponent was the Di Giorgio Corporation, one of the largest grape growers in the Central Valley. In April 1966, owner Robert Di Giorgio unexpectedly announced that he would allow his workers at Sierra Vista to vote on whether the farmworkers wanted a union. However, Di Giorgio did not act in good faith, and his agents set out to intimidate the workers.

Di Giorgio invited the Teamsters to compete with and thus break the NFWA. Di Giorgio held a series of fraudulent elections certifying the Teamsters as the bargaining agent. The NFWA pressured Governor Edmund G. Brown, Sr., to investigate the elections. Brown needed the Chicano vote, as well as that of liberals who were committed to the farmworkers. The governor's investigator recommended a new election, and the date was set for August 30, 1966. Di Giorgio red-baited the union and carried on an active campaign that drained the union's financial resources. This forced Chávez to reluctantly apply for affiliation in the American Federation of Labor and form the United Farm Workers Organizing Committee (UFWOC), which won the election—573 votes to the Teamsters' 425. Field workers voted 530 to 331 in favor of the UFWOC.

In 1967, the UFWOC targeted the Giumarra Vineyards Corporation (the largest producer of table grapes in the United States), boycotting all California table grapes. The result was a significant decline in grape sales. In June 1970, when the strike was approaching its fifth year, a group of Coachella Valley growers agreed to sign contracts. Victories in the San Joaquín Valley and other areas followed.

After the victory in the grape industry, the union turned to the lettuce fields of the Salinas Valley; growers of the area were among the most powerful in the state. During July 1970, the Growers–Shippers Association and 29 of the largest growers in the valley entered into negotiations with the Teamsters. Agreements signed with the truckers' union in Salinas were worse than sweetheart contracts. (A sweetheart contract is one made through collusion between management and labor representatives containing terms beneficial to management and detrimental to union workers.) The contracts provided no job security, no seniority rights, no hiring hall, and no protection against pesticides.

By August 1970, many workers refused to abide by the Teamster contracts, and 5,000 workers walked off the lettuce fields. The growers launched a campaign of violence. Thugs beat Jerry Cohen, a farmworker lawyer, into unconsciousness. On December 4, 1970, Judge Gordon Campbell of Monterey County jailed Chávez for refusing to obey an injunction and held him without bail. This arbitrary action gave the boycott the needed publicity; dignitaries visited Chávez in jail. In the face of mounting pressure, authorities released him on Christmas Eve. By the spring of 1971, Chávez and the Teamsters had signed an agreement that gave the UFWOC sole jurisdiction.[58]

La Casita Farms Corporation Strike of 1966 and the Aftershocks

Texas was a union organizer's nightmare. South Texas's long border ensured growers' access to a constant and abundant supply of cheap labor. The Texas Rangers, the local courts, and right-to-work laws gave growers almost an insurmountable advantage. However, the Chávez movement in California and the growing militancy after the 1963 Crystal City takeover influenced the Texas farmworkers, resulting in the 1966–1967 strikes. Eugene Nelson (who had been with Chávez in California), Margil Sánchez, and Lucio Galván formed the Independent Workers Association (IWA) in May 1966. In June, IWA members voted to affiliate with the NFWA and the UFWOC. More than 400 workers voted to strike the melon growers of Starr

County on June 1, 1966. From the beginning, it was a violent strike, with the Texas Rangers under Captain A. Y. Allee, Jr., spreading a reign of terror.[59]

In the concluding days of June 1967, strikers set out on a march from Rio Grande City to Austin, which ended on Labor Day. Over 15,000 people joined the march in its final days, with thousands more greeting the marchers as they made their way to Corpus Christi, to San Antonio, and then to Austin, the capital of Texas. Not wanting to meet the marchers in the state capital, Governor John Connally, Speaker of the House Ben Barnes, and Attorney General Waggoner Carr had met the marchers in New Braunfels in August. Connally favored agribusiness, and tried unsuccessfully to dissuade the marchers from entering the capitol. Tens of thousands of supporters converged on the Texas state capitol. César Chávez and U.S. Senator Ralph Yarborough participated.[60]

After this action, the marchers wound their way through Starr and Hidalgo Counties. At the Roma Bridge in Starr County, they tried to take control of the bridge to stop the recruitment of undocumented workers to break the strike. Texas Rangers then made mass arrests. On September 30, 1967, a hurricane destroyed the citrus crop, depressing labor conditions and ending all hope of success. Chávez pulled back, saying that the strike had been premature in Texas. Chávez did not have the liberal support that the farmworkers had had in California.[61] Moreover, Texas growers were not as vulnerable to a secondary boycott. Chávez left Antonio Orendain, 37, in charge of membership and placement services in Texas. The strike was supported by Archbishop Robert Lucey of San Antonio, and the congressional hearings drew attention to the Third World–like conditions in the Valley. Throughout the strike, the Rangers and the state bureaucratic establishment favored the growers.

Inspired by the *campesino* (farmworker) movement in California, and more directly by the events in Texas such as the takeover of Crystal City in 1963, Chicano activism increased in the Midwest during the second half of the 1960s. Twenty-two-year-old Jesús Salas, a native of Crystal City, Texas, led Texas-Mexican cucumber workers in Wisconsin. In January 1967, Salas organized an independent farmworkers' union called *Obreros Unidos* (United Workers) of Wisconsin. The organization remained active throughout that year and the next and published *La Voz del Pueblo*. Financial difficulties and the loss of support of the AFL–CIO led to the end of *Obreros Unidos* in 1970.[62] (The student movement in the Midwest was rooted in Texas and influenced by the 1963 Chicano takeover of Crystal City. Leaders such as Salas joined the migrant stream and took memories with them as they confronted racism.)[63]

Michigan used more migrant workers than any other northern state. Led by Rubén Alfaro—a barber from Lansing—migrants, labor, and students from Michigan State marched to Governor George Romney, hoping to get a commitment from him to support their crusade and veto any legislation that would "take away the human dignity of the migrant workers." Michigan attracted more than 100,000 migrants during the harvest season. Romney refused to take a stand. The migrants were supported by the AFL–CIO "in their crusade for better pay, housing, medical care and education for the migrants' children." Alfaro garnered the support of César Chávez and the United Farm Workers (UFW), and of U.S. Senator Robert F. Kennedy, who sent a telegram that ended with the words "*Viva La Causa!*" They marched from Saginaw to Lansing, announcing, "Governor, our feet are sore . . . Some of us have walked more than 70 miles to tell you about our problems," and handed the lieutenant governor their petition. A news reporter described the scene:

> They held American and Mexican flags, and banners depicting the Virgin of Guadalupe—revered saint of Mexico. Hand-lettered signs carried such slogans as "Viva La Causa," "Human Dignity for Migrant Workers" and "Chicken Coops are for the Bird."[64]

In 1967 in Ohio, Mexican farmworkers demanded better wages and enforcement of health and housing codes. Some 18,000–20,000 Mexicans worked in Wallace County, Ohio, and throughout the tomato belt that encircled northwest Ohio, southern Michigan, and northern Indiana. Hunt, Campbell Soup, Libby, McNeil, Vlasic, and Heinz controlled production. Baldemar Velásquez, 21, and his father organized a march in 1968 from Leipsic, Ohio, to the Libby tomato plant and a later march to the Campbell Soup plant. They established a newspaper, *Nuestra Lucha* (Our Struggle), and a weekly radio program. In 1968, the Farm Labor Organizing Committee (FLOC) signed 22 contracts with small growers.[65]

Meanwhile, in the Pacific Northwest *La Raza* was mobilizing against economic injustices. During the peak of the harvesting season, as many as 25,000 migrant Mexicans resided in the state of Washington. Migrant children attended only 21 weeks of school, and the Washington Citizens for Migrant Affairs pointed out that the migrant family had a median of five years of education. The heart of the migrant community was in the agriculturally rich Yakima Valley, where in 1965 the Yakima Valley Council for Community Action (YVCCA) was organized to coordinate War on Poverty programs. The next year, Tomás Villanueva and Guadalupe Gamboa from Yakima Valley College traveled to California where they met with César Chávez. Subsequently, in 1967 Villanueva helped organize the first Chicano activist organization in Washington. The Mexican American Federation was organized that year in Yakima, to advocate for community development and political empowerment in the Yakima Valley. In May 1967, Big Bend Community College raised expectations by receiving a $500,000 grant for the basic education of 200 migrants.[66]

The Road to Brown Power

In 1968, 91 percent of the students enrolled in institutions of higher learning in the United States were white, 6 percent were African American, and just less than 2 percent were Latinos; probably less than half that number were of Mexican origin. Chicanos did not begin to enroll in college in significant numbers until after 1968 following the school walkouts in California and Texas. What set them apart from other students was that most were from working-class families and first-generation college students. The Chicano student revolt beginning in that year challenged and rattled the tactics of middle-class Mexican American organizations.

The first challenge to the old guard by Chicano students came from Texas, where students organized in Kingsville at Texas A&I University in 1964. José Angel Gutiérrez, Ambriocio Meléndez, and Gabriel Tafoya, among others, formed the A&I student group, focusing on the usual issues of admission discrimination, segregated dorms, and poor housing. Organizers emphasized forging a Mexican student community in order to develop broader political power among the Mexican student community as a whole. In 1964, A&I Mexican students attended the PASO state convention; there they met with other Mexican students with similar goals. The students successfully lowered the eligibility age for PASO membership from 21 to 18.[67]

Tejano students formed MAYO at St. Mary's College in San Antonio in 1967. They were energized by PASO's 1963 Crystal City takeover. It was PASO's involvement in La Casita Farms Corporation strike of 1966 in the Rio Grande Valley that Tejano historian David Montejano calls the catalyst for the Chicano movement in Texas—especially for Mexican American students from Texas A&I and future MAYO leaders throughout the state. It was in the heat of the Casitas strike in the spring of 1967 that MAYO was formed in San Antonio. The organizers included José Angel Gutiérrez, Nacho Pérez, Mario Compeán, and Willie Velásquez. Most of the founders were graduate students at St. Mary's College; they were well aware of Student Nonviolent Coordinating Committee (SNCC), strategies of its leader Stokely Carmichael, the Students for a Democratic Society (SDS), and the Port Huron statement. MAYO played a pivotal role in bringing about civil rights for Mexican Americans and developed a master plan to take over boards of education and city councils throughout south Texas. Soon after its formation, other university and high school students started MAYO chapters, mostly as a result of planned high school walkouts beginning in the spring of 1968 and extending into the 1970s. The strategy was to build a cadre of organizers using charismatic leaders from the various school districts and establish beachheads in the campaign to seize political control. As the more than three dozen school walkouts rocked Texas, MAYO formed local chapters, which attracted Chicanas such as Choco Meza, Rosie Castro, Juanita Bustamante, Viviana Santiago, and Luz Bazán Gutiérrez who played leadership roles and helped build consensus in MAYO and later in *La Raza Unida* (the United Race) Party.[68]

MAYO differed from Mexican American student organizations in California. For example, in the mid-1960s there were few Chicano college students in California and elsewhere in the Southwest, whereas Texas, comparatively speaking, had a larger number of second-, third-, and fourth-generation students attending college. In 1964, there were about 1,030 Chicano students, or 25 percent of the total student body, at Texas A&I—not a significant number, but in relation to California or Colorado, for example, substantial. By contrast, San Fernando Valley State (now California State University at Northridge) had less than a dozen

Chicanos. Rampant discrimination and enforced social constraints unified Chicanos at Texas A&I. Though not ideologically united, they socialized together, eventually forming informal networks. This pattern was also evident at other universities, where racism encouraged group organizing. By marked contrast, California institutions favored a dispersion of Mexican students until about 1967.[69]

The next challenge came from California, where Mexican American youth were the most urbanized in the Southwest and thus were subject to fewer institutional and social constraints. When California youth entered the Chicano movement, they did not have to deal with large entrenched organizations such as the American G.I. Forum or LULAC. However, the black and white radical student movements as well as the farmworker movements around them politicized California students. They listened to radio broadcasts teeming with music of social protest. By the mid-1960s, youth in California had become more politically aware—partly because of the national youth revolution and partly because the Mexican American movement itself pushed educational issues to the forefront.

By 1967, more students of Mexican origin filtered into the colleges. That year, students at East Los Angeles Community College formed the Mexican American Student Association (MASA) and on May 13, 1967, Chicano students met at Loyola University (Los Angeles) and founded the United Mexican American Students (UMAS). Most were first-generation college students; most were the children of immigrants.[70] On December 16–17, 1967, the second general UMAS conference was held at the University of Southern California campus.

A majority of Chicano students identified with the UFW; its successes and tribulations became their own. On campus, they joined with the black student movement and the SDS. By the spring of 1969, Chicano college student organizations were beginning to spread throughout California. Priority issues included public education, access to universities, Mexican American studies programs, and the Vietnam War. Speakers such as Corky Gonzales[71] and Reies López Tijerina[72] added to the momentum.

Simultaneously, Chicano student associations formed throughout the country—in places like Tucson, Phoenix, Seattle, and the Midwest—in large part motivated by the UFW boycott and the alienation on campus.[73] In 1968, Alfredo Gutiérrez, who had been with the grape boycott since 1965 and a student at Arizona State University at Tempe, along with graduate student Miguel Montiel, led the Mexican American Student Organization (MASO). Early members included María Rose Garrido and Christine Marín. MASO developed strong ties with Gustavo Gutiérrez and the Arizona Farm. In 1967, in Tucson, Arizona, Salomón Baldenegro, a student with a strong sense of justice and identification with the Civil Rights, antiwar, and labor movements, organized the Mexican American Liberation Committee at the University of Arizona, where he recruited Raúl Grijalva, Isabel García, and Guadalupe Castillo, who were high school students; the committee advocated bilingual and Mexican culture classes. This organization evolved into the Mexican American Student Association (MASA).[74]

In New Mexico, students at Highlands University organized to demand the end of the suppression of Spanish, history classes that reflected the Mexican American experience, more Mexican American teachers, and school counseling programs. By 1968 the protests were taking place against the schools at Albuquerque, Las Vegas, Española, Portales, Roswell, and Santa Fe. That year the Brown Berets and the Black Berets began operating in Albuquerque. The same year in the northern part of the state, *El Grito del Norte* began publication.[75] Also MAYA (later the Chicano Youth Association) began to appear on campuses. Meanwhile, small numbers of Chicano students began filtering into the colleges of the Pacific Northwest and Midwest.

The Making of a Movement

In California and elsewhere the Educational Opportunity Program (EOP) gave Chicanas and Chicanos a tremendous boost; as mentioned, before 1968 colleges could count the number of Chicano students in the dozens. For the first time, many received financial aid and were recruited to go to college—much the same way as athletes were. The added presence of Chicano youth on campuses nurtured the considerable discontent festering in the *barrios* themselves. On the campuses and in the *barrios*, the injustice of the Vietnam War added to the air of urgency. As mentioned, many white and black students were from middle-class backgrounds and thus were very much involved with the Civil Rights and antiwar movements. Many of the white student radicals were red diaper babies, that is, their parents had been involved in radical politics;

many African American students had been involved through their churches. The political involvement of Chicano students was new.

The Vietnam War split many Mexican American organizations, with those opposing the war being accused of unpatriotic motives and even cowardliness. In California in 1966, largely through the work of peace activists, the MAPA executive board passed a resolution condemning the war in Vietnam. In Texas, Chicano public leaders such as Commissioner Albert Peña, Jr., State Senator Joe Bernal, Representative Henry B. González, and Archbishop Robert Lucey opposed the war by 1967, although Hector García of the G.I. Forum continued to support LBJ, sending representatives to the airport to greet the coffins of dead Mexican Americans.

As with the movement as a whole, the 1960s' *veteranos/veteranas* worked alongside recent converts and aided the socialization process. Dolores Huerta became vice president of the UFW, while East Los Angeles Chicana activists like Julia Luna Mount and her sister Celia Luna de Rodríguez, active since the 1930s, continued working for social change. Luna de Rodríguez, a key organizer in the Barrio Defense Committee, spoke out against police abuse. Julia Luna Mount, active in the 40th Assembly District chapter of MAPA, often criticized MAPA leadership. Julia was a driving force in the antiwar movement even before the mid-1960s. She unsuccessfully ran for the Los Angeles School Board in 1967, and was a founding member of the Peace and Freedom Party. Her daughter Tanya was a leader in the 1968 East LA school walkouts.[76]

The Formation of Core Groups

Beginning in 1963, the Los Angeles County Human Relations Commission—staffed by Richard Villalobos, Mike Durán, and others—sponsored annual Chicano junior high and high school student conferences, which pushed identity politics. The commission conducted seminars and invited speakers to motivate student leaders. At these sessions, students not only discussed identity but also compared the grievances they had against their schools. For example, Chicanos had a high school dropout rate of over 50 percent: 53.8 percent of Chicanos dropped out at Garfield and 47.5 at Roosevelt. Many of the seminar participants went on to become leaders in the 1968 student walkouts. High school students such as Vicki Castro, Jorge Licón, John Ortiz, David Sánchez, Rachel Ochoa, and Moctesuma Esparza attended the 1966 conference at Camp Hess Kramer, sponsored by the County Human Relations Commission. These students formed the Young Citizens for Community Action (YCCA) in May 1966. In 1967, the Young Citizens worked for the election of Julian Nava to the Los Angeles School Board.

Student leader David Sánchez was recruited to go to Father John B. Luce's Social Action Training Center at the Church of the Epiphany (Episcopal) in Lincoln Heights. The center was associated with the CSO. Luce introduced Sánchez to Richard Alatorre, a staff member with the Los Angeles Community Services Program, who helped him get an appointment to the Mayor's Youth Council. Moctesuma Esparza, another veteran of the Hess Kramer conference, was also a member. Meanwhile, other members of the Youth Council became politicized by the Training Center, and by meeting people like César Chávez. This transition is reflected in the name change of their organization to the Young Chicanos for Community Action.

Also emerging from the Church of the Epiphany's advocacy efforts was the *La Raza* (The Race, or The People) newspaper, founded by Eleazar Risco, a Cuban national. Risco helped publish *El Malcriado,* the farmworker newspaper. Risco arrived in Los Angeles in 1967 to help organize a grape boycott and soon afterward formed the Barrio Communications Project. Although it had a populist flavor, *La Raza* had a clear focus on *barrio* issues.[77] Father Luce's Social Action Training Center attracted other activists, such as Lincoln Heights Teen Post director Carlos Montes.

The East LA Walkouts

By the 1968–1969 academic year, Latino students in East Los Angeles made up 96 percent of Garfield High School, 83 percent of Roosevelt, 89 percent of Lincoln, 76 percent of Wilson, and 59 percent of Belmont. Sal Castro, a teacher at Lincoln High School who was well known among students, helped them articulate their discontent. As early as September 1967, Castro spoke to students at the Piranya Coffee House about the failure of the schools to provide quality education, access to the latest college prep courses, and counseling. By early 1968, the group formed the Brown Berets, led by David Sánchez. Their goal was to put an end to the discrimination and other injustices suffered by Chicano students. Meanwhile, the Los Angeles sheriff's department harassed them; consequently, the Berets led demonstrations against the police. Sánchez was arrested at a February 20, 1968 demonstration, following which he spent 60 days at Wayside Maximum-Security facility.

Meanwhile, high school and college students held strategy sessions and discussions on the blowout (walkout). As a result of Castro's involvement, the students articulated clear demands. Castro, during the planning stages of the blowouts, worked very closely with UMAS students, who were a bridge to the high school students.

Castro had been in trouble at Belmont High in 1963, when he encouraged Mexican-origin students to form a slate and run for student government. When the slate won, administrators accused Castro of being divisive for telling the students to say a couple of words in Spanish—as John F. Kennedy had done at Olvera Street during his presidential campaign. The transfer of Castro from Belmont to Lincoln High had caused community uproar. School officials thought that Castro and not the schools were the problem.[78]

In March 1968, nearly 10,000 Chicano students walked out of five Los Angeles high schools—Lincoln, Roosevelt, Garfield, Wilson, and Belmont. Following their example, students at Jefferson, a predominantly black school, also walked out. Although high school students formed the core of the walkouts, Chicana college students like Vicki Castro from California State University, Los Angeles, and Rosalinda Méndez (later González) from Occidental College, as well as the leaders of UMAS chapters, also provided leadership. Tanya Luna Mount, a student organizer at Roosevelt High School and a junior, encouraged her fellow students to boycott; she witnessed and wrote about the senseless overreaction of police. Paula Cristóstomo, a senior at Lincoln High who had previously attended the Camp Hess Kramer Youth Conference, and Margarita Mita Cuarón, a sophomore at Garfield High School, urged students to walk out. Police targeted the Brown Berets, who were present only for security, using them as a pretext to brutally suppress the walkout participants. (One of the leaders, Moctesuma Esparza, produced a film, *Walkout* (2006), memorializing the events.)[79]

Prior to the walkout, the school system pushed out more than 50 percent of the Chicano high school students, through either expulsion or transfers to other schools. Eastside schools were overcrowded and run down compared with Euro-American and black schools. The students demanded that racist teachers be removed, charging that school authorities had implemented a curriculum that purposely obscured the Chicanos' culture and programmed students to be content with low-skilled jobs. In 1967, only 3 percent of the teachers and 1.3 percent of administrators had Spanish surnames, and many of these were white women married to Latinos. Whites made up 78 percent of the teachers, 91.4 percent of the administrators, and 54 percent of the students—more than 20 percent of the students were Latinos. Chicano community leaders and supporters formed the Educational Issues Coordinating Committee (EICC) to defend the students and to follow up on their demands.

It was clear that sheriffs' deputies and police had overreacted and treated the protests as insurrections. Police authorities wanted to make an example of Mexican Americans and control and subjugate them. Many activists were caught by surprise; moderates began to question the fairness of the justice system and were radicalized by the events. They were moved by Sal Castro, who said he had walked out with his students because in good conscience he could not remain inside the school knowing that the demands of his students were legitimate.[80]

On June 2, 1968, a Los Angeles grand jury indicted Castro and other activists on charges that included conspiracy to commit misdemeanors. (After two years of appeals, the courts found the counts unconstitutional.)[81] The California Department of Education attempted to revoke Castro's credentials, and he was subjected to frequent and arbitrary administrative transfers. Meanwhile, on September 1968, several thousand protesters, led by the EICC, marched in front of Lincoln High School, demanding Castro's reinstatement to Lincoln. During these confrontations, unexpected help came from the presidential campaign of Robert Kennedy, who met with Chicano leaders. Kennedy hired enlightened Chicanas such as Lupe Anguiano and Polly Baca for his campaign staff, and he was one of the few politicos of any race to reach out to youth.[82]

Chicana/o Student Militancy Spreads

The Los Angeles walkouts, because of the size of the blowouts and the location, called national attention to the Chicanos' plight in education, and encouraged other walkouts throughout the Southwest and the Midwest. On March 20, 1968, students walked out of classes at Denver's West Side High School. They made demands for Mexican teachers, counselors, and courses, as well as for better facilities. Twenty-five people were arrested, including Corky Gonzales.

The perfect storm hit Texas as more than 50 separate walkouts of students occurred. As mentioned, MAYO agitated throughout Texas from the spring of 1968 through the early 1970s. The first walkout in Texas occurred at Lanier High School in San Antonio on April 9, 1968. The student council elections triggered the strike when teachers did not approve the nominees and suspended student council member Elida Aguilar for insubordination. Willie Velásquez of MAYO persuaded the students to form a coordinating committee and to incorporate larger concerns into their demands. Seven hundred students walked out demanding more academic courses, the right to speak Spanish, and more democracy. More pungent was the students' demand for Mexican American history and culture classes. The importance of the walkouts was that they generated considerable community support. Among early supporters were the Neighborhood Youth Corps, the Bishops' Committee for the Spanish Speaking, State Senator Joe Bernal, County Commissioner Alberto Peña, and Councilman Felix Treviño.[83] Peña received a standing ovation when he said "We're handicapped because we have an educational system that doesn't understand bilingual students."[84]

On May 16, students rose once again against racist administrators. A young Willie Velásquez—then a graduate student at St. Mary's University, and later an activist who would earn a national reputation—exhorted the students:

> With the education you get at Edgewood, most of you are going to wind up either in Vietnam or as a ditchdigger. . . . At Jefferson, Alamo Heights or Lee, there is a chance that you'll go to college. But 85 per cent of you will not go—$80 a week is the most you will earn the rest of your life. . . . Tell Stemhauser this is the problem.[85]

The walkout was 80 percent effective. The students ended the boycott on Sunday, May 19, to show that they were not walking out on education.[86] Fundamental to the strike was the district's inability to attract qualified teachers. The all-Mexican Edgewood High spent $356 per student annually versus $594 at Alamo Heights, which was predominantly white. On June 30, Demetro Rodríguez, Martin Cantú, Reynaldo Castañono, and Alberta Snid filed a suit against San Antonio in the federal district court citing the inequality in funding.[87]

Meanwhile, MAYO based its campaign on a brand of Tejano nationalism calculated to take political control of south Texas. Tejano nationalism was based on the Texas experience: a blend of Mexican history, family values, Tejano music, and the Spanish language.[88] The next stepping stone was at Edcouch-Elsa High (and middle) school in Hidalgo County, a town of less than 10,000. This was the first student strike in the rural Rio Grande Valley.[89] Chicano students there suffered numerous indignities. By mid-October 1968, students and parents began informal meetings, with a few MAYO members, VISTA volunteers, and PASO members in attendance. The chair was Jesús Ramírez, a MAYO member. It was supported by State Senator Joe Bernal, and Dr. Hector García, the founder of the G.I. Forum, was present. On November 13, the students rose from their desks and walked out. The school officials bypassed the local police and reported the walkout to county sheriffs, who arrested the walkout leaders. Meanwhile, the superintendent suspended 168 students for three days.[90] Here again students objected to the "No Spanish" rule and wanted classes on Mexican American contributions to Texas history. The students demanded courses and counseling that would prepare them for college. They demanded an end to discrimination.[91] When the students were expelled, the recently organized Mexican American Legal Defense and Education Fund (MALDEF) filed a suit, and board policy was ruled unconstitutional.[92]

According to José Angel Gutiérrez, MAYO led or participated in at least 39 walkouts before the December 1969 Crystal City walkout. Beachheads were established at these venues with local MAYO members leading walkouts in communities where they grew up. The walkouts hit a common nerve that many of the adults identified with. They demanded the right to speak Spanish, the right to learn about Mexican American history, the right to get a quality education, and schools that were free of discrimination. The walkouts made the movement—they had brought to the surface the community's moral outrage.

On May 5, 1970, Chicano students walked out of Delano Joint Union High School in the San Joaquín Valley of California. Protest was centered on the denial of a Chicano speaker at an assembly. On May 7, police encircled the school. The walkout lasted till the end of the school year. Police arrested the strikers when they attempted to enter graduation ceremonies; protesters were beaten up and dragged into padded wagons.[93] The perfect storm, which spread throughout the Southwest, had a tremendous impact on the participants; many of the students remained activists and went on to receive higher education.

The Brown Berets and White Angst

Law enforcement authorities actually believed that the Brown Berets were capable of overthrowing the government—or perhaps they used it as an excuse. The police and sheriff's departments in Los Angeles harassed, intimidated, and persecuted the Brown Berets, a treatment that few other Chicano organizations have experienced in recent times. Police and sheriff's deputies raided the Berets, infiltrated them, libeled and slandered them, and even encouraged countergroups to attack members. The objective was to destroy the Berets and to invalidate them in the public eye.

They branded members as outside agitators while playing down the legitimate grievances of Chicano students. A grand jury later indicted 13 Chicanos on conspiracy charges stemming from the walkouts; 7 were Brown Berets. The defendants appealed, and the appellate court ruled the case unconstitutional, but only after years of legal harassment.

Law enforcement agencies infiltrated the Berets with informers and special agents in order to entrap the members by encouraging acts of violence. Police purposely subverted the Berets, keeping them in a state of flux and preventing the organization from solidifying. Berets dealt with the immediate needs of the *barrios*—food, housing, employment, and education. The conflict and the street molded their ideology. On May 23, 1969, the Berets began publishing a monthly newspaper called *La Causa* (The Cause) to attract new members. Chicanas, such as Gloria Arellanes, the Brown Berets' Minister of Finance and Correspondence, played key roles in the establishment and operation of *La Causa*. Arellanes, along with Andrea Sánchez, organized a free medical clinic that Chicana members of the Berets ran. (Other Beret chapters also established free clinics and free breakfast programs.) The clinic raised issues of sex equality that strained relations between Sánchez and other women, eventually leading to a schism; these women left the Berets.[94]

Brown Berets chapters spread through the Mexican *barrios* of San Antonio, Albuquerque, El Paso, Denver, Seattle, and San Diego—indeed, no one yet knows how many *barrios* had chapters, only that the chapters were small.[95] However, to white America they were the symbols of Brown Power and terrorism. It is unimaginable how reasonable people could see young men and women wearing their brown berets and khaki uniforms and be struck with so much terror and exaggerate their numbers. Texas A&M graduate student Jennifer G. Correa obtained 1,200 pages of Federal Bureau of Investigation (FBI) Surveillance Files, focusing on East Los Angeles, under the Freedom of Information Act. The documents reveal, among other information, that in 1968 FBI Director J. Edgar Hoover had decided to fully investigate the Brown Berets in order to find out if they were a "threat to national security of the United States," admonishing agents in Sacramento and San Diego for not gathering enough information on the Berets. Agents responded that the Berets were under "continuous and aggressive investigative attention." Considering the small numbers of Berets, the FBI reaction can only be labeled as delusional, and their actions as an abuse of authority, since they were directed at spying and controlling a movement.

This abuse mirrored the fears of American society. As late as July 1, 1976, the *Syracuse Herald-Journal* in New York carried headlines such as "Brown Beret Alert Cancelled: Police Playing Down Border Terrorist Warning." The *Herald-Journal* warned its readers about the Brown Berets, a little-known, but according to the newspaper, a heavily armed radical group that reportedly vowed "to kill a cop." Brown Berets were allegedly driving around the East Coast in broad daylight in vans. According to the article, the New York state troopers were in touch with the FBI concerning the Berets and their possible threat to the Montreal Olympics.[96]

Tlatelolco, Mexico

On October 2, 1968, in the Tlatelolco (once an Azteca stronghold) district of Mexico City—just 10 days before the opening of the XIX Olympiad—a massacre occurred, which resulted in a tightening of the Chicanos' emotional bonds with Mexico. Soldiers and riot police opened fire on a demonstration held by thousands of citizens, killing hundreds, if not thousands, of Mexicans, most of them students. The Mexican government tried to play down the slaughter, claiming that "only" a dozen or so were killed; estimates put the figure at more than 500 dead or missing.

Student activists exposed the atrocities in documentaries such as *The Frozen Revolution,* which were played in classrooms and halls throughout the United States. *La matanza* (the massacre) led to movements such as that of Rosario Ibarra, who demanded to know the fate of the more than 500 *desaparecidos* (the disappeared), including her son. Chicano youth supported the Mexicans' struggle, and students hung posters reviving memories of Tlatelolco and, even farther back, the Mexican Revolution. Tlatelolco added to the anger and experiences of Chicano youth, who identified with the Mexican youth.[97]

"Wild Tribes of . . . the Inner Mountains of Mexico"

On January 27, 1960, Los Angeles Police Chief William Parker testified before the U.S. Civil Rights Commission: "Some of these people [Mexicans] were here before we were but some are not far removed from the wild tribes of the district of the inner mountains of Mexico." It caused an uproar, but Police Commissioner R. J. Carreón, Jr., said that he had heard Parker's story and ordered the Mexican American community to drop the controversy. Local newspapers excused Parker, and they even went as far as to censure Edward R. Roybal for demanding an apology and/or Parker's resignation, accusing Roybal of demagoguery.

Parker's racist attitude was replicated in many instances of police brutality in the succeeding years. In 1966, for example, the Los Angeles police called for a backup team when an angry crowd gathered as police attempted to make an arrest. Police fired two warning shots into the crowd. In July, the Happy Valley Parents Association organized a monitoring of police. In September of that year, the American Civil Liberties Union (ACLU), in cooperation with the CSO, opened a center in East Los Angeles. (From September 1966 to July 1968, the ACLU investigated 205 police abuse cases of which 152 were filed by Chicanos.)[98]

In the summer of 1967 some 300 Chicanos attended a conference on police–community relations at Camp Hess Kramer. Police–community relations in Los Angeles reached a new low, and the participants asked the federal government to intervene. The failure of the federal government to protect the rights of the community worsened the situation. Meanwhile, political consciousness increased throughout California. Older activists of MAPA, CSO, LULAC, and the American G.I. Forum, as well as youth, professionals, and poverty workers, criticized the schools and the government's treatment of Mexican Americans. Many new organizations such as the Association of Mexican American Educators (AMEA, 1965) and UMAS (1967) advertised the community's frustrations. Mexican Americans, concerned about their lack of gains made in comparison with African Americans, insisted that more attention be paid to their needs. Nationalism expressed itself as a pride in identity and a rejection of assimilation as a goal.[99]

Meanwhile, tensions rose even higher as the Vietnam War sabotaged Lyndon Johnson's "Great Society" programs. By 1966, the government's commitment to ending poverty was sliding backward; it spent $22 billion on the war in Southeast Asia compared with about $1.5 billion to fight poverty. Nevertheless, as late as 1967, Hector P. García assured LBJ that, "As far as I know, the majority, if not the total Mexican American people, approve of your present course of action in Vietnam."[100]

Gringos and Tejanos

On March 30, 1969, some 2,000 Chicanos assembled at San Felipe Del Rio (about 160 miles west of San Antonio) to protest Governor Preston Smith's cancellation of a VISTA program. Smith had canceled the program because VISTA workers participated in a demonstration against the police beatings of Uvalde resident Natividad Fuentes and his wife. The G.I. Forum, LULAC, and other organizations supported the mass rally.

José Angel Gutiérrez, 24, a MAYO speaker at Del Rio, demanded reinstatement of the VISTA program and protested inequality, poverty, and police brutality throughout Texas. At the rally Gutiérrez said, "We are fed up. We are going to move to do away with the injustices to the Chicano and if the 'gringo' doesn't get out of our way, we will stampede over him." Gutiérrez gave vent to his anger with the gringo establishment at a press conference and called upon Chicanos to "Kill the gringo," by which he meant that the white rule of Mexicans should end, and not literally killing the white people. Nevertheless, Representative Henry B. González from San Antonio called for a grand jury investigation of MAYO and attacked Gutiérrez.[101]

Gutiérrez was a product of Texas culture—a Confederate state with a tradition of southern racism and historical exclusion of Mexican Americans. Texans had never come to grips with the fact that Mexicans had won at the Alamo. Texas also spawned national leaders of the Ku Klux Klan and the White Citizens Council. In the 1960s, whites could still count on the Texas Rangers to keep Mexicans in their place in south Texas, one of the most deprived regions of the country. Gutiérrez and the "we've had enough" rhetoric appealed to many Chicanas/os that society marginalized. Ranger Joaquín Jackson, a long-time adversary, says of Gutiérrez, "He radiated cunning, resourcefulness, intelligence, and charisma. A tireless worker and a gifted, passionate speaker, he was further armed with the conviction that he was right." In his book, Jackson also acknowledges the merit of the Chicano grievances against the system.[102]

Tex-Mexicans lived in a string of dusty, neglected towns on the "wrong side of the tracks." Mexican Americans resented their status and poverty. The intensity of racism fostered nationalism among them, causing frustration at the moderate way older organizations such as LULAC and the G.I. Forum dealt with the gringo establishment. A nucleus of Chicano students was tired of being docile; they knew what black militancy had achieved, and they were influenced not only by the black literature of the time but also by a handful of progressive white professors. José Angel Gutiérrez was one of the leaders who expressed the frustrations of the MAYO generation. His contribution to the Chicano cause was indispensable; it influenced Chicanos throughout the country.[103]

On June 20, 1969, Luz Bazán Gutiérrez,[104] José Angel Gutiérrez, and several young volunteers moved to Angel's hometown of Crystal City (population 8,500), Texas, to organize politically and launch the Winter Garden Project (WGP), which was oriented toward community control and committed to the decolonization of south Texas. Although Chicanos composed more than 85 percent of its Winter Garden area, a white minority, who owned 95 percent of the land, controlled the city's politics. The agribusiness income in Dummit, La Salle, and Zavala Counties totaled about $31 million; yet, in Zavala County, the median family income was $1,754 a year. The median years of education was 2.3 grades for Chicanos. More than 70 percent of the Chicano students dropped out of Crystal City High School. School authorities vigorously enforced a "no-Spanish" rule. Few Mexicans held offices or were professionals; those who received an education moved away. Euro-Americans considered themselves racially and culturally superior to Chicanos. The Texas Rangers patrolled the area, terrorizing Mexicans. Adding to the plight of the Chicanos, a substantial number of them were migrants who had to follow the crops. Many Mexicans routinely left the Winter Garden area in late spring and did not return until the fall. Small hamlets of the region became ghost towns during this period.

A school crisis at Crystal City in November 1969 gave the young volunteers the ideal issue with which to confront the gringo. Although Chicanos comprised the majority of students in the system, school policy excluded them from participating in much of the extracurricular activities. When students complained, the school board ignored them, refusing to even discuss the grievances. Left with no other alternative, parents and students organized a school boycott in December. Student leader Severita Lara published and distributed leaflets and agitated the students. Here again, polemics played a role in agitating parents, and MAYO and the Gutiérrezes were an indispensable part of this discourse on political vocabulary building. Over 1,700 Chicano students participated in the walkout; the students and their parents formed a citizens' organization and decided that Mexicans would take over the school board in the spring election of 1970.[105]

Meanwhile, during the first quarter of 1970, La Raza Unida Party (LRUP) emerged from the citizen action group. Intensive mobilization took place, and in April 1970, LRUP won four of the seven seats on the Crystal City Board of Education; all of the Chicano candidates for city councils in Carrizo Springs, Cotula, and Crystal City were also elected. Cotula also had its first Chicano mayor. The box score for Chicanos in the Winter Garden area was 15 elected with two new mayors, two school board majorities, and two city council majorities. Only one gringo won election. The *Cristal* (Crystal City) victory used the MAYO Plan for Aztlán as a template. They intended to use Cristal as the linchpin across the "Accordion Trail"—the migrants' trail from Texas throughout the Midwest and Northwest—to spread their political revolt.[106]

The Land Struggle

The history of the land grant is rooted in the past. In this system, the holding of land and the peasant farmers' place in the society were central to their identification and social status. The *ejido* (communal land) operated alongside private grants to individuals, with villages holding common lands such as forests or pastures. The community of peasants collectively owned the common land. The *ejido* has been romanticized in Mexican history on both sides of the border, with historical figures such as Emiliano Zapata immortalized for calling for the redistribution of *latifundio* (a large plantation) lands to the peasants. New Mexicans also idealized the collective ownership of communal lands and lamented the loss of ancestral acreage.

The U.S. conquest marked an end to this way of life, as private developers took control of the water, common lands, and finally the villagers' farms. Memories of the past remained strong in the minds of many New Mexicans, who alleged that the gringo had taken the land from them in violation of the Treaty of Guadalupe Hidalgo (1848). Emotions run high to this day.

In 1963, local activist Reies López Tijerina formed *La Alianza Federal de Mercedes* (The Federal Alliance of Land Grants), invoking the Treaty of Guadalupe in the struggle to hold on to common lands. The *Alianza*'s membership jumped from 6,000 in 1964 to 14,000 one year later. A basic premise of the *Alianza*'s demands was that people don't "give away" their lands or rights in treaties. For them, forcing a defeated nation to "sell" territory under duress was intrinsically unjust.

Reies López Tijerina was born in 1926, in Fall City, Texas, where his family lived a marginal existence. Tijerina became a preacher and wandered into northern New Mexico, where he witnessed the poverty of the people. *El Tigre* (the Tiger), as Tijerina was called, became interested in the land-grant question. He studied the Treaty of Guadalupe Hidalgo and became convinced that the national forest in Tierra Amarilla belonged to the Pueblo de San Joaquín de Chama. *Ejido* land belonged to the people in common and could not be sold. Villagers had the right to graze their animals and cut and gather timber in the forestlands.[107]

The Forest Service through the early 1960s had strictly restricted the number of cattle permitted to graze in forestlands. For dryland ranchers, having a permit was a matter of life and death. During the first part of the decade, *Alianza* members staged protests, petitioned government, appealed to public opinion, and sought alliances with African Americans and Native Americans among others. The *Alianza* raised the cry of "*Tierra y Libertad!*" (Land and Liberty!).

On October 15, 1966, Tijerina and 350 *Alianza* members occupied the Echo Amphitheater in the national forest campground, claiming the *ejido* rights of the Pueblo de San Joaquín de Chama. On October 22, *Alianza* members made a citizen's arrest and detained two Rangers for trespassing and being a public nuisance. The "*Alianza* court" found them guilty but suspended the sentence.

After Tijerina was charged with illegal trespassing on national forest land and other crimes, 20 *Alianza* members entered Tierra Amarilla to make a citizen's arrest of District Attorney Alfonso Sánchez. In doing so, the members wounded a jailer. The government sent 200 military vehicles (including tanks), almost 400 soldiers, and scores of police and lawmen to hunt down Tijerina. On November 6, 1967, Tijerina stood trial. A jury convicted him of two counts of assault, and the judge sentenced him to two years in a state penitentiary. Tijerina immediately appealed the verdict.

In May and June of 1968, Tijerina participated in the Poor People's Campaign, threatening to pull the Chicano contingent out if black organizers did not treat them as equals. In the fall, he ran for governor of New Mexico on the People's Constitutional Party ticket. In mid-February 1969, the Court of Appeals for the Tenth Circuit upheld the Amphitheater conviction; Tijerina's lawyer immediately appealed to the Supreme Court.[108] In June, *El Tigre* again attempted to occupy the Kit Carson National Forest at the Coyote Campsite. Tijerina stood trial in late 1968 for the Tierra Amarilla raid and acted in his own defense. Much of the trial centered on the right to make a citizen's arrest. Tijerina proved his point, and the jury entered a verdict of not guilty.

The higher court denied Tijerina's appeal on the Amphitheater case, and Tijerina went to prison. For seven months, prison authorities kept him in isolation. Tijerina became a symbol, convicted of political crimes rather than crimes against "society." Authorities released him in the summer of 1971.

The Crusade for Justice

Rodolfo "Corky" Gonzales symbolized the struggle for control of the urban *barrios*. Born in Denver on June 18, 1928, the son of migrant sugar beet workers, Gonzales grew up the hard way—using his fists. A Golden Gloves champion who turned professional, he was a featherweight contender from 1947 to 1955. He later started a bail bonds business and opened an auto insurance agency. During the 1960s, Gonzales became increasingly critical of the system. In 1963, he organized *Los Voluntarios* (The Volunteers), who protested against police brutality. Two years later he became a director of Denver's War on Poverty youth programs, but he was fired for his involvement in the Albuquerque EEOC walkout. He published his own newspaper, *El Gallo: La Voz de la Justicia* (The Rooster: The Voice of Justice).

Gonzales's epic poem, "I Am Joaquín," was the most influential piece of Chicano movement literature written in the 1960s. Luis Valdez of the Teatro Campesino made the poem into a film documentary. Conditions differed in *barrios* such as those in Denver and Los Angeles, where an identity crisis had developed after World War II. Corky Gonzales understood and summed up this identity crisis in his poem.

Gonzales went on to form a new Denver advocacy organization called the Crusade for Justice; it operated a school, a curio shop, a bookstore, and a social center. The Denver school, named *Tlatelolco: La Plaza de las Tres Culturas* (Tlatelolco: The Plaza of the Three Cultures), had about 200 students, from preschool to college age. On June 29, 1968, the Crusade led a march on Denver police headquarters to protest an officer-related killing of 15-year-old Joseph Archuleta. In 1969, the Crusade participated in a walkout at West Side High School, with parents in support. That same year, the Crusade organized the First Annual Chicano Youth Conference at Denver, where participants adopted *El Plan Espiritual de Aztlán*—a revolutionary plan that promulgated the term *Chicano* as a symbol of resistance.[109]

Every political movement is driven by moral outrage and symbols that inspire unity. Alurista (Alberto Baltazar Urista Heredia), a poet and activist, wrote the *Plan* using the symbol of *Aztlán* as confrontational, saying to white America, "we were here first, so if you don't like it go back to where you came from!" *Aztlán* was the mythical or legendary homeland of the Aztecas. It is significant to point out that the Disturnell Map (1847), considered the most authoritative map of its time, was used as the official map to designate the boundary between the United States and Mexico; it noted the Antigua Residencia de los Aztecas, which it placed north of the Hopi Indians, so this was hardly Alurista's invention.[110] (The Chicano movement was adept at using symbols which some would label nationalistic. One of the most interesting collectives was based in Sacramento, California, and called itself the Royal Chicano Air Force [RCAF]. It was comprised of artists and poets, the most prominent of whom was José Montoya, a poet, artist, and musician. Even the name of the group was in society's face.)[111]

Meanwhile, the Crusade worked with Native American organizations such as the American Indian Movement (AIM), supporting AIM during the Native Warriors' "Era of Indian Power." It maintained close ties with AIM cofounder Dennis Banks and supported AIM in 1972 as it launched its Trail of Broken Treaties caravan, calling attention to the plight of Native Americans. The Crusade perceived Mexicans as native peoples—pointing out that 60 percent of Mexicans were mestizos and another 30 percent were full-blooded Indian. (Less than one percent of Euro-Americans have Native American blood.) The Crusade also strongly supported black activist and scholar Angela Davis. Gonzales and the Crusade assisted in establishing the Colorado branch of LRUP, which ran candidates for state and local offices on November 4, 1970.[112]

El Grito del Norte

The Chicano movement attracted activists such as Elizabeth "Betita" Martínez from the Civil Rights movement. Martínez brought in experiences that helped define oppression in the context of multinational struggle. In the late 1950s, Martínez worked for the United Nations as a researcher on colonialism. In the 1960s, she participated in the Student Nonviolent Coordinating Committee (SNCC) in Mississippi and became coordinator of SNCC's New York office. Martínez played a key role in this movement, editing and discussing the works of major Civil Rights activists. She also worked with the Black Panthers. In 1968, she moved to New Mexico, where she cofounded and published *El Grito del Norte* (The Call of the North) for five years, while working on various *barrio* projects. *El Grito del Norte* was the first internationalist and nationalist Chicano newspaper published and almost totally staffed and run by women. The newspaper was based in Española, New Mexico, which is significant in view of the historic independence of women in this region. New Mexico was a natural starting place, since it was a classic colony. Among other books, Martínez coauthored *Viva la Raza: The Struggle of the Mexican American People* with Enriqueta Vásquez. A theme in Martínez's works is a critique of capitalism and the effects of exploitation.[113]

Enriqueta Longeaux y Vásquez was a New Mexican activist, who coedited *El Grito del Norte*. Vásquez, born in Colorado of farmworker parents, had been involved with Denver activist Corky Gonzales and the Crusade for Justice.[114] Her passionate columns denounced capitalism, the military, the Catholic Church, and "gringo" society. Vásquez wrote vigorously about women's issues, highlighting that women's liberation was possible within the Chicano movement. Some Chicanas later criticized her writing on feminist issues as "loyalist," alleging that she was loyal to male networks of power. However, others point out that Vásquez was working within the Chicano movement at the time, attempting to change it, and that she was one of the first Chicanas to publicly take on the issue of Chicana oppression in the mainstream press as well as in the alternative press. In her column *¡Despierten Hermanos!* Vásquez encouraged the total liberation of both men and women and drew the connection between racism and capitalism.[115]

Other Movement Voices

Discussing all the varied voices of the time would be impossible. There were literally scores of newspapers, magazines, and independently published poems and essays. Further, there were *conjuntos* (small musical groups) that played and composed movement songs. Visual artists like Malaquías Montoya produced politically inspired posters that have become classics. One of the best-known cultural artists was LuisValdez of the *Teatro Campesino*, who contributed greatly to the growth of the new consciousness and to the formation of other *teatros* (theaters). Starting as a farmworker group, the *Teatro Campesino* publicized in one-act plays the struggle of farmworkers and of Chicanos in general. It played *corridos* that popularized the Chicanos' struggle for liberation in the United States.[116] Also important was the publication of *El Grito: A Journal of Contemporary Mexican American Thought,* edited by Professor Octavio Romano of the University of California at Berkeley and Quinto Sol, a publishing collective. It began in the fall of 1967. *El Grito* published, in addition to poetry and art, scholarly articles challenging U.S. scholarship. Its critique of Chicano art helped shape the discourse.[117]

There was a plethora of local activist magazines and newspapers. Francisca Flores, an activist for all of her life, worked on the Sleepy Lagoon case, consulted with Carey McWilliams on *North from Mexico,* and edited *Carta Editorial* in the early and mid-1960s. She was a leader in *la Asociación Mexico Americana* and a critic of Senator Joseph McCarthy. During the 1960s she opposed the Vietnam War and founded *Regeneración,* named after the *Partido Liberal Mexicano*'s newspaper. Francisca played an important role in pushing the progressive agenda of Chicanos during the 1960s and into the 1970s. Based on her experience she brought a clear vision of societal problems and what was to be done. She was at the vanguard of feminist expressions of the time.[118]

Arts flourished during this period. Influenced by the artists of the Mexican Revolution, Chicana/o artists wanted to paint murals with strong political messages; they were also influenced by public murals painted under the auspices of the Works Progress Administration in the 1930s. The art was often raw with strong political messages attached to the UFW and political currents such as the Crusade for Justice and *La Raza Unida*. Frequent themes were *la Virgen de Guadalupe*, Ché Guevara, Zapata, *las adelitas*, and Pancho Villa. The Mural Movement took off in the early 1970s when it entered a semiprofessional stage. More attention has to be paid to murals painted in the late 1960s, like that of Sergio Hernández at San Fernando Valley State, which were painted over. (Sergio also authored a comic strip with *Con Safos,* a *barrio* literary magazine.) Guillermo Bejarano was also an early muralist who worked with the Mexican master Siqueiros. In Texas there were *Festival de Flor y Canto* and *Canto al Pueblo*, as well as many young artists. No one locale had a monopoly on this artistic production that remains one of the most significant footprints of the Chicano movement.[119]

The Chicano Youth Movement Gains Steam

In March 1969, Chicano students from throughout the Southwest and Midwest met in Denver and held the First National Chicano Youth Liberation Conference. The conference adopted *El Plan Espiritual de Aztlán,* setting the goals of nationalism and self-determination for the Chicano Youth Movement. At this conference, the students also adopted the label "Chicano," partly in response to the Black Power movement, which had changed its identification from "Negro" to "Black." The adoption of "Chicano" was an attempt to dedicate the movement to the most exploited sector of the U.S. Mexican community, those whom traditional Mexicans and Mexican Americans pejoratively called "Chicanos."

Shortly after the Denver Conference, the newly formed Chicano Council on Higher Education (CCHE), which was mostly based in California, gathered college and university students, faculty, staff, and community activists at the University of California at Santa Barbara to draw up a plan of action for higher education, called *El Plan de Santa Bárbara.* At that conference, Mexican American student organizations changed their name to *El Movimiento Estudiantil Chicano de Aztlán* (MEChA: the Chicano Student Movement of Aztlán).[120] The militancy of students reinforced attitudes already expressed in the community, and their mass entry into the movement electrified events. At the 1970 Denver Youth Conference, Gonzales pushed for active antiwar involvement.[121] MEChA was at the forefront of the establishment of Chicano studies in California and throughout the nation.

Where Is God?

In 1969, 65 percent of the Catholics in the Southwest were Mexicans; yet there were fewer than 180 priests of Mexican extraction, and there were no Chicano bishops. In Los Angeles, Cardinal James Francis McIntyre, with support from the diocese's Catholic elites, censured priests who participated in Civil Rights activities. The attitude of the powerful Monsignor Benjamin G. Hawkes was, "The rich have souls, too."

In November 1969, Ricardo Cruz, a young law student from Loyola University (Los Angeles), formed *Católicos Por La Raza* (CPLR). Its members became infuriated over the closing of Our Lady Queen of Angels Girls' High School, a predominantly Mexican school, allegedly owing to lack of funds. Cardinal McIntyre had just spent $4 million to build St. Basil's Church in the exclusive Wilshire district of Los Angeles. On Christmas Eve 1969, members of CPLR protested in front of St. Basil's Church. The picketing was peaceful and orderly. When the mass began, demonstrators attempted to enter the church, but sheriffs' deputies posing as ushers locked them out. When a few did gain entry, armed deputies expelled them. Police units arrested 21 demonstrators, 20 of whom stood trial for disturbing the peace and assaulting police officers. The so-called "people" convicted Ricardo Cruz of misdemeanor, and on May 8, 1972, he began serving a 120-day sentence for his conviction.[122]

Simultaneously, changes were taking place within the Chicano clergy itself. Because of the heated discourse surrounding the unequal treatment of Mexicans by the Catholic Church, Mexican American priests in San Antonio formed the group PADRES (*Padres Asociados para los Derechos Religiosos, Educativos, y Sociales*), and in October 1969, 50 Spanish-speaking clergy developed the agenda for a national meeting. Diocesan priests Ralph Ruiz and Henry Casso, Francisco Manuel Martínez, and Jesuit Edmundo Rodríguez were among the leaders. PADRES held its first convention on February 2–5, 1970, in Tucson, Arizona. It successfully lobbied the Church for the appointment of Father Patricio Fernández Flores as the first Chicano bishop in the United States. The group also played a role in resolving labor disputes, establishing various grassroots organizations—among them the Mexican American Cultural Center in San Antonio, founded by Father Virgilio Elizondo, who was a major influence in PADRES.[123]

Las Hermanas was founded in 1970 in Houston by Gloria Gallardo, S.H.G., and Gregoria Ortega, O.L.V.M. (the initials are for religious orders). Both sisters had been heavily involved in community work. In the spring of 1971 they sent out a call to other nuns to join them in Houston for their first organizational meeting. Their primary objective was to raise awareness of the needs of the community and to work for social change. The first national meeting was held in Santa Fe, New Mexico, in November of that year. *Hermanas* were inspired by Liberation Theology and the Vatican Reform. They were committed to the *comunidades de base* concept of empowering the people; and they worked closely with the UFW.[124]

The nuns, while recognizing that racism existed in their orders, were more concerned with service to the poor. The Hermanas organization furnished them with a network to expand their world vision; some sisters studied liberation theology in Quito, Ecuador, where they forged religious and intellectual bonds with Latin American nuns and clergy. The new awareness led to even more involvement with the poor, and many nuns became advocates for the people. Las Hermanas were among the founders of the Mexican American Cultural Center in San Antonio in 1972, which sensitized priests and nuns throughout the country to the needs of Mexican Americans. Many members of *Las Hermanas* became involved in the Communities Organized for Public Service (COPS) in San Antonio, established in 1974 by Ernesto Cortés, a native of San Antonio, and others. The nuns' involvement in social issues represented a new sense of identity among Chicanas/os, which fueled activism. However, the nuns in the Church were especially vulnerable since at that time the Church did not pay into Social Security; many were expelled from their respective orders because of their activism and had to live out old age in poverty.

Violence at Home

Judge Gerald S. Chargin of Santa Clara County (California) Juvenile Court on September 2, 1969, called a 17-year-old Chicano—who had allegedly committed incest—an animal and ordered that he should be sent back to Mexico. The judge concluded: "Maybe Hitler was right. The animals in our society probably ought to be destroyed because they have no right to live among human beings."[125] Throughout the Southwest, Mexicans were deprived of defense counsels and representation on juries. In the County of Los Angeles, where the Chicano population numbered about 1 million, only four Mexicans served on a grand jury in 12 years (grand jurors were nominated by judges). In adjacent Orange County, which had more than 44,000 Mexicans, there had been only one Chicano on the grand jury panel in 12 years. No Chicano had served on the grand jury of Monterey County from 1938 through 1968.

The Mexican American community lacked a legal infrastructure to take on these issues. Tejanos had just formed the Mexican American Legal Defense and Education Fund (MALDEF) in 1968. In the late 1960s, the federal government funded a program called California Rural Legal Assistance (CRLA). Although the CRLA did not handle criminal cases, it represented the poor in various other matters. In Kings County, for example, growers received $10,179,917 from the government in the form of farm subsidies *not* to grow certain crops, but Kings County spent less than $6,000 on food for the poor. The CRLA sued the county on behalf of the poor, charging that it was violating federal statutes. As complaints mounted against the CRLA by reactionary elements such as the California growers, Governor Ronald Reagan became more incensed about the federal government's support of an agency that sued private enterprise. In December 1970, Reagan vetoed the federal appropriation to CRLA, and the work of the agency was curtailed.[126]

Chicanas/os under Siege

The universities played a major role in spreading the antiwar message and transforming public opinion about the Vietnam War. Lea Ybarra, later a professor of Chicano Studies at Fresno State and Johns Hopkins, was active on the Berkeley campus with her friends Nina Genera and María Elena Ramírez, performing *actos* (one-act plays) that criticized the war. The women offered Chicanos draft help through the American Friends Committee, and published an antidraft pamphlet. Betita Martínez was another early voice in comparing the plight of the Vietnamese people to the Chicano experience. Ideas spread like wildfire. Moral outrage against the war in Southeast Asia spread among Chicanos, propelling militancy in the Chicano *barrios*.

The anti–Vietnam War movement united Mexicans and moved even the middle-class and flag-waving groups like the Forum to the left. In Los Angeles, the Congress of Mexican American Unity (CMAU), consisting of some 300 Los Angeles organizations, supported the antiwar effort.

Chicano activists began organizing protests against the war. Rosalio Muñoz, a former student body president at the University of California at Los Angeles (UCLA); Sal Baldenegro of the University of Arizona; Ernesto Vigil of the Crusade for Justice in Denver; and Manuel Gómez, a former member of MASA at Hayward State College, refused military induction. Muñoz had initially set out to organize protests against the draft, not the war. Ramsés Noriega, a fellow student at UCLA and an artist, accompanied Muñoz.

The Brown Berets formed the National Chicano Moratorium Committee, holding its first demonstration on December 20, 1969. Rosalio Muñoz joined as cochairperson with David Sánchez. On February 28, 1970, the group staged another protest, in which 6,000 Chicanos participated, braving the pouring rain.

Simultaneously, mobilizations took place outside Los Angeles. In March, the Second Annual Chicano Youth Conference was held in Denver. A series of Chicano moratoria, climaxing with a national moratorium in Los Angeles on August 29, were planned. Meanwhile, police–community tension increased. On July 4, 1970, a demonstration held at the East Los Angeles sheriff's substation, protesting the death of six Mexican American inmates in the preceding five months, clashed with police. Windows of buildings along Whittier Boulevard were broken; a youth was shot by the police. Twenty-two arrests were made before the rebellion was quelled by 250 deputies and members of the California Highway Patrol. Tension increased as August 29 approached.

Organizational work gathered momentum during the days preceding the August 29 moratorium. According to Rosalio Muñoz, the women of the Brown Berets were especially dedicated. In different locations, mini-moratorium groups were formed to organize the bases; campuses became centers of activity. Chicanas like Irene Tovar, who ran San Fernando Valley College's Community Center, worked relentlessly. Irene had been active in community organization since her teen years. She was a cofounder of the Latin American Civic Association in 1961 and was part of a vast personal network of friends and leaders of organizations. A long-time advocate for quality education for Mexican American children, she testified on behalf of bilingual education throughout the 1960s. It was this credibility of the leaders that drew many from the San Fernando Valley to the protest—this scenario was replicated up and down the state of California.

On the morning of August 29, contingents from all over the United States started arriving in East Los Angeles. By noon, participants' number swelled to just below 30,000. *Conjuntos* blared out *corridos*; *Vivas* and other shouts filled the air; placards read: *"Raza sí, guerra no!"* and *"Aztlán: Love it or Leave it!"* The march ended peaceably as the parade turned into Laguna Park. A minor incident at a liquor store a block away from Laguna Park, where teenagers pilfered some soft drinks, sparked a major confrontation. The police, instead of isolating this incident, rushed squad cars to the park, and armed officers prepared to enter the park area. Their hostile behavior caused a reaction, and a few marchers angrily threw objects at the police. Authorities saw that conference monitors had restrained the few protesters throwing things. However, police had found a pretext to break up the demonstration.[127]

Deputies rushed into the arena, trapping men, women, and children, and causing considerable panic. Wielding clubs, they trampled spectators, hitting those who did not move fast enough. In the main section of the park, the crowd was caught unaware. Numbering more than 500, the deputies moved in military formation, sweeping the park. Wreckage could be seen everywhere: the stampede trampled baby strollers into the ground; four deputies beat up a man in his sixties; tear gas filled the air. The number of police escalated to more than 1,200. Mass arrests followed and sheriffs kept prisoners, chained together in fours, in two buses at the East Los Angeles substation. Sheriffs' deputies did not allow them to drink water or go to the bathroom for about four hours. Deputies killed a 15-year-old boy at Laguna Park.

Late in the afternoon Rubén Salazar and two coworkers from KMEX-TV, the Spanish-language television station, stopped at the nearby Silver Dollar Bar for a beer. Problems for television journalist Rubén Salazar had begun on July 16, 1970, when five Los Angeles detectives and two San Leandro police officers burst into a hotel room in downtown Los Angeles, shooting and killing two Mexican nationals—Guillermo Sánchez, 22, and Beltrán Sánchez, 23, who came to be known as the Sánchez cousins. Police claimed it was a case of "mistaken identity." In the weeks to follow, Rubén Salazar exposed the inconsistencies in police reports. Law enforcement officials called on Salazar and ordered him to tone down his television coverage, alleging that he was inciting the people to violence. A federal grand jury issued an indictment against the officers involved in the Sánchez shootings for violating the civil rights of the two men. When the city of Los Angeles paid for the defense of three of the police officers, a storm of protest arose. A federal court later acquitted the officers.

A month after his exposé of the police brutality issue, Salazar again inadvertently found himself caught in the crossfire, this time literally. Deputies surrounded the bar, allegedly looking for a man with a rifle. When some occupants of the Silver Dollar attempted to leave, police forced them back into the premises. Police claimed that deputies broadcast warnings for all occupants to come out; witnesses testified that they heard no such warning. Sheriffs shot a 10-inch tear-gas projectile into the bar. The missile could pierce 7-inch-thick plywood at 100 yards, and it struck Salazar in the head. Another shot filled the bar with gas. Customers made their way out of the establishment. About 5:30 p.m., two reporters frantically informed deputies that Salazar was still in the bar. Deputies refused to listen, and it was not until two hours later that Salazar's body was discovered.

On September 10, 1970, a coroner's inquest probed the circumstances surrounding Rubén Salazar's death. Officers testified as to the Chicano community's riotous nature. Testimony showing the malfeasance of the deputies was restrained. *La Raza* magazine reporters, eyewitnesses to the events at the Silver Dollar Bar, contradicted the deputies' testimony. For example, deputies claimed that they did not force the customers of the Silver Dollar to return to the bar. *La Raza* produced a photo showing that they had. Shortly afterward, *La Raza* published a special issue featuring the photos taken on August 29. The *Los Angeles Times* obtained permission from the *barrio* publication to reprint many of the photos.[128]

Four inquest jurors found "death at the hands of another"; the three remaining jurors decided "death by accident." After their verdicts, the jurors questioned the officers' recklessness and wondered if they would have acted in the same manner in Beverly Hills. Los Angeles District Attorney Evelle J. Younger announced on October 14, 1970, that he would not prosecute, and there was clearly a cover-up. Many Chicanos posited that Younger decided not to try the officers responsible for Salazar's death out of political opportunism. A candidate for California state attorney general (he was elected), Younger knew the law-and-order mentality of Californians who demanded this response. As usual, the *Los Angeles Times* supported Younger.

On September 16, 1970, a peaceful Mexican Independence Day parade ended in violence when police attacked the crowd as marchers reached the end of the parade route. TV newscasters Baxter Ward and George Putnam inflamed public rage against the demonstrators. Then, on January 9, 1971, Chicanos protested against police brutality, marching to the Parker Center, the LAPD Headquarters. Police incited a riot and arrested 32 people. Chief Davis blamed "swimming pool Communists" and the Brown Berets for the riot.

Numerous minor incidents followed; the last major confrontation took place on January 31, 1971. Contingents arrived at Belvedere Park in East Los Angeles from the four major *barrios* in Los Angeles. The demonstration was peaceful, and as the rally ended, Rosalio Muñoz told supporters, numbering around 5,000, to disperse. Some, however, marched to the sheriff's substation on Third Street and staged a rally. A confrontation ensued, which left one man dead and 19 people wounded by buckshot, two with stab wounds, and numerous people with broken bones. Property damage was estimated at more than $200,000.[129]

The Provocateurs

In October 1971 Louis Tackwood, a black informer, stunned the Los Angeles public by testifying that the Criminal Conspiracy Section (CCS) of the Los Angeles Police Department paid him to spy on militants. The LAPD assigned Tackwood to a group of officers who, in cooperation with the FBI, planned to provoke a disruption of the 1972 Republican convention in San Diego by militants; they planned to kill minor officials to force President Richard Nixon to use his powers to break the militant movement. Tackwood named Dan Mahoney (CCS) and Ed Birch (FBI) as the supervisors of the operation. In private conversations he also described how the police used drug pushers as informers in return for protection from prosecution.

Officer Fernando Sumaya also worked as an undercover agent for the LAPD. In the fall semester of 1968 he attempted to infiltrate the UMAS chapter at San Fernando Valley State College (now California State University at Northridge) during campus protests there. He was ousted from the group because he was unknown and because he came on too strong. Sumaya then moved to East Los Angeles, where he infiltrated the Brown Berets. In the spring of 1969 he was involved in the Biltmore Hotel affair, where Chicanos were accused of disrupting a speech by Governor Ronald Reagan at a Nuevas Vistas Education Conference, sponsored by the California Department of Education and archreactionary California Superintendent of Schools Max Rafferty. Thirteen Chicanos were arrested on the charge of disturbing the peace; 10 of the 13 were charged with conspiracy to commit arson. After two years of appeals the defendants were tried. The key witness for the prosecution was Sumaya. The defendants all denied any involvement with the fires. Some charged that Sumaya set the fires. The jury found the defendants not guilty. Meanwhile, Carlos Montes, a Brown Beret, and his wife, Olivia Montes, had left the area and he was not tried. The Monteses remained at large until the mid-1970s. The LAPD destroyed records documenting Sumaya's role in the Biltmore fires. After relentless hounding, the Montes family was caught, and Carlos was tried. In November 1979, a jury found Montes not guilty—evidently the jury questioned Sumaya's and the LAPD's suspect role. Also questioned by the Berets' *La Causa* was the suspect role of Sergeant Abel Armas in the Special Operation Conspiracy of the LAPD. Freedom of information documents obtained by Professor Ernesto Chávez reveal that the FBI was extremely active in investigating the Berets.[130]

In a press conference on January 31, 1972, Eustacio (Frank) Martínez, 23, revealed that since July 1969 he had infiltrated Chicano groups. A federal agent for the Alcohol, Tobacco, and Firearms Division (ATF) of the Internal Revenue Service recruited Martínez, who, in return for not being prosecuted for a federal firearms violation, agreed to work as an informant and agent provocateur. He infiltrated the MAYO and the Brown Berets in Houston and Kingsville, Texas. He admitted that he committed acts of violence to provoke others. From September 1969 to October 1970 Martínez participated in many protest marches. During the one in Alice, Texas, he tried to provoke trouble "by jumping on a car and trying to cave its top in." He attempted to entice militants to buy guns and to provoke police. He was rebuked by the MAYO members.[131]

In October 1970 ATF agents sent Martínez to Los Angeles, where he worked for agents Fernando Ramos and Jim Riggs. Martínez began spreading rumors against Rosalio Muñoz, accusing him of being too soft, and in November 1970 Martínez ousted Muñoz and became chair of the Chicano Moratorium Committee. Martínez later named officers Valencia, Armas, Savillos, and Domínguez of the CCS as contacts. In other words, when Martínez took part in the Los Angeles rebellions on January 9 and 31, 1971, the Los Angeles police knew of his involvement. He continued in this capacity until March 1971, when he returned to Texas. There Martínez became a member of the Brown Berets and, according to informants, went around waving a carbine and advocating violent tactics.

Upon his return from Texas he was instructed by Ramos and Riggs to infiltrate *La Casa de Carnalismo* to establish links between *Carnalismo* and the Chicano Liberation Front (CLF), which had been involved in numerous bombings. Martínez reported that the main functions of *Carnalismo* were to eliminate narcotics, to sponsor English classes, and to dispense food to the needy; he could find no links with CLF. The officers told him that his "information was a bunch of bullshit." He was to find evidence by any means necessary. They then instructed him to use his influence to get a heroin addict by the name of "Nacho" to infiltrate *Carnalismo*. Martínez refused to take part in the frame-up. He finally became disillusioned when, on the first anniversary of the Chicano National Moratorium, agents told him to plead guilty to charges of inciting a riot. They promised him protection from prosecution.[132]

Although some reporters questioned the reliability of Martínez's disclosures, they did not call for congressional investigations into the provocateur activities of federal and local agencies. Louis Tackwood and Frank Martínez were admitted provocateurs. The latter's revelations cast a shadow on the actions of the police in the Los Angeles Chicano rebellions.

Whatever were their roles, they lie buried in the secret files of the different branches of the federal and local police agencies. Such aspects of history remain closed to historians. The ACLU, in a suit settled in the early 1980s, uncovered extensive police-spying on progressive white, black, and Chicano communities.

Conclusion: The Chicana/o Legacy

The 1960s reached the perfect storm in the mobilization of youth organizations that attempted to transform their constituencies. The relatively small number of Chicano youth succeeded in mobilizing the largest proportion of the community in the history of Mexican Americans in the United States. In part, the success of this mobilization was due to the large number of young people in the Chicano community who listened and nurtured a hope to change society. They integrated with other youth through music; listening to rock and roll bound many together. The Vietnam War tapped an energy that generated anger—anger at the war, anger at society, anger at seeing the disparate treatment of people at home and abroad.

The Chicano movement left legacies, not least of which was a community much more aware of its constitutional rights. Many more persons of Mexican extraction got involved in trying to ensure civil rights for Chicanos and the Spanish-speaking people in the United States. A larger sector joined student organizations such as MEChA and MAYO and mobilized community groups to fight for their rights. Youth activists furthered the Mexican American civil rights tradition of the past, and every subsequent generation of immigrants coming into the country would benefit from this legacy.[133]

Notes

1. Baby Boomers, Ohio History Central, http://www.ohiohistorycentral.org/entry.php?rec=1699.
2. Civil Rights Struggle of the 1960's, http://www.youtube.com/watch?v=EYqsJizN4gI. Today, for example, youth are less homophobic than were the older generation; more youth than those over 55 voted for a black president.
3. "Hearts and Minds," Top Documentary Films, http://topdocumentaryfilms.com/hearts-and-minds/. Ibid, http://www.youtube.com/watch?v=1d2ml82lc7s.
4. America in Ferment: The Tumultuous 1960s, Viva la Raza! 1960s, Digital History, http://www.digitalhistory.uh.edu/era.cfm?eraID=17&smtID=2.
5. Paul Friedländer, *Rock and Roll* (Boulder, CO: Westview Press, 1996), 287. Barbara Ehrenreich, "The Rock Rebellion," http://spiritlink.com/rock-rebellion.html.
6. Leo Grebler, Joan W. Moore, and Ralph C. Guzmán, *The Mexican American People: The Nation's Second Largest Minority* (New York: Free Press, 1970).
7. Grebler et al., *Mexican American People*, 106, 126, 143, 150, 185, 236, 251. Richard W. Slatta, "Chicanos in the Pacific Northwest: An Historical Overview of Oregon's Chicanos," *Aztlán* 6, no. 3 (Fall 1975): 335. Mexicans in the Columbia Basin, http://www.vancouver.wsu.edu/crbeha/ma/ma.htm. "No dogs or Mexicans allowed" ("No Mexicans or dogs allowed"), The Big Apple, http://www.barrypopik.com/index.php/new_york_city/entry/no_dogs_or_mexicans_allowed_no_mexicans_or_dogs_allowed/.
8. Robert Coles and Harry Huge, "Thorns on the Yellow Rose of Texas," *New Republic* (April 19, 1969): 13–17. Robert Garland Landolt, *The Mexican American Workers of San Antonio, Texas* (New York: Arno Press, 1976), 320, 326.
9. Today, Segundo Barrio is fighting for survival. Dr. Lydia R. Otero, Paso Del Sur Group, http://pasodelsur.com/news/plea.html (accessed November 8, 2009). Joe Olvera, "El Segundo Barrio, Cradle of the Chicano Movement," News Paper Tree, http://newspapertree.com/opinion/1007-el-segundo-barrio-cradle-of-the-chicano-movement. "Cultural Life of el Segundo Barrio," http://pasodelsur.com/historia/Culturallife.html.
10. Benjamin Márquez, "Power and Politics in a Chicano Barrio" (PhD dissertation, University of Wisconsin, Madison, 1983), chs 4 and 5. Barry J. Kaplan, "Houston: The Golden Buckle of the Sunbelt," in Richard M. Bernard and Bradley R. Rice, eds., *Sunbelt Cities: Politics and Growth Since World War II* (Austin: University of Texas Press, 1983), 196–212.
11. Because of the size of the Mexican barrios, Los Angeles fostered Chicano sounds. Anthony Macias, *Mexican American Mojo: Popular Music, Dance, and Urban Culture in Los Angeles, 1935–1968* (Durham, NC: Duke University Press, 2008). Steve Loza, *Barrio Rhythm: Mexican American Music in Los Angeles* (Champaign: University of Illinois Press, 1993).
12. Marcos de León, "Statements of Philosophy and Policy as They Pertain to the Acculturation and Education of the Mexican-American" (Unpublished manuscript, 1964) in Rodolfo F. Acuña and Guadalupe Compeán, eds., *Voices of the U.S. Latino Experience*, 3 Vols. (Westport, CT: Greenwood, 2008), 807–9.
13. *Los Angeles Times* (March 8, 1972). Ray Hebert, "L.A. County Latin Population Grows 113 Percent," *Los Angeles Times* (August 18, 1972). *Forumeer* (February 1970). Mike Davis, *City of Quartz: Excavating the Future in Los Angeles* (London: Verso, 1990), 164. Henry Joseph Gutiérrez, "The Chicano Education Rights Movement and School Segregation, Los Angeles, 1962–1970" (PhD dissertation, University of California, Irving, 1990), 35.
14. Rita Arias Jirasek and Carlos Tortolero, *Mexican Chicago* (Chicago, IL: Arcadia Publishing, 2001), 53, 63. The Chicago Mexican community was part of a circuit of Mexican musical events, and they enjoyed traditional music from both Mexico and Texas.

15. Anthony Baker, "The Social Production of Space of Two Chicago Neighborhoods: Pilsen and Lincoln Park" (PhD dissertation, University of Illinois at Chicago Circle, 1995), 30, 42. Louise Año Nuevo Kerr, *The Chicano Experience in Chicago: 1920–1970* (Chicago: University of Illinois at Chicago Circle, 1976), 171–76. Peter T. Alter, "Mexicans and Serbs in Southeast Chicago: Racial Group Formation During the Twentieth Century," *Journal of the Illinois State Historical Society* (January 2001), http://dig.lib.niu.edu/ISHS/ishs-2001winter/ishs-2001winter403.pdf. "Mexicans," *The Electronic Encyclopedia of Chicago* (Chicago: Chicago Historical Society, 2005), http://www.encyclopedia.chicagohistory.org/pages/824.html. Rob Paral and Michael Norkewicz, *The Metro Chicago Immigration Fact Book* (Institute for Metropolitan Affairs, Roosevelt University, June 2003), http://www.robparal.com/downloads/chicagoimmfactbook_2003_06.pdf.

16. 1960: "Harvest of Shame," http://www.youtube.com/watch?v=yJTVF_dya7E.

17. Ibid. Edward Bliss, *Now the News: The Story of Broadcast Journalism* (New York: Columbia University Press, 1992), 391–93. Robert Niemi, *History in the Media: Film and Television* (Santa Barbara, CA: ABC-CLIO, 2006), 323–24.

18. Stoop Farm Labor 1959, http://www.youtube.com/watch?v=BiMjKmuva0I.

19. Grebler et al., *Mexican American People*, 209. Anne Brunton, "The Chicano Migrants," in Livie Isaudro Durán and H. Russell Bernard, eds., *Introduction to Chicano Studies,* 2d ed. (New York: Macmillan, 1982), 260–71. Sara Hoffman Jurand, "Human Rights Group Reports Poor Working Conditions for Child Farmworkers," *Trial* 36, no. 9 (September 2000): 98. Meg Grant, "Still a Harvest of Shame: The Exploitation of Migrant Farm Workers Shocked the Nation 30 Years Ago—But Their Pain Continues," *People Weekly* 34, no. 21 (November 26, 1990): 44–50.

20. George Mowry and Blaine A. Brownell, *The Urban Nation 1920–1980,* rev. ed. (New York: Hill and Wang, 1981), 211–12. Ignacio M. García, *Viva Kennedy: Mexican Americans in Search of Camelot* (College Station: Texas A&M University Press, 2000), 5, 33, 73, 110.

21. Patrick L. Cox, *Ralph W. Yarborough, the People's Senator* (Austin: University of Texas Press, 2002), 233–34. Jan Jarboe Russell, "Henry B. González," *Texas Monthly* 29, no. 1 (January 2001): 204.

22. Interview by José Angel Gutiérrez, Voices Tejanas, Albert Peña, Jr., Tejano Voices, University of Texas Arlington, http://library.uta.edu/tejanovoices/xml/CMAS_015.xml.

23. Political Association of Spanish-Speaking Organizations. *Handbook of Texas Online,* http://www.tshaonline.org/handbook/online/articles/PP/vep1.html.

24. "Revolt of the Mexicans," April 12, 1963, http://www.time.com/time/magazine/article/0,9171,828075,00.html. Rodolfo F. Acuña, *The Making of Chicana/o Studies: In the Trenches of Academe* (New Brunswick: Rutgers University Press, 2011), 22–25.

25. Eligio "Kika" De La Garza II, http://www.loc.gov/rr/hispanic/congress/delagarza.html.

26. Julie Leininger Pycior, *LBJ & Mexican Americans: The Paradox of Power* (Austin: University of Texas Press, 1997), 49, 60, 98, 100, 113, 123, 134. Lorena Oropeza, "La Batalla Esta Aqui! Chicanos Oppose the War in Vietnam" (PhD dissertation, Cornell University, 1996), 105. Charles Ray Chandler, "The Mexican American Protest Movement in Texas" (PhD dissertation, Tulane University, 1968), 157–60, 173–90. Louise Ann Fish, *All Rise: Reynaldo G. Garza, the First Mexican American Federal Judge* (College Station: Texas A&M University Press, 1996), 88–122. "Revolt of the Masses," *Time* (April 12, 1963). Tony Castro, *Chicano Power: The Emergence of Mexican Americans* (New York: Saturday Review Press, 1974), 28. Edwin Larry Dickens, "The Political Role of Mexican Americans in San Antonio" (PhD dissertation, Texas Tech University, 1969), 169.

27. Heather Rose Parker, "The Elusive Coalition: African American and Chicano Political Organization and Interaction in Los Angeles, 1960–1973" (PhD dissertation, University of California, Los Angeles, 1996). Rodolfo F. Acuña, *A Community Under Siege: A Chronicle of Chicanos East of the Los Angeles River 1945–1975* (Los Angeles, CA: Chicano Studies Research Center Publications, 1984), 85. Acuña, *Anything but Mexican: Chicanos in Contemporary Los Angeles* (London: Verso, 1996).

28. California Latino Caucus, Historical Overview of the Latino Caucus, http://www2.legislature.ca.gov/latinocaucus/History.asp.

29. Raphael J. Sonenshein, *Politics in Black and White: Race and Power in Los Angeles* (Princeton, NJ: Princeton University Press, 1993), 55–84. Larry N. George, "Red Wind: Anticommunism and Conservative Hegemony in Cold War Los Angeles," in Gerry Riposa and Carolyn Dersch, eds., *City of Angels* (Dubuque, IA: Kendall/Hunt, 1992), 1–14. Davis, *City of Quartz,* 125–28. *G.I. Forum News Bulletin* (March 1963 and February 1964).

30. Chicago Arts District/Pilsen/Little Village, Brainsnack Tours, http://brainsnack.net/cpg/thumbnails.php?album=62.

31. Kerr, "Chicano Experience," 183–84. William Kornblum, *Blue Collar Community* (Chicago: University of Chicago Press, 1974), 161–87. Baker, "The Social Production of Space," 155, 158, 160.

32. Mowry and Brownell, *Urban Nation,* 213–14. Pycior, *LBJ,* 148–51.

33. Pycior, *LBJ,* 149, 151.

34. Maris A. Vinovskis, *The Birth of Head Start: Preschool Education Policies in the Kennedy and Johnson Administrations* (Chicago: University of Chicago, 2005), 59–68.

35. LBJ State of Union War on Poverty, http://www.youtube.com/watch?v=qfT03Ihtlds.

36. *The Invisible Minority,* Report of the NEA–Tucson Survey on the Teaching of Spanish to the Spanish Speaking, Department of Rural Education, National Education Association, Washington, DC, 1966. Ernesto Galarza, "La Mula No Nacio Arisca," *Center Diary* (September–October 1966): 26–32, reprinted in Acuña and Compeán, *Voices of the U.S. Latino,* 813–18.

37. Graciela Gil Olivarez, Arizona Women's Heritage Trail, http://www.womensheritagetrail.org/women/GracielaGilOlivarez.php.

Mowry and Brownell, *Urban Nation,* 221–22. Biliana María Ambrecht, "Politicization as a Legacy of the War on Poverty: A Study of Advisory Council Members in a Mexican American Community" (PhD dissertation, University of California at Los Angeles, 1973). V. Kurtz, "Politics, Ethnicity, Integration: Mexican Americans in the War on Poverty" (PhD dissertation, University of California, Davis, 1970). This section draws specifically from Greg Coronado, "Spanish-Speaking Organizations in Utah," in Paul Morgan and Vince Mayer, eds., *Working Papers Toward a History of the Spanish Speaking in Utah* (Salt Lake City: American West Center, Mexican American Documentation Project, University of Utah, 1973), 121. Vernon M. Briggs, Jr., Walter Fogel, and Fred H. Schmidt, *The Chicano Worker* (Austin: University of Texas Press, 1977), 38. *Forumeer* (March 1967) states that the Forum almost dropped sponsorship of SER because LBJ was hedging on the White House conference. Pycior, *LBJ,* 152–53, 159, 161.

38. Pycior, *LBJ,* 164, 170, 178–82. Carey McWilliams, *North from Mexico* (New York: Greenwood Press, 1968), 17. *Forumeer* (October 1967). The Forum supported the conference. John Hart Lane, Jr., "Voluntary Associations Among Mexican Americans in San Antonio, Texas: Organization and Leadership Characteristics" (PhD dissertation, University of Texas, 1968), 2. Richard Gardner, *Grito! Reies Tijerina and the New Mexico Land Grant War of 1967* (New York: Bobbs-Merrill, 1970), 231–32. Craig A. Kaplowitz, *LULAC, Mexican Americans, and National Policy* (College Station: Texas A&M University Press, 2005), 98–104.

39. David Nieto, "A Brief History of Bilingual Education in the United States," *Perspectives on Urban Education* (Spring 2009): 61–72.

40. Anguiano, a former nun, had been a national organizer for the United Farm Workers. She later founded, along with Gloria Steinem and Bella Abzug, the National Women's Political Caucus (1971). Jasmin K. Williams, "Lupe Anguiano—A Tireless Warrior Woman," *New York Post* (March 12, 2007).

41. Pycior, *LBJ,* 183–87.

42. Voting Rights Act, 1965, United States Department of Justice, Civil Rights Division, http://www.justice.gov/crt/about/vot/intro/intro_b.php. Mexican Americans were not initially entitled under the Act.

43. Watts Riots Project, https://www.youtube.com/watch?v=aJUS9aa0Yms.

44. Oropeza, "La Batalla," 95, 100–1.

45. Davis, *City of Quartz,* 101–6. Gerald Horne, *Fire This Time: The Watts Uprising and the 1960s* (New York: Da Capo Press, 1997), an excellent presentation of the causes of the uprisings. Meyer Weinberg, *A Chance to Learn: A History of Race and Education in the United States* (Cambridge, England: Cambridge University Press, 1977), 174.

46. Quoted in James T. Patterson, *America's Struggle Against Poverty 1900–1980* (Cambridge, MA: Harvard University Press, 1981), 145–46. Kaplowitz, *LULAC,* 98, 108, 125, 220.

47. Acuña, *Community Under Siege,* 145. Patterson, *America's Struggle,* 148.

48. Morris Singer, *Growth, Equality and the Mexican Experience* (Austin: University of Texas Press, 1969), 31.

49. Ibid., 31. María Fernández-Kelly, *For We Are Sold, I and My People: Women and Industry in Mexico's Frontier* (Albany: State University of New York Press, 1983), 24, 132, 134. Lamar Babington Jones, "Mexican American Labor Problems in Texas" (PhD dissertation, University of Texas, 1965), 33, 35–37.

50. Theodore White, *America in Search of Itself* (New York: Harper Collins, 1984), 363.

51. "The Immigration Act of 1965: Intended and Unintended Consequences of the 20th Century," http://iipdigital.usembassy.gov/st/english/publication/2008/04/20080423214226eaifas0.9637982.html#axzz2BynJjSpp.

52. James Fallows, "Immigration: How It's Affecting Us," *The Atlantic,* 252, no. 5 (November 1983): 45–68. Acuña, *Anything but Mexican,* 114. Mario T. García, *Memories of Chicano History: The Life and Narrative of Bert Corona* (Berkeley: University of California, 1994), 290–300. David G. Gutiérrez, "Sin Fronteras? Chicanos, Mexican Americans, and the Emergence of the Contemporary Immigration Debate, 1968–1978," in David Gutiérrez, ed., *Between Two Worlds: Mexican Immigrants in the United States* (Wilmington, DE: Scholarly Resources, 1996), 175–209. Miriam J. Wells, *Strawberry Fields: Politics, Class, and Work in California Agriculture* (Ithaca, NY: Cornell University Press, 1996), 63.

53. Chávez was a civil rights leader much on par with the Rev. Martin Luther King, Jr., and he used movement symbols to attract a wider constituency. Farmworker Movement Documentation Project, http://www.farmworkermovement.us/phorum/read.php?1,933,940.

54. National Farm Workers Association Collection, Records, 1960–1967, Walter P. Reuther Library of Labor and Urban Affairs, http://microformguides.gale.com/Data/Download/9177000C.pdf.

55. Richard W. Etulain, ed., *César Chávez: A Brief Biography with Documents* (New York: Palgrave Macmillan, 2002), 8–10. "The Fight in the Fields, Cesar Chávez and the Farmworkers' Struggle," PBS. http://www.pbs.org/itvs/fightfields/cesar-chavez.html. Richard Steven Street, "Poverty in the Valley of Plenty: The National Farm Labor Union, Di Giorgio Farms, and Suppression of Documentary Photography in California, 1947–66," *Labor History* 48 (February 2007): 25–48.

56. Dolores Huerta: Labor Leader and Social Activist, http://latino.si.edu/virtualgallery/OJOS/bios/bios_Huerta.htm.

57. Vatican II—Urgent & Essential, http://www.vatican2voice.org/default.htm.

58. Peter Matthiessen, *Sal Si Puedes: César Chávez and the New American Revolution* (New York: Random House, 1969), 41, 50–51, 333–34. Joan London and Henry Anderson, *So Shall Ye Reap* (New York: Crowell, 1971), 146–49. Mark Day, *Forty Acres: César Chávez and the Farm Workers* (New York: Praeger, 1971), 42, 54, 55. Hedda Garza, *Latinas: Hispanic Women in the United States* (New York: Franklin Watts, 1994), 11–13, 114. Vickie Ruiz, *From Out of the Shadows: Mexican Women in Twentieth-Century America* (New York: Oxford University Press, 1998), 134–35. Margaret Rose, "From the Fields to the Picket Line: Huelga Women and the Boycott, 1965–1975," *Labor History* 31, no. 3 (Summer 1990): 272. Samuel R. Berger,

Dollar Harvest: The Story of the Farm Bureau (Lexington, MA: Heath, 1971), 161–63. *Forumeer* (May 1966). Gregory Dunne, *Delano* (New York: Farrar, Straus & Giroux, 1967), 51, 144–45, 147–48. Ronald B. Taylor, *Chávez and the Farm Workers* (Boston: Beacon Press, 1975), 157, 251, 259, 261–69, 287. Sam Kushner, *Long Road to Delano* (New York: International Publishers, 1975), 173.

59. The affiliation with the NFWA was not popular among all the Texans; Sánchez and Galván bolted, forming the Texas Independent Workers Association. Robert M. Utley, *Lone Star Lawmen: The Second Century of the Texas Rangers* (Cambridge, MA: Oxford University Press, 2007), 238–45. "Farmworkers ask help against 'terror campaign,'" Texas Farm Workers Support Committee, http://chavez.cde.ca.gov/Research-Center/DocumentDisplayRC.aspx?rpg=/chdocuments/documentdisplay.jsp&doc=56d6ce%3Aeae63c6e4f%3A-7e83&searchhit=yes. Sons of Zapata: A Brief Photographic History of Farm Workers' Strike in Texas, http://www.farmworkermovement.us/ufwarchives/elmalcriado/Frankel/Strike.pdf. Acuña, *Making of Chicana/o Studies*, 36–38.

60. David Montejano, *Anglos and Mexicans in the Making of Texas, 1836–1986* (Austin: University of Texas Press, 1987), 284. Charles Cotrel interviewed by José Angel Gutiérrez (Tejano Voices, University of Texas, Arlington, San Antonio, July 2, 1992), 4, 6, 9, 16, http://library.uta.edu/tejanovoices/xml/CMAS_020.xml. "Priests Active in Valley Strike," *San Antonio Express* (July 7, 1966).

61. Gilbert Padilla 1962–1980, Interview, 2, http://www.farmworkermovement.us/essays/essays/005%20Padilla_Gilbert.pdf. "U.S. Senate Sub-Committee hearings," *San Antonio Express/News* (July 1, 1966). La Casita Farms strike was called a complete failure. "Farm Strike Could Turn into Social Movement," *Big Spring Herald* (Texas, July 17, 1966). José Angel Gutiérrez, *The Making of a Chicano Militant: Lessons from Crystal* (Madison: University of Wisconsin, 1999), 105. "Melon Packers Did Cross Picket Line," *Brownsville Herald* (July 13, 1967). Timothy Paul Bowman, "What About Texas? The Forgotten Cause of Antonio Orendain and the Rio Grande Valley Farm Workers, 1966–1982" (Master's thesis, University of Texas, Arlington, 2005), 7–10, 45–55. "Orendain Sparks UFWOC Organizing Drive in Texas," *El Malciado*, 3, no. 11 (August 15–September 15, 1969): 13. http://www.farmworkermovement.org/ufwarchives/elmalcriado/1969/August%2015%20-%20Sept%2015,%201969%20No%2011_PDF.pdf.

62. Mark Erenberg, "*Obreros Unidos* in Wisconsin," U.S. Bureau of Labor Statistics, *Monthly Labor Review* 91 (June 1968): 20–23. National Advisory Committee on Farm Labor, *Farm Labor Organizing, 1905–1967: A Brief History* (New York: National Advisory Committee on Farm Labor, 1967), 59. Dennis Nodín Valdés, *Al Norte: Agricultural Workers in the Great Lakes Region, 1917–1970* (Austin: University of Texas, 1991), 189–92. James Maraniss, "Wautoma: New Season, Same Woes," *The Capital Times* (July 31, 1967). *The Post-Crescent* (Appleton, Wisconsin, January 8, 1967). *Oshkosh Daily Northwestern* (August 15, 1966). *The Post-Crescent* (Appleton, Wisconsin, January 8, 1967).

63. Acuña, *Making of Chicana/o Studies*, 29–31. Marc Simon Rodriguez, "Obreros Unidos: Migration, Migrant Farm Worker Activism, and the Chicano Movement in Wisconsin and Texas, 1950–1980" (PhD dissertation, University of Illinois, Evanston, 2000). Marc Simon Rodriguez, *The Tejano Diaspora: Mexican Americanism and Ethnic Politics in Texas and Wisconsin* (Chapel Hill: University of North Carolina Press, 2011).

64. Hob Voces, "Long March Converges on Capitol Steps," *The News-Palladium* (Benton Harbor, Michigan, March 27, 1967). "Migrant Unit Gets Hearing with Romney," *Record Eagle* (Traverse City, Michigan, April 5, 1967). "Romney Aide Works with Migrants," *The Holland* (Michigan, Evening Sentinel, April 5, 1967). "Migrants to Ask Romney to Intervene," *The Holland*, (Michigan, Evening Sentinel April 13, 1967). Acuña, *Making of Chicana/o Studies*, 31–32.

65. National Advisory Committee on Farm Labor, 60. Barbara Jane Macklin, *Structural Stability and Cultural Change in a Mexican American Community* (New York: Arno Press, 1976), vi. Farm Labor Organizing Committee AFL–CIO, http://www.floc.com/.

66. "Governor to Get Report on Migrant Workers," *Walla Walla Union-Bulletin* (May 11, 1967). Timeline: Movimiento from 1960–1985, Seattle Civil Rights and Labor History Project, http://depts.washington.edu/civilr/mecha_timeline.htm.

67. Dr. José Angel Gutiérrez, Tejano Voices, http://library.uta.edu/tejanovoices/gutierrez.php. Acuña, *Making of Chicana/o Studies*, 56–57.

68. Viviana Santiago Cavada, Interview, Tejano Voices, http://library.uta.edu/tejanovoices/xml/CMAS_066.xml. Acuña, *Making of Chicana/o Studies*, 56–58.

69. Armando Navarro, *Mexican American Youth Organization: Avant-Garde of the Chicano Movement in Texas* (Austin: University of Texas Press, 1995), 80–97. J. Gutiérrez, *The Making of a Chicano Militant*, 79.

70. United Mexican-American Students Symposium—UCLA February 1968, Pacifica Radio Archive, http://www.archive.org/details/UnitedMexican-americanStudentsSymposium-UclaFebuary1968. Acuña, *Making of Chicana/o Studies*, 41–42.

71. Rodolfo Corky Gonzales, I Am Joaquin, http://www.latina-mericanstudies.org/latinos/joaquin.htm.

72. Chicano—Quest for a Homeland—Part 1 in 6 parts, http://www.youtube.com/watch?v=RHQ4XS-DrqM.

73. Rosales, *Chicano!*, 211–13. Pedro Acevec, MEChA de UW, Interview, Seattle Civil Rights and Labor Project, http://depts.washington.edu/civilr/acevec.htm. Erasmo Gamboa MEChA; UFW Grape Boycott; Historian; UW Professor, Seattle Civil Rights and Labor Project, http://depts.washington.edu/civilr/Erasmo_Gamboa.htm. Roberto Maestas, El Centro de la Raza, Seattle Civil Rights and Labor Project, http://depts.washington.edu/civilr/maestas.htm. Yolanda Alaniz, MEChA de UW, Radical Women, Freedom Socialist Party, http://depts.washington.edu/civilr/alaniz.htm.

74. Rosales, *Chicano!*, 211–13. Francisco A. Rosales, ed., *Testimonio: A Documentary History of the Mexican American Struggle*

for Civil Rights (Houston, TX: Arte Público Press, 2000), 126–27. Dan Pavillard, "Minorities Like Taste of Honey—Huerta Says," *Tucson Daily Citizen* (October 20, 1967). Maritza De La Trinidad, "Collective Outrage: Mexican American Activism and the Quest for Educational Equality and Reform: 1950–1990" (Tucson: PhD dissertation, University of Arizona, 2008), 150, 162, 183. Acuña, *Making of Chicana/o Studies*, 55–56.

75. Enriqueta Vásquez (Author), Dionne Espínoza (Editor), Lorena Oropeza (Editor), *Enriqueta Vasquez and the Chicano Movement: Writings from El Grito del Norte* (Houston, TX: Arte Público Press, 2006).

76. Navarro, *Mexican American Youth*, 55–66. Juan Gómez-Quiñones, *Mexican Students por La Raza: The Chicano Student Movement in Southern California 1967–1977* (Santa Barbara, CA: Editorial La Causa, 1978), 17–18, 22–23. Gerald Paul Rosen, "Political Ideology and the Chicano Movement: A Study of the Political Ideology of Activists in the Chicano Movement" (PhD dissertation, University of California at Los Angeles, 1972), 248. In Los Angeles, Francisca Flores, a veteran activist, and Ramona Morín (women's auxiliary of the Forum) cofounded the California League of Mexican American Women. Flores published and edited *La Carta Editorial,* which reported on political activism in the mid-1960s, and published *Regeneración,* an activist magazine focusing on women's issues.

77. H. Gutiérrez, "Chicano Education Rights," 53. Gómez-Quiñones, *Mexican Students Por La Raza,* 17. Rosales, *Chicano!,* 186–88.

78. Mario T. Garcia and Sal Castro, *Blowout!: Sal Castro and the Chicano Struggle for Educational Justice* (Chapel Hill: University of North Carolina Press, 2011).

79. "Walkouts," HBOFilms, http://store.hbo.com/walkout-dvd/detail.php?p=100589. Walkout: The True Story of the Historic 1968 Chicano Student Walkout in East L.A., Democracy Now, http://www.democracynow.org/2006/3/29/walkout_the_true_story_of_the.Acuña, *Making of Chicana/o Studies*, 38–42.

80. Blowout Panel 3, http://www.youtube.com/watch?v=hXt8IJZhTM4.

81. *Salvatore B. Castro et al. v. The Superior Court of Los Angeles County*, 9 Cal. App. 3d 675; 88 Cal. Rptr. 500; 1970 Cal. App. LEXIS 1985, July 17, 1970.

82. Dolores Delgado Bernal, "Chicana School Resistance and Grassroots Leadership: Providing an Alternative History of the 1968 East Los Angeles Blowouts" (PhD dissertation, University of California, Los Angeles, 1997), 84–85. Ernesto Chávez, "Creating Aztlán: The Chicano Movement in Los Angeles, 1966–1978" (PhD dissertation, University of California, Los Angeles, 1994), 65, 73. Carlos Muñoz, Jr., *Youth, Identity, Power: The Chicano Movement* (London: Verso, 1989), 64, 68, 132. Rosales, *Chicano!,* 190, 191, 192–94. Sánchez was Prime Minister of the Brown Berets; Carlos Montes, Minister of Information of the Berets; and Cruz Olmeda, Minister of Discipline of the Berets. They had approximately 30 members by mid-1968. H. Gutiérrez, "Chicano Education," 4–5, 56 on the EICC. Along with Castro, the others indicted were Eleazear Risco, editor of *La Raza* newspaper; Joe Razo, co-editor;

Patricio Sánez, community activist; Moctezuma Esparza of UCLA UMAS; David Sánchez and Carlos Montes of the Berets; Ralph Ramírez, minister of defense of the Berets, Fred López of the Berets; and Richard Vigil, Gilberto C. Olmeda, and Henry Gómez. Pycior, *LBJ,* 220–21. Oropeza, "La Batalla," 94.

83. Juan A. Sepúlveda, *Life and Times of Willie Velásquez: Su Voto Es Su Voz* (Houston, TX: Arte Público Press, 2005), 69–72. Doris Wright, "Lanier High Students Get Civic Leader Support," *San Antonio Express* (April 11, 1968).

84. Fern Chick, "Miller Seeks to Calm Lanier 'Revolt'" *San Antonio Light* (April 16, 1968). "Miller Replies to Student Demands," *San Antonio Light* (April 17, 1968). Fern Chick, "Lanier Group Plans to Press Protests," *San Antonio Light* (April 18, 1968).

85. Ron White, "3,000 Ask Reforms in Walkout," *San Antonio Light* (May 16, 1968). "School Chief Insists It's Classes as Usual v. Meet Demands," *San Antonio Light* (May 17, 1968).

86. Ron White, "Edgewood Rally Held," *San Antonio Light* (May 21, 1968). "Edgewood Hearing in Recess," *San Antonio Light* (May 24, 1968). Frank Trejo, "Board Promises Solution to Grievances," *San Antonio Light* (May 24, 1968). Frank Trejo, "School to Act on Grievances," *San Antonio Light* (May 28, 1968).

87. Baldemar James Barrera, "'We Want Better Education!' The Chicano Student Movement for Educational Reform in South Texas, 1968–1970" (PhD dissertation, University of New Mexico, Albuquerque, 2007), 102. Richard R. Valencia, *Chicano Students and the Courts: The Mexican American Legal Struggle for Educational Equality* (New York: New York University Press, 2008), 92–103. Acuña, *Making of Chicana/o Studies*, 37–41.

88. Elaine Ayala, "The Year Latino Students Stood Up, Walked Out," *San Antonio Express News* (May 7, 2008). On March 21, 1973, the Supreme Court in a five-to-four decision ruled against Rodríguez, stating that the system of school finance did not violate the federal constitution. Texas should resolve the issue.

89. David Robles, "Walking Out: The Success of the Edcouch-Elsa Student Walkout of 1968 through the Media," (Master of Arts thesis, University of Texas-Pan American, 2012), 2, 18, makes the valid point that the Edcouch-Elsa walkouts of 1968 "commenced public discourse within the community about the educational practices as well as racism occurring in schools, and opinions over whether or not these students were in the right." Barrera, "'We Want Better Education!,'" is an excellent background to the walkouts.

90. "Valley School Hit by Boycott," *Odessa American* (November 14, 1968), blames the MAYO movement. "Five Arrested in School Boycott," *Galveston Daily News* (November 16, 1968) reported those arrested as Mirtala Villarreal, Homer Trevino, Freddie Sainz, Arnulfo Sustaita, and Xavier Ramírez. Nolene Hodges, "Edcouch-Elsa Students in Class Revolt," *Brownsville Herald* (November 14, 1968). Norma R. Cuellar, "The Edcouch-Elsa Walkout," Mexican-American History 2363, Dr. Rodolfo Rocha (June 29, 1984), 1, http://www.aaperales.com/school/files/walkout/eewalkout.doc. Robles, "Walking Out," 20–22, copy of demands.

91. Cuellar, "The Edcouch-Elsa Walkout," 3.

92. "Refuses Boycotting Pupils," *Big Spring Herald* (Texas, November 19, 1968). Gary Garrison, "Return to School Sought," *Corpus Christi Times* (November 19, 1968). "Edcouch-Elsa Board Hears Each Student," *Brownsville Herald* (November 20, 1968). "Edcouch Student Hearings Scheduled for Wednesday," *Brownsville Herald* (November 26, 1968). "Valley Students Stage Walkout," *Big Spring Herald* (Texas, November 14, 1968). Kenneth Clark, "VISTAs Tied to Boycott," *Brownsville Herald* (November 25, 1968). Cuellar, "The Edcouch-Elsa Walkout," 6–8.

93. Oscar Acosta, "The East L.A. 13 vs. the Superior Court," *El Grito* 3, no. 2 (Winter 1970): 14. London and Anderson, *So Shall Ye Reap,* 25. William Parker Frisbie, "Militancy Among Mexican Americans: A Study of High School Students" (PhD dissertation, University of North Carolina at Chapel Hill, 1972), 4, 143. *Forumeer* (October, December 1968). Eugene Acosta Marín, "The Mexican American Community and Leadership of the Dominant Society in Arizona: A Study of Their Mutual Attitudes and Perceptions" (PhD dissertation, U.S. International University, 1973), 12. Ian F. Haney-López, *Racism on Trial: The Chicano Fight for Justice* (Cambridge, MA: Belknap Press of Harvard University Press, 2004).

94. David Sánchez, *Expedition Through Aztlán* (La Puente, CA: Perspectiva Press, 1978). Rona M. Fields and Charles J. Fox, "Viva La Raza: The Saga of the Brown Berets" (unpublished manuscript). See also G. Rosen, "Political Ideology." David Sánchez himself remained anti-communist throughout his career. Other factions such as La Junta adopted a revolutionary focus. Marguerite Marín, *Social Protest in an Urban Barrio: A Study of the Chicano Movement, 1966–1974* (Lanham, MD: University Press of America, 1991).

95. David Montejano, *Quixote's Soldiers: A Local History of the Chicano Movement, 1966–1981* (Austin: University of Texas Press, 2010).

96. Jennifer G. Correa, "Chicano Nationalism: The Brown Berets and Legal Social Control," (Master's thesis, Texas A&M University, Kingsville, Texas, 2006), 79–97, quoted FBI File #105-178715: March 27, 1968. FBI File #157-2163: March 7, 1968 reported on the ELA Walkouts. Correa also quoted FBI File #105-178715: February 25, 1969.

97. Patrick J. McDonnell, "1968 Massacre in Mexico Still Echoes Across Nation; Activism: Killing of Students Just Before Olympics Radically Changed Country and Questions Continue," *Los Angeles Times* (October 2, 1993). Kate Doyle, "The Tlatelolco Massacre: U.S. Documents on Mexico and the Events of 1968," Posted October 10, 2003, National Security Archive, http://www.gwu.edu/~nsarchiv/NSAEBB/NSAEBB99/. William Kelly, "Nothing Has Happened Here: Memory and the Tlatelolco Massacre, 1968–2008" (PhD dissertation, Texas Christian University, 2010), 35–52.

98. Armando Morales, "A Study of Mexican American Perceptions of Law Enforcement Policies and Practices in East Los Angeles" (DSW dissertation, University of Southern California, 1972), 87, 89, 90. *New York Times* (October 25, 1971). Christopher Rand, *Los Angeles: The Ultimate City* (New York:

Oxford University Press, 1967), 131. Joan W. Moore, *Mexican Americans,* 2d ed. (Englewood Cliffs, NJ: Prentice-Hall, 1976), 93. *G.I. Forum News Bulletin* (March–April 1960). *Eastside Sun* (Los Angeles, February 4, 1960). *Eastside Sun* (February 4 and 11, 1960), see Martin J. Siesl, "Behind the Badge: The Police and Social Discontent in Los Angeles Since 1950," in Norman M. Klein and Martin J. Siesl, *20th Century Los Angeles: Power, Promotion and Social Conflict* (Claremont, CA: Regina Books, 1990), 153–94. *Eastside Sun* (February 11, 1960). "Roybal Comments on Crime Reports of East Los Angeles," *Eastside Sun* (March 10, 1960). "Police Maltreatment Subject at Conference at Biltmore Hotel," *Eastside Sun* (June 16, 1960). Edward J. Escobar, "Bloody Christmas and the Irony of Police Professionalism: The Los Angeles Police Department, Mexican Americans, and Police Reform in the 1950s," *Pacific Historical Review* 72, no. 2 (May 2003): 171–73.

99. Morales, "Mexican American Perceptions," 89, 90. *New York Times* (October 25, 1971).

100. Oropeza, "La Batalla," 109, 113.

101. Congressman Henry B. González's Congressional Speech of April 22, 1969, *Congressional Record,* 91st Cong., 1st Sess. (April 22, 1969). Josh Gottheimer, ed., *Ripples of Hope: Great American Civil Rights Speeches* (New York: Basic Civitas Books, 2003), 331–39.

102. H. Joaquín Jackson and David Marion Wilkinson, *One Ranger: A Memoir* (Austin: University of Texas Press, 2005), 46, 63–75. Acuña, *Making of Chicana/o Studies,* 126–27.

103. José Angel Gutiérrez, *Tejano Voices,* Oral History Collection, University of Texas Arlington, and The José Angel Gutiérrez Papers, 1959–1991, at University of Texas at San Antonio; A Guide to the Jose Angel Gutierrez Papers, 1959–1991, http://www.lib.utexas.edu/taro/utsa/00002/utsa-00002.html; these are priceless for Chicano research.

104. Vicki Ruiz and Virginia Sánchez Korrol, eds., *Latinas in the United States: A Historical Encyclopedia* (Indiana University Press, 2006), 305.

105. Severita Lara, Crystal City Walkout Leader, http://www.youtube.com/watch?v=sQIcz_2HgkE&feature=related. MAYO document, "José Angel Gutiérrez files, Crystal City, Texas," in Rosales, ed., *Testimonio,* 387–88.

106. Jackson and Wilkinson, *One Ranger,* 69. David G. Gutiérrez, *Walls and Mirrors: Mexican Americans, Mexican Immigrants, and the Politics of Ethnicity* (Berkeley: University of California Press, 1995), 186–87. Navarro, *Mexican American Youth,* 100. J. Gutiérrez, *The Making of a Chicano Militant,* 103. *Forumeer* (February, May 1969). Castro, *Chicano Power,* 156–57. José Angel Gutiérrez, "Aztlán: Chicano Revolt in the Winter Garden," *La Raza* 1, no. 4 (1971): 34–35, 37, 39–40. John Staples Shockley, *Chicano Revolt in a Texas Town* (South Bend, IN: University of Notre Dame Press, 1974), 119–21. José Angel Gutiérrez's speech at a meeting in San Antonio, on May 4, 1970, "Mexicanos Need to Control Their Own Destinies," www.clnet.ucla.edu/research/docs/razaunida/control.htm.

107. The Tierra Amarilla Courthouse Raid, http://www.youtube.com/watch?v=phF376VK3ek&feature=related.

108. Malcolm Ebright, *Land Grants & Lawsuits in Northern New Mexico* (Albuquerque: University of New Mexico Press), 11, 14. Fred Rosen, "The Fate of the Ejido (threats to existence of system of communal ownership of agricultural land)," *NACLA Report on the Americas* 26, no. 5 (May 1993): 3ff. Gardner, *Tijerina,* 66–84, 129–30, 208, 265–79. Peter Nabokov, *Tijerina and the Courthouse Raid* (Albuquerque: University of New Mexico Press, 1969), 19, 28, 30, 250–66. Clark Knowlton, "Guerrillas of Rio Arriba: The New Mexico Land Wars," in F. Chris García, ed., *La Causa Politica: A Chicano Politics Reader* (Notre Dame, IN: University of Notre Dame Press, 1974), 333. Reies López Tijerina, "A Letter from the Santa Fe Jail," Reies López Tijerina Collection, University of New Mexico, Albuquerque.

109. *El Plan Espiritual de Aztlán,* http://www.utpa.edu/orgs/mecha/aztlan.html.

110. Aztlan Exploration 2000, http://ttzlibrary.yuku.com/topic/617/Aztec-origins#.UKD2i4bs9nU. "San Ce Tojuan: We Are One: Documentary screening and art exhibit focuses on origins of Uto-Nahuatl people, March 12," LatinoLA: February 24, 2005, http://latinola.com/story.php?story=2442.

111. Guide to the Montoya, José Papers 1969–2001, http://www.oac.cdlib.org/findaid/ark:/13030/kt1m3nf0sm/entire_text/.

112. Stan Steiner, *La Raza: The Mexican Americans* (New York: Harper & Row, 1969), 378–92. Christine Marín, *A Spokesman of the Mexican American Movement: Rodolfo "Corky" Gonzales and the Fight for Chicano Liberation, 1966–1972* (San Francisco: R&E Research Associates, 1977), 1–3, 5. *Forumeer* (November 1965, June 1966). *The Militant* (December 4, 1970). The best book on the Crusade is Ernesto B. Vigil, *The Crusade for Justice: Chicano Militancy and the Government's War on Dissent* (Madison: University of Wisconsin Press, 1999).

113. Elizabeth Martinez, 500 Years of Chicana Women's History Parts 1–3, http://www.youtube.com/watch?v=JzYISUV_Sc8. "Activist Elizabeth 'Betita' Martínez Speaks at Michigan State," http://www.vimeo.com/1211392.

114. Haney-López, *Racism on Trial,* 225.

115. Naomi Helena Quiñonez, "*Hijas de la Maline* (Malinche's Daughters): The Development of Social Agency Among Mexican American Women and the Emergence of First Wave Chicana Cultural Production" (PhD dissertation, Claremont Graduate School, Claremont, California, 1997), 153. Elizabeth Martínez, "'On Time' in Mississippi: 1964–1994: Confronting Immoral Power with Moral Power," *Z Magazine* (September 1994): 37–40. Elizabeth Martínez, *De Colores Means All of US: Latina Views for a Multi-Colored Century* (Cambridge, MA: South End Press, 1998). Dionne Elaine Espinoza, "Pedagogies of Nationalism and Gender: Cultural Resistance in Selected Representational Practices of Chicana/o Movement Activists, 1967–1972" (PhD dissertation, Cornell University, 1996), 147–201.

116. Luis Valdez Profile, http://www.youtube.com/watch?v=C1YylqDIjo. El Teatro Campesino 2008 Actos Promo, http://www.youtube.com/watch?v=8Sr4P6woodk.

117. Felipe de Ortego y Gasca, "Octavio Romano and the Chicano Literary Renaissance," *Chicano Literature Latino Literature— Pluma Fronteriza,* November 6, 2006,

118. Bill Flores, "Francisca Flores: 1913–1996," http://clnet.ucla.edu/research/francisca.html.

119. María Cardalliaguet Gómez-Málaga, The Mexican and Chicano Mural Movements, Yale-New Haven Teachers Institute, http://www.yale.edu/ynhti/curriculum/units/2006/2/06.02.01.x.html. The Chicano Park Historical Documentation Project, http://www.chicanoparksandiego.com/intro.html. Malaquías Montoya, http://www.metroactive.com/papers/metro/08.07.97/art-9732.html. Boyle Heights - Murals - Brooklyn Ave - Footage, http://www.youtube.com/watch?v=f5f9gCGRjvg. Tucson: the City of Murals, http://www.youtube.com/watch?v=j7ksyDL37QI.

120. *El Plan de Santa Barbara,* MEChA, Pan American University, http://www.panam.edu/orgs/MEChA/st_barbara.html.

121. Oropeza, "La Batalla," 115–18, 232–33. The LA Spanish-language newspaper *La Opinion* also supported the antiwar effort. Delfino Varela, "The Making of Captain Medina," *Regeneración* 1, no. 1 (1970): 8–13. Navarro, *Mexican American Youth,* 41–42, 66–70.

122. Albert L Pulido, "Are You an Emissary of Jesus Christ? Justice, the Catholic Church, and the Chicano Movement," *Explorations in Ethnic Studies,* 14, no. 1 (January 1991): 17–34. Acuña, *Anything but Mexican,* 35. *Los Angeles Times* (September 23, 1985). Interviews and conversations with Ricardo Cruz; Cruz passed the California bar, but had to fight to be certified because of his conviction. "Law Students Seek Signatures; Petition Protests Denial of Certification by Bar for Chicanos Active in Barrios," *Belvedere Citizen* (Los Angeles, March 16, 1972).

123. Richard Edward Martínez, *PADRES: The National Chicano Priest Movement* (Austin: University of Texas Press, 2005), 55. Jay Dolan and Allan Figueroa Deck, S.J., eds., *Hispanic Catholic Culture in the U.S.: Issues and Concerns* (Notre Dame, IN: University of Notre Dame Press, 1994), 224–26. Anthony M. Stevens-Arroyo, "The Emergence of a Sacred Identity Among Latino Catholics: An Appraisal," in Dolan and Deck, eds., *Hispanic Catholic Culture,* has a different take. Martin McMurtrey, *Mariachi Bishop: The Life Story of Patrick Flores* (San Antonio, TX: Corona, 1987). Juan Romero, "Charisma and Power: An Essay on the History of PADRES," *U.S. Catholic Historian* 9 (Spring 1990).

124. Lara Medina, "The Challenges and Consequences of Being Latina, Catholic and Political," in Gaston Espinosa, Virgilio Elizondo, and Jesse Miranda, eds., *Latino Religions and Civic Activism in the United States* (New York: Oxford University Press, 2005), 97–108. Lara Medina, *Las Hermanas: Chicana/ Latina Religious-Political Activism in the U.S. Catholic Church* (Philadelphia, PA: Temple University Press, 2004). Las Hermanas, *Handbook of Texas Online,* http://www.tshaonline.org/handbook/online/articles/LL/ixl3.html. Ana María Díaz-Stevens, "The Saving Grace: The Matriarchal Core of Latino Catholicism," *Latino Studies Journal* 4, no. 3 (September 1993): 60–78.

125. Quoted in Morales, "Mexican American Perceptions," 43. Rubén Salazar, "State Calls for Probe of Judge in Latin Slurs," *Los Angeles Times* (October 3, 1969), 3.

126. See previous editions of this book where the treatment of this topic is considerably longer. Morales, "Mexican American

Perceptions," 43, 103–7. U.S. Commission on Civil Rights, *Mexican Americans and the Administration of Justice in the Southwest* (Washington, DC: Government Printing Office, 1970), 4–5, 37–38, 40. *La Raza* 1, no. 2 (1970): 18–19. *Forumeer* (October 1968). On September 1, 1968, Jess Domínguez, 41, was beaten by at least 15 officers and charged with assaulting an officer. On November 9, 1968, Salvador Barba, 13, was beaten by Los Angeles police and received a head wound requiring 40 stitches. On May 5, 1969, Frank Gonzales, 14, of Los Angeles was skipping school and was shot and killed by Officer Thomas Parkham. On September 8, 1968, in Fairfield, California, Sergeant David Huff shot and killed José Alvarado. *Forumeer* (January 19, 1970; March 1970). "Roybal Demands Removal of San Jose Judge," *Belvedere Citizen* (October 16, 1969). "Judge's Intemperate Outburst Against Mexicans Investigated," *Eastside Sun* (October 9, 1969). *Ideal* (February 12–15, 1970). *Los Angeles Times* (February 7, 1972). *Justicia O* 1, no. 3 (January 1971). Gerard J. De Groot, "Ronald Reagan and Student Unrest in California, 1966–1970," *Pacific Historical Review*, LXV, no. 1 (February 1996): 107–29.

127. Quoted in Oropeza, "La Batalla," 133–36, 171–72, 175, 180, 212–16, 221, 226, 228. Mario T. García, ed., *Ruben Salazar, Border Correspondent: Selected Writings, 1955–1970* (Berkeley: University of California Press, 1995). *Los Angeles Times* (July 17, 1970). Gene Blake and Howard Hertel, "Court Won't Drop Case Against Officers in 'Mistake' Slayings," *Los Angeles Times* (April 27, 1971). Letter from Manuel Ruiz, a member of the U.S. Commission on Civil Rights, to Herman Sillas, chairperson of the California State Advisory Committee to the Commission, September 14, 1970, in "A Report of the California State Advisory Committee to the U.S. Commission on Civil Rights: Police-Community Relations in East Los Angeles, California" (October 1970); *Los Angeles Times* (December 18, 1971). Ralph Guzmán, "Mexican American Casualties in Vietnam," *La Raza* 1, no. 1 (1971): 12. *Forumeer* (November 1969). In "Population Control—Weeding Out Chicanos in Vietnam War?," *Forumeer* (April 1970). In the Southwest, out of 2,189 casualties, 316 were Chicanos. *Forumeer* (July 1970). Ralph Guzmán, "Mexican Americans Have Highest Vietnam Death Rate," *Belvedere Citizen* (October 16, 1969). Information about the moratorium is also drawn from the *Belvedere Citizen* (July 9, 1970) and my role as a participant observer.

128. Ruben Salazar, http://www.youtube.com/watch?v=qh7YQtjP4uo. Chicano Moratorium, http://www.youtube.com/watch?v=famNeiosTVk. Enrique Hank López, "Overkill at the Silver Dollar," *The Nation* (October 19, 1970), 365–68.

129. *La Raza,* 3 (Special Issue 1970) features a photo essay of the moratorium, documenting police repression. Armando Morales, *Ando Sangrando! I Am Bleeding* (Los Angeles: Congress of Mexican American Unity, 1971), 105, 117. Chávez, "Aztlán," 118–19, 124. Putnam's transcript on file. "Police Chief Davis Claims Latin Youths Being Used by Reds," *Belvedere Citizen* (January 21, 1971). *Eastside Sun* (February 4, 1971).

130. Chávez, "Aztlán," 82–91. Those arrested were Chris Augustine, Luis Arroyo, Jaime Cervantes, Adelaida R. Del Castillo, Ernest Eichwald, Moctesuma Esparza, Reynaldo Macias, Francisco Martínez, Rene Nuñez, Frank Sándoval, Victor Resendez, James Vigil, Thomas Varela, and Petra Valdez. The ten indicted were Anthony Salamanca, Esmeralda Bernal, Carlos Montes, Ralph Ramírez, Thomas Varela, Rene Nuñez, Ernest Eichwald Cebeda, Juan Robles, Moctezuma Esparza, and Willie Méndoza. Aside from Sumaya, Abel Armas and Robert Avila were listed as infiltrators. Others were Sergio Robledo and Frank Martínez. *Carlos Montes et al. v. The Superior Court of Los Angeles County,* 10 Cal. App. 3d 343; 88 Cal. Rptr. 736; 1970 Cal. App. LEXIS 1845 August 7, 1970.

131. *Los Angeles Times* (July 27, August 18, 1971). *Valley News* (Van Nuys, California, November 27, 1979). Frank Del Olmo, "Provoked. Trouble for Lawmen, Chicano Informer Claims," *Los Angeles Times* (February 1, 1972). *Los Angeles Free Press* (February 4–10, 1972).

132. *Los Angeles Free Press* (February 4–10, 1972). "Chicano Liberation Front Group Claims Bombing Credit," *Belvedere Citizen* (August 19, 1971). "Officials Probe, Seek Links in East LA Bombings," *Belvedere Citizen* (May 6, 1971). "Roosevelt High Bombings Linked to Series of Explosions in Area," *Belvedere Citizen* (June 10, 1971).

133. Briggs, Fogel, and Schmidt, *The Chicano Worker,* 5, 34, 36–38, 44, 53–54, 59–60, 68. Moore, *Mexican Americans,* 60. *Los Desarriagados* (Winter 1976–1977): 6. Castro, *Chicano Power,* 210–11. D. Gutiérrez, *Walls and Mirrors,* 183. Yen Le Espiritu, "Immigration and the Peopling of Los Angeles," in Riposa and Dersch, *City of Angels,* 75.

CHAPTER 14

The 1970s and 1980s: Redefining the 1960s

LEARNING OBJECTIVES

- Show how the 1970s undid many of the civil rights gains of the 1960s.

- List the changes that took place in the 1970s.

- Illustrate how events in Latin America impacted the Chicana/o community.

- Explain how the Bakke decision of 1978 was pivotal in reversing the civil rights gains.

- Discuss the role of immigration during this decade.

- Debate the competing ideologies within the Chicana/o community during this decade.

The timeline calls to mind the impact that the 1960s, the Vietnam War, the youth rebellion, and the Civil Rights movement had on the decade of the seventies. The school walkouts of 1968 politicized thousands of Chicana/o students throughout the country, which led to their involvement in issues such as the Vietnam War and Civil Rights movement in the 1960s. Because of the sacrifices of the Chicana/o and the preceding generations, more Chicanos and Chicanas entered college after this point than at any time in history. The expectations of the community increased as more people started thinking in terms of constitutional rights and control over their own lives. However, the timeline also resembles the decades of the 1920s and the 1950s, which followed the two major wars and were marked by a growing Euro-American xenophobia and a renewal of big businesses' war on the working class.

The intense demands for human and constitutional rights caused a backlash among President Richard Nixon's supporters. The white establishment resisted reform, resulting in friction with Chicanos and other minorities. As the community's awareness expanded, race, gender, and economic issues competed with the Vietnam War for attention. Chicanos became more cognizant of their dependency and their exploitation by the U.S. economy. Finally, many Latinos also shared the dream of the martyred Che Guevara of a united Latin America.[1] They were outraged by world events in general and the complicity of the Central Intelligence Agency in the 1973 overthrow of Chilean President Salvador Allende in particular.[2]

1968	1969	1970	1972	1973	1974	1975	1976	1977	1978	1979

Scores of Chicanos continued to organize along national lines, believing that change was possible through unity among Chicanas/os and through the identity politics of the 1960s. *La Raza Unida* Party (LRUP), founded in 1970, was an expression of this nationalism. It was a political party formed to end the marginalization of the Chicana/o community perpetuated by the two major parties; the two parties elected white candidates and kept Chicanas/os powerless. Some Chicanas/os sought to build revolutionary cells, while others preferred working within established organizations. Large numbers of Mexican immigrants continued to enter the country; they benefited from the entitlements brought about by the struggles of earlier Mexican American and Chicana/o generations, often without understanding their legacy. Meanwhile, the entry of larger numbers of Chicanas and Chicanos into college, and their graduation, brought about a slight widening of the Chicana/o middle class. The end of the 1970s saw the election of more Chicanos to political office. However, the agenda of the movement was also changing.

The 1965 amendments to the Immigration Act dramatically changed the mix of immigrants. In the 1950s, 53 percent of immigrants were from Europe, 25 percent from Latin America, and 6 percent from Asia. By the 1980s, only 11 percent of immigrants came from Europe, whereas 42 percent came from Latin America and 42 percent from Asia.[3] This was a result of changing U.S. admission policy from national origins to family preferences. The bulk of the Latin American immigration was from Mexico—a result of Mexico's high birth rate, modernization of agriculture, and a decline of ruralism. Even more Mexicans would have migrated to the United States had it not been for Mexico's economic growth of the late 1970s based on the "Oil Boom." The presence of more foreign-born people meant an increase in U.S. nativism, as politicos and journalists without substantiation criminalized Mexican immigrants. This racist nativism pressured the Immigration and Naturalization Service (INS) to become more aggressive. Thus, by necessity, immigration took its place along with farmworker issues as a priority among Chicanos.

The redefining of the Chicano identity began even before 1970. Government and the media moved to homogenize all Spanish speakers under the classification of Hispanic, and then Latino. Another attempt at redefinition came from within the Chicano community itself. Large waves of immigrants during the 1970s and 1980s rejected the term *Chicano*, which had been viewed as pejorative among first-generation immigrants since it was first proposed in 1969. In the first part of the 1970s, massive social unrest and ethnic pride increased unity within the movement itself, boosting acceptance for the term Chicano. This unifying moment came in the aftermath of the demonstration of August 29, 1970 (described in Chapter 13). However, it was doused by the police and the media that manipulated the facts of what happened on August 29. The assassination of journalist Rubén Salazar intimidated some, but more tragic was that the media's suppression of the facts repressed the memory of progressives and thus helped institutionalize racism.[4]

Instead of addressing the grievances of youth, the media portrayed young Chicanos as malcontents who wanted to destroy society. This historical distortion allowed for the redefinition of the 1960s; the death of Rubén Salazar thus became merely an unfortunate accident and racism became an aberration rather than a systemic problem. The lack of a coherent memory of the gains of the 1960s led to a fractionalization of the Chicana/o community. The quickness of this reversal caught most Chicanos unprepared and by July 25, 1983, a *Los Angeles Times* poll showed that 25 percent of Chicanos preferred the designation "Mexican"; 23 percent, "Mexican American"; 18 percent, "Latino"; and 14 percent, "Hispanic." The reversal followed a decade of persistent propaganda blurring the definition of the term *Chicano*, or even *Mexican*.[5]

This was not the first time in history that conservatives derailed the nation's commitment to values such as equality and social justice. After World War II, capitalists exaggerated the Communist threat and labeled New and Fair Deal programs as socialistic and a threat to American democracy. Soon after the 1960s, a similar phenomenon was observed: the right wing moved to weaken the Great Society's civil rights legislation and the decade's commitment to equality and justice for all. In order to change the common perception among the Euro-American public, words such as *racism* and *victim* were redefined. For example, during the 1960s many Americans challenged beliefs such as "every American is equal" and claims that "if the poor are poor, it is because the poor do not want to work." Liberals countered that this point of view blamed the victim; they claimed that programs such as affirmative action brought minorities into the mainstream.

Meanwhile, white homeowners and big business led an assault to shift the burden of funding social programs from themselves to the middle class, thus eliminating many social and educational programs. The recessions of the 1970s spawned the so-called taxpayer revolts. California's Proposition 13 in 1978 limited taxation to 1 percent of the full value of the property at the 1975 assessment, or the assessment after a later ownership change or construction, giving tax advantages to property owners who had purchased before the initiative was passed. Proposition 13 represented windfall profits to commercial, industrial, and landlord interests; it cut services to the majority and shifted the property tax burden to renters and those buying homes after 1978. Consequently Proposition 13 ravaged the public school systems where Latino students were in the majority.[6]

The *Bakke v. University of California* case (1978) was a victory for big business. It was part of a well-funded campaign waged by conservatives to manipulate public opinion. They saturated the air ways with the message that the poor were poor because they wanted to be poor, adding a new twist: it was an insult to call anyone a victim because this implied that the poor were passive. With this logic the conservatives concluded that racism was no longer a problem; the problem was programs designed to end racism: these programs ended up discriminating against white males and promoting mediocrity. The result was clichés such as "reverse racism."

Redefining Racism

During the 1960s, *racism* was a dirty six-letter word; to be called a racist was offensive. In the 1970s, popular culture played a role in this watering down of the term *racism*. Symbolic of this change is the television character Archie Bunker in *All in the Family*, which debuted in January 1971.[7] Norman Lear, a man of impeccable liberal credentials and intentions, produced the series, which premiered during the twilight of the Vietnam War protest movement. Archie Bunker, a lower-middle-class hard hat, hated African Americans, Latinos, and Jews, and had a strong antipathy toward social and political reform. Lear intended Archie's son-in-law, Michael, and daughter, Gloria, to ridicule Archie's outlandish prejudices and make the audience laugh at Archie's racism. In retrospect, just the opposite happened as Archie gave bigotry respectability. The fact is that Archie became so popular that there were a few spin-offs and copycats—*Maude, The Jeffersons, Sanford and Son*—all except *Maude* featured African American bigots.[8]

At the same time, Mexican Americans went against the tide, became more sensitive to racial stereotypes, and protested against them. They demanded more Mexican Americans and Latinos in the media.[9] However, they were not as successful as African Americans because they lacked the moral authority that the Civil Rights movement gave blacks. There were other factors too. For example, Mexican Americans were still a regional minority. In 1970, the African American population numbered 22.6 million, about 11 percent of the total U.S. population. That year, the Mexican origin population numbered just under 4.5 million, a fifth of the black population, and thus did not have the national clout to make politicos do the right thing.[10]

Government Legitimizes Racism

In the summer of 1969, presidential advisor Arthur Burns defined *poverty* as an "intellectual concept"; Nixon later appointed Burns to head the Federal Reserve and manage the nation's economy. The Supreme Court also altered its approach, with the Warren Burger Court being less interested than that headed by William Douglas in improving access for minorities. During the 1970s, the courts actively took the teeth out of the *Brown v. Board of Education* case (1954) decision and moved to criminalize the undocumented worker. Both the courts and Congress criminalized unauthorized immigrants. Initially, at least in the field of voting rights and bilingual education, Mexicans and other Latinos fared well in the courts, but by the 1990s these laws and safeguards were neutralized.[11]

Chicanas/os continued to struggle to end discrimination through the courts. However, the nation based its laws on an either-or standard—one was either black or white. At first, Mexican Americans had followed the strategy that they were white and thus entitled to the protections of the constitution. However, the public did not consider them white and the courts accepted subterfuges that Mexicans were separate because of language deficiency. After World War II, Mexican American organizations adopted the "other white" strategy, and in the 1950s it was accepted that Mexican Americans were "a class apart"; consequently, succeeding cases did not include Mexican Americans under the dicta of *Brown v. Board of Education* (1954), and the school districts distorted the status of Mexican children.

In 1968 José Cisneros and other Chicano parents filed suit against the Corpus Christi Independent School District. Attorney James de Anda abandoned the "other white" strategy and argued that Mexican Americans were an identifiable minority group and that the Corpus Christi Schools segregated Mexicans, denying them equal protection under the 14th Amendment of the U.S. Constitution. The court found for the plaintiffs: Mexican Americans were an identifiable minority group based on physical, cultural, religious, and linguistic distinctions, with a history of discrimination against them. *Cisneros v. Corpus Christi Independent School District* was the first case to entitle Mexican Americans under the *Brown* decision. It replaced the "other white" findings of *Hernández v. State of Texas*.[12]

The Politics of Cynicism: Nixon's Hispanic Strategy

In 1968, presidential candidate Hubert Humphrey received 90 percent of the Mexican vote. Analysts concluded that if Nixon had received 5 percent more of the Chicano votes in Texas, he would have carried the Lone Star State. Taking a cue from the 1968 experience, Nixon developed a "Hispanic" strategy: the plan was to court brown Middle America by giving high-level appointments and more government jobs to Mexican Americans.[13]

The next year, President Nixon replaced the Inter-Agency Committee on Mexican American Affairs with the Cabinet Committee on Opportunities for the Spanish-speaking People, broadening the target group from Chicanos to Hispanics. Nixon appointed Martín Castillo the head of the Cabinet Committee. In 1970, Nixon helped form the National Economic Development Association (NEDA), a national organization funded by state and federal agencies to promote private development in low-income areas. Some Mexican American Democrats affectionately called it NADA (nothing). By 1972, Nixon had appointed 50 Chicanos to high federal posts. The president recruited Romana Bañuelos, a Los Angeles food manufacturer, to serve as treasurer of the United States (1971–1974).[14]

The "brown mafia," a network of community leaders tapped by the Nixon administration to capture the Latino vote, played a key role in the Committee to Re-Elect the President (CREEP). Alex Armendaris of South Bend, Indiana, led the brown mafia, which undoubtedly expected to get at least 20 percent of the Latino vote. The Republicans made it clear to the brown mafia that if they did not reach this goal, the administration would cut federal appointments and stop federal funding to Latinos. Nixon received 31 percent of the Mexican vote nationally. Yet, instead of rewarding Latinos, after the election the president dismantled the War on Poverty program (see discussion below). This was a logical political step, since the poorer Chicanos and other so-called Hispanics did not vote for him.[15]

In 1973, Nixon cynically appointed Ann Armstrong, a white woman, to the post of White House Aide on domestic Latino affairs. According to Nixon, Armstrong was qualified because her husband owned a large ranch that employed Mexicans. Nevertheless, because patronage was funneled through Latino Republicans, after this point the Chicanas/os and, especially, Cuban American Republicans gained more influence as power brokers. From 1972 to 1980, the Republican National Hispanic Assembly raised $400,000 to register Republican voters. Nixon promoted programs benefiting the managerial, professional, and business sectors of this community. After reelection in 1972, Nixon launched his New Federalism with renewed vigor. (New Federalism simply meant decentralizing social programs, returning tax moneys to the municipalities and the states, and relying on the city bosses' good faith to care for the poor.)[16]

Dismantling the War on Poverty

Nixon dismantled the War on Poverty and substituted it with block grants to municipalities to spend as they wished. In 1973, Congress passed the Comprehensive Employment and Training Act (CETA), which changed job-training policy. Previous programs had targeted low-skilled, unemployed, nonwhite workers; CETA included other beneficiaries—mostly better-off, white males. The effect of CETA and other government programs was to reduce services to the disadvantaged, giving more control to local politicians and to the private sector. This policy shift was devastating to Chicanas/os as a whole; poverty, inflation, and a sharp rise in the cost of living worsened their plight, and the number of poor and unemployed kept increasing throughout the 1970s and into the 1980s.[17]

Chicano Power

Nationalists of the 1960s felt that they could transform society by organizing around what many called *Chicanismo*. This faction believed that Chicanas/os should continue to organize around Chicano issues and interests and focus on equality for the group. Much like the early utopian societies, they believed that through example, Chicanos would change society. Many supporters of this movement believed unity would come about through embracing a common identity.

A second movement believed that a new understanding of Chicanos' status in the United States had to be placed into the context of historical and materialist explanations. This faction advocated socialist principles, identifying themselves as working-class people, and entered into coalitions with other progressive groups. Equality would come about by totally transforming society—politically, socially, and economically. A third current was perfectly satisfied with society as it was; they believed that with time, Chicanos would be assimilated into the mainstream as racism diminished and more Chicanos became middle class. At the same time, within each of these groups, women were calling for changes in the culture of Chicanos to bring about gender equality.

Nationalists argued that Marxism itself failed to resolve the identity questions—in fact, Marxists undermined the question of identity. Chicanos had to unite around their culture and change society by working to resolve Chicano-specific problems. The counterargument of leftists was that a revolutionary transformation could not be brought about by organizing solely around a Chicano, Chicana, African American, feminist, lesbian, or gay ideology without giving these particular identities an economic definition. The capitalist system must be replaced before equality could be achieved. The assimilation group—or better still, the mainstream group—believed that through individual achievement the group would be lifted; as more educated Chicanos took positions of power, they would resolve many of the ills of society.[18] Chicanas calling themselves feminists were impatient with the persistence of sexism, and the control of the dialogue by males, and they became more vocal—some broke off from these three waves to form a fourth. It is important to note that within each current there was constant agitation and changes that occurred as a result of activism and interaction—not necessarily through theory.

La Raza Unida Party

Early efforts to form LRUP came from Chicanos in Colorado and Texas. On March 30, 1970, activist Corky Gonzales, who had launched the Crusade for Justice organization, announced the formation of the Colorado RUP.[19] At the 1970 Second Annual Youth Liberation Conference in Denver, the 2,500 activists attending endorsed the notion of a Chicano party. The Crusade for Justice Leadership wanted to form the *Congreso de Aztlán*, which would build a Chicano nation. In May, LRUP held a state convention in Pueblo, at which they endorsed candidates for statewide office. Although police authorities continuously harassed this slate, the party was able to run candidates, albeit without success, at all levels of government. LRUP's purpose was not so much to win as to raise the political consciousness of the Mexican-origin community. By 1971, the stress of police interference took its toll; only 500 attended the Third Annual Chicano Liberation Conference.[20]

Texas was a special case. José Angel Gutiérrez raised the notion of LRUP to the Mexican American Youth Organization (MAYO) in 1968; the executive board rejected it. Meanwhile, MAYO's implementation of the Winter Garden Project, the plan to take over south Texas, which was 80 percent Mexican American, led to Chicano electoral victories in Crystal City, Cotula, and Carrizo Springs. Buoyed by success, Tejanos moved to form a third party. The linchpin to the Chicano revolt was the takeover of the Crystal City School Board. In December 1969, at the first and only national MAYO meeting, Chicano activists endorsed the formation of a third party. In 1971, LRUP went statewide as 300 activists gathered in San Antonio on October 31 and formally launched the party.

The Gutiérrezes, José Angel and Luz, had argued that a strong community power base had to be developed before the party went statewide. However, Mario Compeán, a founder of MAYO who was supported by University of Texas professor Armando Gutiérrez, pushed for an immediate statewide party. The Texas LRUP tasted some initial success as it registered 22,388 voters in 1972.[21]

Tejanas were more visible in LRUP than were Chicanas elsewhere, forming *Las Mujeres por la Raza Unida* (Women for the Raza Unida Party), which supported the Equal Rights Amendment. They were led by Marta Cotera, Alma Canales, Rosie Castro, Evey Chapa, and Virginia Múzquiz. The LRUP platform advocated community control of schools, bilingual education, and women's and workers' rights. In 1972, Alma Canales unsuccessfully ran as RUP candidate for lieutenant governor; Cotera unsuccessfully ran for the Texas State Board of Education; and Viviana Santiago successfully ran for the Crystal City Independent School District Board of Trustees. Statewide, attorney Ramsey Muñiz, 29, a former Baylor University football star, ran for governor on the LRUP ticket, accumulating 214,118 votes (6.28 percent). Republicans won the governorship by 100,000 votes.[22]

The California RUP was divided into northern and southern California. Although LRUP registered almost 23,000 voters and ran candidates statewide, the party never really took root in California. Many Chicanos grew disillusioned with LRUP's attempt at electoral politics and gravitated to other groups such as the Labor Committee of LRUP, which became the core of the August 29th Movement (ATM), a Marxist cell. The ATM later merged into the League of Revolutionary Struggle (LRS), which was active almost into the 1990s. Others joined the *Centro de Acción Social Autónoma* (CASA; Autonomous Center for Social Action), which, like the LRS, became an important trainer of union organizers and future politicos in California.

LRUP ran a candidate for the 48th Assembly District on its ticket; the candidate polled 7.93 percent (2,778) of the votes, playing the role of the spoiler and denying Democratic Party candidate Richard Alatorre the victory. The Republican margin of victory was 46.71 percent (16,346 votes) to 42.17 percent (14,759 votes). Alatorre easily won the next election, in which LRUP did not field a candidate. This campaign was controversial because many wanted LRUP to be known more for its principles than as a vehicle for defeating Democrats. They also deplored the lack of consultation with the local LRUP central committee.[23]

Failure to Build a National Third Party

In September 1972, LRUP held its national convention in El Paso. Tragedy marked the event when a white bigot shot and killed Richard Falcón at Orogrande, New Mexico, as he was en route to the convention. Every Chicano leader except César Chávez participated at the convention. (Predictably, Chávez, whose union was part of the AFL-CIO, endorsed George McGovern rather than Richard Nixon.) There was immediate controversy: many delegates wanted to field an RUP presidential candidate, but the majority preferred to stay out of national politics. Another split occurred at the convention when José Angel Gutiérrez defeated Corky Gonzales for the national chair. Although a symbolic show of unity followed, the formation of two camps was irreversible; within two years, the Colorado RUP bolted from the national organization.[24]

Inevitably, factions developed in the Texas RUP. Many within the party looked to Muñiz, a relative newcomer, as leader, while others looked to Mario Compeán, who as a founder of MAYO had a strong following in San Antonio, which had the largest number of Tejanos and voting potential. After Muñiz's unsuccessful run, tension developed between the Compeán and Muñiz camps. Documents obtained by Gutiérrez under the Freedom of Information Act show considerable Central Intelligence Agency (CIA) surveillance of LRUP, suggesting that the CIA considered LRUP an international threat. Moreover, local police provocateurs and an active campaign by the Democratic Party to destroy LRUP accelerated its demise. LRUP was caught in a dilemma: its radical image turned off many U.S. Mexican voters, while efforts to broaden the party's appeal alienated the party's core constituency. LRUP found success in small towns where they had forged a community base for the party, proving that Gutiérrez's original rural strategy was correct. Even in Cristal (Crystal City, Texas), the stress caused by internal divisions was obvious by the mid-1970s. Many Mexican Americans there wanted to be part of the new prosperity—an impossible goal, given the limited resources of the area.

Texas had a larger percentage of second-generation Chicanos than did other states. Outside Texas, LRUP lacked the base and credibility to launch successful candidacies. In New Mexico, progressive Democrats such as Tiny Martínez in Las Vegas, New Mexico, made the launching of a third party impossible. California had capable leaders such as political scientist Armando Navarro and Genaro Ayala, but there was neither the money nor the time to build a base. In California, there were also divisions around the gender question. In the Lone Star State, space was given to women there, and women became candidates. LRUP's legacy cannot be overestimated.[25]

The Last Days of La Raza Unida

Meanwhile, in 1974 the City Terrace chapter unsuccessfully led a drive to incorporate East Los Angeles into a city. Unincorporated East Los Angeles included a population of 105,033 residents, more than 90 percent of whom were Mexican. The initiative lost—3,262 votes to 2,369 votes. There had been other unsuccessful efforts to create a "Chicano city."

As mentioned earlier, Chicanos controlled Democratic Party machines in New Mexico. These state officials branded LRUP members un-American, radicals, and outsiders; in May 1976, Rio Arriba deputies shot two LRUP activists. Since many New Mexicans were already part of the political system, they did not think they needed an alternative party like La Raza Unida to empower them politically.

However, LRUP still exists today. Its national chair is Genaro Ayala, a retired teacher at San Fernando High School, who has served as national chair since 1980. Ayala partly attributes LRUP's failure to "the lack of clarity of ideology."[26]

By 1974, LRUP began to implode, except in limited south Texas enclaves. Ironically, RUP's success led to disunity in Crystal City, Texas, and the party lost its control there in 1977. The emergence of the Southwest Voter Registration and Education Project (founded by Willie Velásquez, a former MAYO activist) led to the defection of some members to the Mexican American Democrats. Meanwhile, the arrest of Ramsey Muñiz on drug charges resulted in a loss of credibility. Nevertheless, a larger core of RUP activists remained in the political arena in Texas than elsewhere. The role played by the Gutiérrezes—both José Angel and Luz—was immeasurable.[27]

Inequality from Within

As in the case of other movements, the question of gender inequality fractionalized the Chicano movement. Some resisted the call for equality of sexes. The reactions differed: Some, like Martha Cotera, criticized LRUP but chose to work within the structure. Others, like Magdalena Mora, a committed student activist and union organizer who died of cancer in 1981 at age 29, chose to work within CASA and write for its newspaper, *Sin Fronteras*, and later for *El Foro de Pueblo*, speaking out against sexism while campaigning for workers' rights. Still others stressed the importance of developing autonomous feminist organizations. Positions often changed, and even when they did not, there were the inevitable personality clashes and egos, which were difficult to untangle. In general, the more to the left the organization, the more inclusive it became of women's issues. To its credit, *The Militant*, published by the Socialist Workers Party, was at the cutting edge of the question of feminism and sexual preferences.[28] By contrast, most leftist groups, while generally progressive in offering lip service to feminist issues, were in the Stone Age when it came to sexual preferences; homophobia was rampant during the 1970s. Nevertheless, the leftist organizations were training grounds for Chicana labor organizers and evolved to extend human rights to all.[29]

Chicana Voices

An important Chicana and Chicano voice was *El Grito del Norte*, a newspaper for which personages such as Enriqueta Longeaux y Vásquez and Elizabeth "Betita" Martínez wrote. In her featured column, Vásquez asked the U.S. Mexican people to "'stand up' and rethink the given social order," including U.S. militarism, interventions in Vietnam and Latin America, the Catholic Church, gringo society, and sexism—forcing many readers to rethink their positions on these issues. Vásquez's work appears as one of the early feminist voices representing the "loyalist" position and supporting nationalism. However, the designation of Vásquez as a loyalist is a distortion. Vásquez, like others, was attempting to reconcile her own evolving political positions with the reality and the political vocabulary of the community of that time, much the same as what Marxists were doing at that time. The question for Vásquez was how to obtain women's liberation, thus transforming the entire nuclear family. Since her involvement lay within Chicano organizations, her focus was on how to change those organizations and the people in them.

Like Marxism and nationalism, feminism had numerous variants. Critics dwell on the fact that Vásquez declared she was a *"Chicana primero,"* claiming that race should take precedence over gender in analyzing oppression. However, within the heat of the debate, myths often crop up. Take, for example, an event at the First National Chicano Youth Conference in Denver, Colorado, in May 1969. When the time came to report on the resolutions formulated at the workshop on the Chicana, Enriqueta Vásquez was shocked at the wording—that the Chicana woman did not want to be liberated. Yet she understood the tremendous pressure from the men in the hall—although she did not agree with the statement. Perhaps the Chicanas present meant that they did not want to be liberated by white women. That this statement was the consensus of the women at the workshop does not hold up.[30]

Inevitable Factions

Every social movement has factions, and the Chicana/o movement is no exception. A series of conferences on the Chicana Question took place in the early 1970s. One of the first activities of Chicanas was the formation of a women's caucus within the Mexican American Political Association (MAPA); women found it necessary to form a pressure group to change MAPA from within. In 1970, the Mexican American National Issues Conference in Sacramento sponsored a workshop on women. Out of this conference formed *La Comisión Femenil Mexicana* (The Mexican Feminist Commission), a group that was important in generating Chicana community programs through government grants; Francisca Flores and Grace Montañez Davis were among the leaders.[31] Meanwhile, Flores edited *Regeneración*, a magazine that published many articles on *la mujer*. That year, local Chicana forums became more popular—for instance, at California State University at Los Angeles, a Chicana forum honored María Cristina de Penichet, Mexico's first woman brain surgeon, and Celia Luna Rodríguez, leader of the Barrio Defense Committee and before that of the Mexican Civil Rights Congress.

In May 1971, over 600 Chicanas from 23 states attended *La Conferencia de Mujeres por La Raza* (the Women's Conference for the Latino People), sponsored by the YWCA in Houston. Some 40 percent of the attendees (300 women)—mostly Tejanas—walked out of the conference and held their own conference in a park. The dissenters charged that the Houston Mexican community had been engaged in a struggle with the YWCA and that, given a lack of Chicanos/as on staff, the YWCA was racist and its staff was elitist and bureaucratic. Those who remained inside claimed that the dissenters were antifeminist, loyalists, and cultural nationalists. Ironically, most agreed on fundamental issues such as abortion but disagreed on tactics and the role of the YWCA.[32]

Chicana groups focused on the special problems of Mexican women. Most topics revolved around male chauvinism, abortion, childcare, and sexism within the Chicano and the white women's movement. The struggle was very intense both within MEChA (*Movimiento Estudiantil Chicano/a de Aztlán*) and within the community. At the universities, because of the establishment of Chicano Studies programs, there was a ready network for the production and consumption of ideas regarding social change. In 1973, Chicanas spearheaded the opposition to the Talmadge Amendment to the Social Security Act, which required mothers on public assistance with children over six years of age to register with the state employment office and to report every two weeks until they obtained work.

As early as 1971, Dorinda Moreno published a journal, *Las Cucarachas* (The Cockroaches). In 1973, she published an anthology, *La Mujer—En Pie de Lucha* (The Woman in Struggle). Moreno also published the newspaper *La Razón Mestiza* (Mestizo Reason) in the San Francisco area in 1974. A recurrent theme in all her works was the unequal status of women.[33] By the late 1970s there was a broader participation of middle-class Chicanas in the women's movement, with Chicana professionals and activists attending the International Women's Year Conference in Mexico City in 1975 and the National Women's Conference in Houston two years later. There was also more popular coverage of the movement in the mainstream press.

Through their actions, women defined a political culture. For example, María Antonietta Berriozábal and Rosa Salazar Rosales set different paradigms for women's role in society. Berriozábal in 1972 founded Mexican American Business and Professional Women, searching for a strategy to empower Chicanas in the business world. Through her involvement with this issue, she developed a support network of women who ultimately got her elected to the San Antonio City Council in the 1980s, where she evolved into one of the most progressive elected officials of her time. (Berriozábal lost her bid for mayor in 1991.)

Rosa Salazar Rosales took another route. Denied entrance to college after high school despite being a brilliant student, she returned to school after becoming a mother and graduated from the University of Michigan. She returned to San Antonio in the late 1970s and became a union organizer; there the work further radicalized her. Both the women had formed strong networks of women and pushed feminist issues within both the Chicana community and the population at large.[34]

Missing in the early Chicana literature were feminist writings in leftist newspapers and journals. The attitude of some Chicanos was that these women gave up their Chicana cultural citizenship when they joined Marxist organizations. However, groups such as the Socialist Workers Party, through their newspaper the *Militant*, published excellent articles on gender and on homophobia, which influenced Chicanas/os during the 1970s and 1980s. The *Militant* was among the first to tackle the abortion issue head on. CASA published *Sin Fronteras*, and the League of Revolutionary Struggle (LRS) published *Unity*. A host of other newspapers were also published; the leftist newspapers far outnumbered the circulation of nationalist newspapers. Although there was tension among many of the groups due to party building, they had a positive impact on the Chicana/o community. The groups' cadres attended conferences and other meetings, pointing out the imbalances of government programs for women's issues. They were very critical of efforts to undo affirmative action programs, as was evident in their campaign against the *Bakke* decision. This body of thought was energized by Rosaura Sánchez and Rosa Martínez Cruz's anthology *Essays on La Mujer*, published by the Chicano Studies Research Center at UCLA in 1977, which gave a materialist interpretation of feminism.[35]

The Birth of Chicano Studies

Chicana/o Studies are one of the few academic programs that were not born within academe. They came together in 1968 as Chicano school walkouts hit California and Texas, and spread throughout the Southwest, Midwest, and Pacific Northwest—receiving much of their initial energy from the farmworker movement and the actions of the Black Student Union that shut down San Fernando Valley State College and San Francisco State College in November 1968 and spread to other colleges.[36] The eye of the storm was in California. In Texas, the MAYO focused on off-campus strategies toward achieving Brown Power and successfully took over local governments and school boards. At the California State Colleges, where most of the Chicano Studies Departments first took root, there were less than 1,000 Chicana/o students enrolled in the spring of 1969 systemwide. The majority of these students had matriculated there in the fall of 1968, as part of the first Educational Opportunity Programs that brought this handful of students to the CSC.[37] The winds that brought Chicano Studies picked up speed after the East Los Angeles school walkouts, and on the campuses Chicano students caught the tailwinds of the black student movement, the farmworker struggle, and the Vietnam War. By the spring of 1969 the small cores of Chicano students were integrated into the National Chicano Student Movement, which, after the Denver Chicano Youth Conference, met at Santa Barbara, California, and formulated the Plan of Santa Barbara that contextualized the disparate efforts of California campuses. For example, California State Colleges at Los Angeles, San Fernando, Long Beach, San Diego, and Fresno had already formulated programs, as had the Universities of California and many junior colleges, where professors such as Gracia Molina de Pick of San Diego Mesa College were pioneers.[38] In general, research institutions formed research centers and state colleges departments. The Plan of Santa Barbara capsulized these movements that spread throughout the Southwest, Pacific Northwest, and Midwest with varying degrees of success.

Centers were more common in Texas, Arizona, and New Mexico. In time, a center was established at the University of Texas, Austin, and at the University of Arizona, while Chicanos elsewhere lobbied for Mexican American programs. Anywhere a handful of Mexicans matriculated, there was the demand for Chicano studies, with varying degrees of success; the most notable efforts were the community colleges. An exception to the general trend of forming Mexican American Research Centers in the Lone Star State was the University of Texas El Paso where a militant but unsuccessful drive for a Chicano Studies department had emerged out of Segundo Barrio after the burning deaths of the three children of Miguel Rosales on January 4, 1967.[39]

What made the formation of Chicano Studies truly extraordinary was that initially it involved so few students. Unlike the Black Studies and Women's Studies programs, Chicanos did not have a large core of middle-class students in college. As mentioned, an overwhelming number of Chicana/o students were first-generation college students, who were children of immigrants. In every southwestern state, with the exception of New Mexico, they comprised less than 5 percent of the students in the state; in the Pacific Northwest and Midwest they formed less than 1 percent of the student community.[40] In 1969, there were an estimated one hundred Mexican Americans with PhDs nationwide. Again unlike the case of Black Studies and Women's Studies, these programs did not have long-standing contacts with the Ford philanthropic foundations, and they received little outside help.

On campus they became foci of Chicano activism and were a training ground for Chicano leaders and cultural workers within the community. Indeed, in the 1980s and 1990s most elected officials and labor and community organizers came out of the Chicano student movement, as did most artists and musicians. The campuses also became laboratories where Chicano and Chicana ideas evolved from a largely nationalist perspective to a more universal school of thought. It was there that sexist and homophobic notions were challenged and in some cases changed. Chicano Studies continuously advocated for the admission of more students of Latino origin, more Chicano Studies programs, appointment of more Chicana/o professors, and financial aid, as well as progressive social causes.

Sterilization: Saving Taxpayers' Money

During the 1970s, the issue of sterilization was a cause of concern. Sterilization has its roots in the social Darwinism eugenics movement of the early twentieth century whereby American eugenicists believed that people could be categorized according to intelligence and that the United States could genetically engineer its racial composition—the extreme position called for sterilization—a notion that was popular through the 1960s. There is evidence that even the members of President John F. Kennedy's Peace Corps, established in 1961, sponsored sterilization programs. Such programs were common in Puerto Rico, and were used as a policy to reduce overpopulation.[41] From 1973 to 1976, medical authorities sterilized one-third of the women of childbearing age in Puerto Rico and more than 3,000 Native Americans.

At the USC/Los Angeles County Hospital (a.k.a. General Hospital), serving the largest Mexican population in the United States, doctors routinely performed involuntary sterilizations during the early 1970s. According to Dr. Bernard Rosenfeld—who strongly objected to the practice as reminiscent of Nazi experimentation with Jews, gypsies, and the mentally retarded—doctors developed the attitude that by sterilizing the breeders the hospital saved the taxpayers millions of dollars in welfare payments.

Los Angeles General Hospital was in the business of training doctors. To gain practice, physicians often persuaded teenagers to authorize tubal ligations and hysterectomies and even rationalized their malpractice: "I want to ask every one of these girls if they want their tubes tied. I don't care how old they are. ... Remember, every one you get to get her tubes tied now means less work for some son of a bitch next time."[42] Some doctors bragged that they waited to seek permission to perform the operations until the anesthesia wore off. Often, the doctors gave English-language forms to patients who spoke only Spanish. Sterilization of poor minority women became a national issue when two black girls, ages 12 and 14, were sterilized in Montgomery, Alabama. Chicanas who spearheaded a suit against the General Hospital vehemently opposed this practice.

The issue of abortion continued to split the community. Many Mexican Americans were Catholic, and they followed the Church teachings that abortion was a sin. Feminists and many activists considered abortion to be a personal matter in which women should have full control of their bodies. Many Chicanas supported *Roe v. Wade* (1973), the U.S. Supreme Court decision legalizing abortion; however, on the matter of sterilization, activists point out that poor women who did not have a personal physician and did not speak English had less choice.

The Road to Delano

The drama of the 1960s, the antiwar movement, the Chicano student movement, the Raza Unida, and the farmworkers eclipsed the rich history of the Chicanas/os in the U.S. labor movement. After an initial resistance, gradually industrial unions such as the autoworkers, steelworkers, electrical workers, and miners had started admitting Chicanos. Mexican-origin workers played a huge role in building these unions, although union leadership often resisted their inclusion. By the 1970s, their numbers were too large to ignore, as were their demands. With the growth of Chicano membership within these unions, the United Farm Workers (UFW) union found ready allies. An example is the United Auto Workers, one of the UFW's staunchest supporters, as leaders such as Pete Beltrán of Local 645/GM Van Nuys championed the farmworker cause.

This alliance helped the UFW withstand the awesome economic and political power of agribusiness. Because of this cooperation and the moral authority garnered by Chávez, the growers were unsuccessful in 1972 in their push for Proposition 22, an initiative to outlaw boycotting and limit secret ballot elections to full-time nonseasonal farmworkers. Meanwhile, the Schenley Corporation refused to renegotiate with the UFW on these issues, sparking a strike in which police arrested 269 strikers. The Nixon administration nudged the Teamsters and the growers to cooperate. In the spring of 1973, the Teamsters' Agricultural Workers Organizing Committee declared war on the UFW in the Imperial Valley. The Seafarers Union offered to help Chávez get rid of the thugs, but Chávez, committed to nonviolence, refused. Teamster terrorists then brutally attacked farmworkers.

Governor Edmund G. Brown, Jr., helped form the Agricultural Labor Relations Board (ALRB) in 1975 to supervise elections and resolve appeals. The board allowed secondary boycotts only if employers refused to negotiate. After Brown left office, however, the Republican-controlled legislature constantly harassed the UFW, intervening on the side of the growers.

In Ohio, the Farm Labor Organizing Committee (FLOC) not only organized Mexicans in the fields of Ohio and Indiana but also sensitized Midwesterners regarding INS abuses. FLOC, with the Ohio Council of Churches, sponsored a conference on immigration in 1977. The Catholic bishops supported FLOC, which called a nationwide boycott of Campbell's Soup products. Also strengthening FLOC was its affiliation with the UFW in the 1980s. This boycott lasted until the spring of 1986, when FLOC signed a contract with Campbell's.

The UFW was unsuccessful at unionizing Texas farmworkers in the 1960s. Although Chávez wanted to expand operations there, difficulties in securing his California base kept his focus elsewhere. For a time, the UFW left Antonio Orendian in Texas to organize farmworkers. A split developed and Orendian left the UFW to organize a new Texas union: Texas Farm Workers (TFW). However, as times worsened and continual recessions swelled the ranks of labor, the TFW became less effective.[43]

The Farah Strike: The Breaking of Labor

Willie Farah had textile plants in both Texas and New Mexico. At his largest facility and headquarters in El Paso, Farah employed some 9,500 workers—85 percent were female, mostly Chicanas. The Amalgamated Clothing Workers Union of America (ACWUA) began organizing workers in Farah's San Antonio plant in the late 1960s. In October 1970, in an NLRB-supervised election, the cutting department voted to affiliate with the union. Willie Farah refused to bargain in good faith and immediately resorted to reprisals such as firing union loyalists or making them sweep floors. Willie erected barbed-wire fences around his five facilities.

By 1972, 4,000 Farah employees in El Paso, San Antonio, Victoria, and Las Cruces, New Mexico, were striking Farah. In July the union called its nationwide boycott of Farah, which lasted for two years and took a tremendous personal toll on the strikers and their families. The backbone of the strike was the women, who created their own group called *Unidad Para Siempre* (Unity Forever). In 1974, Farah signed a contract with the union but continued to harass union activists. By 1976, he closed his San Antonio factory and began to move his operations across the border. Slowly the workers' support of the union eroded. Part of the problem was that the union failed to develop its leadership or to continue the political education of the workers. The International (the national office of the ACWUA) had never fully appreciated or encouraged local Chicana workers. Another problem was the continued negative portrayal of Mexican American women by the media.[44]

Sin Fronteras

The Border Industrialization Program (BIP) reduced Mexico to a sweatshop equivalent of an underdeveloped nation. Since the *maquiladoras* (assembly factories) imported 98 percent of their raw materials from the United States and Japan, they did little to stimulate other domestic industries. By the end of the decade, Mexico would gain the reputation of paying even lower wages and having lower energy costs than the Far East, attracting more multinational factories.

In 1974, 476 *maquiladoras* operated in Mexico. During the recession of 1973–1975, the number of *maquiladoras* dramatically declined. As worker militancy grew, transnational managers, through the American Chamber of Commerce in Mexico, warned Mexican President Luis Echeverría to intervene on the side of capital investors or lose the *maquiladoras*. Mexico was almost bankrupt. The International Monetary Fund (IMF) and the World Bank refinanced Mexico's loans, forcing the country to agree to an austerity plan that provided for reducing the number of public jobs, producing more oil, and devaluing the peso. Devaluation cut wages in half and revived the *maquiladoras* by doubling their profits.

There was an increase in the migration of Mexicans from the interior to the border areas; however, only a few of them could find employment there, and the rest were forced to cross the border to seek employment. The migration furnished electrical and garment factories in the United States with a surplus of cheap labor. Simultaneously, factories in closed-shop (union) states moved to right-to-work states, which weakened the political and economic power of Chicano-dominated locals.[45]

Nativism Is Racism

The recession of 1973–1974 revived the capitalist "Greek chorus," and nativist politicians blamed their favorite scapegoat for the failures of the marketplace. By the mid-1970s, an anti-immigrant hysteria was in full swing. The country had come full circle since the nineteenth century, when Euro-Americans stereotyped the Mexican as a bandit to justify keeping open military forts so that merchants could make a profit from government contracts. In the 1970s, Mexicans again became bandits, blamed for stealing jobs. The purpose of the criminalization was multiple: For one, it justified paying undocumented immigrants less than other workers. Next, treating them like outlaws justified the increasing budget allocation for the INS. Finally, it provided copy for the media, which sensationalized the threat, playing on the Americans' fear of the "other." Even many poor and middle-class Chicanos "believed" that the undocumented immigrants, like aliens from another planet, had invaded their land and taken their jobs. In the face of this hysteria, Chicano leaders experienced their finest hour.

Centro de Acción Social Autónoma–Hermandad General de Trabajadores

Bert Corona, founder of the *Centro de Acción Social Autónoma–Hermandad General de Trabajadores* (CASA-HGT), led the movement to protect the foreign born, first in California and then nationally. Corona, born in El Paso in 1918, had been active in trade unions and civic and political groups since the 1930s. By the late 1960s, Corona had built a mass-based organization to defend the rights of undocumented workers.

CASA grew, establishing chapters in San Diego, San José, San Antonio, Colorado, and Chicago, and claimed a membership of 2,000 undocumented workers. Along with the charismatic Soledad "Chole" Alatorre, Corona developed an understanding of the undocumented immigrant's plight. Indeed, undocumented immigrants were merely scapegoats for failures in the country's unregulated economic structure.

In 1973, under the leadership of barrio lawyer Antonio Rodríguez, who led *Casa Carnalismo*, the Committee to Free *Los Tres* (a national committee formed after the arrest of three *Casa Carnalismo* members for allegedly killing an undercover agent whom they suspected of selling drugs), joined by *Comité Estudiantil del Pueblo* (CEP) became part of CASA. By the mid-1970s, the young cadre took over the organization, and transformed CASA from a mass-based organization to a vanguard Marxist group. At this point, Corona and Alatorre left CASA, and merged their supporters into *La Hermandad Mexicana Nacional* (Mexican National Brotherhood) that had been formed in the San Diego area in 1951 to protect the rights of the foreign born.

With the change in leadership, CASA members devoted less energy to organizing workers and more to movement-building operations in Chicano communities, forming alliances with North American and Mexican radicals. More time was spent on Marxist study and publishing of the newspaper *Sin Fronteras*, whose editorial staff included Isabel Rodríguez Chávez (who became a civil rights attorney) and Chicana activist Magdalena Mora. CASA trained leaders, some Marxists and some not, and gave Chicanos a global view of society. CASA's legacy is that it politicized a cadre of Chicano and Chicana activists who went on to become labor organizers and politicos in California.[46]

Get the Mexican Bandits: Criminalization of Mexicans

The passage of laws criminalizing the undocumented worker became common. In 1971, California passed the Dixon–Arnett Act, fining employers who hired undocumented workers. (The State Supreme Court declared the act unconstitutional because it infringed on federal powers.) The next year, U.S. Representative Peter Rodino (D–New Jersey) proposed a bill that made it a felony to knowingly employ undocumented workers and specified penalties that ranged from warnings for first-time offenders to fines and jail terms for repeat offenders. Senator Edward Kennedy introduced a similar bill that additionally granted amnesty to all aliens who lived in the country for at least three years. Chicanos opposed the Rodino and Kennedy bills. Senator James O. Eastland (D-Mississippi), chair of the Senate Judiciary Committee and a large grower, killed the Rodino bill in committee.

By 1976, Representative Joshua Eilberg (D-Pennsylvania) successfully sponsored a bill lowering the annual number of immigrants entering from any one country from 40,000 to 20,000. Eilberg's bill was a slap in the face to Mexico because at that time, it was the only Latin American country sending more than 40,000 immigrants. The law further granted preferences to professionals and scientists, encouraging a brain drain from Latin America. Lastly, the law made the parents of U.S.-born children ineligible for immigration. Children had the option of being deported and returning when they reached legal age, or becoming wards of the court.

INS commissioner Leonard Chapman, Jr., manufactured statistics to support his myth of a Mexican invasion and to hide the improprieties uncovered during "Operation Clean Sweep." The INS apprehended 348,178 undocumented workers in 1971, 430,213 in 1972, and 609,573 in 1973. News reporters and scholars attribute this stepped-up activity, in part, to the bureau's effort to divert attention from internal problems, including rapes, prostitution, bribery, and the running of concentration camp–like detention camps. At the same time, there were scholars on the payrolls of nativist research foundations: even respected public foundations like the National Endowment for the Humanities funded anti-immigrant research. The federal government gave Mexican specialist Arthur Corwin grant money to conduct a definitive border study, even though Corwin had little to qualify him as a border expert.

Behind the facade of pure research, Corwin launched an attack on Chicano scholars for questioning the role of the INS. On July 16, 1975, he sent Henry Kissinger a letter demanding action and control of migration from Latin America. According to Corwin, the United States was becoming a "welfare reservation," and if the trend were to continue, the Southwest would become a Mexican "Quebec." Corwin recommended that the president mobilize the Army and that Congress appropriate $1 billion to the INS, so that the agency could hire 50,000 additional border officers. Corwin also advocated the construction of an electrified fence. Fortunately, the Corwin letter fell into the hands of the Mexican press, who discredited him.

Scholars F. Ray Marshall, an economics professor at the University of Texas and secretary of labor under Jimmy Carter, and Vernon M. Briggs, Jr., favored restricting undocumented workers. Expressing concern that undocumented workers took jobs from Chicanos, Marshall and Briggs called for fining employers to discourage migration. Like most advocates of employer sanctions, Marshall and Briggs had not adequately studied the role of U.S. capitalism in creating the phenomenon.[47]

The Media Perpetuates Racist Nativism

The media molded this anti-immigrant ideology, legitimizing the myth of the "Mexican invasion" by uncritically reporting INS propaganda and nativist scholarship. The press and television promoted the idea that undocumented workers caused poverty, were criminals, and took jobs away from North Americans. On May 2, 1977, *Time* magazine ran two articles: "Getting Their Share of Paradise" and "On the Track of the Invader." The press uncritically quoted INS sources, reporting that the "invaders came by land, sea, and air," and that U.S. taxpayers spent $13 billion annually on social services for aliens, who sent another $13 billion out of the country annually. As absurd as the INS propaganda was, North Americans believed it. Thus, employers who could buy their labor power at ever-lower rates could deny these stateless workers, who were isolated from the rest of society, their human rights.[48]

Getting Away with Terrorism

While scholars manipulated statistics, the INS committed flagrant abuses of human rights: in October 1972, border patrol officer Kenneth Cook raped Martha López, 26, and threatened to harm her two children. In the summer of 1976, George Hanigan, a Douglas, Arizona, rancher and Dairy Queen owner, and his two sons, Patrick, 22, and Thomas, 17, kidnapped three undocumented workers looking for work. They "stripped, stabbed, burned [them] with hot pokers and dragged [them] across the desert." The Hanigans held a mock hanging for one of the Mexicans and shot another with buckshot. Judge Anthony Deddens, a friend of the Hanigans, refused to issue arrest warrants. Later, an all-white jury acquitted the Hanigans. Activists on both sides of the border protested the verdict and pressured U.S. Attorney General Griffin Bell to indict them. The Hanigan case went to a federal grand jury, which in 1979 indicted the Hanigans for violating the Hobbs Act, involving interference in interstate commerce (obviously the civil rights of the undocumented workers were not at issue). Another all-white jury was deadlocked in a first trial. At the second trial in 1981, the jury found the Hanigan brothers guilty (the father was dead by that time).[49]

In Defense of the Foreign Born

Meanwhile, the INS harassed groups and individuals who were attempting to protect the rights of the undocumented worker. In the spring of 1976, INS authorities broke into the Tucson office of *Concilio Manzo*, an organization that offered free counseling and legal services to undocumented workers. The INS confiscated files and arrested Marge Cowan, Sister Gabriel Marcaisq, Margarita Ramírez, and Cathy Montano. INS authorities accused the *Manzo* workers of not reporting "aliens" to the INS. The court, after an extended period and the expenditure of funds and time, dismissed the case.

Throughout the 1970s, Chicano organizations mobilized their constituencies in defense of undocumented workers. Support came from every sector of the Chicano community, crossing party and class lines. In October 1977, José Angel Gutiérrez and LRUP held a conference in San Antonio attended by 2,600 Chicano activists from all over the country. The conference was held in response to Jimmy Carter's immigration reform legislation. Even organizations such as the League of United Latin American Citizens (LULAC) and the G.I. Forum criticized anti-immigrant legislation.

In San Diego, more than a thousand activists, led by Herman Baca, Rodolfo "Corky" Gonzales, and Bert Corona, marched against the Ku Klux Klan, which had threatened the safety of the undocumented workers. In December 1977, Armando Navarro of the San Bernardino–Riverside area assembled 1,200 community folk for a conference on immigration. Such unanimity on the issue of immigration came not without a price. CASA and the National Coalition for Fair Immigration Laws had become increasingly critical of Chávez because he wanted to stem the flow of undocumented workers to the fields. By the mid-1970s, a rift had developed with Chávez, as the Republican administration attempted to use him to push anti-immigrant legislation. Denouncing the pending anti-immigrant legislation, the coalition—made up of the G.I. Forum, LULAC, and the *Comisión Femenil*—pressured Chávez for a statement. Chávez went on record that UFW was supportive of progressive legislation protecting the rights of undocumented workers—adding, however, that if there were no undocumented workers, "we could win those strikes overnight."[50]

The Growth of the Chicano Middle Class

The growth of the Chicano middle class was neither all good nor all bad. Indeed, this growth was a natural by-product of urbanization, modernization, and the success of pressuring colleges to open their doors to Latino students. The good part was that it gave Chicanos more of a voice in government and society. The bad part was that middle-class Chicanos often developed social and economic interests differing from those of the working class, and they were coopted by the mainstream, making them agents of social control, intermediary gatekeepers, power brokers, or influence peddlers between the Chicano community and the ruling class.

Chicanas/os as Commodities

For some, the growth of the Mexican American population and the widening of the middle class was a market bonanza. Beer companies distributed calendars with photos of "Hispanics," celebrating them as role models for the community. The term *Hispanic* appealed to many of the marketers; it packaged the Mexican American, the Puerto Rican, the Cuban, and other Latin Americans in one innocuous wrapper. Most of the new heroes and heroines were not activists but business executives, politicians, and political appointees—both Democrat and Republican. Newly formed Chicano and Chicana groups followed this pattern of celebrating the success of those selected by the system. The term *Hispanic* also appealed to this new wave of middle-class Mexican Americans, and this identity was much more in line with their class biases and aspirations.

This change in identity laid the foundation for the Colorado-based Coors Brewing Company deal of October 1984, when the so-called Hispanic organizations called off a boycott initiated by the Chicano community in 1968. Over the years, both the American G.I. Forum and LULAC had negotiated with the beer company, trying to end the boycott. In 1975, the Forum reached an agreement with Coors, but Forum members later rejected it because of a recently called AFL–CIO strike against Coors.

In October 1984, the G.I. Forum, the Cuban National Planning Committee, the National Council of La Raza, the National Puerto Rican Coalition, and the U.S. Hispanic Chamber of Commerce signed a contract with Coors, ending the boycott. The agreement supposedly made Coors a "good corporate citizen." The pact pledged that Coors, from 1985 to 1990, would return $350 million to the community in the form of advertisements in Hispanic media, investments in Hispanic businesses, grants to selected community organizations, and some scholarships. Coors tied how much it would give to the organizations on how much beer the "Hispanic" community would drink.

In this cynical agreement, since they were the largest sector of the pseudo-Hispanic community, Chicanos would, of course, be expected to drink the maximum quantity of beer. LULAC's leadership at first refused to ratify the agreement because the contract linked how much money they received to beer consumption. Coors, according to LULAC, did not insist on the beer-drinking clause when it funded other, non-Latino organizations—such as its grant to the Heritage Foundation, an arch-reactionary think tank. Meanwhile, activists and trade union organizations such as the UFW continued with the Coors boycott. Unfortunately, after the election of new officers, LULAC ratified the pact.[51]

Redefinition of the Political Middle

The formation of LRUP had a positive impact on Chicano politics in Texas. But the formation of a leftist party had its downside. LRUP and much of the Chicano left abandoned traditional Chicano organizations to the far right, which resulted in a redefinition of the political middle ground. Without the left, the former right-of-center became the left-of-center, and the far right became the right-of-center. Without a leftist critique, conservatives increasingly controlled many established organizations such as LULAC and the American G.I. Forum, and Republicans gained new respectability. During the presidency of Lyndon Johnson, these organizations had become dependent on patronage; that dependency continued in the 1970s under Nixon and then Gerald Ford. The only thing that changed was the brokers between the organizations and the party in power.

For instance, LULAC and the G.I. Forum had received heavy government funding since the 1960s, and they were wedded to the Democratic Party. In 1964, LULAC and the Forum began administering the Service, Employment, and Redevelopment (SER) agency. By the end of the 1970s, SER supervised 184 projects in 104 cities with an annual budget of $50 million. LULAC and the Forum obtained these grants because of their Washington connections. With Republicans controlling the Executive Branch for most of the 1970s and all of the 1980s, Latino Republicans took over from the Democrats their positions as government liaisons. These factors made easier the Republican penetration of groups like the Forum and LULAC, and Latino Republicans used War on Poverty programs for offering patronage. This dependency on government funding shaped the organizations' agendas. However, a number of Republicans were offended by what they perceived as the racist policies of their party. Concerned about the growing influence of Republicans, LULAC President Rubén Bonilla broke with the Brown Republicans and criticized U.S. immigration policy and Washington's intervention in Central America. According to Bonilla, many LULAC leaders were unwilling to lose friends in the White House and Austin. By the mid-1970s, the media and the public- and private-sector bureaucracies looked almost exclusively to middle-class Hispanics to represent the community's interests.[52]

Political Gains

By the grace of the Voting Rights Act, the Chicano movement, and the population boom, changes eventually took place, in spite of the dismal record of Chicano elected officials in the early 1970s. In Los Angeles, Chicanos remained unrepresented on the City Council and Board of Supervisors. The situation was similar throughout the Southwest. Just getting people elected was not enough, however. In 1974, both Eligio (Kika) de la Garza and Henry B. González voted against extending the benefits of the Voting Rights Act to Chicanos. Arizona Governor Raúl Castro, who was elected in 1974, spent most of his time supporting the state's right-to-work law and placating Arizona's conservatives. In 1977, Castro resigned under a cloud of suspicion involving mismanagement and became U.S. ambassador to Argentina.

To stimulate broader political gains, several Chicano/Latino lobbying groups formed in the 1970s. In the mid-1970s, *El Congreso* (the Congress) functioned as a Latino clearinghouse for President-elect Jimmy Carter, but it faded away owing to lack of funds. In 1975, Representative Edward R. Roybal formed the National Association of Latino Elected Officials (NALEO).[53] Its goals were to lobby, coordinate voter registration, and get out the vote. By 1980, NALEO had 2,500 members, with a potential of 5,000. In addition, in the mid-1970s, the four Latino members of Congress formed the so-called Hispanic Caucus;

by 1984, the caucus had eleven members. The Hispanic Caucus, however, had neither the muscle nor the ideological clarity of the Black Caucus because the ultra-conservative Cuban American cabal held it captive.[54]

In 1976, Carter received 81 percent of the Latino vote. Chicanos gave him a 205,800-vote plurality in Texas. Consequently, the Carter White House appointed more Latinos than did previous administrations. Although the Latino population's growing size was an influencing factor in these appointments, the appointees themselves were accountable only to those who signed their paychecks. Their positions gave neither the community nor the appointees any real say; thus, the poor had no more access to power than in the past. Some officers under Carter, such as the Special Assistant for Hispanic Affairs, a post held first by José Aragón and then by Esteban Torres (both from Los Angeles), had some power—they could control which lobbyists had access to the president.

The most symbolic appointment during the waning days of the Carter administration was that of Julian Nava (a Mexican American) as ambassador to Mexico. Unfortunately, Nava's successor was John Gavin, an actor whose credentials included the fact that his mother was allegedly Mexican. By contrast to Nava, who built bridges with the Mexicans, Gavin played the role of the Reagan administration's hatchetman. Evidently, according to most Mexican pundits, the fact that Gavin spoke Spanish and was presumably half Mexican was intended to soften the blow.[55]

Education: The Stairway to the American Dream

In 1968, Congress passed the Bilingual Education Act. Title VII set the framework for bilingual instruction. In *Lau v. Nichols* (1974), involving the San Francisco Chinese community, the U.S. Supreme Court unanimously ruled that the school district had the duty to meet the linguistic needs of children who had a limited grasp of English. If the district did not, it deprived the children of equal protection under the Civil Rights Act of 1964.

Lau v. Nichols drove the expansion of bilingual classrooms. By the mid-1970s, Mexican Americans believed that bilingual education was the law of the land. Bilingual education, however, was viewed by many nativist teachers and other North Americans as a threat that challenged U.S. institutions. They believed in the supremacy of the English language and culture; but even more important, they were concerned that they would become obsolete. Their basic argument was simple: Spanish-speaking students lived in the United States, and they held the burden of learning English; teachers had no such duty to learn Spanish.

Education failed many Mexican American students. Some 50 percent dropped out of school, and more than three-quarters of twelfth graders fell into the bottom quartile of reading level. Traditional education had indeed failed. In fact, less than 3 percent of Mexican students in the Southwest had access to the new bilingual education, and programs in English as a second language reached less than 5.5 percent. Many conservative critics tried to make bilingual education itself the scapegoat for this failure, rather than the meager implementation of these programs.

The U.S. Civil Rights Commission found that in the early 1970s some school districts still enforced the no-Spanish rule. In California, 13.5 percent of elementary schools discouraged the use of any Spanish; in Texas, the figure was 66.4 percent. The commission report found that 40 percent of the Chicano students in classes for the developmentally disabled spoke no English. The school districts often mislabeled Spanish-speaking children and put them in classes for the developmentally disabled.

Resistance to bilingual education increased during the Ronald Reagan years. At the beginning of the 1980s, federal appropriations had reached $171 million. However, the Reagan Administration appointed strong opponents to the National Advisory and Coordinating Council on Bilingual Education, consequently the Bilingual Education Act of 1984 lowered its appropriation to $139 million. In marked contrast, community support remained solid. In San Antonio, 65 percent of the Mexican population surveyed believed that the federal government and local schools spent too little on bilingual education; only 6 percent believed that the schools overspent on bilingual education. In East Los Angeles, 55 percent said the schools spent too little, and only 9 percent disagreed. A U.S. Commission on Civil Rights survey showed that 89 percent of Chicano leaders favored spending more money, while 2 percent did not. The report continues that in San Antonio, 93 percent of Mexicans favored bilingual education; in East Los Angeles, 87 percent; and for Chicano leaders overall, 96 percent.[56]

Educational Equity

From 1968 to 1974, U.S. Mexicans made gains in education; after this point, they slipped backward. The dropout rate again began to climb. In 1974–1975, the percentage of Chicanos who had dropped out of high school was 38.7 for 20- and 21-year-olds; the number rose to 44.1 percent in 1977–1978. In Texas the state tied funding to teacher and professional salaries. Consequently, Mexican schools received about three-fifths the appropriations of white schools.

In *Serrano v. Priest,* John Serrano, Jr., in 1968 sued the California Department of Education, claiming that his son had received an inferior education in East Los Angeles because local property taxes financed the schools. Serrano alleged that poor districts received less funding than did the wealthier ones, and consequently, the children received unequal treatment. In 1971, the California Supreme Court held that financing primarily through local property taxes failed to provide equal protection under the law. In short, a district's wealth determined the quality of its schools. Therefore, if equal educational opportunity was a right, the rich and the poor had to be funded equally. The U.S. Supreme Court (1976) upheld the California Supreme Court's ruling in *Serrano*, but it limited its decision to California, holding that the financing system violated the state constitution's equal protection clause by denying equal access to education.[57]

In *San Antonio School District v. Rodríguez,* filed in 1968, the Supreme Court had found that the U.S. Constitution did not include equal education as a fundamental right. San Antonio had multiple school districts, segregated along race and class lines. The poorest, Edgewood, was Chicano; the richest, Alamo Heights, was mostly white. Edgewood parents sued under the equal protection clause of the Fourteenth Amendment. During the 1970–1971 school year, the state allocated Alamo Heights $492 per child and Edgewood, $356. In Texas in 1971, the 162 poorest districts paid higher taxes than did the 203 richest districts. For example, the poor spent $130 a year in property taxes for education on a $20,000 home, while the rich paid $46 a year on the same type of home. In 1973, the Warren Burger Court overturned a court of appeals judgment that found in favor of the Edgewood parents. The Burger Court ruled that the Texas method of funding was imperfect but rational. It refused to consider the question of race discrimination. Thus, the Edgewood school district continued to have fewer counselors, fewer library books, and fewer course offerings—all because of unequal funding.[58]

In 1970–1971, Latinos made up slightly more than 20 percent of the student population of the Los Angeles Unified Schools; by the end of the decade, they approached a majority. *Serrano* had brought few changes, because the wealthier districts still had better facilities as well as more experienced and better-educated teachers. Latino and black schools continued to be overcrowded, and year-round schools in the 1980s were almost exclusively in Latino areas. (Year-round schools often split families who had children on different tracks.) The Chicano school buildings were older; they accommodated more students per square foot and offered smaller recreational areas. Thirty years after the *Brown* case (1954), schools remained separate and unequal.[59]

The Continuing Importance of the EOPs

Again, higher education was one of the avenues to upward mobility. As imperfect as they were, the Educational Opportunity Programs (EOPs) recruited and retained more Mexican American students in the universities and colleges than there were at any time before in U.S. history. More important, their presence created the attitude among Chicano students that it was their right to attend college and to be part of academe. This belief engendered an early idealism that opened the door of opportunity for many who had once felt excluded from the realm of higher education. Between 1973 and 1977, more Chicanos entered graduate and professional schools than ever before. However, after this point, the number of

Chicano and Latino graduate and professional students dramatically declined in inverse proportion to an increase in undergraduate enrollment. An explanation for the increase in Chicano student enrollment at the undergraduate level is the dramatic increase in the number of Mexican and Latin American students in the public schools.

The EOP propped up minority enrollment in the late 1970s. The downside was that financial aid decreased and tuition costs zoomed as significant numbers of minorities arrived on campus. Meanwhile, politicos such as Jimmy Carter, to appease middle-class white Americans, cut into the loans and other aid available to the needy. At a time when Chicano student undergraduate enrollment was growing, government policy was spreading financial aid thinner, making, for example, Vietnam refugees eligible for these funds. The allocations remained relatively the same, and the EOP had to serve more students—with the same budget. The increased costs provoked student militancy because they had to work longer hours to pay tuition and survive.

Along with EOPs, Chicano Studies programs (departments, centers, and institutes) were important during the early years, because they offered students a platform to formulate their academic demands—for Chicano professors and courses that not only focused on Chicano identity but also served the needs of the community. These programs politicized Chicanos and served as a reminder of why and how Chicano students got to the universities. Between 1968 and 1973, institutions of higher learning in California established more than 50 programs. However, by 1973, acceptance of Chicano Studies by universities and colleges had declined: a financial squeeze forced cutbacks, and Chicano Studies programs were the first to be cut.[60]

Competing Ideologies

The experiences of Chicano students on the different campuses varied. Academe provided a climate for experimenting with ideas and exposure to various world visions. Some colleges exposed students to political ideas outside the Euro-American paradigm. These ideologies ranged from highly nationalistic to revolutionary models. Within this discourse, Chicano nationalism underwent changes as competing models influenced it. The Marxist critique of capitalism was popular among a small core of students, and Marxist groups competed for the hearts and minds of Chicano students. These groups were in no way homogeneous; in fact, they competed among themselves. The Sino–Soviet split of the 1960s had led to the formation of many Marxist organizations, but these groups often clashed among themselves and with the nationalists. Of course, not everyone took part in this discourse; in fact, most Chicano students were not involved.

During the 1970s and 1980s, white leftist parties often posed a problem for some Chicanos: their party-building (recruiting) activities interfered with the normal flow of business. Nevertheless, they played an important role in forming the discourse and raising the consciousness of students. Early on, there was rivalry between the Socialist Workers Party (SWP) and CASA, and then between CASA and the August 29 Movement (ATM, which later became the LRS), though the differences were minute in the larger context. The SWP followed the writings of Leon Trotsky; CASA members had ties with the Mexican Communist party; and ATM was Maoist. These organizations vied with other Marxist parties and an array of nationalist groups. The salvation of these leftist parties was that they were key to enhancing the political consciousness of Chicano students.

Many of these progressives warned students about being mainstreamed into the university structure. The leftists perpetuated their ideas through their own newspapers and literature, which reported on labor and other community struggles and instilled a sense of idealism in students. These leftist parties wrote about the working class to which most Chicano students belonged. Their arguments, often heated and polemical, inclined the discourse of students to the left. The polemics developed a framework for understanding questions of racism and gender in relation to class oppression. However, except for the SWP, most of the leftist organizations failed to discuss the pervasive fear of homosexuals within the movement. The contribution of the Marxist organizations was that they forced nationalists to cognize the meaning of liberation. Moreover, although exasperating at times, these leftist organizations played a vital role in defining the Chicano issues and agenda of the 1970s.[61]

The "Pochoization" of the Political Vocabulary

The development of students' political ideology can be compared to the improvement of one's vocabulary. The Spanish vocabulary of many Chicanos, for example, remains at a third-grade level owing to the lack of use of Spanish and the lack of reading in the language. In the same way student activists often fail to enrich their political vocabulary because they do not continue their involvement. Their political vocabulary stagnates once they leave the campus. On the other hand, new students who are not involved neither possess nor acquire the basic vocabulary to understand history or societal inequality. They neither know nor learn about the sacrifices of earlier generations of Chicanos and Mexican Americans made to win them their access to opportunities. Most take college admission for granted. Thus, increasingly, students go to college for material gains rather than to benefit society.

Meanwhile, many Chicano professors over time became more involved with their professional lives, and they had less and less contact with student activists. Although some Chicano and Chicana professors continued to be active and worked along with students, others were consumed by profession-related pressures such as publishing and meeting the criteria set by the universities for promotion and tenure. Many new professors never participated in the Chicano movement and consequently did not identify with student concerns and had a difficult time relating to students. Involvement helps develop one's consciousness, or simplistically, one's political vocabulary. Activism determines how one is professionalized or socialized. Often new professors found student demands and methods of communication difficult to handle. A small percentage believed that their research would stimulate the Chicano movement and influence government policy; therefore, they felt that time spent with students detracted from work that was more valuable in the long run. Some let their egos run wild, rationalizing their own interests, or were divisive and attempted to destroy student organizations such as MEChA by forming counter groups.

The Myth of a Color-Blind Society

The *Bakke v. University of California* case (1976) popularized the absurd notion of "reverse racism" and the assumption that affirmative action discriminated against whites. During 1973–1974, Alan Bakke, a 34-year-old engineer, applied to 13 medical schools, all of which rejected him because of his age. A white administrator at the University of California at Davis encouraged Bakke to sue, since allegedly "less-qualified minorities" had been admitted. Bakke challenged the Davis special admission program, initiated in 1970, which set aside 16 out of 100 slots for disadvantaged students. Before this plan began, only three minority students had ever been admitted to Davis's medical school. A lower court found for Bakke, as did the California Supreme Court, which flatly stated that race could not be used as a criterion for admission.

On June 28, 1978, the U.S. Supreme Court, in a 5–4 decision, upheld *Bakke*. It based its decision on the 1964 Civil Rights Act, holding that using race as the sole criterion for admission was unconstitutional. Justice Thurgood Marshall dissented, stating that the Court had come "full circle," returning to the post–Civil War era when the courts stopped congressional initiatives to give former slaves full citizenship. Justice Marshall's dissent was prophetic. The *Bakke* decision gave racist faculties and administrators an excuse for excluding minorities. *Bakke* became the law of the land, and it signaled an assault on affirmative action that continued into the late 1990s. *Bakke* was part of a "culture war" funded by right-wing extremists opposed to the idea of equity in education.

The need for minority doctors and other professionals speaks for itself. In California in 1975, one Euro-American lawyer practiced for every 530 Euro-Americans; for Asians, the ratio was 1:1,750; for African Americans, 1:3,441; for Latinos, 1:9,842; and for Native Americans, 1:50,000. In primary-care medicine, one white doctor practiced for every 990 whites; the ratio for blacks was 1:4,028; for Native Americans, 1:7,539; and for Latinos, 1:21,245. *Bakke* supporters argued that overall there was an oversupply of professionals and that services did not depend on the professional's ethnic or racial background. Admittedly, little research has gone into this latter area. However, Dr. Stephen Keith of the Charles Drew Post Graduate School in Los Angeles had conducted a study, the findings of which suggest that the probability that African American and Latino professionals would work with the poor and minority clients was much higher than that for their white counterparts.[62]

Legacy Admits

The debate over preferential treatment of minorities continues even today. For many, the use of race as a criterion is a bogus argument, so the controversy will remain. On the other hand, Chicanos point out that other groups, such as veterans, the children of alumni, the children of donors to the university, or those over 65 years of age, receive preferential treatment. Today society has ramps for the handicapped, which some people would call preferential treatment. According to Alex Liebman, for Princeton's class of 2001 the overall acceptance rate was 13 percent; the statistic for "legacy admits" (children of alumni) was 41 percent; and that for minorities (which includes Asians) was 26 percent. The assumption was that Latinos and African Americans were not qualified and that the legacy admits were qualified, which was not always the case. At Harvard University during the 1990s, the children of alumni were almost four times more likely to be accepted than other prospective students. Harvard University admitted about 40 percent of its entering class using the criterion that the student was the son or daughter of an alumnus or donor. In the same period, 66 percent of children-of-alumni applicants were accepted by the University of Pennsylvania whereas the overall acceptance percentage was 11. Admissions officers saved 25 percent of Notre Dame's first-year class openings for the children of alumni.[63] The preferential treatment given to legacy admits highlights the hypocrisy and racial bias of those who challenge affirmative action.

Why Progressive Organizations Fail

Documents obtained under the Freedom of Information Act suggest the extent of federal monitoring of progressive political organizations. José Angel Gutiérrez and Ernesto Vigil are among the few Chicano scholars doing research in the field. However, almost no evidence is available on local police spying. An exception was a suit filed by the American Civil Liberties Union (ACLU) in 1978: *CAPA* (Committee Against Police Abuse) *v. Los Angeles Police Department*. Some 141 plaintiffs, individuals and groups, went to court in an attempt to restrain police infiltration of political organizations.

Suing the police is an almost impossible task because of the deep pockets of big cities. For example, *CAPA v. LAPD* almost bankrupted the ACLU, which paid out nearly $1 million in legal costs before the LAPD settled. The plaintiffs argued that responsibility for spying went all the way to Chief Daryl Gates, and that further discovery would yield even more evidence of police spying. The plaintiffs voted to settle because they did not have the money to go on. The negotiated settlement, however, included extensive guidelines calling for outside monitoring of the LAPD. Further, the court set up an independent committee to conduct the audit of the agency, and for the first time, the court ordered the police department not to investigate private individuals or groups "without reasonable and articulated suspicion."[64]

Violence as an Instrument of Control

In 1978 in Duarte, California, a gang member shot at postal officer Jesse Ortiz and his two stepbrothers, killing Ortiz. That same night, Los Angeles sheriffs' deputies raided a party, arresting Gordon Castillo Hall, 16, and dragging him outside to a makeshift lineup with squad car lights shining in his face. The Laras, Ortiz's half brothers, contradicted an earlier description of the murderer and identified Castillo Hall, who was much smaller than the suspect.

The trial proved to be a farce. The Pasadena attorney defending Castillo Hall did not conduct a proper pretrial investigation, nor did he call witnesses to prove that Hall had not been at the scene of the crime. The judge allowed expert testimony documenting the so-called violent nature of Mexican gang members toward white and black gang members. The prosecution underscored that Castillo Hall, a Mexican, belonged to a gang.

Bertha Castillo Hall, Gordon's mother, sold her home to pay for the trial attorney. Convinced of her son's innocence, she approached Chicano attorney Ricardo Cruz, who agreed to take the appeal; but she had no money for expenses. A committee was formed to help her—The Committee to Free Gordon Castillo Hall—which raised more than $60,000.

With proper representation, stories changed. The Laras told authorities that they had made a mistake in identifying Castillo Hall. The investigating deputies urged that the case be reopened. However, the trial judge and District Attorney John Van DeKamp, at that time running for state attorney general, refused. Cruz filed a motion of habeas corpus. After several years, the State Supreme Court appointed a referee to investigate the case. The referee recommended reopening of the case; he cited an overzealous district attorney, trial errors, and an incompetent defense. Finally, Castillo Hall was released: in 1981, the State Supreme Court overturned Hall's conviction and freed him. Castillo Hall simply said, "They took my youth." Hall sued the Sheriff's Department, which avoided payment through legal maneuvering.[65]

Another example of police brutality involved journalist and long-time Chicano activist Roberto Rodríguez. On March 23, 1979, members of the Selective Enforcement Bureau of the Los Angeles Sheriff's Department severely beat up Rodríguez, who had been photographing the deputies beating innocent people. Rodríguez had to be hospitalized, and police also charged him with assault with a deadly weapon. He sued the sheriffs and, after a seven-year ordeal, eventually won the case.[66]

Conclusion: The Final Year of the Decade

The decade had begun full of hope with Chicanas/os assembling the largest march in Los Angeles history to protest the war. However, as the Vietnam War ended, the fervor seemed to dissipate as class and other differences divided the community into special interest groups and organizations. As in other groups, youth represented different interests, and as their numbers grew in the universities and in the professions, separate islands formed in academe and the community. This was further complicated with the arrival of a million immigrants from Mexico who had not been part of the struggles of the 1960s, and who often did not understand the legacy of the Chicana/o generation.

The final year of the 1970s was an eventful one. By that time, the proportion of Mexican Americans living in metropolitan areas (80 percent) relative to their total numbers exceeded the corresponding proportion for the general population. Because of poverty and ghettoization of Chicanos there was a higher incidence of crime and violence among them. In Los Angeles, Mexican Americans and Latinos were 2.3 times more likely than Euro-Americans to become homicide victims. The largest increase in crime statistics—over 166.7 percent—occurred among Chicanos and Latinos; murders went from 11.1 per 100,000 in 1970 to 29.6 per 100,000 in 1979.[67] On July 17, Nicaraguan President General Anastasio Somoza fled to Miami and the Sandinistas formed a new government. Somoza was one among a string of dictators supported by the United States in Latin America.[68] In the years to come, this event would have far-reaching implications for the Mexican-origin population. During the 1970s, the growing foreign-born population was already changing the Chicano community. The decade closed with the Iran hostage crisis, as 3,000 Iranian students invaded the U.S. Embassy in Tehran and took 90 hostages, 63 of whom were American. This crisis was one of several factors that brought to power a succession of ultra-conservative administrations during the 1980s, which would also affect people of Latin American origin in the United States.[69]

Notes

1. Che Guevara Internet Archive, http://www.marxists.org/archive/guevara/index.htm.

2. Classified U.S. State Department Documents on the Overthrow of Chilean President Salvador Allende, 1973, Peter Kornbluh, Chile and the United States: Declassified Documents Relating to the Military Coup, National Security Archive, New Declassified Details on Repression and U.S. Support for Military Dictatorship, http://www.gwu.edu/~nsarchiv/NSAEBB/NSAEBB185/index.htm. "New Kissinger, 'Telcons' Reveal Chile Plotting at Highest Levels of U.S. Government," National Security Archive Electronic Briefing

Book No. 255, http://www.gwu.edu/~nsarchiv/NSAEBB/NSAEBB255/index.htm.

3. David Reimers, "An Unintended Reform: The 1965 Immigration Act and Third World Immigration to the United States," *Journal of American Ethnic History* 3, no. 1 (1983): 9–28.

4. Marjorie Heins, *Strictly Ghetto Property: The Story of Los Siete de La Raza* (Berkeley, CA: Ramparts Press, 1972), 11–12, 49–51, 203–6. In 1969, Central American youth from the Mission District of San Francisco were approached by two plainclothes policemen while moving furniture. An altercation resulted and an officer died from a gunshot wound.

Swarms of officers hit the building and fired automatic rifles and flooded the building with tear gas. Seven youths were arrested in Santa Cruz for murder and attempted murder in the case. Gary Lescallett, Daniel Melendez, Jose Rios, Rudolpho Martinez, Jose Martinez, and Danillo Melendez were acquitted; they included four Salvadorans, one Nicaraguan, and one Honduran. The seventh defendant, George López, was never apprehended. They had been involved in a youth group, the Mission Rebels. The Mission District was a mixed Latino *barrio* held together by La Raza. At trial the stories conflicted and the defendants insisted that the police had drawn their guns. They were in plain clothes. The trial lasted a year and a half, and the seven were acquitted. "Los Siete" Defense Committee helped raise the consciousness of youth.

5. "The Word Chicana/o," Chicana Chicano Public Scholar, http://forchicanachicanostudies.wikispaces.com/Chicana+Chicano+Public+Scholar.

6. Isaac William Martin, "Proposition 13 Fever: How California's Tax Limitation Spread," *California Journal of Politics and Policy*, 1, no. 1 (2009), Art. 17, 1–17. California Chief Justice Rose Bird Loses Election, http://www.youtube.com/watch?v=Kd162US36to.

7. Richard Adler, ed., *All in the Family: A Critical Appraisal* (New York: Praeger, 1979).

8. You can view episodes of these sitcoms. See All in the Family—Archie Bunker Meets Sammy Davis, http://www.youtube.com/watch?v=O_UBgkFHm8o.

9. Culture Clash Show—Lalo Sings No Chicanos on TV, http://www.youtube.com/watch?v=JZt6lZ6RDAU.

10. Rocio Rivadeneyra, "The Influence of Television on Stereotype Threat among Adolescents of Mexican Descent" (Ann Arbor: PhD dissertation, University of Michigan, 2001). Frito Bandito 1, http://www.youtube.com/watch?v=fOUilxJWm24.

11. Michael Harrington, *The Other America: Poverty in the United States* (Baltimore, MD: Penguin Books, 1963), x. George Mowry and Blaine A. Brownell, *The Urban Nation 1920–1980*, rev. ed. (New York: Hill and Wang, 1981), 311. All in the Family—Archie's Civil Rights 3-3, http://www.youtube.com/watch?v=ZDuZQabywjw.

12. *Jose Cisneros et al., Plaintiffs-Appellees, v. Corpus Christi Independent School District et al., Defendants-Appellants*, United States Court of Appeals for the Fifth Circuit August 2, 1972, 467 F.2d 142, http://law.justia.com/cases/federal/appellate-courts/F2/467/142/154342/. Neil Foley, "Straddling the Color Line," in Nancy Foner and George M. Fredrickson, eds., *Not Just Black and White: Historical and Contemporary Perspectives on Immigration, Race, and Ethnicity in the United States* (New York: Russell Sage Foundation, 2004), 351–54.

13. Joan Hoff, *Nixon Reconsidered* (New York: Basic Books, 1995), 97–98. Peter Leyden and Simon Rosenberg, "The 50-Year Strategy," *Mother Jones* (November–December 2007), http://www.motherjones.com/politics/2007/10/50-year-strategy-new-progressive-era-no-really. Deirdre Martínez, *Who Speaks for Hispanics? Hispanic Interest Groups in Washington* (Albany: State University of New York Press, 2009), 32–33.

14. Tony Castro, *Chicano Power: The Emergence of Mexican Americans* (New York: Saturday Review Press, 1974), 103, 199–201; Richard A. Santillán, *La Raza Unida* (Los Angeles, CA: Tlaquila, 1973), 80–81.

15. Frank Del Olmo, "Watergate Panel Calls 4 Mexican Americans," *Los Angeles Times* (June 5, 1974). Report of the Senate Select Committee on Presidential Activities, *The Senate Watergate Reports*, Vol. 1 (New York: Dell, 1974), 345–72. Castro, *Chicano Power*, 7–8, 202–3, 210. See also "La Raza Platform Prohibits Support of Non-Chicanos," *Los Angeles Times* (July 4, 1972). Cindy Parmenter, "La Raza Unida Plans Outlined," *Denver Post* (June 20, 1974). Jim Wood, "La Raza Sought Nixon Cash," *San Antonio Express* (November 18, 1973).

16. "Top Woman Aide Gets U.S. Latin Position," *Los Angeles Times* (March 8, 1977). "Spanish-Speaking Aide Hits Cutbacks," *Santa Fe New Mexican* (March 26, 1973). Julia Moran, "The GOP Wants Us," *Nuestro* (August 1980): 26. Joe Holley, "Leading Texas Republican Anne Armstrong," *Washington Post* (July 31, 2008), http://www.washingtonpost.com/wp-dyn/content/article/2008/07/30/AR2008073002605.html. David Binder, "Charles (Bebe) Rebozo, 85; Longtime Nixon Confidant," *New York Times* (May 9, 1998).

17. Moran, "The GOP Wants Us," 26. Grace A. Franklin and Randall B. Ripley, *C.E.T.A.: Politics and Policy, 1973–1982* (Knoxville: University of Tennessee Press, 1984), 12, 67, 120.

18. Carole A. Stabile, "Postmodernism, Feminism, and Marx: Notes from the Abyss," *Monthly Review* 47, no. 3 (July 1995): 89ff. Ignacio M. García, *Chicanismo: The Forging of a Militant Ethos Among Mexican Americans* (Tucson: University of Arizona Press, 1997), 133–45. Antonia I. Castañeda, "Women of Color and the Rewriting of Western History: The Discourse, Politics, and Decolonization of History," *Pacific Historical Review* 61, no. 4 (November 1992): 501–33. Alma M. García, ed., *Chicana Feminist Thought: The Basic Historical Writings* (New York: Routledge, 1997), 3.

19. Christine Marín, *A Spokesman of the Mexican American Movement: Rodolfo "Corky" Gonzales and the Fight for Chicano Liberation, 1966–1972* (San Francisco, CA: R&E Research Associates, 1977), 17.

20. Armando Navarro, *La Raza Unida Party: A Chicano Challenge to the U.S. Two-Party Dictatorship* (Philadelphia, PA: Temple University Press, 2000), 95.

21. Ibid., 41–48, 153–56.

22. Ibid., 70. Naomi Helena Quiñonez, "Hijas De La Malinche (Malinche's Daughters): The Development of Social Agency Among Mexican American Women and the Emergence of First Wave Chicana Cultural Production" (PhD dissertation, Calremont Graduate School, 1997), 175. Armando Navarro, *Mexican American Youth Organization: Avant-Garde of the Chicano Movement in Texas* (Austin: University of Texas Press, 1995), 75–83. Ignacio M. García, *United We Win: The Rise and Fall of La Raza Unida Party* (Tucson: Mexican American Studies & Research Center, University of Arizona, 1989). Evey Chapa, "Mujeres Por La Raza Unida," in A. García, ed., *Chicana Feminist Thought*, 178–79.

23. Castro, *Chicano Power*, 202. Ernesto Chávez, "Creating Aztlán: The Chicano Movement in Los Angeles, 1966–1978" (PhD dissertation, University of California, Los Angeles, 1994), 152–53, 170–71. Mario T. García, *Memories of Chicano History: The Life and Narrative of Bert Corona* (Berkeley: University of California Press, 1994), 266–69; for Corona's story of what happened, see 308–15. Santillán, *La Raza Unida*, 84–86. Navarro, *La Raza Unida Party*, 46–49, 141–44.

24. Navarro, *La Raza Unida Party*, 236–37.

25. Ibid., 41, 46–48. Oral History Interview of Richard A. Santillán, 1989, by Carlos Vásquez, UCLA Special Collections. Chávez, in "Creating Aztlán," says that Santillán concluded that the Republicans funded the RUP 48th Assembly District race. This charge was denied by the candidate. Good coverage in the *Arizona Republic* in 1972.

26. Navarro, *La Raza Unida Party*, 139, 154, 167–73. Jorge García, "Incorporation of East Los Angeles 1974, Part One," *La Raza Magazine* (Summer 1977): 29–33. Frank Del Olmo, "Early Returns Show East L.A. Incorporation Measure Failing," *Los Angeles Times* (November 6, 1974). Frank Del Olmo, "Defeat of East L.A. Plan Laid to Fear of High Property Tax," *Los Angeles Times* (November 7, 1974).

27. William C. Velásquez: 1944–1988, Willie Velásquez Institute, http://www.wcvi.org/wcvbio.htm. Juan A. Sepúlveda, *Life and Times of Willie Velásquez: Su Voto Es Su Voz* (Houston, TX: Arte Público Press, 2005). Navarro, *La Raza Unida Party*, 70–71, 79.

28. The [Puerto Rican] Young Lords Party, Position Paper on Women (May 1971), *Palante*, 11–14, http://younglords.info/resources/position_paper_on_women.pdf. Young Lords Party, Position on Women's Liberation, *Palante* (May 1971), 16–17, http://younglords.info/resources/position_on_womens_liberation_may1971.pdf.

29. Marta (Martha) Cotera, http://www.umich.edu/~ac213/student_projects05/cf/interview.html. Martha P. Cotera, *Diosa y Hembra: The History and Heritage of Chicanas in the U.S.* (Austin, TX: Information Systems Development, 1976). "Remembering a Revolutionary Mujer: Compañera Magdalena Mora," *!La Verdad!*, http://uniondelbarrio.org/lvp/newspapers/97/janmay97/pg01.html. Rosaura Sánchez and Rosa Martínez, eds., *Essays on La Mujer* (Los Angeles: University of California Los Angeles Chicano Studies Research Center, 1977) and Adelaida R. Del Castillo and Rosa M. Martinez, ed., *Mexican Women in the United States: Struggles Past and Present* (Los Angeles: University of California Los Angeles Chicano Studies Research Center, 1980) were among the first academic contributions on Chicana feminism.

30. Enriqueta Vásquez, *Enriqueta Vásquez and the Chicano Movement: Writings from El Grito del Norte* (Houston, TX: Arte Público, 2006). Alma M. García, "The Development of Chicana Feminist Discourse, 1970–1980," *Gender & Society* 3, no. 2 (June 1989): 174, 218, 224, 232. Dionne Elaine Espinosa, "Pedagogies of Nationalism and Gender: Cultural Resistance in Selected Representational Practices of Chicana/o Movement Activists, 1967–1972" (PhD dissertation, Cornell University, 1996), 149, 150, 152, 155. Enriqueta Vásquez,

"The Woman of La Raza," *El Grito del Norte* (July 6, 1969). F. Arturo Rosales, *Chicano! The History of the Mexican American Civil Rights Movement* (Houston, TX: Arte Público Press, 1996), 183.

31. Maylei Blackwell, "Contested Histories: Las Hijas de Cuauhtémoc, Chicana Feminisms, and Print Culture in the Chicano Movement, 1968–1973," in Gabriela F. Arredondo, Aida Hurtado, Norma Klahn, Olga Nájera-Ramírez, and Patricia Zavella, eds., *Chicana Feminisms: A Critical Reader* (Duke University Press, 2003), 77–78.

32. Lucy R. Moreno Collection, 1971–1997, University of Texas Austin, http://www.lib.utexas.edu/taro/utlac/00103/lac-00103.html. Vicki L. Ruiz, *From Out of the Shadows: Mexican Women in Twentieth-Century America* (New York: Oxford University Press, 1999), 108–9. Marta Cotera, "La Conferencia De Mujeres Por La Raza, Houston, Texas, 1971," in A. Garcia, ed., *Chicana Feminist Thought*, 155–57.

33. *Dictionary of Literary Biography* on Dorinda Moreno, *Book Rags*, http://www.bookrags.com/biography/dorinda-moreno-dlb/. Flor Y Canto, University of Southern California 1973, http://readraza.com/florycanto/index.htm.

34. Rosa Rosales, Interview by José Angel Gutiérrez, University of Texas Arlington, Tejano Voices, http://library.uta.edu/tejanovoices/xml/CMAS_045.xml. Key profiles, Bios & Links Blog, http://key-profiles.blogspot.com/2006/10/profile-rosa-rosales-lulac-national.html. President of LULAC on Homies Nation TV, http://www.youtube.com/watch?v=2JB63EseIJ4.

35. A. García, ed., *Chicana Feminist Thought*, 8. Marta Cortera, "Chicana Identity (platica de Marta Cortera)," *Caracoal* (February 1976), 14–15, 17, 108–09. Quiñonez, "Hijas De La Malinche," 182. Espinosa, "Pedagogies," 176–81. Benita Roth, "On Their Own and for Their Own: African-American, Chicana, and White Feminist Movements in the 1960s and 1970s" (PhD dissertation, University of California, Los Angeles, 1998), 180. Jim Wood, "Report on Bias Against Latinos in Welfare," *San Francisco Chronicle* (July 2, 1972). Rodolfo Rosales, *Illusion of Inclusion* (Austin: University of Texas Press, 2000), 159–77. Beverly Padilla, "Chicanas and Abortion," *The Militant* (February 18, 1972) quoted in A. García, ed., *Chicana Feminist Thought*, 121. Statement by Elma Barrera, First National Chicana Conference-Workshop Resolutions, in Mirta Vidal, *Chicanas Speak Out! Women: New Voice of La Raza* (New York: Pathfinder Press, 1971).

36. Fabio Rojas, *From Black Power to Black Studies: How a Radical Social Movement Became an Academic Discipline* (Baltimore, MD: Johns Hopkins University Press, 2007), 79. SF State Third World Student Strike, http://www.youtube.com/watch?v=7ar2i-G5O-0&feature=related.

37. CSUN student political activism 1960s/70s "The Storm at Valley State" http://www.youtube.com/watch?v=NB3s_3RDEIc. On the Formation of Chicano Studies at Northridge see Miguel Durán, Unrest Documentary: Full Movie, http://www.youtube.com/watch?v=erf3j3UOmWE. Rodolfo F. Acuña, *The Making of Chicana/o Studies: In the Trenches of Academe* (New Brunswick: Rutgers University Press, 2011).

38. Javier Rangel, "The Educational Legacy of El Plan de Santa Barbara: An Interview with Reynaldo Macías," *Journal of Latinos and Education*, 6, no. 2 (2007): 192. Ruben Salazar, "Chicanos Set Their Goals in Education," *Los Angeles Times* (May 4, 1969), G8. *El Plan De Santa Bárbara: A Chicano Plan for Higher Education,* Analyses and Positions by the Chicano Coordinating Council on Higher Education (Oakland, CA: La Causa Publications, October 1969).

39. Acuña, *The Making of Chicana/o Studies.*

40. Adapted Urban Education Inc., Office for Civil Rights Data, pg. 130, Office of Civil Rights, Racial and Ethnic Enrollment Data from Institutions of Higher Education, Fall 1972, OCR-74-12 (U.S. Department of Heath, Education, and Welfare, 1974), 79–80, in Ronald W. López, Arturo Madrid-Barela, and Reynaldo Flores Macias, *Chicanos in Higher Education: Status and Issues.* The National Commission on Higher Education, Monograph No. 7 (Los Angeles: Chicano Studies Center Publications, University of California, Los Angeles, 1976), 63–64, 67–68.

41. "Cabinet Meeting Decisions" (Puerto Rico). October 6, 1960. Women in World History, http://chnm.gmu.edu/wwh/modules/lesson16/lesson16.php?menu=1&s=12. Harriet B. Presser, "Puerto Rico: The Role of Sterilization in Controlling Fertility," *Studies in Family Planning*, 1, no. 45 (September 1969): 8.

42. Norma Solis, "Do Doctors Abuse Low-Income Women?" *Chicano Times* (April 15–29, 1977). "Doctor Raps Sterilization of Indian Women," *Los Angeles Times* (May 22, 1977). "Puerto Rican Doctor Denounces Sterilization," *Sin Fronteras* (May 1976). Dr. Helen Rodrigues, head of pediatrics at Lincoln Hospital in San Francisco, said that by 1968, 35 percent of the women in Puerto Rico had been sterilized. See also Bernard Rosenfeld, Sidney M. Wolfe, and Robert E. McGarrah, Jr., *A Health Research Group Study on Surgical Sterilization: Present Abuses and Proposed Regulation* (Washington, DC: Public Citizens, 1973), 1, 7. Robert Kistler, "Women 'Pushed' into Sterilization, Doctor Charges," *Los Angeles Times* (December 2, 1974). See also Robert Kistler, "Many U.S. Rules on Sterilization Abuses Ignored Here," *Los Angeles Times* (December 3, 1974). Georgina Torres Rizk, "Sterilization Abuses Against Chicanos in Los Angeles" (Los Angeles Center for Law and Justice, December 2, 1976). Richard Siggins, "Coerced Sterilization: A National Civil Conspiracy to Commit Genocide upon the Poor?" (Chicago, IL: Loyola University School of Law, January 15, 1977), 12. Forced Sterilizations of American Indian Women, http://www.youtube.com/watch?v=WadjMamG4eQ. Reproductive Justice for Latinas: Coerced, Forced, and Involuntary Sterilization, http://www.youtube.com/watch?v=tShnkBmoe3Y.

43. Ronald B. Taylor, *Chávez and the Farm Workers* (Boston: Beacon Press, 1975), 278, 289. "A Boost for Chavez," *Newsweek* (May 26, 1975). "California Compromise," *Time* (May 19, 1975). "Chavez vs. the Teamsters: Farm Workers' Historic Vote," *U.S. News & World Report* (September 22, 1975): 82–83. American Friends Service Committee, *A Report of Research on the Wages of Migrant Farm Workers in Northwest Ohio* (July, August 1976), 1–9. Baldemar Velásquez, interview by Rodolfo Acuña, Toledo, Ohio, August 8, 1977. "Statement of Problem," *Farm Labor Organizing Committee Newsletter* (January 1977). "FLOC: Both a Union and a Movement," *Worker's Power* (May 9, 1977). Thomas Ruge, "Indiana Farm Workers, Legislative Coalition Fights H.B. 1306," *OLA* (April 1977). Jim Wasserman, "FLOC Goal Is Power Base for Migrants," *Fort Wayne Journal-Gazette* (September 14, 1976). Fran Leeper Buss, ed., *Forged Under the Sun/Forjada bajo el sol: The Life of Maria Elena Lucas* (Ann Arbor: University of Michigan Press, 1993). Anon., *The Struggle of the Texas Farm Workers' Union* (Chicago, IL: Vanguard Press, 1977), 4, 14–15. Ignacio M. García, "The Many Battles of Antonio Orendian," *Nuestro* (November 1979), 25–29.

44. Irene Ledesma, "Texas Newspapers and Chicana Worker's Activism, 1919–1974," *Western Historical Quarterly* 26, no. 3 (Fall 1995): 327 Laurie Coyle, Gail Hershatter, and Emily Honig, *Women at Farah: An Unfinished Story* (El Paso, TX: Reforma, 1979). Bill Finger, "Victoria Sobre Farah," *Southern Exposure* 4, nos. 1–2 (1976): 5, 46, 47–49. Numerous articles ran in *San Antonio Express* and *El Paso Times* during 1972 and 1973 on the Farah strike, the boycott, and the closing of the plant. "Fury Stands Pat on Farah," *San Antonio Express* (December 14, 1973), is a solid article that lays out reasons for the bishops' support of the boycott. Laura E. Arroyo, "Industrial and Occupational Distribution of Chicana Workers," *Aztlán* 4, no. 2 (1973): 358–59. Philip Shabecoff, "Farah Strike Has Become War of Attrition; The Worst Part," *New York Times* (June 16, 1973).

45. Peter Wiley and Robert Gottlieb, *Empires in the Sun* (Tucson: University of Arizona Press, 1982), 257, 265. Gay Young, "Gender Identification and Working-Class Solidarity Among Maquila Workers," in *Ciudad Juarez: Stereotypes and Realities*, in Vicki L. Ruiz and Susan Tiano, eds., *Women on the U.S.–Mexico Border: Responses to Change* (Boston: Allen & Unwin, 1987), 105–28. Devon Peña, "Tortuosiadad: Shop Floor Struggles of Female Maquiladoras Workers," in Ruiz and Tiano, *Responses to Change*, 129–54.

46. Chávez, "Creating Aztlán," 179–86, 199, 200–01. David G. Gutiérrez, *Walls and Mirrors: Mexican Americans, Mexican Immigrants, and the Politics of Ethnicity* (Berkeley: University of California Press, 1995), 191. David G. Gutiérrez, "Sin Fronteras? Chicanos, Mexican Americans, and the Emergence of the Contemporary Mexican Immigration Debate, 1968–1978," in David G. Gutiérrez, ed., *Between Two Worlds: Mexican Immigrants in the United States* (Wilmington, DE: Scholarly Resources, 1996), 175–209. M. García, *Bert Corona*, 290–95. Carlos Muñoz, Jr., *Youth, Identity, Power: The Vhicano Movement* (London: Verso, 2007), 92–94. See Juan Gómez-Quiñones, *Chicano Politics: Reality and Promise 1940-1990* (Albuquerque: University of New Mexico Press, 1990). Gómez-Quiñones, *Mexican Students For La Raza: The Chicano Student Movement in Southern California 1967-1977* (Santa Barbara, CA: Editorial La Causa, 1978).

47. Rodolfo F. Acuña, *Occupied America: A History of Chicanos,* 2d ed. (New York: Harper & Row, 1981), 168–71. Vernon M. Briggs, "Labor Market Aspects of Mexican Migration to the

United States," in Stanley R. Ross, ed., *Views Across the Border* (Albuquerque: University of New Mexico Press, 1979), 21, 211, 221. Ronald Bonaparte, "The Rodino Bill: An Example of Prejudice Toward Mexican Immigration to the United States," *Chicano Law Review* 2 (Summer 1975): 40–50. Frank Del Olmo, "Softer Penalties in Alien Cases Urged," *Los Angeles Times* (April 20, 1977). Arthur F. Corwin, *Letter to Henry Kissinger* (July 16, 1975), 2–3, 20, 21, 39; photocopy in possession of Professor Jorge Bustamante, University of Nortre Dame, Indiana.

48. David S. North and Marion Houston, "Illegal Aliens: Their Characteristics and Role in the U.S. Labor Market," study conducted for the U.S. Department of Labor by Linton and Co. (November 17, 1975). Vic Villalpando, "Abstract: A Study of the Impact of Illegal Aliens in the County of San Diego on Specific Socioeconomic Areas," in Antonio José Ríos-Bustamante, ed., *Immigration and Public Policy: Human Rights for Undocumented Workers and Their Families*, Chicano Studies Center Document no. 5 (Los Angeles: Chicano Studies Center Publications, University of California Los Angeles, 1977), 223–31. Jorge Bustamante, "The Impact of the Undocumented Immigration from Mexico on the U.S.–Mexican Economics: Preliminary Findings and Suggestions for Bilateral Cooperation," Forty-sixth Annual Meeting of the Southern Economic Association, Atlanta, Georgia, November 1976.

49. Bill Curry, "Alien-Torture Case Ends in Mistrial for 2 Ranchers," *Los Angeles Times* (July 30, 1980). "The Nation; Judge Sets 3rd Trial in Alien Torture Case," *Los Angeles Times* (September 3, 1980). Tom Miller, *On the Border* (New York: Ace Books, 1981), 158–79. *Arizona Republic*, "Third Trial to Begin in Beating of Aliens: Two Arizona Ranchers Have Been Acquitted Once and a 2d Jury Could Not Reach a Verdict," *New York Times* (January 20, 1981). "Rancher in Plea to High Court in Case of Tortured Mexicans," *New York Times* (December 5, 1982). *United States of America, Plaintiff-Appellee, v. Patrick W. Hanigan, Defendant-Appellant*, No. 81-1262. 681 F2d 1127 (1982), http://openjurist.org/681/f2d/1127/united-states-v-w-hanigan.

50. See Ron Dusek, "Aliens Given Deportation Reprieve by Chicago Judge," *El Paso Times* (March 25, 1977). James Sterba, "Alien Ruling Snarls Migrant Job Inquiry," *New York Times* (August 14, 1977). Robert Kistler, "No Effort to Block KKK 'Patrol' of Border Planned," *Los Angeles Times* (October 10, 1977). *CCR Newsletter* (San Diego, October 29, 1977).

51. Gutiérrez, *Walls and Mirrors*, 199. David Reyes, "In Pursuit of the Latino American Dream," *Los Angeles Times* (July 24, 1983), Orange County section. Armando Navarro, *Mexicano Political Experience in Occupied Aztlán: Struggles and Change* (Lanham, MD: Altamira Press, 2005), 519.

52. Juan Gómez Quiñones, *Chicano Politics: Reality & Promise 1940–1990* (Albuquerque: University of New Mexico Press, 1990), 166. Moises Sándoval, "The Struggle Within LULAC," *Nuestro* (September 1979): 30. Navarro, *Mexicano Political Experience*, 519–22. Craig A. Kaplowitz, *Lulac, Mexican Americans, and National Policy* (College Station: Texas A&M University Press, 2005), 153, 194.

53. NALEO Education Fund, http://www.naleo.org/.

54. Congressional Hispanic Caucus Institute, http://www.chci.org/.

55. Ron Ozio, "The Hell with Being Quiet and Dignified, Says Rubén Bonilla," *Nuestro* (September 1979): 31–32. "3 Million Chicanos Voiceless in California," *Forumeer* (October 1971). In California in 1971, out of 15,650 elected and appointed officials, 310—or 1.98 percent—were Chicanos. None of the 46 state officials and none of the advisors to the governor were Mexican. Castro, *Chicano Power*, 106. Andrew Hernández, *The Latin Vote in the 1976 Presidential Election* (San Antonio, TX: Southwest Voter Registration Education Project, 1977), i, 1–2, 9. Choco González Meza, *The Latin Vote in the 1980 Presidential Election: Political Research Report* (San Antonio, TX: Southwest Voter Registration Education Project, January 1, 1981), 13. Julian Nava Collection, Urban Archives, California State University Northridge, http://digital-library.csun.edu/LatArch/.

56. Keith J. Henderson, "Bilingual Education Programs Spawning Flood of Questions," *Albuquerque Journal* (June 11, 1978). Meyer Weinberg, *Minority Students: A Research Appraisal* (Washington, DC: U.S. Department of Health, Education and Welfare, 1977), 287. U.S. Commission on Civil Rights, *The Excluded Student: Educational Practices Affecting Mexican Americans in the Southwest*, Mexican American Education Study, Report iii (Washington, DC: Government Printing Office, 1972); bilingual education reached only 2.7 percent of the entire Chicano population.

57. *Serrano v. Priest*, 5 Cal. 3d 584; 96 Cal. Rptr. 601; 487 P.2d 1241 (1971). David C. Long, "Litigation Concerning Educational Finance," in Clifford P. Hooker, ed., *The Courts and Education* (Chicago, IL: University of Chicago, 1978), 221–29.

58. *San Antonio Independent School District v. Rodriguez*, 411 U.S. 1 (1973), Appeal from the United States District Court for the Western District of Texas, No. 71-1332 Argued: October 12, 1972—Decided: March 21, 1973. *Rodríguez v. San Antonio ISD*. Handbook of Texas Online, http://www.tshaonline.org/handbook/online/articles/RR/jrrht.html.

59. Alexander W. Astin, *Minorities in American Higher Education* (San Francisco, CA: Jossey-Bass, 1982), 29. Meyer Weinberg, *A Chance to Learn: A History of Race and Education in the United States* (Cambridge, UK: Cambridge University Press, 1977), 164, 340–45. Thomas Carter and Roberto D. Segura, *Mexican Americans in School* (New York: College Examination Board, 1979), 233–35.

60. See Astin, *Minorities*. Donald J. Bogue, *Population of the United States* (Glencoe, IL: Free Press, 1959), 570 gives an excellent synthesis of historical trends up to 1980. Alexander W. Astin, *Assessment For Excellence: The Philosophy and Practice of Assessment and Evaluation in Higher Education* (Westport, CT: Oryx Press, 1993), 196, 199.

61. Peter Camejo, (September 14, 2009), http://asitoughttobe.wordpress.com/2009/09/14/peter-camejo/.

62. Rodolfo F. Acuña, *Sometimes There Is No Other Side: Chicanos and the Myth of Equality* (Notre Dame, IN: University of Notre Dame Press, 1998), 21–32. Minority Admissions Summer

Project, sponsored by the National Lawyers Guild and the National Congress of Black Lawyers, *Affirmative Action in Crisis: A Handbook for Activists* (Detroit, 1977); hereafter referred to as *Minority Admissions*. Celeste Durant, "California Bar Exam—Pain and Trauma Twice a Year," *Los Angeles Times* (August 27, 1978). Robert Montoya, "Minority Health Professional Development: An Issue of Freedom of Choice for Young Anglo Health Professionals" (paper presented at the Annual Convention of the American Medical Student Association, Atlanta, Georgia, March 4, 1978). *Regents of the University of California v. Bakke*, 438 U.S. 265 (1978); No. 76–811.

63. Stephen N. Keith, R. M. Bell, A. G. Swanson, and A. Williams, "Effects of Affirmative Action in Medical Schools: A Study of the Class of 1975," *New England Journal of Medicine* 313 (1985): 1519–25. Rodolfo F. Acuña, *US Latinos Issues* (Westport, CT: Greenwood Press, 2004), Chapter 5 on affirmative action. Alex Liebman, "How'd That Guy Get In, Anyway?" *Argos* 1, no. 2 (Summer 1998); hyperlink no longer available.

64. The Federal Bureau of Investigation (FBI), http://www.zoklet.net/totse/en/politics/federal_bureau_of_investigation/index.html. Ernesto B. Vigil, *The Crusade for Justice: Chicano Militancy and the Government's War on Dissent* (Madison: University of Wisconsin Press, 1999). José Angel Gutiérrez, *The Making of a Chicano Militant: Lessons from Cristal* (Madison: University of Wisconsin Press, 1999).

65. The author was part of the Committee to Free Gordon Castillo Hall. Frank del Olmo, "The System Can Be Murder," *Los Angeles Times* (July 16, 1981). Henry Mendoza, "For Gordon Castillo Hall, First Steps Taken in Freedom Are Frightening," *Los Angeles Times* (July 15, 1981). George Ramos, "Justice Takes a Tortuous Route for Latino Man," *Los Angeles Times* (August 9, 1993).

66. Roberto Rodriguez, *Justice: A Question of Race* (Tempe, AZ: Bilingual Review Press, 1997).

67. Homicide-Los Angeles, 1970–1979, *Morbidity and Mortality Weekly Report* 35, no. 5 (February 7, 1986), 61–65, http://www.cdc.gov/mmwr/preview/mmwrhtml/00000841.htm.

68. S. O. B., http://www.youtube.com/watch?v=odRqoMZRm_Y. Anthony Lake, *Somoza Falling* (Boston: Houghton Mifflin, 1989), 94, 186, 260, 273. Anastasio Somoza Debayle, http://www.youtube.com/watch?v=TDRWSFroSbk&feature=related.

69. People and Events: The Iranian Hostage Crisis, November 1979–January 1981, http://www.pbs.org/wgbh/amex/carter/peopleevents/e_hostage.html. U.S. Interventions: 1945–2000, http://www.metacafe.com/watch/1181268/u_s_interventions_1945_2000/.

CHAPTER 15

Becoming a National Minority: 1980–2001

LEARNING OBJECTIVES

- Compare the causes and effects of the massive U.S. immigration from Mexico and Central America.

- Discuss the reasons for deindustrialization and globalization, and the impact on Mexican Americans.

- Tell how immigration became the overwhelming issue in the Mexican American community.

- Explain how immigrants had a positive impact on the American economy.

- Discuss the impact of population growth on the Mexican American community.

- Recognize Propositions 187, 209, and 227 and tell their importance.

- List the most important issues of the period 1980–2001 in a timeline.

The timeline covers two decades—two very hectic periods. For Mexican Americans, population growth contributed to a transformation that saw the community take center stage nationally. In 1980 fewer than 9 million Mexican Americans were counted; they grew to 12.6 million by 1989; and to 20.6 million by 2000. The Latino population as a whole increased from 22.4 million in 1990 to 35.3 million in 2000.[1] The reason for combining decades has to do with history—the events of these two periods are fairly recent, and it takes a bit of distancing for the historian to view the events unfolding decade after decade. Too often historians find themselves so close to the events that the picture blurs.

The population growth put emphasis on the adage *Gobernar es poblar* (to govern is to populate), which in reference to Latinos meant increased involvement in the political process.[2] Increased immigration came from Mexico due to the collapse of the Mexican economy in the 1980s; the civil wars in

1979	1980	1981	1982	1983	1984	1985	1986	1987	1988	1989

1990	1991	1992	1993	1994	1995	1996	1997	1998	1999	2000

Central America uprooted millions of people that joined the polyglot of Spanish-surname people living in the United States. Almost immediately they became the targets of well-funded xenophobic organizations and a rabid press. Most of the media since the 1970s were shallow and pandered to racist nativists. They stereotyped Mexican and Central American immigrants as criminals. Television, radio, and the print media were the important forms of mass communication in the 1980s and 1990s, and viewers, listeners, and readers all depended on them for news.

In 1971 Lewis Powell's political manifesto was a call to action. Over the next years Corporate America created the Heritage Foundation (1973), the Manhattan Institute (1978), the Cato Institute (founded as the Charles Koch Foundation in 1974), Citizens for a Sound Economy (1984), Accuracy in Academe, and other powerful organizations. Massive corporations moved to control communication and war with the reformers. By the 1980s, many of these foundations played on the fears of an aging white population and made war on trade unions and immigrants. To the credit of Latinos as a community, they did not abandon the foreign born.[3]

A study of the files of the *Los Angeles Times* index shows that it first used the term *illegal alien* to refer to immigrants on September 25, 1901. The first reference to Mexicans as illegal aliens was in January 26, 1930; it was only the fourth time it used the term. By 1970, the *Los Angeles Times* had used the phrase 100 times. But from 1970 to mid-1985 it used it more than 6,200 times and by 2006, in an estimated 20,000 documents. By contrast, the *New York Times*, which began publishing in 1851, did not use the term until 1926, when it reported that a man on a bicycle made an unauthorized entry on the Canadian border. By 1970, the *New York Times* had used the term 74 times. From 1970 to 2003, it used the phrase 4,382 times, far less often than the *Los Angeles Times*.[4]

The Decade of the Hispanic

At the beginning of the decade, a prominent Mexican American national leader called the 1980s the "Decade of the Hispanic," suggesting that Mexican Americans would reap the fruits of their struggle for equality. Not quite! Congressional Representative Edward R. Roybal[5] responded at the G.I. Forum Convention in 1980:

> *We have been told over and over that the 1980s will be the Decade of the Hispanics. But, we all remember we were told the same thing at the start of the 1970s. The real answer, my friends, is that we have no clout.*

The theme of the conference was "Merchandising the Mexican American Market in the United States."[6] In California, despite the hype, Mexicans still had only one congressman, and in Los Angeles, with millions of Mexican Americans, the community did not have representation at the city or county levels.

Later in the 1980s, this disparity was somewhat narrowed thanks to the Voting Rights Act of 1965 and lawsuits brought by the Mexican American Legal Defense and Education Fund [MALDEF].[7] However, many Latino leaders and business persons were oblivious to the inequality and became cheerleaders, hyping the 1980s as the Decade of the Hispanic as if the community were a commodity. *Latino* organizations multiplied, and many Mexican American organizations broadened their trajectory to include new immigrants in order to create a national market. The numbers, rather than a sense of civil rights history or struggle, were the standard for representation. Consequently, Latinos failed to educate the new immigrants about the fact that their entitlements came not from the numbers alone but the struggles of the Mexican American, Chicano, and Puerto Rican movements. The entitlements did not come through the covers of fashion magazines.

The election of Ronald Reagan in 1980 ushered in an era of political and economic privatization and conservatism; like the 1920s and the McCarthy era in the aftermath of World War II, it was a war on the poor, immigrants, and unions. The deindustrialization of the economy, that is, the downsizing of heavy manufacturing, was a blow to the working class, increasingly composed of minorities.[8] Some of the impact on Latinos and minorities was absorbed by the increased numbers in higher education, brought about by affirmative action. Reagan's policies of privatization and deregulation would in the next 20 years dismantle this access. Big Business would refuse to pay for the social costs of production, and transfer the support of public higher education to the middle class and poor in the form of increased tuition fees.

The expansion of farm employment and the growth of light industries during the 1980s attracted immigrants. These sectors paid minimum wages, and most often they did not provide health benefits. What was disturbing to many Euro-Americans was the color of the skin of many of the new immigrants. The Immigration Act of 1965 had opened the door for nonwhite groups. The act also allowed more political refugees to enter the country. As a result, the foreign-born population increased from 9.6 million in 1970 to 22.8 million in 1994—a jump of 137 percent. In 1988, 43 percent of authorized immigrants came from Latin America, 41 percent from Asia, and only 10 percent from Europe; the preferred destinations of 70 percent of these immigrants were in just six states. Increased numbers of darker-skinned people triggered rabid racist nativism, a xenophobia agitated by right-wing think tanks and foundations, as well as by fanatics and conservative extremists. They built their organizations on fear and made a lot of money in the process.[9]

Immigration in the 1980s

The Central American Wave

It is important to reiterate that the reason large waves of immigrants from Central America arrived in the 1980s was not the Immigration Act of 1965, but the civil wars in their countries, principally funded by the United States. Moreover, prior to the civil wars, there was a population explosion in Central America. From 1950 to 1990 the population of the region swelled from just over 9 million to almost 29 million. El Salvador and Guatemala went from 4.1 million and 6 million, respectively, in 1975 to 5.3 million and 9.1 million in 1990. The population explosion led to a flight to the cities, as farming was nearly impossible owing to the monopolization of land by elite families and foreign coffee and banana conglomerates. U.S. corporations owned 400,000 acres in Honduras alone—land obtained free of cost through arrangements with friendly dictators at the beginning of the twentieth century. Owing to the lack of a manufacturing infrastructure, the cities could not absorb displaced Salvadoran and Guatemalan rural workers. These conditions produced unrest, and civil wars followed. In Salvador an estimated 5–20 percent of the total population fled to the United States.[10]

U.S. intervention in Central America was a major cause of the diaspora. The fall of U.S.-anointed Nicaraguan dictator Anastasio Somoza in 1979 intensified civil wars in Central America—especially in El Salvador, Guatemala, and Nicaragua. Central American immigrants differed from the Mexican immigrants in that most Central Americans were political refugees. The overthrow of Somoza weakened North American hegemony in the region, and a domino effect followed as other Central Americans began demanding sovereignty and democracy.

El Salvador had been in a state of flux since the 1920s; peasants wanted land and were tired of exploitation by the *latifundista* (large plantation owners). Farabundo Martí, aided by the Communist Party, led a revolt, which the Salvadoran military sadistically suppressed in 1932. More than 12,000 peasants (mostly Indians) died; Martí was murdered. During the 1960s, influenced by Liberation Theology, Catholic clergy and lay persons formed base communities where the question of inequality was discussed and many peasants were politicized. This led to a reaction by elite groups, and in the early 1970s, the ruling elite subverted elections and sponsored the rise of Roberto D'Aubuisson, a neo-Nazi, who headed death squads that conducted a campaign of terror.[11] In 1977, D'Aubuisson's White Warriors machine-gunned Jesuit Father Rutilio Grande and ordered all Jesuits out of the country. Archbishop Oscar Romero began to speak out against injustice, and in 1980, assassins murdered Romero as he celebrated mass. That year, the Salvadoran National Guard tortured, raped, and killed four North American churchwomen.[12]

In 1980, a coalition of Christian Democrats, Social Democrats, minor parties, trade unions, students, and others formed the *Frente Democrático Revolucionario* (FDR), which joined hands with the *Farabundo Martí Liberación Nacional* (FMLN), the military wing heading the armed struggle. At the same time, to give the government an air of legitimacy, a centrist party took the national presidency. Meanwhile, the right controlled the legislature. The United States financed military operations against the FMLN. Some 50,000 Salvadorans—most of whom were civilians—died during this civil war. Still, unable to find peace at home, hundreds of thousands of Salvadorans fled north.

The U.S. government sent the Salvadoran military $4.2 billion to conduct the war and, consequently, destroy any semblance of a free market. The military, through its surrogate Arena Party, controlled a large bloc of votes during the 1991 elections—which it subverted, committing gross fraud. Nevertheless, the warring factions signed peace accords that year.[13]

Meanwhile, in Nicaragua, the rebels under the leadership of the Sandinista National Liberation Front (*Frente Sandinista de Liberación Nacional*, or FSLN) successfully set up a revolutionary government.[14] The United States, fearing that a Marxist or left-of-center government would threaten its economic and political interests, backed counterrevolutionaries with the purpose of overthrowing the FSLN. (Nicaragua numbered 2.4 million people. The United States had a population of 226.6 million in 1980.) The United States intensified the war in Nicaragua, under the pretext that Nicaragua was a threat to the security of the United States and it was supplying arms to El Salvador's insurgents. Ronald Reagan's 1980 election escalated the war against the Sandinistas. Reagan stationed 2,000 troops in Honduras, where the CIA—with the Contras (the ultraright opposition)—led military operations against the Nicaraguan government. Thus, the CIA openly violated the Boland Amendment, which prohibited the use of U.S. funds to overthrow a foreign government.[15]

Reagan insisted that Soviet and Cuban influence in Nicaragua threatened U.S. security. But just as it did in 1954 in Guatemala, the Dominican Republic in 1963–1965, and Chile on 9/11/1973, the U.S. moved to overthrow the Nicaraguan government. Reagan dubbed the Sandinistas undemocratic. In 1984, the Sandinistas held elections. While Western European and Latin American nations praised the elections for being open, Reagan labeled them a sham. Reagan and then George H. W. Bush isolated Nicaragua, and in 1990, the Nicaraguan people, weary of war, voted for the United Nicaraguan Opposition. The Sandinistas peacefully relinquished power. This ended the dirty little war, which led to an indictment of Ronald Reagan's former Defense Secretary Caspar W. Weinberger on charges that he lied to Congress about his knowledge of arms sales to Iran and efforts by other countries to help underwrite the Nicaraguan war. It was also charged that the CIA allowed illegal drugs to be imported into the United States by the Contras, which were sold and the proceeds used by Contra leaders to buy arms. President George H. W. Bush pardoned Weinberger and five others, thus preventing an airing of evidence that Bush, while he was Reagan's vice president, was involved in the conspiracy. The media called this unconstitutional operation *Iran Contra*.[16]

During 1966–1968, President Lyndon Johnson sent Green Berets to Guatemala, to train government forces against insurgents. U.S.-supported government troops crushed a revolution, which resurged again in the 1980s. Knowing that the rebels had peasant support, the military embarked on a strategy of burning indigenous villages, corralling the natives into key cities. A secret army unit, financed and trained by the United States, operated in the country in the early 1980s, kidnapping, torturing, and executing Guatemalans in a violent campaign against leftists suspected of subversion. This was the longest and bloodiest butchery in Central America, killing more than 200,000 people. Well over 50,000 disappeared in a nation of 11 million. The war displaced about a million and a half Guatemalan peasants as the army pursued a strategy of "permanent counterinsurgency" against the nation's 5 million Maya.[17]

The Mexican Wave

Mexican immigration accelerated in the 1980s. The underlying causes were population growth and a movement of large number of Mexicans to the cities due to the continued commercialization of agriculture. An international crisis devastated Mexico's economy in 1982 and accelerated the push. Outgoing President José López Portillo dramatically devalued the peso, which in the next three years fell from 12.5 pesos to the dollar to more than 700 pesos to the dollar. The reason for the devaluation was to supposedly stop the flight of dollars from Mexico. The country's external debt, both private and public, climbed to $85 billion. Mexico needed the dollars to pay its debt, which by 1986 was approaching $100 billion.

The minimum wage in Ciudad Juárez in 1978 was 125 pesos ($5.30) a day. Three years later 600 *maquiladoras* (assembly plants) operated south of the border, 90 percent of them along the border. They employed 130,000 workers, 75–90 percent of them women, 70 percent of whom were single. The system supported 80,000 workers in Juárez alone and another 5,000 white-collar jobs in El Paso. Mexican *maquila* wages averaged $2 an hour in 1982 before the devaluation; in 1987, they averaged $0.67 an hour, which was lower than Asian wages. By 1986, Ciudad Juárez became a *maquiladora* boomtown. Corporations such as General Motors, which assembled wire harnesses there, maintained large operations all along the border.

By 1986, Mexico defaulted on the loans or declared a repayment moratorium. Mexico's domestic situation worsened—it could no longer comply with the International Monetary Fund (IMF) demands without facing severe internal consequences. The situation was rendered almost impossible by the nearly 50 percent plunge in the price of oil, which furnished 70 percent of Mexico's export exchange and 50 percent of government revenues. Hence, the rich got richer, and by the end of the millennium, there were 13 Mexican billionaires, the highest by far in Latin America (France was 16).[18]

Reaction to the Little Brown Brothers and Sisters

Since the Alien and Sedition Acts of 1798, there has been a pattern of irrational Euro-American angst fed by the notion that someone was taking America away from them. The panic was worse during periods of uncertainty; generally the fear was fanned by the media. As in the case of a horror movie like *Friday the 13th*, the audience's fear reaches its height over anticipated situations. In the case of white suburban women, the fear was that the inner city would catch up to them and dark men would stalk them. The argument that unauthorized immigrants took jobs away from "Americans," and in some way were stealing their "American Dream," was disproven. Americans refused to listen to the evidence and there was a disconnect between reality and myth. For example, California benefited from immigration. In 1984, the Urban Institute of Washington reported that 645,000 jobs had been created in Los Angeles County since 1970; immigrants took about one-third of the jobs. Without immigrants, the factories hiring them would have left the area, resulting in the loss of higher-paying jobs.[19]

Although the availability of an immigrant labor force spurred economic activity for the nation as a whole, nativism became more strident in 1986, as Californians passed the "English Is the Official Language" Proposition 63, which voters approved by a 3 to 1 margin. The campaign was a look into the future; it was based almost entirely on half truths and hate. Within a year, seven other states passed similar measures, and 31 more were considering English Only measures. Yeshiva University Psychology Professor Joshua Fishman questioned the good faith behind the sudden concern for the "functional protection of English." He asked how English was endangered in a country where 97 percent of the population spoke the language. Fishman raised the probability of a "hidden agenda."[20]

About the same time, Congress responded to nation's jingoism by passing the Immigration Reform and Control Act (IRCA), which was a compromise that included employer sanctions as well as amnesty for unauthorized immigrants who had been residents since January 1, 1981, or could prove they had done farmwork for 90 days, from May 1, 1985, to May 1, 1986. By January 1989, some 2.96 million applied for amnesty (about 70 percent of them were Mexican). IRCA allocated $1 billion a year for four years to fund English, U.S. history, and government classes to be administered by the State Legislation Impact Assistance Grant. The classes were mandatory for all amnesty applicants, and organizations such as *Hermandad Mexicana Nacional* and One-Stop Immigration hoped to use the funds to teach the new immigrants English and to assimilate them into the social and political life of Chicanos. The antiamnesty forces were spearheaded by groups such as the American Immigration Control Foundation (AICF) and the Federation for American Immigration Reform (FAIR) whose opposition was ideological rather than based on reason. The Center for New Community reported:

> *Much of the AICF leadership crosses the thin ideological line separating xenophobic nativism and outright white nationalism. Former AICF board chair Sam Francis (1992–1995 . . .), for example, is well-known for his racist and biological determinist positions. Longtime AICF board member Brent Nelson is on the Editorial Advisory Board of the Citizens Informer, the flagship*

publication of the white nationalist Council of Conservative Citizens (C of CC) and often pens articles for this publication, as does AICF President and Immigration Watch editor John Vinson. Moreover AICF has received strong financial support from the Pioneer Fund, a foundation which has been linked to eugenics and other "racial" research.[21]

Equally to blame for spreading panic were elected officials who had nothing to lose, and a lot to gain, by taking cheap shots at immigrants. For instance, Dallas Mayor Pro Tem Jim Hart exploited the fears of the voters and warned that aliens had "no moral values," and that they were destroying Dallas neighborhoods and threatening the security of the city. California Congressman Elton Gallegly (R–Simi Valley) proposed a constitutional amendment to deny citizenship to U.S.-born children of undocumented immigrants. Even California Representative Anthony Bielenson (D–San Fernando Valley), considered a progressive Democrat, raised the bogus prospect of a Mexican invasion.[22] This tension emboldened far-right racists, who began to abuse the initiative and referendum process with impunity. An example was the campaign to dump California Supreme Court Justice Rose Bird and Associate Justices Joseph Grodin and Cruz Reynoso, a highly respected Chicano jurist who had a long history of involvement in public interest law. Nativists lied and exaggerated the votes of these justices against the death penalty to whip up public angst and hatred of the "other." *Los Angeles Times* columnist Frank de Olmo put the campaign to remove Reynoso in the context of Proposition 63.

> *The campaign against Reynoso and his colleagues, including Chief Justice Rose Elizabeth Bird, is being pushed by law-and-order advocates who claim that the "liberal" justices are lenient on crime. It has been waged for several years and has been analyzed more than any other issue on the state ballot—except for a troubling undercurrent that Californians have become too polite to discuss openly: racism.*
>
> *I don't mean the ugly racism that motivates some people to burn crosses. The campaign against Reynoso is more subtle. It indirectly suggests that because Reynoso came from a large family of farm workers he is not quite as capable as judges with a different (that is, "better") social background. And it slyly hints that a Mexican-American judge can't analyze cases affecting poor people dispassionately.[23]*

The Militarization of the Border

Shortly after the Berlin Wall, separating East and West Germany, came down in 1989, the United States built its own wall separating it from the Third World. Border Patrol abuse increased, as did the military swagger of the agency. The official line—that the Border Patrol was fighting a war on drugs—gave the agency tremendous latitude in violating human rights. In 1990, one year after the Berlin Wall came tumbling down, the Defense Department built an 11-mile fence in the San Diego area as part of its war on drugs. Two years later, the Army Corps of Engineers announced plans to place scores of floodlights along a 13-mile strip of border near San Diego to "deter drug smugglers and illegal aliens." A 1992 *Atlantic* piece posited, "It would not require much killing: the Soviets sealed their borders for decades without an excessive expenditure of ammunition," adding that a systematic policy of shooting illegal immigrants would deter most Mexicans, but "adopting such a policy is not a choice most Americans would make. Of course, there would be no question of free trade."[24]

President Bill Clinton, mindful that he had been defeated in his reelection for Arkansas governor because he allegedly did not act quickly enough to put down a riot of Cuban inmates at Fort Chaffee, Arkansas, played Mr. Tough Guy and followed the policies of Reagan and George H. W. Bush. He manufactured a war against undocumented immigrants, ordering Attorney General Janet Reno to begin blockades and roundups in the El Paso and San Diego areas. By the end of the Clinton administration, San Diego became ground zero in the anti-immigrant war. The Clinton administration called it "Operation Gatekeeper": sealing the border in western San Diego County and forcing undocumented immigrants to cross the deadly terrain to the east. The government increasingly commingled crackdowns on immigrants and the war against drugs—falsely equating immigration and drug smuggling and, thus, further criminalizing the immigrant. However, as described later in this chapter, immigration hysteria lessened considerably by 1998—partially because of improved economic conditions, but in good part because of the backlash within the Mexican American and other Latino communities.[25]

Mexican American Labor

Never before in the history of Chicanos were labor unions needed more than in the 1980s and 1990s. The poverty rate went on climbing throughout the late 1970s and 1980s to reach a 27-year high in 1991, with 35.7 million people living below the poverty line—the highest poverty rate since 1964. Frequent economic recessions during the 1980s and early 1990s especially hurt women, most of whom possessed few job skills. From 1973 to 1990, the median salary of female heads-of-households under the age of 30 fell 32 percent in real dollars—more than 50 percent of the Mexicanas in the workforce earned less than $10,000. Close to 50 percent (47.7 percent) of the Mexican households with an absent father lived in poverty; and close to 40 percent (37.3 percent) of Mexican-origin workers who did not have a high school education lived in poverty, versus 16.7 percent in the non-Latino community.

While the white population increased its college enrollment from 31.8 to 39.4 percent during the 1980s, and African American enrollment went from 27.6 to 33 percent, the Latino enrollment fell from 29.8 to 29 percent. And, unlike black school segregation, which had fluctuated within a narrow range over the previous 25 years, Latino segregation kept increasing. In 1970, the typical black student attended a school where enrollment was 32 percent white; by 1994, it was 33.9 percent. On the other hand, for schools attended by Latino students, white enrollment went down—from 43.8 to 30.6 percent. The harshness of the new economy and the growing gap between the rich and poor did not escape Archbishop Roger Mahoney, who in 1985 said, "we cannot evaluate our economy primarily by the extraordinary opportunities it offers a few."[26]

It is not that history repeats itself, it is that we forget its lessons. During the 1950s Republicans sought to dismantle the protections of the New Deal, though the memory of the Great Depression was still fresh. By the 1980s, those memories either faded or were repressed. This historical amnesia gave Reagan the opportunity that reactionaries had waited for 40 years—to dismantle the safety nets for the average American and make the country business friendly. Reagan declared in 1982, as he signed the Garn–St. Germain Depository Institutions Act, lessening regulations on savings and loans and banks, "This bill is the most important legislation for financial institutions in the last 50 years. It provides a long-term solution for troubled thrift institutions. . . . All in all, I think we hit the jackpot."[27] Reaganomics made all but certain the financial disaster of 2008.

Capitalists hit the jackpot with Reagan's labor policies when in 1981 Reagan declared war on organized labor by firing 11,400 air traffic controllers, decertifying the Professional Air Traffic Controllers Organization (PATCO), and replacing its members with scabs—labor was paralyzed. As a result, during 1980–1987, strike activities fell some 50 percent in selected unions, and the number of strikers that were replaced jumped 300 percent. Union membership declined nationally, with overall union participation in the private sector falling below 15 percent. In the face of this repression, the trade union movement became more submissive, reluctant to strike or fight back.[28]

Much of the credit for organizing during these lean years has to go to immigrant workers. The historical attitude of labor since the nineteenth century has been anti-immigrant. Even progressive unions such as the Western Federation of Miners in the early twentieth century sought to limit immigration and exclude Mexican laborers as retarded and not having a working-class consciousness. As late as the 1980s, labor federations such as the Los Angeles County Federation of Labor lobbied to crack down on undocumented labor. However, amnesty and the waves of immigrants changed this.

Beside the militancy of the immigrant workers, there emerged a new class of organizers, many of whom had been involved in student and popular activism of the 1960s. Some were white and African American, but a large core was comprised of the Chicano student movement leadership of the 1960s and 1970s. For example, the hotel and restaurant labor had a core of Chicano activists: For María Elena Durazo, whose parents were immigrants, her interest in the protection of the foreign born began when she was a student at St. Mary's College and member of CASA (Center for Autonomous Social Action). Durazo worked alongside Magdalena Mora, a dedicated UC Berkeley student from Mexico who died very young of cancer (see Chapter 14). After working for the International Ladies Garment Workers Union (ILGWU), Durazo was hired in 1983 by Local 11, the Hotel Employees and Restaurant Employees Union (HERE), as a worker representative. Four years later Durazo won the presidency of the local; however, the international put the local into receivership. In 1989, Durazo was reelected as president. Under her leadership, HERE took on business giants such as the Hyatt Hotel chain. The union returned to the basics of militant unionism, picketing and courting arrest to call attention to the plight of the workers. Local 11 played hardball, relentlessly pressuring politicos to support the union. As of 2013, Local 11 is still in the trenches, fighting for immigrant workers. Meanwhile, Durazo was elected Executive Secretary of the Los Angeles Federation of Labor, one of the most powerful positions in California Labor.[29]

Immigrant workers in the cleaning service sector, although one of the most vulnerable workforces, organized across the country. Like the hotel and restaurant workers, they fought not only for decent wages but medical coverage. Membership in Los Angeles Local 399, Justice for Janitors, plunged 77 percent in the 1980s, and by 1987, only 1,500 janitors remained under contract. With the assistance of white and Mexican college graduates, the workers began to organize. The movement also produced rank-and-file organizers such as Salvadoran Ana Navarette and Chicana Patricia Recino. Navarette was active in the Salvadoran liberation struggle; Recino, a product of the Chicano student movement, had been active in various social justice organizations since her teens.

Fearing permanent replacement of its desperately poor members, Local 399 formulated the strategy of going directly to the streets—making it financially dangerous for the subcontractors to get in the union's way. Among the targets were Century City and the International Service System, Inc. (ISS), the world's largest commercial cleaning contractor. On May 15, 1990, 150 armed LAPD officers attacked janitors and their supporters. The officers gave the order to picketers to disperse in English only. A police riot ensued, which resulted in 40 arrests and 16 injuries, with two women having miscarriages after being beaten. The Century City massacre was more vicious but less publicized than the Rodney King beating a year later. The janitors sued the LAPD, and in September 1993 they settled for $2.35 million.[30]

Confrontational tactics helped union organizers in recruiting low-paid minority workers and renewing the cycle of activism. The percentage of union janitors working in major Los Angeles commercial buildings rose from 10 percent in 1987, when Local 399 launched its campaign, to about 90 percent in the mid-1990s. However, tensions between the members and the union leadership began to surface. In June, a 21-member dissident slate called "Multiracial Alliance" won control of the union's executive board. Once in power, the dissident slate "cleaned the house." Regretfully, it fired many leaders who contributed to the success of the union. The new Latino officers (Salvadoran, Guatemalan, and Mexican) accused the former leadership of being paternalistic and racist. Charges and countercharges followed.

When the international headquarters of the janitors' union responded by placing the local union in receivership and naming Mike García of San Jose as the interim head, most of the so-called dissidents left the union, bitter because they won a fair election and were then dismissed. The old guard, in turn, rationalized that nationalism had produced the rupture. In reality, the labor movement was largely to blame for this and other ruptures, for its failure to employ adequate resources where the labor movement was expanding most—among immigrants and Latinos.[31]

In the 1970s, Los Angeles, once known as the Detroit of the West, employed 15,000 autoworkers producing a half million cars annually. Automakers then began to dismantle their California operations; the Ford Pinto factory in Pico Rivera geared down, as did the General Motors plant in South Gate. By 1982, Van Nuys workers saw the handwriting on the wall. They knew it was only a matter of time before GM would shut down that plant.

Led by the United Auto Local 645 president, Pete Beltrán, the workers and the community built a coalition that threatened a boycott if the GM plant was closed. Although the labor/community strategy bore fruit, the UAW international capitulated and sold workers on the notion that if they cooperated the plant would remain open. In the summer of 1991, General Motors announced the shutdown of the Van Nuys plant. Some GM workers, forced to sell their houses, moved to other states where GM employed them;

others collected severance pay for a year while the community inherited a worsening economic situation as more businesses closed down.

Despite the closing, the "Keep G.M. Van Nuys" campaign begot the Labor/Community Strategy Center, under the leadership of Eric Mann, who had spearheaded the campaign to keep the plant open.[32] The center has done outstanding environmental work. In 1992, the Strategy Center initiated a transportation policy group. Two years later, the group began organizing bus riders in the "Billions for Buses" campaign to confront the racism reflected in the policies of the Metropolitan Transportation Authority of Los Angeles (MTA). Membership in the Bus Riders Union has since grown to more than 3,000 dues-paying members and 50,000 self-identified members on the buses. Most of the riders are Latinos and women.[33]

In eastern Arizona, the cradle of the Chicana/o labor movement, in July 1983, 13 unions, led by the steelworkers' Local 616 at Clifton-Morenci, Arizona, struck the workers' old nemesis Phelps–Dodge.[34] Trouble broke out when Phelps–Dodge imported scabs to break the strike. The National Labor Relations Board (NLRB), under the Reagan administration, sided with management, and it conducted a poll in which it allowed only the scabs to vote; they voted to decertify the union. The mineworkers attempted to gain support from outside the area. A ladies' auxiliary led by activists such as Jessie Téllez toured the Southwest, talking to Chicano and labor groups. Despite insurmountable odds, the miners continued to strike, facing eviction and harassment. However, by 1987—still led by the union's president, Angel Rodríguez—the Morenci strike was all but dead. Only the diehards remained, learning from their mistakes and rebuilding their union. Barbara Kingsolver, in her book *Holding the Line: Women in the Great Arizona Mine Strike of 1983*, captures the feelings of women both inside and outside the mine who struggled for their space in the movement.[35]

In San Antonio, Texas, Levi Strauss, the world's largest apparel manufacturer, closed its plant in 1990, resulting in 1,100 layoffs. The plant, acquired in 1981, was the main domestic production facility for the Dockers line of casual pants, which required twice the labor as was needed for jeans. The company produced $70 million worth of Dockers and Officers Corp jeans. The San Antonio plant made record profits in 1989, and it was Levi's largest operation in Texas. To cut costs, Levi transferred the work previously done in San Antonio to independent contractors in the Caribbean and Costa Rica, where wages ranged from 30 cents to $1 an hour, compared with $6–$7 per hour in the United States. The company notified workers 90 days before closing the plant, 30 days more than is required by law. Levi laid off 10,400 workers between 1981 and 1990, and it shut down 26 plants nationwide from 1985 to 1993. The city of San Antonio lost 10,000 jobs in 1990 alone.

Virginia Castillo, a sewing machine operator at Levi Strauss, was still bitter four years after the San Antonio plant closed. The shutdown abruptly ended Castillo's employment of 16 years and began the unraveling of her life as a factory worker, wife, mother, and grandmother. Castillo, 52, was left unemployed. She had limited job and language skills. Her health deteriorated owing to nerve damage to her back and wrists caused by factory work. Her marriage failed. Yet her experiences made Castillo a labor activist. Like many others, she moved to San Francisco to take on Levi Strauss and to tell the world that, despite its socially conscious image and record of philanthropy, the company continues to exploit workers in the United States and abroad.

Castillo belonged to a movement called *Fuerza Unida* (United Strength), a 480-member group of former San Antonio Levi Strauss workers. *Hispanic* magazine voted Levi Strauss one of the hundred best companies in the United States for Hispanic workers, and *Vista* magazine placed it among the top 50 companies for Latina women. The fact remained, however, that Levi Strauss did not act in a socially responsible way toward the San Antonio workers. Most of the women lacked education. Paid on a piece rate, they worked extremely fast and hard. The shutdown caused vast unemployment. The women, hard hit, lost their homes and cars.[36]

Fuerza Unida said that Levi Strauss cheated the former employees of some severance pay, profit sharing, and other pay from pensions, vacation time, holiday overtime, and $500 Christmas bonus promised to each employee the December before the layoffs. In total, the company owed the workers about $4 million. Levi Strauss responded that it had properly compensated its former employees, and a federal lawsuit by Fuerza Unida was dismissed in 1993. Levi Strauss continued its restructuring throughout the decade. In November 1997, it shut down 11 plants in the United States, laying off another 6,395 workers— one-third of its U.S. manufacturing force. The bottom line, according to former Levi workers in San Antonio, was that the 1997 shutdowns alone saved Levi Strauss $200 million. Even before the 1997 shutdowns, Levi made profits, for example, of $357 million on nearly $5 billion in sales in 1991. Closing their plant was not an economic necessity, the former workers say, but a tactic to earn more profits. Meanwhile, under the leadership of Chicanas, *Fuerza Unida* continued its fight-back campaign.[37]

Although César Chávez symbolized the struggle of the Mexican American people for justice, many Americans by the mid-1980s wanted to forget about the sacrifice of farmworkers, and Chávez's personal contributions were eclipsed by those of Julio César Chávez, a boxing champion. It was symptomatic of the times. The two men symbolized different values and different legacies.[38]

A 1985 poll revealed that 53 percent of the general public still favored Chávez, and only 21 percent opposed him. Chávez's organizational problems, related to the length and intensity of the struggle, led to personality clashes and dissatisfaction with the United Farm Workers' (UFW) direction among a minority of the organizers. Compounding the UFW's woes, California Governor George Deukmejian, heavily indebted to agricultural capitalists, torpedoed the Agricultural Labor Relations Board (ALRB) by appointing David Stirling, a grower hatchetman, as general counsel to the board. Under Stirling only 10 percent of the cases reached the ALRB, compared with 35 percent under the appointees of Governor Edmund G. Brown, Jr. Deukmejian cut the ALRB's budget by one-third; by 1986 the board became inoperative when, because of the governor's appointees, it was totally under the growers' control. Government continued to conspire against the UFW.

Simultaneously, President Reagan appointed John R. Norton—head of J. R. Norton Company, one of the largest lettuce producers of the world—as the U.S. deputy secretary of agriculture. This template of Republican–grower complicity continued at the state and national levels through the administrations of California Governor Pete Wilson and President George H. W. Bush.

In 1985, 4,000 farmworkers walked out of the fields in the Imperial Valley. The growers hired armed guards and attack dogs that injured many strikers. A grower's car struck Isauro López and permanently crippled him. Thugs hired by growers shot Rufino Contreras through the head and killed him. Judge William Lehnhardt refused to disqualify himself from the case, even though his wife had worked as a strikebreaker. Lehnhardt ruled that the union was responsible for the violence and crop loss and did not prosecute growers' agents for murder. The union, on the other hand, raised $3.3 million to appeal this perversion of justice and wait for years to get its day in court. The UFW continued to struggle against all odds to organize workers.[39]

The Movement for Inclusion: The Politicos

An essential part of any struggle is political representation—it is a measure of not only the unity within a group but also the group's acceptance by others. Numbers usually determine the success of the out-groups; however, they do not tell the entire story. The majority culture makes the rules, and therefore the dice are loaded in their favor. In the case of Mexican Americans, gerrymandering and other political gimmickry diluted their voting strength. But there were also other factors such as immigrants not being eligible to vote and the relatively lower median age of Mexican Americans. Moreover, white people would not vote for Mexicans. So the Mexican American community took a long arduous path through the courts to get new rules.

One of the few areas where the Reagan administration helped Mexican Americans was in the enforcement of the 1965 Voting Rights Act. Reagan signed the 1982 amendment to the Voting Rights Act into law, and his justice department vigorously enforced the law. This was not an altruistic gesture though. While redistricting, Republicans often sided with Latinos in disputes between them and Democratic incumbents. Mexican Americans took full advantage of these tensions between Republicans and Democrats by using the 1965 Voting Rights Act, and its subsequent amendments by Republicans, as the basis of the Mexican American electoral revolution of the 1990s. Again, as in the case of labor leadership, throughout the country the Latino candidates for office emerged out of the activist core of the 1960s and 1970s.

The Southwest Voter Registration and Education Project (SVREP) and the MALDEF were major players in the movement. The former registered Chicanos to vote, and the latter used court challenges to give them a fighting chance. For example, MALDEF sued the city of Los Angeles for violations of the Voting Rights Acts in its redistricting plans; the result was the formation of two Latino-friendly council districts. SVREP increased Chicano registration from 488,000 in 1976 to over 1 million by 1985. The project published reports and analyses of Chicano voting potential and trends. Along with MALDEF and sympathetic lawyers, the SVREP challenged reapportionment and at-large voting practices that diluted electoral strength of Latinos. Meanwhile, amendments to the Voting Rights Act in 1975 and 1982 made it easier for the SVREP and MALDEF to persuade local municipalities to restructure their electoral units, *por las buenas o las malas* (literally, "the easy way or the hard way").[40]

In 1981, 19 Chicano candidates were elected to local offices in Salinas and the San Joaquín Valley. Latino population increased in 16 districts. The following year, Mario Obledo, former California secretary of health and welfare and cofounder of MALDEF, who had considerable credibility within the mainstream Mexican American community, decided to enter the Democratic Party primary for governor. Liberals criticized Obledo for running against Los Angeles Mayor Tom Bradley. The unsuccessful campaign, however, mobilized Mexican American activists throughout the state, stimulating aspirations about offices statewide. Unfortunately, the new awareness and the relative success of redistricting also started political infighting in East Los Angeles, as elected officials attempted to forge a political machine. An early defector was Gloria Molina, who ran successfully for the State Assembly in 1982.[41]

Assemblyman Art Torres caused some raised eyebrows by successfully challenging State Senator Alex García for his seat. Although criticized at the time, Assemblyman Richard Alatorre, as chair of the Assembly Elections and Reapportionment Committee, managed to add a new congressional seat. Another congressional seat was vacant as an incumbent had retired. Former White House aides Esteban Torres and Matthew Marty Martínez ran successfully for the open congressional seats in 1982.[42]

The prize that everyone wanted was the Los Angeles City Council seat held by Art Snyder for a decade and a half. His political base scared off most Latino challengers. However, in 1983 a relatively unknown urban planner, Steve Rodríguez, challenged Snyder and almost beat him. (The Los Angeles political establishment did not support Rodríguez because he had once been a member of *La Raza Unida* Party [RUP].) This close race raised expectations—especially as Larry González, 27, beat ultraconservative Richard Ferraro for an LA Unified Board seat. Consequently, in 1986, Richard Alatorre was elected to the Council, replacing Snyder, making him potentially the most powerful Chicano politico in California.[43]

Chicanos pressured the Justice Department to file a suit against the City of Los Angeles—*U.S. v. City of Los Angeles* (1985)—alleging that the city violated civil and voting rights guarantees of Latinos under the Fourteenth and Fifteenth Constitutional Amendments and the Voting Rights Acts of 1965, 1975, and 1982. The suit forced the Los Angeles City Council to submit a new plan to the court in 1986. A compromise was reached, and an additional Chicano district was formed, which opened the possibility of another future seat in the San Fernando Valley. Redistricting made it possible for Gloria Molina to be elected to the Council—a second Latino-held seat. Statewide, other patterns were emerging: The Latino population of the San Gabriel Valley, east of East Los Angeles, and of small cities along the San Bernardino Freeway, grew by almost 50 percent. This area was more middle class than the Los Angeles Eastside and was a base of funding support for Chicano politicos.[44]

In 1986, Texas led the nation in the number of Latino elected officials: 1,466, compared with 588 in New Mexico and 450 in California. Tejanos in the Lone Star State made up one-fifth of the voting-age population that year. Tejanos comprised 12.9 percent of the electorate in November 1988, but only 5.6 percent of the Texas city council members were Chicanos. In 1986, 50 percent of Texas first graders were Tejanos, but again only 6.6 percent of Texas school board members were of Mexican origin.

Henry Cisneros was the best known Chicana/o politico in the country in terms of offices held and his national visibility.[45] He rose to become a member of President Bill Clinton's cabinet, as Secretary of Housing and Urban Development. Mexican-dominated San Antonio elected Cisneros to the San Antonio City Council in 1975. He was a crossover candidate favored by the Euro-American elite and their Good Government League (GGL). That year, Mexicans comprised 51.8 percent of the city but only 37 percent of the registered voters; whites made up 39 percent of the population and almost 56 percent of the registered voters. The Cisneros victory inspired more Tejano political participation, and two years later Chicanas/os and African Americans took over the San Antonio City Council.

Mexicans received a big boost from the Justice Department in 1976 when the department halted San Antonio annexations of surrounding areas. Whites used annexation as a device to dilute the voting power of minorities. In Texas, municipalities annexed surrounding neighborhoods to include more whites, invariably absorbing white areas to neutralize the Mexican and black population increases. The rise of the Communities Organized for Public Service (COPS) also played a determining role in politicizing and registering Mexican voters.

In 1981, Henry Cisneros became the first Mexican American mayor of San Antonio since the 1840s. Born in San Antonio, Cisneros attended Central Catholic High and then graduated from Texas A&M. An urban planner, Cisneros received his doctorate from George Washington University and then returned in 1974 to San Antonio, where he solicited GGL sponsorship. Cisneros's father, a retired Army Reserve colonel, worked at Fort Sam Houston; his mother, Elvira Mungía Cisneros, came from an elite family who fled Mexico during the revolution. Cisneros's maternal grandfather, Henry Romulo Mungía, ran a print shop and had close ties with other exiled families, which included a surprising number of the present generation of San Antonio's Chicano leaders. Cisneros was ideologically more Republican than Democrat. He was one of the few politicos who did not have roots in the 1960s era. Cisneros emphasized economic growth, participation in the technological revolution, and the necessity of attracting high-tech business to San Antonio. Cisneros appealed to educated middle-class Mexican Americans, who were becoming a larger proportion of the community.

By the mid-1980s, Texas had 3 Tejanos who were members of Congress, 4 state senators, and 21 state representatives. In 1986, Texas also led in the number of Chicanas elected to public office. As for electoral politics, Texas had a higher percentage of native-born Mexican Americans than any state outside of New Mexico. In 1980, 83 percent of the Latino population of San Antonio was born in the United States, in contrast to 43 percent of the Latino population in Los Angeles. One hundred and fifty years of housing segregation resulted in residential bonding.[46]

The electoral strength of Tejanos stemmed from the activities and the leadership development of the Mexican American Youth Organization and the political successes of *La Raza Unida* Party that pressured the Democratic Party to open its doors wider. In addition, Texas developed a healthy organizational network; the League of United Latin American Citizens (LULAC), the American G.I. Forum, RUP, SVREP, MALDEF, and followers of Saul Alinsky—who founded the Industrial Areas Foundation (IAF) in Chicago and trained community organizers for organizations such as COPS—all originated in Texas. COPS is part of a network of IAF organizations, which have units throughout the Southwest. In the Latino community, the IAF organizations were heavily involved in Catholic Church networks. Ernesto Cortez, head of the IAF, was a major power, negotiating with state politicos to end the "legacy of neglect." Cortez organized in the barrios of the Rio Grande Valley, Houston, San Antonio, and El Paso.[47]

By the 1980s Chicago ranked second in the United States in terms of a Mexican-origin population. It had a unique history, and Chicago Chicanos functioned within a well-defined "patronage system." Its wards clearly defined the boundaries of the city's ethnic neighborhoods. By 1986, Chicago's Latino population was close to 540,000—19 percent of the city's total population; residents of Mexican origin comprised about 60 percent of the Latino group as a whole. In 1983, Harold Washington, an African American, was elected the mayor of Chicago, supported by Mexicans as well as Puerto Ricans, African Americans, and progressive whites. The Pilsen district remained the principal port of entry for Latinos, and housed the greatest concentration of Mexicans. The South Side barrios of Pilsen, Little Village, and South Chicago numbered more Mexicans than other Latinos. A Mexican minority also lived in the North Side, where they shared space with Puerto Ricans and other Latino groups. Although a large percentage of the Mexican population was foreign born, in the mid-1980s the Latino Institute found that 83 percent of the Latino youth were born in the United States.

In 1981, not a single Latino served on the Chicago City Council; that year, council members blatantly gerrymandered the districts, making the future election of a Latino almost impossible. The following year, MALDEF sued the Chicago City Council under the 1965 Voters Rights Act as amended in 1982. The remapping of the district, according to MALDEF, diluted Latino voting strength. Four years later, the court issued a judicial order that created four Latino wards—the 22nd, 25th, 26th, and 31st; the 22nd and 25th were predominantly Chicana/o. A special election took place in March, in which Jesús García and Juan Solíz were elected from the 22nd and 25th Wards, respectively. The creation of the Latino wards was crucial to the growing power of Chicanos and Latinos in Chicago.[48]

In 1982, Mexican Americans and organized labor turned out heavily to elect Toney Anaya governor of New Mexico. Anaya, the former state attorney general, received 85 percent of the manito vote. Anaya was an energetic governor who took strong and controversial stands opposing the death penalty. He declared New Mexico a sanctuary for Central American political refugees, and was pro–foreign born, condemning racist nativism. He was highly criticized for focusing on Latino issues. A bold step in his career was that he appointed manitos to key posts to protect their interests. For instance, Anaya appointed John Páez to the University of New Mexico's Board of Regents in 1983, giving Latinos a majority for the first time. The next year he appointed Jerry Apodaca and Robert Sánchez to the board of regents.

New Mexico was also the home to newcomer Representative Bill Richardson, who was elected to Congress two years after he arrived in 1980. He made friends with the New Mexican power brokers, who supported his rise. Richardson, under Clinton, was named U.S. ambassador to the United Nations and Energy Secretary in 1998. Richardson, a Democrat, was elected to the House of Representatives from New Mexico in 1982 and reelected seven times. Richardson's mother was Mexican, and his Euro-American father was born in Nicaragua, grew up in Boston, and worked for Citibank as an executive in Mexico. Richardson was raised in Mexico City, but moved to Massachusetts at age 13 to attend a Boston-area high school.

Latinos in New Mexico rivaled Mississippi for the highest percentage of children who lived below the poverty line. San Miguel County rivaled the Rio Grande Valley in claiming the worst poverty. How could this be? Nativists could not blame it on the immigrant, as they did in California. The tragedy was that the old *patrón* politics of the nineteenth century still victimized New Mexican politics. People there largely voted according to personal and family loyalties rather than for issues. Sadly, by the 1980s, outsiders—primarily elderly Euro-Americans—were migrating into the state, and the ability to make substantive changes was slipping away.[49]

Not as nationalistic as Texas, Colorado was divided into north and south, with the latter being more like New Mexico than were Denver and the north. Federico Peña, Denver's first Mexican American mayor, was an exile. Born in Laredo in 1947 and raised in Brownsville, Texas, Peña attended St. Joseph's Academy and received his law degree from the University of Texas in 1971. After law school, he moved to Denver, where he was first elected as state representative in 1978 and then as mayor in 1982—79,200 votes to 74,700. At this time, Mexicans made up only 18 percent of the city's population and 12 percent of its voters.

Peña was a young, upwardly mobile urban Latino who migrated to Denver from Texas and built a rapport with the young building developers, who supported economic development. No doubt Peña, a world apart from the Crusade for Justice Chicanos of the 1960s, was a welcome relief to the white establishment. Peña also enjoyed the support of unions and construction companies because he promoted the expansion of Denver's infrastructure, which to them meant contracts and jobs. Although Peña benefited from being Mexican American, attracting national press, locally he played down his ethnicity. Peña did not promote a Mexican agenda, stating, "I am not an Hispanic candidate. I just happen to be Hispanic." Still, Peña's success encouraged other Latinos nationwide. Peña went on to become secretary of transportation in the Clinton administration.[50]

The 1990s was a decade in which Mexican American and Latino candidates made significant electoral gains. The exuberance was expressed by Xavier Hermosillo, a Mexican American Republican from California who said, "We're taking it back, house by house, block by block. . . . We have a little saying here: 'If you're in California, speak Spanish.' . . . People ought to wake up and smell the refried beans: Not only are we the majority of the population, but we're not going anywhere."[51] Because of the growth in population of Mexican-origin people and the enlargement of the Central American population, there was a dramatic increase in the voting power of Latinos. And numbers count in politics. For instance, a presidential candidate needs 270 electoral votes to win an election. Eighty-three percent of Latinos were concentrated in eight states that alone accounted for 187 electoral votes: Arizona held 8 electoral votes; California, 54; Colorado, 8; Florida, 25; Illinois, 22; New Mexico, 5; New York, 33; and Texas, 32. Of these eight states, Latino population was the highest in three—California, Illinois, and Texas.

The growth in Latino population did not immediately translate into elected officials at the national level. There were no Latinos in the 100-member U.S. Senate in 1999, and only 18 Latinos of 435 voting members in the House of Representatives. Eleven of them were from Texas and California. African Americans, on the other hand, that was slightly larger in numbers had 39 seats. Nevertheless, Latino visibility was increasing. As already mentioned, in 1993, Transportation Secretary (later Energy Secretary) Federico Peña and Housing and Urban Development Secretary Henry Cisneros served on the Clinton cabinet. Clinton later appointed UN Ambassador Bill Richardson as Energy Secretary.[52]

The Glass Ceiling

Some scholars characterized Latinas as invisible in politics, which was often true—and often not—before the 1980s. For example, Olga Peña, wife of Bexar County Supervisor Albert Peña, Jr., in Texas, is generally credited with putting together her husband's political machine and getting him elected. By the 1980s large numbers of Mexican American women were attending universities or working outside the household. Their voices grew louder and more persistent in pursuing their interests. Chicanas were developing a profile quite distinct from that of their male counterparts: in Texas and California, for instance, Mexican American women were less likely than Mexican American men to identify with the Republican Party, a trend that was to continue through the end of the century. Studies in the 1990s showed that there was an 18-percentage-point gender gap in party identification among Latino voters: 69 percent of Latinas claimed Democratic Party affiliation compared with 51 percent of Latino men. In 1986, the number of Latino elected officials grew to 3,314, and the number of Latino women in office jumped to 592—a 20 percent increase in one year. Women accounted for 18 percent of all elected Latino officials.[53]

By 1980, 51 percent of Latinas were either unemployed or underemployed; Latinas earned 49¢ to every dollar made by white males, versus 58¢ for white women and 54¢ for black women. Half completed less than 8.8 years of education. Some 67 percent of households were headed by women with children under 18 and they lived below the poverty line. This statistical profile did not change much throughout the next two decades.

Just over 18 percent of Latinas, and 16 percent of Mexican-origin females, were professionals. More than 50 percent were white-collar workers. Between 1980 and 1990, the percentage of Latinas with BA degrees increased from 7.7 to 10. However, not all the statistics were rosy; only a fraction of 1 percent of all PhDs at the University of California were awarded to Latinas in the late 1970s, and universities nationwide awarded Latinas barely 0.4 percent of the doctorates. The achievements were small, but they represented an important avenue for the change of traditional female roles. The growth of this sector produced a market, and by the mid-1980s, even Chicana Republicans claimed space in the "Hispanic women's movement."[54]

Conscious of the disparities, Chicanas challenged inequalities. In 1982, Gloria Molina ran successfully against Richard Polanco in the Democratic primary race for the California Assembly. Chicano politicos tried to dissuade her from contesting, warning that a woman could not win in East Los Angeles, that she was not tough enough to negotiate with the heavyweights, and that she could not raise sufficient funds without their support. Molina was a field representative to Assemblyman Art Torres and had participated in the founding of the national *Comisión Femenil* (Feminist Commission).

The issue that catapulted Molina into local prominence was her opposition to building a prison in downtown Los Angeles. This issue pitted Molina against recently elected Assemblyman Richard Polanco, who had promised that he would vote against the prison but changed his vote. Molina's leadership in the struggle against the prison attracted a constituency of grass-roots activists. Among them were the Mothers of East Los Angeles, a lay Catholic group from Resurrection Parish headed by Father John Moretta, and St. Isabel Parish, whose women members were led by Juana Gutiérrez. During the summers of 1986 and 1987, these groups attracted 1,500–3,000 protesters at their weekly marches.[55]

The coalition fought Governor George Deukmejian for six years, enlisting the support of Archbishop Roger Mahoney for the "Stop the Prison in East Los Angeles" effort. The prison issue provided a springboard for Molina, who in the fall of 1986 announced her candidacy for the newly created First Council District. Molina registered a landslide victory in the contested race in February 1987. In February 1991, Molina was elected to the Los Angeles County Board of Supervisors. At 48, Molina represented 1.9 million people and became one of the five people overseeing a $13 billion budget. Molina developed her own network, surrounding herself with women such as Antonia Hernández, the chief council of MALDEF; Mónica Lozano, publisher of *La Opinión*, perhaps the largest Spanish-language newspaper in the country; and Vilma Martínez, a prominent attorney and former chief counsel of MALDEF.

Texas differed from California and other states. For example, as mentioned, the RUP had a much greater impact on Chicanos in Texas than in California, and Tejanas were more quickly integrated into mainstream politics. The 1970s saw the rise of grass-roots political activists such as San Antonian Rosie

Castro, who in 1971 was one of the first candidates for city council when she ran on a slate with Gloria Cabrerra and two Tejano males. Castro was very active in demanding equality and forging political space for Chicanas in the process. Another activist was María Antonietta Berriozábal, who successfully ran for the San Antonio City Council in 1981—supported by a network of grass-roots Chicanas. This victory led to the election of Yolanda Vera to the council in 1985. Berriozábal's procommunity stances put her at odds with the rest of the council, which tended to favor business interests. In 1991, Berriozábal ran for mayor and came close to becoming the first Chicana mayor of a major city.[56]

In San Antonio Chicanas enjoyed a measure of success in politics; but even there, the success was limited. Outside San Antonio, the problem of exclusion was even more marked. For example, in Texas the most powerful elected position within local government is the county judge. In 1998, Texas had 254 county judges, of whom 23 were white women and 7 were Chicano. Only one, Norma Villarreal of Zapata County, was a Tejana. An obvious impediment was that the election for county judge ran countywide, not only making the race expensive but also diluting the Mexican American voting numbers.

In 1986 in Crystal City, Texas, Severita Lara ran against an incumbent for county judge. On the first count, she won by one vote. On a recount, she lost by two votes. Although there was foul play, Lara did not have the funds to challenge the verdict of the electoral panel, which the incumbent heavily influenced. Lara ended up $7,000 in debt, an amount she had to pay from her pocket. Unlike Molina, she did not have access to funding from feminist groups. Lara was later elected to Crystal City Council and then served as mayor.[57]

Alicia Chacón from El Paso and Enriqueta Díaz from Eagle Pass won races for county judge in the early 1990s; however, both were defeated in reelection. One impediment was that they never became part of the old-boys' network and did not conduct politics in the usual way, which was to go down to the local bar for informal sessions. Chacón was later elected to the City Council.[58]

Norma Villarreal Ramírez made a successful bid for county judge of Zapata County in 1994. Armed with a $20,000 loan from her father, she challenged the county's count in an election, which she lost by 40 votes. The courts found fraud and ordered a recount, which Villarreal won by several hundred votes. However, once she took office, few people came forward to help Villarreal. "The collegial arrangements between male members from the same political affiliation and/or ethnic group do not extend to women either. The men simply do not want the women in charge."[59]

By the 1980s there was a critical mass of Chicanas in politics. Fewer belonged to the generation that was active in *La Raza Unida* or the 1960s and more to the generation that benefited from those earlier struggles. They cut their teeth in more traditional political routes working in campaigns of others before running themselves. Many, such as Elvira Reyna, learned their politics under the tutelage of white politicos. (Reyna later became a state representative.) What they shared with the previous generation was life experiences which in Texas were formed more by the Confederate culture of the state. The socialization of this generation was different: racism was different—you could choose where you would live and what you would join. Elvira was raised in Dallas, picked cotton, but became a Republican. She was married with two kids before she went to college. She began working part time for law-and-order State Representative Bill Blackwood and became a Republican. Elvira first ran for office in 1993. This experience was much different from that of a Rosie Castro or Severita Lara, who formed their worldviews through activism.[60]

Immigrant Women Workers

Due to a lack of education and the absence of skill development programs for immigrant women, the odds of their achieving success were low. Clearly, deindustrialization affected Latinas, as did their defined class roles. Female immigrants provided a large, motivated, inexpensive, and specialized workforce for service and manufacturing sectors, which supported the expanding export-oriented economy of places like Los Angeles, San Antonio, and Chicago. In 1980, only 8 percent of recently arrived European females worked in blue-collar occupations, compared with 62 percent of Mexican female immigrants. Seventy-five percent of the Mexican female immigrants worked in part-time occupations that paid extremely poor wages. They had little education and a limited ability to speak English, and their situation did not improve over time.[61]

Chicanas and Mexican immigrant women had different characteristics. For instance, in 1980 the mean years of schooling among Chicanas was 11.3, compared with 8.3 years among established immigrant women and 6.8 for recently arrived immigrants. Some 36.3 percent of Chicanas did not have a high school diploma, compared with 64.5 percent of established immigrants and 83.8 percent of recently arrived Mexican female immigrants. Of the Chicanas, 4.8 percent held college degrees, compared with 2 percent of the established immigrant women and 1.7 percent of the recently arrived. The only advantage of age was that the older female workers were more likely to organize. Younger workers were generally more passive and naïve, probably not yet realizing they would be subject to the glass ceiling.

Not all immigrant Latina workers were Mexican. In the 1980s, an estimated 500,000 men and women migrated from El Salvador alone. In 1985, 32.4 percent of the Salvadoran population in the United States was under 10 years of age and 57.3 percent was under the age of 20. More than 89 percent of Salvadoran refugees and 95 percent of the immigrants (those arriving before 1980) lived in family-based households. Labor force participation among Salvadoran males was 74 percent for refugees in 1988. For Salvadoran females, it was 66.7 percent, which was higher than the 52 percent for other Latinas. Salvadoran female refugees had the highest unemployment at 16.7 percent. Median age was 27.7 for females and 25.6 for males. In addition to economic deprivation, these refugees suffered from the experiences of civil war, oppression, and trauma.

Latinas of all nationalities engaged in self-help. Libertad Rivera, 28, from Tepic, Nayarit, in Mexico, worked for the Coalition for Humane Immigration Rights of Los Angeles (CHIRLA), educating and uniting domestic servants. Women also worked in AIDS programs. In the United States, 18 percent of all teenagers infected with HIV are Latinos. In Los Angeles, 38 percent of the babies and children infected with AIDS are Latino—more than double the Latino share of adult AIDS cases. At least 40 percent of Latinas with AIDS contracted it through their husbands or boyfriends. Fear of deportation kept many undocumented Latinas away from healthcare systems and other support services.[62]

¿Gobernar Es Poblar?

The 1990 Census showed that 25 percent of California's 29,760,021 inhabitants (an undercount) were Latinos, an increase from 4,544,331 (19.1 percent) in 1980 to 7,687,938 (25.8 percent) 10 years later. This population was heavily concentrated in 10 assembly districts, yet Latinos represented only four of the districts. (The California Assembly had 80 seats.) At stake in any redistricting were seats in both houses of the state legislature and in Congress. The basic problem was that Chicana/os and Latinos did not always vote, for various reasons: many were not citizens, a substantial number were under 18, and 18- to 35-year-olds, which made up a large proportion of the Latino population, overall had lower registration and turnout rates. In 1990, only 844,000 Latinos voted out of a population of 4,739,000 Latinos who were 18 or older. Some 2,301,000 adults were citizens, 1,218,000 of whom were registered to vote. Another problem was incumbency: white politicos stayed in office for years, and it took substantial efforts to win their seats. As always, Democrats in the California legislature protected their own. Meanwhile, Governor Pete Wilson vetoed three proposed redistricting bills, giving the excuse that the Democratic majority was seeking an "unfair partisan advantage."

Because the legislature and the governor could not agree on a plan, the chief justice of the California Supreme Court appointed a panel of three jurists. They remapped districts for the state legislature and Congress. The maps devised by the court made it possible for Latinos to increase their representation by 40 percent in the state legislature. The 1992 elections made room for gains in the Assembly, where seven Latinos won election. Latinos did not do as well in Congress and gained only one additional seat. The Chicano community believed that with proper redistricting it could have gained another congressional seat. Even so, the first Chicana elected to Congress was Lucille Roybal-Allard, the daughter of retiring Congressman Edward R. Roybal. Nationwide, the 1992 election marked the entry of 17 Latinos to Congress. An estimated 1 million Latinos voted in California alone. And, in the spring of 1993, Latinos won some 60 city council elections in Los Angeles County alone.[63]

Up to this point, population growth and the Voting Rights Act of 1965 and its amendments drove Chicano political victories. In Texas, population clusters made it almost impossible to prevent Mexican

Americans getting elected. However, California in 1990 was a closed shop with incumbents monopolizing the election process. In 1990, by a margin of 52 percent to 48 percent, California voters passed Proposition 140, which put term limits on most state offices. Pushed by Republicans in the days when the Democrats held sway over the California legislature, the proposition reflected the mood of Californians, who trusted neither themselves nor politicos to govern. In their usual self-righteous way, California voters thought that by passing an initiative they would empower themselves merely by forcing incumbents out of office.

Term limits opened the door for more Latinos to become involved in politics. The proposition resulted in the election of Cruz Bustamante as the first Chicano speaker of the California Assembly, and term limits forced him to seek higher office. He was elected California Lieutenant Governor in 1998—a first in the twentieth century. His successor as speaker was Antonio Villaraigosa, and the so-called Latino Caucus, for the first time in history, was a "power broker" in the true sense of the word.[64]

During the 1990s, the population of Texas grew by 23 percent, while that of the nation grew by 13 percent. The number of Latinos increased from 4.3 million in 1990 to almost 6.7 million in 2000, a 53 percent rise—one of every three Texans identified as a Latino/a. The white population grew by only 6 percent. Latinos became the largest ethnic group in Houston, Dallas, San Antonio, and El Paso. Seven Tejanos sat in the state legislature in 1960, 6 in 1965, 15 in 1974, 19 in 1983, and 25 in 1992. Elected women officials among Mexican Americans ran ahead of women officials from other groups. The first Chicana elected to the Texas state legislature was Irma Rangel from Kingsville in 1976, and the first elected to the state senate was Judith Zaffirini from Laredo in 1984. Other changes took place, such as most *La Raza Unida* activists joining Mexican American Democrats (MAD). "[By] 1990 more than 1,000 Mexican Americans (not all MAD members) attended the state convention."[65]

The number of Tejano elected officials increased to 2,030 in 1993, more than in any other state. It is estimated that Texas had 40 percent of all Latino elected officials in the country. Latinos, mostly Mexican Americans, made up a quarter of the state's 17 million residents. Some 2,684,000 Latinos were eligible to vote in Texas; 40 percent (1,073,600) were registered. In 1994 the Texas congressional delegation included five Mexican Americans, all members of the House. However, the question remained: Did numbers automatically translate into political power?

Most pundits assume that Mexican American support for the Democratic Party was a matter of fact. However, as José Angel Gutiérrez pointed out during the 1994 national congressional elections, Latino support for the Democratic Party dropped from 72 percent in 1992 to 61 percent in 1994. There was a spillover to state legislative races; of 140 Latino incumbents in nine states, four lost their seats. Nevertheless, as a group, they were effective and brought about reforms. For example, during George W. Bush's terms as governor, the legislative Latino caucus successfully lobbied him for increased funding for education and bilingual programs.[66]

Outside California and Texas, it was more difficult to get Latinos elected to office. For instance, in Iowa the population of Latinos grew 153 percent during the 1990s. They aspired to be represented in the famed Iowa Caucus, since that would have been an indicator of the power of the Latino vote. The numbers were not large enough, however, for representation. Latinos—especially Mexican Americans—were young, with almost 40 percent of the nation's Latinos not yet voting age. Another factor was that many Latinos were not yet citizens.

How important are numbers then? University of Maryland political science professor James G. Gimpel has shown that as of 2004, 70.2 percent of U.S. House campaign contributions came from outside the candidates' districts. So it is no wonder that as much as 90 percent of campaign contributions in Los Angeles City Council is estimated to come from outside the councilmatic districts.[67]

The North American Free Trade Agreement

The North American Free Trade Agreement (NAFTA) was proposed formally in 1991. The Bush administration pressured Congress to put the negotiations for free trade with Mexico on the "fast track"—implying that congressional debate and criticism of the treaty would be minimal. Mexican President Carlos Salinas de Gortari hailed the treaty as the key to Mexico's future. Advocates for NAFTA dismissed questions about its effects on the environment, human rights, political reform,

Mexican workers, and the indigenous populations. The most controversial provision was a change in Article 27 of the Mexican Constitution, the basis for the nation's *ejidos* (communal lands): NAFTA made it possible for *ejido* members to sell or mortgage their land—thus burying the outcome of the Mexican Revolution. As one Mexican scholar put it, "the death of the Mexican Revolution at least deserved a formal farewell."

The debate over NAFTA split the Latino community into ideological camps. Union activists, environmentalists, and human rights groups campaigned against NAFTA. They argued that NAFTA would take U.S. jobs away, threaten environmental laws, and hurt Mexican farmers and workers by privatizing the Mexican economy. Their campaigns, for the most part, were ineffective and often bordered on racism. U.S. labor in general was mainly concerned about job loss and depressed wages. Meanwhile, Bill Clinton became president and brought the hedging Latino organizations into line through aggressive use of patronage. On November 18, 1993, the U.S. House passed NAFTA by 234–200 votes, 16 more than the needed 218; 102 Democrats voted for and 156 voted against it.[68] As expected, the Senate voted for the accord. The Latino vote in the House of Representatives (which was essentially Chicano) included two Chicanos against it— Henry B. González and Marty Martínez.

On January 1, 1994, the day the NAFTA went into effect, the *Ejercito Zapatista de Liberación Nacional* (EZLN; Zapatista National Liberation Army) rebelled in the southern Mexican state of Chiapas, citing the passage of NAFTA and the changes in Article 27 of the Constitution. Their rebellion was logical since NAFTA would encourage the influx of cheap corn into Mexico, underselling the small farmer. The indigenous peoples argued that the privatization of land would lead to the death of their culture.[69]

The Zapatistas raised the "Land and Liberty" banner of Emiliano Zapata. The impact of liberation theology is suggested by the support of Monsignor Samuel Ruiz García.[70] In 1974, Ruiz convened an Indigenous Congress in an attempt to improve conditions for Mexico's indigenous population. The catechisms raised the consciousness of the indigenous communities and encouraged them to organize and to fight for their rights. In 1989, Ruiz García founded the Fray Bartolomé Human Rights Center, which investigates human rights cases and conflicts over land and religion. He saw the NAFTA agreement as the final straw in the systematic destruction of indigenous communities. For his work, Ruiz was labeled a subversive. He became the target of assassination attempts, and his sister also was attacked and wounded.

December 22, 1997, witnessed an event that horrified the world—the Acteal massacre—enacted with the concurrence of government officials. Masked gunmen from a paramilitary group murdered 45 unarmed Tzotzil Indians seeking refuge in a camp on the road to the village of Acteal, some 20 miles north of San Cristobal. Children, women, and old people were massacred while praying and fasting for peace in the chapel of Acteal. The Mexican government charged that the murdered villagers belonged to the Abejas, many of whom were sympathetic to the Zapatistas.

The Zapatista identity was based on the preservation of their communal culture. Being an agrarian, grass-roots peasant movement, they believed that the neo-liberal policies of the Mexican government would destroy their way of life. Hence, they engaged in "low-intensity warfare" to preserve it. They pursued, as much as possible, a nonviolent struggle. They took inspiration as well as their name from Emiliano Zapata, who said, "It is better to die on your feet than to live on your knees!" The Mexican government was duplicitous in its negotiations with the Zapatistas. A stalemate resulted, which still continues, but the Mexican government so far has not mobilized the army to totally crush the movement for fear of worldwide rebuke.

Meanwhile, a demoralization and skepticism spread among Mexicans. They realized that contemporary Mexico was in the hands of extremely wealthy narco-traffickers, or drug lords. Social scientist James Cockcroft likened "the 'narcotics rush' of the late twentieth century . . . [to the] gold rush of the sixteenth century in Mexico." Shortly before President Carlos Salinas de Gortari left office, drug scandals broke out involving his family and his brother Raul was implicated. It was uncovered that Raul Salinas had placed more than $120 million in foreign banks.[71] However, just as NAFTA is in the hands of Euro-American capitalists, which most people in Mexico are aware of, so is control of the drug trade, which depends on a U.S. market and U.S. bankers to launder the money.

"Don't Mourn, Organize!"

In 1993, César Chávez died in his sleep while on union business in Arizona. More than 40,000 mourners attended Chávez's funeral in Delano, California. Chávez followed a Franciscan regimen: he exercised regularly; he ate healthy, vegetarian, pesticide-free food; and he often fasted. However, he died of exhaustion, having pushed his body to its limits. César told his son-in-law the night before his death, "I'm tired . . . I'm really very tired."[72] Chávez's son-in-law, Arturo Rodríguez, assumed the UFW presidency. The union immediately stepped up activity in the fields, launching a major campaign to organize farmworkers in California; the struggle was often bitter. The UFW still relied heavily on its vast network of boycott volunteers. The workers, most of them poor Latinos, earned an average of only $8,500 a season for up to 12-hour days with no overtime or benefits. Growers continually sprayed fields with a cancer-causing pesticide. The first target was California's strawberry industry, producing 80 percent of all berries eaten in the United States and grossing more than $550 million. More than 10,000 workers were concentrated in the Watsonville–Salinas area alone.[73]

The Political Refugees from Central America

The Salvadoran and Guatemalan communities in the United States formed political refugee organizations and integrated themselves into the Protestant and Catholic refugee relief network. North American groups such as the Committee in Solidarity with the People of El Salvador (CISPES) worked full time to counter Reagan's propaganda. Angela Sanbrano, a Chicano originally from the El Paso area, worked as the national director of CISPES. Another Chicano who worked with refugees was Father Luis Olivares, originally from San Antonio, Texas. An adamant critic of U.S. involvement in El Salvador, in 1985 Olivares declared his Placita church in Los Angeles (Our Lady Queen of the Angels) a sanctuary to Central American refugees. Father Olivares died in March 1994 of AIDS. He contracted the disease when he was injected with an unsterilized needle on a visit to Central American refugee camps.[74]

Meanwhile, successive presidential administrations and Congress gave ultraright refugees preferential treatment in immigrating to the United States. Congress passed the 1997 Nicaraguan Adjustment and Central American Relief Act (NACARA) to protect Nicaraguans and Cubans from deportation if they could prove they had fled communism. By contrast, U.S. government policy excluded thousands of Salvadorans and Guatemalans entering the United States without documents. These refugees routinely applied for political asylum and were just as routinely denied. Eventually, Salvadorans and Guatemalans, through Temporary Protected Status (TPS), won the right to go before an immigration judge to prove, on a case-by-case basis, that returning to their countries would cause them to suffer "extreme hardship." Under new rules, the U.S. government presumed that returning refugees to their countries of origin would in itself pose an extreme hardship for them. An Immigration and Naturalization Service (INS) official would hear the cases rather than a judge.

Forging Communities

Central Americans founded organizations such as the Central American Resource Center (CARECEN), *El Rescate* (the Rescue), the Oscar Romero Health Clinic, and the Coalition for Humane Immigrant Rights of Los Angeles (CHIRLA), among others. Many Central Americans were involved in street vending, day labor, and domestic work, and were prime candidates for exploitation by some employers. CHIRLA instructed the workers about the laws that govern all employers, including individual homeowners who routinely hired them for odd jobs.

Apart from a cluster in Los Angeles, Central Americans were spread out in the United States. The Salvadorans were among the most organized groups, and in the early 1980s the FMLN sent organizers without documents to Washington, D.C., to lobby Congress and organize information centers. After the end of hostilities in 1991, most of them stayed and lobbied for domestic programs. In that year, riots broke out in the Mt. Pleasant neighborhood of Washington, D.C., a *barrio* made up mostly of Salvadorans and

Dominicans. A confrontation between residents and the police ensued when police shot a migrant in a *barrio* street. Several days of rebellion followed, which led to confrontations between Latinos and African Americans. (This happened a year before the South Central Los Angeles Uprisings.) Meanwhile, Central American women played a key role. In the Langley Park area of Washington, D.C., Salvadoran women pushed grocery carts loaded with home cooking, selling to immigrant laborers who live in the area. Langley Park's "pupusa ladies" fed their tired, hungry neighbors for a dollar a dish. Most of the women were unwilling to put a sign on their chest begging for work. Many of them came to the United States during and after the war, leaving children behind with grandparents and other relatives, and were sending money back to give them a better life. Guilt about being separated from their children and fear that they might never see them again consumed many mothers.[75]

Believers: Chicana/o Studies

By 1990, the Mexican American student population on university and college campuses had grown dramatically. This was a new generation that did not come of age in the 1960s and did not necessarily call themselves Chicanas/os. They were children of immigrants entering the country during and after the 1960s, who did not know about the sacrifices it took to get them on campus. Others did, but escalating costs of education forced them to drop out of political activities. Along with the Mexican-origin core, there were growing numbers of Central Americans who might call themselves Hispanic in public but sought their own national identification. The generational change and the other factors mentioned above brought about a reduction in the number of activists on campus, and MEChA as an organization shrank as more Latinos joined sororities and fraternities—some in established organizations and others in Latina/o-specific Greek organizations.

Those calling themselves Chicanas or Chicanos were passionate about seeking an identity and getting more Latina/o faculty hired. On many campuses student groups such as CAUSA (Central American United Student Association) were formed, and a few campuses such as California State University Northridge began to call for a Central American Studies Department.[76] Among Mexican American students, a core sought to expand their programs and recapture the mission of Chicana/o Studies, which was to serve the community.[77]

Within this activity a perfect storm was occurring that would affect the history of Latinas/os. The number of students brought here by their undocumented parents had grown dramatically since 1970. Until the 1990s, California colleges and universities allowed undocumented immigrant students to attend as if they were citizens if they could show residence for a year and a day when they applied and declare that they intended to make California their residence. This resulted from a successful 1985 lawsuit known as *Leticia A. v. Board of Regents* brought against the University of California and the California State University Systems for the right of undocumented students to attend as residents.

The backlash began almost immediately; a UCLA employee named David Paul Bradford sued the University of California, alleging that he was coerced to quit because he would not implement the *Leticia A.* ruling. By 1991 the courts found in favor of Bradford; many *Leticia A.* supporters justifiably claimed that the UC system folded under this intense right-wing pressure. The University of California said that after June of 1991 it would classify undocumented students as nonresidents. In 1992, the California Student Aid Commission followed Bradford and stopped awarding Cal Grants to undocumented students. Then the California Community Colleges (CCCs) adopted the UC policy although they were not mentioned in the Bradford ruling. The CSU appealed the decision but lost and in 1995 began implementing it. Many *Leticia A.* supporters believed that all was lost with the passage of California Proposition 187 in 1994. However, a nucleus was growing daily that did not give up hope or abandon their dreams.[78]

Meanwhile, one of the most dramatic events in Chicana/o Studies history was the UCLA Hunger Strike of 1993, which led to the foundation of the Chicana/o Studies Department (the César Chávez Center) at the University of California Los Angeles (UCLA). The hunger strike in May 1993 was led by Marcos Aguilar and Minnie Fergusson who worked about four years to get a Chicano Studies Department. It was an impossible journey in which they braved opposition to the department by Chancellor Charles Young, associate vice-chancellor Raymundo Paredes, and the institution itself. With the exception of Juan

Gómez-Quiñonez and later Leo Estrada, most of the Chicano faculty was divided and did not support the push for a department. In the years preceding the hunger strike, Minnie and Marcos gathered community support, studied curriculum, and held conferences on campus—helping to organize the United Community and Labor Alliance, which was also involved in the campaign to preserve Olvera Street as Mexican cultural space.[79] Marcos was so adamant about a department that after four years he was expelled from MEChA; its members were increasingly concerned that the issue was polarizing faculty members and students, and consequently reducing its membership and influence.

After three years of controversy, Chancellor Young announced on April 28, 1993, that *Chicano* studies "will not be elevated to an independent department at the Westwood campus."[80] For Marcos and Minnie it became a now-or-never moment. Young announced his decision on the eve of the funeral of César Chávez—a slap in the face of the Chicano community.

Without internal support, Marcos and Minnie went on the offensive and formed Conscious Students of Color, a multiracial group of students, most of whom had never been active in campus politics. A rally began at noon on May 11, which attracted about 200 participants. According to the *Los Angeles Times*, "When they were denied entrance to the faculty center, some of the demonstrators broke windows with hammers, chairs and backpacks and about 80 began a sit-in inside." UC campus police, assisted by 200 LAPD officers, arrested 89 students on felony charges. On the second day a rally drew a crowd of 1,000 people to the front of Royce Hall, and, seeing their friends arrested, some Mechistas returned to the fold. Because the quarter end was fast approaching, most observers speculated that the drive to get a department was kaput and that Marcos and Minnie would be scapegoated.[81]

Pushed to the edge by an intransigent administration, on May 25, Marcos, Minnie, sisters Cindy and Norma Montañez, Balvina Collazo, and María Lara—along with Jorge Mancillas, an assistant professor of medical biology, and two other students—started a hunger strike that lasted 14 days.[82] The strike attracted the citywide support of hundreds of thousands of Chicano and Latino students in surrounding high schools and universities, who sporadically walked out of school. Tensions mounted as a 20-mile march from Olvera Street to UCLA in support of the hunger strikers began on the 12th day to pressure UCLA administration to meet with the hunger strikers. The march stimulated community support, and a thousand supporters marched into UCLA. The strike was settled two days later, and UCLA got the César Chávez Center for Interdisciplinary Instruction in Chicano/Chicana Studies. It functioned as a department but was not given full departmental status—Chancellor Young and Paredes were vengeful to the last. When their journey toward a Chicano Studies Department began four years earlier, someone told Marcos and Minnie that it was doable, but that it would take at least five years. They did it before that deadline.[83]

The success of the UCLA strike motivated student hunger strikes at the University of California at Santa Barbara, Columbia, and Princeton, the Claremont Colleges, the University of Texas at Austin, the University of California at Berkeley, and other schools. However, much of the momentum generated by the UCLA Hunger Strike was diverted by the crises in the Chicano community as community activists, labor leaders, politicos, and students turned their attention to combating the siege on the foreign born. The question of immigration eclipsed all other issues.[84] There was the emergence of racists such as California Governor Pete Wilson and media features such as Glenn Spencer's *American Patrol* website, CNN's *Lou Dobbs*, and Fox's *O'Reilly Factor*, which took every opportunity to label MEChA a terrorist organization. By the turn of the century, this rabid right-wing reaction rivaled the McCarthy witch hunts of the 1950s. These hate groups' anti-immigrant, anti–affirmative action, and pro-racist policies took their toll on Chicano student activists, and their numbers temporarily receded.

The Renaissance in Chicana/Chicano Thought and Arts

The impact of Chicana/o Studies goes beyond the formation or lack of formation of Chicana/o Studies programs or even their influence on the campuses. A large number of the murals, paintings, literature, and music in the communities owe their geneses to Chicana/o Studies. For example, El Centro De La Raza in Seattle, the murals on the walls of Chicano park in San Diego, the National Mexican Art Museum in Chicago's Pilsen District, mariachi and Mexican Folk dance groups throughout the country, and many theatre groups have been nourished by Chicana/o Studies. It is the largest market for Chicana/o literature of all forms. Indeed, the main mission of the disparate study programs has been to organize and produce a Mexican American corpus of knowledge. Moreover, these programs have been a source of support for progressive causes such as the Zapatistas. Chicana/o Studies went beyond the walls of academe.[85]

The content of Chicana/o Studies has changed over the years. In the late 1960s and 1970s, the symbol of the farmworker's eagle and the face of César were ubiquitous. Although initially it was an almost all-male club, since the 1990s the main scholarly current has been that of Chicanas. In 1991, a cursory survey of Proquest's 72 dissertations and a smattering of theses in Chicana/o Studies shows that 49 were written by women. In 2008, out of 94 dissertations/MA theses, 70 were written by women; they are also an indicator as to who will be teaching in those programs. Dissertations are important in synthesizing the existing fund of knowledge. Besides the implications of the hegemony of Chicanas in the area of Chicana/o Studies, much of the ideological energy came from Chicanas who raised questions and pushed the parameters.

Historian Emma Pérez, who authored *The Decolonial Imaginary: Writing Chicanas into History*, intertwines modernist and postmodernist theory. Perez analyzes the self-colonization and institutionalization which Chicanas internalize (something that also applies to males). A Chicana lesbian, Pérez writes in a restless style that is reminiscent of African American writers such as Langston Hughes.[86] Noteworthy are the essays, poetry, and playwriting of Cherríe Moraga. She teaches Creative Writing, Chicano/Latino literature, Xicana-Indigenous Performance, Indigenous Identity in Diaspora in the Arts, and Playwriting at Stanford and other universities. She was a founding member of La Red Xicana Indígena, "a network of Xicanas organizing in the area of social change through international exchange, indigenous political education, spiritual practice, and grass roots organizing." Moraga's use of symbols enriches her writing with brilliant colors not frequently found in Euro-American society.[87] It would be easy to draw a shopping list of cutting-edge Chicana scholars, among them Yolanda Broyles-González of the University of Arizona and historian Antonia Castañeda. But this would only take time away from the Great Gloria Anzaldúa.[88]

Gloria Anzaldúa (1942–2004) was a product of the border; she blended this reality with history. A postmodernist, a feminist, and a lesbian, she enjoyed more influence on these fields than any other Chicana/o writer of her time. She was a major force in Chicana cultural theory and queer theory. Anzaldúa was part of those communities, collaborating with writers such as Moraga. Her *New Mestiza* calls for an awareness of conflicting and meshing identities; her point of conflict is the border. Many feminists have interpreted her "new mestiza" as a way of understanding postcolonial feminism. Anzaldúa talked about consciousness and boldly trespasses into space thought to be reserved for indigenists. Anzaldúa was spiritual in a field that was once dominated by materialists, thus resolving the past with the present. She is one of the few Chicana/o scholars to have universal appeal. In a sense she is one of the few Chicanas/os with appeal outside the Latino sphere. Chicano artist Harry Gamboa has said that some artists are weak painters with great messages, and some are great painters with weak messages; Anzaldúa practiced great artistry that expressed great messages.[89]

Hate Is Tax Deductible

Racist nativist anti-immigration groups have spent millions of dollars in framing the immigrant debate—talking incessantly and irresponsibly about the "illegal alien" threat. These organizations received unlimited funds through conservative think tanks that in turn were financed by reactionaries such as Richard Mellon Scaife, Cordelia Scaife May, Charles and David Koch, and Joseph Coors among other billionaires.[90] In a manner, taxpayers pay for the hate campaigns, since the donations to the think tanks are tax deductible. They financed the English Only political campaigns; Scaife May donated $650,000 to U.S. English. She used the severe recession of the early 1990s to fan an anti-immigrant hysteria—encouraging opportunistic politicos and racist nativists to play on the fears of "Americans." As mentioned, supporters contributed hundreds of millions of dollars to these hate groups, which subsidized the research of right-wing scholars. For example, the Heritage Foundation helped fund *The Bell Curve: Intelligence and Class Structure in American Life* (1994) by Richard Hernstein and Charles Murray, a book that argues that inherited intelligence is a prime determinant of success or failure in society. The authors tied the question of intelligence to race and concluded that African Americans were unsuccessful not because society did not invest in them, but because they lacked intelligence.[91]

These and other foundations actively poisoned public opinion toward affirmative action, immigration, and bilingual education by funding vicious campaigns. The Hoover Institution at Stanford sponsored the work of John Bunzell, one of the intellectual godfathers of the anti-affirmative action movement. The Hoover Institution held ties with the National Association of Scholars (NAS), a right-wing professional organization founded with a gift of $100,000 from the Smith Richardson Foundation. The Center for Individual Rights, founded in 1989, also held close ties with the NAS; it led the fight in *Hopwood v. Texas* (1996), a case filed against the University of Texas Law School in 1992, which resulted in a decision that severely limited affirmative action programs nationally. The U.S. Court of Appeals for the Fifth Circuit found that the University of Texas School of Law violated the equal protection clause of the Fourteenth Amendment by denying admission to Cheryl Hopwood, a white woman, and three white men while admitting African American and Mexican American students with lower grade-point averages and test scores. The court held that race could not be used as a "factor in deciding which applicants to admit."[92]

In police code the number 187 means "Murder," referring to the California Penal Code section for *Murder* or *Homicide*. It became an insider joke among the supporters of Proposition 187. The Proposition 63 campaign laid the groundwork for Proposition 187; more than $1 million was spent on the 63 campaign—$500,000 of it from U.S. English, the largest English-first organization in the country. From this point on, the anti-immigrant movement started to pick up speed with angst dollars pouring in from small contributors. The FAIR and extremist groups such as Voices of Citizens Together (VCT) spun statistics manufactured by the INS and the think tanks. Internet fund-raising was also a bonanza for many immigrant hate groups that collected tax-deductible donations.

The draconian SOS (Save Our State) Initiative, Proposition 187, appeared on the November 1994 California ballot. It proposed denying health and educational services to undocumented immigrants. Governor Pete Wilson immediately supported the proposition. Supporters of the breakup of the Los Angeles Unified School District, the voucher campaign, and the "3 strikes and you're out" proposition joined him. Even Democratic candidates opposed to 187 took potshots: in July, U.S. Senate candidate Diane Feinstein ran an ad claiming that 3,000 "illegals" crossed the border each night. "I'm Diane Feinstein and I've just begun to fight for California."

Chicano organizations and individuals in Los Angeles, led by activists from the 1960s, responded to the anti-immigrant hate crimes by going to the streets. In February 1994, a pro-immigrant march in Los Angeles drew 6,000. On May 28, another march attracted about 18,000 people who trekked up Broadway to City Hall. On October 16, more than 150,000 protesters marched down Avenida César Chávez to City Hall. Some Latino leaders feared that the large number of Mexican flags seen on the march would turn off white voters.

On the eve of the election, spontaneous massive walkouts of high school students who opposed 187 caught most people by surprise. Some Latino politicos, worried that the walkouts would turn off white voters, opposed the demonstrations. Walkouts took place at Huntington Park, Bell, South Gate, Los Angeles, Marshall, and Fremont High Schools, and throughout the San Fernando Valley. Police were called out in Van Nuys as students took to the main street; 200 officers were on tactical alert. News sources estimated that 10,000 (on the low side) students walked out of 39 schools.

A September 1994 *Los Angeles Times* poll showed that 52 percent of Latinos supported Proposition 187. However, Latinos were increasingly alarmed by the racist tone of the anti-immigrant rhetoric, and a field poll about a month before the election showed Latinos in California sharply divided over Proposition 187: Latinos opposed the measure by a slight margin of 48 to 44 percent, and white voters favored it by 60 to 17 percent. White support for 187 remained constant, and another *Los Angeles Times* poll showed that Californian whites favored 187 by 65 to 35 percent, and Latinos by 52 to 48 percent. As expected, on November 8 California overwhelmingly passed 187. Only the San Francisco Bay Area voted against—by 70 percent. Los Angeles voted for 187 by a 12-point margin. Exit polls showed Latinos opposing the proposition 77 percent to 23 percent statewide.

Before the election, Cardinal Mahoney said that the measure would undermine "clear moral principles"—stopping just shy of calling it a mortal sin. The victory of 187 was a blow to the moral authority of the Catholic Church. White Catholics voted 58 to 42 percent for 187. To those supporting racism, Catholic bishops did not deny the sacraments, as they did in the case of the abortion issue. Most Protestant churches remained silent on the issue.[93]

On November 5, 1996, California voters passed Proposition 209. The California Association of Scholars, funded by ultraconservative foundations, placed Proposition 209 on the ballot. It said that "preferential treatment" because of race, sex, ethnicity, or national origin was forbidden. In effect, Proposition 209 made anti-discrimination laws moot. Institutions were not required to recruit or enroll minorities; consequently, there were no damages if they discriminated. Proponents of 209 argued that affirmative action went too far and now was resulting in discrimination against whites who were better qualified. The United States was supposedly a color-blind society.

African Americans voted against Proposition 209 by 73 percent and Latinos by 70 percent. Asian Americans also voted against it, although only by 56 percent. Whites made up three-fourths of the voters; white males voted for 209 by a 66 percent margin and white females by 58 percent. The death of an idea such as social justice does not happen by accident. Indeed, it is very difficult to reverse public policy and change basic commitments to ideals such as civil rights.

Proposition 209 was driven by mean-spirited and extremist organizations and people. They ranged from opportunists such as the VCT, led by Glenn Spencer, who ranted and raved about the Mexican invasion of the United States, and the California Association of Scholars, an affiliate of the NAS, which led a well-funded, well-thought-out campaign designed to change the definition of fairness. The message was, "We live in a classless society; there is equal opportunity for all; work hard enough and you'll make it to the middle-class heaven."

Unfortunately, the Latino community did not organize marches of any size against Proposition 209 in California. Latinos, however, held a march in Washington, D.C., in October 1996. More than 50,000 people marched through the capital in support of Latino and immigrant rights. Although it was successful, the march in Washington was criticized. Many activists felt that a march in Los Angeles to protest Proposition 209 would embarrass President Clinton. It was not until the end of the presidential campaign in California, when Clinton was certain to win by a landslide, that the Democratic Party took a more visible stance.[94]

In June 1998, Californians overwhelmingly approved Proposition 227, insidiously called the "English for the Children" initiative. Californians based their vote not so much on the merits of bilingual education, but on numerous untested assumptions that bilingual education was a failure.

Ron Unz, the man behind Proposition 227 and a Silicon Valley millionaire with dreams of running for governor, had opposed 187. He knew that the core constituency of anti-immigrant, anti-minority voters in California was still very much alive, and he did nothing to mute it. Unz was also a contributor to the Heritage Foundation Policy Review. (Ironically, the Heritage Foundation, while against most progressive agendas, favored the family reunification immigration policy.)

Proposition 227 did not enjoy the near-unanimous Republican support that existed for 187 and 209. First, nativism subsided because of the improving economy and the defections among Republicans running for statewide offices or districts with a sizable Latino constituency. Republican candidates were becoming aware of the backlash in the Chicano/Latino community in the aftermath of Propositions 187 and 209. Their nativism was tempered by the realization that they were losing Latino voters, who once marginally supported them.

Exit polls of Proposition 227 showed that the Latinos opposed 227—in fact, some 63 percent of the Latino electorate voted against Proposition 227. Because of the perception that the proposition was racist, some Republican candidates began to distance themselves from the anti-immigrant, anti-affirmative action, and anti–bilingual education sentiments of their party. Attorney General Dan Lungren, aware of the growing antipathy of Chicanos and Latinos toward Republicans, came out against Proposition 227 to try to stem the loss of their support.

Spanish-language media were crucial in informing the public about 187 and 227. Spanish-language reporters identified with the issue. In the Greater Los Angeles area, 9.74 million radio listeners divided their attention among 81 stations, 12 of which broadcast in Spanish. Two of the 10 TV broadcast channels were Spanish in a "designated market area" that encompassed Los Angeles County; all of Orange, San Bernardino, and Ventura Counties; and parts of Kern, Riverside, and San Diego Counties. Los Angeles–based Univision KMEX Channel boasted higher ratings for its 6 p.m. and 11 p.m. newscasts than those for its English-language competitors.[95]

The National Scene: Census 2000

The 2000 U.S. Census counted 35,305,818 U.S. Latinos; Mexicans comprised 20,640,711 or 58.5 percent; the next largest group was "All other Hispanic or Latino," 6,211,800 or 17.6 percent—meaning that the Mexican-origin population was probably larger. While the Puerto Ricans continued to have a presence, for large numbers of peoples other than Mexican and Puerto Rican, the question of identity was much more complex. Taken as a whole, the U.S. Latino population in 2000 was approaching that of Spain, 39.9 million, and would surpass it by 2008. The Mexican American population alone qualified as one of the largest in the United States. This was a far cry from 1970 Census.[96]

According to the 2000 Census, about three out of four U.S. Latinos lived in California, Texas, New York, Florida, Illinois, Arizona, or New Jersey. Half of the nation's Latinos lived in California or Texas, whose populations were heavily Mexican in origin. Although the largest Mexican populations lived in Los Angeles, Chicago, Houston, San Antonio, and Phoenix, countless Mexicans and Latinos were living in small hamlets throughout the Southwest, Midwest, and Northwest. Latinos' voting strength was growing, although at a snail's pace compared to their dramatic jump in numbers. Youth and citizenship remained obstacles, though the Latino population grew everywhere from Oregon to the rural South, which by 2000 was 12 percent Mexican. Nationally, the U.S. Mexican population grew by 53 percent, with registered Latino voters increasing from 5.5 million in 1994 to 8 million in 2000. Hence, the potential for an increased influence of Latino voters became stronger, since the three largest Latino-population states—California, Texas, and Illinois—have nearly half (108) of the 270 electoral votes needed to elect the president.[97]

Latinos cast 1.61 million votes in the 2000 election, representing 15.2 percent of the total votes cast in California and turning out at a rate of 70.4 percent—far higher than the national average of 51 percent. According to the Willie C. Velásquez Institute, "We estimate California Latino registration at 2.3 million as of October 10, 2000. We estimate that U.S. Latino registration is between 7.2 million and 7.7 million." In 2000, the city of Los Angeles was 46 percent Latino, 30 percent Anglo, 11 percent African American, and 10 percent Asian. California had a total population of 33,871,648 residents, of which 10,966,556 were Latino, including 8,455,926 of Mexican origin. There were a significant number of Central Americans: 576,330. Statewide, white non-Latinos comprised only 47 percent of the population; however, they made up 71 percent of the people who voted in the 2000 presidential election. And, with 54 electoral votes, California wields enormous power.

California, Texas, and New York were considered "out of play" in the race of the presidential election of 2000. Al Gore did little campaigning in California, where support for the Democratic Party was thought to be a given, and Texas, where the opposite was true, and committed few resources to the Latino voter, who was largely ignored. Democrats conceded Texas to George W. Bush. This neglect resulted in the building of some support for Bush among all voters. It demonstrates the opportunistic side of politics and a tendency in the Democratic Party since the time of Franklin D. Roosevelt to ignore or take for granted the Mexican American/Latino vote. It takes money and time to maintain an ethnic voting bloc, something that the machine politicians of old understood. The trend has been for Latinos to vote for Spanish surnames, with a lessening of party loyalty. Incredibly, in places like California, Latino politicos who back white candidates over Latino candidates—for personal reasons or because they want support from the white politico—are diluting this unity. A lot more water or "grease" (in dollars) has to be put on the beans before Latinos can fry them.[98]

Latino voting increased nearly 40 percent from 1990 to 1996. New citizens became a factor as more than 250,000 Latinos became citizens in 1996. That year saw four new Latinos elected to the legislature, including the first Latino Republican. There were now 13 Latinos in the California Assembly. The elections elevated Chicanos to significant leadership positions, such as committee chairs. That same year, a Chicano became Speaker of the Assembly, and another, Senate majority floor leader. State Senator Richard Polanco played a key role in molding the Latino Caucus into an influential power bloc.

In Orange County, Loretta Sánchez (D–Garden Grove) defeated right-wing Republican icon Representative Bob Dornan by 984 votes. Sánchez won reelection handily two years later. In 1999 there were 20 Democrats in the two houses, nine of them Latinas. Two years later, there were 15 Latinos in the

Assembly—four of them were women and four others were Republicans. In the State Senate, there were five Latinos, three of whom were women. GOP strategist Tony Quinn acknowledged, "Republicans simply cannot win in California without one-third of the Latino vote."[99]

In 2000, there were 6,669,666 Latinos in Texas: 32 percent of the state population. Victor Morales was a candidate for the U.S. Senate; although Morales lost, he received more than 80 percent of the Latino vote. Despite the bloc voting, Tejanos were still suckers for the old Texas proverb that went "never trust a Mexican smoking a cigar, or a gringo speaking Spanish." Republican Texas Governor George W. Bush pinned his hopes of winning the White House on wooing the Mexican vote. Bush won reelection to the governorship by more than a 2-to-1 margin; he took half the Latino vote and more than a quarter of the black vote, both of which were normally Democratic. (Although the figure is open to scrutiny, Southwest voters' exit polls placed the Latino support at 39 percent.)

By November 2000 the effect of the growth in Mexican population was evident. Mexican American representatives from Texas to the U.S. Congress numbered six (five Democrats and one Republican). In the Texas Senate there were seven Tejanos and in the House, 28. Meanwhile, the campaign for redistricting heated up in Texas. The G.I. Forum and the MALDEF submitted plans that would boost Latino representation in Congress. Crucial was the pairing of candidates with a sufficient percentage of Latinos in a district to ensure the candidate a winning chance. Many districts had a majority Latino population, but because a large number of the residents were under 18 or were not citizens, only 40 percent of the registered voters would have Spanish surnames. Both parties were aware of the dramatic growth in the Latino population, forcing Republicans to look for Mexican American candidates. The stakes were higher than those after the 1980 and 1990 redistricting when Republicans sided with Latinos to ensure Latino districts at the expense of white Democratic incumbents—in 2000 that was not enough. There were now enough Latinos in Republican districts to turn an election, and Mexican American votes were vital statewide: numbers were redefining Tejano politics.[100]

The year 2001 saw the election of a brown diaper baby—Julian Castro—to the San Antonio City Council; in 2002, his twin brother Joaquin was elected to the Texas House of Representatives. Twenty-six years old in 2001, they graduated from Harvard and Stanford Law Schools. Their mother Rosie Castro, a Raza Unida activist who had run for the city council in 1971, inspired the Castro brothers.[101]

The 2000 Census recorded that, of the 35 million Latinos, 4.7 million resided in the Midwest. Since 1990 the Latino population increased by 107 percent in Wisconsin, 166 percent in Minnesota, and 153 percent in Iowa. Organizations such as the National Council of La Raza continued a strong presence in the Midwest and advocated for education, civil rights, the census, welfare reform, economic and community development, health issues, migrant labor, and youth leadership.

Illinois was the state with the third highest Mexican-origin population after California and Texas. By 2000, 63 percent of its counties possessed a Latino population of 5 percent or more. Chicago remained the capital for the Mexican-origin population in the Midwest. According to the *New York Times*,

> *The biggest change in Chicago's population mosaic is the increase in Hispanics, up more than 200,000 from 1990. While partly the result of better counting efforts, demographers say there has been a rapid stream of Mexicans coming from Mexico and from other American cities, and a growing influx of immigrants from El Salvador, Guatemala, Colombia and other countries.*[102]

The first Latino elected to the Chicago City Council—in 1915—was William Emilio Rodríguez, son of a Mexican immigrant father and a German mother. In Chicago in the 1990s, a gauge of power was the vote you brought in—the living and the dead (an allusion to the Daly political machines voting the living and the dead). In the late 1990s, Representative Luis V. Gutiérrez (D–IL), a Puerto Rican, personified coalition politics. Gutiérrez took strong stands for undocumented immigrants. Latino voter turnout had been terrible; but during the 1990s, it began to improve, and Latinos began to make gains. Seventy-eight percent of the white community was of voting age, versus 68 percent of the African American community, and barely 60 percent of the Latino community. This fact and the fact that a high percentage of the voting-age population is recent immigrants and/or undocumented keep the voting strength of Mexicans and other Latinos just a potential rather than a reality.

By 2000, the Latino population began to move to the suburbs, a change that caused another set of problems. During the 1990s, 32 Illinois towns saw their minority populations grow by nearly 45 percent. Although these areas included more than 30 percent Latinos in 2000, only one Latino was elected to office, a trend that would continue into the 2000s. In 2000, seven aldermen on the 50-member Chicago City Council were Latinos—four were U.S. Mexican and three were Puerto Rican. According to the 2000 Census, almost two-thirds of Chicago Latinos were of Mexican origin; 15 percent were Puerto Rican; just fewer than 8 percent were Cuban; 10 percent were of Central and South American heritage.

The political situation of the Chicago area resembled that of most of the United States. Redistricting was on the minds of the Latino political players, who thought that their growth would offset the decline in African American and white populations. Chicago numbered 175,793 Latino registered voters by the year 2000. However, as in Los Angeles, even when they comprised a majority of a ward, they would be outvoted by a minority of white, and sometimes black, voters: a large proportion of the community was too young to vote or undocumented. And the chances of Latinos winning in wards where they were a minority were still remote. In Chicago, there were five wards that had a majority of Latino voters; MALDEF wanted another such ward, and it sued the city.

The court dealt Latinos a setback in 1998, when the U.S. Court of Appeals for the Seventh Circuit ruled that only residents of voting age who are citizens should be counted for remapping purposes. This criterion was of concern, since 60 percent of the Latinos would not be counted, thus drastically reducing their political clout. Taken as a whole, Latinos comprised more than one in five Chicagoans (in a city of 2,896,016 residents), with some 530,462 of the Mexican born making up 75 percent of the Latino population. Of concern to non-Latinos was that any growth in Latino representation would come at the expense of African Americans and whites. Increased gentrification also threatened Latino political power.[103]

The Northwest, once largely a Texas affair, with most migrants coming from the Lone Star State, included more of a mix of Texans and immigrants by 2000. By the 1980 Census the Latino population in Washington had grown to 3 percent of the state's total population—approximately 123,000; by the end of the decade it nearly doubled. The 2000 Census showed it had increased to 441,509. Similarly, neighboring Oregon by 2012 grew to 450,062, which was 11.7 percent of the total population, up from 8 percent in 2000.[104] It is a community in transition, with the Latino population doubling every decade. Although Mexican-origin people make up approximately 80 percent of the Latino population, other Latinos are growing in numbers. The changes taking place are interesting. For example, the number of Mexican *tortillerías* that have sprung up in places like the Yakima Valley of Washington amazes the outsider. Indeed, Latino-owned companies in Washington grew 64 percent between 1992 and 1997, employing 18,830 persons by 1997. The number of Latino farmers there also grew from 378 in 1992 to 625 four years later. Two-thirds of the farmers owned and operated their own farms, 120 were part-time owners, and only 79 were tenants. No longer is the region a stopping-off place for migrants; established communities were formed.

Looking at the Mexican-origin population in the Pacific Northwest, from the vantage point of numbers, they are growing dramatically—this is made more significant by the fact that the percentage of the white population is declining. In 1990 just over 380,000 Latinos, of whom over 80 percent were of Mexican origin, lived in Washington, Oregon, and Idaho (they were 4.4 percent of the total population). Ten years later the Mexican portion had grown to 623,000. Unlike in many other regions of the country, the growth is in agricultural communities where the Latino population is still growing.

In 1980, whites were 90.2 percent of Washington's population. Just two decades later it would dip to 76.2. It was not so much that the white population was falling but that the Latino population, which remained overwhelmingly of Mexican origin, was skyrocketing. Asian and Latino immigration played a huge role, too. In 1980, 5.8 percent of Washingtonians were foreign born; it would double in the next two decades. By 2000, 67.2 percent of Washington's Asian population and 45.6 percent of Latinos were foreign born. However, the 2000 Census indicated 88.64 percent were classified as white.

The Yakima Valley continued to be a major entry port for Mexican migrants. For instance, the town Wapato, according to the 2000 Census, numbered 4,572, of which 76 percent were Latino—and this is not counting undocumented residents.[105] Whites call it "Mexican Town." Mexican residency goes back to World War II when undocumented workers, *braceros*, and Tejanos and Mexican sugar beet workers came to pick crops. In the 1970s cold-storage facilities in Wapato and Union Gap opened new opportunities and made possible year-round employment. In the 1980s Mexican immigrants displaced Chicano migrants as the primary farm workforce. The landscape took on more diversity as local restaurants and tortilla plants run by Mexican immigrants and the cantinas run by Chicanos multiplied. Some Mexicans own farms, but agriculture is still dominated by Euro-Americans.[106]

The largest state in the Northwest is Washington. In 2000, its total population was 5,894,121—of which 441,509 (or 7.5 percent) were Latinos. Mexicans made up 329,934 or just fewer than 75 percent of the Latino population. Puerto Ricans were the next largest group (16,140), followed by Central Americans (12,126). As with other states, the Latino population of Washington doubled during the 1990s. Some 40 percent were under 18, making it the youngest ethnic group. Adams and Franklin Counties in eastern Washington were 50 percent Latino, and Yakima County was 35 percent Latino. Central Americans became more numerous as Guatemalans moved into Shelton and Salvadorans into Aberdeen.

Besides this resident population, 100,000 migrants arrived in Washington annually. Another trend was the in-migration of indigenous Mexicans who knew little Spanish or English. The Spanish-speaking were bound together by a chain of Spanish-language radio stations playing Spanish music. Despite some economic progress achieved, the low educational attainment, with corresponding low income, has contributed to low rates of home ownership in comparison with other groups. The big banana in Washington is Seattle, home of Microsoft. It is a white city, ranking last in terms of percentage of minorities among the 25 most populous cities. "The Times [Seattle] analysis also shows Seattle has earned a distinction as a city short on children. Only about one in six Seattlites is under age 18." Sixty-eight percent of Seattle's population is white. It ranked second in the Pacific Northwest behind Portland, Oregon.

In 2000, Latinos made up at least 20 percent of the school enrollment in 26 Oregon towns—and 65 percent in Woodburn, Oregon. The Latino population of Oregon was expected to grow to 500,000 by 2025. Nevertheless, Latinos lacked political representation.[107]

The town of Salem, Oregon, has experienced dramatic growth in the Mexican-origin population since the 1970s. As in other places in the Pacific Northwest, the roots of the Mexican population extend back into the nineteenth century—but up until recently they have not been strong in terms of numbers. World War II was a turning point, with significant numbers of migrants and *braceros* finding their way into Oregon. By the 1970s, immigrants arrived from Michoacán and Oaxaca to work in tree farms and canneries. A similar growth occurred in surrounding areas, and, by the beginning of the twentieth century, 55,000 Latinos lived in Marion and Polk Counties and over 100,000 lived in Clackamas, Multnomah, and Washington Counties alone.[108] By the beginning of the twenty-first century, the proportion of whites in the population was declining and the growth in the Latino population was taking up the slack. As in the Southwest and Midwest, the Mexican and Latino communities were increasingly divided into those with green cards and those without. On the one hand, more Mexican American students attended universities; on the other hand, like California, Oregon attracted thousands of Mixtec and other Mexican migrants coming to work in the fields. They differentiate themselves from other Latinos, and many do not speak Spanish or English and are the victims of exploitation, living in fear.[109]

As with Oregon and Washington, Mexicans migrated to Idaho for agricultural work.[110] The sugar beet companies recruited Mexicans around World War I as Central European labor was restricted. Mexicans also worked on the railroads. During World War II *braceros* entered the state, as did the Mexican American migrants. The Mexican population changed in the 1960s, 1970s, and 1980s, with the existing Mexican American population settling in and the state's economy diversifying. Mexican American and Latino businesses became more common, and distinct communities formed. These communities grew more conscious of their rights. Migrant workers continued to work in Idaho, where as many as 100,000 arrived in the summer months. The Tejanos continued to be a significant part of the workforce. By 1991, the Idaho Migrant Council estimated that the Mexican-origin population reached more than 58,000 in the southern Snake River Valley.[111]

Political Roundup: 2000

In 2000, Antonio Villaraigosa lost the election for mayor of Los Angeles partially because the then Assemblyman Tony Cárdenas, Los Angeles City Councilman Alex Padilla, and Congressman Xavier Becerra supported Jim Hahn. The rift was personal. Villaraigosa supported a white liberal to replace him as Speaker of the Assembly. This schism gave many white liberals and African Americans an excuse to support Hahn, who ran racist ads associating Villaraigosa with gang members and drug dealers.

California Latinos as a whole were entering a new era, one where money beyond the means of an ordinary politician carried the day. To run successfully for city council or mayor required more money than the Mexican/Latino community could raise independently. To attract such huge amounts of funds, compromises were made with the business community, whose interests did not always coincide with those of Mexican Americans and other Latinos. Term limits, personal ambitions, and the need to raise campaign funds were changing the direction of Chicano politics.

In the years past, nationalism disciplined politicians such as Richard Alatorre. However, times had changed, and by 2000 Mexican Americans and Latinos wanted to believe that they were players. While the redistricting processes in 1980 and 1990 were contentious, this time around the Mexican American community assumed that it was part of the establishment, given its power in Sacramento. Latinos were now incumbents, and incumbents in both parties worked out a bipartisan redistricting plan that protected incumbents. It kept intact 13 seats (7 state senators; 6 members of Congress) currently held by Latinos. The legislature would also create a new Chicano congressional district in Los Angeles County. MALDEF disputed the plan. Considering the growth and size of the Latino population, it was entitled to more.

According to Chicano elected officials, the benefits of multiracial coalitions were huge. They said that in 2002 there were 26 Latino legislators, proof of the effectiveness of coalition politics. Evidently, many elected officials forgot that Chicanos leveled the political field in the courts. In fact, it cost the community a lot of political capital to get them elected.

In June 2002, the Ninth Circuit Court found that the redistricting plan—a blatant deal—was not unreasonable. In effect it held that rules protecting minorities were no longer necessary because of the dramatic political progress Latinos had made in California in recent years—such as winning dozens of seats in Congress and the California legislature and nearly electing a Latino mayor in Los Angeles. This decision was significant since it came from the court's most liberal judges. In the space of just under three decades, society returned to the era of legal gerrymandering.[112]

The success of George W. Bush in cultivating Latino voters formed his base in Texas. Whereas Latinos were not a factor in California, where Gore was the overwhelming favorite, they were much more of a factor in Texas and New York. Nationally, the U.S. Latino community took a huge leap during the 1990s, growing by 58 percent to 35.3 million people; they were 12.5 percent of the population while constituting 7 percent of all voters. However, in some cases increased numbers did not result in Latino representation: despite a 2000 Census count of 30 percent Latino citizens in Fort Worth, Texas, there were no Latinos on the City Council. They did better on the Fort Worth school board where they held three of the nine seats. It was estimated that Latinos needed at least a 60 percent majority to elect a candidate.[113] This was a pattern for Latino politics throughout the country.

Some Things Never Change: Police Brutality

Twenty-five years after the assassination of Rubén Salazar (described in Chapter 13), the justice system was still not protecting the rights of Mexican Americans. In 1995 in Sun Valley, California (a suburb of Los Angeles), William Masters II, 35, killed an 18-year-old tagger named César Rene Arce and wounded his friend, David Hillo, 20. Both taggers were unarmed. Many Euro-Americans applauded Masters, while the Chicano community remained largely indifferent. In the end, the district attorney did not indict Masters for the murder; still the community remained silent.

In 1999, the Los Angeles Police Department's (LAPD) Rampart scandal began when Officer Rafael Pérez, who served as a Rampart Community Resources Against Street Hoodlums (CRASH) antigang officer, copped a plea bargain for having stolen drugs from LAPD evidence lockers—in return for evidence of widespread corruption and brutality in the Rampart CRASH unit. Dozens of police were implicated in numerous crimes and acts of brutality committed while waging a systematic war and shooting down youth in the Pico-Union neighborhood. Only a few Chicanos and Central Americans protested this gross violation of human rights; many Latino elected officials sided with the police.

In Bellevue, a suburb of Seattle, Washington, police killed Nelson Martínez Méndez, 24, an unarmed Guatemalan accused of domestic violence against a cousin. *El Centro de la Raza* of Seattle, led by Roberto Maestas, organized protests against the injustice. In January 2002, an inquest jury ruled it justifiable homicide, and the district attorney refused to prosecute the officer.

In 2005, an LAPD SWAT team killed 19-month-old Susie Lopez Peña in an exchange of gunfire with her father, who was holding her. Police fired over 60 shots at the father, with numerous bullets hitting and killing Susie. Not one politico challenged Police Chief William J. Bratton, who defended his officers.[114]

Race continued to be a factor in society. At the trial of Jessy San Miguel, the prosecutor made a point of emphasizing the so-called Mexican Macho culture. The prosecutor made a reference to "those that cross the border and commit crimes." San Miguel, 28, died from lethal injection, after George Bush refused a stay of execution.[115]

Conclusion: The Problem of Becoming the Nation's Largest Minority

As mentioned at the beginning of the chapter, the timeline encompasses two decades—two very hectic decades. Not only had the population grown dramatically, but no longer could it be assumed that Latinos were a homogeneous population—there were Mexicans, there were Puerto Ricans, and, to a lesser extent, there were Cuban Americans. Neither did these peoples live in exclusive pockets—all Mexicans did not live in the Southwest; Puerto Ricans, in New York; or Cubans, in Florida. By 2000, most Latino groups were scattered throughout the country, with the most dramatic shift taking place in the South. A report of the Pew Hispanic Center wrote:

> *The Hispanic population is growing faster in much of the South than anywhere else in the United States. Across a broad swath of the region stretching westward from North Carolina on the Atlantic seaboard to Arkansas across the Mississippi River and south to Alabama on the Gulf of Mexico, sizeable Hispanic populations have emerged suddenly in communities where Latinos were a sparse presence just a decade or two ago.[116]*

These new settlement areas differed from California, Texas, and New York, where migrants joined well-established Latino communities with networks of organizations. They posed new challenges to national Latino organizations, a majority of which were still Mexican American. There would also be the challenge of how the member communities of this amorphous group called "Latinos" would relate to each other and how they could find unity and the consensus to develop a common agenda.

Notes

1. Betsy Guzmán, The Hispanic Population: Census 2000 Brief May 2001, http://www.census.gov/prod/2001pubs/c2kbr01-3.pdf.
2. Ibid. Rafael Valdivieso, "Demographic Trends of the Mexican-American Population: Implications for Schools. ERIC Digest," ERIC Clearinghouse on Rural Education and Small Schools, Charleston WV. ED321961 (September 1990), http://www.ericdigests.org/pre-9217/trends.htm.
3. The Powell Memo (also known as the Powell Manifesto). The Powell Memo was first published August 23, 1971. Confidential Memorandum: Attack of American Free Enterprise System, August 23, 1971, TO: Mr. Eugene B. Sydnor, Jr., Chairman, Education Committee, U.S. Chamber of Commerce. FROM: Lewis F. Powell, Jr., In Reclaim Democracy, http://reclaimdemocracy.org/powell_memo_lewis/. Lewis was later appointed to the Supreme Court. Jean Stefanic and Richard

Delgado, *No Mercy: How Conservative Think Tanks and Foundations Changed America's Social Agenda* (Philadelphia, PA: Temple University Press, 1996).

4. Amy Goodman, "The Criminalization of Immigration," *Democracy Now* (September 11, 1997), http://www.democracynow.org/1997/9/11/the_criminalization_of_immigration.

5. Edward R. Roybal, "Hispanic Americans in Congress, 1822–1995," http://www.loc.gov/rr/hispanic/congress/roybal.html.

6. David Reyes, "GI Forum Address," *Los Angeles Times* (August 7, 1980).

7. MALDEF, Mexican American Legal Defense and Education Fund, http://www.maldef.org/.

8. Deindustrialization is the reduction of heavy industry and manufacturing within the country's borders and sending the production abroad. Paul L. Street, *Racial Oppression in the Global Metropolis: A Living Black Chicago History* (Lanham, MD: Rowman & Littlefield Publishers, Inc., 2007), 132. Joan Moore, "Latina/o Studies: The Continuing Need for New Paradigms," Occasional Paper No. 29, Julian Samora Research Institute, December 1997, http://www.jsri.msu.edu/pdfs/ops/oc29.pdf.

9. Jorge Chapa, "The Burden of Interdependence: Demographic, Economic, and Social Propects for Latinos in the Reconfigured U.S. Economy," in Frank Bonilla, Edwin Meléndez, Rebecca Morales, and María de los Angeles Torres, eds., *Borderless Borders: U.S. Latinos, Latin Americans and the Paradox of Interdependence* (Philadelphia, PA: Temple University Press, 1998), 71–82. Stefanic and Delgado, *No Mercy*.

10. Robert W. Fox, "Neighbors' Problems, Our Problems: Population Growth in Central America," Negative Population Growth (NPG) Forum Series, http://www.npg.org/forum_series/BalancingHumansInTheBiosphere.pdf. Thomas F. O'Brien, *The Revolutionary Mission: American Enterprise in Latin America, 1900–1945* (Cambridge, UK: Cambridge University Press, 1999), 51–53. Charles D. Brockett, *Land, Power and Poverty: Agrarian Transformation and Political Conflict in Central America* (Boulder, CO: Westview Press, 1990), 70–76.

11. El Salvador in the 1980s, http://www.youtube.com/watch?v=1bEpEK7uKzE&feature=related. David Kirsch, "Death Squads in El Salvador: A Pattern of U.S. Complicity," *Covert Action Quarterly*, Summer 1990, http://www.thirdworldtraveler.com/US_ThirdWorld/deathsquads_ElSal.html. El Salvador: Civil War, PBS, http://www.pbs.org/itvs/enemiesofwar/el-salvador2.html. Ron Rhodes, "Christian Revolution in Latin America: The Changing Face of Liberation Theology," Part One in a Three-Part Series on Liberation Theology, Reasoning from the Scriptures Ministries, http://home.earthlink.net/~ronrhodes/Liberation.html. Roberto D'Abussion [*sic*] interview (1984), http://www.youtube.com/watch?v=0e-jnwAwIKE&feature=related.

12. Massacre in El Salvador During Oscar Romero's Funeral, http://www.youtube.com/watch?v=EN6LWdqcyuc&feature=related.

13. I was in El Salvador in the spring of 1991 before the peace accords. Rodolfo F. Acuña, "Column Left; Latin Generals Count on the Wages of War," *Los Angeles Times* (April 1,

1991). Tom Gibb, "US Role in Salvador's Brutal War," *BBC News/America* (March 24, 2002), http://news.bbc.co.uk/2/hi/americas/1891145.stm.

14. Nicaraguan Sandinistas, Latin American Studies, http://www.latinamericanstudies.org/sandinistas.htm.

15. Boland Amendment—Definition and Overview, WorldIQ.com, http://www.wordiq.com/definition/Boland_Amendment. Secrets of The CIA—Nicaragua, http://www.youtube.com/watch?v=zKXZfwG43pU.

16. Lawrence E. Walsh, Independent Counsel, "Final Report of the Independent Counsel for Iran/Contra Matters," in *Volume I: Investigations and Prosecutions*, August 4, 1993 (Washington, DC, United States Court of Appeals for the District of Columbia Circuit Division for the Purpose of Appointing Independent Counsel, Division No. 86–6), http://www.fas.org/irp/offdocs/walsh/. Iran Contra Coverup: Part 1 (All eight can be found on YouTube), http://www.youtube.com/watch?v=35KcYgMPiIM. CIA, Guns, Drugs, Fraud, Iran Contra, http://www.youtube.com/watch?v=bbt9PsaSUiI.

17. Ginger Thompson and Mireya Navarro, "Rights Groups Say Logbook Lists Executions by Guatemalan Army," *New York Times* (May 20, 1999). Rachel Cobb, "Guatemala's New Evangelists," *Natural History* 107, no. 4 (May 1998): 32ff. "Guatemala Civil War 1960–1996," GlobalSecurity.org, http://www.globalsecurity.org/military/world/war/guatemala.htm.

18. "Maquiladoras," *Handbook of Texas Online*, http://www.tshaonline.org/handbook/online/articles/MM/dzm2.html. María Patricia Fernández-Kelly, *For We Are Sold. I and My People: Women and Industry in Mexico's Frontier* (Albany: State University of New York Press, 1983), 45–84. Devon G. Peña, *The Terror of the Machine: Technology, Work, Gender, & Ecology on the U.S.-Mexico Border* (Austin: CMAS Book, University of Texas Press, 1997). James M. Cypher, "Mexico: Financial Fragility or Structural Crisis?" *Journal of Economic Issues* 30, no. 2 (June 1996): 454–55.

19. Thomas Muller, *California's Newest Immigrants: A Summary* (Washington, DC: Urban Institute Press, 1984), ix–x, 7, 13, 28.

20. James Crawford, "California Vote Gives Boost to 'English-Only' Movement," *Education Weekly* (April 1, 1987), http://www.edweek.org/ew/articles/1987/04/01/27useng.h06.html.

21. Leo R. Chávez, "The Power of the Imagined Community: The Settlement of Undocumented Mexicans and Central Americans in the United States," *American Anthropologist* 96, no. 1 (1994): 52–73. Margo De Ley, "Taking from Latinos to Assist Soviet Immigrants—an Affront to Fairness," *Los Angeles Times* (March 19, 1989). A Look at the Forces Behind the Anti-Immigrant Movement, Democracy Now! May 2, 2007, http://www.democracynow.org/2007/5/2/a_look_at_the_forces_behind.

22. Terry Maxon, "Hart Angers Hispanics with Letter on Aliens," *Dallas Morning News* (February 5, 1985). Stephen Moore, "A Pro-Family, Pro-growth Legal Immigration Policy for America," Backgrounder no. 735, The Heritage Foundation (November 6, 1989): 1–7. Elton Gallegly, "Just How Many Aliens Are Here Illegally?" *Los Angeles Times* (March 13, 1994).

23. California Chief Justice Rose Bird Loses Election, http://www
.youtube.com/watch?v=Kd162US36to. Cruz Reynoso Honored for Civil Rights Commitments, http://www.youtube.com/
watch?v=wViKbfS_Gds&feature=related. Frank del Olmo, "Ugly
or Polite, It's Racism," *Los Angeles Times* (October 30, 1986).

24. William Langwiesche, "The Border," *Atlantic Monthly* (May
1992), 69. Sebastian Rotella, "Border Abuses Continue 2
Years, Study Says," *Los Angeles Times* (February 26, 1992).
Sebastian Rotella, "INS Agents Abuse Immigrants, Study
Says," *Los Angeles Times* (May 31, 1992).

25. Stuart Silverstein, "Years Later, Many Scoff at Immigration Act,"
Los Angeles Times (August 29, 1993). Dan Freedman, "U.S. to
Boost Border Patrols," *Los Angeles Daily News* (February 3,
1994). "Southern Exposure—Perspective," *California Journal*
(May 1, 1998). "U.S. Border Patrol in S. California Developing
Deadly But Ineffective Operation Gatekeeper," *In Motion
Magazine*, http://www.inmotionmagazine.com/rm99.html.

26. Robert R. Brischetto and Paul A. Leonard, "Falling Through
the Safety Net: Latinos and the Declining Effectiveness of
Anti-Poverty Programs in the 1980s," *Public Policy Report 1*,
Southwest Voter Research Institute, 1988. Rebecca Morales
and Frank Bonilla, "Restructuring and the New Inequality,"
in Rebecca Morales and Frank Bonilla, eds., *Latinos in a
Changing U.S. Economy. Comparative Perspectives on Growing
Inequality* (Newbury Park, CA: Sage Publications, 1993), 11–12.
Roger M. Mahoney, "Democracy's Obligated to the Poor," *Los
Angeles Times* (October 23, 1985). Jason DeParle, "Poverty
Rate Rose Sharply Last Year as Incomes Slipped," *Los Angeles
Times* (September 27, 1991). James Risen, "History May Judge
Reaganomics Very Harshly," *Los Angeles Times* (November 8,
1992). Harry Bernstein, "Closing the Wage Gap: Job Equality,"
Los Angeles Times (April 8, 1993).

27. Paul Krugman, "Reagan Did It," *New York Times* (June 1, 2009).

28. Harry Bernstein, "Put Teeth Back in Worker's Right to Strike,"
Los Angeles Times (July 5, 1993). "Patco: Ex-Controllers
Regret Striking in 1981," *Los Angeles Times* (July 17, 1991).
Bob Baker, "Workers Fear Losing Jobs to Replacement in
Strikes," *Los Angeles Times* (June 7, 1990). Jane Slaughter,
"What Went Wrong at Caterpillar?" *Labor Notes* (May 1991).
Bob Baker, "Union Buster Turns to 'A Labor of Love,'" *Los
Angeles Times* (September 5, 1993).

29. Marita Hernandez, "Latina Leads Takeover of Union from
Anglo Male," *Los Angeles Times* (May 6, 1989). "*Raiz Fuerte
que no se arranca,*" pamphlet paying homage to Magdalena
Mora (Los Angeles, CA: Editorial Prensa Sembradora, 1981).
Steve Proffitt, "María Elena Durazo," *Los Angeles Times*
(September 27, 1992). Bob Baker, "Union, Hyatt Hotels Still
at Odds," *Los Angeles Times* (July 23, 1991). See Rodolfo F.
Acuña, *Anything but Mexican: Chicanos in Contemporary Los
Angeles* (London: Verso, 1996). Patrick J. McDonnell, "Hotel
Boycott Is a High-Stakes Battle for Union. . . ," *Los Angeles
Times* (February 3, 1996).

30. Justice for Janitors actions (1990 through 2006), http://www
.youtube.com/watch?v=WKfQgUn7UNg. Stronger Colorado/
Justice for Janitors Denver Rally, http://www.youtube.com/
watch?v=WV_1vb0JDHg. NOW "Janitor Justice?"; PBS,

(October 26, 2007), http://www.youtube.com/watch?v=kdK7
Chg7Dm4&feature=related.

31. Sonia Nazario, "Janitors Settle Suit, Involving Clash in 1990,"
Los Angeles Times (September 4, 1990). Rodolfo F. Acuña,
"America Retreats on Labor Laws," *Los Angeles Times* (July
16, 1990). Bob Baker, "Tentative Accord Ok'd to End Janitor's
Strike," *Los Angeles Times* (June 26, 1990). Sonia Nazario,
"For Militant Union, It's a War," Los Angeles Times (August
19, 1993). Harry Bernstein, "It's a Fine Line Between Profit
and Greed," *Los Angeles Times* (January 2, 1994).

32. Labor Community Strategy Center, http://www.thestrategy-
center.org/project/bus-riders-union.

33. Bob Baker, "L.A.'s Booming Auto Industry Now a Memory,"
Los Angeles Times (July 20, 1991). Henry Weinstein, "Boycott
by UAW of GM Threatened," *Los Angeles Times* (May 15,
1983). Eric Mann, *Taking on General Motors: A Case Study
of the UAW Campaign to Keep GM Van Nuys Open* (Los Angeles: Center for Labor Research and Education, Institute of
Industrial Relations, University of California Los Angeles,
1987), 7–9, 219–50. James F. Peltz, "General Motors Plant in
Van Nuys to Close," *Los Angeles Times* (July 2, 1991).

34. Rodolfo F. Acuña, *Corridors of Migration: The Odyssey of
Mexican Laborers, 1600–1933* (Tucson: University of Arizona
Press, 2007).

35. Robert B. Reich, "Business Dynamism Gone Overboard,"
Los Angeles Times (November 17, 1985). Barbara Kingsolver,
*Holding the Line: Women in the Great Arizona Mine Strike
of 1983* (Ithaca, NY: ILR Press, Cornell University, 1996).
Jonathan D. Rosenblum, *Copper Crucible: How the Arizona
Miners Strike of 1983 Recast Labor-Management Relations in
America* (Ithaca, NY: ILR Press, Cornell University, 1995) 4,
no. 2 (Summer 1988): 251–68.

36. The Women of "Fuerza Unida," http://www.youtube.com/
watch?v=TllODcghnHk.

37. "Texas Plant Closure Still Haunting Levi's" (November 1, 1992).
Reese Erlich, "Former Levi Strauss Workers Protest Texas
Plant Closing," *Christian Science Monitor* (November 9, 1992).
Alexander Cockburn, "Merciless Cruelties of Bottom Line,"
Arizona Republic (Phoenix, May 23, 1993). Suzanne Espinosa
Solis, "Rare Shadow on Company's Image: Ex-Workers Take
on Levi Strauss," *San Francisco Chronicle* (July 18, 1994). Fuerza
Unida, http://fuerzaunida.freeservers.com/.

38. Cesar Chavez Trilogy Cut Version, http://www.youtube.com/
watch?v=jZt7g1t1iAo.

39. Harry Bernstein, "Farm Workers Still Mired in Poverty," *Los
Angeles Times* (July 25, 1985). Harry Bernstein, "The Boycott:
Chávez Gets a Slow Start," *Los Angeles Times* (July 25, 1985).
Harry Bernstein, "Growers Still Addicted to Foreign Work-
ers," *Los Angeles Times* (October 2, 1985). Harry Bernstein,
"Ruling May Devastate Chávez's Union," *Los Angeles Times*
(February 25, 1987).

40. Rochell L. Stanfield, "Reagan Courting Women, Minorities,
But It May Be Too Late to Win Them," *National Journal* 15,
no. 22 (May 28, 1983): 1118ff. *Dallas Morning News* (October
19, 1984). Juan Vásquez, "Watch out for Willie Velásquez,"
Nuestro (March 1979), 20.

41. Robert Gnaizda, "Mario Obledo, Latino Vote: The 'Sleeping Giant' Stirs," *Los Angeles Times* (November 13, 1983). Gloria Molina interviewed by Carlos Vásquez (1944), Courtesy of the Department of Special Collections/UCLA Library, Calisphere (1990), http://content.cdlib.org/xtf/view?docId=hb8b69p65d&chunk.id=div00011&brand=calisphere&doc.view=entire_text.

42. Chip Jacobs, "Return of the Native," *Los Angeles City Beat* (April 7, 2005), http://chipjacobs.com/articles/profiles/return-of-the-native/. John P. Schmal, "Chicano Representation: Coming into their own (1975–1984)," HispanicVista.com, http://www.hispanicvista.com/HVC/Columnist/jschmal/071805jpschmal1.htm. Acuña, *Anything but Mexican*, 56, 74, 98.

43. Frank del Olmo, "Snyder's Narrow Victory Gives Latino Political Activists a Rude Awakening," *Los Angeles Times* (April 28, 1983). Janet Clayton, "Snyder's Decision Throws Eastside Seat Up for Grabs," *Los Angeles Times* (January 3, 1985). Frank del Olmo, "Alatorre Vs. Snyder . . . " *Los Angeles Times* (January 31, 1985).

44. Douglas Johnson, "Latinos and Redistricting: 'Californios for Fair Representation' and California Redistricting in the 1980s," The Rose Institute of State and Local Government, Claremont McKenna College, July 1991.

45. Douglas Johnson, "Latinos and Redistricting: 'Californios for Fair Representation' and California Redistricting in the 1980s," The Rose Institute of State and Local Government Claremont McKenna College, July 1991. Henry Cisneros Interview: Charlie Rose: July 26, 1996, no longer available on internet.

46. Kemper Diehl and Jan Jarboe, *Henry Cisneros: Portrait of a New American* (San Antonio, TX: Corona Publishing, 1985). Rodolfo F. Acuña, *Occupied America: A History of Chicanos*, 3d ed. (New York: Harper & Row, 1988), 430–37. Marshall Ingersol, "San Antonio's Mayor Is Simply 'Henry' to Everyone," *Christian Science Monitor* (March 24, 1984). James García, "Cisneros Fall Wasn't a Tragedy," *Dallas Morning News* (January 4, 1998).

47. "Where Minority Mayors Ride High," *U.S. News & World Report* (April 22, 1985), 12. Peter Skerry, "Neighborhood COPS; The Resurrection of Saul Alinsky," *New Republic* (February 6, 1984), 27. Peter Skerry, *Mexican Americans: The Ambivalent Minority* (New York: Free Press, 1993), 66. Robert Reinhold, "Mexican-Americans in Texas Move into Political Mainstream," *New York Times* (September 15, 1985).

48. Rita Arias Jirasek and Carlos Tortolero, *Mexican Chicago* (Chicago, IL: Arcadia Publishing, 2001), 135–45. Ray Hutchison, "Historiography of Chicago's Mexican Community," Urban and Regional Studies University of Wisconsin-Green Bay, April 1999, http://tigger.uic.edu/~marczim/mlac/papers/hutchison.htm. Chicago Activist Voices Opinion on Immigration, Online News Hour, PBS, http://www.pbs.org/newshour/bb/social_issues/july-dec06/immigration_08-18.html. Karen Mary Davalos, "Ethnic Identity Among Mexican and Mexican American Women in Chicago, 1920–1991" (PhD dissertation, Yale University, 1993). Latino Institute, *Al Filo/At the Cutting Edge: The Empowerment of Chicago's Latino Electorate* (Chicago, IL: Latino Institute, 1986), 1–6, 11, 14–15, 18–19, 24–26.

49. "New Mexico Offers a Preview of Mobilization," *New York Times* (September 1, 1983); interview with nine academicians within the state. Ted Robbins, "1980 Race Set Tone for Richardson's Political Future," NPR, September 13, 2007, http://www.npr.org/templates/story/story.php?storyId=14361319.

50. Chip Martínez, "Federico Peña: Denver's First Hispanic Mayor," *Nuestro* (August 1983), 14–17. Steve Padilla, "In Search of Hispanic Voters," *Nuestro* (August 1983), 20. "A Mile High: Denver Buys Peña's Dream," *Time* (July 4, 1983), 22. Kenneth T. Walsh, "Minority Mayors on Fast Track," *U.S. News & World Report* (April 7, 1986), 31–32.

51. Bill Boyarsky, "Battle Over Hermosillo: It's Just the Start," *Los Angeles Times*, August 25, 1993.

52. Acuña, *Anything but Mexican*, 152–53. Mark Z. Barabak, "Latinos Struggle for Role in National Leadership, Politics . . . " *Los Angeles Times* (July 7, 1998).

53. Rodolfo F. Acuña, *Sometimes There Is No Other Side: Chicanos and the Myth of Equality* (Notre Dame, IN: University of Notre Dame Press, 1998), 66. Lisa J. Montoya, Carol Hardy-Fanta, and Sonia Garcia, "Latina Politics: Gender, Participation, and Leadership," *PS: Political Science & Politics* 33, no. 3 (September 2000): 555–61. Mary Benanti, "Hispanic Officeholders 'Barometer' of Progress," *USA Today* (September 18, 1987).

54. Sarah Deutsch, "Gender, Labor History, and Chicano/a Ethnic Identity," *Frontiers* 14, no. 2 (1994): 1–9. Virginia Escalante, Nancy Rivera, and Victor Valle, "Inside the World of Latinas," *Los Angeles Times* (August 7, 1983). "For Business: Making Full Use of the Nation's Human Capital. Fact-Finding Report of the Federal Glass Ceiling Commission Release by the Department of Labor," March 1995, Washington, DC, http://digitalcommons.ilr.cornell.edu/cgi/viewcontent.cgi?article=1118&context=key_workplace.

55. Mary Pardo, *Mexican American Women Activists: Identity and Resistance in Two Los Angeles Communities* (Philadelphia, PA: Temple University Press, 1998). Rodolfo F. Acuña's Herald-Examiner articles on the Mothers of East Los Angeles are in his collection at the California State Northridge Library.

56. José Angel Gutiérrez, Michelle Meléndez, and Sonia Adriana Noyola, *Chicanas in Charge: Texas Women in the Public Arena* (Lanham, MD: Rowman & Littlefield, 2007), 106–12. María Antonietta Berriozabal, Tejano Voices, http://library.uta.edu/tejanovoices/interview.php?cmasno=033.

57. Severita Lara, Tejano Voices, UT Arlington, http://library.uta.edu/tejanovoices/interview.php?cmasno=013. Gutiérrez et al., *Chicanas in Charge*, 113, 121.

58. Alicia Chacón, Tejano Voices, UT Arlington, http://library.uta.edu/tejanovoices/interview.php?cmasno=002. Gutiérrez et al., *Chicanas in Charge*, 47–55.

59. Norma Villarreal Ramírez, Tejano Voices, http://library.uta.edu/tejanovoices/interview.php?cmasno=007. José Angel Gutiérrez, "Experiences of Chicana County Judges in Texas Politics: In Their Own Words," *Frontiers* 20, no. IL

(July–August 1999): 181ff. See Tejano Voices, http://library .uta.edu/tejanovoices/gallery.php.

60. Gutiérrez et al., *Chicanas in Charge*, 131–35, 144.

61. Rebecca Morales and Paul Ong, "Immigrant Women in Los Angeles," *Economic and Industrial Democracy* 12, no. 1 (February 1991): 65–81. Benjamin Mark Cole, "Do Immigrants Underpin L.A. Business World?" *Los Angeles Business Journal* (May 27, 1991). Elaine M. Allensworth, "Earnings Mobility of First and '1.5' Generation Mexican-Origin Women and Men: A Comparison with U.S.–Born Mexican Americans and Non-Hispanic Whites," *Internal Migration Review* 31, no. 2 (Summer 1997): 386–410. Elizabeth Martínez and Ed McCaughan, "Chicanas and Mexicanas within a Transnational Working Class," in Adelaida R. Del Castillo, ed., *Between Borders: Essays on Mexicana/Chicana History* (Los Angeles, CA: Floricanto Press, 1990), 31–52. Pierrette Hondagneu-Sotelo, *Gendered Transition: Mexican Experiences of Immigration* (Berkeley: University of California Press, 1994). Rebecca Morales and Paul M. Ong, "The Illusion of Progress," in Morales and Bonilla, eds., *Latinos*, 69–70.

62. Morales and Ong, "The Illusion of Progress," 64–77. Claudia Dorrington, "Central American Refugees in Los Angeles: Adjustment of Children and Families," in Ruth E. Zambrana, ed., *Understanding Latino Families: Scholarship, Policy, and Practice* (Thousand Oaks, CA: Sage, 1995), 111. Claire Spiegel, "Prenatal Care in L.A. Worsening, Report Concludes," *Los Angeles Times* (July 12, 1988). Jill L. Sherer. "Neighbor to Neighbor: Community Health Workers Educate Their Own," *Hospitals & Health Networks* 68, no. 20 (October 20, 1994): 52. Leo R. Chaves, Estebán T. Flores, and Marta López-Garza, "Undocumented Latin American Immigrants and U.S. Health Services: An Approach to a Political Economy of Utilization," *Medical Anthropology Quarterly* 6, no. 1 (March 1, 1992): 6–26. David James Rose, "Coming Out, Standing Out: Hispanic American Gays and Lesbians," *Hispanic* (June 1994): 44ff.

63. Marita Hernandez, "Gloria Molina," *Los Angeles Times* (February 13, 1989). Virginia Escalante, Nancy Rivera, and Victor Valle, "Inside the World of Latinas," in *Southern California's Latino Community. A Series of Articles Reprinted from the Los Angeles Times* (Los Angeles, CA: Los Angeles Times, 1983), 82–91. Daniel M. Weintraub, "Remap Bills Are Vetoed by Wilson," *Los Angeles Times* (September 24, 1991). "Proposed Redistricting in Los Angeles County," *Los Angeles Times* (January 3, 1992). Frederick Muir, "Reapportionment Shuffles the Political Deck," *Los Angeles Times* (January 3, 1992). "Latino Voters in California," *Nuestro Tiempo* (April 30, 1992).

64. "World Politics and Current Affairs," *The Economist* (September 29, 1990). Madeleine May Kunin, "Give Everyone a Turn at the Game; Term Limits . . . " *Los Angeles Times* (September 13, 1991).

65. Britney Jeffrey, "Rangel, Irma Lerma," *Handbook of Texas Online* (http://www.tshaonline.org/handbook/online/articles/ fra85), accessed December 5, 2013, Cynthia Orozco, "Mexican American Democrats," *Handbook of Texas Online*, http:// www.tshaonline.org/handbook/online/articles/wmm02.

66. José Angel Gutiérrez and Rebecca E. Deen, "Chicanas in Texas Politics" (Occasional Paper No. 66, Julian Samora Research Institute, October 2000). Roberto R. Calderón, "Tejano Politics," *Handbook of Texas Online*, http://www .tshaonline.org/handbook/online/articles/TT/wmtkn.html . Guillermo X. García, "Texas Surpasses N.Y. as Second Most Populous State," *USA Today* (March 13, 2001).

67. Lee Drutman, "The Rise of the Political Donor Class," *Miller-McCune* (August 28, 2008), http://www.psmag.com/ politics/the-rise-of-the-political-donor-class-4305   http:// www.miller-mccune.com/politics/the-rise-of-the-political-donor-class-562.

68. Marie Claire Acosta, "The Democratization Process in Mexico: A Human Rights Issue," *Resist* (January 1991), 3–6. Bob Howard, "U.S. Latinos Speak up on Free Trade Accord," *Nuestro Tiempo* (November 7, 1991). "The U.S. and Mexico: A Close Look at Costs of Free Trade," *Business Week* (May 4, 1992), 22. Joel D. Nicholson, John Lust, Aljeandro Ardila Manzanera, and Javier Arroyo Rico, "Mexican-U.S. Attitudes Toward the NAFTA," *International Trade Journal* 8, no. 1 (1994): 93–115. Acuña, *Anything but Mexican*, 231–49.

69. North American Free Trade Agreement (NAFTA), Public Citizen, http://www.citizen.org/trade/nafta/. "1994—60 Minutes—Subcomandante Marcos," part#1 of 2, http://www.youtube .com/watch?v=Ali_88YoUFk. Denise Bedell, "Revisiting Nafta." *Global Finance*, 23, no. 3 (2009): 22–24. Garrett Zehr, "On NAFTA." *This*, 42, no. 2 (2008): 20–21.

70. David Agren, "Bishop Samuel Ruiz Garcia, 86, champion of indigenous, dies in Mexico," Catholic News Service, http:// www.catholicnews.com/data/stories/cns/1100290.htm.

71. Denise Dresser, "A Painful Jolt for the Body Politics," *Los Angeles Times* (January 12, 1994). Juanita Darling, "With Chiapas Cease Fire, Political Fallout Begins," *Los Angeles Times* (January 14, 1994). Michael Lowy, "Sources and Resources of Zapatism," *Monthly Review* 49, no. 10 (March 1998): 1ff. Catherine Capellaro, "My Visit with the Bishop of Chiapas; Bishop Samuel Ruíz García; Interview," *Progressive* (November 1998), 26ff. J. C. Seymour, "Two-Hearted in Chiapas: After the Massacre; Relations between Indians of Chiapas, Mexico, and the Mexican Government," *Christian Century* (April 1, 1998), 333ff. James D. Cockcroft, *Mexico's Hope: An Encounter with Politics and History* (New York: Monthly Review Press, 1998), 221–22, 336. Andy Gutierrez, "Codifying the Past, Erasing the Future: NAFTA and the Zapatista Uprising of 1994," *West-Northwest Journal of Environmental Law & Policy* 14 (2008): 883–1703.

72. A History of Hispanic Achievement in America—Cesar Chavez, Cesar Chavez Foundation, http://www.chavezfoundation.org/_ cms.php?mode=view&b_code=001013000000000&b_no=472 &page=4&field=&key=&n=11.

73. Miriam J. Wells, *Strawberry Fields: Politics, Class, and Work in California Agriculture* (Ithaca, NY: Cornell University Press, 1996). David Bacon, "Fruits of Their Labor: In Steinbeck Country, the United Farm Workers Are Battling the Strawberry Growers in the Fields and in the Suites," *LA Weekly* (August 8, 1997).

74. Charles Nicodemus, "FBI Agents Get Training About Rights; Decree Ends 'Spying' Case Here," *Chicago Sun-Times* (December 15, 1997). The FBI admitted misconduct during its probe of CISPES, which sued the FBI in 1988. In March 1983, the FBI accepted unsubstantiated—later discredited—charges by an undercover informant who insisted that CISPES was providing financial support to Salvadoran terrorists. Court documents showed that the local FBI probe targeted dozens of Chicagoans through infiltration; analysis of phone, utility, and banking records; and other covert activities. "Olivares' Legacy," *Los Angeles Times* (March 1, 1994).

75. Little Central America LA—Pico Union/Salvadoran Culture, http://www.youtube.com/watch?v=ylAxy8xYXa0. Salvadoran Riots 1991 Mount Pleason [*sic*] Washington, D.C. Riots, http://www.youtube.com/watch?v=-gpjiUSRA38. José Cardenas, "State Official Tells Day Laborers How Laws Can Work for Them; Jobs: Exploitation All Too Common, Labor Commissioner José Millan Says in Outreach Program Held to Educate Workers," *Los Angeles Times* (June 30, 1998). Pamela Constable, "Central Americans Protest Uncertain Future Under Refugee Amnesty Program," *Washington Post* (October 23, 1994). Philip Pan, "Honorable Work or Illegal Activity? In Langley Park, It's 'Pupusa Ladies' vs. County Agencies, with Latino Officers Caught in Middle," *Washington Post* (August 24, 1997). Lisa Leff, "Sacrifice Through Separation; Salvadoran Women Grieve for Children They Left Behind," *Washington Post* (March 31, 1994). Making pupusas at Chicago's Pupuseria Las Delicias, http://www.youtube.com/watch?v=qe96acRppe0&feature=related. Ana Patricia Rodríguez, *Dividing the Isthmus: Central American Transnational Histories, Literatures, and Cultures* (Austin: University of Texas Press, 2009), 184–85.

76. CAUSA, http://www.csun.edu/cas/causa.html. CSUN Central American Studies, http://www.csun.edu/catalog/centralamericanstudies.html.

77. National Association for Chicana/o Studies, History of NACCS, http://www.naccs.org/naccs/History.asp. Gary M. Stern, "TRENDS: Minority Students Outnumber Whites," *Hispanic Outlook in Higher Education* 6, no. 8 (1995): 6.

78. Dennis López, "Chicano/Latino Coalition for Educational Equity & English Learners of the Inland Empire Practical Issues in Serving Undocumented Immigrant Students," Latino Educational Advocacy Day @ CSU San Bernardino, March 29, 2010. "Undocumented Immigrant Students: A Very Brief Overview of Access to Higher Education in California," http://tcla.gseis.ucla.edu/reportcard/features/5-6/ab540/pdf/UndocImmigStud.pdf.

79. George Ramos, "UCLA Cuts in *Chicano Studies* Hit Education: Protests Have Spread off Campus to Involve Latino Leaders . . ." *Los Angeles Times* (January 9, 1991), 1. Chancellor Young told LA Times editor Frank del Olmo that there would never be a department as long as he was chancellor.

80. Larry Gordon, "*UCLA* Resists Forming *Chicano* Studies Department," *Los Angeles Times* (April 29, 1993), B1.

81. Larry Gordon and Marina Dundjerski, "Protesters Attack UCLA Faculty Center Education: Up to $50,000 in Vandalism Follows the University's Refusal to Elevate *Chicano studies* Program to Departmental Status. Police Arrest 90," *Los Angeles Times* (May 12, 1993), 1. Larry Gordon and Marina Dundjerski, "*UCLA* Has 2nd Day of Protest over Program," *Los Angeles Times* (May 13, 1993), B1. "UCLA Students Demand Chicano Studies Department," *San Francisco Chronicle* (May 13, 1993), A7. "Reassessment, Please, in UCLA Controversy: Rethinking *Chicano studies* Issue in Wake of Protest," *Los Angeles Times* (May 13, 1993), 6. Rodolfo F. Acuña, *The Making of Chicana/o Studies: In the Trenches of Academe* (New Brunswick: Rutgers University Press, 2011), 179–187.

82. "Chicano Studies Activists Begin Hunger Strike at UCLA," *Los Angeles Times* (May 26, 1993), 4. Mary Anne Perez, "A Hunger for Change Protest: Students from the Central City Join the Fight for Chicano Studies Department . . . " *Los Angeles Times* (June 6, 1993). Raymundo Paredes, "Chicano Studies at UCLA: A Controversy with National Implications," *Hispanic Outlook in Higher Education* 2, no. 3 (November 30, 1991): 10.

83. "A hunger strike ends, a center is born," UCLA History Project, June 7, 1993, http://www.uclahistoryproject.ucla.edu/Fun/ThisMonth_JunTent.asp. Semillas Community Schools, Winter 2008, http://www.dignidad.org/index.php?option=com_content&view=article&id=81&Itemid=55. Acuña, *Anything but Mexican*, chap. 12. Robert A. Rhoads, "'Immigrants in Our Own Land': The Chicano Studies Movement at UCLA," in *Freedom's Web: Student Activism in an Age of Cultural Diversity* (Baltimore, MD: Johns Hopkins Press, 1998), 61–94, http://orion.neiu.edu/~tbarnett/102/race.htm. Marcos Aguilar and Minnie Fergusson interviewed by Rodolfo F. Acuña (August 12, 2009) in El Sereno, California. The César Chávez Center has since achieved full department status. Marcos and Minnie continue to work in the community. They are the founders and directors of the Semilla Charter School, which teaches indigenous cultures along with Spanish, Nahuatl, and Mandarin. Routinely they are libeled by KABC Radio and other right-wing forces.

84. Rodolfo F. Acuña, "Forty Years of Chicana/o Studies: When the Myth Becomes a Legend," http://forchicanachicanostudies.wikispaces.com/Chicana+Chicano+Studies.

85. El Centro de La Raza, Transcript: El Centro de la Raza, NOW, PBS, http://www.pbs.org/now/transcript/transcript_laraza.html. The History of Chicano Park, San Diego, California, http://www.chicanoparksandiego.com/. Mexican Art in the Pilsen District of Chicago, http://artpilsen.blogspot.com/. Harry Gamboa, Chicano Art, http://www.harrygamboajr.com/.

86. Emma Pérez, *The Decolonial Imaginary: Writing Chicanas into History* (Bloomington: Indiana University Press, July 1, 1999), 20. Emma Pérez, "Queering the Borderlands: The Challenges of Excavating the Invisible and Unheard," *Frontiers: A Journal of Women Studies* 24, nos. 2 & 3 (2003): 122–31.

87. About Cherríe Moraga, http://www.cherriemoraga.com/index.php?option=com_content&view=section&layout=blog&id=5&Itemid=53.

88. The title "the Great" is used sparingly, as in the case of La Gran Lola Beltrán.

89. Borderlands/LaFrontera, http://www.youtube.com/watch?v=c2jvSN_-JS4. Gloria Anzaldúa, *Borderlands/La Frontera, The New Mestiza*, 3d ed. (San Francisco, CA: Aunt Lute Books, 2007). Gloria Anzaldua, http://almalopez.com/projects/ChicanasLatinas/anzalduagloria5.html.

90. Who is Richard Mellon Scaife? http://www.youtube.com/watch?v=km_yDCfDNn0. Behind The Veil: America's Anti-Immigration Network, http://www.youtube.com/watch?v=qpiq1nAK4a0. Make Coors pay for funding racism! Defend Affirmative Action Defend the Victory in *Grutter v. Bollinger!* http://www.bamn.com/boycott-coors/. Codewords of Hate, http://www.youtube.com/watch?v=5kCpoXbCpqQ&feature=related. Stefancic and Delgado, *No Mercy*, name most of the early benefactors.

91. "A Look at the Forces Behind the Anti-Immigrant Movement," Democracy Now, http://www.democracynow.org/2007/5/2/a_look_at_the_forces_behind. Excerpt James Crawford, "Hispanophobia," Chapter 6, in *Hold Your Tongue: Bilingualism and the Politics of "English Only"* (Reading, MA: Addison Wesley, 1993), http://www.languagepolicy.net/archives/HYTCH6.htm. An important work in understanding the extent of the new-rights' financing of the "culture war" is Stefanic and Delgado's *No Mercy*. Alexander Cockburn, "In Honor of Charlatans and Racist," *Los Angeles Times* (November 3, 1994). Nina J. Easton, "Linking Low IQ to Race, Poverty Sparks Debate," *Los Angeles Times* (October 30, 1994). Richard Hernstein and Charles Murray, *The Bell Curve: Intelligence and Class Structure in American Life* (New York: Free Press, 1994).

92. Laura C. Scanlan, "Hopwood v. Texas: A Backward Look at Affirmative Action in Education," *New York University Law Review*, 71, no. 6 (1996): 1580–1633. Lawrence S. Wrightsman, *Judicial Decision Making: Is Psychology Relevant?* (Springer 1999), 29–30.

93. Wilson's Re-Election Ads on Illegal Immigration, http://www.youtube.com/watch?v=o0f1PE8Kzng&feature=related. Barbara Sellgren, "California's Proposition 187: A Painful History Repeats Itself," *U.C. Davis Journal of International Law & Policy*, 1 (1995): 153–331. Richard D. Lamm and Robert Hardway, "Pro 187 Opposition Has Origins in Racism," *Daily News* (November 22, 1994). Patrick J. McDonnell, "March Just 1st Step, Latino Leaders Vow," *Los Angeles Times* (June 4, 1994). Ed Mendel, "Voters Still Favor Pro 187 but Field Poll Finds Latinos Split on Issue," *San Diego Union-Tribune* (September 27, 1994). Paul Feldman, "Times Poll: Pro 187 Is Still Favored Almost 2 to 1," *Los Angeles Times* (October 15, 1994). Howard Breuer, "Voters Approve Pro 187, Lawsuits to Follow," *Los Angeles Daily News* (November 9, 1994). John Dart, "187 Shows Clergy's Weak Influence on Electorate," *Los Angeles Times* (November 19, 1994).

94. Acuña, *Sometimes There Is No Other Side,* chap. 1. Juan González, "In Washington, Latino Chorus Lifts Its Voice," *New York Daily News* (October 15, 1996). Amy Pyle, Patrick J. McDonnell, and Hector Tobar, "Latino Voter Participation Doubled Since '94 Primary," *Los Angeles Times* (June 4, 1998). Patrick J. McDonnell and George Ramos, "Latino Voters Had Key Role in Some States . . . ." *Dallas Morning News* (November 10, 1996). Linda O. Valenty and Ronald D. Sylvia, "Thresholds for Tolerance: The Impact of Racial and Ethnic Population Composition on the Vote for California Propositions 187 and 209," *Social Science Journal* 41, no. 3 (2004): 433–46.

95. Pyle et al., "Latino Voter Participation." McDonnell and Ramos, "Latino Voters." Dave Lesher and Mark Z. Barabak, "Gubernatorial Hopefuls Hold Landmark Forum . . . ," *Los Angeles Times* (May 24, 1998). Jeffrey L. Rabin, "Elusive Univision Chairman Spreads Wealth Around in Gubernatorial Race," *Los Angeles Times* (March 2, 2001); the chair of Univision was A. Jerrold Perenchio, an Italian American. He donated $1.5 million to defeat 227. However, he also donated $1,040,000 in support of vouchers for private schools, and $425,000 to support school board members for the L.A. school districts who were on a slate supported by L.A.'s former Republican mayor, Richard Riordan. A Proposition 227 Story, http://www.youtube.com/watch?v=TQwKrz_6dRY.

96. Center for Latin American, Caribbean, and Latino Studies: Latino Population of the U.S. Data Bases, Census 2000, http://web.gc.cuny.edu/lastudies/census2000data/Latinodatabases.htm.

97. The Hispanic Population: Census 2000 Brief (May 2001), http://www.census.gov/prod/2001pubs/c2kbr01-3.pdf. "Latino-Origin Populations Revisited: Estimating the Latino-Origin Group Populations at the National Level and for Selected States, Counties, Cities, and Metro Chicago," Research Reports, Vol 2005.1, Inter-University Program for Latino Research, see http://latinostudies.nd.edu/publications/.

98. Diane G. Thomas, "Hispanic Voter Project at Johns Hopkins University," http://learningtogive.org/papers/paper242.html. Antonio Gonzalez, The Rise of the California Latino Vote, Willie Velasquez Institute, www.wcvi.org/data/election/PR_021108_CALatinoVote.doc.

99. Jodi Wilgoren, "California and the West; Sanchez Elated as Probe Is Dropped . . . ," *Los Angeles Times* (February 5, 1998). Roxanne Roberts, "House Mates Loretta and Linda Sanchez Are Congress's First Sister Act . . . ," *Washington Post* (December 11, 2002). Phil García, "Latino Voters Showing Strength," *Sacramento Bee* (November 14, 1996). Anthony York, "Latino Politics," *California Journal* (April 1, 1999). Hugo Martin, "Power of Polanco Evident in Alarcón's Victory . . . ," *Los Angeles Times* (June 22, 1998).

100. John P. Schmal, "The Tejano Struggle For Representation," Hispanics in Government, Houston Institute for Culture, http://www.houstonculture.org/hispanic/tejano4.html. R. G. Ratcliffe, "Congressional Fate in Hands of Court/Democratic Judge Has Until Oct. 1 to Rule on State Redistricting Plans," *Houston Chronicle* (September 23, 2001). Eduardo Porter, "Hispanics Seek Increased Representation, and Republicans are Very Eager to Help," *Wall Street Journal* (April 2, 2001).

101. Dane Schiller, "Castro Upholds Family's Involvement Tradition," *San Antonio Express-News* (May 6, 2001).

102. Illinois Hispanic Population as a Percentage of Total Population (2012), Illinois Hispanic Population as a Percentage of Total Population (2000). Pam Belluck, "Chicago Reverses 50 Years of Declining Population," *New York Times* (March 15, 2001).

103. Georgia Pabst, "La Raza Meeting to Draw 12,000," *Milwaukee Journal Sentinel* (July 8, 2001), 1B. Danielle Gordon and Natalie Pardo, "Hate Crimes Strike Changing Suburbs," *Chicago Reporter* (September 1997). Manuel Galvan, "Hispanics in Chicago from Central America Take First Steps to Political Empowerment," http://www.lib.niu.edu/1993/ii931134.html. Juan Andrade, "Latinos Must Beware of Redistricting," *Chicago Sun-Times* (January 4, 2002). Rick Pearson, "Latinos Seek More Power in Remap," *Chicago Tribune* (Internet Edition, July 25, 2001). "State Profile—Illinois" http://www.cnn.com/ALLPOLITICS/1996/states/IL/IL00.shtml. The Chicago Reporter, 2001 Back Issues, http://www.chicagoreporter.com/issue/index.php?y=2001. Nacho González, "Latino Politics in Chicago," *CENTRO: Journal of the Center for Puerto Rican Studies* 2, no. 5 (1990): 47–57. "Gentrification in West Town: Contested Ground," University of Illinois at Chicago, Nathalie Voorhees Center of Neighborhood and Community Improvement (September 2001), http://www.uic.edu/cuppa/voorheesctr/Publications/Gentrification%20in%20West%20Town%202001.pdf.

104. Jerry Garcia, "History of Latinos in the Northwest," https://www.k12.wa.us/CISL/pubdocs/HistoryLatinoPacificNorthwest.pdf. Nikole Hannah-Jones, "Oregon's 2010 Census Shows Striking Latino and Asian Gains," *The Oregonian* (February 23, 2011), http://www.oregonlive.com/pacific-northwest-news/index.ssf/2011/02/2010_census.html.

105. Washington County Selection Map, U.S. Census Bureau, http://quickfacts.census.gov/qfd/maps/washington_map.html.

106. Carlos Arnaldo Schwantes, *The Pacific Northwest: An Interpretive History*, Revised and Enlarged ed., (Lincoln: University of Nebraska Press, 1996), 6, 450. Gonzalo Guzmán, Wapato—Its History and Hispanic Heritage, HistoryLink.org 7937, September 16, 2006, http://www.historylink.org/index.cfm?DisplayPage=output.cfm&file_id=7937. Mexican Americans in the Columbia Basin, Washington State University, http://www.vancouver.wsu.edu/crbeha/ma/ma.htm. Chicano/Latino Archive, Evergreen State College Library, http://chicanolatino.evergreen.edu/introduction_en.php.

107. Florangela Davila, "Spanish Definitely Spoken Here: State's Hispanics Gain Numbers, Clout," *Seattle Times* (Online, March 26, 2001). U.S. Census Bureau, Grant County, Census 2000 PHC-T-10, Hispanic or Latino Origin for the United States, Regions, Divisions, States, and for Puerto Rico: 2000. Florangela Davila and Susan Gilmore, "Big Racial Gap Remains in State Homeownership," *Seattle Times* (Online, July 16, 2001). Stuart Eskenazi, Justin Mayo, and Tom Boyer, "Seattle Behind Other Cities When It Comes to Diversity," *Seattle Times* (Online, March 31, 2001). Steve Suo, "Oregon Surge Has Mexican Roots," *Oregonian* (Portland, May 10, 2001).

108. Oregon County Selection Map, http://quickfacts.census.gov/qfd/maps/oregon_map.html.

109. Latinos in Salem, http://www.salemhistory.net/people/latinos.htm. Modern Society in the Pacific Northwest: The Second World War as Turning Point, http://www.washington.edu/uwired/outreach/cspn/Website/Classroom%20Materials/Pacific%20Northwest%20History/Lessons/Lesson%2020/20.html. Oregon State University, Bracero Collection, http://library.state.or.us/repository/2008/200805231544055. Gosia Wozniacka, "Hispanic Surge Is Reshaping Oregon," *Oregonian* (May 13, 2009), OregonLive.com, http://www.oregonlive.com/washingtoncounty/index.ssf/2009/05/2008_census_estimates_hispanic.html. Robert Bussel, ed., *Understanding the Immigrant Experience in Oregon: Research, Analysis, and Recommendations from University of Oregon Scholars* (Eugene: University of Oregon, [No Year]), http://library.state.or.us/repository/2008/200805231544055/index.pdf. Lynn Stephen, "Globalization, the State, and the Creation of Flexible Indigenous Workers: Mixtec Farmworkers in Oregon," The Center for Comparative Immigration Studies, University of California, San Diego, Working Paper 36, April 2001, http://escholarship.org/uc/item/4wd691zw.

110. Idaho County Selection Map, http://quickfacts.census.gov/qfd/maps/idaho_map.html.

111. Errol D. Jones, Invisible People: Mexicans in Idaho history, http://web1.boisestate.edu/research/history/issuesonline/fall2005_issues/1f_mexicans.html. Mexicans figured in Idaho events of Frontier Days, Idaho Digital Resources, http://idahodocs.cdmhost.com/cdm/singleitem/collection/p4012coll2/id/103. Amando Alvarez, The Mexican Experience in Idaho, http://www.angelfire.com/journal2/luz/cuentos04.htm. Idaho History, Raices, http://raices2.obiki.org/approach/cluster_sites/idaho.html.

112. David Rosenzweig, "Judges Asked to Postpone Voting in 4 House Districts . . . ," *Los Angeles Times* (November 1, 2001). Thomas B. Edsall, "A Political Fight to Define the Future; Latinos at Odds over California's Two New Democratic Congressional Districts," *Washington Post* (October 31, 2001). Carl Ingram, "Davis OKs Redistricting That Keeps Status Quo . . . ," *Los Angeles Times* (September 28, 2001). Frank del Olmo, "Getting away with a Blatant Gerrymander for the Record," *Los Angeles Times* (June 16, 2002).

113. Ambika Kapur, "Encouraging the Latino Vote," *Carnegie Reporter* 1, no. 3 (Fall 2001): http://carnegie.org/publications/carnegie-reporter/single/view/article/item/38/. Richard Gonzales, "Where Are the Latino Office Holders?" *Fort Worth Star-Telegram* (December 9, 2001).

114. Stuart Eskenazi, "150 Years of Seattle History: Familiar Landscape Lured Scandinavians," *Seattle Times* (Online, November 4, 2001). Robin Fields and Ray Herndon, "Segregation of a New Sort Takes Shape; Census: In a Majority of Cities, Asians and Latinos Have Become More Isolated from Other Racial Groups," *Los Angeles Times* (July 5, 2001). Gordy Holt, "Hetle Again Spurns Shooting Review; But Bellevue Officer Meets Arbitrator on Another Matter," *Seattle Post-Intelligencer* (January 11, 2002).

115. T. Christian Miller, "Race Issues Raised in Latest Texas Death Penalty Appeal," *Los Angeles Times* (June 29, 2000).

116. Rakesh Kochhar, Roberto Suro, and Sonya Tafoya, "The New Latino South: The Context and Consequences of Rapid Population Growth," Pew Hispanic Center (July 26, 2005), http://pewhispanic.org/reports/report.php?ReportID=50. "U.S.-Born Hispanics Increasingly Drive Population Developments," Pew Hispanic Center, http://pewhispanic.org/files/factsheets/2.pdf.

CHAPTER 16

Losing Fear: Decade of Struggle and Hope

LEARNING OBJECTIVES

- Discuss the chapter title, "Losing Fear: Decade of Struggle and Hope."

- Analyze the impact of the Afghanistan and Iraq wars on Mexican Americans.

- Show how the economy contributed to a backlash to Mexican/Latino immigration.

- Describe how the dramatic growth in the Mexican/Latin American population in the United States changed the politics of the group.

- Interpret the changes in the attitudes of Latino immigrants by 2012.

- Analyze the importance of the Dream Act movement.

- Compare the impact of past right-wing movements on Chicanas/os to that at the beginning of the twenty-first century.

The timeline tells us that we have passed through the first decade of the twenty-first century and gone beyond. Events are fresh in our memory: George W. Bush's reelection in 2004, Barack Obama's historic election in 2008 and reelection in 2012, the 9/11 terrorist attacks, the Middle Eastern wars, and the economic crisis beginning in 2008. It is difficult to be objective since most of us have not only lived through the decade, but we have developed strong views and attachments. As mentioned in the previous chapter, the closeness to the events blurs our judgment—much like when we hold a dime too close to our eye and the only thing we can see is the dime. Concentrating too much on the present makes us forget the past. We fail to learn from the mistakes of our parents—history teaches us a lot but we refuse to learn. This is unfortunate: just think of the number of inept decisions that we could have avoided. Perhaps if we had learned from our errors in Vietnam, we could have avoided the current wars in the Middle East. Could the present economic crisis have been averted? Who's to blame? Was it George W. Bush, Bill Clinton, or Ronald

| 2001 | 2002 | 2003 | 2004 | 2005 | 2006 | 2007 | 2008 | 2009 | 2010 | 2011 | 2012 |

Reagan? The purpose of timelines is to help us find answers by putting these events into context. What we are doing is moving that dime away from our eye so we can see the bigger picture.

When Numbers Count

The Latino population in 2011 numbered an estimated 52 million—a growth of over a million a year.[1] In California alone Latinos numbered 14 million. Texas followed with 9.7 million, Florida with 4.2 million, New York with 3.4 million, and Illinois with 1.2 million. The U.S. Latino population grew by 43 percent from 2000 to 2010, four times the national growth rate; Latinos comprised 26.3 percent of the population younger than age one.[2] An estimated two-thirds to 70 percent of these totals are of Mexican origin. The numbers were significant in the presidential elections of 2008 and 2012. Add the fact that in 2012, Latinos were concentrated in three states with large Electoral College votes: California (55), Texas (38), and Florida (29). In the first two states, the Mexican-origin population reached a plurality of the total state population; that is, larger than any other ethnic or national-origin group.

The growth of this population caught politicians and educators off guard. In 1990, the Mexican American population alone was projected at 13,174,000, only 1.5 million shy of all Latinos counted in 1980. Latinos account for over half the nation's population growth (50.5 percent). The Census Bureau has projected that by 2050 the U.S. population will climb to 438 million, and the Latino population will triple to 29 percent of the U.S. population with whites comprising 47 percent.[3] By that year, Latinos will be the largest school-age population in the country.[4] The immensity of the U.S. Latino and Mexican American population is demonstrated in Table 16.1.

If U.S. Latinos were a nation, they would be the third largest Latin American country—the second largest Spanish-speaking nation in the world. The U.S. Latino population would be larger than that of either Spain or Argentina. U.S. Mexicans alone would be the sixth largest Latin American nation and the fifth largest Spanish-speaking nation. It would seem reasonable that the American academy entrusted with the search for the truth would want to study the group—if for no other reason but to learn its impact on the nation's identity. It cannot be assumed that 50 years from now most Americans will be homogenized and that

TABLE 16.1 Populations of Selected Latin American and Spanish-Speaking Nations

Brazil	199,321,413 (July 2012 est.)
Mexico	114,975,406 (July 2012 est.)
U.S. Latinos	**50.5 million (2010)**
Colombia	45,239,079 (July 2012 est.)
Spain	47,042,984 (July 2012 est.)
Argentina	42,192,494 (July 2012 est.)
U.S. Mexican Origin	**34,000,000 (est.)**
Peru	29,549,517 (July 2012 est.)
Venezuela	28,047,938 (July 2012 est.)
Chile	17,067,369 (July 2012 est.)
Ecuador	15,223,680 (July 2012 est.)
Guatemala	14,099,032 (July 2012 est.)
Honduras	8,296,693 (July 2012 est.)
El Salvador	6,090,646 (July 2012 est.)
Nicaragua	5,727,707 (July 2012 est.)
Uruguay	3,316,328 (July 2012 est.)

Source: *CIA: The World Fact Book*, https://www.cia.gov/library/publications/the-world-factbook/docs/profileguide.html.

Mexicans will go the way of Italian Americans. (Look at the maps: where is Italy and where is Mexico? What does location tell you?) This is a very threatening proposition to many white people—everyone, according to them, should want to meet the white-male norm. Since the creation of the nation of the United States of America, white-male values have been the standard. That is why some white senators reacted so irrationally when they learned what Judge Sonia Sotomayor said: "I would hope that a wise Latina woman with the richness of her experiences would more often than not reach a better conclusion than a white male who hasn't lived that life." The reason it was so controversial is that it challenges the accepted truth.

How Else Can You Teach Them a Lesson?

There are contradictions in society that the student must deal with. Comedian Mort Sahl, for instance, said of capital punishment: Sure, execute them, "how else could you teach them a lesson?" As of January 1, 2009, there were 376 Latinos sitting on death row. California and Texas led the pack. In the Golden State, 148 of the 678 prisoners on death row were Latinos, in Texas, 104 of 358. It surprises many people to learn that this is one of the longest-standing civil rights controversies between Mexicans and the law. Studies have found that the race of the victim is a determining factor in a decision to sentence a defendant either to death or to life in prison. Realizing this and the fallibility of the court system, New Mexico Governor Bill Richardson signed a law that abolished the death penalty. Supreme Court Justice John Paul Stevens, who was among the Supreme Court justices reinstating the death penalty in 1976, in 2008 called it "anachronistic." But the truth is that the death penalty plays a role similar to that of horror films in white suburbia—they alleviate society's fears of the inner city. According to Amnesty International, in 1999, the United States—along with China, Congo, Iran, and Saudi Arabia—accounted for 85 percent of the world's executions. Because a disproportionate number of Latinos are poor and young, the death penalty also disproportionately affects them. Occasionally, a defendant successfully challenged the system, as in the case of Manuel Salazar, a young Chicano on death row in Illinois whose sentence for the 1984 murder of a white Joliet police officer was overturned. A new jury found Salazar guilty of involuntary manslaughter in the case, and he was freed because he had served more than twice the sentence for that charge.[5]

In January 2000, Republican Governor of Illinois George Ryan declared a moratorium on executions. The fact that Illinois had exonerated 13 death-row inmates since 1976 shook the conservative governor's faith in the fairness of the system. A case that weighed in his decision was that of Rolando Cruz, whom the state freed after 12 years on the Illinois death row for the 1983 murder and rape of a 10-year-old girl. Cruz and Alejandro Hernández were charged with the murder of the small girl—although police had arrested a repeat sex offender and murderer named Brian Dugan, who confessed to the crime. DNA testing linked Dugan to the crime. At Cruz's first trial, an expert claimed that she could tell a person's class and race by shoe imprints. At the third trial in 1995, a police officer admitted that he had lied when he testified that Cruz had confessed to a "vision" about the girl's murder. The judge declared Cruz not guilty. An investigation led to criminal charges against the authorities that prosecuted Cruz, and resulted in the identification of the actual killer.[6]

Texas and Virginia accounted for almost half of all executions in the United States. During his term as governor of Texas, George W. Bush, the "compassionate conservative," refused to grant stays of execution in death penalty cases riddled with evidence of racial bias. When the Republican presidential candidate was asked how he could be so certain that in all of the executions the defendants were guilty, he replied that nothing like what happened in Illinois had happened on his watch: "I'm confident of the guilt of the person who committed the crime." (Bush presided over more than 135 executions, a record for any governor in U.S. history.) The Chicago Tribune cast doubt on Bush's statement, and its investigative reporters found that of the 131 death-row executions in Texas under Governor George W. Bush, 43 were the result of trials using defense attorneys who were publicly sanctioned for misconduct, either before or after their work on the cases. Forty of the executions involved trials during which the defense attorneys presented no evidence or only one witness during the sentencing phase. Twenty-nine cases included testimony by psychiatrists whom the American Psychiatric Association categorized as unethical and untrustworthy. Twenty-three included jailhouse informants, who were considered among the least credible of witnesses. Twenty-three included visual hair analysis, which has consistently been proved unreliable. Incidentally, Texas ranked 40th among states in money spent for indigent defense.[7]

Between 1992 and 1997, 47 states passed laws making it easier to try children as adults. Of the 38 death penalty states, 19 sanction the execution of 16- and 17-year-olds and 4 permit the execution of those aged 17 and older. In 1988, the U.S. Supreme Court held that executing children under the age of 16 violated the Eighth Amendment's ban against "cruel and unusual punishment." This ruling has recently been challenged. Former Governor Pete Wilson, the architect of California's Proposition 21, which passed in 2000, said that the age for the death penalty should be lowered to 14; Texas legislator Jim Pitts proposed lowering of the age to 11.The Bureau of Justice Statistics reports that the number of youths under the age of 17 committed to adult prisons has more than doubled, rising from 3,400 in 1985 to 7,400 in 1997. Two-thirds of the youths in the juvenile system nationally are minorities; African American youth make up 62 percent, although they comprise only 17 percent of U.S. youths.[8] In 2009, the Bureau of Justice Statistics reported that approximately 2,778 youth under age 18 were held in in adult state prisons.[9] However, by 2007, national opinion was shifting, and the U.S. Supreme Court in a 5-4 ruling abolished the execution of anyone convicted of murder who was 17 years or younger when the crime was committed. In that year more than 70 people sat on death rows for committing capital crimes when they were 16 or 17.

Mexican Americans and 9/11

On September 11, 2001, 19 al-Qaeda operatives hijacked four commercial passenger airliners and crashed two of them into the Twin Towers of the World Trade Center in New York City, which collapsed within two hours. The third airliner was crashed into the Pentagon in Arlington, Virginia, and the fourth plane into a field in rural Somerset County, Pennsylvania. The attacks claimed 2,974 lives in addition to the 19 hijackers. The United States retaliated and launched a "War on Terrorism."

On October 7, 2001, the United States, supported by a handful of NATO nations including the United Kingdom and Australia, invaded Afghanistan under Operation Enduring Freedom. The invasion was allegedly launched to capture Osama bin Laden, the leader of al-Qaeda accused of being the architect of the September 11, 2001, attacks. In March 2003, a U.S.-led "coalition of the willing" invaded Iraq; the pretext was that Iraq had weapons of mass destruction, which ploy was later proved to have been manufactured. It was alleged that there were ties between al-Qaeda and Iraqi leader Saddam Hussein—this was proven to be untrue.

These wars had a devastating impact on the Mexican American and Latino communities and almost bankrupted the country. From 2003 to 2012, the total cost for wars in Iraq, Afghanistan, and Pakistan was at least $3.2 to $4 trillion in direct and indirect costs. As with the Vietnam War, many of the first casualties were Chicanos and Latinos, many of whom were not citizens. Indeed, some 37,000 of the combat troops held only green cards. Latinos made up 27 percent of all Marine fatalities in Iraq, although they comprised 14 percent of the Corps. California contributed nearly one of every three green-card soldiers. In some Los Angeles neighborhoods, Army and Marine recruiters estimated that 50 percent of the enlistee pool were not citizens.[10]

The trillions of dollars spent on the wars was diverted from much-needed projects such as education and the rebuilding of a crumbling infrastructure and an economy that has been made even more dependent on Chinese loans. Programs such as Bush's "No Child Left Behind" mandated the so-called reforms, but lacked proper funding support. The wars suppressed reasonable discussion of issues such as immigration.

President Bush, before the attacks, was open to this dialogue on immigration reform, despite opposition from his party's racist nativist agenda. Bush might have been incompetent, but he was not a racist. Regrettably most Americans believed that the nation's problems could be solved by wearing a flag pin. Indeed, they were not prepared to sacrifice, and taxes on the rich were lowered during time of war, putting the wars on a credit card. It also gave voice to racist nativist commentators and fearmongers such as Lou Dobbs, Pat Buchanan, and the former Republican congressman from Colorado Thomas Gerard Tancredo, all of whom scapegoated the immigrant.[11]

Because of the Vietnam experience, the middle class resisted and still resists the military draft—and volunteers, heavily recruited from poor areas, are increasingly fighting these wars. At first the all-volunteer army consisted mostly of men and women who joined the armed forces or the National Guard in peacetime. Minorities made up about 30 percent of the United States population and 35 percent of the armed forces. In order to fight sustained wars, it was evident that larger numbers of Latinos would have to be recruited. In 2000, the median age of Americans (including minorities) was about 36 years. The U.S. Census in 2000 reported the median age of Latinos as 25.9 years, and that of the Mexican-origin population as 24.3 years. (In the event of a prolonged war, half the Latino population would be eligible for the armed forces.) In 2010, the median age for Latinos was 27 years while the median age for the U.S. population was 37 years; for Mexicans, 25 years, Puerto Ricans, 27 years, and Guatemalans, 27 years.[12]

As the war became more unpopular, Latinos for a time were the recruits of choice.[13] Between 2001 and 2005, Army recruitment among Latinos rose by 26 percent. By 2006, Latinos comprised 11 percent of enlisted men; Latinas were 12 percent of enlisted women; they constituted 4.8 percent and 5.3 percent respectively of the commissioned officers. They made up 15 percent of the Marine Corps and 6 percent of the Air Force. Statistics are deceiving, though: Latinos made up 16 percent of the workforce; however, excluding immigrants they comprised 8.2 percent of the qualified civilian workforce. All in all, although the military continued to recruit heavily among Latinas/os the results were not significant largely because of the failure of the education system to graduate Latinos, who continued to drop out in record numbers.[14] The Solomon Amendment was passed by the Republican-led Congress in 1996. It withheld federal funding from schools that did not provide adequate access to military recruiters.[15] The Solomon Amendment was an assault on the autonomy of institutions of higher learning, and its consequences went beyond Reserve Officers' Training Corps (ROTC) and military recruiting. In 1999, the Republican-controlled Congress set up the Student and Exchange Visa Program/Coordinated Interagency Project Regulating International Students to help track certain foreign students electronically. After 9/11, the Homeland Security on Research and Education Acts further curtailed civil liberties—often in secret. Because universities were whipped in line (they became part of the military–industrial complex), the government raised the issue of a security clearance for university administrators and professors.

Meanwhile, Section 9528 of the No Child Left Behind Act was passed on January 8, 2002, that included a section titled "Armed Forces Recruiter Access to Students and Student Recruiting Information," which says "each local educational agency receiving assistance under this Act shall provide," upon request of military recruiters, access to the high school students' names, addresses, and telephone listings.[16]

What is wrong with Latinos joining the service and bettering their education? First, only a few of the soldiers gain civilian-world skills. Second, the law undercuts the authority of some local school districts. In effect, the law makes school authorities snitches. Third, the military is not targeting students in the lower halves of their classes. It targets those who would normally be eligible for a college education but, because of economic disadvantages, find attractive the illusions pressed by the military.

If the area of conflict gets expanded in the future, who will pay and who will fight the wars? It is no secret that the so-called Red states that voted for Bush were the most hawkish on the war. However, of the 18 Blue states who voted against Bush and were either against the war or lukewarm, 14—or more than three-quarters—paid more taxes to the federal government than they got back. Of the 32 Red states, only 12 states paid more than they got back. Thus, only 37 percent of the Red states are not losers in terms of taxes paid. In 2002, California's share of the nation's $6.2 trillion debt was 14.2 percent; New York was second with $145 billion. California received 78 cents in federal payments and services for every dollar sent to Washington. In the fiscal year 2003, the states that benefited most from the federal government were New Mexico, which received $1.99 in federal handouts for every $1.00 it sent to Washington; Alaska, $1.89; Mississippi, $1.83; and West Virginia, $1.82. It should be noted that all of these were Red states in 2004. The lowest beneficiaries were New Jersey with 57 cents; New Hampshire, 64 cents; Connecticut, 65 cents; Minnesota and Nevada, 70 cents; Illinois, 73 cents; and California and Massachusetts, 78 cents. All except Nevada were Blue states. The Blue states paid some $82 billion for a war that most of their residents probably did not support. As of May 2004, the Red states contributed $49.1 billion to the Iraq War. Just the states of California, New York, Illinois, New Jersey, and Washington paid $51.5 billion for the war, $2.4 billion more than the 32 free-loading Red states. The plot thickens when you consider that California and New York, which are paying a large portion of these war costs, have only four senators between them versus 64 senators in the Red states.[17]

Coming back to the draft, let us look at the 10- to 15-year-old pool. According to the outdated 2000 U.S. Census, California had a pool of almost 3 million Latinos in the age group of 10–24 years—this includes females as well—or 41 percent of the California pool. This number is all the more significant because the Latino population growth from 2000 to 2010 doubled. By 2012 Latinos comprised 38.2 percent of the California pool of 38,041,430. The Texas Latino portion was also 38.2 percent of the total 26,059,203 pool in that state. Arizona Latinos were 30.2 percent of the total pool of 6,553,255. New Mexico Latinos were 47 percent of a total pool of 2,085,538. The Latino populations in these states were at least 10 years younger that the median age of white citizens. California's Latino community itself would potentially contribute more draftees than Red states Alaska, Arkansas, Idaho, Georgia, Iowa, Montana, Nebraska, North Dakota, South Dakota, West Virginia, and Wyoming combined. Factoring in the growth of the Latino population nationally, this portrait becomes grimmer.[18]

The costs of the wars need to be evaluated from various angles. For instance, could the monies spent on wars be better spent on programs that will ameliorate and eventually wipe out poverty? Latinos who have or do not have documents pay taxes—federal, state, and local. Moreover, military recruitment competes with college recruiters. What also has to be computed is the damage done to the Constitution by the hysteria and passage of the Patriot Act, which was signed into law on October 26, 2001. In his first term, President Barack Obama did not correct the threats to the Constitution caused by the hysteria. The American Civil Liberties Union (ACLU) underscores its threat:

> There are significant flaws in the Patriot Act, flaws that threaten your fundamental freedoms by giving the government the power to access to your medical records, tax records, information about the books you buy or borrow without probable cause, and the power to break into your home and conduct secret searches without telling you for weeks, months, or indefinitely.[19]

Indeed, under the guise of Homeland Security the Latino community was put under siege. Even in normal circumstances, the Mexican-origin community suffers from the excesses of the border patrol. The Homeland Security Act of 2002 authorized the U.S. Immigration and Customs Enforcement (ICE) agency, which has the duty of identifying, and investigating possible violations of 400 federal statutes within the United States and has attachés at major U.S. embassies overseas much the same as the Central Intelligence Agency has. ICE supposedly protects the United States and upholds public safety. It is the second largest contributor to the Joint Terrorism Task Force. Besides criminal investigation, protection of federal buildings within the United States also comes under ICE's purview. It is ICE with this War-on-Terror mentality that conducts raids on undocumented workers and sweeps workplaces throughout the country.

Raids have taken on a Special Weapons and Tactics (SWAT) Team aura, and often children are afraid to go to school fearing that they will return to a home without parents. In places such as San Francisco, communities have organized to prevent abuses. A good part of the work of the Equal Justice Society and the San Francisco Immigrant Legal and Education Network has been devoted to this pursuit. "Last September [2008], Fugitive Operations Teams made more than 1,157 arrests, including 436 in northern California. Twenty percent of those in custody had criminal histories and were in the country illegally, according to ICE." The agency can and does racially profile and is empowered to make raids on homes without warrants. Often citizens such as Hector Véloz, 37, of Los Angeles get caught in the raids: "My case was so ironic," said Véloz. "I am a U.S. citizen, but was held for 13 months and placed on deportation procedure. Because the prison is in Arizona and my family lives in California, I didn't see my son Gerónimo even once in those 13 months." Véloz had been picked up for receiving stolen property and had served six months. He showed ICE his birth certificate but the authorities did not bother to investigate; he had no right to counsel and was released only because of the involvement of Amnesty International and immigrant rights groups.[20]

As we shall see, currently Democrats are pushing for immigration reform. It seems as if they have marginal support from Republican congressional representatives. The reason for this sudden shift is the growth of the Latino population, primarily Mexican-origin people. As in the case of California, a Republican running for national office will have a difficult time being elected without a significant portion of Latino votes.

The Stairway to Heaven: Electoral Politics

The proportion of immigrant Latinos applying to become naturalized citizens rose during the first years of the twenty-first century to 52 percent by 2010. This increased the pool of Latino voters, who were generally young voters compared to their white counterparts. Most spoke Spanish, but English was their primary language. In 2012, "According to the Pew Hispanic survey, seven-in-ten (70%) Hispanic registered voters say they identify with or lean toward the Democratic Party while 22% say the same about the Republican Party. In the November 2000 election, an estimated 5.9 million Latinos voted, comprising 5 percent of the total vote." In 2012, the Washington Post reported: "Hispanics make up 17 percent of voters; they were 15 percent in 2008. Among all Hispanics, President Obama leads 60 to 39 percent. Among non-Cuban Hispanics, he leads Mitt Romney 68 to 32 percent."[21] A gap exists between voting potential and actual turnout of an overwhelmingly young population. However, the gap is closing and more Latinos are getting elected in state and local races.

In 1998 Latinos were a majority minority in the City of Los Angeles. By 2013 Latinos had elected four Latinos to the City Council, among them the first Latina, Nury Martínez.[22] Throughout California voters elected Latinos to city governments and school boards; it was a trend that had accelerated in the 1990s when Latinos elected a critical mass in the state legislature and senate. The 1998 elections increased the number of Latino elected officials in the state legislature to 24, including a historic high of 4 Latino Republicans. That year Antonio Villaraigosa was elected speaker of the Assembly. Cruz Bustamante became lieutenant governor. The engineer of this growth was State Senator Richard Polanco, who was chair of the Latino Caucus. These gains did not come without pain.

By the 2000 Census, Latino elected officials had lost some momentum and some of the elected began to act like incumbents rather than part of a movement. This change was evident during the reapportionment triggered by the census. As a result, the Mexican American Legal Defense and Education Fund (MALDEF) sued the state over new election boundaries that would protect incumbents. The new boundaries were supported by 23 of the California's 26 Latino lawmakers—a deal that strengthened their election prospects. They defended their vote, calling MALDEF racially divisive and saying that elections were no longer about race. MALDEF responded "[MALDEF is] representing the interests of the Latino community, while Latino lawmakers are trying to 'protect themselves.'" State Senators Marta Escutia and Gloria Romero criticized MALDEF, defending the deal in the name of multiracial cooperation. "More and more, California is reaping the benefits of multiracial coalitions. The voice of Latinos in California is stronger because electoral politics and issues are no longer just about race." The Chicana senators failed to address how they were elected to office as well as the undemocratic outcome of the redistricting.[23]

There were other splits caused by Mexican American officeholders supporting white candidates largely to further their own career growth. In a few instances this appeared logical because the white or black candidate was the best choice. Term limits opened up local and state offices to Latinos, African Americans, and Asians, but office holding quickly became a game of musical chairs. Previously, incumbents stayed in office for life, and they were buoyed by corporate sponsors who contributed to their campaigns. The one positive thing that could be said of the old process was that incumbents learned their craft. Latino politicos under the old system were very skilled. Under the new system, the politicos are swept out of office about every eight years, so they spend the second half of their incumbency looking for a new office and donors. Money does the talking, and a race for a Los Angeles School Board membership costs over $200,000. For statewide elections the stakes are even higher, and building a constituency outside the Latino base often involves trading off the interests of Latinos in other districts by supporting candidates of another color. As mentioned in Chapter 15, such multiracial coalitions often result in the promotion of self-interest.[24]

Tejanos continued their infatuation with electoral politics. *Los Angeles Times* columnist Frank del Olmo commented:

> *Recently, former state Atty. Gen. Dan Morales, of San Antonio, and Tony Sanchez, a Laredo oilman and rancher, faced off in televised debates with a uniquely Tejano twist. The first hour was in English, the second in Spanish.*[25]

That spring, Texas Republican Congressman Tony Bonilla ran unopposed in the Republican primary; former Texas Secretary of State Henry Cuellar never stood a chance in the November election. It was clear that there were realignments in the political landscapes. In Texas, San Antonio was no longer the uncontested Mecca, with Latinos becoming the largest ethnic group in Houston and Dallas.

In November 2002, Texas Republican Governor Rick Perry beat his Democratic Party opponent Tony Sánchez by 18 points. Sánchez had spent $60 million of his personal fortune, which was estimated to be as high as $600 million. Amid controversy surrounding why Sánchez lost, mainstream pundits speculated that Sánchez did not excite Latino voters, which votes he needed in order to have a chance. Republicans claimed that Rick Perry received about 35 percent of the Latino vote; the Southwest Voter Registration Education Project disagreed, reporting that Perry received only 12 percent of the Latino vote. The truth is that many factors may have contributed to confusion among Latino voters. Many Latinos saw Sánchez more as a Republican than as a Democrat; many Chicano Democrats resented that he had been a heavy contributor to George W. Bush's candidacy; and some Latinos, as well as Texas liberals, did not like him because of his business dealings—including those with Enron. However, all said and done, the fact remains that more than 70 percent of white voters cast their ballot against Sánchez. The banker/oilman was the first Mexican American gubernatorial candidate in U.S. Texas, and evidently many people still remembered the Alamo.[26]

In 2002, Bill Richardson, a former ambassador to the United Nations, who had served on Bill Clinton's cabinet as secretary of energy, ran successfully for governor of New Mexico. Richardson had served for 15 years in the U.S. Congress before joining the Clinton administration. (In 2008, he would run unsuccessfully for President.) Neighboring Colorado elected Ken Salazar the junior senator from Colorado in January 2005. Salazar, who had been the state attorney general, was considered a moderate. President Barack Obama appointed him to the cabinet post of secretary of interior.[27]

Meanwhile, Latino numbers zoomed in the state of Washington; in 2002 the Latino population numbered 490,448, rising to 11.6 percent out of 6,830,038 residents by 2011. In the early part of the century, Antonio Ginatta, executive director of the Washington State Commission on Hispanic Affairs in Olympia, predicted, "It's just a matter of time before the Latino groups organize to exercise their political power." However, as elsewhere the road to power was difficult. In 2012 it was reported that while the Latino vote had grown in importance, representation remained at mid-1990 levels.[28] The rise in Latino numbers also revived a "dying South" where the percentage of growth led to increased national representation. "The Lone Star State's population swelled to 25,145,561 [in 2010], a 20.6 percent increase since 2000."[29] In 2011, 38.1 percent of Texas' population was Latino; it had 34 electoral votes, a growth of 2 since 2000. Similar changes were occurring elsewhere.

Between 2000 and 2010, the Old South grew at a clip of 9.8 to 19.3 percent. Much of this growth was spurred by the Latino population. The percentage of growth in Georgia was 16.8 from 2000 to 2002, and by 2011 9.1 percent of the state was Latino. A similar boost occurred in North Carolina (8.6 percent Latino), Kentucky (3.2 percent), South Carolina (5.3 percent), Virginia (8.2 percent), and Alabama (4.0 percent). Other states such as Mississippi benefited from heavy seasonal migration into the state. The Latino was the fastest-growing population sector in Oklahoma, where from 2000 to 2004 it increased by 24.4 percent, and by 2011 Latinos made up 9.2 percent of Oklahoma. Latino political successes lagged in these states considering the population, and the requirement for a "super majority" to elect Latinos was the rule of thumb.[30] Slowly, nativists were learning what Argentine President Domingo Faustino Sarmiento said in the nineteenth century, "To govern is to populate." An economy cannot be built on an aging population.

In 2003, Lieutenant Governor Cruz M. Bustamante made an unsuccessful bid for governor of California after the recall of Governor Gray Davis. Bustamante grew up south of Fresno, California. He had to drop out of college and make his way as a butcher. Along the way, he became an intern to the local congressman; returning to Fresno, he enrolled in the local state college and was active in MEChA, which advocated the recruitment of Latinos to the campus. During the campaign, although he was to the right of moderate, his opponents distorted the affiliation in the Chicano student organization and outrightly red-baited him. To his credit, he did not disavow the past as some of his Latino colleagues did. After a vicious campaign, he lost to Republican Arnold Schwarzenegger.[31]

In Arizona, Latinos comprised a quarter of the state's 5.5 million residents. The National Association of Latino Elected and Appointed Officials (NALEO) reported that there were 369 Latinos serving in elected offices in Arizona, which included school boards, city councils, boards of supervisors, the state legislature, and the U.S. Congress.[32] In 2003, Raúl M. Grijalva went to Washington to represent Arizona's seventh congressional district. Grijalva had been active in Tucson politics since his youth, serving on the local school board and as a consistent voice for educational reform. Grijalva's parents were farmworkers; his father had migrated into southern Arizona as a *bracero*. As a congressman, he is a favorite whipping boy of the racist nativists who accuse him of having been a member of MEChA and blame him for "terrorists" coming into the country.[33]

The 2004 presidential election was a milestone. Out of a U.S. population of 289,362,000, 41,300,000 were U.S. Latinos. Between 2000 and 2004, the U.S. Latino population had increased by 5.7 million, accounting for half of the population growth in the United States but only one-tenth of the increase in the total votes cast. Exit polls conducted for the Associated Press and television networks found that Bush in 2004 won 44 percent of the Latino vote, up from 35 percent in 2000. Kerry won 53 percent, down from 62 percent won by Democrat Al Gore four years earlier. One-third of "Hispanics" self-identified as born-again Christians, and nearly 20 percent listed moral values as their top issue, suggesting that in some areas they have more in common with Republicans than with Democrats. These religious conservatives supported Bush by more than a 3-to-1 margin. According to the William C. Velásquez Institute (WCVI), over 7.6 million Latinos went to the polls in 2004, up 1.6 million from the 2000 presidential election.[34]

The election of Antonio Villaraigosa as mayor of Los Angeles in 2005 was historic. Villaraigosa was the first Latino mayor of Los Angeles since 1872. The city had a total population of 3,845,541, nearly half of whom were Latinos. However, Los Angeles's influence included a metropolitan area twice that size. Villaraigosa came out of the liberal tradition of the Chicano community. Since his college years, he had been a member of MEChA and *CASA Hermandad Mexicana*, an organization for the protection of the foreign born. There was a world of difference between him and his opponent, James Hahn, who was conservative and was not above race baiting. Villaraigosa won handily. The African Americans who had supported Hahn in the previous election moved away from him when Hahn did not retain Los Angeles Chief of Police Bernard Parks, an African American.

In 2006, Latino voters continued to support Democratic congressional candidates over the Republican candidates by a margin of 63.0 percent to 33.2 percent. The latter was disappointing as it contradicted the class interests of most Latinos; in the 1950s the figure would have been 90 percent Democrat.[35] In places such as Chicago, where Mexicans shared space with Puerto Ricans and increasingly with other Latinos, the number of Latinos reached 1,722,843 residents and the Mexican-origin population stood at 1,357,353 or 78.79 percent of the Latino total. Puerto Ricans were next at 153,206 (8.89 percent). Eighty-nine percent of Latinos under the age of 18 were born in the United States compared to 37 percent of Latinos over the age of 18—a pattern recurring in most places. Some 200,000 Latinos did not have documents, and a third were not citizens. Much of the growth was in the Chicago suburbs.[36]

There was a dramatic growth of the Mexican-origin population in New York: the city's Latino population increased by 2.5 percent between 2006 and 2007, numbering 2.3 million in 2007. Puerto Ricans were the largest Latino group comprising about a third of the total. Dominicans were next at 602,093, or a quarter of the total, followed by Mexicans at 289,755. The Mexican population was the fastest-growing national group, increasing by 9.8 percent between 2006 and 2007—it had mushroomed by 57.7 percent since 2000. Most studies attributed the dramatic growth of the Mexican-origin population to high fertility rates; this may be one factor, but more compelling arguments are the proximity of the United States to Mexico, cheaper land transportation, the historic corridors of scores of years of migration, and the fact that Mexico has a much higher population than most other Latin American nations.[37]

The 2008 presidential election in many ways reminds one of the political strategies of Gore and Kerry; they professed to love Latinos but campaigned only in the larger electoral states and focused on Latinos where they represented the swing vote. The race was between Arizona Senator John McCain and Illinois Senator Barack Obama. Even in the primaries, the Latino vote was contested and split by Senator Hillary Clinton and Obama. Support varied according to age group. (Mexicans generally like to buy branded products.) In the November 2008 elections, 76.3 percent of the total 131 million people who voted were white, versus 12.1 percent black, 7.4 percent Latinos, and 2.5 percent Asians. Latinos supported Obama and Joe Biden over Republicans John McCain and Sarah Palin more than two to one overall. Latinos voted 56–41 percent for Obama even in McCain's home state of Arizona. In Illinois, Obama's home state, the Latino vote was 72–27 percent in favor of Obama. In battleground states, the Latino votes favoring Obama were: Colorado 61–39 percent, Florida 57–42, Michigan 65–33, Nevada 76–22, Pennsylvania 72–28, and Virginia 65–34. In the non-battleground states, Obama's Latino percentages were just as dramatic: California 74–23, New Mexico 69–30, New Jersey 78–21, Illinois 72–27, and Texas 63–35. Even Latino evangelicals supported Obama 57–43 percent. From all accounts, the Latino vote kept the immigration reform issue from becoming a football game.[38]

In 2009 Congresswoman Hilda Solis (D-CA) was appointed secretary of labor by Obama, and an election to replace her followed in Los Angeles's 32nd Congressional District. It was a dividing moment. The 32nd was a Latino district—drawn in 1982 as a result of the pressure from the Latino community, which sued under the Civil Rights Voting Act. At least 62 percent of the population was Latino, and 18 percent Asian; of the 126,000 registered voters 53 percent were Latino, and 17 percent Asian. The 32nd includes parts of East Los Angeles and has a large immigrant base. State Senator Gilbert Cedillo, a longtime activist who since his youth had been involved in the pro-immigrant rights and labor movements, ran for the office. Former State Assemblywoman Judy Chu challenged him. Chu as chair of the appropriations committee had not supported Cedillo's legislation for driver's licenses for undocumented workers, thus killing the bill. Nevertheless, Latino politicos split in their support of the two candidates, mostly around personalities and self-interest. It was a dirty campaign with opponents of Cedillo running multiple Spanish-surnamed candidates. On May 19, 2009, Cedillo lost and so did the community; it lost its most persistent and effective voice for immigrant rights.[39]

The 2012 presidential election was a replay of 2008. Latinos, for the first time, were major players, and a key part of the Obama strategy was to form a coalition and carry groups such as single women, African Americans, Asian Americans, and Latinos by substantial margins. Although Latinos had been critical of Obama's deportation policies and failure to put through a meaningful immigration reform act, the alternative was Republican Mitt Romney, who said the undocumented should self-deport themselves. In mid-June Obama made up ground by issuing an executive order temporarily addressing the needs of young undocumented youth in danger of being deported "to a country they never knew, having been brought here by their parents." His actions were in marked contrast to Romney, who up to the end referred to the Dreamers (the youth who benefited from Obama's order) as "illegal aliens."[40]

They were called Dreamers because they were mostly undocumented students who dreamt about being Americans. As mentioned in Chapter 15, the civil rights movement of undocumented students had begun in 1985 with the successful *Leticia A.* suit to be counted as residents for educational purposes. They received a blow with the 1994 passage of California Proposition 187; however, they never gave up hope.

By 2000, approximately 2.5 million undocumented youth under the age of 18 were living in the United States. Their numbers had increased substantially, and although they were in their majority Latinas/os, they included large numbers of Asians, Caribbean African Americans, and Europeans. Today approximately 65,000 undocumented students graduate from U.S. high schools each year (roughly 40 percent are from California). These networks began to coalesce at the turn of the century and united to pass legislation.

Many of these activists had been in the United States since they were infants. Following the example of the Civil Rights movement, they began to press government for their human rights. In 2001 Assembly Bill (AB) 540 was passed and signed into law in California. It allowed undocumented students who had completed three years of a California high school to pay in-state tuition. Although this fell short of the *Leticia A.* ruling that gave them access to financial aid, it was a victory. Dreamers continued to press for an expansion of the Dream Act.

In August 2001, a federal Development, Relief, and Education for Alien Minors Act (Dream Act) was proposed in the U.S. Senate. It would have required five years' residence prior to the passage of the act, that the recipient be under 15 at the time of entry, and of good character. A qualifying student would then be given six years of documented status. It left it up to the states to determine tuition. In 2007 another unsuccessful bill was proposed to cancel the removal and adjustment of students who had been in the United States for a long period and had been brought to the United States as children.

At each step, the Dreamers became more persistent and better organized. With each defeat, the Dreamers' resolve increased. By the 2012 presidential election the Dreamers' civil rights tactics were embarrassing Democrats and human rights advocates. On June 15, President Obama announced the Deferred Action for Childhood Arrivals (DACA), using his executive power to implement the DREAM Act, in effect giving students amnesty until their status could be regularized. Thirteen states as of November 2013 passed versions of the DREAM Act: Texas, California, Illinois, Utah, Nebraska, Kansas, New Mexico, New York, Washington, Wisconsin, Massachusetts, Maryland, and Minnesota. Success has not spoiled the youths' dreams.

Meanwhile, there was a notable presence of Latinos in national politics: San Antonio Mayor Julian Castro delivered the keynote address at the Democratic National Convention in Charlotte, North Carolina, in 2012. His twin brother, Texas State Representative Joaquín Castro, 37, ran successfully for U.S. Congress. The Castros were raised by a single mother, Rosie Castro, a Raza Unida organizer and activist, in San Antonio's West Side.[41] As a student Julian wrote of his mother, "[My mother] sees political activism as an opportunity to change people's lives for the better. Perhaps that is because of her outspoken nature or because Chicanos in the early 1970s (and, of course, for many years before) had no other option. To make themselves heard Chicanos needed the opportunity that the political system provided. In any event, my mother's fervor for activism affected the first years of my life, as it touches it today."[42]

According to exit polls taken by the Pew Hispanic Center, "Latinos voted for President Barack Obama over Republican Mitt Romney by 71% to 27." This was the highest margin since the Bill Clinton–Bob Dole election in 1996. Latino youth voted for Obama over Romney by 74 percent versus 23 percent. "Among Latino voters whose total family income is below $50,000, 82% voted for Obama while 17% voted for Romney. Among Latino voters with family incomes of $50,000 or more, 59% voted for Obama while 39% voted for Romney."[43]

In 2012 Texas elected Tea Party favorite Ted Cruz as the first "Hispanic" U.S. senator from the Lone Star state. By this time it was politically incorrect to mention that Cruz was not Mexican American but a scion of a conservative Cuban family whose interests were not compatible with the majority of working-class Mexican American and Latino families. Cruz, Florida Republican Senator Marco Rubio, who was also from a conservative Cuban background, and Republican New Mexican Governor Susana Martinez, a Mexican American, are ascending stars in the Republican Party. As a result of the presidential election, Republicans were scurrying to find binders with Latino names.

Protection of the Foreign Born

The one issue that was overwhelming supported by Latino leaders and Latino politicos was the protection of the foreign born. In 2008, 12.7 million Mexican immigrants lived in the United States, 17 times more than in 1970—more than half were undocumented, comprising 32 percent of all immigrants. As of 2008, almost half of all Latinos owned their homes. It came with incredible sacrifice—27.6 percent of the loans to Latinos were higher priced, versus 33.5 percent to blacks and 10.5 percent to whites, in 2007.[44]

Because those without papers were discriminated against, exploited, and harassed by governmental agencies and ordinary citizens, Mexican Americans have a long history of forming associations for the protection of immigrants. Beginning in the 1890s, they organized *La Alianza Hispano Americana* in Tucson, Arizona; again in the 1910s, *La Liga Protectora Latina* was founded to fight against the 80 percent rule; and in the 1960s, *CASA Hermandad Mexicana* was formed. Chapter 8 put this into the context of Mexican *mutualistas* and immigrant newspapers that crusaded against capital punishment and unequal treatment of their compatriots. Up until very recently, Mexican Americans and Chicanos protected the rights of the immigrants even when the Mexican government and its intellectuals shunned the immigrant as a traitor of the homeland.

In 2005, the media went wild. Almost nightly, CNN's Lou Dobbs—who is married to a Mexican woman—told horror stories of a Mexican invasion. On November 28, *U.S. News & World Report* carried a cover titled "Border Wars," and a cover story, "Border wars: More illegal immigrants. More violence. More death. The public has had it. Now the Bush administration has a new plan. Will it matter?" These inflammatory media statements climaxed a year in which more than a thousand vigilantes ran around with guns, trying to pick off brown people who were entering the country to survive. Adding to the hysteria was California Governor Arnold Schwarzenegger cheering on these border criminals called "minutemen." By December 2005, Republican congressmen were calling for a constitutional amendment that would deprive children of citizenship if they were born in the United States to undocumented parents.[45]

It is evident that the motivation of the racist nativists was to keep America white and divert attention from the excesses of Corporate America. For this, they had to get rid of "family preferences" in the U.S. immigration policy. Never before in U.S. history has the nativist movement been so robust. It is kept alive by hundreds of think tanks, foundations, and hate groups through their literature and Internet sites. The Internet allows a core of nativists to communicate and to stay informed about the anti-immigrant propaganda spewed by think tanks and reactionary groups playing on the fear of Euro-Americans.

A recent study funded by the National Cancer Institute of the National Institutes of Health "traced the roots of the Tea Party's anti-tax movement back to the early 1980s when tobacco companies began to invest in third party groups to fight excise taxes on cigarettes, as well as health studies finding a link between cancer and secondhand cigarette smoke."[46] The Tea Party, far from being a grassroots organization, has attacked immigrants and unions throughout the country, especially in Arizona where it has supported draconian laws.

The reality is that immigrants are not taking away jobs, nor are they a drag on the economy. Latinos use emergency health care because "American" employers refuse to pay the social costs of production for their workers. They did not create the health crisis in the United States that is threatening millions of U.S. working families. Undocumented workers are not taking the high-paying jobs that are being outsourced to Asian and other Third World countries. And certainly immigrants did not defraud the public and cause the implosion of the American economy in 2008.

Still, a solution to heavy Mexican and Central American migration is possible and necessary in the interest of those countries. For example, the fertility rate among Mexican women of childbearing age has fallen dramatically from 7.2 children in 1965, to 2.5 today. This has led many scholars to suggest that Mexican population growth is under control. Hence, creating decent jobs in Mexico could drastically reduce push factors. However, this does not mean there should be more *maquiladoras* or more U.S. corporations such as Monsanto doing business in Mexico. Historically the United States has manipulated the flow of labor into the country from Latin America, destabilizing those countries' economies.[47]

By the year 2025, one out of two children born in the United States will be Latino. They will comprise 30 percent of the nation's population, and in that year, it is estimated that whites will be a minority: 47 percent. At the same time, the nation's elderly population will double in size, and they will be disproportionately white. Even today one of four children under five is Latino. Like it or not, someone has to work to pay for social benefits. Immigrants are part of the solution, and they are no longer hidden in the Southwest. With this in mind, it is in the nation's self-interest to ensure quality healthcare and good schools for this population and to integrate them into the mainstream society. A first step is equitable pay.[48]

The policy of the United States toward Mexico and Central America is based on the delusion that a free market is the key to solving poverty there. However, the free market works like the game of Monopoly. If you own all of the good property, you are going to clean the other person out. In reality, trade with Mexico creates more billionaires and accelerates people's move to the cities where the flimsy infrastructure cannot absorb them. Among the 15 Mexican billionaires named by *Forbes* magazine for 2013, the leader is Carlos Slim, the richest man in the world.[49]

The Europeans have a different and more intelligent approach toward solving migration problems. Thirty years ago, Spain was a major exporter of workers to northern Europe. Today, Spain has become wealthy enough to lure foreign workers. Spain needs foreign workers to compensate for shortages in certain sectors and keep the retirement pension system alive. Even though Spanish unemployment is among the highest in the European Union, there are jobs Spaniards will not do. Only the future will tell how it will recover from the World Economic Crisis, which many blame on the excesses of Wall Street. Today, Spain's fertility rate is 1.3 children per woman, and the population is growing old. In the United States, the fertility rate fluctuates between 2.0 and 2.1 births per woman, down from a high of almost 3.8 in 1957.

Spain turned around its economy and rebuilt its infrastructure with the support of the European Union that, unlike the United States, took a comprehensive approach to helping member states. It initiated programs to improve the commercial environment, using economic, political, and market approaches. Through the European Regional Development Fund (ERDF), regional growth was encouraged by allocations from the wealthier states to the poorer regions of the continent. The wealthier states provided funds for improving farming infrastructure and for training and retraining the workers, particularly those who were unemployed.[50]

Without regional solutions, Mexicans and Central Americans will continue to migrate to the United States. As it is today, if undocumented immigration were to be eliminated, Mexican and Central American economies would be badly destabilized. In 2003, Mexico received nearly $13.3 billion in workers' remittances, an amount equivalent to about 140 percent of foreign direct investment and 71 percent of oil exports. Remittances from Salvadorans reached an all-time high of $2.5 billion in 2004—approximately 17.1 percent of the gross domestic product (GDP).

In 2008, "the money Mexican migrants sent home fell for the first time in history last year, from $26 billion to $25 billion." Remittances are the second largest source of foreign income after oil. And even among Latinos sending money home, more than seven in 10 reported they were sending less back in 2008 than in the previous year. This money that has somewhat stabilized the economy of Mexico is entirely earned by tax-paying workers. It is sent back by people like María, 33, who migrated to Milwaukee in 2005; "she worked two jobs and sent as much as $2,000 to Mexico every two months." Without such remittances from workers abroad, Mexico's and Central America's economies would implode. As it is, they are much more susceptible to the growing drug trafficking that runs wild because of the U.S. drug market. A positive effect is that the Mexican government policy has become much more proactive in the defense of the immigrants, recognizing them as an economic and political asset.[51] However, the economic depression starting in 2008 affected not only remittances but the flow of Mexicans into the United States.

Meanwhile, because of inequality, corruption and violence are rampant on the Mexican side of the border. The U.S. drug market and the concentration of *maquiladoras* further magnetized the border. Drug wars spill over into border towns such as Laredo, Juárez, and Nogales while U.S. banks get richer from money-laundering profits. Violence ebbed and flowed, and in Juárez, at least 370 women, 24 per year on average, succumbed to violence from 1993 through January 2004. Police authorities ignored these homicides/disappearances until women activist groups pressured them for some kind of action. The annual female homicide/disappearance and homicide rates were higher than for the entire United States and 38 times the total homicide rates for all of the Canadian provinces combined. Many critics speculated that the motives behind these crimes were sexual or related to serial murders, drug crimes, or slavery or they were killed for body part transplants.[52]

Many informed persons on both sides of the border criticize the War on Drugs, charging that it is used by the United States like the so-called War on Terror, to frighten people into supporting assaults on basic freedoms. They point to a contradicting and ineffective police. Hundreds of million dollars were spent to shut down ocean drug corridors, diverting the corridors through Central America and Mexico, corrupting their governments and civil societies. It resembles the closing off of the corridors migrants took through Texas and California, channeling them through the deserts of Sonora and Arizona, leaving men, women, and children to die of hunger and thirst. Critics point out that what drives the drug trade is the huge demand in the U.S. drug market. The situation is worsened by the deportation of thousands of gang members to their homelands in Central America and Mexico. Most of the deportees were raised in the United States and inducted into crime in the U.S. prison system. The enormous profits in drugs have spawned cartels and caused internal wars among the cartels and with local, state, and federal authorities. As of November

2, 2009, the number of people killed since January 2007 in Mexico as a result of this war was 9,903; still the United States blames Mexico for this war![53]

The Firewall?

Racist xenophobia is as American as apple pie, dating back to the Alien and Sedition Acts (1798). Since the early 1970s it has been picking up steam once more, and California launched Proposition 187 in 1994. The only reason that nativists did not run wild in California is because of the Latino electorate that has made Republicans pay a price for their racism. In 2012, Republican candidate for governor Meg Whitman spent more than $141.5 million of her own money in an unsuccessful bid to defeat Democrat Jerry Brown. Republican Carly Fiorina, the former CEO of Hewlett Packard, also unsuccessfully challenged U.S. Senator Barbara Boxer. Democrat Boxer won 65 percent of the Latino vote while Fiorina won 29 percent. In California's gubernatorial race, Democrat Brown won 64 percent of California's Latino vote while Republican Whitman won 31 percent.[54] Fiorina and Whitman paid for the anti-immigrant rhetoric they had engaged in during their party primaries.

In contrast, Arizona does not have a firewall similar to that of California. Latino elected officials as a group are weak, and could not or would not pressure the Barack Obama administration to enforce Constitutional protections in the areas of human rights or education. Since the 1970s Tucson has been under a court order to desegregate, which it has avoided enforcing. Xenophobia and anti-Mexican hysteria have been virulent since the late 1960s in Arizona. It reared its ugly head in 2012 with the passage of Arizona Senate Bill (SB) 1070, an anti-immigrant law, and Arizona House Bill (HB) 2281 that made the teaching of ethnic studies and Mexican studies in particular unlawful. The rationale was the securing of the border and the allegation that Mexican American Studies divided races and was subversive. The Tucson Unified School District even banned books including the one you are reading and William Shakespeare's *The Tempest*.[55] In the documentary "Outlawing Shakespeare," Tom Horne, then superintendent of public instruction and now state attorney general, made the accusation that the TUSD's Mexican American Studies program was part of a Mexican conspiracy to retake "Aztlan," the Southwest or the territory that the United States took from Mexico.[56]

Since the 1970s Arizona has been the poster child for xenophobia in the United States. Arizona is the second fastest growing state in the country, and this is one of the reasons predators have been able to exploit the fears of white residents. The population in Arizona grew 50 percent from 1990 to 2004 (from 3.6 to 5.6 million). By 2015, the Arizona population is projected to increase by more than 30 percent (to 7.9 million). The migration to Arizona brought many retired white people who did not know about Mexican heritage and considered them outsiders, not caring that many Mexican American families had lived in the state for generations. From 1990 to 2000, the Latino population grew 88 percent (from about 700,000 to 1.3 million). From 2000 to 2004, Latinos grew 22 percent (to 1.5 million), which alarmed white colonists. The Latino population is young, with a median age of 24 versus 38 for white residents. (Some figures say 24 and 44). These statistics frightened many colonists who knew that in time Latinos would outvote them and that the Euro-Americans would depend on their labor. Add to this that by 2013–2014, Latinos were expected to represent more than 40 percent of all public high school graduates. Meanwhile, Latinos have not kept pace with the rest of the population educationally or economically. Although the Latino community grew more than 100 percent from 1990 to 2004, Latinos with bachelor's degrees only increased 3 percent. Simply put, Latinos have been priced out of the education market; the cost of higher education is too high for low-end wage earners in general.[57]

This shifting population brought out the worst in white citizens who resented paying for the education of other people's children. Meanwhile, the border became a lightning rod with white residents blaming "Mexicans" for the violence there and the drug traffic, although statistics show that fewer Mexicans are migrating northward, and that there is less violence at the border than elsewhere in the state. The shift unnerved the white colonists, and white vigilante groups such as the Minutemen and the Tea Party openly agitated for stricter enforcement of the laws. In many instances this led to violence. On May 30, 2009, a Minuteman contingent burst into a home where a child, Bisenia Flores, "was sleeping with her puppy." They identified themselves as law enforcement. After shooting the father, one of the intruders shot Brisenia as she begged for her life, crying, "Please don't shoot me!" The Minuteman shot the nine-year-old point-blank twice in the head. For two years there was very little coverage in the press about this outrage.[58]

For the past five years Arizona has been a nightmare, taken over by corporate predators such as the Koch brothers and ALEC—the American Legislative Exchange Council—that have moved into Arizona. The latter controls over 50 state legislators and has written legislation such as SB 1070. It is in league with the prison industry that has spearheaded the privatization of prisons and reaped a bonanza from incarcerating undocumented and other Latinos. The infamous Koch brothers have funded the Tea Party and agitated racial hatred within the state. In the process these predators seized control of the Republican Party, and silenced Democrats who are prominent in the ranks of the Blue Dogs. In this environment Mexicans were under siege, especially Arizona's highly touted Mexican American Studies Program, which the predators labeled subversive, unpatriotic and racially divisive based on no proof other than state Superintendent of Schools John Huppenthal and state Attorney General Tom Horne saying it was. Very expensive studies conducted by the state and federal government proved otherwise.[59]

Thus far the only shift toward enforcing the constitutional rights of Mexican Americans has been the Obama administration's taking greater interest in the plight of Mexican Americans beginning about two months before the 2012 election. Up to this time the Tea Party and the Minutemen were running around unchecked. This interest in the civil rights of Mexican Americans is mainly due to the growing national presence of Mexican American voters, who make up more than two-thirds of the Latino bloc. Behind the scenes more Mexican American leaders outside Arizona became critical of the national government and Arizona Latino politicos for not constructing a firewall to protect the rights of the foreign born and the Latino community.

This criticism is both good and bad. Local Arizona Latino organizations will be bypassed with a growing number of Latinos outside the state believing that Arizona politicos cannot protect Latino interests and so the national community should. Members of the Hispanic Congressional Caucus expressed this concern to me: The national threat is present. A majority of white Americans side with Arizona's racist anti-immigrant laws. Arizona is a model for them.[60] It has encouraged stereotyping: in South Carolina a Mexican restaurant is selling T-shirts depicting "how to catch an illegal immigrant"—with an image of an old-style box trap using tacos as bait.[61] In the South, there are no firewalls like in California.

Losing Fear

Even before the economic crisis unfolded in 2008, Latinos were losing their fear. Fewer relied on politicos to protect them. Unlike in the first half of the twentieth century, they did not nurture the illusion that the Mexican government would protect their human rights. Latinas spoke out and sought support from legal aid agencies and battered women shelters. Latino and Latina homosexuals demanded space that belonged to them as members of society. They formed their own groups but also demanded space in the larger Latino community.

In San Antonio, Texas, *Casa Esperanza* fought for freedom from "domination and inequality—[for] women, people of color, lesbians and gay men, the working class and poor. We believe in creating bridges between people by exchanging ideas and educating and empowering each other. We believe it is vital to share our visions of hope . . . we are esperanza [hope]."[62]

In 1987 a group of queer and straight Chicanas organized *Esperanza;* they wanted a place where community-based organizers, activists, and cultural artists could meet and engage in dialogue against all forms of social, political, and economic oppression.

> *The organization has been active in women's reproductive choice, human rights, and the rights of Spanish-speaking workers. Esperanza has organized antiwar protests, low-cost housing actions, and demonstrations against the Klu [sic] Klux Klan. Esperanza has presented the work of hundreds of artists and cultural workers, particularly those who have been ignored or silenced*

in mainstream arenas. Individually, the women and men of Esperanza have done the work at home. They have talked, challenged, and learned with their own families and with neighborhood friends. With great courage, they have strived to live the changes they advocate and to empower the people they love.[63]

In the mid-1990s, it threatened the establishment by advocating a broader definition of diversity. Responding to the pressure of those on the religious right and homophobes, the City of San Antonio cut funding for its cultural arts programs in 1997. San Antonio then tried to isolate *Esperanza* by threatening the funding of other gay/lesbian, Latino, and African American groups. Although San Antonio has a Confederate mentality, it also has a network of progressives—many of them women like those in Fuerza Unida, who organized the Levi's boycott. Meanwhile, *Esperanza* was reluctant to sue because it threatened the funding for other worthy programs; however, it was now or never.

It began a *Todos Somos Esperanza* dialogue that "brought the issues of cultural diversity and public funding for cultural arts to discussions throughout the city." It brought a suit in federal court against the city, which went to trial in 2001. At the trial,

Esperanza Executive Director Graciela Sánchez identified herself as a lesbian and a woman who had grown up working class in San Antonio's Westside barrio. Graciela used numerous Spanish words as she testified about the work of Esperanza, speaking in a bilingual weave that is familiar among Chicanos in San Antonio. Judge Garcia listened closely, and the courtroom filled with the power of Spanish spoken openly, without translation, in the formal atmosphere of federal court. The audience was completely silent in recognition of the moment. Sánchez testified to the judge and to her family, friends, and allies. The determined, engaged presence of community members was essential as a testament to that moment.[64]

Federal Judge Orlando García found in *Esperanza*'s favor.

On April 10, 2006, millions of people, mostly immigrants, took to the streets of 140 cities across the nation. It was one of a series of marches. They were tired of being afraid, intimidated by ICE and pot-bellied bullies who called themselves "minutemen." The protests began in response to proposed legislation known as U.S. House of Representatives Bill (H.R.) 4437, an extreme measure that would criminalize not only unauthorized immigrants but anyone who helped them. The undocumented would be classified as felons, among other punitive measures. Over a million people showed up in Los Angeles, several hundreds of thousands in Dallas, and upwards of 300,000 in Chicago. Despite provocation by some racist nativists, the marches were peaceful. Marches held on March 26 had paved way for these marches that not only protested H.R. 4437 but also called for immigration reform.[65]

Prior to these marches, thousands of students walked out of school to protest H.R. 4437. Key Chicana/o activists—such as Javier Rodríguez in Los Angeles and Armando Navarro in Riverside—supported the organization of events throughout the country. However, the protest was organized largely by a network of immigrant resources. For example, Spanish-language radio and other media supported the marches. There was a backlash with the right-wing media ranting that many of the marchers waved Mexican and Salvadoran flags instead of *American* flags—ironically, they did not complain when other groups did the same. The scenario was the same everywhere: in April 2006, in Dallas, Texas, 900,000 people marched through the streets of the city and thousands more students left their classes to protest the proposed anti-immigrant legislation; on May 1, 700,000 participated in a march in Chicago. Los Angeles was divided as politicos, labor, and the Catholic Church called an alternative march. Even so, thousands marched, and a confrontation broke out in MacArthur Park; Los Angeles police overreacted and beat up the protestors.[66]

The marches brought about a sense of solidarity, not only in the Latina/o communities, but among progressives throughout the country. The protection of the foreign born was on the agenda of human rights struggles. More important is the transformation that is taking place in people who are barely making it economically, who have no papers, and who have been constantly harassed by ICE and are threatened by racists, yet who walk out of their employment, often at the risk of losing their job, to fight back. Although the economic bad times have dampened much of this energy, it sends the message that if pushed too far, the powerless will defend themselves. This is what the people of Mexican origin and other Latinos have done throughout their history in this country. What they want is what every other human being wants—food, shelter, and clothing—and the opportunity to earn them. They have no other choice but to fight back![67]

Conclusion: Toward an Ideology

The year 2001 began the decade and a new millennium. Like everyone else, modern Mexican Americans also were full of hope at the dawn of the decade; they believed that the Sleeping Giant had awakened. They rationalized that now that Mexican Americans, Latinos, or whatever they called themselves, were entitled to a piece of the pie, things were going to be different. However, the reality is that no matter how much the "Latino" is hyped, and no matter how many more Latino businesses gross in the millions, and no matter how many more Latinos are elected to office, things remain the same for the masses of Mexican Americans and other Latinos. The true stairway to heaven continues to be education. Hence, it is at the root of the proverbial Catch-22—despite the hype, it is becoming much harder for students from *barrio* schools to climb that stairway.

In 1956 the author worked as a janitor and bought his first home. Today, how many janitors qualify to own their home? College fees were less than $10 a semester then. In 2008, tuition reached $8,000 at most University of California campuses and half of that amount at California State Universities—and the rates are projected to increase by more than 30 percent annually! Back then, successive generations knew that they would have it better than their parents; but not any more. Today students leave graduate schools $100,000 in debt! This trend began well before the 2000s, but the first decade of the twenty-first century cemented it. Bailouts are for rich people, not the working class—someone has to pay for it.

The only ones who do not seem discouraged are undocumented students who hang on by the tips of their fingernails—often paying nonresident fees that they and their parents scrape together. They have won some battles: through the efforts of elected officials such as California State Senator Gilbert Cedillo and Texas State Senator Roberto Alonzo, they were granted the privilege of paying resident tuition fees. However, even this is becoming impossible, with tuition skyrocketing. Most elected officials lack the courage to raise taxes for essential services, so that the heavy burden of tuition fees can at least partly be lifted off the shoulders of the poor students. The myth that these officials try to perpetuate is that education is less costly and more accessible in the United States than elsewhere—when the reality is that Europeans have better lower-cost higher education than Americans do.

As we have seen, the only ones that seem to believe in the American Dream are the undocumented youth. Throughout the decade they hung on to the illusion that America cared and that Congress would pass the Development, Relief and Education for Alien Minors Act (the "DREAM Act"). The bill would allow undocumented students who graduate from U.S. high schools—provided they arrived in the United States as children, are of good moral character, and had been in the country continuously for at least five years before the bill's enactment—the opportunity to earn conditional permanent residency. They would be given temporary residence while they earn their degree. Since 2001 immigrant youth have lobbied for the bill, often traveling to state capitols and Washington, D.C., at their personal risk and cost.[68] So what is the motivation behind this struggle of undocumented immigrants? The truth is that poor people have few options. The U.S. drug market and policies destroyed Mexico's economy and civil society, so there is no question of returning to their home country.[69] Although physically they were not born in what is today the United States, this is their home.

The Dreamers, as they are called, won a phenomenal victory in getting President Obama to pass an executive order stabilizing their status. "September 21, 2012—President Obama, speaking at the Latino town hall in Coral Gables, Fla. last night during the Univision News Forum, reaffirmed his belief in the American Dream for Dreamers, the young undocumented immigrants, who are still fighting to get the DREAM Act passed through Congress. . . . What stands between them and that dream is a Republican Congress that has thwarted both President Obama and Democrats to pass legislation to make that dream a reality."[70] It was a victory for undocumented students who began coming out in greater numbers, and at real personal sacrifice flaunting their undocumented status. This along with the overwhelming support of Latino voters gave President Obama an offer he could not refuse. The refusal of Republican candidate Mitt Romney to moderate his anti-immigrant position cost him dearly.

Mexican American and Latino organizations try to advocate for the interests of their constituents—only the most cynical among us would dispute this. However, their success is measured by the growth of the middle class and it is not viewed from the bottom. Very few students or working families have access to the new elites who run these organizations, whose banquets run as high as $500 a pop. One of the major barriers to communication is Mexican Americans and Latinos who believe the hype and, as the cheerleaders, like to remind anyone who will listen that Latinos are the nation's No. 1 minority. However, it is useful to remember what Edward R. Roybal said in 1980: "We have been told over and over that the 1980s will be the Decade of the Hispanics. But, we all remember we were told the same thing at the start of the 1970s. The real answer, my friends, is that we have no clout."[71] We forget that the political and economic centers of the country are still in the East and only the rich and the lawmakers have time and money to reach these centers.

Not every Latino who is suffering today is an immigrant, although most are children of immigrants. Consequent to the immigration marches, the new generation of youth has learned to take on the system and fight for justice. Indeed, most of the youth who participated in school walkouts were born in this country and are citizens, who will vote one day. Their protest is instigated by bitterness: some are bitter about the plight of their parents; many are bitter that they have to sacrifice so much to get an education, whereas it was open to the earlier generations. The marches have achieved one thing for certain: many participants have lost their fear. These walkouts are similar to the 1968 East Los Angeles and Texas school walkouts—they politicize the younger generation. The simile does not end there—even into the second generation, they are children of immigrants and first-generation college students. It is projected that by the year 2050 U.S. Latinos will number 102.6 million. But what good will it be if they are the majority—or that they are No. 1—if they do not have access to that stairway to a better life? And if access does not improve, how long will it be before the base begins to revolt—first by not voting and then by becoming more vociferous?

Notes

1. "U.S. Hispanic Population Surpasses 45 Million, Now 15 Percent of Total," U.S. Census Bureau Press Release, May 1, 2008, http://www.census.gov/newsroom/releases/archives/population/cb08-67.html. "Hispanic Herit-age Month 2012: Sept. 15-Oct." Profile America Facts, U.S. Census, August 6, 2012, http://www.census.gov/newsroom/releases/archives/facts_for_features_special_editions/cb12-ff19.html.

2. "U.S. Hispanic Population Surpasses 45 Million, Now 15 Percent of Total," U.S. Census Bureau Press Release, May 1, 2008, http://www.census.gov/newsroom/releases/archives/population/cb08-67.html. Hispanic Voters 2012, *Resurgent Republic*, http://www.hispanicvoters2012.com/. "16.3%—Hispanic Population in the U.S." Pew Hispanic Center, November 29, 2012, http://pewresearch.org/databank/dailynumber/?NumberID=1224. Vanessa Cárdenas and Sophia Kerby, "Although This Growing Population Has Experienced Marked Success, Barriers Remain," Center for American Progress (August 8, 2012), http://www.americanprogress.org/issues/race/report/2012/08/08/11984/the-state-of-latinos-in-the-united-states/.

3. "U.S. Hispanic Population to Triple by 2050," *USA Today* (February 11, 2008), http://www.usatoday.com/news/nation/2008-02-11-population-study_N.htm. Hispanic Voters 2012,

Resurgent Republic, http://www.resurgentrepublic.com/hispanic-voters. 'Hispanic Population in the U.S.," Pew Hispanic Center (November 29, 2012), http://pewresearch.org/databank/dailynumber/?NumberID=1224. Vanessa Cárdenas and Sophia Kerby, "Although This Growing Population Has Experienced Marked Success, Barriers Remain," *Center for American Progress* (August 8, 2012).

4. A Francesca Jenkins, "Students: A Statistical Survey," *Hispanic Outlook in Higher Education. Paramus* 19, no. 7 (January 5, 2009), 54–56.

5. National Statistics on the Death Penalty and Race, Race of Death Row Inmates Executed Since 1976, Death Penalty Information Center, http://www.deathpenaltyinfo.org/race-death-row-inmates-executed-1976%23defend. Citing Race and Regional Bias, Latino Leaders Join Call for Halt to Federal Executions, ACLU, June 13, 2001, http://www.aclu.org/capital/unequal/10570prs20010613.html. James Oliphant, "In a Reversal, Justice Stevens Calls the Death Penalty 'Anachronistic,'" *Los Angeles Times* (April 17, 2008).

6. Governor George Ryan's Clemency Speech, http://www.youtube.com/watch?v=Cv75EcK1arI. Steve Mills and John Chase, "Rolando Cruz Seeks Pardon: Petition Criticizes Ryan on Nicarico," Chicago Tribune (September 19, 2002).

7. Alexander Cockburn, "George W. Bush: The Death Penalty Governor," *San Jose Mercury News* (February 9, 2000). "Death Penalty in America, Executions in America," *Chicago Tribune* Special Issue (2012), http://www.chicagotribune.com/news/nationworld/chi-dpdpamerica-special,0,4453522.special.

8. "Juvenile Justice," Children's Defense Fund, State of America's Children (2011), http://www.childrensdefense.org/child-research-data-publications/state-of-americas-children-2011/pdfs/jj.pdf, J-2.

9. Ibid., J-9.

10. "Cost of War," National Priorities Project, http://costofwar.com/. Deborah White, "Iraq War Facts, Results & Statistics at January 31, 2012," U.S. Liberal Politics, http://usliberals.about.com/od/homelandsecurit1/a/IraqNumbers.htm. 4,487 US Soldiers Killed, 32,223 Seriously Wounded.

11. William G. Gale and Peter Orszag, "Bush Administration Tax Policy: Revenue and Budget Effects," Urban Institute and Brookings Institution, October 4, 2004, http://www.taxpolicycenter.org/publications/url.cfm?ID=1000695. Tom Tancredo on illegal immigration and race, http://www.youtube.com/watch?v=FIXehNC65Y0&feature=related.

12. Hispanics in the Military, The Pew Hispanic Center (March 27, 2003), http://pewhispanic.org/files/reports/17.pdf. Median Age for Hispanics is Lower Than Median Age for Total U.S. Population, The Pew Hispanic Center (July 2, 2012), http://www.pewresearch.org/daily-number/median-age-for-hispanics-is-lower-than-median-age-for-total-u-s-population/.

13. Bill Berkowitz, "Latinos on the Front Lines: US Military Targets Latinos for Iraq and Future Twenty-First Century Wars," *Dissident Voice* (October 16, 2003), http://dissidentvoice.org/Articles8/Berkowitz_Military-Latinos.htm.

14. Mady Wechsler Segal and David R. Segal, "Latinos Claim Larger Share of U.S. Military Personnel," October 2007, Population Reference Bureau, http://www.prb.org/Articles/2007/HispanicsUSMilitary.aspx. Alfredo Gonzalez, "Filling the Ranks: Latinos and Military Combat Occupations" (paper presented at Western Political Science Association annual meeting, Portland, Oregon, 23 March 2012), 1. "Most of the data concerning minorities in the military has been concentrated on the African-American experience." One reason more minorities were not recruited was because of the high unemployment that made the military an attractive option. "Yo Soy El Army: US Military Targets Latinos with Extensive Recruitment Campaign," *Democracy Now* (May 18, 2010), http://www.democracynow.org/2010/5/18/yo_soy_el_army_us_military.

15. Solomon Amendment, http://www.yalerotc.org/Solomon.html.

16. No Child Left Behind Act (Public Law 107-110), Sec. 9528. Armed Forces Recruiter Access to Students and Student Recruiting Information, http://prhome.defense.gov/rfm/MPP/ACCESSION%20POLICY/docs/no_child_act.pdf. What Are Some Criticisms of No Child Left Behind? Wise Geek, http://www.wisegeek.com/what-are-some-criticisms-of-no-child-left-behind.htm. Linda Darling-Hammond, "Evaluating 'No Child Left Behind,'" *The Nation* (May 21, 2007), http://www.thenation.com/article/evaluating-no-child-left-behind.

17. Rodolfo F. Acuña, "Política: Impuestos sí, pero representación no," *La Opinión* (28 de noviembre de 2004). Historical Debt Outstanding—Annual 2000–2012, Treasury Direct, http://www.treasurydirect.gov/govt/reports/pd/histdebt/histdebt_histo5.htm Federal Taxes Paid vs. Federal Spending Received by State, 1981-2005. Tax Foundation (October 19, 2007), http://taxfoundation.org/article/federal-taxes-paid-vs-federal-spending-received-state-1981-2005. Federal tax revenue by state. Free Republic(March 17, 2011) http://www.freerepublic.com/focus/f-chat/2690371/posts Federal tax revenue by state, Wikipedia, "Federal tax revenue by state," http://en.wikipedia.org/wiki/Federal_tax_revenue_by_state

18. State & County QuickFacts, 2012 Census, United States Census Bureau, http://quickfacts.census.gov/qfd/states/04000.html.

19. [quote] Jack Tripper, "It's Official the US is a Police State," *General News* (September 20, 2012), http://www.opednews.com/articles/It-s-Official-the-US-is-a-by-Jack-Tripper-120919-551.html. USA Patriot Act (11/14/2003), http://w2.eff.org/patriot/. HR 3162 RDS, 107th Congress, 1st Session, H. R. 3162, In the Senate of the United States, October 24, 2001, Electronic Privacy Information Center, http://epic.org/privacy/terrorism/hr3162.html.

20. [quote] Tyche Hendricks, "U.S. Citizens Wrongly Detained, Deported by ICE," *SFGate* (July 27, 2009), http://www.sfgate.com/news/article/U-S-citizens-wrongly-detained-deported-by-ICE-3291041.php. Steve Saldivar, "ICE 101: Immigration on the Legal Front Line," March 26, 2009, http://missionlocal.org/2009/03/ice-101/. Julia Preston, "No Need for a Warrant, You're an Immigrant," *New York Times* (October 14, 2007). Albor Ruiz, "ICE Locks 'em up, Throws Away Key: Immigration Becomes a Human Rights Scandal," *New York Daily News* (March 26, 2009). ICE-U.S. Immigration & Customs Enforcement, http://www.youtube.com/watch?v=TRYfJAnUkHM&feature=PlayList&p=21BA2291F7BA4375&index=0. Smash ICE Northwest Detention Center—docushort, http://www.youtube.com/watch?v=bTrR1s7du6s&feature=PlayList&p=21BA2291F7BA4375&index=2. Postville, Iowa Struggles on After ICE Raid, http://www.youtube.com/watch?v=JYwG6Z6NvsA&feature=PlayList&p=21BA2291F7BA4375&index=3. ICE Arrests Illegal Immigrants, http://www.youtube.com/watch?v=5Vory6-IGdE&feature=PlayList&p=21BA2291F7BA4375&index=5.

21. "Latino Voters Showing Strong Turnout in Election 2012," *Washington Post* (November 6, 2012).

22. Tony Castro, "Nury Martinez Becomes Los Angeles' First Latina Elected To City Council in 25 Years," *Huffington Post* (August 5, 2012), http://www.huffingtonpost.com/2013/08/05/nury-martinez-los-angeles_n_3707410.html.

23. Karin Mac Donald. "Adventures in Redistricting: A Look at the California Redistricting Commission," *Election Law Journal: Rules, Politics, and Policy* 11, no. 4 (December 2012): 472–89, doi:10.1089/elj.2012.1148. Antonio Olivo, "Special Report: They Have Opened Up Legislative Seats, But Also

Created Some Bitter Political Rivalries, Making . . .; Term Limits a Mixed Blessing for Latinos," *Los Angeles Times* (July 2, 2000). Marta Escutia and Gloria Romero, "MALDEF's Lawsuit Is Racially Divisive," *Los Angeles Times* (November 1, 2001).

24. Laura Mecoy, "MALDEF Ripped over Remap Fight," La Prensa San Diego (November 16, 2001), http://www.laprensa-sandiego.org/archieve/november16/MALDEF.HTM. Leo F. Estrada, "Redistricting 2000: A Lost Opportunity for Latinos," La Prensa San Diego (June 7, 2002), http://www.laprensa-sandiego.org/archieve/june07-02/lost.htm

25. Frank del Olmo, "Commentary; The Lucha Libre That Is Latino Politics," *Los Angeles Times* (March 10, 2002): M5.

26. "Articles about Tony Sanchez," *New York Times*, http://topics.nytimes.com/topics/reference/timestopics/people/s/tony_sanchez/index.html.

27. Governor Bill Richardson, http://www.billrichardson.com/about-bill/biography. Kenneth Salazar, U.S. Congress Votes Base, *Washington Post*, http://projects.washingtonpost.com/congress/members/s001163/.

28. Regina Graham, "Washington State's Latinos Find 'Politics Has Not Changed with the Population,'" Guardian (UK), (October 7, 2012). "Washington," State & County Quick-Facts, U.S. (2012) Census, http://quickfacts.census.gov/qfd/states/53000.html. "Hispanic Population Jumps 10 Percent in Washington," RedOrbit (September 18, 2003), http://www.redorbit.com/news/science/10835/hispanic_population_jumps_10_percent_in_washington/. Manuel Valdes, "Lack of Diversity in New Wash. Legislature," *Seattle Times* (November 24, 2012).

29. [quote] Steve Campbell, "Texas' Population Reaches 25.1 Million," *Fort Worth Star-Telegram* (December 22, 2010), http://www.mcclatchydc.com/2010/12/22/105663/texas-population-reaches-251-million.html.

30. Campbell, "Texas' Population Reaches 25.1 Million." "Hispanic Population Fastest Growing in State of Oklahoma," RedOrbit (August 11, 2005). Halimah Abdullah, "Hispanic Population Growth Could Realign South's Politics," McClatchy Newspapers (April 22, 2011). Tony Pugh, "New 2010 Census Data Alter Balance of Power in Congress," McClatchy Newspapers (December 21, 2010), http://www.mcclatchydc.com/2010/12/21/105625/us-population-grows-at-slowest.html.

31. Lowell Ponte, "Bustamante: The Racist in the Race?" *FrontPageMagazine.com* (August 11, 2003), http://www.frontpagemag.com/readArticle.aspx?ARTID=16840.

32. Nicole Greason and Willy Diaz, "Voting Power Trails Demographic Might: Population Growth Outpacing Political Gains," *Latino Perspectives Magazine* (October 2004).

33. Mexican Reconquista: Raul Grijalva in the U.S. Congress, American Patrol, http://www.americanpatrol.com/REFERENCE/Grijalva-Raul.html. Members of Congress/Raul Grijalva, "U.S. Congress Votes Data Base," *Washington Post*, http://projects.washingtonpost.com/congress/members/g000551/.

34. C. J. Karamargin, "Bush Owes 'Gracias' to Latino Voters," *Arizona Daily Star* (November 8, 2004). Dee Allsop, "Election Results and Implications for Regional Stewardship," *Wirthlin Worldwide* (November 12, 2004). "More Than 7.6 Million Latinos Vote in Presidential Race," Press Release, Willie C. Velasquez Institute, November 4, 2004. http://wcvi.org/press_room/press_releases/2004/us/nat_to_110404.html.

35. Latino Voters Show Strong Democratic Support in Congressional Races, "Split Democratic Support in Governor's Race," Press Release, WCVI, November 9, 2006, http://wcvi.org/press_room/press_releases/2006/exitpoll_TX2006.htm.

36. Esther J. Cepeda, "Chicago's Latino Landscape 2008: A Statistical Portrait of Chi-Town Hispanics," *Huffington Post* (March 20, 2009), http://www.huffingtonpost.com/esther-j-cepeda/chicagos-latino-landscape_b_177169.html. City of Chicago, Institute for Latino Studies, Notre Dame University, http://www.nd.edu/~chifacts/chicago.html.

37. Laura Limonic, *The Latino Population of New York City, 2007*, Center for Latin American, Caribbean & Latino Studies, Latino Data Project—Report 20—(December 2008), 3, http://web.gc.cuny.edu/lastudies/latinodataprojectreports/The%20Latino%20Population%20of%20New%20York%20City%202007.pdf. Mexican Population Distribution, City of New York Queens Community Board 3 East Elmhurst—Jackson Heights—North Corona, http://www.cb3qn.nyc.gov/page/54812/.

38. Mark Hugo López and Paul Taylor, "Dissecting the 2008 Electorate: Most Diverse in U.S. History," Pew Hispanic Research Center (April 30, 2009), http://pewhispanic.org/reports/report.php?ReportID=108. James G. Gimpel, "Latino Voting in the 2008 Election: Part of a Broader Electoral Movement," Center for Immigration Studies (January 2009), http://www.cis.org/latinovoting.

39. Javier Rodriguez, "Gil Cedillo, The Activist Politician and the Latino Wars to Replace Hilda Solis" (May 19, 2009), http://forchicanachicanostudies.wikispaces.com/News+Items. Immigrant Student Adjustment/DREAM Act, National Immigration Law Center, http://www.nilc.org/econ_bens_dream&stdnt_adjst_0205.html. "CA Democrats shelve driver's licenses for illegal aliens," http://24ahead.com/blog/archives/005448.html. hecubus, Worldpress, "Morons Want to Reward Illegal Immigrants . . . Again" (August 23, 2006), http://hecubus.wordpress.com/2006/08/23/morons-want-to-reward-illegal-immigrants-again/.

40. "DREAM Act: Questions and Answers about President Obama's Immigration Order for Undocumented Children," *Washington Times* (June 22, 2012).

41. The Reliable Source, "Julian Castro's Twin Brother Joaquin: Rising Stars Have Democrats Seeing Double," *Washington Post* (September 4, 2012). Charles Johnson, "Julian Castro: A Radical Revealed," *Breitbart* (September 4, 2012), http://www.breitbart.com/Big-Government/2012/09/04/Julian-Castro-A-Radical-Revealed.

42. Johnson, "Julian Castro."

43. Mark Hugo Lopez and Paul Taylor, "Latino Voters in the 2012 Election," Pew Hispanic Center (November 7, 2012).

44. Mexican Immigrants in the United States, 2008, "Fact Sheet," Pew Hispanic Center, April 15, 2009, 1, http://pewhispanic.

org/files/factsheets/47.pdf. Rakesh Kochhar, Ana Gonzalez-Barrera, and Daniel Dockterman, "Through Boom and Bust: Minorities, Immigrants and Homeownership," Pew Hispanic Center, May 12, 2009, http://pewhispanic.org/reports/report.php?ReportID=109.

45. Warren Vieth, "GOP Faction Wants to Change 'Birthright Citizenship' Policy," *Los Angeles Times* (December 10, 2005). Ronald Brownstein, "Immigration May Again Drive a Wedge Between GOP, Latinos," *Los Angeles Times* (December 16, 2005). Marc Cooper, "The 15-Second Men," *Los Angeles Times* (May 1, 2005). Rick Sanchez vs Lou Dobbs on immigration, http://www.youtube.com/watch?v=cG_vHkm-C9E. Lou Dobbs - National Council of La Raza (The Race), http://www.youtube.com/watch?v=7kmTLk2Fgas&feature=related.

46. Brendan DeMelle, "Study Confirms Tea Party Was Created by Big Tobacco and Billionaire Koch Brothers," *Huffingtonpost* blog (February 12, 2013).

47. "Census Figures Show Mexicans Accounted for 44 Percent of Influx," *Dallas Morning News* (January 24, 2002). Sonia M. Perez, *Beyond the Census: Hispanics and an American Agenda* (Washington, DC: National Council of La Raza, August 2001), 18–19. Sam Dillon, "Mexico's Birth Rate Drops as Families Seek a Better Life," *New York Times* (June 14, 1999).

48. Karen Bernick, "Tapping into the Hispanic Workforce," National Hog Farmer, September 15, 2008, http://nationalhogfarmer.com/human-resources/0915-tapping-hispanic-workforce.

49. Allan Wall, "Eleven Mexicans Make Forbes 2012 List of Billionaires," Mexidata.info (March 19, 2012), http://mexidata.info/id3299.html.

50. Andrew Evans, *The E.U. Structural Funds* (New York: Oxford University Press, 1999), 62–65, 112. Paul Pierson and Stephan Leibfried, *European Social Policy: Between Fragmentation and Integration* (Washington, DC: Brookings Institution Press, 1995), 140–47. Spain, CIA World Fact Book, https://www.cia.gov/library/publications/the-world-factbook/geos/sp.html.

51. "Workers' Remittances to Mexico," *Business Frontier*, Issue 1, 2004, Federal Reserve Bank of Dallas, El Paso Branch, http://www.dallasfed.org/assets/documents/research/busfront/bus0401.pdf. Mark Hugo Lopez, Gretchen Livingston, and Rakesh Kochhar, "Hispanics and the Economic Downturn: Housing Woes and Remittance Cuts," January 8, 2009, http://pewresearch.org/pubs/1073/hispanics-and-the-economic-downturn-housing-woes-and-remittance-cuts. Georgia Pabst, "Economic Crisis Hits Latinos Helping Relatives Abroad," *Milwaukee Journal Sentinel* (February 18, 2009), http://www.jsonline.com/news/milwaukee/39820472.html.

52. "Resolution on Violence Against Women in Ciudad Juárez," Washington Office on Latin America, http://www.wola.org/es/node/383. John Burnett, "Explosive Theory on Killings of Juarez Women: Journalist Hints Wealthy Drug Lords Behind Scores of Murders," *NPR* (February 22, 2003), http://www.npr.org/templates/story/story.php?storyId=1532607. Bordertown—Jennifer Lopez, http://www.youtube.com/watch?v=NvZrbLjJowA. The Dead of Juarez, http://www.youtube.com/watch?v=2jvvk7AKKq4. Stop the Killing of the Women of Juarez, National Organization of Women, http://www.now.org/issues/global/juarez/.

53. "Mexico Under Siege: The Drug War at Our Door Steps," *Los Angeles Times*, http://projects.latimes.com/mexico-drug-war/#/its-a-war. The "War on Drugs" is a joke . . . (part 1), http://www.youtube.com/watch?v=4cefoV_A878. The Global Addiction—40 minutes documentary, http://www.youtube.com/watch?v=6SOvTdpQJwo&feature=related. War on drugs and Mexico's demise, http://www.youtube.com/watch?v=Yj7LKauVzro.

54. Mark Hugo Lopez, "The Latino Vote in the 2010 Elections," Pew Hispanic Cnter (November 2, 2010).

55. Jeff Biggers, "Yes, Virginia, They Still Ban Books in Tucson, Arizona," *Huffingtonpost* (September 28, 2012), http://www.huffingtonpost.com/jeff-biggers/yes-virginia-they-still-b_b_1923928.html. Mari Herreras, "TUSD Banning Books? Well Yes, and No, and Yes," (January 17, 2012), http://www.tucsonweekly.com/TheRange/archives/2012/01/17/tusd-banning-book-well-yes-and-no-and-yes.

56. "Outlawing Shakespeare: The Battle for the Tucson Mind," The Nonprofit Network, Video, Posted: Nov 16, 2012, http://newamericamedia.org/2012/11/outlawing-shakespeare-the-battle-for-the-tucson-mind.php.

57. "Arizona's Human Capital: Latino Students and their Families" (No date), www.edexcelencia.org/system/files/AZ-ACHE-FINAL.pdf. Demographic Profile of Hispanics in Arizona, 2010, Pew Hispanic Center (2012), http://www.pewhispanic.org/states/state/az/. Teresa Wiltz, "Expanding Age Gap Between Whites and Minorities May Increase U.S. Racial Divide," *America's Wire*, http://americaswire.org/drupal7/?q=content/expanding-age-gap-between-whites-and-minorities-may-increase-us-racial-divide. America's Wire states, "In Arizona, the median age for whites is 43 compared with 25 for Latinos, who comprise 31 percent of the state's population. On per-pupil spending for education, census data show that Arizona ranks 49th among the states and the District of Columbia. In terms of spending on transportation, the state is in the bottom quarter of all states, according to Dominique Apollon, research director at the Applied Research Center, which has offices in New York, Chicago and Oakland."

58. Raul A. Reyes, "Brisenia Flores Was a Victim of Border Vigilantes and Media Indifference," Huffington Post (March 8, 2011), http://www.huffingtonpost.com/raul-a-reyes/brisenia-flores-was-a-vic_b_832416.html. Vanessa Williamson, Theda Skocpol, and John Coggin, "The Tea Party and the Remaking of Republican Conservatism," *Perspectives on Politics* 9, no. 1 (March 2011), 28–43, http://scholar.harvard.edu/files/williamson/files/tea_party_pop.pdf.

59. Rodolfo F. Acuña, "Giving Hypocrisy a Bad Name: Censorship in Tucson," *CounterPunch* (February 7, 2012). I have written several dozen articles on the situation in Tucson, which can be found in CounterPunch and ThreeSonorans.com. Also see Jeff Biggers, *State Out of the Union: Arizona and the Final Showdown Over the American Dream* (New York: Nation Books, 2012). Cambium Report, May 2, 2011,

http://saveethnicstudies.org/assets/docs/state_audit/Cambi-um_Audit.pdf. Nolan L. Cabrera, Ph.D., Jeffrey F. Milem, Ph.D., Ronald W. Marx, Ph.D., "An Empirical Analysis of the Effects of Mexican American Studies Participation on Student Achievement within Tucson Unified School District, Report Submitted June 20, 2012, to Willis D. Hawley, Ph.D., Special Master for the Tucson Unified School District Desegregation Case." In effect the Special Master found for the program. However, the question is what the implementation of the decision will be like.

60. Yvonne Wingett Sanchez, "Arizona Immigration Law Still Supported, Poll Suggests SB 1070 Viewed Favorably by 65 Percent of Those Surveyed," *Arizona Republic* (April 23, 2012).

61. "UPDATE: SC Mexican restaurant responds to uproar over racist T-shirts," Palmetto Public Record (February 15, 2013), http://palmettopublicrecord.org/2013/01/07/sc-mexican-res-taurants-offensive-t-shirt-how-to-catch-an-illegal-immigrant/

62. Esperanza Peace and Justice Center, http://www.esperan-zacenter.org/.

63. Amy Hilsman Kastely, "Esperanza v. City of San Antonio: Politics, Power, and Culture," *Frontiers: A Journal of Women Studies* 24, nos. 2 & 3 (2003): 189, 190. Esperanza Peace and Justice Center, a Non-Profit Corporation, The San Antonio Lesbian & Gay Media Project, an Unincorporated Association, and VAN, an Unincorporated Association, Plaintiffs, v. City of San Antonio, and Howard Eak, in his official capacity as Mayor of the City of San Antonio, Defendants. Cause No. Sa-98-ca-0696-og United States District Court for the Western District of Texas, San Antonio Division 316 F. Supp. 2d 433; 2001 U.S. Dist. Lexis 6259 May 15, 2001, Decided.

64. Kastely, "Esperanza v. City of San Antonio," 195.

65. "Pro-Immigrant Marches Surging Nationwide," *The Nation* (April 10, 2006). http://www.thenation.com/blog/pro-immi-grant-marches-surging-nationwide. Jennifer Ludden, "Hundreds of Thousands March for Immigrant Rights," National Public Radio, http://www.npr.org/templates/story/story.php?storyId=5333768.

66. "Ku Klux Klan Rebounds with New Focus on Immigration, ADL Reports," *PR Newswire* (February 6, 2007). Cynthia Leonor Garza, "Immigration Debate Reached the Point of Protests, Walkouts," *Houston Chronicle* (December 31, 2006), 1. Leslie Fulbright, "Huge Crowd Marches Through L.A.," *San Francisco Chronicle* (May 2, 2006), A8. Gong Lin II and Arin Gencer, "The Immigration Debate; Gearing Up, and Girding for, Protests; Around the U.S., Cities Brace for Marches. In L.A., a Huge Crowd Is Expected Along Wilshire," *Los Angeles Times* (May 1, 2006), A1. Kevin Roderick, "Police Fighting with Protestors," *LA Observed* (May 1, 2006).

67. Immigration March in Dallas, CBS, April 20, 2006, http://www.cbsnews.com/video/watch/?id=1483046n. MacArthur Park LAPD Police Riot 2007 Mexica Movement, http://www.youtube.com/watch?v=QYVWAqSRBUU&feature=PlayList&p=0F7E18335ECC3073&playnext=1&playnext_from=PL&index=38. 05/01/06 Police Shooting Mexican Protest Chief Bratton Riot, http://www.youtube.com/watch?v=CLfWLp4C8e0. Immigrants March NYC (May 1, 2006), http://www.youtube.com/watch?v=oTHoA-0TjYg. César Chávez and Immigrants' Rights (March 2006), Sacramento, http://www.youtube.com/watch?v=-3mkPF0WTH8. Immigration March in Seattle (May 1, 2006), http://www.youtube.com/watch?v=g2km0cyWQnQ. [LA] Immigration March, http://www.youtube.com/watch?v=4markP8B4Vg. Dallas Mega-March Movie, April 9, 2006 (producer Bill Millet), http://www.youtube.com/watch?v=U0PiTtZdvAM. Second Day of North Texas Student Walkouts, http://www.youtube.com/watch?v=ucL_mARah2I&feature=related.

68. Growing Activism: Undocumented Students/DREAM Act, University of California Television, http://www.uctv.tv/search-details.aspx?showID=12488.

69. War on drugs and Mexico's demise, http://www.youtube.com/watch?v=Yj7LKauVzro. Mexico Drug War, http://www.youtube.com/watch?v=pLlrbAZv9Do.

70. "DREAM Act: President Obama Reaffirms Unwavering Support for DREAM Act at Univision's Latino Forum," *Washington Times* (September 21, 2012).

71. David Reyes, "GI Forum Address," *Los Angeles Times* (August 7, 1980).

EPILOGUE

The Chicana/o Legacy

LEARNING OBJECTIVES

- In your own words tell the legacy of the Chicana/o movement to the Chicanas/os/Latinos of today.
- Show where the disparate Latino groups live in the United States.
- Explain how funded right-wing movements have fueled racism and xenophobia.
- Calculate what the future will bring for Mexican American/Latino groups in the United States by 2050.

A major mistake made by the Chicana/o generation was not explaining its legacy to Mexican and Latino immigrants who are the beneficiaries of the rights and benefits that they take for granted. These rights were won by previous generations of Chicanas/os. Indeed, many students and their parents immigrated to the United States because of the failure of the Mexican and other Latin American governments to take care of their working poor. Once in the United States, immigrants were unwanted and often lacked legal protections. The first haven for most Latino immigrants was and is Mexican barrios where they work alongside Mexican workers who in their time overcame similar barriers. During the 1960s Chicana/o student and community organizations fought for the right of immigrant students to pursue a higher education. The protection of the foreign born became a priority for the community.

The legal struggle of Mexican Americans goes back to before *In Re Ricardo Rodriguez* (1897) that affirmed Rodríguez's right to citizenship and the right to vote if naturalized. Those opposing Ricardo Rodríguez's citizenship said he was disqualified under the law because Mexicans were not a "white person, nor an African, nor of African descent, and is therefore not capable of becoming an American citizen." A federal statute (1872) specified that only whites and Africans had the right to be citizens; however, the statute did not specifically deny Mexicans that right. The court found for Rodriguez based on the Texas Constitution and the Treaty of Guadalupe Hidalgo.[1]

The racial status of Mexicans, and what rights they held under the 14th Amendment, was litigated for most of the twentieth century. Organizations such as La Alianza Hispano Americana, the League of United Latin American Citizens, and the American G.I. Forum were at the vanguard of this legal struggle. The definition of race as it pertained to Mexican Americans, and by inference other Latinos, was intensely argued in the courts during the 1950s and 1960s. At stake was not only a definition but also entitlements and protections under law established in cases such as *Brown v. the Board of Education* (1954) and by the Voting Rights Act (1965).

The constitutional debate over these and other issues continue to this day. It is an arduous struggle, and as late as the 1960s some Americans questioned the eligibility of Chicanas/os to benefit from the War on Poverty and other programs of the decade. Chicana/o veterans are quick to add that aside from the courts, Chicanas/os won their rights in three major wars. By the twenty-first century it was clear that Mexican Americans were entitled to equal protection under the 14th Amendment and civil rights legislation. In the broadest sense, the term Chicanas/os included anyone of Mexican and Latino origin. They are protected by *Brown* and other court cases. For example, they cannot be legally segregated in the schools, and children born in the United States to undocumented parents cannot be deported. In Arizona, U.S.-born children of undocumented immigrants were derisively labeled "anchor babies," a pejorative term. Mexican American organizations are struggling to protect this right of birth.

Under the 14th Amendment, a child born in the United States is automatically an American citizen, and Mexican and Latino organizations have fought attempts to take citizenship away from them. In 2010 Arizona Republican State Senator Russell Pearce and Republican Representative John Kavanagh tried to formally introduce a bill challenging the 14th Amendment's citizenship clause. National Public Radio reported, "Sen. Lindsey Graham (R–South Carolina) has argued that illegal immigrants come [to] the U.S. with the intent to have babies, who are automatically granted citizenship under the 14th Amendment."[2]

Strengthening these constitutional arguments is the holding in *Jose Cisneros v. Corpus Christi Independent School District* (1970) that broke the discrimination barrier for Mexican Americans and other Latinos. It extended the protections of *Brown v. the Board of Education* to Mexican Americans. It recognized them as a minority group that could be and frequently was discriminated against. Discrimination such as segregation was ruled unconstitutional. Cisneros replaced the "other white" argument of *Hernández v. State of Texas* (1954). Mexican Americans "were legally defined as an identifiable group that had suffered historic discrimination."[3]

> *Mexican-Americans, or Americans with Spanish surnames, or whatever they are called, or whatever they would like to be called, Latin-Americans, or several other new names of identification—and parenthetically the court will take notice that this naming . . . phenomena is similar to that experienced in the Negro groups: black, Negro, colored, and now black again, with an occasional insulting epithet that is used less and less by white people in the South, fortunately. Occasionally you hear the word "Mexican" still spoken in a derogatory way in the Southwest—it is clear to this court that these people for whom we have used the word Mexican-Americans to describe their class, group, or segment of our population, are an identifiable ethnic minority in the United States, and especially so in the Southwest, in Texas and in Corpus Christi.*[4]

In other words, Mexican Americans explicitly or implicitly endured and suffered a history of discrimination.

The *Cisneros* ruling goes beyond the definition of race—white and black have historically been the standard used in determining rights and in who was deserving of legal protections to correct inequalities caused by historical racism. *Cisneros* raised the principle of equity in considering whether an individual or group suffered a history of discrimination. This is important today when increasing numbers of upper-middle-class Latin Americans are immigrating to the United States, and some claim group identification. The problem is that many do not have the same experiences as working-class Latinos.

The question then is, who should be treated as a minority under the *Cisneros* standard? This problem surfaced during the 2001 nomination of Miguel Estrada, a 40-year-old native of Honduras, to the U.S. Court of Appeals for the District of Columbia. Republicans claimed that Estrada's nomination marked a milestone for Latinos. Estrada was from an upper-middle-class immigrant family and immigrated to the United States as a teenager, and he did not identify with Latinos in this country or did he acknowledge the history of racism toward them. His father owned a small plantation in Honduras and Estrada attended private schools there.[5]

Estrada's experiences contrast with those of Sonia Sotomayor, who was born in Puerto Rico and was raised by a single mother after her father died when she was nine. She grew up in a public housing project in the South Bronx; she attended Princeton where she graduated summa cum laude. At Yale Law School, she was the editor of the Yale Law Review. She worked as a prosecutor, trial judge, and appellate judge. Sotomayor's life experiences qualified her under the rule of *Cisneros* (the Jones-Shafroth Act granted Puerto Ricans U.S. citizenship in 1917).[6]

Whether or not a person agrees with the politics of Alberto Gonzales, former attorney general under George W. Bush, it cannot be denied that the *Cisneros* case applies to him. Born in San Antonio, Texas, he is the second of eight children. His father, who died in 1982, was a construction worker. His grandparents may or may not have been undocumented. Gonzales graduated from Harvard Law School.[7]

Why is this discussion important? It is because the way we acquire knowledge determines the questions we ask, and the questions determine the outcome. How we acquire knowledge is called epistemology, and life experiences add to how we deal with the problems of all sectors of society. This is why Supreme Court Justice Sonia Sotomayor said: "I would hope that a wise Latina woman with the richness of her experiences would more often than not reach a better conclusion than a white male who hasn't lived that life."

Remember that words and life experiences are important in forming identity. The fact that most Supreme Court justices come from upper-middle-class families and attended Harvard, Yale, or other Ivy League law schools makes a difference in how they see things. Life experiences define interests and expose the funds of knowledge that individuals have. The bottom line is that not all Americans have the same economic and political interests, just as they don't have similar life experiences. There are differences of class, ethnicity, gender, and sexuality. Identity goes beyond a surname or color; our past has shaped us, the past is us.[8] For this reason it is important to examine the life experiences and interests of politicians such as Marco Rubio, Ted Cruz, or Miguel Estrada—ethnicity has nothing to do with it.

Who Are Latinos? Where Do They Live?

The Census Bureau, the media, and institutions seem to refer to anyone with brown hair and brown eyes or whose name ends in a vowel as Hispanic or Latino. However, each group has its own identity and personality. In 2000, 32.8 million Latinos resided in the United States, representing 12 percent of the total U.S. population. In 2012 the number climbed to 53 million Latinos, comprising 17 percent of the total U.S. population. The 2010 Census registered 33 million Mexican-origin residents (64.9 percent of Latinos); Puerto Ricans within the United States numbered 4.7 million (9.2 percent); Cuban Americans, 1.9 million (3.7 percent); Salvadorans, 1.8 million (3.6 percent); Dominicans, 1.5 million (3 percent); Guatemalans, 1.1 million (2.2 percent); Colombians, 972,000 (1.9 percent); Hondurans, 731,000 (1.4 percent); Ecuadorans, 665,000 (1.3 percent); and Peruvians, 609,000 (1.2 percent).[9]

> A majority (51%) say they most often identify themselves by their family's country of origin; just 24% say they prefer a pan-ethnic label . . . by a ratio of more than two-to-one (69% versus 29%), survey respondents say that the more than 50 million Latinos in the U.S. have many different cultures rather than a common culture. Respondents do, however, express a strong, shared connection to the Spanish language. More than eight-in-ten (82%) Latino adults say they speak Spanish, and nearly all (95%) say it is important for future generations to continue to do so.[10]

In March 2012, 11.1 million unauthorized immigrants resided in the United States. Just over 37.1 percent of Latinos in 2012 were foreign born; 36 percent of Mexicans, 59 percent of Cubans, 57 percent of Dominicans, and 62 percent of Salvadorans were foreign born—suggesting strong ties with their mother countries.[11]

The Mexican population, although it has spread throughout the United States, has huge concentrations in California where 11.8 million live, followed by Texas with 8.4 million Mexicans. These two states account for 61 percent of the total Mexican American population. Latinos are concentrated as national-origin groups in four counties, as listed in Table 1.[12]

TABLE 1 Top U.S. Counties, by Hispanic Origin Group

Origin Group	County	Population	Share of National Hispanic Origin Group Population (%)
Mexicans	Los Angeles County, CA	3,510,677	11
Puerto Ricans	Bronx County, Ny	298,951	6
Cubans	Miami-Dade County, FL	856,007	48
Salvadorans	Los Angeles County, FL	358,82	22
Dominicans	Bronx County, Ny	240,987	17
Guatemalans	Los Angeles County, FL	214,939	21
Colombians	Miami-Dade County, FL	114,701	13
Hondurans	Miami-Dade County, FL	54,192	9
Ecuadorians	Queens County, Ny	98,512	17
Peruvians	Miami-Dade County, FL	40,701	8

Note: "Share if national Hispanic Origin group population" shows the share of a Hispanic origin group's national population in a signal county. For Example, 11% of the nation's Mexicans-origin population lives in Los Angeles County and nearly half (48%) of the nation's Cuban-origin population lives in Miami-Dade County.

Source: Adapted from Pew Research Center, originally from 2010 U.S. Census Summary File 2

PEW RESEARCH CENTER

A different way of looking at the distribution is to note that more than one in five Latinos live in just four counties: Latinos comprise 48.1 percent of Los Angeles County's 9.9 million people; Miami-Dade, Florida, 64.5 percent of 2.5 million; Harris County, Texas, which includes Houston, 41.9 percent of 4.2 million; and Cook County, Illinois, which includes Chicago, 16.2 percent of 12.9 million. U.S. Mexicans were the overwhelming majority of Latinos in three of these four counties.[13]

Latino groups share many characteristics. Except for Cubans, most Latinos are much younger than white Euro-Americans. The median age of Latinos nationally is 27 years, 10 years below the national median of 37. The median age of Mexicans nationwide was 25 years; Puerto Ricans, 27 years; Salvadorans, 29; Dominicans, 29; and Cubans, 40. The young age of Mexicanas contributed to a higher birthrate. Based on this internal growth, demographers project that by the year 2030, Latinos will comprise half of Texas. "The majority of babies now being born in California are of Hispanic descent, forecasting Latinos will be a majority sometime in the future." Though the numbers of U.S. Mexicans seem overwhelming, other U.S. Latino groups have a strong and unique presence. Significant for future elections is that "[The Latino] median age is 27 years—and just 18 years among native-born Hispanics—compared with 42 years for that of white non-Hispanics."[14]

The major characteristic of the Latino population as a whole is growth, with a doubling in size from 2000 to 2010. Although Latinos are concentrated in the West, and are an urban population, since the 1990s this population has spread nationally. Most Latinos continued to live in nine states: Arizona, California, Colorado, Florida, Illinois, New Mexico, New Jersey, New York, and Texas. However, the decade saw a shift with Latinos moving beyond city borders. The top five fastest-growing Latino counties in the country are Luzerne, Pennsylvania (479 percent change); Henry, Georgia (339 percent change); Kendall, Illinois (338 percent change); Douglas, Georgia (321 percent change); and Shelby, Alabama (297 percent change). Moreover, Latinos are now in Arkansas, Kentucky, Maryland, Mississippi, North Carolina, South Carolina, Tennessee, and South Dakota. Most of these are conservative, former Confederate states.[15]

The Ramifications of Growth and Spreading Nationally

While cities such as Los Angeles, San Antonio, Chicago, and New York have well-established organizational infrastructures, the protection of the rights of Latinos living in the periphery is problematic, and it is often difficult to get basic medical care or the resources to counter racism.[16] This organizational problem makes it hard to organize from the ground up, and to network with other regions in relationships that extend beyond the acquaintance level. The absence of a defense complex is true even in Arizona where Mexican Americans have resided since before the Euro-American takeover, and where Latinos comprise a third of the state. Local Latino organizations are overwhelmed and stunted by the rush of outside money from special interests.

Therefore, it is important in the age of Citizens United (2010) to consider the impact of corporate money on Latinos and other working-class people. In Citizens United the Supreme Court ruled 5-to-4 that the government "may not ban political spending by corporations in candidate elections." According to the majority, the ban violated the First Amendment's most basic free speech principle. In essence it ruled that the government was regulating political speech. The dissenters countered that this case licenses corporate money to flood the political marketplace.[17] This is, however, nothing new; the hijacking of the 14th Amendment dates back to the 1870s and 1880s; in a series of cases the Court ruled that corporations were persons entitled to protection from state regulation.

Arizona state and local governments are controlled by special interests such as oil billionaires David H. Koch and Charles G. Koch and the American Legislative Exchange Council (ALEC).[18] This cabal is joined by local and business groups such as the Southern Arizona Leadership Council (SALC) (Tucson) that own the Republican Party and Blue Dog Democrats. These special interests mobilize the fears of an aging white and politically backward population. The tactic is similar to that used successfully by the Republican Party in exploiting social issues such as gay marriage and gun rights to mobilize their base. In the case of Arizona, it is the fear of the Mexican. This fear enabled a 30-year avoidance of court desegregation rulings, and resulted in a minimal per capita expenditure per child, in which Arizona ranks last among the states. Arizona SB 1070 targeted Latino undocumented workers and their families, and HB 2281 licensed the dismantling of the Tucson Unified School District's Mexican American Studies department. Instead of "The Russians Are Coming," the cry is "The Invasion of Illegal Aliens" who, like the body snatchers, are out to do white people harm.[19]

It is no coincidence that Arizona State Senator Russell Pearce, a lackey of ALEC, introduced SB 1070. The stakes are high, and it comes down to profit: much of Arizona's public services and resources are privatized. "Private prisons in Arizona have housed DUI offenders and other low- and medium-security inmates since the early 1990s." By the late part of the first decade of this century, state legislators were moving to privatize maximum security prisons. The prizes are tremendous profits from warehousing inmates and control of employee pension funds.[20] SB 1070 ensures a bonanza in the form of additional prison inmates.

The Corrections Corporation of America, one of the largest private prison corporations in the US, earned over $1.7 billion in revenue in 2009, 40% of which came from ICE, the US Marshalls Office and Federal Bureau of Prisons. In Arizona specifically, the Governor's office proposed a budget that set aside $98 million for private prison corporations alone, mostly to accommodate the influx of undocumented immigrants with new private and state prison beds, according to the Arizona Education Network.[21]

This corruption leads to abuses such as those by Maricopa County Sheriff Joe Arpaio.

ICE has relied on local police, like Sheriff Joe Arpaio, to meet its goal to detain hundreds of thousands of immigrants. This has led to the detention of more than 380,000 people in FY 2009 in unsafe and inhumane conditions with no meaningful access to lawyers or hope for a fair day in

> *court. It has also resulted in the deportation of 387,000 people, tearing apart countless families.*
> *SB 1070 will be effective at one thing: continuing to fill Arpaio's jails and driving the growth of*
> *the detention industry across the country.*[22]

SB 1070 and poor schools further ensure that large numbers of Mexican and Latino inmates will fill the jails as long as the round-up mentality persists and Mexicans keep dropping out of school. It is dangerous because like any other form of hysteria it is unreasonable and innocent people get hurt. In Chapter 16 we saw how Minutemen shot down nine-year-old Brisenia Flores. This assassination is not an aberration.

Racism led to other shootings that the press and the media have not reported. This contrasts to the media's irresponsible coverage of the shooting of border patrol personnel; more often than not the media jumps to unfounded conclusions when reporting the shooting of border patrol officers. Hatred abets these outrages, and it encourages Arizonans to ignore the corporate takeover of their state. The injustices are hidden by the irrationality of the Tea Partiers that run wild, holstering guns and intimidating progressives and minorities. These groups are financed by predators such as the Koch brothers, the third richest men in the United States who fund Tea Party groups through front organizations such as Americans for Prosperity, Freedom Works, and Citizens for a Sound Economy ($12 million).[23] The chaos also serves the purpose of keeping the National Rifle Association and gun dealers prosperous. Many of the drug cartels shop in Arizona where gun dealers do not register the guns or ammunition they sell to the cartels. In turn, U.S. banks launder the profits.[24]

Education and government jobs are also a source of patronage, providing well-paid employment for people such as Tucson Unified School District (TUSD) Superintendent John Pedicone, who did the predators' bidding. A former vice-president of the Southern Arizona Leadership Council (SALC) Pedicone had three years of experience in a small district, but is paid a salary comparable to that of a much larger California school district. Pedicone dismantled the TUSD Mexican American Studies program. Ironically, this happened while the TUSD is under a court order to desegregate. The Tucson superintendent in defiance of this order also allowed the proliferation of privatized charter schools, which in Arizona were approved in the 1990s; charter schools are heavily white. Blogger David Safier writes,

> *No question, our traditional public schools suffer from racial, ethnic and economic segregation,*
> *too often creating separate-but-unequal schools. It's a huge problem. But charter schools prom-*
> *ise to make the problem far worse. That's the dirty little secret about the push for charters. The*
> *unstated mission of the conservative "education reform"/"school choice" movement is to create*
> *publicly funded, good-to-great schools for students coming from middle class to affluent homes*
> *while the rest of the student population attends educational holding tanks which teach them*
> *basic skills and little else.*[25]

The fear machine keeps charter schools stocked with students by spreading fear propaganda on the violence in the public schools, and exaggerating so-called racial tensions. Mexicans and other minorities, according to them, diminish the quality of education. The outcome is bad schools that ensure future inmates for the prisons. Lastly, Mexican-baiting elects failed white politicians to office who are easily bought.

These special interest groups and individuals, or predators as they are called by Arizona progressives, have huge amounts of money and resources. Local groups cannot muster these kind of resources. There is also the problem of communication with groups outside of Arizona. The reason the word got out about SB 1070 was because of trade unions and a national network of pro-immigrant groups.

However, it is more difficult to communicate attacks on Mexican American education to organizations outside Arizona. In this case, word was spread mostly through tedious person-to-person contact through the Internet; national Latino groups ignored the attack against a pedagogy that had stemmed the dropout problem, and they ignored the censorship of books. Thus the struggle resembles Sisyphus's rolling the boulder up the hill.

Arizona is not alone in the assault on immigrants and as in the case of other states the prisons have been privatized. Incarcerating immigrants has brought a rainfall in profits. The Internet has reported attacks on the foreign-born nationally. The bloggers have kept the public apprised since the mainstream media ignore the problem. An equally present danger is the excuse of that budgetary problems make it necessary to eliminate or weaken programs serving minorities and the poor. The latter is asking to privatization, which has not been slowed by the economic depression beginning in 2008.

Throughout the country Republican governors and even Latino politicos are cooperating in privatizing education and public resources. They call the Wall Street predators job creators although they took the country to the brink of disaster. They propose privatizing social security, the post office, public lands, and everything and anything of value. In Los Angeles, attorney Richard Riordan made a fortune by speculating in municipal and county properties and downtown Los Angeles real estate. He became mayor in 1993, and moved to privatize everything in sight, even making an unsuccessful move to privatize the main city library. Riordan along with billionaire Eli Broad control a host of politicos including most of the Los Angeles City Schools Board of Education. Charter schools are part of his mantra.

In 2012 the predators in California worked against Proposition 30 and for Proposition 32.[26] The predators' assault on 30 was to avoid $6 billion in taxes on the rich to repair California's embattled and decaying public schools. The purpose of the opposition to Proposition 30—the "No" people—was destroy teacher unions by making sure that the public school system went over the fiscal cliff. Yes on Proposition 32 was about destroying trade unions; it was a power grab designed to empower the super rich to take over California as they have Arizona. It denied unions the right to contribute to elections thus giving corporations a freehand. Not surprisingly, money flowed from Arizona to help fund Proposition 32 and other corporate-friendly California propositions.

Propositions 30 and 32 must be put into a historical context. The genesis of the propositions dates back to post–World War II. American corporations moved to regain the political and economic hegemony that they lost during the Great Depression. The nation's plutocracy wanted to continue looting the national treasury while returning to the laissez-faire relationship with government that they enjoyed in the 1920s. The first step was to destroy the unions. After World War II, the plutocracy engineered the passage of the Taft–Hartley Act of 1948 that weakened unions and purged militants from labor.

Organized labor continued to be a thorn in the side of the plutocracy that resented the high taxes necessary to educate Americans after World War II. During the 1960s, a war broke out over the funding of public education, which continues to the present. The plutocrats or predators slowly but surely eroded the public funding of higher education. In most states it transferred the social cost of production from the plutocracy to the middle class and working poor.

The direct assault on the public schools came about with the passage of California Proposition 13 (1978) that underfunded K–12 and higher education in California. It dismantled a premier educational system that resulted in California joining Mississippi and Arizona in low levels of school funding. Locally, the cost of funding schools was transferred from wealthy home and commercial property owners to the poor. No longer did municipalities fund education; this responsibility was shifted to the state's General Fund. Since the year 2000 the plutocrats have waged an unrelenting war on trade unions. They have warred against teachers and public employees, blaming them for the fiscal crisis. With the Citizens United court ruling, the only obstacle in their takeovers are the unions. As mentioned, money poured into California from Arizona to support Proposition 32. People like the Koch brothers joined California privatizers such as former LA City Mayor Richard Riordan and billionaire Charles Munger, Jr. The only thing that stood and stands in the way of a corporate takeover of California is the trade unions. Although the plutocrats lost Proposition 32, they showed strength in recruiting current and past Latino elected officials, many of them liberals, to act as spokespeople for the proposition. If you want to know what motivates them, follow the money. Latino support for plutocrats' position on Propositions 30 and 32 should not be a surprise.

Quo Vadis? What Will the Future Bring?

Education pays tremendous dividends to Latinos and other communities. A recent article by Professors Anne-Marie Nuñez and Elizabeth Murakami-Ramalho underscores that in 2010, María Hernández Ferrier was inaugurated as the first president of the new Texas A&M University campus in San Antonio. She was the first Latina college president in the nation. The article points out that there is still discrimination, however, citing Arizona. Despite this,

> *Although the number of Latino students in US higher education has increased in recent decades, and Latinos have now surpassed African Americans as the largest minority group in US higher education (currently constituting 22 percent of total enrollment), Latinos as a group still have the lowest educational attainment of any racial or ethnic group. According to Pew Hispanic Center data, only about 13 percent of Latinos age twenty-five and over hold college degrees (compared with 18 percent of African Americans, 31 percent of whites, and 50 percent of Asian Americans). Latinos consequently tend to work in low-skill occupations. Pew data show that only about half as many Latinos (19 percent) as whites (39 percent) are employed in management, science, engineering, law, education, entertainment, the arts, and health care.*[27]

The strongest point in the article is its call for collective responsibility, which will be needed just to maintain our present levels, and frankly those levels are unacceptable. From personal experience I can say that we Latinos or Chicanas/os, which I still use, have come a long way. When I arrived at San Fernando Valley State College in 1969, between 50 and 100 students of Mexican origin attended SFVSC. Today, there are 11,000 Latinos of which over 8,200 are Mexican Americans. However, times have changed. Chicana/o Studies offers 166 sections of CHS per semester. However, 75–80 percent of the CSUN departments don't have a single Mexican American professor. Despite numerical changes there is no cohesive value system that binds the *majority* of Latino students. Membership in Latino fraternities and sororities far outnumbers that in Chicana/o political organizations.

The dramatic progress of Mexican Americans took place as the result of the historic rise in the Chicana/o and other Latino population of the late 1960s and early 1970s. It was a groundswell with students throughout the Southwest criticizing high schools for not offering college prep classes, and pressuring guidance counselors not to discourage Mexican American students from applying to college. Simultaneously, they pressured colleges to initiate special programs such as EOP (the Educational Opportunity Program) to offer students from disadvantaged areas' special admissions, counseling, and outreach services. Further, the environment in California and some other places was such that cost of education was not prohibitive. Community colleges were free and at the California State Colleges the state paid 100 percent of instructional costs. When I attended Los Angeles State College in the late 1950s I paid no tuition. By 1970 the cost was $50 a semester; today it is over $3,200.[28]

The student walkouts in Texas and California as well as the rest of the country created a mind set that education was not a privilege but a right. In sum, the students were taking back their history, and took pride in it. At a forum circa 1970, Dr. Ernesto Galarza, a renowned Chicano scholar, and one of the few academicians that I do not begrudge calling "doctor," was asked why we didn't just forget about the Alamo and the atrocities committed by groups such as the Texas Rangers. Galarza replied that it was necessary to know the past, warts and all, if only to fend off inane questions such as, "Well, the Italians made it, so did the Jews and the Irish, so what's wrong with the Mexicans?" According to Galarza, working Mexican families always struggled for justice and a better life. Mexicans struggled for decent housing; they fought against racial discrimination and demanded integrated schools. History shows that Mexicans fought back!

Galarza made the remarks in the context of his *Spiders in the House and Workers in the Field* (1970), and another book he was writing, *Alviso: The Crisis of a Barrio*[29] (1973). In the former, Galarza showed how the government joined agribusiness during the Di Giorgio Strike to break the strike. He related "Alviso" to this incident, and pressed the urgency of saving the Alviso community. To paraphrase Galarza, "Without a community people lose their historical memory," allowing history to be rewritten to make it seem as if Mexicans are the problem.

This theme goes back to Galarza's 1966 address before the Center for the Study of Democratic Institutions in Santa Barbara, California—an institute formed by Robert Maynard Hutchinson to bring about democratic reforms. The title was "La Mula No Nacio Arisca," or in English, "The mule was not born stubborn . . . it was made this way." A manito brother, Estevàn Arellano, told me that in New Mexico the saying went, "La mula no era arisca los chingasos la hicieron así." The moral is that Mexicans and blacks are not sullen or resentful because they are born that way but because society makes them that way.[30] Relating this to Alviso, Galarza said that in order to fight injustice we had to have a historical memory, without which there is no unity of purpose.

As mentioned, this scenario is currently being acted out in Tucson where so-called custodians of public education are trying to erase Mexican American history. They have made it subversive for Mexicans and other minorities to know the past. According to them, learning about injustice contributes to un-Americanism, divides races, and is unpatriotic. Ironically, it is Tucson and the state of Arizona that stand accused of segregation and offering Mexican Americans bad school.

Saving Humpty Dumpty

A lot more thought has to be paid to the question, "Why Chicana/o Studies?" CHS are not a whim; they are not a fad. They are part of the historical reasons for the struggle of the Mexican American community to obtain equality of opportunity. If these reasons are forgotten, CHS will be minimized—reduced to whims and fads, obfuscating why institutions of higher learning continue to exclude Latinos, and what role this plays in keeping them powerless.

The failure to ask "why" perpetuates the myth that higher education is dedicated to a search for the Truth, and open to all Americans. Chicana/o Studies are tolerated because it is politically expedient. They are tolerated to placate Mexican American and Latino students and a growing Latino electorate. Latinos therefore should not take for granted that their growth in voting power will alone result in correcting society's injustices. It was great that President Barack Obama conceded to Dream Act activists in June of 2012 giving them a temporary amnesty; but we must remember that it was expedient for that moment in time and it will take much more to make this executive order permanent.

Numbers matter, since 1970, the Mexican American population grew from 5 million to over six times that number in 2012. It went from a regional to a national minority. In 1970 the Mexican/Latino student population in the mammoth Los Angeles Unified School District was 22 percent; today it exceeds 75 percent. In the City of Los Angeles the Latino population has zoomed from about 15 percent to just over 50 percent. We have more Latino elected officials than at any time in our past, but what does that mean? Are these elected officials any more effective than those in the past? Do they identify with the interests of the community? I am certain, given the 2012 election results, that there will be more *light* brown faces at the Republican Conventions, but is this necessarily good? Babies constantly ask, Why? However, the schools and other institutions suppress the spirit of "why." Even historians who are supposed to be skeptical generally go along with the program.

Bonding and forging a sense of community goes beyond one's skin color or surname. There has to be a sense of caring. In 1966, I was personally moved by an essay written by a 13-year-old Tucson student in a National Education Association study, *The Invisible Minority* (1966). It began:

> Me To begin with, I am a Mexican. That sentence has a scent of bitterness as it is written. I feel if it weren't for my nationality I would accomplish more. My being a Mexican has brought about my lack of initiative. No matter what I attempt to do, my dark skin always makes me feel that I will fail. Another thing that "gripes" me is that I am such a coward. I absolutely will not fight for something even if I know I'm right. I do not have the vocabulary that it would take to express myself strongly enough.[31]

I almost cried when I read the essay. Most Mexican American professionals of my generation suffered inferiority complexes. The dropout rate among youth was horrendous, but I stayed active because I cared. How can you rectify society if you do not feel the injustices? But also, how can you fill the epistemological gap between that generation and today's? Reading and listening to educators such as George I. Sánchez was important. There was a consensus among Mexican American scholars regarding the essentiality of identity in motivating Mexican American students who had become disaffected with the schools. The dropout challenge kept me in the movement and in Los Angeles.

The first priority of Chicana/o educators was not exclusively to reach the upper third of the student community who already possessed the necessary skills to succeed. The goal was to reach the bottom two-thirds who just needed the opportunity to get ahead or, for that matter, fail. (Today because of the rising cost of tuition, students can't afford to fail.) It was the lower two-thirds that needed motivation and skill development. As mentioned, for all of the obstacles, it was easier then than now. The main obstacle in 1969 was institutional racism. Today under the guise of fiscal savings and the depression beginning in 2008, the lower two-thirds of Latin students are being denied access by rising tuition costs. The pretext is that these sectors are not being excluded because they can always go to community colleges, which is not true. The myth of the American Dream is kept alive; forget that community colleges are severely overcrowded and their costs have skyrocketed.

There were few Chicana/o educators in the 1960s; there were less than a hundred Mexican American PhDs nationally. The goal was mass education. Coming out of a public school teaching background, I always reminded myself that my priority was to teach the child, not the subject. Progressive educators from the beginning of large immigrant waves adhered to this principle. They advocated for compulsory school attendance, and the formation of labor and ethnic schools. Reformers espoused mass education as the linchpin of a democratic society. This was the mission reflected in the 1960 California Master Plan for Higher Education that has today been scrapped.

Hardly any mention is made today of the fact that if the commitment to mass education is abandoned, class differences will proliferate within the Mexican American and Latino communities and social stratification will become more pronounced. Hypocritically, society will claim that there is equal opportunity for Mexican Americans because it is open to the upper third of the community. In just over 40 years, the stairway to middle-class heaven is being dismantled.

In this conclusion, I am not calling for ideological purity but instead for an ideological coherence. As recipients of the legacy of Chicana/o struggle and sacrifices, we must renew our commitment to mass education. It is not just our obligation but our duty to keep access to higher education open. The fact is that working-class students are being priced out of public and private nonprofit colleges. Recent spikes in tuition and the overcrowding of colleges and universities impact Latinos and minorities most. In recent years growth of for-profit schools has occurred; it is claimed that they have picked up some of the slack for the overcrowding. Indeed, the for-profit colleges have outpaced the growth of public and private not-for-profit institutions. From 2000 to 2008, public college and university enrollment increased 19 percent; private, not-for-profit enrollment rose 15 percent over this eight-year period—contrasted with for-profit enrollment that tripled. While this growth is impressive, the for-profit schools enroll only about 7 percent of all undergraduate students. Full-time students at for-profit schools paid an average of $30,900 annually for tuition in the 2007–2008 academic year. This was almost double the $15,600 average paid at public universities. The average cost of attending a private nonprofit college was $26,600. The problem is that the student default on loans is much higher at the for-profit schools with fewer earning degrees. The result is that disillusionment has set in, especially among Latino males who are not pursuing a higher education. Following the pattern among African Americans, the ratio between Latin males and Latinas is 30-70 in California state universities.

As mentioned, the private sector is refusing to pay for higher education, although the private sector profits most from a trained workforce. Education subsidizes the private sector. The privatization is not the answer as shiwb by the record of for-profit colleges. Alternative models have to be examined since getting a higher education determines social and economic mobility.

We have entered a period of steady of decline, and we are in for bad times. While 9 in 10 Latinos say it is "necessary" to get a college education to get ahead in life, less than half of Latino 18- to 25-year-olds say they plan to earn a Bachelor of Arts degree. Of those surveyed, three-quarters listed the need to help their families financially as a reason not to go to college; over 40 percent cited the high costs of higher education.[32] The choice is to do something now or write off several generations of poor working-class Latinos.

Meanwhile, we should take inspiration from the Dreamers that counter Republicans and their extremist allies. Almost daily, the Dream Act Movement grows in size and militancy. After years of fear, these young people have come out and wear their immigration status on their chests. No longer afraid, they have taken the struggle to another level by committing acts of civil disobedience. They also have numerous web sites that explain the justice of their cause and announce activities. At CSUN "Dreams to be Heard" works with other networks in the community and on other groups on other campuses such as the California Dream Network founded in 2003. (http://www.cadreamnetwork.org/). Two of my former graduates Lizabeth Mateo and Alma de Jesús have joined a more proactive group of dreamers. Mateo was one of the nine activists known as "Dream 9" who crossed over into Nogales, Mexico and sought to re-enter without documentation. They were held and released while their asylum cases come before a court. Throughout the book there are examples of profiles of courage and changes made as a result of the sacrifices of the few—who realize that dreams have a price.

In conclusion, the obstacles to equality and equity in society almost seem insurmountable for those on the bottom rung. In dealing with the macro problems confronting us, we should not forget to correct the imperfections within our first lines of defense—the community and ourselves. We should correct our own defects—machismo, sexism, homophobia, and racism toward other groups. Teaching for over 50 years, I am struck by how these imperfections become worse with the consumption of alcohol. Imperfections cannot be cured with a bironga in our hand. Sexual harassment, rape, spousal and child abuse, domestic violence, and violence all become worse. Uncontrolled use of alcohol is equivalent to an assault weapon, it is deadly. So while some of you may be inspired to save humanity, don't forget about your own imperfections and those in your communities—leadership requires discipline.

Notes

1. Teresa Palomo Acosta, "In Re Ricardo Rodriguez," Handbook of Texas Online, http://www.tshaonline.org/handbook/online/articles/pqitw, accessed December 8, 2012. Published by the Texas State Historical Association.

2. Nathan O'Neal, "'Anchor Baby' Phrase Has Controversial History," ABC News (July 3, 2010), http://abcnews.go.com/Politics/anchor-baby-phrase-controversial-history/story?id=11066543#.UMSY0Hf8e20. "The Debate Over 'Anchor Babies' and Citizenship," NPR-National Public Radio (December 9, 2012), http://www.npr.org/templates/story/story.php?storyId=129279863.

3. John Albert Treviño, "'Cisneros v. CCISD': The desegregation of the Corpus Christi Independent School District," (PhD dissertation, Texas A&M University, Corpus Christi, 2010), 11–30.

4. *Cisneros v. Corpus Christi ISD*, 324 F. Supp. 599, 607 (S.D.Tex., 1970). Steven H. Wilson, "Brown over 'Other White': Mexican Americans' Legal Arguments and Litigation Strategy in School Desegregation Lawsuits," *Forum: Whiteness and Others: Mexican Americans and American Law, Law and History Review* 21, no. 1 (Spring 2003): 70. Jeffrey Passel and Paul Taylor, Who's Hispanic? Pew Hispanic Center, May 28, 2009, http://pewhispanic.org/reports/report.php?ReportID=111. Treviño, "Cisneros v. CCISD," 49–51.

5. "Estrada Withdraws as Judicial Nominee: Bush Slams 'Disgraceful Treatment,'" CNN.com, September 4, 2003, http://www.cnn.com/2003/ALLPOLITICS/09/04/estrada.withdraws/. Rodolfo F. Acuña and Guadalupe Compeán, eds., *Voices of the U.S. Latino Experience*, 3 vols. (Westport, CT: Greenwood, 2008), 997–99. John Nichols, "Filibustering on Estrada," *The Nation*, 276, no. 8 (2003): 5.

6. Nico Pitney, "Sonia Sotomayor, Supreme Court Nominee: All You Need To Know," *Huffington Post* (May 26, 2009).

7. "Profile: Attorney General Alberto Gonzales: From Humble Beginnings to Harvard to the White House," *ABC News*, http://abcnews.go.com/Politics/Inauguration/story?id=241596.

8. James Clifford, "Taking Identity Politics Seriously: 'The Contradictory, Stony Ground . . .'" in Paul Gilroy, Lawrence Grossberg, and Angela McRobbie, eds., *Without Guarantees: Essays in Honour of Stuart Hall* (London: Verso, 2000), 94–112. "The Word Chicana/o," http://forchicanachicanostudies.wikispaces.com/Chicana+Chicano+Public+Scholar.

9. Seth Motel and Eileen Patten, "The 10 Largest Hispanic Origin Groups: Characteristics, Rankings, Top Ten Counties," Pew Hispanic Center (Updated: July 12, 2012).

10. Paul Taylor, Mark Hugo Lopez, Jessica Hamar Martínez and Gabriel Velasco, "When Labels Don't Fit: Hispanics and Their Views of Identity," Pew Hispanic Center (April 4, 2012).

11. "Latinos in America: A Demographic Overview," Immigration Policy Center (April 2012), http://www.immigrationpolicy.org/sites/default/files/docs/latinos_in_america_-_a_demographic_overview_042612.pdf.

12. Seth Motel and Eileen Patten, "The 10 Largest Hispanic Origin Groups: Characteristics, Rankings, Top Counties," Pew Hispanic Center (July 12, 2012).

13. "State & County QuickFacts," United States Census Bureau, http://quickfacts.census.gov/qfd/states/17000.html.

14. "Median Age for Hispanics is Lower Than Median Age for Total U.S. Population," Pew Hispanic Center (December 7, 2012), http://pewresearch.org/databank/dailynumber/?NumberID=1533. Paul Taylor, Ana Gonzalez-Barrera, Jeffrey Passel, and

Mark Hugo Lopez, "An Awakened Giant: The Hispanic Electorate Is Likely to Double by 2030," Pew Hispanic Center (November 14, 2012), http://www.pewhispanic.org/2012/11/14/an-awakened-giant-the-hispanic-electorate-is-likely-to-double-by-2030/.

15. Sam Stein, "Hispanic Population, Rising Faster Than Anticipated, A 'Huge Weapon' For Obama," *Huffington Post,* July 3, 2011, http://www.huffingtonpost.com/2011/05/31/hispanic-population-rising-faster-than-anticipated_n_869209.html. Jeffrey Passel, D'Vera Cohn, and Mark Hugo Lopez, "Census 2010: 50 Million Latinos: Hispanics Account for More than Half of Nation's Growth in Past Decade," Pew Hispanic Center (March 24, 2011).

16. Richard Fausset, "New Latino South," *Los Angeles Times* (The series began on December 30, 2011), http://www.latimes.com/news/nationworld/nation/new-latino-south,0,565070.storygallery. "The Latino population in the South has grown dramatically over the last decade. The Times' occasional series chronicles the lives of Latinos in a changing region."

17. Adam Liptak, "Justices, 5-4, Reject Corporate Spending Limit," *New York Times* (January 21, 2010). Tom Hayden, "Participatory Democracy: From the Port Huron Statement to Occupy Wall Street," *The Nation* 294, no. 16 (2012): 11–19.

18. Ellen Dannin, "Privatizing Government Services in the Era of ALEC and the Great Recession. (American Legislative Exchange Council) (Public Sector Labor Law at the Crossroads Symposium)," *University of Toledo Law Review* 43, no. 3 (2012): 503–1005.

19. Brendan DeMelle, "Study Confirms Tea Party Was Created by Big Tobacco and Billionaire Koch Brothers," *Huffington Post,* The Blog (February 11, 2012).

20. Jeremy Duda, "Privatization Proposal for Maximum Security Prisons Raises Concerns," AzCapitolTimes (June 18, 2009), http://azcapitoltimes.com/news/2009/06/18/privatization-proposal-for-maximum-security-prisons-raises-concerns/#ixzz2EUGOrbaY. "Gender and the Prison Industrial Complex (2012)," Arizona Prison Watch: A community resource for monitoring, navigating, surviving, and dismantling the prison industrial complex in Arizona, http://arizonaprisonwatch.blogspot.com/. Beau Hodai, "Private Prison Companies Behind the Scenes of Arizona's Immigration Law," *Prison Legal News* (December 2012), https://www.prisonlegalnews.org/displayArticle.aspx?articleid=22734&AspxAutoDetectCookieSupport=1.

21. Seth Hoy, "Prisonomics 101: How ALEC and the Prison Industry Got Arizona's SB1070 onto Gov. Jan Brewer's Desk," *LA Progressive* (no date), http://www.laprogressive.com/sb1070-gov-jan-brewers-desk/#sthash.jW9xqAfK.dpuf.

22. "Detention and Deportation Consequences of Arizona Immigration Law (SB 1070): Why Is Arizona SB 1070 a Problem?," *Detention Watch Network* (no date), http://detentionwatchnetwork.org/SB1070_Talking_Points. Carlos Galindo, "The Business Side of SB1070," *Tucson Citizen* (June 26, 2012), http://tucsoncitizen.com/arizona-unapologetic-liberal/2012/06/26/the-business-side-of-sb1070/.

23. Peter Fenn, "Tea Party Funding Koch Brothers Emerge from Anonymity," *USNews & World Report* (February 2, 2011), http://www.usnews.com/opinion/blogs/Peter-Fenn/2011/02/02/tea-party-funding-koch-brothers-emerge-from-anonymity.

24. Jeremy Pelofsky, "Gun Lobby Fights Mexico Border Rifle Sale Control," Reuters (August 3, 2011), http://www.reuters.com/article/2011/08/03/us-usa-mexico-guns-idUSTRE7725DB20110803. David Neiwert, "Mexican drug cartels go shopping for their guns in Arizona," Crooks and Liars (January 27, 2011), http://crooksandliars.com/david-neiwert/mexican-drug-cartels-go-shopping-the.

25. David Safier, "Charter schools: the new segregation?" Blog for Arizona.com, http://www.blogforarizona.com/blog/2012/11/charter-schools-the-new-segregation.html. Casey D. Cobb, and Gene V Glass. "Ethnic Segregation in Arizona Charter Schools," *Education Policy Analysis Archives* 7, no. 1 (1999): 1. Anthony M. Garcy, "High Expense: Disability Severity and Charter School Attendance in Arizona," *Education Policy Analysis Archives* 19, no. 6 (2011): 1–26. Beau Hodai, "ALEC and Its Tea Party Sugar Daddies," *In These Times,* 35, no. 8 (2011): 16.

26. "Take a Stand—Yes on Prop. 30," http://www.youtube.com/watch?v=RtO1xsnWsw4. "Progressive Caucus on Prop. 32—California, November 2012," http://www.youtube.com/watch?v=CwgVTPSyQzo.

27. Anne-Marie Nuñez and Elizabeth Murakami-Ramalho, "The Demographic Dividend: Why the Success of Latino Faculty and Students Is Critical," Academe Online (January–February 2012), http://www.aaup.org/AAUP/pubsres/academe/2012/JF/Feat/nune.htm.

28. Mark Engberg and Daniel Allen, "Uncontrolled Destinies: Improving Opportunity for Low-Income Students in American Higher Education," *Research in Higher Education* 52, no. 8 (2011): 786–807. Greg G. J. Duncan, "Does Money Really Matter? Estimating Impacts of Family Income on Young Children's Achievement with Data from Random-assignment Experiments," *Developmental Psychology* 47, no. 5 (2011): 1263–79.

29. Ernesto Galarza, *Spiders in the House & Workers in the Field* (Notre Dame, IN: Notre Dame University Press, 1970); Galarza, *Alviso: The Crisis of a Barrio* (San Jose: Mexican American Community Service Agency, 1973).

30. Ernesto Galarza, "La Mula No Nacio Arisca," *Center Diary,* September–October 1966, pp. 26–32. In Rodolfo F. Acuña and Guadalupe Compeán, eds., *Voices of the U.S. Latino Experience* [Three Volumes] (Westport, CT: Greenwood Press, 2008), 814–18.

31. "The Invisible Minority: Report of the NEA-Tucson Survey on the Teaching of Spanish to the Spanish-Speaking," Dept. of Rural Education, National Education Association (Washington DC, 1966), 5.

32. Kim Clark, "49 States Flunk College Affordability Test: California, the only state that passed in the study, scraped by with a C minus," *US News & World Report,* December 3, 2008, http://www.usnews.com/education/articles/2008/12/03/49-states-flunk-college-affordability-test. "Fewer Latinos pick 4-year colleges," http://communitycollegespotlight.org/content/fewer-latinos-pick-4-year-colleges_1147/. Tamar Lewis, "What's the Most Expensive College? The Least? Education Dept. Puts It All Online," *New York Times,* June 30, 2011.

INDEX